Reference and Information Services

Recent Titles in the Library and Information Science Text Series

Collection Management Basics, Sixth Edition
G. Edward Evans and Margaret Zarnosky Saponaro

Library and Information Center Management, Eighth Edition
Barbara B. Moran, Robert D. Stueart, and Claudia J. Morner

Information Resources in the Humanities and Arts, Sixth Edition
Anna H. Perrault and Elizabeth Aversa, with contributing authors Cynthia Miller and Sonia Ramírez Wohlmuth

The School Library Manager, Fifth Edition
Blanche Woolls, Ann C. Weeks, and Sharon Coatney

Young Adult Literature in Action: A Librarian's Guide, Second Edition
Rosemary Chance

Children's Literature in Action: An Educator's Guide, Second Edition
Sylvia M. Vardell

Internet Technologies and Information Services, Second Edition
Joseph B. Miller

Library Programs and Services: The Fundamentals, Eighth Edition
G. Edward Evans, Margaret Zarnosky Saponaro, Carol Sinwell, and Holland Christie

The Complete Guide to Acquisitions Management, Second Edition
Frances C. Wilkinson, Linda K. Lewis, and Rebecca L. Lubas

Introduction to Cataloging and Classification, Eleventh Edition
Daniel N. Joudrey, Arlene G. Taylor, and David P. Miller

The Collection Program in Schools: Concepts and Practices, Sixth Edition
Marcia A. Mardis

Libraries in the Information Age: An Introduction and Career Exploration, Third Edition
Denise K. Fourie and Nancy E. Loe

REFERENCE AND INFORMATION SERVICES

An Introduction

Fifth Edition

Linda C. Smith and Melissa A. Wong, Editors

Library and Information Science Text Series

LIBRARIES UNLIMITED™
An Imprint of ABC-CLIO, LLC
Santa Barbara, California • Denver, Colorado

Library of Congress Cataloging-in-Publication Data

Names: Smith, Linda C., editor. | Wong, Melissa Autumn, editor.
Title: Reference and information services : an introduction.
Description: Fifth edition / Linda C. Smith, Melissa A. Wong, editors. | Santa Barbara, CA : Libraries Unlimited, [2017] | Series: Library and information science text series | Includes bibliographical references and index.
Identifiers: LCCN 2016013108 (print) | LCCN 2016032711 (ebook) | ISBN 9781440836961 (paperback) | ISBN 9781440836978 (eBook)
Subjects: LCSH: Reference services (Libraries) | Information services. | BISAC: LANGUAGE ARTS & DISCIPLINES / Library & Information Science / Cataloging & Classification. | LANGUAGE ARTS & DISCIPLINES / Library & Information Science / Collection Development.
Classification: LCC Z711 .R443 2017 (print) | LCC Z711 (ebook) | DDC 025.5/2—dc23
LC record available at https://lccn.loc.gov/2016013108

ISBN: 978-1-4408-3696-1
EISBN: 978-1-4408-3697-8

21 20 19 18 17   1 2 3 4 5

This book is also available as an eBook.

Libraries Unlimited
An Imprint of ABC-CLIO, LLC

ABC-CLIO, LLC
130 Cremona Drive, P.O. Box 1911
Santa Barbara, California 93116-1911
www.abc-clio.com

This book is printed on acid-free paper ∞

Manufactured in the United States of America

Contents

PART III: The Future of Reference Service

Preface

The fifth edition of *Reference and Information Services* reflects the dramatic changes shaped by rapidly developing technologies and increasing volumes of digital content over the past five years. This edition takes the introduction to reference sources and services significantly beyond the content of the previous edition. In Part I, "Concepts and Processes," chapters have been revised and updated to reflect new ideas and methods in the provision of reference service in an era when many users have access to the Web. New chapters in this part provide coverage of consortia and cooperation, models of reference services, and marketing and promotion of reference services. Two chapters provide more thorough coverage of services for specific populations, by dealing separately with children and young adults and with a wider range of diverse populations. In Part II, "Information Sources and Their Use," discussion of each source type has been updated to encompass a much more extensive list of Web resources, both freely available and licensed. New chapters in this part cover licensing electronic sources, search strategies for electronic sources, sources for data and statistics, readers' advisory services and sources, business sources, health and medicine sources, primary and archival sources, and legal sources. A final chapter makes up Part III, exploring how professionals can create the future of reference service.

A number of new authors are contributors to the fifth edition, bringing to their chapters their experience as teachers of reference or as practitioners in various types of libraries. Throughout the text, boxes are used to generate thought and discussion. Despite these updates and changes, the fifth edition has the same goal as its predecessors, to provide students and practitioners with an overview of current reference sources, issues, and services.

Linda C. Smith
Melissa A. Wong

Acknowledgments

A number of individuals assisted the editors or authors in the creation of the fifth edition of *Reference and Information Services*. We would like to express our gratitude for their valuable contributions here.

First, we would like to thank the editorial and production staff of Libraries Unlimited, an imprint of ABC-CLIO, for their support in publishing this new edition.

The authors of several chapters in the fifth edition built on the work of authors who contributed to the fourth edition. We would like to acknowledge our debt to David A. Cobb, Prudence W. Dalrymple, Eric Forte, Jim Hahn, Frances Jacobson Harris, Lisa Janicke Hinchliffe, Josephine Z. Kibbee, Kathleen M. Kluegel, Lori S. Mestre, Carol Bates Penka, Richard E. Rubin, Joseph E. Straw, Jo Bell Whitlatch, and Lynn Wiley for helping shape earlier editions of this text.

Thanks go to Holly Soboroff for creating the Venn diagram figures in Chapter 15 and to Matthew Beth for his assistance.

We are deeply indebted to Richard E. Bopp (1944–2011), who first proposed the idea of a collaboratively authored reference textbook in the late 1980s and served as the lead editor for the first four editions published in 1991, 1995, 2001, and 2011.

Melissa would like to thank her family, Bob, Erica, and Craig, for their patience and support while she worked long hours on this project. You make it a wonderful world every day.

Part I

Concepts and Processes

Chapter 1

History and Functions of Reference Services

Dave A. Tyckoson

INTRODUCTION

We are living in the information age, where information is available everywhere all the time. With devices that we carry in our purses and pockets, we are able to find, collect, and utilize the information that we need—no matter when we need it or where we are located. The tools for connecting to a vast array of types and quality of information are always at hand—meaning that the information we want is also always at hand. We can collect statistics on climate change, quote *Macbeth*, watch the rise and fall of the stock market, read news stories from around the corner and around the world, listen to our favorite music, find out when the bus will reach our stop, figure out which store has the best price on the product we want to purchase, and watch cat videos—all at the same time. Every person has the power to retrieve the information that he or she needs—so why do we still need libraries? And why do we still need reference librarians?

There are obviously many answers to those questions—and this book will provide a variety of opinions, options, and actions that will keep libraries and reference services growing and thriving. But ease of use does not always equal ease of understanding. And too much information can cause some of the same problems as too little information. To fully understand the roles, responsibilities, and continuing need for reference librarians, we need to look back at the reasons that reference service was established, the things reference librarians have done traditionally, and how those activities have evolved to the present day. And to start, we need to understand the role of the library within the broader community that it serves.

THE LIBRARY AND THE COMMUNITY

Libraries do not exist in isolation. Every library serves a specific, defined community. The library is not an independent institution in and of itself, but exists to serve and support the community for which it was established. Public libraries serve the residents of a certain geographical area, most often a city or county. Academic libraries serve the faculty, staff, and students at the college or university. School libraries serve the teachers and students attending a specific school. Medical libraries serve the doctors, nurses, staff, and patients of the hospital. Law libraries serve the attorneys and staff of the firm. Corporate libraries serve the management and employees of a specific company.

In each case, the function of the library is to provide information to its parent community. When members of the community need information services, the primary objective of the library is to fill that need. Whether that need relates to research, business, or entertainment, members of the community often turn to the library. Most libraries, especially public and academic libraries, also allow people from outside the primary community to use their collections, facilities, and services. However, the primary focus needs to be on the people who make up the parent community. If a library fails to serve its primary clientele, it will not remain in business. A library that is perceived as vital to its community will receive the support, staff, and funding to maintain its role as an information utility for the community. A library that does not fill the needs of its parent community will slowly wither, will become marginalized, and may even close. To serve the community effectively, librarians must learn who composes that community, what their information needs are, and how those needs are changing. Know the community, and one will know what the library should contain, which services to offer, and what level of support to expect in return.

WHAT LIBRARIES DO

Libraries perform three basic functions in order to fill the information needs of their communities. Each is extremely detailed and highly complex, yet all of the activities of the library can be reduced to one of these three functions. The functions of the library have evolved over time as libraries and their parent communities have coevolved. In many libraries, a new function has taken root, and in some, this new function is flourishing. To fully understand reference service, one first needs to understand the basic functions of the library.

Collections

Historically, the first function of libraries was to select, collect, and preserve information. From ancient times, librarians have collected and retained documents of interest to their parent communities. From the scrolls in the Great Library of Alexandria to the books chained to the desks of the Bodleian Library, to the scientific journals of the National Library of Medicine, to the children's books of the local public library, every library has had and continues to have as its first role the accumulation of information of interest to its community. This information takes many forms, which today include books, journals, microforms, photographs, compact disks, videos,

DVDs, websites, MP3s, computer files, and any other form of information storage that has been used in the past. In response to the needs of the community, librarians will also collect any new information formats that will be developed in the future. The popular image of the library as a warehouse for materials—whether those materials are row after row of books on shelving, cabinets of microfilm or audio CDs, or a Web page full of links—comes directly from this collection function. This is the oldest historical function of libraries: to find, select, acquire, and preserve documents of interest to the community. It remains a vital role to this day. Part II (Chapters 13–28) of this book discusses collections for reference service.

Organization

The second function of libraries is to organize the information they collect. The fact that librarians organize information is intuitively obvious, but it is a much more recent function than collecting. Historically, this was the second function to arise in libraries, evolving as a corollary to the first function. As libraries grew in size, it became more and more difficult for users (and librarians) to find the information in which they were interested. When libraries were very small, the user could simply browse the entire collection to find what was needed. As the size of libraries grew, other methods of organization were required.

From alphabetical order to RDA and from MARC to metadata, librarians have developed a wide variety of methods for organizing and finding materials in their collections. Most of these tools were initially developed by librarians primarily for self-assistance. As libraries grew larger, it became much more difficult for librarians to know where to find specific documents or pieces of information within the overall collection. As a result, librarians developed concepts such as subject headings, main entries, authority files, call numbers, metadata tags, and controlled vocabularies. Although libraries must have always had some kind of organization, the first true catalogs were developed as inventory control devices in the latter half of the 15th century (Hanson and Daily 1970). The first published catalog was the book catalog of the Bodleian Library in Oxford, which was published in 1620. Although no precise date can be given for when librarians began to organize information on a large scale, they have been doing so for at least 500 years.

Over time, our organizational tools became more and more sophisticated, with author, title, and later even subject entries included. By the early 19th century, librarians had developed a number of codes that described how such information would be organized, resulting in the publication of the famous 91 rules of Panizzi in 1841 and Cutter's *Rules for a Dictionary Catalog* in 1876. Today we use RDA, MARC records, HTML, XML, EAD, OpenURL, and metadata coding to describe our collections. Tomorrow, new schema will be developed that will be applied to as-yet-undeveloped forms of information or that will better organize materials in our collections. However, the central function remains the same: to tell the users what information is included in the library and to help them retrieve that information.

Librarians have become quite sophisticated in organizing and indexing the materials contained within their collections. Using the technology of the times, from scrolls to books to cards to databases, librarians have been and continue to be leaders in the theory and practice of indexing and cataloging information. *Google* may tell library users what exists out on the Web, but librarian-developed tools and guides tell people where the useful information is located. Although

Google will always provide the searcher with lots of websites, it relies on automatic linking and indexing, whereas library guides include only sources that have been evaluated by the librarian. For more on the organization function of libraries, see Chapter 13.

Publishing

The third function of libraries is newer and is a direct extension of the organization role—that is, to serve as a publisher and distributor of information produced by its community. Many communities are digitizing their unique materials and making them available to the world—and it is often the library that takes the lead in these projects. In an age when information is everywhere, it is hard to find information that has the highest value. For many communities, that hard-to-find information is contained in the special collections area of the local library. In many communities, it is only the library that has made the effort to retain and preserve these materials. With new digitization technology, the library now has the ability to share those local resources with the rest of the world—and many libraries are doing exactly that.

Service

However, it is the fourth function of libraries that is most relevant for this book—and that is to provide direct assistance to users in their search for and retrieval of information, which is what librarians now call reference service. This aspect of librarianship began in the mid- to late 1800s. Although everyone today has grown up with reference service and tends to take this service for granted, it was truly a revolutionary concept when first introduced. To understand how revolutionary the idea of reference service really was, a look back in time at what society was like in that era is required.

HISTORICAL DEVELOPMENT OF REFERENCE SERVICES

Universal Education and Public Libraries

The fact that reference service was developed at all is linked to two different, yet related 19th-century ideals: universal education and public libraries. These two movements transformed the fabric of American society and had a lasting impact that remains today. Universal education was the concept that all children in the United States, no matter what class, race, or religion, would be able to receive free public education. Reasons for establishing universal education for all school-age children varied widely and were often at cross-purposes to each other (Gutek 1970, 51–52). Business leaders saw universal education as a way to attain better workers. Labor leaders saw it as a way for people to move up in society. Religious leaders saw it as a way to enable more people to read the Bible. Politicians saw it as a way to create a single national identity among a varied immigrant population. Regardless of the true motivations for establishing universal education, state and local governments throughout the nation established free public schools, which did in fact result in a more highly educated society. As a direct result of universal education, the literacy rate in the United States rose significantly.

Precise data on literacy prior to 1870 are difficult to obtain, and rates varied widely from region to region (Soltow and Stevens 1981). Estimates of literacy rates in the 1850s range from 90 percent in Massachusetts to 60 percent in the Southern states. However, these figures count only white males. Female literacy rates tended to be lower than that for males, ranging from 2–4 percent less in the Northeast to 10–15 percent less in the South. Literacy among the free black population was estimated at 50 percent, and the literacy rate of slaves was 5–10 percent. The literacy rate for Native Americans would have been even lower. By 1870, the literacy rate had risen to 88.5 percent in the white population and 20.5 percent in the nonwhite population (U.S. Bureau of the Census 1975, 1: 382). As more and more people learned to read, they became more and more interested in doing so.

At the same time as universal education was becoming the norm, the concept of the free public library was being established. To convince the city fathers that such an institution would be a necessary and valuable component of the community, the trustees of the Boston Public Library made these arguments: "The question is not what will be brought about by a few individuals of indomitable will and an ardent thirst for improvement, but what is most for the advantage of the mass of the community. In this point of view we consider that a large public library is of the utmost importance as the means of completing our system of public education" (Trustees [1852] 1975, 9). The fact that the public library was viewed as a component of universal education is emphasized again later in that same report (emphases in the original document):

> And yet there can be no doubt that such reading ought to be furnished to all, as a matter of public policy and duty, on the same principle that we furnish free education, and in fact, as a part, and the most important part, of the education of all. For it has been rightly judged that,—under political, social and religious institutions like ours,—it is of paramount importance that the means of general information should be so diffused that the largest possible number of persons should be induced to read and understand questions going down to the very foundations of social order, which are constantly presenting themselves, and which we, as a people, are constantly required to decide, and do decide, either ignorantly or wisely. That this *can* be done,—that is, that such libraries *can* be collected, and that they will be used to a much wider extent than libraries have ever been used before, and with much more important results, there can be no doubt; and if it can be done *anywhere*, it can be done *here* in Boston; for no population of one hundred and fifty thousand souls, lying so compactly together as to be able, with tolerable convenience, to resort to one library, was ever before so well fitted to become a reading, self-cultivating population, as the population of our own city is at this moment.
>
> To accomplish this object, however,—which has never yet been attempted,—we must use means which have never before been used; otherwise the library we propose to establish, will not be adjusted to its especial purposes. Above all, while the rightful claim of no class,—however highly educated already,—should be overlooked, the first regard should be shown, as in the case of our Free Schools, to the wants of those, who can, in no other way supply themselves with the interesting and healthy reading necessary for their farther education. (Trustees [1852] 1975, 15–16)

The Boston Public Library did, in fact, become a reality and opened its doors to the public—all of the public—on March 20, 1854. It was an instant success. In less than six months of operation, more than 35,000 volumes were borrowed

(Stone 1977, 158). When given an opportunity to read, the public responded at an overwhelming rate, borrowing an average of one book for every two people living in the city, and this at a time when the concept of borrowing books was new to the majority of the population and not yet a common practice. The concept of the free public library was rapidly adopted by other municipalities, with 188 such libraries having been established in 11 different states by 1876 (Poole 1876).

Reference service came about as a direct result of these two innovations. Universal education taught the public to read, and public libraries offered material to read. As Melvil Dewey put it,

> The school teaches them to read; the library must supply them with reading which will serve to educate, and so it is that we are forced to divide popular education into two parts of almost equal importance and deserving equal attention: the free school and the free library. (1876, 6)

The newly literate members of society knew how to read and sought out materials that would allow them to practice that newly learned skill. Unlike today's society, where information is ubiquitous, information was somewhat scarce in that time period. Few families owned reading materials, and books were relatively expensive, so people turned to the newly formed public libraries. However, they had no idea how to use a library. Naturally, they asked the librarians for advice. By 1876, the idea of reference service had been born.

Samuel Green and the Founding of Reference Service

The first discussion of any type of direct service by librarians to help library users was in a paper presented by Samuel Swett Green at the first conference of the American Library Association in Philadelphia in 1876. His paper, "Personal Intercourse and Relations between Librarians and Readers in Popular Libraries," outlined the concept of the librarian interacting with and assisting the reader; he did not use the phrase "reference service" because that term had not yet been developed. His paper was published with a shorter title in the first volume of *Library Journal* and is universally recognized as the first professional discussion of what we now call reference service.

The fact that reference service originated in public libraries is proof positive of the democratic ideals on which those institutions were founded. Instead of being developed within the walls of academe, where students were theoretically seeking to build upon the knowledge of the past, it was in the *people's university*, the *free public library*, that the concept took hold. Samuel Rothstein, who studied the development of reference services in academic libraries, accounts for the lack of interest among academics as follows: "Actually, the student of that era was little inclined to make much use of the college librarian in any case. The idea of research had as yet scarcely reached American universities, and the teaching methods in undergraduate courses still emphasized the traditional reliance upon the textbook. The student had little occasion to borrow books from the library, and his demands for personal assistance must have been even more rare" (Rothstein 1953, 4).

However, some positive reaction to the concept of personal assistance was found in academic institutions. In the discussion that followed Green's presentation, Otis Robinson of the University of Rochester heartily endorsed the concept (1876, 123–24). At the London Conference the following year, Reuben Guild of

> **Box 1.1 Why Do We Call It "Reference Service"?**
>
> When the idea of helping library users was first proposed, the terms "reference service" and "reference librarian" had yet to be coined. However, the term "reference book" was already widely in use. Reference books earned that name because they were the books, such as catalogs, indexes, and bibliographies, that one consulted to find references to other sources. By the 1870s, any library book that did not circulate was being called a reference book.
>
> In the first paper discussing reference service, Samuel Green called it "personal intercourse between librarians and readers." Fortunately, that phrase was quickly shortened to "aid to readers." Later, the term "assistance to readers" came into more widespread use as the service end of reference began to be more widely recognized. Because the librarians who helped readers tended to use the books that were located in the reference collection, they gradually became known as reference librarians. In 1885, Melvil Dewey became the first to hire staff with the title of "reference librarian" when he organized the first multiple-librarian (i.e., two-person) reference department at Columbia College. "Reference work" was what "reference librarians" did. That name caught on, and the rest, as they say, is history.
>
> (Rothstein 1972, 25–27)

Brown University described the availability of librarians to the public (faculty and students) at his university (1878, 278). Within a decade of Green's paper, Melvil Dewey had embraced the idea of reference service in the Columbia College (now Columbia University) Library. Dewey was the first to establish a team of librarians to provide personal assistance to users and was the first to use the phrase "reference department" when referring to that team. Rothstein indicates, "Under Dewey's dynamic and positive leadership, the Columbia College Library had already recognized that such assistance was more than just another aid or subsidiary activity, that the personal help given to individual readers was a necessary and integral part of the library's educational function" (1972, 27–28). As the teaching methods used in colleges and universities evolved into a more research-based model, the use of the library by students increased to the point where reference service became established in academic libraries. More traditional academic institutions took longer to adopt this idea, but eventually reference service was available in virtually any public or academic library in the United States.

Original Functions of the Reference Librarian

So what exactly does a reference librarian do? Green's (1876) original paper on the topic consists primarily of examples of the types of questions asked by the variety of users of his public library. However, embedded within those examples are four distinct functions of the reference librarian. They include:

1. *Teach people how to use the library and its resources.* Although some scholars may have known their way around catalogs, indexes, and the stacks, most of the newly literate members of the society were unfamiliar with what libraries

contained and how to find it. The first function of the librarian providing personal assistance to readers was to teach them how to find things in the library. Green states, "Give them as much assistance as they need, but try at the same time to teach them to rely upon themselves and become independent" (80).

2. *Answer readers' questions.* Green's paper provides a myriad of examples of the types of questions asked by users of the public library, ranging from simple factual queries to in-depth research projects. The librarian was expected to be able to answer—or more accurately, to provide sources that would answer—all of these types of questions. As Green states so succinctly, "persons who use a popular library for purposes of investigation generally need a great deal of assistance" (74). He then presents three pages of examples of the type of assistance that readers in his library have needed.
3. *Aid the reader in the selection of good works.* People wanted to read but did not know what was worth reading. One of the major roles of the librarian was to serve as a readers' advisor, recommending material that fit each reader's interests and ability. Green, in discussing his reference librarian, comments, "I am confident that in some such way as this a great influence can be exerted in the direction of causing good books to be used. . . . Only let her aim at providing every person who applies for aid with the best book he is willing to read" (79).
4. *Promote the library within the community.* Underlying all of Green's examples is the concept that by being personally available to members of the community, the librarian would generate support from the community, which of course would lead to more use of the library and greater financial support. Green closes his paper by stating, "The more freely a librarian mingles with readers, and the greater the amount of assistance he renders them, the more intense does the conviction of citizens, also, become, that the library is a useful institution, and the more willing do they grow to grant money in larger and larger sums to be used in buying books and employing additional assistants" (81). In other words, if you help them, they will come—and provide funding!

Changes since 1876

Technology

Of course, society has changed significantly since 1876. The area that is most obviously different is the technology used in libraries. While librarians in Green's time had essentially two formats, books and periodicals, librarians today use a wide range of resources. The reference librarian today almost always consults a computer rather than a book when responding to a question. A wide range of types of machines are found throughout the library. Technology has transformed the way that libraries operate and the way that readers use the library. Over the decades, the library has gone from a place that relied on paper and pencil to one that uses silicon chips and electrons. Figure 1.1 illustrates the parade of technology through libraries by decade.

Although this is a vast array of technologies, each of which has had a profound impact on libraries, all of these technologies can be broken down into three distinct categories: technology that stores information, technology that reproduces information, and technology that communicates information. The technologies in Figure 1.1 can be divided into these three categories as illustrated in Figure 1.2.

1890s	Typewriter	1980s	Personal computer
1920s	Telephone		Printer
	Radio		Floppy disk
1930s	Phonodisc		Audio compact disc
1940s	Television		CD-ROM
	Microfilm		Email
1950s	Tape recording		Electronic mailing lists
	Punch card	1990s	World Wide Web
	Slide		Internet Chat
	Thermofax copier		E-commerce
1960s	Photocopier		Laptop computer
	Filmstrip		Wireless telecommunication
	Microfiche	2000s	iPod
	Microcard		USB storage device
	Telex		Smart Phones
1970s	Mainframe computer		Text messaging
	Modem	2010s	Social Media
	Video recording		Tablets
	Cassette tape		
	Telefacsimile		

FIGURE 1.1 Technology arranged chronologically

Storage	**Reproduction**	**Communication**
Phonodisc	Typewriter	Telephone
Microfilm	Thermofax copier	Radio
Punch card	Photocopier	Television
Tape recording	Mainframe computer	Telex
Slide	Telefacsimile	Modem
Filmstrip	Personal computer	Telefacsimile
Microfiche	Printer	Email
Microcard	Laptop computer	Electronic mailing lists
Video recording	Tablet	World Wide Web
Cassette tape		Internet Chat
Mainframe computer		E-commerce
Personal computer		Wireless telecommunication
Floppy disk		Smart phones
Audio compact disc		Text messaging
CD-ROM		Social Media
Laptop computer		
iPod		
USB storage		
Tablet		

FIGURE 1.2 Technology arranged by function

Some of these technologies are used to perform more than one of the three listed functions (e.g., the computer), but each technology enhances the ability of the library to function in one or more ways. While each of these technologies is a tool that enhances library service, it does not fundamentally change the nature of that service. The next several years will undoubtedly bring about even more technological developments, and libraries will adopt those technologies that help them improve service to their communities. The chapters in Part I (Chapters 2–12) of this book address many aspects of reference and include a discussion of how technology continues to influence reference services.

Diversity

The other major change in libraries over the past 130 years has been in the nature of the populations that libraries serve. Since the 19th century, the population of the United States has become much more diverse. While the users of libraries in Green's time were primarily English speakers of European descent, users of libraries in the United States today come from all over the world and speak hundreds of languages. As our communities have changed to incorporate immigrants from Asia, Africa, and Latin America, our libraries also have changed to include more materials about other cultures in more and more languages.

Diversity is not only ethnic in nature. In the 1870s, libraries existed to serve adults. During the ensuing years, libraries have established a number of specialized services and departments for various segments of the population, including children, teens, senior citizens, veterans, persons with disabilities, students, teachers, the business community, unemployed persons, and virtually any other discrete population not served by basic library programs. Diversity has had an impact on reference service by creating the need to respond to these demographic changes. For more on diversity and reference service, see Chapters 11 and 12.

FUNCTIONS OF THE REFERENCE LIBRARIAN TODAY

So what do reference librarians do today? With all of these changes in technology and the growing diversity of our users, what is reference like now? Surprisingly (or perhaps not), the actual functions of the reference librarian have changed very little over the years. A century after Green first discussed reference service, Thomas Galvin (1978, 25: 220–21) listed the functions of the modern reference librarian as follows:

- Assistance and instruction (formal or informal) in the use of the library
- Assistance in the identification and selection of books, journals, and other materials relevant to a particular information need
- Provision of brief, factual information of the "ready reference" variety

In the 1980s, a series of essays was commissioned in honor of Margaret Monroe, the esteemed library science educator at the University of Wisconsin. The main body of the work consists of four survey articles that present the state of reference and public service at that time. These chapters are titled simply "Information," "Instruction," "Guidance," and "Stimulation" (the latter referring to promotion of the use of the library's human and material resources) (Schlachter 1982).

More recently, in her dictionary of librarianship, Joan Reitz (2004, 602) has dcfined reference services as:

> including but not limited to answering substantive questions, instructing users in the selection of appropriate tools and techniques for finding information, conducting searches on behalf of the patron, directing users to the location of library resources, assisting in the evaluation of information, referring patrons to resources outside the library when appropriate, keeping reference statistics, and participating in the development of the reference collection.

The role of the reference librarian today is also reflected in the definitions of a reference transaction and reference work, adopted by the Reference and User Services Association (RUSA) (2008a) of the American Library Association:

> **Reference Transactions** are information consultations in which library staff recommend, interpret, evaluate, and/or use information resources to help others to meet particular information needs. Reference transactions do not include formal instruction or exchanges that provide assistance with locations, schedules, equipment, supplies, or policy statements.
>
> **Reference work** includes reference transactions and other activities that involve the creation, management, and assessment of information or research resources, tools, and services.

Although these definitions do not mention the public relations role of the librarian, the functions described today are otherwise essentially the same as those mentioned by Green. While technology and information sources today are entirely different than they were in Green's era, the process and function are essentially the same.

REFERENCE WORK: VARIETIES AND APPROACHES

Styles of Reference Service

Although what librarians do has remained fairly constant over the years, the relative importance of those functions has varied tremendously. Ever since librarians began providing direct assistance to users, the librarian has had to determine whether it is appropriate to *conduct* research for the patron or to *instruct* the patron in how to do that research. This debate has raged for at least a century and is one that is still appropriate today. In one of the early textbooks on reference service, James Wyer (1930, 6–7) described three different philosophies of reference service, which he labeled "conservative," "moderate," and "liberal." In his landmark history of reference service, Samuel Rothstein (1961) calls these same philosophies "minimum," "middling," and "maximum." No matter what one calls them, these philosophies define the range of possible reference services. Simply stated, these alternatives are as follows:

1. *Conservative or minimum.* The primary role of the librarian is to teach patrons how to use the library. The librarian helps users find sources but does not read or interpret those sources for the user. The library is seen as an

extension of instruction. Not surprisingly, this approach is most common in academic libraries.

2. *Moderate or middling.* The librarian not only teaches the user how to use sources but also provides answers to many questions. The librarians do not do homework assignments for students but will search exhaustively to find answers for research and factual questions. This model is most common in public libraries.
3. *Liberal or maximum.* The librarian takes the user's question, conducts the research, finds appropriate material, and presents it to the user. In some cases, the librarian even writes a summary or analysis of the information found. This type of reference service is most often found in special libraries, including medical libraries, law libraries, and corporate libraries.

The conservative/minimum philosophy emphasizes instruction over answers, the liberal/maximum philosophy emphasizes answers over instruction, and the moderate/middling philosophy comprises equal parts of each. All reference services fall somewhere within this overall spectrum; exactly where depends on the needs and expectations of the parent community.

Types of Reference Service

Within these philosophies and functions of the reference librarian, several particular types of reference service have been developed. Some common forms of reference service include readers' advisory, ready reference, research consulting, subject specialists, bibliographic verification and citation, interlibrary loan and document delivery, instruction, literacy programs, and outreach and marketing.

Readers' Advisory

Readers' advisory is the process of recommending titles, particularly fiction, for leisure reading to library users. In her dictionary, Joan Reitz (2004, 592) defines this service as: "a readers' advisor recommends specific titles and/or authors, based on knowledge of the patron's past reading preferences, and may also compile lists of recommended titles."

Commercial information suppliers have also jumped on the popularity of readers' advisory services by creating their own recommendation services. Shopping sites use aggregated data to recommend additional titles to consumers, music streaming sites recommend similar artists or styles to listeners, and video sites recommend similar themes to viewers. Recommendation has become a ubiquitous component of the always-online information age and is an example of how work originally done primarily by reference librarians has evolved into a standard service in a wide range of environments. For more on readers' advisory, see Chapter 24.

Ready Reference

Ready reference is the provision of short factual answers to highly specific questions. Answers to these questions are verifiable as accurate or inaccurate. The following are examples of ready-reference questions: "What is the population of

Chicago?" "How many apples were grown in Washington State in 2014?" "Who played the role of Stella in the film version of *A Streetcar Named Desire*?" "What is the address of the headquarters of Microsoft?" "In what year did Yugoslavia cease to be a single nation?"

Answering ready-reference questions is the most common image of the reference librarian. This image has been popularized by media, as in the portrayals by Katharine Hepburn and her staff in the film *Desk Set* (Lang 1957). However, ready reference has never been the primary function of reference service and is rapidly becoming an even smaller component of the reference librarian's duties. In the past, reference librarians did more ready reference simply because the sources required to answer such questions were in library collections and not in the hands of the users. With the development of the Web and search tools such as *Wikipedia* and *Google*, users have the tools to find this type of information on their own. As a result, there is less need to consult a librarian for ready reference. This is another example of how today's information age has changed reference services.

Research Consulting

A more common form of reference service is assisting users with research questions. These questions do not have single, factual answers but have many possible results that vary depending on the researcher's interests and needs. In this case, the librarian may suggest sources, search terms, and pathways that will lead to material relevant to the research project. The following are some examples of research questions: "Why did the various ethnic groups in Chicago settle in the neighborhoods that they now occupy?" "What is the effect of pesticides on apple production?" "What is Stella's psychological background in *A Streetcar Named Desire*?" "How did Microsoft grow into a company that dominates the information industry?" "What political, economic, and social issues led to the breakup of Yugoslavia?"

Each of these examples corresponds to one of the ready-reference examples in the previous section, but in each case, the question touches on issues that are much more complex. With research questions, there is not one single answer that can be verified as categorically correct or incorrect. Instead, a wide range of possible approaches, search strategies, and potential sources are available, each leading in a different direction. The role of the librarian as a research consultant is to find out what aspects of the problem the user is interested in and to suggest possible search strategies that will lead the user toward the best solution. As a research consultant, the librarian may get the user started in the research, but the user will do most of the actual searching, potentially returning to the librarian for additional assistance several times during the process. Research consulting is more common in academic and research libraries than in other types, but it is becoming the dominant form of reference service in all libraries.

Subject Specialists

Many large libraries hire librarians to be specialists in a specific subject field or discipline. These librarians immerse themselves in the subject area, usually selecting materials for the collection as well as assisting users with specialized research. Although subject specialists can be assigned to cover any discipline, they are most common in areas that society sees as requiring more specialized knowledge to succeed, such as law, medicine, the sciences, and business. Subject specialists often have advanced degrees within their field of specialization. They work closely with the researchers who comprise their community and often handle very complex questions. Subject specialists are most often found in academic libraries, large public libraries, and special libraries.

Bibliographic Verification and Citation

Bibliographic verification is the process of reading, identifying, and interpreting citations to information sources. Those sources include books, journals, theses, Web pages, manuscripts, or any other form of publication. In the process of verification, the librarian usually finds other reference sources that cite the same publication, corrects errors, and determines where to find the desired information. As information becomes more and more complex, verification is a growing activity for reference librarians. A newer function related to bibliographic verification is helping users to correctly cite the information sources that they have used. Students, researchers, and the general public all need to be able to provide accurate citations to their sources so that others will be able to find those same sources. With the wide range of available citation styles, such as APA (from the *Publication Manual of the American Psychological Association*), MLA (from the *MLA Handbook for Writers of Research Papers*), and Chicago (from *The Chicago Manual of Style*), and an ever-growing number of information formats, users find it increasingly difficult to accurately cite the information sources that they use. Add to that the ubiquity of information on the Web, and users are very confused about citations. Aiding users with citations is probably the single most rapidly growing function of the reference librarian. This is extremely common in academic and school libraries, where students are learning how to cite material, but citations are also frequent inquiries in public and special libraries. Reference librarians are often the people behind the scenes who are most responsible for maintaining good standards in citations and references.

Interlibrary Loan and Document Delivery

Interlibrary loan is the process of sharing materials among and between libraries. One library may loan a physical item to another library for a specific period of time or may copy the original and deliver it to the requesting library. Interlibrary loan is a common service in most libraries of all types because it extends the range of material available to users beyond the home library's collection. Most libraries belong to consortia that determine which materials may be borrowed or photocopied using established codes (Reference and User Services Association 2008b). When cooperative union catalogs such as OCLC were adapted for interlibrary loan, the process was made significantly easier, and the volume of traffic among lending libraries rose tremendously.

Interlibrary loan librarians spend a lot of time doing bibliographic verification. Their primary responsibility is to search for material requested by users, verify that the information is accurate, determine that the home library does not own it, and identify potential lending partners who can provide the material. Software such as OCLC's ILLiad makes the processing of requests much easier for the librarian, allowing the same staff to handle an increasing volume of requests.

Instruction

Green's first function of the reference librarian was to instruct readers about the library, and that instructional role continues well into the 21st century. Instruction tends to take two forms: direct and indirect. Direct instruction is characterized by the librarian communicating directly to the user and may be delivered through any of a number of channels. It may come in a one-on-one situation in which the librarian teaches the user as they work together on a query; it may be done in a voluntary group environment, through workshops or classes that teach general or specific skills to those who choose to attend; or it may be a required part of a specific course or assignment in which the instructor wants all students to use library resources. Required instruction is more common in academic libraries, whereas voluntary and one-on-one instruction are features of reference service in all libraries.

In indirect instruction, the librarian does not communicate directly with the user, but communicates through instructional tools. In order to assist users with common problems, librarians create guides or tutorials that describe how to approach typical research problems. These guides range from printed handouts to videos to interactive modules. Some cover specific issues, such as how to use the catalog, a specific database, or a specific reference source, while others may be directed at specific disciplines or topics, such as biology, music, or education. Guides may be in print or electronic form and are updated as needed. Indirect instruction is provided in anticipation of user needs. For more about instruction, see Chapter 4.

Literacy Programs

In addition to providing resources for the literate segment of society, libraries have continued to play a role in education itself. Many librarians conduct literacy programs that are designed to teach reading and writing skills to those members of the community who have not acquired such skills through other channels. Frequently, these programs are aimed at adults who have not completed their schooling, for whom English is a second language, or who are new immigrants to the community. Literacy programs are most common in public libraries. These programs continue the historic role of the public library in educating members of the communities that they serve.

Outreach and Marketing

Public relations is as important in today's libraries as it was back in Samuel Green's time. Green realized the value of having the public interact directly with librarians, and this type of personal interaction has been a symbol of reference service ever since. However, librarians today have gone beyond a passive approach of waiting for users to come to the library and now work to generate interest in their communities. Academic and public libraries frequently have staff whose primary responsibility is to work with specific segments of the community to increase library awareness and use within those populations. In the academic environment, the library may target outreach efforts at specific disciplines or departments, or toward specific types of users, such as faculty or graduate students. In public libraries, outreach is often directed at segments of the community, such as teens, senior citizens, particular ethnic or cultural groups, or members of clubs or interest groups. Outreach activities continue to grow in libraries and are often a part of the reference librarian's duties.

Some reference librarians spend more time on outreach and marketing than they do in ready reference and research consulting. This is a growing responsibility in all types of libraries. See Chapter 10 for more on outreach and marketing.

Models of Reference Service

Samuel Green saw great value in having the librarian interact directly with the users of the library. The method by which that interaction happens may take many different forms, including service at a reference desk, roving reference, tiered reference, reference by appointment, and service to remote users. Chapter 6 discusses models of reference service in more detail, so the following provides a brief overview.

Reference Desk

In this traditional model of reference service, the librarian staffs a desk or counter at a fixed location within the library. The location is usually in a prominent position within the building so that users can easily find it. The materials consulted by the reference librarians—books, indexes, computers, and so on—are usually found adjacent to the librarian for easy access. Users approach the desk when they have a question. The librarian may work with the user at the desk or take the user to the appropriate sources or facilities elsewhere in the building. One distinguishing characteristic of the reference desk model is that the user initiates the transaction, not the librarian.

Roving Reference

In order to provide more proactive reference service, some reference librarians wander through the library looking for users who may have questions. This has the advantage of offering assistance to users where they are already working on their questions, of allowing more hesitant users to be helped, and of eliminating any physical barriers that the desk itself poses to users. The roving method is distinguished by the fact that the librarian is the one who initiates the reference transaction by approaching the potential user. The main problems with roving are that users sometimes are unsure of whether the person who approaches them really is a librarian and that users who do have a question do not know where to go if they want to find the librarian. Roving is used in many libraries, often as an adjunct to the traditional reference desk.

Tiered Reference Service

Tiered service is a model in which staff members with varying levels of skills answer different levels of queries. The theory behind tiered reference is that staff will answer questions that best fit their training. Paraprofessionals or student assistants staff an information desk and answer directional questions and basic questions regarding library holdings, as well as ready-reference questions, freeing up reference librarians to answer all of the research-level questions. When a user comes to the desk with a complex question, that user is referred to the reference librarian on duty, who is often in a private office or another area of the building, away from the busy atmosphere of the information desk. A benefit of tiered reference is that high-level staff is not wasted on routine directional questions. The problem with this method is that many users simply accept the information provided at the first level of service and do not follow through with the referral. This method of reference service is also known as the Brandeis method because it was first popularized at Brandeis University (Massey-Burzio 1992). Although tiered reference is not a widespread service model, it is used in many academic libraries.

Reference by Appointment

A more extreme version of tiered reference is reference service by appointment. In this method, users who wish to consult a reference librarian make an appointment to meet with the librarian. The benefit of this method is that the individual has the full attention of the librarian for an extended period of time. The disadvantage of appointment-based service is that many users do not want to wait for an appointment and simply accept whatever information they can find on their own. Appointment-based reference service is most often used with subject specialists in research and special libraries.

Service to Remote Users

All of the service models mentioned earlier require that the user be physically in the library building in order to receive assistance. In Green's day, that was always the case. Unless a user wrote a letter to the librarian, the only way to make any use of the library was to go in person to the physical library building. In today's environment, advances in telecommunications have made it very easy for people to use just about any library from almost any physical location. Using technologies such as the telephone, e-mail, chat, instant messaging, and social networking tools, individuals can communicate instantly with librarians at a distance. As a result, many libraries have developed special reference services based on those technologies.

Reference service has been available by telephone for many years. This is such a popular service in urban public libraries that such libraries often have separate telephone reference departments handling hundreds or thousands of calls each day. More recently, most libraries have established e-mail accounts or Web forms that allow users to submit questions. Some have initiated virtual reference services using chat, instant messaging, or other software that allows the librarian to communicate over the Web with users. Because of the technical requirements of some of these virtual reference services, they are often established in cooperative ventures with other libraries or with commercial companies. These services succeed when the community members served by the library are frequent users of those communication technologies. Virtual reference is now offered by many libraries of all types and has grown to become a standard service in many libraries.

THE PERSONAL NATURE OF REFERENCE SERVICE

Whether they are physically present or not, people who ask reference librarians for assistance are often at a psychological disadvantage. In today's information environment where information is available everywhere all the time, people feel that if they cannot find what they want, then they have failed. In the user's mind, there is a feeling that they are inadequate because they could not retrieve what they wanted. Having to approach another person for help implies that they have to admit that they are a failure, which some users are not willing to do. Of course, the librarian does not see the user as a failure—but the user does not know that. Because users are not certain how to proceed, they rarely state exactly what they want.

It is very important that people feel comfortable in asking for the reference librarian's help and that each user is treated with dignity and respect. Most of the time, reference librarians are not helping users find specific factual information but are helping the user to identify sources and suggesting search strategies. In this regard, reference service is more like counseling the user than providing answers. Reference service is about developing a relationship between the user and the librarian, not about a specific answer to a question. In order to help librarians work with users, RUSA (2013) has developed a set of guidelines to assist librarians with the behavioral nature of the reference process. This is where the reference interview comes into play.

The reference interview is a set of questioning skills that enables the librarian to work with the user to figure out what the query really is. A good interview is a conversation between the librarian and the user that identifies and clarifies what the user is looking for. In many cases, the user has not thought deeply about the topic, and the librarian helps the user determine the parameters of the information need. By using good interview skills, the librarian can help the user define the information need and come up with some search possibilities to satisfy that need. For more information on the reference interview, see Chapter 3.

Even the most skilled reference librarians have limits to what they can offer. In some subject areas, especially law and medicine, the librarian needs to be very careful about giving advice to users. Even in his original paper, Green (1876, 78) recognized that librarians cannot provide answers to all questions: "There are obvious limits to the assistance which a librarian can undertake to render. Common-sense will dictate them. Thus no librarian would take the responsibility of recommending books to give directions for the treatment of diseases. Nor would he give legal advice nor undertake to instruct applicants in regard to the practical manipulations of the workshop or laboratory." In light of recent events and the current political climate, formerly theoretical ethical issues for reference librarians have become practical realities. Ethical questions such as the provision of information that has the potential to harm society (e.g., how to build a bomb) are now concrete issues that reference librarians encounter in their daily lives. For more on the ethics of reference service, see Chapter 2.

HOW ARE REFERENCE LIBRARIANS DOING?

Reference service has become a standard component of library services, but is it achieving its goals? Are reference librarians really effective in teaching people to use the library, answering their questions, recommending resources, and promoting the library in the community? Evaluation and assessment of reference service present a number of challenges.

On a superficial level, reference staff can easily measure the quantity of reference transactions. Most reference departments keep statistical tallies that indicate how many users ask questions. These data are used to fill annual reports and are an indication of the busy-ness of the reference department. Sometimes these statistical tallies are divided by type of question, by subject field, or by type of user. Many different methods of tracking statistics are used, from simple tick marks to data-tracking software. No matter what method of statistics collection is being used, a disturbing trend has emerged: fewer and fewer reference transactions are occurring each year.

The decline in reference statistics first emerged as a trend in the 1990s and, in the beginning, was reported anecdotally. More detailed analysis of reference statistics indicates that the decline in questions was a reality. A 2006 statistical report from the Association of Research Libraries showed a steady and dramatic decline in reference transactions from the mid-1990s through 2005, with 48 percent fewer questions recorded in 2005 compared with 1991 (Kyrillidou and Young 2006, 8–9). Other studies indicate a similar, although perhaps not as dramatic, decline. Collectively, reference librarians are answering many fewer questions than a decade ago.

Statistics such as this are measures of quantity, but how can one also measure quality? In the 1970s, the idea of unobtrusive testing of reference service was developed. This assessment method involves asking questions of librarians and comparing the answers received with the previously known correct answer. This method was popularized by Peter Hernon and Charles McClure in the 1980s. The results of these studies were disturbing: reference librarians gave correct answers only slightly more than one half of the time. This gave rise to what Hernon and McClure (1986) called the "55 percent rule": whenever a user asks a question, there is a 55 percent chance of getting the correct answer. This is clearly not very good. The results of unobtrusive testing have pointed out areas in which improvement can be made through staff training, collection enhancement, and other techniques to improve the accuracy of responses to factual questions. For more on reference assessment, see Chapter 8.

Because assessment techniques were producing such discouraging results, reference librarians went through a crisis of conscience during the 1980s and 1990s. This era was bracketed by two classic articles on the state of reference service: William Miller's (1984) "What's Wrong with Reference?" and the follow-up 15 years later by David Tyckoson (1999), "What's Right with Reference?" In between these two publications, reference librarians did a lot of collective soul searching. The most critical viewpoint about reference service was expressed by Jerry Campbell (1992), who attempted to shake reference to its conceptual foundation by proposing that libraries essentially eliminate the reference component of library service.

Some of the most prominent efforts to review reference services were the "Rethinking Reference" institutes organized by Anne Lipow (1993). These seminars reexamined each of the roles traditionally played by reference librarians, from the reference desk to instruction to management. Some librarians, including Steve Coffman (1999), looked to the commercial sector for ideas about customer service. Some very innovative new services came out of this period of reflection, most notably the concept of cooperative 24/7 virtual reference. Reference librarians may not only answer fewer questions now than in the past, but also handle more complex questions in more innovative ways.

THE FUTURE OF REFERENCE

What will happen next in reference service? Will this now common role of the library remain a standard feature for years to come, will it fade into history, or will something else take its place? In another century, will reference service be viewed as an aberration of the 20th century, or will it still be a common service offered by libraries to their future communities? Of course, no one can say for sure. Many have made an attempt to predict what reference service will be like in future years, including a panel of experts who were invited to write papers for ALA/RUSA on this topic (Rockman 2003). The best indication of the value of reference service comes from the most important critics, the users. When asked, users consistently rate reference service as one of the most important features of the library. In survey after survey in every type of library, it is clear that users still place a very high value on Samuel Green's "personal intercourse between librarians and readers."

However, the fact that reference is popular now does not necessarily mean it will remain so in the future. Following are three possible scenarios in which the current model of reference service will cease to exist:

1. *Information tools become so easy to use that people no longer need assistance using them.* Although users currently have the ability to find and retrieve more information than at any previous time in human history, they still need help finding the information that they actually want amid the torrent of results. Although new tools do get better and make information easier to get, reference librarians still have a role in teaching people how to use them and in evaluating the results. In addition, the quantity and complexity of information are so vast that people will always need assistance in finding and using that information. Despite the advances in technology and tools, this scenario is extremely unlikely to occur.
2. *Information becomes entirely commercialized, requiring each user to pay for any and all information obtained.* This scenario is slightly more likely than the first, but still highly unlikely. Although information has become more of a commodity in the past few decades, libraries serve as information utilities, purchasing information collectively for the use of all members of their communities. In addition, in a democratic society, federal and state governments will have an obligation to make information produced by government agencies widely available. Even when some information is privatized, other sources are available that will provide similar information at no cost. *Wikipedia* is the prime example of this phenomenon. Although it may not be as good an encyclopedia as *Britannica* or *World Book*, it is the single most heavily used reference source in human history. And it has achieved that status because it is free, instantly available, and up to date. Those factors outweigh the scholarship—and the cost—of commercial encyclopedias. Information that is free is the information that will be used.
3. *Parent communities no longer value libraries and the services that they provide.* Sadly, this is the most likely scenario to occur. A few public libraries have closed or threatened to close in places ranging from Corning, New York, to Salinas, California. Many corporations have already closed their libraries in efforts to reduce costs. Some students (and a few professors) have the idea that everything that they need is on the Web. If reference service is to wither away, it will be due to the decline of the library as a useful institution in the community. For this reason, Green's concept of promoting the value of the library to the community will become ever more important. Marketing and outreach activities are designed to prevent this scenario from occurring.

So in this information age, do we still need reference librarians? The answer is a definite yes. And reference librarians will continue to instruct users, answer questions, recommend sources, and promote the library within the community. The amount of each activity will vary, most likely with answering questions going down and marketing and instruction going up—but the reference librarian of the future will continue to provide direct personal service to members of the community. And the personal nature of that service is what will bring people back to the library, ensuring that it remains a vital institution in the mind of the community.

Box 1.2 Why Do We Still Need Reference Librarians When We Have *Wikipedia* and *Google*?

It is the question that we have all heard before in one variation or another. After all, we live in a world in which every individual has instant access to more information than at any previous time in human history. With any networked device, we can all find information, take classes, make purchases, listen to music, watch videos, get directions, see what our friends are doing, and find out about just about anything. In this connected world, why do we need libraries—or reference librarians?

It is a valid, but naive, question. The popular image of the reference librarian is of someone who dispenses answers. The question assumes that what librarians do is dispense facts. Do you need to find a biography of Einstein? The dates of the Norman invasion? The distance to the closest star? The names of the seven dwarfs? You used to ask a reference librarian. But with the Internet, people no longer need to ask those questions—they can find that information themselves. So they naively make the assumption that reference librarians are no longer needed.

The problem with the question is that it misses the more subtle—and more important—nature of libraries and reference service. Yes, we sometimes give out factual answers. But most of the time, the questions that we get have no single answer. Is global warming real? Does listening to music while asleep improve memory skills when awake? Do diet soft drinks increase a risk of cancer? Are the beaches nicer in the Caribbean or in Hawaii? We help our users with many more of those kinds of questions than we do for factual ones—and we always have. Finding facts is easy—answering complex questions is difficult. And it is for those complex questions that reference librarians are needed.

Reference librarians know how to search and how to evaluate information. We understand how to judge which sources are credible, and we know search techniques that find resources that simple searching cannot. We know how to determine an author's biases. We know how to identify the underlying political aspects of a document. And we never tell anyone else what we helped you with.

But the biggest impact of the reference librarian—and of the library—is on the community.

Some of that value comes from the library collections, which provide access to specific information resources that support the community. Yes, we purchase sources, build guides, and link to sites that meet the needs of members of our specific community. But the real value comes from the librarians who guide users to their information. Reference librarians serve as advisors, recommending the best information sources for each community member. Reference librarians serve as searchers, using specialized skills to retrieve the best information from the overwhelming number of documents available. Reference librarians serve as evaluators, identifying which sources are credible and which are not. And reference librarians serve as instructors, teaching community members skills to make them information independent.

The library and the reference librarian exist to serve the community. By interacting with reference librarians, community members become more information literate. And when a community is composed of members with a higher degree of information literacy, it becomes a better community. Libraries and reference librarians help the community learn and grow. Libraries and reference librarians help the community survive. Communities become better places when libraries and reference librarians are part of them. And that is why we still need reference librarians.

Adapted from Dave Tyckoson (2014)

REFERENCES

Campbell, Jerry D. 1992. "Shaking the Conceptual Foundations of Reference: A Perspective." *Reference Services Review* 20 (Winter): 29–35.

Coffman, Steve. 1999. "Reference as Others Do It." *American Libraries* 30 (May): 54–56.

Dewey, Melvil. 1876. "The Profession." *American Library Journal* 1 (September 30): 5–6.

Galvin, Thomas J. 1978. "Reference Services and Libraries." In *Encyclopedia of Library and Information Science*, vol. 25, edited by Allen Kent and Harold Lancour, 210–26. New York: Marcel Dekker.

Green, Samuel S. 1876. "Personal Relations between Librarians and Readers." *American Library Journal* 1 (November 30): 74–81.

Guild, Reuben A. 1878. "Access to Librarians." *Library Journal* 2 (January–February): 278.

Gutek, Gerald Lee. 1970. *An Historical Introduction to American Education.* New York: Crowell.

Hanson, Eugene R., and Jay E. Daily. 1970. "Catalogs and Cataloging." In *Encyclopedia of Library and Information Science*, vol. 4, edited by Allen Kent and Harold Lancour, 242–305. New York: Marcel Dekker.

Hernon, Peter, and Charles McClure. 1986. "Unobtrusive Reference Testing: The 55 Percent Rule." *Library Journal* 111 (April 15): 37–41.

Kyrillidou, Martha, and Mark Young. 2006. *ARL Statistics 2004–2005.* Association of Research Libraries. http://www.libqual.org/documents/admin/2012/ARL_Stats/2004-05arlstats.pdf.

Lang, Walter, dir. 1957. *Desk Set.* 20th Century Fox.

Lipow, Anne G. 1993. *Rethinking Reference in Academic Libraries.* Berkeley, CA: Library Solutions Institute.

Massey-Burzio, Virginia. 1992. "Reference Encounters of a Different Kind." *The Journal of Academic Librarianship* 18 (November): 276–86.

Miller, William. 1984. "What's Wrong with Reference?" *American Libraries* 15 (May): 303–6, 321–22.

Poole, William F. 1876. "Some Popular Objections to the Public Libraries." *American Library Journal* 1 (November 30): 45–51.

Reference and User Services Association. 2008a. "Definitions of Reference." American Library Association. http://www.ala.org/rusa/resources/guidelines/definitions reference.

Reference and User Services Association. 2008b. "Interlibrary Loan Code for the United States." American Library Association. http://www.ala.org/rusa/resources/guide lines/interlibrary.

Reference and User Services Association. 2013. "Guidelines for Behavioral Performance of Reference and Information Service Providers." American Library Association. http://www.ala.org/rusa/resources/guidelines/guidelinesbehavioral.

Reitz, Joan M. 2004. *Dictionary for Library and Information Science.* Westport, CT: Libraries Unlimited.

Robinson, O.H. 1876. "Librarians and Readers." *American Library Journal* 1 (November 30): 123–24.

Rockman, Ilene, ed. 2003. "Special Issue: The Future of Reference." *Reference Services Review* 31: 7–104.

Rothstein, Samuel. 1953. "The Development of the Concept of Reference Service in American Libraries, 1850–1900." *The Library Quarterly* 21 (January): 1–15.

Rothstein, Samuel. 1961. "Reference Service: The New Dimension in Librarianship." *College & Research Libraries* 22 (January): 11–18.

Rothstein, Samuel. 1972. *The Development of Reference Services through Academic Traditions, Public Library Practice and Special Librarianship.* ACRL Monographs 14. Boston: Gregg Press.

Schlachter, Gail A., ed. 1982. *The Service Imperative for Libraries: Essays in Honor of Margaret E. Monroe.* Littleton, CO: Libraries Unlimited.

Soltow, Lee, and Edward Stevens. 1981. *The Rise of Literacy and the Common School in the United States: A Socioeconomic Analysis to 1870.* Chicago: University of Chicago Press.

Stone, Elizabeth W. 1977. *American Library Development, 1600–1899.* New York: H.W. Wilson.

Trustees of the Public Library of the City of Boston. (1852) 1975. *Upon the Objects to Be Attained by the Establishment of a Public Library,* City Document no. 37. Boston: J.H. Eastburn, Printer. Reprint, G.K. Hall. Citations refer to the Hall edition.

Tyckoson, Dave. 2014. "Talking Shop with Dave Tyckoson: The Importance of Being a Reference Librarian." *Booklist Online.* http://www.booklistonline.com/Talking-Shop-with-Dave-Tyckoson-The-Importance-of-Being-a-Reference-Librarian-Tyckoson-Dave/pid=7112623.

Tyckoson, David A. 1999. "What's Right with Reference?" *American Libraries* 30 (May): 57–63.

U.S. Bureau of the Census. 1975. "Percent Illiterate in the Population, by Race and Nativity: 1870–1969." *Historical Statistics of the United States: Colonial Times to 1970.* Series H: 664–68. Washington, DC: Government Printing Office.

Wyer, James I. 1930. *Reference Work: A Textbook for Students of Library Work and Librarians.* Chicago: American Library Association.

SUGGESTED READINGS

Anderson, Byron, and Paul T. Webb. 2006. *New Directions in Reference.* New York: Haworth.

With 10 chapters written by contributors from academic, public, and special libraries, this collection covers topics relating to the role of the reference librarian, services provided, and new technologies.

Cassel, Kay Ann, and Uma Hiremath. 2013. *Reference and Information Services: An Introduction,* 3rd ed. Chicago: Neal-Schuman.

Based on the premise that reference librarians must commit to an ongoing understanding of the fundamental concepts, essential resources, search techniques, and managerial tasks inherent to reference, this book provides a basic handbook of library reference work today.

Janes, Joseph. 2003. *Introduction to Reference Work in the Digital Age.* New York: Neal-Schuman.

Although the discussion of digital reference comprises much of this book, the focus of this work is more on how we can incorporate digital reference into our already existing reference practices.

Mulac, Carolyn. 2012. *Fundamentals of Reference.* Chicago: American Library Association.

Mulac provides a review of reference sources and services, including policies, standards, and the evaluation of reference services.

Radford, Marie L., and R. David Lankes. 2010. *Reference Renaissance: Current and Future Trends.* New York: Neal-Schuman.

This work contains 22 papers based on presentations given at the two-day Reference Renaissance Conference, with topics ranging from philosophy and foundations to practices, and technology.

Saunders, Laura, Lillian Rozaklis, and Eileen G. Abels. 2015. *Repositioning Reference: New Methods and New Services for a New Age.* Lanham, MD: Rowman & Littlefield.

This work provides textbook-like chapters on reference services in libraries that examine the roles of reference librarians and the technologies and issues that affect them.

Steiner, Sarah K., and M. Leslie Madden. 2008. *The Desk and Beyond: Next Generation Reference Services*. Chicago: Association of College and Research Libraries.

This collection is intended to provide inspiration for potential new digital and physical reference services at academic libraries, with chapters providing introductions to innovative service concepts and an annotated list of sources for additional research.

Thomsen, Elizabeth. 1999. *Rethinking Reference: The Reference Librarian's Practical Guide for Surviving Constant Change*. New York: Neal-Schuman.

Thomsen provides an overview of reference service in modern times, covering all aspects of reference service, including the history of reference, communication skills, answering questions, instruction, and the Internet.

Tyckoson, David A., and John Dove, eds. 2015. *Reimagining Reference in the 21st Century*. West Lafayette, IN: Purdue University Press.

This book examines how library services meet user needs, with perspectives from librarians and publishers, along with a variety of case studies demonstrating current innovations in reference services.

Zabel, Diane, ed. 2011. *Reference Reborn: Breathing New Life into Public Services Librarianship*. Santa Barbara, CA: Libraries Unlimited.

This collection addresses the current issues in reference, from changing users to new roles for reference librarians to the role of technology in reference and the education and training of reference librarians.

Chapter 2

Ethics

Emily J. M. Knox

MAKING ETHICAL JUDGMENTS

Though many equate the job of reference librarians with simply politely answering patrons' questions all day, reference librarians make professional ethical judgments both large and small every day. Even the prosaic act of answering questions can involve ethical dilemmas that are not always readily apparent. Some of the ethical judgments that reference librarians make concern larger social and community issues such as what types of information to include in the collection and how to manage patrons' records, while others center on the questions that an individual patron might ask regarding, for example, health information. These decisions might seem to have little consequence, but even minor choices can have a huge accumulated impact. This chapter is a very short introduction to some of the ethical challenges that a reference librarian might encounter on the job. It is hoped that the information presented here will provide some understanding of the principles that guide contemporary librarianship. However, the chapter is not intended to be comprehensive, and readers are strongly encouraged to explore the additional materials listed at the end of the chapter.

In *Our Enduring Values: Librarianship in the 21st Century*, Michael Gorman defines values as "something that is of deep interest . . . to an individual or a group" (2000, 5). For Gorman, librarianship's enduring values are stewardship, service, intellectual freedom, rationalism, literacy and learning, equity of access to recorded knowledge and information, privacy, and democracy. Ethics, or the application of values is, along with metaphysics, logic, epistemology, and aesthetics, one of the major areas of study in philosophy. Ethics in the workplace is known as applied ethics and has long been the concern of scholars and practitioners of library and information science (LIS). Information ethics and its close and more recent counterpart, computer ethics, have a long history of scholarship. As will be seen later, because LIS is fundamentally concerned with the storage, organization, and circulation of knowledge, ethics in the field is also closely related to epistemology or the study of knowledge. Debates over what sort of information should be provided in libraries; whether or not librarians should protect the privacy of all patrons, regardless of status; and how librarians should weigh their competing obligations to society, the profession, their institutions, and individuals have been part of the landscape of LIS since its inception.

One of the best historical examples of information ethics discourse in LIS concerns the so-called fiction question. Although librarians are now known for their commitment to provide all of their patrons with access to information, this was not always the case. As a profession, librarianship has often wavered between paternalism and autonomy with regard to patrons. Evelyn Geller notes that "the freedom to read as it has come to be perceived, had little to do with the aspirations of the founders of the first public libraries, for the knowledge relevant to their goals was linked to quite different preoccupations. In a period that predated widespread secondary and higher education, the diffusion of knowledge meant certified knowledge of value to elites . . . Libraries were established in opposition not to censorship but to [social] privilege" (1984, 11). Libraries were intended to be places of social assimilation, and in order to fulfill this mission, they were expected to include only "good" reading material in their collections. In the late 19th and early 20th centuries, librarians held what might be called a traditional–modernist view of the effects of new knowledge on individuals and society wherein reading good books would lead to good outcomes while reading bad books would lead to the opposite (Knox 2014a, 11–26). As a result, "immoral" books, especially popular naturalistic fiction, were excluded from libraries.

This attitude slowly started to shift during the early and mid-20th centuries. Geller attributes this to new ideas regarding the library as an educational institution; educational freedom required an open shelf. According to Joyce M. Latham (2009), the Chicago Public Library Board passed the first statement on intellectual freedom in the United States in 1936 followed by the Des Moines Public Library policy, which is often cited by historians as the basis for the American Library Association's (ALA) first code. This growing commitment to intellectual freedom and other liberal information ethics principles was eventually codified in the profession when the ALA adopted its first code of ethics in 1939. In 1950, Leon Carnovsky, a professor of library science at the Graduate Library School at the University of Chicago, wrote that the public library has "no nobler function" than to "put teeth to the principle of free speech" (1950, 25). Over the latter part of the 20th century, librarians solidified their commitment to intellectual freedom primarily because they accepted two ideas. First, they accepted the epistemology of reader-response theory, which holds that different readers have different responses to the same text. Second, they accepted an agnostic–postmodernist view of reading effects wherein it is impossible to know how any one person might be affected by reading a particular text (Knox 2014a). Acceptance of these two premises gave librarians the philosophical foundation to invite any and all ideas into their collections.

Other ethical issues would gain importance in librarianship depending on current events. For example, the development of the copier in the 1960s and 1970s spearheaded the discussion regarding the rights of creators and protecting the rights of patrons to access information. After 9/11 and the passage of the USA PATRIOT Act and again with the revelations regarding federal surveillance of electronic information by Edward Snowden in 2013, protecting patron privacy moved to the fore. However, as will be shown later, even though these events have been the catalyst for various ethical discussions in the literature, librarians have remained committed to providing the best service possible for their patrons while weighing their various obligations to society, the profession, and their institutions.

MAJOR ETHICAL CODES FOR REFERENCE LIBRARIANS

Librarians do not work in a vacuum. As part of the profession, they receive both training and guidance to make ethical judgments in their work. Training happens in workshops, classes, continuing professional education, and on the job. Institutionalized guidance is provided through the codes of ethics and other statements of values and principles by various professional organizations including the ALA, the Association for Information Science and Technology (ASIS&T), and the Medical Library Association (MLA). These statements are the codification of the values of the profession (Knox 2014b).

Although each of these codes of ethics has a slightly different emphasis, they all have several themes in common. All espouse four levels of obligation: to the individual, to the profession, to the organization or institution, and to society (Rubin 2011, 40). The individual level refers to the obligations that the librarian has to each individual patron. The professional level refers to the idea that librarians should promote and adhere to the standards and principles of professional conduct that have been established by the professional organizations that have created the codes of conduct. The institutional level refers to the obligations that librarians have to uphold the mission of their institutions, while the societal level refers to the obligations that librarians have to serve the best interests of their society.

It should not come as a surprise that these obligations can sometimes conflict with each other. This is where training and practice becomes of the utmost importance, as it is the only way that librarians can gain the knowledge to balance the competing obligations enumerated in the codes of ethics discussed here. It should be noted that codes of ethics tend to be reactionary documents; an accumulation of outside events, such as changes in technology or the law, will eventually spur a change in one of the levels of obligation, and the organizations will respond to that change by revising their codes.

The Code of Ethics of the American Library Association (2008)

The code of ethics that is most familiar to members of the information profession is the Code of Ethics of the American Library Association (see the appendix at the end of this chapter), most recently amended in 2008. The ALA originally adopted the code in 1939 in response to the spread of propaganda in the run-up to World War II and has amended it three times since then. It is considered by many to be the most general statement of ethics in librarianship.

ASIS&T (1992)

The ASIS&T approved a set of professional guidelines instead of a code of ethics (see the appendix). As noted in the document, because ASIS&T's membership has a less institutionally focused membership than the ALA's, the guidelines address information professionals who might work outside of traditional information institutions. The guidelines have not been amended since their initial adoption in 1992.

Medical Library Association (MLA) (2010)

The MLA's code of ethics addresses a particular subset of librarians whose work may come in conflict with the expertise of another group of professionals, members of the medical community (see the appendix). It was most recently updated in 2010 and addresses not only librarians in traditional medical settings but also those who work in academic libraries and research organizations. MLA's code specifically addresses the impact that access to knowledge can have on health.

American Association of Law Libraries (AALL) (1999)

The AALL updated its statement of ethical principles in 1999. Like the MLA code, the AALL document (see the appendix) specifically addresses a particular subset of librarians, those who provide legal information services to both the legal profession and the public. Members of the organization work in law firms, academic law libraries, and other legal settings.

Society of American Archivists (SAA) (2011)

Unlike the earlier statements, the SAA's code addresses a group of information professionals whose guiding principles are somewhat different from those found in traditional librarianship. It is divided into both a statement of principles available on the SAA website and a code of ethics (see the appendix) that is intended to be used in tandem. Although access to information is still a guiding principle for archivists, the framework differs in that emphasis is placed on providing access to specific aspects of humankind's cultural heritage.

OTHER ETHICAL PRINCIPLES AND GUIDELINES

Along with the codes of ethics statements discussed earlier, there are other guidelines and statements of principles that librarians use to guide their ethical practice. These vary according to country but are often mentioned when discussing ethics and librarianship.

The Library Bill of Rights (1980)

The Library Bill of Rights (see the appendix) is also a document from the ALA. It is often used as a guiding principle in many different library settings for developing policy along with the Code of Ethics. It differs from codes of ethics in that it addresses the purpose of the library as an institution rather than the various levels of obligations of the librarian. Many libraries also adhere to the Freedom to

Read statement (see the appendix), which enumerates the principles of intellectual freedom. It was first adopted in 1953 and last amended in 2004.

The First and Fourth Amendments to the U.S. Constitution

Many libraries in the United States include a reference to the First Amendment of the U.S. Constitution in their policies along with the Code of Ethics and Library Bill of Rights. The familiar words of the First Amendment (see the appendix) cover many freedoms granted to U.S. citizens. Most importantly for libraries and ethics in librarianship, it prohibits the U.S. government from passing any law that curtails the freedom of speech. As noted earlier, many in American society consider the library to be the embodiment of this amendment in their local communities. The Fourth Amendment (see the appendix), while not often explicitly stated in library policy, protects the privacy of U.S. citizens.

The Universal Declaration of Human Rights

Outside of the United States, many libraries base their policies on the Universal Declaration of Human Rights. This document, which was passed by the General Assembly of the United Nations in 1948, enumerates the rights of all human beings including, for example, the right to a fair hearing by a court (see the appendix). Articles 18 and 19 of the Declaration are most directly related to ethics in librarianship and discuss the right to freedom of thought and to freedom of expression.

The IFLA Code of Ethics

In 2012, the Committee on Freedom of Access to Information and Freedom of Expression of the International Federation of Library Associations and Institutions (IFLA) developed an international code of ethics for information professionals. Like the ALA Code of Ethics, it includes several levels of obligation. Librarians outside of the United States often base their policies on this statement of ethics. There are two versions—one long, one short. The long version discusses each of the enumerated principles in depth and is available on the IFLA website. The short version is found in the chapter appendix.

All of these guidelines and principles can be used as a framework for ethical conduct for reference librarians. In particular, these statements are used in the development of policy in information settings. The process for moving from a statement of guidelines to policy is discussed here.

WRITING ETHICAL POLICY AND COMPETENCIES

Although policy is often considered to be a dry subject, it is the written embodiment of an institution's values. Without thorough written policies, it is impossible to know, for example, what a particular library's stance on privacy is or how staff are expected to treat patrons. In essence, policies transform values into action (Nelson, Garcia, and Public Library Association 2003). They may be dry, but written policy provides guidance for many different stakeholders to understand the purpose of an institution and how it will enact this purpose in everyday transactions. Policies should be current, truthful, and accessible. That is, they must be updated on a regular basis, they should match what is actually done in an institution and should not discuss ideals, and they should be accessible both on the institution's website and, if feasible, in hard copy.

In their book on developing library policy, Sandra S. Nelson and June Garcia note that there are four different elements in policy documents: guidelines, statements, regulations, and procedures (2003, 4). Guidelines are the codes of ethics and other statements of principles listed earlier. They are philosophical in nature and provide a framework for the policy. Guidelines like the ALA Code of Ethics and the Library Bill of Rights are often referenced in the preamble to policies in libraries. Statements describe why an institution provides a particular service. For example, reference departments often include a statement of objectives that addresses the information services the department provides to patrons. Regulations define the policy statement and are what is generally understood as "policy" although, as mentioned earlier, all four elements constitute policy for institutions. Reference services department policies often detail such regulations as the mode of delivery, how much time staff will spend answering a question, and sometimes which types of questions staff will not answer. Finally, procedures are step-by-step instructions for carrying out tasks, such as steps for answering questions using a chat reference client. Taken as a whole, policies provide guidelines for ethical behavior of librarians within a particular institution.

Along with policies, reference librarians are also subject to certain competencies. These are lists of behaviors and best practices that reference librarians should exhibit in their work. Many information organizations have published competencies, including the Special Libraries Association, the MLA, and the SAA. The competencies from the Reference and User Services Association (RUSA), a division of the ALA, serve as guidelines for reference librarians in many different settings and institutions. RUSA's competencies discuss five areas: access, knowledge base, marketing/awareness/informing, collaboration, and evaluation and assessment of resources and services. These competencies specifically refer to behaviors that a librarian must be able to exhibit in order to succeed at his or her job and are available in full on the RUSA website (Reference and User Services Association 2003). It is important to note that reference librarians are not expected to have these skills on their first day of work; instead they are expected to apply the knowledge they have learned in their coursework and should be open to "learning on the job" and further continuing education.

MAJOR ETHICAL AREAS AND ISSUES

Right of Access and Protecting Individuals and Society from Harm

Few areas of ethics are more at the forefront of reference librarianship than protecting the right of individuals to access information and protecting both individuals and society from harm. Note that many of the codes of ethics as well as the RUSA competencies have some reference to access to information. For example, the ALA Code of Ethics states that "we are members of a profession explicitly committed to intellectual freedom and the freedom of access to information" (see the appendix). Providing this access can take many different forms, and reference librarians are often the key to matching an information seeker with the material that meets his or her information need. Richard Rubin notes that librarians are often seen as neutral arbiters of information. That is, when someone asks any question, the ALA Code of Ethics, Library Bill of Rights, and the Freedom to Read statement hold that librarians must answer the question to the best of their ability and "resist all efforts to censor library resources" (American Library Association 2008). However, it is important to note that this is not, in fact, a neutral stand. By answering any and all questions, reference librarians take a stand, one that holds that all questions should be answered (Jensen 2008). Instead of being neutral, librarians must define what it means to provide access to information for all and navigate the various tensions between providing information and serving both individual and societal interests.

These tensions manifest themselves in several ways. First, one of the most persistent situations focuses on the harm that the questioner might cause to himself or herself. The case study in Box 2.1 focuses on a patron who is giving signs of being depressed and asks for a book about suicide. Other questions that involve harm to the individual include when patrons ask about information that concerns drug use or for materials that include extreme violence. According to the Code of Ethics and the Library Bill of Rights, no judgments should be made regarding the appropriateness of these materials for any individual (see the appendix). As discussed earlier, because it is impossible to know how any one person might react to information, it is best to err on the side of providing access.

Box 2.1 Activity: To Be or Not to Be

Melissa, a 15-year-old, comes into the Jonestown Public Library from time to time. None of the reference librarians in the library know her well, but when Melissa passes the desk, she usually says "hi" as she goes by to any staff member who is stationed there. She is not a behavioral problem, although rarely a staff member may have to tell her to keep her voice down. The reference staff are aware that Melissa has had "some problems," and there is a rumor that last year she tried to hurt herself.

Melissa approaches the reference librarian. She looks like she has been crying; her eyes are a little red, and her face is slightly puffy. In a slightly shaky voice, she asks, "I've been looking for a book, but it's not on the shelf. It's called *Final Exit*. Can you tell me where it is?" You know that *Final Exit* is a book on how to commit suicide. You also know that it has just been returned and is on a cart ready for reshelving.

Questions for Reflection and Discussion:

1. Should the librarian retrieve the book from the cart and give it to Melissa?
2. Should any other actions be taken?
3. Exactly what would you say to Melissa?
4. How would your reaction differ if you are a state-designated mandatory reporter?

(Based on a scenario developed by Richard Rubin 2011)

Another tension concerns the issue of how much and what kinds of information should be available to patrons of the library, as illustrated by the case study in Box 2.2. This has become particularly salient with the rise in the ubiquity of the Internet in everyday life. Almost all libraries provide some sort of patron access to the Internet, and these computers often become a contested space in the library, especially those that provide services to children and young adults. In 2000, the U.S. Congress passed the Children's Internet Protection Act and held that institutions that use the E-rate to provide access to the Internet (usually public libraries and schools) must filter the Internet for information that might cause harm to children. The Supreme Court held that this is legal as long as adults are permitted to ask for the filters to be removed. Internet filters are clearly a violation of the ALA Code of Ethics; however, there are often good reasons for libraries to use them (Caldwell-Stone 2013). For example, libraries may be unable to afford to provide Internet access to their patrons without using E-rate. In this case, providing even limited access to resources on the Internet might outweigh the restrictions that filters impose on patrons.

With regard to harming society, one of the most often debated situations concerns patrons asking for information about explosives and other massively destructive materials. In 1976, Robert Hauptman went to 13 different reference desks and asked for information on how to build a bomb. All of the librarians gave him the information (Hauptman 1976). Hauptman was quite horrified by this and stated in an interview from 2008 that he was "aghast" that they helped him (Buchanan 2008, 252). The Hauptman case is the embodiment of the tensions that exist between protecting the needs of the individual while also protecting the needs of society. Most librarians, strictly following the Code of Ethics, would choose to answer patrons' questions even if the questions seem suspect. Librarians hold that since it is impossible to know what any one person might do with the information, one must err on the side of protecting individual rights (Knox 2014a).

Box 2.2 Activity: "Trashy" Books in the School Library

Mrs. Smith, a parent of one of the ninth graders at your affluent suburban public high school, approaches the reference desk holding a copy of Lauren Myracle's *yolo*. Her daughter brought the book home last night, and Mrs. Smith is appalled that the school library would include such "poorly written trash." The book is written in a series of texts and chat messages and employs "text speech." You know that all of the books in Myracle's Internet Girls series circulate well.

Questions for Reflection and Discussion:

1. How would you respond to Mrs. Smith?
2. What resources would you use to support your response?
3. What other actions might be taken?

Equality of Access

Another ethical issue that affects both individuals and society concerns equality of access to information. It should also be noted that there is a difference between equity and equality of access. Equality means that all things are equal, that all libraries have the same services, while equity means the level of service is equal. As Betty J. Turock and Gustav W. Friedrich note, "Equity adds the denotation of fairness, impartiality, freedom from favoritism, and justice" (Turock and Friedrich 2009, 24).

One of the most important issues regarding equality of access in the 21st century is the digital divide. The digital divide (or, more accurately digital divides) is a complex issue that can be understood on many different levels. For example, there is a divide among nations (how many citizens have access to the Web) and also among different types of communities within a nation (which communities lack broadband access). There have been many attempts to close the digital divide across the world. For example, UNESCO is highly involved in programs to create inclusive knowledge societies, particularly through the implementation of the goals of the World Summit on the Information Society held in 2005 (Souter 2010). In the United States, the American Recovery and Reinvestment Act of 2009 included provisions for expanding broadband access across the country (National Telecommunications and Information Administration). Libraries are an integral part of bridging access divides in the digital age and provide information for patrons in many different forms. In some respects, the presence of a library as an institution within a community can help alleviate this divide and facilitate equality of access. Noninformation professionals often focus on books in library collections, but libraries also provide information through many types of media (magazines, newspapers, the Internet) and for many different purposes. Technology in libraries also supports patrons engaged in all aspects of the information cycle including creation, for example, using a word processor to write a novel, and interaction, for example, providing access to e-mail, job sites, and coursework.

Another aspect of equality of access concerns levels of service that libraries provide. Should libraries provide an equal level of service to all individuals regardless of status? This is often harder to do than it might seem, as the library itself has its own interests. Discussions regarding whether or not public libraries should provide services for fees or the types of services that should be given to children are always a part of the LIS landscape. What is most important for reference librarians is to consider who or what benefits when policies are written that are onerous on the poor or deprive children from accessing particular types of information. The answers to these questions are not always straightforward, but they are important to keep in mind when developing ethical policies and guidelines for information institutions.

Copyright Issues

Copyright issues are ubiquitous in the information profession. Article IV of the ALA Code of Ethics states that librarians must "respect intellectual property rights and advocate balance between the interests of information users and rights holders" (American Library Association 2008). This has proven a thorny area in the digital age. Now that most serials and many books are available electronically, previous methods of balancing between rights of users and creators are proving untenable. For many years, the fair use guidelines of the 1976 copyright law found in Title 17 of the U.S. Code and Title 37 of the Code of Federal Regulations have been seen as out of date. Seven different sections of the copyright code apply to libraries. One is the right of first sale, which was recently under scrutiny by the U.S. Supreme Court in the *Kirtsaeng v. John Wiley & Sons, Inc.* case. Another is Section 108, which describes how librarians may copy a work for use in their collections. Fair use, found in Section 107, is an exception to copyright, meaning that although the right to copy remains with the owner, when material is used under "fair use," this is an exception to these laws.

It is imperative that reference librarians understand Section 107 and "fair use." Although the vagaries of copyright law and fair use are too complex to go into detail here, it is important to at least be aware that there are four factors that must be considered whenever one is judging whether or not materials can be used under the fair use guidelines. These factors are purpose, nature, amount, and effect. Purpose refers to how the entity that wants the material will use it, including whether it is for noncommercial or educational use. Nature refers to the type of work. How the law considers books, images, videos, and journal articles differs. Amount refers to how much of a particular work the entity wants to use. Obviously, there are different considerations for longer works such as books or movies as opposed to images or articles. Effect concerns the effect that using the copyrighted work will have on market value of the work. Intellectual property law is complex, and reference librarians are not expected to be attorneys; thus, there are guidelines, such as the National Commission on New Technological Uses of Copyrighted Works, that librarians follow to guide the copying and sharing of works.

Confidentiality, Privacy, and Security

Concerns with confidentiality, privacy, and security have long been of interest to librarians. The 1939 ALA Code of Ethics stated that "it is the librarian's obligation to treat as confidential any private information obtained through contact with library patrons." In the United States, privacy is protected in the First and Fourth Amendments to the U.S. Constitution (see the appendix). With the rise of the Internet, the passage of the USA PATRIOT Act in the wake of 9/11, and the revelations of Edward Snowden regarding the National Security Administration's surveillance of private citizens, this area of ethics has become even more salient (Greenwald and MacAskill 2013).

Note that there is a difference between privacy and confidentiality. Privacy refers to the person, while confidentiality refers to data. That is, a librarian keeps facts about a person such as their address and birthdate private, but records of the books that they read are confidential. Before the digital age, librarians were primarily concerned with keeping patrons' records confidential. In *Library Ethics*, Jean Preer discusses privacy as the paradox of access. In order to know what someone needs, they must be willing to open up about their need (2008, 183).

Reference librarians protect their patrons' privacy in many different ways. Chat reference is conducted anonymously, and any personal information that is shared by the patron should be purged from the records. However, note that these records are often kept on nonlibrary servers, which may lead to additional privacy issues. Virtual reference is discussed in more detail in Chapter 6. Librarians do not discuss individuals' questions with other people including their fellow librarians in ways that will identify the patron. For example, when sending an e-mail to colleagues for help on a question, the e-mail writer usually writes, "a patron asked. . . ." This is often done automatically, but this is an important aspect of protecting a patron's privacy. With the revelations by Snowden and the ubiquity of sharing data online, it often falls to frontline librarians to inform patrons of what it means to agree to the terms of service for social media sites like Facebook or Twitter or Internet services and product corporations like *Google*.

The issues involved in confidentiality, privacy, and security explore the tensions between information professionals' obligations to individuals and to society. In this area, librarians tend to lean on the side of protecting individuals from harm by society. Daniel Solove (2007) argues that privacy is made up of a plurality of things that mitigate the power relationship between the individual and the modern state. Although in common parlance privacy is about concealment and hiding things, Solove argues that privacy is actually about power and it is important for reference librarians to both know and inform their patrons of what is happening with their data.

Box 2.3 Activity: A Case of Honor or Privacy

Mary Smith is a reference librarian at the Martinville College Library, a small liberal arts college. Recently, a college student came into the library and requested help on the Internet terminal. The student indicated she was looking for help on preparing a term paper on James Joyce because she had to do one in Dr. Jones's introductory literature class. Mary knows Dr. Jones very well and considers her a good friend.

The student brought with her the name of a particular website, and she wanted to know how to find it. Mary recognized the name of the site because it had become popular among some of the students. It was a site that provided access to copies of term papers prepared by students around the country.

Mary took the student to the terminal and briefly instructed her regarding how to use the search engines to locate the website. The student stayed at the terminal for about 20 minutes. The last 10 minutes were spent printing off a fairly lengthy document. Just before the student left, she approached the desk and thanked Mary for the help. Mary could see that she had a copy of a paper in her hand.

Not long after the student left, Mary went to the terminal and saw that the student had printed off a term paper on James Joyce titled "James Joyce: Portrait of an Artist as an Old Man." The paper was authored by Patricia Van Doren. Mary felt some pangs of guilt. A clear plagiarism policy at the college says that students and staff must report evidence of plagiarism. Mary wondered whether she should say anything, but she didn't.

Several weeks later, Dr. Jones came into the library to talk to Mary about some term papers that worried her. The names of the students had been removed. Dr. Jones pointed out that the style and quality of writing far exceeded the students' regular performances, and she feared that someone had written their papers for them. The papers were finely written, and she simply didn't think that these students could do that kind of work. Dr. Jones expressed frustration that she couldn't really do much about it. Mary saw that one of the papers was the one by Van Doren that a student printed out earlier in the semester.

Questions for Reflection and Discussion:

1. What are Mary's ethical obligations?
2. What, if anything, should Mary say to the student?
3. What, if anything, should Mary say to Dr. Jones?
4. Should she mention the student specifically?
5. Should she mention the term paper database without mentioning the student?
6. If Dr. Jones mentions that she had heard of term paper databases and asks Mary if she knew whether they were being used by her students, what should Mary say?

CONCLUSION

Earlier discussions have probably raised more questions for the reader than they answered. In some respects, this is always true of ethical discussions. Making ethical choices pervades every aspect of library service and is a continually moving target. New technologies and service models change some aspects of how the various levels of obligations mentioned in the information codes of ethics are weighed against one another. Although learning to make ethical decisions and keeping up with changes in the field can seem daunting, it is important to remember that, as discussed earlier, everyone makes ethical decisions every day. In a profession dedicated to acting in an ethical manner, LIS provides many different resources and tools to aid librarians in making these decisions in their professional lives.

REFERENCES

American Library Association. 2004. "Freedom to Read Statement." http://www.ala.org/advocacy/intfreedom/statementspols/freedomreadstatement.

American Library Association. 2008. "Code of Ethics." http://www.ifmanual.org/codeethics.

Buchanan, Elizabeth. 2008. "On Theory, Practice, and Responsibilities: A Conversation with Robert Hauptman." *Library & Information Science Research* 30 (4): 250–56.

Caldwell-Stone, Deborah. 2013. "Filtering and the First Amendment." *American Libraries* 44 (3/4): 58–61.

Carnovsky, Leon. 1950. "The Obligations and Responsibilities of the Librarian Concerning Censorship." *The Library Quarterly* 20 (1): 21–32.

Geller, Evelyn. 1984. *Forbidden Books in American Public Libraries, 1876–1939: A Study in Cultural Change*. Westport, CT: Greenwood.

Gorman, Michael. 2000. *Our Enduring Values: Librarianship in the 21st Century*. Chicago: American Library Association.

Greenwald, Glenn, and Ewen MacAskill. 2013. "NSA Prism Program Taps in to User Data of Apple, Google and Others." *The Guardian*. June 7. http://www.theguardian.com/world/2013/jun/06/us-tech-giants-nsa-data.

Hauptman, Robert. 1976. "Professionalism or Culpability? An Experiment in Ethics." *Wilson Library Bulletin* 50 (8): 626–27.

Jensen, Robert. 2008. "Myth of the Neutral Professional." In *Questioning Library Neutrality*, edited by Alison Lewis, 89–96. Duluth, MN: Library Juice.

Knox, Emily J. M. 2014a. "Intellectual Freedom and the Agnostic-Postmodern View of Reading Effects." *Library Trends* 63 (1): 11–26.

Knox, Emily J. M. 2014b. "Supporting Intellectual Freedom: Symbolic Capital and Practical Philosophy in Librarianship." *The Library Quarterly* 84 (1): 1–14.

Latham, Joyce M. 2009. "Wheat and Chaff: Carl Roden, Abe Korman, and the Definitions of Intellectual Freedom in the Chicago Public Library." *Libraries & the Cultural Record* 44 (3): 279–98.

National Telecommunications and Information Administration. "BroadbandUSA." Accessed June 10, 2015. http://www2.ntia.doc.gov/about.

Nelson, Sandra S., June Garcia, and Public Library Association. 2003. *Creating Policies for Results: From Chaos to Clarity*. Chicago: American Library Association.
Preer, Jean. 2008. *Library Ethics*. Westport, CT: Libraries Unlimited.
Reference and User Services Association. 2003. "Professional Competencies for Reference and User Services Librarians." American Library Association. http://www.ala.org/rusa/resources/guidelines/professional.
Rubin, Richard E. 2011. "Ethical Aspects of Reference Services." In *Reference and Information Services: An Introduction*, edited by Richard E. Bopp and Linda C. Smith, 4th ed., 29–56. Santa Barbara, CA: Libraries Unlimited.
Solove, Daniel J. 2007. "'I've Got Nothing to Hide' and Other Misunderstandings of Privacy." *San Diego Law Review* 44: 745–72.
Souter, David. 2010. "Towards Inclusive Knowledge Societies: A Review of UNESCO's Action in Implementing the WSIS Outcomes." UNESCO. http://www.unesco.org/new/en/communication-and-information/resources/publications-and-communication-materials/publications/full-list/towards-inclusive-knowledge-societies-a-review-of-unescos-action-in-implementing-the-wsis-outcomes/.
Turock, Betty J., and Gustav W. Friedrich. 2009. "Access in a Digital Age." In *Encyclopedia of Library and Information Sciences*, 3rd ed., 23–33. New York: Taylor & Francis.

SUGGESTED READINGS

American Library Association. 2015. *Intellectual Freedom Manual*, 9th ed. Chicago: American Library Association.

This handbook provides a comprehensive overview of the American Library Association's official positions on many issues related to intellectual freedom. The Code of Ethics, Library Bill of Rights, and the Freedom to Read Statement as well as the myriad interpretations of each are included. The 9th edition includes 17 new or updated policy statements. Historical documents are now published in a separate supplement.

Besnoy, Amy L., ed. 2009. *Ethics and Integrity in Libraries*. New York: Routledge.

This anthology of articles from the *Journal of Library Administration* provides a wide range of views on various aspects of information ethics in libraries including fair use law and plagiarism. It is particularly concerned with maintaining the integrity of the library as an institution that provides access to information for all.

Buchanan, Elizabeth A., Kathrine A. Henderson, and Robert Hauptman. 2009. *Case Studies in Library and Information Science Ethics*. Jefferson, NC: McFarland.

Case Studies includes both theoretical and practical insight into ethical issues in LIS. It has more than 100 case studies and discussion questions in the areas of intellectual freedom, privacy, intellectual property, professional ethics, and intercultural information ethics.

Fallis, Don. 2007. "Information Ethics for Twenty-first Century Library Professionals." *Library Hi Tech* 25 (1): 23–36.

This article provides general background on various ethical concepts in the information professions. Fallis argues that information ethics is primarily concerned with providing access to information. He notes that codes of ethics are valuable resources for librarians and other information professionals even though their meaning is sometimes unclear, and they do not always provide guidance when there are conflicts among obligations.

Hauptman, Robert. 2002. *Ethics and Librarianship*. Jefferson, NC: McFarland.
Hauptman, who conducted the famous research question experiment described in the chapter, offers a normative view of professional ethics in librarianship. The monograph covers many topics including intellectual freedom, technical and access services, and reference.

International Review of Information Ethics. Stuttgart, Germany: International Center for Information Ethics, 2004—. Semiannual. http://www.i-r-i-e.net/index.htm.
The *International Review of Information Ethics* is the official journal of the International Center for Information Ethics. It is primarily focused on information technology and ethics in an international context. The journal is available free of charge online, and articles may be published in English, French, German, Portuguese, and Spanish.

Isaacson, David. 2004. "Is the Correct Answer the Right One?" *Journal of Information Ethics* 13 (1): 14–18.
This article deftly explores how one might resolve dilemmas that occur when a patron is provided with the correct answer but is not happy with it.

Journal of Information Ethics. Edited by Robert Hauptman. Jefferson, NC: McFarland, 1992–. Semiannual.
This journal, published in the United States, focuses on many different ethical issues including privacy, human rights, copyright, and professional values.

Moore, Adam D., ed. 2005. *Information Ethics: Privacy, Property, and Power*. Seattle: University of Washington.
This book provides a short introduction to ethical theory and several short frameworks for analyzing ethical issues including excerpts from John Stuart Mill's *Utilitarianism* and Immanuel Kant's *The Metaphysics of Morals*. It then covers specific areas of information ethics including intellectual property, privacy, and freedom of speech.

Preer, Jean. 2008. *Library Ethics*. Westport, CT: Libraries Unlimited.
Preer's text endeavors to provide an ethical framework for decision making that endures even when the values of librarianship are reexamined. It offers many historical cases to examine the issues of access, conflicts of interest, and confidentiality.

Reference and User Services Association. 2003. "Professional Competencies for Reference and User Services Librarians." American Library Association. http://www.ala.org/rusa/resources/guidelines/professional.
RUSA's guidelines offer standards for professional behavior in reference services. The guidelines have implications for ethics and cover areas such as access, marketing, and evaluation. Other organizations such as ASIS&T, AALL, MLA, and SAA offer guidelines for educational objectives in their respective areas. These are easily obtained online and also provide guidance for ethical behavior.

Rubin, Richard E., and Thomas J. Froehlich. "Ethical Aspects of Library and Information Science." In *Encyclopedia of Library and Information Sciences*, 3rd ed., 1743–57. New York: Taylor & Francis.
Rubin and Froehlich's article provides an excellent introduction to ethics in LIS. It takes the perspective that information professionals operate as both members of staff for a particular institution and members of a profession. The article covers privacy, selection, reference, copyright, administrative, access, technology-related, conflicting loyalties, and societal issues.

Solove, Daniel J. 2007. "'I've Got Nothing to Hide' and Other Misunderstandings of Privacy." *San Diego Law Review* 44: 745–72.
Solove offers a theory of privacy as a plurality of things that mitigate the power relationships between people and the modern state.

Zaïane, Jane Robertson. 2011. "Global Information Ethics in LIS." *Journal of Information Ethics* 20 (2): 25–41.

This article compares and contrasts 10 national codes of ethics. The author found nine patterns including references to human rights, copyright, and privacy but not much mention of technology.

Appendix
Code of Ethics of the American Library Association

As members of the American Library Association, we recognize the importance of codifying and making known to the profession and to the general public the ethical principles that guide the work of librarians, other professionals providing information services, library trustees and library staffs.

Ethical dilemmas occur when values are in conflict. The American Library Association Code of Ethics states the values to which we are committed, and embodies the ethical responsibilities of the profession in this changing information environment.

We significantly influence or control the selection, organization, preservation, and dissemination of information. In a political system grounded in an informed citizenry, we are members of a profession explicitly committed to intellectual freedom and the freedom of access to information. We have a special obligation to ensure the free flow of information and ideas to present and future generations.

The principles of this Code are expressed in broad statements to guide ethical decision making. These statements provide a framework; they cannot and do not dictate conduct to cover particular situations.

Adopted at the 1939 Midwinter Meeting by the ALA Council; amended June 30, 1981; June 28, 1995; and January 22, 2008.

I. We provide the highest level of service to all library users through appropriate and usefully organized resources; equitable service policies; equitable access; and accurate, unbiased, and courteous responses to all requests.

II. We uphold the principles of intellectual freedom and resist all efforts to censor library resources.

III. We protect each library user's right to privacy and confidentiality with respect to information sought or received and resources consulted, borrowed, acquired or transmitted.

IV. We respect intellectual property rights and advocate balance between the interests of information users and rights holders.

V. We treat co-workers and other colleagues with respect, fairness, and good faith, and advocate conditions of employment that safeguard the rights and welfare of all employees of our institutions.

VI. We do not advance private interests at the expense of library users, colleagues, or our employing institutions.

VII. We distinguish between our personal convictions and professional duties and do not allow our personal beliefs to interfere with fair representation of the aims of our institutions or the provision of access to their information resources.

VIII. We strive for excellence in the profession by maintaining and enhancing our own knowledge and skills, by encouraging the professional development of co-workers, and by fostering the aspirations of potential members of the profession.

ASIS&T Professional Guidelines

Dedicated to the Memory of Diana Woodward

ASIS&T recognizes the plurality of uses and users of information technologies, services, systems and products as well as the diversity of goals or objectives, sometimes conflicting, among producers, vendors, mediators, and users of information systems.

ASIS&T urges its members to be ever aware of the social, economic, cultural, and political impacts of their actions or inaction.

ASIS&T members have obligations to employers, clients, and system users, to the profession, and to society, to use judgement and discretion in making choices, providing equitable service, and in defending the rights of open inquiry.

RESPONSIBILITIES TO EMPLOYERS/CLIENTS/SYSTEM USERS

- To act faithfully for their employers or clients in professional matters
- To uphold each user's, provider's, or employer's right to privacy and confidentiality and
- To respect whatever proprietary rights belong to them, by limiting access to, providing proper security for and ensuring proper disposal of data about clients, patrons or users.
- To treat all persons fairly.

Adopted 5/30/92

RESPONSIBILITY TO THE PROFESSION

To truthfully represent themselves and the information systems which they utilize or which they represent, by

- not knowingly making false statements or providing erroneous or misleading information
- informing their employers, clients or sponsors of any circumstances that create a conflict of interest
- not using their position beyond their authorized limits or by not using their credentials to misrepresent themselves
- following and promoting standards of conduct in accord with the best current practices
- undertaking their research conscientiously, in gathering, tabulating or interpreting data; in following proper approval procedures for subjects; and in producing or disseminating their research results
- pursuing ongoing professional development and encouraging and assisting colleagues and others to do the same
- adhering to principles of due process and equality of opportunity.

RESPONSIBILITY TO SOCIETY

To improve the information systems with which they work or which they represent, to the best of their means and abilities by

- providing the most reliable and accurate information and acknowledging the credibility of the sources as known or unknown
- resisting all forms of censorship, inappropriate selection and acquisitions policies, and biases in information selection, provision and dissemination
- making known any biases, errors and inaccuracies found to exist and striving to correct those which can be remedied.

To promote open and equal access to information, within the scope permitted by their organizations or work, and to resist procedures that promote unlawful discriminatory practices in access to and provision of information, by

- seeking to extend public awareness and appreciation of information availability and provision as well as the role of information professionals in providing such information
- freely reporting, publishing or disseminating information subject to legal and proprietary restraints of producers, vendors and employers, and the best interests of their employers or clients.

Information professionals shall engage in principled conduct whether on their own behalf or at the request of employers, colleagues, clients, agencies or the profession.

MLA Code of Ethics for Health Sciences Librarianship

GOALS AND PRINCIPLES FOR ETHICAL CONDUCT

The health sciences librarian believes that knowledge is the *sine qua non* of informed decisions in health care, education, and research, and the health sciences librarian serves society, clients, and the institution by working to ensure that informed decisions can be made. The principles of this code are expressed in broad statements to guide ethical decision making. These statements provide a framework; they cannot and do not dictate conduct to cover particular situations.

SOCIETY

- The health sciences librarian promotes access to health information for all and creates and maintains conditions of freedom of inquiry, thought, and expression that facilitate informed health care decisions.

CLIENTS

- The health sciences librarian works without prejudice to meet the client's information needs.

- The health sciences librarian respects the privacy of clients and protects the confidentiality of the client relationship.
- The health sciences librarian ensures that the best available information is provided to the client.

INSTITUTION

- The health sciences librarian provides leadership and expertise in the design, development, and ethical management of knowledge-based information systems that meet the information needs and obligations of the institution.

PROFESSION

- The health sciences librarian advances and upholds the philosophy and ideals of the profession.
- The health sciences librarian advocates and advances the knowledge and standards of the profession.
- The health sciences librarian conducts all professional relationships with courtesy and respect.
- The health sciences librarian maintains high standards of professional integrity.

SELF

- The health sciences librarian assumes personal responsibility for developing and maintaining professional excellence.
- The health sciences librarian shall be alert to and adhere to his or her institution's code of ethics and its conflict of interest, disclosure, and gift policies.

AALL Ethical Principles

Approved by the AALL membership, April 5, 1999

Preamble

When individuals have ready access to legal information, they can participate fully in the affairs of their government. By collecting, organizing, preserving, and retrieving legal information, the members of the American Association of Law Libraries enable people to make this ideal of democracy a reality.

Legal information professionals have an obligation to satisfy the needs, to promote the interests and to respect the values of their clientele. Law firms, corporations, academic and governmental institutions and the general public have legal information needs that are best addressed by professionals committed to the belief that serving these information needs is a noble calling and that fostering the equal participation of diverse people in library services underscores one of our basic tenets, open access to information for all individuals.

Service

We promote open and effective access to legal and related information. Further we recognize the need to establish methods of preserving, maintaining and retrieving legal information in many different forms.

We uphold a duty to our clientele to develop service policies that respect confidentiality and privacy.

We provide zealous service using the most appropriate resources and implementing programs consistent with our institution's mission and goals.

We acknowledge the limits on service imposed by our institutions and by the duty to avoid the unauthorized practice of law.

Business Relationships

We promote fair and ethical trade practices.

We have a duty to avoid situations in which personal interests might be served or significant benefits gained at the expense of library users, colleagues, or our employing institutions.

We strive to obtain the maximum value for our institution's fiscal resources, while at the same time making judicious, analytical and rational use of our institution's information resources.

Professional Responsibilities

We relate to our colleagues with respect and in a spirit of cooperation.

We distinguish between our personal convictions and professional duties and do not allow our personal beliefs to interfere with the service we provide.

We recognize and respect the rights of the owner and the user of intellectual property.

We strive for excellence in the profession by maintaining and enhancing our own knowledge and skills, by encouraging the professional development of co-workers, and by fostering the aspirations of potential members of the profession.

Code of Ethics for Archivists

INTRODUCTION

Statements of ethics emerge from the core values of a profession. The Core Values of Archivists and the Code of Ethics for Archivists are intended to be used together to guide archivists, as well as to inform those who work with archivists, in shaping expectations for professional engagement. The former is a statement of what archivists believe; the latter is a Code of Ethics for Archivists.

(*Approved by the SAA Council February 2005; revised January 2012.*)

Archives are created by a wide array of groups and provide evidence of the full range of human experience. Archivists endeavor to ensure that those materials, entrusted to their care, will be accessible over time as evidence of human activity and social organization. Archivists embrace principles that foster the transparency of their actions and that inspire confidence in the profession. A distinct body of ethical norms helps archivists navigate the complex situations and issues that can arise in the course of their work.

The Society of American Archivists is a membership organization comprising individuals and organizations dedicated to the selection, care, preservation, and administration of historical and documentary records of enduring value for the benefit of current and future generations.

The Society endorses this Code of Ethics for Archivists as principles of the profession. This Code should be read in conjunction with SAA's "Core Values of Archivists." Together they provide guidance to archivists and increase awareness of ethical concerns among archivists, their colleagues, and the rest of society. As advocates for documentary collections and cultural objects under their care, archivists aspire to carry out their professional activities with the highest standard of professional conduct. The behaviors and characteristics outlined in this Code of Ethics should serve as aspirational principles for archivists to consider as they strive to create trusted archival institutions.

PROFESSIONAL RELATIONSHIPS

Archivists cooperate and collaborate with other archivists, and respect them and their institutions' missions and collecting policies. In their professional relationships with donors, records creators, users, and colleagues, archivists are honest, fair, collegial, and equitable.

JUDGMENT

Archivists exercise professional judgment in appraising, acquiring, and processing materials to ensure the preservation, authenticity, diversity, and lasting cultural and historical value of their collections. Archivists should carefully document their collections-related decisions and activities to make their role in the selection, retention, or creation of the historical record transparent to their institutions, donors, and users. Archivists are encouraged to consult with colleagues, relevant professionals, and communities of interest to ensure that diverse perspectives inform their actions and decisions.

AUTHENTICITY

Archivists ensure the authenticity and continuing usability of records in their care. They document and protect the unique archival characteristics of records and strive to protect the records' intellectual and physical integrity from tampering or corruption. Archivists may not willfully alter, manipulate, or destroy data or records to conceal facts or distort evidence. They thoroughly document any actions that may cause changes to the records in their care or raise questions about the records' authenticity.

SECURITY AND PROTECTION

Archivists protect all documentary materials for which they are responsible. They take steps to minimize the natural physical deterioration of records and implement specific security policies to protect digital records. Archivists guard all records against accidental damage, vandalism, and theft and have well-formulated plans in place to respond to any disasters that may threaten records. Archivists cooperate actively with colleagues and law enforcement agencies to apprehend and prosecute vandals and thieves.

ACCESS AND USE

Recognizing that use is the fundamental reason for keeping archives, archivists actively promote open and equitable access to the records in their care within the context of their institutions' missions and their intended user groups. They minimize restrictions and maximize ease of access. They facilitate the continuing accessibility and intelligibility of archival materials in all formats. Archivists formulate and disseminate institutional access policies along with strategies that encourage responsible use. They work with donors and originating agencies to ensure that any restrictions are appropriate, well-documented, and equitably enforced. When repositories require restrictions to protect confidential and proprietary information, such restrictions should be implemented in an impartial manner. In all questions of access, archivists seek practical solutions that balance competing principles and interests.

PRIVACY

Archivists recognize that privacy is sanctioned by law. They establish procedures and policies to protect the interests of the donors, individuals, groups, and institutions whose public and private lives and activities are recorded in their holdings. As appropriate, archivists place access restrictions on collections to ensure that privacy and confidentiality are maintained, particularly for individuals and groups who have no voice or role in collections' creation, retention, or public use. Archivists promote the respectful use of culturally sensitive materials in their care by encouraging researchers to consult with communities of origin, recognizing that privacy has both legal and cultural dimensions. Archivists respect all users' rights to privacy by maintaining the confidentiality of their research and protecting any personal information collected about the users in accordance with their institutions' policies.

TRUST

Archivists should not take unfair advantage of their privileged access to and control of historical records and documentary materials. They execute their work knowing that they must ensure proper custody for the documents and records entrusted to them. Archivists should demonstrate professional integrity and avoid potential conflicts of interest. They strive to balance the sometimes-competing interests of all stakeholders.

Library Bill of Rights

The American Library Association affirms that all libraries are forums for information and ideas, and that the following basic policies should guide their services.

I. Books and other library resources should be provided for the interest, information, and enlightenment of all people of the community the library serves. Materials should not be excluded because of the origin, background, or views of those contributing to their creation.

II. Libraries should provide materials and information presenting all points of view on current and historical issues. Materials should not be proscribed or removed because of partisan or doctrinal disapproval.

III. Libraries should challenge censorship in the fulfillment of their responsibility to provide information and enlightenment.

IV. Libraries should cooperate with all persons and groups concerned with resisting abridgment of free expression and free access to ideas.

V. A person's right to use a library should not be denied or abridged because of origin, age, background, or views.

VI. Libraries which make exhibit spaces and meeting rooms available to the public they serve should make such facilities available on an equitable basis, regardless of the beliefs or affiliations of individuals or groups requesting their use.

Adopted June 19, 1939, by the ALA Council; amended October 14, 1944; June 18, 1948; February 2, 1961; June 27, 1967; January 23, 1980; inclusion of "age" reaffirmed January 23, 1996.

Freedom to Read Statement

The freedom to read is essential to our democracy. It is continuously under attack. Private groups and public authorities in various parts of the country are working to remove or limit access to reading materials, to censor content in schools, to label "controversial" views, to distribute lists of "objectionable" books or authors, and to purge libraries. These actions apparently rise from a view that our national tradition of free expression is no longer valid; that censorship and suppression are needed to counter threats to safety or national security, as well as to avoid the subversion of politics and the corruption of morals. We, as individuals devoted to reading and as librarians and publishers responsible for disseminating ideas, wish to assert the public interest in the preservation of the freedom to read.

Most attempts at suppression rest on a denial of the fundamental premise of democracy: that the ordinary individual, by exercising critical judgment, will select the good and reject the bad. We trust Americans to recognize propaganda and misinformation, and to make their own decisions about what they read and believe. We do not believe they are prepared to sacrifice their heritage of a free press in order to be "protected" against what others think may be bad for them. We believe they still favor free enterprise in ideas and expression.

These efforts at suppression are related to a larger pattern of pressures being brought against education, the press, art and images, films, broadcast media, and the Internet. The problem is not only one of actual censorship. The shadow of fear cast by these pressures leads, we suspect, to an even larger voluntary curtailment of expression by those who seek to avoid controversy or unwelcome scrutiny by government officials.

Adopted June 25, 1953, by the ALA Council and the AAP Freedom to Read Committee; amended January 28, 1972; January 16, 1991; July 12, 2000; June 30, 2004.
Used with permission from the American Library Association.

Such pressure toward conformity is perhaps natural to a time of accelerated change. And yet suppression is never more dangerous than in such a time of social tension. Freedom has given the United States the elasticity to endure strain. Freedom keeps open the path of novel and creative solutions, and enables change to come by choice. Every silencing of a heresy, every enforcement of an orthodoxy, diminishes the toughness and resilience of our society and leaves it the less able to deal with controversy and difference.

Now as always in our history, reading is among our greatest freedoms. The freedom to read and write is almost the only means for making generally available ideas or manners of expression that can initially command only a small audience. The written word is the natural medium for the new idea and the untried voice from which come the original contributions to social growth. It is essential to the extended discussion that serious thought requires, and to the accumulation of knowledge and ideas into organized collections.

We believe that free communication is essential to the preservation of a free society and a creative culture. We believe that these pressures toward conformity present the danger of limiting the range and variety of inquiry and expression on which our democracy and our culture depend. We believe that every American community must jealously guard the freedom to publish and to circulate, in order to preserve its own freedom to read. We believe that publishers and librarians have a profound responsibility to give validity to that freedom to read by making it possible for the readers to choose freely from a variety of offerings.

The freedom to read is guaranteed by the Constitution. Those with faith in free people will stand firm on these constitutional guarantees of essential rights and will exercise the responsibilities that accompany these rights.

We therefore affirm these propositions:

1. *It is in the public interest for publishers and librarians to make available the widest diversity of views and expressions, including those that are unorthodox, unpopular, or considered dangerous by the majority.*

   Creative thought is by definition new, and what is new is different. The bearer of every new thought is a rebel until that idea is refined and tested. Totalitarian systems attempt to maintain themselves in power by the ruthless suppression of any concept that challenges the established orthodoxy. The power of a democratic system to adapt to change is vastly strengthened by the freedom of its citizens to choose widely from among conflicting opinions offered freely to them. To stifle every nonconformist idea at birth would mark the end of the democratic process. Furthermore, only through the constant activity of weighing and selecting can the democratic mind attain the strength demanded by times like these. We need to know not only what we believe but why we believe it.
2. *Publishers, librarians, and booksellers do not need to endorse every idea or presentation they make available. It would conflict with the public interest for them to establish their own political, moral, or aesthetic views as a standard for determining what should be published or circulated.*

   Publishers and librarians serve the educational process by helping to make available knowledge and ideas required for the growth of the mind and the increase of learning. They do not foster education by imposing as mentors the patterns of their own thought. The people should have the freedom to read and consider a broader range of ideas than those that may be held by any single librarian or publisher or government or church. It is wrong that what one can read should be confined to what another thinks proper.

3. *It is contrary to the public interest for publishers or librarians to bar access to writings on the basis of the personal history or political affiliations of the author.*

   No art or literature can flourish if it is to be measured by the political views or private lives of its creators. No society of free people can flourish that draws up lists of writers to whom it will not listen, whatever they may have to say.
4. *There is no place in our society for efforts to coerce the taste of others, to confine adults to the reading matter deemed suitable for adolescents, or to inhibit the efforts of writers to achieve artistic expression.*

   To some, much of modern expression is shocking. But is not much of life itself shocking? We cut off literature at the source if we prevent writers from dealing with the stuff of life. Parents and teachers have a responsibility to prepare the young to meet the diversity of experiences in life to which they will be exposed, as they have a responsibility to help them learn to think critically for themselves. These are affirmative responsibilities, not to be discharged simply by preventing them from reading works for which they are not yet prepared. In these matters values differ, and values cannot be legislated; nor can machinery be devised that will suit the demands of one group without limiting the freedom of others.
5. *It is not in the public interest to force a reader to accept the prejudgment of a label characterizing any expression or its author as subversive or dangerous.*

   The ideal of labeling presupposes the existence of individuals or groups with wisdom to determine by authority what is good or bad for others. It presupposes that individuals must be directed in making up their minds about the ideas they examine. But Americans do not need others to do their thinking for them.
6. *It is the responsibility of publishers and librarians, as guardians of the people's freedom to read, to contest encroachments upon that freedom by individuals or groups seeking to impose their own standards or tastes upon the community at large; and by the government whenever it seeks to reduce or deny public access to public information.*

   It is inevitable in the give and take of the democratic process that the political, the moral, or the aesthetic concepts of an individual or group will occasionally collide with those of another individual or group. In a free society individuals are free to determine for themselves what they wish to read, and each group is free to determine what it will recommend to its freely associated members. But no group has the right to take the law into its own hands, and to impose its own concept of politics or morality upon other members of a democratic society. Freedom is no freedom if it is accorded only to the accepted and the inoffensive. Further, democratic societies are more safe, free, and creative when the free flow of public information is not restricted by governmental prerogative or self-censorship.
7. *It is the responsibility of publishers and librarians to give full meaning to the freedom to read by providing books that enrich the quality and diversity of thought and expression. By the exercise of this affirmative responsibility, they can demonstrate that the answer to a "bad" book is a good one, the answer to a "bad" idea is a good one.*

   The freedom to read is of little consequence when the reader cannot obtain matter fit for that reader's purpose. What is needed is not only the absence of restraint, but the positive provision of opportunity for the people to read

> the best that has been thought and said. Books are the major channel by which the intellectual inheritance is handed down, and the principal means of its testing and growth. The defense of the freedom to read requires of all publishers and librarians the utmost of their faculties, and deserves of all Americans the fullest of their support.

We state these propositions neither lightly nor as easy generalizations. We here stake out a lofty claim for the value of the written word. We do so because we believe that it is possessed of enormous variety and usefulness, worthy of cherishing and keeping free. We realize that the application of these propositions may mean the dissemination of ideas and manners of expression that are repugnant to many persons. We do not state these propositions in the comfortable belief that what people read is unimportant. We believe rather that what people read is deeply important; that ideas can be dangerous; but that the suppression of ideas is fatal to a democratic society. Freedom itself is a dangerous way of life, but it is ours.

This statement was originally issued in May of 1953 by the Westchester Conference of the American Library Association and the American Book Publishers Council, which in 1970 consolidated with the American Educational Publishers Institute to become the Association of American Publishers.

United States Constitution

FIRST AMENDMENT

Congress shall make no law respecting an establishment of religion, or prohibiting the free exercise thereof; or abridging the freedom of speech, or of the press; or the right of the people peaceably to assemble, and to petition the Government for a redress of grievances.

FOURTH AMENDMENT

The right of the people to be secure in their persons, houses, papers, and effects, against unreasonable searches and seizures, shall not be violated, and no Warrants shall issue, but upon probable cause, supported by Oath or affirmation, and particularly describing the place to be searched, and the persons or things to be seized.

Universal Declaration of Human Rights

ARTICLE 18

Everyone has the right to freedom of thought, conscience and religion; this right includes freedom to change his religion or belief, and freedom, either alone or in community with others and in public or private, to manifest his religion or belief in teaching, practice, worship and observance.

ARTICLE 19

Everyone has the right to freedom of opinion and expression; this right includes freedom to hold opinions without interference and to seek, receive and impart information and ideas through any media and regardless of frontiers.

IFLA Code of Ethics for Librarians and Other Information Workers (Short Version)

PREAMBLE

This Code of Ethics and Professional Conduct is offered as a series of ethical propositions for the guidance of individual librarians as well as other information workers, and for the consideration of Library and Information Associations when creating or revising their own codes.

The function of codes of ethics can be described as

- encouraging reflection on principles on which librarians and other information workers can form policies and handle dilemmas
- improving professional self-awareness
- providing transparency to users and society in general.

This code is not intended to replace existing codes or to remove the obligation on professional associations to develop their own codes through a process of research, consultation and cooperative drafting. Full compliance with this code is not expected.

Endorsed by the IFLA Governing Board, August 2012.

The clauses of this code of ethics build on the core principles outlined in this preamble to provide a set of suggestions on the conduct of professionals. IFLA recognises that whilst these core principles should remain at the heart of any such code, the specifics of codes will necessarily vary according to the particular society, community of practice or virtual community. Code making is an essential function of a professional association, just as ethical reflection is a necessity for all professionals. IFLA recommends the Code of Ethics for IFLA to all its member associations and institutions and to individual librarians and information workers for these purposes.

IFLA undertakes to revise this code whenever appropriate.

1. ACCESS TO INFORMATION

The core mission of librarians and other information workers is to ensure access to information for all for personal development, education, cultural enrichment, leisure, economic activity and informed participation in and enhancement of democracy.

To this end, librarians and other information workers reject censorship in all its forms, support provision of services free of cost to the user, promote collections and services to potential users, and seek the highest standards of accessibility to both physical and virtual services.

2. RESPONSIBILITIES TOWARDS INDIVIDUALS AND SOCIETY

In order to promote inclusion and eradicate discrimination, librarians and other information workers ensure that the right of accessing information is not denied and that equitable services are provided for everyone whatever their age, citizenship, political belief, physical or mental ability, gender identity heritage, education, income, immigration and asylum-seeking status, marital status, origin, race, religion or sexual orientation.

To enhance access for all, librarians and other information workers support people in their information searching, assist them to develop their reading skills and information literacy, and encourage them in the ethical use of information (with particular attention to the welfare of young people).

3. PRIVACY, SECRECY AND TRANSPARENCY

Librarians and other information workers respect personal privacy, and the protection of personal data, necessarily shared between individuals and institutions. At the same time they support the fullest possible transparency for information relating to public bodies, private sector companies and all other institutions whose activities affect the lives of individuals and society as a whole.

4. OPEN ACCESS AND INTELLECTUAL PROPERTY

Librarians and other information workers' interest is to provide the best possible access for library users to information and ideas in any media or format, whilst recognising that they are partners of authors, publishers and other creators of copyright protected works. Librarians and other information workers seek to ensure that both users' rights and creators' rights are respected. They promote the principles of open access, open source, and open licenses. They seek appropriate and necessary limitations and exceptions for libraries and, in particular, seek to limit the expansion of copyright terms.

5. NEUTRALITY, PERSONAL INTEGRITY AND PROFESSIONAL SKLLS

Librarians and other information workers are strictly committed to neutrality and an unbiased stance regarding collection, access and service. They seek to acquire balanced collections, apply fair service policies, avoid allowing personal convictions to hinder the carrying out of their professional duties, combat corruption and seek the highest standards of professional excellence.

6. COLLEAGUE AND EMPLOYER/EMPLOYEE RELATIONSHIP

Librarians and other information workers treat each other with fairness and respect. To this end they oppose discrimination in any aspect of employment because of age, citizenship, political belief, physical or mental ability, gender, marital status, origin, race, religion or sexual orientation. They support equal payment for equal work between men and women, share their professional experience, and contribute towards the work of their professional associations.

Chapter 3

The Reference Interview

M. Kathleen Kern[1] and
Beth S. Woodard

INTRODUCTION

The concept of the reference interview has been around since early in the 20th century, but it was often called the librarian–user "conversation," and it focused more on the information needed to supply the user with resources and not on the interpersonal skills necessary to conduct the interview. It was not until 1954, when David Maxfield applied interviewing principles from the counseling field to the reference interview, that acceptance, understanding, communication, and collaboration were identified as important to a successful reference interview.

Some writers describe the reference interview as a dialogue, with the reference librarian taking the responsibility for finding out the information need of the user and providing the information for him or her. Others (Mabry 2003) suggest that this interaction should be described as a "partnership" in which both partners are equals and have mutual goals. The reference interview is a dialogue between the user and the librarian in which the librarian's objective is clarification and understanding of the user's question as a means to meet the user's information need, and the user's objective is to have the librarian understand and meet the information need.

The reference interview is where library science becomes an art. It is about the skills of listening and communicating. A good searcher, a librarian skilled at information retrieval, may not necessarily be good at interactions with users. Fortunately, communication skills can be developed, and many minds in library science have contributed to researching and documenting the communication skills that librarians need to complement their knowledge of information sources. Like painting, there are both process and talent involved in the reference interview. Knowledge of technique is essential, but each librarian will develop his or her own style.

Reference interviewing has been the subject of much research and analysis. This scrutiny has resulted in evidence that the quality of the interaction the user has with the librarian is important. Some studies have even found that a positive interaction, one in which the user feels that the librarian has listened and been concerned, is more important to the user's willingness to return with another question than the accuracy of the answers that are received (Dewdney and Ross 1994; Durrance 1995; Radford 1999).

Some reference questions are straightforward and do not require a high degree of interaction between the reference librarian and the user to be successful. Others require a great deal of negotiation. Experienced librarians can provide examples of instances in which users with seemingly simple questions had more complex information needs that they have not yet acknowledged or realized. Robert Taylor (1968, 182) called these needs that are felt but not yet consciously formulated "visceral needs." The librarian's ability to help the user verbalize these needs and clarify their exact nature has been identified as an important aspect of user satisfaction with reference service (e.g., see Dewdney and Ross 1994).

This chapter considers the reference interview as a dialogue between the librarian and the user and provides exercises to learn and improve this foundational reference skill. Other topics beyond the basics of the reference interview are covered including adapting the reference interview for remote and online interactions, working with special situations that arise in libraries, and identifying the characteristics of a good reference librarian.

OVERVIEW OF THE REFERENCE INTERVIEW PROCESS

The Reference and User Services Association (RUSA) of the American Library Association (ALA) has studied the reference interview process in great detail. The RUSA "Guidelines for Behavioral Performance of Reference and Information Service Providers," excerpted in Box 3.1, outlines in a linear way the elements of best practice in reference interviewing. However, because the reference interview is a process and, like most processes, is iterative with steps repeated and returned to as necessary, the guidelines alone do not give an accurate picture of the process. The diagram in Figure 3.1 is based on the RUSA behavioral guidelines and attempts to illustrate that communication techniques such as asking questions, paraphrasing, and providing information are appropriate throughout the reference interview, not merely at certain stages.

To be complete, a "reference interview" extends beyond the stage of interviewing users about their information needs. The interaction does not end with the confirmation that the librarian understands the user's inquiry; it encompasses searching, presentation of results, and follow-up. In many ways, it is better to think of this as the "reference interaction," or perhaps the "reference dialogue," because it is a two-way communication between a user and a librarian in which both contribute to the process. The user brings the question and the understanding of what is needed. The librarian brings understanding of available resources and asks questions to encourage the user to explain any expectations and to help the librarian match available resources with the user's information needs. It is only the user who can determine the extent to which the information provided is relevant or accurate. Thus, the reference interaction starts and ends with the user, regardless of which person speaks the first or last word.

Box 3.1 Excerpts from the RUSA "Guidelines for Behavioral Performance of Reference and Information Service Providers" (2013)

1.0 Visibility/Approachability

A successful reference transaction requires a high level of visibility. Reference assistance should be available through a variety of technologies at a patron's point of need.

In order to have a successful reference transaction, it is essential that the reference librarian be approachable. Whether acting in a traditional/in-person role or a remote/virtual role, the librarian's first step in initiating the reference transaction is to make the patron feel comfortable in a situation that can be perceived as intimidating, confusing, or overwhelming. The librarian's initial response in any reference situation sets the tone for the entire communication process, and influences the depth and level of interaction.

2.0 Interest

A successful librarian demonstrates a high degree of objective, nonjudgmental interest in the reference transaction. While not every query will be of interest to the librarian, the librarian should embrace each patron's informational need and should be committed to providing the most effective assistance. Librarians who demonstrate a high level of interest in the inquiries of patrons will generate a higher level of satisfaction among users.

3.0 Listening/Inquiring

The reference interview is the heart of the reference transaction and is crucial to the success of the process. The librarian should effectively identify the patron's information needs in a manner that puts the patron at ease. Effective listening and questioning skills are necessary for a positive interaction.

4.0 Searching

The search process is the portion of the transaction in which behavior and accuracy intersect. Without an effective search, not only is the desired information unlikely to be found, but patrons may become discouraged as well. Many aspects of searching that lead to accurate results are dependent on the behavior of the librarian.

5.0 Follow-up

Supplying information is not the end of the reference transaction. The librarian is responsible for determining if the patron is satisfied with the results of the search, and referring the patron to other sources including those not available through the local library.

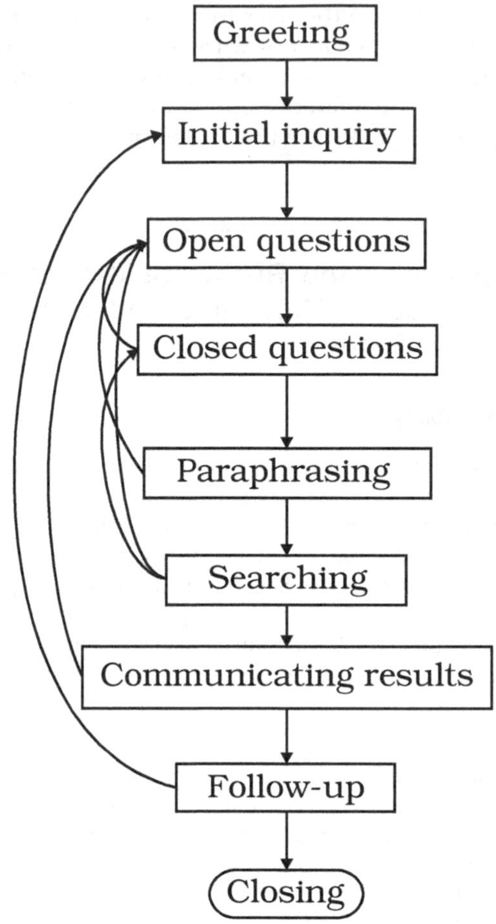

FIGURE 3.1 Reference interaction process

OPENING THE INTERVIEW

Greeting and Engaging

First impressions are said to be lasting ones. How the librarian first appears to users will affect their attitude toward the librarian and may shape the phrasing of their questions; it may sway a user's decision to ask a question at all. The reference librarian should always appear welcoming. Some users may feel that their questions are stupid or that they are bothering the librarian by asking for assistance. A smile goes a long way and encourages reluctant or shy users to approach the reference desk and ask their question. Making eye contact with users as they come near the reference desk establishes a connection and expresses that the librarian is there to help. In some cases, a verbal greeting might be necessary to reassure the hesitant patron that he or she is in the right place for assistance.

A simple greeting delivered in a pleasant tone such as "Hi, how may I help you?" will establish that the librarian is available to help the user and allay any fears that she or he is in the wrong place or that the librarian is busy. Professionalism dictates that librarians sound enthusiastic about providing assistance even if the heat in the building has failed or they are covering a colleague's shift and have been working at the reference desk for several hours. Each user should be treated as a new and interesting interaction.

It is important not to appear involved in other work because this will increase user perception that the librarian is too busy or important to answer questions. Users often open an interaction with "Sorry to bother you. . . ." Users should never feel that their questions are bothersome or an interruption. It is, after all, exactly why the reference librarian is available. Libraries' policies differ on whether librarians are allowed to take other work, such as collection development or report writing, with them to the desk, but if other projects are worked on while at the reference desk, the librarian must be even more aware of approachability factors and look up frequently from other tasks and be conscious of users in the area.

Library and clientele will dictate the formality of the greeting, and telephone greetings are often a little more formal than in person. With experience, a reference service provider can learn to adapt his or her communication style to one more consistent with the user's preferences.

Online greetings for chat and instant messaging (IM) are often pre-scripted but should avoid sounding too automated and cold. It is frequently effective to follow up a pre-scripted greeting with a personalized one, incorporating the user's name or screen ID to establish rapport. The interaction might look like this:

RefLibrarian:	Hi, welcome to the Library's Ask-A-Librarian Service. How may I help you?
SportsFan1:	Who won last night's baseball game?
RefLibrarian:	Hi, SportsFan! Which baseball game are you interested in?

Sometimes the reference desk is busy and a queue forms. Users may linger farther from the desk if they see that the librarian is involved in helping someone else. Smiling at and greeting the waiting users is a way to let them know that they have been seen and that someone will be with them presently. Again, a simple statement such as "Hi, I'll be with you soon" reassures the users that they have been noticed. When working with multiple people via telephone or IM, it is more polite to pick up the incoming call and ask the user to hold or offer to call back than to let the call go unanswered.

Expressing Interest Verbally and Nonverbally

The need for a friendly demeanor extends beyond the initial contact with the users. For the reference interaction to be successful, the users must feel that they have the reference librarian's attention and that the librarian is truly listening to what is said. Undoubtedly, there will be questions in which the librarian has no personal interest or that have been encountered 10 times already that day. The librarian should engage the same way as when listening to a friend: nod, smile, encourage.

The body language of the service provider can go a long way toward communicating an openness and willingness to listen to a user's query. Maintaining an open stance, facing the user squarely instead of at an angle, and leaning forward in the chair are all positive nonverbal messages that the service provider is ready to pay attention to the other person. Other considerations include being at the same eye level, which might mean standing if the person approaches the desk in a standing posture, or taking a seat if the individual is in a wheelchair. Reducing reference-desk clutter also allows the service provider to concentrate attention on the question at hand. Roving, or walking around the service area to where the users might have questions, is another way of inviting queries with positive body language. Simple things such as taking fingers off the computer keyboard or putting down a held pencil can also reduce the distractions perceived by the user.

Showing interest during in-person encounters is primarily nonverbal. The user can see that someone is paying attention when that person is looking at him or her and appears focused and alert. When the user is remote, reaching the reference service by telephone or online communications, these visual cues are missing. Verbal expressions of interest are very important in telephone conversations; an "okay" or an "I see" can substitute for a nod. When the interaction occurs via online communications, typing must substitute for verbal and visual indicators of interest. The librarian should be sure not to leave the user hanging. The librarian can break apart long sentences with ellipses and send the fragments of thought, indicate to the user that a few minutes are needed to search or to think, and send some type of communication at least every two minutes, even if it is just to say that the search is still in process. The librarian does not want to give the impression that he or she has given up or gone away.

NEGOTIATING THE INFORMATION NEED

Through the questioning process, the librarian seeks to (1) elicit the user's question in his own words; (2) obtain knowledge that the user has about the query to enable effective searching and evaluation of information; and (3) verify that the librarian and the user share the same understanding of the information need. Only after this shared understanding is confirmed can the search process begin. Several communication strategies are used during question negotiation: *open questions*, *closed questions*, *encouragers*, and *active listening*. The first two strategies encourage users to describe their information needs in their own terms and to provide the librarian with specifics required to match the vast array of available information with those needs. As Mary Ellen Bates (1998, 19) has observed, "The time you invest in the reference interview is time you don't spend later re-doing your work when you finally figure out what your client really wanted."

The strategies of active listening and use of encouragers make users aware that the librarian is interested, concerned, and attentive to their question. Noncommittal acknowledgments of what the user is saying indicate that one is listening and can encourage the user to continue talking. Even short phrases such as "Yes?" or "Okay, what else?" can be very effective ways of getting the user to further explain the question so that the librarian can begin thinking about where to start in the search for an answer. These types of short phrases are sometimes called "encouragers" (Ross and Nilsen 2013, 27). Nonverbal encouragers can include head-nodding, eye contact, and facial expressions that match what the speaker is saying.

Encouragers keep the user talking and help the librarian to gain more insight into the background that produced the question.

Gathering the Evidence

What is it that the librarian needs to know in order to successfully assist a patron? The Ohio Library Council (2014) states that "At the conclusion of a good reference interview, you should have the six pieces of evidence." The traditional questions of who, what, when, where, why, and how, which can be remembered with the mnemonic 5W1H, are a good framework to think about the "six pieces of evidence" that will enable a successful reference interaction.

- *Who* is the patron? Characteristics about the patron can help the librarian determine how to best assist the patron. Is this person a new student? A small business entrepreneur? What is the person's level of experience with finding information? Do not make too many assumptions based on how the patron looks or sounds or types. Find out as much as possible through dialogue.
- *What* is the basic question? Note: the basic question is the core of the information need and the most critical thing that the librarian needs to understand.
- *When* does the user need the information? Is there a deadline?
- *Where* has the patron already looked for information? Or *where* did the patron learn about the topic?
- *Why* is this question being asked? For what purpose will it be used? The information needed for a research paper on the history of French cuisine will be different from information on how to make a soufflé.
- *How* much information is needed? Are particular types of information needed? How broad, specific, or technical?

This is a method to remember the types of evidence that will be useful when assisting a user, and not an exhaustive list of questions. 5W1H is a mnemonic and not an ordered list, although as the most basic questions, *Who* and *What* are typically determined early in the interaction and the other evidence, which is more narrowly focused, is gathered later. This list is a jumping-off point to help with determining open and closed questions to ask during the reference interview.

Open Questions

After the greeting and the user's initial question, the reference interview almost always starts with the librarian asking an open question. An open question is one to which there is no fixed answer; it cannot be answered with a yes or no and does not draw its response from a set of predetermined choices, as in multiple choice responses. Open questions encourage users to talk about the information need using their own terms (King 1972, 159). There are many possibilities for open questions, and some inquiries will naturally present obvious questions to ask. For example, the user who approaches the desk needing travel guides prompts the librarian to inquire, "What part of the world are you interested in?" Open questions seek to elicit descriptive answers and typically begin with "what," "when," "where," and "how." Box 3.2 lists some possible open questions.

Box 3.2 Activity: Asking Open Questions

The following list presents typical open questions used by librarians; however, everyone has his or her own style of asking questions. How would you phrase these? Are there other questions you would ask?

If asking open questions feels awkward or unfamiliar, it can be useful to think about a discussion with a friend about a new hobby or an upcoming vacation. In addition, as you think about asking open questions, consider how you can simultaneously express interest in the patron's query.

- That is a broad topic. Do you have something more specific in mind?
- Is there a particular aspect of or type of information about [topic] that you are interested in finding information on?
- What materials have you already examined?
- What do you already know about this subject?
- We have a number of books/articles about [topic]. Was there something in particular you were looking for?
- I'm not sure if I know what [topic] is/means. Could you tell me some more about it?
- How much information are you looking for?

At times, the user's question may be unfamiliar, and the open questions will seek to draw out more explanation as well as inform the librarian about the topic area. An example of this is the user who says, "I need to write a paper about top quarks." An open question to ask here might be "Could you tell me more about top quarks? What field of study does that relate to?" If the librarian is comfortable doing so, it is okay to let the user know if terms are unfamiliar; it is better to ask for clarification than to blunder ahead without direction.

Closed Questions

After the user's topic is known, often the librarian needs to know more before searching for an answer. How much information does the user need? Is he or she interested in articles or books, or does it matter? Is there a particular time period for the information: recent or historical? Closed questions ask for a yes or no response or present the user with options from which to choose. Closed questions tend to focus narrowly and distinctly on a particular subject or source and help further the librarian's understanding of the user's information need.

Closed questions are asked after the open questions to avoid leading the user in a particular direction or narrowing the options too soon. Even if the user's initial question is very broad or not yet well formed, it is the user who needs to define the information need. Users view librarians as the authorities of information and may think that the information they want is not available if the librarian uses closed questions too soon in the process and the suggestions given are not what they have in mind.

Consider this scenario:

Patron: Do you have anything on athletes and drugs?
Librarian: Are you looking for legislation or statistics?

Patron: Well, I wanted to read athletes' stories. What they've written. I don't know if you have anything like that. So, statistics, I guess.

This user did reveal a preference, but not all users will. Users often do not know what is available from the library and will try to match their question with what they think they will be able to find. When presented with a list of options, users may be hesitant to say something that is not on the list, even if that is what they want. It is good practice when presenting a list to leave an "other" option. For example, "Are you interested in Canada, England, or somewhere else?" Box 3.3 gives sample closed questions and provides some questions for discussion.

Box 3.3 Activity: Closed Questions

The following are examples of common closed questions.

- Do you need books or magazine and journal articles?
- Are you looking for current or historical information?
- What time period does your information need to be about?
- Are you interested in information on [topic 1] or [topic 2]?
- Do you want advanced material or something basic?
- What material have you already looked at? *Or* Where have you already looked?

Questions for Reflection and Discussion:

1. How could asking these questions too early misdirect the rest of the reference interaction?
2. The general guidance is to ask closed questions later in the reference interview process; however, when might it be appropriate to use closed questions early in the negotiation process?
3. Would it ever be appropriate to ask an open question at the end of a reference interview? Can you think of examples?

Neutral Questions

When direct questions might offend the user, a technique called *neutral* or *sense-making questioning* can be used to elicit further information. By using questions such as "If you could tell me the kind of problem you are working on, I will get a better of idea of what would help you" (Dervin and Dewdney 1986, 511), the librarian can gain valuable background information. Questions about why the information is needed and to what use the information will be put help the librarian understand the context from which the information need arose.

Like open questions, neutral questions strive to get the user to talk more fully about the information need. Although neutral questions, according to Brenda Dervin and Patricia Dewdney (1986), are most effective early in the interview process to help the librarian see the question more in the way the user does, they can also be used later in the process when materials judged by the librarian to be useful are not seen as relevant by the user. In general, neutral questions help the librarian to avoid reaching premature and inaccurate conclusions about the user's need based on the librarian's experience, biases, or history with that user.

Asking Why

Depending on the environment and the user's inquiry, neutral questions from the librarian might not seem neutral to the patron. Because many questions, such as those regarding health, legal issues, or even about kinds of services, have their roots in personal and private situations, asking how information will be used or why the user needs it may seem intrusive to the user. This type of question can destroy the trust established throughout the interview process, and there is no consensus in the literature on whether or how the librarian should ask the user why the information being sought is needed. Alfred Benjamin, in *The Helping Interview* (1981, 85–96), discusses his objections to the use of asking why because of the tension caused in the interview and the frequent withdrawal by the interviewee. Dewdney and Michell (1997) explore speech act theory to understand that "why" questions are often misinterpreted because the user does not understand the relevance to the reference interview. However, sometimes, in order to better serve the user, the librarian needs to determine "the level of treatment and amount of information needed" (Oser 1987, 72) and needs to ask "why."

If possible, dealing solely with the question and information volunteered by the user is the best strategy for the librarian to follow. In situations where the librarian needs to make a recommendation for a tool to use and does not have adequate information to make a decision, one possibility is to employ neutral questioning techniques such as asking how the information is going to be used. Although this is not as abrupt as asking why, it is very close and could still give offense or make the patron uncomfortable. Careful phrasing such as "I can help you better if I know something more about how you will use this information" makes it clear that the question is not nosy but an attempt to offer the best customer service. Suggesting several possible sources and allowing the user to choose the appropriate material is another method and illustrates the cyclical nature of the reference interview process. Librarians can also elicit feedback from the user to fill in for asking "why." For example, when looking at search results, the librarian can ask which articles are most like what the user wants and which are not useful. The librarian can then infer a why while also creating an opportunity for the user to offer whether the articles are useful or not.

Setting the Tone

For the reference interaction to be successful, the user needs to be comfortable in what might be an unfamiliar environment. There are conversational considerations to keep in mind when asking questions and imparting information or instructions, such as clarity, careful word choice, and tone, as well as some more advanced skills such as using encouragers and active listening.

Each librarian has his or her own style of speech, and each service provider develops his or her own approach to asking questions. It is important to realize that the reference interview is a dialogue, not an interrogation. The user is not (likely) willfully withholding information, but may not have provided everything that the librarian needs to know to meet the information need. The questions asked should display interest and maintain approachability. The librarian should avoid using any words that are judgmental and may cause the user to back away from communication, such as saying that a question is "too broad" or that the user needs "to focus" on an area. This is particularly true in text-based conversations such as e-mail and chat, where there is no tone of voice or body language to help the user interpret the librarian's intent. In addition to keeping the choice of words and tone positive, librarians can add constructive comments that provide context to questions. For example, "That topic is too broad" could become "That topic is very broad. You will have an easier time finding information and writing your paper if you narrow your focus. Is there an aspect of this topic that interests you the most?"

Language

Librarians have the responsibility to use clear language, free of jargon, so that users can understand. Dina Cramer (1998) notes that "the reference interview is supposed to elicit the real questions, but it can't if people mean different things by the words they use." So when a questioner uses a word in the commonly understood sense, but the librarian uses the same word to mean something else, the librarian must be aware that misunderstandings can occur. Such words as "bibliography" and "biography" are commonly recognized as problematic. Dina Cramer further suggests that librarians not use the word "citation" because to the user it might refer to a traffic ticket.

Active Listening

Because good communication involves both getting the message across and understanding what the other person is saying, the use of active listening techniques helps ensure not only that the message is received accurately, but also that it is understood. Research shows that people listen at about 25 percent efficiency (Burley-Allen 1995, 3), meaning that of everything one hears, only 25 percent is likely to be interpreted correctly. In order to turn hearing into listening, one must focus on what a person is saying, pay attention to what is said, and concentrate on understanding. So a mere restatement of the perceived message is not enough. The message needs to be restated in one's own words, or paraphrased. Active listening involves not only paraphrasing but also asking clarifying questions and understanding the nature of the problem fully before attempting to assist with the user's information need. Feedback from the user, then, is also an essential element of active listening. With straightforward questions, the librarian may simply need to paraphrase the question before beginning the search. In more complex questions, however, the librarian may need to renegotiate the question several times during the interview and the search process. Box 3.4 provides an opportunity to practice active listening along with the other reference interview skills discussed in the chapter.

Box 3.4 Activity: Bringing It All Together: Practice Getting to the Real Question

The following exercise will help you practice the reference interview.

Divide into pairs. Each person should think of a reference question to ask their partner. The initial question should not express the full information need. For example, one partner might ask, "Where are your books on China?" when what she really needs is resources on international adoption. Take turns being the user who asks a reference question and the librarian who conducts a reference interview to determine the user's information need.

Guidelines:

- Keep in mind the different types of questioning skills used in the reference interview.
- Focus on the question-negotiation part of the reference interview. Do not focus on the searching aspect. Try *not* to think about sources that you would use to answer the question. What follow-up questions would you ask to clarify what the user wants? What information do you need to know?

Assessment (to be performed by the "user" and the "librarian"):

- Was the user welcomed/greeted?
- How was interest in the user's question shown?
- Were open-ended questions asked? Was more than one open-ended question asked?
- Were neutral questions or encouragers used to keep the user talking?
- Was sensitivity to "why" the user needed the information shown? How did the librarian get to this information?
- Were closed questions used appropriately?
- Has the user's question been restated or paraphrased in the process?

The user and librarian should compare and discuss assessments.

SEARCHING FOR THE ANSWER

It is important not to start searching too early in the interview process. If the librarian jumps ahead to searching before establishing a shared understanding of what the user wants, then a lot of time can be wasted, and frustration may result for both the user and the librarian. Once the search process has been started, however, the librarian can continue to ask questions, refining what the user wants and adjusting the search strategy accordingly. This can be a helpful approach particularly when the user has been cryptic or uncertain, when the user has declined to narrow a broad topic, or when there is a lot of available information on a topic.

Asking the user what the final answer might look like is a technique suggested by Tim Buckley Owen (2012, 42). For example, if the user is asking about migration patterns, does the user want the information in the form of statistics, graphs, charts, or diagrammatic maps? Knowing the kind of answer the user is expecting can help guide the selection of the tools or resources that will provide that kind of answer.

Sometimes searching is done without the user present, and this presents its own set of challenges in the reference interview. Ideally, more of the communication must be done up front, and then communication should be continued when the results are presented to the user to avoid constant back-and-forth delays in the searching while waiting for the user to respond. When compiling a lot of information or when there are ambiguities, sending a sample article or book and asking the user to comment on the usefulness of the item can help guide the search process before it is too far along. Be judicious with this technique and package samples and follow-up questions to avoid a volley of e-mails or phone calls that might seem scattered and overwhelm the user.

Involving the User

Just like questioning, searching is a joint process with the user. What form and extent this collaboration takes is affected by the reference environment (discussed later in this chapter). A basic principle for most situations is that the search process should be transparent for the user, so that the user can see and understand what the librarian is doing. This keeps the dialogue open and allows the user to offer further information and the librarian to continue to ask questions.

In most environments, and when possible and appropriate, the librarian should explain the search process as it is happening. Discretion should be used here to match the level of user involvement in the search process with the time the user is willing to spend. In some situations, it may be appropriate to show a user how to find a call number for a book; in others, it is more appropriate to provide the call number. In some libraries, particularly corporate libraries, where the librarian performs the research for the user with minimal involvement from the user, the search process is explained in a very brief summary when the requested information is delivered.

One of the most effective ways to involve the users is to work alongside them at a table with reference books or at a computer terminal with access to the library's databases. In this way, users can be instructed how to search or can be shown search results and can provide immediate feedback as to the relevance of what has been found. For example, when users see that there is a lot of information about their chosen topic, they may narrow the topic, and the search results can be used to spark ideas for a more refined search. Remember that it is difficult for users to frame their questions because they are often not aware of what information might be available on their topic. Catherine Ross, Kirsti Nilsen, and Marie Radford (2009, 112; see also Michell and Harris 1987; White 1981) call this "inclusion" and suggest that it involves these basic steps: restating the problem; describing briefly what steps are going to be taken and why these are the appropriate steps; and, if appropriate, indicating the amount of time these steps might take. Box 3.5 is a sample reference scenario, where the librarian tells the user what to do rather than involving the patron in the search and evaluation of results.

Box 3.5 Activity: Involving the User

As you read the following scenario, think about how involving the user in the selection of search terms, viewing results with the user, or asking questions to help the user evaluate the appropriateness of the results might have changed the outcome of this reference interaction. Individually, or as a small group, write up a new scenario that involves the user. At the end are additional discussion questions to help you with adapting your reference interview techniques to the variety of environments and users that you might encounter.

Scenario:

User:	I need to find information on students who are homeschooled and their interests. Where would you suggest I look? I tried using the online catalog but didn't get any results so I must be doing something wrong.
Librarian:	No problem! I can help you with that.
Librarian:	What type of information are you looking for?
User:	Articles and statistics.
Librarian:	When you say you are looking for articles on homeschooled children's interests, do you mean hobbies, or educational interests, because that would help us narrow down our search?
User:	Yes, how they spend their spare time.
Librarian:	Okay, so from the ERIC database, I am going to put the term homeschooling in the first search box . . . and hobbies in the second box directly under that.
Librarian:	We may have to try some different things and see what works.
Librarian:	Okay, actually we got no results for that search. There are results for just homeschooling, so it's a matter of picking a second keyword that might work.
Librarian:	Actually, I got results from trying the word interests in the second box.
User:	Okay, I'll give that a try.
Librarian:	Also, the term activities worked.
Librarian:	Let me know if you need further assistance.
User:	All right, I will, thanks again.
Librarian:	No problem! Happy to help!

Questions for Reflection and Discussion:

1. How might the interaction have changed if the librarian knew more about the user's demographics, such as age or status as a university student or a homeschooling parent?
2. How might different library settings affect the decision to instruct the user?
3. Is it always better to instruct? How would you determine the teachable moment?

If a question may have been misinterpreted by the librarian, searching with the user provides a comfortable opportunity for realignment. Users may be hesitant to reapproach a librarian to point out that a mistake has been made because they fear seeming rude, but when librarian and user are viewing and discussing the same search results or reference book, it is easier to continue the dialogue.

Presenting Answers

In recent years, librarians have found that they are asked factual "ready-reference" questions less often and receive a higher proportion of questions that involve assisting users with finding information where there is not a single brief answer. There seems to be a trend of moving away from asking for the number of a specific hotel in Virginia Beach to asking how they can research lodging and travel options for their next vacation. In these cases, the answer is really providing the user with a set of options about where to look and some strategies for doing research. Returning to the example of the user looking for information on athletes and drug use, the answer is the librarian's guidance with choosing and using one or two databases, an article index, and the library's catalog perhaps, in which the user will be able to search, examine results, and determine appropriateness of content.

When the question has a definite factual answer, the answer should be given to the user, and a source for the information provided. If the user was not present during the searching part of the process, some communication regarding what was done to find the information, such as search terms and other sources consulted, may be presented as well. When providing information, it is important to cite the source. Authority is an important aspect of information. Because a source may have a particular bias or perspective, knowing the source is vital to users' evaluation of the information, whether or not they requested identification of the source. Speak clearly, particularly via telephone, spelling unusual or difficult terms, and check to see whether the answer is understood.

Providing context is vital to the user's understanding of the information. This is true for assistance in searching as well as for providing factual answers. Knowing why the librarian chose a database or particular search terms will help the user by hopefully increasing his or her information literacy. Context is often obvious to the librarian but not to the user who is less immersed in the complex information environment. These explanations can happen organically during an in-person or chat conversation, particularly during the searching and evaluating phases. When the user is not present and results are sent via e-mail, the librarian should provide information about what resources were used and why the results presented were chosen as most relevant. Further context might include what was not included and notes on overall volume and selectivity. For example, the librarian might say, "These results do not include news articles, since you wanted to focus on Congressional reports and scholarly articles. Out of the hundreds available, here are five reports and five articles from the most recent two years that focus most specifically on the Affordable Care Act post-enactment. Please let me know if these are useful and if you would like me to expand or modify my search."

CLOSING AND FOLLOW-UP

Librarian:	Does this information answer your question?
User:	Yes, I think that this is good for now.
Librarian:	Great. If you think of anything else, just ask. We are here today until 10.
User:	Okay. Thanks!

Closing the reference interview properly is important because it is the last communication with the user and can affect the way that the user remembers the entire interaction. The end of the reference interview should always leave open the opportunity for the user to say more. Asking, "Does this completely answer your question?" or "Is there anything else that I can help you with today?" gives the user the opportunity to ask for further information or to say that something different is required than what was found. Although the early stages of the reference interview ideally would have determined the scope of the information need, it is professional and polite to verify that the information presented is what was expected. A user might hesitate to ask for something more without this prompt from the librarian, but during the search process, he or she may have modified the original inquiry or determined that more information is needed. Asking appropriate follow-up questions has been demonstrated to improve the accuracy of the answer provided by the librarian (Dyson 1992; Gers and Seward 1985; Isenstein 1992). Similarly, an invitation to return reminds the user that there is always the opportunity to ask for more or different information. It is also a pleasant reminder that librarians are always available to help with the user's information needs.

Follow-Up

If the user remains in the library, it is a nice touch for the librarian to follow-up with the user to confirm that the information was adequate and nothing else is required. In a corporate setting, or one where librarians have a close connection with their remote users, a follow-up telephone call may achieve the same end. In other settings, this type of follow-up would seem intrusive, so whether to do this is at the discretion of the librarian, based on how it fits with the library environment.

Referrals

Sometimes the librarian or library will not have the answer that the user needs. In these cases, it is appropriate to refer the user to another person, library, or organization. It is kind to the user to first confirm that the referral destination can indeed help the user and that someone is available. Users resent being treated like footballs passed from one person to another.

Confirming that a referral is appropriate not only helps the user; it helps the next person or organization that works with the user because that helper will be prepared, and the user will not be upset over being misdirected. Librarians, in their zeal to be helpful, may find it difficult to let go of a question and can have the tendency to hang on too long to questions that could be better or more quickly answered by other librarians or experts in the field. A call to verify that there is another expert willing and available to help the user can ease the librarian's anxiety over parting with a question. Christopher Nolan (1992) suggests that an unsuccessful interview should always end with a referral.

Negative Closure

When a reference interview is ended abruptly without a real examination of the user's question or an adequate attempt to meet the user's information need, this is called *negative closure* (Ross and Dewdney 1998). Nolan (1992) suggests that there are three reasons interviews terminate prematurely: (1) the librarian was unsuccessful in answering the user's query and did not make an appropriate referral; (2) the interview was not going well whether because of frustration or futility, lack of patience, or poor communication skills; or (3) the librarian was constrained by policy or institutional factors such as time of day, queues of other users waiting, or costs.

Everyone has experienced negative closure in some service interaction, whether in a library, a retail store, or elsewhere. Some classic examples and their library manifestations include pointing ("the encyclopedias are over there") and vague unhelpful responses ("try looking in the 700s"). Box 3.6 illustrates other ways in which negative closure can occur.

Negative closure also encompasses taking the user's question at face value, bypassing the reference interview, and beginning to work without asking questions or providing explanations. Research consistently finds that reference interviews are conducted in only about 50 percent of reference interactions. Mary Jo Lynch (1978) found that about 50 percent of library staff chose to conduct a reference interview, while Patricia Dewdney (1986) found that of 629 nondirectional questions, only 332 cases, or 57 percent, had interviews. Ross and Nilsen (2000) found that of 261 transactions, 129 reference interviews were conducted. Other types of negative closure are blind or unmonitored referrals without confirming that the other person can help and providing a call number without follow-up confirmation with the user that the information was actually helpful. Ross (2003, 41) found that this error happens in about one-third of the accounts of negative closure.

Too often the librarian's questions relate to the library system instead of the context of the user's information need. In these instances, the librarian asks questions that may be answered by the user but that may not be understood by the user or that have little bearing on the user's question. An example is asking the user whether an answer from an encyclopedia or a dictionary is needed, without providing context as to how information in one would differ from information in the other. Or the librarian may respond to the user's request for *Time* magazine by asking, "Are you looking for the unbound periodicals section?" rather than asking what date is needed. With these examples, closed questioning has become a type of negative closure.

Box 3.6 Examples of Negative Closure

Ross and Dewdney (1998) have identified numerous practices that lead to negative closure.

- Implying that the user should have done something else before asking for reference help.
- Trying to get the user to accept more easily found information instead of the information requested.
- Warning the user to expect defeat because the topic is too hard, obscure, large, elusive, or otherwise unpromising.
- Encouraging the user to abort the transaction voluntarily.
- Signaling nonverbally that the transaction is over by turning away, by tone of voice, or by starting another activity.
- Stating explicitly that the search has reached a dead end.
- Claiming that the information is not in the library or else does not exist at all.
- Telling the user that he or she will track down a document but then never returning.

In general, then, the closure of the reference interview is extremely important, and care should be taken to ensure that the answer provided is to the question intended by the user, both throughout the interview process and at the end of the interaction.

Self-Reflection on the Interaction

Another aspect of follow-up is the reference librarian's self-reflection concerning the interaction. Particularly in instances where the interaction did not go well, or the librarian was unsuccessful in finding an answer, an analysis of each aspect of the reference interview can point out areas for improvement. Box 3.7 provides an evaluation sheet that can be used for self-evaluation or in conjunction with a trusted peer.

Box 3.7 Reference Interview Evaluation Sheet

1. Approachability and Interest
   - Was a greeting given beyond the standard welcome message? Y N
   - Was interest shown (via attentive comments, etc.) to the user's questions? Y N
2. Question Negotiation
   - Was there any question negotiation or a reference interview? Y N
   - Number of open questions asked: ____________
   - Number of closed questions asked: ____________
   - Was the user's question restated or paraphrased before searching began? Y N
3. Searching
   - Was the user kept updated on the status of the search? Y N
   - Were sources cited to the user (e.g., names of databases, books, etc.)? Y N
   - Appropriateness of sources:
     1 (not appropriate)—2 (appropriate)—3 (extremely appropriate) ____________
   - Amount of information given:
     1 (too little)—2 (just right)—3 (too much) ____________
   - When appropriate, amount of library instruction given:
     N/A—1 (none)—2 (basic instruction)—3 (sufficient instruction) ____________
   - How completely was the question answered?
     1 (not answered)—2 (somewhat answered)—3 (fully answered) ____________
4. Follow-Up
   - Did the librarian confirm that the answer was understood? Y N
   - Was a follow-up question asked that addressed the specific question? Y N
   - Was the user asked to check back, when appropriate? Y N N/A
   - If referrals were given, were they appropriate and monitored? Y N

Source: Adapted from an evaluation sheet developed by David Ward, Reference Services Librarian, Undergraduate Library, University of Illinois at Urbana-Champaign.

INTERVIEWS FOR SPECIFIC SITUATIONS

Dealing with Multiple Users and Queues

Sometimes the reference desk is busy, and more than one user is waiting for an answer. It is of little consequence whether these users are all at the desk in person, one is on the telephone, or another has contacted the library via instant messaging (IM). The result is that the librarian will need to make a decision about which individual to help first and how to make all users contacting the library feel like their questions are important. Unlike banks and the post office, the reference desk does not have stanchions and numbers are not taken, and of course no one likes to wait in line even when there are such queuing devices. What is a librarian to do?

Acknowledging waiting users is vital. The librarian should smile and nod at users waiting in line, verbally greet them, and let them know that someone will assist them shortly. For telephone queries, the librarian should pick up the ringing phone, warmly greet the caller, and ask whether he or she can hold. Electronically, the librarian should respond to the IM or chat and let the user know that staff members are assisting other users and will be with the user soon. These actions reassure users that they are not being ignored, and for remote users, the acknowledgment confirms that the library is open and staffed with helpful people.

Users may be helped on a "first come, first served" basis. This is easy but not always practical for the librarian or the user. A user waiting for directions may be frustrated by waiting behind a user who is working on research for a 10-page paper. Therefore, asking waiting users how they could be helped is effective. If all questions are of an in-depth nature, ask the later-arriving users to wait; if some questions are easy or quick to answer, handle those first, and then full attention can be devoted to the more complicated questions. It is possible to start with one user, get to the search stage, and then help another user while the first user looks over search results. Obviously, there are limits to how long users can be expected to wait. It might be more considerate to take a phone number and return the call of the telephone user, perhaps with an answer if the question was taken. Constant interruptions while the librarian is helping with that 10-page paper may be interpreted as lack of interest.

Some libraries have tiered reference services where short questions are handled at one desk and longer questions at another. This may alleviate some juggling of questions of various types, but any reference desk can get busy at any time with any type of question, necessitating judgment about priorities. Most libraries do not set priorities by a formal policy, but strive to be equitable in how they treat all users and place equal importance on all inquiries regardless of mode of communication, type of user, or content of question. It is then up to the librarian working the desk at a given moment to determine the appropriate way in which to serve a queue of users.

Owen (2012, 84–86) suggests some alternatives to immediately providing answers to users including suggesting sources rather than finding answers, suggesting alternative libraries or individual sources of information, asking for thinking time, offering a "quick and dirty" answer, and giving the user reports on the progress of the search. Certainly, if any of these techniques are utilized, follow-up becomes even more important so that the interaction does not feel like a brush-off to the user. See Box 3.8 for a scenario where the reference provider is dealing with three different questions simultaneously.

Box 3.8 Activity: Whom Would You Help in What Order and Why?

Imagine you are at the reference desk and receive the following queries:

Telephone call:	User wants to know whether the library owns a particular book.
In person:	User is looking for articles on how media images affect anorexia in teenage girls.
Instant messaging:	User is encountering difficulty in accessing one of the library's online journal subscriptions.

Questions for Reflection and Discussion:

1. What would you do if all three of these users contacted you within the space of three minutes?
2. Does it matter whether the instant messaging question is from a prominent community member or whether the in-person user is a student or teacher?
3. How might your approach be different if all of the users were in person?
4. What approaches and alternatives to immediate assistance might be appropriate?

Angry or Upset Users

The complexity of information and the variety of ways in which libraries organize and provide access to their collections can cause confusion, frustration, and even anger on the part of library users. Whether it is restrictive library policies that cause irritation, incomplete collections, inadequate services by library staff, or a frustrating event prior to the library visit, library users can be quite angry and upset when dealing with reference staff. In such a situation, individuals in public services positions are vulnerable to angry reactions by library users for even minor irritations. For whatever reason, reference staff will need to be ready to deal effectively with a user who is difficult to handle.

Nowhere is professional judgment more in evidence than when a librarian is confronted with an angry or upset user. The library literature offers a variety of resources to help librarians prepare themselves to deal with such situations (Rubin 1990; Sarkodie-Mensah 2002; Willis 1999). In general, these works suggest using not only general communication skills, including the active listening and questioning techniques discussed throughout this chapter, but also using *empathetic listening*.

Empathetic listening requires acknowledging the feelings of others. This acknowledgment is uncomfortable for most people (Burley-Allen 1995, 128), but when strong emotions stand in the way of resolving an issue, these feelings need to be addressed. In general, the librarian should acknowledge the user's feelings and link them with the specific facts of the situation in a statement. The statement should include acknowledgment of responsibility, the reflection of emotion or feeling, and the description of the event and facts. "You [responsibility] feel [insert feeling word] when [event]." For example, "You feel frustrated when you can't download an audiobook." This statement acknowledges the credibility of the user and demonstrates that the librarian as a listener accepts the user as a person as well. These statements exhibit empathy, not sympathy. By contrast, "absorbing or agreeing with the sentiments of the patron" (McGuigan 2002, 201) has the potential to interfere with the librarian's helping role (Quinn 2002, 188). Box 3.9 provides practice with formulating reflective statements.

Box 3.9 Activity: Reflective Statements

Practice acknowledging the user's feelings in the following situations. Use simple, reflective statements. Do not try, in the exercise, to solve the user's problem; just work on exhibiting an understanding of the user's frustration. Do this exercise with another person, if someone is available. This exercise will work for any mode of communication: online, in person, or telephone.

- The books that I want are always checked out. The library never has anything that I need.
- Why does the library close so early? You used to be open later.
- I can't believe that you charge for printing. Where I used to live, they didn't charge for printing.
- This catalog is stupid. I can't find anything!
- You canceled the most important journal in my field. How can the library do that?
- These DVDs are inappropriate for the library. You shouldn't spend money on that.

Once the user's feelings have been acknowledged, then the librarian must take some action to address the user's problem, starting with asking what the user wants the librarian to do to solve the problem. Often, the librarian cannot take the action that the user wants and will have to identify alternative solutions or bring in a supervisor with greater authority to clarify library policies or to review whether an exception can be made to the current policy.

If an exception cannot be made or alternative solutions found to satisfy the user, the librarian can promise to review the policies and procedures in light of the user's frustrations. Willingness to rethink policies and procedures acknowledges that these need constant updating and that libraries are responsive to users' needs.

Written policies available to users and to staff members are essential to minimize conflicts (Rubin 1990, 47; Willis 1999, 109–17). Without written policies, users may attempt to intimidate librarians into deviating from established policy for their benefit. Other staff members may unwittingly cause problems by deviating from established policy without informing the users that they are making an exception, which thus allows the user to establish an unrealistic expectation of the services the next staff member can and should provide.

Reference staff should also explore opportunities to discuss conflict situations and look for ways to avoid similar problems in the future. After each difficult situation, staff should discuss mechanisms to respond. Sometimes the user simply wants more than the library can provide, but repeated complaints, such as inadequate access to computers and electronic databases or unhappiness over canceled reference sources, should be referred to administrators for further consideration or review. Whether or not expressions of frustration and anger are justified, a user-centered reference service will be willing to regularly reexamine its responses to expressed user needs.

Imposed Queries

Questions asked by a user on behalf of another person, called *imposed queries* (Gross 1995; Gross 1999; Ross, Nilsen, and Radford 2009, 138–43), are seen in all types of libraries. Individuals ask questions to glean information for someone else, such as their children, spouses, parents, friends, employers, or other individuals, or for situations that do not arise out of their own curiosity, such as with school assignments or work projects. Gross's survey of public libraries found that about 25 percent of questions were imposed queries (1995; 1999); the Transform Inc. survey in Maryland revealed that 90 percent of children's reference questions were school related (Blatchford et al. 1998). Because such users often have incomplete or misunderstood information regarding the information requested, it is more important than ever for librarians to seek to understand the context from which the question arose. "When questions are imposed and not self-generated, they are very apt to be presented to reference staff as an 'ill-formed query' . . . because the person asking the question might not fully understand it" (Ross, Nilsen, and Radford 2009, 139).

When librarians in school, public, or academic libraries encounter a number of questions from different students related to the same topic, it is easy to jump to the conclusion that the questions arise from some sort of homework assignment. It is important, even if it appears that the question is one heard before, to conduct a reference interview.

Children tend to have broad initial requests more frequently than adults, so when their initial queries are vague, it is important for the librarian to not jump to the immediate conclusion that the question is related to a homework assignment. However, when children's questions are generated from someone else rather than out of their own curiosity, they often do not have the additional information the reference librarian would like to have.

Not surprisingly, there are differences of opinion regarding whether a librarian should ask whether the question arises from a homework assignment, just as there are about asking "why." The 1997 Maryland study suggests asking open questions of the child to elicit more information and asking about an assignment only if the child cannot provide enough information about the question. This same study found that reference interviews started with broad initial questions about 70 percent of the time, but that "librarians appear to have a problem using more than one open probe in questioning children" (Blatchford et al. 1998), indicating the need to use more open questions in working with children in the reference interview.

When it is obvious that the questioner is working from a homework assignment, it is certainly appropriate to ask whether the student has a copy of the teacher's written instructions to look at. Sometimes talking to the teacher, the person who asked the original question, is appropriate, to avoid placing the student in the middle. Likewise, it is important when dealing with children to talk to the child rather than an accompanying parent in negotiating the question. Further explorations of reference interviews with children can be found in Chapter 11, and more discussion of other special populations are found in Chapter 12.

Ross, Nilsen, and Radford (2009, 142–43) point out, "when a user says that the material is needed 'for a friend,' sometimes this formulation is a defensive strategy to avoid self-disclosure about a sensitive topic." If so, then the individual is in a good position to answer questions about the information need because it is in reality his or her own. Also problematic are the situations in which the individual is acting as an "information gatekeeper," bringing information to others. Again, asking for ways in which the other person will be using the information will be helpful.

When an employee asks a question on behalf of a boss or supervisor, the individual may not know the context of the information need. Bates (1998, 20) suggests, "One approach in handling the issue of getting past the intermediary to the ultimate client is to provide the go-between, often a secretary or administrative assistant, with a written list of questions you need answered before you can proceed with the research." The librarian may need to teach the individual elements of the reference interview in order for that person to go back to the originator of the question for more information. Another alternative is to create a search form. Ross, Nilsen, and Radford's advice for creating an e-mail reference form works equally well in this situation: eliciting information on the user's eligibility for the service, history of the question, gaps in current information, how the information will be used, features of the perfect answer, and time constraints (2009, 220–22).

REMOTE USERS

Telephone

Libraries have been receiving questions by telephone for more than 130 years (Kern 2003). Communication via telephone in the reference environment has its own challenges. As mentioned previously, the lack of nonverbal cues is an impediment in the telephone interview. Although some emotions are easily communicated via tone of voice, such as annoyance or anger, others, such as interest or confusion, are not as easily communicated by vocal inflection. Further, in the absence of facial expressions and body language, it is easier to misinterpret another's tone of voice. This works both ways, with the potential for the librarian to misunderstand the user and for the user to misunderstand the librarian. Unhelpful awkwardness might arise if the user perceives the librarian as uninterested or the librarian thinks that the user sounds annoyed.

It is effective when answering the phone to smile because this affects the tone of voice and sounds more welcoming. A typical telephone greeting such as "Hello" or "Good morning" starts the conversation off in a friendly manner. Additionally, telephone greetings usually contain the name of the library or reference desk, to assure the user that the correct number has been reached. An open question such as "How may I help you?" invites the user to state his or her question.

The rest of the question negotiation is really the same via telephone as it is in person. Open and closed questions and paraphrasing are still good practice. It is even possible to instruct inquirers in the use of library resources while they are on the telephone. This is particularly true when the inquirer is using the online library catalog or electronic databases and is able to work at a computer while talking on the telephone with a librarian. For other questions, the librarian and inquirer may not want to stay on the telephone that long. If the question requires extensive instruction, it is polite to offer the user an option to meet in person or arrange a phone call consultation at a more mutually convenient time. When it will take the librarian more than a couple of minutes to find an answer, it is kindest to ask inquirers whether they would prefer a callback or would like to hold. No one enjoys waiting on hold for a long time, so inquirers who are on hold should be reassured every few minutes that the librarian is still working on their question and given the option for a callback.

Ambient noise and inaudible inquirers can be a problem with telephone calls. A reference desk may have too much in-person activity to allow the librarian to hear someone on the phone clearly, or the acoustics of the room may be bad. A particularly busy telephone also may make it difficult to work with in-person users. Libraries deal with staffing telephone reference in different ways. Some have a desk that is in a different location, staffed separately from the in-person reference desk. It is more common for libraries to staff the telephone from the same desk as in-person queries and to have a volume control to help them better hear callers on the telephone.

E-mail, Mail, and Fax

Reference queries received via e-mail, mail, and fax all have an asynchronous nature in that the librarian cannot interview the user in real time. All three interactions can result in substantial delays in responses to users. All three are appealing because users can submit the question whenever it occurs to them. Those who live at a distance, who have mobility constraints, or who are more comfortable using written rather than verbal communication because of language skills or shyness may prefer to use these types of written communications. For librarians, these transactions have some advantages. It has been suggested that the users formulate and present their questions more effectively when they formally write them out rather than speak them (Abels 1996).

Because the user is not present in person or in real time, there is more time for thought and reflection, and questions can be deferred to quieter times. It is easier to refer questions to the appropriate person or expert, and the workload is more easily distributed to others. E-mail software can capture and save the queries and responses for later analysis or evaluation. Some back-and-forth communication may be needed to clarify the question, but this can be difficult to achieve via e-mail because the user may view a request for clarification as being put off or may become frustrated with the amount of time that the interaction is taking. Ultimately, as Joseph Straw writes, "reference librarians must be able to write messages that are organized, concise, and logical. A well-written response not only answers a question eloquently, but it also tells the user about the importance that the library places on the question" (Straw 2000, 376–79).

Chat and Instant Messaging

Real-time chat and instant messaging (IM) services augment but do not replace e-mail services in libraries. Chat reference services have been around since about

1999, and IM has recently become a popular communication technology in libraries. These terms can be confusing as they are often used interchangeably. A simple explanation is that "chat" is a broader term that encompasses a variety of different software protocols for synchronous text communication including IM. Sometimes "chat" is used to refer to commercial software that supports virtual reference although that has become blurry as some commercial virtual reference software incorporates IM. As it relates to the reference interview, IM is similar to chat in the way that communication occurs and in best practices to be used by the librarian in interacting with the user, with the exception that some chat software allows screensharing or co-browsing so that user and librarian can see the same computer screen.

One advantage that virtual reference services have over e-mail, mail, and fax is the ability to conduct the reference interview in real time and to eliminate the waiting time. Other advantages of virtual transactions are the ability to escort the user through complex searches, provide instruction in using resources, and assist in evaluating the results. Cooperative ventures even allow answers to be given 24/7 by librarians not in the library where the user is a patron. The librarian may be at home, on another campus, or even on another continent. The disadvantages of this communication mode are that there are no visual or aural cues, and the communication is more labor-intensive because typing requires more time and concentrated effort than speaking. Electronic reference interviews require the same skills as traditional reference interviews, but some additional considerations should be taken into account.

Chat interactions utilize a more casual tone than that to which most librarians are accustomed. The exchanges of text utilize shorter phrases than in speech and often incorporate commonly accepted abbreviations. Hirko and Ross state that "economy of phrase is invaluable, along with the ability to break a longer answer into brief one- or two-line parts that can be quickly sent" (2004, 12). Although the abbreviations used in online communication initially may be unfamiliar, sources such as NetLingo provide explanations; these may be bookmarked or distributed to staff for their reference. Use of abbreviations may be less frequent than expected because there are varying levels of formality in online communication, just as in spoken discourse. As with any reference interview, the librarian should be aware of and responsive to the user's formality, but should not feel obligated to use abbreviations or slang because this may come across as contrived.

Keeping the user informed is one of the most challenging aspects of the virtual environment, with the librarian needing to let the user know what he or she is doing. Appropriate responses to common questions and situations can be selected from pre-scripted messages, such as initial greetings, prompts for additional information, search instructions, technical messages, and advising the user to please wait or that the librarian is still searching. In one study of chat communication, "lengthy, formal scripts were seen as impersonal, and overuse of them implied lack of either interest or interview skills on the part of the library operator" (Hirko and Ross 2004, 13). Scripts should be used to facilitate the flow of conversation but should not become the conversation. Attention to the tone of the scripts is important to avoid a robotic or unwelcoming tone.

The availability of chat transcripts has been useful both for research into the reference interview and interpersonal communication and as training tools within libraries. Marie Radford examined transcripts to investigate rapport-building techniques used by both librarians and inquirers in chat communication as well as barriers to effective communication (Radford 2006). Although Radford's suggestions came from analyzing chat transcripts, most are more broadly applicable to any reference encounter. The individual librarian will find reviewing transcripts for successful and unsuccessful communication strategies to be useful as a self-assessment tool, and library trainers may use them to discuss way to improve communication in the reference interview. For example, the self-reflection form presented in Box 3.7 could also be used with chat transcripts to improve reference skills.

New communications technologies are continually explored by the general public and libraries. Voice-over IP technology, such as Skype or Google Voice, and online videoconferencing technologies that deliver real-time voice and video over the Internet have yet to gain significant use by the general population and so have not been incorporated into reference services by many libraries. If these technologies are implemented by libraries, librarians will need to adapt reference interview techniques to these new environments.

PERSONALITY QUALITIES OF REFERENCE LIBRARIANS

The communication skills necessary to conduct good reference interviews can be learned with appropriate study and training, but not everyone can be an effective reference librarian. In an attempt to summarize several authors, Charles Patterson (1984, 167) listed good memory, thoroughness, orderliness, accuracy, imagination, an inquisitive mind, logicalness, an outgoing personality, the ability to interact, and a desire to help people. Certain qualities from Patterson's list may be traits developed over a lifetime or part of someone's personality rather than skills that can be learned efficiently and effectively. The list of personality qualities presented in this chapter is not exhaustive, but focuses on areas that can be developed by the reference librarian through training, practice, and active reflection.

Service Orientation

"Service orientation" is a phrase used in many advertisements for reference positions (Allen and Allen 1992, 68), referring to an innate desire or commitment to helping others. This desire to help is expressed through approachability, friendliness, open-mindedness, and interest in each user as an individual. It is not necessary to be an extrovert to be a reference librarian, and people who define themselves as quiet may enjoy working with people in the structured environment of the reference interaction. Conversely, people who are outgoing are not always accepting and service-oriented. Enjoying the "give-and-take of human interaction" is highlighted by Elaine Z. Jennerich and Edward J. Jennerich (1997, 37) as extremely important, given that many reference librarians do not have private offices and must deal with people during most of their working day. Individuals who like people are more likely to accept people as they are and resist making assumptions based on superficial observations.

This interest in helping should be accompanied by flexibility in working with people of diverse personalities, appearances, and backgrounds. If the librarian is open and self-revealing, users will respond correspondingly and be more forthcoming and thus be more satisfied with the human relations aspect of the reference service provided (Markham, Stirling, and Smith 1983, 372–73).

Patience and Persistence

Successful reference librarians exhibit a great deal of patience with individuals who have difficulty expressing themselves or with frustrated, angry, impatient, arrogant, insensitive, or shy individuals. Reference librarians will help all of these users at some point. In such situations, the librarian may need to spend more time eliciting information and listening to the user talk, and the user needs to feel that the librarian is not in a hurry to go do something else.

Reference librarians also need to have patience with their own inadequacies in the search process, realizing that no one person can possibly know everything and be everything to everyone. In dealing with difficult questions, whether because of delicate negotiations or complex or puzzling queries, the librarian needs to remain calm and composed, so that the user does not lose trust in the librarian or regret asking the question. When faced with questions that seem insurmountable, librarians may need to tell users that they have to get back to them later in the day or week because of the complexity of the question. The librarian may wish to discuss the question with colleagues to broaden the range of options to pursue.

Sensitivity and Adaptation

Richard E. Bopp (2001, 50) suggested that "sensitivity is the surest way to transform the desire to help into effective results." A sensitive individual can adapt to the communication style preferred by the individual being interviewed and sense whether a more formal and objective approach is needed or whether casual conversation and a more obvious personal interest in the question will result in the best interaction. Issues in communication that may arise from differences between the librarian and the user, such as age, level of education, native language, and familiarity with the library, are more readily addressed when the librarian is open to the uniqueness of the individual. An insensitive reference librarian can destroy the chance to negotiate the reference interview successfully by not perceiving the unique needs and concerns that must be addressed.

Self-Control

Negotiating a successful reference interview requires a certain amount of discipline, or self-control. Discipline helps counteract the impulse to skip the reference interview and take the question at face value. It can be very tempting to treat the sixth person who asks a seemingly simple question differently from the first one. Discipline is also needed to give each user the proper amount of concentration in the midst of a variety of distractions in the reference environment. Particularly in hectic atmospheres, it is important for users to feel that they have the librarian's full attention.

The exercise of self-control to encounter the next reference query without the baggage of the previous one, especially with time constraints, failed search strategies, or a difficult librarian–user interaction, is important. Every librarian has shifts when he or she hits the right tone in almost every encounter. Conversely, every reference librarian has times when nothing seems to go right. Martin Seligman, in *Learned Optimism* (1991), talks about optimists' and pessimists' views of good and bad events as permanent, pervasive, and personal, and he stresses that individuals can change their viewpoints by monitoring their self-talk. For example, after a difficult reference encounter, does one say, "Man that was a tough one! What was it about that interaction that was so difficult?" (temporal, isolated, external to self). Or does one say, "I really blew that one; I'll never be a good reference librarian!" (permanent, pervasive, personal). This self-control results in handling negative emotions and false leads in a way that does not compromise the user's trust in the librarian as a competent provider and also will help the librarian maintain a more positive frame of mind about the job. The librarian who interprets difficulties (with the user, the resources, or his or her own skills) in a reference interaction as permanent, pervasive, and personal is more likely to give up on a reference question or send the user away out of frustration. The librarian who is sure that he or she can affect a satisfactory outcome is more likely to stay with the task and explore alternative solutions to help the user.

Flexibility

The ability to jump quickly from one subject to another is another good trait for a reference librarian, whether in a specialized setting or a general one (Neill 1975, 314). Handling in-person and virtual reference questions at the same time, a combination of telephone and virtual inquiries, or three virtual queries at once can be challenging and stressful and requires the flexibility to handle more than one query at the same time and the ability to move from one to the other smoothly. Flexibility can be thought of as another aspect of imagination and creativity, the ability to change directions by looking at the question from another perspective or to borrow ideas from other contexts.

Sense of Humor

A sense of humor is often cited as a good quality for a reference librarian (Jennerich and Jennerich 1997, 36; Osborne 1992). In general, the use of humor can help relieve stress, put people at ease, and establish rapport. Care should be taken, however, not to make individuals the focus of that humor.

Good Judgment

Librarians must continuously make decisions in their interactions with users. Deciding which sources to consult is actually among the easier decisions faced by reference librarians. Communicating with users requires the application of professional judgment to determine appropriate questions and responses based on the interaction so far as well as the content and tone of the user's communication. This is not about jumping to conclusions or making snap judgments about a user, but about careful consideration of all that has been observed during the interaction and the ability to remain open to new cues from the user.

A few of the areas requiring professional judgment are matching the level of the answer to the user, determining the teachable moment, and knowing when to not ask too much. Examining each of these areas in turn, matching the level of the answer to the user, requires being aware of the user's comfort with the library and the amount of previous library experience. It also includes knowing how much information the user is seeking. Some of this can be ascertained through questioning during the reference interview, but attention to the user's level of facility with using the library resources and to the degree of sophistication in how the question is framed and presented is vital. Librarians can easily overwhelm users with resources about a topic or information about libraries and research. Impatience, boredom, or glassy eyes are extreme indicators that the user either has lost interest or is overwhelmed.

Teaching is a primary mission in some libraries and not employed at all in others. Library type is always a factor in determining whether it is appropriate to instruct the user. Of equal importance is the user's willingness to learn. If the user is impatient or uninterested, the librarian can teach, but it is unlikely that the user will retain any learning. It may be more suitable to provide the information needed and tell the user the search process being used, for example, "I will look up that book in the catalog, using the 'title' search." Some searches are complex or convoluted because of the nature of the information being sought, and these are rarely good opportunities for learning unless the user is a dedicated researcher or openly expresses interest. Nonetheless, in many settings, it is necessary to have users research for themselves and evaluate the results of the findings. In these cases, the librarian should present the research process in steps, working with the user and paying attention to nonverbal cues and signs of understanding or frustration. Librarians can leave the user to examine the results of the first part of the search (e.g., finding newspaper articles) and return later to explain the next step (e.g., finding books) or invite the user to return to the desk when ready to move to the next part of the research process.

Sometimes users have questions that may be of a sensitive or personal nature. This can be uncomfortable for both users and librarians. It is imperative that librarians remain impartial and not let personal beliefs or experiences affect their responses. Avoid forming opinions about the user's needs or uses for the information. That is not to say that the librarian should be uncaring, but caring is best exemplified by avoiding intrusions into the user's privacy. Medical, legal, and social or personal welfare questions are the most frequent examples in this category. Good judgment is needed to know how to navigate the line between privacy and empathy and to allow the user to retain control over what details to share. Questions should be neutral; the librarian should ask about the type of information needed and avoid "why" questions as discussed earlier in this chapter. Occasionally, a user may divulge more than the librarian wishes to know, in which case it is prudent to bring the user back to questions that the librarian can help with while still maintaining a caring disposition.

Knowledge and Confidence

A good reference librarian has the ability to match users' queries to available resources and knows how to use resources effectively. In order to achieve this, the librarian should develop a broad knowledge of resources by reading a daily newspaper and possibly a weekly newsmagazine, or by subscribing to a news blog to keep up with current events (Dilevko and Dolan 1999). Bopp suggested that because many humanities graduates are drawn to reference work and they work at general reference desks, a specialized source for nonspecialists, such as *Scientific American*, might be included in the librarian's regular reading (2001, 51).

Similarly, a thorough knowledge of reference sources is necessary for selecting the resource appropriate in a particular situation. Time and experience in dealing with these sources are necessary to gain mastery over them. The successful reference professional is familiar with a broad range of reference sources in different formats. There are, in reality, a relatively small number of multipurpose reference sources, but knowing the content of these materials will give the librarian confidence to know when to go beyond them to other resources. Knowledge of local collections, and the broader availability of resources in distant or remote collections, is also important. Good knowledge of information sources inspires the confidence of the user and contributes to the trust that is needed to enter into a successful reference transaction.

CONCLUSION

The effectiveness of reference service depends on the ability of library staff to conduct a successful reference interview. This is a constant, regardless of the mode of communication. Ross, Nilsen, and Radford state, "(t)he process of finding out what the user really wants is the bedrock of successful reference service upon which everything else depends. The most comprehensive understanding of the sources is wasted if the information intermediary is looking for the wrong thing. The need to understand what the user really wants to know remains the same, whether the reference transaction is face-to-face, over the telephone, or online" (2009, ix).

Successful reference interactions require a variety of interpersonal skills and traits in addition to questioning, including genuine interest in users' information needs, the ability to establish trust and confidence, flexibility, professional judgment, and knowledge of research tools and reference sources. User satisfaction not only with the answer provided but also with the interaction with the librarian is the ultimate goal. As research by Durrance (1995) and others has shown, personal interaction is as significant a factor in user satisfaction and willingness to return as being given the correct answer. Thus, just as approachability is the beginning of a reference interview, facility with the reference interview is the beginning of an excellent reference librarian.

NOTE

1. The views expressed are the author's own and do not reflect the official policy or position of the National Defense University, Department of Defense, or the U.S. Government.

REFERENCES

Abels, Eileen G. 1996. "The E-Mail Reference Interview." *RQ* 35 (Spring): 345–58.

Allen, Gillian, and Bryce Allen. 1992. "Service Orientation as a Selection Criterion for Public Service Librarians." *Journal of Library Administration* 16 (4): 67–76.

Bates, Mary Ellen. 1998. "Finding the Question behind the Question." *Information Outlook* 2 (7): 19–21.

Benjamin, Alfred. 1981. *The Helping Interview*, 3rd ed. Boston: Houghton Mifflin.

Blatchford, Mary Lee, Marjorie Ann Crammer, Susan Paznekas, and Stacey Aldrich. 1998. "Quality of Reference Service to Children: A Pilot Study from Maryland." Paper presented at the Public Library Association Conference, Kansas City, MO. Quoted in Melvin K. Burton. 1998. "Reference Interview: Strategies for Children." *North Carolina Libraries* 56 (3): 110–13.

Bopp, Richard E. 2001. "Reference Interview." In *Reference and Information Services: An Introduction*, edited by Richard E. Bopp and Linda C. Smith, 3rd ed., 47–68. Santa Barbara, CA: Libraries Unlimited.

Burley-Allen, Madelyn. 1995. *Listening: The Forgotten Skill: A Self-Teaching Guide*, 2nd ed. New York: Wiley.

Cramer, Dina C. 1998. "How to Speak Patron." *Public Libraries* 37 (6): 349.

Dervin, Brenda, and Patricia Dewdney. 1986. "Neutral Questioning: A New Approach to the Reference Interview." *RQ* 25 (Summer): 506–13.

Dewdney, Patricia. 1986. "The Effects of Training Reference Librarians in Interview Skills: A Field Experiment." PhD diss., University of Western Ontario.

Dewdney, Patricia, and B. Gillian Michell. 1997. "Asking 'Why' Questions in the Reference Interview: A Theoretical Justification." *Library Quarterly* 67 (January): 50–71.

Dewdney, Patricia, and Catherine Sheldrick Ross. 1994. "Flying a Light Aircraft: Reference Service Evaluation from a User's Viewpoint." *RQ* 34 (2): 217–30.

Dilevko, Juris, and Elizabeth Dolan. 1999. "Reference Work and the Value of Reading Newspapers." *Reference & User Services Quarterly* 39 (1): 71–81.

Durrance, Joan C. 1995. "Factors That Influence Reference Success: What Makes Questioners Willing to Return?" *The Reference Librarian* 49/50: 243–65.

Dyson, Lillie Seward. 1992. "Improving Reference Services: A Maryland Training Program Brings Positive Results." *Public Libraries* 31 (September/October): 284–89.

Gers, Ralph, and Lillie J. Seward. 1985. "Improving Reference Performance: Results of a Statewide Study." *Library Journal* 110 (November 1): 32–35.

Gross, Melissa. 1995. "The Imposed Query." *RQ* 35 (2): 236–43.

Gross, Melissa. 1999. "Imposed versus Self-Generated Questions: Implications for Reference Practice." *Reference & User Services Quarterly* 39 (1): 53–61.

Hirko, Buff, and Mary Bucher Ross. 2004. *Virtual Reference Training: The Complete Guide to Providing Anytime Anywhere Answers*. Chicago: American Library Association.

Isenstein, Laura. 1992. "Get Your Reference Staff on the STAR Track." *Library Journal* 117 (April 15): 34–37.

Jennerich, Elaine Z., and Edward J. Jennerich. 1997. *The Reference Interview as a Creative Art*, 2nd ed. Englewood, CO: Libraries Unlimited.

Kern, M. Kathleen. 2003. "Have(n't) We Been Here Before? Lessons from Telephone Reference." *The Reference Librarian* 41 (85): 1–17.

King, Geraldine B. 1972. "The Reference Interview: Open & Closed Questions." *RQ* 12 (2): 157–60.

Lynch, Mary Jo. 1978. "Reference Interviews in Public Libraries." *The Library Quarterly* 48 (2): 119–42.

Mabry, Celia Hales. 2003. "The Reference Interview as Partnership: An Examination of Librarian, Library User, and Social Interaction." *The Reference Librarian* 83/84: 41–56.

Markham, Marilyn J., Keith H. Stirling, and Nathan M. Smith. 1983. "Librarian Self-Disclosure and Patron Satisfaction in the Reference Interview." *RQ* 22 (4): 369–74.

McGuigan, Glenn S. 2002. "The Common Sense of Customer Service: Employing Advice from the Trade and Popular Literature of Business to Interactions with Irate Patrons in Libraries." *The Reference Librarian* 36 (75/76): 197–204.

Michell, Gillian, and Roma M. Harris. 1987. "Evaluating the Reference Interview: Some Factors Influencing Patrons and Professionals." *RQ* 27 (1): 95–105.

Neill, S.D. 1975. "Problem Solving and the Reference Process." *RQ* 14 (4): 310–315.

"NetLingo List of Chat Acronyms & Text Shorthand." 2015. NetLingo. Accessed September 26, 2015. http://www.netlingo.com/dictionary/r.php.

Nolan, Christopher W. 1992. "Closing the Reference Interview: Implications for Policy and Practice." *RQ* 31 (4): 513–23.

Ohio Library Council. 2014. "Six Pieces of Evidence." Ohio Reference Excellence on the Web. http://web.archive.org/web/20151015043101/http://www.olc.org/ore/2pieces.htm.

Osborne, Nancy S. 1992. "Librarian Humor in Classroom and Reference." ERIC Document ED349018.

Oser, Fred. 1987. "Referens Simplex or the Mysteries of Reference Interviewing Revealed." *The Reference Librarian* 6 (16): 53–78.

Owen, Tim Buckley. 2012. *Successful Enquiry Answering Every Time*, 6th rev. ed. London: Facet.

Patterson, Charles D. 1984. "Personality, Knowledge, and the Reference Librarian." *Reference Librarian* 3 (9): 167–72.

Quinn, Brian. 2002. "How Psychotherapists Handle Difficult Clients: Lessons for Librarians." *The Reference Librarian* 36 (75/76): 181–96.

Radford, Marie L. 1999. *The Reference Encounter: Interpersonal Communication in the Academic Library*. Chicago: Association of College and Research Libraries.

Radford, Marie L. 2006. "Encountering Virtual Users: A Qualitative Investigation of Interpersonal Communication in Chat Reference." *Journal of the American Society for Information Science and Technology* 57 (8): 1046–59.

Reference and User Services Association. 2013. "Guidelines for Behavioral Performance of Reference and Information Services Providers." American Library Association. http://www.ala.org/rusa/resources/guidelines/guidelinesbehavioral.

Ross, Catherine Sheldrick. 2003. "The Reference Interview: Why It Needs to Be Used in Every (Well, Almost Every) Reference Transaction." *Reference & User Services Quarterly* 43 (1): 38–43.

Ross, Catherine Sheldrick, and Patricia Dewdney. 1998. "Negative Closure: Strategies and Counter-Strategies in the Reference Transaction." *Reference & User Services Quarterly* 38 (2): 151–63.

Ross, Catherine Sheldrick, and Kirsti Nilsen. 2000. "So Has the Internet Changed Anything in Reference? The Library Visit Study, Phase 2." *Reference & User Services Quarterly* 40 (2): 147–55.

Ross, Catherine Sheldrick, and Kirsti Nilsen. 2013. *Communicating Professionally*, 3rd ed. New York: Neal-Schuman.

Ross, Catherine Sheldrick, Kirsti Nilsen, and Marie L. Radford. 2009. *Conducting the Reference Interview: A How-To-Do-It Manual for Librarians*, 2nd ed. How-to-Do-It Manuals for Librarians, no. 166. New York: Neal-Schuman.

Rubin, Rhea Joyce. 1990. "Anger in the Library: Defusing Angry Patrons at the Reference Desk (and Elsewhere)." *The Reference Librarian* 14 (31): 39–51.

Sarkodie-Mensah, Kwasi, ed., 2002. *Helping the Difficult Patron: New Approaches to Examining and Resolving a Long-Standing and Ongoing Problem*. New York: Haworth Press.

Seligman, Martin E.P. 1991. *Learned Optimism*. New York: Alfred A. Knopf.

Straw, Joseph E. 2000. "A Virtual Understanding: The Reference Interview and Question Negotiation in the Digital Age." *Reference & User Services Quarterly* 39 (4): 376–79.

Taylor, Robert S. 1968. "Question-Negotiation and Information Seeking in Libraries." *College & Research Libraries* 29 (3): 178–94.

White, Marilyn Domas. 1981. "The Dimensions of the Reference Interview." *RQ* 20 (4): 373–81.

Willis, Mark R. 1999. *Dealing with Difficult People in the Library*. Chicago: American Library Association.

SUGGESTED READINGS

Durrance, Joan C. 1995. "Factors That Influence Reference Success: What Makes Questioners Willing to Return?" *The Reference Librarian* 49/50: 243–65.

Durrance seeks to expand the evaluation of reference encounters beyond the provision of successful information service (accuracy of answers) to include other aspects such as the quality of the reference interview and the provision of instruction and guidance. In her "Willingness to Return" study, she uses the willingness of users to return to the same librarian at a later time with another question to study what factors users consider important in the reference interaction. She found that interpersonal qualities such as approachability, ability to listen, and interest in the user's question were among the behaviors most often associated with success as judged by users.

Fine, Sara. 1995. "Reference and Resources: The Human Side." *Journal of Academic Librarianship* 21 (1): 17–20.

In this short but thought-provoking essay, Fine discusses librarians' assumptions about themselves and their users and how these assumptions can affect the service provided. She argues that better awareness of their own assumptions about themselves and their users will help reference librarians improve their service to those users.

Gross, Melissa. 1995. "The Imposed Query." *RQ* 35 (2): 236–43.

Gross, Melissa. 1999. "Imposed versus Self-Generated Questions: Implications for Reference Practice." *Reference & User Services Quarterly* 39 (1): 53–61.

In these two thought-provoking articles, Melissa Gross discusses reference interviewing when the question asked is posed not by the originator of the question but by an agent of that person, such as a secretary, student, family member, or other individual. In the first article, she reviews some of the relevant literature and develops a model for imposed queries. The second article delves more specifically into the problems associated with these questions and suggests solutions.

Harmeyer, David. 2014. *The Reference Interview Today: Negotiating and Answering Questions Face to Face, on the Phone, and Virtually*. Lanham, MD: Rowman & Littlefield.

This field guide provides a series of different reference interview scenarios set in different modes demonstrating a specific principle. Each scenario includes an overview of the principle, a script of the reference interview, and learning questions designed to demonstrate the principles.

Howze, Philip C., and Felix E. Unaeze. 1997. "All in the Name of Service: Mediation, Client Self-Determination, and Reference Practice in Academic Libraries." *RQ* 36 (3): 430–37.

Howze and Unaeze apply the concept of "client self-determination" (or self-empowerment), borrowed from social work, to the field of reference librarianship. They argue that the reference librarian's role as a mediator between users and information sources is best carried out when the librarian encourages users to "become full participants in their own outcomes."

Knoer, Susan. 2011. *The Reference Interview Today*. Santa Barbara, CA: ABC-CLIO.

Knoer covers the skills needed for traditional face-to-face reference and how they can be applied in 2.0 media. Best practices for culturally diverse, disabled, and "difficult" patrons; strategies for public and academic libraries; and virtual technologies like Twitter and Second Life are also described.

Luo, Lili. 2007. "Chat Reference Competencies: Identification from a Literature Review and Librarian Interviews." *Reference Services Review* 35 (2): 195–209.
Based on a thorough review of the chat reference literature and interviews with experienced librarians, three types of chat reference competencies are identified: core competencies for general reference, competencies for general reference but highlighted in the chat environment, and competencies specific to chat reference service.

Murphy, Sarah Anne. 2005. "The Reference Narrative." *Reference & User Services Quarterly* 44 (3): 247–52.
This article examines the reference interview using the rhetorical narrative or "text." Reference, like medicine, is a human endeavor requiring interpretation of objective, subjective, and ambiguous texts. There are three types of texts that come together in the reference interview: the user's text, the librarian's text, and the institution's text. These make up the narrative through which the librarian may interpret the user's information needs, empathize with the user's experience in using the library, and collaborate with the user to focus the information need to achieve the desired outcome.

Radford, Marie L. 1996. "Communication Theory Applied to the Reference Encounter: An Analysis of Critical Incidents." *The Library Quarterly* 66 (2): 123–37.

Radford, Marie L. 1999. *The Reference Encounter: Interpersonal Communication in the Academic Library*. ACRL Publications in Librarianship, no. 52. Chicago: American Library Association.
Both of these Radford titles report qualitative studies of reference interactions, using detailed interviews with both the librarian and the user to understand their perceptions of the encounter. Radford found that librarians were likely to talk about issues of content, such as the amount or quality of information, whereas users looked at relational factors such as pleasantness, helpfulness, and similar qualities in determining the success or failure of a reference transaction. These two works are foundational in the study of interpersonal communications between users and librarians.

Ross, Catherine Sheldrick, and Kirsti Nilsen. 2013. *Communicating Professionally: A How-To-Do-It Manual for Librarians*, 2nd ed. New York: Neal-Schuman.
Ross and Nilsen discuss the skills required for effective communication and apply them to various library activities, from group activities and formal presentations to the one-to-one communication found in the reference interview. Of most relevance here are the sections on listening and question negotiation and on the types and stages of reference interviews. The book is very readable, and the annotated readings appended to each section are very helpful.

Ross, Catherine Sheldrick, Kirsti Nilsen, and Marie L. Radford. 2009. *Conducting the Reference Interview: A How-To-Do-It Manual for Librarians*, 2nd ed. How-to-Do-It Manuals for Librarians, no. 166. New York: Neal-Schuman.
An outgrowth of years of research on reference interview effectiveness and countless workshops on conducting the reference interview, this work provides excellent summaries of the research as well as some practical suggestions for individual study or group interactions to improve the librarian's ability to understand what the user wants. The use of case studies, checklists, and exercises makes this a valuable tool for training on the reference interview, engaging the reader in active learning.

Taylor, Robert S. 1962. "The Process of Asking Questions." *American Documentation* 13 (4): 391–96.

Taylor, Robert S. 1968. "Question-Negotiation and Information Seeking in Libraries." *College & Research Libraries* 29 (3): 178–94.

These seminal articles are among the most frequently cited discussions of the application of communication principles to the reference interview. Taylor focuses on the ways questions are formulated by the user and how they are presented to the reference librarian. The second article, in particular, discusses principles of question negotiation that librarians should follow to accurately understand the user's information need.

Chapter 4

Instruction

Wendy Holliday

INTRODUCTION

Instruction has been an essential part of reference service in libraries since at least the late 19th century. According to John Mark Tucker, the modern notion of the librarian as educator emerged in 1876; Otis Richard Hall and Melvil Dewey both espoused that librarians were teachers and that libraries were not simply places to hold books (1980). This role has evolved in conjunction with the changing mission of libraries and broader educational institutions and with new frameworks for teaching and learning. Over the past century, user education has been central to efforts to promote an educated democratic citizenry, to reform education in response to various historical contexts, and to address the new challenges brought on by the Internet and a proliferation of content and information channels. Spurred by different events and impulses, instructional services over time have consistently been dedicated to a common goal: to understand users' learning needs and abilities and to design effective instructional interventions to meet those needs. In this broad frame, instruction is a core reference service function.

Instruction has a long history in reference librarianship, but it truly blossomed as a central mission for libraries in the 1970s. In 1974, Paul Zurkowski first coined the term "information literacy." He described an information-literate individual as one who has "learned techniques and skills for utilizing the wide range of information tools as well as primary sources in molding information solutions to their problems" (Zurkowski 1974, 6). The American Library Association (ALA), the American Association of School Librarians (AASL), and the Association of College and Research Libraries (ACRL), along with various international library and educational groups, have since developed standards, best practices, and outreach efforts to promote the role of libraries and librarians in the development of information literacy. While there are still debates about specific standards, practices, and approaches to instruction, the teaching role of librarians is generally acknowledged as central to promoting more productive and empowered societies.

According to UNESCO (2014), "Empowerment of people through Media and Information Literacy (MIL) is an important prerequisite for fostering equitable access to information and knowledge and promoting free, independent and pluralistic media and information systems."

INSTRUCTION IN LIBRARIES

The Reference and Instruction Relationship

Throughout the modern history of libraries, there has been an ongoing tension about the relationship of instruction and reference services hinging on this basic question, "Should librarians provide instruction to promote more independent users or should they provide information directly?" Tucker (1980, 19–20) describes three main schools of thought:

- *Instructional*: The purpose of the reference librarian is to teach the user to help himself or herself.
- *Informational*: The patron does not want instruction but information, and it is the responsibility of the reference librarian to retrieve it.
- *Situational*: As personnel and materials become increasingly expensive, the reference librarian cannot and should not provide complete service but should exercise his or her professional judgment in providing information to some and instruction to others. What the librarian does in a given situation depends on his or her particular library environment.

Tucker suggests that a variety of philosophical and practical considerations contribute to these basic classifications of reference service. For some, providing instruction to an individual user compromises more complete reference service, allows the user to retain autonomy, and is a response to limited personnel resources. In this view, librarians are teachers, and the primary goal for librarians should be the development of self-sufficient lifelong learners (Katz 1969; Schiller 1965; Tucker 1980). James K. Elmborg, for example, suggests that reference librarians should treat reference interactions as teachable moments. Borrowing from constructivist learning theory, he argues that reference as information provision takes the process out of the hands of the student: "We must unlearn that definition of our job in order to teach at the reference desk. Instead, we must see our job as helping students to answer their own questions" (2002, 459).

Traditionally, there has been a stronger role of librarian as educator in academic and school libraries and a more prominent information service model in public libraries (Schiller 1965). While firmly established in formal school settings by the 1980s, Roma M. Harris (1989) notes that, in public libraries, the role of instruction was still a matter of debate. Recently, there has been wider acknowledgment of public libraries' educational role in the context of budget cuts, the closure of school libraries, and the growing needs of adult learners seeking to retool their job skills or meet other personal learning needs. As the Institute of Museum and Library Services (IMLS) suggests, these factors place public libraries at the center of their communities' educational needs: "Skills like critical thinking and problem solving are not only relevant for K–12 students and schools. Millions of adult learners not in formal education programs are looking to refine workplace skills. Even school-aged children spend the overwhelming majority of their waking hours in non-school settings, and increasingly they spend this time in organized out-of-school settings such as afterschool, museum, and library programs" (2009, 4).

The history of instruction as a part of reference service has been shaped by numerous factors. Questions of professional status for librarians, for example, have an influence on the instruction vs. information provision debate. On the information provision side of the debate, librarians seek the status implied in a professional–client relationship such as in the medical profession. For proponents of an instructional philosophy of reference, especially in the academic and school context, teaching aligns with the status conferred on faculty (Nielsen 1982).

Technology influences the debate as well. The growth of mediated online searching in the 1970s and 1980s contributed to a shift back toward expert information provision by librarians. Eventually, the emphasis shifted back to instruction by the 1990s with end-user searching and freely available Internet resources (Atlas 2000). Current debates over whether to teach users a wide range of skills unrelated to information seeking per se, such as workshops on resume writing, software coding, or makerspaces, are therefore not new, but have a long history in the philosophical trajectory of reference services.

Instructional Models in Libraries

Given that the philosophical and professional definitions of instruction in libraries have shifted over time, it comes as little surprise that there are numerous models for designing and delivering user education. The basic models have developed through the years and represent something of an evolution: library orientation, library instruction, bibliographic instruction, and information literacy. These models are neither completely linear nor mutually exclusive. Library orientations, for example, might be a vital part of an information literacy program in K–12 or higher education, but, in this context, they are one method of delivery, rather than an overarching pedagogical model. In law schools, librarians often teach first-year students a "process approach," with elements of bibliographic instruction and information literacy, as part of the regular first-year curriculum. But they also provide workshops that fit more in a tools-based model akin to library instruction (Peura 2014). Similarly, a public library program for small business might include instruction in library tools (as in the library instruction model) and critical information literacy components related to free Internet resources (consonant with information literacy instruction). Furthermore, while information literacy replaced bibliographic instruction as the dominant model in academic and school library settings in the 1990s, many librarians, in all types of libraries, refer to what they do as "library instruction." Public librarians, who often teach during individual reference transactions, might use an array of approaches that do not fit neatly into these more formal educational models. Thus, the outline of each of the following models highlights the primary focus and purpose of instruction in group settings, even though general terms like "orientation" and "library instruction" might be used across all four models.

Library Orientation

Library orientations focus on introducing users to the library. Traditionally, orientations focused on the library as physical place and emerged as a need when libraries became larger and harder to navigate at a glance. Today, orientation activities might include an online tour of the library website, as this virtual library "space" has become increasingly complex for the end users. Print materials, such as handouts, maps, and brochures, also serve as orienting material by providing overviews of library resources, services, and space. Orientations also include an emotional element of welcoming users, rather than focusing solely on cognitive or intellectual goals. Orientations are designed to make the library a welcoming place and to introduce users to a helpful, friendly staff. These affective goals can be important elements of an instruction program because of the well-documented phenomenon of library anxiety (Mellon 1986). Understanding that librarians are available with expertise and a commitment to users can remove a significant barrier to learning for many students.

Library Instruction

Library instruction, sometimes also called user education in the literature, is focused on "know-how" and library-centered tools and resources. When libraries held only print collections, librarians trained users how to access library collections using specific tools, such as catalogs, indexes, and reference books. Library orientation and instruction often went hand in hand, although instruction in the use of library collections continued to become more diverse as collections grew in scope and complexity. By the 1970s, library instruction was a well-established (if still contested) function of most libraries. In academic libraries in particular, the 1970s witnessed a growth in practical approaches to instruction, professional infrastructure, and theoretical underpinnings. In 1971, the Library Orientation Exchange (LOEX) was established, providing a clearinghouse for instructional materials and an annual conference (LOEX 2014). Rader (1974) created the first bibliography of research and professional publications related to library instruction.

Bibliographic Instruction

The key difference between library instruction and bibliographic instruction is the movement away from teaching users only about tools and resources. Proponents of bibliographic instruction, beginning in the mid-1970s, argued that collections, resources, and the information needs of users were becoming more complex. By the 1980s, bibliographic instruction was the term used to describe more conceptual approaches to teaching information seeking and use. Librarians should teach transferable skills, given that learning a single strategy or library tool could not serve all of their users' future needs. Furthermore, new online searching technologies were changing the nature of both mediated and end-user searching. Forecasting a concern that many associate more closely with the rise of the Internet, Constance A. Mellon argued, "The need to develop sound information-seeking and research skills among clients still will be necessary to insure that the college-educated public of the future does not become dependent on the information provided by easy-to-use sources only" (1987, 15).

The 1980s witnessed a growing body of theoretical and research-based literature, as well as greater professional recognition for the role of teaching in libraries. According to Mellon, advocates of bibliographic instruction were concerned with "consolidating the discipline by fostering research, publication, critical analysis, and development of an underlying pedagogy of bibliographic instruction" (1987, 6).

This underlying pedagogy was informed by greater attention to learning theory. Pamela Kobelski and Mary Reichel (1981) argued that bibliographic instruction needed to help learners build cognitive structures, following David Ausubel's learning theory, because students did not have knowledge of the underlying bibliographic structures in libraries. For example, bibliographic instruction might focus on the concept of classification schemes rather than on the steps to search a library catalog. Bibliographic instruction also emphasized search strategies and processes. Carol Collier Kuhlthau's (1992) work on the Information Search Process, building on George Kelly's constructivist theory of learning, was particularly influential in school and academic libraries, providing an empirically derived model of how information seekers move cognitively and affectively through a search process.

Information Literacy Instruction

Although the term was first coined in 1974, information literacy became the dominant user education paradigm by the 1990s. It marks a departure from bibliographic instruction in that it emphasizes a wider range of information sources than traditional library resources. The goal of information literacy is to teach specific skills related to finding, evaluating, and using information. The ALA Presidential Committee on Information Literacy states in its final report: "Information literacy is a survival skill in the Information Age" (American Library Association 1989). A common image in the information literacy discourse is one of users being flooded with too much information. Thus, instead of requiring skills to successfully access finite sources stored in a library building, libraries can best serve users by helping them learn the skills to navigate, or keep from drowning, in the sea of information.

> Libraries, which provide a significant public access point to such information and usually at no cost, must play a key role in preparing people for the demands of today's information society. Just as public libraries were once a means of education and a better life for many of the over 20 million immigrants of the late 1800s and early 1900s, they remain today as the potentially strongest and most far-reaching community resource for lifelong learning. Public libraries not only provide access to information, but they also remain crucial to providing people with the knowledge necessary to make meaningful use of existing resources. (American Library Association 1989)

In addition to the information age, information literacy emerged from numerous educational, social, and economic trends. In school libraries, for example, the "skills crisis" described in the *A Nation at Risk* report in 1983 generated a broad interest in information skills needed for competitive advantage in a knowledge or learning society (National Commission on Excellence in Education 1983). Similar questions were raised by the American Bar Association (ABA) about whether law students were adequately prepared for practice (American Bar Association 1992). School library media professionals began exploring ways to both define and integrate information skills into K–12 school curriculums. In *Information Power: Building Partnerships for Learning*, the AASL formally outlined guidelines for school librarians for promoting information literacy skills in their libraries, classrooms, and school curricula (American Association of School Librarians and Association for Educational Communications and Technology 1998). The standards include skills for finding, evaluating, and using information as well as computer or technology skills (Eisenberg, Lowe, and Spitzer 2004). The AASL released the "Standards for the 21st-Century Learner" in 2007. These standards include three main categories: information literacy, independent learning, and social responsibility.

Similarly, information literacy in higher education was framed as a response to the needs of a knowledge economy and a broadly educated citizenry. Themes of abundant information and rapid advances in technology were found in the higher education discourse as well. The introduction to the ACRL "Information Literacy Competency Standards for Higher Education" reads:

> Because of the escalating complexity of this environment, individuals are faced with diverse, abundant information choices—in their academic studies, in the workplace, and in their personal lives. Information is available through libraries, community resources, special interest organizations, media, and the Internet—and increasingly, information comes to individuals in unfiltered formats, raising questions about its authenticity, validity, and reliability. In addition, information is available through multiple media, including graphical, aural, and textual, and these pose new challenges for individuals in evaluating and understanding it. The uncertain quality and expanding quantity of information pose large challenges for society. The sheer abundance of information will not in itself create a more informed citizenry without a complementary cluster of abilities necessary to use information effectively. (Association of College and Research Libraries 2000)

The 1990s witnessed numerous efforts to define information literacy and codify national standards of what it meant to be information literate. The ALA developed an early definition of information literacy in 1989: "To be information literate, a person must be able to recognize when information is needed and have the ability to locate, evaluate, and use effectively the needed information." Since the 1990s, numerous library and professional associations across the world have developed definitions, standards, and learning outcomes for information literacy, including the ACRL, the AASL, the Society of College, National and University Libraries in Great Britain, and the Australian and New Zealand Institute for Information Literacy. Information literacy also began to appear in academic accreditation standards (Eisenberg, Lowe, and Spitzer 2004). The ABA, for example, includes legal research skills in the standard learning outcomes that all accredited law schools must address (American Bar Association 2014). Most of these standards include statements related to the basic definition outlined by the ALA Presidential Committee on Information Literacy. These standards all address formal school settings. The IMLS provides a broader list of competencies in their 21st Century Skills project, aimed at supporting museums and public libraries in their educational role. In addition to information literacy, the IMLS skills include areas of digital, financial, health, environmental, and civic literacies. See Boxes 4.1, 4.2, and 4.3 for examples.

In the 1990s, information literacy also became an object of academic study by both library and information science faculty and professional librarians. In 1993, Christina Doyle published a groundbreaking Delphi study that documented expert consensus on the definition of information literacy skills. Her work provided the basis for the AASL Information Literacy Standards for Student Learning (published in full in *Information Power*) as well as numerous other definitions and standards (American Association of School Librarians and Association for Educational Communications and Technology 1998; Marcoux 1999).

Box 4.1 Association of College and Research Libraries "Information Literacy Competency Standards for Higher Education"

1. The information literate student determines the nature and extent of the information needed.
2. The information literate student accesses needed information effectively and efficiently.
3. The information literate student evaluates information and its sources critically and incorporates selected information into his or her knowledge base and value system.
4. The information literate student, individually or as a member of a group, uses information effectively to accomplish a specific purpose.
5. The information literate student understands many of the economic, legal, and social issues surrounding the use of information and accesses and uses information ethically and legally.

(Association of College and Research Libraries 2000)

Box 4.2 AASL "Standards for the 21st-Century Learner"

Learners use skills, resources, and tools to:

1. Inquire, think critically, and gain knowledge
2. Draw conclusions, make informed decisions, apply knowledge to new situations, and create new knowledge.
3. Share knowledge and participate ethically and productively as members of our democratic society.
4. Pursue personal and aesthetic growth.

Excerpted from "Standards for the 21st-Century Learner" by the American Association of School Librarians, a division of the American Library Association, copyright © 2007 American Library Association. Available for download at www.ala.org/aasl/standards. Used with permission.

Christine Bruce (1997) employed phenomenography to describe how individuals conceive of and experience information literacy, rather than relying on externally derived or expert opinions. She discovered that individuals experience information literacy in seven variations, or faces:

1. Information technology
2. Information sources
3. Information process
4. Information control
5. Knowledge construction
6. Knowledge extension
7. Wisdom

Box 4.3 IMLS "Museums, Libraries, and 21st-Century Skills"

Skills identified as aligned with public library and museum priorities:

- Critical Thinking and Problem Solving
- Creativity and Innovation
- Communication and Collaboration
- Visual Literacy
- Scientific and Numerical Literacy
- Cross-Disciplinary Thinking
- Basic Literacy
- Information Literacy
- Media Literacy
- Information and Communication Technology Literacy
- Global Awareness
- Financial, Economic, Business and Entrepreneurial Literacy
- Civic Literacy
- Health Literacy
- Environmental Literacy

(Institute of Museum and Library Services 2015)

Instead of defining information literacy as successful mastery of discrete skills, Bruce defined an information literate person as one who understands variations in ways of experiencing information literacy and can reflect on and apply these varied experiences to different contexts.

Much of the practitioner literature on information literacy addresses issues of pedagogy and teaching methods, models of delivery, faculty perceptions of information literacy and the role of librarians, and conversations about the value and limits of specific frameworks for information literacy instruction. There has been an ongoing debate, especially in academic libraries, over the very term "information literacy," for example. Several authors have argued that the term is limited, lacks clarity, and means very little outside of librarianship. The politically loaded nature of the term "literacy" is also problematic in this view, as it implies a deficit, or illiteracy, as the starting point for individuals who have not mastered all of the requisite skills (Arp 1990). Loanne Snavely and Natasha Cooper outline the pros and cons of the debate and suggest that information literacy is the best of a wide range of alternatives (1997). Edward K. Owusu-Ansah argues that the debate over the term distracts librarians from deeper questions about executing effective instruction programs in the larger context of higher education: "The controversies and uncertainties surrounding the conceptual delineation of information literacy therefore suggest a deeper professional dilemma, one that concise definitions and elaborate standards have failed to resolve. That dilemma involves not definitional uncertainties but rather difficulties of execution, arising within the dynamics of the educational environment, the deliberations of its power brokers, and the influence and results the relative image and power of the participating interests allows" (2003, 226).

Since the 1990s, librarians have also debated the merits of particular avenues of delivery, especially in academic settings. The most vigorous debate in the literature was over course-integrated instruction, a series of sessions or learning activities integrated into an existing course, vs. credit-bearing information literacy courses taught by librarians and not tied to a particular academic department or curriculum. Proponents of credit-bearing courses suggest that information literacy can be addressed in greater depth, and librarians can develop close relationships with students. They might also benefit librarians politically because they position librarians as faculty peers. Critics of information literacy credit courses argue that they detach information skills and practices from the context in which they will be used: courses in the disciplines. Students often see these kinds of courses, akin to required writing courses, as busy work and extra credits they are forced to take. Students might be less motivated in this context (Davis, Lundstrom, and Martin 2011). Law schools have a long tradition of librarians teaching first-year legal research courses, with many of the advantages that an in-depth credit course offers. But these courses are often electives and not part of the core curriculum, so they do not necessarily reach all students (Peura 2014).

Advocates for course-integrated instruction argue that it provides a richer context for learning information literacy. Librarians tailor their instruction to the content and assignments in the course and provide instructional interventions at the most appropriate points of need. Integrating into courses also potentially promotes better collaborations with faculty, and students see the direct value of librarians and information literacy skills in relation to course assignments and their major disciplines (Davis, Lundstrom, and Martin 2011). Some academic librarians argue for an even more integrated approach, embedded librarianship, a model in which librarians are present throughout the entire course, either in person or online, and are seen as resources or fixtures throughout research-intensive classes (Kobzina 2010; Kvenild and Calkins 2011).

Critics argue that course-integrated instruction, while possibly ideal in the abstract, is hard to implement. It requires a great deal of political clout to get faculty to give up course time and add collaborative instructional design with a librarian to their already busy workloads. It is also difficult to integrate across entire campuses, so only those students in select courses or majors with a high degree of integration are exposed (Davis, Lundstrom, and Martin 2011). These questions of integration play out differently in school libraries, where librarians are often certified teachers with deep knowledge of the curriculum and clear instructional roles in their schools. Questions of integration and models of delivery are also different in public libraries, where structures like courses and curricula do not exist.

While much of the discussion in the United States focused on practical questions of standards, definitions, and instructional delivery, researchers outside of the U.S. context, especially in Australia and Europe, explored more situated models for information literacy, especially in the last decade. These researchers argued that information literacy is not a discrete skill that can be understood, taught, or learned outside of a specific sociocultural context. In the situated model, information literacy learning is a collaborative process of solving authentic problems in communities of practice (Lupton and Bruce 2010).

Sociocultural approaches to information literacy have led to greater attention to nonacademic contexts. Annemaree Lloyd's work on information literacy and firefighters suggests that information literacy is learned not just through formal texts, but through a social apprenticeship as well. A novice firefighter uses formal texts to develop a basic understanding, but then watches and learns from other firefighters how different sources of information are useful. Mastery comes through the ability to "read" a fire corporally, through the body (Lloyd 2007). This work has led to greater attention to workplace information literacy and the need to understand how novices learn in a wide range of settings beyond school. This work is especially important to public librarians as they expand services to support local businesses, entrepreneurs, and other adult learners outside of a formal school context. Creating communities of practice through teen reading or software coding clubs might be informed by this work on situated learning.

In *Informed Learning*, Christine Bruce writes that librarians need to pay more attention to the context of learning. She critiques mainstream generic models of information literacy that focus on "the acquisition of technological skills, library skills, and information skills," arguing that these skills are important but limiting: "All these skills are necessary, but sometimes we stop with the skills and do not focus on how students and others must use information to learn" (2008, 5). Understanding the learner's perspective of both information literacy and learning can, consequently, lead to improved learning (Bruce 2008; Bruce, Edwards, and Lupton 2006). Other researchers have found similar connections between the learners' goals and assumptions about learning. Students who perceive information seeking as "scrutinizing and analyzing" achieve learning outcomes more effectively than those who view research as fact-finding or seeking evidence (Limberg 2000; Lupton 2008).

Critical information literacy is another significant trend, particularly in academic libraries (Accardi, Drabinski, and Kumbier 2010; Elmborg 2006, 2012; Kapitzke 2003). Borrowing from critical theory more broadly, proponents argue that traditional information literacy approaches tend to treat information, learning, knowledge, and even an "information-literate student" as neutral and universal concepts. According to Christine Pawley (2003), this approach tends to reify these concepts, or make them into things themselves. She notes how the contradiction between the stated goals of information literacy standards to promote a more broadly educated citizenry with the seemingly fixed ideas of "good vs. bad" sources and "efficient" information retrieval can narrow the possibilities for individuals learning how to decide what is authoritative and valuable. James K. Elmborg (2006), building on the work of Paulo Freire, argues that critical theory can help librarians move away from the "banking concept" of education that assumes that teachers deposit knowledge into the heads of students and that learning is the product of the accumulation of this intellectual capital. Critical information literacy also proposes that librarians should address the socioeconomic underpinnings of our current information environment and issues of access, the digital divide, and information privilege, as well as broader issues of social justice (Accardi and Vukovic 2013; Gregory, Higgins, and Samek 2013).

Future Directions

The shift from library orientation to more situated and critical information literacy instruction opens new possibilities and challenges for librarians. Educating users about information is no longer an activity confined to the physical library, focused on specific tools, or even taught by librarians. A new emphasis on communities of practice and workplace literacy potentially brings information literacy out of formal educational settings. Issues of economics and information privilege provide new opportunities for public librarians to serve the needs of their community, as seen in library programs on job skills and entrepreneurship, services to homeschooled students, or broader technology instruction in makerspaces.

Information literacy in K–12 and higher education is drawing on a rich literature incorporating both information literacy and learning theory. ACRL adopted the "Framework for Information Literacy for Higher Education" in 2015. The Framework builds on the educational theory of threshold concepts (Townsend, Brunetti, and Hofer 2011). Threshold concepts are defined as "foundational concepts that, once grasped by the learner, create new perspectives and ways of understanding a discipline or challenging knowledge domain. Such concepts produce transformation within the learner; without them, the learner does not acquire expertise in that field of knowledge" (Association of College and Research Libraries 2015, 3). While these more situated and less formal contexts for instruction are potentially powerful, they can also be challenging in their diversity, complexity, and lack of foundational definitions. School librarians face similar issues with the Common Core standards, which do not separate information literacy as a discrete skill. Instead, the standards infuse language about inquiry, research, and critical thinking throughout all of the core subject areas, even math. This not only provides opportunities for school librarians to integrate information literacy in new ways, but also provides challenges, including the need for even greater coordination with classroom teachers and a greatly expanded role in nearly all areas of the curriculum. What information literacy might look like in the future, then, very much depends on how librarians and other educators enact and reframe the long-standing tradition of libraries helping patrons, in Christine Bruce's words, "use information to learn" (2008, 3).

DEVELOPING AND IMPLEMENTING INSTRUCTION

While education goals, contexts, and philosophies might differ among librarians and institutions, developing and implementing instruction and instructional programs requires a common range of skills that include teaching methods, classroom management, technology and multimedia creation, and evaluation and assessment. It also requires a firm grounding in educational theories and frameworks for information literacy and use. In essence, it requires "know-how" in addition to a strong disciplinary grounding in library and information science.

Instructional Design

Instruction is more than just presenting information in front of a group of learners. Instruction is like an iceberg. Learners might see only what is above the surface: the learning activities and materials, the assignments, and so on. But effective instruction involves a great deal more that lies below the surface. Steven J. Bell and John D. Shank (2007) argue that all library services, including reference and instruction, must be intentionally designed, using processes of analysis and understanding, rapid prototyping and revision, and evaluation and assessment. Instruction is essentially a process of designing learning experiences and materials to meet a learner's need. It is about making informed choices at every stage, from determining learning outcomes to assessment. There is no recipe or one-size approach to all content and all learning situations. However, frameworks and models guide educators, including librarians, in making wise choices and assessing the effectiveness of those choices.

Each instructional design model includes different elements, steps, or features, but all share some commonalities. They frame the values and assumptions about learning and learners, the context or conditions of learning, the outcomes of learning, and methods. There is no one best model. Some emphasize affective or motivational outcomes, while others are better suited to goals of efficiency. Some focus on designing discrete interventions, while others are intended to design sequenced curricula (Oswald and Reigeluth 2002). Some models provide excellent guidance on developing learning materials (handouts, guides, etc.) intended for self-paced and independent use. Other models pay more attention to the particular challenges and opportunities that online learning provides. One of the foundational skills for effective instruction, then, is the ability to select the models or tools that are most appropriate to the situation. For example, a complex model meant to help design K–12 curricula might not be suited for designing a workshop on using genealogy resources in a small public library or historical society.

Robert M. Gagné (1985) developed one of the first instructional design models, and his work is still influential today. He categorized learning objectives into three broad domains: cognitive, affective, and psychomotor. Benjamin S. Bloom (1956) also developed a well-known taxonomy of learning that outlined a hierarchy of learning goals, ranging from remembering to evaluating and creating. The taxonomy was revised in 2001 and still remains a widely used tool in instructional design (Anderson, Krathwohl, and Bloom 2001). See Box 4.4 for an overview of Bloom's taxonomy. In both of these taxonomies, the teacher should design instruction to meet the category of outcome desired, rather than addressing only the subject content to be learned. Thus, if one is trying to teach an intellectual skill, such as the ability to classify concepts (Bloom's "Understanding"), one should use a different strategy than if the goal is to teach someone to memorize and recite a poem (Bloom's "Remembering"). Paul D. Callister (2010) provides a useful model for using Bloom's taxonomy for legal research skills.

Box 4.4 Bloom's Revised Taxonomy of Learning

1. *Remember*: Recall relevant knowledge (e.g. recognize, recall, identify)
2. *Understand*: Construct meaning from content (e.g. interpret, classify, summarize, infer, compare, explain)
3. *Apply*: Use a procedure in a specific situation (e.g. execute, implement)
4. *Analyze*: Break content or concepts into parts and determine relationships and purpose (e.g. differentiate, organize, deconstruct, parse, select)
5. *Evaluate*: Make judgments based on criteria (e.g. critique, test)
6. *Create*: Combine or reorganize pieces together to form coherent whole or new patterns (e.g. generate, plan, design, hypothesize, construct)

(Anderson, Krathwohl, and Bloom 2001, 67–68)

Gagné (1985) outlines nine instructional events, or conditions of learning:

1. Gaining attention
2. Informing learners of objectives
3. Stimulating recall of prior learning

4. Presenting the stimulus
5. Providing learning guidance
6. Eliciting performance or demonstrating learning
7. Providing feedback
8. Assessing performance
9. Enhancing retention and transfer

This is a linear model and assumes that an instructor should run through this entire sequence in order to enhance learning.

Other models outline specific steps in the design process that one should take when designing learning. The ADDIE model is one of the most widely used. It focuses on the process of iterative design and assumes that designers should view instruction as rapid prototyping: try something, evaluate, and refine the design. The phases of the ADDIE model (Hodell 2006) are:

1. *Analysis*: Understanding the learners' needs and learning context.
2. *Design*: Creating a learning activity, intervention, or product that will address the learners' needs.
3. *Develop*: Create the activity, intervention, or product.
4. *Implement*: Deliver the instruction.
5. *Evaluate*: Assess the effectiveness of the instruction and the impact on student learning.

ADDIE is particularly useful for designing discrete interventions, such as workshops, training materials, online tutorials, and short lessons and learning activities, and might be particularly appropriate for designing the learning experiences in public libraries.

The Understanding by Design (UbD) (Wiggins and McTighe 1998) model can be useful for more academic and curricular approaches that include a series of lessons and learning activities over time. UbD poses three basic questions:

- What do you want learners to be able to know and do?
- How will you know they learned it?
- How will you design learning to address your goal?

UbD, sometimes called "backwards design," is based on the premise that instructors need to understand the end goal in order to design effective instruction. Grant P. Wiggins and Jay McTighe argue that teachers often begin with lesson plans and outlines about content to cover and techniques to use (lecture, discussion, etc.) and then realize at the end of the process that they failed to cover what students actually needed to learn (Wiggins 2005; Wiggins and McTighe 1998). An essential feature of the UbD model is articulating "enduring understandings," or the things that are essential for a student to comprehend or be able to do in order to achieve his or her goal. It is also essential to identify common misunderstandings in order to address those in the instructional process. Then the designer determines what performance or assessment methods to use in order to determine whether students have met the goals outlined in the first step. One cannot design instruction without knowing what successful learning looks like.

Char Booth adapted several models to address issues specific to designing instruction in the library context. Like the ADDIE model, her approach involves an iterative process of analysis, development, and reflection and evaluation. It also includes "backwards" assumptions in that librarians have to understand goals and the learner as the first step of the process. As shown in Figure 4.1, the USER model includes four basic stages (Booth 2011, 95–96):

1. *Understand*: Identify the problem or challenge that learners face and analyze the situation, including learner characteristics, the context of instruction, and self-reflection on the educator's own understanding and assumptions.
2. *Structure*: Create goals or targets and identify methods to effectively engage the learners.
3. *Engage*: Create and deliver instruction.
4. *Reflect*: Assess the impact of instruction and think about ways to revise and reuse instructional approaches and materials in future instruction.

Booth also includes the analysis of technology affordances and constraints as an essential part of the design process. If using technology, designers should select the tools that enable or afford users to reach the specific instructional goal. For example, if collaboration is a goal, librarians need to select a communication or authoring tool that is simple and easy for users to access and use collectively. Booth also pays attention to issues of scalability, which is why planning for reuse is an important element of her model. Instructors do not have to reinvent these things each time they create instruction if reuse is part of the design. This is especially useful for teaching librarians because instruction is rarely the only function of their work, and in many settings, librarians teach similar content multiple times (Booth 2011).

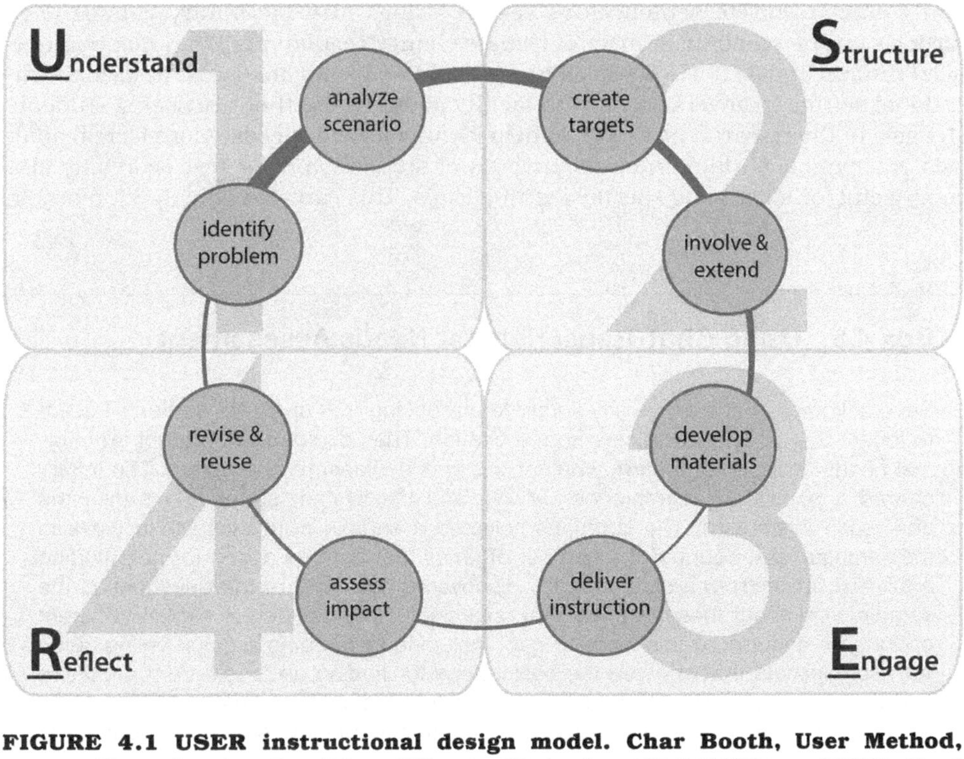

FIGURE 4.1 USER instructional design model. Char Booth, User Method, page xviii, *Reflective Teaching, Effective Learning* (ALA Editions, 2011). Used with permission.

While all of these models work from different assumptions and for different purposes, they have several commonalities that can guide any instructional design effort: understanding needs, understanding learners and their context, having clear learning goals, designing for purpose, and using an iterative process of evaluation and assessment to improve future design and, ultimately, improve student learning.

Understanding Needs

Effective instructional design starts with a process of analysis. Instructors have to begin with a clear understanding of what their students need to learn, including gaps in knowledge or skills, community needs and interest, and curricular requirements in formal educational settings. There are a variety of ways that an individual librarian might approach assessing the needs of learners in order to develop effective instruction. In some cases, the needs are presented to librarians in formal requests from teachers, faculty members, students, or community members.

In other cases, informal scans of the environment can yield clues about learning gaps. Common reference or other questions, collected informally through discussion with other librarians or more formally through chat transcript analysis, can highlight common difficulties that library users have with a particular resource, skill, or technology. See Box 4.5 for an example of using common questions to identify user needs. Search logs of library catalogs, websites, and search tools can yield similar information. Some of these problems might be addressed through improved interface design, but there are often conceptual misunderstandings that could be addressed with some type of instruction. For example, if users consistently enter complete sentences as search strings into the library catalog (e.g., "articles on the economic impact of climate change regulations"), a quick point-of-need tutorial about effective search terms might help educate users. In formal educational settings, conversations with faculty about where they are seeing students struggle in the research process can help identify learner needs. More formal analysis of assessment data, such as analysis of student work or test scores, is also very useful for identifying specific learning gaps. This can also help develop buy-in

Box 4.5 Using Chat Transcripts for Needs Assessment

Several librarians at a university library kept noticing that students could not seem to locate the full text of articles from a citation. They decided to conduct an informal needs analysis to confirm whether this was a widespread problem. The library offered a popular chat reference service, and the system stored the transcripts after each interaction. The librarians selected a sample from every third week in the semester and counted the number of times that patrons asked for help finding a full-text article from a citation. They discovered that 10% of the questions in the sample were about these "known item" searches. They decided to explore different options for addressing this learning gap, including developing a quick online guide with screenshots that showed the basic steps for finding an article from a citation and developing a bookmark that could be distributed in library instruction sessions for point-of-need help. They analyzed the chat transcripts a year later and found that "known-item" search questions declined.

from potential faculty collaborators. The library literature, such as the Project Information Literacy reports (2014), also contains general information on trends in student attitudes toward and use of information. Business organizations, think tanks, and other researchers have also produced reports that outline learning or skills gaps in the workforce that are useful for public libraries to identify the needs of adult learners (American Management Association 2012; Partnership for 21st Century Learning 2006; Peura 2014).

Once the general need is understood, this must be translated into learning goals and outcomes. There are a variety of definitions of the differences between learning goals and outcomes. Char Booth describes goals, objectives, and outcomes as *targets* for instruction. They provide more specific guidance so that librarians can structure learning activities and assessments more effectively. Some use the terms interchangeably, but Booth suggests that the key difference is based on whether the teacher or learner perspective is being addressed. Goals define the proposed impact of the instruction on the learner from the teacher's perspective, while objectives and outcomes are described from the perspective of the learner (Booth 2011, 118).

Learning outcomes are often defined as what the instructor will be able to see students doing as the result of instruction. According to Debra Gilchrist and Anne Zald, "Learning outcomes are specific statements that express our hopes for our students' learning" (2008, 168). Developing clear outcomes from the student perspective can help guide the instructional design process and enhance learning in a number of ways. Outcomes help the instructor make better instructional choices because one can focus attention only on those areas that are essential and remove unnecessary content in order to manage cognitive load. These issues are heightened with online instruction, whether synchronous online presentations or self-paced instructional material, because the instructor does not have the benefit of visual feedback that is available in a face-to-face class or reference interview to help pace teaching in the moment. In addition, clear outcomes are important because evidence suggests that students learn more effectively when they understand the goal of instruction (Wiggins and McTighe 1998). Mark Battersby (1999, 1) argues, "Learning outcomes are best viewed in the context of an approach to thinking about teaching and learning rather than a formula or a change in course outline terminology. . . . Such reflection will lead instructors to focus on a broad synthesis of abilities that combine knowledge, skills and values into a whole that reflects how people really use knowledge." This approach to outcomes is especially useful for information literacy instruction, given that it encompasses such a broad synthesis of knowledge, skills, and attitudes.

There are several criteria for creating good learning outcomes. Outcomes should be clear not just to the instructor but to the student as well. The verbs in an outcome should be specific and clear about what a student will actually be doing to demonstrate that outcome. If designing more than one outcome for a particular intervention, it can be helpful to use more than one level of learning. Bloom's taxonomy can provide guidance to ensure that higher-order thinking skills are included, such as those requiring synthesis and analysis, rather than only outcomes that require remembering or restating. For the benefit of the learner, effective outcomes tell students not just what they will be learning but why it is important. Outcomes also have to be measurable or "judge-able" using professional expertise. If one cannot really tell whether someone has achieved an outcome, then there is no way for the teacher or student to assess the learning and make adjustments (Gilchrist and Zald 2008). See Box 4.6 for examples of learning outcomes for school, academic, and public library settings.

Box 4.6 Sample Learning Outcomes

For a fourth-grade class:

> Students will be able to use the index in a print encyclopedia to locate a specific entry in order to summarize background information on their native species research project.

For a self-publishing workshop at a public library:

> Participants will be able to locate images licensed for commercial reuse in order to legally, ethically, and affordably include illustrations in their manuscripts.

For a reference question in a public library:

> The patron, in this case a local business owner, will be able to locate economic data in order to evaluate her business plan every year without having to return to the library for help each time.

For an online tutorial created by a Special Collections and Archives department:

> Participants will be able to locate historical photographs, download the most appropriate version for use in multimedia, and assign geographical metadata based on photograph locations in order to create engaging local history materials.

For a workshop provided by a medical librarian for first-year physician assistant students:

> Students will be able to evaluate an empirical research study in order to identify what level of evidence it provides for making a clinical decision.

Understanding Learners

Understanding learners is just as important as understanding learning needs. Instruction is more effective if teachers base their approaches on what they know about how people learn. This includes an understanding of learning theory, learning styles, and other factors and characteristics that might shape the learning experience.

Learning theory is valuable not because it provides simple rules to follow about how people learn, but because it provides a framework for making informed choices about the instructional design. According to Stephen D. Brookfield, reflection enables teachers to uncover their own assumptions about learning and solve instructional problems that they encounter in practice. Learning theory is one useful lens for educators to analyze and reflect on their teaching. It provides coherence and explanatory power to what teachers often view as individual experiences and anecdotes. Brookfield writes, "Theory can help us 'name' our practice by illuminating the general elements of what we think are idiosyncratic experiences. It can provide multiple perspectives on familiar situations" (1995, 36).

Learning theories communicate assumptions about the definition of learning and the role of the teacher. The three most common, sometimes called "classic," learning theories are behaviorism, cognitivism, and constructivism. Some break constructivism into two schools, cognitive and social. Table 4.1 summarizes some of the key assumptions and definitions of the three theories.

Behavioral learning theories define learning as an outward change in behavior. In this model, learners are passive recipients of knowledge, and the teacher's role is to transmit that knowledge and help the learner practice until he or she

TABLE 4.1 Summary of Learning Theories

	Behaviorism	Cognitivism	Constructivism
Definition of learning	Change in behavior.	Change in mental structures to make sense of new information.	Construction of knowledge based on problem solving, activity, and social interaction.
Role of the teacher	Transmit information and provide stimulus and feedback.	Provide explanations and examples to provide students with new mental models or schema.	Create learning experiences that provide real problems and opportunities to learn from experts.
Role of the learner	Receive knowledge.	Create individual meaning.	Novice in a community of practice.
Focus of information literacy instruction	Definitions of source "types." Rules for searching. Formal and ordered procedures.	Developing a recursive process of information seeking.	Introduction to "valued" information in a discipline, workplace, or community.
Methods of information literacy instruction	"One-shot" demonstrations of sources and tools in classroom.	Multiple instruction sessions integrated into course. Reflective, process-oriented assignments.	Expert navigation of disciplinary tools. Identifying authority or disciplinary expertise. Problem-based learning.
Mastery defined	Demonstration of skills.	Moving through process with greater confidence and independence.	Understanding of information environments. Participation in community discourse.

masters the specific behavior through processes of trial and error or stimulus and response. For behaviorists, there is a correct answer. Memorizing the multiplication tables is a good example of something that is often taught and learned from a behaviorist perspective. In libraries, behaviorism can often be seen in online tutorials or handouts that transmit to users the "proper" or most effective steps to search a library database (Booth 2011, 38–39).

Cognitivists define learning as changing cognitive structures in order to facilitate sense-making. Cognitive theories focus on internal information processing, rather than outward behavior. David Ausubel, for example, focuses on the issue of prior learning. He defined learning as the process by which individuals integrate new information into existing knowledge structures and make connections between new and existing concepts in order to create meaning (Ausubel, Novak, and Hanesian 1986). The role of the teacher in a cognitive framework is to help students build effective mental models or schema so that they can efficiently process new information and knowledge. Jerome S. Bruner (1956; 1960) argues that the teacher needs to align his or her teaching with the students' understandings of concepts and that students will learn more effectively if they understand the structure of what they are learning, such as the concepts and relationships between them. These theories had a strong influence on the bibliographic instruction tradition, but they also continue to influence information literacy instruction. For example, teaching students to develop an accurate mental model of the search process is a cognitive approach (Kobelski and Reichel 1981; Kuhlthau 1992).

While the literature sometimes refers to constructivism as a single learning theory, it is more accurately described as a range of theories. Jean Piaget (1953), for example, is sometimes classified as a cognitive theorist because of his ideas about children's progressive development of schemata to process and assimilate new knowledge. He is also regarded as a constructivist because of his emphasis not just on cognitive information processes but also on the idea that children build new mental schemata through doing, rather than passively taking in information (D'Angelo, Touchman, and Clark 2009). John Dewey was also an early constructivist theorist. He argued that learning did not happen passively, either through observation or receiving information from a teacher, but was an active process of constructing knowledge and meaning in the context of actual problems. Those problems could arise from purely academic inquiry, or they could be authentic life problems. For Dewey, teachers should be facilitators and guides through an active process of questioning and discovery. He also argued that school was an extension of society and that the ultimate goal was to help students become self-directed learners so that they could shape and support a more ethical and democratic society (Dewey 1915, 1916). Dewey's work is the inspiration for many constructivist pedagogies, including problem-based learning (PBL) and experiential learning (D'Angelo, Touchman, and Clark 2009).

Social constructivists assume that learning is a process between people and are widely influenced by the work of Lev Vygotsky. In this view, learning is the process of developing psychological tools through activity and engagement with others (fellow teachers and students) in a community of practice. The role of the teacher is to design learning experiences that help learners develop the most appropriate psychological tools for the object or goal of learning and at the most appropriate developmental level of the learner. Vygotsky called this the "zone of proximal development" or the space between what a learner can do with help and what they can do independently (Vygotsky 1978). Social constructivists emphasize situated learning, or learning with and through others in specific social contexts. Jean Lave and Etienne Wenger (1991) developed the idea of communities of practice and legitimate peripheral participation. Novices learn by observing others, modeling, and practicing on low-stakes tasks or activities, and then eventually become experts in the community through this process of social learning. Annemaree Lloyd's work on information literacy and firefighters is an example of this kind of situated learning. Teachers and learners in this view are much more fluid, with experts taking on the role of teaching through modeling and socializing novices to the assumptions, vocabulary, and valued knowledge of the group.

More recently, educators are exploring how learning works from the perspective of psychology and neuroscience. Research on attention, memory, thinking process, and motivation can also shape the choices librarians make in designing instruction. Understanding the research on attention, for example, can help librarians design classroom sessions or online modules that take into account the limits of human attention. Understanding, for example, that people are poor judges of their own attention processes and are easily distracted can help designers of online learning minimize the number of tasks required in a single learning module (Miller 2014).

Learning *theories* can help illuminate our assumptions about the process of learning. Learning *styles* can help librarians analyze the individual needs of their learners. Learning styles are defined as the ways in which individual learners prefer to learn. As with learning theories, there are many competing models. Some emphasize basic modalities of learning (verbal, visual, kinesthetic, etc.), while others suggest more complex categories based on how individuals process information. David A. Kolb, for example, developed a learning style inventory based on his research on experiential learning. Kolb (1984) argues that learning happens in a cycle of concrete experience, reflective observation, abstract conceptualization, and active experimentation. The four styles based on individual preferences or strengths (Kolb and Kolb 2005, 5) are:

- *Diverging*: Prefer concrete experience and reflective observation.
- *Assimilating*: Prefer abstract conceptualization and reflective observation.
- *Converging*: Prefer abstract conceptualization and active experimentation.
- *Accommodating*: Prefer concrete experience and active experimentation.

Kolb argues that teachers need to provide opportunities to engage in all four processes in order to move learners through the cycle. Teachers should also be aware of students' preferences, not necessarily to cater to all of them, all of the time, but also to understand students' challenges throughout the learning process.

In recent years, there has been some controversy about the empirical basis for learning styles. The crux of the controversy is the "matching thesis," which states that teachers need to match their instruction to each learner's style in order to improve learning. Critics contend that learning styles tend to be simplistic and that trying to meet everyone's learning style can paralyze instructors trying too hard to address each learner's individual style. A meta-analysis conducted in 2008 found no conclusive evidence from empirical studies of the matching thesis, and few studies of learning styles met a high standard of methodological rigor. The authors argue that this does not mean that learning styles are invalid, but suggest that resources would be better spent on developing educational practices based on solid empirical evidence (Pashler, McDaniel, Rohrer, and Bjork 2008). Others argue that while the matching thesis might be too overdetermined, there is value in trying to use a variety of teaching methods to enliven the classroom and ensure that all students experience learning in multiple ways (Felder 2010).

Assessing Learning

Paul Black and Dylan Wiliam (2010, 82) define assessment as "all those activities undertaken by teachers—and by their students in assessing themselves—that provide information to be used as feedback to modify teaching and learning activities." Beginning in K–12 education and now firmly established in higher education, assessment is a multifaceted effort to measure what students know and can do in order to improve teaching practice, provide feedback to students so that they can assess their own learning and make improvements, and provide evidence of learning and achievement to a variety of stakeholders, including local school administrators, governments and funding agencies, accrediting bodies, and the general public. In many formal educational settings, especially in K–12 schools, assessment is a mandatory activity.

Assessment is often seen as something that comes at the end of learning, but as the backwards design model suggests, it should be at the front and center of instructional design. Once learning outcomes have been established, the next step is to outline the ways in which learners can demonstrate those outcomes. Only then can one design learning activities with the end in mind. According to backwards design models, instructors need to determine what evidence of learning they need to collect, as well as the criteria for evaluating that evidence, before designing any learning activities. If not, instructors risk the danger of reaching the end of the instructional activity with no usable evidence (Wiggins 2005, 8).

Assessment is not just a measure of learning for accountability. It is an essential part of the learning process. Alverno College (2001) calls this Assessment-as-Learning, defined as:

- A process integral to learning
- Involving observation and judgment of each student's performance
- Based on public criteria
- With self-assessment
- With feedback for student improvement of learning and faculty improvement of teaching

Assessment should not be restricted to the end of the learning activity or course. Formative assessment happens in the midst of learning and provides learners with feedback throughout the process. This kind of feedback is an essential element of learning, so that both students and teachers can check their understandings, identify areas for improvement, and make necessary adjustments. Formative assessments should be low stakes. Formative assessments do not have to take much time or require substantial grading. Even asking questions throughout a class or monitoring online discussion boards for common misunderstandings and then providing students corrective feedback is a formative assessment technique. Other options include one-minute papers in which students write down their clearest and muddiest point from a lecture, polls using classroom response systems such as clickers and Web based, or quizzes (Stiggins 2003). Effective reference interview techniques, such as checking the understanding of the patron to make sure the librarian is providing appropriate explanations, are a kind of formative assessment that can take place in one-on-one learning situations.

Summative assessment evaluates what students learned by the end of an activity or course of instruction. It is often more high stakes. Formative assessment might focus on smaller sets of concepts or knowledge, but summative assessment is usually more comprehensive and performance based. For example, a formative assessment might help students check their understanding of plagiarism and research ethics, but a final term paper will show whether the students can attribute their sources in actual practice. Summative assessment is often used for grading purposes, but instructors can also use it as part of their formative teaching assessment. Analyzing students' final performance on a test, writing assignment, or project can help identify common learning bottlenecks or problem areas. This information can then be cycled back into the instructional design process in order to improve instruction (Stiggins 2003).

Gilchrist and Zald (2008, 168) have developed a practical template for developing effective assessments based on clear learning outcomes. The template consists of the following five questions:

1. *Outcome*: What do you want the student to be able to do?
2. *Information Literacy Curriculum*: What does the student need to know in order to do this well?
3. *Pedagogy*: What type of instruction will best enable the learning?
4. *Assessment*: How will the student demonstrate the learning?
5. *Criteria for Evaluation*: How will I know the student has done this well?

Box 4.7 provides an example of using this model in a school library setting.

Numerous assessment techniques can help librarians assess student learning. Thomas A. Angelo and K. Patricia Cross (1993) provide dozens of ideas for classroom assessment techniques, and many of them are highly suitable for instruction

Box 4.7 Designing Outcomes and Assessment

For an eighth-grade class:

1. Outcome
   Students will be able to determine whether statements are common knowledge or require a source attribution in order to ethically attribute information in their own writing.
2. Information Literacy Curriculum
   The definition of common knowledge and the reasons for citing outside sources, including plagiarism.
3. Pedagogy
   A quick lecture. An interactive common knowledge polling contest.
4. Assessment
   Students will code a *Wikipedia* entry of their choice and identify whether each statement is attributed properly or whether it is common knowledge.
5. Criteria for evaluation
   The level of successful mastery is defined as 80% of the statements properly coded.

in libraries, especially in cases where assessment can happen only during a public library workshop or instruction session. Some of these techniques include short writing assignments, like the one-minute paper, or incomplete outlines, in which students are given part of an outline of content and have to fill in the rest at the end of class. Many of these techniques can be used in online instruction as well. Tests and quizzes, including some standardized information literacy tests, such as TRAILS (Kent State University Libraries 2015), can provide feedback on students' conceptual knowledge. Authentic performance-based assessments are more effective at demonstrating whether students can locate, evaluate, integrate, and use information effectively. Librarians can sometimes get copies of student papers in formal education settings and assess student learning through the use of a rubric that includes clear criteria for levels of performance for each learning outcome. Sample information literacy rubrics appropriate for higher education and, in some cases, secondary education, are available from the Rubric Assessment of Information Literacy Skills project ("Rubrics" 2014). The Association of American Colleges & Universities also developed an information literacy rubric (Rhodes and Finley 2013). Kathy Schrock (2015) maintains a comprehensive collection of K–12 rubrics, including several for research and writing projects in elementary school settings.

Designing Learning

Designing learning activities is the process of determining the content, delivery mode, and methods that will best address the learning outcomes and the needs of the learners. Many novice teaching librarians might assume that teaching methods are the most important determinant of effective instruction. There are also popular myths or sentiments that all lectures are bad and active learning is always required. But effective instructional design is more strongly influenced by alignment. The instructional approaches should align with the learning outcomes, the assessments that provide evidence of learning, and the context of learning.

Grant Wiggins (2005, 9) suggests some of the key questions for planning learning activities and sequences:

- What content should we cover? What content needs to be "uncovered?"
- When should the "basics" come first? When should they be on a "need-to-know" basis?
- When should I teach, when should I coach, and when should I facilitate student "discovery"?
- What can I do to make the work maximally engaging and effective?

One of the essential issues in designing learning is what to cover. In many cases, teachers try to cover too much content, especially in the library context where a single workshop, class session, or online tutorial might be the only avenue to reach learners. Clear learning outcomes can mitigate against this. Wiggins and McTighe suggest placing potential content into three categories: enduring understandings, things that are important to know and be able to do, and things that are worth being familiar with. Then librarians can determine how to organize this material. For enduring understandings, students will need to be engaged actively in the process of questioning, analyzing, and applying in order to develop that deeper understanding. Such content can be taught and assessed best through complex and authentic tasks and performance activities, such as writing, projects, simulations, debates, and discussions. See Boxes 4.8 and 4.9 for examples.

Box 4.8 Designing Instruction for Enduring Understanding

For a high school government class

A school librarian has been asked by the government teacher to show students how to find credible sources for an upcoming term paper assignment on the Electoral College. The librarian had lectured and demonstrated database searching in the past, but students were bored and did not do well on the assignment. She decided to try a more active scenario-based approach, using the following prompt:

> The presidential election is a toss-up. One candidate won the popular vote and one won the Electoral College. There are debates over the validity of ballots in one state. Some members of Congress are fed up and pass a bill to get rid of the Electoral College. The class will hold a Congressional floor debate and then vote.

Students were given 15 minutes, with no advance instruction, to find the best information that they could to make a two-minute speech for or against the Electoral College. During the debate, the students were told to listen to the evidence presented by their classmates and be ready to summarize the best evidence and explain their criteria for evaluating the evidence. In the next class, each student presented his or her criteria, and this list was then used as the guide for the students' independent research. The librarian then showed students how to locate information that matched their most sought-after criteria.

Box 4.9 Designing Instruction for Enduring Understanding

For a college history class

A librarian and a faculty member discuss their mutual dissatisfaction with last semester's final research papers in a 300-level history class. Students tended to use sources to back up "facts" rather than explore the arguments that historians were making about the topic over time. They decided to try a new approach. Instead of a standard research paper, students would write a paper tracing the impact of one historian's work using the metaphor of scholarship as a conversation. The librarian developed a session showing students how to use the citations in books and articles to trace ideas backwards through time and how to use citation indexes to trace them moving forward. The history professor spent several class sessions showing students ways to analyze how historians use secondary sources to have a conversation with each other. Based on the instructors' grading rubric, the final papers were much more critical and engaging. More important, the professor of the capstone class, the next year, noticed that students wrote much better final projects, especially in their ability to summarize and analyze historical arguments.

For the "need to know and be able to do," one might consider readings, online tutorials, and lectures to convey essential concepts, definitions, and procedural knowledge. The "flipped" classroom is based on the premise of "off-loading" content transmission to online and dedicating classroom time to guided facilitation (Baker 2000). For things that fall in the "worth being familiar with" category, readings, guides, handouts, and online tutorials can be provided for point-of-need reference.

Different teaching methods are particularly suited to certain kinds of learning processes, as well as student engagement and motivation. There is no right or wrong answer, and most instruction will employ a variety of strategies. Variety is also important for meeting the needs of learners with different learning styles and linguistic preferences and for accommodating different abilities. Universal Design for Learning (UDL) standards suggest that teachers need to address the multiple needs of learners from the very beginning of the design process, rather than as an accommodation after the fact. Instructional designs should provide multiple means of representation of content, multiple means of expression by the students, and multiple means of engagement, all in order to remove barriers to learning (National Center on Universal Design for Learning 2014). While UDL is an effective practice for any student, it is often associated with students with learning disabilities (King-Sears 2014). According to Margaret King-Sears (2009), one central advantage of using a UDL framework is more natural integration into the wider classroom environment, rather than being a separate accommodation, such as those outlined in an individualized education program in the K–12 environment. King-Sears also notes that UDL is not just about technology solutions or accommodations, but embraces larger pedagogical practices as well. Thus, not only might UDL include providing audio texts for students with reading or visual disabilities, but it also might involve the teacher providing multiple explanations and opportunities for practice for all students. For librarians teaching in primarily a reference context, UDL might require that extra attention be paid to the design of printed or online guides and other instructional support material, in order to provide multiple formats and explanations.

Lectures, either in person or recorded, provide one-way transmission of information to large groups of students. They are useful for conveying large amounts of conceptual or factual information. They are less useful for promoting interactivity. Lectures do not need to take an entire class session, but can be broken down into smaller chunks and interspersed with more active learning approaches like small group discussions. In strategic doses, they can be very useful for reinforcing essential concepts, facts, and vocabulary.

Demonstrations are useful for conveying procedural, or know-how, content. They are especially common in certain types of library instruction focused on search tools and mechanics. Demonstrations are often more effective if coupled with the opportunity for students to follow along during the demonstration and/or have immediate hands-on practice. Demonstrations can be passive and might not enable a great deal of student engagement. In many cases, demonstrations can be offered to students through handouts or short online tutorials for point-of-need help, rather than as the central focus of in-person instruction.

Active learning techniques afford more interaction, student engagement, and higher-order learning outcomes that involve synthesis, analysis, and application. Passive techniques might be appropriate when the goal is to transmit basic content, but active learning techniques can help students develop deeper understandings and integrate new knowledge into their existing knowledge. Active learning can also help students transfer knowledge from one situation to another. There are a variety of active learning techniques, but most focus on having students doing and thinking about the object of instruction.

Discussions are a simple active learning technique and can take place in person or online. They promote interaction, critical thinking, and the application of concepts to questions or problems and social engagement between students in the classroom. They are best suited for smaller classes, but even large classes can use small group discussions in the middle of a lecture, to have students test and apply their understandings. Discussions can also take place in online courses through discussion boards, wikis, blogs, and other social media.

Problem-based learning, project-based learning, and *case-based learning* are all variations of an active learning technique in which students learn through the process of solving a problem, developing a project, or working through a case or scenario. PBL does not provide students with subject content up front. Instead, students work in groups and are assigned a problem to figure out. They must determine what they need to know to address the problem and find, evaluate, and apply information and knowledge in order to solve the problem. As an information-intensive process, PBL is well suited for information literacy learning outcomes. The role of the instructor in PBL is to serve as a guide throughout the process, rather than as a source of answers. Developed by McMaster University for medical education, PBL is now common across many disciplines and in both higher education and K–12 (Hmelo-Silver 2004). Project- and case-based learning are similar. In business and teacher education, for example, students are often given real cases or scenarios and then must apply tools and concepts from the course, as well as independent research, to make a recommendation about what the actors in the case should do (Harrington 1995; Helms 2006). Project-based learning might be particularly effective in public libraries for teaching skills like software coding or multimedia creation.

There are many more active learning techniques, such as simulations, classroom debates, and games. Some tactics are as simple as having the patron in a reference transaction or a student in a class navigate online resources, rather than the librarian doing all of the "driving." Online classes provide opportunities for active practice, with short low-stakes quizzes or activities that require learners to actively do something, rather than passively consume content. Combining active learning techniques with more passive information transmission and reflective activities can help provide variety and an effective pace. Too much active learning at once can overwhelm learners who need time to reflect and process. As with instruction generally, the most appropriate method is the one that matches the goal.

Not all instruction needs to happen face-to-face or synchronously in order to address the desired learning goals. Research guides, handouts, and online tutorials can be the primary mode of instruction, and they should be created with the same attention to instructional design principles. Print and online learning materials are often the most appropriate way to meet certain learning goals. For procedural knowledge, quick point-of-need instruction is more effective than demonstrating a database long before a student will actually need to use one. Principles for developing good print and online materials include:

- *Format*: Select the most appropriate format for the learners. For definitions, text might be more appropriate, but for procedural or tool-based instruction, visuals such as screenshots or short videos will be more appropriate.
- *Length*: Students might not have the patience to watch a long video about every possible advanced database feature or detailed search process. Chunk the

information into smaller bits so that students can easily process the information, not get lost, and quickly go back if they need to repeat something again.
- *Clarity*: Avoid jargon, distracting fonts or visuals, and clutter. Stay focused on conveying the most essential content in the most concise way possible. Have an outside reader or viewer review the content for clarity.
- *Accessibility*: For video or online content in particular, make sure that the content meets accessibility guidelines for learners with disabilities, such as video captioning.

Technology is an important consideration for effective instructional design because a great deal of teaching and learning is enhanced by or takes place completely via technology. Michelle Miller argues that understanding the psychology of learning can help us improve teaching in an online environment and use technology more effectively to enhance face-to-face instruction. Miller writes, "I *don't* believe that instructional technology promotes learning by its mere presence. Nor does it let us evade some of the apparently immutable truths about how we learn—especially the fact that learning requires focused attention, effortful practice, and motivation. Rather, what technology allows us to do is amplify and expand the repertoire of techniques that effective teachers use to elicit the attention, effort and engagement that are the basis for learning" (Miller 2014, xii). Miller notes some of the ways that technology can support good teaching practice, such as enabling frequent low-stakes testing, presenting material in different ways for different learners, providing varied practice options, and including gamification components to improve motivation.

Making wise choices about instructional technology is, therefore, an essential element in the design process. Booth (2011, 64–65) outlines a practical strategy for assessing the value of technology in various instructional situations and for making effective choices. She developed a list of affordances to consider when evaluating technology:

- *Assessment*: Does it provide templates or enable you to develop integrated assessments of learning?
- *Collaboration*: Does it promote cooperation and/or crowdsourcing?
- *Communication*: Does it promote exchange between learners?
- *Customization*: Does it enable learners to customize or personalize the product or learning environment?
- *Documentation*: Does it enable recording information for future use?
- *Play*: Does it promote playfulness and creativity?
- *Portability*: Can you use it in a mobile context?
- *Productivity*: Does it promote task and time management?
- *Sharing*: Does it enable public sharing or publication?
- *Visualization*: Does it promote the visual display of information?

Most technologies will have more than one affordance. They will have specific constraints as well, and some of these might not be technology related. For example, complex visualization tools or technology that is highly customizable might have a steep learning curve and be less appropriate for a quick workshop. Using affordance analysis to make technology choices promotes good learning design in a number of ways. It keeps instructors from focusing only on the newest and shiniest technologies because they are interesting and appealing. It can also help librarians keep from feeling overwhelmed by trying to keep up with every new gadget and tool. Affordances provide clear criteria for evaluating new products and applying older technologies to new purposes. As in all instructional design, alignment is the central criterion for making technology choices: will this technology best help to meet the learning outcomes? See Box 4.10 for an example of using affordances to analyze technology choices.

Box 4.10 Analyzing Technology Affordances

In a public library

A librarian is planning a series of workshops for a teen reading and writing group. The librarian would like them to use some type of software to comment on each other's writing. She would like the students to be able to see everyone's comments and suggestions, and the technology needs to be readily available in the library for those who do not have computers at home. She conducted an affordance analysis and decided that her most important criteria were collaboration, customization, documentation, and public sharing. It also had to be free and easy to use. After looking at a series of wiki, blogging, and other products, she decided to use the *Google* Docs platform. It was free, could be used on the library computers and tablets, was simple to use, included collaborative commenting and editing features, and final work could be publicly shared with a link. It also had versioning capabilities so that if someone made a change accidentally, he or she could go back and find the previous version of the work.

Management and Administration

Effective instruction efforts in libraries are more than collections of teaching activities. Ideally, instruction efforts are conducted programmatically, with clear outcomes that support the larger institution's strategic goals and purpose. Few librarians, especially those early in their careers, will have direct oversight of a large instruction program, but all librarians can contribute to program effectiveness. Also, in many small libraries, one or two librarians are responsible for leading instructional efforts, even without managerial authority. Thinking programmatically can help all instructional efforts meet the needs of users more effectively.

Needs Assessment and Planning

Individual librarians can conduct small-scale and informal needs assessments to determine the learning needs of their users. This can also be done on a wider and more formal basis at the program level. A needs assessment at the program or community level should identify gaps or deficiencies the library might help fill. In the case of instruction, needs assessments will most likely focus on gaps in learning that keep members of the community from achieving their full potential in some way (Royse 2009). At a public library, for example, the closing of school libraries might mean that the public library can identify and fill in a gap for information literacy instruction that will help students succeed in school. Needs assessments should also focus on areas that the program or library can effectively fill. In academic settings, librarians might notice a gap in math skills in the student population, but a student services or tutoring center might be a more appropriate unit to address that gap.

Several resources can help identify processes and methods for conducting needs assessments and using the results for strategic planning (Altschuld et al. 2010; Royse 2009). Many needs assessments use basic social science research methods, including surveys, focus groups, and interviews. In academic libraries, ethnographic research methods have produced significant insights into the ways in which students use library services and approach the research process. These studies, and others, can be analyzed for important information about gaps in student learning (Foster and Gibbons 2007). Using existing data can save time, which is important for smaller institutions that cannot engage in complex research projects. Public libraries can mine local economic and social data to identify pressing needs in their communities. Large-scale assessments of student learning from other libraries and institutions, such as Project Information Literacy, can also provide useful information to the needs assessment process.

Once data have been collected in a needs assessment, they can be used to develop strategic priorities for an instruction program. Creating program-level goals or outcomes can help librarians prioritize the actions to be taken as a result of the needs assessment. AASL (2009) provides general planning and assessment goals in *Empowering Learners: Guidelines for School Library Programs.* The ACRL *Standards for Libraries in Higher Education* (2011) provide an outcomes-based model for setting program goals. The Public Library Association is currently undertaking "Project Outcome," an effort to define measurable program outcomes for public libraries. Outcomes are defined as the ways in which the user will be changed as a result of his or her interaction with a program. For example, if one of the goals of a program is closer integration into the academic curriculum because a needs assessment identified little coordination between librarians and faculty, the following program outcome might be appropriate: "Students and faculty consult with librarians on work requiring information resources" (Association of College and Research Libraries 2011). Librarians would then design actions and activities to promote greater collaboration on assignment design, rather than, for example, having librarians work in isolation on information literacy instruction workshops. Success could be measured by the number and quality of collaborative assignments developed.

Logic models can provide another framework for planning. A logic model "links outcomes (both short- and long-term) with program activities/processes and the theoretical assumptions/principles of the program" (W.K. Kellogg Foundation 2006). Logic models have been employed widely in the nonprofit sector and might be particularly suited to the public library environment.

Program Structures

Instruction programs are organized in different ways depending on the type and size of the library and the particular context of the larger institution. In smaller institutions, especially smaller public, school, and special libraries, an instruction program might involve one or two librarians who also provide reference service and even some technical service functions. In these settings, the reference desk might be the primary environment for instruction, with most instruction happening in a one-on-one interaction between a librarian and a patron. In larger K–12 settings, school librarians might manage a small staff of paraprofessionals and work closely as a member of the larger instructional team. In academic libraries, there are a variety of models.

Smaller academic libraries might look like their school and public counterparts, with one or two people doing much of the public services work, including instruction. At larger academic libraries, reference and instruction are often functions in a single department, with multiple librarians sharing the teaching and instructional design load. In some cases, there might be an instruction coordinator who oversees the planning and management of the program, but he or she might not be the department head or have formal authority. Another common model is the subject liaison model, in which librarians across the library serve particular academic departments and combine reference, outreach, instruction, and collection development duties for that department. In some cases, libraries have created instruction departments separate from the liaison or reference librarians, with a few personnel dedicated to instructional design and university-wide instructional initiatives such as general education. All of these models have advantages and disadvantages. Dedicated instruction librarians have strong pedagogical expertise, for example, but liaison librarians, with a full complement of duties, can often develop strong relationships with departmental faculty.

Infrastructure

Effective instruction programs require physical and technical infrastructure to support teaching and learning. In many cases, libraries have a dedicated classroom or training room, with computers so that learners can do hands-on activities during a session. Effective classroom design should ensure that these computers provide good sight lines to the instructor, are accessible to all users, and have up-to-date technology. Some libraries, especially in higher education, are building technology-rich classrooms that enable flexible group work and interactivity, and public libraries are building makerspaces to promote hands-on learning, problem-solving, and other critical 21st-century skills (Kroski 2013; MIT 2015).

Technology is needed not just in classrooms, but to support online learning and the creation of instructional materials as well. Librarians might need access to software to create multimedia materials, including videos, as well as standard productivity software for word processing. In higher education, universities are using sophisticated learning management and assessment and learning analytic systems. Librarians should have access to these as academic personnel and be provided training and professional development to deploy them effectively.

Professional Development

Librarians enter the profession with a diverse background in educational theory and practice. Many school librarians are certified teachers with extensive pedagogical knowledge and experience. By contrast, many new librarians in academic, public, and special libraries are exposed to basic information about teaching and learning in the course of their library school programs, and some programs include opportunities to take dedicated courses on instruction and information literacy. Despite this formal training, some librarians feel ill-prepared for their new instructional roles and require on-the-job training and continuing professional development (Julien and Genuis 2011).

The skills required for instruction librarians are diverse. When school librarians are certified teachers, they must meet the professional licensing requirements of individual states (American Association of School Librarians 2015b). For academic librarians, ACRL outlined the Standards for Proficiencies for Instruction Librarians and Coordinators (2007). The proficiencies include:

- Administrative skills
- Assessment and evaluation skills
- Communication skills
- Curriculum knowledge
- Information literacy integration skills
- Instructional design skills
- Leadership skills
- Planning skills
- Presentation skills
- Promotion skills
- Subject expertise
- Teaching skills

The Medical Library Association (2015) includes the understanding of "curricular design and instruction and . . . the ability to teach ways to access, organize, and use information" as a core competency for medical librarians. ALA's Reference and User Services Association (RUSA) defines several instruction-related professional competencies, including knowledge of current information competency standards and a respect for "the right of users to determine the direction of their research by empowering them to pursue their own preferences" (2003). RUSA also outlines broad competencies for marketing and promotion, understanding the needs of users, and keeping up with the professional literature, all of which have broad application to the role of librarians as teachers in any context. Reference interview skills are also an essential component for teaching in one-on-one reference situations.

Library managers and school administrators can provide professional development for all of their teaching librarians through activities like journal clubs, in which everyone reads and discusses a current professional or academic work, and staff presentations in which "expert" staff members teach colleagues. In formal school settings, librarians can often participate in the professional development opportunities provided to the larger teaching staff. These can also be useful for developing relationships with teaching faculty and getting a better understanding of their needs. National education conferences, such as the annual conference of the National Association for the Education of Young Children, often include programming especially relevant for school librarians. For librarians in smaller institutions, especially if they are solo librarians, these collaborative learning opportunities can be harder to develop. Local and state library associations often provide learning activities related to instruction, and many of these are now online if travel to a conference or workshop is not possible. ALA, RUSA, ACRL, and AASL all offer a wide range of conference programming and online professional development, including frequent webinars. There are also small conferences dedicated to library instruction, mainly in an academic context, such as LOEX in the United States and the Workshop for Instruction in Library Use in Canada.

Advocacy and Publicity

Building instruction programmatically requires strong allies across the library and across the institution and community. Instruction is a resource-intensive effort that requires personnel to design, deliver, and assess instruction. Instruction is also more effective if it closely aligns with the needs of the institution, especially in the case of formal school settings, where instruction is ideally a shared responsibility of librarians and faculty or teachers. Public librarians face the challenge of advertising their offerings to users who are not "captive" in the same ways as students in schools and colleges. Marketing of instruction should follow general marketing principles and guidelines. It should be clear, concise, and consistent. It should send a clear message that the instructional offerings align with the institution's goals. There are several useful guides to marketing general library programs, including the use of social media and strategies for marketing instruction programs specifically (Lederer 2005; Potter 2012).

Outreach can also be a form of advocacy and marketing, one that engages directly with users in a meaningful way. Emily Ford argues that instead of viewing marketing and outreach as a separate function, "As professionals we should all be talking about the library in our communities and fostering relationships. We should be offering satellite services and, yes, we should all have down pat our 30 second 'why the library is important' elevator speech. These are essential aspects of a library and of any librarian's job. They are not separate nor should they be contained in a different or a sole unit or entity" (2009, 2).

For librarians in K–12 and higher education, serving on committees, engaging with student service activities, and collaborating with faculty on instructional design or assessment projects can all be an effective form of advocating for the role of libraries in instruction. For public librarians, participating in community groups can provide avenues for promotion. Even hosting community events in the library can be a simple way to market library services. In essence, showing rather than telling might be the most effective marketing strategy and one that all teaching librarians can engage in.

FUTURE CHALLENGES

Rapid change, new technologies, changing user needs, and crisis are themes that recur throughout the library literature. The current challenges for instruction in libraries echo earlier concerns about ill-prepared students, the need to filter an abundance of possibly "bad" information sources, debates over the professional status and the educational role of librarians, and declining support for public goods such as libraries and universities. The current situation certainly mirrors this past discourse in several ways.

The financial challenges are significant. Since 2008, states have "disinvested" in higher education, for example, at a substantial rate (Hiltonsmith and Draut 2014). School libraries are closing in large numbers, and many school librarians are being replaced by classified staff (Santos 2011). In addition, accountability and educational reform movements are asking schools and universities to make learning outcomes more transparent and be accountable if their students fail to meet these outcomes. The Lumina Foundation (2014) has developed a general Degree Qualification Profile to define outcomes that all college graduates should have, and information literacy is one of the stated goals. But many faculty and institutions find such reform proposals to be overdetermined, top-down, too focused on job preparation rather than liberal education, and limiting to an institution's autonomy in addressing the specific learning needs of their population. Similarly, the Common Core standards in K–12 remain controversial because of fears of federal control on the one hand and criticism of standardized testing regimes on the other (Baker 2014; Common Core State Standards Initiative 2015). Many educational institutions are being asked to do and "prove" more in an era of declining resources.

The key challenge for teaching librarians today, then, is how to navigate an educational environment that is very much in flux, with competing interests and even definitions of success. One of the most essential skills for librarians will be the ability to read the local environment to identify opportunities, partners, and language that can help further the goals of their educational programs, while at the same time avoiding destructive political pitfalls and battles. At some institutions, developing degree program learning outcomes might be an excellent opportunity to work with campus leaders to integrate information literacy across the curriculum, while at other institutions, it might be politically unwise. In that case, a more grassroots approach with a few faculty partners would yield more benefits. For school librarians, the Common Core Standards might provide a structure for integrating high-order information literacy skills into the school's curriculum and learning activities (American Association of School Librarians 2015a). In other cases, resistance to high-stakes testing might limit the efficacy of this approach. In public libraries, limited funding means paying special attention to the language of local political leaders, boards, and potential advocates in the business community. Being able to analyze these situations and make strategic decisions requires much deeper knowledge of the context of education and learning needs at all levels. Environmental scanning might be the most essential skill for teaching librarians so that they can find effective partners and align their efforts with their institutions and communities.

While information literacy calls for librarians to move beyond library-centered education, it is even more urgent now for librarians to understand the learning needs of their patrons and stakeholders, the curriculum in formal school settings, and other contextual influences that shape their local communities. The IMLS 21st Century Skills initiative provides a potentially useful framework for all libraries. Their list of skills is intentionally extensive, ranging from specific areas, such as financial literacy, to broad critical thinking and communication skills. IMLS invites each library to identify and prioritize the skills that best meet its community needs, and these might not even be "traditional" library or information literacy skills (Institute of Museum and Library Services 2015). There have always been calls for librarians not to "own" information literacy and to share the responsibility with a wide of range of teaching partners. These partners might be found in some of the usual places (teachers in K–12 and higher education), but they might also be found in local community or business groups interested in addressing science and technology education needs outside of a formal school setting. Removing barriers between different kinds of libraries might also provide new paths forward, such as movements to better align K–12 and higher education information literacy programs or partnerships between public and school librarians on after-school services. According to the IMLS (2009, 6), libraries have always been engaged in education, but we need to make this function more visible and intentional: "All libraries and museums—and the people they serve—stand to benefit from becoming more intentional and purposeful about accommodating the lifelong learning needs of people in the 21st century, and doing this work collaboratively in alignment with community needs."

The challenge for the future is to think creatively about the most productive roles that teaching librarians from all kinds of institutions might engage in, both within and beyond our walls, to make further progress toward weaving libraries into the fabric of our local communities.

REFERENCES

Accardi, Maria T., Emily Drabinski, and Alana Kumbier. 2010. *Critical Library Instruction Theories and Methods*. Duluth, MN: Library Juice Press.

Accardi, Maria T., and Jana Vukovic. 2013. *Feminist Pedagogy for Library Instruction*. Sacramento, CA: Library Juice Press.

Altschuld, James W., David D. Kumar, J. Nicholls Eastmond, Jeffry L. White, Laurie Stevahn, and Jean A. King. 2010. *Needs Assessment*. Thousand Oaks, CA: SAGE Publications.

Alverno College. 2001. "Assessment Essentials." http://depts.alverno.edu/saal/essentials.html.

American Association of School Librarians. 2007. "Standards for the 21st-Century Learner." American Library Association. http://www.ala.org/aasl/sites/ala.org.aasl/files/content/guidelinesandstandards/learningstandards/AASL_LearningStandards.pdf.

American Association of School Librarians. 2009. *Empowering Learners: Guidelines for School Library Programs*. Chicago: American Association of School Librarians.

American Association of School Librarians. 2015a. "Learning Standards & Common Core State Standards Crosswalk." Accessed April 24. http://www.ala.org/aasl/standards-guidelines/crosswalk.

American Association of School Librarians. 2015b. "Library Education & Licensing." American Library Association. Accessed April 24. http://www.ala.org/aasl/education/recruitment/licensing.

American Association of School Librarians and Association for Educational Communications and Technology. 1998. *Information Power: Building Partnerships for Learning*. Chicago: American Library Association.

American Bar Association. 1992. *Legal Education and Professional Development—An Educational Continuum*. http://www.americanbar.org/content/dam/aba/publications/misc/legal_education/2013_legal_education_and_professional_development_maccrate_report).authcheckdam.pdf.

American Bar Association. 2014. "Program of Legal Education." In *ABA Standards and Rules of Procedure for Approval of Law Schools*, 15–25. Chicago: American Bar Association. http://www.americanbar.org/content/dam/aba/publications/misc/legal_education/Standards/2014_2015_aba_standards_chapter3.authcheckdam.pdf.

American Library Association. 1989. "Presidential Committee on Information Literacy: Final Report." http://www.ala.org/acrl/publications/whitepapers/presidential.

American Management Association. 2012. "AMA 2012 Critical Skills Survey." http://www.amanet.org/uploaded/2012-Critical-Skills-Survey.pdf.

Anderson, Lorin W., David R. Krathwohl, and Benjamin S. Bloom. 2001. *A Taxonomy for Learning, Teaching, and Assessing: A Revision of Bloom's Taxonomy of Educational Objectives*. New York: Longman.

Angelo, Thomas A., and K. Patricia Cross. 1993. *Classroom Assessment Techniques: A Handbook for College Teachers*. San Francisco: Jossey-Bass.

Arp, Lori. 1990. "Information Literacy or Bibliographic Instruction: Semantics or Philosophy?" *RQ* 30 (1): 46–49.

Association of College and Research Libraries. 2000. "Information Literacy Competency Standards for Higher Education." American Library Association. http://www.ala.org/ala/mgrps/divs/acrl/standards/informationliteracycompetency.cfm.

Association of College and Research Libraries. 2007. "Standards for Proficiencies for Instruction Librarians and Coordinators." American Library Association. http://www.ala.org/acrl/standards/profstandards.

Association of College and Research Libraries. 2011. "Standards for Libraries in Higher Education." American Library Association. http://www.ala.org/acrl/standards/standardslibraries.

Association of College and Research Libraries. 2015. "Framework for Information Literacy for Higher Education." American Library Association. http://www.ala.org/acrl/sites/ala.org.acrl/files/content/issues/infolit/Framework_ILHE.pdf.

Atlas, Michel C. 2000. "The Rise and Fall of the Medical Mediated Searcher." *Bulletin of the Medical Library Association* 88 (1): 26–35.

Ausubel, David P., Joseph D. Novak, and Helen Hanesian. 1986. *Educational Psychology: A Cognitive View*. New York: Werbel & Peck.

Baker, Al. 2014. "Common Core Curriculum Now Has Critics on the Left." *New York Times*. February 16. http://www.nytimes.com/2014/02/17/nyregion/new-york-early-champion-of-common-core-standards-joins-critics.html.

Baker, J. Wesley. 2000. "The 'Classroom Flip': Using Web Course Management Tools to Become the Guide by the Side." In *Selected Papers from the 11th International Conference on College Teaching and Learning*, 9–17. Jacksonville, FL: Center for the Advancement of Teaching and Learning, Florida Community College at Jacksonville.

Battersby, Mark. 1999. "So, What's a Learning Outcome Anyway?" http://eric.ed.gov/?id=ED430611.

Bell, Steven J., and John D. Shank. 2007. *Academic Librarianship by Design: A Blended Librarian's Guide to the Tools and Techniques*. Chicago: American Library Association.

Black, Paul, and Dylan Wiliam. 2010. "Inside the Black Box: Raising Standards through Classroom Assessment." *Phi Delta Kappan* 92 (1): 81–90.

Bloom, Benjamin S. 1956. *Taxonomy of Educational Objectives: The Classification of Educational Goals*. New York: Longman.

Booth, Char. 2011. *Reflective Teaching, Effective Learning: Instructional Literacy for Library Educators*. Chicago: American Library Association.

Brookfield, Stephen D. 1995. *Becoming a Critically Reflective Teacher*. San Francisco: Jossey-Bass.

Bruce, Christine. 1997. *The Seven Faces of Information Literacy*. Adelaide, Australia: Auslib Press.

Bruce, Christine. 2008. *Informed Learning*. Chicago: Association of College and Research Libraries.

Bruce, Christine, Sylvia Edwards, and Mandy Lupton. 2006. "Six Frames for Information Literacy Education: A Conceptual Framework for Interpreting the Relationships between Theory and Practice." *Innovation in Teaching and Learning in Information and Computer Sciences* 5 (1): 1–18.

Bruner, Jerome S. 1956. *A Study of Thinking*. New York: Wiley.

Bruner, Jerome S. 1960. *The Process of Education*. Cambridge, MA: Harvard University Press.

Callister, Paul D. 2010. "Time to Blossom: An Inquiry into Bloom's Taxonomy as a Hierarchy and Means for Teaching Legal Research Skills." *Law Library Journal* 102: 191–218.

Common Core State Standards Initiative. 2015. "Preparing America's Students for Success." Accessed April 24. http://www.corestandards.org/.

D'Angelo, Cynthia M., Stephanie Touchman, and Douglas P. Clark. 2009. "Constructivism: Overview." In *Psychology of Classroom Learning: An Encyclopedia*, edited by Eric M. Anderman and Lynley H. Anderman, 262–68. Detroit: Macmillan.

Davis, Erin D., Kacy Lundstrom, and Pamela N. Martin. 2011. "Librarian Perceptions and Information Literacy Instruction Models." *Reference Services Review* 39 (4): 686–702.

Dewey, John. 1915. *The School and Society*. Chicago: University of Chicago Press.

Dewey, John. 1916. *Democracy and Education: An Introduction to the Philosophy of Education*. New York: Macmillan.

Doyle, Christina. 1993. "The Delphi Method as a Qualitative Assessment Tool for Development of Outcome Measures for Information Literacy." *School Library Media Annual* 11: 132–44.

Eisenberg, Michael, Carrie A. Lowe, and Kathleen L. Spitzer. 2004. *Information Literacy: Essential Skills for the Information Age*. Westport, CT: Libraries Unlimited.

Elmborg, James K. 2002. "Teaching at the Desk: Toward a Reference Pedagogy." *portal: Libraries & the Academy* 2 (3): 455–64.

Elmborg, James K. 2006. "Critical Information Literacy: Implications for Instructional Practice." *The Journal of Academic Librarianship* 32 (2): 192–99.

Elmborg, James K. 2012. "Critical Information Literacy: Definitions and Challenges." In *Transforming Information Literacy Programs: Intersecting Frontiers of Self, Library Culture, and Campus Community*, edited by Carroll Wetzel Wilkinson and Courtney Bruch, 75–95. Chicago: Association of College and Research Libraries.

Felder, Richard. 2010. "Are Learning Styles Invalid? (Hint: NO!)." http://www4.ncsu.edu/unity/lockers/users/f/felder/public/Papers/LS_Validity(On-Course).pdf.

Ford, Emily. 2009. "Outreach Is (un)Dead." *In the Library with the Lead Pipe*. http://www.inthelibrarywiththeleadpipe.org/2009/outreach-is-undead/.

Foster, Nancy Fried, and Susan Gibbons. 2007. *Studying Students: The Undergraduate Research Project at the University of Rochester*. Chicago: Association of College and Research Libraries.

Gagné, Robert M. 1985. *The Conditions of Learning and Theory of Instruction*, 4th ed. New York: Holt, Rinehart and Winston.

Gilchrist, Debra, and Anne Zald. 2008. "Instruction & Program Design through Assessment." In *Information Literacy Instruction Handbook*, edited by Christopher N. Cox and Elizabeth Blakesley, 164–92. Chicago: Association of College and Research Libraries.

Gregory, Lua, Shana Higgins, and Toni Samek. 2013. *Information Literacy and Social Justice: Radical Professional Praxis*. Duluth, MN: Library Juice Press.

Harrington, Helen L. 1995. "Fostering Reasoned Decisions: Case-Based Pedagogy and the Professional Development of Teachers." *Teaching and Teacher Education* 11 (3): 203–14.

Harris, Roma M. 1989. "Bibliographic Instruction in Public Libraries: A Question of Philosophy." *RQ* 29 (1): 92–98.

Helms, Marilyn M. 2006. "Case Method of Analysis." In *Encyclopedia of Management*, edited by Marilyn M. Helms, 67–70. Detroit: Thomson/Gale.

Hiltonsmith, Robert, and Tamara Draut. 2014. "The Great Cost Shift Continues: State Higher Education Funding after the Recession." http://www.demos.org/sites/default/files/publications/TheGreatCostShift2014-Brief_0.pdf.

Hmelo-Silver, Cindy E. 2004. "Problem-Based Learning: What and How Do Students Learn?" *Educational Psychology Review* 16 (3): 235–66.

Hodell, Chuck. 2006. *ISD from the Ground Up: A No-Nonsense Approach to Instructional Design*. Alexandria, VA: ASTD Press.

Institute of Museum and Library Services. 2009. "Museums, Libraries, and 21st-Century Skills." http://www.imls.gov/assets/1/workflow_staging/AssetManager/293.PDF.

Institute of Museum and Library Services. 2015. "21st Century Skills Definitions." Accessed April 6. http://www.imls.gov/about/21st_century_skills_list.aspx.

Julien, Heidi, and Shelagh K. Genuis. 2011. "Librarians' Experiences of the Teaching Role: A National Survey of Librarians." *Library & Information Science Research* 33 (2): 103–11.

Kapitzke, Cushla. 2003. "Information Literacy: A Positivist Epistemology and a Politics of Outformation." *Educational Theory* 53 (1): 37–53.

Katz, William A. 1969. *Introduction to Reference Work*. New York: McGraw-Hill.

Kent State University Libraries. 2015. "TRAILS: Tool for Real-Time Assessment of Information Literacy Skills." http://www.trails-9.org/.

King-Sears, Margaret. 2009. "Universal Design for Learning: Technology and Pedagogy." *Learning Disability Quarterly* 32 (4): 199–201.

King-Sears, Margaret. 2014. "Introduction to Learning Disability Quarterly Special Series on Universal Design for Learning: Part One of Two." *Learning Disability Quarterly* 37 (2): 68–70.

Kobelski, Pamela, and Mary Reichel. 1981. "Conceptual Frameworks for Bibliographic Instruction." *The Journal of Academic Librarianship* 7 (2): 73–77.

Kobzina, Norma G. 2010. "A Faculty—Librarian Partnership: A Unique Opportunity for Course Integration." *Journal of Library Administration* 50 (4): 293–314.

Kolb, Alice, and David Kolb. 2005. "The Kolb Learning Style Inventory—Version 3.1: 2005 Technical Specifications." Haygroup: Experience Based Learning Systems Inc. http://learningfromexperience.com/media/2010/08/tech_spec_lsi.pdf.

Kolb, David A. 1984. *Experiential Learning: Experience as the Source of Learning and Development*. Englewood Cliffs, NJ: Prentice-Hall.

Kroski, Ellyssa. 2013. "A Librarian's Guide to Makerspaces: 16 Resources." *OEDB.org*. http://oedb.org/ilibrarian/a-librarians-guide-to-makerspaces/.

Kuhlthau, Carol Collier. 1992. *Seeking Meaning: A Process Approach to Library and Information Services*. Norwood, NJ: Ablex.

Kvenild, Cassandra, and Kaijsa Calkins. 2011. *Embedded Librarians: Moving beyond One-Shot Instruction*. Chicago: Association of College and Research Libraries.

Lave, Jean, and Etienne Wenger. 1991. *Situated Learning: Legitimate Peripheral Participation*. New York: Cambridge University Press.

Lederer, Naomi. 2005. *Ideas for Librarians Who Teach: With Suggestions for Teachers and Business Presenters*. Lanham, MD: Scarecrow Press.

Limberg, Louise. 2000. "Is There a Relationship between Information Seeking and Learning Outcomes?" In *Information Literacy around the World: Advances in Programs and Research*, edited by Christine Bruce and Philip Candy, 200–201. Wagga Wagga, Australia: Centre for Information Studies, Charles Sturt University.

Lloyd, Annemaree. 2007. "Learning to Put Out the Red Stuff: Becoming Information Literate through Discursive Practice." *The Library Quarterly* 77 (2): 181–98.

LOEX. 2014. "About LOEX." Accessed December 2. http://www.loex.org/about.php.

Lumina Foundation. 2014. "Degree Qualifications Profile." http://www.luminafoundation.org/files/resources/dqp.pdf.

Lupton, Mandy. 2008. "Evidence, Argument and Social Responsibility: First-Year Students' Experiences of Information Literacy When Researching an Essay." *Higher Education Research & Development* 27 (4): 399–414.

Lupton, Mandy, and Christine S. Bruce. 2010. "Windows on Information Literacy Worlds: Generic, Situated and Transformative Perspectives." In *Practising Information Literacy: Bringing Theories of Learning, Practice and Information Literacy Together*, edited by Annemaree Lloyd and Sanna Talja, 3–27. Wagga Wagga, Australia: Centre for Information Studies, Charles Sturt University.

Marcoux, Betty. 1999. "Developing the National Information Literacy Standards for Student Learning." *NASSP Bulletin* 83 (605): 13–19.

Medical Library Association. 2015. "Competencies for Professional Success." Accessed April 24. https://www.mlanet.org/education/policy/index.html.

Mellon, Constance A. 1986. "Library Anxiety: A Grounded Theory and Its Development." *College & Research Libraries* 47 (2): 160–65.

Mellon, Constance A. 1987. "Bibliographic Instruction Think Tank I: Looking Back and the Challenge for Think Tank II." In *Bibliographic Instruction: The Second Generation*, edited by Constance A. Mellon, 5–23. Littleton, CO: Libraries Unlimited.

Miller, Michelle D. 2014. *Minds Online: Teaching Effectively with Technology*. Cambridge, MA: Harvard University Press.

MIT. 2015. "TEAL—Technology Enabled Active Learning." *iCampus*. Accessed April 24. http://icampus.mit.edu/projects/teal/.

National Center on Universal Design for Learning. 2014. "About UDL." Accessed December 8. http://www.udlcenter.org/aboutudl.

National Commission on Excellence in Education. 1983. "A Nation at Risk: The Imperative for Educational Reform." http://www2.ed.gov/pubs/NatAtRisk/risk.html.

Nielsen, Brian. 1982. "Teacher or Intermediary. Alternative Professional Models in the Information Age." *College & Research Libraries* 43 (3): 183–91.

Oswald, Daniel, and Charles Reigeluth. 2002. "Instructional Design: Overview." In *Encyclopedia of Education*, edited by James Guthrie, 1146–51. New York: Macmillan.

Owusu-Ansah, Edward K. 2003. "Information Literacy and the Academic Library: A Critical Look at a Concept and the Controversies Surrounding It." *The Journal of Academic Librarianship* 29 (4): 219–30.

Partnership for 21st Century Learning. 2006. "Are They Really Ready to Work?: Employers' Perspectives on the Basic Knowledge and Applied Skills of New Entrants to the 21st Century U.S. Workforce." http://www.p21.org/storage/documents/FINAL_REPORT_PDF09-29-06.pdf.

Pashler, Harold, Mark McDaniel, Doug Rohrer, and Robert Bjork. 2008. "Learning Styles: Concepts and Evidence." *Psychological Science in the Public Interest* 9 (3): 105–19.

Pawley, Christine. 2003. "Information Literacy: A Contradictory Coupling." *The Library Quarterly* 73 (4): 422–52.

Peura, Christina Elizabeth. 2014. "Electronic Legal Research Tools: An Examination of the Resources Available, Training of New Attorneys, and Employer Expectations." *Legal Reference Services Quarterly* 33 (4): 269–91.

Piaget, Jean. 1953. *The Origin of Intelligence in the Child.* London: Routledge & Paul.

Potter, Ned. 2012. *The Library Marketing Toolkit.* London: Facet Publishing.

Project Information Literacy. 2014. Accessed December 5. http://projectinfolit.org/.

Public Library Association. 2015. "Project Outcome: Measuring the True Impact of Public Libraries." Accessed April 24. http://www.ala.org/pla/performancemeasurement.

Rader, Hannelore B. 1974. "Library Orientation and Instruction—1973: An Annotated Review of the Literature." *Reference Services Review* 2 (1): 91–93.

Reference and User Services Association. 2003. "Professional Competencies for Reference and User Services Librarians." American Library Association. http://www.ala.org/rusa/resources/guidelines/professional.

Rhodes, Terrel L., and Ashley P. Finley. 2013. *Using the VALUE Rubrics for Improvement of Learning and Authentic Assessment.* Washington, DC: Association of American Colleges & Universities.

Royse, David D. 2009. *Needs Assessment.* New York: Oxford University Press.

"Rubrics." 2014. *RAILS: Rubric Assessment of Information Literacy Skills.* Accessed December 8. http://railsontrack.info/rubrics.aspx.

Santos, Fernanda. 2011. "In Lean Times, Schools Squeeze Out Librarians." *The New York Times.* June 24. http://www.nytimes.com/2011/06/25/nyregion/schools-eliminating-librarians-as-budgets-shrink.html.

Schiller, Anita R. 1965. "Reference Service: Instruction or Information." *The Library Quarterly* 35 (1): 52–60.

Schrock, Kathy. 2015. "Assessment and Rubrics." Accessed April 24. http://www.schrockguide.net/assessment-and-rubrics.html.

Snavely, Loanne, and Natasha Cooper. 1997. "The Information Literacy Debate." *The Journal of Academic Librarianship* 23 (1): 9–14.

Stiggins, Richard. 2003. "Classroom Assessment." In *Encyclopedia of Education*, edited by James W. Guthrie, 123–28. New York: Macmillan Reference USA.

Townsend, Lori, Korey Brunetti, and Amy R. Hofer. 2011. "Threshold Concepts and Information Literacy." *portal: Libraries and the Academy* 11 (3): 853–69.

Tucker, John Mark. 1980. "User Education in Academic Libraries: A Century in Retrospect." *Library Trends* 29 (1): 9–27.

UNESCO. 2014. "Information Literacy." Accessed November 25. http://www.unesco.org/new/en/communication-and-information/access-to-knowledge/information-literacy/.

Vygotsky, Lev Semenovich. 1978. *Mind in Society: The Development of Higher Psychological Processes*. Cambridge, MA: Harvard University Press.

Wiggins, Grant. 2005. "Overview of UbD & Design Template." http://www.grantwiggins.org/documents/UbDQuikvue1005.pdf.

Wiggins, Grant P., and Jay McTighe. 1998. *Understanding by Design*. Alexandria, VA: Association for Supervision and Curriculum Development.

W. K. Kellogg Foundation. 2006. "Logic Model Development Guide." https://www.wkkf.org:443/resource-directory/resource/2006/02/wk-kellogg-foundation-logic-model-development-guide.

Zurkowski, Paul G. 1974. "The Information Service Environment Relationships and Priorities. Related Paper No. 5." http://eric.ed.gov/?id=ED100391.

GUIDELINES, STANDARDS, AND DEFINITIONS

American Association of School Librarians. 2015. "Learning Standards & Program Guidelines." American Library Association. Accessed April 24. http://www.ala.org/aasl/standards-guidelines.

This website provides links to the current AASL "Standards for the 21st-Century Learner," as well as other valuable material, such as crosswalks between the AASL Standards and the Common Core, a lesson plan database, and other practical resources for teaching information literacy in the K–12 environment.

American Association of School Librarians and Association for Educational Communications and Technology. 1998. *Information Power: Building Partnerships for Learning*. Chicago: American Library Association.

Information Power remains an essential handbook for school librarians. While the AASL learning standards have been updated since the initial publication of this book, it still contains valuable information on issues related to collaboration with classroom teachers, leadership, and program management.

American Library Association. 1989. "Presidential Committee on Information Literacy: Final Report." http://www.ala.org/acrl/publications/whitepapers/presidential.

A foundational document for information literacy that outlines a basic definition and need for information literacy programs and instruction across all libraries.

Association of College and Research Libraries. 2000. "Information Literacy Competency Standards for Higher Education." American Library Association.
http://www.ala.org/ala/mgrps/divs/acrl/standards/informationliteracycompetency.cfm.

The official learning standards for information literacy in academic libraries. These remain in place as one of the constellation of documents, including the "Framework for Information Literacy for Higher Education" (2015), designed to guide academic librarians in their information literacy programs.

Association of College and Research Libraries. 2015. "Framework for Information Literacy for Higher Education." American Library Association. http://www.ala.org/acrl/sites/ala.org.acrl/files/content/issues/infolit/Framework_ILHE.pdf.

Officially filed by ACRL in 2015, this document provides "frames" of essential understandings. Strongly influenced by threshold concepts, the *Framework* includes concepts and dispositions intended to enable students to deepen their information literacy skills in the context of higher education.

SUGGESTED READINGS

Booth, Char. 2011. *Reflective Teaching, Effective Learning: Instructional Literacy for Library Educators*. Chicago: American Library Association.

An approachable introduction to instructional design for librarians teaching in any setting. Includes useful frameworks and tools for designing a wide range of learning activities and materials, including face-to-face classes, print or online material, and technology-rich learning objects.

Bruce, Christine. 2008. *Informed Learning*. Chicago: Association of College and Research Libraries.

Bruce provides an alternative view of information literacy based on how learners and teachers view and experience the process of using information to learn. The book includes a summary of the research base for this approach, as well as examples and scenarios for designing instructional interventions that call learners' attention to the use of information, rather than only the process of finding information.

Institute of Museum and Library Services. 2009. "Museums, Libraries, and 21st-Century Skills." http://www.imls.gov/assets/1/workflow_staging/AssetManager/293.PDF.

This document provides an overview of the 21st Century Skills initiative by the IMLS. It calls for libraries and museums to take a more active and purposeful role in addressing the multifaceted needs of learners in formal and informal educational settings. It is particularly strong in advocating for public libraries and museums to be educational leaders because they are essential in extending formal schooling and meeting the needs of adult learners.

Miller, Michelle D. 2014. *Minds Online: Teaching Effectively with Technology*. Cambridge, MA: Harvard University Press.

Miller's focus is online learning, but this book provides a readable and coherent overview of the current state of knowledge on the psychology of learning, including attention and memory. Each chapter summarizes the literature and then provides practical examples and suggestions about how to leverage technology to enhance learning in both online and face-to-face settings.

Wiggins, Grant P., and Jay McTighe. 1998. *Understanding by Design*. Alexandria, VA: Association for Supervision and Curriculum Development.

A classic in instructional design, this book outlines a backwards design method that begins with learning goals in order to develop effective assessments and learning activities. Wiggins and McTighe argue for designing instruction to promote "essential understandings" of the content. The book is intended for designing instruction at the curricular level, so is especially useful in the K–12 setting, but also contains insights into making effective instructional choices that might be applied to workshops and other small-scale instructional efforts.

Chapter 5

Cooperation and Consortia

Rick Burke

INTRODUCTION

Library consortia have been a crucial, yet often overlooked, part of the library landscape for many years. Consortia form part of the foundations undergirding and building up libraries' collections and services. They function like businesses or agencies, and they are largely nonprofit. Consortia play a major role as intermediaries between libraries and other library-related businesses, not only in the acquisition of online resources and discovery tools, but also in interlibrary loan (ILL) and other forms of resource sharing, cooperative reference services, and more. Growth in consortial activity has been significant during the past 20 years, largely because of the shift of library material acquisitions from print to electronic and the shrinking of library budgets. Many librarians find that their library's membership in a consortium impacts their day-to-day work on a regular basis. This chapter details the variety of needs fulfilled by library consortia and suggests ways in which a librarian may establish productive connections with them.

The official definition of a consortium reads: "any local, statewide, regional, interstate, or international cooperative association of library entities which provides for the systematic and effective coordination of the resources of school, public, academic, and special libraries and information centers, for improved services for the clientele of such library entities" ("Library Consortium Law and Legal Definition" 2015). This definition is comprehensive and reflective of the variety of shapes and sizes of library consortia. They can be statewide, state-funded legal entities. They can be quasi for-profit or nonprofit business entities. They might be regional in focus, covering a broad geographical area across multiple states, or national in scale, as often occurs in Europe and Asia. And they might serve multiple types of libraries, or a single type of library, such as an academic library consortium.

A common phrase among consortium directors is that consortia are like snowflakes, each unique in its purpose and focus. Thus, it is not easy to cover all types of consortia in a single book chapter, and this chapter will not attempt to do so. This chapter provides an overview of the history of library consortia and their current role in resource acquisition and sharing, with a focus on how these activities impact the work of reference librarians.

HISTORY OF LIBRARY COOPERATION

Consortia have long played a role in library innovation. Starting with the Ohio College Library Center (now the Online Computer Library Center or OCLC), the Research Libraries Group (which merged with OCLC in 2006), and Washington Library Network (which merged with OCLC in 1999) in the 1970s, libraries began collaborating on a large scale to form bibliographic utilities for shared cataloging. Large OCLC-subsidized multistate networks also formed during this time. These networks performed a number of services for their member libraries, such as consulting, technology assistance, online catalogs, and continuing education (Horton 2013).

A second burst of consortial activity occurred in the mid-1990s as a result of the emergence of networked electronic resources. This process was magnified and accelerated by the growth of competing search engines such as *Yahoo!*, the now defunct *Altavista*, and the eventually dominant *Google*, all of which fundamentally shifted the focus of the research process from the local library catalog and reference shelf to a networked environment where researchers had easy access to a much wider array of information. Commercial publishers of all sizes and a variety of start-ups moved from publishing print materials to producing online resources. Along with this shift in format came a new form of acquisition of library resources, site licensing. Following in the footsteps of personal computer software licensing, for the first time librarians found themselves confronted by the prospect of licensing rather than purchasing content, and they realized that this new environment required guidelines and standards to ensure ongoing access to information that was acquired by the library.

The second wave of library consortia built on the collaborative environment engendered by the bibliographic utilities and their associated consortial networks. Consortia multiplied, appearing globally in Europe, Central and South America, Asia, Australia, and Africa. During this second wave, cooperative efforts that had focused on bibliographic utilities evolved to include a plethora of resource-sharing activities including ILL and shared licensing of online resources. Over time, these cooperative efforts grew to include shared discovery systems, coordinated purchasing of print materials, cooperative archival projects, and more (Box 5.1 provides a case study illustrating how a meeting of local library directors in southern California grew to a statewide consortium involved in a wide variety of activities).

While most consortia engage in a variety of activities, some have become leaders in a particular area. For example, the Orbis Cascade Alliance in the Pacific Northwest is distinguished for its highly successful and tightly knit set of resource-sharing activities and systems. It has recently become one of the first major consortia to implement a fully shared next-generation library system and discovery service for all 37 of its member libraries. Other consortia offer a variety of training services, while some analyze usage statistics to provide their libraries with return-on-investment data. Some do all of the earlier-mentioned activities (see Box 5.2).

Box 5.1 Case Study: Statewide California Electronic Library Consortium

The development of the Statewide California Electronic Library Consortium (SCELC) illustrates patterns of growth and activities seen at other library consortia. The author of this chapter first discovered a local library consortium in California when he was the director of a small, private, sectarian, liberal arts college library. While much of the consortial activity had originated with large research libraries, there are a larger number of smaller yet vital private academic colleges and universities that are part of the larger higher education landscape. California in particular has more than 100 such institutions, but in the then extant consortial landscape of California, only the large state-funded systems (University of California, California State University system, and the community colleges) had organized into their own respective library consortia.

SCELC was founded by the University of Southern California in Los Angeles in 1986 to help network selected private colleges in southern California only. In 1994, the author joined SCELC in order to meet other library directors and share concerns and expertise regarding issues raised by the electronic resource world. By 1995, the library directors were beginning to figure out how to share costs for site licenses of emerging eResource databases. By 1998, this activity was beginning to expand rapidly and required more attention and focus. Representatives of SCELC began attending the nascent Consortium of Consortia (COC; now the International Coalition of Library Consortia, or ICOLC) meetings to engage with other library consortia and their staffs, and better understand how to cope with this new environment. By 2001, SCELC expanded its scope statewide, incorporating as a 501(c)(3) nonprofit organization. This process moved it from being an informal association of library directors meeting to discuss library issues to one with a governance structure and a part-time director whose focus was on working with library vendors to negotiate optimal pricing and terms for the acquisition of eResources. By attending many library conferences and meetings with library vendors of all sizes, SCELC focused on building a strong foundation of relationships with vendors to help insure an ongoing stream of product offers and acquisition opportunities that were advantageous to its member libraries. Negotiation skills were key in this process. In this context, SCELC, which now employs a full-time director as well as other staff, might be seen as a "buying club" type of consortium, and while that is its principal activity, it has branched out to provide other services, much like the consortia noted in the following text.

The role of vendors in helping consortia grow cannot be discounted. Many vendors have small sales forces, and in consortia, they found partners who could help them advertise and market their resources and consolidate licensing, billing, and order fulfillment. For those consortia with a business model built to manage licensing transactions, this was a boon, and it led to rapid growth of consortia and increased licensing activity among all types of libraries (see Chapter 14 for more detail).

However, if there was one common activity among most consortia from the late 1990s through the first decade of the 21st century, it was the cooperative licensing of electronic resources. Later this chapter will cover trends in library consortia, and while the licensing of eResources has become more regularized than it was 10 years ago, it does remain a major activity of library consortia.

Box 5.2 Activity: Examples of Consortial Activities

Library consortia engage in a wide variety of activities, including:

- Resource licensing
- Print and electronic purchasing
- ILL/document delivery
- Cooperative reference
- Shared catalogs and/or discovery systems
- Archival projects
- Training and continuing education
- Member consulting

Questions for Reflection and Discussion:

1. Which of these activities would you find most helpful as a reference librarian? As a library director?
2. Think about the resources and services libraries might develop in the future. What role could consortia play in supporting these efforts?
3. This chapter provides examples of how a library might benefit from being part of a consortium. Can you think of an instance where a library might not benefit?
4. Library consortia have proliferated in the past 20 years. Under what circumstances might they begin to consolidate and what impact would this have on libraries?

VARIETIES OF CONSORTIA

It is estimated that there are approximately 120 different consortia in the United States alone (Box 5.3 provides a small sampling of consortia in the western United States). Many are formally organized, while others are loosely organized and lack governance or other specific structural frameworks. Historically, consortia were formed to serve specific geographical regions or types of libraries or formed as a result of particular funding models; however, modern consortia are likely to cross over one or more of these historic classifications.

Traditionally, one way to classify consortia was by the geographical region served, but as consortia have expanded their services, they have often found themselves moving far beyond their original geographical borders. SOLINET, based in Atlanta, Georgia, became LYRASIS when it became the umbrella organization for the merger of several other former OCLC network consortia. As the largest consortium in terms of the number of member libraries in the United States, LYRASIS now serves libraries in 49 states. SCELC's affiliate program has extended its reach into 30 states. Other consortia can also point to coverage in more than half of the states in the United States. This overlap makes it harder to distinguish consortia by region or state alone, and it has increased competition among consortia while providing more choice for libraries.

Another way to classify consortia is by the audience served. As noted earlier, some consortia, such as Amigos, provide services and support to all types of

Box 5.3 Examples of Library Consortia

Amigos: a multi-type consortium that covers the southwestern region of the United States and was one of the OCLC networks.

- Cataloging services
- Collection sharing
- Resource licensing
- ILL/document delivery
- Preservation
- Training
- Union lists/shared catalogs
- OCLC systems training and implementation
- Most recently, Amigos developed a hosted eBook platform, Amigos eShelf

Califa: a multi-type consortium that primarily serves public libraries in California.

- Resource licensing
- Enki, a hosted eBook platform developed by Califa and the Contra Costa County Library system
- Administration of a host of grant-funded projects sourced through federal grants, such as providing broadband access to public libraries through the Corporation for Education Network Initiatives in California (CENIC) program

California Digital Library (CDL): serves 10 University of California campuses.

- Resource licensing
- Digital repository services
- Union catalog
- Preservation
- Digitization of books (partnered with Google)
- Administration of the Western Regional Storage Trust (WEST), a distributed retrospective print journal repository program

Colorado Alliance of Research Libraries: a consortium of primarily academic libraries in Colorado and Wyoming, plus one major public library, Denver Public Library.

- Shared catalog
- Resource licensing
- Digital repository services
- Gold Rush eResources management and access system
- Inter-consortium borrowing system with Mobius consortium in Missouri

Greater Western Library Alliance (GWLA): serves 33 Association of Research Libraries members in the central and western United States

- Resource licensing
- Shared eBook collections
- eBook ILL pilot project with *Occam's Reader*
- Discovery and resource-sharing tools
- Consortial print and electronic collection management
- Managing research data
- Shared student learning outcomes—best practice methodologies

Orbis Cascade Alliance: an academic library consortium covering both public and private colleges and universities in the Northwest.

- Resource licensing
- Collection sharing
- Shared discovery system
- ExLibris Alma, shared library management system

Statewide California Electronic Library Consortium (SCELC): serves private academic libraries and nonprofit research libraries.

- Resource licensing
- Grants and scholarships
- Fee-free ILL
- Patron-initiated borrowing system
- Digital Library Program
- Monograph archiving
- Continuing education programs, including Vendor Day, Research Day, and Colloquium

TexShare: a multi-type consortium funded by the state of Texas to serve all libraries in Texas.

- Resource licensing
- ILL
- Shared courier delivery service
- Competitive funding for digitization projects

libraries. Others, such as GWLA, are limited to large research libraries located at major universities. Some serve a specific class of academic libraries, such as SCELC's private academic libraries. One national consortium, NELLCO, serves only law libraries throughout the United States, while the Arizona Health Information Network (AZHIN) is limited to hospital and medical libraries. Some of these lines are blurring with time. Upon incorporation, SCELC added nonprofit research institutions to its membership portfolio. Many consortia might also serve a group of affiliated libraries that are not dues-paying members, but for a small fee, they can use a specific consortial service, such as access to discounted eResource offers.

A third way to look at library consortia is to understand the funding approach that underwrites their cost of operation. Some consortia are funded solely by membership dues, which, depending on the principal activity of a consortium, can be considerable. For example, a consortium that runs a shared integrated library system for all of its libraries would need significant dues to underwrite the cost of system support. Another funding model is to have lower dues, but in the instance of eResource licensing, an administrative surcharge will be collected for each business transaction. These surcharges can underwrite the cost of consortium operations when the consortium's principal activity is licensing of eResources for its members. Other consortia may have an outside funding source, such as a state legislature, and no dues or administrative surcharges. However, with public funding cuts in recent years, this model is not as prevalent as it once was.

As new library consortia emerged to grapple with the issues resulting from site licensing, an informal association, the Consortium of Consortia (COC), emerged to tackle these problems directly and to inform library vendors as to the preferred practices in this new marketplace. The COC later evolved into the International Coalition of Library Consortia (ICOLC). ICOLC now hosts an autumn meeting in Europe and a spring meeting in North America, and these meetings and an ICOLC listserv continue to be the principal venues where library consortia share information, compare consortium management strategies, and examine future trends that will impact libraries.

ICOLC is significant because of the large number of consortia it represents. Approximately 170 consortia are profiled on the ICOLC website, while more than 200 consortia globally are represented in the ICOLC listserv. Outside of the United States, many consortia represent entire countries, and they are often government affiliated or supported (Feather 2015).

As shown in Box 5.2, libraries and their consortia engage in a wide variety of cooperative activities. The remainder of this chapter will focus on these activities, including ILL and resource sharing, shared cataloging, eResource licensing and purchasing, print and digital collections projects, cooperative reference, member consulting, training and continuing education, and promoting open access (OA).

INTERLIBRARY LOAN AND RESOURCE SHARING

Resource sharing enables librarians to provide patrons with access to materials and resources beyond their local collections. Technology plays a critical support role in this process, and that technology may be hosted or underwritten by a consortium to support its libraries' resource-sharing activities. These technologies can support a variety of resource-sharing collaborations for two essentially different types of materials: "returnables," or circulating items such as books, and "nonreturnables," such as copies of journal articles or chapters from eBooks.

Traditionally, ILL required the intervention of library staff. Patrons would request an item, such as a book, video, or journal article; ILL staff would locate the item at a nearby library; request it; and when it arrived, give the item to the patron. If the item was a returnable, ILL staff would also be responsible for return shipping. Because of the cost of shipping as well as the cost of maintaining a dedicated staff, ILL was often fee based, with the requesting library paying a fee to the lending library.

Online services such as ILLiad and WorldShare ILL also streamlined the ILL process, allowing librarians to place and track requests online and send some materials, such as copies of journal articles, electronically. This efficiency, along with the decreased costs associated with transmitting some items electronically, has led to a decrease in or an elimination of ILL fees. Recent developments in this area include RapidILL, a service conceived and run by the Colorado State University Library. A popular low-cost option for the delivery of articles, RapidILL is praised for its fast turnaround, typically seven to nine hours or less, for the average ILL request, at a fraction of the cost of traditional ILL. Another service from Canada, Relais, has been deployed by some consortia as a cooperative approach to ILL.

While technological advances have streamlined ILL, the growth in eJournals and online databases has complicated the process at the same time. As discussed in Chapter 14, license terms need to allow ILL transactions, and consortia play an important role in enabling such arrangements through their license negotiation. If a library wishes to lend an article or other document from its licensed collection, the eligibility to lend those materials has to be tracked, as does the copyright associated with those documents. Document delivery software, such as the Copyright Clearance Center's Infotrieve, or another service, Reprints Desk, makes the processing of these transactions relatively seamless by documenting the lending library's holdings and permission to lend. New technology, such as ProQuest SIPX, enables end users and librarians to share materials locally and, through resource sharing, to other libraries by verifying copyright status and automating payment to those who hold the copyright to the materials.

Early on, some libraries, often those located near one another or those with similar patron needs, developed reciprocal borrowing agreements where they would lend one another materials at no cost. These agreements led to the development of patron-initiated ILL, where patrons can search a shared catalog, identify an item not held locally, request it, and have it delivered to their home library. The only human intervention required here is for a member of the lending library's staff to pull the item from the shelf, see that it has been processed in the circulation system of the lending library, and prepare it for courier pickup. Likewise, reciprocal borrowing systems have been established that enable patrons to visit and borrow directly from participating libraries.

In all of its forms, ILL is a complex process that requires interoperability between many disparate systems to enable a streamlined transaction. Some consortia, Orbis Cascade Alliance being the most outstanding example, have helped reduce this technological overhead by implementing a shared library system among member libraries. In 2015, the California State University System announced a similar move to one common library system to better enable resource sharing. A shared library system lowers overall technology costs by eliminating the need for interoperability among disparate local library systems. This approach requires strong consortial leadership and an ability to negotiate lending policy agreements among all participating libraries, while still balancing local library independence. Successful models such as these will no doubt encourage other consortia to pursue this path.

Consortia are also involved in the development of pay-per-view arrangements as another mechanism to deliver needed materials to patrons. In this scenario, the patron will locate the desired article directly from the publisher, order it, and the cost, with perhaps a negotiated consortial discount, will be charged directly to the library. The digital rights negotiated by the library or consortium will then determine the permissions the patron has to use the article or chapter.

Although librarians can contract directly with a publisher for such a service, there are aggregator services that bring together articles from multiple publishers and can offer access at a lower cost. ReadCube works with articles from selected publishers and allows a short-term rental or a higher-cost download. Another service, Get It Now from the Copyright Clearance Center, will deliver downloadable articles from a set of participating publishers and offers consortial discounts. The aforementioned Reprints Desk also offers article downloads.

SHARED CATALOGING

Shared cataloging was a very early consortial activity dating back to the formation of OCLC in 1967, and the funding of the various OCLC network consortia soon thereafter, that coincided with the emergence of the early online catalog systems. Prior to the rise of OCLC, librarians had to manually catalog every new title they received and enter the records into their own circulation and catalog database. The development of the OCLC database allowed for "copy cataloging," in which librarians could access the database and, for a small fee, download the record for an item and add it to their library's system. Although some libraries now receive catalog records directly from their book vendors, copy cataloging from OCLC is still in wide use today.

More recently, some consortia have created shared technical services, including cataloging, to help relieve local library pressure and allow for the reallocation of staff from traditional library services like cataloging to newer services, such as data curation, faculty outreach, and intensive information literacy programs. In some cases, libraries collaborate to achieve efficiency in cataloging or share expertise in niche areas like foreign-language cataloging, but maintain separate catalogs (Larsen and Arkoosh 2013).

In other cases, shared technical services have become the backbone for a shared catalog system, further facilitating resource-sharing efforts. The Triangle Research Libraries Network (TRLN) in North Carolina implemented a shared platform for discovery in 2007 called Search TRLN. This platform enabled search and discovery of the consortium's collection of more than 16 million volumes, and resource sharing of the collections increased 70 percent. Search TRLN also led to the recognition of duplicative cataloging processes and expenditures among their libraries, so the Search TRLN platform was used to reduce this duplication and share cataloging expertise across the consortium (Pennell, Sommerville, and Rodriguez 2013).

ELECTRONIC RESOURCE LICENSING AND PURCHASING

Resource licensing has historically been one of the foremost activities of library consortia and has reshaped the acquisitions marketplace for library electronic resources. As will be discussed in Chapter 14, consortia are able to help member libraries achieve discounted or stable pricing and negotiate fair license terms when licensing eResources. Representatives of major library vendors regularly schedule meetings with consortia staff to discuss renewals and new products, pricing, licensing terms, new programs, and more. For many consortia, a strong partnership with their vendors is an essential part of resource licensing, and it is important to recognize that consortia foster cooperation not only among libraries, but also between libraries and vendors.

Even before the emergence of eResources and licensing, library consortia have coordinated collaborative purchasing. Prior to the emergence of electronic resources, consortia, particularly those who were also OCLC networks, supported the purchasing of the hardware and software associated with cooperative cataloging. In the current era of electronic resources and a host of digital publishing efforts, many consortia support the purchase of shared collections of eBooks, eJournal backfiles, and archival collections, and the development of shared licenses to build digital library collections.

For selected consortia, electronic resource licensing and purchasing go hand in hand. At one consortium recent licensing patterns have shifted in the past three years to more purchases than subscriptions. This shift to purchases might be attributed to the fact that subscription costs are ongoing and outpace inflation, whereas a purchase represents a more fixed and predictable cost. Additionally, for libraries that have engaged in licensing resources for many years, their subscription budgets have largely been exhausted, yet they may find "end of the year money" for one-off purchases. However, for libraries newer to licensing through a consortium, subscriptions still tend to outpace direct purchases of content.

For purchased eResources, one of the more contentious issues for librarians is that of annual access fees. Many electronic resources that are purchased might be enhanced with new content annually; others might be fixed archival collections. In both instances, there is typically an annual access fee that, while relatively modest, represents an ongoing cost to the library much like that of an annual subscription. Access fees are typically not discounted, even through consortia, but consortia still play a valuable role in helping member libraries explore cost-effective options for access, whether licensed or purchased, and negotiate fair license terms.

PRINT AND DIGITAL COLLECTION PROJECTS

Shared print projects are a very active area for consortia, driven by several pressures within libraries. Many librarians, particularly in academic libraries, are weeding collections of print books to make room for other services, such as information commons, makerspaces, and group study rooms. In addition, the move in library acquisitions to a demand-driven model and usage analysis has led librarians to carefully analyze usage patterns in collections (Knievel, Wicht, and Connaway 2006). In some cases, these analyses have demonstrated that a large portion of some academic library collections have rarely or never circulated, prompting librarians to move unused materials from the library. Shared print projects enable librarians to coordinate weeding decisions so that copies of these low-use items are preserved at some libraries within the consortium, while enabling other libraries to remove the items to make room for higher-use collections or other services.

Consortia are especially important for shared print because they provide an existing network of trusted libraries through which to build relationships. Working collaboratively on collections can be challenging for librarians as it goes against the grain of the traditional model of building and maintaining notable local collections. Librarians in a consortium are accustomed to developing mutually beneficial services such as those noted in this chapter, and the shared print projects that are proliferating rely on existing consortial relationships as the foundation for their work.

While shared print often focuses on retrospective print collection management and archiving issues, some consortia, such as the Virtual Library of Virginia and the Central-Iowa Collaborative Collections Initiative, are pursuing cooperative development of print collections. In such instances, librarians collaborate when purchasing print materials, ensuring that while some libraries in the consortium hold desirable titles, unnecessary duplication is minimized. This allows librarians to use limited budgets to select new print purchases in their preferred subject areas, working cooperatively with others in the group to insure that the broad spectrum of subjects is covered by the group as a whole.

Similarly, some consortia focus on shared electronic resource collection development, particularly where a trusted repository of electronic texts already exists. One form of shared collection development for eResources revolves around demand-driven acquisition (DDA)/patron-driven acquisition (PDA). Since approximately 2010, this has emerged as a primary form of acquisition for eBooks. Essentially, a librarian might negotiate access to a large collection of eBooks with terms of use that allow free access to the materials until a certain agreed-upon number of uses triggers a purchase of the eBook. Variations in the usage models trigger a purchase, and models for DDA or PDA can vary among publishers and vendors. In a consortial environment, a resource-sharing agreement might enable the sharing of content, where each library's particular subject focus is reflected within the consortium's greater book collection.

A similar arrangement might apply to the joint purchase of shared eBook or eJournal collections. Within a consortium, libraries might agree to purchase a "big deal" package of eJournals and share access to those journals across the consortium. A rare but innovative approach to cooperative collection development is where a consortium works with a publisher to share subject-based collections of eBooks. Imagine a publisher publishes several hundred eBooks divided into many subject areas. In this consortial model, the libraries cooperate by each agreeing to purchase one subject collection. The participating libraries then share access to all of the subject collections by virtue of having purchased one of each collection through the consortium. Such an arrangement requires the cooperation of the content provider, and unfortunately this model is quite rare.

Librarians also collaborate to develop and share digital collections. In this instance, resource sharing occurs as a result of digital preservation activities. Libraries utilize software such as OCLC's popular CONTENTdm to digitize locally held archives of unique items. These original items are generally not published material, but reflect the focus of a library's local special collections. Consortia work with librarians to bring these collections together under one Web interface, underwriting the cost of the software, hardware, or interface construction to provide a common home for these materials. Examples of such efforts include Plowshares Digital and Callimachus.

As noted earlier, collective acquisition agreements among multiple libraries are difficult to negotiate, as each library has traditionally attempted to distinguish itself through the depth and breadth of its local collections. With the explosion of digital information came the recognition that no library can stand alone in this mission to acquire the broadest collection possible. Via consortial cooperation, librarians have found ways to network and collaborate as they build and manage both print and online collections.

A side effect of shared print is that it leads to greater resource sharing in general. Shared print programs utilize technology to facilitate the discovery of retained items across institutions. A delivery mechanism, such as a courier service, may also be built into the program. Once these discovery and delivery tools are in place, every library's collection is visible, and librarians can focus on what collection areas are key to their local needs.

Shared print also leads to large-scale cooperative collection development, where resources are shared on a consortium-wide, regional, national, or even international level. HathiTrust, a partnership of academic and research institutions offering a collection of millions of titles digitized from libraries around the world, demonstrates the broad scope of shared print at the international level. Regional programs such as Maine Shared Collections Cooperative and PALCI Distributed Print Archive also reflect a high level of local consortial activity.[1]

COOPERATIVE REFERENCE

Cooperative reference was a popular consortial service in the late 1990s and early 2000s. When virtual reference first emerged, librarians would invest in a virtual reference platform that allowed them to transfer questions between libraries; identify a group of interested colleagues, often through their existing regional consortium; and create a shared schedule to handle reference questions at all hours. Many of these early cooperative efforts merged with or joined QuestionPoint, a software tool and collaborative service codeveloped by OCLC and the Library of Congress (Weak and Luo 2013, 83–84). QuestionPoint remains a popular tool for providing virtual reference services, and subscribing libraries can choose to participate in the 24/7 Reference Cooperative, which provides a cooperative reference service for libraries across the United States and in other countries.

Springshare's LibGuides was created to help librarians format topical research guides and bibliographies for the Web using a simple Web-based interface. The system enables librarians to borrow and build on the work of colleagues at other institutions, another form of interlibrary cooperation. A later product, LibAnswers with LibChat, supports FAQs and virtual reference services and has emerged as a popular tool at many libraries. Consortia have commonly worked with Springshare to market their products to librarians.

MEMBER CONSULTING

Some consortia employ experts in certain areas in order to help their librarians from smaller libraries with fewer staff resources solve problems posed by the new electronic resource era. For example, some consortia will manage usage data to help librarians calculate their return on investment in selected eResources. Using standards such as Project COUNTER and Standardized Usage Statistics Harvesting Initiative (SUSHI), publishers can provide raw usage data to libraries, but assimilating these data into a usable format can be formidable. Other common areas for consulting are in the area of building digital collections, utilizing new technology, care and preservation of library collections, institutional repositories, understanding OA, and collection weeding and storage planning for libraries. In some cases, consortia have also assisted schools in organizing and de-duplicating their online resources after institutions have merged.

TRAINING AND CONTINUING EDUCATION

Continuing education for librarians is an essential activity for many consortia to help their members cope with change and trends in electronic resource acquisition, digital libraries, shared print, and more. Some consortia host symposia or colloquia to bring member libraries together and provide a venue for mutual education and the exchange of ideas. Another useful activity is a "vendor day," where librarians and vendors come together for a day devoted to exposure to new resources and interfaces, updates to current resources, and more. Both parties find this extremely useful and educational, and it provides a rare opportunity for face-to-face contact for both parties without the usual distractions of the big library conferences such as ALA Annual.

One consortium, SCELC, also provides training in professional research design for librarians. Created and developed in cooperation with one of their member institutions, the consortium presents an annual Research Day to help librarians hone their professional research skills and publish scholarly work in the field. An associated nine-day institute, the Institute for Research Design in Librarianship, sponsored by Loyola Marymount University in Los Angeles with some support from the library school at San Jose State University and SCELC, is a unique example of continuing education partially supported by a consortium.

Training is another core activity for many consortia, particularly those whose roots lie in the old OCLC networks model. An excellent example of the breadth of training courses offered to libraries of all types is provided by Amigos. A look at their listings reveals a broad range of courses, from "Basic Digitization" to "EBook Collection Development for Public and Academic Libraries." Likewise, LYRASIS offers a large number of classes for members.

PROMOTING OPEN ACCESS

Open access (OA) continues to be an evolving publication model. Approaches to OA vary. In some cases, researchers publish in a traditional journal, while also making their manuscript freely available in an institutional or disciplinary repository either as a preprint or following an embargo period. In other cases, researchers publish in an OA journal, bypassing traditional subscription-based journals. While some OA journals are completely free, relying on institutional support for server space and volunteer reviewers and editors, many OA journals charge a publication fee to authors. For fee-based publications, one of the features of OA is that it shifts the cost of publication from the end user, such as libraries as subscribers, to the authors. An "author-pays" model places the economic burden on the author or their institution to subsidize the cost of publication by paying for each article published, often in the form of page fees.

As OA publication grows, some libraries, particularly smaller ones with a limited budget for eJournals, may find that OA provides them with enhanced access to research literature. However, Kimberly L. Armstrong and Jay Starratt (2015) found that librarians had not canceled any journal subscriptions as a result of OA opportunities and reported no or minimal impact on their library collections budget due to OA. Overall, Armstrong and Starratt found that while librarians think OA is good, it is currently expensive for the libraries to maintain due to the new and different models that need to be integrated into collection workflows. They believe that there may be a tipping point where OA will provide savings, but it is unclear when that tipping point will occur.

However, at the October 2015 ICOLC meeting, there was much discussion about a more comprehensive move from the subscription model to an OA model in the libraries represented by major European consortia. Backed by mandates from the European Union and the government in the United Kingdom, European consortia are leading the charge for support of new OA models designed to replace the subscription model. In the United States, the California Digital Library is working on a similar program called Pay It Forward. Consortia are also working with major journal publishers to assure that OA article publication in hybrid subscription/OA journals results in subscription cost reductions over time. Such hybrid journals will contain a significant number of articles already paid for by the author-pays model, and the consortia are pushing to ensure that such prepayment of the cost of publication is offset in the total subscription cost, resulting in a net savings to the libraries.

One challenge for some consortia is how to adapt the economic model of negotiating discounts for electronic resources to the OA environment. For example, for the fee-based OA publications, consortia might provide subsidies to support the author-pays model. Such an approach might increase the visibility and value of the library on campus, as this would place libraries squarely in the middle of helping faculty publish in OA publications. Consortia might also support OA simply as an extension of their mission to help libraries provide access to information in all formats and models.

For many consortia, OA is core to their mission of helping libraries broaden access to peer-reviewed content at a reasonable cost, or even free of cost to the end user. By removing the commercial vendor from the middle and placing publication in the hands of researchers who produce the content, consortia are helping to underwrite and promote these new models of scholarly communication. Overall, OA still makes up only a fraction of the whole of publishing, but by promoting OA, consortia are continuing their mission of bringing innovation to the library marketplace.

CONCLUSION

Library consortia first worked to help libraries make the transition from print to electronic resources, then to make the commercial market for electronic resources more compatible with library practice. Collaboration among consortia, as reflected in the activities of ICOLC, helped lay the groundwork for the business models most commonly used for online content and library services. The standards and practices that consortia have helped establish for working with the commercial publishers have saved libraries money and provided guidelines for effective licensing practices. Consortia now play a significant role in print and electronic collection development, resource sharing, and many other services, while also working toward new models of scholarly publishing through support of OA.

Reference librarians need to be aware of consortia because of the impact they have on the collections and tools used in the provision of reference services. While services like virtual reference service can directly impact reference work, as this chapter demonstrates, consortia enable much-expanded access to eResources and ILL, which in turn enable reference librarians to respond to a wider variety of patron needs in more depth.

NOTE

1. For a more complete list of shared print programs, see the Print Archives Preservation Registry.

REFERENCES

Amigos. https://www.amigos.org.
Arizona Health Information Network. http://www.azhin.org/home.

Armstrong, Kimberly L., and Jay Starratt. 2015. "Is Open Access the Golden Ticket? The Real Cost of OA for the Library." ER&L Conference, Austin, TX, March 2015.
Califa. http://califa.org.
California Digital Library. http://www.cdlib.org.
Callimachus. http://scelc.org/callimachus.
Central Iowa—Collaborative Collections Initiative. https://ci-cci.org.
Colorado Alliance of Research Libraries. https://www.coalliance.org.
CONTENTdm. http://www.oclc.org/en-US/contentdm.html.
Feather, Celeste. 2015. "The International Coalition of Library Consortia: Origins, Contributions and Path Forward." UKSG Insights 28 (5). http://insights.uksg.org/articles/10.1629/uksg.260/.
Get It Now. Copyright Clearance Center. http://www.copyright.com/academia/get-it-now.
Greater Western Library Alliance. http://www.gwla.org.
HathiTrust. https://www.hathitrust.org.
Horton, Valerie. 2013. "Whither Library Consortia?" *Collaborative Librarianship* 5 (3): 150–53.
ILLiad. https://www.oclc.org/illiad.en.html.
Infotrieve. http://www.infotrieve.com/document-delivery-service.
Institute for Research Design in Librarianship. http://irdlonline.org.
International Coalition of Library Consortia. http://icolc.net.
Knievel, Jennifer E., Heather Wicht, and Lynn Connaway. 2006. "Use of Circulation Statistics and Interlibrary Loan Data in Collection Management." *College & Research Libraries* 67 (1): 35–49.
Larsen, Tom, and Rachel Arkoosh. 2013. "Adventures in Collaborative Technical Services: Past, Present, and Future with the Orbis Cascade Alliance." ALA Annual 2013, Next Generation Technical Services Program, Chicago, IL, June 29, 2013.
LibAnswers with LibChat. http://springshare.com/libanswers.
LibGuides. http://springshare.com/libguides.
"Library Consortium Law and Legal Definition." 2015. *USLegal.* Last accessed November 12. http://definitions.uslegal.com/l/library-consortium/.
LYRASIS. https://www.lyrasis.org/Pages/Main.aspx.
Maine Shared Collections Cooperative. http://www.maineinfonet.org/mscs.
NELLCO. http://www.nellco.org.
OCLC. https://www.oclc.org.
Orbis Cascade Alliance. https://www.orbiscascade.org.
PALCI Distributed Print Archive. http://palci-ccd.pbworks.com/w/page/13784118/PALCI%20Distributed%20Print%20Archive%20(PDPA).
Pay It Forward. http://icis.ucdavis.edu/?page_id=286.
Pennell, Charles, Natalie Sommerville, and Derek A. Rodriguez. 2013. "Shared Resources, Shared Records: Letting Go of Local Metadata Hosting with a Consortium Environment." *Library Resources & Technical Services* 57 (4). https://journals.ala.org/lrts/article/view/5586/6886.
Plowshares Digital. http://palni.contentdm.oclc.org/cdm/about.
Print Archives Preservation Registry. http://papr.crl.edu/.
Project COUNTER. http://www.projectcounter.org/.
QuestionPoint. http://www.questionpoint.org.
RapidILL. http://rapidill.org.
ReadCube. https://www.readcube.com.
Relais International. http://www.relais-intl.com.
Reprints Desk. http://info.reprintsdesk.com.
SIPX. http://www.sipx.com.
Statewide California Electronic Library Consortium. http://scelc.org.
SUSHI. http://www.niso.org/workrooms/sushi.

TexShare. https://www.tsl.texas.gov/texshare/index.html.
Triangle Research Libraries Network. http://www.trln.org/.
The Virtual Library of Virginia. http://www.vivalib.org/.
Weak, Emily, and Lili Luo. 2013. "Collaborative Virtual Reference Service: Lessons from the Past Decade." *Advances in Librarianship* 37: 81–112.
WorldShare ILL. https://www.oclc.org/worldshare-ill.en.html.

SUGGESTED READINGS

American Library Association. 2013. "Interlibrary Loans: ALA Library Fact Sheet 8." http://www.ala.org/tools/libfactsheets/alalibraryfactsheet08.

This summary fact sheet from the American Library Association provides a succinct overview of ILL along with references to a variety of resources.

Breeding, Marshall. 2013. "Introduction to Resource Sharing." *Library Technology Reports* 49 (1): 5–11.

Breeding provides a concise summary of resource sharing, covering issues of technology, workflow, consortial management, document delivery, and the role of discovery systems.

Esposito, Joseph. 2015. "Libraries and Consortia in the Context of a Publisher's Strategy." *The Scholarly Kitchen*. September 30, http://scholarlykitchen.sspnet.org/2015/09/30/libraries-and-consortia-in-the-context-of-a-publishers-strategy/.

A management consultant to publishers, Esposito provides an interesting point of view on the impact of consortia on small publishers and scholarly communication from the perspective of the publishers. This essay and the comments that follow provide an interesting interchange on the topic.

Horton, Valerie, and Greg Pronevitz, eds. 2015. *Library Consortia: Models for Collaboration and Sustainability*. Chicago: American Library Association.

Horton and Pronevitz cover the history, current landscape, management approaches, trends, and services that define library consortia.

Kaufman, Paula. 2012. "Let's Get Cozy: Evolving Collaborations in the 21st Century." *Journal of Library Administration* 52 (1): 53–69.

Kaufman provides a rationale for collaboration among academic libraries and consortia for resource sharing and shared print.

Kieft, Robert H., and Lizanne Payne. 2010. "A Nation-Wide Planning Framework for Large-Scale Collaboration on Legacy Print Monograph Collections." *Collaborative Librarianship* 2 (4): 229–33.

The authors discuss collaborative management and preservation of print journals, newspapers, legal materials, and government documents, with a focus on print monographs. Monographs present complex challenges at a time when libraries want to ensure the preservation of the print record but have increasing incentives to divest of older, less used print materials and take advantage of the affordances of electronic text.

Machovec, George. 2013. "Library Networking and Consortia." *Journal of Library Administration* 53 (2–3): 199–208.

Machovec summarizes consortial activities, funding models, and challenges facing consortia.

Machovec, George. 2014. "Consortial E-Resource Licensing: Current Trends and Issues." *Journal of Library Administration* 55 (1): 69–78.

The author, executive director of the Colorado Alliance of Research Libraries, provides a summary of current licensing issues with a focus on trends of greatest concern to libraries and consortia, such as new licensing terms addressing data mining and metadata extraction, as well as other topics such as the overlap between consortia.

Maskell, Catherine A. 2008. "Consortia: Anti-Competitive or in the Public Good?" *Library Hi-Tech* 26 (2): 164–83.

The author examines the potential effects of academic library consortia on the scholarly publishing cycle with a focus on Canadian libraries and asks the questions, "Do consortia effectively promote barrier-free access to scholarly information?"

Read, Kim Marsh. 2010. "Collective Voice for Collective Good: Library Consortia, Open Access, and the Future of Scholarly Communication." *Oregon Library Association Quarterly* 16 (3): 23–28.

The author provides a brief overview of the role of librarians and consortia in the open access movement.

Reference and User Services Association. "Interlibrary Loan Code for the United States." American Library Association. http://www.ala.org/rusa/resources/guidelines/interlibrary.

This document provides guidelines and standards for ILL in the United States. A linked explanatory supplement provides additional detail.

Wiser, James. 2011. "Playing Well with Others: New Opportunities for Library Consortia." *Theological Librarianship* 4 (1): 43–47.

Wiser gives an overview of the variety of consortia with advice on when and how a library should use the services of a consortium.

Chapter 6

Models of Reference Services

Lili Luo

INTRODUCTION

For over a hundred years, ever since Samuel Green defined the relations between librarians and library users, human-intermediated assistance provided by reference librarians has been considered a pivotal function of reference departments (Green 1876). An essential part of reference work is to help users find information to fulfill their information needs by every possible means.

Traditionally, reference service takes place in a reference room, or an otherwise designated area in the library, at a desk staffed by librarians and close to the reference collection. During the pre-digital age, people relied on reference librarians substantively for access to information. Since the advent of the Internet, personal computers, and other communication/networking technologies, the accessibility and availability of information have been greatly enhanced. Search engines like *Google* and *Bing*, and free Web reference resources like *Wikipedia*, have become the first stop in many people's information-seeking process. Nowadays, with the rapid development of mobile technologies, people can search for information even more easily and conveniently using various apps on their mobile devices. On one hand, the exponential expansion of information access has reduced people's dependence on reference service; on the other hand, it offers more possibilities for reference service to be delivered beyond brick-and-mortar buildings in response to the incessantly evolving information landscape. In the past half century, reference service has migrated from a print resource-oriented service limited to a certain physical space, to a diversified service portfolio that can reach more people with more resources and less restriction of time and space.

Instead of sitting idly behind the reference desk waiting for people to visit, librarians have adopted the "going where users are" motto and offer reference service via digital venues that people commonly use for communication, such as e-mail, online real-time chat, and texting. A group of proactive reference librarians have even ventured into social Q&A sites like Quora and Yahoo! Answers, hoping to represent librarianship in a new venue, encounter users beyond the library, provide well-sourced dependable answers to people's questions, and make people aware that librarians and libraries can be valuable sources not just for books, videos, and other materials, but also for intermediated answers to questions and referral to appropriate sources and organizations (Luo 2014).

An important part of contemporary reference service is to constantly evaluate the role reference librarians can and should play in helping people fulfill their information needs. Understanding how and where people seek information in the wired world and how their information-seeking experience can benefit from librarians' intermediation or assistance is key to the vitality of reference service and determines how reference service is delivered. Currently, there are two main models of reference service: in person and remote/virtual. In-person venues consist of the reference desk, research consultations, and roving reference. Remote/virtual venues include telephone, e-mail/Web form, online real-time chat, and texting.

The reference desk offers a convenient access point for users to seek assistance from librarians, but over the years, the decline of reference transactions has led to challenges about its value. New staffing arrangements such as tiered reference, where paraprofessionals handle simple directional questions and refer in-depth queries to librarians, are being employed to increase efficacy. Research consultations allow library users to schedule individual meetings with a librarian. Though time consuming, such consultations are opportunities for librarians to help users deeply engage with their research projects and develop a wide range of information literacy skills. Roving reference enables librarians to be proactive, reach out to users, and provide service at their point of need, but careful planning and staff preparation are needed in order for roving to be successful.

E-mail reference service makes it possible for patrons to ask questions anytime and anywhere, as long as they have an Internet connection. It is an asynchronous service and good for nonurgent queries, where an immediate response is not expected. A downside of e-mail reference is the difficulty to conduct an in-depth reference interview. To compensate, libraries offer online real-time chat reference services, where users can engage in a text-based chat session with a librarian for reference assistance. Text reference service allows users to send in queries and receive answers via texting on their mobile device. Due to the 160-character limit in each text message, this service is usually used for short and simple queries.

While expanding the reach of library services, virtual reference also brings new challenges such as technological issues, concerns about privacy, and the increasing number of frivolous questions due to anonymity. In order to successfully plan and implement a suite of reference services, it is important to understand the characteristics of each in-person and remote/virtual venue as well as its advantages and disadvantages in delivering reference service.

Box 6.1 provides a summary of the two models. This chapter discusses the basics of delivering reference service under these models and concludes with a discussion of ways to keep current and stay relevant as librarians strive to meet users' needs and optimize their experience.

Box 6.1 Models of Reference Services

In person:

- Reference desk
- Research consultations
- Roving reference

Virtual:

- E-mail/Web form
- Online real-time chat
- Texting

IN-PERSON REFERENCE SERVICE

In-person reference services are provided through face-to-face interactions with librarians and are the most direct way for users to receive assistance in their information-seeking process. However, some library users may be reluctant to approach librarians if they are not comfortable with in-person conversations or do not speak English as their first language. If librarians at the reference desk appear to be busy or aloof, users may also feel discouraged from asking them for assistance. Thus, the first item in the Reference and User Services Association's (RUSA) "Guidelines for Behavioral Performance of Reference and Information Service Providers" is visibility and approachability, highlighting the importance of making users "feel comfortable in a situation that can be perceived as intimidating, confusing, or overwhelming" (Reference and User Services Association 2013).

Face-to-face interaction allows for the exchange of nonverbal information, enables librarians to transmit interpersonal relational messages of empathy and interest found to be important to the user, and builds rapport between librarians and users (Selby 2007). The richness of communication in in-person reference services makes it the best platform for librarians to address in-depth and complex queries and to provide instruction. This section introduces three models of in-person reference service—the reference desk, research consultations, and roving reference.

Reference Desk

The focal point of the reference area has been the reference desk, staffed by one or more librarians, in proximity to a reference collection that contains many of the titles described in this book. For easy recognition and approachability, the reference desk is usually located prominently in the library and properly labeled—popular signage includes "Reference & Information," "Ask Here," and "Research Help." To better facilitate the reference transaction, some desks have an extra monitor facing outward for users to see the librarians' searches in action so they can feel more connected and informed.

To many, the reference desk is viewed as a cornerstone of reference service and reflects values that are identified to be core to reference librarianship: convenient and equitable service to users, individually tailored personal assistance, and high professional standards (Bunge and Ferguson 1997). It represents "a critical mass of resources—human, printed, and now electronic, so configured for a convenient and predictable location so that library patrons can find the service and can find someone to help them" (Swanson 1984, 89). However, not all people believe in the value of the reference desk. Barbara Ford was one of the first to question the efficiency and effectiveness of the service provided from the reference desk and challenged the idea of the reference desk as the center of reference service (Ford 1986). Over the years, opponents of the reference desk have claimed that it is only a symbol of reference service, not the service itself (Bell 2007) and advocated the elimination of the reference desk for the following reasons:

- *Decline of reference transactions*: The shift to the online world has dramatically increased people's ability to search for information and reduced the need for reference service. For example, from 1994 to 2008, academic libraries experienced a 50 percent decline in reference transactions (American Library Association 2015).
- *Trivialization of queries*: Most of the queries received at the reference desk are directional (e.g., "where is the group study room?") or technical (e.g., how to fix a printer jam) questions that are routine and repetitive. Such questions ignore librarians' expertise and contribute to job dissatisfaction (Aluri and St. Clair 1978; Freides 1983; Massey-Burzio 1992).
- *Expanding responsibilities of reference librarians*: With the transition to an online information world, reference librarians are faced with growing responsibilities to keep up with massive electronic resources (e.g., databases and specialized Web resources), to deliver reference service via digital venues, to provide instruction, and to conduct outreach through liaison work, embedded services, and social media (Giordano, Menard, and Spencer, 2001). Sitting behind the reference desk is no longer an efficient use of their time.
- *Emergency-style service in a nonemergency situation*: Users are inclined to view the reference desk as intended for quick replies and under the impression that librarians function more as clerks at a service counter rather than as professionals. When the reference transaction involves an in-depth query, both user and librarian experience frustration when ringing phones and queues of users with short-answer questions compete for the librarians' attention, making the reference desk an unideal venue for consultations that could truly benefit from librarians' expertise (Freides 1983; Summerhill 1994).

The listed problems point to the rejection of the reference desk, not the idea of human-intermediated reference service. The opponents of the reference desk believe that it is an outmoded method of service delivery, and greater emphasis should be placed on the potential for virtual reference service to address quick-answer and repetitive queries and appointment-based individual consultations to handle complex queries (Nolen 2010). Proponents of the reference desk, on the other hand, champion the value of "human contact," as indicated in Michael Gorman's statement, "We must maintain the vital human-to-human component that typifies reference service across our history. This is an age in which human values are under strain; human contact and sympathy become more and more prized as they become rarer" (Gorman 2001, 182).

Still, they recognize the problems of the reference desk. Instead of elimination, their solution is to reorganize it to enhance its efficiency. As a result, the tiered service model has been implemented to maximize use of the librarian's expertise and time, reduce stress and burnout, present an appropriate professional image, and optimize the use of human resources. Under this staffing model, multiple types of staff are arranged to answer user queries. In some cases, paraprofessionals or trained students staff the reference desk alongside librarians, and they are responsible for answering simple queries like directional and technical questions and refer more in-depth and complex queries to reference librarians. In some other cases, they operate from a separate service point, often called the "Help Desk" or "Information Desk," to handle simple queries and make necessary referrals to librarians at the reference desk.

While the tiered service model allows differentiation of reference services and supports more effective and efficient use of librarians' time and expertise, it has its own challenges. Small libraries are unlikely to have the manpower, resources, and facilities to support multiple service points. A considerable amount of time is needed for defining the mission of the separate information desk and for training the staff. In addition, the line between simple quick-answer queries and complex queries can be ill-defined, and inadequately trained paraprofessional staff may misjudge the nature of user queries and fail to make referrals, which ultimately will undermine the user's library experience. Furthermore, the public is rarely aware of the difference between the service points, and thus the service model may not achieve its intended effect (Mosley 2007). Some libraries combine the reference desk with other service points like the circulation desk into one location to help facilitate a "one-stop shop" to improve service access (Aho, Beschnett, and Reimer 2011; Schulte 2011). The frontline service staffs are usually paraprofessionals, and they are responsible for fielding user queries and making proper referrals to on-call librarians who operate from their offices. Such a single service point often requires significant cross-training of library staff.

Despite the debate about the reference desk, a recent survey by Dennis Miles shows that it is still prevalent in libraries with 66.4 percent of academic libraries still using the reference desk to offer reference services, and 77.2 percent with a professional librarian at the reference desk all or some of the time (Miles 2013). Librarians in the study indicated that the face-to-face interaction with users is the most important reason why librarians still want to offer service from the desk. They also offer other modes of reference service such as roving reference and consultations, but these services are offered in addition to the reference desk, not in place of it. While the study indicates librarians' commitment to service at the reference desk, it is worth noting that the libraries surveyed in the study were midsize college and university libraries. Libraries of other types may have different experiences. There is no "one-size-fits-all" solution when it comes to deciding the fate of the reference desk. Careful analysis based on the library's constituents, budget, and culture is indispensable to determining the reference service model most appropriate for the library.

Research Consultations

Research consultations are individual meetings between a librarian and a user or a group of users (e.g., several students working together on a group project). Such meetings are appointment based and take place in a private room (e.g., the librarian's office). Length of the meetings varies, often depending on the specific needs of the user. Research consultations are particularly popular among academic libraries, where students get in-depth research assistance from librarians in a quiet environment, and librarians can focus exclusively on an individual student's needs (Gale and Evans 2007; Jastram and Zawistoski 2008).

Library users schedule research consultations with librarians in many different ways. Recently, a scheduling tool called YouCanBook.me has been more widely adopted. It is an external appointment booking service that links directly with an individual's *Google Calendar*. Google users can log in via *Google*, and YouCanBook.me will connect to the user's *Google Calendar*. From there, a user can choose which calendar to use, and a grid of available time slots will be generated. They can then click an available time slot, fill out a reservation form, and submit it to schedule an appointment. Confirmation will be sent to both the user and the librarian, and the appointment will be displayed on the linked *Google Calendar* (Hess 2014).

Research consultations can be time consuming, especially when the demand is high. Librarians often have to prepare for the meeting by reviewing resources and consulting with colleagues. At the same time, many benefits have been identified. Research consultations are believed to be an important venue to address "student needs that were not sufficiently covered in a classroom setting" (Yi 2003, 349) and the "unique concerns of each student in a way that is not possible in larger groups" (Reinsfelder 2012, 263). If librarians consciously integrate information literacy objectives into such encounters with students, the quality of their research assistance can be greatly enhanced. Research consultations may also help promote the value of the library and nicely complement information literacy programs as some students need individual reinforcement of newly learned information skills (Gale and Evans 2007; Faix, MacDonald, and Taxakis 2014).

Trina J. Magi and Patricia E. Mardeusz (2013), in their study of students' experience with research consultations, described a number of ways that students are helped in these meetings—receiving assistance in choosing databases, identifying keywords, using search interfaces, interpreting their professors' assignments, brainstorming about how to approach their project, discussing possible topics, sharing knowledge about the subject, evaluating results for relevance and credibility, determining how disparate pieces of information could be used in a paper, and understanding how to stay organized during a semester-long research project. Students also appreciate watching the librarian work through a problem so that later they can replicate the research process. If librarians are concerned about helping students deeply engage with their research projects and develop a wide range of information literacy skills, they should consider making research consultations a component of their reference services.

Roving Reference

Roving as a means of providing reference service started in the late 1980s and early 1990s when an increasing number of online catalog terminals and CD-ROM stations were installed in the library. More and more library users were using library computers for research, engendering a need for a more convenient way to receive help from librarians as they navigated through an overwhelming array of online information resources. A roving librarian presents a helpful human presence in the increasingly electronic environment as he or she circulates in the general reference area to approach library users (especially those who look confused and might be in need of help) to offer assistance. Rather than waiting for users to come to the reference desk, roving allows librarians to be proactive, reach out to users, and provide service at their point of need. Particularly, users who are reluctant to use the reference desk for various reasons may benefit from the assistance offered by a friendly roving librarian (Courtois and Liriano 2000).

Although roving is an extension of the reference desk, it brings to play interpersonal dynamics that can be quite different from the encounters at the reference desk. Martin P. Courtois and Maira Liriano (2000) provided a series of strategies to successfully implement roving reference:

- *Prepare staff to rove.* Rovers need to project confidence and a helpful attitude, and all roving librarians need to be adequately prepared.
- *Schedule times for roving.* If the library's staffing level allows a designated rover, it is ideal to schedule roving during the busiest times as the rover can help relieve the burden of the reference desk staff, enabling them to work with users on in-depth questions.
- *Use the best people as rovers.* It is more effective to use librarians or experienced support staff as rovers in order to win trust of users and engage them in a reference transaction.
- *Use assistants for backup or tech support.* Having assistants available to handle basic technical questions will free rovers to concentrate on helping users with more complex information needs.
- *Create an atmosphere of active learning.* On one hand, there is a concern that roving violates user privacy; on the other hand, the reference area can be a place for active learning, where the focus is on dialogue and interaction.
- *Refer queries from the reference desk to the rover.* When queries received at the reference desk involve a follow-up on a library computer, it is more efficient to refer them to the rover.
- *Employ useful roving techniques*: (1) wear a nametag/badge; (2) be mobile and do not stay too long with any one user; (3) follow up with users to check on their progress; (4) be discreet, and address users before addressing their screen even when their screens are displaying ineffective search statements or error messages; (5) think in terms of welcoming behaviors that could put users at ease; (6) address each user instead of announcing an offer of assistance to a group of users; and (7) be prepared for indifference when assistance is declined.
- *Keep statistics to monitor the content and number of roving reference transactions.* Such statistics can be used to determine needed staffing.

In recent years, mobile technologies have been increasingly used in supporting roving reference. Portable voice communication devices allow roving librarians to communicate with other reference staff and consult with them while roving. The Vocera Badge is one such device, about the size of a large USB drive, usually worn around the neck like a security tag. It is often linked to telephone systems, runs on a wireless network, and works with voice commands. It is extensively used in hospitals, and now some public libraries also use it to assist with staff communication as well as for roving reference (Forsyth 2009). iPads and other tablets are also gaining popularity among roving librarians as they allow them to access the library's online resources (e.g., online catalog and databases) and demonstrate searches while assisting users (May 2011).

Roving reference does not necessarily have to be limited to the library. Some academic librarians rove around campus to provide assistance. Such campus-wide roving services usually take place in locations frequented by students and faculty like a campus café or a residence hall. Since librarians are outside of the library, it helps to bring some printed help guides (e.g., searching the online catalog or submitting an interlibrary loan request) for dissemination. Laptops with wireless connections and cell phones can also be helpful. The primary benefit of roving outside of the library is the informal spontaneous engagement with faculty, students, and staff, especially those who do not necessarily visit the library. It helps reduce barriers to library interactions, build librarians' relationships with the user community, convey the librarians' collaborative spirit, and market library services in a high-profile way (Holmes and Woznicki 2010).

REMOTE/VIRTUAL REFERENCE SERVICE

When reference service is provided remotely, it enables users to receive assistance from librarians without having to be physically in the library and provides an opportunity for the library to reach out to users who shy away from in-person reference services. Before the Internet, the use of mail, telephone, and Teletype were all incorporated in remote reference service delivery (Ryan 1996). Nowadays, telephone reference is still a popular service, particularly in urban public libraries, where there are staff specially designated to handle reference calls.

As libraries adopted computing and networking technologies (especially the Internet) in the 1980s, digital media started becoming a popular choice to deliver reference services to reach a far wider audience. Digital-media-based reference services are usually referred to as either "digital reference services" or "virtual reference services." RUSA chose to use "virtual reference" for reference services provided digitally and defined it as the "reference service initiated electronically, often in real-time, where patrons employ computers or other Internet technology to communicate with reference staff, without being physically present. Communication channels used frequently in virtual reference include chat, videoconferencing, Voice over IP, co-browsing, e-mail, and instant messaging" (Reference and User Services Association 2004). Although some researchers tend to also incorporate digital/electronic resources in their definition of "virtual reference" (Tenopir and Ennis 2002), RUSA clarified this distinction by stating that "while online sources are often utilized in provision of virtual reference, use of electronic sources in seeking answers is not of itself virtual reference" (Reference and User Services Association 2004). Thus, resources created and distributed in digital means are not considered part of "virtual reference." Only human-intermediated reference service provided via digital media is considered "virtual reference."

Using virtual reference services, users can send their queries by e-mail or by filling out a Web form and then receive answers via e-mail, or engage in an online real-time chat reference session where they can interact with librarians synchronously and receive immediate help from the librarians. In recent years, libraries have started offering text reference service, where users can text their queries to librarians and receive answers in texts as well.

Virtual reference services are often named "Ask a Librarian" or "Ask Us" on the library website. In a virtual reference transaction, the query can be seen and referred to as the answer is sought, which is convenient for librarians. Queries and answers can also be stored easily for statistical tracking or other record-keeping purposes. Frequently asked questions can help librarians decide what information should be made more accessible and available on the library website. Online information can easily be incorporated into the answers, which may help users become more aware of the vastness of the library's electronic resources. In addition, libraries can provide virtual reference services collaboratively and take turns staffing the service, making it possible to reduce cost and extend service hours.

While expanding the reach of library services, virtual reference also brings new challenges such as concerns about privacy and the increasing number of frivolous questions due to anonymity. Libraries have to reconsider their service policies in response to these challenges. Librarians also have to acquire new skill sets to most successfully help users fulfill their information needs via virtual reference services. In this section, three types of virtual reference services are introduced—e-mail/Web form reference, chat reference, and text reference service, and strategies for successfully providing virtual reference services are discussed.

E-mail/Web Form Reference Service

The use of e-mail was adopted by libraries as an extension of the reference desk as early as the 1980s (Schardt 1983). These early e-mail reference services were mostly provided through e-mail systems linked to online catalogs or campus-wide information networks (Ford 2002). A survey conducted by the Association of Research Libraries (ARL) in 1988 indicated that 20 percent of ARL libraries offered e-mail reference services by then (Still and Campbell 1993). One decade later, this number rocketed up to 96 percent, due to the widespread availability of the Internet and personal computers (Ford 2002).

E-mail reference services are provided either through an e-mail address to which users can send their questions directly or through a Web form that users can fill out to submit their questions. In both ways, users will receive the answer to their questions by e-mail (White 2001). While libraries were making e-mail reference services available for their users, some independent Internet-based services, usually called "AskA" services, also started offering e-mail reference services to answer questions from the general public (Lankes 1998). These services are mostly subject specialized (Pomerantz 2003). For example, Ask Dr. Math focuses on mathematics, Ask the Space Scientist answers questions about astronomy and space science, and Ask a Linguist helps people seek information related to language and linguistics.

E-mail reference service has freed users from the limitations of time and location, making it possible for them to ask questions anytime and anywhere, as long as they have an Internet connection (Bushallow-Wilber, DeVinney, and Whitcomb 1996). They do not have to know whom to contact at the library, and for those whose first language is not English, it might be more comfortable to compose queries in a written message than speak to a reference librarian.

Since e-mail is an asynchronous communication means, librarians are not expected to provide an immediate response. Certain pressures of time and place fall away, and user queries may be answered away from the busy reference desk, allowing librarians more time to conduct thorough searches and consult colleagues when composing the answer. The service turnaround time is usually stated on the page of the e-mail reference service; although it varies from library to library, the majority of the libraries promise to return an answer to the user's query within one to two business days.

The downside of asynchronicity is that it inevitably prevents librarians from conducting in-depth reference interviews with users (Janes and Hill 2001) and thus may lead to inadequate understanding or even misinterpretation of the user's information needs. Despite the challenges of the medium, librarians still make efforts to conduct a reference interview in e-mail reference service. Eileen Abels (1996) summarized these efforts and developed the following approaches to the e-mail reference interview:

- *The piecemeal approach*: Questions are asked on an ad hoc basis as they occur to the librarian.
- *The feedback approach*: The e-mail medium, with time lags between responses, permits the librarian to jump from the question negotiation stage to the feedback stage and back again. This approach tends to be used when responses to questions posed are not received quickly.
- *The bombardment approach*: The librarian asks a series of questions in one e-mail message, formatted in one long paragraph.
- *The assumption approach*: The librarian may make assumptions as to the true nature of the information need.
- *The systematic approach*: The interview is initiated when the user sends an unstructured query statement. This message is followed by a response from the librarian that poses all related questions in an organized fashion.

However, the interview process in e-mail reference can be very lengthy. It might take weeks to conclude the reference negotiation conducted through e-mail exchanges.

Another remedy for the lack of interactivity inherent in e-mail reference service is the use of well-designed Web forms to elicit users' information needs. A structured Web form encourages users to fill in pertinent information that might have otherwise been left out but is useful for librarians answering their questions (Haines and Grodzinski 1999). Common items on a Web form include user's name and address (sometimes library card number if the service is provided only to library cardholders), user status (e.g., faculty or student), and content of the user query. A more structured Web form may also ask users to provide information on the type of query (e.g., accounts or library website), subject of the query, or resources already examined. The advantage of a well-structured Web form is that it compensates for the lack of a reference interview and provides better context for users' information needs. The disadvantages include the following: users may not want to go through the trouble of filling out a form with many required fields and hence choose not to use the service, users may have difficulty in assigning subject categories to their questions and determining whether their questions are factual or require information sources for assistance, and the effectiveness of Web forms may be undermined by users' inappropriate understanding of the items on the form (Carter and Janes 2000). Therefore, when designing a Web form, it is important to keep a well-balanced structure that could elicit as much information from the user as possible without confusing or overwhelming them.

Figure 6.1 is a screenshot of the Web form at San Jose State University Library. The question field is listed first to allow users to enter their question before submitting information like their name and e-mail address. Such a design is more welcoming and encouraging for users to fill out the form and submit their query.

Since it is difficult to conduct a reference interview via e-mail, in their response to user queries, librarians tend to recommend patrons use other modes of reference service where they can interact with librarians in real time (e.g., desk, telephone, online real-time chat) if they have more complex queries. Such a recommendation may be included in the signature of librarians' e-mail response to user queries.

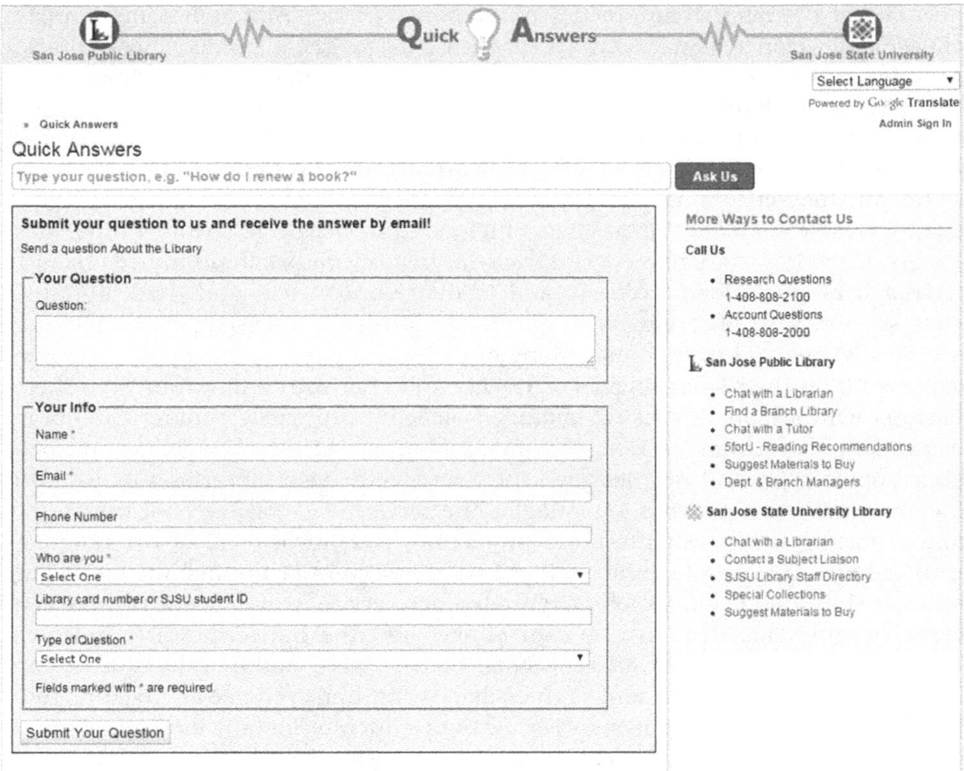

FIGURE 6.1 San Jose State University Library virtual reference Web form

It not only promotes the variety of reference services offered by the library, but also helps users better understand what types of information needs can be appropriately addressed by which modes of service and therefore use reference services more effectively and efficiently.

Online Real-Time Chat Reference Service

Libraries have experimented with real-time communication technologies, such as videoconferencing, to provide synchronous reference services to users since the 1990s. Using a videoconferencing system, librarians and users could see each other through Web cameras installed on both of their computers and have a conversation through microphones, as well as exchange typed messages. While several videoconferencing-based reference projects were implemented in the mid- and late 1990s, the technological shortcomings such as poor video transmission quality, limited bandwidth, and limited access to the supporting infrastructure made it difficult for "a critical mass of users" to develop for the services (Sloan 1998).

In the early 2000s, libraries adopted a simpler technology that allowed librarians and users to "chat" with each other by exchanging written messages without any visual and audio feed, and started providing online real-time chat reference service. Chat reference services have since become increasingly popular and are now one of the mainstream modes of reference service. Although some libraries choose to develop in-house software for their chat reference service, most libraries provide the service via software developed by others. There are two primary categories of chat reference software: simple, and usually free, text-based chat applications like instant messengers, and more full-fledged commercial software with advanced features like page-pushing or whiteboarding (Ronan 2003).

Instant messengers are applications that offer online real-time text transmission. Examples of instant messengers include AIM, Google Talk, and Yahoo! Messenger. Providing chat reference service via instant messaging, libraries need to have a user name for patrons to add to their contact list, and there initiate a chat session with librarians. The advantage of instant messengers is that they are mostly free and easy to use. Many of them also have mobile apps that users can install on their smartphones or tablets and chat with a librarian from there. Patrons who are already using instant messaging can easily contact the library from a familiar technology. However, since instant messengers are general-purpose chat applications and not designed for reference service, librarians may find it inconvenient when it comes to managing the service (e.g., logging chat transcripts and reporting usage statistics) and protecting user privacy. All of the reference transactions are recorded and archived on the servers of the instant messaging services that a library uses for virtual reference service, which poses privacy concerns because libraries have no control over how the transcripts are protected. Meanwhile, users may use different instant messengers, and therefore, the library needs to accommodate as many of them as possible and even use aggregating tools like Trillian to support chatting with users on different instant messengers from one single application. Less tech-savvy users may shy away from using the service because it requires them to download and install an instant messenger, which may be beyond their realm of technical knowledge. Another concern is that the library's information technology department may have issues with free software because of security risks. Librarians cannot exercise any control as the software changes, grows, or disappears. For example, when Meebo, a free and popular instant messenger among libraries, abruptly discontinued its service in 2012, it caused much inconvenience as libraries hurried to find a replacement in order to continue their chat reference service.

An alternative to instant messengers is commercial virtual reference software. Such software is specially designed for virtual reference service and seeks to meet the needs of delivering and managing not only chat reference, but also e-mail and text reference service. They are usually subscription based, and libraries use a log-in name to access the software service through a Web browser.

QuestionPoint, provided by OCLC, is representative of commercial virtual reference software. Using QuestionPoint, each library obtains a master account, within which it can create subaccounts for all the librarians staffing chat reference service. Each librarian may use his or her own subaccount to log in during the shifts, and multiple librarians can be logged in simultaneously. Users can access the service by typing in a widget on a Web page, or by formally initiating a chat session within a Web browser, after entering their name, e-mail address, and the query. Librarians can monitor the user queue on their end and are alerted when new users are online.

When engaged in a chat session with users, librarians are provided with more functionality than the simple exchange of texts. For example, librarians may push pages to the user's screen—if they enter a URL in their message, the Web page the URL leads to will open on the user's screen. The chat reference interface on the user end consists of two parts. About one-fourth of the screen displays the transcript of the chat session between the librarian and the user, and the other three-fourths of the screen displays the Web pages sent over by the librarian. Page-pushing allows librarians to more effectively escort users in the information searching process and makes it easier for librarians to transmit electronic information to users and guide them in the navigation, given the fact that virtual reference services utilize electronic resources extensively in answering user queries (Tenopir and Ennis 2001). Another useful feature is pre-scripted messages—librarians can create frequently used scripts for their responses, such as greetings, follow-ups, and URLs of popular Web resources. This helps save typing time and thus makes the transaction more efficient. Figure 6.2 is a screenshot of the librarian interface in QuestionPoint, where the right-hand side displays the e-mail exchange between the librarian and the user, the upper left-hand side shows the queues of users waiting to use the service, and the lower left-hand side provides the various tools such as scripts that librarians can access to facilitate the chat session.

When each chat session ends, a transcript of the session will be saved and e-mailed to the user as well. This is convenient for users to refer back to the sources provided by the librarian in their future information-seeking efforts. A resolution code will be assigned to the session to indicate whether the query is fully answered, referred to another party, or to be followed up with, which can be helpful for libraries to keep track of how the service is addressing users' information needs. In addition, QuestionPoint enables the reporting of various service statistics such as the number of chat sessions in a specified time frame, the distribution of resolution codes, and queries from repeat users.

Since QuestionPoint supports multiple simultaneous log-ins, librarians can communicate with each other and consult each other when answering queries. They can also transfer users to librarians from their home institution, which often happens in a collaborative virtual reference service. Virtual reference software like

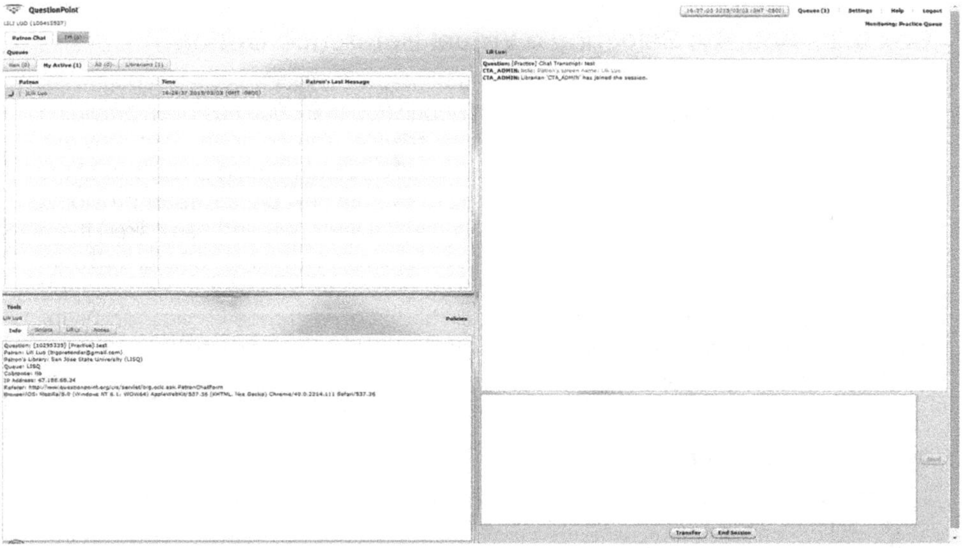

FIGURE 6.2 Librarian interface in QuestionPoint

QuestionPoint allows libraries to form a consortium in providing the service, reaping the benefits of reduced cost and extended service hours. In such a collaborative virtual reference service, participating libraries take turns staffing the service, and therefore users may be connected to librarians from institutions other than their home institution. In order to best answer queries requiring local knowledge (e.g., queries pertaining to particular libraries' policies as well as the location of items within the libraries), librarians often have to transfer users to a librarian from their home institution.

Although QuestionPoint offers more functionality to support chat reference service than instant messengers, there are drawbacks as well. Some libraries may find the software too costly and the learning curve too steep. There are other commercial virtual reference software options on the market; for example, LibraryH3lp is a popular alternative to QuestionPoint. Using LibraryH3lp, users submit their queries through various ways (e.g., through a customizable chat widget or through a mobile app), and librarians are able to answer them using a single LibraryH3lp interface. Multiple librarians can operate at the same time, sharing expertise with each other, and users can be routed to all available staff, to targeted staff subgroups, or even individuals.

Nevertheless, no matter which software a library chooses as the platform for chat reference service, it is important to consider the following factors: usability both for users and for librarians, software stability, cost, customizability, training support, customer service support, support for staffing flexibility, compatibility with other modes of reference service, support for mobile apps, and the need for providing chat reference service collaboratively. Clear service goals, a detailed picture of the library's wants and needs, and a thorough understanding of what each virtual reference software offers are key for a library to select a proper platform to support chat reference service. Box 6.2 provides a hypothetical scenario for discussion related to selecting a virtual reference option.

Box 6.2 Activity: Selecting a Virtual Reference Option

A library at a public university with a student population of 21,000 has been providing chat reference using a free instant messenger service. The company that provides the service has just announced that the service will be discontinued at the end of the month. The library director has asked her staff to explore new platforms for providing virtual reference, including both free and commercial services, and has asked them to consider the following factors: usability both for users and for librarians, software stability, cost, customizability, training support, customer service support, support for staffing flexibility, compatibility with other modes of reference service, and support for mobile apps. She would also like the staff to consider whether joining a consortium would be a good option for the library.

Questions for Reflection and Discussion:

1. Which factors would you consider most important when evaluating platforms for virtual reference?
2. If you were given this task, how would you approach it?

As mentioned earlier, libraries' attempts at offering virtual reference service via videoconferencing did not succeed in the 1990s because of limitations of the technologies. In recent years, such technologies have advanced tremendously, and VoIP software like Skype has gained wide popularity as a tool for voice and video chat. Libraries have started exploring the use of Skype in the provision of virtual reference service. Advantages of Skype include (1) bringing visual and nonverbal cues back to virtual reference; (2) the ability to send links, pdf files, articles, or Jing videos via instant messages while video chatting with users; and (3) sharing screens with users. Disadvantages include the need for installing the Skype software on one's computer, the awkwardness factor of being "on screen," and a low level of interest in the use of Skype for reference service among undergraduates (Beaton 2012). However, Skype has not yet gained ground as part of the virtual reference suite, and some early adopters such as Ohio University Libraries have discontinued the service. The lack of interest among users could be the primary cause. Skype, in the eyes of library users, may be a tool for informal communication between friends and family, but not suitable for interacting with librarians, as Chad Boeninger commented when discussing Ohio University Libraries' experiment with Skype, "our patrons may never be comfortable enough to want to call us face-to-face" (Boeninger 2010). Still, libraries and librarians should keep experimenting with new technologies to deliver enriched and enhanced reference service to users. The experiments may not all be successful, but they are valuable experiences nonetheless, as Chad Boeninger (2010) summarized, "in the process, we learned about video calling software options, how to configure pages to close automatically with javascript, discovered how flaky wireless connections and computer applications can be, and much more. We also learned to be flexible, patient, and try different things to improve the service. I believe our experiences with the service have prepared us well for our next technology/reference endeavor (whatever that may be), and you can't put a price on that knowledge."

Text Reference Service

Text messaging, or texting, has become an increasingly popular communication venue. In recent years, libraries have started providing text reference service, which enables library users to send in queries and receive answers via texting. Although this service, like other types of virtual reference service, makes it possible for users to use the library remotely, people often text librarians from within the library, frequently including information about exactly where they are (Pearce, Collard, and Whatley 2010). It appears that many users prefer to communicate via text even when other options for seeking assistance are available. Reasons may range from practical considerations related to what is most convenient at a given moment to a more general preference on the part of a user for a certain form of communication. For instance, patrons who are working at a library computer may find it more convenient to text a librarian than pack up their things and log out in order to visit the reference desk.

Librarians can deliver text reference service two ways. One relies on a dedicated mobile device (usually a smartphone) and the other utilizes computer applications like e-mail or instant messenger to process users' texted queries. The mobile-device-based delivery model is quite simple. A library needs to purchase only a cell phone with a monthly texting plan to enable text reference service. At some libraries, the cell phone is stationed at the reference desk along with other reference service points during business hours and monitored by librarians covering the reference desk; it is stashed away when it is not in use. When the reference desk is busy, an information hierarchy of importance is employed to determine query priority. Text reference questions may come after in-person, telephone, and chat reference queries (Kohl and Keating 2009). At some other libraries, the cell phone is operated independently of any other service point; it is not kept at the reference desk, and texting shifts are not connected to any other reference shifts. A different schedule is made for librarians to monitor the service, and the phone travels with the individual librarian when it is his or her shift. Librarians coordinate the hand-offs among themselves rather than according to a formalized procedure.

Since a cell phone is associated with a straightforward 10-digit phone number, users can easily store it in their own devices and text to this number without any special instructions. Librarians are able to communicate to users through the same technology and hence are able to experience the service from the user's perspective (Pearce 2010). Certain cell phones (e.g., smartphones like iPhone) display text messages in threaded mode, enabling librarians to see all the exchanges associated with a particular phone number. This establishes a context for each transaction, which helps librarians answer users' questions better. Furthermore, cell phones can be set to vibrate or emit an alert sound when new messages arrive and thus lead to more timely responses.

Regarding cost, it is relatively inexpensive to purchase a cell phone with a calling and texting plan (Kohl and Keating 2009). Since the phone is used primarily for the purpose of texting, minimal calling minutes should be sufficient. As for the texting plan, libraries can choose what they need based on their budget and anticipated service traffic.

One of the prominent drawbacks of depending on a cell phone is that it cannot be integrated into any of the existing virtual reference services and thus poses extra work for librarians. They have to master yet another technology to deliver reference service and may be reluctant to embrace this new service venue. Meanwhile, typing on a cell phone keyboard, even the most user-friendly kind, is far less comfortable than typing on a computer keyboard and may slow down the service's response time. Staffing can also be a challenge when the cell phone is not stationed at the reference desk. Without effective staffing and shift management, it will be difficult to ensure consistent and reliable service quality.

An alternative is using computer applications such as instant messenger or e-mail to receive and respond to text reference queries, allowing librarians to work with a potentially familiar interface while offering reference service via a new venue. The learning curve is as flat as possible in terms of technology, and hence text reference service may be greeted with a more positive attitude among librarians.

Some libraries choose a free computer application that supports texting and interacts with text messages, and have users text their questions directly to this computer application, such as AIM and Gmail. This is a great way for budget-conscious libraries to explore new technologies for reference service. However, a significant concern about such free applications is privacy. It is known that Google archives all the data on its servers, which means users' phone numbers and their text messages stored in a Gmail account can also be accessed by Google. Additionally, AIM and Gmail are general-purpose applications, lacking certain features useful for the specific purpose of providing text reference service. Also, as mentioned previously, libraries have no control over these free service providers and are subject to whatever changes they make. In the long run, this can create serious issues in sustaining the service.

If a library already uses commercially developed software for its e-mail and chat reference service, the software often supports text reference service as well. For example, QuestionPoint and LibraryH3lp cover the whole spectrum of virtual reference service, allowing text reference service to be integrated into the library's existing e-mail or chat reference service. This integration can help minimize technology training among librarians and keep the library's virtual reference service suite streamlined with the new service addition.

Some software limits the length of librarians' responses to users' questions (Jensen 2010). Usually a reply cannot exceed two or three text messages (320 or 480 characters), and if it does, the extra part will be truncated and will not be displayed on the user's phone. However, built-in features like a character counter and a URL shortener (Weimer 2010) may also be available to help librarians to compose their responses concisely.

Most commercial software allows libraries to have a dedicated phone number that users can store in their cell phone. Generally, no special instructions are needed for texting to this number. More importantly, users' privacy is better protected as the service is run on software vendors' private servers, and access to user information is strictly limited. Some software even masks users' phone numbers and replaces them with a unique patron ID in order to further alleviate privacy concerns. Again, determining the delivery method or choosing the software for text reference is contingent upon a number of factors, and careful analysis of the library's staffing level, librarian preparedness, budget, and users' texting philosophy and behavior (not all users feel comfortable with texting librarians as they consider texting an informal way of communication among family and friends) is key to deciding on the best way to offer text reference service.

Providing Virtual Reference Services Successfully

There are two staffing models for virtual reference services. The more commonly adopted model is that reference librarians staff the service in their own offices or other locations away from the reference desk. This arrangement allows them to focus on virtual reference transactions without much distraction or interruption, which is especially advantageous when the query is complex and requires an in-depth reference interview. For libraries with an understaffed reference department, it could be challenging to have enough personnel to cover virtual reference service (particularly the synchronous chat reference service where users expect an immediate response) shifts during all library hours. Instead of limiting service hours, some libraries choose to form a consortium to provide the services collaboratively. The less popular staffing model is to staff virtual reference services from the reference desk. Under this model, priority is always given to in-person patrons, so the information needs of online users may not be satisfactorily addressed when the reference desk is busy.

Which model to choose depends on the library's culture, user needs, budget, and staffing capacity. The most important thing is to have a well-prepared staff who are competent in providing virtual reference services. The changes in service venues have brought new challenges that require updated or new skills. For example, reference interview skills, indisputably, have been acknowledged to be one of the core skills in reference work. But conducting the reference interview is a different experience in each service venue. Although chat reference service enables the synchronous interaction between librarians and users, it cannot completely model the reference interview in the face-to-face encounter and is not an effective service venue for queries requiring in-depth question negotiation. Thus, techniques in the reference interview that could help librarians avoid a lengthy and cumbersome transaction become particularly important in chat reference service. Such techniques include having the ability to make appropriate referrals and recognize the need to follow up with the user. In the meantime, some of the traditional reference values like thoroughness ought to be modified in chat or text reference service. Virtual reference is viewed as a convenient access point toward a vast amount of reference expertise where complex questions can be handled more efficiently and thoroughly. Librarians need to learn to "let go" at a certain point when it comes to a complex question. Particularly, in text reference, queries tend to be those seeking brief and simple answers (e.g., "who wrote the *Great Gatsby*?") (Luo and Weak 2011). It is not practical to engage in in-depth reference transactions via the exchange of text messages, and hence librarians need to be perceptive and efficient in determining what users are looking for, and be clear and succinct in providing the information. This can be challenging as reference librarians are usually expected to be thorough and detail oriented when assisting library users. Therefore, it is as important to help librarians understand the shift in expectation and make the proper mind-set adjustment, as it is to equip them with requisite knowledge and skills (e.g., how to use a character counter and URL shortener as well as how to write concisely without appearing brusque and impatient).

A large part of reference librarians' expertise comes from the knowledge of general and subject-specific resources. In virtual reference, such knowledge has a particular emphasis on resources in electronic format. Librarians' familiarity with resources on the Internet and in subscription databases plays a critical role in delivering virtual reference service since users expect immediately available answers in a chat or text reference transaction; answers have to be provided electronically in order to be delivered immediately (Coffman 2003).

Commitment to user services has always been an essential competency in reference work; in virtual reference, there is no exception. As a matter of fact, it is even more important in the virtual environment given that there are no nonverbal cues and users can be completely anonymous. Misunderstandings arise and inappropriate user behaviors occur, and still, librarians need to maintain a professional presence and have a customer service mentality when dealing with users from all sorts of backgrounds and with all sorts of needs.

Every line of work has pressure. In reference service, a considerable proportion of stress comes from dealing with human beings while under time pressure, such as encountering rude users and receiving tough questions. With the advent of virtual reference, a number of new sources of pressure have come into the picture and aggravated the stress level. For instance, the lack of verbal and visual cues can complicate the librarian–user communication and even cause anxiety and misunderstanding on both ends. Unexpected situations, like technology failure or the sudden disappearance of users in the middle of a chat session, can make librarians panic. Sometimes librarians have to staff both virtual reference services and the reference desk simultaneously and juggle virtual and physical user queries, which can increase the stress level. All the pressure inherent in the virtual environment requires librarians to be able to multitask, think quickly, manage time effectively, and be flexible and calm when dealing with difficult situations.

In virtual reference, particularly chat reference service, the ability to keep users informed by constantly notifying them of what the librarian is doing is critical to a successful transaction. In a face-to-face reference encounter, the physical presence of both the librarian and the user makes it easier to communicate the process of searching for an answer to the user's question. However, in a chat session, where no audio or visual cues exist and the entire communication is based on the exchange of written messages, librarians are faced with a more critical need to stay connected to the user. Telling the user what search activities the librarian is engaged in is an effective technique for the librarian to assure users of the "connectedness" and avoid making the user feel ignored.

The ability to use virtual reference software effectively is indispensable, especially when the service is offered through software like QuestionPoint. While software skills ensure the technical operation of a virtual reference session, it is online communication skills that produce the content of a successful transaction. In order to maintain a professional and yet friendly virtual presence, librarians need to be able to communicate effectively via e-mail, chat, or text, which requires a clear understanding and appreciation of online culture and etiquette and the ability to use online or texting language appropriately.

In a virtual reference consortium where members take turns staffing a collaborative service, librarians are expected to know other participating libraries' resources as well as their own so that users of other participating libraries can be well served. Usually users come to use a collaborative service with the expectation to be connected to a librarian from their own library and anticipate a conversation with a professional who knows the local library's resources well. Thus, in order for users to receive the best possible service, librarians of a virtual reference consortium should expand their expertise to include knowledge of member libraries' resources.

An effective way to prepare librarians and help them provide virtual reference service successfully is to review transcripts of virtual reference sessions. Such transcripts will provide a concrete view of how users frame their questions in e-mail, chat, and text, and what the common communication patterns are. This enables librarians to interpret user information needs more effectively and precisely, and provide appropriate assistance in addressing them.

GOING WHERE USERS ARE

Reference service, since it began in the late 19th century, has evolved greatly in the way it is delivered. Nowadays it is a multimodality service where personal assistance is provided not only in person, but also remotely and virtually via different venues. These venues have their own advantages and disadvantages in supporting reference transactions, and it is important that librarians have a solid understanding of them and make the best use of each venue. For example, in-person reference services at the reference desk and via research consultations are more effective in handling complex queries than virtual reference services. It would be helpful to put a statement on the library's virtual reference page, informing users that e-mail, chat, and text reference services are most effective when their queries are brief and straightforward, and if they need in-depth assistance, they are welcome to visit the reference desk or schedule an appointment for research consultation.

Providing users with optimal service experience is both the impetus and the goal of reference service. Users' information behavior will always change as new developments emerge in the information landscape. Librarians need to be keenly aware of this change and how this change has transformed reference services. It is imperative to constantly consider and address questions like what are users' information-seeking processes, what search strategies do they use for different information needs, where are the roadblocks, and what are their concerns when accessing digital information and services (e.g., privacy), in order to acquire a solid understanding of the evolving user information behavior and identify the best ways to provide assistance to users via various reference venues.

Being flexible, being prepared, and being creative are three indispensable factors contributing to a successful journey of "going where users are." The rapid development of information and communication technologies requires that librarians have the flexibility to recognize and explore new service potential and adapt to new service models. Effective and efficient responses to changes in service organization and delivery cannot be achieved without being fully prepared. More often than not, librarians, faced with limited budget and staff resources, have to be creative in utilizing technologies and making staffing arrangements to conduct outreach and provide services. Going where users are, and offering services in the ways most needed, welcomed, and appreciated by them, will always remain the key for reference services to stay current and relevant.

REFERENCES

Abels, Eileen. 1996. "The E-mail Reference Interview." *RQ* 35 (3): 345–56.

Aho, Melissa K., Anne M. Beschnett, and Emily Y. Reimer. 2011. "Who Is Sitting at the Reference Desk?: The Ever-Changing Concept of Staffing the Reference Desk at the Bio-Medical Library." *Collaborative Librarianship* 3 (1): 46–49.

Aluri, Rao, and Jeffrey W. St. Clair. 1978. "Academic Reference Librarians: An Endangered Species?" *The Journal of Academic Librarianship* 4 (2): 82–84.

American Library Association. 2015. "Academic Libraries in the United States—Statistical Trends." Accessed January 30. http://www.ala.org/ala/research/librarystats/academic/academiclibraries.cfm.

Ask a Linguist. http://www.linguistlist.org/ask-ling/.

Ask Dr. Math. http://mathforum.org/dr.math/.

Ask the Space Scientist. http://image.gsfc.nasa.gov/poetry/ask/askmag.html.

Beaton, Barbara. 2012. "New Technologies for Virtual Reference: A Look at Skype and Twitter." http://www.lib.umich.edu/files/departments/SkypeTwitter%20112912.pdf

Bell, Steven J. 2007. "Who Needs a Reference Desk?" *Library Issues: Briefings for Faculty and Administrators* 27 (6): 1–9.

Boeninger, Chad. 2010. "So Maybe This Is Why No One Uses Our Skype Reference Service." http://libraryvoice.com/technology/so-maybe-this-is-why-no-one-uses-our-skype-reference-service.

Bunge, Charles, and Chris Ferguson. 1997. "The Shape of Services to Come: Values-Based Reference Service for the Largely Digital Library." *College & Research Libraries* 58 (May): 252–65.

Bushallow-Wilber, Lara, Gemma DeVinney, and Fritz Whitcomb. 1996. "Electronic Mail Reference Service: A Study." *RQ* 35 (3): 25–36.

Carter, David, and Joseph Janes. 2000. "Unobtrusive Data Analysis of Digital Reference Questions and Service at the Internet Public Library: An Exploratory Study." *Library Trends* 49 (2): 251–65.

Coffman, Steve. 2003. *Going Live: Starting & Running a Virtual Reference Service.* Chicago: American Library Association.

Courtois, Martin P., and Maira Liriano. 2000. "Tips for Roving Reference: How to Best Serve Library Users." *College & Research Libraries News* 61 (4): 289–90, 315.

Faix, Allison, Amanda MacDonald, and Brooke Taxakis. 2014. "Research Consultation Effectiveness for Freshman and Senior Undergraduate Students." *Reference Services Review* 42 (1): 4–15.

Ford, Barbara J. 1986. "Reference beyond (and without) the Reference Desk." *College & Research Libraries* 47 (5): 492–94.

Ford, Charlotte. 2002. "An Exploratory Study of the Differences between Face-to-face and Computer-Mediated Reference Interactions." PhD diss., Indiana University at Bloomington.

Forsyth, Ellen. 2009. "Fancy Walkie Talkies, Star Trek Communicators or Roving Reference?" *The Australian Library Journal* 58 (1): 73–84.

Freides, Thelma. 1983. "Current Trends in Academic Libraries." *Library Trends* 31 (3): 457–74.

Gale, Crystal D., and Betty S. Evans. 2007. "Face-to-Face: The Implementation and Analysis of a Research Consultation Service." *College & Undergraduate Libraries* 14 (3): 85–101.

Giordano, Peter, Christine Menard, and Rebecca Ohm Spencer. 2001. "The Disappearing Reference Desk: Finding New Ways to Support the Curriculum of a Small Liberal Arts College." *College & Research Libraries News* 62 (7): 692–94.

Gorman, Michael. 2001. "Values for Human-to-Human Reference." *Library Trends* 50 (2): 168–82.

Green, Samuel S. 1876. "Personal Relations between Librarians and Readers." *American Library Journal* 1 (November 30): 74–81.

Haines, Annette, and Allison Grodzinski. 1999. "Web Forms: Improving, Expanding and Promoting Remote Reference Service." *College & Research Libraries News* 60 (4): 271–72.

Hess, Amanda Nichols. 2014. "Scheduling Research Consultations with YouCanBook. Me." *College & Research Libraries News* 75 (9): 510–13.

Holmes, Claire, and Lisa Woznicki. 2010. "Librarians at Your Doorstep." *College & Research Libraries News* 71 (1): 582–85.

Janes, Joseph, and Chrystie Hill. 2001. "Finger on the Pulse: Librarians Describe Evolving Reference Practice in an Increasingly Digital World." *Reference & User Services Quarterly* 42 (1): 54–65.

Jastram, Iris, and Ann Gwinn Zawistoski. 2008. "Personalizing the Library via Research Consultations." In *The Desk and Beyond: Next Generation Reference Services*, edited by Sarah K. Steiner and M. Leslie Madden, 14–24. Chicago: Association of College and Research Libraries.

Jensen, Bruce. 2010. "SMS Text Reference Comes of Age: The My Info Quest Collaborative." *The Reference Librarian* 51 (4): 264–75.

Kohl, Laura, and Maura Keating. 2009. "A Phone of One's Own: Texting at the Bryant University Reference Desk." *College & Research Libraries News* 70 (2): 104–6.

Lankes, David. 1998. *Building & Maintaining Internet Information Services: K-12 Digital Reference Services*. Syracuse, NY: ERIC Clearinghouse on Information & Technology.

Luo, Lili. 2014. "Slam the Boards: Librarians' Outreach into Social Q&A Sites." *Internet Reference Services Quarterly* 19 (7): 33–47.

Luo, Lili, and Emily Weak. 2011. "Texting 4 Answers: What Questions Do People Ask?" *Reference & User Services Quarterly* 51 (2): 133–42.

Magi, Trina J., and Patricia E. Mardeusz. 2013. "Why Some Students Continue to Value Individual, Face-to-Face Research Consultations in a Technology-Rich World." *College & Research Libraries* 74 (6): 605–18.

Massey-Burzio, Virginia. 1992. "Reference Encounters of a Different Kind: A Symposium." *The Journal of Academic Librarianship* 18 (5): 276–81.

May, Fiona. 2011. "Roving Reference, iPad-Style." *Idaho Librarian* 61 (2). http://theidaholibrarian.wordpress.com/2011/11/23/roving-reference-ipad-style/.

Miles, Dennis. 2013. "Shall We Get Rid of the Reference Desk?" *Reference & User Services Quarterly* 52 (4): 320–33.

Mosley, Pixie Ann. 2007. "Assessing User Interactions at the Desk Nearest the Front Door." *Reference & User Services Quarterly* 47 (2): 159–67.

Nolen, David S. 2010. "Reforming or Rejecting the Reference Desk: Conflict and Continuity in the Concept of Reference." *Library Philosophy and Practice* (May): 1–8.

Pearce, Alexa. 2010. "Text Message Reference at NYU Libraries." *The Reference Librarian* 51 (4): 256–63.

Pearce, Alexa, Scott Collard, and Kara Whatley. 2010. "SMS Reference: Myths, Markers, and Modalities." *Reference Services Review* 38 (2): 250–63.

Pomerantz, Jeffrey. 2003. "Question Taxonomies for Digital Reference." PhD diss., Syracuse University.

Quora. http://www.quora.com.

Reference and User Services Association. 2013. "Guidelines for Behavioral Performance of Reference and Information Service Providers." American Library Association. http://www.ala.org/rusa/resources/guidelines/guidelinesbehavioral.

Reference and User Services Association. 2004. "Guidelines for Implementing and Maintaining Virtual Reference Services." American Library Association. http://www.ala.org/rusa/resources/guidelines/virtrefguidelines.

Reinsfelder, Thomas L. 2012. "Citation Analysis as a Tool to Measure the Impact of Individual Research Consultations." *College & Research Libraries* 73 (3): 263–78.

Ronan, Jana. 2003. *Chat Reference: A Guide to Live Virtual Reference Services*. Westport, CT: Libraries Unlimited.

Ryan, Sara. 1996. "Reference Service for the Internet Community: A Case Study of the Internet Public Library Reference Division." *Library & Information Science Research* 18 (3): 241–59.

Schardt, Connie M. 1983. "Electronic Mail Service: Applications in the Pacific Northwest Region." *Bulletin of the Medical Library Association* 71 (4): 437–38.

Schulte, Stephanie J. 2011. "Eliminating Traditional Reference Services in an Academic Health Sciences Library: A Case Study." *Journal of the Medical Library Association* 99 (4): 273–79.

Selby, Courtney. 2007. "The Evolution of the Reference Interview." *Legal Reference Services Quarterly* 26 (1/2): 35–46.

Sloan, Bernie. 1998. "Service Perspectives for the Digital Library: Remote Reference Services." *Library Trends* 47 (1): 117–43.

Still, Julie, and Frank Campbell. 1993. "Librarian in a Box: The Use of Electronic Mail for Reference." *Reference Services Review* 21 (1): 15–18.

Summerhill, Karen Storin. 1994. "The High Cost of Reference: The Need to Reassess Services and Service Delivery." *The Reference Librarian* 43: 71–85.

Swanson, Patricia. 1984. "Traditional Models: Myths and Realities." In *Academic Libraries: Myths and Realities: Proceedings of the Third National Conference of the Association of College and Research Libraries*, edited by Suzanne Dodson and Gary L. Menges, 84–97. Chicago: American Library Association.

Tenopir, Carol, and Lisa Ennis. 2001. "Reference Services in the New Millennium." *Online* 25 (4): 40–45.

Tenopir, Carol, and Lisa Ennis. 2002. "A Decade of Digital Reference: 1991–2001." *Reference & User Services Quarterly* 41 (3): 264–73.

Yahoo! Answers. https://answers.yahoo.com/.

Yi, Hua. 2003. "Individual Research Consultation Service: An Important Part of an Information Literacy Program." *Reference Services Review* 31 (4): 342–50.

Weimer, Keith. 2010. "Text Messaging the Reference Desk: Using Upside Wireless' SMS-to-Email to Extend Reference Service." *The Reference Librarian* 51 (2): 108–23.

White, Marilyn Domas. 2001. "Diffusion of Innovation: Digital Reference Service in Carnegie Foundation Master's (Comprehensive) Academic Institution Libraries." *The Journal of Academic Librarianship* 27 (3): 173–87.

SUGGESTED READINGS

Bridgewater, Rachel, and Meryl B. Cole. 2008. *Instant Messaging Reference: A Practical Guide*. Oxford: Chandos.

This book focuses on the practical implementation of instant messaging (IM) in delivering virtual reference service. It provides basic information about starting and running a virtual reference service using IM. Also included is a discussion of the broader issues such as privacy, security, and the future potential of IM in the virtual reference arena.

Gorman, Michael. 2001. "Values for Human-to-Human Reference." *Library Trends* 50 (2): 168–82.

Gorman gives a brief history of how human-to-human reference service has evolved and provides a discussion of its future. Particularly, it elaborates on the eight values (stewardship, service, intellectual freedom, rationalism, literacy and learning, equity of access, privacy, and democracy) derived from the author's earlier work and how each relates to the practices of human-to-human reference.

Janes, Joseph. 2003. *Introduction to Reference Work in the Digital Age*. New York: Neal-Schuman.

Janes discusses how reference work has evolved and will continue to evolve in the digital age, and how librarians should embrace the digital reference revolution and choose the best approaches to identify and meet users' needs.

Janes, Joseph, and Chrystie Hill. 2001. "Finger on the Pulse: Librarians Describe Evolving Reference Practice in an Increasingly Digital World." *Reference & User Services Quarterly* 42 (1): 54–65.

The authors examine librarians' experiences in adapting reference practice to the digital environment and their own views about virtual reference. Issues such as the reference interview, service quality and standards, and types of questions are also discussed in the context of virtual reference.

Kern, M. Kathleen. 2009. *Virtual Reference Best Practices: Tailoring Services to Your Library*. Chicago: American Library Association.

Kern outlines the tools and decision-making processes that will help libraries evaluate, tailor, and launch virtual reference services that are appropriate for their specific user communities. The book departs from general guidelines and focuses on making concrete decisions about integrating virtual with traditional reference.

Lankes, R. David, Scott Nicholson, Marie L. Radford, Joanne Silverstein, Lynn Westbrook, and Philip Nast, eds. 2008. *Virtual Reference Service: From Competencies to Assessment*. New York: Neal-Schuman.

This useful volume, part of the *Virtual Reference Desk* series, presents experts' best practices, forward-looking models, and advice on new developments in virtual reference. Chapters feature both practical guidance and the latest thinking about virtual reference work in libraries. Topics discussed include the building of consortia, motivational and coaching techniques for staff, instant messaging options, creation of subject-specific taxonomies, interpersonal communications improvement, methods of assessment, and competencies and training.

Luo, Lili, and Emily Weak. 2011. "Texting 4 Answers: What Questions Do People Ask?" *Reference & User Services Quarterly* 51 (2): 133–42.

This article provides a detailed view of how patrons use text reference service, especially what kinds of questions they ask and what types of information needs are fulfilled by text reference. Additional analysis of characteristics such as transaction length and interactivity provides a more in-depth picture of the nature of text reference. It strengthens the professional understanding of how to best deliver reference service via this emerging reference venue.

Magi, Trina J., and Patricia E. Mardeusz. 2013. "Why Some Students Continue to Value Individual, Face-to-Face Research Consultations in a Technology-Rich World." *College & Research Libraries* 74 (6): 605–18.

This article explores the value of research consultations from students' perspective. It examines students' views on why they schedule consultations, the kinds of assistance they receive from librarians during consultations, and what they find valuable about the consultations.

Miles, Dennis. 2013. "Shall We Get Rid of the Reference Desk?" *Reference & User Services Quarterly* 52 (4): 320–33.

This article studies the use of the reference desk in 119 academic libraries at universities offering master's level programs. It provides an empirically grounded view on the role of the reference desk at academic libraries.

Nolen, David S. 2010. "Reforming or Rejecting the Reference Desk: Conflict and Continuity in the Concept of Reference." *Library Philosophy and Practice* (May): 1–8.

Nolen provides a historical examination of the debate about the reference desk and challenges the assertion that there are two camps with diametrically opposed views of reference. He suggests that the protagonists and antagonists of the reference desk actually agree in their vision of reference, although their approaches are different.

Pomerantz, Jeffrey. 2005. "A Conceptual Framework and Open Research Questions for Chat-Based Reference Service." *Journal of the American Society for Information Science and Technology* 56 (12): 1288–1302.

Pomerantz focuses on the creation and discussion of theoretical frameworks to unite emerging standards and best practices in providing chat reference service. A model of the provision of chat reference service is developed at a high level of abstraction and may serve as a conceptual framework for future virtual reference research and development.

Ronan, Jana. 2003. *Chat Reference: A Guide to Live Virtual Reference Services*. Westport, CT: Libraries Unlimited.

This volume is a useful guidebook in establishing virtual reference services. Through the discussion of online real-time chat reference software and human and organizational issues, the author lays out the many decisions and considerations involved in implementing virtual reference services. Case studies are included to provide readers with concrete examples of how a virtual reference service is set up.

Chapter 7

Management of Reference Services

JoAnn Jacoby and
M. Kathleen Kern[1]

INTRODUCTION

> Some people are born to be library directors [or reference service managers]. Not me . . .
>
> My entire goal was to be the best reference librarian I could possibly be. (Olver 2011, 6)

Aspiring reference librarians may wonder what relevance management has to them. Those who do may not realize that most professional library positions, including those at the entry level, involve a range of management and/or supervisory responsibilities. Most librarians are also involved with a variety of formal and informal leadership roles in professional organizations and at their home institutions. This means that almost everyone pursuing a career involving reference will have the opportunity to provide leadership for reference-related initiatives or participate directly or indirectly in the management of reference services.

Reference managers take the lead in their institution for defining what reference is, what primary and secondary services are included, how those services are staffed, and how they are assessed. Outlining the four foundational functions of reference services—teaching users how to use the library and its resources, answering specific informational queries from users, recommending sources to users that fit their needs, and promoting the library to the community—David A. Tyckoson defines the core responsibilities of the reference manager as making decisions about "how much focus should be placed on each of those functions, what staff and resources should be expended to support them, and how to ensure the best and most current materials are available" (2011, 276). Elsewhere in this volume, Tyckoson (Chapter 1) traces some of the varieties of reference services that have developed throughout library history, and Lili Luo (Chapter 6) describes contemporary models of reference services. The current chapter provides an orientation to reference management through an overview of managerial roles and expectations, a discussion of managers as leaders, and an exploration of specific responsibilities and competencies of reference managers. Pointers to resources that are available to help both "accidental" managers[2] as well as those who are intentionally preparing to take on this role are included throughout.

Box 7.1 Sample Position Description: Head of Reference

The core responsibilities of a reference manager are outlined later, adapted from a job posting Felix Unaeze identified as representative in an article on 21st-century reference leadership (2003, 113):

- Provide the leadership to develop comprehensive, first-class reference services to the community
- Supervise reference services, including:
  - Scheduling
  - Monitoring and evaluating service quality
- Develop goals and objectives for the unit/service
- Envision and implement innovative projects and services in response to needs of the community
- Identify and evaluate emerging technologies
- Formulate policies
- Coordinate documentation of procedures and services
- Prepare and submit reports
- Develop outreach initiatives
- Coordinate collection development and management

Questions for Reflection and Discussion:

1. Does this description meet your perception of current needs in reference management?
2. What was included that was unexpected? What was lacking?
3. How well does this position description apply to different types of libraries?

The core responsibilities of a reference manager are outlined in Box 7.1. As G. Edward Evans and Camila Alire observe, "management is an art as well as a science" (2013, xv). This chapter explores the art and the science, the roles and responsibilities, and the characteristics and skills needed to be a successful manager. The exceptions are those areas covered in other chapters in this volume: developing and managing collections, covered in Chapter 13; outreach and promotion, discussed in Chapter 10 as well as in Chapters 11–12, which address working with specific communities; evaluation and assessment, covered in Chapter 8, and service models, covered in Chapter 6.

MANAGERIAL ROLES AND EXPECTATIONS

Select good people, trust them, delegate authority while retaining responsibility, build true teams, and be supportive. (Evans and Alire 2013, 7)

Librarians with responsibilities for managing reference services do so in a variety of contexts and organizational structures. Learning the organizational culture and the managerial and leadership expectations that relate to the position is an important step in becoming an effective manager. Where oversight of reference services is positioned in the institution's hierarchy (or lack thereof) will shape both the scope of the reference manager's responsibilities and what management style and approaches will be most effective. Within different types of organizational structures, the specific title given to positions with reference management responsibilities varies accordingly, with common examples ranging from "head" (implying oversight of a department within a hierarchical structure and direct reports), "manager" (generally denotes direct reports within a functional unit), to "coordinator" or "team leader" (which usually means a team-based or matrix organization with staff at different levels devoting a certain amount of time to reference services). "Head of Reference" positions are increasingly less common, with responsibility for overseeing reference services more typically assigned to a middle manager, coordinator, or team leader.

Responsibilities and Roles

Some roles and responsibilities are common to all managers whether the position is in a traditional hierarchical organization as a head of a reference department, a flat organization as a reference team leader, or in an entirely different environment. One of the most frequently cited descriptions of the manager's role, Luther Gulick and Lyndall Urwick's (1937) POSDCoRB model, focuses on core functional responsibilities:

1. *Planning*: Determining goals and deciding how they will be met.
2. *Organizing*: Dividing work among units, establishing procedures to accomplish tasks.
3. *Staffing*: Making all personnel decisions, including staff hiring and evaluation.
4. *Directing*: Overseeing and assigning work to individuals.
5. *Coordinating*: Coordinating activities between units.
6. *Reporting*: Reporting on unit activities and accomplishments, keeping upper management informed about progress.
7. *Budgeting*: Determining how the unit's budget will be allocated and ensuring that unit stays within budget.

Recent studies have found that these responsibilities are still salient in today's workplace, but with some key differences including a heavier managerial workload, a contact pattern more oriented toward staff working in group or team settings, and a greater emphasis on giving information (Martin 2006; Moran, Stueart and Morner 2013, 270). In addition to the concrete responsibilities in the POSDCoRB model, Joan Giesecke and Beth McNeil observe that in the current environment in many libraries, the role of managers and supervisors has become "more of a coach than director, more of a facilitator than a commander" (2010, 6). Changes to managerial expectations move away from the limits of the POSDCoRB responsibilities and focus on roles that are more contextualized within the organization, more interpersonally oriented, and more collaborative. Giesecke and McNeil enumerate new roles such as mentoring staff, facilitating conflict management, serving as a broker or negotiator for the staff or unit with upper management and other library units, and acting as an innovator who plans and manages change (2010, 6–14).

While there is an overlap with the POSDCoRB model, Giesecke and McNeil emphasize the characteristics and soft skills expected of library managers by focusing on the role of the person (facilitator, creator) rather than on the task or activity (organizing, overseeing). These higher-level roles and competencies are the starting point for considering good management and leadership, and after that foundation, this chapter will focus on specific areas of responsibility and tools and resources for day-to-day reference management activities.

Competencies and Skills

Success as a manager or leader requires more than executing a set of responsibilities. The skills and competencies needed to be a reference librarian—the ability to gather, organize, and analyze information; to develop a clear understanding of other's information needs; and to connect people to appropriate resources and tools—provide an excellent foundation for developing the soft skills needed to be a successful manager. One of the best statements of professional competencies for librarians is provided in Giesecke and McNeil's "Core Competencies and the Learning Organization" (1999, 160). These competencies, summarized in Chapter 9, include a number of skill areas—such as resource management, organizational understanding, and global thinking—in which managers should work to gain deep competence. These high-level skills align with the expanded roles of managers as facilitators and creators. Soft skills such as communication, time management, and initiative serve to support the specific responsibilities discussed later in the chapter and are an important factor in providing the type of leadership often expected of reference managers.

MANAGERS AS LEADERS

> Managers do things right; while leaders do the right things. (Bennis and Nanus 2007, 45)

> If your actions create a legacy that inspires others to dream more, learn more, do more and become more, then, you are an excellent leader. (Dolly Parton, quoted in Adrain 1997)

Leading leadership theorist John P. Kotter argues that management and leadership are distinctive but complementary modes of action (1990b). Kotter describes leadership as a process that involves developing a vision and strategy for the future and mobilizing others to realize that vision. The overall effect is to produce change and to develop new services and approaches. By contrast, management involves planning and using resources efficiently to produce the intended results. These two modes need to be in balance for an organization to be effective. Organizations that develop strong leaders without equally strong management will falter as key operational functions are neglected. Conversely, organizations with strong management and weak or absent leadership can find themselves doing things the right way, but not necessarily doing the right things (Kotter 1990a). For reference services, this might mean continuing to provide quality dependable services that are relevant only to a small handful of legacy users while missing new opportunities for more meaningful engagement. While Kotter views leadership and management as distinct roles that cannot and should not be combined, other management theorists disagree. Regardless of the theory, in practice, most reference managers are expected to both manage and lead. Moreover, the techniques of leadership that focus on motivating, inspiring, and aligning people are valuable skills for anyone who wants to influence future directions in the workplace or the profession.

Some people are lucky to have developed skills in both leadership and management, to apply as the situation demands, but a single individual is usually stronger in one or the other. Each individual will need to undertake a frank assessment of his or her own strengths and weaknesses and then work to develop a strong group of people whose strengths complement his or her own weaknesses. Those who are more comfortable managing than leading can make a point of listening to more visionary coworkers or enlisting charismatic colleagues to help them motivate and inspire others. They can arrange opportunities for group brainstorming or other events such as charrettes or hack-a-thons to elicit innovative ideas that they can then work to implement using their managerial skills. Another strategy managers can use is developing processes for gathering input from their community of users (e.g., through focus groups or advisory committees) and trying approaches like scenario-based planning or environmental scans that can help keep the bigger picture in focus. Conversely, strong leaders will want to build a team of people around them who are empowered to establish procedures and deadlines, organize the work of other staff or team members, and monitor and evaluate progress toward the intended result.

Developing a Leadership Style

Management and leadership theories abound, and there are more books and articles (both scholarly and popular) than anyone could read. Readings on leadership vary from the promotion of different styles as the best approach to ones that help people to determine their own leadership style. Choosing something to read is a place to exercise reference skills in finding what has been well reviewed. There are books that are considered classics of leadership, although styles can come in and out of vogue. Determining which books to read can also be a way to connect with others. Asking administrators or supervisors for suggestions on management and leadership books is a good place to start as their choices will help you to learn about the organizational culture, or at least their aspirations for the organizational culture. Box 7.2 outlines an exercise for developing an individual management philosophy based on conversations with other professionals, individual reflection, and research.

Box 7.2 Activity: Develop Your Own Management Philosophy

"Select good people, trust them, delegate authority while retaining responsibility, build true teams, and be supportive" is a concise statement of the management philosophy held by Evans and Alire, authors of *Management Basics for Information Professionals* (2013, 7).

New and aspiring managers will be well served to begin developing a concise statement of their own management philosophy. To get started:

- Reflect on the good, and the not so good, managers you have worked for in the past. What are some of the traits you would like to emulate? And that you want to avoid?
- Talk to colleagues you admire in management or leadership positions and ask them about their management philosophies and approach. Listen for the variety of ways different leaders face similar challenges and the varied definitions of what constitutes a good result.
- Use the sources identified through the process suggested at the beginning of this section to examine some management and leadership approaches in more depth. The *Harvard Business Review* is also a great place to browse for inspiration. Which approaches resonate with you? Which fit best with your core values? With your particular strengths?

Style inventories can be a useful tool for a manager. Style inventories assess and categorize people's traits into groups that can then be used to examine common ways in which people of different styles relate, how working relationships can be improved, and how to make one's own approach to the workplace more effective. For example, learning that a supervisee prefers concrete direction can help the manager who prefers to provide staff with the ability to make their own decisions and processes. Often these preferences are not voiced or even fully realized but can be revealed through style inventories. These typologies can also depersonalize character traits to make talking about them less about the individual and more on making changes that improve communication and work between people and within groups. While all team members may learn and benefit from the exercise, it is the manager who must "understand, recognize, and accommodate different work styles of the people that they supervise" (Giesecke and McNeil 2010, 106–7) and adapt to bring out the best in the people that he or she supervises. Even where a manager is not a direct supervisor, learning how to adapt to others' work styles is a quality that a leader should develop.

Some inventories aim to be holistic personality assessments such as the Myers–Briggs Type Indicator (Myers and Briggs 2009) and others are specific to the workplace or other situations like the DiSC Profile (2015). Use an inventory that is well researched, even though there may be a fee, as the time that has gone into their development makes for tools that are balanced, thoughtful, and present even traditionally negative traits as challenges and opportunities. Some people find inventories to be invaluable in learning about themselves and their colleagues. Not everyone likes to be "typed" into categories, however. When using a style inventory with a team, an outside facilitator who knows the tool is advisable. The facilitator can frame the uses and limitations of the tool, remind people that there are no "bad" types but only differences among types, and keep team members focused on how to use the information in the workplace.

Organizational Cultures and Leadership Expectations

Every organization has a culture that affects how decisions are made, the managerial structures, and the expectations on staff at all levels. Being successful, particularly as a manager, requires understanding the organization's culture. Carol Shepstone and Lyn Currie (2008) offer a formal process for analyzing current organizational culture, noting that organizational culture is the behaviors and norms (often unspoken) that govern how things are done and decisions get made. These aspects may not be apparent from the organizational structure, but are equally important in learning how to work effectively with colleagues in order to make things happen. Time and observation, along with talking with longer-term employees, are informal ways to learn an organization's culture. When moving to a new organization, or when assuming a new role, it is advisable for the leader to give thought to how to adapt personal style to the new workplace culture. For example, top-down decisions in a collaborative culture might appear heavy handed and meet resistance, whereas a lengthy collaborative process might be seen as slow and indecisive in a culture more accustomed to leaders who are out in front with their decision making.

Defining a Vision for Reference Services

> Everyone here has the sense that right now is one of those moments when we are influencing the future. (Steve Jobs, quoted in Sheff 1985)

Vision and the ability to translate that vision into words and actions that inspire others are the hallmarks of leadership. Where does that vision come from? Keeping up with conversations in the profession can provide inspiration or spark new ideas, but merely following trends can lead down a rabbit hole of contradictory proclamations and perspectives. Numerous articles over the past decade have reflected on the future of reference (Carlson 2007; O'Gorman and Trott 2009; Tyckoson and Dove 2015), some heralding the imminent death of reference (Campbell 1992; Kelley 2011) and others its rebirth through new technologies or its transformation from transaction-based reference services to relationship-based research support services (Gibson and Mandernach 2013; Murphy 2011; Radford 2012; Saunders, Rozaklis, and Abels 2014; Steiner and Madden 2008; Zabel 2007; Zabel 2011). The first and last chapters of this volume, on the history and future of reference services respectively, also reflect on where we have been and where we might be heading. There are rich ideas here, but no single path, which is not unexpected given the variety of settings and approaches taken by various librarians exploring new models of service provision and dealing with financial uncertainty and volatility.

Finding an individual path and developing vision involves at least three things on the part of the manager. First, it involves touching bases with the fundamentals, including the professional philosophy of service articulated in sources such as Ranganathan's Five Laws (1931), the American Library Association's (ALA) Code of Ethics and Library Bill of Rights, discussed in Chapter 2, and the reflections on the core functions of reference offered by Tyckoson and others in the sources cited earlier. Next, it involves developing a deep knowledge of the library's community of users, looking at both current needs and needs that are likely to emerge given changing technologies, work habits, and demographics. Finally, it involves learning to trust instincts and judgment, which is the key to developing an authentic vision.

Planning

Effective management involves planning for the future and implementing that vision of reference services. Planning necessitates assessing present needs and anticipating future needs through knowledge of the broader environment and providing the resources to successfully implement services. Assessment is an important tool in both determining future directions and appropriately allocating resources. Chapter 8 provides an in-depth examination of assessment methods and tools. The following are a few types of decision-making approaches for planning in reference services.

Librarians should pay attention to what is happening outside of the library's walls, both within the local community and in the world. This includes not only an awareness of trends at other libraries, but factors that might affect local users and their information habits such as demographics, economics, and technology trends as well. It would be a lot for a single librarian to gather and examine these data on his or her own, but there are some excellent sources for awareness such as the Pew Internet reports on libraries and related technology trends (Pew Research Center), Public Library Data Service annual survey (Reid 2014), and the Association of College and Research Libraries' (ACRL) Top Trends in Academic Libraries (ACRL Research Planning and Review Committee 2014). National and state organizations and listservs, discussed more in the section on Professional Development Resources, are good places for information on what is happening at other libraries. Trends that are observed by the manger or staff should not be overlooked: Are there a lot of tablet users in the library? How might that affect services such as the library's website, and how people contact the reference librarian? Awareness of trends does not necessitate being on the leading edge of changes. The "Accidental Technologist" column in *Reference & User Services Quarterly* has columns on finding and choosing reference technologies that may be helpful in keeping abreast of relevant innovations.

Knowledge of local reference use patterns enables the reference manager to plan changes that make the most of limited resources while offering services that are appropriate to the local user group. To be useful to decision making, reference statistics should be more than just a tally of the number of questions received each day or each hour. Tracking reference questions by factors such as time of day, patron type, nature or subject of question, day of week or month, and mode of communication, can be used to determine the best way to utilize staff. Attention to changes over time can inform the creation of a new service point or the combination of service points or changes in who is staffing a service (Todorinova et al. 2011; Ward and Phetteplace 2012). For example, if evenings are when the most challenging reference questions are received, it would make sense to staff that time of day with librarians or experienced staff. Tracking information about subjects of the questions received at the reference service desk and through consultations can also inform training and collection development. Reading chat reference transcripts and e-mails is more time consuming than analyzing meta-data collected about reference interactions, but can also be a rich source of information for training and collection development.

Statistics about the nature of reference questions received and changes over time are a good decision-making tool, but they do not tell a complete story. Gathering information from users and the staff who work the frontlines of the reference service can support richer decision making. Examination of trends and statistics may reveal what else needs to be known to make a well-reasoned decision. If a lot of people in the library are observed using tablets, what are they doing? Are they checking out eBooks? Asking reference questions? Playing games? If there is a new technology for reference that other libraries have adopted, is this something of interest to the local user population? Surveys or focus groups can take observed trends and supply additional information from end users. Frontline staff are another group whose ideas and opinions are important to decision making. Those working the reference desk daily are best situated to alert management to emerging patterns such as a particular shift becoming busier, an increase in questions from off-campus students, or a decline in questions that require the use of traditional reference sources. These observations can lead to an examination of existing data or the collection of additional information to take initial impressions to the point where they can be the basis of a change in operations.

HIRING AND MANAGING STAFF

Categories of Staff

In every organization of more than one person, there are different staff roles and titles. Some organizations will be fluid about who can take on responsibilities, but in many library settings, positions are defined by level of education, training, and experience. The terms "professional" and "paraprofessional" or "professional" and "clerical" are traditionally used to delineate between those with an MLIS degree (professional) and those without. Changes in hiring are affecting those categories as MLIS degree holders take nonlibrarian staff positions and professionals with other degrees work in libraries in specialized roles.

How staff members at different levels relate and how expectations are set are a matter of organizational culture, as discussed earlier. It can also be a human resources and legal matter. In public universities, municipal libraries, and public schools in particular, staff may be unionized, and in those cases, "working within class" becomes important. The manager must know the rules for working with staff and the guidelines for work of staff at each level. For example, staff classification may stipulate that only staff at a certain level or classification can work at a reference desk or as a frontline supervisor. Assigning a staff person at a lower level these responsibilities would violate the workplace rules and risk an employee grievance or initiate the need to reclassify that staff person to a higher level (including a higher level of pay). If the work needs to be done and that staff person is qualified and capable, the case should be made in advance for a reclassification rather than running afoul of the contract. These are important issues for the reference manager given changes to reference services configurations and which staff are providing the frontline of service (see Chapter 6). Some staff are motivated by challenging work, and in a rigidly classified environment, the supervisor must put thought into finding work that is interesting but within the bounds of the contract.

Hiring and Recruitment

One of the most important jobs of a manager is to hire good people. Hiring can be a daunting responsibility for a new manager, in part because of this importance. There are rules and procedures in almost every organization that facilitate the process, but the final hiring recommendation is often up to the manager or search committee. A first step when hiring is to meet with Human Resources to find out the procedures and what templates and tools they have available; this will not only save the manager work but also make sure that the standard practices of the organization are followed. Even if specifics differ across organizations, there are some standard types of work that are part of most hiring processes; these are justifying the need for the position, developing a position description, recruiting candidates, forming a search committee, and interviewing and making a final hiring decision.

When positions become vacant or new positions are created, the need to fill them must be communicated to administration or whoever has budgetary authority over positions and salaries. This requires vision and the ability to communicate the importance of the position not just today, but for the future. A good tactic is to articulate what vital work will not be done if the position is not filled as well as the benefits of filling the position. This justification of the position is also a good time to examine if the position that is needed is exactly the position that was vacated or if it is time to rethink and reconfigure the position. Sometimes a newly structured position can not only meet the needs of the reference department better, but also incorporate needs from elsewhere in the library, making the position easier to justify, particularly when budgets are tight and filling positions is a competitive process. The newly defined position should still be coherent, able to be filled by one person, and not so big in scope and responsibilities as to be unmanageable. In some cases, writing the formal position description is part of the justification process, while at other libraries, it may be a later step.

The formal position description informs the candidate of the responsibilities of the position as well as the required and preferred qualifications. Consider carefully what is required, as candidates who do not meet those requirements may be ineligible for interviews and hiring. Place anything that is not essential into a desired or preferred list. The position description should be detailed enough for potential candidates to understand the work and the requirements, but not so comprehensive as to be off-putting. Including everything that might possibly be desired in a candidate could narrow the field of applicants too much and also read as a position that is not cohesive or an organization that wants more than is realistic. To develop a strong position description, read other similar position descriptions with an eye to what positions will attract the candidates that your organization would also want. Keep in mind that the position description will often serve as an internal document post-hire to guide the work of the position as well as the foundation of the job announcement.

After a position is approved for hiring, a job vacancy announcement needs to be posted. Where the position is posted and for how long will affect who applies. Find out the standard recruiting process for the organization and discuss to what extent that can be augmented to increase diversity and depth of the candidate pool. There might be limitations on some types of positions that first must be filled internally if possible before being posted or requirements to post only locally or to recruit nationally. In addition to posting the job announcement, recruit specific qualified candidates by contacting them and inviting them to apply. This is not a promise of employment or even of an interview, but it does indicate that the person is thought to be well qualified. Some candidates who would not otherwise be looking for a job might apply if contacted directly so this method is used more frequently, but not exclusively, for non-entry-level positions. It is important to know the rules of the organization around recruiting, but many organizations consider recruitment a way to build the depth and diversity of the candidate pool.

Depending on the organization and situation, hiring may be a solo decision of the person managing the position or may involve administrative or board approval or a search committee that brings multiple perspectives to hiring. When composing a search committee, think about representation from inside and outside of the department, as there may be people external to the department who will work with the individual and who could offer a valuable perspective.

The interview process, much like other parts of hiring, can vary dramatically depending on the organization and may take from one hour to multiple days. Two rounds of interviews, telephone and in person, are common for some organizations and are particularly useful if there is a large number of highly qualified candidates. Regardless of format, number, and length of interviews, the most important aspect is what questions are asked of the candidate and the information that the candidate receives about the position and organization during the interview. When crafting interview questions, move beyond what is likely to be on the resume and spend time on questions likely to elicit specific examples and reveal characteristics of how the candidates think and work. Questions like "what techniques do you find most effective when conducting a reference interview?" can be helpful in assessing how well the candidate's approach matches your expectations.

Building and Fostering Diversity

Historically, the majority of library employees have been white and female. In order to better reflect their communities, libraries are actively recruiting a more diverse workforce across categories such as race, ethnicity, and physical ability. A diverse workplace also is inclusive of people of varying religions and sexual orientations. People from a range of backgrounds and experiences will bring in a wider variety of ideas and approaches. From a reference service perspective, this can have a positive impact on outreach and connection with user populations as well as enhance the learning environment among staff. When recruiting and hiring, check with human resources about diversity statements to include in the position announcement, venues for recruiting, and equal opportunity guidelines.

Encouraging diversity extends beyond the hiring process, and it is the role of the manager to ensure that the work environment is inclusive and supportive. Communication and listening skills as well as an awareness of how everyone in the department relates to one another are an important part of the manager's toolset for fostering diversity. It is not necessary for everyone to be friends, but everyone should be respected and listened to by every other person and not just by the manager. If there is discord in the department, the manager should seek to understand the causes and mitigate appropriately. Is the source of tension differences in culture or interpersonal communication style? Are the causes based on biases against a group of people? Are the causes related solely to divergent opinions about work matters? Intolerance and discrimination can be overt or subtle, but must be dealt with and documented by the manager. Consultation with human resources is also appropriate. Differences in communication style or opinions about work issues could be culturally based or personality based. An organization's human resources office may be able to suggest resources on developing cultural sensitivity; working with varied personality and work styles are addressed later in this chapter.

Performance Expectations and Supervision

The position description is the starting place for setting expectations about employee responsibilities and performance, but it is certainly not the end. Position descriptions are generally overviews that do not provide measurable goals. There may be standards within the library for employee reviews and goal setting, or it may be up to the individual supervisor. Yearly or twice-yearly meetings to set goals and review performance will allow alignment of work activities to organizational priorities and a formal assessment of progress. Performance expectations should include not only a focus on projects and concrete outcomes, but also areas of importance to the position such as punctuality and reliability, communications, customer service, and teamwork.

Meeting with employees should not be limited to formal review cycles. Frequency of meetings between the supervisor and the employee will depend on the needs of the employee (and the manager) and the type of work being supervised. Delegated projects may require closer communication in order to support the employee doing the work. New employees may need more mentoring than long-term employees.

When employees are not meeting expectations or are struggling with assigned work, documentation and regular meetings are necessary. It can be difficult and uncomfortable to tell employees that they are not meeting expectations. However, avoiding the issue makes it only worse. Performance issues should be addressed immediately so that they are fresh in the memory of the employee and so it does not seem like the manager has stockpiled issues that then come as a surprise to the employee. Chapter 9 on training discusses competencies and providing feedback in more depth. The main point for now is to be clear and impartial in the communication of any issues, to seek and respect the perspective of the employee, to work with the employee to develop a plan to remediate the issues, to follow-up as a manager and provide training or support for improvement, and to document the process fully.

Empowering Staff and Building Teams

> Trusted, empowered employees provide better services (and otherwise do better) than those that are required to report to their manager before making the smallest of decisions. [Staff] appreciate managers who provide direction while they allow autonomy (Gordon 2005, 159)

Job Aids

Job aids include things like procedure manuals, opening and closing checklists, and computer help screens—basically, anything that helps people do their job better and provides crucial information and documentation when and where it is needed. Job aids are mentioned in Chapter 9 as a method to infuse training into daily practice. Providing staff with the information they need to do their jobs well and make appropriate decisions independently is essential to maintaining service quality, as well as creating productive and empowered staff at all levels. Well-designed job aids save the time of staff, the manager, and most importantly the library user.

Job aids can take many forms, utilizing a range of formats and media, as described in Joe Willmore's how-to guide to creating and using job aids (2006). Some reference-specific examples are listed in Box 7.3.

Box 7.3 Activity: Job Aids for Reference Work

- An alarm bell—a reminder to check the e-mail queue for incoming questions or to take the room count.
- Troubleshooting guide—a flowchart of questions to ask and things to try when a user reports problems accessing an online resource.
- Images—a photo or map showing the meeting spot for building evacuations.
- Dashboard—an easily used Web page of links or set of bookmarks to key resources needed to provide reference services. This might include links to key databases and catalogs, as well as to desk schedules, individuals' schedules, software, log-ins, procedures, and the like.
- Canned answers—prewritten answers to commonly asked questions that can be used as a customizable template for responding to chat, e-mail, and other inquiries.
- FAQs—automatically generated or cooperatively developed lists or databases where staff share information for common (and not so common) questions.

Questions for Reflection and Discussion:

1. What are additional ways that these job aids could be used?
2. What software or other formats might support the creation and sharing of these aids?
3. Are there other types of job aids that you have used or that come to mind?

It is important to consider what users (in this case staff members) are trying to accomplish, and how and where they will be working, so the material can be readily available at the point of need, and novice and experienced staff alike can quickly find what they need to know. Whenever possible, job aids should be integrated into existing workflows. For instance, if everyone checks the e-mail queue at the start of the reference desk shift, that would be a good place to include information about a student assignment that is generating questions.

Delegating

Effective delegation requires good communication in order to make sure the person to whom the responsibility is assigned has the information and resources he or she needs to complete the assignment and a clear picture of the goals and parameters of the project or task. Delegation, when done right, conveys to the person receiving the assignment that he or she is trusted and empowered. In a chapter entitled "Field Guide to Mistakes Managers Make," Charles Curran and Lewis Miller (2005, 252–53) outline questions to ask in order to assess the risks that come with delegating and not delegating:

- Do we have people who can/want to grow? Can we surrender some authority, responsibility, and a little bit of glory?
- Do we believe if we want the job done correctly, we have to do it ourselves?
- Do we understand that delegation refers to the handing over of important, growth-producing tasks, not the transferring of work we hate?
- Are we at peace with the risk that sometimes delegatees, and therefore we, will err? Is it true that "Everyone in your unit will be better at something than you are?"

Team Building

In many libraries, the responsibility for coordinating services is distributed throughout the organization among teams and individuals who exercise leadership in different ways. Reference services may be led by a coordinator with few or no direct reports. Even in more hierarchical organizations, important functional and decision-making responsibilities, including oversight of specific areas or initiatives relating to reference services, may be assigned to teams, working groups, or committees. Regardless of the setting, the principles involved in building effective teams are widely applicable when working with groups as well as when delegating specific tasks and responsibilities to individuals. As Rachel Singer Gordon explains, teamwork is an essential part of "a climate that encourages collaboration, cooperation, and communication [and] allows people to use individual strengths together in pursuit of library goals" (2005, 138).

What does it take to build an effective team? Giesecke and McNeil use a definition of "team" from Jon Katzenbach and Douglas Smith (1993, 45) as "a small number of people with complementary skills who are committed to a common purpose . . . for which they hold themselves accountable" (2010, 24). They suggest the following five factors that impact team effectiveness (50–51):

- *Goals* set the direction for the group and need to be clear, specific, and shared. The team as a whole takes responsibility for achieving the goal.
- *Roles* clarify who does what, including the manager. These should be clear to all members of the team.
- *Processes* are the internal procedures that determine how the team does its work, how decisions will be made, and how the meeting should be run. Documentation of processes enables a shared understanding.
- *Relationships* in the workplace are supported by roles and processes. Teams work best when they have agreed-upon guidelines defining how different opinions and viewpoints will be addressed and how disagreements will be handled.
- *Environmental influences* are external forces that impact teamwork, including reward systems, organizational structures, resources, and policies. Managers should ensure that teams have the resources necessary to accomplish the task at hand.

Teams can be effective ways to organize and accomplish work. Teams also pose leadership challenges that leave them open to failure. Elaine Russo Martin's

(2006, 275–77) study of team effectiveness in medical libraries found that while focus group participants were uniformly positive about the use of teams in the libraries, all reported that they could name at least one problematic team at their institution. In some cases, a team leader assumed too much authority and did all the work, while in others, team leaders were uncomfortable assuming the authority given to them or cited unclear lines of authority. Participants in Martin's study emphasized the need for leaders to intervene when there was a conflict or teams were struggling, while team leaders often reported being unwilling to confront conflict with colleagues and thus risk damaging collegial relationships. Team leaders universally identified the need for more training in leadership skills and more coaching.

Sometimes the team leader, or manager, will be able to assemble a team. At other times, the team may be preexisting or assembled by administration or based on roles within the organization. Ideally, a team will be comprised of members with a complementary variety and depth of skills. This not only supports completion of the work but also team members can learn cross-functionally and from more experienced colleagues.

Successful teams have a clear purpose and articulated goals. The goals should be shared, well defined, achievable, and relevant to the organization. Inevitably, there will be multiple priorities and goals, and it is the role of the manager to provide vision to help the team in setting priorities and even changing or dropping goals.

Teams typically work in a participatory way rather than through top-down management, although that does depend on the organization. Setting the goals, roles, and processes mentioned earlier as a group can cement the team early on and also increase adherence to the guidelines. The manager or team leader still is responsible for setting a tone and maintaining awareness of both the work output of the team and team dynamics (Giesecke and McNeil 2010, 55; Trotta 2006, 55–56). As addressed throughout this chapter, communication and information flow are key managerial roles. This includes internal team communications and communication with other teams and parts of the organization.

One of the most rewarding parts of being a manager is developing people. Good managers structure the work of teams to both highlight people's skills and allow them to grow and develop skills. Celebrating the work of individuals and the work of the team encourages good work, and most people appreciate recognition of accomplishment. This recognition can be standard within an organization (employee of the month) or something created by the manager that might be more specific to the team. Celebrating employees' lives through birthdays or other life-events acknowledges them as people outside of their work role and can foster more connection between team members. An understanding of individual team member's preferences and motivations can help the manager to come up with appropriate recognition.

COMMUNICATION

Communicating up, down, and across the organization is an essential part of every reference department head or team leader's responsibilities. It is vital to be able to communicate with different groups and to be active in listening as well as sharing information and ideas. Henry Mintzberg's (1980) classic model of managerial work, based on long-term observations of managers on the job, identifies three informational roles that most managers play:

1. *Monitor*: Seek out information related to the broader organization and the user community as well as to professional developments in reference services and related areas, looking for relevant changes in the environment; pay attention to one's staff or team members' performance and well-being.
2. *Disseminator*: Serve as a conduit of information, sharing, interpreting, and integrating information of potential value to the reference department or team and colleagues.
3. *Spokesman*: Represent and speak for the reference department or team, transmitting information about plans, accomplishments and policies, and so on, to people outside the team.

These roles frame how communication and management roles intersect.

Communication with Staff

Good communication within the reference department or team helps develop staff who are fully engaged in providing service, are empowered to share ideas, and work together to solve problems. It also helps to ensure that effort is focused toward broader goals and outcomes. In the *Accidental Library Manager*, Rachel Singer Gordon quotes one respondent to a survey about effective management practices in libraries, "Managers need to share enough information with employees so that everyone understands what is happening and their place in the overall scheme of things. When employees understand the why and how of something, they are apt to do things correctly and to take ownership, responsibility for, and satisfaction from the job" (2005, 163).

Meetings

In a connected and highly scheduled world, meetings may seem unnecessary, and communicating via e-mail or some other means might appear to be a more efficient way to share information. This is especially true for reference, where finding a time for the whole group to meet can be challenging given the demands of service schedules and other commitments. If the purpose is one-way communication, for instance, when making an announcement, e-mail or a similar technology may be appropriate, but meetings actually allow for more efficient group discussion. Meetings, be they in person or online, provide a venue uniquely suited to sharing information, generating ideas, problem solving, and decision making. Regularly coming together as a group to focus on shared work and goals empowers staff and creates a positive work environment.

That said, calling a meeting just for the sake of meeting is not a productive approach, and running a good meeting requires some preparation and structure. Giesecke and McNeil (2010, 146–57) provide some excellent guidelines for running good meetings, including skills for handling problem behaviors and how to decide when a meeting is not necessary. One key to running meetings that all participants will find valuable is to focus on getting things done and making decisions. Being productive, however, can be successfully paired with a relaxed collegial atmosphere, as explained by this employee describing the weekly meetings convened by one of her best managers: "One manager I had . . . had Friday morning meetings and usually someone brought bagels . . . We'd hash out workflows, plans for the fiscal year and interdepartmental issues while enjoying a good nosh. I looked forward to these meetings, not only because of the food, but because . . . we were actually productive and felt energized and motivated to do a successful job afterward" (Gordon 2005, 164).

Small work groups or teams focused on agile work might benefit from more frequent, but less lengthy, group communication. Even groups not identified as "agile" can adapt and benefit from the shorter style of meeting. Some examples are: stand-up meetings, scrums (also called circle-ups or huddles), or even regular 15-minute coffee breaks where team members briefly check in to share progress, identify issues or next steps, and assign work priorities (Bluedorn, Turban, and Love 1999; Sutton 2012).[3] Whatever the meeting methodology, a reference team that is in the habit of working through issues together will also be better prepared for times of crisis or of major change, when open communication, trust, and the habit of working together to solve problems become even more essential.

Walking Around

Simply walking around and observing how things are functioning at the reference service point or in people's offices can be an important way to maintain awareness and stay in contact with staff. It can be an important diagnostic tool, providing an informal opportunity to work with staff to troubleshoot problems, develop a sense of how services could be improved, and what could be done differently. Doing this at least daily keeps managers in close contact with staff and the services provided.

Communication with Other Units and Partners

Managers have a responsibility to bring information in from the rest of the organization, work with other teams and departments to align efforts toward larger organizational goals, and represent the goals and needs of their group externally (Giesecke and McNeil 2010, 57). As with many areas of their work, reference managers are in the middle of communications and must manage down, up, and across the organization.

Reference managers will want to develop supportive relationships with allied departments and functions across the organization. This may include functions inside the library that are closely related to reference services, such as access services or cataloging and discovery systems, as well as partners outside the library like teachers, faculty, or community organizations that are (or can become) key partners in outreach or educational initiatives. Kay Ann Cassell and Uma Hiremath talk about "messy partnerships" becoming increasingly common in reference services, with reference playing important, but not always clearly defined, roles in areas like electronic resource management, website management, and marketing (2013, 394–97). These often involve informal partnerships with other parts of the organizations, and reference staff contributions to these areas may not be well recognized if care is not taken to make them readily apparent. Reference departments work in a variety of ways to coordinate efforts and develop shared service programs with partners inside and outside the library, including partnering with Information Technology departments to develop learning commons, with tutoring or writing services to provide integrated support for student learning, or with community organizations to provide services related to health care, small business development, or other community needs. Opportunities to develop these services often arise as a result of ongoing relationships developed with key stakeholders throughout the organization and community, nurtured through formal and informal communication around shared goals and community needs. If the decision is made to develop a formal partnership, working relationships need to be developed using the team-building techniques discussed earlier, as well as more formal mechanisms like drafting written partnership agreements (Walters and Van Gordon 2007).

Institutional and Community Stakeholders

In addition to formal reports, which are discussed later, informal conversations can be an opportunity to generate excitement, interest, and support for any new initiatives or projects related to reference services. Reference managers should look for opportunities to communicate the importance of reference services to key institutional stakeholders including higher-level managers or administrators, influential faculty or community members, and others in order to build an awareness of the ways reference services impact outcomes they care about, such as resilient communities or student success. Fostering this awareness can help ensure that needed resources are available to sustain and support reference activities. Start developing an "elevator speech," a simple, succinct, and memorable statement of what your reference service does and why key stakeholders should care. The Association for Library Service to Children (ALSC) has developed a template for crafting an effective elevator speech, as well as a longer "coffee shop conversation," as part of their Everyday Advocacy project. There are many other models and guidelines available specifically for libraries on the Web. An example from the ALSC website is illustrative: "I help kids and families unpack their curiosity at the library so that the kids can go out and change our world for the better" (Association for Library Service to Children 2014). Similarly, Christine Dettlaff (2008) outlines some key arguments for the importance of reference services targeted at administrators, including some answers to the question, "Why do we still need reference services when students can find the answers so easily using the Web?" Statements like these can be customized for higher impact by mapping them directly to the mission and strategic goals of your university, college or school, or other parent organization.

In conversations with stakeholders and community members, also listen for trends or new directions that may influence how to best grow and develop the library's reference services. Are there new strategic directions the institution is taking that create opportunities for reference-related services, like a distance education program, a shift in curriculum, or an expanded community center?

User Communities

The same sort of two-way communication that builds strong teams within the organization is equally important to foster with the community of current and potential users. Some techniques apply equally well in both environments; walking around, observing, and making the most of day-to-day interactions is just as effective for engaging with users as it is with staff. From informal approaches such as attending lectures and events and scheduling lunches and coffee meetings to more formal methods of engaging with groups such as running focus groups and surveys, the reference manger can create opportunities for himself or herself and the staff to develop relationships with the broader community of current and potential users.

Managing Conflict

> The best manager that I worked for allowed for open communication, even of difficult issues. She was open and honest and made herself available to employees to discuss whatever might come up in the workplace. (Gordon 2005, 161)

Between Staff

Conflicts inevitably arise between coworkers. Whether one is a supervisor with direct reports or a reference team leader coordinating a group of peers, it is one's responsibility to manage these conflicts. Conflict can be productive—the open discussion of divergent views can be an opportunity to generate new ideas, clarify and refine the group's shared service values, resolve underlying tensions, or reach a clearer understanding of another point of view. Conflict can also be damaging or unhealthy for individuals and the group as a whole, especially when left unaddressed. Box 7.4 outlines approaches that are commonly used to respond to conflict with an exercise for exploring which approaches are best suited to specific situations and individuals.

Interpersonal conflicts need to be addressed as soon as they surface as an issue. Unresolved conflict can continue to fester, eventually undermining the effectiveness of the department or team. Roger Fisher, William L. Ury, and Bruce Patton (2011) outline a method for getting to the root of conflicts that focuses on each person's interests rather than their positions. According to their model, people in a conflict situation tend to communicate their positions—the concrete and specific things they want. By shifting the frame to their underlying interests—the unexpressed motivation behind the position—it becomes possible to achieve the collaboration-based style of conflict resolution mentioned in Box 7.4. Just as when trying to develop a full understanding of a user's information need, using open-ended questions that encourage staff to "tell their story" helps build a clearer understanding of their underlying interests. Avoid closed-ended questions, which require a response of "yes" or "no." For example, "Do you have a good relationship with Jane?" is a closed-ended question, while "Tell me about your relationship with Jane," is open-ended. Examples of open-ended questions to use to get a better understanding of the underlying interests in a conflict include:

- What is your basic concern about . . . ?
- Could you help me understand . . . ?
- How could we fix . . . ?
- What do you want to do next?
- What have you tried before?
- How else could you do . . . ?
- How can I be of help?

Box 7.4 Activity: Responding to Conflict

The Thomas-Kilmann Conflict Mode Instrument (Thomas 1992) identifies five styles for responding to conflict:

- *Competition*: This approach focuses on gaining control and pressuring a change even at another's expense. It may be appropriate when you have to implement an unpopular decision, make a quick decision, or let others know that an issue is important to you. Repeated use can damage relationships and may lead others to use covert methods to get their needs met.
- *Collaboration*: This approach addresses conflicts as problems to be solved and looks for solutions satisfying all parties' concerns by identifying underlying concerns, testing your own assumptions, and understanding the views of others. It takes time and requires good interpersonal skills. It may be appropriate when optimal outcomes are important, and there is time available to work through the issues.
- *Compromise*: This approach seeks a mutually acceptable "middle-ground" solution that partially satisfies all parties' concerns. It may be appropriate when expediency and quick resolution is needed, but outcomes are usually suboptimal. Repeated use can lead to game playing.
- *Avoidance*: This approach tries to avoid, ignore, or withdraw from conflict. It may be appropriate when you need more time to decide how to respond, confrontation might hurt a relationship or be damaging to you personally, or there is little chance of satisfying your needs. The style may be perceived as not caring enough to engage, and repeated use allows conflict to simmer, usually resulting in anger, resentment, or a negative outburst.
- *Accommodation*: This approach involves setting aside your own needs to keep the peace and preserve relationships. It can result in a false solution, and accommodators who harbor resentments may come to play the role of complainers, saboteurs, or martyrs. This style may be appropriate when you realize you are wrong or you want to minimize losses. Used frequently, accommodation can result in reduced creativity and increased power imbalances.

None of these is inherently right or wrong, but a particular style might be inappropriate for a given conflict and, in some more extreme cases, result in a situation quickly spiraling out of control. Most people have one or more styles that they feel more comfortable using or that feel more natural. Becoming comfortable responding with a range of styles and being intentional about choosing what response style to deploy in a given situation can be a powerful tool.

Questions for Reflection and Discussion:

1. What style do you find is most natural for you?
2. What style do you think would be most effective for resolving a difference with another manager over allocation of an open office?
3. Is there a style that you might choose as most appropriate to handle a conflict with a library user?

Keep in mind that different styles are appropriate not only to the nature of the conflict but also to the organizational culture and the individuals involved, so these are not questions with one right answer but are a matter of preference and meant to generate thought and discussion.

Open-ended questions often elicit ideas on the specific steps all parties need to take to resolve the current conflict and prevent recurrences, including the ways one can be of help. Gordon (2005) also provides practical advice for novice managers on how to resolve conflict as well as ways to distinguish between one-time conflicts and long-running arguments or patterns of destructive behavior, and Barbara B. Moran, Robert D. Stueart, and Claudia J. Morner (2013) outline some additional techniques and approaches to conflict management.

Upset Users

All reference staff should be trained and ready to deal effectively with users who become upset, following the strategies discussed in Chapter 3, but managers will often need to help resolve more difficult cases, and staff should know that they can make this referral. Reference managers will also want to be aware of any complaints or expressions of dissatisfaction with services so that they can monitor for any patterns that suggest a service adjustment might be needed and identify frustration points that could be fixed systemically.

Staff should feel comfortable contacting managers to see whether they are available to respond immediately and know how and when to call on higher levels of the administration. Frequently, simply being offered the opportunity to talk to the person in charge can itself help defuse the situation when a patron becomes upset. The offer to bring a manager into the conversation (or another colleague, if the manager is not available) signals to the person that he or she is being heard and that the issue or frustrations have been recognized as being important enough to be referred up.

When called in to help resolve a situation with an upset user, be careful not to undermine the competence or authority of any other staff or departments. Casting blame does not help solve the problem, and the priority should be to present a positive view of the library as a whole. If exceptions are made to standard practice or policy, explain that the exception is contingent upon the particular situation at hand (e.g., "We don't normally print things for people, but since I already have this page up on the screen . . ."). This helps reduce the expectation that this will be repeated in the future and helps clarify that the exception is being made due to the circumstances rather than in response to the person becoming upset. For additional techniques for handling upset patrons, see the strategies in Chapter 3, as well as Michelynn McKnight (2010), who outlines a process of conducting a "complaint interview" following the techniques of the classic reference interview that is focused on understanding and solving the patron's problem; Marcia Trotta (2006), who outlines techniques for managing and defusing heightened emotions; and G. Edward Evans and Thomas L. Carter (2009), who summarize best practices from a range of sources.

Sometimes situations involving angry or frustrated users simply cannot be resolved, even with the most adept handling of the situation. Anger or frustration may escalate into abusive or threatening behavior. The safety and security of library staff and users is always paramount, and security personnel should be called before the situation escalates further. Most libraries or their home institutions will have policies defining inappropriate patron conduct that can serve as a guideline for determining when behavior crosses this line. If such a policy is not in place, work with appropriate people to develop one drawing on the policy development resources described later in this chapter.

BUDGETING AND FINANCIAL MANAGEMENT

Reference managers may or may not have direct oversight of specific budgets other than the funds allocated for materials or collections, covered in Chapter 13. This section will therefore be limited to a brief overview of some key concepts related to managing expenditures, resources for learning more about budgeting and financial management, and developing budget requests for specific projects or grants.

Monitoring Budgets

Each library will have its own systems for reporting on budgets, and practice will vary on what costs (salaries, supplies, equipment, etc.) are assigned to the department and program and what is paid centrally. Reference managers will most likely be responsible for monitoring monthly reconciliation reports showing balances for what funds have been expended, encumbered (i.e., committed but not yet paid, e.g., items on order), or remain available. Knowing how to read and interpret these reports is essential, so do not hesitate to ask other managers or the library's budget office for assistance. If the library does not provide reports, or the standard reports do not provide the detail needed, fund managers and supervisors will need to develop their own internal systems to track funds. Microsoft Excel spreadsheets can be used to track specific expenses, as well as to work with figures to calculate percentages or create graphs. Managers can delegate responsibility to someone else in the department or team familiar with the software, but as the person responsible for budgetary oversight, managers will want to be sure to review and understand any reports created by others.

Why does this matter? As Giesecke and McNeil explain, "it is crucial to have accurate records and anticipate change" (2010, 140) as this will allow the reference manager to provide advice to senior management and respond proactively in case of budget cuts. A manager who understands the budget and knows what funds are still available will have the flexibility to take advantage of opportunities that may arise, like hiring an hourly employee for a special project or buying equipment with funds left over near the end of the year.

Making Special Purchases

When planning a purchase or negotiating a license, such as for a new chat software, it is important to consult with the budget office early in the process. There may be local procurement guidelines that need to be considered or, in government institutions, regulations that stipulate rules governing contact with vendors. Knowing about these procedures and rules sooner than later saves everyone's time.

Developing Budget Requests

Special projects and new initiatives often require special funding or at least pose an opportunity to request nonrecurring money or apply for a grant. Requests should include a convincing statement of need, clearly defined goals, and objectives that highlight the impact the project will have on the target user community; a plan for evaluating the outcomes; an accounting of any existing resources that will be leveraged to support the project; and a budget based on sound estimates of the costs, including staff time, equipment, and any licensing or contractual fees. Granting agencies will have specific requirements and guidelines, so be sure to follow them closely and consider seeking out examples of successful requests as a model. Blanche Woolls, Ann C. Weeks, and Sharon Coatney (2014, 184–91) provide a step-by-step guide to developing proposals to fund new programs, and M. Kathleen Kern (2009) provides a useful overview of the process of estimating both the budget (new allocations) and costs (total costs, including existing staff time that may be reallocated) needed to support new services.

Evaluating Services

Ongoing service evaluation is a fundamental part of stewarding resources and making sure that staff time and other resources are being allocated toward services that are meaningful to users and that have the outcomes that were intended. Service evaluation and assessment can also play an important role in demonstrating the value and impact of reference services to key stakeholders, including administrators and community leaders who make decisions about allocating the funding to support reference services. The evaluation and assessment of reference services, covered in depth in Chapter 8, is an important part of the reference manager's toolkit.

SPACE PLANNING

Most reference managers have some degree of responsibility for or influence on both staff and user spaces. For staff spaces, this involves making sure that the equipment and furniture needed to complete their work is available and may also include making decisions about space and office assignments. Giesecke and McNeil recommend that supervisors "begin by examining their employee's work area and try to see the space from the point of view of the employee" (2010, 140).

Reference managers may also have an opportunity to be involved in space planning for their service points as well as for surrounding user spaces. See Chapter 6 for ideas on how to make the most of these opportunities to ensure that service points are placed in the flow of the users and that any redesign of service points is flexible enough to be adapted to evolving models of service delivery.

POLICIES

Many, but not all, libraries find it useful to develop a general reference service policy that provides an overarching statement of purpose, including goals and objectives, as well as a broad strategy that will be followed to reach those goals and objectives (Katz 2002, 184–86). These policies help situate the reference services within the broader institutional mission, clarify the primary audiences served by the service, establish service priorities, let users know what they can expect from the library, and serve as a touchstone for staff. The best service policies are grounded in a shared philosophy of service and stem from a thoughtful consideration of what reference means at that institution (Kern 2009, 32).

Professional guidelines and standards provide invaluable guidance when developing policy and can support staff if a policy is challenged. The Madison Public

Library's "Reference Assistance Policy," for instance, specifically cites both state statutes regarding the confidentiality of library records and the ALA Code of Ethics (Madison Public Library Board 2001). Professional principles should inform all policies developed for reference services, and care should be taken to ensure that policies align with librarians' core values. Figure 7.1 illustrates the many factors that contribute to reference service policies, including user needs, institutional mission, legal requirements, institutional regulations, and available resources, as well as professional standards and ethics.

In addition to an overarching reference service policy, reference managers may be involved in creating policies regarding new modes of service delivery, such as virtual reference services, geared either to the public or staff (or in some cases, both), in order to clarify the scope of the service. Specific policies can help govern

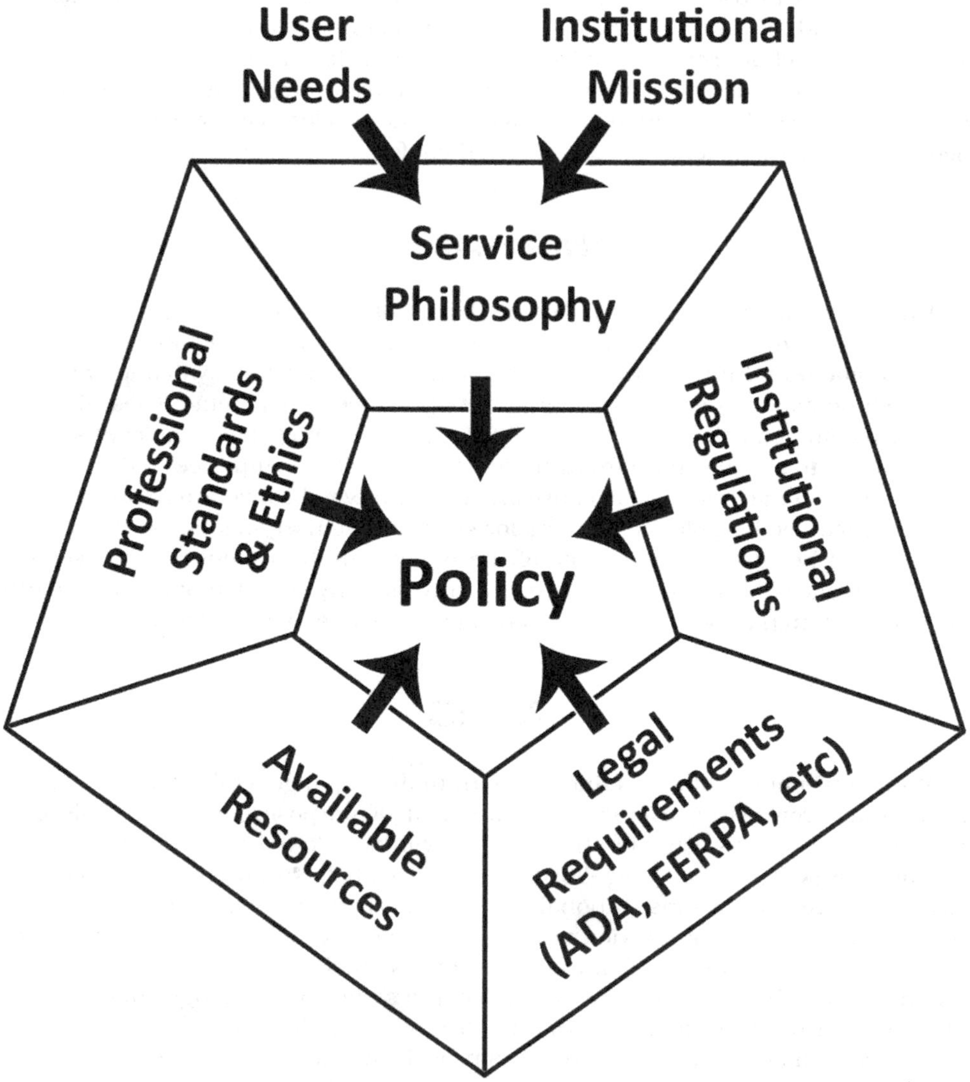

FIGURE 7.1 Factors that shape reference policy development

access to limited resources, like Internet use, in the interest of making sure that all have equal access to high-demand services. Reference managers may also be involved in the development or revision of policies concerning general customer service issues, like patron behavior or unattended children. Please see the list of Suggested Readings for resources on writing policy.

Box 7.5 Policy in Action: Balancing Principles, Politics, and the Service Imperative

Scenario 1

A university library has a reference service policy that prioritizes service to students, faculty, and staff of the university, as well as the broader community of scholars and researchers utilizing unique or less commonly held materials in their collection. They regularly receive questions from librarians and library school students not affiliated with their university requesting help cataloging and classifying books.

Questions for Reflection and Discussion:

1. Are there ways to provide a helpful response without diverting staff time away from the core service mission?
2. What new policy might you write that acknowledged the library-wide policy but provides a way for reference staff to connect unaffiliated users with high-quality freely available resources for cataloging?
3. Who would you consult with in developing this policy?

Scenario 2

The high school library reference desk receives a request for instructions for making a bomb from a teenage boy who says he is working on a project for a class.

Questions for Reflection and Discussion:

1. How would you use policy to provide guidance to staff about responding to such inquiries?
2. Would your policy include reporting this to others, for example, a counselor or security? Does this change if you are at a public library rather than in a school setting?
3. How do broad issues like intellectual freedom and confidentiality of patron records factor into local policy development?

Scenario 3

Patrons in a public library complain about a man who is viewing pornography at a computer that they passed by on the way to the children's area.

Questions for Reflection and Discussion:

1. If no policy existed at your library, how would you tell staff to respond to this situation?
2. How would you explain your position on what the policy should be to your director and emphasize the need for a policy? Is this policy the responsibility of the director or of the reference manager?
3. What factors might you consider in developing a policy that balances open access to information with maintaining a pleasant environment for library users and staff?

Sandra Nelson and June Garcia note that one of the primary functions of policies is to provide a mechanism for library managers and staff to translate the library's service priorities into actions (2003, 8). Policies can indeed provide an invaluable guide to action, but as with all guides, they provide only a sense of direction and are not an inviolable set of rules. As indicated in Chapter 9, managers and staff should be prepared for likely challenges and exceptions to policies. Staff should be given explicit guidance on when rules can be modified to help users and who is empowered to make decisions about exceptions (e.g., permanent staff may be able to make exceptions within certain guidelines, but not student staff). Generally, policies will be modified in the interest of providing more or better service. Be sure to be clear that exceptions are being made in response to the particular situation at hand (e.g., "We don't usually retrieve books for visiting scholars, but since we have staff available and your time on campus is so brief, we'll be able to have the book ready for you at the desk when you stop in tomorrow").

Even with the best-written policy and a clear sense of service priorities, things can get muddy on the ground. There are times when professional judgment will be needed. Box 7.5 provides a few such examples.

DEVELOPING MANAGEMENT AND LEADERSHIP SKILLS

Drawing on 30 years of experience managing public and academic libraries, teaching management courses, and observing colleagues, J. Robert Verbesy concludes: "Managing people is an art. . . . You can only learn it well by carefully observing, by doing, making errors, learning from those errors, mending your ways, picking the brains of successful experienced managers, and thereby incrementally improving" (2009, 192). Indeed, the nuances will come with experience, but time and experience are complemented by other modes of learning. As Evans and Alire contend, "Reading about management, taking a course, or attending some workshops on the subject improves your chances of being better at it. . . . Course work and workshops will not ensure you will be a good manager, but these tools can improve your managerial skills" (2013, 4–5). Some resources for building skills as a reference manager are provided in Box 7.6.

Build a Support Network

New managers, and indeed all managers, should build a network of peers, colleagues, and mentors from whom they can get advice and inspiration and with whom they can share experiences and ideas. Participating in professional associations and attending workshops and leadership or management training institutes can be a way to further build this network. Listservs, blogs, and other social media help build a virtual network. These sources for professional development serve a dual purpose by providing structured learning opportunities and a space for informal learning.

Other Libraries

Surfing the websites of other libraries, both similar and different, as well as other service organizations and businesses, can suggest ideas and models. When contacted, libraries may share their internal policies, procedures, annual reports,

Box 7.6 Professional Development Resources for Library Managers

Professional Associations

Library Leadership & Management Association (LLAMA): LLAMA is a division of ALA focused on advancing outstanding leadership and management practices and developing excellence in current and aspiring library leaders. LLAMA brings together librarians from all types of libraries.

Reference and User Services Association (RUSA): RUSA provides an excellent venue for connecting with others involved in the provision of reference services in every type of library. The Reference Services Section of RUSA includes a Management of Reference committee.

State and regional library associations are a good way to network with those close geographically. Many offer conferences or workshops that can be attended without lengthy travel, and some offer online webinars as well.

Listservs

Joining the organizations listed earlier will give you membership on their listservs, and some may allow nonmembers to join the list. Another list you may want to join:

> *LibRef-L*: This discussion list deals with issues in reference services and is a good place to monitor issues and trends and seek information and advice.

Institutes and Webinars

Numerous training institutes and workshops are available for library leaders. The following list identifies nationally available opportunities geared toward managers rather than administrators. Many state libraries or regional or state library organizations offer workshops or multiday institutes for managers, sometimes focused on a specific type of library, such as the Statewide Public Library Management Institute sponsored by the Illinois State Library.

WebJunction: Sponsored by OCLC, this "learning place for libraries" hosts free webinars and courses related to library technology, management, and services. A topically organized archive of past sessions, along with links to related resources, supports self-directed learning on demand.

TRLN Management Academy: This is an experiential learning program focusing on preparing mid-level academic library managers to manage complex and diverse resources with emphasis on the sound management of staff, budgets, and technology.

or other documentation. Most librarians are pleased to share this information, and it can be another way to build a professional network as well as helping with an immediate need for managerial information.

Books and Journals

Reference managers should also keep up with journals specific to the type of library in which they work, such as *portal: Libraries and the Academy*, *Public Libraries*, or *School Library Research*, as well as the standard reference journals like *Reference Services Review*, *Reference & User Services Quarterly* (RUSQ), and *The Reference Librarian*. Management-specific journals such as *Library Administration and Management*, *Library Management*, *Journal of Library Administration*, and *The Bottom Line* explore topics of interest to library managers. Professional trade publications like *American Libraries* and *Library Journal* provide an overview of developments and emerging topics across the profession. The books listed in the Suggested Readings section at the end of the chapter will also be useful to both new and experienced managers.

CONCLUSION

> Management means making things happen, and the more people know how to make things happen, the more successful the library as a whole will be. (Applegate 2010, 4)

Reference services, in all their various forms and "messy partnerships" (Cassell and Hiremath 2013, 394), are a pivotal place where users and librarians engage together in the process of discovery, and reference managers help ensure that libraries continue to meet users when, where, and how services are needed. Managing reference services is an awesome responsibility, in all senses of that word. Reference managers play a central role in their organizations, with responsibility for making decisions that help shape the future of the services that provide personalized guidance in an increasingly complex information landscape. Growing into this role—developing skills as a manager and an individual voice as a leader—is a process that unfolds over time and deepens with experience. Whether a reference manager by design or accident, embrace the role, and you will learn and grow with every new challenge and opportunity.

NOTES

1. The views expressed are the author's own and do not reflect the official policy or position of the National Defense University, Department of Defense, or the U.S. Government.
2. See the introductory chapter in Rachel Singer Gordon (2005) for an overview of the many paths to "accidentally" becoming a library manager, drawn from stories shared by respondents to her 2003 survey of library managers.
3. "How-to" approaches are provided by Verne Harnish (2013) and Joseph Yip (2011).

REFERENCES

ACRL Research Planning and Review Committee. 2014. "Top Trends in Academic Libraries." *College & Research Libraries News* 75 (6): 294–302.

Adrain, Lorne A. 1997. *The Most Important Thing I Know: Life Lessons from Colin Powell, Stephen Covey, Maya Angeou and Over 75 Other Eminent Individuals*, 60–61. New York: Cader Books.

Applegate, Rachel. 2010. *Managing the Small College Library*. Santa Barbara, CA: Libraries Unlimited.

Association for Library Service to Children. 2014. "Elevator Speech." American Library Association. http://www.ala.org/everyday-advocacy/speak-out/elevator-speech.

Bennis, Warren G., and Burt Nanus. 2007. *Leaders: Strategies for Taking Charge.* New York: HarperCollins.

Bluedorn, Allen C., Daniel B. Turban, and Mary Sue Love. 1999. "The Effects of Stand-Up and Sit-Down Meeting Formats on Meeting Outcomes." *Journal of Applied Psychology* 84 (2): 277–85.

Campbell, Jerry D. 1992. "Shaking the Conceptual Foundations of Reference: A Perspective." *Reference Services Review* 20 (4): 29–36.

Carlson, Scott. 2007. "Are Reference Desks Dying Out? Librarians Struggle to Redefine—and in Some Cases Eliminate—the Venerable Institution." *The Reference Librarian* 48 (2): 25–30.

Cassell, Kay Ann, and Uma Hiremath. 2013. *Reference and Information Services: An Introduction.* 3rd ed. New York: Neal-Schuman.

Curran, Charles, and Lewis Miller. 2005. *Guide to Library and Information Agency Management.* Lanham, MD: Scarecrow Press.

Dettlaff, Christine. 2008. "Managing to Keep Academic Reference Service." In *Defining Relevancy: Managing the New Academic Library,* edited by Janet McNeil Hurlbert, 161–69. Westport, CT: Libraries Unlimited.

DiSC Profile. 2015. Personality Profile Solutions, LLC. https://www.discprofile.com/.

Evans, G. Edward, and Camile Alire. 2013. *Management Basics for Information Professionals.* 3rd ed. New York: Neal-Schuman.

Evans, G. Edward, and Thomas L. Carter. 2009. *Introduction to Library Public Services.* 7th ed. Westport, CT: Libraries Unlimited.

Fisher, Roger, William L. Ury, and Bruce Patton. 2011. *Getting to Yes: Negotiating Agreement without Giving In.* New York: Penguin.

Gibson, Craig, and Meris Mandernach. 2013. "Reference Service at an Inflection Point: Transformations in Academic Libraries." In *Imagine, Innovate, Inspire: The Proceedings of the ACRL 2013 Conference in Indianapolis, Indiana, April 10–13, 2013,* edited by Dawn M. Mueller, 491–99. Chicago: ACRL.

Giesecke, Joan, and Beth McNeil. 1999. "Core Competencies and the Learning Organization." *Library Administration and Management* 13 (Summer): 158–66.

Giesecke, Joan, and Beth McNeil. 2010. *Fundamentals of Library Supervision.* 2nd ed. Chicago: American Library Association.

Gordon, Rachel Singer. 2005. *The Accidental Library Manger.* Medford, NJ: Information Today.

Gulick, Luther, and Lyndall Urwick. 1937. *Papers on the Science of Administration.* New York: Institute of Public Administration, Columbia University.

Harnish, Verne. 2013. "How Do You Keep Your Team Focused?" *Fortune.* December 13. http://fortune.com/2013/12/16/how-do-you-keep-your-team-focused/.

Katz, William A. 2002. *Introduction to Reference Work.* 8th ed., 2 vols. New York: McGraw-Hill.

Katzenbach, Jon, and Douglas Smith. 1993. *The Wisdom of Teams.* Boston: Harvard Business School Press.

Kelley, Michael. 2011. "Geeks Are the Future: A Program in Ann Arbor, MI, Argues for a Resource Shift toward IT." *Library Journal,* April 26. http://lj.libraryjournal.com/2011/04/technology/geeks-are-the-future-a-program-in-ann-arbor-mi-argues-for-a-resource-shift-toward-it/#.

Kern, M. Kathleen. 2009. *Virtual Reference Best Practices: Tailoring Services to Your Library.* Chicago: American Library Association.

Kotter, John. P. 1990a. *A Force for Change: How Leadership Differs from Management.* New York: Free Press.

Kotter, John. P. 1990b. "What Leaders Really Do." *Harvard Business Review* 68 (3): 103–11.

Library Leadership and Management Association. http://www.ala.org/llama/.

LibRef-L. https://listserv.kent.edu/cgi-bin/wa.exe?A0=LIBREF-L.

Madison Public Library Board. 2001. "Reference Assistance Policy." http://www.madisonpubliclibrary.org/policies/reference-assistance.

Martin, Elaine Russo. 2006. "Team Effectiveness in Academic Medical Libraries: A Multiple Case Study." *Journal of the Medical Library Association* 94 (3): 271–78.

McKnight, Michelynn. 2010. *The Agile Librarian's Guide to Thriving in Any Institution*. Santa Barbara, CA: Libraries Unlimited.

Mintzberg, Henry. 1980. *The Nature of Managerial Work*. New York: Harper & Row.

Moran, Barbara B., Robert D. Stueart, and Claudia J. Morner. 2013. *Library and Information Center Management*. 8th ed. Santa Barbara, CA: Libraries Unlimited.

Murphy, Sarah Anne. 2011. *The Librarian as Information Consultant: Transforming Reference for the Information Age*. Chicago: American Library Association.

Myers, Isabel Briggs, and Katharine Cook Briggs. 2009. *Myers-Briggs Type Indicator® Assessment (Form M)*. CPP, Inc. https://www.cpp.com/products/mbti/index.aspx.

Nelson, Sandra, and June Garcia. 2003. *Creating Policies for Results: From Chaos to Clarity*. Chicago: American Library Association.

O'Gorman, Jack, and Barry Trott. 2009. "What Will Become of Reference in Academic and Public Libraries?" *Journal of Library Administration* 49 (4): 327–39.

Olver, Lynne. 2011. "So You're the New Director? Twelve Points to Help You Survive the First Year." *Public Libraries* 50 (2): 6–7.

Pew Research Center. http://www.pewinternet.org/.

Radford, Marie L., ed. 2012. *Leading the Reference Renaissance: Today's Ideas for Tomorrow's Cutting-Edge Services*. New York: Neal-Schuman.

Ranganathan, Sarada. R. 1931. *The Five Laws of Library Science*. Madras, India: The Madras Library Association.

Reference and User Services Association. http://www.ala.org/rusa/.

Reid, Ian. 2014. "The 2013 Public Library Data Service Statistical Report: Characteristics and Trends." *Public Libraries*, March/April. http://publiclibrariesonline.org/2014/05/2013-plds/.

Saunders, Laura, Lillian Rozaklis, and Eileen G. Abels. 2014. *Repositioning Reference: New Methods and New Services for a New Age*. Lanham, MD: Rowman & Littlefield.

Sheff, David. 1985. "Playboy Interview: Steve Jobs." *Playboy*. February. http://longform.org/stories/playboy-interview-steve-jobs.

Shepstone, Carol, and Lyn Currie. 2008. "Transforming the Academic Library: Creating an Organizational Culture That Fosters Staff Success." *The Journal of Academic Librarianship* 34 (4): 358–68.

Statewide Public Library Management Institute. Illinois State Library. http://www.cyberdriveillinois.com/departments/library/libraries/splmi.html.

Steiner, Sarah K., and M. Leslie Madden. 2008. *The Desk and Beyond: Next Generation Reference Services*. Chicago: Association of College and Research Libraries.

Sutton, Bob. 2012. "The Virtues of Standing Up in Meetings and Elsewhere." *Work Matters*. April 3. http://bobsutton.typepad.com/my_weblog/2012/04/the-virtues-of-standing-up-in-meetings-and-elsewhere.html.

Thomas, Kenneth W. 1992. "Conflict and Conflict Management: Reflections and Update." *Journal of Organizational Behavior* 13 (3): 265–74.

Todorinova, Lily, Andy Huse, Barbara Lewis, and Matt Torrence. 2011. "Making Decisions: Using Electronic Data Collection to Re-Envision Reference Services at the USF Tampa Libraries." *Public Services Quarterly* 7 (1–2): 34–48.

TRLN Management Academy. http://www.trln.org/academy2015/.

Trotta, Marcia. 2006. *Supervising Staff: A How-To-Do-It Manual for Librarians.* New York: Neal-Schuman.

Tyckoson, David A. 2011. "Issues and Trends in the Management of Reference Services: A Historical Perspective." *Journal of Library Administration* 51 (3): 259–78.

Tyckoson, David A., and John G. Dove, eds. 2015. *Reimagining Reference in the 21st Century.* West Lafayette, IN: Purdue University Press.

Unaeze, Felix E. 2003. "Leadership or Management: Expectations for Head of Reference Services in Academic Libraries." *The Reference Librarian* 39 (81): 105–17.

Verbesy, J. Robert. 2009. "What I've Learned from 30 Years of Managing Libraries." *Catholic Library World* 79 (3): 192–94.

Walters, Carolyn Mary, and Elizabeth Ann Van Gordon. 2007. "Get It in Writing: MOUs and Library/IT Partnerships." *Reference Services Review* 35 (3): 388–94.

Ward, David, and Eric Phetteplace. 2012 "Staffing by Design: A Methodology for Staffing Reference." *Public Services Quarterly* 8 (3): 193–207.

WebJunction. https://www.webjunction.org/.

Willmore, Joe. 2006. *Job Aids Basics: A Complete How-To Guide to Help You Understand Basic Principles and Techniques, Create and Use Job Aids Effectively, Enable Top Performance.* Alexandria, VA: ASTD Press.

Woolls, Blanche, Ann C. Weeks, and Sharon Coatney. 2014. *The School Library Manager.* 5th ed. Westport, CT: Libraries Unlimited.

Yip, Joseph. 2011. "It's Not Just Standing Up: Patterns for Daily Standup Meetings." *Martin Fowler.* August 29. http://martinfowler.com/articles/itsNotJustStandingUp.html.

Zabel, Diane. 2007. "A Reference Renaissance." *Reference & User Services Quarterly* 47 (January): 108–10.

Zabel, Diane, ed. 2011. *Reference Reborn: Breathing New Life into Public Services Librarianship.* Santa Barbara, CA: Libraries Unlimited.

SUGGESTED READINGS

Bryson, Jo. 2006. *Managing Information Services: A Transformational Approach.* Aldershot, England: Ashgate.

British author Bryson focuses on transformational management and the role of the information manager in supporting the learning organization and institutional change. The tone is corporate, but the points are well taken in any library context where library managers must have a vision that communicates their services as vital in a broader institutional environment.

Evans, G. Edward, and Camile Alire. 2013. *Management Basics for Information Professionals.* 3rd ed. New York: Neal-Schuman.

Evans and Alire provide a good balance between practicalities of hands-on management and the broader philosophical and professional issues, further supplemented with sidebars highlighting the real-life experiences of the authors and an advisory board. The chapter on "Managing Money" is a good guide to understanding library-wide budgeting processes and cycles.

Evans, G. Edward, and Thomas L. Carter. 2009. *Introduction to Library Public Services.* 7th ed. Westport, CT: Libraries Unlimited.

This textbook covering all aspects of public services librarianship includes an extensive discussion of staffing, including working with different categories of staff, hiring and recruitment, training, retention, and performance appraisals. The chapter on "Reference Services" includes a brief discussion of the administration of reference services.

Giesecke, Joan, and Beth McNeil. 2010. *Fundamentals of Library Supervision.* 2nd ed. Chicago: American Library Association.

This book provides a practical introduction to the issues and strategies of library supervision in all areas of library work. The emphasis is on building supervisory skills and in turn creating a better working environment with motivated and productive staff. New managers in particular will find this work approachable and helpful with concrete suggestions.

Gordon, Rachel Singer. 2005. *The Accidental Library Manger.* Medford, NJ: Information Today.

Gordon provides advice and inspiration for librarians who did not plan to become managers, but her book will be equally useful to those who are intentionally preparing for this role. In addition to drawing on her own experience and the literature, Gordon interweaves results of a survey of managers and employees that elicited real-life perspectives on the best and worst approaches to management.

Kern, M. Kathleen. 2009. *Virtual Reference Best Practices: Tailoring Services to Your Library.* Chicago: American Library Association.

In the chapter on "Policies: Setting Expectations of Who, When, and What," Kern outlines questions that should guide the development of virtual reference policies, many of which are applicable to reference service policies more generally.

McKnight, Michelynn. 2010. *The Agile Librarian's Guide to Thriving in Any Institution.* Santa Barbara, CA: Libraries Unlimited.

Addressing librarians at all stages of their careers who want to develop skills and practices that will allow them to effectively demonstrate their worth, McKnight emphasizes evidence-based decision making as well as strategies for communicating effectively, expanding influence, marketing, setting priorities, and managing time.

Mid-Hudson Library System. 2015. "Policies." Accessed June 19. http://midhudson.org/topics/director-resources/policies/.

Developed for use by public library directors and library boards, this Web guide includes excellent tips on writing and reviewing policies and testing whether a policy is enforceable, as well as links to example policies.

Moran, Barbara B., Robert D. Stueart, and Claudia J. Morner. 2013. *Library and Information Center Management.* 8th ed. Santa Barbara, CA: Libraries Unlimited.

This is an exhaustive text with an emphasis on the fundamentals of management processes. The chapter on "Fiscal Responsibility and Control" provides a useful overview of the types of library budgets and budgeting processes, along with examples, statements, and reports.

Nelson, Sandra, and June Garcia. 2003. *Creating Policies for Results: From Chaos to Clarity.* Chicago: American Library Association.

This guide to creating new polices or systematically reviewing existing policies includes specific questions to address when developing various types of policies.

Sarkodie-Mensah, Kwasi, ed. 2003. *Managing the Twenty-First Century Reference Department: Challenges and Prospects.* Binghamton, NY: Haworth Information Press. Also published in 2003 as *The Reference Librarian* 39 (81).

This special issue of *The Reference Librarian,* simultaneously published as an edited volume, brings together articles focusing on core competencies, management and leadership approaches, supervision, and training for reference managers. While uneven in quality and scope, the collection provides an overview of issues in reference management.

Wisconsin Department of Public Instruction. 2015. "Wisconsin Public Library Policy Resources." Accessed June 19. http://pld.dpi.wi.gov/pld_policies.

This website includes guides to developing policies as well as links to policies used by public libraries in Wisconsin. The links are organized both by library and by type of policy, such as "Behavior" and "Reference/Information Services."

Woolls, Blanche, Ann C. Weeks, and Sharon Coatney. 2014. *The School Library Manager*. 5th ed. Santa Barbara, CA: Libraries Unlimited.
A comprehensive and easy-to-follow overview of everything the school library manager needs to know, as well as some solid practical advice that would be useful for reference managers in other contexts. The chapter on "Managing the Budget" is particularly noteworthy, with guidelines for writing proposals to expand programs and examples of specifications for equipment requests.

Chapter 8

Evaluation and Assessment of Reference Services

Laura Saunders

INTRODUCTION

Evaluation and assessment refer to processes by which librarians gather and analyze data in order to measure things like the quality of resources and services, customer satisfaction, or progress toward goals. As this book demonstrates, reference librarians engage in a wide range of activities and provide a host of services and resources to support their users' information needs, all of which can and should be evaluated and assessed. Through a variety of techniques, reference librarians can evaluate the effectiveness and quality of their services and resources as well as the satisfaction level of users, and assess progress toward goals and the impact of services. Evaluation and assessment are both linked to accountability, or the process of providing stakeholders with evidence of quality, improvement, and progress toward mission and goals.

While the terms are often used interchangeably, evaluation and assessment are "separate but connected concepts and processes" (Hernon, Dugan, and Nitecki 2011, 2). Evaluation involves "identifying and collecting data about specific services or activities, establishing criteria by which their success can be judged, and determining the quality of the service or activity and the extent to which the service or activity is economically efficient and accomplishes stated goals and objectives" (Hernon and Schwartz 2012, 79). Evaluation is a managerial activity and can have political implications, as managers can use evaluation data to make decisions about allocation of staff and resources. Assessment, on the other hand, refers to a process of measuring progress toward a specific outcome or goal. While often associated with measuring learning, assessment is "any activities that seek to measure the library's impact on teaching, learning, and research, as well as initiatives that seek to identify user needs or gauge user perceptions or satisfaction. The overall goal is data-based and user-centered continuous improvement of library collections and services" (Ryan 2006, 78). Assessment centers on understanding the current state and impact of a program or service and providing feedback for improvement, while evaluation engages in measurement for the purpose of judging a program or service and determining its overall value or quality (Starr 2014). In an era of increased accountability, when stakeholders are demanding that institutions provide evidence of their value and accomplishment of mission and goals, it is crucial for librarians to engage in both evaluation and assessment in order to demonstrate their contribution to their communities.

Box 8.1 Definitions

Evaluation is the process of determining the quality of a library's collections or services or the level of patron satisfaction with those collections or services; evaluation asks questions like "Does the library have appropriate print and online resources to answer the majority of patron inquiries?" and "Are patrons satisfied with the service they receive at the circulation desk?"

Assessment is the process of measuring the impact of a library's services and educational programs; assessment asks questions like "How has the library's new outreach program improved access to healthcare information?" and "After attending a workshop on resume writing, are participants using action verbs to describe their past work experience?"

Evidence-based librarianship involves incorporating research data and evidence into professional practice in order to make informed decisions; evidence-based practice asks questions like "What are best practices for providing virtual reference services?" and "How might the latest research on undergraduates' information literacy skills inform changes to the library's instruction program?"

Questions for Reflection and Discussion:

1. As a student, you may have read studies that librarians have undertaken to learn about and improve library services. Think of one such article. Would you characterize the study as evaluation or assessment? Why? How were the results used to improve services to patrons or the efficiency of library operations?
2. Think about the type of library or information center you would like to work in. What programs and services are typically offered? How could librarians evaluate the quality of these services? How could the library assess the impact of those programs or services?
3. Think about a library and information science research article you have read (or try finding a new one) and examine the findings of the study. How might the librarians involved in the study use the findings to improve services and programs? Think about a library or information center with which you are familiar. Are the results of this study applicable to that setting? If you were director of that library, how might you use these findings to inform your own practice?
4. Imagine you have been hired as manager of a large reference department. Before making any major decisions, you would like to learn more about the department, and its staff and services. What kinds of questions might you ask? Try formulating two evaluation questions and two assessment questions that would help you to gain a better understanding of the overall quality and impact of the department. How might you go about gathering evidence and data to answer these questions?

In addition to providing proof of performance, evaluation and assessment underpin evidence-based practice. Evolving from the health sciences field, evidence-based practice entails using data to inform decision making. In library science, evidence-based practice is described as "a means to improve the profession of librarianship by asking questions as well as finding, critically appraising and incorporating research evidence from library science (as well as other disciplines) into daily practice. It also involves encouraging librarians to conduct high quality qualitative and quantitative research" (Crumley and Koufogiannakis 2002, 62). By conducting research, including engaging in evaluation and assessment, librarians can gather the kind of data necessary to make good decisions regarding their programs and services. If they share their findings, they can provide colleagues at other institutions with information for evidence-based practice as well. Box 8.1 provides brief definitions of evaluation, assessment, and evidence-based practice.

This chapter examines the concepts of evaluation and assessment as applied specifically to reference services. It begins with a general overview of evaluation and assessment practices and trends, followed by specific applications to reference services. The focus of this chapter is on methods for evaluating face-to-face and virtual reference services. Other chapters will examine evaluation and assessment in relation to related areas such as instruction and collection development. For ease of reading, this chapter will use the terms "evaluation" and "assessment" interchangeably, since the models and methods discussed can be applied to both activities.

WHY ARE EVALUATION AND ASSESSMENT IMPORTANT?

The goal of evaluation research is to better understand the library's communities and services and to make informed decisions to continuously improve those services (Oakleaf 2010). Too often, librarians rely on anecdotal evidence. While it is true that, as frontline service providers, reference librarians interact with patrons on a daily basis and should have a sense of their patrons' opinions and perceptions of services, that sense is simply not the same as hard data. Only when librarians systematically ask for and collect feedback can they be sure that they understand the wants and needs of their community and the impact library services and programs have on that community. By engaging in evaluation and assessment research, librarians can produce the data needed to guide their decisions, continue to improve services and programs, and provide evidence of the library's value to stakeholders.

At one time, the library was the only option for most people to access information. Currently, the Internet, along with smartphones and other mobile devices, has made vast amounts of information instantly accessible. Patrons have many other options for accessing information, some of which may be more convenient and easier to use than the library. Libraries are facing greater competition for patrons' attention, and many libraries have seen dramatic declines in the number of reference questions asked (Martell 2008). In fact, at a time when people can answer many of their questions seemingly effortlessly through a *Google* search, some critics question why libraries and reference services are even necessary. As a result, the communities that support libraries are pressuring them to gather evidence that demonstrates their value and justifies continued support. If librarians hope to attract and retain patrons and to satisfy stakeholders, they need to know whether patrons are satisfied with the quality and content of library resources and services. Librarians can use the results of evaluation and assessment to support expenses and to demonstrate value by illustrating the ways in which their work supports the educational and entertainment needs of their users.

THE EVALUATION AND ASSESSMENT CYCLE

The evaluation and assessment process is often depicted as a loop or cycle, in which data are gathered and interpreted to measure progress toward goals, and then to inform decision making and establishment of new goals (Oakleaf 2009). In this sense, evaluation and assessment are iterative, meaning that as one cycle concludes, a new one begins. Figure 8.1 depicts one version of the process, involving five steps: choosing a focus and setting goals, gathering and analyzing data, making decisions, sharing results, and revisiting goals.

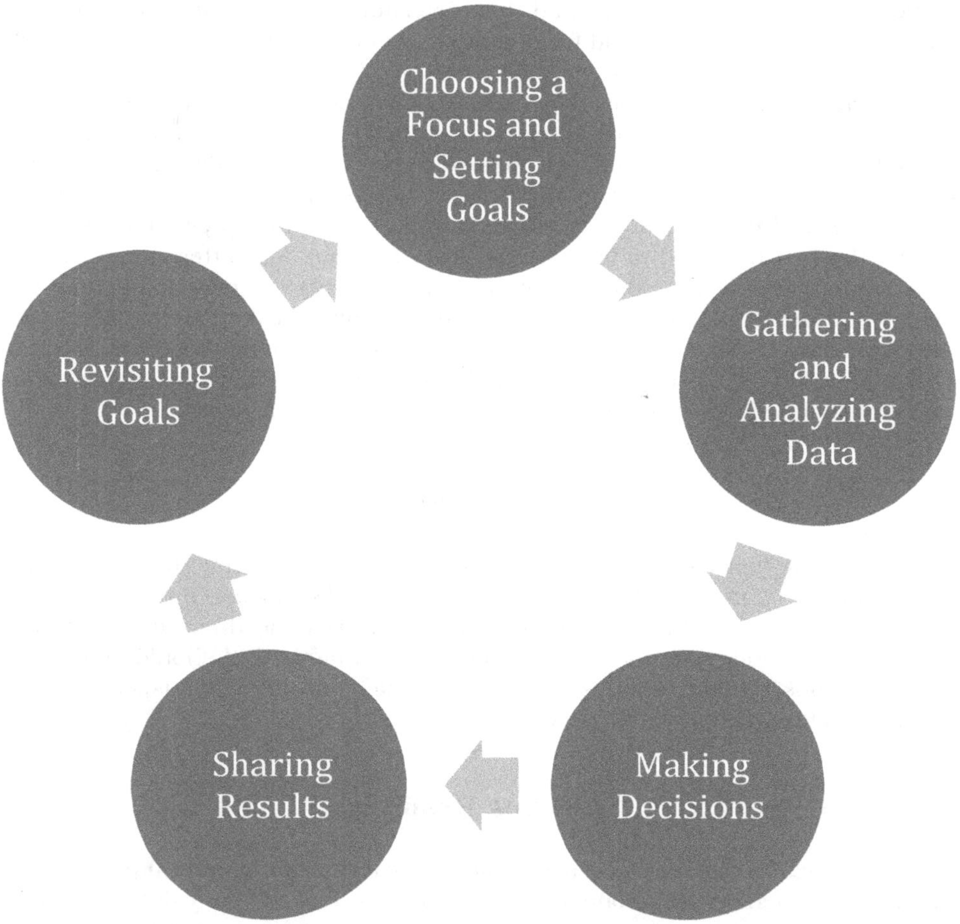

FIGURE 8.1 The assessment cycle

Choosing a Focus and Setting Goals

The first step in any assessment project is to determine what questions need to be answered, or what the goals are. To begin with, the librarians involved have to define which aspects of the service they plan to study. For instance, perhaps they are interested in levels of customer satisfaction with virtual reference services and want to achieve a 90 percent satisfaction rate. Or maybe they want to test how well students in their instruction sessions are learning the concepts presented. Or maybe they want to examine how accurate staff are when providing answers to questions. Knowing the goal of the research is important because that will determine what kind of data is needed, as well as what methods are most appropriate for gathering that data.

Gathering and Analyzing Data

Once the research questions and goals have been identified, data collection can begin. There are many different methods for collecting data, some of which are described in more detail later. The most important consideration when choosing a method of data collection is to consider what kinds of data are needed—customer opinions? workflow processes?—and then determine what method will yield that data. For instance, surveys and focus groups are often good ways of getting feedback and opinions from users.

It is important to remember that this step does not end with the collection of data. Once the data have been gathered, it must be reviewed and analyzed. The method of analysis will depend to some extent on the type of data gathered. For instance, quantitative data from surveys can be summarized using percentages and averages. If the data are qualitative, such as focus group or interview transcripts, the text will need to be read and reread to look for patterns and themes in the content. Most important, however, is determining the meaning behind the data. What does it mean if 75 percent of patrons say that they are satisfied with reference services? Are there patterns or consistencies among those who are less than satisfied? How closely do these results meet the goals that staff set for themselves, or how well do they answer the research questions asked?

Making Decisions

The ultimate purpose of assessment research is to take action. In other words, simply gathering and analyzing data is not enough. As discussed earlier, librarianship is one of several fields that have adopted an evidenced-based approach to practice. Thus, once data have been gathered and analyzed, it should be used to make decisions, whether about staffing, budgeting, continuing or suspending programs, or setting new goals for service improvement.

Sharing Results

Communicating the results of assessment research is an important part of closing the assessment loop and one that is too often overlooked. Many different stakeholder groups, from patrons to trustees to local government agencies or college provosts and presidents, will be interested to know what was learned from the research, and what will be done with that information. In some cases, some of those stakeholders will have also participated in the research by filling out surveys or taking part in focus groups, and sharing results is one way of letting them know that their feedback is being taken seriously and that their opinions matter.

Revisiting Goals

Assessment is an iterative process. Once the results have been analyzed in order to determine how well the library is meeting goals, and decisions have been made about services based on the research, the cycle begins again.

WHAT SHOULD BE EVALUATED OR ASSESSED?

Librarians have always gathered data about their resources and services. Traditionally, most libraries focused on inputs and outputs. Inputs describe the resources and infrastructure needed to create and maintain library resources and services, such as the staff and budget. Outputs are the products and services the library offers (Dugan and Hernon 2002). Outputs can include the numbers of reference questions asked and answered, the number of volumes in the reference collection, or the number of instruction sessions held. Such data are valuable for tracking the activities of the library, for benchmarking against peer institutions, and for comparing the activity of a single library over time. In addition, data such as the number of reference questions received on different days and at different times of the day can help librarians plan staffing for the reference desk (Dugan and Hernon 2002). A weakness of inputs and outputs as a source of data, however, is that they focus solely on the library's perspective and do not provide a sense of the quality of the resources or services being measured, or of the patron's opinions and perceptions. Inputs and outputs answer "how much," but not "how well." As Lynn Silipigni Connaway (2014, 1) explains:

> Input measures evaluate the library's raw materials (budget, space, collection, equipment, and staff) against standards, but are insufficient for overall assessment. Output measures quantify the work done, such as the number of items circulated, the number of reference questions answered, or the number of individuals who attended library instruction sessions, but do not relate these factors to the overall effectiveness of the library. Output measures suggest demand, performance efficiency, and customer satisfaction, but do not describe performance or identify the outcomes or benefits resulting from the use of library services and systems.

As stakeholders put greater pressure on libraries to demonstrate their value, there has been a shift in the focus from tallying inputs and outputs to evaluating quality and assessing outcomes. "Quality" refers to how good a resource or service is, either as measured by outside standards or as measured by the perceptions of the people using the resource or service. Quality in reference could be measured by outside standards, such as adherence to the Reference and User Services Association's (RUSA) "Guidelines for Behavioral Performance of Reference and Information Service Providers" (2013), or by self-reported levels of customer satisfaction. "Outcomes" refers to the results of a library's resources or services, such as the impact on an individual or community. The Institute of Museum and Library Services (IMLS) defines outcomes as "benefits to people: specifically, achievements or changes in skill, knowledge, attitude, behavior, condition, or life status for program participants ('visitors will know what architecture contributes to their environments,' 'participant literacy will improve')," and outcome-based evaluation as "observations that can credibly demonstrate change or desirable conditions ('increased quality of work in the annual science fair,' 'interest in family history,' 'ability to use information effectively')" (2015a). Outcomes for reference services could be related to learning from the reference transaction or from instruction sessions and workshops. Patrons could also benefit from a librarian's expertise in efficiently and effectively finding resources for an information need or for entertainment.

As this book demonstrates, reference librarians engage in a wide range of services and activities; all of these can and should be scrutinized. Evaluation of quality and assessment of outcomes in reference services could focus on a variety of areas, including customer satisfaction with service at virtual and physical reference desks, quality of collections and online resources, quality and effectiveness of services, and learning outcomes of reference interactions and instruction sessions. Librarians could also examine usability aspects of virtual reference services, library Web guides, and other library-created content, or of physical space devoted to reference services, including design and signage. Some librarians have also engaged in cost–benefit and return-on-investment evaluation, attempting to show the economic value of the library to its community (Kelly, Hamasu, and Jones 2012). Finally, evaluation research can focus on staff performance, which could also involve assessing training programs for support staff and student workers, and could encompass areas such as job satisfaction.

In addition to determining what will be evaluated, librarians must consider which perspective they will take in their evaluation. In their book, *Viewing Library Metrics from Different Perspectives* (2009), Robert E. Dugan, Peter Hernon, and Danuta A. Nitecki elaborate on these possible perspectives, including those of the patron, the stakeholder, and the library itself. They note, for instance, that when studying resources and services from the library perspective, librarians might focus on inputs and outputs, as those become surrogates for library use. At the same time, things like library space and facilities could be studied from a librarian's perspective to see how space impacts things like workflow or collaboration. To gain the patron's perspective, librarians must ask patrons for their opinions, perceptions, and overall satisfaction with the resources and services they use. In addition to asking patrons for their opinions, librarians could study the patron perspective indirectly, for instance by observing how patrons use the physical library space or reviewing transaction logs from electronic resources to understand how patrons are accessing and using those resources. Stakeholders might not be direct users of libraries, but they care about the services and resources those libraries provide. Stakeholders could include citizens whose tax dollars support the public library, parents whose children will be using the resources and services of school and academic libraries, or local, state, and federal governments that provide financial support to libraries. If stakeholders are not using libraries themselves, then their interest will be more focused on how the library is benefiting those who do use it. Since many stakeholders have a financial interest in the library, they might be interested in return-on-investment or cost–benefit data.

The choice of what to evaluate and assess is really a local one. While virtually any service or resource could (and probably should) be examined, evaluation and assessment can be intensive processes that demand an investment of time and resources. It would be impossible to evaluate all reference services and/or resources at once. Rather, each individual library and reference department will need to determine which areas to focus on. The decision of what to evaluate should be driven by local needs, the mission of the library and parent institution, and the interests of library stakeholders. An academic or school library might begin by focusing on student learning through reference interactions or instruction sessions, since that is likely the main focus of their parent institution, while a city government might be most interested in the return on tax dollars invested in the public library, or satisfaction of public library patrons. One possible approach for nearly any library setting is to begin with a general survey to gather feedback from users on the range of reference services and resources, and use the results to prioritize future research areas. For instance, perhaps such a survey would show that users are generally satisfied with the service they receive from staff, but are unhappy with the space and facilities. The reference department would be able to plan a future study to probe why users are dissatisfied with the space and determine what can be improved. The following sections outline some traditional and emerging areas for reference evaluation: number and type of reference questions, accuracy, patron satisfaction, service quality, learning, and usability.

Counting Reference Questions

Tracking the number and types of reference questions asked is a common activity for reference librarians in all types of settings. Librarians report these statistics to agencies such as IMLS and the National Center for Education Statistics (NCES). The Integrated Postsecondary Education Data System (2015) through the NCES makes academic and school library statistics available, allowing libraries to benchmark activity against peers and making it possible to see aggregate trends in usage over time. The IMLS provides similar data for public and state agency libraries (Institute of Museum and Library Services 2015b).

Reference desk statistics can be tracked in a number of ways. In addition to the overall number of questions asked, librarians might track the format of the interaction (face-to-face, e-mail, chat, telephone, etc.). Many libraries also classify questions by type. At the simplest level, questions might be categorized as reference, directional, or equipment. In this sense, reference questions are generally defined as "an information contact that involves the knowledge, use, recommendations, interpretation, or instruction in the use of one or more information sources by a member of the library staff" (Hodgson 2013). This definition differentiates reference questions from directional or equipment questions (e.g., "where is the bathroom?" or "can you put more paper in the printer?"), which do not require specialized knowledge or the use of information resources.

Questions classified as reference can be further broken down by type, as described in Chapter 1. For instance, ready-reference questions have known factual answers and are often best answered by traditional sources such as dictionaries, encyclopedias, and almanacs. Bibliographic verification involves helping users track down a particular item such as a book or journal article, often starting with an incomplete citation. Research consultations refer to in-depth questions that tend to take a substantial amount of time, involving recommendations on search strategies and instruction in the use of resources. Readers' advisory centers on helping patrons find leisure reading based on their reading history and their particular likes and dislikes. Another model of classifying reference questions is the READ scale, which attempts to classify reference questions by the amount of knowledge, effort, and time required by the librarian to answer the question (Gerlich and Berard 2007). Finally, the Warner (2001, 53) classification system organizes reference questions around the strategies for answering the question. In this system, questions are categorized as:

1. *Non-resource based*: Questions that do not require a resource to answer, and might be answered by a sign or help sheet (e.g., geographical or policy questions), usually answered at the service desk.
2. *Skill-based*: Questions that require a demonstration to answer (i.e., "how-to" questions that might be answered by a well-developed set of directions). Most often, the library staff have to move to a location and demonstrate a skill. The same question should always get the same answer.
3. *Strategy-based*: Questions that require the formulation of a strategy to locate an answer and require selection of resources and may require individualized subject approaches.
4. *Consultation*: Usually longer encounters outside of regular desk duty and may be for the selection of curriculum materials. The librarian will often have to research recommendations or prepare reports for consultation work.

Data about the number and type of reference questions fielded can inform the allocation of resources and staffing. Knowing peak days and times, and also knowing when more in-depth questions are typically asked, can assist reference managers in planning coverage for different service points. Librarians can also use that data to track and evaluate their own professional activities (Garrison 2010). In addition, tracking question types can provide insight into patrons' information needs and behaviors (Olszewski and Rumbaugh 2010). While useful, counting reference questions is an output measure and does not offer any insight into the quality of the service, or patron satisfaction. Librarians will continue to track these statistics for staffing and benchmarking purposes, but as noted earlier, the trend is to move past input and output measures to measure quality and outcomes.

Accuracy

One classic study attempted to move beyond inputs and outputs (Hernon and McClure 1986). For this study, proxies (individuals recruited and trained by the researchers) were sent to a variety of reference desks where they asked one of several predetermined reference questions. The researchers had already confirmed that each institution had a resource that could answer the question being asked. Nevertheless, nearly half of the time, the staff member at the reference desk was unable to fill the patron's request. In some cases, the librarian failed to engage in a reference interview and thus may not have understood the patron's question fully. In other cases, the librarian incorrectly indicated that the institution did not have the information needed to answer the question in its collection, or admitted that she did not know whether they had it, and did not provide a referral or other options to the patron. The results of this study led the researchers to conclude that the librarians in the study were able to provide a correct answer only just over half of the time. They coined the phrase the "55 percent rule" to describe the rate at which librarians provided an accurate answer to a question.

This study was an important one, as it moved beyond inputs and outputs to evaluate the accuracy of the service being provided. The authors also gauged the quality of the service from the patron's perspective by examining the librarians' behaviors, including whether they engaged in a reference interview or offered a referral. However, the study has also been criticized for being too limited in its approach. In the end, the measure of success of the reference transaction was based solely on the accuracy of the librarian's answer. Issues such as the librarian's demeanor and helpfulness, and the patron's satisfaction, were not considered as part of the results. As described in more detail in the following text, later researchers have focused more on customer satisfaction and librarian behaviors as factors in the overall success of the reference interview.

Patron Satisfaction

Good customer service is crucial to any organization. People usually share good customer service experiences only with a few friends. On the other hand, when they have a poor customer service experience, they are likely to tell many more people about it. One survey found that 75 percent of people would tell family, friends, and coworkers about a bad customer service experience (Estep 2011). Further, 48 percent of people who had a bad customer service experience were likely to tell 10 or more people about that experience (Dixon, Freeman, and Toman 2010). In this way, customer service can have a ripple effect, with one bad experience deterring others from using the service or engaging with a program.

While librarians want patrons to be satisfied with the whole range of resources and services provided, customer service is particularly important for the person-to-person reference transaction, whether in a face-to-face or a virtual environment. In fact, Joan Durrance (1989) found that for most library patrons, a good customer service experience was one of the most important factors in determining whether a patron would return to the reference librarian with another question. Durrance found that patrons who rated the reference librarian's interpersonal skills highly were more likely to say that they would return to that reference librarian for help in the future. Patrons were much less likely to return to a librarian whom they perceived to be judgmental, uninterested in them, or who made them feel uncomfortable, even if that librarian answered their question accurately. Other studies similarly found that when describing whether a reference transaction was successful, patrons were much more likely to focus on "relational aspects," such as whether the librarian was perceived to be friendly and pleasant (Radford 1996), and that the librarian's friendliness strongly correlated with the patrons' overall satisfaction (Dewdney and Ross 1994). Similar criteria held true for studies of virtual reference services (Connaway and Radford 2010). These studies demonstrate the importance of patron satisfaction to the overall success of reference services, making this a crucial area for reference librarians to study and understand.

Service Quality

Quality refers to the overall attributes or characteristics that make up a product or a service, and that would influence a person to use that service initially and to return to it in the future (Pass et al. 2006). For instance, a good quality car should run well, last a long time, and not need repairs beyond general maintenance. While customer service relies solely on the customer's opinions—that is, the customer's subjective perception of how good a resource or service is—quality can be measured from different perspectives. In the examples given earlier for customer service, many studies found that library patrons made judgments about the quality of reference transactions based on the friendliness of the librarian. These results show that from the customer's perspective, interpersonal skills are an important aspect of quality. On the other hand, librarians often judge the success or quality of reference transactions differently. Marie Radford (1999) found that when discussing the success of a reference encounter, librarians tended to focus on the content of the question, and the amount and quality of the resources available. From the librarian's perspective, providing a complete and accurate answer to the question seems to be one of the most important factors in determining quality.

When the focus of quality research is on the services provided, it is referred to as service quality. While quality can be viewed from both internal (library) and external (patron) perspectives, service quality places the emphasis on the patron. Service quality is related to satisfaction in that it relies on the patron's judgment and perceptions of their experience, and quality is generally a factor in whether a patron is satisfied. In evaluation and assessment research, however, service quality is differentiated from satisfaction. Satisfaction usually focuses on a single instance, or transaction, whereas service quality is a more general concept, encompassing the patron's overall experience (Parasuraman, Zeithaml, and Berry 1988). According to Peter Hernon and Ellen Altman, service quality in libraries "encompasses the interactive relationship between the library and the people whom it is supposed to serve. A library that adheres to all the professionally approved rules and procedures for acquiring, organizing, managing, and preserving material but has no customers cannot claim quality because a major element is missing: satisfying people's needs, requests, and desires for information" (1996, 2). Basically, service quality means meeting (or exceeding) patron expectations on a consistent basis and across a variety of service points (Lewis and Booms 1983). When an organization fails to meet a patron's expectations, the failure is identified as a gap in service, and actions are taken to improve (Bannock et al. 2003).

The focus on discrepancies, or gaps, between a patron's expectations and the perceived level of service is perhaps best described by the Gap Model of Service. This model, first proposed by A. Parasuraman and later adapted for libraries, identifies five potential gap areas:

Gap 1: Between customers' expectations for excellent service and management's perceptions of those expectations (i.e., the extent to which the managers know what the customers expect)

Gap 2: Between management's perceptions of customers' expectations and service quality specifications (i.e., the extent service standards are designed to meet understood quality expectations)

Gap 3: Between service quality expectations and service delivery (i.e., the service performance in terms of its standards)

Gap 4: Between service delivery and external communications to customers about the service (i.e., the degree to which service promises are delivered)

Gap 5: Between the customers' expectations for service excellence and their perceptions of service delivered (i.e., the operational definition of service quality) (Dugan, Hernon, and Nitecki 2009).

While gaps 1 through 4 include library or management perspectives, gap 5 is focused solely on the patron's perception. The central idea of gap 5 is that patrons have an expectation or desire for a certain level of quality when they interact with a service provider. There is also a minimum level of quality that a patron will tolerate before he or she chooses not to return to that provider. Finally, there is the actual level of service that the patron perceives or experiences. The Gap Model of Service attempts to measure the discrepancy between the patron's desired and perceived levels of service quality. If they are equal, then the organization has met the patron's expectations. If the patron perceives better service quality than they desired, the organization has exceeded expectations, and if the patron perceives lower service quality than desired, the organization has failed to meet expectations.

Because it relies on patron opinions, service quality is different from what might be considered more "objective" measures of quality, such as those applied in manufacturing to determine whether to accept or reject a prototype. While some might be uncomfortable with the subjective nature of service quality, ultimately, the patron's perception is their reality. Regardless of how the library or even another patron might rate the same service, if an individual believes that he or she has received a lower-quality service than anticipated, the person will be dissatisfied. In other words, "[if] customers say there is quality service, then there is. If they do not, then there is not. It does not matter what an organization believes about its level of service" (Hernon and Altman 1996, 6).

Box 8.2 Activity: Quality Service

Consider this quote: "If customers say there is quality service, then there is. If they do not, then there is not. It does not matter what an organization believes about its level of service" (Hernon and Altman 1996, 6).

Questions for Reflection and Discussion:

1. Do you agree? Why?
2. Are there any circumstances in which the organization's beliefs about its service might be more valid than those of its users?

Libraries have been attempting to measure service quality for a number of years. LibQUAL+® is a standardized survey instrument based on the Gap Model of Service, which asks participants to rate their minimum, desired, and perceived levels of quality across a range of library services (LibQUAL 2015a). The survey is administered locally, but data are submitted to and analyzed by a central service. The library then receives a report identifying where it is meeting or exceeding patron expectations, as well as areas of gap where it is falling short of expectations. With relation to reference services, LibQUAL asks a series of questions about staff behaviors and attitudes. In one study, researchers conducted a meta-analysis of the results from over 200,000 LibQUAL respondents from a variety of libraries across the United States and Europe from the years 2004 to 2006 to look for trends in patrons' expressed desires (Thompson, Kyrillidou, and Cook 2008). Librarians at the University of Mississippi were able to do a longitudinal analysis after using the LibQUAL survey for 10 years and found that their customer's perceptions of staff had improved over time (Greenwood, Watson, and Dennis 2011). Although LibQUAL has been quite popular, with over 1,400 libraries around the world participating (LibQUAL 2015b), some critics have noted its limitations, including its lack of attention to certain populations such as patrons with disabilities (Dugan, Hernon, and Nitecki 2009).

More recently, Counting Opinions (2015) has emerged as an alternative approach to measuring customer service in libraries. Counting Opinions offers a suite of products, including a customizable survey designed to gather ongoing data about customer service, which can then be used to benchmark performance over time and inform improvements. Unlike most surveys, which usually take place over a specific limited time period, Counting Opinions allows libraries to implement the survey on a continuous basis. According to its website, Counting Opinions helps to reduce response bias and provide reliable data by offering its surveys in multiple languages as well as in Web, phone, and paper-based formats, and it offers a reliable and valid question set.

Learning

Assessing the extent to which patrons have learned something from their encounter with a reference librarian has become increasingly important, especially for school and academic libraries. Learning is the central mission of schools, colleges, and universities, and in this era of accountability, these institutions are demanding to know how all of their departments and resources, including reference, contribute to accomplishing that mission. Reference librarians are taking on greater responsibility for teaching, often in more formal settings such as classes, courses, and workshops. Much of the assessment for learning will be tied to those more formal instructional roles, often using classroom assessment techniques. Assessment related to such instruction is covered in Chapter 4.

This section focuses on learning that might take place through more traditional reference transactions. While some reference transactions might result in the librarian finding and supplying an answer for the patron, often the librarian has an opportunity to guide the patron through the information search process. This guidance could include demonstrating the use of different kinds of search strategies, helping the patron to understand and use subject headings, and helping the patron to evaluate different sources, among other things. During such an interaction, it is possible that the patron will learn some new strategies and techniques that he or she could apply to future searches. By assessing the extent to which learning takes place during reference encounters, librarians can demonstrate how reference services contribute to the learning mission of their institutions.

Several studies use virtual reference transcripts to assess the extent to which librarians engage in instructional activities or behaviors during the reference encounter (Passanneau and Coffey 2011; Taddeo and Hackenberg 2006). While the focus of these studies is on teaching, librarians at Wartburg College found that over 90 percent of students surveyed indicated that the librarian had taught them something during their reference encounter. Further, nearly three-quarters saw a connection between what they learned at the reference desk and what they had been taught in information literacy sessions, showing some retention of content (Gremmels and Lehmann 2007). Similarly, librarians at Indiana University analyzed and classified reference questions as a way of assessing the information literacy levels of the patron asking the question. They correlated that analysis with a survey asking whether the patron had attended an information literacy course, in order to determine whether patrons who had taken the class asked more sophisticated questions (Cordell and Fisher 2010). Overall, these students perceived the reference interaction to be a learning experience. Megan Oakleaf and Amy VanScoy highlight the need for librarians to demonstrate their support of the educational missions of their schools and encourage them to "explore the direct impact of librarian instructional strategies [during virtual reference transactions] on student learning" (2010, 386).

Usability

Usability is defined as "how effectively, efficiently and satisfactorily a user can interact with a user interface" (Usability.gov 2015a). Usability is a part of the overall user experience, which examines the ease of use and satisfaction of a user with a system. Usability.gov (2015b) identifies six factors that impact usability:

1. *Intuitive design*: A nearly effortless understanding of the architecture and navigation of the site.
2. *Ease of learning*: How fast a user who has never seen the user interface before can accomplish basic tasks.
3. *Efficiency of use*: The speed with which an experienced user can accomplish tasks.
4. *Memorability*: Whether a user can remember enough to use the site effectively in future visits.
5. *Error frequency and severity*: How often users make errors while using the system, how serious the errors are, and how users recover from the errors.
6. *Subjective satisfaction*: Whether the user likes using the system.

As more reference services and resources move online, librarians are recognizing the need to evaluate the usability of those services and resources. Usability is also an issue because patrons will compare library websites and online services to the ease, speed, and convenience they are used to from popular online sources like *Google* and *Amazon*. If library sites seem too complicated or clunky, the patrons are not likely to use them. One usability study compared several formats of remote and virtual reference using usability measures and found that chat seemed to be the preferred method, scoring highest for efficiency, effectiveness (in terms of task completion), and satisfaction (Chow and Croxton 2014). Librarians at the University of Saskatchewan employed a user-centered design approach to usability testing as a way to plan the overall design and labeling of their virtual reference service (Duncan and Fitcher 2004). In addition to virtual reference services, usability testing can be implemented for online reference tools such as research guides (Vileno 2010).

HOW TO ASSESS

Each evaluation or assessment project has five distinct aspects that must be defined before the project is undertaken: what will be studied, who will be the focus of the study, where the study will take place, when the study will take place, and how the data will be gathered. As a whole, these five areas are sometimes referred to as the logical structure of the research project.

What

The "what" of the logical structure refers to the focus of the study: what, specifically, is being evaluated or assessed. The first step to evaluation research is deciding what, exactly, will be evaluated. As outlined earlier, almost any resource (e.g., website, pathfinders, collections) or service (e.g., virtual or face-to-face reference, instruction) can be evaluated. In addition to choosing an area of focus for evaluation, it is important to define what aspect of the resource or service will be evaluated (e.g., customer satisfaction, quality, learning) and which perspective will be taken (e.g., patron's, library's).

Who

The "who" is the population being studied. In some cases, the population could be very broad, such as library cardholders, students, or genealogists. In other cases, the population might be more limited, such as students of a certain age or enrolled in a certain class. The important thing is to make sure that the population aligns with the focus of the study. Depending on its size, it might not be possible or practical to study an entire population. At such times, the librarians will draw a sample of the population, often trying to take a random sample or otherwise taking care to make the sample representative of the population. While a detailed explanation of sampling is outside the scope of this chapter, the additional readings listed at the end of the chapter offer good overviews of how to draw an appropriate sample for a study.

Where

The "where" of the study refers to the organization, or place, on which the study focuses, or to which it is connected. Because evaluation research is generally local in nature—that is, it is undertaken to study local services and inform decision making within the organization—the "where" of an evaluation research project is usually the library or information setting carrying out the research.

When

"When" defines the timetable in which the research will be carried out. Selecting an appropriate time frame is important. If, for instance, a reference department wants to study customer service at the reference desk, it will need to find a time when there will be plenty of activity, with a range of patrons and questions being asked. For this reason, an academic library typically would not want to carry out a study during spring break, when many students will not be on campus.

How

"How" refers to the methods that will be used to collect data. There are numerous methods for studying reference services. A comprehensive review of those methods is outside the scope of this chapter. However, a few of the more popular methods are discussed later. The additional readings at the end of this chapter offer more in-depth explanations of these methods, as well as overviews of additional methods not discussed here.

Definitions and Standards

Part of setting up an evaluation or assessment project involves clarifying each aspect of the study, including vocabulary, and how each aspect of the study will be measured. The first step is to define the terms of the study, a process sometimes referred to as operationalization. For instance, several of the studies described earlier employed different definitions of reference success. Joan Durrance and Patricia Dewdney and Catherine Sheldrick Ross defined success at the reference desk in terms of the patron's willingness to return to the librarian, whereas Peter Hernon and Charles McClure measured reference success by the accuracy or completeness of the answer supplied by the librarian. The point with operationalization is to ensure that it is clear to those engaged in or using the results of the study how all aspects of the research are being defined.

Once terms have been defined, the librarians will need to decide how to measure each area under study. For instance, continuing with the example of reference service success, Durrance and Dewdney and Ross needed to know not just whether patrons were willing to return to the reference desk, but also what factors made them more likely to return. To that end, they had patrons rate the reference interactions across a number of criteria, including the different behavioral aspects of the librarian and the helpfulness of the answer provided. Those criteria are the standards against which the librarian's performance was measured.

Although it is possible to define local measures, it is usually possible and often preferable to find externally defined measures. Many professional associations like the American Library Association (ALA), the Public Library Association (PLA), and the Association of College and Research Libraries (ACRL) publish definitions, standards, and metrics that can be used for evaluation and assessment. For instance, the RUSA offers the "Guidelines for Behavioral Performance of Reference and Information Service Providers" (2013), which are often used to assess librarians' performance during reference encounters. Similarly, ACRL's "Information Literacy Competency Standards for Higher Education" (2000) or the more recently published "Framework for Information Literacy for Higher Education" (2015) are often used to assess learning related to library instruction. In addition, researchers have proposed additional standards based on studies of reference services. For instance, the Warner classification for reference questions described earlier was proposed by Debra Warner after an extended study of question types received at an academic health sciences library. Similarly, R. David Lankes, Melissa Gross, and Charles R. McClure (2003) proposed six quality standards that could be used to evaluate virtual reference services, which are courtesy, accuracy, satisfaction, repeat users, awareness, and cost. External standards save librarians the time and effort of developing their own measures. They also allow for benchmarking and comparison across research studies that have used the same standards, allowing librarians to see whether results hold true across different studies.

EVALUATION AND ASSESSMENT METHODS

Evaluation research can be carried out through a wide variety of methods. Most methods fall into one of two basic categories: quantitative or qualitative. As the name implies, quantitative methods focus on information that can be represented numerically and might include frequency counts, percentages, and ratios. Common types of methods for gathering quantitative measures include surveys, questionnaires, or polls (with closed-ended questions); transaction log analysis (including reviews of analytics of website and eResource use); and bibliometrics (including citation analysis). Qualitative research, on the other hand, relies on observation and description. Some common types of qualitative research include interviews, focus groups, document analysis, critical incident questionnaires, and unobtrusive observation.

Each methodological approach has its strengths and weaknesses. Quantitative methods can often be applied to larger groups, meaning there is more likelihood of getting a representative sample whose results are generalizable to the larger population. On the other hand, qualitative methods can usually probe deeper and get at the context behind quantitative results. For instance, while a survey might tell us that patrons are generally satisfied with reference services, a focus group could find out why people are more or less satisfied with different aspects, and probe the reasons for satisfaction and dissatisfaction. As such, it is often recommended to use both quantitative and qualitative methods together to get a fuller picture of the area under research. The following sections offer an overview of some of the more common research methods applied to reference services studies.

Surveys

Surveys are a popular method for evaluation research. They take less time to administer than qualitative methods, and since quantitative data can generally be analyzed more quickly, surveys are a good choice for large populations. Surveys are often administered online, usually with software that can analyze the results itself or export results to programs such as Excel or SPSS for statistical analysis. If surveys are administered on paper, the data must be manually entered into an online program for analysis. Surveys can elicit a range of information, including demographics, knowledge, opinions, and awareness. In general, surveys are made up of closed-ended questions, meaning questions with a fixed set of answers from which the participant must choose. In addition, however, surveys can include open-ended questions that allow participants to write in their own responses. These questions offer participants an opportunity to elaborate on or clarify answers to closed-ended questions and thus add qualitative aspects to the study.

Surveys are used regularly for customer service feedback, but they have also been implemented in other ways. For instance, Gillian S. Gremmels and Karen Shostrom Lehmann (2007) used a survey to assess patrons' perceptions of learning during reference transactions. Surveys have also been used to study patrons' information-seeking behaviors in order to better understand how to support their needs through reference services (Mokhtari 2014; Project Information Literacy 2015) and to determine the extent to which patrons use certain technologies such as mobile devices so that services can be tailored to support access on such devices (Becker, Bonadie-Joseph, and Cain 2013; Dresselhaus and Shrode 2012). Surveys can also focus on the employee, and several libraries have used surveys to assess the job satisfaction of their reference staff (Hendricks and Buchanan 2013; Landry 2000).

While these surveys focus on a single perspective, it is also possible for surveys to gather feedback from multiple perspectives in order to compare and contrast. For instance, the Wisconsin–Ohio Reference Evaluation Program (WOREP), developed in the 1980s by Marjorie Murfin, Gary Gugelchuk, and Charles Bunge, consisted of two surveys in one that were completed at the end of a reference transaction (Murfin and Gugelchuk 1987). One half of the survey was completed by the patron and asked whether they found the materials they were seeking, whether they were satisfied and why, and included some questions about the affect and behaviors of the librarian. The other half of the survey was completed by the librarian and asked about the content of the question, how fully the question was answered, and included questions about any special considerations such as whether there were other patrons waiting for attention or whether the question was outside of the scope of the library's collection. The two portions of the survey were coded, so they could be recombined and compared.

Having the two perspectives allowed the librarians to see whether their opinion of the success of the transaction matched the patron's, and if not, where the discrepancies were. For instance, librarians at the Pattee Library of Pennsylvania State University discovered that staff were overestimating the patrons' satisfaction with reference transactions (Novotny and Rimland 2007). This discovery was crucial because without it, librarians would have continued to assume that the service was functioning well and would not have seen a need to take any steps toward improvement. Further, dissatisfied patrons who had no outlet for expressing their frustration might have simply decided not to return to the library and might have shared their dissatisfaction with fellow students thereby discouraging their use of the library. Thus, evaluation research enabled librarians to identify a problem and to make an informed decision to correct that problem.

Based on their findings, the librarians implemented a training session encouraging librarians to use more resources when answering questions, to spend more time with the patron, and to offer alternatives when the desired resource was not available. A follow-up study showed that overall satisfaction improved after the training was implemented. Although the WOREP project was discontinued in 2011, the questions are available in the Pattee Library study (Novotny and Rimland 2007). Whether one uses the specific questions or format laid out in that article, however, WOREP offers a good model for collecting data from multiple perspectives and could guide the development of local surveys. For instance, librarians at Hillman Library of the University of Pittsburgh used elements of LibQUAL+® and WOREP to create their own survey of reference services. As with the Pattee Library study, the researchers found that patrons tended to rate the success of transactions lower than staff. However, the patrons' satisfaction was generally higher when they were served by a professional librarian, rather than by paraprofessionals or students (Miller 2008).

Deciding whether to use an existing survey or to create a local one is an important consideration. There are established surveys like LibQUAL+® and Counting Opinions that offer valid instruments and assistance with data analysis. Many surveys are also included in research articles published in the library and information science literature or are available from the authors upon request. Still, many librarians choose to develop their own survey, perhaps for budget reasons (standardized instruments can be expensive) or in order to tailor the questions to a local audience. Generally, surveys are somewhat less time and resource intensive to develop than other data collection instruments. However, creating a survey that will elicit reliable and valid data is not necessarily easy.

Survey creators must think carefully about question wording, survey length, and an appropriate mix of questions. When creating survey questions, it is important to avoid common pitfalls such as leading questions, double-barreled questions, assumptions, and ambiguous wording. Leading or biased questions are worded in such a way that they might influence the respondent to answer in a certain way. For instance, asking "how good was the service you received today?" suggests the service was, in fact, good, while asking "how would you rate the service you received today?" is more neutral. Double-barreled questions ask about two separate items in a single question, as in "how satisfied are you with library services and resources?" It is possible that respondents might feel differently about the services than they do about the resources, but this question forces them to choose one answer to represent their satisfaction level with both items. Such questions should be broken into two separate questions. Sometimes survey questions have embedded assumptions. For instance, asking "how many times did you use the library this month?" assumes that the respondent did use the library. Finally, ambiguous questions include wording that could be interpreted in different ways by different people, which could affect how people answer the question. An example would be whether one asked "do you use resources when you come to the library?" For some, resources might refer to books and magazines, to others online resources, and to still others it could mean facilities like the bathrooms. Thus, it is important to be clear and specific about what is being asked. Box 8.3 shows some more examples of poorly worded survey questions and suggestions for rewording.

Box 8.3 Creating Good Survey Questions

Avoid double-barreled questions:

Are reference librarians friendly and helpful?

Better:

Are reference librarians friendly?
Do you find reference librarians to be helpful when you have a question?

Avoid making assumptions:

How often do you ask questions at the reference desk?

Better:

Do you ask questions at the reference desk?

Avoid leading questions:

How convenient are the virtual reference services?

Better:

What is your opinion of the virtual reference services?

Avoid using jargon:

How user-friendly is the OPAC?

Better:

The online catalog is the part of the library website where you search for books and other materials. What is your opinion of the usability of the online catalog?

In addition to the wording of questions, answer choices must be carefully crafted. It is important to be sure that all possible options are represented and, whenever possible, that answer options are mutually exclusive. Asking someone to indicate their age range and offering options such as "10–20, 20–30, 30–40" presents a problem for someone aged 20 or 30, as their age is listed in two answer options. Thus, it is better to offer ranges like "10–19, 20–29, 30–39," and so on. For potentially sensitive questions such as race or income, it is recommended to include a "prefer not to answer" option. This allows the respondent some measure of privacy, without deterring them from completing the rest of the survey. Including an "other, please specify" option can be useful if you are concerned that respondents might not fit into predetermined categories, but it is important to remember that those write-in answers must then be analyzed and categorized manually. Finally, it is important to be clear about the type of answer category. In other words, are respondents supposed to choose only one answer, or can they choose all that apply? If the question asks respondents to rate agreement, satisfaction, or other opinions on a number scale, the scale should be labeled to indicate which numbers represent positive opinions and which are negative.

Overall, surveys are an excellent way of gathering feedback on almost any topic from a wide range of community members. They are not necessarily time or resource intensive to execute, and software packages like Excel can make analysis relatively easy. On the other hand, surveys can be limited. The closed-ended nature of surveys means that they can offer a snapshot of a situation, but they cannot usually probe deeper into the explanations behind the situation. In addition, people receive surveys from many different sources, which can lead to survey burnout. If they are tired of answering surveys, patrons might not be as thorough in their answers, might not persist until the end, or might choose not to answer the survey at all. Finally, the nature and format of the survey can create barriers to response. Since surveys are written and require a certain reading level, young children, nonnative speakers, and patrons with low literacy levels may be unable to participate. People without reliable Internet connections may be unable to access online surveys. On the other hand, paper surveys usually are distributed only within the physical library, thus eliminating nonusers, remote users, or anyone who simply does not visit the library during the time the survey is being distributed. Researchers must consider all of these limitations when planning surveys and decide how best to reach the largest number of patrons.

Focus Groups

While surveys can be good for large samples, but tend to be limited with closed-ended questions, focus groups allow for greater depth by bringing together the perspectives of a group of individuals and giving them space to explore their thoughts, bounce ideas off of each other, agree, disagree, and question or challenge one another (Liamputtong 2011). Participants often learn from each other during the discussion, and researchers can see how participants' opinions influence each other. Unlike surveys, it is also possible to ask follow-up questions if a participant's answer is unclear, or if they raise a particularly interesting point. In addition, focus groups can be a marketing tool in and of themselves, as participants "really appreciate the opportunity to be heard and the library is viewed as being caring enough to solicit their experiences" (Massey-Burzio 1998, 214).

Focus group methodology can be applied to any type of research problem or question, but because it emphasizes direct and open-ended feedback from participants, it can be useful for probing patrons' awareness about reference services as well as their satisfaction and opinions about those services. One study found that patrons were uncomfortable asking questions and that when they did use reference services they found them unhelpful. Further, they complained of poor signage and indicated that they found the librarians to be generally unavailable or hard to identify (Massey-Burzio 1998). Conversely, focus group participants in another study indicated that their needs were being met by the reference desk (Fitzpatrick, Moore and Lang 2008). Focus groups have also been used to gauge patrons' preferences for different service formats. For instance, some studies have explored patron preference for face-to-face, phone, and chat interactions (Granfield and Robertson 2008; Naylor, Stoffel, and Van der Laan 2008), while others have examined patrons' use of mobile devices for reference support (Owen 2010).

Pamela B. Kleiber (2004) offers a thorough and straightforward introduction to focus group design. Focus groups should be made up of 7–12 participants with a moderator whose role is to facilitate the discussion and encourage participation. The purpose of the group is not to arrive at consensus, but to explore opinions and get at the underlying beliefs and attitudes. In order for participants to feel comfortable expressing their opinions to the group, the moderator has to establish an atmosphere of respect and trust. The moderator can help to foster that atmosphere by establishing ground rules and by asserting each participant's right to privacy.

Generally, focus groups will last from an hour to an hour and a half. The discussion should be organized around four to six open-ended questions. Part of the moderator's role is to ensure that all participants are active in the discussion, which might involve gently drawing out the quieter participants. The moderator must also be careful not to reflect any bias or assumptions when asking the discussion questions or by reacting to participants' answers. Finally, the moderator must work to keep the discussion on course, without leading it toward a particular end. In other words, if the discussion goes off course and the participants begin pursuing irrelevant topics, it is up to the moderator to guide the discussion back to the topic of the focus group.

Because focus groups rely on open-ended discussion, they generate detailed data. Taping the sessions ensures that one captures an accurate record of the conversation to enable review of the material and extraction of exact quotations. Videotaping will also capture nonverbal cues that might provide insight into participants' thoughts and reactions. However, it is important to remember that video- and audiotapes will likely need to be transcribed or otherwise converted to text for analysis, which can be time consuming. They may also require additional consent from the participants. If taping the sessions is not feasible, the researcher should try to arrange for one or more notetakers at the session. This way, the moderator can focus on facilitating the dialogue.

Focus groups are an extremely useful methodology. They tend to elicit deeper explanations and beliefs behind opinions than that can be easily captured through a survey. Also, the discussion can lead to new understandings or opinions as the participants learn from one another. Finally, focus group participants tend to feel appreciated by the library and believe that the library is interested in their opinion, which can make the groups a good public relations exercise. However, with just 7–12 participants per session, focus groups reach far fewer people than surveys, meaning that the findings are limited as well. One way to maximize the strengths of each methodology while minimizing its disadvantages is to pair the two together.

A survey can be used to get an overview of the community's perspectives, while follow-up focus groups can probe into the questions or concerns raised by the survey.

Box 8.4 Activity: Patron Satisfaction

A library has just conducted a satisfaction survey, and the results show that patrons are not as satisfied with reference services as the staff would like them to be. When asked to rate their satisfaction with the service they receive at the reference desk, with 1 being poor and 5 being excellent, the mean response was 3.5, and the mode, or most common response, was 3. The library director has asked the head of the reference department to do some follow-up to discover more about the reasons why patrons are less than satisfied.

Question for Reflection and Discussion:

1. What methods could be used to study reference transactions, and why? Identify three or four questions that could be used to guide your study.

Observation

Observation has long been a popular method for studying reference services. As the name implies, this method involves a systematic approach to observing reference librarians in action and comparing or benchmarking their actions and behaviors against a predetermined set of criteria. Observation can be either obtrusive, meaning the subject of the study knows he or she is being observed though the individual may not know when it will happen, or unobtrusive, meaning the subject does not know he or she is being observed or studied. For instance, Peter Hernon and Charles McClure (1986) used unobtrusive observation when they established the 55 percent rule, as did both Joan Durrance (1989) and Patricia Dewdney and Catherine Sheldrick Ross (1994) when they tested patrons' willingness to return. In each of these studies, the researchers engaged observers to ask questions at the reference desk and then report back on their experiences.

Mystery shopping is a form of unobtrusive observation that some libraries have employed more recently. Originally used in retail settings, mystery shopping involves using trained surrogates who use the services of the library in order to assess the effectiveness of the service and/or the communication, behaviors, and customer service orientation of the employees. Mystery shoppers are not necessarily current patrons of the library, but have been recruited and trained to use the library services as a regular patron would (Jankal and Jankalova 2011). For reference services, these shoppers would ask a reference question and then evaluate the librarian against a set of predetermined criteria, such as RUSA's (2013) "Guidelines for Behavioral Performance of Reference and Information Service Providers." This approach has been used successfully to evaluate customer service aspects of both academic (Kocevar-Weidinger et al. 2010) and public (Backs and Kinder 2007) libraries. The Kent Libraries in Australia offer a video describing a mystery shopping program in which learning disabled adults act as the mystery shoppers and offer insight into how the library can better support patrons with certain needs (CILIP 2011).

Although researchers tout unobtrusive observation and mystery shopping as effective methods that can lead to actionable results, some practitioners are uncomfortable with the approach. For one thing, research involving people, known as human subjects research, typically requires the informed consent of the people involved. However, for unobtrusive observation to work, the subject has to be unaware that he or she is being observed. Otherwise, they are unlikely to act naturally. Librarians who decide to implement unobtrusive observation can meliorate the problem by letting their staff know that observations are being undertaken and by discussing the purpose, without telling the librarians exactly when the observations will be done, or by whom.

Another issue arises from the fact that in some industries, mystery shopping routinely identifies individual employees, and in some cases, poor results are held against the individual. The approach can also be used to assess overall staff performance on a larger scale, however. In such cases, rather than reviewing individual performance, the researchers will look for trends and patterns that can then be addressed generally with all staff. As Elizabeth Kocevar-Weidinger and colleagues note, "identifying problems that are generally observed—rather than focusing on specific employees' behaviors—would allow us to design more effective refresher sessions for our current workers and training programs for new workers" (2010, 30–31). In order for staff to feel comfortable with the process, researchers will need to be clear that observation and mystery shopping are intended to diagnose general problems and not to target specific staff.

Box 8.5 Activity: Mystery Shopping

A library has decided to set up a mystery shopping study of its reference department. The director is interested in finding out how well patrons' questions are being answered (in other words, are they given full and accurate answers insofar as the librarian is able to do so) and whether they are receiving a good customer service experience. Develop a list of questions or observation criteria for the mystery shopper to respond to after their interaction. For instance, should they note the number of sources the librarian consults? Whether the librarian makes eye contact and greets the patrons as they arrive? Create a list of 5–10 things for mystery shoppers to respond to and report on.

Transcript Reviews

Reference interactions that take place by chat or e-mail usually generate a transcript that documents the transaction. These transcripts will show every aspect of the interaction, from the librarian's greeting, to the reference interview questions asked, any attempts at instruction, the format of the answer provided, sources cited, and how the interview is closed. As such, virtual reference transcripts can be useful in evaluating the reference interview and the overall quality of the reference service. A number of studies have compared reference transcripts with RUSA's (2013) "Guidelines for Behavioral Performance of Reference and Information Service Providers" to see whether the librarians engaged in the recommended behaviors. Among other things, these studies have looked at whether the librarian offered a friendly greeting at the beginning of the transaction, whether the librarian used jargon or technical terminology that might have confused the patron, and whether the librarian maintained a professional yet friendly tone (Maness, Naper, and Chaudhuri 2009; Zhou et al. 2006). These reviews can also examine elements such as whether the librarian is engaging in a reference interview to uncover the full information need, whether the librarian engages in any instruction, and whether the librarian cites sources when providing answers.

Box 8.6 Activity: Transaction Analysis

Following is an excerpt from a chat reference transaction. Read through and critique it, keeping the reference interview and the RUSA "Guidelines for Behavioral Performance of Reference and Information Service Providers" in mind. Does the librarian convey a welcoming tone and interest in the question? Does she ask good follow-up questions to clarify the patron's need? Are there additional questions she could have asked? How well does she seem to answer the patron's question? Does she provide a good closure to the interview?

Patron: Hi I'm looking for information for books on minerals and rocks for elementary school kids.

Librarian: Hello! Thanks for using reference chat! Let me take a minute to look through some of our resources, and I'll let you know what I find.

Patron: Thanks! That sounds great.

Librarian: I found some books that might be of interest to you. If you go to the library homepage, and then click on "Research & Resources," you can then browse the databases that we have. From there you can select "Children's Core Collection" from the Library and Information Science drop down menu. Doing a keyword search for minerals and rocks will give you many results for books on the subject for elementary school kids. Unfortunately, it doesn't seem that the library owns very many of these. You can, however, request these materials through interlibrary loan. And that can be done by clicking "full-text" and then "request via interlibrary loan."

Patron: This sounds great, thank you. I'm also looking for lesson plans for students on how to identify rocks and minerals in the classroom. Are there any websites where I can find them?

Librarian: Sure. A good place to start might be http://www.dlese.org/library/index.jsp. A search for minerals and rocks brings up many results, but a good one to note is result number 24 "USGS Education." Here's the direct link: http://education.usgs.gov/. From there you can search educational resources for grades K-6. Let me see if I can find any lesson plans from here. If you scroll down towards about the middle of the page, there's a section on Rocks and Minerals. Some of these resources include lesson plans. (Which is indicated with a yellow square next to the resource). Here's an example of one Web resource that includes a lesson plan, called Schoolyard Geology: http://education.usgs.gov/lessons/schoolyard/index.html

Patron: This is fantastic. Thank you for your help.

Librarian: You're very welcome. Are there any other resources you're looking for?

Patron: Thank you very much, I think I got everything I needed!

Librarian: Excellent! Glad I could help.

In a different approach, Joanne B. Smyth and James C. MacKenzie (2006) analyzed chat reference transcripts against satisfaction surveys that users submitted upon completing a reference transaction. Comparing the two documents allowed the researchers to see what aspects of the reference transaction might influence the patron's satisfaction. Nahyun Kwon (2007) found that the quality of the answers provided to public library patrons through chat reference varied depending on the type of question, concluding that librarians performed less effectively when answering locally based questions for libraries other than their own. Finally, reference librarians have also found chat transcripts to be effective for training purposes. Staff can review and analyze their own transcripts to identify areas for improvement (Ward 2003).

While chat reference transcripts appear to be useful assessment tools, it is important to remember that they might contain personally identifying information about patrons and/or librarians. Transcripts might automatically insert the person's name as they type, or the people involved might identify themselves within the body of the conversation. In order to protect the privacy and confidentiality of anyone involved, it is good practice to anonymize transcripts before reviewing them by removing names or any other personal information first. This is important not only to protect patrons, but also to reinforce the idea for staff that the purpose of the review is not to target individual staff members, but to look at and improve the service as a whole.

CLOSING THE LOOP

It is important to remember that the purpose of evaluation and assessment research is to take action. Simply gathering data is not enough. Once data have been collected, they must be analyzed in order to inform decision making. For instance, if a transcript review of chat reference services reveals that librarians seem to be missing opportunities to offer instruction during the interactions, the department head could develop a training session to help them integrate more instruction. The focus should always be on taking steps to continually improve services, not to target and take action against individuals (staff training and other efforts to improve reference services are discussed in more detail in Chapter 9). Each time a new decision, project, or service is implemented, the librarians should set new goals and then begin the assessment process again.

Another aspect of closing the assessment loop is to share the results of studies with others. Because assessment is tied to improvement, and because the data from assessment studies can be evidence of the library's value to the communities, it is wise to share assessment activities and results with stakeholders such as city managers, deans, provosts, or others who have oversight of the library. Sharing results with the communities served, especially people who directly participated in the study, shows that the library takes their feedback seriously and could encourage more participation in future studies. Finally, librarians should consider sharing results with colleagues in other institutions, so that they can learn from each other's experiences.

A CULTURE OF ASSESSMENT

Libraries continue to face greater competition from other information providers and increased scrutiny from stakeholders and critics. Assessment and evaluation of services like reference allows librarians to generate evidence and demonstrate their value to their communities. Assessment and evaluation are also critical for checking progress toward goals, informing decisions, and continuously improving services. Given the importance of these activities, it is crucial that librarians develop a culture of assessment, making evaluation and assessment an integral part of everything they do. This means that responsibility for assessment should be a part of all job descriptions. Library directors and managers should model behavior by stressing the importance of assessment activities and by providing staff with the resources they need to engage in assessment. Reference services should be assessed regularly, and any new programs or initiatives should be developed with a plan for assessment. With such an organization-wide commitment, librarians can ensure that their services are of high quality and their patrons will continue to be satisfied.

REFERENCES

Association of College and Research Libraries. 2000. "Information Literacy Competency Standards for Higher Education." American Library Association. http://www.ala.org/acrl/standards/informationliteracycompetency.

Association of College and Research Libraries. 2015. "Framework for Information Literacy for Higher Education." American Library Association. http://www.ala.org/acrl/standards/ilframework.

Backs, Stephen M., and Tim Kinder. 2007. "Secret Shopping at the Monroe County Public Library." *Indiana Libraries* 26: 17–19.

Bannock, Graham, Evan Davis, Paul Trott, and Mark Uncles. 2003. "Perceived Service Quality." *The New Penguin Business Dictionary*. London, UK: Penguin.

Becker, Danielle Andre, Ingrid Bonadie-Joseph, and Jonathan Cain. 2013. "Developing and Completing a Mobile Technology Survey to Create a User-Centered Mobile Presence." *Library Hi Tech* 31: 688–99.

Chow, Anthony S., and Rebecca A. Croxton. 2014. "A Usability Evaluation of Academic Virtual Reference Services." *College & Research Libraries* 75: 309–61.

CILIP: Chartered Institute of Library and Information Professionals. 2011. "Kent Libraries and Archives." YouTube video, 3:08. June 8. http://www.youtube.com/watch?v=f69sfZXEkZs.

Connaway, Lynn Silipigni. 2014. "Why Libraries? A Call for User-Centered Assessment." *BiD* 32: 1–4.

Connaway, Lynn Silipigni, and Marie L. Radford. 2010. "Virtual Reference Service Quality: Critical Components for Adults and the Net Generation." *LIBRI: International Journal of Libraries & Information Services* 60: 165–80.

Cordell, Roseanne M., and Linda F. Fisher. 2010. "Reference Questions as an Authentic Assessment of Information Literacy." *Reference Services Review* 38: 474–81.

Counting Opinions. 2015. "FAQ." Accessed February 23. http://www.countingopinions.com/faq.html.

Crumley, Ellen, and Denise Koufogiannikis. 2002. "Developing Evidence-Based Librarianship: Practical Steps for Implementation." *Health Information & Libraries Journal* 19: 61–70.

Dewdney, Patricia, and Catherine Sheldrick Ross. 1994. "Flying a Light Aircraft: Reference Service Evaluation from a User's Viewpoint." *RQ* 34: 217–30.

Dixon, Matthew, Karen Freeman, and Nicholas Toman. 2010. "Stop Trying to Delight Your Customers." *Harvard Business Review* 88: 116–22.

Dresselhaus, Angela, and Flora Shrode. 2012. "Mobile Technologies and Academics: Do Students Use Mobile Technologies in Their Academic Lives and Are Librarians Ready to Meet This Challenge?" *Information Technology and Libraries* 31: 82–101.

Dugan, Robert E., and Peter Hernon. 2002. "Outcomes Assessment: Not Synonymous with Inputs and Outputs." *The Journal of Academic Librarianship* 28: 376–80.

Dugan, Robert E., Peter Hernon, and Danuta A. Nitecki. 2009. *Viewing Library Metrics from Different Perspectives: Inputs, Outputs, and Outcomes*. Santa Barbara, CA: ABC-CLIO.

Duncan, Vicky, and Darlene M. Fitcher. 2004. "What Words and Where? Applying Usability Testing Techniques to Name a New Live Reference Service." *Journal of the Medical Library Association* 92: 218–25.

Durrance, Joan. 1989. "Reference Success: Does the 55 Percent Rule Tell the Whole Story?" *Library Journal* 114 (April 15): 31–36.

Estep, Meredith. 2011. "New Survey Shows Unhappy Customers Spread the Word." *Intelligent Help Desk* (blog), *Unitiv*, May 16. http://www.unitiv.com/intelligent-help-desk-blog/bid/64134/New-Survey-Shows-Unhappy-Customers-Spread-the-Word.

Fitzpatrick, Elizabeth B., Anne C. Moore, and Beth W. Lang. 2008. "Reference Librarians at the Reference Desk in a Learning Commons: A Mixed Methods Evaluation." *The Journal of Academic Librarianship* 34: 231–38.

Garrison, Judith S. 2010. "Making Reference Service Count: Collecting and Using Reference Service Statistics to Make a Difference." *The Reference Librarian* 51: 202–11.

Gerlich, Bella Karr, and G. Lynn Berard. 2007. "Introducing the READ Scale: Qualitative Statistics for Academic Reference Services." *Georgia Library Quarterly* 43: 7–13.

Granfield, Diane, and Mark Robertson. 2008. "Preference for Reference: New Options and Choices for Academic Library Users." *Reference & User Services Quarterly* 48: 44–53.

Greenwood, Judy T., Alex P. Watson, and Melissa Dennis. 2011. "Ten years of LibQUAL: A Study of Qualitative and Quantitative Survey Results at the University of Mississippi 2001–2010." *The Journal of Academic Librarianship* 37: 312–18.

Gremmels, Gillian S., and Karen Shostrom Lehmann. 2007. "Assessment of Student Learning from Reference Service." *College & Research Libraries* 68: 488–501.

Hendricks, Arthur, and Sherry Buchanan. 2013. "From Exhaustion to Exhilaration: Assessing Librarian Job Satisfaction with Virtual Reference." *Library Hi Tech* 31: 42–63.

Hernon, Peter, and Ellen Altman. 1996. *Service Quality in Academic Libraries*. Norwood, NJ: Ablex Publishing.

Hernon, Peter, and Charles R. McClure. 1986. "Unobtrusive Reference Testing: The 55 Percent Rule." Library Journal 111 (April 15): 37–41.

Hernon, Peter, and Candy Schwartz. 2012. "The Assessment Craze." *Library & Information Science Research* 34: 79.

Hernon, Peter, Robert E. Dugan, and Danuta Nitecki. 2011. *Engaging in Evaluation and Assessment Research*. Santa Barbara, CA: Libraries Unlimited.

Hodgson, Cynthia. 2013. "ANSI/NISO Z39.7–2013, Information Services and Use: Metrics and Statistics for Library and Information Providers Data Dictionary." *National Information Standards Organization*. http://www.niso.org/apps/group_public/download.php/11283/Z39-7-2013_metrics.pdf.

Institute of Museum and Library Services. 2015a. "Outcome Based Evaluation: Basics." *Institute of Museum and Library Services*. Accessed June 27. https://www.imls.gov/grants/outcome-based-evaluations.

Institute of Museum and Library Services. 2015b. "Research." Accessed February 22. http://www.imls.gov/research/.

Integrated Postsecondary Education Data System. 2015. U.S. Department of Education. Accessed June 29. https://nces.ed.gov/ipeds/.

Jankal, Radoslav, and Miriam Jankalova. 2011. "Mystery Shopping: The Tool of Employee Communication Skills Evaluation." *Business: Theory and Practice* 12: 45–49.

Kelly, Betsy, Claire Hamasu, and Barbara Jones. 2012. "Applying Return on Investment (ROI) in Libraries." *Journal of Library Administration* 52: 656–71.

Kleiber, Pamela B. 2004. "Focus Groups: More Than a Method of Qualitative Inquiry." In *Foundations for Research: Methods of Inquiry in Education and the Social Sciences*, edited by Kathleen Bennett DeMarrais and Stephen D. Lapan, 87–102. Mahwah, NJ: L. Erlbaum Associates.

Kocevar-Weidinger, Elizabeth, Candice Benjes-Small, Eric Ackermann, and Virginia R. Kinman. 2010. "Why and How to Mystery Shop Your Reference Desk." *Reference Services Review* 38: 28–43.

Kwon, Nahyun. 2007. "Public Library Patrons' Use of Collaborative Chat Reference Service: The Effectiveness of Question Answering by Question Type." *Library & Information Science Research* 29: 70–91.

Landry, Marie B. 2000. "The Effects of Life Satisfaction and Job Satisfaction on Reference Librarians and Their Work." *Reference & User Services Quarterly* 40: 166–77.

Lankes, R. David, Melissa Gross, and Charles R. McClure. 2003. "Cost, Statistics, Measures, and Standards for Digital Reference Services: A Preliminary View." *Library Trends* 51: 401–13.

Lewis, Robert C., and Bernard H. Booms. 1983. "The Marketing Aspects of Service Quality." In *Emerging Perspectives on Services Marketing*, edited by G. Lynn Shostack, Leonard L. Berry, and Gregory D. Upah, 99–107. Chicago: American Marketing Association.

Liamputtong, Pranee. 2011. *Focus Group Methodology: Principles and Practice*. Thousand Oaks, CA: Sage Publications.

LibQUAL+®. 2015a. "FAQs." Accessed February 23. https://www.libqual.org/about/about_survey/faq_survey.

LibQUAL+®. 2015b. "Service Enhancements." Accessed February 23. http://www.libqual.org/about/enhancements.

Maness, Jack M., Sarah Naper, and Jayati Chaudhuri. 2009. "The Good, the Bad, but Mostly the Ugly: Adherence to RUSA Guidelines during Encounters with Inappropriate Behavior Online." *Reference & User Services Quarterly* 49: 151–62.

Martell, Charles. 2008. "The Absent User: Physical Use of Academic Library Collections and Services Continues to Decline 1995–2006." *The Journal of Academic Librarianship* 34: 400–407.

Massey-Burzio, Virginia. 1998. "From the Other Side of the Reference Desk: A Focus Group Study." *The Journal of Academic Librarianship* 24: 208–15.

Miller, Jonathon. 2008. "Quick and Easy Reference Evaluation: Gathering Users' and Providers' Perspectives." *Reference & User Services Quarterly* 47: 218–22.

Mokhtari, Heidi. 2014. "A Quantitative Survey on the Influence of Students' Epistemic Beliefs on Their General Information Seeking Behavior." *The Journal of Academic Librarianship* 40: 259–63.

Murfin, Marjorie E., and Gary M. Gugelchuk. 1987. *Development and Testing of a Reference Transaction Assessment Instrument.* College and Research Libraries 48 (4): 314–39.

Naylor, Sharon, Bruce Stoffel, and Sharon Van der Laan. 2008. "Why Isn't Our Chat Reference Used More? Findings of Focus Group Discussions with Undergraduate Students." *Reference & User Services Quarterly* 47: 342–54.

Novotny, Eric, and Emily Rimland. 2007. "Using the Wisconsin-Ohio Reference Evaluation Program (WOREP) to Improve Training and Reference Services." *The Journal of Academic Librarianship* 33: 382–92.

Oakleaf, Megan. 2009. "The Information Literacy Instruction Assessment Cycle: A Guide for Increasing Student Learning and Improving Librarian Instructional Skills." *Journal of Documentation* 65: 539–60.

Oakleaf, Megan. 2010. *The Value of Academic Libraries: A Comprehensive Research Review and Report.* Chicago: Association of College & Research Libraries.

Oakleaf, Megan, and Amy VanScoy. 2010. "Instructional Strategies for Virtual Reference: Methods to Facilitate Student Learning." *Reference & User Services Quarterly* 49: 380–90.

Olszewski, Lawrence, and Paula Rumbaugh. 2010. "An International Comparison of Virtual Reference Services." *Reference & User Services Quarterly* 49: 360–68.

Owen, Victoria. 2010. "Trialling a Service Model of the Future: Mobile Technologies in Student Support." *Multimedia Information & Technology* 26: 26–27.

Parasuraman, A., Valarie A. Zeithaml, and Leonard L. Berry. 1988. "SERVQUAL: A Multiple-Item Scale for Measuring Consumer Perceptions of Service Quality." *Journal of Retailing* 64: 12–40.

Pass, Christopher, Bryan Lowes, Andrew Pendleton, Malcolm Afferson, and Daragh O'Reilly. 2006. "Quality." In *Collins Dictionary of Business.* London: Collins.

Passanneau, Sarah, and Dan Coffey. 2011. "The Role of Synchronous Virtual Reference in Teaching and Learning: A Grounded Theory Analysis of Instant Messaging Transcripts." *College & Research Libraries* 72: 276–94.

Project Information Literacy. 2015. Accessed February 23. http://projectinfolit.org/.

Radford, Marie L. 1996. "Communication Theory Applied to the Reference Encounter: An Analysis of Critical Incidents." *The Library Quarterly* 66: 123–37.

Radford, Marie L. 1999. *The Reference Encounter: Interpersonal Communication in the Academic Library.* Chicago: Association of College & Research Libraries.

Reference and User Services Association. 2013. "Guidelines for Behavioral Performance of Reference and Information Service Providers." American Library Association. http://www.ala.org/rusa/resources/guidelines/guidelinesbehavioral.

Ryan, Pam. 2006. "EBL and Library Assessment: Two Solitudes?" *Evidence Based Library and Information Practice* 1 (4): 77–80. http://ejournals.library.ualberta.ca/index.php/EBLIP/article/view/136/177.

Smyth, Joanne B., and James C. MacKenzie. 2006. "Comparing Virtual Reference Exit Survey Results and Transcript Analysis: A Model for Service Evaluation." *Public Services Quarterly* 2: 85–99.

Starr, Susan. 2014. "Moving from Evaluation to Assessment." *Journal of the Medical Library Association* 102: 227–29.

Taddeo, Laura, and Jill M. Hackenberg. 2006. "The Nuts, Bolts, and Teaching Opportunities of Real-Time Reference." *College & Undergraduate Libraries* 13: 63–85.

Thompson, Bruce, Martha Kyrillidou, and Colleen Cook. 2008. "Library Users' Service Desires: A LibQUAL+ Study." *The Library Quarterly* 78: 1–18.

Usability.gov. 2015a. "Glossary." Accessed February 23. http://www.usability.gov/what-and-why/glossary/u/index.html.

Usability.gov. 2015b. "Usability Evaluation Basics." Accessed February 23. http://www.usability.gov/what-and-why/usability-evaluation.html.

Vileno, Luigina. 2010. "Testing the Usability of Two Online Research Guides." *Partnership: The Canadian Journal of Library and Information Practice & Research* 5: 1–21.

Ward, David. 2003. "Using Virtual Reference Transcripts for Staff Training." *Reference Services Review* 31: 46–56.

Warner, Debra G. 2001. "A New Classification for Reference Statistics." *Reference & User Services Quarterly* 41: 51–55.

Zhou, Fu, Mark Love, Scott Norwood, and Karla Massia. 2006. "Applying RUSA Guidelines in the Analysis of Chat Reference Transcripts." *College & Undergraduate Libraries* 13: 75–88.

SUGGESTED READINGS

Babbie, Earl. 2015. *The Practice of Social Research*, 14th ed. Belmont, CA: Wadsworth.
Babbie offers a clear and straightforward overview of social science research. This edition covers basic quantitative and qualitative research design, including operationalization, defining metrics, and sampling. More depth is given to some of the more common methodological approaches, such as surveys and observation, and a section is devoted to evaluation research. A substantial section of the book (Chapters 13–17) delves into analyzing and presenting data, including some statistical analysis. Although not specific to library research, this classic book offers a solid introduction to research.

Connaway, Lynn Silipigni, and Ronald R. Powell. 2010. *Basic Research Methods for Librarians*, 5th ed. Santa Barbara, CA: Libraries Unlimited.
Although useful as a textbook for LIS students, this handbook is tailored for practicing librarians. While it includes some sections on qualitative and historical research, the primary focus is on quantitative methods, including survey research and experiment design, as well as attention to some newer and emerging research areas such as social networking and other Web-based approaches. Like many of the other titles listed here, this book includes sections on statistical analysis, writing up results, and publishing research.

Creswell, John W. 2014. *Qualitative, Quantitative and Mixed Methods Approaches*, 4th ed. Thousand Oaks, CA: SAGE.
As the title implies, Creswell's work covers the range of research methodologies, with an emphasis on mixed methods. Like Babbie's book, given earlier, *Qualitative, Quantitative and Mixed Methods Approaches* is not specific to library and information science, but it is both thorough and general enough to be easily adapted to LIS projects. Creswell delves into the theory and philosophy, including ethical considerations in research design. He also provides detailed guidance on developing a purpose statement and research questions or hypotheses. However, the book does not offer much detail on any one approach. For instance, the section on surveys does not cover issues like question design. Nevertheless, this is a solid practical guide to overall research design.

Harmon, Charles, and Michael Messina, eds. 2013. *Customer Service in Libraries: Best Practices*. Lanham, MD: Scarecrow.
Although not a research guide, this volume presents nine case studies of customer service models across different types of libraries. Specific customer service topics range from technology planning to collection organization, to social media. Since much evaluation research in libraries centers on customer service and experience, this book provides ideas for focusing research on customer service topics, as well as offering some guidance on developing customer service programs.

Hernon, Peter, and Joseph R. Matthews. 2011. *Listening to the Customer*. Santa Barbara, CA: Libraries Unlimited.
Listening to the Customer focuses exclusively on tools, data gathering, and research from a library patron's perspective. Hernon and Matthews draw on theories from marketing and business to frame research as a tool for a user-centered approach. In addition to standard chapters on methodologies, the book offers chapters devoted to regaining lost customers and effective communication. The ultimate focus of the book, however, is using research methods to gather and analyze data in order to improve the customer experience.

Hernon, Peter, Robert E. Dugan, and Joseph R. Matthews. 2013. *Getting Started with Evaluation*. Royersford, PA: Alpha Publication House.
Written by some of the biggest names in library evaluation research, *Getting Started with Evaluation* is a practical guide emphasizing evidence-based practice and the

use of evaluation data for decision making and planning purposes as well as continuous improvement. The volume addresses stakeholder perspectives and the development and definition of library metrics for gathering data. Separate chapters are devoted to satisfaction, service quality, and return-on-investment studies.

Hernon, Peter, Robert E. Dugan, and Danuta A. Nitecki. 2011. *Engaging in Evaluation and Assessment Research.* Santa Barbara, CA: Libraries Unlimited.

Engaging in Evaluation and Assessment Research offers a clear and comprehensive guide to designing a research study. Although they can be read as standalone texts, the chapters move sequentially from the planning process to the presentation and use of findings. Hernon, Dugan, and Nitecki devote an entire chapter to operationalizing key concepts such as efficiency, effectiveness, and satisfaction. Subsequent chapters focus on research design, including sampling, reliability, and validity issues, and experiment design. Attention is given to both quantitative and qualitative approaches.

Manuel, Karen, and Susan E. Beck. 2009. *Practical Research Methods for Librarians and Information Professionals.* Chicago: Neal-Schuman.

This book provides a concise and user-friendly guide to conducting research, with library-specific examples. Manuel and Beck give step-by-step guidance for designing a research project, with chapters addressing interviews, focus groups, and usability testing as well as classroom and action research.

Matthews, Joseph R. 2007. *The Evaluation and Measurement of Library Services.* Santa Barbara, CA: Libraries Unlimited.

Although somewhat older than most of the other titles listed here, this handbook is still one of the clearest roadmaps to evaluation research in libraries. The book begins with an introduction to evaluation research, followed by an overview of several methodologies. Unique among the books listed here, however, Matthews includes a section of examples of evaluation research placed in the context of various library programs and services. For example, there are sections devoted to the evaluation of collections, reference services, and circulation, making this a very practical guide for librarians and administrators.

Matthews, Joseph R. 2014. *Library Assessment in Higher Education.* Santa Barbara, CA: Libraries Unlimited.

With a focus on academic libraries, Matthews draws on models from different colleges and universities to illustrate exemplary approaches to assessment. For each example, Matthews elaborates not just on how the assessment is carried out, but also on the ways in which the libraries use the data to demonstrate their impact on the wider campus, thus emphasizing the role of assessment in accountability to stakeholders. Less of a step-by-step guide, this book offers a broad overview of the assessment landscape in academic libraries, encouraging practitioners to develop their own culture of assessment.

Pickard, Alison Jane. 2013. *Research Methods in Information*, 2nd ed. Chicago: Neal-Schuman.

Pickard's book offers a solid and broad overview of various research methods with a focus on application in the information professions. She includes approaches to the research process, such as formulating questions and crafting research proposals, as well as attention to a range of data collection tools and instruments such as case studies, Delphi method, and ethnography, and sections on quantitative and qualitative data analysis. This handbook also includes chapters on using existing external data sets and managing research data.

Thayer-Hart, Nancy, Jennifer Dykema, Kelly Elver, Nora Cate Schaeffer, and John Stevenson. 2010. *Survey Fundamentals: A Guide to Designing and Implementing Surveys*. Madison, WI: University of Wisconsin. http://oqi.wisc.edu/resourcelibrary/uploads/resources/Survey_Guide.pdf.

This brief (20 page) open-source guide offers a solid overview on survey creation. In addition to an overview of determining the purpose of the survey and analyzing the data, the guide offers a number of tips for writing good questions and enhancing the reliability and validity of the study.

Trochim, William M. K. 2006. "Social Research Methods." *Web Center for Social Research Methods*. October 10. http://www.socialresearchmethods.net/.

Another open-source guide described as an online hyper-textbook, this website provides a thorough overview of social research methods, beginning with background on the language of research. The guide also covers foundational philosophies and ethics, followed by detailed sections on design. Although it includes sections on surveys and qualitative research, the main focus is on experimental and quasi-experimental designs. There is also a comprehensible section on basic statistical analysis.

Wallace, Danny P., and Connie J. Van Fleet. 2012. *Knowledge into Action: Research and Evaluation in Library and Information Science*. Santa Barbara, CA: Libraries Unlimited.

In this volume, Wallace and Van Fleet focus on evaluation research for evidence-based practice. They offer step-by-step guidance for developing a research project, including looking for funding. Separate sections are devoted to historical, descriptive, and experimental research methods, with detailed guidance on implementing the method, as well as an analysis of the pros and cons of each method. The authors briefly cover some basic statistical analysis and include a section on communicating results.

Wildemuth, Barbara M. 2009. *Applications of Social Research Methods to Questions in Library and Information Science*. Santa Barbara, CA: Libraries Unlimited.

Written in a clear and straightforward manner, this book makes research design and implementation accessible for students and practitioners. Wildemuth introduces a variety of research methods, examines their strengths and weaknesses, and provides illustrative examples. The author details a number of data collection approaches, including surveys and interviews, document analysis, transaction log analysis, and diary studies. The chapters function well as stand-alone texts, so readers can go directly to the relevant sections.

Williamson, Kirsty, and Graeme Johanson, eds. 2013. *Research Methods: Information, Systems, and Contexts*. Prahran, Australia: Tilde University Press.

This book pulls together contributions by a number of notable authors, offering a similar approach to many of the earlier texts by starting with an overview of research methods and ethics, followed by overviews of research tools and methods, and a section on quantitative and qualitative data analyses. The book includes attention to some research methods not often covered in other texts, including bibliometrics.

Chapter 9

Training and Continual Learning for Reference Staff

Beth S. Woodard

INTRODUCTION

In "The Making of a Reference Librarian," Samuel Rothstein (1983) argues that whether one believes that reference librarians are "made" or "born," for more than 100 years, a small industry has been devoted to improving their performance at the reference desk. Most librarians agree that merely working with library users and reference sources on a daily basis does not ensure that reference librarians will acquire a thorough knowledge of a wide variety of sources, that they will understand users' requests accurately, or that they will translate the users' requests appropriately. While some people have natural abilities in working with others and good instincts regarding how to approach reference questions, both asking appropriate questions and listening for what is not expressed, all reference librarians need nurturing and training to expand and complement these innate abilities.

New reference librarians often begin their careers with only the required library and information science courses to support them, occasionally reinforced with paraprofessional or preprofessional work (Powell and Raber 1993). Beginning reference courses generally cover specific reference sources, types of print and electronic sources, reference query negotiation, selection and evaluation of reference sources, and searching strategies (Broadway and Smith 1989). Only one of these five topics is directly related to the service aspect of reference work. To use this basic knowledge effectively, Nakano and Morrison (1992) suggest that reference librarians must be trained to apply their professional education to a particular library setting.

Although there are examples in the literature of how students can get a glimpse of what it is like to work with reference queries (Roy 2010), the reality is that relatively few students have actual reference experience when they leave library school. It is unreasonable to expect new graduates to perform today's sophisticated reference services successfully, or even adequately, without an investment of time and effort on the part of the employing library. These graduates need careful orientation, training, retraining, development, and continuing education to maximize their potential for providing effective reference service.

In a pilot study conducted in Ohio (Deputy 1995), almost all librarians surveyed felt that the skills needed to conduct a reference interview successfully can be taught. Most of them indicated that their formal training in conducting interviews had been given by their employer.

Reference librarians rarely see themselves as educators or administrators, even though they often perform traditional educational and administrative functions, such as teaching individuals how to use the library catalog or an online database and supervising clerks, students, paraprofessionals, volunteers, or other librarians. These supervisory responsibilities usually include training employees. The average reference librarian is generally only vaguely aware of the librarian's role in training, either as a recipient or as a facilitator for others. This chapter describes the role of training in preparing reference staff to provide effective service and in maintaining skill levels.

As reference departments continue the process of "rethinking reference," recognizing limitations on the roles that professionals can play in providing reference service, there has been more of an emphasis on the use of paraprofessionals in reference services. Subsequently, there has been greater interest in designing training programs and in sharing information about the training process (Morgan 2009, 1–7). In addition, there has been enormous interest generated in training as a result of studies indicating that reference service is not always accurate (see Chapter 8).

When reference department personnel rely only on informal apprenticeships, serious gaps in reference staff training occur. Commonly, trainees, whether new reference librarians, reference assistants, students who shelve books, or volunteers, learn a few specific tasks and never understand the rationale for what they are doing or how these tasks fit into the overall mission of the library. Employees not only need to be trained in specific skill areas related to their direct responsibilities, but they also must have a knowledge base broad enough to understand the larger context. A broad knowledge base also allows them to learn the new skills they need to respond to the rapidly changing environment of reference and information services.

Today's reference staff are expected to handle changes, which occur with increasing frequency. Reference personnel must live with uncertainty and must adapt to new management styles, changing user demands, and advances in technology, and their own expanding roles in creating Web pages or participating in networked campuses or organizations, community outreach, and distance education. Unless training ensures that librarians are committed to the value of reference service, are able to provide instruction to users regarding available services, and are flexible in responding to changes, reference librarians will be limited to using traditional tools, and they will not be able to approach reference service in the context of changed user needs or new technologies (Creth 1986, 6).

The terms "training," "education," and "development" are often used interchangeably. Leonard Nadler and Zeace Nadler introduced the term "human resource development" in 1969 and defined it as "organized learning experiences in a definite time period to increase the possibility of improving job performance growth" (Nadler and Nadler 1990, 1.3). Current practice defines it as "the activities that encompass workplace learning" (Chalofsky, Rocco, and Morris 2014, xxxix). Nadler went on to make fine distinctions between training, education, and development, which Suellyn Hunt further clarified for librarians: "Training = job-related learning experiences; Education = individual-related learning experiences; Development = organizational-related learning experiences" (1983, 227). The various aspects of these three activities are explored in this chapter.

ORIENTATION

All staff members, whether part-time workers, temporary workers, or experienced individuals who plan to stay for a while, need *orientation*, or an introduction to the job environment. *Staff orientation* is "an initial training process designed to acquaint new employees with various aspects of the organization, including established goals, policies, and procedures; the physical environment; other personnel and working relationships, job duties and responsibilities; and fringe benefits" (Young 1983, 214). Typically, this type of training is not transferable to another setting and provides little that employees could use if they took jobs in other libraries.

Enculturation

Orientation provides a sense of support, defines the employee's singular role in the library, and establishes the individual as a part of the team. Dorothy Jones (1988, 222) stresses that the training of new librarians should address the political setting, the work organization of the department, the details of each task, and the path to promotion and job retention. The orientation program's ultimate goal is to promote a feeling of self-worth, a sense of belonging, an attitude of pride and confidence in both self and the library, and a desire to succeed. H. Scott Davis (1994, v) stresses that research has indicated that the first few weeks in a new job are important to establishing future job satisfaction and productivity in new employees and in capitalizing on the excitement and anticipation felt in the first few days. One objective should be to address typical issues and answer typical questions before they cause frustration or inhibit productivity. *Enculturation* should be a part of orientation programs, communicating the culture, the expectations for dress and behavior (both the formal and the informal rules of behavior), and the importance of each individual in the organization.

To give the new staff member a sense of the organizational culture, including areas of authority and expertise, individuals should meet with key personnel throughout the organization. This allows them to discover how each unit functions and the interrelationships between units (Weingart, Kochan, and Hedrich 1998, 157). The personal connection also allows the individual to feel comfortable in returning to the expert to ask questions when needed.

Socialization

Socialization is also an important aspect of the reference orientation session, according to Angela Ballard and Laura Blessing (2006). Employees need time to get acquainted with their coworkers in an informal setting, to discuss their activities in an unstructured environment, and to reflect on and absorb what they have already been told. In any training program, reference staff, as well as staff in other departments with which the trainee comes in daily contact, should be formally introduced, but they should also have some opportunity to meet on a less-formal basis, such as a coffee hour or other informal gathering. This is particularly important for reference staff who must work together as a team and make referrals to other service points in the library.

Expectations

The first day of orientation is the appropriate time to discuss both the employee's expectations and the employer's. "Time spent here can prevent many misunderstandings and counterproductive situations later" (Weingart, Kochan, and Hedrich 1998, 157). Anne May Berwind (1991) stresses the need for staff to discuss the local philosophy of reference service. This discussion should include the nature of the population of users served and the primary purpose of the reference service, whether it is to find answers as rapidly as possible or to teach users how to find information independently. Priorities for service should be agreed upon, and reference librarians need to know whether they are expected to work independently or together to provide service. This is particularly important for new librarians, whose preexisting expectations can differ radically from the job reality (Oud 2008, 254).

Linda A. Jerris (1993, 3) suggests that orientation is "a process, not just a program" and goes on to state that orientation should communicate the values and priorities of the organization. It should focus on alignment with the organization's mission statement, have a quality and customer focus, and emphasize accountability and teamwork. In order to accomplish this, she urges the participation of supervisors and senior management in orientation programs, fostering two-way communication between new employees and decision makers. She also discusses the importance of conducting follow-up and review (Jerris 1993, 6).

Environments Conducive for Ongoing Learning

Orientation is only the first step in a continuing process. A positive upbeat orientation program extending over a period of several weeks or even months can be very effective in helping the new employee to become an efficient, productive member of the library staff (Oliver 1972, 140). An effective period of induction will help the new staff member become more receptive to continuing training, absorb the details of the job, become a better team player, and feel comfortable in the new position.

A planned orientation also helps to establish an atmosphere that facilitates learning. Orientation reduces stress when opportunities are given for individuals to share work-related problems and questions. When similarly situated individuals share feelings of frustration and isolation, those feelings are reduced, and work relationships can also improve. Orientation can also be a motivator. When individuals see the library as an organization that is willing to put time and effort into orientation and training, they are likely to feel more a part of the organization and make a commitment to it.

Departmental		
First 2 weeks	First Month	Within first 6 months
Review training plan. Tour of employee's work area. Tour of reference department. Review of job duties and expectations.	Policies and procedures and why they were written. How to handle user complaints. How feedback/evaluation is provided.	When it is appropriate to make exceptions and/or refer to supervisor. Individuals outside unit who can help solve problems. At least one formal session providing feedback to date.
Enculturation		
First 2 weeks	First month	Within first 6 months
Arrange for individual meetings with each person in the unit. Arrange introductions to key personnel from other units. Tour building.	Ask a variety of individuals to arrange more informal coffee or lunch sessions. Arrange tours of other units.	Introduce staff member during various meetings. Arrange a more formal "meet and greet" library-wide. Arrange tours of units in other buildings.
Organizational Issues		
First 2 weeks	First Month	Within first 6 months
Institutional mission. Library mission. Unit mission.	Structure of responsibility: reporting, responsibility. Decision-making structure: Who participates; how decisions made. Governance structure: Role, structure, and membership of the Board or other governing group; actual powers of administrators, Physical/geographical structure: Locations of desks and/or other buildings and/or locations.	History of the organization. Review of current organizational challenges.
Working the Reference Desk		
First 2 weeks	First Month	Within first 6 months
Basic desk procedures. Library hours. Emergency procedures. How to keep desk statistics.	How to operate equipment. How to complete necessary forms. Phone system tricks.	Directions to frequently requested campus or local locations.

FIGURE 9.1 Sample library orientation outline (inspired by Bessler 1994, 15)

Online Searching		
First 2 weeks	First Month	Within first 6 months
How to do simple searches and/or most frequently requested kinds of searches. How to find the right tool for typical undergraduate research needs. How to examine an online database for features offered. Basic troubleshooting for problems with online resources, remote access, and printing or scanning.	How to do complicated keyword searches. How to use online thesauri. How to use primary indexes. How to be a better "Googler." Begin introduction to more-in-depth resources, starting with the sources in more popular academic subject area that has "user friendly" reference sources. Typical online problems encountered by remote users.	How to use the more-complex sources in various academic disciplines and special collections, such as government documents, business, and law. Ask the individual to identify a subject area in which they would provide training for others.
Familiarization with Collection and Types of Questions		
First 2 weeks	First Month	Within first 6 months
Types of reference sources. Analyzing reference questions. Location of the most frequently requested sources. Introduction to READ scale (readscale.org) for documenting reference transactions.	Training in use of the READ Scale. Procedures for requesting purchase of new reference materials.	Ask the individual to identify a reference source for which they would provide training for others. Ask individual to examine one area of collection with the idea of updating or weeding the collection.
Interpersonal Skills		
First 2 Weeks	First Month	Within first 6 months
Reference interview training, if necessary. Customer service standards. Greeting patrons. Encouraging patron follow-up. Phone techniques. Treating staff as patrons.	Listening skills. Working collaborative with others at the desk. Making referrals. Receiving referrals. Awareness of cultural differences. Coping with stressful individuals and situations. How to incorporate instructional techniques in the reference exchange.	Dealing with angry or upset patrons. Saying "no." Institutional resources for assisting with patrons with special needs. Intervening when another staff member is not providing correct information. Reviewing chat transcripts in order to improve ability to ask appropriate questions.

FIGURE 9.1 (Continued)

When planning orientation and training activities, trainers should attempt to create environments that facilitate learning. Trainers need to remember that research about how adults learn (Imel 1994; Knowles 1996, 253–56) suggests that the following elements need to be incorporated into the design of a training program:

- Involve participants in mutual planning
- Provide for active involvement
- Promote individual discovery
- Recognize the personal and subjective nature of learning
- Accept differences
- Recognize people's right to make mistakes
- Tolerate ambiguity
- Allow cooperation and self-evaluation
- Permit confrontation

BASIC TRAINING: LEARNING THE ESSENTIALS

Basic training in job requirements is mainly concerned with helping staff members learn fundamental job skills, but it also covers some skills that employees may be able to take to other jobs. The *ALA Glossary* (Young 1983, 231) defines training as "the process of developing the knowledge, skills, and attitudes needed by employees to perform their duties effectively and to meet the expectations and goals of the organization. This diverse process, which may be performed by supervisors, fellow employees, and personnel officers, involves planning, preparation, execution, and evaluation."

Defining Competencies

If supervisors fail to define performance expectations, employees will establish their own acceptable performance levels, either individually or as a group (Roethlisberger and Dick 1939, 522). Staff members will observe colleagues and draw their own conclusions regarding the kind of behavior that is expected if expectations are not clearly articulated.

The mutual development of performance expectations and objectives will avoid hidden expectations of standards. If clear standards and specific models of performance are described, individuals will know what is expected of them and how they are to be evaluated. If librarians, or any group of library workers, are asked to participate in establishing these objectives, the objectives are more likely to be accepted by the group.

After a consensus of what constitutes adequate performance has been established, the next important step is to write a competency description, which describes the correct performance of a job and delineates behaviors that signal when it is done right. *Competencies* are knowledge, skills, or attitudes that enable a person to function satisfactorily in a work situation, either alone or with others. The profession has made great strides to come to consensus about competencies for reference service. The Reference and User Services Association's (RUSA's) "Professional Competencies for Reference and User Services Librarians" (2003) includes competencies in access; knowledge base; marketing, awareness, and informing; collaboration; and evaluation and assessment of resources and services. When answering questions, librarians must know about available reference sources, be able to find proper sources to answer the questions, be familiar with the library's collection, and use appropriate technology. Although these are only a few of the functions that reference librarians perform, they definitely need to be competent in these areas. See Box 9.1 for an example.

Box 9.1 A Portion of the RUSA "Professional Competencies for Reference and User Services Librarians"

Responsiveness:

Goal: A librarian provides services that are responsive to user needs.

Strategies:

1. Determines the situational context of the individual information needs of users when interacting with each user in person or through another communication channel.
2. Analyzes information sources recommended to users in the context of the attractiveness, interests, and content level for each user.
3. Suggests specific works that relate to what the user said is important.
4. Utilizes the *Behavioral Standards for Reference Librarians* on Approachability, Interest, and Listening/Inquiring when providing reference service in a traditional in-person service setting.
5. Engages users in discussions about experiences related to their information needs and communicates interest in every user's experiences.
6. Respects the right of users to determine the direction of their research by empowering them to pursue their own preferences.

(Reference and User Services Association 2003). Used with permission from the American Library Association.

Some other reference competencies can be derived from the various functions performed by reference librarians. In the reference interview, reference staff need to have excellent communication skills, including listening, instructing others, and giving clear directions. Virginia Massey-Burzio (1991, 73) emphasized that reference librarians need communication skills: "In addition to verbal skills, writing skills are also needed since a considerable part of a reference librarian's life is spent preparing brochures, pathfinders, flyers, point-of-use instruction guides, grant proposals, articles in the campus newspaper and in library newsletters, and other written communication." Reference staff need to be able to work well in teams and foster ways of sharing knowledge. They must deal with angry and frustrated users as well as diversity issues. They must prioritize when confronted with multiple demands and long lines of users. They must know when to give information, how far to go in providing information, when to stop, when to refer, and when to teach. Reference staff increasingly must develop presentation skills for instructing groups.

When answering questions, librarians must know about available reference sources, both electronic and print, be able to find proper sources to answer questions, be familiar with the library's collection and local resources, and use appropriate technology. They also have to maintain awareness of community resources and optional delivery services through interlibrary loan, consortial agreements, fax, and full-text services. Only minimal skill levels in searching online systems and the Web are not sufficient. Today's reference staff need to be able to think creatively about searching and finding resources.

Mary Nofsinger (1999) identifies six major categories of competencies: reference skills and subject knowledge, communication and interpersonal skills, technological skills, analytical and critical thinking skills, management and supervisory skills, and commitment to user services. Although these are only a few of the functions that reference librarians perform, they illustrate the diversity of competencies required. Anne Roberts (1984, 402) gives further discussion of areas of competencies for reference librarians.

Competencies can be identified for specific staff levels or for particular services. For example, certain groups of staff may provide all levels of reference service, from providing directional assistance to complex bibliographic verification and research consultation. Other staff members may provide only directional and ready-reference assistance, referring all other queries to a more experienced staff member, to a different level of staff, or to another service point (see Chapter 6 for a discussion of models of reference service). Box 9.2 provides an excerpt of core competencies needed in an academic library besides the kinds of communication and interpersonal skills one typically considers.

Assessing Training Needs

Reference departments frequently hire new staff members. Because no department has unlimited time or funds to train, it needs to determine how to get the most from training. Therefore, it is essential to conduct a *needs assessment*. A needs assessment is important in order to plan, manage, and allocate scarce training dollars, as well as to evaluate training results. Training needs are competencies required or desired but which have not yet been developed. Training should never be conducted without identifying its purpose or need.

A great deal of discussion continues about what reference librarians need to know from a general liberal arts and sciences background that gives a basis of knowledge to comprehensive knowledge of reference sources. A public service attitude, communication skills, teaching ability, an ability to evaluate information, a knowledge of the structure of literature, and the ability to formulate search strategies effectively are all aspects of reference service that most reference librarians would include as requirements.

Analyzing Tasks

Analyzing what goes on at the reference or information desk can be a good beginning for identifying needs of reference librarians or paraprofessionals. Reference interview techniques; knowledge of reference sources; ability to manipulate online catalogs, local files, community information, and online databases;

Box 9.2 Excerpt of Core Competencies from the University of Nebraska-Lincoln

Analytical Skills/Problem Solving/Decision Making

Recognizes patterns, draws logical conclusions, and makes recommendations for action. Uses a well-ordered approach to solving problems and sound judgment in making decisions despite obstacles or resistance.

Creativity/Innovation

Looks for opportunities to apply new and evolving ideas, methods, designs, and technologies.

Flexibility/Adaptability

Performs a wide range of tasks, responds to changes in direction and priorities, and accepts new challenges, responsibilities and assignments.

Leadership

Sets and models high performance standards characterized by integrity. Earns trust and respect of others by coaching, inspiring, and empowering teams of people to achieve strategic objectives.

Organizational Understanding and Global Thinking

Demonstrates an understanding of the institution in its entirety and works to achieve results across disciplines, departments, and functions. Develops and maintains supportive relationships across the organization.

Ownership/Accountability/Dependability

Accepts responsibility for actions, results, and risks. Gets the job done.

Planning and Organizational Skills

Anticipates and predicts internal and external changes, trends, and influences in order to effectively allocate resources and implement appropriate library initiatives.

Resource Management

Demonstrates a consistent focus on minimizing expenses while maximizing results.

(Giesecke and McNeil 1999, 160). Used with permission from the American Library Association.

working as a team with colleagues; and sharing knowledge in a constructive way are all areas in which any staff member who works at a reference or information desk should be competent. Although analysis of reference desk activities is a good method to identify basic training needs for new reference desk workers, many other techniques are available. Geary A. Rummler (1987) discusses alternative needs assessment techniques, and Mel Silberman (2006, 32–34) identifies advantages and disadvantages of nine basic needs assessment techniques.

Interviews

Interviews, either with individuals or in groups, are particularly useful in determining the needs of experienced librarians (Conroy 1976, 19). From interviews, it may be determined that librarians have specific ongoing training needs, such as further practice in asking open-ended questions and achieving closure in the reference interview. Other areas in which experienced personnel generally identify training needs are in using new equipment or systems, learning new sources and tools, and reviewing little-used reference sources. Box 9.3 provides a sample list of the training needs of a reference assistant.

Box 9.3 Sample List of Training Needs of a Reference Assistant

Task: "Responds to routine and directional questions in person, over the telephone, and via electronic reference service."

Needs to know:

- Responses to questions that are "routine"
- Location of all library service points
- Layout of all library floors
- How to navigate the library's Web page
- How to use online catalog
- How to use the telephone properly
- Location of phone numbers
- How to utilize virtual reference software
- Communication techniques
- Guidelines and procedures for referrals

(Morgan 2009, 24)

When Needs Do Not Point to Training

When skill deficiencies exist, certain questions must be answered to determine the best course of action. If the job is one the employee used to do, have procedures changed? If not, then feedback and practice may be the answer. If procedures have changed or if it is a new job, then procedures may be simplified, training may be done on the job, or formal training may have to be arranged. If there is no skill deficiency, then the obstacles to adequate performance must be examined and corrected. One obstacle may be that procedures are unrealistic or have not been clearly communicated. Creating practice sessions, a job aid, or finding guide, or combining them, can be a more practical approach to helping people to perform infrequently used complex tasks. Not all deficiencies in performance can be addressed with training; some performance problems are associated with environmental or attitudinal factors that prevent or discourage optimum performance. Other techniques, such as providing feedback on observed behaviors or planning practice sessions, can also be used to improve performance at the reference desk. Some reference departments have found success with having individuals become "the resident expert" in certain areas, resources, or databases, and then have the responsibility of teaching others.

Box 9.4 Activity: Is This a Training Problem?

A large university reference department provides occasional reference assistance in using the library's collection of British Parliamentary Papers. The staff has received training, which consists of reviewing the types of access tools, discussing formats, and examining a bibliography prepared by an experienced librarian. One particular staff member has trouble dealing with these questions. She ordinarily panics and turns to the person who prepared the bibliography. When that person is not available, she can generally muddle through to answer the question.

Questions for Reflection and Discussion:

1. Is this a training problem?
2. What are the obstacles to adequate performance?

Training Needs of Staff Groups

Every reference department has a variety of individuals who make up the staff and provide varying levels of service. From the students shelving books and the clerical persons who check in the books, to the paraprofessional who works the reference desk a few hours a week, to the senior reference librarian or head of the department, everyone has training needs that need to be addressed.

Volunteers

Although the use of volunteers to provide reference service is a managerial decision that may or may not come under the purview of the individual entrusted with training, the training of volunteers requires flexibility and individuation. Volunteers can range from unemployed librarians, to staff members in other departments, to well-meaning community members with little or no skills or background in libraries. Consequently, this makes it extremely difficult to lump them into a single category. The kind of responsibilities they have in the department will determine the kind of training they will need. Museums and other nonprofit organizations use volunteers very successfully in their educational programs, and there is certainly no reason why libraries cannot do the same.

Students and Clerical Workers

Students and clerical workers have similar needs in that they often come to their jobs without library backgrounds or familiarity, so they often need more than basic orientation to know where they fit into the system. They need to understand the terminology and the service mission of the department, with the understanding that they represent the library to many users.

Paraprofessionals

Paraprofessionals often come with a wide variety of backgrounds and skills. Some may have little or no library experience and little formal education; others may have extensive library experience; yet others may have advanced degrees in other subject areas. With such inconsistency, trainers must either test for each person's knowledge or assume no knowledge and begin from scratch.

Reference interview behaviors, as well as general information on how materials are physically and intellectually accessed in the library, need to be included, along with specific tools and sources paraprofessionals are expected to know. Generally, training should include an introduction to and practice sessions on the library's catalog and specific tools such as indexes in all formats that are appropriate. In addition, types of information frequently in demand, such as biographical information, statistics, government information, or current events, or special types of materials such as newspapers or government publications, should be covered in a manner determined by the individual library. The chapters of this book on sources can provide suggestions for these sessions or modules of training. Paraprofessionals also need guidance regarding how to examine a new reference source, and how to identify strengths and weaknesses of specific sources. In addition, paraprofessionals will need written policies and procedures indicating when it is appropriate to refer users to professional librarians in the department or in other departments, other libraries, or outside agencies.

Because most paraprofessionals do not have the benefit of a library school education, they will need guidance in the process of approaching a reference question. For example, they need to learn how to analyze a question so that when they do not find the answer in the first source they try, they can devise an alternate strategy.

Writing Objectives for Training

If training objectives are to be useful, they must describe the kind of performance that will be accepted as evidence that the learner has mastered that particular task. This definition by behavior is used to measure whether the trainees have achieved the goal of the training and whether the training is successful.

Three kinds of objectives, *acquiring knowledge*, *learning skills*, and *reinforcing attitudes*, are described. Examples of knowledge in the reference setting include information and understanding about the reference collection, the general collection, library services, and policies. Skills of reference librarians include the ability to translate that knowledge into performing tasks, such as conducting reference interviews, instructing users, and communicating in a clear and concise way. Steven Carr (2013, 113) asserts that a "customer service attitude was a key ingredient to any organization's success."

As with other educational sessions (see Chapter 4), if objectives are to be useful in developing training, Robert F. Mager (1975, 21) suggests that three elements are necessary: *performance*, *conditions*, and *criteria*. Performance describes what is to be done—what the trainee should be able to do. Conditions describe the situation and the kinds of tools that can be used. Criteria describe the quality and quantity of work expected and the time allowed to complete the job. In reference work, this means the quality of service, including accuracy and completeness.

Selecting Methods

Selection of the most suitable instructional strategy is based on several considerations. One of the most important is congruency with the stated training objective. The strategy should recognize the need for trainees to respond and to receive feedback, should adapt to individuals' different learning styles, and should approximate what happens on the job. Factors that restrict the choice of strategy include the instructor's level of skill, the size of the group, costs, time, and equipment available.

Knowledge

Some methods are more suitable than others in helping trainees attain the objective. Objectives that stress knowledge acquisition, such as "describe the structure of biological literature," are appropriately reached through lecture, discussion, and assigned readings. Lectures and films require only that people listen and watch, while programmed texts and computer-aided instruction are specifically designed to require that a choice be made before the trainee can move to the next question, page, or screen. John Newstrom (1980, 58) reports that research has shown that teaching materials based on the principles of programmed learning—small steps, self-pacing, and immediate feedback—are the first choice of trainers for knowledge retention because of the activity involved. Today, the format of programmed learning materials is frequently found in online tutorials. Lynda.com represents these principles well. A number of good online training resources are available through clearinghouses such as WebJunction.

Skills

The use of videos has been increasingly popular in training, but it is often difficult to find quality clips. For communication and management skills, videos can model appropriate behavior. For technical procedures that apply step-by-step processes, videos not only demonstrate appropriate techniques, but also allow slow motion and replay functions that will deepen comprehension. Gwen Arthur (1992) suggests that when used to record trainees' behaviors, video can provide opportunities for self-observation and evaluation. Phillippa Dolphin (1986) uses *trigger videos*, or short episodes, to raise a large number of issues, including sexual harassment, handling aggression or other problems, or behaviors that affect the image of the library, and stimulate or trigger discussions.

Skills generally cannot be learned and applied without some sort of practice. While the general concepts behind the application of skills, such as the steps involved in the reference interview, can be learned through lectures, demonstrations, or other passive forms of teaching, reference staff must *use* a skill if they are to apply it consistently.

Role-playing, in which situations are outlined and individuals assume roles to try out behaviors in a realistic manner, is one technique that simulates the job environment. Other methods that simulate job behavior include case studies, management games, practice sessions, and workshops. Often, reference departments compile questions that have really been asked at their desks and ask trainees to identify sources to answer these questions (Isaacs 1969). If the training objective is to select an appropriate search strategy to find a known item in the online catalog, effective methods might include online tutorials, or a combination of reading, lecture, and discussion, as well as practice sessions. Because this objective requires that a choice be made, a method requiring a response will be more effective.

In introducing new staff to database searching, general searching techniques can be explained through lecture and demonstration. This can be followed by a set of practice searches for specific databases. Other databases, search software, and more specific search techniques can again be demonstrated with lectures and demonstration and followed by hands-on practice. As training proceeds over the course of several days with several different databases, trainees should start to ask when they would go to a particular source. Training people *how* to use a particular resource does not guarantee that they will know *when* to use it appropriately. After a discussion of the advantages and disadvantages of each system, the trainees can be divided into small groups and given a series of questions. They can be asked to try them in different systems and report back to the group what worked and what did not. Providing an environment in which it is acceptable to make mistakes, but simulating the kinds of questions they will be asked at the information or reference desk, helps them learn for themselves when it is appropriate to examine a particular tool.

The best training promotes self-discovery, recognizing that "the most important things cannot be taught but must be discovered and appropriated for oneself" (Schön 1987, 92). As an ancient proverb puts it: "Tell me, I forget. Show me, I remember. Involve me, I understand." Adults learn best with active involvement, by solving realistic problems. If adults work things out for themselves, they are more likely to be able to work out a similar problem on the job. Active learning promotes the use of ingenuity and imagination rather than performance of a task in a set manner. Problem-solving skills can be learned effectively in this way, using

Box 9.5 Activity: Write Guidelines for Preparing Training

The introduction to and updating of the information staff, which consists of 12 library assistants, to online databases has gotten out of hand. There are just too many databases and too many software vendors for one person to keep track of. The reference training coordinator has decided to ask each of the 12 library assistants to be responsible for training the others. A small committee of reference librarians has been assigned to help the training coordinator come up with guidelines for the training.

Questions for Reflection and Discussion:

1. What should be included in the documentation that each assistant develops?
2. Should they also be asked to develop handouts for users?
3. How much autonomy will each assistant have in creating these training materials?

case studies or in-basket exercises to simulate decisions that must be made on the job. Asking staff to take on training another person can have similar benefits.

Attitudes

Attitudes can be influenced in a variety of ways, and experts differ in the approaches they suggest. With adults, interaction again is important, so sensitivity training, role-playing, and discussion groups are useful means of changing attitudes. Trigger videos, or dramatic vignettes illustrating a dilemma, a problem, or a situation with which the audience is familiar without providing the answer as to what should be done to resolve the situation, are useful in stimulating discussions. They are particularly useful for handling issues that are hard to describe or replicate, such as sexual harassment, the handling of aggression, or other problems or behaviors that affect the image of the library (Dolphin 1986).

Factors in Strategy Selection

The availability or lack of experienced trainers, instructional space, facilities, equipment, and materials can do much to facilitate or hinder the training process, and all influence the choice of instructional strategy. The time and costs of development, the size of the group, and the learning styles of the trainee population also restrict the choices the trainer can make. A number of training experts, including Jonassen, Grabinger, Duncan, and Harris (1990), Bean (2014), and Sites, Green, and Allen (2014), have written excellent guides to facilitate selection of training methods for the new trainer. Instruction experts have also identified approaches to teaching library skills to users; these approaches transfer well to training situations.

In planning training events, trainers should consider known educational principles. Although individual study and reflection are excellent ways that people learn, one should also take into consideration that cooperative learning is a good practice. One study on training library technicians to take on reference responsibilities found that relying too heavily on self-paced study proved difficult with hectic schedules. The program was revised to include more formal courses (Bandys, Daghita, and Whitmore 2002).

Box 9.6 Activity: Identify Training Activities

The reference librarian and the circulation librarian at a small college library have been asked to improve the staff's dealings with angry patrons. In doing research, they identified three steps: (1) calming the patron, (2) identifying the problem, and (3) providing relief. Staff members have more difficulty with steps one and three.

Questions for Reflection and Discussion:

1. What training activities could be used in this situation?
2. What are the strengths and weaknesses of each?

Box 9.7 Activity: Develop a Case Study

In small groups, identify a problem area in reference services training and develop a case study. Share the case study with another group and ask them to work through the problem. Have them consider the perspectives of both staff and users in determining an approach. Ask the group to identify the strengths of this case study and offer suggestions for improvement.

Example:

You are working alone at a very busy information desk at Green County Public Library. The mayor's secretary calls and says that the mayor needs the names and addresses of the publishers of about 20 periodicals and that she needs it now. Although the source of this information is at your service desk, the information will require multiple lookups. Furthermore, you see three restless users circling your desk area. Identify three ways to handle this call that could satisfy the mayor and also tend to your on-site users.

(Example from Bessler 1994, 30)

Facilitating Retention of Skills

In learning almost any skill, people go through an awkward phase when the newly acquired skill does not feel natural and does not achieve results. This period, called the "results dip" or "incorporation lag," is particularly difficult. Initially, when reference librarians attempt to substitute a new behavior for an old one, it feels uncomfortable and results suffer. Some studies have found that up to 87 percent of the skills actually acquired by a training program may be lost if attention is not paid to making sure that these skills are retained (Rackham 1979, 14). Combating the problem of transferring learned skills to the job environment can take several forms, both during the training itself and back on the job.

Practice

Techniques that simulate the behavior used on the job are more likely to teach skills that will actually be used in that setting. The training program itself should include a sufficient amount of time to practice, which may be as much as a third of the instruction time (Chellino and Walker 1983, 12). Practice away from the job provides an opportunity to fail in a controlled environment without the normal consequences, a frame of reference for tasks to be performed, and an ability to apply new skills learned more easily and readily.

Role-playing, although not a particular favorite with trainees, continues to be one of the best approaches to allow the learner to take part in a realistic, but simulated and therefore nonthreatening, situation. Role-playing is an excellent way to demonstrate appropriate techniques to use with difficult patrons and in question negotiation. Role-playing exercises in isolation do not produce skilled performers. They do, however, help ensure that trainees learn the steps appropriate for skilled performance. This technique has been used successfully at Baylor University, where Janet Sheets (1998) developed a role-playing exercise she called "The Reference Game." In this game, the emphasis is on the interaction with users rather than on the selection of a particular reference tool. For virtual reference, practice is particularly important, given that unfamiliarity with the software may make the interaction more difficult (see Box 9.8).

Box 9.8 Activity: Answering Questions Using Chat

Instructions:

During the interaction, you will take turns asking a question (patron) and answering a question (librarian). Once in the chat system, the patron will send a chat invitation to the librarian. The patron can select a question from the list below or make up one.

If you are the patron with a question:

- Determine what role you are playing, such as a person with a personal information need, someone with a trivia question, or a student with an assignment.
- Keeping your role in mind, phrase your questions and responses accordingly.
- To make sure you don't lose the chat conversation, open another browser window to input any URLs the librarian may send you.
- When asked, respond to the librarian's query about whether or not you are satisfied with the answer.

If you are the librarian answering the question:

- Use a reference interview to find out what the patron wants.
- Search for the answers to the question in a separate browser session.
- Maintain contact with the patron, informing him or her of your process and progress.
- Send the URL for the answer you have found to the patron via the chat program.
- Ask if the patron finds the answer satisfactory.

Then switch roles.

Practice Questions:

1. Bonnie and Clyde. When and where did they commit most of their crimes and when and where were they killed?
2. When was the last big tsunami in the Indian Ocean?
3. When will Muslims pilgrimage in 2025?
4. I am writing a paper on teenage drug use. I would like to find testimonials of those who got help and quit.
5. My son wants to dress up as Kirby for Halloween. Who is Kirby and what does he look like?
6. What are the seven wonders of the Ancient World, and how do we know about them?
7. What is the origin of the quote, "Give a man a fish and feed him for a day; teach a man to fish and feed him for a lifetime"?
8. Where will the 2020 world's fair be held?
9. I'm writing a paper on crime reduction strategies and need some examples of some successful programs. Are there any statistics that prove that they are successful?
10. In what year was the St. Valentine's Day massacre in Chicago? Who was Al Capone trying to trap?
11. When is Disability Awareness Week?
12. Why do you poke holes in baking potatoes? Does it help them cook faster?
13. What is equine therapy? How far do I have to travel to find someplace that offers it?
14. When was the first Pulitzer Prize given? How many categories are currently honored?
15. Who was the last person to walk on the Moon?

(Adapted from Hirko and Ross 2004, 134–35)

Drills, or short repetitive exercises, can be used to master skills in small steps. As skills are practiced under a variety of circumstances, the trainee's ability to perform consistently improves. During these drills, trainees function as coaches for each other, helping to critique as each element or move is practiced and then combined into a series of moves. Drilling then provides confidence and "confidence builds 'ownership' of the skill. And ownership must occur *during* the training course in order for the skill to transfer to the real job" (Georges 1988, 46).

Several other techniques can be used during the training session to facilitate retention of skills learned. *Action plans*, where the participants reflect on program content and write goals of intended implementation, are useful techniques for maintaining behavior. These can take the form of a letter to oneself or an "ideas and applications" notebook. Other activities that can be incorporated into training sessions include *guided practice* (as opposed to turning trainees loose for independent practice) and *question-and-answer sessions* that involve some sort of systematic pattern to include everyone.

Other ways to improve the transfer of skills to the on-the-job setting include highlighting similarity of the new information to something that the participants already know, as in illuminating a framework or pattern. Sometimes this can be a completed matrix or a grid that is handed out, or it can be an empty frame where the participants can complete the form for themselves (West, Farmer, and Wolff 1991, 58–92). The other advantage to this kind of activity is that it provides specific items to look for. Figure 9.2 illustrates this in the context of comparing the contents of two databases.

Feedback

One of the most important methods of facilitating retention of skills on the job is *feedback*. There are two basic types of feedback. The first recognizes good work, general competence, or exemplary performance, and encourages employees to keep up the good work. This kind of feedback is important in maintaining

Content Evaluation		
	Name of Database 1	Name of Database 2
Publisher/provider?		
How many periodicals are indexed?		
Are periodicals indexed cover to cover?		
Approximate % of English language material?		
What type of information is included (bibliographic, full text, other)?		
What time period is covered (year range)?		
Are there any particular subject strengths applicable to your library? (list)		
Are there any particular gaps in coverage? (list)		

FIGURE 9.2 Online database comparison

skill levels, because behaviors can lapse through lack of reinforcement. Addressing the upkeep of these strengths is as important as fixing problems. The other kind of feedback is *improvement feedback*, which sends the message that change is needed. This feedback calls attention to poor work, areas of incompetence, or problem behavior.

Effective feedback is immediate, clear, accurate, specific, and positive. Behaviors should be reinforced as quickly as possible. Trainees need to be informed of the trainer's awareness of their behavior as soon as it happens, through attention, recognition, or praise. Negative feedback is better than no feedback at all, but positive feedback produces the best results. Employees tend to remember longest what they hear first and last in a message, and are more likely to apply suggestions if the feedback is personal and private. Approval of or agreement with ideas and behavior is communicated by the absence of feedback, so it is very important for people to be informed when their behaviors are not appropriate.

Box 9.9 Activity: Giving Effective Feedback

Mary, a new reference assistant, is handling the reference desk while the reference librarians are in an extended meeting. An abusive caller telephones the reference desk and demands to speak to a reference librarian. Mary tells the caller that none are available and asks whether she can help in any way. He curtly says no and continues to be abusive without actually swearing. Mary hangs up.

When the reference librarians return from their meeting, the abusive individual immediately calls the reference head. After taking the call, John, the reference head, calls Mary into his office and says, "I hear you hung up on one of our users; tell me about it." Mary relates the story in detail. John says, "I think you did the right thing. No one should have to put up with that kind of abuse. However, based on what you told me, I think there may have been a better way to handle the situation. What do you think it might be?"

Question for Reflection and Discussion:

1. Was this feedback effective?

Feedback on the job can be provided in several ways. Performance can be examined through personal diaries and self-reporting by individuals; through observations and interviews with supervisors, either informally or in a performance appraisal; or through buddy systems, support groups, coaching, or job aids. Very few of these methods have been reported as having been applied in reference settings. *Coaching*, which is basically one-on-one counseling, is one technique that has been used to provide feedback on reference staff performance in reference interviews, notably in public libraries. Coaching is one of the best ways to make sure that newly learned skills are transferred and maintained on the job, but it is a feedback technique that has only recently been applied in reference situations. Informal coaching situations can be established, however, merely by providing an environment in which an experienced person works with an inexperienced one.

Other Interventions

Alternatives to giving feedback include *review sessions*, which give trainees opportunities to refine and polish skills learned and encourage continued use of the skill; *further practice time*, particularly for skills like searching online databases; or the use of *job aids*. The use of informational job aids or performance aids helps to transfer skills learned in training. The idea behind job aids is to eliminate the need for people to remember details by providing assistance in the form of checklists, reference manuals, flowcharts, databases, templates for keyboards or telephones, and so forth (Zemke and Gunkler 1985, 62). These performance aids give trainees a better chance to use new skills by providing the minimal guidance that is so badly needed in the early stages of attempting to apply a newly learned skill on the job. See Figure 9.3 for more intervention techniques.

Evaluating Training

Without evaluation, it is impossible to know whether the training program has done what it was designed to do. Has the performance of the reference staff member improved? If so, is it because of the training program? It is important to build evaluation into the program from the very beginning. Chapter 4 discusses the assessment of learning, while more information on the evaluation of reference services in general is available in Chapter 8.

Who Evaluates?

Experts suggest that evaluation be done by as many people as possible to eliminate biases. This means that the supervisor, the trainer (if not also the supervisor), the employee who received the training, coworkers, and outsiders (who could be library users) may be involved in evaluation.

Otherwise excellent staff development programs often fail to provide built-in opportunities for participants' self-assessment. Thomas Shaughnessy argues that "staff development programs which include a self-assessment component should focus on providing each participant with the tools and materials necessary for the individual

IMPROVE PERFORMANCE	ESTABLISH PERFORMANCE
Action research Business planning Coaching Feedback Training	Employee selection Job aids Mentoring Modeling Training
MAINTAIN PERFORMANCE	**EXTINGUISH PERFORMANCE**
Compensation Feedback Performance standards Work schedules	Outplacement Upward evaluation Withholding information Withholding rewards

FIGURE 9.3 Sample interventions for performance problems (Langdon, Whiteside, and McKenna 1999, 20)

to test himself or herself and to score the test" (1988, 7). Programs that provide for self-assessment ease staff anxiety concerning test results and increase accuracy of results. Videotaping has been suggested as "a useful, and surprisingly comfortable, self-evaluation technique, because it captures actions in context otherwise lost to the person acting" (Mucci 1976, 33). The results of self-evaluation are difficult to validate, however, and should be used in conjunction with other approaches.

William Young believes that peers working together at a reference desk are those in the best position to judge reference behaviors and that this is the most promising and realistic approach to evaluating reference desk performance (1985, 73). *Behaviorally anchored rating scales* (BARS) are frequently used to assist in defining degrees of performance on the job. Several libraries have used these satisfactorily. Most have extracted behaviors, skills, and knowledge from a service standard to create a checklist of desirable behaviors, such as a reference librarian asking for assistance in certain situations or suggesting alternative sources of information to the user (Adams and Judd 1984, 141–42; Schwartz and Eakin 1986, 6). Figure 9.4

II. Interactions with Users	Seldom	Not Frequently Enough	Sometimes	Frequently	Almost all the Time	Cannot Respond
Maintains a Professional Posture						
1. Looks alert, confident, and interested.						
2. Manifests openness (e.g., is approachable).						
3. Works to minimize initial barrier between patron and staff member.						
4. Establishes good eye contact (e.g., looks up as patron approaches desk).						
Desk Service Priorities						
1. Gets people started.						
2. Acknowledges the presence of users not yet served.						
Effective Communication						
1. Uses good grammar.						
2. Gears expression to user's understanding.						
3. Avoids unexplained or unnecessary jargon.						
4. Speaks in a positive, relaxed, appropriately loud tone of voice.						
Helps Shape Questions						
1. Listens well.						
2. Seeks definitions.						

FIGURE 9.4 A portion of an instrument used in peer evaluations by staff at an information desk

shows BARS that are a portion of an instrument used in peer evaluations of an information desk staff in an academic library.

The supervisor's evaluation is the most subjective and can be difficult to rely on in training situations, unless testing, observation, or interviews accompany it. Also, since supervisors have a number of other areas of job performance to attend to, the particular performance concerned with training may be difficult to determine.

Although library users' consistently high ranking of satisfaction with reference services calls into doubt their ability to evaluate reference performance (Young 1984), it has been suggested that library users can evaluate librarians' attitudes, degree of self-confidence, and ability to instruct individuals in the use of reference sources (Schwartz and Eakin 1986). See Chapter 8 for further information on seeking user evaluation data.

What Is Evaluated and How?

Evaluating training can be very difficult. Decisions have to be made not only concerning how to evaluate but also on what can and should be evaluated. Four different levels can be evaluated in a training program: *reactions*, *learning*, *job behavior*, and *results* (Kirkpatrick and Kirkpatrick 2014, 473).

Although attendees do not necessarily have to enjoy a session, it is important that a positive reaction to the training sessions occur if learning is to take place. A positive reaction to training is a precondition to learning, but it is not a guarantee that learning will transpire. Participants must feel a commitment to training—must feel it is valuable—in order to learn. Most often, reactions are assessed by asking trainees to complete rating scales for individual sessions. Verbal comments or nonverbal cues can also be observed. In order to supplement the attendees' comments, the supervisor or an observer should also record comments.

Learning, the acquisition of knowledge, skills, or attitudes, within the training context can be tested through programmed instruction, objective tests, essays, and pen-and-pencil tests. Testing may also be built into the training, such as judgment of performance in practice sessions or in-class exercises. To determine whether skill improvement can indeed be attributed to the training program or whether it results from outside influences, training experts recommend the use of *pretests*, *posttests*, and *control groups* (Hamblin 1974, 8). All those attending a training session, as well as those in a control group, which does not receive training, are given a pretest, to see what skills and knowledge they already possess. After a period of time has elapsed since the training was administered, both groups are again tested to see whether skills improved through training, or merely from working on the job. Most librarians, of course, have difficulty finding the time to administer tests in this way. Chapter 4, on instruction, talks about assessing learning.

Although trainees may learn the skills and be able to perform them in the training session, they may not be able to perform them on the job. If the trainee did achieve the criteria during training sessions, the application exercises may not have been similar to the on-the-job environment. For example, when given citations with the author and title identified, reference assistants may be able to search the online catalog correctly. However, they may not be able to do so effectively on the job because they are unable to identify those key items from a citation that does not have the elements labeled. The evaluation itself can affect the result of training, so if trainers or supervisors wish to reinforce that training, they should use *obtrusive methods*, or testing that is known to the trainee. If it is important that outside factors be limited, *unobtrusive methods*, in which the trainees do not know they are being tested, should be used. Terry L. Weech and Herbert Goldhor (1982) have shown that reference librarians correctly answer a larger proportion of reference questions when they know they are being evaluated. Chapter 8 discusses the advantages and disadvantages of unobtrusive and obtrusive methods in more detail.

When on-the-job benefits of training programs are hard to measure or are unclear, or when outcomes are not adequately measured with simple quantitative methods, as is the case in reference librarianship, interviews can be useful. Interviews and group discussions are more informal ways of assessing the effectiveness of a training program. Robert O. Brinkerhoff (1983, 61) discusses using "success cases," and Sumru Erkut and Jacqueline P. Fields (1987, 74) explore using focus groups to see how training is effective.

The final results, or benefits to the organization, should be the last stage of evaluation. Benefits such as users' satisfaction with library service, or their ability to access needed information, are difficult to measure. If the goal is to determine the effect that training has had on these outcomes, it becomes even more complicated; for this reason, libraries rarely evaluate at this level (Kirkpatrick and Kirkpatrick 2014, 480).

BEYOND THE BASICS: CONTINUAL LEARNING

Training for reference staff should be a continuous process that is never really finished. Although the library can complete its induction phase to orient new staff members and finish on-the-job training for basic job skills, the basic level of skills constantly changes as resources, technology, user needs, and services evolve. Donna Cromer and Andrea Testi assert that "cultivating an atmosphere of lifelong learning, continuing education, and self-evaluation for reference personnel is essential in responding to and anticipating change" (1994, 51). Reference staff members have an additional need to go beyond basic-level competencies to mastery of their field, or expertise in a particular area. "Today's dynamic environment of reference work demands that reference staff, whether newly-hired or seasoned professional or paraprofessional, engage in ongoing professional development opportunities" (Block and Kelly 2001, 208).

Two different approaches to continual or lifelong learning can be identified. While the two approaches use similar methods, and have similar purposes of improving the competence of individuals, each has a different focus. *Staff development* is the "system of providing opportunities for employees within an organization to reach their full potential (through improving skills and competency) and become of greater value to the organization" (Heery and Noon 2008, 124). *Staff development* is organizationally centered and directed, while *continuing education* is individually centered and directed. They are, however, not mutually exclusive and are in fact complementary approaches. Both approaches are actually beneficial in helping staff members avoid technological obsolescence, develop expertise and knowledge in specialized areas, and widen experiences and practical knowledge.

Mastery or Expertise

A common practice in new employee orientation and training efforts is to have the new employees spend a lot of individual time with other staff members at the beginning of the employment period. Once the overview is given and a foundation is laid, they are often left to jump in and "sink or swim." Because they do not know yet how to choose the most important information out of all they are hearing, they often reach information overload, and "later portions of the orientation process may not even be heard" (Caputo 1991, 134). Alternating tasks with early orientation sessions and providing continuing training and review sessions can help new staff members build full knowledge or mastery of the content more gradually and more interactively.

Expertise in specific areas should also be encouraged. In developing expertise in reference, staff members deepen their understanding of resources and technology, and learn how to transfer existing skills to a new environment, a crucial skill in a constantly changing environment.

Change Management

Multiple paradigm shifts in the world economic, political, and cultural order, and simultaneous shifts in organizations, businesses, and information technology are having a significant impact on library and information services. Joan Giesecke and Beth McNeil suggest that "to succeed, libraries must now be agile, flexible, and able to adjust to a world that resembles an amusement park roller-coaster ride or white-water rafting" (1999, 158).

The sources that record information and the tools that provide access to these sources are revised and updated or appear in different forms. In such a time of profound change, the knowledge that individuals bring initially to their work can become obsolete rapidly. The effort required to maintain current knowledge and understanding is immense.

"In the print era the reference librarian could turn to the Mudge/Winchell/Sheehy *Guide to Reference Books*, or locate an index for a given journal through the listings in *Ulrich's* or other specialized guides. In the online era, new tools will have to be built that can deal comprehensively with a dynamic environment" (Force 1994, 113). Reference librarians will always have to keep up with new information, new reference sources and access tools, and the changing needs of their users (Bunge 1982, 228). The summer 2015 announcement that the classic *Guide to Reference Books* will no longer be updated is confirmation that no one source can keep track of all of the resources that reference librarians have at their disposal.

Reference librarians have traditionally been conservators or caretakers of the library's collections. These roles are evolving as reference librarians become mediators between users and materials, information counselors, and educators in teaching how to find and evaluate information. Mary Nofsinger notes that, "(T)he reference librarian must not only be able to find relevant information or documents, but must be able to evaluate them on the criteria of availability, ease of access, authority, presence of biases, scope, and timeliness—regardless of electronic or print format or location. In addition, a critical thinking librarian must estimate the quantity and intellectual level of information required by the user" (1999, 15).

Julie Parry is concerned with how staff will deal with a constantly changing environment. She states, "Clearly, ongoing training is necessary to enable staff to keep up-to-date with changes. In responsive service, processes and procedures will be constantly monitored and modified to meet changing needs. Managers and supervisors need to ensure that staff understand new procedures and are able to put them into practice" (1996, 23).

Job Stress

Continual learning should help reference librarians deal with the stress that accompanies any kind of frontline position (see Box 9.10). Tina Roose points out that "reference librarians are among the few researchers of this world who are expected to perform with an audience in the midst of many other demands and distractions" (1989, 166). Four factors contribute to stress at the reference desk: technology, users, environment, and staffing.

Box 9.10 Reference Service as Combat: Fighting Job Stress

Some experts suggest that jobs with a high emotional labor content, jobs where the performer's persona goes on the line time and time again at the customer interface, should be treated as combat. And like combat soldiers, people in high-stress service jobs need to be rotated off the front line frequently—and sometimes permanently. As one expert puts it, "In Vietnam we *knew* come hell or high water, that after so many months, we were out of there. You need to do that for service people. They have to know there is a light at the end of that tunnel—and it isn't from an oncoming train."

(Zemke 1986, 44)

Technology

Computers have assumed a central role in librarianship. Librarians need to maintain basic knowledge of operating systems, learn hardware and communications troubleshooting techniques, and develop deep understanding of software used every day (Marmion 1998). "When libraries dealt with only one or two database vendors, it was comparatively simple for an individual to remember what databases were available. For unfamiliar subject areas, a quick reference to the paper directories supplied by the online vendor yielded the needed information. As the sources of online information have multiplied one person can no longer keep a mental catalog of the likely places where individual pieces of information may be found" (Force 1994, 112–13). In addition to the variety of sources available, in an online environment, available resources can change overnight. Technological obsolescence can occur when individual competence holds constant while professional standards advance (Stone 1985, 65).

Users

The technological age has brought further complications in raising the expectations of users about libraries and the ability of library staff to provide information immediately. Users often expect reference staff to provide data that may not be collected or that by nature is confidential. When advised by reference staff on a course of action, the user may not be willing to follow that advice if it seems like too much work. For example, individuals wanting information on a topic from the 1960s are incredulous when told they will have to use print indexes to find information. They may go to the next person on duty in the hope of getting a different answer to their question.

Reference staff is increasingly dealing more directly with diverse populations, including individuals with physical, emotional, and health limitations who may have been served by special agencies before, or individuals with different cultural expectations (see Chapter 12). Without adequate training in cross-cultural communication and/or highly developed skills to communicate effectively with people from a wide variety of backgrounds, the reference staff member may experience significant stress from the additional pressures of dealing with this wide range of users.

Environment

Local collections necessarily have limitations, and with today's information explosion, no one institution can be expected to acquire everything its users could reasonably ask about. Additionally, the arrangement of the reference collection, the physical desks, and equipment can negatively affect the reference transaction (Donnelly 1995). If desks are cumbersome to use or inhibit the use of a particular kind of source, service is affected. Aging or constantly breaking equipment can also be a stress factor. Service philosophies can vary tremendously from one service desk to another even within the same institution. This, too, can contribute to users' expectations or frustrations and thus the librarian's stress.

Staffing

Individuals have a limit on how much they can work with the public, and this time factor is different for each person. Some individuals work better in small stretches of time, while others do well working on the desk for longer periods of time. Departments should have limits on the number of hours that staff members are expected to work. Inappropriate staffing can also create stress. Boredom from staffing professionals during slow periods and anxiety from single staffing during busy times are equally problematic. Lack of backup to handle technology problems and troubleshooting, especially on nights and weekends, can be another problem.

Burnout

Burnout is an overwhelming feeling of frustration, apathy, and exhaustion regarding one's work (Roose 1989, 167). It is not a problem unique to reference service providers, but it is very intense and pervasive. "Reference librarians seem most particularly at risk for burnout because of their assignment of general direct availability for an unpredictable stream of requests and demands and their high visibility in most libraries" (Caputo 1991, 59). Various individuals have attributed the problem to:

- Too many new services and activities added to traditional reference desk service with no increase in staff to handle the new activities (Miller 1984, 303).
- "[A] gap between the ideals of reference librarianship that [librarians] believe and espouse and the realities of reference service that can be practiced" (Bunge 1984, 131).
- *Technostress*, or the anxiety and psychological pressure created by the continually expanding range of electronic tools that reference librarians must master.

It is important to note that the four stages of burnout—*enthusiasm*, *stagnation*, *frustration*, and *apathy*—start with enthusiasm. The challenge to libraries and to individuals is to rekindle the fire of enthusiasm and not let it burn out, but to feed it with challenges, new environments, new information, and new techniques, without letting it engulf reference staff members. Staff development and continuing education can provide the kindling for the fire by presenting new information and techniques of approaching the reference process. When someone is removed from the desk, even temporarily, to attend a development activity, it gives that person breathing room and a chance to reflect upon what has happened. The sessions are intended to provide new insights into desk service and new ways of coping with stress by improving knowledge, skills, or attitudes. Nancy McCormack and Catherine Cotter (2013) provide more in-depth discussion about managing and overcoming burnout for information professionals.

Organizational Responses

"The organizational costs of burnout are high. Lost motivation, increased staff turnover, poor delivery of services, increased employee theft, increased tardiness, and greater absenteeism all result in significant indirect costs to organizations" (Caputo 1991, 32). Luckily, the organization has a variety of ways to prevent burnout and to help combat it once it has developed.

Managerial Decisions

The library reference manager can take control of some of the issues that contribute to stress and burnout. By establishing an atmosphere of support and trust, by balancing the kinds of service activities in which reference librarians are engaged, and by establishing service standards and policies and communicating them effectively, the reference department head can help keep burnout from developing. Once burnout has occurred, the department head can change job assignments or institute cross-training to change the environment in which the burnout was initiated.

Janette Caputo identifies "a high level of mutual trust" as the single most important facet to the effective supervisory relationship in terms of burnout prevention. "Supervisors who see themselves as trainers or coaches have the best success in counteracting burnout, as they encourage individual growth and development and open the door for group applications of theoretical knowledge to practical situations" (1991, 136). Individuals with good support systems with colleagues develop better coping mechanisms.

Supervisors can keep reference desk hours at a reasonable level, minimizing excessive contact with the public. Reference managers need to respond when demands are high. Joanne Bessler (1994, 33) suggests using a "floater" position to assist in areas with higher workloads, identifying low-priority work that can be deferred or eliminated, and creating a team that can work across units when needed.

Department heads can develop reference service policy statements that recognize reasonable limits to service that librarians are expected to provide. "When training staff to apply policies, you should also prepare staff for likely challenges and exceptions. Discussing exceptions at staff meetings is helpful. A staff member who knows why a policy was written and how it has been interpreted is well-prepared to make a reasonable judgement" (Bessler 1994, 38). Explicitly stating to staff at all levels when rules can be modified in providing help to users is important in defining levels of empowerment. For example, volunteers or student staff who work very limited schedules may not have the comprehensive understanding of overall library operations to be able to judge special user requests, while nonsupervisory staff may be able to bend policies within certain guidelines.

Managers can redesign the content of a job through job rotation or exchange or can provide assignments that allow individuals to gain authority, personal achievement, recognition, growth, responsibility, and advancement. They can encourage employees to undertake new and different assignments periodically to assure that their jobs do not become too routine or lacking in challenge (Huang 1990). Staff development programs that help service providers see their job as playing a role for the organization can also provide concrete assistance with job burnout and stress.

"Cross-training is valuable because it helps employees become familiar with co-workers' contributions and get a better idea of how the institution works as a whole. In addition, cross-trained staff members can pinch-hit for each other when the need arises" (Weingart, Kochan, and Hedrich 1998, 157). Lothar Spang states that "(l)ibrarian participants have agreed that the cross-training opportunities have substantially improved their ability to provide accurate and convenient service to an increasingly cross-discipline user population" (1996, 84).

Staff Development

The goal of staff development is to improve the organization's effectiveness, or service to its users, by increasing the competence of its staff. Much of the training that has been discussed up to this point is encompassed by the term "staff development"; orientation and on-the-job training are certainly included. The library management has a responsibility to improve staff performance, and it is to the library's benefit to produce employees who are committed to the library.

Merely providing the training for basic job skills is not enough. The library administration should provide continual training for reference librarians that develops and maintains competence, updates basic professional foundations, and introduces new concepts. Staff development should emphasize attitude shaping, people-handling skills, dealing with users' feelings, listening skills, and thinking on one's feet. "Given the scope and pace of present and prospective change, training, by itself, will not provide librarians with a satisfactory framework for new understandings, or the basis for responding to the changed environment" (Harris 1996, 48). An ongoing development program is necessary.

Libraries as Learning Organizations

While individual learning is important, it needs to impact the overall organizational performance in order to have a long-range benefit. Although a particular individual may become an expert in a specific area, if that information and expertise are not shared with the organization, the organization will lose that expertise when the individual leaves. On the other hand, if individuals share this expertise in such a way that they train others and the information learned is incorporated into organizational documentation, then the expertise remains in the organization after the individuals leave. Libraries that promote this kind of transfer of knowledge and expertise can call their libraries *learning organizations*.

A learning organization is one that has an enhanced capacity to learn, adapt, and change, and is "skilled at creating, acquiring, and transferring knowledge and insights" (Garvin 1993, 80). It is characterized by:

- Using information technology to inform/empower the many rather than the few.
- Collaborating rather than competing, making comparisons of the organization's best practices with the practices of others.
- Encouraging self-development opportunities for everyone in the organization and encouraging individuals to take responsibility for their own learning and development.
- Exchanging information—getting closer to customers and suppliers.
- Using the people in contact with customers to bring back useful information about needs and opportunities (Harris 1996, 51).

Personal Responses: Continuing Education

Individuals must also accept some of the responsibility for refueling the fire by planning their own continuing education activities. Continuing education activities center on the individual's personal interests and include those that promote personal development and growth as an individual, whether to increase personal job satisfaction or to prepare for a promotion. Continuing education includes learning experiences that will introduce new concepts and skills, update basic professional foundations, refresh or reemphasize aspects of professional training, provide additional competencies to make career advancement or change possible, and furnish the individual with an overview of his or her profession as a changing and evolving discipline (Stone 1985, 62).

Reference librarians must constantly keep updated on their reference knowledge and skills. Commonly used strategies include reading professional literature, reference staff meetings, and staff sharing. Attendance at conferences, workshops, and other meetings outside the individual's library is a much-used method for reference librarians. Subscribing to appropriate listservs and reading relevant blogs are other strategies. Librarians can start a "journal club," where individuals share what they have learned through professional reading. There are many opportunities to interact with individuals at other institutions using technological options such as webinars and online chat sessions, offered through the American Library Association or other professional organizations.

Opportunities for continuing education originate from many different sources. Courses offered at local community colleges, colleges, or universities range from those in computer and software management to courses in supervisory and teaching skills to courses in subject-related topics that may or may not lead to an advanced degree. Outside groups, such as online database vendors, often offer basic and advanced training in the use of their software, with refresher courses and updates on specific databases. Library professional organizations make many contributions to continuing education for reference librarians. Local interest groups often provide forums for discussing mutual problems, challenges, and potential solutions with peers. State associations sponsor conferences, workshops, and programs in more convenient locations than many nationally sponsored programs. The American Library Association and associations of special groups provide numerous activities that can promote the individual reference librarian's development. The American Library Association's "Continuing Education" Web page has numerous resources and suggestions.

CONCLUSION

The results of a thorough and responsive training program that involves staff in decision making and uses participatory educational methods will be a highly motivated staff who have high morale and good self-esteem, identify with their peers, cope with changes and stress, make fewer mistakes, and solve problems. On the other hand, unplanned on-the-job training may result in ill-trained unmotivated employees, with the added danger that necessary skills may not be learned or that undesirable methods and approaches will be reinforced and low standards set. "Employees (new or old) learn, whether we wish it or not. If we are disorganized, indifferent, or sloppy in our approach, the employee will absorb the standards. No amount of future lecturing will erase these standards" (Shea 1981, 61).

The act of training itself motivates and builds employee confidence and self-esteem, regardless of the actual content of training. Training reduces stress and turnover, improves work relationships, and increases adaptability. Without training, reference librarians cannot keep up with change, develop expertise, or learn how to transfer what they already know to new environments.

Reference librarians are truly in the knowledge business, both on behalf of their users and for themselves. Librarians cannot help users fulfill their information needs if they themselves are ignorant of the sources, lack the ability to access the information they know exists, or are unwilling to go that extra step to gain that knowledge and skills. A well-planned program of training, development, and continuing education will give the reference staff the tools they need to tackle the tasks at hand and strategies for approaching new problems as they arise.

REFERENCES

Adams, Mignon S., and Blanche Judd. 1984. "Evaluating Reference Librarians Using Goal Analysis as a First Step." *The Reference Librarian* 11 (Fall/Winter): 131–45.

Arthur, Gwen. 1992. "Using Video for Reference Staff Training and Development: A Selective Bibliography." *Reference Services Review* 20 (Winter): 63–68.

Ballard, Angela, and Laura Blessing. 2006. "Organizational Socialization through Employee Orientations at North Carolina State University Libraries." *College & Research Libraries* 67 (May): 240–48.

Bandys, Barbara, John Daghita, and Susan Whitmore. 2002. "Raising the Bar or Training Technicians to Assume Reference Responsibilities." Paper presented at the Special Libraries Association Conference, Los Angeles, CA, June 9–12.

Bean, Cammy. 2014. *The Accidental Instructional Designer: Learning Design for the Digital Age.* Alexandria, VA: ASTD Press.

Berwind, Anne May. 1991. "Orientation for the Reference Desk." *Reference Services Review* 19 (Fall): 51–54, 70.

Bessler, Joanne M. 1994. *Putting Service into Library Staff Training.* LAMA Occasional Papers Series. Chicago: American Library Association.

Block, Karla J., and Julia A. Kelly. 2001. "Integrating Informal Professional Development into the Work of Reference." *The Reference Librarian* 72: 207–17.

Brinkerhoff, Robert O. 1983. "The Success Case: A Low-Cost, High Yield Evaluation." *Training and Development Journal* 37 (August): 58–59, 61.

Broadway, Marsha D., and Nathan M. Smith. 1989. "Basic Reference Courses in ALA-Accredited Library Schools." *The Reference Librarian* 25–26: 431–48.

Bunge, Charles A. 1982. "Strategies for Updating Knowledge of Reference Resources and Techniques." *RQ* 21 (Spring): 228–32.

Bunge, Charles A. 1984. "Potential and Reality at the Reference Desk: Reflections on a 'Return to the Field.'" *The Journal of Academic Librarianship* 10 (July): 128–32.

Caputo, Janette S. 1991. *Stress and Burnout in Library Service.* Phoenix: Oryx Press.

Carr, Steven. 2013. "Refining the Customer Service Attitude." In *Staff Development: A Practical Guide*, edited by Andrea Wigbels Stewart, Carlette Washington-Hoagland, and Carol T. Zsulya, 4th ed., 113–26. Chicago: American Library Association.

Chalofsky, Neal E., Tonette S. Rocco, and Michael Lane Morris, eds. 2014. *Handbook of Human Resource Development.* Hoboken, NJ: Wiley and Sons.

Chellino, Susan N., and Richard J. Walker. 1983. "Merging Instructional Technology with Management Practices." In *Strengthening Connections between Education and Performance*, edited by Stanley M. Grabowski, 11–19. San Francisco: Jossey-Bass.

Conroy, Barbara. 1976. "The Structured Group Interview: A Useful Tool for Needs Assessment and Evaluation." *Mountain Plains Journal of Adult Education* 4 (March): 19.

"Continuing Education." 2015. American Library Association. http://www.ala.org/tools/atoz/continuing-education.

Creth, Sheila D. 1986. *Effective On-The-Job Training: Developing Library Human Resources.* Chicago: American Library Association.

Cromer, Donna E., and Andrea R. Testi. 1994. "Integrating Continuing Education for Reference Librarians." *Reference Services Review* 22 (Winter): 51–80.

Davis, H. Scott. 1994. *New Employee Orientation.* How-To-Do-It Manual for Librarians, no. 38. New York: Neal-Schuman.

Deputy, Michele M. 1995. "A Study of Librarians' Attitudes towards the Reference Interview." ERIC Document 401919, December.

Dolphin, Phillippa. 1986. "Interpersonal Skill Training for Library Staff." *Library Association Record* 88 (March): 134–35.

Donnelly, Anna M. 1995. "Reference Environment." In *The Reference Assessment Manual*, 47–50. Ann Arbor, MI: Pierian Press.

Erkut, Sumru, and Jacqueline P. Fields. 1987. "Focus Groups to the Rescue." *Training and Development Journal* 41 (October): 74–76.

Force, Ron. 1994. "Planning Online Services for the 90s." *The Reference Librarian* 43: 107–15.

Garvin, David. 1993. "Building a Learning Organization." *Harvard Business Review* 70 (4): 78–91.

Georges, James C. 1988. "Why Soft-Skills Training Doesn't Take." *Training* 25 (April): 42–47.

Giesecke, Joan, and Beth McNeil. 1999. "Core Competencies and the Learning Organization." *Library Administration and Management* 13 (Summer): 158–66.

Hamblin, A. C. 1974. *Evaluation and Control of Training.* London: McGraw Hill.

Harris, Howard. 1996. "Retraining Librarians to Meet the Needs of the Virtual Library Patron." *Information Technology and Libraries* 15 (March): 48–52.

Heery, Edmund, and Mike Noon. 2008. *A Dictionary of Human Resource Management*, 2nd ed. Oxford: Oxford University Press.

Hirko, Buff, and Mary Bucher Ross. 2004. *Virtual Reference Training: The Complete Guide to Providing Anytime, Anywhere Answers.* Chicago: American Library Association.

Huang, Samuel T. 1990. "The Impact of New Library Technology on Reference Services." *Illinois Libraries* 72 (November): 601–2.

Hunt, Suellyn. 1983. "A Structure and Seven-Step Process for Developing In-House Human Resources Programs." *Bookmark* 41 (Summer): 227–32.

Imel, Susan. 1994. "Guidelines for Working with Adult Learners." *ERIC Digest* 154. ERIC Document 377313. http://www.ericdigests.org/1995-2/working.htm.

Isaacs, Julian M. 1969. "In-Service Training for Reference Work." *Library Association Record* 71 (October): 301–2.

Jerris, Linda A. 1993. *Effective Employee Orientation.* New York: AMACOM.

Jonassen, David H., R. Scott Grabinger, N. Duncan, and C. Harris. 1990. "Analyzing and Selecting Instructional Strategies and Tactics." *Performance Improvement Quarterly* 3 (2): 29–47.

Jones, Dorothy E. 1988. "I'd Like You to Meet Our New Librarian: The Initiation and Integration of the Newly Appointed Librarian." *The Journal of Academic Librarianship* 14 (September): 221–24.

Kirkpatrick, Jim, and Wendy Kayser Kirkpatrick. 2014. "Implement the Four Levels of Evaluation to Demonstrate Value." In *The ASTD Handbook: The Definitive Reference for Training and Development*, edited by Elaine Biech, 471–87. Alexandria, VA: ASTD Press.

Knowles, Malcolm S. 1996. "Adult Learning." In *ASTD Training and Development Handbook: A Guide to Human Resource Management*, edited by Robert L. Craig, 4th ed., 253–65. New York: McGraw-Hill.

Langdon, Danny G., Kathleen S. Whiteside, and Monica M. McKenna, eds. 1999. *Intervention Resource Guide: 50 Performance Improvement Tools.* San Francisco: Jossey-Bass.

Lynda.com. http://www.lynda.com. [subscription required for full access]

Mager, Robert F. 1975. *Preparing Instructional Objectives*, 2nd ed. Belmont, CA: Fearon Publishers.

Marmion, Dan. 1998. "Facing the Challenge: Technology Training in Libraries." *Information Technology and Libraries* 17 (December): 216–18.

Massey-Burzio, Virginia. 1991. "Education and Experience: Or, the MLS Is Not Enough." *Reference Services Review* 19 (1): 72–74.

McCormack, Nancy, and Catherine Cotter. 2013. *Managing Burnout in the Workplace: A Guide for Information Professionals.* Oxford: Chandos.

Miller, William. 1984. "What's Wrong with Reference: Coping with Success and Failure at the Reference Desk." *American Libraries* 15 (May): 303–6, 321–22.

Morgan, Pamela. 2009. *Training Paraprofessionals for Reference Service: A How-To-Do-It Manual for Librarians*, 2nd ed. How-To-Do-It Manual, no. 164. New York: Neal-Schuman.

Mucci, Judith. 1976. "Videotape Self-Evaluation in Public Libraries: Experiments in Evaluating Public Service." *RQ* 16 (Fall): 33–37.

Nadler, Leonard, and Zeace Nadler. 1990. *Handbook of Human Resource Development*, 2nd ed. New York: Wiley.

Nakano, Kimberly L., and Janet Morrison. 1992. "Public-Service Experience in the Introductory Reference Course: A Model Program and Survey of Accredited Library Schools." *Journal of Education for Library and Information Science* 33 (Spring): 110–28.

Newstrom, John W. 1980. "Evaluating the Effectiveness of Training Methods." *Personnel Administrator* 25 (January): 55–60.

Nofsinger, Mary M. 1999. "Training and Retraining Reference Professionals: Core Competencies for the 21st Century." *The Reference Librarian* 61: 9–19.

Oliver, Mary W. 1972. "Orientation of New Personnel in the Law Library." *Law Library Journal* 65 (May): 140–42.

Oud, Joanne. 2008. "Adjusting to the Workplace: Transitions Faced by New Academic Librarians." *College & Research Libraries* 69 (3): 252–67.

Parry, Julie. 1996. "Continuing Professional Development." In *Staff Development in Academic Libraries: Present Practice and Future Challenges*, edited by Margaret Oldroyd, 21–28. London: Library Association Publishing.

Powell, Ronald R., and Douglas Raber. 1993. "Education for Reference/Information Service: A Quantitative and Qualitative Analysis of Basic Reference Courses." *The Reference Librarian* 43: 145–72.

Rackham, Neil. 1979. "The Coaching Controversy." *Training and Development Journal* 33 (November): 12–16.

Reference and User Services Association. 2003. "Professional Competencies for Reference and User Services Librarians." American Library Association. http://www.ala.org/rusa/resources/guidelines/professional.

Roberts, Anne F. 1984. "Myth: Reference Librarians Can Perform at the Reference Desk Immediately upon Receipt of MLS. Reality: They Need Training Like Other Professionals." In *Academic Libraries: Myths and Realities: Proceedings of the Third National Conference of the Association of College and Research Libraries*, 400–404. Chicago: ACRL.

Roethlisberger, F.J., and W.J. Dick. 1939. *Management and the Worker*. Cambridge, MA: Harvard University Press.

Roose, Tina. 1989. "Stress at the Reference Desk." *Library Journal* 114 (September 1): 166–67.

Rothstein, Samuel. 1983. "The Making of a Reference Librarian." *Library Trends* 31 (Winter): 375–99.

Roy, Loriene. 2010. "Engaging LIS Students in Reference Work through Online Answer Boards." *The Reference Librarian* 51 (2): 97–107.

Rummler, Geary A. 1987. "Determining Needs." In *Training and Development Handbook*, edited by Robert L. Craig, 3rd ed., 217–47. New York: McGraw-Hill.

Schön, Donald A. 1987. *Educating the Reflective Practitioner: Toward a New Design for Teaching and Learning in the Professions*. San Francisco: Jossey-Bass.

Schwartz, Diane G., and Dottie Eakin. 1986. "Reference Service Standards, Performance Criteria, and Evaluation." *The Journal of Academic Librarianship* 12 (March): 4–8.

Shaughnessy, Thomas W. 1988. "Staff Development in Libraries: Why It Frequently Doesn't Take." *Journal of Library Administration* 9: 5–12.

Shea, Gordon F. 1981. *The New Employee: Developing a Productive Human Resource*. Reading, MA: Addison-Wesley.

Sheets, Janet. 1998. "Role Playing as Training Tool for Reference Student Assistants." *Reference Services Review* 26 (Spring): 37–41.

Silberman, Mel. 2006. *Active Training: A Handbook of Techniques, Designs, Case Examples, and Tips*, 3rd ed. San Francisco, CA: Pfeiffer.

Sites, Richard, Angel Green, and Michael Allen. 2014. *Leading ADDIE for SAM: An Agile Model for Developing the Best Learning Experiences*. Alexandria, VA: American Society for Training & Development.

Spang, Lothar. 1996. "A Staff-Generated Cross-Training Plan for Academic Reference Librarians: The TQM Approach at Wayne State University Libraries." *Reference Services Review* 24 (Summer): 77–85.

Stone, Elizabeth W. 1985. "Towards a Learning Community." In *Continuing Education for the Library Information Professional*, edited by William G. Asp, Suzanne H. Mahmoodi, Marilyn L. Miller, and Peggy O'Donnell, 52–82. Hamden, CT: Library Professional Publications.

WebJunction. OCLC. http://webjunction.org.

Weech, Terry L., and Herbert Goldhor. 1982. "Obtrusive versus Unobtrusive Evaluation of Reference Service in Five Illinois Public Libraries: A Pilot Study." *The Library Quarterly* 51: 305–24.

Weingart, Sandra, Carol A. Kochan, and Anne Hedrich. 1998. "Safeguarding Your Investment: Effective Orientation for New Employees." *Library Administration and Management* 12 (Summer): 156–58.

West, Charles K., James A. Farmer, and Phillip M. Wolff. 1991. *Instructional Design: Implications from Cognitive Science*, 58–92. Englewood Cliffs, NJ: Prentice Hall.

Young, Heartsill, ed. 1983. *The ALA Glossary of Library and Information Science.* Chicago: American Library Association.

Young, William F. 1984. "Evaluating the Reference Librarian." *The Reference Librarian* 11 (Fall/Winter): 123–24.

Young, William F. 1985. "Methods for Evaluating Reference Desk Performance." *RQ* 25 (Fall): 69–75.

Zemke, Ron. 1986. "Contact! Training Employees to Meet the Public." *Training* 23 (August 1): 41–45.

Zemke, Ron, and John Gunkler. 1985. "28 Techniques for Transforming Training into Performance." *Training* 22 (April): 56–63.

SUGGESTED READINGS

Allan, Barbara. 2013. *The No-Nonsense Guide to Training in Libraries.* London: Facet Publishing.

Allan provides a succinct discussion of developing workplace learning environments along with three main approaches: content centered, learner centered, and social. She explores a variety of learning and teaching methods to make training interesting, including action planning, group work, guest speakers, hands-on sessions, inquiry-based learning, problem-based learning, and the use of stories and metaphors. Additionally, she provides an overview of different ways in which current technologies can be incorporated into training, while acknowledging that the speed of change in this area makes it difficult to keep up to date.

Auster, Ethel, and Donna C. Chan. 2004. "Reference Librarians and Keeping Up-To-Date: A Question of Priorities." *Reference & User Services Quarterly* 44 (Fall): 57–66.

The authors studied the professional development activities of reference librarians in large urban public libraries in Ontario, finding that most were consciously developing and updating their technological skills, about half were updating communication and interpersonal skills, and smaller portions were improving instructional and management skills. No respondents mentioned problem-solving and analytical skills as topics of professional development activities. The most significant deterrents were inconvenient scheduling or lack of information, as well as the perceptions of the library environment as not encouraging information sharing and innovation. The authors suggest that librarians need to take more responsibility for their own professional development.

Ballard, Angela, and Laura Blessing. 2006. "Organizational Socialization through Employee Orientations in North Carolina State University Libraries." *College & Research Libraries* 67 (May): 240–48.

Ballard and Blessing discuss the importance to the organization of including socialization in the employee orientation program. This particular program has three components: (1) orientation sessions that encourage participation in sharing knowledge about work in other departments, overview of computing environment, tours of the building and units, a safety presentation, and exploration of the mission and vision statements of the organization; (2) orientation checklists; and (3) one-on-one meetings with appropriate personnel.

Davis, H. Scott. 1994. *New Employee Orientation.* How-To-Do-It Manuals for Librarians, no. 38. New York: Neal-Schuman.

The author, a practicing librarian, wrote this book as a practical guide to the process of effectively orienting new library employees. A menu of program options and activities is presented. Good examples of gathering staff suggestions through surveys, brainstorming, and focus groups for determining the content of and need for orientation are included. Scott includes an excellent section on anticipating and handling problems such as ineffective participants, short notice, dropouts, resistance, and mismatching of mentors.

Donovan, Georgie L., and Miguel A. Figueroa, eds. 2004. *Staff Development Strategies That Work! Stories and Strategies from New Librarians*. New York: Neal Schuman.

Focused primarily on the development of leadership skills, 18 new librarians tell their stories of what was done to help them feel satisfied in their jobs to build leadership skills and to transform them into leaders, managers, and supervisors. Strategies include coaching, mentoring, expressing trust, cultivating relationships outside the library, developing as researchers, and using professional service as a development tool.

Hirko, Buff, and Mary Bucher Ross. 2004. *Virtual Reference Training: The Complete Guide to Providing Anytime, Anywhere Answers*. Chicago: American Library Association.

This practical and hands-on approach to creating training for virtual reference includes guidance in developing curricula, assessment tools, and enjoyable learning activities.

Massis, Bruce E. 2004. *The Practical Library Trainer*. Binghamton, NY: Haworth Press.

This text examines types of staff training, strategies for recruiting and retaining staff, online training, in-house training, how to use professional conferences as continuing education opportunities, and evaluation of training programs.

Morgan, Pamela J. 2009. *Training Paraprofessionals for Reference Service*, 2nd ed. How-To-Do-It Manuals, no. 164. New York: Neal-Schuman.

Morgan provides a practical approach to assist librarians in training paraprofessionals for library reference work. Reviewing briefly the planning process, she reviews orientation, basic skills that include using online catalogs and Web services, evaluating Internet sources and understanding call numbers, advanced skills on article databases, federated searching link resolvers and SuDoc call numbers, and ready-reference skills on encyclopedias, international information, statistics, and government, company and consumer medical and health information. She goes into depth on communication skills and the reference interview, and covers managing performance as well as evaluating and revising training.

Nofsinger, Mary M., and Angela S.W. Lee. 1994. "Beyond Orientation: The Roles of Senior Librarians in Training Entry-Level Reference Colleagues." *College & Research Libraries* 55 (March): 161–70.

The authors suggest that more experienced staff members can play four vital roles in training entry-level reference librarians: as teachers or coaches; as interpreters or advisers for the institution's culture; as role models for interpersonal skills and cooperation among professional colleagues; and as mentors in professional development.

Staff Development: A Practical Guide. 2013. Edited by Andrea Wigbels Stewart, Carlette Washington-Hoagland, and Carole T. Zsulya, 4th ed. Chicago: American Library Association.

This edition addresses needs assessment, goal setting, establishing competencies, and working within the library's strategic plan in developing your staff. This work takes a more holistic approach to staff training, considering cross-functional training as well as developing a culture of collaboration, an attitude of customer service, and leadership potential and succession planning. Of course, it also addresses planning a training program, instructional design, ensuring transfer of learning, and assessing performance and coaching for performance.

Todaro, Julie, and Mark L. Smith. 2006. *Training Library Staff and Volunteers to Provide Extraordinary Customer Service.* New York: Neal-Schuman.

Todaro and Smith focus on the specific concerns that libraries have about customer service that are different than those of for-profit organizations. They emphasize the need to create a framework for gathering customer feedback and building a system of continuous learning.

Trotta, Marcia. 2011. *Staff Development on a Shoestring.* How-To-Do-It Manuals, no. 175. New York: Neal-Schuman.

This work is based on the assumption that the most cost-effective way to accomplish good staff training "is to design in-house training programs that turn experienced staff into proficient trainers" (p. ix), so is focused on developing individualized training programs. In addition to coverage of assessing needs, developing training, using technology, and assessing training, this book also discusses the manager's role in customizing job descriptions, helping staff solve problems, internal marketing, mentoring employees, evaluating performance, and recognizing effective performance. Also included are model training programs.

Chapter 10

Marketing and Promotion of Reference Services

Elisabeth Leonard and
Rosalind Tedford

WHAT IS MARKETING?

For every type of library—public, academic, school, special, governmental, tribal, corporate—it is essential to develop and deliver products and services that are relevant to library users. While some users will discover library services unaided, many, perhaps even most, users will need to have the services promoted to them before they will be aware of what modern reference services have to offer. Marketing is the activity through which librarians develop the right products and services, decide how to deliver the services, determine how best to communicate the value of those products and services, and then promote the relevant services to the right user group.

For many consumers, marketing has a tarnished reputation associated with advertising and selling in an inauthentic way, with the aim of persuading consumers to buy goods and services they do not really need or want. When done well, however, marketing is a holistic approach to examining the library's existing services, planning new services, making changes to existing services, ceasing existing services that have outlived their utility, communicating internally and externally about library services, and measuring success, ideally with the needs of the user population intersecting with the goals of the organization. More formally, according to Philip Kotler, marketing is "the science and art of exploring, creating, and delivering value to satisfy the needs of a target market. . . . Marketing identifies unfulfilled needs and desires. It defines, measures and quantifies the size of the identified market and the profit potential. It pinpoints which segments the company is capable of serving best and it designs and promotes the appropriate products and services" (2005, 3). This approach to marketing includes market research, market segmentation, market communications, and product development, and while the definition refers specifically to the potential for profit, this does not mean marketing must result in financial gains. Marketing can also result in a wide variety of other gains, including increased usage of a service, increased awareness of a service within a target population, or even serving an unmet need. In short, marketing is an essential approach for any organization hoping to effectively evaluate and manage its products and services, regardless of whether the organization is for-profit or nonprofit.

To better understand how to apply marketing principles to reference services, it is useful to extend Kotler's definition by examining nonprofit marketing and services marketing. Nonprofit marketing is a mind-set in which the organization considers its programs and services as well as how the organization impacts the world and how the world impacts the organization (Wymer, Knowles, and Gomes 2006, 4). This removes profit as a motive and instead focuses marketing efforts on goals that are specific to nonprofits, such as maintaining positive relationships with donors or taxpayers or furthering literacy.

However, not all libraries operate within nonprofit organizations. In these cases, it is useful to consider the literature on service marketing. The focus on services provides a theoretical structure and real-world examples that work well when planning marketing for reference services, although the structure may not be broad enough to encompass marketing reference products such as databases. However, examining the literature on services marketing serves as a reminder that reference departments need to consider the emphasis on customer relationships, marketing to internal stakeholders, and assessing and addressing service quality (Baron 2010).

Effective marketing can reap significant benefits for the organization and the people the organization serves. This chapter draws upon the framework of both nonprofit and services marketing to examine why and how librarians market information services to internal and external stakeholders. After introducing the Seven Ps as a marketing framework, the chapter presents the steps of the marketing process and looks at several channels to showcase the desired marketing messages. While the examples in the chapter are drawn heavily from the reference realm, the distinctions that differentiate reference from other library services are rapidly becoming obsolete in the library profession. The consolidation of service points and the movement of services online have made traditional distinctions between the different "desks" much more blurry over the last decade. The advice presented here on marketing reference is applicable to any area of the library that is marketing a product or service, including interlibrary loan, technology assistance, circulation, library collections, and digital repositories.

A FRAMEWORK FOR MARKETING

Librarians of all types can use the framework of the marketing mix to examine their information services. The marketing mix was established for commercial organizations selling products or services, but can be easily adapted to libraries. Classically, the marketing mix is presented as the Seven Ps: product, price, promotion, place, packaging, positioning, and people. For libraries, products are the available services and resources; price is recognizing what a user must give up

TABLE 10.1 Defining the Ps for Reference and Information Services

	Question	Example
Product	What is the library providing?	For most reference departments, this is the suite of reference and instruction services, such as chat reference, research consultations, and mediated searching.
Price	What does the user give up to use the services?	For many users, this includes time, confidential information or privacy, or pride, often due to information anxiety issues.
Promotion	How is the library going to tell users about services and persuade them to use those services?	This includes techniques such as events, direct mail, and banners on Web pages and within databases.
Place	Where will they find or how will they use services—do they have to come into the library or can they use services virtually? Where are users mentally—how can the library's service be the first thing they think of, rather than the last?	This can be from links within a course management system, in an office, via space in other buildings like a community center, in a virtual meeting room, or through a video call.
Packaging	What is the look and feel of the service?	Reference looks different for a school library than a corporate library. It can also look very different from one academic library to another. Not only should the service look and feel like the library, but it may also need to be packaged differently for different users.
Positioning	What is the value proposition for the user?	This is the elevator pitch for the service. If a librarian has 30 seconds with a target user, what would he or she say to convince the user to change his or her behavior? Try this formula, written from the user's point of view: What do I get? Why do I need it—what unique solution does it provide for *my* problems? What do I need to do to get it?
People	Who will provide the service? Do they have the right disposition? Do they have the right training?	Responsibility for some services, such as instruction, can be shared by multiple librarians. Training can be a key component of a successful service.

when choosing a library service (and for some libraries includes setting a monetary price); promotion is the mix of activities that increases awareness or use of a service; place is where the service is made available; packaging is the appearance of the product or service; positioning is creating a value proposition for a service that acknowledges the competition; and people is a focus on training and recruiting the right people within the organization. Each of the Ps comes with a question; answering these questions can help a marketing effort take shape. Table 10.1 outlines the Seven Ps and defines them for reference and information services.

Box 10.1 provides a case study showing the Seven Ps in action. This case study illustrates how the Ps look when applied to a specific situation as well as how marketing efforts can be aligned with library and organizational goals.

Box 10.1 Case Study: Setting Objectives That Support Organizational Goals

In a medium-sized academic library, the research conducted for the campus strategic plan identified the library as an intellectual and social hub. However, the campus is shifting from a residential campus where all freshmen and sophomores live to a distance education campus. Campus administration has asked the library to find ways to maintain the feel of the library as a place, even for students who may never come to campus.

The library identified the following objectives:

- Ensuring faculty know what resources are available for their distance students.
- Ensuring distance students feel included in the library's zeitgeist.
- Ensuring students in online programs recognize the library as the place to go for research assistance.

From these objectives, librarians tailored the Seven Ps into customized questions. Because the library's objectives were matched to campus goals, the answers to these questions will help librarians address the concerns of campus administration.

- *Products*: What products and services will aid the connection between distance education students and the library, including efforts that further study and socialization?
- *Price*: What are the impediments for a distance education student in using the library's key services? Where else does he or she go to satisfy these needs?
- *Promotion*: How can librarians make the faculty teaching online courses aware of the library services available to them and their students? How can students be alerted to library content and services?
- *Place*: In the absence of in-person chances to talk to students, where can information about library services be placed? On the library website? Within the course management system?
- *Packaging*: How will the message grab the attention of the online student? Can the website be updated? Could a logo/brand be developed for services specifically for online students?
- *Positioning*: How can librarians position the value of the library's space, services, and products like subscription databases, especially when situated against spaces like local cafes or a product like *Google*?

STEPS TO SUCCESSFUL MARKETING

Regardless of the type of library, the following steps provide a focused and strategic approach to marketing:

1. Define goals and objectives.
2. Determine the product.
3. Conduct an environmental scan.
4. Create a marketing plan.

Depending on the scope of the library's marketing efforts, the marketing goals and plan for the reference department may include adding new products and services and/or altering existing products and services. What is most important is to start with a clear direction and the support of the administration so that the marketing efforts receive full support.

DEFINING GOALS AND OBJECTIVES

The first step in any marketing effort is to define the goal. Is it launching a new service? Is it increasing use of an existing service? There are times when marketing goals are very personal and individual and other times when marketing goals are broad and involve multiple people and departments. In a solo library, the efforts will focus on a single person who may need to market himself or herself and the individual's services, even though the person represents the library. At other times, there will be broader library goals and a preexisting library-wide marketing plan, of which reference services will be a single line within a 10-page document. More often, there is a strategic plan that alludes to reference or information services; in these cases, the marketing plan for reference should align with the library's strategic plan. The main benefit of defining a goal early on is that it can save time, money, and frustration in the long run.

Just as when a reference librarian begins a reference consultation there is uncertainty if the posed question is the "real question," the same can be true as the reference department's goals are drafted for a marketing project. The "real" goals become clear as the process continues; the initial goal may be representative of the true end goal, or it may be a red herring. As librarians proceed through the process, they should keep an open mind and continue to challenge internal assumptions while allowing the original goal to serve as a touchstone in case too many alternate possibilities pose a distraction.

Librarians can conduct internal reference interviews to define the library's goals. For example, the head of reference could receive a request from administration to produce a market research plan for "reference." Rather than taking the request at face value and creating a massive effort to promote all of the reference services to the library's entire user population, the head of reference should ask for clarification. Upon further investigation, she might learn that the director has heard that the library's new online virtual reference service is not well known or well used and has assumed that none of the library's services are being marketed well. Once the context of the request is understood, marketing efforts can be directed at improving the awareness and use of that one particular service (and making the director aware that it is a new service and will likely need some extra marketing to make it effective), rather than spending time on a marketing plan for all services. By asking for clarification, the head of reference can ensure that any marketing efforts focus on what is needed to solve the one specific problem at hand.

> **Box 10.2 Tip: Defining Goals**
>
> Define the library's marketing goals and objectives before beginning any marketing efforts, including who should be involved, what the budget is, how much time there is for planning, how much time there is before results are needed, or how the work will be assessed.

DETERMINING THE PRODUCT

The next step after determining goals is to determine what is being marketed. While the question of *what* can seem like a simple one, some forethought can increase chances of fulfilling the desired goals without unnecessary confusion or delays. Is the department introducing a new service? A new space? Is there an existing service that is not getting well utilized that needs to be highlighted to the right user group? Whatever the answer, defining the service accurately can help the reference department gather the necessary information to market or promote it. Keep in mind that whatever the service is, it likely will not be the *only* service the library offers, and librarians should take time to think about how the service fits in with existing services. Is the library now offering online homework help in addition to face-to-face help? Or perhaps the library is now offering drop-in research sessions for student papers that complement the existing help given through scheduled meetings. If a new service is being promoted, librarians should be careful not to focus so much on promoting the new service that the current service is seen as nonexistent. Instead, co-brand and cross-promote the existing service while raising awareness of the added benefits of the new service. This should allow both services to thrive.

Before promoting any service, librarians need to know exactly what the service is and who the target audience is. A single service can serve multiple market segments, just as a single market segment can use multiple information services (including services provided by market competitors). Librarians can consider the following questions to contextualize the service and focus on *what* it is before the service is promoted:

- What will the service be called? If it is an existing service, should it be renamed?
- Who is/will be responsible for managing the service?
- Why is the service needed?
- Who is the target audience?
- Does this audience already use other services provided by the library?
- Does the service require outreach to a population of patrons that has not benefited from this service before?
- What other services in the library relate to this service?
- What other services in the library target this audience?

CONDUCTING AN ENVIRONMENTAL SCAN

The third step is to understand the environment in which the service is being offered. Any marketing effort is not going to be effective if it does not match the organization's goals and personality or if it does not fit in with the current culture or ongoing efforts. An environmental scan does not have to be a formal assessment; it can be casual or observational in nature. But depending on the environment of the institution, a more formal scan might be needed, especially if a significant change is going to be proposed. Assessing current and previous efforts, organizational culture, patron culture, and the available resources (human and otherwise) can give a broad picture into which to paint (or repaint) the service.

Assessing Current Marketing Efforts

Librarians should talk to the people in the organization who are tasked with marketing in some way, either officially or unofficially. In recent years, there has been a trend for larger libraries to hire dedicated outreach or marketing librarians, but even if the library does not have someone dedicated to getting the word out, there are always unofficial evangelists of library services to be found.

- Who currently markets services?
- What services are currently marketed?
- What channels are used? Print, e-mail, social media?
- Who are these marketing efforts directed toward?
- Who *should* these marketing efforts be directed toward?
- Are they reaching the intended audience?
- What are the strengths of the current efforts?
- What are the weaknesses of the current efforts?

Assessing Previous Marketing Efforts

Librarians should also look at previous marketing efforts. If the library has tried and failed at something in the past, suggesting it again may meet with resistance. This does not mean it cannot be done, but librarians will need to know how and why it was tried and how it failed in order to make a case for trying it again.

- Who coordinated previous marketing efforts?
- What shape did these previous efforts take?
- What services were marketed?
- When did these previous efforts occur?
- Why were these efforts started?
- What were the strengths of the previous efforts?
- What were the weaknesses of the previous efforts?

Understanding Organizational Culture

Perhaps the most important part of the environmental scan is to fully understand the politics and personality of the library. Marketing will not be successful if it is for a service or has a message that is inconsistent with the organization's culture. Organizational culture can be a difficult thing to understand, but once done, it will pay dividends for a long time. Few libraries have an existing statement that conveys this kind of information, but new librarians can look for it in mission statements, in staff meetings, and through conversations with other people.

- What rules or restrictions are in place that would affect marketing efforts?
- What assumptions about marketing exist that would impact efforts?
- What official channels or policies must be followed?
- Are there graphic or branding restrictions?
- Who are the stakeholders in the marketing effort?
- Who gives the final OK (hint, they are also a stakeholder)?

Understanding Patrons

Understanding the patron culture, especially those you want to attract to new services, is equally important. Demographics, cultural traditions, and technology habits all play into how they will be informed about and attracted to a new service. More about the specifics of market research will come later in the chapter, but for the purposes of an initial environmental scan, keep this informal. Always keep in mind, however, that if the goal is to reach a new audience, just talking to existing patrons will not be enough. Research into where the desired audience for the service is and how they can be reached will need to be done.

- Who currently uses similar services at the library? In the community?
- How do they find out about these services?
- Would these patrons be interested in the new service?

Identifying Available Resources

Finally, no environmental scan would be complete without gauging what resources will be available. Resources can and often do mean money, but more often than not, the most critical resources in marketing efforts are people and time.

- Who will do the marketing?
- How much time is going to be involved?
- Is marketing part of this person's prescribed job duties?
- If not, have accommodations been made to allow the person to spend time on the effort?
- Is there a budget?

As with everything, going slowly can be key, and librarians should take time to evaluate the environment. Many new librarians, and many veterans as well, can feel deflated coming into an organization that is rigid or behind the times in terms of marketing efforts. The way to change the culture, however, is not to proclaim it rigid and behind the times. Small steps are often much more effective than trying an all-out change offensive. A new service marketed in a slightly new way may be just the thing to relax a bit of the rigidity and create an environment open to trying new things.

CREATING A MARKETING PLAN

Once the librarian has a clear list of goals, knows what product is being marketed, and has a sense of the environment in which the marketing will take place, it is time to assemble a marketing plan. This chapter outlines a detailed list of procedural steps that are classically part of a marketing plan. Some projects will benefit from all the steps, but other projects can be approached by skipping a step or two and still be successful. Librarians can think of each step as part of a marketing toolkit and not as a prescriptive linear process. Each librarian should utilize what makes sense for his or her environment, considering the desired timeline, the staff involved, and the circumstances.

1. Market research
    a. Primary research
    b. Secondary research
2. Environmental scan or SWOT analysis
3. Value propositions
4. Promotion or communication plan
5. Timeline
6. Budget
7. Assessment
8. Sunsetting a service

Market Research

In order to make decisions about the marketing mix, market research is necessary. Market research is often done as part of the library's strategic planning process, but even if the library has just done market research for the strategic plan, additional research is necessary for marketing. Primary research is done to discover what patrons want and need, what they are likely to respond to, and how they would like for the library to communicate with them. Secondary research is found in published reports and statistics about target audiences, such as reports about Generation X. The best market research uses a combination of methods and sources, as each method provides a different piece of information about the target users and the environment in which the library is competing for the target users' time and attention.

Primary Research

There are many ways for librarians to find out what patrons and community members think about the library and its services. In addition to the quantitative data that libraries keep (door count, circulation statistics, reference statistics, interlibrary loan statistics, etc.), the most popular qualitative market research methods are focus groups, interviews, surveys, and observational studies (see Chapter 8 for more on quantitative and qualitative research methods). Before conducting research, go back to the goals for marketing and then think about what knowledge is needed in order to deliver on those goals. Is the library trying to attract new patrons? Existing patrons? Is there a particular segment of the population that needs to be reached? Does the library want to know about beliefs, behaviors, or attitudes? Match the type of research desired with the kind of information needed. If the library's users are nothing like the national average, then do not waste time searching for and reading aggregate reports. Instead, look for local sources and conduct research locally.

A focus group typically consists of gathering three to ten people in a room where they are asked about their opinions, beliefs, and attitudes. The focus group can be for a single niche group, like teens, instructors, or business students, or it can be a representation of every target group. Often, focus groups begin with a wide range of population types and narrow as the library learns more about whom they are trying to reach and what else the library wants to know. Sometimes focus groups are conducted by an outside interviewer who is trained in the method. If the library cannot afford this, the staff should find someone who is able to remain neutral no matter what the group says about the library and who is good at asking probing questions. Focus groups last for one to two hours and should be recorded so they can be analyzed later.

It is crucial to carefully plan the questions that will be posed in order to get useful data. "Do you like the library?" is not going to be as useful as "How do you find out about library events?" or "Where do your peers study if they aren't coming to the library?" However, some flexibility in allowing the discussion to wander a bit can be revealing. Sometimes more can be learned when the conversation veers a bit than when the moderator sticks to a strict script. It is also important to remain open to what participants have to say, even if it does not match what librarians were hoping to hear.

Focus groups can be used after surveys to delve into some topics more deeply or before large surveys or personal interviews in order to figure out what to ask. They are a relatively simple way to get at important, and very often surprising, information about users. Offering food, and for an adult audience even drinks, can aid in attendance and opening up participants to the experience.

Interviews allow the library to delve more deeply into opinions, behaviors, and attitudes than focus groups or surveys. Interviews are typically between a single librarian and a single patron. They can be done as follow-ups to information gained from surveys and focus groups. Interviews range in length, but rarely last longer than two hours and are recorded so they can be analyzed later. If interviews are used, it is important to recognize that they are a limited source of opinion. Do not make major decisions about a service on the basis of a single interview or a small focus group. At the same time, in-depth conversations are often more revealing than a multiple choice survey so they have a valuable place in any marketing plan. As with focus groups, intentional questions prepared beforehand will help ensure that the interview is a good use of time.

Surveys are an efficient way to quickly gather information from a large number of people. Unlike focus groups or interviews, respondents can remain anonymous, something that can help get candid feedback on a sensitive topic, but that can also lead to answers without any context.

As with all of these methods, determining what data are needed and how they will be used before deploying the survey can save time and frustration. Exploring research conducted at other libraries may reveal an existing survey that could be adapted for use. In addition, reviewing the work of other libraries can reveal what questions were not particularly successful at getting to the desired information. The biggest drawback to a survey is that the questions are fixed and may not allow for patrons to share everything they want to. Librarians should include at least one open-ended question where respondents can provide feedback on anything from the survey or give feedback about any library issue.

Response rates for surveys vary, and it is advisable to do what is needed to get as many responses as possible. Incentive gifts are a good way to attract survey takers, as are messages targeted directly to particular user groups. If part of the plan is to follow up the survey with a focus group or interview, the survey should ask respondents to identify themselves if they would be willing to participate further.

Observation can determine behaviors that patrons may be unwilling to verbalize or may be unaware they have and is something every reference librarian does, even though it is rarely intentional. Ask a librarian how patrons use the catalog, and every librarian will have an answer based on what he or she observes at the reference desk. But unsystematic observation is prone to observer bias, where the observer thinks he or she sees what the person wanted or expected to see. Objective observation research can illustrate how people really use the library and can be especially informative about when and how people are getting frustrated as well as what they find easy to use. If methods are used that eliminate observer bias, observation can be one of the most revealing types of research. Observation for Web interfaces or services is often conducted as part of a usability study, and there are many potential methods for those that range from usability labs to software that tracks all keyboard activity to direct person-to-person observational sessions. Sometimes, however, more anthropological methods are used in observational research, including setting up cameras, monitoring room usage, and time-lapse photography.

Box 10.3 Tip: Human Subjects Research

In some organizations, any research done with people is called "human subjects research," and an institutional review board must review and approve the research plan before any research is conducted. Before conducting primary research, consult your organizational policies.

Secondary Research

In addition to interacting directly with users, librarians can access research about the target population, including articles and presentations done by other librarians, market research reports available through library databases, and research conducted by organizations such as OCLC Research, Ithaka S+R, and the Pew Research Center (see Box 10.4). For most reference librarians, this kind of research comes easily, and the sources uncovered in a literature search can be invaluable. For small libraries without the resources to conduct primary research, relevant secondary sources can serve a similar purpose with less time and money expended. In addition to presentations, journal articles, and other research produced by librarians, commercial market research reports can help librarians understand general consumer behavior, such as when and why Millennials use cell phones or why and how people use bookstores and coffee shops.

Often, this kind of research about population groups can be extremely helpful in working out a strategy to market to them. If users all have cell phones, then a service that is mobile friendly might be worth investigating; if they are generally distrustful of technology, then face-to-face information and classes might be better.

Box 10.4 Activity: Researching Patron Behavior

The Pew Research Center publishes numerous studies that examine how Americans use libraries, the Internet, and technology. Access one of the following reports:

- "Mobile Messaging and Social Media 2015"—http://www.pewinternet.org/2015/08/19/mobile-messaging-and-social-media-2015/.
- "Parents and Social Media"—http://www.pewinternet.org/2015/07/16/parents-and-social-media/.
- "Public Libraries and Hispanics"—http://www.pewhispanic.org/2015/03/17/public-libraries-and-hispanics/.

Alternately, select a recent report of interest at http://www.pewinternet.org/category/publications/report/.

Questions for Reflection and Discussion:

1. What does this report tell you about the population segment it studied?
2. If you were trying to develop and market services for this population segment, how could the report inform your work?

SWOT Analysis

Looking inside and outside the library to provide context to the problems the marketing efforts are intended to resolve can be crucial at the beginning of the process. One of the most popular ways to do this is through a strengths, weaknesses, opportunities, and threats (SWOT) analysis. A SWOT analysis is beneficial at the beginning of a planning process. It helps isolate the resources available (strengths), the limitations faced (weaknesses), the places where new ground could be broken (opportunities), and the obstacles that stand in the way of success (threats). Librarians should enter into a SWOT analysis with an open mind and gather the perspectives of multiple people in the organization. Often what one person sees as a weakness (outdated computer equipment), others might see as an opportunity (chance to reach out to a community partner for a donation). Often, gathering SWOT input from a variety of stakeholders can begin to shift perspectives and create a narrative as the project moves forward (Table 10.2). Box 10.5 takes a closer look at how a SWOT analysis might be applied to library marketing.

Box 10.5 Example of a SWOT Analysis

A group of academic librarians has been charged with adapting the library's reference services to accommodate an increasing number of online students at the institution. As part of their work, they conduct a SWOT analysis.

TABLE 10.2 SWOT Example

Strengths	Weaknesses
• Large number of online resources available already • Librarians who are skilled in the use of online resources • Librarians who have received degrees from online programs themselves • Library with a good reputation among faculty and students • Provost willing to make online education work on campus	• Lack of staff experience with troubleshooting problems from a distance • Staffing models that do not take into account students in multiple time zones • Reliance of some disciplines on print resources • Website focused on residential student needs • Staff resistance to change
Opportunities	**Threats**
• Chance to open up services to a wider range of students • Money available to acquire online resources for programs with online degrees • Chance to develop new marketing strategy aimed at online students that can serve all students • Chance to rethink Web presence to meet the needs of all students better • Chance to be more integrated in the university's course management system	• Online students may not realize they have access to library services and use *Google* instead • Online faculty who do not reside on-campus could fail to recommend library services to students • Programs could fail, and budget would be cut

Value Propositions

Value propositions illustrate the benefit a target group can receive from a library's service. It is rarely true that every market segment wants the same thing from the same service. Writing value propositions for each target group will codify what has been learned about each group and will help to communicate not only with patrons, but also with staff and internal stakeholders.

Each value proposition should communicate the most important benefits to the patron. It is key to remember to write these from the patron's point of view and not to try to force organizational values and organizational language onto users. Charles Doyle's (2011) Attention, Interest, Desire, and Action (AIDA) marketing formula can be used to write value propositions from the user's point of view.

- What do I get? (What is the attention getter?)
- Why do I need it? (What about this will interest them?)
- What unique solution does it solve for *my* problems? (Why should they desire it?)
- What do I need to do to get it? (What action should they take?)

For example, if the library has always promoted the personal research session as a way for students to get individual attention and to be pointed to quality information, but transfer students do not use that service, questions about why that is the case should arise. If it turns out that transfer students are overwhelmed in general by the transition from the local community college to the university and that they feel a large amount of information anxiety in their first year at the university, then the library may need to approach transfer students differently than how they approach traditional students. Imagine that after conducting several focus groups, interviewing a few outspoken transfer students, and looking at the demographic information the registrar provides, it turns out that more than anything, the students need to feel welcomed by the library. The library needs to convey in its value proposition to transfer students that the library is there to help them and that individual assistance is available.

To be clear, the value proposition is for internal guidance. What is in the actual messaging should have similar points to what are found in the value proposition, but applying creative license typically means that the messages and promotional material users see are less factual and more inviting. Ideally, the value proposition would be tested with each user group so the library can be sure to capture accurately what matters to them and in a style to which they are receptive.

Promotion or Communication Plan

After the value proposition has been developed and tested, it is time to put the goals, the market research, and the value proposition together into a plan for promoting the service. Some popular ways that libraries advertise services include print (ranging from table tents, flyers, brochures, postcards, newsletters, ads in local papers, and bookmarks), online (via social media, Web banners, videos, e-mail, blog posts, and highlights on the library's website), and at events (contests, open houses, lecture series). However, guerilla marketing and word of mouth are both very effective ways to increase awareness and use of reference services. Guerrilla marketing embeds the library's marketing efforts into the places where the users/customers are. For example, libraries in New York benefited from a guerrilla campaign where people could read a small portion of a book while in the subway, but after the first 10 pages, they were "informed [of] the nearest library where they can borrow the book" (Cruz 2013). While guerrilla marketing does not have to be initiated by the library's patrons, it is most effective when the campaign looks and feels like the people the library aims to attract.

Timeline

A timeline not only establishes what work needs to be accomplished and when, but also illustrates whose responsibility that work is. This helps with making sure that no staff person will suddenly become overwhelmed with his or her part in the marketing plan and helps remind those involved of what work needs to be done so that they can manage their time effectively.

Once the timeline is established, a manager can see whether the reference staff is trying to do too much marketing in one month with no marketing efforts in another month. The manager or the marketing lead can then spread out the work more evenly so that it is easier to accomplish, and so that in no single month will any target audience be overwhelmed by the marketing messages from various members of the reference staff.

What can make the timeline truly impactful is presentation as a snapshot that shows how messaging will be targeted and what key events and tasks librarians need to complete. In this way, the timeline can serve as a mini project plan (see Box 10.6 for an example).

Box 10.6 Sample Marketing Timeline

A small public library would like to increase enrollment in its summer reading program. It develops a marketing plan that includes the following timeline:

- *May 1*: Hold open house to show off fiction collection and reader services to parents and teachers. At the event, promote the upcoming workshops on the summer reading program.
- *May 15*: Hold workshops for parents and teachers to inform them of the summer reading program and its benefits. Send them home with marketing materials that they can hand out to their children or students.
- *May 20*: Place posters on school and library bulletin boards.
- *May 20*: Add an enrollment form to the circulation desk. The circulation member with the most sign-ups wins a prize.
- *May 25*: Put bookmarks and table tents out in each reading room in the library.
- *May 30*: Summer reading program begins.
- *June 5*: Have a campaign ready to e-mail parents and teachers if there are not enough children enrolled. Check benchmarks to see whether goals have been met.

Budget

Any marketing plan should include a realistic budget. Even though administrators may seem enthusiastic about marketing, it is unlikely that there is an unlimited budget, and the initial budget may need to be adjusted before plans are shared more widely. For the draft budget, show who is doing the work for each part of the plan and provide costs for the work. For example, if there is no one on staff capable of designing graphics, estimate how much it will cost to hire a graphic designer to create brand images. Costs such as prizes for a survey, promotional materials for campus events, and catering for receptions would also need to be included. Librarians should also budget for ongoing expenses, such as a print brochure that will need to be updated and printed annually. If users want new services, the plan should show how the reference department could respond to those desires, including the costs to begin a new service, and how much time and money might be saved by ceasing a service that no one wants or needs anymore.

Once administrators are ready to move forward, librarians should formalize how much time and money it takes to implement that plan. The budget becomes part of the marketing plan and is updated as tasks and events are completed.

Assessment

Assessment is perhaps the hardest area of marketing and is, unfortunately, often an afterthought rather than something that is planned from the beginning. It is important to articulate what "success" looks like for the marketing campaign from early on in the process as well as how that success will be measured.

There is no single measurement to apply to all marketing goals. Instead, there are a variety of measurements that can be used based on the library's needs. For example, if the goal of a marketing campaign is to increase use of a service, then librarians can track usage of the service both before and after the marketing campaign. They will also need to determine whether any of the use is *because* of the marketing campaign. If a new service is starting from scratch, it is crucial to define what metrics will be used to deem that service a success and then determine the role the marketing effort played in the outcome. This section describes several available metrics and how they are used.

If the goal for an event is to have a certain number of people in the audience, measuring success is quite easy. Simply set the target audience size and count heads. This is not an example of strategic marketing, however; so as marketing efforts grow, goals should indicate a more direct tie to the library's mission or to the larger goals of the marketing plan. What exactly is the event intended to do? Raise community awareness about an issue, such as literacy? Create a relationship with a target audience? Goals should be set before an event, and any evaluation should be based on whether it met those goals.

Libraries keep innumerable statistics about use. If any marketing goals are about increasing use, librarians can take a close look at what statistics the library already keeps. A new measurement may not be needed, and the library can instead use the tools that are already in place. For example, circulation statistics can often be gathered that illustrate by market segment (undergraduate, graduate student, alumni, faculty, staff) how often and what type of materials are circulating. Depending on what integrated library system the library uses, generating the data could be very easy or could take time. Librarians involved in marketing efforts should be sure the data are really needed before asking someone to run a time-consuming report.

LibQUAL+, a widely used survey administered by the Association of Research Libraries, is used by libraries around the world. It surveys patrons about the disparity between the level of service a patron desires and the perceived level of service offered by the library. Given that libraries are in the service business and that marketing is about customer relationships, LibQUAL+ offers a means to measure patron satisfaction with current services as well as what services they have the highest expectations for. In addition, because LibQUAL+ is designed to be done at regular intervals, a survey done a year or two after the implementation of a new service or a substantial change in the marketing of an existing service can provide strong evidence of the impact of a marketing plan.

Advertising effectiveness is another way to measure the success of marketing. Advertising can include paid media, such as a poster on campus buses or an ad in the student paper or radio, and free media, such as a video on YouTube or a banner on the library's Web page or school's course management system. Popular metrics to measure how widely advertising is working include impressions, click-throughs, response rate, and recall (see Box 10.7).

Box 10.7 Metrics to Measure Advertising Effectiveness

Impressions: Impressions are the number of times the marketer assumes that a message has been seen. The premise of using advertising this way is based on AIDA, where part of what a marketer wants to do is get the patron's attention. Thus, if the goal for the advertising campaign is simply having the message seen, impressions can be used to help determine how many people you have reached. Impressions are hard to measure in print marketing although building counts, ridership, number of addresses, and so on can be useful for estimates. For electronic marketing, there are a variety of ways to measure, including things like Google Analytics for measuring Web page traffic, read receipts for e-mail newsletters, and click-throughs.

Click-throughs: Click-throughs arose as an advertising metric in the 1990s when Internet advertising became a popular and inexpensive way to advertise. Advertisers use click-throughs, or the number of people who click on an ad on a Web page, to determine not just whether someone has seen the message, but whether he or she was interested enough to click and learn more or to use the service. For libraries, click-throughs can be a valuable way to discover which method of access is driving traffic to resources. If increasing use of a database is your goal, click-through data from Google Analytics or a database provider can track usage before and after an advertising campaign.

Response rate: Response rate is similar to click-through in that it measures whether a patron is taking action on the message. This measurement can be used if mailers have been sent or coupons have been issued for services, such as an ad for a free research consultation that the patron needs to bring in with him or her. In this case, collecting the coupons will show how many were used in conjunction with the service. Alternatively, asking at the point of use how the patron had heard about the service can provide valuable data. Asking for information like this at the point of service does require the respondent to be honest and that staff ask persistently until the end of the data collection period.

Recall: Recall measures how many people were able to remember advertising or how many people can say that they have heard of a service. This can be a useful baseline for establishing advertising's impact throughout the duration of an advertising campaign. It is difficult to gather though and should be used with caution. If only five people have been asked and they all say they heard of a service by seeing an ad on a bus, that does not mean that everyone else heard of the service this way.

More likely than not, librarians will need to create measures that more directly reflect individual goals. If the goal is to change patrons' perceptions of the library, then measuring their perceptions before any marketing efforts and again after marketing efforts will be the right path. The return on investment would then be based on the percentage of people whose minds were changed as a result of the campaigns. Clearly, this is not as easy as it sounds. In a clinical setting, the messages a population views can be tightly controlled along with other factors that can impact change. In the real world, it may be necessary to create multiple measures of success and then assess impact. By using multiple measures, realistic conclusions are more likely to be arrived at than relying on a single measure, but when it comes to marketing, there is rarely a clear and easy assessment.

Sunsetting a Service

While it would be satisfying if every service was successful and could continue on indefinitely, the truth is that library services come and go, and this is how it should be. As patrons and organizations change, it is often better to stop a service than to let it limp along. Letting a service go can be an effective way, or even the only way, to free up resources such as people, space, and time to introduce a new service or to make an existing service even better.

Before letting a service end, however, be sure that it is not needed. A service may be underutilized because it is truly not needed anymore (remember the banks of typewriters libraries used to have) or it may be that the service simply needs to be promoted to the right people. There are several questions to ask when faced with the choice of whether or not to sunset a service:

- How long has the service been around?
- Why was it instituted in the first place?
- What is the history of its use?
- Who was its target audience?
- Why is it not successful now? Do people know about it and just not use it? Do people not need it?
- What would the library gain if the service ended?
- What would the library lose if the service ended?
- What would it take to resuscitate the services, assuming it is still needed by patrons?
- Are there political ramifications to ending it?

Before sunsetting a service, librarians should recognize that ending the service will require marketing in and of itself. If some patrons still check out VHS tapes, but not enough to justify the space they take up or the effort they require to maintain, a bit of marketing to those invested patrons about why the library plans to end the service will be needed. It is critical that everyone who would come in contact with those patrons is giving consistent answers, so sometimes the target audience for a sunsetting marketing plan is really library employees. Be prepared ahead of time for any negative reactions that come from ending a service and have good responses for those patrons who may complain.

ADVERTISING CHANNELS

While marketing encompasses the whole process, advertising is the final step in getting the word out. There are numerous ways to do it, none inherently better than any others. If the library has done the right research and preparation for its marketing efforts, choosing the right channel or channels for advertising should be the easy, and fun, part. If the target audience is primarily mobile phone users, then social media might be the best route. If they are older and prefer print information, a print newsletter could be preferable. If they are professionals, an e-mail newsletter might reach them most effectively. Or if the entirety of the community needs to know about a new service, the library will want to use multiple channels.

Logos, titles, and color schemes are all visual cues about the library and can grab attention. Regardless of the advertising channel used, it is always best if there is some continuity among channels. At the very least, use the same library branding on all communications.

The following section discusses the most common advertising channels used by libraries. The list is not comprehensive, but should serve for most libraries.

Print

Despite media declarations to the contrary, print is not actually dead as a means of communication. Even in the digital native world of college campuses, print flyers are still nearly ubiquitous for getting out specific information about events quickly. But compared with the other options, print is relatively expensive, and librarians should proceed with caution.

Print flyers or posters placed around the library or community in places the target audience is likely to visit can be excellent attention-grabbers. Be sure to include the needed details, but no more. People do not tend to absorb long blocks of text from a flyer hanging in a stairwell or at a community center, but a who–what–when–where approach can grab their attention. Having a place on your flyer where patrons can go for more information, usually a website, is a way to economize on text.

Newsletters were more common a decade or two ago and were sent out via regular mail to library patrons and friends groups or left out on a circulation desk for pickup. Newsletters allow for longer discussion of events than flyers do, so more detail can be added. Getting a new service or service reminder into an existing newsletter can be an excellent way to spread the news.

Newsletters can still be useful tools if the library has a history of providing them and an up-to-date mailing list. However, starting a print newsletter from scratch is unlikely to serve most libraries well, simply due to the cost and time involved. Instead, librarians can consider an eNewsletter or blog; these allow for a similar long-form description of a service without the cost of printing and mailing.

Electronic

Electronic modes of communication are usually the chosen routes for a good deal of library marketing efforts because they are, in general, less expensive and more far-reaching than print. Electronic information can also be updated more easily and changed when the need arises. For example, if homework help hours change, it is easy to change a Web page and post updates to social media, but much more difficult to bring back in flyers or newsletters with the old information on them.

Similar to print newsletters, eNewsletters allow for longer descriptions of services and are effective if the audience uses e-mail heavily. An easy e-mail sign-up on the home page can be used to gather the e-mails of patrons that want to be updated about services. Then, librarians can develop a publication plan (e.g., monthly, quarterly, semiannually) and proceed from there. Companies exist that will help manage e-mail communications with options for formatting, pulling in Web content and reminders, storing e-mail lists, and more. While these services do cost money, they can be an enormous time-saver when the time comes for sending out e-mails.

Most libraries today have a website. While part of their purpose is to get users to library services, another important use is as a marketing device. Libraries should make sure that the website has a way to display marketing information when needed. A blog on the home page can be updated with a variety of library information and news. Alternatively, a "what's new" banner could be placed at the top of the page or a social media feed incorporated on the home page. Whatever avenue is chosen, the website should have all the information about the services the library provides and highlight those that are the focus of current marking efforts.

Using social media for marketing in libraries is a double-edged sword. On the one hand, it is an easy way to push information out to users. On the other hand, a staff member must be willing to administer and monitor all of the library's social media accounts. Facebook, Twitter, Instagram, Tumblr, and GoodReads are just some of the social media platforms patrons are active on today, but their use changes over time. Libraries need someone on the staff to keep up with the demographics of social media platforms as well as the logistics of using each one.

If a library has no social media presence, it might be best to start small by getting an account on a single social media platform and experiment (see Box 10.8). If a library already has a number of accounts, there are ways to streamline activity. Services like IFTTT can be used to connect all of the library's accounts; if a librarian posts something on one platform, it will cascade out to others. No single social media platform will reach all users, so librarians will need to be strategic. Since most patron groups expect to be able to connect to a library via some form of social media, finding out which could be a good use of a focus group.

Box 10.8 Activity: Using Social Media to Promote Library Services

Pick a social media service such as Twitter, Instagram, or Tumblr, and search for library accounts.

Questions for Reflection and Discussion:

1. What types of libraries were present?
2. What types of services were being promoted?
3. Could you see librarians advancing "value propositions"? If so, what were those value propositions, and how were they communicated using the unique features of the social media service?
4. Do you think these promotion efforts were effective? Why or why not?

CONCLUSION

"The culture of assessment" is a frequently touted phrase in libraries. It is used to convey the message that in order for a library to succeed, not only does assessment need to be consistent, but also every member of the staff must be aware of how what he or she does helps the patron. The same is true for marketing. Libraries must arrive at a culture of marketing, where everyone on the staff understands what relationship the library wants to have with its patrons and how the library is working on those relationships. The reference department is one of the public faces to that relationship and is often central to marketing efforts.

Marketing is a cyclical process for identifying patron needs, creating services and products based around those needs and the library's mission, determining value propositions, communicating those value propositions, and monitoring to see whether the promised value was noticed by and delivered to the patron. Marketing should be embedded into the daily work of the library and its staff. Library patrons change every year, and library products and services are not stagnant; therefore, efforts at promoting services should not be stagnant either (Box 10.9 provides sources of inspiration). A library that implements the full promise of marketing will find itself a ubiquitous and integral part of its patrons' lives.

Box 10.9 Further Inspiration

Several resources can provide inspiration for marketing campaigns, some of which are specific to libraries. Each of these is intended to help with brainstorming. Some can easily be adapted into a library's marketing campaign, but it is a rare moment that users will be engaged with the library and its services by seeing or hearing a message intended to serve a different population. Keep users at the forefront of your mind, and you will not go wrong.

- *Library award winners*: Every year, the Library Leadership and Management Association (LLAMA) sponsors an idea exchange and issues awards for best public relations campaigns. In addition, EBSCO offers the John Cotton Dana Library Public Relations Award. While every library is unique, it can be useful to see what other libraries have done. Having someone explain what worked and did not work about his or her own efforts can help any librarian understand what pitfalls and rewards there can be to an approach before getting too far along.
- *Advertising websites and awards*: *Advertising Age* and other trade publications regularly report on advertising campaigns. Reading what efforts are being made to target consumers similar to a patron population should help place the library's efforts into a broader context and may help librarians think about similar messages to reach the same audience.
- *Observation*: Watching people in the grocery store and other "natural" environments where people are using technology, gathering information, and shopping with a mission can provide insights about how people interact with their environments.

REFERENCES

Advertising Age. 1930–. New York: Crain Communications. Weekly.

Baron, Steve, ed. 2010. *Service Marketing*. 4 vols. London: SAGE Publications.

Cruz, Xath. 2013. "New York Public Library Creates Subway Libraries." *Creative Guerrilla Marketing*. May 10. http://www.creativeguerrillamarketing.com/guerrilla-marketing/new-york-public-library-creates-subway-libraries/.

Doyle, Charles, ed. 2011. "AIDA." *Dictionary of Marketing*. New York: Oxford University Press. http://www.oxfordreference.com.

Facebook. http://www.facebook.com.

GoodReads. http://www.goodreads.com/.

IFTTT. https://ifttt.com/.

Instagram. http://instagram.com.
Ithaka S+R. http://www.sr.ithaka.org/.
John Cotton Dana Library Public Relations Award. EBSCO. https://www.ebscohost.com/academic/john-cotton-dana.
Kotler, Philip. 2005. *According to Kotler: The World's Foremost Authority on Marketing Answers Your Questions.* New York: AMACOM.
LibQUAL+®. 2015. "General Information." Accessed August 17. https://www.libqual.org/about/about_lq/general_info.
Library Leadership and Management Association. "PR Xchange Awards." American Library Association. http://www.ala.org/llama/awards/prxchange_bestofshow.
OCLC Research. http://www.oclc.org/research.html.
Pew Research Center. http://www.pewinternet.org/.
Tumblr. http://tumblr.com.
Twitter. http://twitter.com.
Wymer, Walter, Patricia Knowles, and Roger Gomes. 2006. "Introduction to Nonprofit Marketing." In *Nonprofit Marketing: Marketing Management for Charitable and Nongovernmental Organizations*, 3–24. Thousand Oaks, CA: SAGE Publications.

SUGGESTED READINGS

Alman, Susan, and Sara Swanson. 2014. *Crash Course in Marketing for Libraries*, 2nd ed. Santa Barbara, CA: Libraries Unlimited.

This book is exactly what the title implies—a quick crash course in marketing, public relations, and advocacy. Targeted specifically for small libraries, but relevant to all, the book briefly looks at the basics of planning for and developing a marketing plan, communication strategies and techniques, and fund-raising. Then in the appendices, examples of marketing plans, fund-raising appeals, annual reports, and more are provided to help get any librarian going in marketing endeavors.

Barber, Peggy, and Linda Wallace. 2010. *Building a Buzz: Libraries & Word of Mouth Marketing.* Chicago: American Library Association.

This book combines general marketing principles with case studies and step-by-step guides to present a well-rounded look at why and how to build buzz around a library using word of mouth. From the importance of a marketing plan, to examples from many libraries and sample scenarios, this book covers all the bases for librarians wanting to use this more informal but critical method of spreading the word about their resources and services.

Brodie, Roderick J., Linda D. Hollebeek, Biljana Juric, and Ana Ilic. 2011. "Customer Engagement: Conceptual Domain, Fundamental Propositions, and Implications for Research." *Journal of Service Research* 14 (3): 252–71.

This article looks specifically at customer engagement (CE) from a theoretical and academic perspective. Customer engagement is critical for the success of libraries, and this article helps library marketers define what they mean by CE and develop strategies that will specifically target an increase in CE. It helps distinguish CE from simple participation and will give librarians a way to define the value that customer engagement practices provide to the organization.

Kennedy, Marie R., and Cheryl LaGuardia. 2013. *Marketing Your Library's Electronic Resources: A How-To-Do-It Manual for Librarians.* Chicago: ALA Neal-Schuman.

Marketing the library's online resources is often much more difficult than marketing flashy events or new books. The audience for these resources may not be in the library, so creativity in getting the word out is key. This book is a How-To-Do-It manual guiding readers through developing, implementing, and evaluating plans to market eResources. With a focus on promoting underutilized resources and creative ways of getting the word out, this book should offer library marketers good ideas for spreading the word about online resources.

Koontz, Christie, and Lorri Mon. 2014. *Marketing and Social Media: A Guide for Libraries, Archives, and Museums*. Lanham, MD: Rowman & Littlefield.

This book walks readers through the process of examining the internal and external environment of their organization so they can begin to create a thoughtful, deliberate marketing campaign. It is both an introductory textbook and a guide for working professionals that covers the SWOT analysis, identifying and involving stakeholders, a four-step marketing model, market research, market segmentation, market mix strategy, and evaluation. Examples from libraries, archives, and museums are all included.

Lucas-Alfieri, Debra. 2015. *Marketing the 21st Century Library: The Time Is Now*. New York: Chandos Publishing.

This book is a systematic look at marketing in the 21st-century library. It looks at marketing holistically from the perspective of benefiting patrons as well as the library. It looks at marketing concepts and the history of library marketing, and provides tools and resources for library practitioners to use as they market their resources and services.

Mathews, Brian. 2009. *Marketing Today's Academic Library: A Bold New Approach to Communicating with Students*. Chicago: American Library Association.

Focused specifically on academic libraries, this book takes a bold look at how librarians communicate with a transient, mercurial patron base—college students. Based on many real-world trials and experiences, this book challenges academic librarians to listen to their students and match services to the needs of those students rather than trying to force those students into well-established pathways and practices.

Potter, Ned. 2012. *The Library Marketing Toolkit*. London: Facet Publishing.

This guide offers coverage of various elements of library marketing and branding for different sectors including archives and academic, public, and special libraries. It looks at strategic marketing, marketing inside and outside the library, and using technologies and social media to market. It also includes discussions of using national campaigns and library advocacy in marketing plans. It is suitable for those who are involved in promoting their library or information service, whether at an academic, public, or special library or in archives or records management.

Scott, David Meerman. 2014. *The New Rules of Marketing and PR: How to Use News Releases, Blogs, Podcasting, Viral Marketing, & Online Media to Reach Buyers Directly*. Hoboken, NJ: John Wiley & Sons.

This book is not library specific but has a good deal to offer librarians. By looking at the most current trends in marketing in the broader world, the book provides realistic ways and step-by-step plans for organizations to leverage the technologies at hand to increase awareness of their products or services. Grounded in marketing theory and relevant enough to include the most current trends, this book can be of great use to librarians who want to broaden their reach.

Thomsett-Scott, Beth C. 2014. *Marketing with Social Media: A LITA Guide*. Chicago: American Library Association.

In addition to discussing libraries and technologies more broadly, this book takes each of nine social media platforms and discusses using them for marketing by the library. Facebook, Pinterest, Google+, Wikis, video sharing, Foursquare, blogs, QR Codes, and Twitter are all discussed in separate chapters, which use examples from libraries across the country and what they are doing with social media.

Watson-Lakamp, Paula. 2015. *Marketing Moxie for Librarians: Fresh Ideas, Proven Techniques and Innovative Approaches*. Santa Barbara, CA: Libraries Unlimited.

This book is focused on offering low- and no-budget ideas for marketing library resources and services. The book provides an overview of the basics of marketing and continues through the numerous channels that should be incorporated into a modern-day marketing strategy mix. Branding, merchandising, and media relations are covered, as are social media, new technologies, fund-raising, and advocacy. More recent tools such as data-driven information gathering and e-mail segmentation are also discussed as ways to make marketing more efficient and effective.

Zdravkovic, Srdan, Peter Magnusson, and Sarah M. Stanley. 2010. "Dimensions of Fit between a Brand and a Social Cause and Their Influence on Attitudes." *International Journal of Research in Marketing* 27 (2): 151–60.

This study looks at marketing efforts around particular causes and what it takes to make them successful. The authors find that it is not enough to market particular causes, but one needs to explain why the organization is the right fit for marketing that cause. This "fit" is essential in making the campaign successful. While not explicit about libraries, it has resonance because so often librarians market things that, on the surface, may not seem the right "fit" for a library, such as makerspaces, gaming, or financial assistance.

Chapter 11

Reference Services for Children and Young Adults

Marcia A. Brandt

INTRODUCTION

The face of reference services for children and young adults is evolving as quickly as the patrons themselves. The reference desk is morphing into a tablet-wielding mobile librarian, while collection development may mean selecting a set of wrenches for a makerspace. With the increased use of digital reference resources, providing physical access to technology hardware and Internet, especially for those without adequate access at home, becomes integral to service. Still, reference service for children and young adults continues to fall into the traditional three categories: readers' advisory, ready reference, or research (Harper 2011, 12). School and public libraries have complementary roles, along with shared challenges, in providing these services to young patrons.

In this chapter, children are defined as persons from birth to age 14, or infancy through junior high school, and young adults are defined as persons from age 12 through 18, or middle school and high school students. There is an intentional overlap in the definitions of children and young adults to account for the variety of ways in which public libraries and schools choose to serve persons of junior high or middle school age. Students are defined as those children and young adults whose needs are specifically focused on learning.

Librarians serving children and young adults have varied titles. "Children's librarian," "youth services librarian," or "teen services librarian" are common titles in public libraries large enough to have staff dedicated to serving youth, while "school librarian," "teacher librarian" (reflecting recent emphasis on the instructional role), and "library media specialist" are common titles in school libraries.

UNIQUE CHALLENGES

Reference services to children and young adults hold unique challenges. To begin with, the word "reference" is not even in their vocabulary, seemingly replaced by "I'll just Google it!" The smartphone has young people connected 24/7 to massive amounts of information on the Internet, and the ease of "googling" has given false confidence, particularly to young adults. Doug Johnson jokes that, "The challenge for today's librarian is not to keep kids from abusing the library's stuff, but to get kids to use the library at all" (Johnson 2014, 62).

Reference queries from children and young adults are unique in that a large portion of their need for information is often imposed. Children's questions often arise from what others (usually teachers) ask them to find out and do not necessarily reflect what children themselves find intrinsically interesting. While identified as a distinct information query by Melissa Gross (1995), the imposed query impacts the reference interview. Imposed queries can lead not only to a lack of motivation, but also to a lack of understanding regarding their own information-seeking assignment, and as Gross posits, imposed queries often mutate. Like a game of telephone, the necessary details surrounding the original query imposed on a student are not always communicated to the library professional accurately.

Children and young adults are also unique in that they are often powerless. Physical access to the library is problematic for children and young adults. Children are often dependent on adults for transportation to the public library; the reference interview may need to be short because the adult providing transportation is impatient. In the school setting, access to the library is dictated by schedules; bells ring before information seeking is completed. Students may come from homes where their needs are not supported, are supported, or are helicopter supported. (Helicopter parents are those who cannot cease hovering, and their over-involvement can complicate their child's information seeking.) Sadly, digital resources that could resolve transportation and time issues may not be an option in homes that lack Internet access or only have access via a slow connection or mobile device. Children and young adults are often helpless, lacking authority over their own constraints; it is important to be cognizant and sensitive to the needs that surround their situations and look for ways to effectively provide service to each individual.

CATEGORIES OF REFERENCE SERVICES

Reference services for children and young adults include readers' advisory, ready reference, and research support. Each of these is discussed in more detail in the following text.

Readers' Advisory for Children and Young Adults

"Can you help me find a good book to read" is the traditional and cherished role for the librarian. Children especially need to practice their reading skills with the goal of helping them develop lifelong reading skills and habits. Librarians today are in competition with Goodreads and online vendors' read-alike/buy-alike suggestions.

The library advantage is that libraries are free and librarians are a human face; libraries and library staff need to be sure that it is always an inviting and friendly face. Chapter 24 provides more information on the readers' advisory interview and sources, but this chapter provides tips for readers' advisory focused specifically on children and young adults.

Getting children and young adults to define "a good book" takes skill in questioning. Asking what they read and liked recently is often a good starting point. Naming genres in library jargon is less effective than describing a genre; science fiction means nothing to most 10-year-olds, but a book with aliens or gadgets that defy known science holds appeal. Rather than asking a young adult to think like a librarian, the reference interview requires good listening and interpretation. Cartoonist Jeff Stahler deftly illustrated this challenge (Figure 11.1).

FIGURE 11.1 STAHLER © 2013 Jeff Stahler. Reprinted by permission of Universal Uclick for UFS. All rights reserved.

Box 11.1 Activity: Translation, Please?

Reference interviews with children take not only probing but often require translation. Every children's librarian needs his or her super powers when asked for "the green book I read last year."

Attempt to translate the following requests. Answers are provided at the end of the chapter in Box 11.16.

Transaction One:

Third grader:	Mrs. Brandt, do you have any books on geometry?
Librarian:	Geometry? You want a book on math?
Third grader:	Math? No.
Librarian:	Why do you want geometry?
Third grader:	I want to make a present for my mom. Her birthday is today.

What does the student want?

Transaction Two:

Fifth grader: I need a book on cancer.
Librarian shows student books on diseases in the Dewey 571.978 shelf.
Fifth grader: No, this isn't what I need. I have a report for my social studies class.

What does the student want?

Transaction Three:

Child:	I'm looking for a book on Greece.
Librarian:	Sure, are you looking for books on Ancient Greece, current-day Greece, or something else?
Child:	Um, music.
Librarian:	Oh, you're looking for Greek music?
Child:	Um, no . . . not exactly.

What does the student want?

Readers' Advisory: Web 2.0 and Social Media

Young adult librarians are embedding readers' advisory in social media. They are creating websites and wikis, writing blogs, using Twitter, posting to Pinterest, and creating Facebook pages as tools for connecting students and books. All of these Web 2.0 tools will enhance face-to-face readers' advisory, not take its place, but as larger and larger numbers of young adults are connected to the Web 24/7 through their phones and tablets, it only makes sense that we use current (and future) digital tools to connect them to books and reading opportunities.

Readers' Advisory: Computerized Reading Programs and Text-Leveling Systems

Computerized reading programs such as Accelerated Reader (AR) or Scholastic's Reading Counts are commercial technology-based programs for K–12 students intended to promote independent reading practice through book lists, levels, and software-based reading assessments. Points are earned based on books read and comprehension tests passed. The goal of the computerized reading systems is to encourage students to read and to give schools a way to build comprehension skills and to provide some sort of reading progress assessment.

Among the common text-leveling systems are both Fountas & Pinnell and Lexile. The Fountas & Pinnell (2015) system of leveling books assigns gradients from A to Z, leveling a text for the purposes of guided reading or scaffolded reading instruction. The Lexile Framework for Reading (2015) uses an algorithm to assess a book's difficulty, simultaneously measuring sentence length and vocabulary. A numeric Lexile scale then matches reader ability and text difficulty.

Reading lists intended to guide and develop student reading can potentially result in children and young adults not utilizing the full scope of the school library collection as they feel compelled (or sometimes are required) to select resources only from their reading level or a specific list. The American Library Association (ALA) speaks strongly against librarians using such lists or levels to limit students. "Restricting access to library materials based on age or grade level does not respect the individual needs, interests, and abilities of users and violates the Library Bill of Rights" (American Library Association 2010).

When making reading recommendations to children and young adults, it is important to remember that their age or grade level does not represent their total reading ability and their reading ability (as determined by standardized tests) may not reflect their emotional and maturity level. For example, an elementary school child reading three or four years above grade level may be capable of reading the text in the novel *Tree Girl* by Ben Mikaelsen (2004), but she is *not* ready for the intensity of what the protagonist experiences in Guatemalan civil war. Computerized reading programs and text-leveling systems are criticized for not successfully taking this into account. And when that same young student is *required* to read from an advanced list or level, it can be extremely challenging to find a book that meets list requirements *and* matches individual, age-specific interests.

It is important to remember that, while collaborative, the purposes of a school library are distinct from the purposes of reading instruction. School librarians should avoid the pressure to label or organize their libraries to correlate to Lexile levels or to match computerized reading programs such as AR (2015) or Reading Counts (2015). Neither Lexile nor AR levels factor in the maturity level of a title's content when determining reading level. Labeling, dividing the collection, or color-coding creates a false sense of security; this is *not* readers' advisory. The ALA strongly advises against this as well. "While some parents and teachers may find housing books by grade or reading levels helpful in guiding developing young readers, a library should not use such labels as a classification system, or to promote any restrictive or prejudicial practice. Most computerized reading programs list books by grade or reading levels on their Web sites and parents and teachers may consult these if they wish to seek such information" (American Library Association 2010).

School librarians who want to support the various programs of reading instruction can utilize the 521 Target Audience field of the MARC record, which allows for inclusion of AR, Reading Counts, Lexile, or F&P levels. As searchable fields in the online catalog, rather than labeled and collated collections, these numbers become tools and not rules. The computerized reading programs and the various text-leveling systems can be wonderful tools, but they should never rule organization of the school library collection, limit student self-selection, or serve as readers' advisory.

Public libraries are likewise impacted when AR and similar programs are used in the local schools. How the program is implemented and managed at individual schools makes a difference, but regardless, the unintended result of reading only for points is problematic for readers' advisory in public libraries as well. Children's services librarians may find their patrons asking for a five-point book rather than a "good" book. Librarians report that students will often refuse to read a book *not* on the AR list, because they won't receive points. Reading choices are based not by what truly attracts and interests the child, but by how many points he or she will get. The joy of selection based on individual interests is devastatingly impacted. Points, levels, and lists cannot replace a living librarian who is committed to keeping current on authors and titles and knowing the students in order to match readers with books. Reading *and* readers' advisory is an art, not a science of lists or numbers.

Box 11.2 Activity: A Closer Look at Labeling and Leveling

Compare the AR and Lexile levels on *The Poky Little Puppy* and *The Color Purple* using Accelerated Reader's Bookfinder (http://www.arbookfind.com/UserType.aspx) and the Quick Book Search (https://lexile.com/). Then compare *Diary of a Wimpy Kid* with *Fahrenheit 451*; and *Gossip Girl: A Novel* with *The Great Gilly Hopkins.*

Title	AR Level	Lexile Level
The Poky Little Puppy	BL 4.0	640
The Color Purple	BL 4.0	670
Diary of a Wimpy Kid		
Fahrenheit 451		
Gossip Girl: A Novel		
The Great Gilly Hopkins		

Question for Reflection and Discussion:

1. Consider the impact of titles with low Lexile scores and mature themes on young readers. How could a librarian make reading recommendations to a young reader with very strong reading ability?

Ready Reference

Ready reference can be defined as questions or inquiries that can be answered quickly. Print reference collections were formerly maintained at a reference desk for this purpose, but Web-based resources are increasingly replacing them. *School Library Journal's* 2014 Spending Survey reports that in school libraries, "print reference use is on the decline" and that "nearly half (45 percent) of school librarians say they're purchasing more digital reference materials than they did two years ago" (Barack 2014, 34). School libraries are weeding the print reference section, sometimes reclassifying worthwhile titles to circulate in the general collection. Digital resources are selected, vetted, and curated on bookmark tools, Web pages, and wikis for the professional use of the librarian in providing ready-reference services. Increasingly, school and public librarians are walking the floor with tablet in hand for both ready reference and readers' advisory rather than sitting at a reference desk.

The reference desk preferred by young adults may involve Twitter, Facebook, or whatever social media tool is next on the horizon. Ask the Librarian can be virtual with reference questions answered via chat, e-mail, phone, fax, and texting, as well as social media. Synchronous communication such as chat or texting allows for a reference interview and live feedback, but that is a luxury that takes larger staffs and budgets. Asynchronous communication like answering reference questions via e-mail remains more common in small and rural libraries due to staffing and budget constraints.

An additional advantage of moving ready reference to websites and wikis is that it also provides opportunity to reach those patrons who do not (or will not) ask for help directly from library staff. School librarians with budget, time, and staffing constraints can put most of their energies into clearly and efficiently organizing online reference resources for student self-service. Every opportunity should then be used to promote these digital reference resources to students, giving both formal and informal (individual, point of need) instruction whenever possible.

Web 2.0 virtual reference is not a one-size-fits-all solution, but school and public librarians serving teens, especially, need to find what forum will be effective given their constraints. An annual survey of students regarding their favored communication methods can help library staff target what will be worthwhile. Less is more with students in the online environment. Short answers given in the online environment and basic self-service Web-based reference can be used as a hook into the fuller resources and services the library can provide.

Box 11.3 Activity: Digital Reference Services

Explore current practice by searching the Internet for school library websites and children or teen sections of public library websites. Three noteworthy sites to start with are:

- Joyce Valenza's exemplary Springfield Township High School Virtual Library: http://springfieldlibrary.wikispaces.com/home.
- Chicago Public Library Teens page is an example of how public libraries are approaching both readers' advisory and virtual reference: http://www.chipublib.org/browse_audience/browse-audience-teens/.
- New York State Library maintains a useful website of "Selected Ready Reference Resources": http://www.nysl.nysed.gov/reference/readyref.htm.

Research

Children and young adults are not skilled at information seeking; research projects assigned in school settings are intended as learning experiences to help them develop their skills. Instruction must be embedded in every information-seeking encounter when dealing with children and young adults. In schools, school librarians should be in a collaborative, if not leadership, role when developing opportunities for information literacy instruction.

Information-Seeking Behaviors

Children cannot always articulate their own information needs. The previously mentioned challenge of the imposed query means the child may not truly understand his or her information need; librarians may need to help students interpret their assignment before reference needs can be ascertained. Librarians who work with children need to be skilled at the reference interview (discussed in more detail in Chapter 3), particularly in using open-ended questions and applying probing techniques. In addition, children may need to be given more time to respond and rephrase. Much more instruction and guidance are necessary with children and young adults, which makes providing reference assistance to students of all ages very different than providing reference assistance to adults.

Children bring limited background knowledge and vocabulary skills to their information seeking. Unless the topic is the child's personal interest or a topic about which he or she is passionate, children rarely have enough background knowledge or vocabulary to construct a good search. Since constructing keywords requires both background knowledge and vocabulary, lack of these presents huge challenges for children when researching. Children's librarian Sharon Hrycewicz (pers. comm.) explains further, "Children have a limited window to the world. They don't know what they don't know, which makes it hard for them to ask for what they want. Children don't often have context to know that a picture of a real dinosaur isn't plausible."

Children's inability to spell also hampers their ability to search successfully both in print and online. Although it may be tempting to tell children to "look it up in the dictionary," this can be difficult for a poor speller, may not be an effective use of time constraints, and can detract from the original research goals. Librarians should be prepared to spell words for younger patrons and demonstrate the use of database features that offer corrected spellings and suggested terms.

In the school setting, it becomes the role of the librarian to find ways to mediate these challenges. School librarians can be proactive with classroom teachers, developing a school information-seeking culture with instructional scaffolding. For example, students can be assigned preliminary reading on their topic in a print or online encyclopedia to begin building background knowledge. Following construction of background knowledge, time should be spent brainstorming for keywords and validating correct spelling to prepare for further searching. Even when the child is an expert on a topic, the librarian must help with the correct terminology or the controlled vocabulary used by reference tools and resources. Students can then begin an information-seeking session with terms already written and spelled correctly. Instructional scaffolding procedures such as this create a research culture that will build skills and make students successful in independent information seeking.

As students progress through the grades, research projects become more challenging, and even young adults are hindered by a less-than-ideal understanding of their topics. While teens may be comfortable with the process of searching thanks to information literacy instruction and librarian-created tutorials, the librarian remains necessary for help with correct terminology and controlled vocabulary for specific tools and sources. In addition, while librarians may know almost nothing about the research topic, they will have an understanding of the resources available, experience with search strategies, and skills in the evaluation of resources. Young adults are rarely so capable; while it may appear that they are so comfortable in the digital search environment that they no longer need the information professional, they are not experienced at finding *quality* information.

Conferring

Conferring is an important research process tool for the school librarian, particularly when working with older students. Whether it is called the reference interview, conferencing, conferring, or coaching, one of the main goals is to model how to tackle a difficult research task. Students do not learn skills in information seeking by doing a research project or paper; they learn by being mentored in the process. Rather than simply evaluating research projects when completed, the librarian (in collaboration with the classroom teacher) monitors student work throughout the research, providing instruction and correction as part of the process.

Information Literacy and Instruction

The name "school library" itself has evolved along with changing collections and methods of instruction. When nonprint resources became part of the information landscape in the 1980s, the school library was often renamed the Library Media Center or Library Resource Center. Instruction evolved as well, with "library skills" morphing into "information literacy." More recently, the library has been referred to as the Information Commons, Learning Commons, or Library Learning Commons, reflecting the current model of collaborative and embedded learning for information literacy instruction.

Current best practices reflect the librarian and the classroom teacher collaborating on the creation of information-seeking projects. Information literacy skills are embedded in content learning rather than taught as separate "skill" lessons. Research shows that "skills taught at the moment of need raise achievement significantly" (Loertscher 2012, 57). No longer in isolation, the librarian is co-teaching content and learning process as the information specialist.

Foundational skills can be embedded during read-aloud sessions with students as young as kindergarten and first grade; skills such as identifying the title page, copyright, and organization of informational text (table of contents and index) in print materials can be introduced as part of the experience. Once is not enough with children; concepts and terms should be reinforced continually. When instruction is constantly embedded, consider impacting the school culture by referring to sessions with children as "Library Literacy Time" as opposed to "Storytime." While many individuals can skillfully read aloud to children in a "Storytime," there is information literacy content woven throughout "Library Literacy Time" with a professional school librarian.

The basics of copyright should be introduced when second and third graders are first taught digital copying and pasting. "Don't use what doesn't belong to you without permission or giving credit" is a lesson they can understand. Students can be simultaneously introduced to the idea that they own what *they* create by introducing them to the concept of Creative Commons.

Most second and third graders are not ready to use search engines to find resources. They must first learn to read for information as well as learn about the organization and navigation of both print and digital reference sources. It should be noted that readability is often an issue when using both print and digital resources. Some online resources adjust the interface for children, but results returned are at a high reading level. On the other hand, some online resources, such as *World Book Online*, not only offer various interfaces for different age groups, but also adjust content for readability. Librarians should search for and provide links to appropriate sources for emerging researchers.

As third-, fourth-, and fifth-grade students are introduced to using the library's online catalog, foundations can be laid for understanding the differences between subject and keyword searching as well as advanced search skills. The online catalog is a valuable and safe tool for children practicing search skills. Instruction in using the library's catalog leads to lessons on the organization of the library and the skills to independently locate print materials.

Box 11.4 Suggestions for Teaching Children Organization of the Library

- Introduce the basics of library organization, including alphabetical and Dewey arrangements.
- Do not assume that reading shelves left to right and up to down is intuitive; include it in instruction.
- Use the online game *Order in the Library*[1] to allow students to practice skills alphabetizing and ordering decimal numbers. (Fourth- and fifth-grade students are introduced to decimals in their math classroom so this is an excellent opportunity for collaboration in content teaching.)
- Print individual citations with call numbers for fiction and Dewey numbered titles. Have students find one or two of each. Students locate the books on the shelf and then raise their hand when the book is found. Staff verifies success and assists as needed.
- Appreciate actual statements from students such as: "This is fun, now I can find stuff myself!", "This is like a treasure hunt!", and "Thank you for making me learn this!"

If children and young adults are introduced early to criteria for quality resources (authority, reliability, currency, completeness, relevancy), this provides a strong foundation for research. A useful proverb when instructing students in the reliability of information is "You get what you pay for!" An honest introduction to the strengths and weaknesses of *Wikipedia* and googling can be concluded with a question: "If the information doesn't cost anything, what is it worth?" Students recognize that it is potentially worthless or possibly wonderful and that the researcher always has to evaluate his search results. Children can quickly be convinced that using the vetted subscription resources provided by the library saves a lot of time and trouble.

Combating the Principle of Least Effort and Satisficing

The application of the principle of least effort to information-seeking behaviors and use of library resources is easily observed in children and young people. When researching, many students will do what is easy even if it produces low-quality results. Their preferred tool is *Google*, and assuming that top results equate with quality, they use the first page of results or the results with the most bold hits on their search term(s).

A related behavior, satisficing (a portmanteau of satisfy and suffice), is selecting the first available answer rather than searching for the best or most complete answer. Satisficing students will fill in the blank with whatever pops up on the screen without thinking or evaluating, using convenience over quality as the primary criterion.

A successful method for demonstrating the need for evaluation of search results is to do an image search of a familiar adult, such as the librarian or another staff member. Test results in advance to be sure the point will be successfully communicated, but usually only one or two of the images returned will be the familiar face students expected to see. Demonstrating obviously bad results, as in this exercise, communicates clearly to children and young adults.

Both public and school librarians must keep least effort and satisficing behaviors in mind when giving instruction and designing access to subscription sources. School librarians can collaborate with instructors to create a LibGuide (2015) for a specific research project, directing students to high-quality sources. Students will tune out long instructional sessions; use small pieces of instructional content such as podcasts, screenshots, and screencasts, and locate them adjacent to source links or, if possible, embed them directly into sources. Free online tools such as Guide on the Side (2015), Screencast-o-matic (2015), Screenr (2015), and Drupal (2015) can be used to create instructional content. In addition, vendors of subscription databases often have video tutorials; linking to the best of these tutorials not only is effective but also saves the time and effort of creating them in-house.

Box 11.5 Suggested Tutorial Topics

- Finding sources
- Using a database
- Narrowing and focusing research topics
- Developing keywords
- Developing search strategies
- Evaluating sources
- Citing sources
- Connecting ideas

TECHNOLOGY

The way children and young people find, access, and use information has been changed by technology. It is embedded in everything one currently does in reference, resources, tutorials, and communications. But as noted by Microsoft cofounder Bill Gates (Ratcliffe 2014), "Technology is just a tool. In terms of getting the kids working together and motivating them, the teacher [or librarian] is the most important." It is also important to emphasize again that while these "digital natives" are comfortable with technology, their searching and evaluation skills are often lacking (see Figure 11.2 for one librarian's lamentation of this fact).

Access

Librarians must be mindful of those students who do not have hardware or Internet access at home and are dependent on their school or public library for access to e-mail, school materials, and research resources. Both economically disadvantaged students and students in rural areas, where home Internet options are limited to satellite or dial-up, benefit from access to the school library before and after school and the public library on nights and weekends. Libraries can also provide access to technologies that students are less likely to have at home, such as specialized hardware and software for schoolwork, learning, and creative pursuits.

Safety and Policies

Librarians must also remember that they may have a responsibility to protect children and young adults using the Internet. The Children's Internet Protection Act (CIPA) was enacted by Congress in 2000 to address concerns about children's access to obscene or harmful content over the Internet. Imposed in early 2001 and updated in 2011, CIPA is overseen by the Federal Communications Commission.

Sara Kelley-Mudie
@skm428
Following
I'm helping students upload video files and I would like to smack everyone who has ever uttered the phrase "digital natives" with a fish
10:56 AM - 11 Nov 2014

FIGURE 11.2 Digital natives and searching skills. Used with permission.

To qualify for the E-rate, a federal program that makes certain communications services and products more affordable, CIPA requires libraries to filter their Internet service.

CIPA continues to be controversial as the Internet filtering software it requires can *overprotect* students from the information they need. For example, a filter set tightly to block the word "sex" will also block information on the poet Anne Sexton. ALA strongly condemns this as censorship and an intellectual freedom issue for students. The tension between access and filtering is discussed in Chapter 2, and many helpful links can be found on ALA's "Filters and Filtering" page (American Library Association 2009).

The Intellectual Freedom Committee from ALA has developed a useful toolkit to use in conjunction with the *Intellectual Freedom Manual* (2015). *Libraries and the Internet Toolkit: Tips and Guidance for Managing and Communicating about the Internet* can be downloaded and used freely by libraries (American Library Association 2013). The toolkit recommends that for children 10 years of age and under, Internet use should be supervised, and children should be using age-appropriate portals, search engines, and applications. While major search engines blindly crawl the Web, kid-safe search engines and directories use people to search and review appropriate resources, filtering out sites that would be objectionable. A search for "search engines for kids" will provide librarians with options to test and review.

The *Libraries and the Internet Toolkit* warns that young adults "are knowledgeable about using the Internet safely but they do not always have the judgment needed to determine what constitutes safe behavior" (American Library Association 2013, 16). Internet predators are a rare but highly publicized threat; cyberbullying and identity theft are more likely threats to young adults as they are often unaware that they are revealing too much personal information online. This *digital footprint* is a growing concern, so much so that the term has shifted to *digital tattoo* because, like a tattoo, it is difficult if not impossible to erase.

Schools and libraries need appropriate policies in place that protect but also respect intellectual freedom. School districts refer to their policies as Acceptable Use Policies. Often simply called AUPs, students *and* parents must sign the AUP before students are allowed access to hardware or networks. School librarians should be involved in developing and updating these AUPs, making sure that intellectual freedom is represented. The Association for Library Service to Children has collected resources to help librarians; "Children and the Internet: Policies That Work" is an electronic publication with links to guidance as well as exemplary policies (Braun 2015).

Librarians should also be instrumental in providing ongoing lessons and programs to educate children, young adults, and parents on Internet safety. Librarian and author Christopher Harris summarized this effectively: "Filter a website, and you protect a student for a day. Educate students about online safety in the real world environment, and you protect your child for a lifetime" (Harris 2006).

Web 2.0 as a Tool for Reference

Many librarians are creating Web 2.0 spaces as tools for connecting with students. Facebook pages and Twitter accounts make the library and staff seem approachable and accessible, serving to develop rapport and a sense of community, and giving students another forum for requesting assistance with information seeking.

It is necessary to be aware of any institutional policies regarding social media. Whether required by policies or not, keeping these accounts separate from personal accounts is advisable; they should reflect the library and not the librarian, personally. Inform students that the library social media accounts are available, but avoid directly soliciting young adults as "friends" or "followers"; allow the social media to spread organically.

As previously mentioned, podcasts, screenshots, and screencasts are useful formats for tutorials. LibGuides, pathfinders, wikis, and Web pages can organize reference resources and tutorials to make them easy to find, while QR codes can be used on handouts and signage to point toward resources, bibliographies, or tutorials.

Citation management tools should be introduced to middle and high school students. Such tools will create bibliographies, format citations, and help the student manage and organize citations. Citations can be imported from databases, websites, and academic library catalogs. Some products integrate note-taking and allow for collaboration.

Box 11.6 Activity: New Tools for Reference Work?

Skype

Kate Messner writes that "Skype has gone from being a novelty to an everyday tool, as much a part of the school day as whiteboards and textbooks" (2014, 28). Consider the use of Skype or other videoconferencing platforms as a tool for reference with young adults. What merits and constraints do you see?

QR Codes

Brainstorm reference applications for QR codes. What might be problematic for young adults?

Instagram

Consider the use of Instagram as an outreach tool for youth services. What could it be used for? What might be problematic?

Usability

Young adult authors have long recognized that they need to hook young readers with the first page if not the first line of text; digital library resources need to do the equivalent. Simple interfaces, convenience of use, and immediate results will hook and keep users. Interfaces should look familiar to students, for example, by placing the search box in the middle of the page similar to *Google*. Young adults want to figure it out for themselves quickly, or they will move on to something more intuitive and convenient. In addition, young adult information seekers want full-text results that they can use immediately.

What seems intuitive to a library professional may not be intuitive to students. To know how young users utilize the library's resources, librarians can conduct usability studies, develop personas (fictional characters created to represent different types of users) and test sites, and employ Web analytics. For the librarian with limited time and resources, over-the-shoulder testing (silently observing a young person using the library website or tools, then adjusting tools accordingly) can be as effective as in-depth studies.

Box 11.7 Activity: Think Usability

Explore the "Learning Tools" website from The School District of Palm Beach County, a collaborative project between the Educational Technology Department and Library Media Services, at http://www.palmbeachschools.org/learning_tools/. Evaluate the content, organization, and usability, and consider usage by different ages and audiences.

Questions for Reflection and Discussion:

1. What is intuitive?
2. What is problematic?

TRENDS IMPACTING EDUCATION

Trends in education impact the library, both school and public, and will be reflected in collection development and reference inquiries. How librarians approach reference with children and young adults needs to adapt to and support current education and library standards and practices.

Standards

Common Core

Common Core State Standards (2015), commonly abbreviated and referred to as CCSS, are academic standards created by the federal government and currently available for mathematics and English-language arts/literacy (ELA). Previously, individual states created and adopted their own unique standards, but the overarching goal of CCSS is that, regardless of where a student lives, the standards will outline what K–12 students should know and be able to do at the end of each grade. As of spring 2015, 43 states, the District of Columbia, four territories, and the Department of Defense Education Activity had adopted the CCSS. Individual states, schools, and educators will determine how the standards look in practice as they develop curriculum and pedagogy to support student achievement of the standards.

In their public comments on CCSS, the American Association of School Librarians (AASL) noted that the role of the school librarian is critical in the areas of inquiry-based learning, critical thinking, information literacy, digital literacy, and exposure to literature and informational text—all prime pieces of Common Core (2010). Numerous studies continue to find that a full-time school librarian makes a critical difference in boosting student achievement and that the neediest learners benefit the most from trained librarians and quality library programs (Kachel and Lance 2013, 28). A close look at the ELA anchor standards for writing in both K–5 and 6–12 immediately reflects the connection between the standards and library reference services; the words "research," "text," "read," "write," "technology," and "information" are all prevalent in the standards (see Box 11.8 for examples).

Box 11.8 College and Career Readiness Anchor Standards for Writing (K–5) and (6–12)

Research to Build and Present Knowledge

7. Conduct short as well as more sustained research projects based on focused questions, demonstrating understanding of the subject under investigation.
8. Gather relevant information from multiple print and digital sources, assess the credibility and accuracy of each source, and integrate the information while avoiding plagiarism.
9. Draw evidence from literary or informational texts to support analysis, reflection, and research.

CCSS impacts collection development with its increased emphasis on informational text. As students progress through the grades, CCSS sets expectations for what they will be reading. Fourth graders should be reading equal amounts of informational text and fiction, or "literary" texts. By eighth grade, it is 55 percent informational text and 45 percent literary. By the senior year of high school, students are expected to read 70 percent informational texts. It is no surprise, then, that *School Library Journal's* 2014 spending survey noted that nearly half of their respondents have "spent more on nonfiction materials, compared to what they spent just two years ago, particularly at elementary schools" (Barack 2014, 34).

Public libraries also feel the impact, reporting an increase in buying books to assist with school assignments as a result of curriculum changes brought by CCSS. Teen Services Librarian Heather Booth (pers. comm.) notes the impact CCSS is having on reference. "I see teens asking much more thoughtful questions, or at least I'm fielding much more complex reference requests. Schools are asking teens to integrate and understand more information these days instead of collecting it and repeating it. It's a good change, but it's one that requires more time and resources on our end."

Standards for the 21st-Century Learner

The Common Core State Standards and the AASL's "Standards for the 21st-Century Learner" (2007) have strong similarities. AASL's standards are based on a foundation of "Common Beliefs" such as the importance of reading, inquiry, ethical use of information, and skills in technology emphasizing the school library's importance in providing equitable access. The "Standards for the 21st-Century Learner" are meant to provide a foundation for information literacy instruction.

Box 11.9 AASL "Standards for the 21st-Century Learner"

Learners use skills, resources, and tools to:

1. Inquire, think critically, and gain knowledge.
2. Draw conclusions, make informed decisions, apply knowledge to new situations, and create new knowledge.
3. Share knowledge and participate ethically and productively as members of our democratic society.
4. Pursue personal and aesthetic growth.

Excerpted from "Standards for the 21st-Century Learner" by the American Association of School Librarians, a division of the American Library Association, copyright © 2007 American Library Association. Available for download at www.ala.org/aasl/standards. Used with permission.

The AASL's four foundational standards are further broken down into skills, dispositions in action, responsibilities, and self-assessment strategies. AASL and Common Core's language differ, but they are essentially pointing to the same skills. AASL has a useful tool called "Crosswalk" (American Association of School Librarians 2015), which aligns the two.

Technology Standards

The International Society for Technology in Education (2007) developed the "ISTE Standards". Formerly known as the NETS (National Education Technology Standards), the "ISTE Standards" address learning, teaching, and leading in the digital age. With standards for students, teachers, and others, the ISTE Standards correspond to CCSS and AASL, particularly Standard 3: Research and Information Fluency.

The Institute of Library and Museum Services also offers a list of 21st-century skills (2015). A blend of information literacy and technology skills, these standards are aligned with library and museum priorities. Public librarians in particular may find the IMLS standards helpful.

Impact

The number of standards and organizations writing them can be overwhelming; however, documents such as AASL's "Crosswalk", which align the various standards, can make them more manageable to understand and put into practice. In addition to "Crosswalk", a good resource for an overview of three of the standards touched on in this chapter (CCSS, AASL, and ISTE) is the Illinois Standards Aligned Instruction for Libraries (2015), commonly called I-SAIL.

The earlier-mentioned standards represent and reflect a "sea change" in education. It is important for librarians working with children and young adults to have a grasp on the skill set that these standards require. Reference service today is less focused on helping students find answers and more focused on helping them to frame questions, evaluate resources, and think critically. Librarians should not focus on simply providing and pointing toward sources, but instead on teaching skills and strategies that will help students become safe, responsible, productive, and independent users of information.

Primary Sources

The Common Core State Standards require students to use primary and secondary sources. Primary sources are original unfiltered materials created at the time of a historical event. Secondary sources are generally written after the fact and are interpretations and evaluations or commentaries on primary sources. Primary sources provide authentic materials for students to practice critical thinking, analysis, and inquiry by using the raw materials of history such as photographs, newspapers, film, and documents. Primary sources are typically the more difficult of the two for classroom teachers and students to understand and locate. Librarians need to be familiar with available primary source collections and be prepared to assist students and teachers with locating materials.

The Library of Congress has taken a leadership role in providing and promoting its many primary source resources to educators with Web pages, databases, and their Teaching with Primary Sources (2015) program aimed at K–12 classroom educators. Another resource for primary sources is the Digital Public Library of America. Expertise with primary and secondary sources creates an excellent opportunity for the librarian to collaborate with classroom content teachers.

Box 11.10 Activity: Primary Source Practice

Select a topic (e.g., slavery in the United States, Scopes "Monkey Trial," Revolutionary War music) and locate relevant primary sources. Use a LibGuide, wiki, or other tool to organize, evaluate, and annotate the sources for student use.

Option: If you have the opportunity to work with classroom students, flip the project. Create a shared digital space and assist students as *they* locate the primary sources and contribute to the shared space. Collaborate with the teacher as students practice critical thinking, analysis skills, and inquiry. Think about ways your shared space could function for project purposes beyond collecting resources.

STEM and Makerspaces

In 2010, in response to the growing concern that comparatively few American students excel in the fields of science, technology, engineering, and mathematics (STEM) and that the number of teachers skilled in those subjects is inadequate, "President Obama set a priority of increasing the number of students and teachers who are proficient in these vital fields" (U.S. Department of Education 2015). While people have long associated libraries with their traditional roles related to books and reading, modern libraries have moved into also providing technological resources in the form of computers and other digital equipment. Yet libraries are still thought of as focused on writing and literature as opposed to science, technology, engineering, and mathematics. But President Obama's *Educate to Innovate* (2015) and the Obama-supported nonprofit *Change the Equation* (2015) campaigns have impacted libraries as well as classrooms. Research and growing practice demonstrates that librarians' expertise with technology and their training in inquiry and evaluation of resources and results put them in a prime position to interest and engage students in STEM subjects.

A relative of STEM, makerspaces are a new facet of library services impacting children and young adults. Public libraries have led the way in developing makerspaces; school libraries are not far behind. Makerspaces in libraries are all unique, but the emphasis is on hands-on creation, often with technology. Three-dimensional printers get a lot of attention, but libraries are also supporting maker activities with Arduino, Snap Circuits, Sphero Robotic Ball, and even familiar objects like sewing machines. The goal is to make resources available to students that will help guide their inquiry and exploration. Librarians need not be the expert on these technologies; they can facilitate connecting experts with young people in makerspaces. Given a little space (or a rolling cart) and money, the possibilities are limited only by the interests and imaginations of students and staff. The Make it @ Your Library (2015) website is a good resource for getting started.

SCHOOL LIBRARIES AND REFERENCE

Reference services hold some distinctive characteristics in the school setting. Above all, the reference role of the school librarian cannot be separated from instruction. School librarians represent the integration of reading, writing, and research while providing support and leadership in the effective use of available technologies. AASL's "Position Statement on the Role of the School Library Program" states it should "enable students to become efficient and effective in the pursuit of information" (American Association of School Librarians 2012).

Effective school librarians are proactive in the design of research projects and instruction on copyright and plagiarism, working with teachers to create non-googleable questions. They communicate to students the power of information and model critical thinking skills. Authority, bias, critical examination of information, currency, and relevance are issues that must be taught in the context of the school curriculum at the point of learning and in collaboration with the classroom instructor (for more on instruction in libraries, see Chapter 4).

Effective school librarians teach students to use technology tools by focusing on the process and principles, not the tool itself. This includes teaching principles of word processing rather than a particular piece of software such as Word; principles and best practices of presentation software rather than Prezi or Powerpoint; and principles of citation management, not just RefWorks or NoodleTools. Teaching the concepts needed to be effective users of technology allows students to teach the actual tool to themselves, both now and in the future, preparing students to be lifelong learners.

BYOD

In schools where students are allowed or encouraged to bring their own technology devices (BYOD or bring your own device), school librarians can provide equity. Librarians must always advocate for students who cannot afford to purchase laptops and mobile devices for at-school use. Soliciting donations of used or new hardware or creating a collection of circulating hardware purchased by the library will assist those students without their own devices. The librarian may also need to be well versed in different technology platforms and devices in order to assist with troubleshooting connection issues as well as to function as an advocate for students with information technology staff on issues like firewalls and filters. BYOD also impacts resources: library online content needs to be developed with multiple platforms in mind.

1:1 Technology Initiatives

One-to-one computing (abbreviated as "1:1") is an initiative where each enrolled student is issued an electronic device to access the Internet and digital resources. Success of 1:1 initiatives depends on changing the learning culture, not simply distributing hardware. "Adding a digital device to the classroom without a fundamental change in the culture of teaching and learning will not lead to significant improvement. Unless clear goals across the curriculum—such as the use of math to solve real problems—are articulated at the outset, one-to-one computing becomes 'spray and pray.'" "Spray" on the technology, and then "pray" that you get an increase in learning will not gain the desired outcomes (November 2013).

School librarians must be involved in school improvement plans and committees where districts implement 1:1. The library collection must be evaluated to ensure that digital resources are available to support the shift, with the school librarian advocating early for a resource budget that will support these needs. Administrators and others may need to be educated to the continued need for print along with digital; CCSS clearly states that students need to "gather relevant information from multiple *print* and digital sources." Dropping print because a school has moved to 1:1 is not an option.

Flipped Classrooms and Flipped Learning

Flipping the classroom means changing when and where learning content is delivered to students. Teachers assign videos, other digital instruction, or readings to be completed at home, while class time is spent applying learning through discussion, inquiry, and creation. Flipped learning is where direct instruction moves from the group learning space to the individual learning space. Group time is spent in an interactive learning environment where the educator guides students as they apply concepts and engage creatively in the subject matter. The terms "flipped classroom" and "flipped learning" are not considered interchangeable. Regardless, in both of these approaches, students are expected to be responsible for their own learning, often through online content. The impact of these learning models on reference services is not usually a demand for information resources but a need to access technology if students do not have it at home.

The flipped classroom approach is very effective for library instruction. Students can complete recorded lessons (e.g., videos, podcasts) on topics such as how to develop search terms, search a database or other digital resource, or manage citations before they come to the school library. Time in the library and with the librarian can then be hands-on with more opportunities for conferring or conferencing with individual or small groups of students rather than delivering direct lecture-style instruction. This hands-on flipped style of learning can be very effective.

Inquiry-Based Learning and Learning Commons

School library, Library Media Center, and now, Learning Commons; libraries that successfully serve students are evolving in more than name. According to David V. Loertscher and Carol Koechlin, "a Learning Commons is a common, or shared, learning *space* that is both physical and virtual. It is designed to move students beyond mere research, practice, and group work to a greater level of engagement through exploration, experimentation, and collaboration" (2012, 20). Sometimes called Information Commons, an Information or Learning Commons is a space for traditional research and more. It is a gathering space for learning, project collaboration, and team effort. It is a place where collaborative media can be created, with the tools and the space to do the creating.

The *Virtual* Learning Commons is the online extension where not just the librarian, but also the whole learning community participates. Loertscher and Koechlin caution that "it is *not* a library website that only provides a one-way stream of useful information" (2012, 20). It is a space that invites many contributors to build information and collaborate. Related in spirit to flipped learning, the Virtual Learning Commons depends on collaborative content built by administration, staff, and students rather than a website built in isolation by administration or the librarian.

Inquiry-based learning, with its emphasis on asking questions and critical thinking, fits naturally with information literacy instruction and the Learning Commons approach. Reference services that reflect inquiry-based learning go beyond the typical "research" lessons on locating and accessing resources, taking notes, creating citations, and following copyright. Instead inquiry invites students to formulate and ask the questions, find and make sense of information, and communicate what they learn in ways that reflect the work world for which they are preparing. Inquiry-based learning is about the experience of learning and not about top-down instruction.

Staff as Patron

A final distinctive consideration for school libraries is an awareness that teaching staff also need reference services. Their needs can include resources for continuing education or personal queries, or sometimes extend to reference needs for their "home" children. Staff often need instruction in searching and evaluating resources as much or more than the students; staff can be guilty of satisficing as much as students. The effective school librarian provides staff development on search skills and resources, collaborating on assignments to ensure that they meet current standards. The effective school librarian also demonstrates leadership with technology and is available to staff through both formal and informal instructions in using and applying technology to learning.

PUBLIC LIBRARIES

While there are many similarities in how public and school libraries serve the reference needs of children and young people, there are differences in approach. In general, school librarians are focused on curriculum and improving student achievement. Public librarians serve broader needs that reflect not only the children and young people's academic needs, but also their personal interests.

Information Literacy Role

The public librarian's role in reference instruction is a challenging topic. The father of reference, Samuel Swett Green, said, "Be careful not to make inquirers dependent. Give them as much assistance as they need, but try at the same time to teach them to rely upon themselves and become independent" (Green 1876, 80). It is a struggle for the public librarian to balance inquiry and instruction. Teen Services Librarian Heather Booth (pers. comm.) explains the conflict, "Every time teens come in and ask a reference question, I feel compelled to help them understand the library, its resources and how to access them to their best advantage. Most of them just want an answer."

Children and young adults are learners by definition of their young age and lack of experience. Never assuming knowledge, talking the process and modeling good search skills while assisting students with reference needs are common approaches for public librarians. Children's librarian Sharon Hrycewicz (pers. comm.) shares that ". . . the role a public librarian plays in information literacy is to model good behaviors. I'll recite out loud why I'm looking in the index vs. the table of contents and oftentimes it falls on deaf ears. If the book has a weird index I'll explain it."

Homework

Serving the reference needs of children and young adults at the public library often involves helping with homework. Homework assistance in the public library can be as limited as providing access to resources and technology or as encompassing as offering a homework center where staff or volunteers are available. Libraries can also contract with services like Tutor.com to provide homework help. In fact, in ALA's 2013 Digital Inclusion Survey, 95.6 percent of public libraries reported offering online homework assistance (American Library Association 2014). When helping young patrons with homework, it can be difficult to know how much assistance to give. Helping them understand the assignment, locate needed resources, and use them effectively enable students to succeed academically and should be the goal of any transaction. A policy on homework assistance can give helpful direction to public library staff.

Box 11.11 Activity: Online Homework Help

View the "Homework Help Site" section of the Los Angeles Public Library's *Teen Web* http://ya.lapl.org/ya/homework/index.html. View the promotional video and explore and discuss what services are offered.

Next, explore the online services offered at the Chicago Public Library http://www.chipublib.org/news/free-homework-help/ and the Indianapolis Public Library http://www.imcpl.org/resources/guides/education/homework/.

Contrast these sites with what can be offered by rural and small public libraries.

Question for Reflection and Discussion:

1. What is the implication of the statement from ALA's Digital Inclusion Survey that "there is an urban/rural digital divide in public libraries"?

Trends in Queries

Young patrons often do not understand the difference between conducting Internet searches with a search engine and using the library's online resources. Public librarians report that they see patrons come to the library for really difficult questions and when their own search with *Google* or another search engine has failed to provide results. Teen Services Librarian Heather Booth (pers. comm.) notes that a lot of the teens she sees requesting reference assistance do so at the "urging of their teachers or parents. When they do seek assistance on their own, I find that many of their requests are of a personal nature."

As schools adjust their curriculum for Common Core, public librarians are reporting an increase in reference queries in addition to their usual readers' advisory requests. Traditional research topics for children (e.g., elementary school fall reports on Native Americans, inventions, and explorers) are changing due to CCSS and inquiry-based learning. The implementation of Common Core has caused a shift in the kinds of books being requested (Maughan 2014, 32). Where collection development once could center on those predictable local research topics, current requests and queries are less predictable as more districts and teachers bypass published instructional materials and use teacher-developed materials, either locally created or from websites such as *Teachers Pay Teachers* or *Share My Lesson* (DelGuidice and Luna 2015a, 16).

Reference questions for teens are becoming more complex as schools are now asking teens to integrate and understand more information instead of collecting it and repeating it. This is a positive change, but one that requires more time and resources for the public library. As with children's services, resources that were heavily used in the past by teens for assignments now collect dust; literary criticism, for example, is rarely assigned although in the recent past, it was a common query, Booth reports (pers. comm.). Another change Booth reports is seeing "a significant increase in teens needing help for AP projects. This is extraordinarily frustrating as public libraries are not equipped to serve the needs of college level classes, regardless of whether they are taught in college or in a high school."

Box 11.12 Advice from a Children's Services Librarian

To work in reference services for children and young adults in a public library, you need "the ability to take children's requests seriously. Be an advocate for the children in your library. If someone says that libraries shouldn't help kids with homework, question it. Library service to children and teens means equal service."

(Sharon Hrycewicz, children's services librarian)

Perhaps in the near future, as instruction becomes adjusted for Common Core and other shifts in education, patterns in queries will once again emerge. Until then, public librarians in children's and teen services will need to respond to a wider variety of questions and needs than in the past. For now, unpredictable is the norm.

COLLABORATION

"Collaborative efforts in providing reference service are beneficial to both school and public libraries" (Harper 2011, 14). Collaboration takes time and organization, but more importantly, it takes relationship building. Trust and communication are necessary for successful collaboration. The bottom line is that reference services are better for children and young people if their teachers and school and public librarians work cooperatively.

Cooperative Collection Development

As reference queries shift with the rollout of Common Core, a different and a wider variety of resources are needed. At the same time, both school and public library children's and young adults' budgets are declining. Collaboration in collection development is wise. "Two-fifths of school libraries report they're communicating with the local public library about decisions such as book purchases to ensure they're not doubling up on titles" (Barack 2014, 34). Collaboration on digital resources also makes sense, especially in states where statewide consortial access to larger databases and encyclopedias is not provided free to school and public libraries.

Academic Support

Approaching inquiry-based research and reference projects in a Learning Commons environment requires collaboration between the librarian and the classroom teacher. Ideally, research assignments are created together, but when that is not the reality, the school librarian needs to solicit information about the assignment from the classroom teacher. The school librarian should concurrently be cognizant of the needs of the local public library, e-mailing or faxing the assignment to the public library staff.

Collaboration between the public library and the school is dependent on the attitudes of those involved. Some teachers and school librarians are wonderful and welcoming and see the public library and its librarians as resources and allies. But children's and teen services librarians also report encountering school personnel who see the public library as one more organization that is just trying to get in and promote its own agenda. Booth reports being told to contact teachers directly to gain access to classrooms because she does not have a teaching certificate. "On the public side, we want to be of service. We see educating the kids in the community as the job of everyone in the community and are here to help. We don't always have all of the time we wish we had to do school visits, but we are here" (pers. comm.).

Box 11.13 Teachers and Public Librarians in Conversation

In a contribution to the Teen Librarian Toolbox blog, librarian Heather Booth (2014) posted a summary of an insightful conversation she had with a teacher regarding collaboration.

Here's what she told me that I think every public librarian should hear:

- She reminds her students not to wait till the last minute to do their research.
- Her students often need a nudge . . . or more than a nudge, a LOT more than a nudge . . . to get into the library.
- Sometimes the road block isn't the students, but their parents.
- She values the library and wants her students to value it and printed books too.
- She knows print isn't the only way to get information and is encouraging her students to find reputable sources online too.
- She recently learned a bit more about the differences between our databases, and why we sometimes say "It IS from a book" even if we accessed it online.
- She wants her students to succeed in their research.

Here's what I told her that I think every teacher should hear:

- Your students often come to the library not really understanding how information is organized differently in books than it is online.
- We try to give your students both the books they need, and a mini lesson on information organization while they're here, because it's often difficult to convince them that a book on anatomy will actually be a useful resource for their paper on arthritis.
- We buy databases not because we think the Internet is better, but because it's more economical and space saving than buying the equivalent reference books in print.
- We know you're busy, but we can give your students a much better experience if we have a heads-up that dozens of them will be coming in asking for the same thing.
- We would love to work with you, visit your classroom, or provide support materials—just say the word!

Used with permission.

MARKETING

Library anxiety among children and young people is a very real thing, although apathy and satisficing play a role in not using the library as well. "Sometimes the most important goal of instruction and outreach is getting students comfortable with the idea of using the library. . . . putting an empathetic human face on the library can go a long way toward encouraging help-seeking and library use" (Farkas 2012, 29). As with any other patron group, librarians must market themselves to children and young adults. This "Age of Information Plenty," as Doug Johnson (2014) calls it, with its information overload, is the librarian's opportunity. As information *specialists*, it is the knowledge of available resources and skills with the tools that gives librarians value.

Rather than competing, view *Google* and *Wikipedia* as opportunities. Providing instruction to students on evaluating "free" Internet resources secretly promotes use of library resources. Once students see the difficulties in thorough website evaluation and understand that there is an invisible Web that search engines do not see, they will realize the value of the library's subscription-based resources. Contrast the capricious reliability of *Wikipedia's* wiki environment with *Encyclopaedia Britannica*, which is updated every 20 minutes under quality editorial direction. As long as the link is easily accessible and log-in is simple, the library can harness students' satisficing behaviors to promote the library's quality reference tools. Market the *value* library resources bring to children and young people rather than only teaching use of those resources.

Social Media

Scott Stone argues (2014, 44), "It is hypothesized that the creation of personal relationships with library users through social media helps to alleviate library anxiety and increases the amount of library interaction during the users' information seeking process." It is not enough to redesign a website no one uses; instead go where the users are. Facebook, Instagram, and Twitter all have a credible presence with young adults. Use social media to push information, resources, and services, linking to engaging online content, instruction, blog posts, or the redesigned website.

Box 11.14 Activity: What Would Dad Think?

Samuel Swett Green, considered the "father of reference work," published an article in *American Library Journal* (1876) entitled "Personal Relations between Librarians and Readers." Read the entire article (available at http://polaris.gseis.ucla.edu/jrichardson/DIS245/personal.htm).

Discuss what Samuel Green might have thought of using Facebook and other social media for reference work with young adults, focusing on Green's thesis statement, "Personal intercourse and relations between librarian and readers are useful in all libraries. It seems to me that in popular libraries they are indispensable."

(Green 1876, 80)

Safe Space

In this high-tech world, where librarians become invisible behind the seamless user experiences they create, it is important not to lose the personal touch, the human face of the library that librarians provide for patrons. British novelist Matt Haig (2013) said it best. "Librarians are just like search engines, except they smile and they talk to me and they don't give me paid-for advertising when they are trying to help. And they have actual hearts." In order for children and young adults to come to librarians for their information needs, the library needs to feel safe and welcoming. Be proactive in developing relationships with students: know their interests, their problems, and their fears. Most of all, remember their names. Remain professional in the interest of student safety and privacy, but bear in mind that giving a young person a form to fill out on his or her interests is *not* a relationship. Reference interviews and book recommendations can create unique opportunities to connect with students. "Often, it is the school librarian who becomes the confidant and first line of defense for a student in crisis, and who initiates professional intervention for that child" (DelGuidice and Luna 2015b, 16).

Box 11.15 Advice from a Teen Services Librarian

"Don't blow it. Library service is holistic. Every piece works with all of the others. If you mess up or only put forth halfhearted effort for a simple homework request there's no way that teen is coming back to ask you about how to write an essay that will get them into the college of their dreams, or how to find resources on their life's great passion for surfing, or how to get out of an abusive relationship. Every interaction we have with teens is an opportunity to make a difference in their lives, either by being the one person that smiled at them today or being the one to give them the perfect resource for their paper. All of it matters. Every day."

Heather Booth (pers. comm.)

Visual Learners and Infographics

Children and young adults are visual learners accustomed to online images and videos. Children can have short attention spans, and teens are more comfortable with brief communications such as texting, Twitter, and Instagram. Employ infographics in instruction and signage to attract young patrons. Infographics are a combination of text, visuals, and design, a way to represent information through images (see Figure 11.3 for an example). When information must be explained simply and quickly, infographics excel. Vendors may have images that can be included in an infographic when providing instructions for accessing databases. Library rules, book displays, and library procedures could successfully be communicated to children and young adults via infographics.

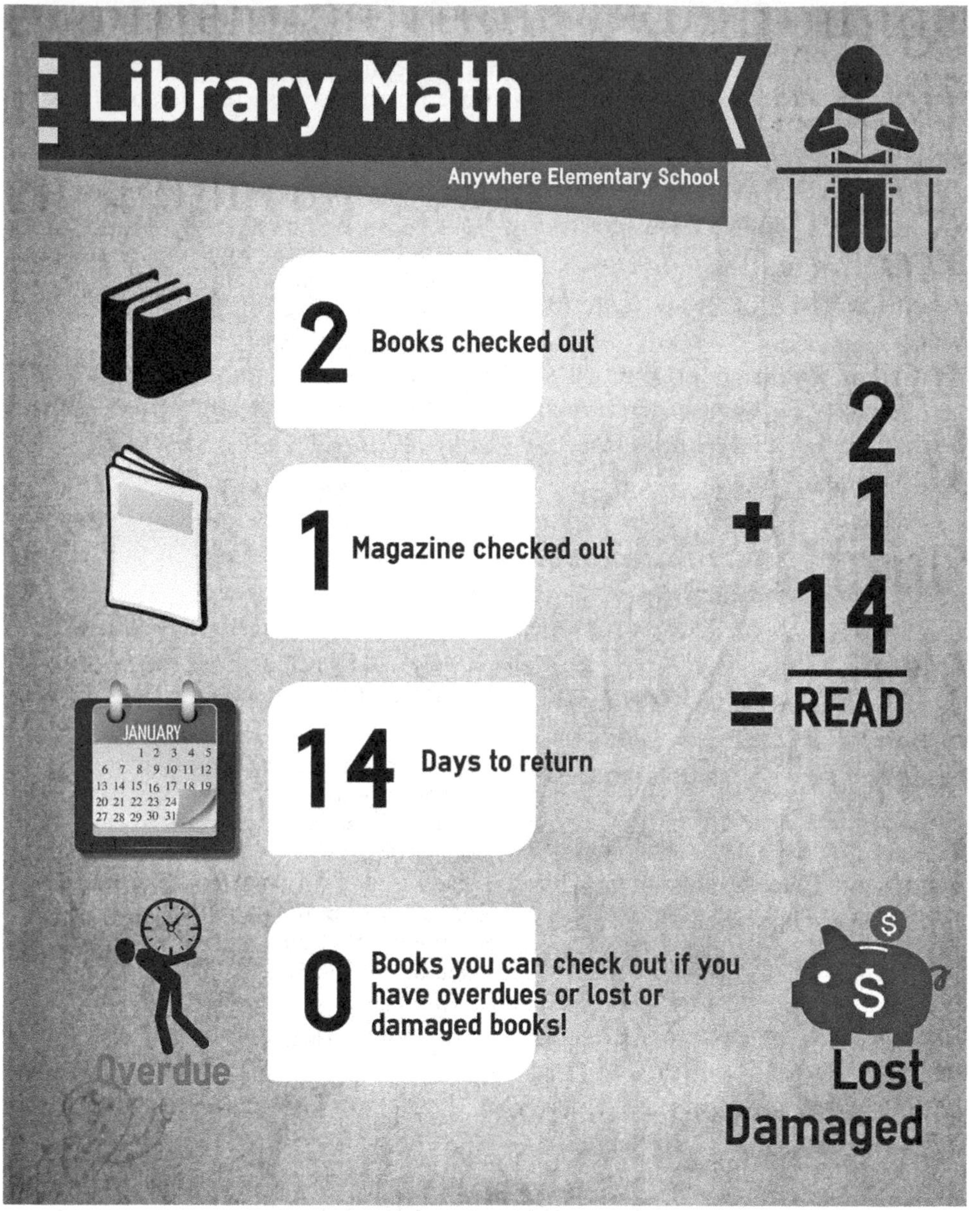

FIGURE 11.3 Infographic © 2015 Marcia A. Brandt. All rights reserved.

CHILDREN'S RIGHTS

In their "Position Statement" *on the Role of the School Library Program*, AASL states, "The school library represents for students one of our most cherished freedoms—the freedom to speak our minds and hear what others have to say. Students in America have the right to choose what they will read, view, or hear and are expected to develop the ability to think clearly, critically, and creatively about their choices, rather than allowing others to do this for them" (American Association of School Librarians 2012). Intellectual freedom for students impacts not only collection development and filtering issues, but also AR-type lists and levels that limit student selection.

The ALA Code of Ethics reminds librarians that "We protect each library user's right to privacy and confidentiality with respect to information sought or received and resources consulted, borrowed, acquired or transmitted" (American Library Association 2008). This statement applies equally to children and young adults. State and national laws, such as the Family Educational Rights and Privacy Act (FERPA), and the individual school's Acceptable Use Policy may address privacy issues, but "library usage information may fall outside the parameters of legally or policy defined 'educational records.' Circulation records, internet use histories, and other professional observations generally do not fit the description of an 'educational record'" (Johnson 2014, 62).

Designed to be used internally for administrative purposes, library circulation records of minor age students are considered confidential records and should not be released without parental consent. To further protect students' rights related to library materials usage as well as provide clear guidance to staff, a clear board-approved privacy policy stating who can access library patron records and under what circumstances they may be released is needed. Notice of overdue materials should remain private and not be posted or read aloud in the library or classroom setting. Consider what records the circulation system keeps, limit access to them through password protection, and regularly purge patron records (Adams 2011, 34).

Service to young adults needs to be mindful that adolescents can be extremely self-conscious. The Reference and User Services Association's "Guidelines for Library Services to Teens" states, "reference librarians need to assure courteous service and confidentiality. Teenagers will not ask certain questions if they fear that other adults or kids can find out what they're asking" (Reference and User Services Association 2008). Librarians should reassure young adults that any inquiries or conversations with the librarian will remain private. In busy libraries, librarians can provide privacy during the reference interview by inviting patrons to step to a quiet corner of the library and publicizing the availability of service options like e-mail and chat reference.

Using Internet and Web 2.0 technologies to serve children and young adults offers additional challenges to protecting the privacy of children and young adults. This was addressed earlier in the chapter, but a reminder that the youngest patrons may be creating "digital tattoos" is in order. The Suggested Readings, in particular Johnson (2014), provide additional information on privacy, safety, and intellectual freedom for children and young adults.

FUTURE

The phrase "the future is now" applies to reference services to children and young adults. Librarians must see change as normal and adjust services and resources accordingly. To remain current, join school library and youth services professional organizations, attend conferences, and join and monitor listservs. Read professional journals and follow blogs written by leaders in the field of children's and young adults' services (the best blogs to follow are often written by the contributors to the journals).

Those imposed queries that bring children and young adults through the library doors hold opportunity. The library has the chance to make those imposed information-seeking experiences so valuable that young patrons will turn to a library and library resources for their needs throughout their school years and into their adult lives. Working with children and young adults is a chance to *influence* the future.

Box 11.16 Answers to Box 11.1: Translation, Please?

Transaction One: The student wanted a book on origami.
Transaction Two: The student needed to research the Tropic of Cancer.
Transaction Three: The child was looking for the soundtrack from *Grease*.

NOTE

1. *Order in the Library* was developed in 2002–2004 by software engineering students at The University of Texas at Austin in collaboration with an elementary school librarian. Its simple design has made it popular around the country and kept it in demand. It can be found at https://www.ischool.utexas.edu/resources/order_in_the_library_game.swf.

REFERENCES

Accelerated Reader. 2015. Renaissance Learning. https://www.renaissance.com/products/accelerated-reader.

Adams, Helen R. 2011. "The Privacy Problem: Although School Librarians Seldom Discuss It, Students' Privacy Rights Are under Attack." *School Library Journal* 57 (4): 34–37.

American Association of School Librarians. 2007. "Standards for the 21st-Century Learner." American Library Association. http://www.ala.org/aasl/sites/ala.org.aasl/files/content/guidelinesandstandards/learningstandards/AASL_LearningStandards.pdf.

American Association of School Librarians. 2010. "Position Statement on the Common Core College and Career Readiness Standards." American Library Association. http://www.ala.org/aasl/advocacy/resources/statements/common-core.

American Association of School Librarians. 2012. "Position Statement on the Role of the School Library Program." American Library Association. http://www.ala.org/aasl/advocacy/resources/statements/program-role.

American Association of School Librarians. 2015. "Learning Standards & Common Core State Standards Crosswalk." American Library Association. Last accessed June 21. http://www.ala.org/aasl/standards-guidelines/crosswalk.

American Library Association. 2008. "Code of Ethics." http://www.ifmanual.org/codeethics.

American Library Association. 2009. "Filters and Filtering." http://www.ala.org/advocacy/intfreedom/filtering.

American Library Association. 2010. "Questions and Answers on Labeling and Rating Systems." http://www.ala.org/advocacy/intfreedom/librarybill/interpretations/qa-labeling.

American Library Association. 2013. "Libraries and the Internet Toolkit." http://www.ala.org/advocacy/intfreedom/iftoolkits/litoolkit/librariesinternet.

American Library Association. 2014. "Public Libraries Lead the Way to Digital Inclusion." http://www.ala.org/offices/ors/public-libraries-lead-way-digital-inclusion.

American Library Association. 2015. *Intellectual Freedom Manual*, 9th ed. Chicago: American Library Association.

Barack, Lauren. 2014. "Spending Smarter, Stretching Further." *School Library Journal* 60 (4): 34.

Booth, Heather. 2014. "Help Me Help You Help Them." *Teen Librarian Toolbox* (blog). http://www.teenlibrariantoolbox.com/2014/05/help-me-help-you-help-them-by-heather-booth/.

Braun, Linda. 2015. "Children and the Internet: Policies That Work." American Library Association. http://www.ala.org/alsc/issuesadv/internettech/childrentheinternetpoliciesthatwork.

Change the Equation. 2015. http://www.changetheequation.org/.

Common Core State Standards Initiative. 2015. http://www.corestandards.org/.

DelGuidice, Margaux, and Rose Luna. 2015a. "Cut to the Core: The Common Core Controversy and the Materials Market." *Publishers Weekly* 262 (2): 16.

DelGuidice, Margaux, and Rose Luna. 2015b. "Cut to the Core: Education Reform Must Include Support for School Libraries." *Publishers Weekly* 262 (25): 16.

Digital Public Library of America. http://dp.la.

Drupal. 2015. Dries Buytaert. Last accessed June 20. https://www.drupal.org/.

Educate to Innovate. 2015. The White House. Last accessed June 20. https://www.whitehouse.gov/issues/education/k-12/educate-innovate.

Farkas, Meredith. 2012. "The DIY Patron." *American Libraries* 43 (11): 29.

Fountas & Pinnell Leveled Books. 2015. http://www.fountasandpinnellleveledbooks.com/.

Green, Samuel S. 1876. "Personal Relations between Librarians and Readers." *American Library Journal* 1 (November 30): 74–81.

Gross, Melissa. 1995. "The Imposed Query." *RQ* 35 (2): 236–43.

Guide on the Side. 2015. University of Arizona Libraries. http://code.library.arizona.edu/.

Haig, Matt. 2013. "Matt Haig: Why I Love My Library." *The Guardian*. February 8. http://www.theguardian.com/childrens-books-site/2013/feb/08/matt-haig-why-i-love-my-library.

Harper, Meghan. 2011. *Reference Sources and Services for Youth*. New York: Neal-Schuman Publishers.

Harris, Christopher. 2006. "Dealing with DOPA." *Infomancy* (blog). http://web.archive.org/web/20080629151455/http://schoolof.info/infomancy/?p=212.

Illinois Standards Aligned Instruction for Libraries. 2015. Illinois School Library Media Association. http://www.islma.org/ISAIL.htm.

Institute of Museum and Library Services. 2015. "Museums, Libraries and 21st Century Skills". http://www.imls.gov/about/21st_century_skills_list.aspx.

International Society for Technology in Education. 2007. "ISTE Standards: Students." http://www.iste.org/standards/iste-standards/standards-for-students.

Johnson, Doug. 2014. "Head for the Edge." *Library Media Connection* 33 (2): 62.

Kachel, Debra E., and Keith Curry Lance. 2013. "Librarian Required." *School Library Journal* 59 (3): 28.

The Lexile Framework for Reading. 2015. MetaMetrics. https://lexile.com/.

LibGuides. 2015. Springshare. Last accessed June 20. http://www.libguides.com.

Loertscher, David V. 2012. "At the Center of Teaching and Learning, or Isolated Again, It's Time to Decide." *Teacher Librarian* 39 (5): 57–58.

Loertscher, David V., and Carol Koechlin. 2012. "The Virtual Learning Commons and School Improvement." *Teacher Librarian* 39 (6): 20.

Make it @ Your Library. 2015. Last accessed June 20. http://makeitatyourlibrary.org.

Maughan, Shannon. 2014. "What's the Buzz?" *Publishers Weekly* 261 (7): 32.

Messner, Kate. 2014. "The Skyping Renaissance." *School Library Journal* 60 (11): 27–29.

Mikaelsen, Ben. 2004. *Tree Girl.* NY: HarperTeen.

November, Alan. 2013. "Why Schools Must Move beyond One-to-One Computing." *November Learning* (blog). http://novemberlearning.com/educational-resources-for-educators/teaching-and-learning-articles/why-schools-must-move-beyond-one-to-one-computing/.

Order in the Library. 2015. University of Texas. Last accessed June 20. https://www.ischool.utexas.edu/resources/order_in_the_library_game.swf.

Ratcliffe, Emma. 2014. *Oxford Essential Quotations*, 2nd ed. Oxford: Oxford University Press. http://www.oxfordreference.com.

Reading Counts. 2015. Scholastic. http://teacher.scholastic.com/products/independent_reading/scholastic_reading_counts/.

Reference and User Services Association. 2008. "Guidelines for Library Services to Teens." American Library Association. http://www.ala.org/rusa/resources/guidelines/guidelinesteens.

Screencast-o-matic. 2015. Screencast-O-Matic. Last accessed July 8. http://screencast-o-matic.com/.

Screenr. 2015. Articulate Global. Last accessed July 8. https://www.screenr.com/.

Stone, Scott. 2014. "Breaking the Ice." *Reference & User Services Quarterly* 54(1): 44–49.

Teaching with Primary Sources. 2015. Library of Congress. Last accessed June 20. http://www.loc.gov/teachers/tps/.

U.S. Department of Education. 2015. *Science, Technology, Engineering and Math: Education for Global Leadership.* Last accessed July 8. http://www.ed.gov/stem.

SUGGESTED READINGS

Booth, Heather, and Karen Jensen. 2014. *The Whole Library Handbook: Teen Services.* Chicago: ALA Editions.

This handbook provides a comprehensive introduction to the background and day-to-day realities of teen librarianship. While there is not a section specifically aimed at reference, sections on communicating with teens, technology, readers' advisory, collection development, and marketing apply.

Farmer, Lesley S.J. 2014. *Introduction to Reference and Information Services in Today's School Library.* Lanham, MD: Rowman & Littlefield.

Focusing on reference and information services in schools, this resource contains more in-depth discussions and information on topics such as information-seeking behaviors in the context of the current digital and information age. It is recommended for those wanting more on information services provided by school libraries.

Harper, Meghan. 2011. *Reference Sources and Services for Youth.* New York: Neal-Schuman.

Harper provides a comprehensive work on reference with youth in both school and public libraries, addressing what is developmentally appropriate in K–12 reference services as well as providing services to students with special needs. She includes valuable discussion on developing a core reference collection and integrating information literacy. This work also includes skill-based exercises and case study scenarios in each chapter.

Intner, Carol F. 2011. *Homework Help from the Library: In Person and Online.* Chicago: American Library Association.
The author, an experienced English teacher and tutor, focuses this work on practical advice for helping children and young adults with their homework. Collaboration with teachers, integrating and using current technologies, staff training, and community outreach are important topics covered.

Johnson, Doug. 2013. *The Indispensable Librarian: Surviving and Thriving in School Libraries in the Information Age*, 2nd ed. Santa Barbara, CA: Linworth.
Written especially for K–12 school librarians, Johnson focuses on changes needed in the field of school librarianship. This work includes topics such as program assessment, planning, advocacy, digital intellectual freedom, and the librarian's role in curriculum development. Both readable and often humorous, Johnson gives emphasis to harnessing the popularity and effectiveness of technology to build strong school library programs.

Krashen, Stephen D. 2004. *The Power of Reading: Insights from the Research*, 2nd ed. Westport, CT: Libraries Unlimited.
Stephen Krashen reviews the research on reading and continues his case for free voluntary reading in this second edition. Included in the work are the role and responsibilities of librarians, both school and public, and Krashen's conclusions on the research on Accelerated Reader and other electronic reading programs.

Lanning, Scott. 2014. *Reference and Instructional Services for Information Literacy Skills in School Libraries.* Santa Barbara, CA: Libraries Unlimited.
Lanning emphasizes reference service and instruction in the information-seeking process. Methods for teaching information literacy and cultivating electronic resources to support reference and instruction are included. The work also includes topics such as inquiry, critical thinking, building core reference skills, electronic and Web resources, leadership skills, virtual reference services, and the current impact of the various standards.

Lanning, Scott, and John Bryner. 2010. *Essential Reference Services for Today's School Media Specialists.* Westport, CT: Libraries Unlimited.
An introduction to reference services for school librarians, this book focuses on the current model of empowering students rather than locating resources for them.

Latham, Don, and Melissa Gross. 2014. *Young Adult Resources Today: Connecting Teens with Books, Music, Games, Movies, and More.* Lanham, MD: Rowman & Littlefield.
This book is a very useful title for understanding youth services, focusing on information-seeking behaviors as well as resources and programming.

Riedling, Ann Marlow, Loretta Shake, and Cynthia Houston. 2013. *Reference Skills for the School Librarian: Tools and Tips.* Santa Barbara, CA: Linworth.
An overall guide to reference in the K–12 school setting, the authors cover both resources and practice along with tools and strategies.

Valenza, Joyce Kasman. 2012. "The Flipping Librarian." *Teacher Librarian* 40 (2): 22–25.
A good resource for further insight into "flipping" instruction, Valenza promotes librarians as leaders in "flipping."

Chapter 12

Reference Services for Diverse Populations

Nicole A. Cooke

INTRODUCTION

An underlying philosophy of this book, articulated most explicitly in Chapter 2, is a commitment to quality reference service for *all*. Because "all" encompasses individuals with a variety of needs, successful reference service must accommodate those needs. "All," however, does not mean that all reference services are appropriate for all user groups. "One size" does not fit all when it comes to reference. No standard blueprint for reference services exists that is appropriate in all situations. Developing specialized reference services for specific, or diverse, populations within our communities is an essential corollary to developing service for the majority. Beyond the provision of basic reference services to an obvious primary group of users, librarians need to identify special groups of users with common and equally important needs and tailor reference service to these groups.

The basis of concern for reference service to specific populations is ethical as well as legal. Reference librarians often must be advocates for members of these groups to ensure equitable access to information and materials. As noted in Chapter 2, the profession has created the "Library Bill of Rights" to emphasize its commitment to fair use of resources and openness to all users. In particular, Article I says that materials should be provided for all members of the community and "should not be excluded because of the origin, background, or views of those contributing to their creation." Article V continues by saying that people, no matter their "origin, age, background, or views" should have complete and equal access to the library (American Library Association 1996). Broadly interpreted, these articles argue that library services, which include reference services, should be made available to any and all patrons and should reflect the needs and interests of members of the community. In addition, libraries supported by public funds have a legal obligation to provide service without discrimination based on class, race, gender, sexuality, religion, or other defining social or physical characteristics.

This chapter examines models of reference service delivery to a *selection* of groups whose needs are not always recognized or well defined, and not always met. This chapter does not address the reference needs of those in the business or technical sector, who would typically be served by special libraries. Instead, the focus is on groups who are defined in terms of socioeconomic, ethnic, or physical characteristics. The specific groups discussed throughout the chapter are differentiated on the basis of *cultural, social, and gender identities*, which may include language facility (non-English-speaking and the adult illiterate) and sexual orientation, *disabling conditions* (physical and developmental disabilities), and *age* (in this case, adult learners and seniors; for more on serving children and young adults, see Chapter 11). For each of these groups, defining characteristics are described, and reference techniques and policy issues associated with the group are discussed.

GENERAL PRINCIPLES FOR SERVING DIVERSE PATRONS

Within any library service community, there are nontraditional or even invisible groups to consider (e.g., institutionalized populations, specific ethnic or religious groups, and others), and not every group discussed here may be part of a given library's service population. And unfortunately, this chapter cannot encompass every potential diverse population libraries serve around the world. The intent of this chapter is to give an overview of issues associated with reference service to a sampling of diverse groups. The assumption is that service to any one group is a microcosm of general reference service—that the basics of reference service are present, and the task is to adapt good reference skills and collections to serve each group. Satia Marshall Orange and Robin Osborne (2004) argue that librarians need to shift their focus from developing special services for specific user groups (with funds that are limited and may disappear) to sustaining quality services for all user groups. They suggest that librarians reframe the idea of outreach so that it is based on equity rather than on underserved populations per se. If the focus is on certain underserved or "special" populations, these services could be marginalized and are the first to be cut in times of budget crisis. But if the focus is on equitable service delivery, then service to specific populations is part of the whole, part of a systemic approach that serves all and gives librarians the knowledge and ability to tailor and customize services when necessary. This approach requires more of librarians and library staff; it requires flexibility, cultural competence, openness, and empathy toward the many diverse users who patronize libraries. It is in this spirit that this chapter is written.

Although public, academic, school, and special libraries may vary in the degree to which certain reference services are provided, an equitable and responsive reference service model for diverse populations should aim to include these components:

1. Assessing the problems a member of a diverse group experiences when trying to access information and services provided by the library.
2. Conducting research that includes contact with associations and service providers about how to improve services for diverse categories of users (and how to attract nonusers).
3. Planning how to adapt the reference interview, collection development, and delivery of service.

4. Training staff to work with users with special needs or cultural differences.
5. Implementing periodic evaluation of reference services to members of diverse groups. (Based in part on Fitzgibbons 1983, 5–6)

To this end, library professionals poised to serve diverse users in these capacities should be cognizant of differences that may exist between themselves and the people they are serving. Patrons from diverse groups may have a variety of visible and invisible differences (or perhaps barriers) that could require extra attention, consultation of different resources, intercultural understanding, empathy, and so on, and could result in reluctance to use the library. This reluctance is above and beyond the library anxiety that many library users (and nonusers) experience. It becomes that much more important that the reference transaction, and other library interactions, strives to make the patron feel at ease and as though he or she is welcome and can be assisted.

Library professionals should strive to develop empathy and cultural competence (see Box 12.1), exhibit patience, encourage patrons, and ensure that patrons are aware of the helping role of the library (e.g., yes, it's ok to ask questions!), follow up with patrons, and admit any limitations (e.g., no, we don't have that book, but we have something similar). In addition, library professionals should be ready, willing, and able to work with the differing work styles, language barriers, accents, and cultural norms that patrons may possess (e.g., a man of the Muslim faith may be uncomfortable speaking with a female librarian and might be more comfortable speaking with a male colleague) (Brothen and Bennett 2013). These professional attributes benefit all patrons, and particularly those from diverse user groups.

Box 12.1 Cultural Competence

A concept referenced in many disciplines, including nursing, counseling, social work, and public health, cultural competence is also important for library and information science professionals. The American Library Association (2010) defines cultural competence as "the acceptance and respect for diversity, continuing self-assessment regarding culture, and the ongoing development of knowledge, resources, and service models that work towards effectively meeting the needs of diverse populations. Cultural competence is critical to the equitable provision of library and information services."

Key articles about cultural competence in LIS include Patricia Montiel Overall (2009) and Ghada Elturk (2003).

Reference Services in a Pluralistic Society

This chapter highlights several diverse user groups, and the intersections of these groups are worth noting (see Figure 12.1). Diverse user groups do not exist in silos; rather, most users represent multiple diversities (e.g., an African American homeless veteran is suffering from PTSD and needs assistance applying for benefits). Recalling that a one-size-fits-all approach to reference is not desirable, learning how to compassionately and competently serve diverse user groups will enable library professionals to serve *all* users.

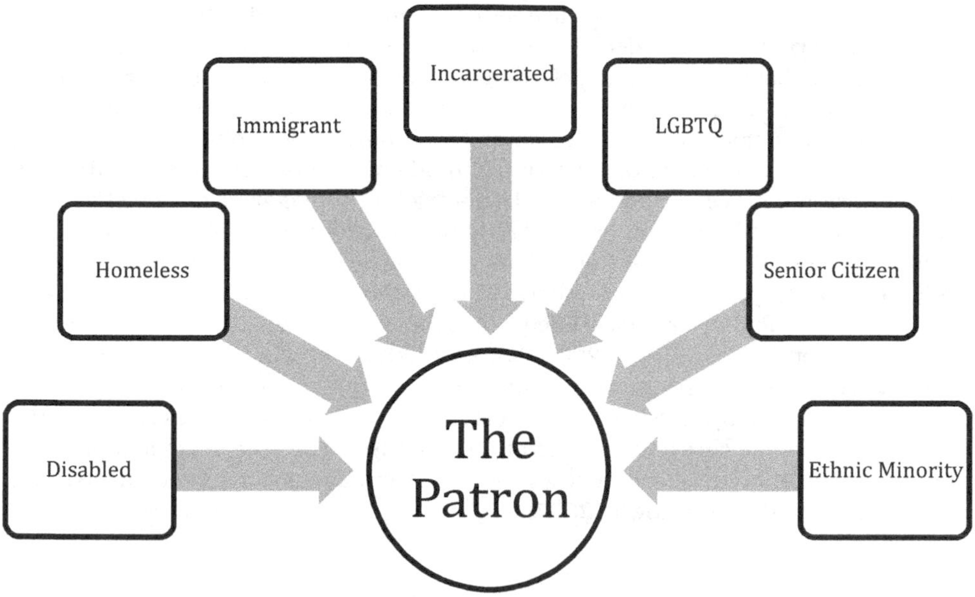

FIGURE 12.1 The intersectionality of diverse users

The Reference Interview

Fundamentally, how the professional librarian conducts the reference interview is no different with diverse users than it is with other users (Saunders and Jordan 2013). As stressed in Chapter 3, the librarian should treat all people and queries with respect and seriousness. However, with diverse users, it is especially important to anticipate some timidity and a possible reticence toward public institutions and asking for assistance. It is crucial to be aware of and to understand both cultural and individual differences. Although most Hispanics in the United States are of Mexican descent, many are from Puerto Rico, the Dominican Republic, Cuba, and countries in Central and South America. Each cultural grouping has its own traditions, value systems, and social classes. Hispanics may be of any race and also include the indigenous peoples whose native language is something other than Spanish. Within this array of cultural identities, it is *individuals* with unique needs and questions who come to the reference desk for help.

It is also important not to make assumptions regarding what diverse users know about libraries. Donna L. Gilton (1994) suggests that culture shock (or clash) can occur when diverse users are new to library use, not unlike the clash or discomfort that may occur when anyone visits a foreign land or engages in an unfamiliar environment. This can occur in addition to any library anxiety many users experience when using the library. "Five aspects of culture can lead to culture shock or clash: verbal communication; nonverbal communication; orientation modes, or the use of time and space; social value patterns, which include written and unwritten rules of social behavior; and intellectual modes, which include learning styles valued by the culture" (Gilton 1994, 55). All of these are applicable to library use and reference interactions.

Depending on circumstances, diverse users may not understand the concept of call numbers, be able to decipher commonly used library terms, or know how to distinguish between printed first names and surnames. In answering reference questions, slang should be avoided and the use of the library's materials explained and demonstrated, giving users the opportunity to observe and then to imitate. Whenever possible, the librarian should escort a new library user through to the end of the process, such as locating a book or a magazine on the shelf. It is easy to mistake nods and smiles as signifying comprehension. This pitfall can be avoided by asking open-ended questions that allow users to communicate more precisely what they do or do not understand. It is very easy to misunderstand body language, eye contact (or lack thereof), attempts at humor, and other common communication habits (Strong 2001; Walker 2006). The librarian must abandon assumptions and concentrate on the intent of the user's question. After a question is answered, follow-up is especially important and is vital to proper closure of the interview. The same care and consideration extended to diverse users in a physical library setting should be extended to diverse users seeking reference assistance virtually (Shachaf and Horowitz 2007).

REFERENCE SERVICES TO PATRONS OF DIVERSE ETHNIC BACKGROUNDS

Anecdotal evidence and observation suggests that society is more diverse than it has ever been, and this diversity is more than reflected in the communities served by libraries, especially public libraries. Population projections from the U.S. Census Bureau indicate that by 2020, Hispanics will make up 17.8 percent of the U.S. population, African Americans 13.5 percent, and Asians 5.4 percent. Hispanics have already replaced African Americans as the country's largest minority group. The percentage of non-Hispanic whites in the population will continue to decrease, and by 2050, non-Hispanic whites will be at 50.1 percent of the total population (U.S. Census Bureau 2015). Despite becoming the "emerging majority" (Turock 2003, 494), in 2009, 25.8 percent of African Americans and 25.3 percent of Hispanics lived below the poverty line, in stark contrast with the 12.3 percent of the white population who lived below the poverty line (14.3% of the total population lived below the line) (U.S. Census Bureau 2012, Table 713). Religious and ethnic diversity have also increased and become more prominent. In 1990, 527,000 Americans identified themselves as Muslim. By 2008, that number had risen to 1,349,000, a 156 percent increase (Table 75). During the same period, the number of self-identified Hindus rose from 227,000 to 582,000, also a 156 percent increase, whereas the total Christian population rose from 151,225,000 to 173,402,000 (Table 75). Although Christians are still the overwhelming majority, these latter figures represent only a 15 percent increase in that population.

Such significant data compel librarians to provide reference service that is responsive to different needs and, as stated earlier, does not have a formulaic "one-size-fits-all" approach. Mengxiong Liu (1995) notes that patrons from diverse backgrounds may not even understand how North American libraries work, as it may be a different, strange, or even unwelcome model of education and service. As individuals, their information-seeking behavior is affected by "different cultural experiences, language, level of literacy, socioeconomic status, education, level of acculturation and value system" (124).

Phoebe Janes and Ellen Meltzer (1990) suggest that library professionals be trained so that they will be able to address the needs of diverse users and individualize or adapt reference services as necessary. The authors suggest that invisible barriers and implicit assumptions could impact services to these users, even unintentionally. For example, reference staff could assume that their experiences, habits, and communication styles in libraries are the same for everyone and that there is little chance that they would be misunderstood. This assumption of homogeneity not only exists among individual staff, but is also often a larger issue of organizational culture. If the organization is not welcoming or understanding of patrons who are marginalized or somehow exist outside the norm of the accepted culture, these potential users will not frequent the library, no matter how wonderful the programs or extensive the collection (Elteto, Jackson, and Lim 2008). Yolanda J. Cuesta (2004) advises that staff training cover three types of techniques: techniques for engaging the community, techniques for effective communication with a diverse customer base, and techniques for analyzing the library from the community's perspective. Training could include cultural awareness and sensitivity training, cultural knowledge, and linguistic competence to help staff convey information in a manner that is easily understood by diverse audiences. Cuesta states, "everything and anything the library does communicates a message to the community" and staff should be aware of this and be willing to plan accordingly (113). Training could also teach staff how to conduct a community analysis (see Box 12.2), which would provide rich insight into the communities being served (for more on community analysis, see Giesecke and McNeil 2001; Goodman 2011; Grover, Greer, and Agada 2010; McCleer 2013; and McDonald 1981).

Box 12.2 Activity: Community Analysis

Community analysis is a mixture of formal and informal techniques that gives librarians a comprehensive view of their community's needs and habits; this insight can inform reference services, in addition to other services such as collection development and programming.

Using the *Community Analysis Scan Form* located on the Library Research Service website (http://www.lrs.org/public/ca_form.php), consider the community in which you live or work.

Questions for Reflection and Discussion:

1. What is the makeup of your community?
2. How well is your local public library currently addressing the represented diverse populations?
3. What improvements or enhancements would you suggest?

Ultimately, the information needs of minorities do not differ primarily because of race or ethnicity, but rather because of an individual's life situation, which may include factors associated with race or ethnicity, such as cultural experiences, language, literacy, recent arrival in the United States, socioeconomic status, education, and most generally, levels of acculturation (Carlson 1990) (see Box 12.3 for an example). Gillian D. Leonard (1993) extends this argument by stating that the reference requests and information needs of minority groups should pose no special challenges to a professionally trained librarian. Rather, as Patrick Andrew Hall (1991) suggests, the role of *affectivity*, which is "the more intangible qualities of personal rapport and empathy," is just as important as familiarity with specific cultural experiences and sensitivity to diversity (320). Thus, although it is useful to know that people of color may regard professional distance as "a sign of rudeness or contempt" (322), it is the specific *relationship* between librarian and user that builds an effective interaction, more so than a well-intentioned, albeit blanket "politically correct" or culturally competent approach.

Box 12.3 Activity: Avoiding the Reference Desk: Stereotype Threat

Consider this scenario posed by Patricia Katopol (2014, 1). After previous negative and frustrating experiences, Keisha again entered her school's library because she really needed some help to complete her research paper. "She looked up at the workers; some of them looked kind of young—were they real librarians? Student workers? And, as usual, they were all Caucasian, so that Keisha questioned whether she should bring her topic on black Americans to one of them. Would they understand what she was doing and would they really be able to help her? Would they think her questions were elementary and not worthy of a graduate student? She sighed and gathered her things for the long trek to the reference desk."

Question for Reflection and Discussion:

1. If you were the librarian in line to help Keisha, how would you work with her?

REFERENCE SERVICE TO INTERNATIONAL STUDENTS AND IMMIGRANTS

America is proverbially known as a "melting pot," and as such, libraries are very familiar with international and immigrant patrons. In particular, these diverse users often come to the United State with little, or no, proficiency in the English language. Known as English as a second language (ESL), English for speakers of other languages (ESOL), English as an additional language, or English as a foreign language learners, these populations are frequent library users and perhaps have the hardest time receiving information because they cannot communicate easily with library staff.

International Students

Academic librarians are particularly familiar with international students studying at their colleges and universities. Successful scholars in their native tongues, a lack of English mastery and different cultural norms may inhibit them while studying in the United States. "Culture can be a veil that prevents us from understanding students from other backgrounds and cultures, and it also can prevent them from understanding us. Unfamiliarity with cultural communication differences can lead to misinterpretations, misunderstanding, and even unintentional insult" (Osa, Nyana, and Ogbaa 2006, 23). Studies also suggest that international students have limited knowledge of libraries in an American context, including the idea of female librarians (Carder, Pracht, and Willingham 1997), and may not understand that the reference desk and librarians are there to assist and should be consulted for information (Dunbar 1986; Lewis 1969). As such, these patrons may be less likely to ask for assistance at an American library reference desk without outreach and training (Ganster 2011; Ishimura and Bartlett 2014; Knight, Hight, and Polfer 2010; Pyati 2003). Anxious about possible communication failures, international students are less likely to seek in-person assistance, instead relying on the Internet and friends for information.

Research about the information behaviors of international students has revealed that these users "are accustomed to lecture, recitation, rote memory, and recall, while American students are accustomed to analyzing, synthesizing, critiquing, and expanding" (Macdonald and Sarkodie-Mensah 1988, 426). With a predilection toward print materials, international students are receptive to library instruction sessions and orientation tours, particularly those who are accompanied with print handouts, guides, slides, and visual aids. When working with international students, library professionals should be consistently checking for comprehension and making eye contact.

Immigrants or New Americans

Libraries, especially public libraries, have a long history of welcoming and serving immigrant, or New American, populations (Shen 2013; Wang 2012). According to the New York Public Library (2013), one of the largest and most diverse library systems in the United States, 40 million people living in the United States are immigrants, approximately 13 percent of the population. New Americans are often financially and information poor, and consequently, this diverse user group often relies on the library for access to the Internet and computers, and other basic information necessary for everyday life. Additionally, New Americans can require assistance with learning English (ESL classes), basic education (GED or equivalency courses), and information about citizenship. The library is also a prime source of community, health, employment, and legal information.

Using the New York Public Library as an example, particularly the Queens Public Library, which serves New American populations in 59 different languages (Berger 2012), libraries can serve as sites of acclimation and integration for these users. In order to be effective, which in turn facilitates the provision of reference services, librarians should survey their communities and incorporate these users into the library as much as possible (e.g., bring teenagers as pages or volunteers, invite community gatekeepers to serve on boards and committees), and establish community partnerships (New York Public Library 2013). Zhang emphasizes the need to be familiar with the communities being served and developing cultural literacy; for example, there are many different and culturally distinct communities of Spanish speakers and 22 separate ethnic groups that make up the larger Asian community (Zhang 2001). Each group could have different language and information needs. When providing reference services to those with limited English proficiency, "It is crucial that librarians remain open-minded, patient, and persistent.

Keep in mind that these students come from a variety of backgrounds and cultures. They may have little experience with libraries and librarians, or they may be perfectly comfortable in this setting. They may view the services offered in the library as privileges or as rights. They may speak or write perfect English or struggle with grammar or vocabulary. Of course, they may fall somewhere in the middle of all these extremes, and it is the librarian's responsibility to assess and meet their research needs appropriately" (Walker and Click 2011, 23).

For both International and New American users, who may experience barriers due to language, it is helpful if library staff speak simply and at an easily understandable pace and avoid slang, colloquialisms, or library jargon. Language barriers can cause self-consciousness and prevent patrons from asking for assistance. Ajit Pyati (2003) suggests that libraries have extra outreach for these diverse patrons, including special resources on the library's website. Other low-stakes accommodations and actions librarians can make include having dedicated Web pages and tutorials, specialized instruction, and orientations in other languages (Knight, Hight, and Polfer 2010); having foreign-language materials in the reference and circulating collections; creating multilingual signage and handouts; and gesturing and pointing (gesturing and pointing are often perceived as rude, but can actually be helpful when there is a language barrier). Other investments, which require more time and financial commitment, involve hiring bilingual library staff and creating multilingual online catalogs.

REFERENCE SERVICES TO THE HOMELESS AND IMPOVERISHED

Libraries have often had tenuous relationships with those who are homeless, or otherwise hungry or impoverished. The homeless in particular are a diverse user group who are often viewed as problematic or troublesome, particularly if they have strong body odor, carry all of their belongings with them, stay in the library during all open hours, or use the public restrooms to bathe. In the early 1990s, the library world witnessed a public library and homeless patron engaging in a series of high-stakes lawsuits. The library ejected the patron after intense encounters and complaints from other members of the community who said the homeless man smelled, used the library as a personal lounge, and created an uncomfortable environment for others. The homeless man countered, saying that by ejecting him they were denying him his basic rights to access information (Hanley 1992). This case is oft cited and characterizes the relationships many libraries have had with their homeless patrons.

The homeless are often mentally ill, but these two circumstances do not always co-occur. The homeless, like the mentally ill, are not inherently violent or less intelligent than other patrons. The homeless are also an especially intersectional group—there are high proportions of homeless teens (Eyrich-Garg and Rice 2012; Woelfer and Hendry 2011), particularly those who are gay, lesbian, or transsexual/transgendered (Winkelstein 2014). Many homeless are veterans who have been unable to find sufficient employment, many homeless are elderly or immigrants, and the homeless span every racial and ethnic group. There are many homeless people with jobs, but perhaps are underemployed and do not earn enough to secure and maintain a residence. With the country in times of economic strain and high rates of unemployment, the homeless population is more diverse than ever. In 2013 and 2014, there were two nationally covered news stories that brought this fact to bear, one a five-part *New York Times* article that featured a homeless girl named Dasani and her family (Elliott 2013), and the other, a *Chicago Sun Times* article that revealed one of the players on the world championship Little League baseball team was homeless (Sfondeles 2014). These accounts emphasize just how pervasive homelessness is and that not everyone "looks" or acts homeless. Should these children be singled out or treated any differently in the library because they are homeless? Homeless patrons, of all ages, require quality reference services in all types of libraries (Hersberger 2003; Hersberger 2005; Muggleton and Ruthven 2012). Keith A. Anderson, Chaniqua D. Simpson, and Lynette G. Fisher (2012, 180) concur by stating: "The challenges of serving the needs of homeless library patrons are complex. Library staffs are professionally and ethically compelled to meet the informational and support needs of homeless patrons, while maintaining the decorum of the library and serving the needs of other library patrons."

Interacting with the homeless, mentally ill, or otherwise impoverished in a compassionate yet effective manner can be assisted with training. Many feel that serving these diverse populations is the domain of social workers, and indeed, there is much overlap between librarianship and social work. Additionally, there are library systems that employ social workers and public health nurses to work *with* library staff and these diverse users (see American Library Association 2012; Blank 2014; Jenkins 2014; Knight 2010; Nemec-Loise 2014; and Shafer 2014). However, this can be considered a luxury that most libraries will not have. But librarians, with proper training, can be effective as providers of information and referral services. Library staff can assist homeless patrons with their financial, physical, family, work, emotional, substance abuse, and mental health issues by referring them to appropriate resources and by being empathic human beings (Anderson, Simpson, and Fisher 2012). To emphasize the point that the homeless and impoverished are no less deserving of quality and dignified services, Glen E. Holt (2006, 184) states: "The wrong library question that many public libraries might ask at this point is 'What services should my library offer to the poor?' The right question is more complex: How can my library develop and fit its services into the lives of the poor so they will benefit from what we know how to do? The differentiation is not mere words. The first question is marked by passive 'supply-side' thinking about library services, that is, 'If we offer them (i.e., services), they will come.' The second question is proactive, involving process (finding out what is needed) and outcomes."

To this end, John Gehner suggests that library professionals get out of the library and get to know this diverse user group in such a way that enables them to look beyond appearance to understand deprivation and the causes (and not the symptoms) of poverty and homelessness. This deeper understanding of circumstances can assist in the removal of barriers that socially exclude certain groups. Library staff need to "understand that charity is not dignity; dignity is inclusion" (2010, 45). Other suggestions for providing reference services to the homeless and impoverished include delivering services at times and places that may be more convenient to these users, focus on services to homeless and poor families, and publicize these initiatives (Holt 2006). Peter Willett and Rebecca Broadley (2011) even propose that libraries should evaluate their policies, particularly those that require proof of residency to acquire a library card; for the homeless, this may not be possible. Are there other alternatives or temporary memberships available? Julie Ann Winkelstein (2014) concurs and suggests that staff be trained specifically to work with members of this community, create partnerships with the surrounding community, and create a glossary of terms to be used in conjunction with other appropriate resources. Overall, the goal should be to create a safe and welcoming environment.

REFERENCE SERVICES TO THE INCARCERATED

Library services to the incarcerated or detained are important and often overlooked, in part because of the diverse population being served, the library locations, and a lack of resources and staff. Prison libraries are often referenced as a social justice issue and can support curriculum, hobbies and recreational reading, legal endeavors, and overall learning and improvement for those utilizing their services. Prison libraries also provide information about treatment programs (e.g., substance abuse, anger management) and can serve a much-needed space of quiet and provide a sense of normalcy for the detained (Lehmann 2011). A marginalized population that overlaps with the mentally ill, homeless, LGBTQ, young adult, minority, and other diverse populations, the incarcerated particularly benefit from library services as the information gained can aid in rehabilitation, which in turn can aid in their release, reentry into society, and avoidance of recidivism (Clark and MacCreaigh 2006). Once individuals are released, libraries can also assist with the development of employment skills and computer skills. An exemplar is the Denver Public Library, which works with the formerly detained and supports them in three areas: "job search skills and readiness, computer and Internet skills, and library awareness and understanding" (Morris 2013, 120). The library trains staff to work with this diverse population in such a way as to diffuse shame and build confidence in patrons.

Prison libraries often lack dedicated staff; some are manned with part-time staff, volunteers, or mobile librarians who enter the facility on an ad hoc basis (Rubin and House 1983). Other services are supported by volunteer organizations that do readers' advisory or answer basic reference questions off-site and through postal mail. Reference services can be particularly challenging in this setting. Rebecca Dixen and Stephanie Thorson (2001) state that reference can be abbreviated and sporadic, depending on the librarian's schedule and the availability of resources. Reference interactions could last between 5 and 10 minutes, and could happen as infrequently as once a month. This makes the reference interview vitally important, and supplemental reference, via forms in the mail, is often necessary. Sheila Clark and Erica MacCreaigh (2006) speak to the range of questions that occur, from both male and female inmates, many of whom have trust (and alternately attachment) issues. The authors state that libraries are fulfilling basic information needs for these patrons, information that aids in informed decision making about their criminal charges, their children and families, and their legal counsel. They caution library professionals providing reference assistance by stating, "while librarians cannot and should not answer any of these questions, we believe that we are duty-bound to provide our patrons with the research tools they need to answer the questions for themselves" (194).

These circumstances are even more challenging when trying to assist with legal information and research. The authors continue by discussing the need for compassion, flexibility, respect, and confidentiality while working with this population, who range greatly when it comes to backgrounds, communication skills, and educational levels. "Along with a sense of fairness, other qualities are required of all librarians who deal with the public; flexibility, high tolerance, good communication skills, awareness of cultural issues and lack of bias toward any group, emotional maturity, and a sense of humor. These skills are even more necessary for a prison librarian because of the extreme circumstances and pressured context surrounding the patrons who come to her. And often, the limited communication skills of some prisoners bring a special challenge, making the reference interview especially important" (Clark and MacCreaigh 2006, 51).

Ready reference, readers' advisory, and legal information are especially important to this population. Glennor L. Shirley (2003, 71) cautions about material that is deemed dangerous, in that it could unduly incite inmates who are violent, who are sex offenders, or who have psychological issues. To that end, prison libraries experience censorship of materials, further limiting the librarian's reach and abilities. Librarians who work within prisons or detention centers, or those who work in public libraries, can aid members of this community by forging relationships "with community partners, especially with halfway houses, government agencies, correctional facilities, and other organizations that provide services to felons" (Morris 2013, 120) (see Box 12.4). Partnerships are especially important for this user group in order to maintain their progress and help them reenter society.

Box 12.4 Activity: Books to Prisoners

UC Books to Prisoners (http://www.books2prisoners.org) is a volunteer project in Urbana, Illinois, that provides books to inmates around the state. Inmates are able to write to the organization's volunteers and request reading material. Such an initiative benefits jails and prisons with library services, but is particularly necessary for facilities without libraries and staff. Similar organizations exist in Seattle (http://www.bookstoprisoners.net), New York, Louisiana, Oregon, and other states around the country (http://prisonbookprogram.org/resources/other-books-to-prisoners-programs/). *LGBT Books to Prisoners*, located in Madison, Wisconsin (http://lgbtbookstoprisoners.org), extends this idea further by sending reading materials to LGBT inmates across the United States.

Questions for Reflection and Discussion:

1. What services exist to the meet the information needs of the incarcerated and/or recently released in your community or region?
2. If no such services exist, how would you propose that your community's library get involved with serving the incarcerated and/or recently released?

REFERENCE SERVICE TO THE LGBTQ COMMUNITY

Another growing population of diverse users is lesbian, gay, bisexual, transgender, and queer/questioning individuals (LGBTQ). There is debate about this label, as it is not felt that it is inclusive enough of the sexual diversity even *within* this community. Other identities include transsexual, intersexed, non-heterosexual, and non-cisgender. For the purposes of this brief introduction, LGBTQ will be used to discuss reference services to this community. In addition to internal diversity, the LGBTQ community is particularly intersectional, and there is a growing and integral connection with services to this community particularly as it pertains to homeless, mentally ill, or incarcerated LGBTQ individuals. As Becky McKay notes, "LGBT people have been grouped together for the purposes of research and advocacy, but LGBT communities are immensely diverse, comprising individuals of every gender, race/ethnicity, age, socioeconomic class, religion, and geographical area, just to name a few dimensions of difference. However, stigma remains one circumstance that unites these diverse constituencies" (2011, 394). She states that the LGBTQ community is especially prone to physical and mental health concerns because of fear of the medical system, and as a result, there are high rates of suicide (for more on the nuances of the LGBTQ community, see Greenblatt 2011; Taylor 2002; Thompson 2012).

Ann Curry (2005), Jeanie Austin (2012), and other authors focus on LGBTQ youth, but the best practices that apply to serving them in a library setting apply to the entire LGBTQ community. Curry also discusses the implicit biases that may impact library professionals when serving patrons from the LGBTQ community. She suggests that even if librarians at the reference desk do not outright refuse to serve these patrons or interact with them in a purposefully rude way, their demeanor and body language can indicate discomfort, hostility, or even judgment. Such nonverbal communication can deter or stifle reference interviews and interactions. Body language and subsequently search strategies (or lack thereof) and a lack of a concluding statement or follow-up can convey a lack of objectivity and hesitancy to help LGBTQ patrons. A failed reference encounter can be compounded when the library's collection and/or public catalog are not current or representative of the community, or even exclude the LGBTQ community and its needs and interests. Cal Gough and Ellen Greenblatt (1992, 61) refer to this as "systemic bibliographic invisibility," when a library's collection lacks appropriate materials because they do not fit in with existing collection and classification schemes.

Curry's study found that the best librarians were welcoming and "personal but not nosy," conducted a good reference interview, portrayed a level of comfort when using the words "gay" and "lesbian," found appropriate resources, worked with the patron as opposed to telling them what to do, and referred the patron when more information was required (2005, 72). In general, when working with LGBTQ youth or adults, librarians should: appear interested in the question; appear comfortable with LGBTQ topics; maintain eye contact; demonstrate a relaxed body posture; give their full attention to the patron; maintain confidentiality by being discrete; and make the patron feel at ease during the interaction (Curry 2005, 73). These best practices should of course be present in all types of libraries.

Libraries and their staff should also reflect on their behaviors and resources by conducting a SWOT analysis (strengths–weaknesses–opportunities–threats) and adjust accordingly (Mehra and Braquet 2011). An important, and possibly overlooked, option for interacting with this community is to develop and maintain robust virtual services and resources, including chat reference, article databases, and online tutorials. Finding aids and library guides, both general and specific to LGBTQ issues, can be displayed in the library and put on the library's website. These resources allow patrons to find information privately and independently; these are qualities important to the LGBTQ community. "Owing to fear of stigma and rejection, LGBTQ individuals find the anonymity of online reference safer and easier for asking questions than broaching the subject face to face" (Thompson 2012, 11).

Finally, Kelly J. Thompson (2012) suggests libraries train their staff to effectively work with this diverse user group and work toward making the library a welcoming environment overall, and Gough and Greenblatt (1992) recommend that librarians strive to handle materials and questions neutrally and equally, and stop the assumptions, stereotypes, and biases that are inherent in the larger heterosexist society.

REFERENCE SERVICES TO USERS WITH DISABILITIES

Among the specific populations for whom librarians need to develop a full range of reference services are individuals with physical and mental disabilities; this includes those with visual impairments (Davies 2007), hearing impairments (Day 2000; Saar and Arthur-Okor 2013), and various mobility impairments (some of which could be invisible to an observer). In 1990, the Americans with Disabilities Act (ADA) was signed into law, representing "a milestone in America's commitment to full and equal opportunity for all its citizens" (U.S. Equal Employment Opportunity Commission and U.S. Department of Justice 1992). Title II of the ADA governs public services for individuals with disabilities. It states that "library services must be provided in a manner that allows *each* eligible user with a disability to equally benefit from the local library. . . . Every decision about ADA compliance must be made on a case-by-case basis, taking into consideration the elements involved in the service or program and the needs of the library patron with a disability" (Gunde 1991, 99). A particular service for persons with disabilities can be denied only if a library can prove that it would incur an undue burden were it required to offer the service. However, thinking in terms of "requirements" masks a simple reality. As Katy Lenn observes, it "is important to remember that the purpose of legislation for the disabled is not to create special rights but equal rights" (1996, 14).

Persons with Physical Impairments

Developments in adaptive technology, such as speech recognition systems, screen enlargement software, and computerized Braille embossers have transformed access to information for users with many types of disabilities. But lack of funding for high technology should not inhibit service to disabled users. Many aspects of ADA compliance are not technology intensive and serve the able-bodied population as well. A magnifying glass and an adjustable piece of furniture are two such examples. Other solutions involve forethought more than cost. If a workstation is set up on a push-button adjustable-height table with an adjustable keyboard tray, with a keyboard that has large-type black-on-white keys, and with two pointing devices such as a conventional mouse and a trackball, the workstation will meet the needs of wheelchair users and people who have computer-related repetitive strain injuries or carpal tunnel syndrome, as well as other dexterity disabilities (Goddard 2004). Rob Imrie (2004) advocates principles of universal design, in which products, environments, and communication systems are designed for the broadest spectrum of users. He stresses that social, attitudinal, and political shifts must first take place so that design principles and technical adaptations take place within an ethos of inclusiveness. By following this advice, libraries simultaneously meet the needs of able-bodied users as well as clientele with disabilities.

Some services and technologies that are new to mainstream audiences have engendered unexpected benefits for persons with disabilities; for example, live online chat reference service is an improvement on traditional TTY reference service. However, other unanticipated consequences have not been so welcome, such as how networked public computing workstations are often difficult to reconfigure or customize for individual users (Goddard 2004, 4). Voice recognition software requires users to build a voice file that the computer learns to "recognize," another challenge in a shared-use environment. Some technologies create noise, such as Braille embossers and voice output systems (although headphones can mitigate problems with the latter). Conversely, a workstation that is intended for users with learning disabilities should be installed in a quiet location with a minimum of distractions.

Each library needs to formulate its own service policies, using the ADA as a guideline along with publications that have been written specifically to help libraries through this process.[1] A library, for example, may adopt the policy that when its employees are unable to provide equal immediate delivery of service, such as photocopying the information in answer to a reference question, they will provide the material within 24 hours. The goal to work toward is equal treatment of all persons, the key ingredient being a positive attitude on the part of the staff. In any library, the reference department will certainly play a central role in developing and implementing services for persons with disabilities.

Both legally and ethically, librarians should evaluate the reference services they offer from the perspective of the user with a disability. This is a challenging task, given that there are numerous disabling conditions, and in any community served, the incidence of any one disabling condition may be relatively low.

Persons with Developmental Disabilities

Persons who have developmental disabilities fall into a wider variety of categories; characteristics that are often common to these disabilities are difficulties with language, communication, perception, and cognition. Some individuals may also experience problems with emotional and social development. Because of the potential for confusion and misunderstanding, it is recommended that the term "developmentally disabled" be defined whenever it is used. Obviously, with such a variety of characteristics, reference needs will vary, and librarians need to plan accordingly.

Despite a limited ability to manipulate information, individuals with cognitive disabilities have a right to information, and reference librarians can adapt services to meet their needs. Reference interview sessions will need to be short and focused. Rephrasing or repetition may be necessary, and listening creatively will facilitate communication. The most successful materials are those that have large print, brief texts, and uncluttered pictures. Although children's materials often prove to be good reference tools, adults with developmental disabilities have the full range of adult concerns, such as vocation, social relationships, sexuality, money management, and parenting; thus, they frequently need to go beyond the resources of a children's reference collection. The adult reference collection can include titles from among the increasing number of materials available for the adult new reader. Because the developmentally disabled user may be slow in processing information, it is important to have useful reference materials that circulate or to have space so that the materials may be used for extended periods of time in the library.

It is important for librarians to recognize that they may serve developmentally disabled users through intermediaries, such as parents or attendants. Libraries should provide information about developmental disabilities, including the identification of relevant local and national organizations and agencies, so that family and caregivers can understand the conditions as well as make appropriate decisions about care. Reference librarians may offer to create bibliographies and special informational brochures about library services to be used by care providers, educators, and organizations for individuals with developmental disabilities.

Persons with Mental Illness

Another category of mental disability is mental illness, which is included in the ADA's definition of disability. With the deinstitutionalization of large numbers of seriously mentally ill individuals without the provision of sufficient community resources to accommodate them, many have become marginalized in society and even homeless. Libraries have seen an influx of these displaced people in their reference and reading rooms. Thomas E. Hecker (1996) suggests that libraries' "problem patron" response be replaced by casting the situation in terms of disability, where services and protections are provided as appropriate. But he does not intend for libraries to serve as social service agencies in the face of extreme situations: "Rather, I suggest that librarians apply the disability model to patrons with mental illness who have retained, or who have regained, a level of functioning which is still within the pale of society. Such people may exhibit symptoms which 'stretch the envelope' of our tolerance, but if tolerance will allow them to live an acceptable life within society, tolerance is the accommodation which must be accorded them" (1996, 10).

In her book on handling problem situations in libraries, Anne M. Turner (2004, 12) proposes that it is possible to deal with the unanticipated consequences of social policy such as the presence of mentally ill patrons (a broad and intersectional category of people) in the library without compromising professional ethics and principles, and also without creating draconian policies and procedures that attempt to address every conceivable situation. She suggests that libraries consider some overarching themes in their approach to library services: everyone has a right to use the library; staff should be flexible in their approach when dealing with these diverse populations; and the task of the library and its staff is to learn how to handle problem situations and *not* problem patrons.

The Association of Specialized and Cooperative Library Agencies (ASCLA) reminds library professionals that mentally ill patrons are no more or less prone to violence than any other member of the population and should not be automatically discriminated against. ASCLA makes suggestions for treating those with mental illness with the same respect and tolerance as with other patrons, including: do not be quick to assume that these patrons are a problem or security risk; do not assume that mental illness equates to deviant or criminal behavior; allow extra time and patience for those easily disoriented; become familiar with the wide range of behaviors associated with mental illness and encourage other patrons to do the same; be liberal with the library's signage (which allows patrons to be independent); do not overempathize in an attempt to relate to the patron; and establish community partnerships that may be able to provide additional resources (e.g., mental health clinics, group homes, homeless shelters, social workers) (Association of Specialized and Cooperative Library Agencies 2010).

REFERENCE SERVICES FOR OLDER ADULTS

Service to adults is not addressed here because the basic reference services described elsewhere in this book focus on services to the general adult audience. Services to children and young adults are also addressed in this text (see Chapter 11). However, this chapter explicitly considers older adults (or senior citizens or the elderly) as a diverse population. Librarians should be cognizant of the particular needs of adult learners (Cooke 2010), and this holds true for older adults who frequent the library. Indeed, older adults may have additional special needs that require accommodating and unassuming services from the library. According to the Census, the term "elderly" refers to adults who are 65 years of age or older. This is one of the fastest-growing segments of our population, constituting 12.9 percent of the population in 2010 (U.S. Census Bureau 2012, Table 9); this percentage is projected to rise to 20.2 percent by 2050 (Table 9). Libraries should be adapting reference services to meet the needs of this growing population whose needs will be coming to the forefront in the next 35 years (Decker 2010).

In working with older adults, it is important to approach each person as an individual who may not share the characteristics or interests commonly associated with the elderly. One should avoid assuming that older adults experience a decline in cognitive ability because many do not. Indeed, unless disease attacks the brain, intellectual capacities can improve with age (Mates 2003, 13). Other assumptions must also be avoided, for example, reading interests may or may not change as individuals grow older. Older adults are not necessarily retired; they may be working full-time or part-time, or they may be underemployed and actively looking for work. Finally, many grandparents are now raising their own grandchildren and consequently are very involved in technology, gaming, and other activities not readily associated with this age group. These older adults have reference needs that do not fit the mold of the stereotypical senior citizen.

Good reference service for elderly individuals includes all the basic components of good reference service for the general adult population, with particular attention to the individual needs of elderly users. In its guidelines for library service to older adults, the Reference and User Services Association (1999) exhorts libraries to provide a full slate of integrated library services to the elderly. The ALA Office for Diversity, Literacy and Outreach Services (2015) provides suggestions for serving older adults, which include having large print materials and magnifying equipment; having comfortable and supportive seating; having accessible shelving (so as to eliminate excessive bending or reaching for materials); having relevant information in a central location (e.g., agency brochures and flyers); and taking care that the physical building is conducive and accessible (e.g., bathrooms, elevators, and checkout stations should have support rails, computer stations should be ADA compliant, and computers might have cordless mouse devices for those suffering from arthritis) (Reference and User Services Association 1999; Perry 2014).

Reference librarians need to avoid stereotyping or patronizing older users and should develop effective communication skills so as to encourage them to ask questions and to ensure that each answer is fully understood by the user.

Some older adults, for example, have had limited exposure to computers and may experience more computer anxiety than younger library users. While the library was once a friendly, welcoming physical place for recreation and leisure, it now feels intimidating and impersonal. Special online catalog instruction sessions (or word processing classes, or workshops dedicated to e-mail, Internet searching, and social media) tailored for older individuals will create a comfortable atmosphere, where users can ask questions and experience self-paced practice and one-on-one coaching.

Because computer use in libraries has become so important, Barbara T. Mates (2003) devotes two full chapters of her book to the subject as it relates to seniors. She discusses hardware considerations, the problems seniors tend to have with navigation and coordination, training and marketing approaches, and website design recommendations (with special attention to color and font choices), and emphasizes the importance of teaching online safety and evaluation skills, given that many seniors may not be prepared for the preponderance of online misinformation and scam artists. Information access and training in regard to health information (including information about sex and sexual health) is also increasingly pertinent (Xie and Bugg 2009). As baby boomers continue reaching retirement age, they are changing the picture of how senior citizens relate to computers.

To provide reference service to older adults, it may be necessary to offer remote delivery of materials and service. Certainly the most common form of remote delivery of reference service to seniors is by telephone. In libraries where in-person reference service is busy and takes precedence over answering questions over the telephone, special provisions must be made to serve the homebound and the institutionalized elderly. The general rule of serving walk-in users before answering the telephone is logical but may make it difficult for the older adult to access the library. It may be necessary to set up a special telephone service for elderly (or disabled) persons who cannot easily get to the library. Also, it may be possible to take reference service to elderly individuals by including reference materials in the bookmobile collection when making stops at retirement homes, assisted living facilities, nursing homes, or senior citizen centers or by providing chat and e-mail reference service to these agencies. Training bookmobile staff in basic reference service and teaching care-facility staff to assist with online reference services would ensure that questions could be answered in a timely and predictable fashion.

It is important to communicate to older adults the reference services that are available to them and to make them feel welcome. The library can effectively market services of particular interest to older persons through library brochures, specific informational programs held in the library, and outside agencies. Reference librarians should cultivate communications with other service agencies in the community; often, specialists in services to the elderly can provide training for library staff in working with the elderly and make appropriate referrals to the library if interagency cooperation is practiced. Careful assessment of what use older citizens make of a library may reveal a need to publicize existing reference services or a way to adapt services to meet the needs and capacities of older adults. The library should not be a place where older adults encounter ageism, but rather a place that encourages and facilitates lifelong learning and healthy, independent living. In order to achieve this kind of atmosphere, Connie Van Fleet (1995) suggests that librarians serving older adults need patience, should be sensitive to unspoken needs, and need to be flexible when implementing service (e.g., in the event of diminishments in vision, hearing, or mobility).

CONCLUSION

Reference services should be offered to all persons in a library's service community regardless of their circumstances or identifying characteristics. There are several issues to be addressed by librarians responsible for ensuring that specific groups in their service community have equal access to reference service. First, librarians need to acknowledge that reference services *do* need to be adapted, or at least assessed, with respect to the needs and abilities of particular groups. Librarians need to identify groups within their community that might face obstacles to free and full access to information (see Box 12.5). It should be stressed that this assessment needs to go beyond polling or observing current users of library reference materials or services. If impediments such as physical or communication barriers exist, members of a group affected by the barriers often are nonusers of the library and thus are invisible to the librarian who observes only the behavior of the user group.

Box 12.5 Activity: Other Diverse Populations

Every community is different and dynamic; in fact, a diverse user group can be very small and unique to a particular community. This chapter covers some, but certainly not all, diverse populations that use libraries. For example, the town of Arthur, Illinois, has a large Amish community that has particular information needs (Miller and Aguilar 1984). The Oakland (California) Public Library has made a notable investment to serve their Asian teen population. And many communities have a significant number of children who are homeschooled and rely heavily on their local libraries (Jennings 2013).

Questions for Reflection and Discussion:

1. What diverse populations are present in your community?
2. How would you apply the aforementioned best practices and service recommendations to members of these groups?
3. If you are unfamiliar with the needs of this group, how could you learn more?

Once groups are identified, librarians need to create a plan of service for meeting the special needs of individuals in each. This plan would include determining the adaptations needed by each group, assessing the library's ability to meet identified needs, and establishing priorities for actions to be taken by the library. It is important to work with other agencies, including local ones and regional or national organizations, both to identify needs of special users and to design collections and services that meet groups' reference needs (Box 12.6 lists some professional organizations that librarians can consult). The library should have policies and procedures, including staff training, which enhance access to full reference services. Special adaptations to library procedures to accommodate the needs of identified groups should be incorporated in library handbooks or manuals. Librarians should work diligently with patrons of various diverse user groups without judgment or assumptions; instead, empathy and openness should guide all reference interactions, and library services in general. Finally, librarians should plan regular evaluation of services and facilities for targeted groups, so that they can keep up with—or even anticipate—changes in the population of those groups, as well as relevant changes in library technology.

Librarians need to plan reference services, assemble reference collections, and develop reference skills appropriate to the various groups in their community of users. This planning process must begin with an understanding of the diverse groups that constitute that community.

Box 12.6 Professional Organizations Related to Diversity

Not all of these organizations pertain explicitly to reference services, but they are organizations focused in some way on diversity and culture, and comprise and/or serve professional librarians who engage in reference and related activities in their libraries.

American Indian Library Association (AILA)
http://ailanet.org

Asian Pacific American Librarians Association (APALA)
http://www.apalaweb.org

Association of Specialized and Cooperative Library Agencies
http://www.ala.org/ascla/

ASCLA Library Services to the Incarcerated and Detained Interest Group
http://connect.ala.org/node/155875

ASCLA Library Services for Youth in Custody Interest Group
http://connect.ala.org/node/159343

Association of Tribal Archives, Libraries, & Museums (ATALM)
http://www.atalm.org/

Black Caucus of the American Library Association (BCALA)
http://www.bcala.org

Chinese American Librarians Association (CALA)
http://cala-web.org

Ethnic and Multicultural Information Exchange Round Table (EMIERT)
http://www.ala.org/emiert/

The National Association to Promote Library & Information Services to Latinos and the Spanish Speaking (REFORMA)
http://www.reforma.org

NOTE

1. For example, see Rubin (2001) and Deines-Jones (2007). Some older guides (e.g., Foos and Pack 1992) are still useful for information on staff training and building accommodation, but they do not address newer concerns such as website compliance.

REFERENCES

American Library Association. 1996. *Library Bill of Rights*. http://www.ala.org/advocacy/intfreedom/librarybill.

American Library Association. 2010. "B.3 Diversity (Old Number 60)." http://www.ala.org/aboutala/governance/policymanual/updatedpolicymanual/section2/diversity.

American Library Association. 2012. "Extending Our Reach: Reducing Homelessness through Library Engagement." http://www.ala.org/offices/extending-our-reach-reducing-homelessness-through-library-engagement-6.

American Library Association. 2015. "Outreach Resources for Services to Older Adults." Office for Diversity, Literacy and Outreach Services. Accessed August 6. http://www.ala.org/advocacy/diversity/outreachtounderservedpopulations/.

Anderson, Keith A., Chaniqua D. Simpson, and Lynette G. Fisher. 2012. "The Ability of Public Library Staff to Help Homeless People in the United States: Exploring Relationships, Roles and Potential." *Journal of Poverty and Social Justice* 20 (2): 177–90.

Association of Specialized and Cooperative Library Agencies. 2010. American Library Association. "People with Mental Health Issues: What You Need to Know Library Accessibility Tip Sheet 7." http://www.ala.org/ascla/sites/ala.org.ascla/files/content/asclaprotools/accessibilitytipsheets/tipsheets/7-Mental_Illlness.pdf.

Austin, Jeanie. 2012. "Critical Issues in Juvenile Detention Libraries." *The Journal of Research on Libraries and Young Adults*. July 26. http://www.yalsa.ala.org/jrlya/2012/07/critical-issues-in-juvenile-detention-center-libraries/.

Berger, Joseph. 2012. "Libraries Speak the Mother Tongue." *The New York Times*. January 3. A18.

Blank, Barbara Trainin. 2014. "Public Libraries Add Social Workers and Social Programs." *The New Social Worker*. October 2. http://www.socialworker.com/feature-articles/practice/public-libraries-add-social-workers-and-social-programs/.

Brothen, Erin, and Erika Bennett. 2013. "The Culturally Relevant Reference Interview." In *Library Services for Multicultural Patrons: Strategies to Encourage Library Use*, edited by Carol Smallwood and Kim Becnel, 297–302. Lanham, MD: Scarecrow Press.

Carder, Linda, Carl Pracht, and Robert Willingham. 1997. "Reaching the Whole Population: Adaptive Techniques for Reaching Students Who Fall through the Cracks." Paper presented at the Twenty-Fourth National LOEX Library Instruction Conference, Ann Arbor, MI, May 16–18.

Carlson, David. 1990. *Adrift in a Sea of Change: California's Public Libraries Struggle to Meet the Information Needs of Multicultural Communities*. Sacramento: California State Library Foundation.

Clark, Sheila, and Erica MacCreaigh. 2006. *Library Services to the Incarcerated: Applying the Public Library Model in Correctional Facility Libraries*. Westport, CT: Libraries Unlimited.

Cooke, Nicole A. 2010. "Becoming an Andragogical Librarian: Using Library Instruction as a Tool to Combat Library Anxiety and Empower Adult Learners." *New Review of Academic Librarianship* 16 (2): 208–27.

Cuesta, Yolanda J. 2004. "Developing Outreach Skills in Library Staff." In *From Outreach to Equity: Innovative Models of Library Policy and Practice*, edited by Robin Osborne, 112–15. Chicago: American Library Association.

Curry, Ann. 2005. "If I Ask, Will They Answer? Evaluating Public Library Reference Service to Gay and Lesbian Youth." *Reference & User Services Quarterly* 45 (1): 65–75.

Davies, J. Eric. 2007. "An Overview of International Research into the Library and Information Needs of Visually Impaired People." *Library Trends* 55 (4): 785–95.

Day, John Michael, ed. 2000. *Guidelines for Library Services to Deaf People*. The Hague, Netherlands: The International Federation of Library Associations and Institutions.

Decker, Emy Nelson. 2010. "Baby Boomers and the United States Public Library System." *Library Hi Tech* 28 (4): 605–16.

Deines-Jones, Courtney, ed. 2007. *Improving Library Services to People with Disabilities*. Oxford: Chandos Publishing.

Dixen, Rebecca, and Stephanie Thorson. 2001. "How Librarians Serve People in Prison." *Computers in Libraries* 21 (9): 48–53.

Dunbar, H. Minnie. 1986. "Bibliographic Instruction for Freshman Students at Florida International University." Paper presented at the National Conference on the Freshman Year Experience, Columbia, SC, February 18.

Elliott, Andrea. 2013. "Invisible Child." *The New York Times*. December 9. http://www.nytimes.com/projects/2013/invisible-child/.

Elteto, Sharon, Rose M. Jackson, and Adriene Lim. 2008. "Is the Library a 'Welcoming Space'?: An Urban Academic Library and Diverse Student Experiences." *portal: Libraries and the Academy* 8 (3): 325–37.

Elturk, Ghada. 2003. "Diversity and Cultural Competency." *Colorado Libraries* 29 (4): 5–7.

Eyrich-Garg, Karin M., and Eric Rice. 2012. "Cyber Behavior of Homeless Adolescents and Adults." In *Encyclopedia of Cyber Behavior*, edited by Zheng Yan, 284–91. Hershey, PA: IGI Global.

Fitzgibbons, Shirley. 1983. "Reference and Information Services for Children and Young Adults: Definition, Services, and Issues." *The Reference Librarian* 2 (7/8): 1–30.

Foos, Donald D., and Nancy C. Pack. 1992. *How Libraries Must Comply with the Americans with Disabilities Act*. Phoenix: Oryx Press.

Ganster, Ligaya. 2011. "Reaching Out to International Students: A Focus-Group Approach to Developing Web Resources and Services." *College & Undergraduate Libraries* 18 (4): 368–84.

Gehner, John. 2010. "Libraries, Low-Income People, and Social Exclusion." *Public Library Quarterly* 29 (1): 39–47.

Giesecke, Joan, and Beth McNeil. 2001. "Core Competencies for Libraries and Library Staff." In *Staff Development: A Practical Guide*, edited by Elizabeth Fuseler, Terry Dahlin, and Deborah A. Carver, 49–54. Chicago: American Library Association.

Gilton, Donna L. 1994. "A World of Difference: Preparing for Information Literacy Instruction for Diverse Groups." *Multicultural Review* 3 (3): 54–62.

Goddard, Marti. 2004. "Access through Technology." *Library Journal Net Connect* 129 (Spring): 2–6.

Goodman, Valeda Dent. 2011. "Applying Ethnographic Research Methods in Library and Information Settings." *Libri* 61 (1): 1–11.

Gough, Cal, and Ellen Greenblatt. 1992. "Services to Gay and Lesbian Patrons: Examining the Myths." *Library Journal* 117 (1): 59–63.

Greenblatt, Ellen, ed. 2011. *Serving LGBTIQ Library and Archives Users: Essays on Outreach, Service, Collections and Access*. Jefferson, NC: McFarland.

Grover, Robert, Roger C. Greer, and John Agada. 2010. *Assessing Information Needs: Managing Transformative Library Services*. Santa Barbara, CA: Libraries Unlimited.

Gunde, Michael G. 1991. "Working with the Americans with Disabilities Act." *Library Journal* 116 (December): 99–100.

Hall, Patrick Andrew. 1991. "The Role of Affectivity in Instructing People of Color: Some Implications for Bibliographic Instruction." *Library Trends* 39 (Winter): 316–26.

Hanley, Robert. 1992. "Library Wins in Homeless-Man Case." *The New York Times*. March 25. http://www.nytimes.com/1992/03/25/nyregion/library-wins-in-homeless-man-case.html.

Hecker, Thomas E. 1996. "Patrons with Disabilities or Problem Patrons: Which Model Should Librarians Apply to People with Mental Illness?" *The Reference Librarian* 53: 5–12.

Hersberger, Julie. 2003. "Are the Economically Poor Information Poor? Does the Digital Divide Affect the Homeless and Access to Information?" *Canadian Journal of Information and Library Science* 27 (3): 45–64.

Hersberger, Julie. 2005. "The Homeless and Information Needs and Services." *Reference & User Services Quarterly*, 44 (3): 199–202.

Holt, Glen E. 2006. "Fitting Library Services into the Lives of the Poor." *The Bottom Line: Managing Library Finances* 19 (4): 179–86.

Imrie, Rob. 2004. "From Universal to Inclusive Design in the Built Environment." In *Disabling Barriers—Enabling Environments*, edited by John Swain, Sally French, Colin Barnes, and Carol Thomas, 2nd ed., 279–84. London: Sage.

Ishimura, Yusuke, and Joan C. Bartlett. 2014. "Are Librarians Equipped to Teach International Students? A Survey of Current Practices and Recommendations for Training." *The Journal of Academic Librarianship* 40 (3–4): 313–21.

Janes, Phoebe, and Ellen Meltzer. 1990. "Origins and Attitudes: Training Reference Librarians for a Pluralistic World." *The Reference Librarian* 30: 145–55.

Jenkins, Mark. 2014. "D.C. Adds a Social Worker to Library System to Work with Homeless Patrons." *The Washington Post.* August 27. http://www.washingtonpost.com/local/dc-adds-a-social-worker-to-library-system-to-work-with-homeless-patrons/2014/08/26/2d80200c-2c96-11e4-be9e-60cc44c01e7f_story.html.

Jennings, Cynthia. 2013. "Homeschoolers and Public Libraries: A Synergistic Relationship." *Maine Policy Review* 22 (1): 92–93.

Katopol, Patricia F. 2014. "Management 2.0: Stereotype Threat." *Library Leadership & Management* 28 (3): 1.

Knight, Heather. 2010. "Library Adds Social Worker to Assist Homeless." *San Francisco Chronicle* (San Francisco). January 11. http://www.sfgate.com/bayarea/article/Library-adds-social-worker-to-assist-homeless-3275950.php.

Knight, Lorrie, Maryann Hight, and Lisa Polfer. 2010. "Rethinking the Library for the International Student Community." *Reference Services Review* 38 (4): 581–605.

Lehmann, Vibeke. 2011. "Challenges and Accomplishments in US Prison Libraries." *Library Trends* 59 (3): 490–508.

Lenn, Katy. 1996. "Library Services to Disabled Students: Outreach and Education." *The Reference Librarian* 53: 13–25.

Leonard, Gillian D. 1993. "Multiculturalism and Library Services." *The Acquisitions Librarian* 5 (9–10): 3–19.

Lewis, Mary Genevieve. 1969. "Library Orientation for Asian College Students." *College & Research Libraries* 30: 267–72.

Liu, Mengxiong. 1995. "Ethnicity and Information Seeking." *The Reference Librarian* 23 (49–50): 123–34.

Macdonald, Gina, and Elizabeth Sarkodie-Mensah. 1988. "ESL Students and American Libraries." *College & Research Libraries* 49 (5): 425–31.

Mates, Barbara T. 2003. *5-Star Programming and Services for Your 55+ Library Customers.* Chicago: American Library Association.

McCleer, Adriana. 2013. "Knowing Communities: A Review of Community Assessment Literature." *Public Library Quarterly* 32 (3): 263–74.

McDonald, Martha J. 1981. "Structural Approaches to Community Analysis." *Indiana Libraries* 1 (2): 51–59.

McKay, Becky. 2011. "Lesbian, Gay, Bisexual, and Transgender Health Issues, Disparities, and Information Resources." *Medical Reference Services Quarterly* 30 (4): 393–401.

Mehra, Bharat, and Braquet, Donna. 2011. "Progressive LGBTQ Reference: Coming Out in the 21st Century." *Reference Services Review* 39 (3): 401–22.

Miller, Jerome K., and William Aguilar. 1984. "Public Library Use by Members of the Old Order Amish Faith." *RQ* 23 (3): 322–26.

Morris, Jen. 2013. "Free to Learn: Helping Ex-Offenders with Reentry." *Public Library Quarterly* 32 (2): 119–23.

Muggleton, Thomas H., and Ian Ruthven. 2012. "Homelessness and Access to the Informational Mainstream." *Journal of Documentation* 68 (2): 218–37.

Nemec-Loise, Jenna. 2014. "A Little Extra Help—Why Public Libraries Need Social Workers." *Public Libraries Online*. September 23. http://publiclibrariesonline.org/2014/09/a-little-extra-help-why-public-libraries-need-social-workers/.

New York Public Library. 2013. "New York City Celebrates Immigrant Heritage Week." http://www.nypl.org/help/community-outreach/immigrant-heritage-week.

Oakland Public Library. 2015. "Asian Branch." Accessed August 6. http://www.oaklandlibrary.org/teens/your-library/teen-zones/asian-branch.

Orange, Satia Marshall, and Robin Osborne. 2004. "Introduction." In *From Outreach to Equity: Innovative Models of Library Policy and Practice*, edited by Robin Osborne, xi–xvii. Chicago: American Library Association.

Osa, Justina O., Sylvia A. Nyana, and Clara A. Ogbaa. 2006. "Effective Cross-Cultural Communication to Enhance Reference Transactions: Training Guidelines and Tips." *Knowledge Quest* 35 (2): 22–24.

Overall, Patricia Montiel. 2009. "Cultural Competence: A Conceptual Framework for Library and Information Science Professionals." *The Library Quarterly* 79 (2): 175–204.

Perry, Claudia A. 2014. "Information Services to Older Adults: Initial Findings from a Survey of Suburban Libraries." *The Library Quarterly* 84 (3): 348–86.

Pyati, Ajit. 2003. "Limited English Proficient Users and the Need for Improved Reference Services." *Reference Services Review* 31 (3): 264–71.

Reference and User Services Association. 1999. "Library Services to Older Adults Guidelines." American Library Association. http://www.ala.org/ala/mgrps/divs/rusa/resources/guidelines/libraryservices.cfm.

Rubin, Rhea Joyce. 2001. *Planning for Library Services to People with Disabilities*. Chicago: American Library Association.

Rubin, Rhea Joyce, and Connie House. 1983. "Library Service in US Jails: Issues, Questions, Trends." *Library Journal* 108 (3): 173–77.

Saar, Michael, and Helena Arthur-Okor. 2013. "Reference Services for the Deaf and Hard of Hearing." *Reference Services Review* 41 (3): 434–52.

Saunders, Laura, and Mary Jordan. 2013. "Significantly Different?" *Reference & User Services Quarterly* 52 (3): 216–23.

Sfondeles, Tina. 2014. "Family of Little League Champ without a Home Base of Their Own." *Chicago Sun Times*. August 28. http://www.suntimes.com/news/metro/29504225-418/family-of-little-league-champ-without-a-home-base-of-their-own.html#.VI38h4fyBYc.

Shachaf, Pnina, and Sarah Horowitz. 2007. "Are Virtual Reference Services Color Blind?" *Library & Information Science Research* 28 (4): 501–20.

Shafer, Scott. 2014. "Urban Libraries Become De Facto Homeless Shelters." *NPR News around the Nation*. Podcast audio. April 23. http://www.npr.org/2014/04/23/306102523/san-francisco-library-hires-social-worker-to-help-homeless-patrons.

Shen, Lan. 2013. "Out of Information Poverty: Library Services for Urban Marginalized Immigrants." *Urban Library Journal* 19 (1): 1–12.

Shirley, Glennor L. 2003. "Correctional Libraries, Library Standards, and Diversity." *Journal of Correctional Education* 54 (2): 70–74.

Strong, Gary E. 2001. "Teaching Adult Literacy in a Multicultural Environment." In *Literacy & Libraries: Learning from Case Studies*, edited by GraceAnne A. DeCandido, 110–15. Chicago: American Library Association.

Taylor, Jami Kathleen. 2002. "Targeting the Information Needs of Transgender Individuals." *Current Studies in Librarianship* 26 (1/2): 85–109.

Thompson, Kelly J. 2012. "Where's the 'T'?: Improving Library Service to Community Members Who Are Transgender-Identified." *B Sides* 1–17. http://ir.uiowa.edu/bsides/22.

Turner, Anne M. 2004. *It Comes with the Territory: Handling Problem Situations in Libraries*. Jefferson, NC: McFarland & Company.

Turock, Betty J. 2003. "Developing Diverse Professional Leaders." *New Library World* 104 (11/12): 491–98.

U.S. Census Bureau. 2012. *Statistical Abstract of the United States 2012*. Washington, DC: Government Printing Office. http://www.census.gov/compendia/statab/.

U.S. Census Bureau. 2015. *Projections of the Size and Composition of the U.S. Population: 2014 to 2060*, by Sandra L. Colby and Jennifer M. Ortman. Washington, DC: Government Printing Office. http://www.census.gov/content/dam/Census/library/publications/2015/demo/p25-1143.pdf.

U.S. Equal Employment Opportunity Commission and the U.S. Department of Justice. 1992. *Americans with Disabilities Act Handbook*. Washington, DC: Government Printing Office.

Van Fleet, Connie. 1995. "A Matter of Focus: Reference Services for Older Adults." *The Reference Librarian* 23 (49–50): 147–64.

Walker, Billie E. 2006. "Using Humor in Library Instruction." *Reference Services Review* 34 (1): 117–28.

Walker, Claire, and Amanda Click. 2011. "Meeting the Reference Expectations of ESL Students: The Challenges of Culture." *College & Research Libraries News* 72 (1): 20–23.

Wang, Hong. 2012. "Immigration in America: Library Services and Information Resources." *Reference Services Review* 40 (3): 480–511.

Willett, Peter, and Rebecca Broadley. 2011. "Effective Public Library Outreach to Homeless People." *Library Review* 60 (8): 658–70.

Winkelstein, Julie Ann. 2014. "Public Libraries: Creating Safe Spaces for Homeless LGBTQ Youth." Paper presented at the 2014 IFLA Conference, Lyon, France, August 8.

Woelfer, Jill Palzkill, and David G. Hendry. 2011. "Homeless Young People and Living with Personal Digital Artifacts." In *Proceedings of the SIGCHI Conference on Human Factors in Computing Systems*, 1697–706. New York: ACM.

Xie, Bo, and Julie M. Bugg. 2009. "Public Library Computer Training for Older Adults to Access High-Quality Internet Health Information." *Library & Information Science Research* 31 (3): 155–62.

Zhang, Xiwen. 2001. "The Practice and Politics of Public Library Services to Asian Immigrants." *Contributions in Librarianship and Information Science* 97: 141–50.

SUGGESTED READINGS

Brazier, Helen, and David Owen, eds. 2007. "Library and Information Services for Visually Impaired People." *Library Trends* 55 (4): 757–993.

This collection of articles offers an international perspective on library services for the visually impaired. The scope includes national models for service delivery and the use of specific technologies to enhance resource discovery and Web accessibility.

Clark, Sheila, and Erica MacCreaigh. 2006. *Library Services to the Incarcerated: Applying the Public Library Model in Correctional Facility Libraries*. Westport, CT: Libraries Unlimited.

Clark and MacCreaigh present a comprehensive look at prison librarianship, especially when viewed through the perspective of public librarianship, which stresses a variety of services and material provision. The authors are lighthearted at times, but go to great lengths to describe all the character types that can be found in this specialized library setting.

Cuban, Sondra. *Serving New Immigrant Communities in the Library*. 2007. Westport, CT: Libraries Unlimited.

Cuban discusses strategies for enhancing services to new immigrant communities, including assessment of needs, addressing these needs through library services, and connecting new immigrants to learning opportunities.

Deines-Jones, Courtney, ed. 2007. *Improving Library Services to People with Disabilities*. Oxford, England: Chandos Publishing.

This compilation includes chapters on improving library services to individuals with visual impairments, hearing impairments, and physical disabilities. A chapter by Deines-Jones discusses low-cost/no-cost ways to improve services through strategies such as addressing staff attitudes. The book concludes with a guide to resources, including publications, websites, and organizations.

Greenblatt, Ellen, ed. 2011. *Serving LGBTIQ Library and Archives Users: Essays on Outreach, Service, Collections and Access*. Jefferson, NC: McFarland.

Greenblatt is an expert in this area, and this anthology contains case studies from others in the field that work with LGBTQ populations. Chapters also specifically address the collection development, classification, and censorship of LGBTQ materials, and concerns of LGBTQ library professionals.

Jacobson, Trudi E., and Helene C. Williams, eds. 2000. *Teaching the New Library to Today's Users: Reaching International, Minority, Senior Citizens, Gay-Lesbian, First-Generation, At-Risk, Graduate and Returning Students, and Distance Learners*. New York: Neal-Schuman.

Though focused on instruction in the academic library, this book models how library services should be adapted to meet the needs of diverse users. The text is now dated, but gives good information about the fundamentals of dealing with several categories of diverse users.

Moller, Sharon Chickering. 2001. *Library Service to Spanish Speaking Patrons: A Practical Guide*. Englewood, CO: Libraries Unlimited.

Moller first provides a historical background for the need for service to Spanish-speaking populations and then addresses her topic by age level. The appendix of this useful guide contains glossaries of library and computer terms translated into Spanish and Spanish-language forms that are commonly used in libraries. This text is dated, but remains useful and is one of the only books on this specific topic.

Vogel, Brenda. 2009. *The Prison Library Primer: A Program for the Twenty-First Century*. Lanham, MD: Scarecrow Press.

Vogel has worked and written extensively in this area. Her text is a guidebook detailing the social, political, and physical environment of the prison system, essential information for professionals working in (or thinking of working in) a prison library.

COMPETENCIES, STANDARDS, AND GUIDELINES

Alter, Rachel, Linda Walling, Susan Beck, Kathleen Garland, Ardis Hanson, and Walter Metz. 2007. *Guidelines for Library Services for People with Mental Illnesses*. Chicago: Association of Specialized and Cooperative Library Agencies, American Library Association.

American Library Association. 2010. "Prisoners' Right to Read." http://www.ifmanual.org/prisoners.

Association of College and Research Libraries. 2012. "Diversity Standards: Cultural Competency for Academic Libraries." American Library Association. http://www.ala.org/acrl/standards/diversity.

Association of Specialized and Cooperative Library Agencies. 1999. *Guidelines for Library Services for People with Mental Retardation.* Chicago: Association of Specialized and Cooperative Library Agencies.

Association of Specialized and Cooperative Library Agencies. 2011. *Revised Standards and Guidelines of Service for the Library of Congress Network of Libraries for the Blind and Physically Handicapped.* Chicago: Association of Specialized and Cooperative Library Agencies.

Bayley, Linda. 1981. *Jail Library Service: A Guide for Librarians and Administrators.* Chicago: Association of Specialized and Cooperative Library Agencies.

Goddard, Martha L., ed. 1996. *Guidelines for Library and Information Services for the American Deaf Community.* Chicago: Association of Specialized and Cooperative Library Agencies.

Lehmann, Vibeke, and Joanne Locke. 2005. *Guidelines for Library Services to Prisoners.* IFLA Professional Reports, No. 92. The Hague, Netherlands: International Federation of Library Associations and Institutions.

Reference and User Services Association. 2007a. "Guidelines for Library Services to Spanish-Speaking Library Users." American Library Association. http://www.ala.org/rusa/resources/guidelines/guidespanish.

Reference and User Services Association. 2007b. "Guidelines for the Development and Promotion of Multilingual Collections and Services." American Library Association. http://www.ala.org/rusa/resources/guidelines/guidemultilingual.

Reference and User Services Association. 2008. "Guidelines for Library and Information Services to Older Adults." American Library Association. http://www.ala.org/rusa/resources/guidelines/libraryservices.

Part II

Information Sources and Their Use

Chapter 13

Selection and Evaluation of Reference Sources

Carol A. Singer

REFERENCE SOURCES

The varied types of services that make up the work of reference librarians were the focus of Part I of this text. However, a reference librarian can provide excellent reference service only if an equally excellent reference collection is available to be consulted. As Rosanne Cordell wrote, "The selection and management of these sources continues to be a time-consuming part of reference work, but these are essential for timely and accurate reference assistance. One cannot depend exclusively on open Web searching on-the-fly to provide the highest quality of assistance" (Cordell 2014, 53). This chapter reviews the most common types of reference sources used in reference work and also discusses how to develop and manage a reference collection. It will list and discuss the criteria used to evaluate reference sources and introduce resources that assist in the development of a reference collection. This chapter introduces types of reference sources and models of collection development and explores the similarities and differences in the inclusion of print materials, licensed electronic sources, and freely available Internet resources.

What Is a Reference Source?

A wide variety of sources might be included in a reference collection. Even when reference collections were expected to include only one format, print resources, they were still composed of many kinds of resources. Given the current incredible variety of electronic resources, both paid and free, that could be considered to be part of the reference collection, deciding what reference resources to acquire is guaranteed to be time consuming and complex.

In an article published in *Library Journal* in 1893, E.C. Richardson defined a reference book as "a book which is to be consulted for definite points of information (rather than read through), and is arranged with explicit reference to ease in finding specific facts" (254). This definition would have been sufficient for decades. In 2009, Carolyn Wilcox, editor of *Choice*, wrote, "Reference works serve as a go-to resource, a jumping-off point, a sure foundation for research. Though an exact definition remains elusive, most people think of dictionaries, encyclopedias, bibliographies, and the like" (iv).

Current definitions reflect the inclusion of nonprint resources in reference collections. The *ALA Glossary of Library and Information Science* defines "reference source" as "Any source used to obtain authoritative information in a reference transaction." Reference sources can include, but are not limited to, printed *materials*, *databases*, *media*, the *Internet*, other *libraries* and institutions, and persons both inside and outside the library. Synonymous with *reference work*" (Levine-Clark and Carter 2013). Most reference collections continue to include print sources, although many print collections have diminished substantially in size in recent years, as libraries transition to a reference collection that is increasingly composed of online resources. It is not uncommon for the books that remain in reference collections to include a supplementary CD-ROM or to include access to an online resource that may contain the same content as the print book or provide supplementary resources such as additional readings, graphs, charts, spreadsheets, audio and/or video files, interactive materials, links to Internet sites, or other resources. Many titles that were originally published as print books are now available in an electronic format. Also many reference sources were never available as a print product, but were produced initially as licensed online resources. The number of online reference sources that are freely available on the Internet continues to increase, making it even more difficult to define the boundaries of the reference collection. Because of the ability to search online resources, these materials are not necessarily traditional reference works as almost anything online is a potential reference source. Margaret Landsman wrote, "The ability to search full text, though, turns every collection of online texts into a reference collection and provides an automatic concordance for every title. Titles can no longer be tidily separated into 'reference works' and 'general collection'" (Landsman 2005, 19).

Types of Sources

Reference sources may be categorized by format. These would include paper, microform (e.g., microfiche or microfilm), tangible electronic formats (e.g., CD-ROM), or online-accessible formats (e.g., the Internet). Another method of classifying reference sources would be to group them loosely into two categories. Some compilations contain facts, definitions, essays, data, citations, or other information. Other compilations refer the user to the source of the information. Of course, these are just loose categories. Some of the compilations that contain information also provide referrals to other sources of information, while compilations that primarily refer the user to other sources sometimes contain sufficient information without looking at the source being referenced. These distinctions become even fuzzier when the sources are online. Compilations that provide information that can be directly accessed include encyclopedias, dictionaries, almanacs, statistical compendiums, atlases, gazetteers, handbooks, yearbooks, and rule books.

Compilations that primarily refer the user to the source of information include indexes and abstracts, catalogs, and bibliographies. However, it is very common for encyclopedia articles to include lists of recommended sources for further research. The *Statistical Abstract of the United States* has long functioned as an index to statistical sources because the source of each table is given and the user can frequently identify additional data by consulting the cited source. Many of these types of sources will be treated in later chapters of this book. Government publications, although not a single type of source, will be treated in a separate chapter, as these publications are frequently housed in a separate collection. In the past, many libraries collected pamphlets, clippings, and other ephemera in a vertical file. These files frequently emphasized items of local interest. Much of this type of material has moved to the Internet, and vertical files have often been replaced with online research guides.

Trends in Reference Publishing

In many libraries, the print reference collection has continued to diminish in size, while the number and variety of online reference resources has expanded. Online indexes and abstracts have been available since 1971, when the National Library of Medicine made *Medline* available (Neufeld and Cornog 1986, 184). Other types of online reference works have proliferated since then, to the point that many librarians and library users think first to use online resources when searching for information. Some librarians refer to the print reference collection as the legacy print collection as so many of their current purchases are for online resources.

Many online reference sources contain the full text of traditional reference sources, such as encyclopedias, dictionaries, handbooks, or atlases. Some aggregated databases feature the publications of a single publisher, while others include the works of many publishers. One example of a database that provides access to reference sources of many publishers is *Credo Reference.* In 2015, the database included more than 3,400 reference books, on a wide variety of subjects, from more than 100 publishers, all available in a single search.

Box 13.1 Advantages of Aggregated Databases

Adam Hodgkin, who developed *xrefer*, which became *Credo Reference*, defined what he saw as the advantages of this type of aggregated database:

1. By combining reference works together at one URL, the reference service becomes much better known to potential users and easier to find.
2. By tackling a number of reference works, there are economies of scale in production and development.
3. The user's search session is likely to be much more powerful and fruitful, since a collection of reference resources "behind" a common interface can be meta-searched. By firing a search term at the "collection of books," the user finds hits across the whole library, and this is a procedure impossibly time-consuming with any modest collection of print books.

(Hodgkin 2002)

Other databases that include only reference books provide information about a single broad subject area, such as *Science Online*, which aggregates the content of science encyclopedias such as the *Encyclopedia of Space and Astronomy* and *African Americans in Science, Math, and Invention*. It also displays illustrations from reference works such as *Human Anatomy on File*.

Many other types of full-text databases are available that mix reference materials with other resources such as periodicals, newspapers, poems, plays, pamphlets, manuscripts, letters, audio and video files, or dissertations. *SBRnet*, the *Sports Business Research Network*, features market research, directories, data, facility reports and news, and full-text periodical articles. The *Berg Fashion Library* provides not only access to the 10-volume *Berg Encyclopedia of World Dress and Fashion*, but also access to additional reference books, eBooks, links to journal articles, essays written exclusively for this database, and images. Some databases aggregate both reference works and other materials. EBSCO's *Consumer Health Complete* includes reference works such as the *American Medical Association Complete Medical Encyclopedia*, plus periodical articles and medical images.

Some databases aggregate primary source materials and other resources, such as the *Rock and Roll, Counterculture, Peace and Protest: Popular Culture in Britain and America, 1950–1975* database, which provides access to manuscripts, government files, underground magazines, fanzines, letters, photographs, pamphlets, video files, posters, and memorabilia. *Accessible Archives* compiles a series of databases that may be searched individually or collectively, including historical newspapers and magazines, county histories, and books.

This rapidly expanding variety of databases is invaluable to the reference librarian. It allows librarians and library users to access resources that would have previously been unavailable. Aggregators of reference materials can make it possible to provide access to a wider variety of resources than would be available if each were purchased individually. However, the use of these aggregators can also end the practice of carefully choosing each book in a reference collection. If an already acquired online resource that aggregates reference books includes an encyclopedia of food science, the library might not be able to also afford a similar title that is deemed to be superior. Because aggregators are expensive and include only the publications of a select group of publishers, one unintended result of acquiring aggregated databases could be a reference collection with less diversity of content and viewpoint.

REFERENCE COLLECTION DEVELOPMENT AND MAINTENANCE

It is the responsibility of reference librarians to select a collection of appropriate reference sources and to arrange and maintain these sources so that they support the reference services of the library. Planning is extremely important to ensure that the collection matches as closely as possible the needs of the library users and of the reference staff.

Components of the Collection

Most reference collections are composed of a variety of formats, although an increasing number of libraries are making the majority of purchases in electronic formats. Nevertheless, most libraries retain a print reference collection, even if they have downsized this collection. There are various reasons for continuing to purchase new print reference books. Some sources may only be available in print, may be considerably less expensive in print, or may be easier to use in print. A library may also have a substantial number of users who do not want to use a computer, or the library may have inadequate or nonexistent Internet service.

Even when the content of the various formats is identical, the online format may offer superior functionality, or library users may have a strong preference for online resources. This superior searching capability that is often found in online formats is one reason many reference collections are transitioning to a heavier dependence on online resources, resulting in the cancellation or non-purchase of print sources. In addition to comparing the content of the various formats, librarians must consider the comparative cost, the desirability of a purchase or a subscription, ease of use, search capabilities, unique features of each format, and the potential reaction of library users to the available formats. Because circumstances change, these decisions must be made as each new acquisition decision is made.

Reference Collection Development

Because reference materials are quite expensive, budgets tight, and the available resources seem more abundant than ever before, it is imperative that the reference collection is carefully planned and not assembled in a haphazard manner. This text will describe many of the most common types of resources found in a reference collection, but remember that there is no such thing as a one-size-fits-all reference collection. The reference collection manager must always plan a reference collection that will serve the needs of the library's user community. Box 13.2 identifies the many collection development decisions that reference collection managers must make.

Box 13.2 Collection Development Decisions

Reference collection managers must decide whether or not to:

- Purchase or subscribe to newly published titles
- Acquire a resource in a tangible or virtual format
- Buy a new edition of a title already in the collection
- Buy a supplement to a title already in the collection
- Cancel a title that is freely available on the Internet
- Cancel a title that is now contained in an aggregated database
- Continue to receive serials or standing orders
- Acquire online resources as an Internet resource or load the material locally
- Coordinate collection development decisions with other libraries
- Purchase resources as part of a consortium in order to save money
- Repair a book or purchase a replacement
- Remove materials from the collection in response to a complaint
- Weed or review the collection

(Singer 2012, 19–20)

A collection development policy can provide guidance for these decisions and help ensure that decisions are made in a fair and equitable manner. However, some librarians think that a reference collection development policy is a waste of time because, after being written, it is rarely consulted. In 2010, Jane Kessler published the results of a survey of academic and public libraries in New York. The survey revealed that 58.6 percent of responding libraries did not have a written reference collection development policy (36). Such a policy serves several purposes, in addition to being the basis for decision making about the collection. It defines the purpose of the collection and describes what should and what should not be included. Because it serves as a written record of the collection decisions that have been made, it encourages continuity when there are personnel changes. It can provide justification for a requested budget. If the reference collection manager is asked why materials are included in or excluded from the collection, the policy can provide an explanation. If there is a challenge to any materials in the collection, it can be used to explain and, if necessary, justify the resource being questioned.

In addition to the value of the policy itself, the process of writing a reference collection development policy can be a valuable exercise. Daniel Liestman wrote, "The actual process of creating a policy is beneficial as it forces the library staff to consider unspoken/unrecorded assumptions about the reference collection. In order to successfully manage a reference collection, a library's staff must possess a shared understanding of their reference philosophies as well as the users' current and anticipated information needs. . . . Developing such a document provides the opportunity for those involved to come to a consensus about major goals for the collection and reference service" (2001, 86). Box 13.3 identifies potential parts of a reference collection development policy.

Box 13.3 Collection Development Policies

Reference collection development policies may include:

- Purpose of the collection development policy
- Who has responsibility for collection development
- Purpose of the reference collection
- Target audience(s)
- Budgeting and funding
- Selection criteria
- Resources to aid in selection of materials
- Preferred format(s)
- When, or if, to purchase duplicates
- Preferred language(s)
- Circulation of tangible reference materials
- Treatment of specific resource groups
- Resource sharing with other libraries
- Collection maintenance
- Weeding and reviewing the collection
- Timeline for revision of the policy

Box 13.4 Activity: Evaluating a Collection Development Policy

Many library collection development policies can be found on the Web. Reviewing some of these policies can provide you with valuable experience before you begin writing a collection development policy for your library. Begin this exercise by locating and reading a reference collection development policy.

Questions for Reflection and Discussion:

1. Does the policy include sections that were not on the list in Box 13.3?
2. Does the policy exclude sections that were on the list in Box 13.3?
3. Does the policy clearly define who is responsible for collection development?
4. Who is the target audience for this collection? Do the selection criteria make sense when choosing resources for this audience?
5. Does the policy include directions for when and how to weed the collection?
6. Is there a section of this policy that you might want to use as a model when you write your own reference collection development policy?
7. If you were the manager of this reference collection, what changes would you make to this policy?

Maintenance of any reference collection is a continuous process. Some types of materials in the collection can become swiftly outdated, such as directories, statistics, road maps, or rule books. Some print resources are updated on a regular schedule, such as monthly or annually. Others may be updated on an irregular schedule by supplements, pocket parts, or transmittal sheets. The librarian must be alert for Internet resources that are more current than the available tangible resources. The collection should be regularly evaluated to ensure that information is as current as necessary.

Arrangement of the Collection

Reference collections may be arranged in a variety of ways. Many libraries arrange all, or part, of the tangible collection in call number order regardless of type of resources. Some libraries divide the collection by type of book, such as encyclopedias, dictionaries, atlases, biographical sources, indexes and abstracts, legal materials, or job hunting materials. The majority of the collection may be arranged in call number order, with a few categories of specific materials in separate spaces, such as atlas cases or dictionary stands. Most reference collections designate a section of shelving near the reference desk as a ready-reference collection, which contains resources that are used so frequently they ought to be easily retrieved by the reference librarians.

Inclusion of special formats such as CD-ROMs, microforms, or maps should be carefully considered to ensure maximum ease of access and use for both reference librarians and library users. This is particularly true of formats that require the use of specialized equipment. Appropriate signage and directions for use are essential to ensure that these resources and the equipment needed to use them will be easy to identify and use.

Even as many libraries are decreasing the size of their tangible reference collection, they are increasing the size of their virtual reference collection. As a result, reference librarians are frequently involved in the redesign of the library's user interface or the part of the library's Internet presence that provides access to electronic resources in order to assist library users in identifying the most appropriate databases or other online sources for their needs.

Box 13.5 Activity: Organizing Databases

Electronic resources must be organized in order to be discoverable and accessible. Not all libraries choose to organize these resources in the same fashion. Look at the following Web pages to see how some libraries have organized their online resources:

Boston University http://www.bu.edu/library/research/collections/databases/.
Toledo Lucas County Public Library http://web2.toledolibrary.org/research/research-tools.
Oakland Public Library http://oaklandlibrary.org/online-resources/articles-and-databases.
University of North Florida http://libguides.unf.edu/az.php.
University of New Hampshire https://www.library.unh.edu/find/databases.

Questions for Reflection and Discussion:

1. What are the advantages and disadvantages of each?
2. Which organizational scheme is better for a public library? Would that scheme also be the best for a college or university library?
3. Which organizational scheme would you choose for your own library?

Weeding the Collection

Weeding, or deselecting, is an extremely important part of maintaining a usable current collection. Maria Isabel Fernandes defines weeding as "the process of removing materials from the collection. It is the process by which librarians control the overall health of a collection" (2008, 205). Although weeding is such an important function of collection maintenance, some librarians find weeding difficult or distasteful. This reluctance can result in a print collection that is dusty, cramped, and out of date. An online collection may not get dusty, but the list of online resources can certainly get crowded with incorrect URLs, out-of-date editions, resources that no longer serve any useful purpose, and resources that have lost significant functionality. It is difficult to maintain excellent reference service when the reference staff cannot find the information they need.

When weeding either the print or online collection, taking the time to plan before acting is critical. A number of questions should be answered before beginning to weed. Will the entire collection be weeded or only a portion? Who will do the weeding? Who will assign the areas to be weeded? Will people outside the reference department be involved? What criteria will be used to determine what to keep and what to remove? Who will make the final decision if there are disagreements about what should be weeded? What will happen to the books that are removed from the reference collection? Who will decide which books to replace with newer editions? What will be done about missing books?

It is essential to notify any department in the library whose workload will be affected by the project, so they will be able to plan. If the weeding project will cause a significant disruption to the work of other departments, this must be taken into consideration when planning the timeline. Communication is one of the most important aspects of planning and managing a weeding project. All those who are involved or affected by the project need to be kept informed.

If the collection will be weeded as a continuous project, with only a small section being weeded at one time, planning may not need to be as elaborate. In a continuous weeding project, there might only be a single person to make the initial decisions about what should be weeded. These books may be placed where others can review the books recommended for removal and indicate any disagreement with the recommendation. Those who review the books may include other reference librarians, subject specialists within the library, or constituencies outside the library. Once the review period is over, the books can be transferred to the circulating collection, sent to off-site storage, or withdrawn. Depending on the policies of the library, withdrawn items might be sold at the next book sale, sold to a used book dealer, given to a charitable organization, sent to recycling, or put in the trash.

In a major weeding project, the collection to be weeded might be divided into sections, and each person involved be given the responsibility of making initial weeding decisions in one or more sections. It is not unusual in a large library for every member of the reference department to be involved at this level. At this point, the basic steps listed earlier will be followed. In a major weeding project, managing the process is crucial. One or more people must be designated to keep track of which sections have been weeded, make sure that books are not sent to the next step until the agreed-upon review time has expired, resolve disagreements over individual titles, ensure that each weeded book is sent to the correct destination, decide what must be done about books that are missing, and, if necessary, order replacement copies or more current books.

The criteria for removing books from the collection will vary, depending on the goals of the project and the mission of the library. See Box 13.6 for some common reasons for weeding books.

Box 13.6 Reasons for Weeding Reference Books

Reasons for weeding reference books can include:

- Lack of use or lack of recent use
- Availability of online or other formats
- Not being listed in the selection aids used to select books for the collection
- Not being sufficiently comprehensive
- Duplicating information in other sources
- Not citing sources for further exploration
- Out-of-date information
- Availability of a new edition
- Duplicate copies in the collection
- Poor condition
- Would be more useful in the circulating collection
- Written in a language that few library users can read

(Singer 2012, 96–97)

Box 13.7 Activity: Evaluating Reference Books

A university library reference department has in its collection a multivolume encyclopedia published in the 1950s in the European duchy of Transmogrania. Of course, it is written in Transmogranian, a language that none of the reference staff can read. This encyclopedia remains in the lists of reference works because it is a standard authoritative work on all aspects of Transmogranian life and culture. A survey of the reshelving of reference works in the department shows that no volumes of this work were reshelved during the six months in which the survey was conducted. As always, the reference library is finding that its shelf space is inadequate, and one reference librarian suggests removing the encyclopedia from the reference collection.

Questions for Reflection and Discussion:

1. Would you (1) keep the encyclopedia in reference, because it is a standard reference work; (2) transfer the encyclopedia to the general stacks, where it will become a circulating title; or (3) get rid of the encyclopedia by donating it to the only faculty member on campus who can read Transmogranian?
2. Are there alternative solutions?

Now suppose that one of your expert Web-surfing librarians has discovered that the government of Transmogrania has established a website that contains very thorough current information about the duchy of Transmogrania in both Transmogranian and imperfect English.

Question for Reflection and Discussion:

- Does the availability of this resource affect your decision about the encyclopedia?

Weeding the online reference collection may be more difficult than weeding the print collection. Librarians are more likely to feel empowered to weed the print collection because they own the books in the collection and they have physical possession of them. Online materials, on the other hand, are frequently not owned and may not be loaded on local servers. If eBooks were purchased as part of an aggregated database, the library may not be able to remove individual titles from the database. This may be one of the reasons that weeding the library's collection of eBooks receives so little attention. In 2009, a survey published by the Association of Research Libraries revealed that only 4 percent of respondents had a policy on weeding eBooks (Anson and Connell 2009, 32).

The first step in weeding the eBook collection is to determine which books are able to be removed from the collection or from the access points to the collection. It is a waste of time to identify eBooks that ought to be removed if there is no mechanism for the librarian to remove them in any way. Once those that can be removed or whose presence in the collection can be suppressed have been identified, the process for weeding will be similar, allowing for the difference between working with tangible and virtual books. In order to review these books, there must be some type of list of the books that will be reviewed. It may be more practical to make several lists, with a list for each eBook vendor or a list for each method of removing any indication that the library makes the eBook available. Once weeding decisions have been made, the method used to remove the eBook from the collection will vary depending on how the library acquired the eBook, the way(s) in which library users access the eBook, and the license agreement. If the eBook is on a library server, the eBook itself can be removed from the server. However, most eBooks will be on servers controlled by the database vendor. In these cases, the library will not have the choice of removing the eBook itself and can remove only evidence of the eBook from the library catalog and from any other media the library used to provide access to the eBook.

Some of the criteria used will be similar to those used to weed the print collection, such as lack of use, not being listed in the selection aids used by the library, not being sufficiently comprehensive, duplicating information in other sources, not citing sources for further exploration, containing outdated information, availability of a new edition, or written in a language that few library users can read. However, other criteria are important when reviewing online resources, such as the adequacy of the methods available for library users to identify and access the eBook or the usefulness of the user interface.

Reference databases should also be reviewed regularly. This might be performed by a single person, there may be a meeting of reference librarians to review all reference databases, or there may be an annual meeting of all stakeholders within the library to consider all databases. With the proliferation of databases and the amount of work that must go into preparing for a database review, it is very easy to put off this important task. If possible, all databases should be examined as a group to ensure that duplication is kept to a minimum. Participants should examine changes in content or usability that may alter the need for the database. This is also a good time to consider new databases that might be added to the suite of available databases or might replace a currently available database. Before the meeting, a list of all databases should be prepared that includes at least the title of the database, the database producer, annual cost, and any usage data. Knowing usage and cost per use are important factors in making an informed decision. It is also essential to review usage over an appropriate length of time and from an appropriate time period. For instance, making decisions based on summer usage in a school library, or intersession usage in an academic library, will not be as effective as reviewing usage during the semester. Participants should also know before the meeting whether the budget must be reduced and, if so, by how much, or whether the reference department is in the fortunate position of having additional funds to spend. Even if the budget remains the same, databases normally increase in price, so one or more databases may need to be cancelled.

Numerous articles discuss how reluctant some librarians are to weed the collection. One way to overcome this reluctance is to use onion weeding, that is, to weed, or peel off, one layer at a time. Librarians can choose any category that they perceive is easier to review. This category will vary from librarian to librarian and collection to collection. If the reference collection contains many old travel guides, that might be a good place to start. Or the collection might include books that have not been reshelved within the most recent 10 years. Other possible categories might be directories that are more than 10 years old, old medical guides, old computer manuals, duplicate volumes, books that are also available online, or books that do not get used because the information they include is now available on the

Box 13.8 Activity: Which Databases to Cancel?

Cancelling a database or subscription is rarely an easy decision. Many factors may be considered, but one common one is the usage of the resource. Usage figures may be evaluated as straightforward numbers or may be used in conjunction with the cost of the resource to compute the cost per use.

For this exercise, assume your library subscribes to the databases on the list provided by the Wyoming State Library at http://will.state.wy.us/wyld/statistics/. It is time to decide which of these databases will be renewed; however, the budget is not going to be sufficient to pay for all of them. Review the usage statistics on that website and choose two to three databases to cancel.

Questions for Reflection and Discussion:

1. Why did you choose these particular databases?
2. What did you learn from the usage data?
3. What other information would have improved your ability to make an informed decision?

Now, for each database you chose to cancel, look at the data listed under the Summaries category. Compare the data for a particular calendar or fiscal year for at least three libraries.

Questions for Reflection and Discussion:

- Would you make the same cancellation decision for each of those libraries, or would you keep the database for one or more of the libraries? Why?

Internet. Remember, the decision was made to review the category, not to weed everything within that category without examining it. Some of the books within that category may be kept because they still serve a useful purpose. Once the first category of books has been reviewed, the librarian can choose another category to review. For most librarians, onion weeding can be a way to ease into weeding because weeding usually becomes easier with practice.

EVALUATION OF SOURCES

As part of developing a reference collection, each source must be evaluated to see whether the material is appropriate for the collection and to ensure the collection is composed of works of high quality. This evaluation should take place for all sources of any format. Because most libraries are spending a significant portion of the budget on online resources and these resources tend to be more expensive, there are sometimes fewer selection decisions than when the collection was composed mostly of books. In the not-too-distant past, a reference librarian would have made a decision about each reference title in the collection. Now, the reference librarian might instead make a decision about an aggregated database in which there are hundreds of titles. This chapter will cover general evaluation criteria that apply to many types of reference resources. Chapters 16 through 28 include sections on the evaluation of particular types of sources. Using these criteria will assist the reference librarian in developing a superior reference collection that meets the needs of the library. Box 13.9 identifies the evaluation criteria for print and/or electronic resources.

Box 13.9 Evaluation Criteria

Evaluation criteria that may be used for all formats:

Content
Authority
Format

Evaluation criteria that may be used for electronic resources:

User interface
Branding and customization
Provision of full text
Accessibility
Cost and licensing

Evaluation criteria that may be used for print resources:

Physical attributes
Indexing
Cost

Content

The first thing most librarians consider when choosing reference materials is the relevancy of the content to the reference collection. Most budgets are insufficient to purchase all the desired titles. The reference collection manager must consider the collection holistically, thinking about what areas need additional or current resources. The librarian should also try to anticipate necessary changes in the content of the collection. A school or college might be adding new courses, the composition of a public library's constituency might be changing, or a company or organization might be altering the type of business it performs, any of which might cause changes in the demands made upon the library's reference services.

When looking at the content, the librarian should consider the scope and intent of the resource and whether it is accurate, complete, and current. Since most reference books that are ordered are not available to be examined, the librarian must frequently rely on book reviews or other selection aids to assist in making decisions about what titles to acquire. The needed degree of completeness of the content will vary, depending on the purpose the book will play in the reference collection and on the intended audience. When choosing an encyclopedia about the care of cats and kittens, the librarian of a school library would choose a volume with considerably less technical information than the librarian at a veterinary school library, but both might feel that the book they purchased was complete, given their user population. The currency of all reference books is not equally important. A book about the meaning of people's names might be perfectly usable, even if it had been published 10 years earlier. However, a medical encyclopedia or a travel guide would need to be much more current. If a print reference book is updated by pocket parts, transmittal sheets, supplements, or yearbooks, it is advisable to subscribe to these additions or to place a standing order for the necessary publications so the title will remain current. Some libraries prefer to order online versions of reference sources that require regular updates.

Illustrations should support the content of the book or online resource and enhance the usefulness of the content for the library user. They should also be of excellent quality. Black-and-white illustrations may be appropriate to the content of the book, but for some topics and some audiences, color will be mandatory.

The content of the book or online resource should match the age and/or reading level of the intended audience. Reference books that are appropriate for a college student are unlikely to be very usable for a sixth grader. Publishers who produce books intended for a school audience frequently indicate the age or grade level of intended users, although librarians should still use professional judgment in selecting titles. If the library serves a diversity of ages or reading levels, the reference collection should reflect that diversity.

Authority

Ideally, the author, publisher, and/or database producer should have an excellent reputation for producing reference materials. If desired, academic credentials or publishing history can be checked. The catalog or website of the publisher can be explored to see what types of books or online resources are issued by this company and whether any of these have received awards. The library may already own titles by the author or publisher that can be examined. The library may already have access to online resources from a database vendor that will give some indication of the level of quality typical of that organization.

If the book or eBook includes multiple articles or entries, such as a subject encyclopedia, the librarian can check the credentials of the authors of individual entries. There may be a list of authors, with academic credentials, included in a book. Each entry of a subject encyclopedia should be signed and include a list of resources for further exploration.

Format

Reference sources come in various formats. Although most reference sources are print or electronic resources, reference sources might also include microforms, maps, CD-ROMs, globes, or field identification cards. The format should contribute to the usability of the content and enhance the user's proficiency in finding pertinent information in the source.

As a result of research conducted for a SAGE white paper, Elisabeth Leonard described the results of a survey of librarians, who were asked their preference for print or online reference sources. Sixty percent of librarians from public libraries stated they had no preference, while 35 percent preferred online reference sources. Only 22 percent of academic librarians showed no preference, while 68 percent preferred online sources. Thirty-one percent of special librarians said they had no preference, while 50 percent preferred online sources (Leonard 2014, 12).

Participants in a 2010 Association of Research Libraries survey were asked to list what criteria were most important in assessing whether or not to acquire an electronic resource. The results are shown in Box 13.10.

Box 13.10 Selection Criteria for Electronic Resources

Respondents to a 2010 Association of Research Libraries survey listed the most important selection criteria for electronic resources as:

Cost (39%)
Compatibility with library systems (12%)

The criteria rated as very important were:

Relevance to current curricula (49%)
Relevance to current faculty research (47%)
Uniqueness of content (46%)
Inflation history (43%)
Cost per use (42%)

(Bleiler and Livingston 2010, 58–59)

Online Resources: User Interface

User interfaces can vary enormously depending on the type of online resource. One constant is that most people prefer a user interface that is graphically clean, well-organized, and easy to read. The user interface should be appropriate for the content of the online resource and the intended audience. Over time, users' expectations will change, so the user interface of a resource should reflect contemporary graphical and functional preferences. If the user interface remains the same, over time it begins to look outdated. The functionality should be updated and enhanced as new and improved technologies become available.

Many databases offer a Basic Search page that may be as simple as a search box with a Search button. They may also offer an Advanced Search page that includes multiple search boxes, limiters, and other search options. Some offer alternative types of search pages, such as a visual search or a Boolean search page. Databases that index any type of text usually offer at least the ability to search by author, title, and keyword. However, there may be many other types of search fields, such as subject terms, names of people mentioned in the text, geographical locations, company names, or the institutional affiliations of the author(s). These specialized search fields should be appropriate to the content and also to the intended user group. A business database might offer the ability to search by the company name, the North American Industry Classification System (NAICS) code, or stock ticker symbol. A database of children's books might allow the user to search by reading level, name of the illustrator, or name of the awards won by the book.

Some online resources offer the ability to search a controlled vocabulary. The quality of the thesaurus, including the existence of subject term definitions, cross-references, and pertinent subheadings, should be examined. Linwood DeLong investigated the utility of the controlled vocabulary in various databases. He cited the use of a controlled vocabulary by *Project Muse* "because it is essential for reliable and comprehensive user searching, that there be consistent terminology, devoid of inflections or other spelling variations, that is applied consistently, with adequate concern for both broadness and precision, to the articles that are indexed in databases" (2007, 105).

The help screens should be easy to locate and easy to negotiate. They should also be context sensitive, so that clicking on the Help link on a page of search results will display a selection of Help topics related to search results.

Lists of search results should be consistently organized, and the fields in the entries should be easily identifiable. It should be obvious how the result list was sorted, whether by relevance or by some other method, and be simple to change the method of sorting. If the online resource provides search limiters on the results page, they should enhance the user's ability to identify and retrieve the most pertinent results.

The ability to work with search results in varied ways may be crucial to users. Frequently, the user can save, print, or e-mail individual entries from the result list or a group of entries that have been placed in a virtual folder. Users will want to have the ability to print a range of pages with a single command. Some users may wish to export citations to a bibliographic management software program.

Online Resources: Branding and Customization

When people come to the library to use reference sources, they are reminded they need and want resources provided by the library. When they can access reference sources from their home or business, it is easy for them to forget that the resources they are using were acquired and managed by the library. This is particularly true for users who connect directly to the online resources they use most often, bypassing the library website. Most libraries want to remind library users and the people who fund the library that these resources were provided by the library. One way to do this is to brand their online resources. Many online resources make some provision for the library to add a logo or text that indicates that the source is part of the library collection.

Many databases also offer opportunities for libraries to further customize the user interface of an online resource. It is common for the library to have the opportunity to add a logo and/or text that provides access to the library's chat reference service. The library may also be able to choose some of the ways in which the database's home page, search page, or results page are organized. There may be some aspects of functionality that can be customized. For instance, if there is more than one search form, the library may be able to choose which form will be on the landing page that is first displayed when the user enters the database from the library's website. Librarians may be able to alter the text on some of the buttons of the user interface, choose which limiters will appear on the search page, choose the order in which limiters appear, or make other types of customizations.

Online Resources: Provision of Full Text

If the database indexes full text, the convenient availability of the full text may be one of the most important factors in selection. Library users typically want to be able to easily find the full text of articles, books, dissertations, company reports, or other textual sources once that source has been identified. The most convenient method for users to find the full text is for the database in which the item has been identified to also supply the full text. However, not all databases supply full text for all of the items indexed. When the full text of the item identified is not available in a database, the ability to link to the full text from another of the library's databases is the next most desirable option. At the very least, the database should have the ability to indicate whether the library owns the full text of the item being indexed, whether that item is online, in print, in microform, or another format.

Linking to the full text of an item when it is available in another database is frequently accomplished by the use of an open URL link resolver. This uses the metadata from the record in the database that identified the item to search other databases to look for the full text. The user can then click on the link to that full text and be taken into the other database, ideally to the full text of the exact item. In some cases, the link may be to a search form in the database that includes the full text of the item, and the user will need to perform a search to find the full text. The ability to identify and access full text may be a deal-breaker when choosing online resources because so many library users have become accustomed to the convenience of instant full text online. In response to this, databases from most major database producers are open URL compliant.

Even when the entry for an item indicates that it is available full text, some or all of the text may be missing. Sometimes other articles from the title are available, but the article the searcher wants is missing. If the article is available full text, it may be missing some illustrations, or the article may be continued on another page that is missing. If the item is an eBook, it may be missing appendices or other materials that were present in the print volume.

Databases that supply full text usually provide an HTML and/or a PDF file. HTML files are usually smaller and load more quickly, but might not include the illustrations. The HTML file might also not indicate the presence of page breaks, making proper citation problematic. The PDF file will generally be a much larger file, but should be an exact image of the print page, so that students will be able to cite the exact page on which a particular text is found. Some databases offer the option of listening to audio files of full text and even allow the user to choose the gender or accent of the reader. Sue Polanka wrote, "Visualizing information, hearing the pronunciation of a word, or listening to the content in its entirety can be a tremendous help, particularly to those with learning or physical disabilities and ESL learners" (2010, 116).

The currency of any resource that indexes library materials can be crucial. Some journals have an embargo period before the full text is available. This can be very inconvenient if the library is relying on the database to provide access to the full text and the embargo period is one year or even longer. Currency is more important if the source is issued daily, such as a newspaper or the *Federal Register*. Reference eBooks sometimes also have currency problems. If an eBook is replaced by a new edition, it might be replaced by the newer edition or the new edition may simply be added to the database. If the library must purchase the new edition, the older edition may remain in the database or it may be removed from the database as soon as the new edition is available. If the new edition replaces the older edition in the database and the library does not purchase the new edition, library users would have access to neither edition. The policy for retaining sources in an online format will depend on the terms of the license that was signed by the library and the vendor.

Online Resources: Accessibility

A number of types of accessibility may be important when selecting online reference sources. The ability to access online resources when away from the library is frequently a deal-breaker. The provisions made for accessibility for those who are blind or have a visual handicap may be an important factor in selecting resources. An increasing number of library users want to use library resources on their mobile device. The library may have subscribed to a Web-scale discovery service and want all online resources to be available through that service. The library may have a service that indexes the entries in eBooks.

For many libraries, if a database cannot be accessed remotely, it is not a desirable purchase. College and university students need to be able to use materials from off campus. Public libraries acquire resources that can be accessed by users in a city or county area. Some states provide a suite of databases for all residents of the state. Companies and other organizations must provide employees with online resources that are available while traveling. However, there are a number of remote-access software programs, and not all online resources work equally well with each of these programs. These problems are usually solvable, but it may require some consultation between the library's computer staff and that of the database vendor or producer.

Online resources have made various provisions so users who are visually handicapped are able to use the resource successfully (Tatomir and Tatomir 2012). This might involve text-only Web pages, audio files for full-text articles, provision for the site to interface with particular software, or other types of accommodation.

An increasing number of library users choose to access library databases on their smartphones, tablets, or other handheld devices. The demand for this ability will vary by the user population, but the demand for mobile access is now so widespread that most databases from major database producers will offer a mobile-optimized Web page and/or a mobile app.

The *2014 Pearson Student Mobile Device Survey* revealed that 62 percent of students in grades 4–12 used a smartphone regularly and 53 percent used a tablet regularly. Smartphones were regularly used by 44 percent of students in elementary school, 58 percent of those in middle school, and 75 percent of those in high school. Tablets were used by 66 percent of students in elementary school, 58 percent of those in middle school, and 42 percent of those in high school (Pearson 2014b, 24). The same survey revealed that 83 percent of college students used a smartphone regularly and 45 percent used a tablet regularly (Pearson 2014a, 20).

If the library has subscribed to a Web-scale discovery service, all library reference sources will ideally be accessible from that service. Print reference books may be discoverable only to the extent of the information that is in the library catalog. If possible, online resources should be accessible to the article or entry level. Some librarians find that online resources accessible through the Web-scale discovery service experience significant increases in use. In some cases, accessibility by the library's Web-scale discovery service may be a deal-breaker, or librarians may find that use of online resources not accessible through the discovery service declines so much that they decide to cancel the database.

Addition of *Reference Universe* to the library's suite of online resources allows the user to search the contents of the library's collection of subject encyclopedias. If the library subscribes to this service, reference librarians would certainly prefer to purchase subject encyclopedias that are included in this database.

Online Resources: Cost and Licensing

Cost models vary widely for online resources. The acquisition of an online resource might be a purchase, a subscription, a lease-to-own purchase, or some more creative arrangement. An online resource that has been purchased, or for which the perpetual access has been purchased, might require payment of an annual maintenance fee. Some online resources that seem to be a single database might actually be a group of separate databases or titles with the content available in units, each of which can be acquired individually. The library might have purchased perpetual access for some portions of the overall online resource, but have a subscription for other portions of the resource.

Pricing of online resources can be influenced by such variables as the number of FTE students, the number of library branches, the number of majors in an academic department, the number of residents in a library district, the number of simultaneous users, the number of computers that have access to the resource, or the ability to provide remote access. The price may also be negotiable, particularly in a poor economy when fewer libraries can afford to acquire new online resources. Membership in a library consortium, discussed in detail in Chapter 5, can help a library manage costs for online resources.

Most online resources require the library to sign a license with the database provider. A license will usually define who is allowed to use the online resource; any restrictions to using such features as printing, saving, or e-mailing; the ability to use items in the resource for electronic reserve or interlibrary loan; the availability of technical support; the library's liability; and provision of usage data. If the library has already acquired at least one online product from the database vendor, it is sometimes possible to modify the existing license to include the new resource rather than negotiate a new license. If the online resource was acquired through a consortium, the consortium might negotiate and administer the license, relieving the librarian of that responsibility. Because the license is a legal instrument, it may be desirable to consult an attorney, particularly if some of the elements of the license are problematic. Whether or not an attorney is required, in many libraries, there will be only one person who is authorized to negotiate licenses. Chapter 14 provides additional information on price models and licensing for online resources.

Print Resources: Physical Attributes

Reference books that are expected to last for many years should have sturdy binding that will withstand use by numerous people. The quality of the binding is more important for a book such as an encyclopedia on the Civil War or a biographical directory of children's authors because they might be expected to have a long shelf life. An oversized book is more prone to binding damage if it is shelved on its spine as this will sometimes cause the binding to crack or break.

Box 13.11 Activity: Choose a Database

In this scenario, you'll be responsible for choosing databases for a particular library. You can choose to work for one of the following (imaginary) libraries:

- James R. Weir Public Library in Whittier, California
- Margaret Whitlinger Memorial Library at Freeport State University, Kentucky
- Franz Holscher High School Library in Augusta, Georgia

You are trying to decide whether your library should subscribe to one of the following imaginary databases. Although the databases are not in the same subject area, you have sufficient funds for only one of them. Which would you choose and why?

Note that you can devise additional information about your library and/or the sources, if that will support your decision.

- *Hot Topics Pro & Con*: A database that provides full-text sources on multiple sides of important current issues.
- *Movie Abstracts*: A searchable database of scholarly articles on film.
- *People & Places*: A collection of information about countries and cultures worldwide.
- *Languages to Go*: Lessons for more than 20 languages, emphasizing everyday conversation.
- *Green Issues*: Books and articles on a wide variety of environmental topics.
- *Marketing Full Text*: A collection of marketing research reports.
- *All the News*: Clips of television news stories that aired during the past year.

Thick reference books are also liable to binding damage as the spines are more likely to crack during use. Photocopying can damage any book, even if it has been hardbound. However, the quality of the binding is less likely to be important for a book that is expected to be useful for only a few years, such as a weather almanac, a travel guide, or a list of the members of the U.S. Congress. Paper binding may be acceptable for sources such as a monthly issue that is replaced by an annual bound volume. If a book is expected to be rebound, the inner margins of the book should be sufficiently generous for the book to be rebound without losing part of the text.

The quality of the paper is more likely to be important for a book that is expected to have a long shelf life because deteriorating paper may not be able to be rebound, if rebinding is necessary. Poor quality paper may also become brittle and fall out of the book, or the page may be creased and split at the point of the crease so that part of the page falls out.

Print Resources: Indexing

Indexes and other finding aids in a reference book or set may be particularly important as library users may have no other way to identify individual entries in the print volume. The indexes should be easy to locate and appropriate to the content and the target audience. The language used in these finding aids should enhance the ability of the intended user population to identify and access the desired information. If the indexes cover a multivolume set, it is essential that index entries include both volume and page numbers so library users aren't forced to hunt through multiple volumes in order to find the correct page. Some multivolume sets are issued one volume at a time. In these sets, the index may not arrive until the entire set has been received, which may be years after the first volume is published. If the multivolume set received in this fashion is a newer edition of a title already in the reference collection, it may be necessary to retain the older edition, with its indexing, until the entire new edition has been received.

Print Resources: Cost

Print reference books are usually purchased one at a time. The library may obtain a discounted price by buying books on sale, purchasing from a company that will offer a reduced price as the library's regular purchasing agent, or receive a discount as a member of a consortium. Reference books received as part of an approval plan are usually discounted. If a multivolume set is received one volume at a time, the individual volumes may be cheaper if the library places a standing order for the series. Some reference books are accompanied by access to the eBook edition, although this access may be only for a limited time.

Materials such as annuals and yearbooks are frequently purchased as a subscription or standing order. Subscriptions are usually an annual fee that pays for everything received during the year. This is more appropriate for materials in which the library knows how many items will be received during the subscription period, such as a monthly or annual publication. Libraries use standing orders for items that are received irregularly because the library is billed as materials are received. Standing orders are usually used for items such as pocket parts or transmittal sheets because the number of these received in a year will vary. A standing order may also be used for a multivolume set received one volume at a time. Standing orders can represent a budgeting challenge because the cost for the entire year is uncertain. If the standing order has been in effect for one or more years, the reference collection manager can look at the total cost for the previous several years and use that data to predict the cost for the current year.

COLLECTION DEVELOPMENT OF FREE INTERNET SOURCES

The number of reliable freely available Internet sites that can be used for reference work continues to expand. In some cases, these sources are so heavily used that they compete with long-established reference works. For many years, libraries relied on *Books In Print* to provide information about books they wished to purchase. Now many librarians use online booksellers, such as *Amazon.com* to obtain purchasing information about books. Company and organization information is easy to locate on the Internet, causing some libraries to cancel their subscription to the *Encyclopedia of Associations*. Instead of purchasing movie review guides, a library might use *IMDb*, the *Internet Movie Database*.

Many titles of freely available textual and multimedia resources are on the Internet. Some are produced by a government agency, such as *PubMed* from the National Library of Medicine; *ERIC* from the U.S. Department of Education; *AGRICOLA* from the U.S. Department of Agriculture; *Homeland Security Digital Library* from the Naval Postgraduate School; and *National Criminal Justice Reference Service*

(NCJRS) from the U.S. Department of Justice. A few of the free sources that are privately produced and maintained are *Google Scholar*; *Independent Voices*, which provides full-text alternative press materials; *Hip Hop Archive*; *RoJaRo*, an index to music magazines; *WorldWideScience.org*; and *Media History Digital Library*.

Some encyclopedias, dictionaries, thesauruses, statistical compendiums, and many other reference resources are freely available. The availability of some of these free resources has led to the demise of vertical files, company annual report files, and telephone books in many library reference collections. Heather Hill and Jenny Bossaller asked public libraries to name online resources that had resulted in the library canceling print reference resources. Among the titles were the CIA's *The World Factbook*, the *Occupational Outlook Handbook*, and the *Kelley Blue Book* (2012, 108–9).

A major problem with freely available Internet sources is that they vary enormously in quality. They may disappear without notice or they may remain on the Internet, but cease to be updated. Ideally, a reference librarian would use the same selection criteria when choosing freely available Internet resources as when choosing licensed online resources. In actual practice, many librarians will use less strict criteria when selecting freely available online resources. Some criteria cannot be used because they are usually not applicable to freely available resources. For most of these sites, branding, customization, and usage data are not available.

One advantage to listing some freely available Internet sites and databases in the list of library-provided resources is that they are available to all. This can be very helpful when providing reference service to those who are outside the boundaries of the public library district or those who are not faculty, staff, or students of a college or university library. These sources really prove their usefulness for the many libraries that provide some level of reference service via telephone, chat, e-mail, or texting.

SELECTION AIDS

A number of tools will provide assistance in selecting reference resources. Review sources, issued periodically, provide critical and descriptive reviews of newly issued print and/or electronic titles. Guides to reference sources identify important reference titles and can also be useful when reviewing the reference collection to identify gaps. Both types of sources are invaluable in identifying high-quality reference materials. However, the reference librarian must still have a thorough knowledge of both the reference collection and the needs of the library's users in order to build a collection that will fully support reference service for the library's clientele.

Sources of Reviews

In an ideal world, the reference librarian would be able to personally examine each reference source before ordering it. That is rarely possible, but there are a number of sources of reviews that will assist the librarian. The best sources of reviews for a library will vary by type of library, as each of the sources in this section is intended for a particular target audience.

American Reference Books Annual is a very comprehensive compilation of reviews for reference sources. It attempts to provide reviews for every English-language book and online reference resource released in the United States and Canada. Some English-language resources published outside the United States and Canada are also reviewed if they have an exclusive North American distributor. Annual publications, such as directories, yearbooks, or almanacs, are reviewed every three or four years or if the content has significantly changed. As of July 2015, the accompanying online database, *ARBAonline*, included more than 19,500 reviews published from 1997 to the present.

Booklist, a semimonthly publication, includes long signed reviews of English-language reference books and electronic reference sources. The reviews of reference works, along with reviews of non-reference resources, are then made available in a searchable database at the *Booklist Online* website.

The *Charleston Advisor: Critical Reviews of Web Products for Information Professionals*, a quarterly journal, publishes extensive reviews of both licensed and free online resources. The *Charleston Advisor* website, a licensed product, includes an index to the electronic sources that have been reviewed, which shows the score given to the product by the reviewer.

Choice: Current Reviews for Academic Libraries publishes brief signed reviews of reference books and online resources of interest to college and university libraries. The reviews are made available online at the *Choice Reviews Online* website.

Library Journal publishes a section of brief signed reviews of print and online reference sources. These reviews are also available on the *Library Journal* website. *Library Journal* publishes an annual supplement on new and forthcoming reference resources that usually accompanies one of the November issues.

School Library Journal also publishes a section of signed reviews of print and online reference sources, although the focus is on reviews of reference resources that are suitable for school libraries. The reviews are also available on the *School Library Journal* website.

Reference & User Services Quarterly (RUSQ) publishes a section of signed reviews of print and online reference sources. These reviews also appear on its website, which is accessible to subscribers. *RUSQ* began publishing exclusively digitally with Volume 51, number 1 (Fall 2011). *RUSQ* publishes several annual lists of reference materials chosen by various committees of the American Library Association's (ALA) Reference and User Services Association (RUSA). The Emerging Technologies Section's (ETS) Best Free Web Sites Committee chooses an annual list of particularly valuable freely available websites. These reviews are also posted on the ETS website, which includes a combined index to all of the reviews from this list published from 1999 to the present. Committees of the Business Reference and Services Section (BRASS) choose an annual list of the best business information sources and a list of the best business websites, both published in *RUSQ*.

This is only a sample of the available reviews in serials. Many serials include reviews of reference books about the subject covered by the journal.

If the library orders books from an online vendor database, that database might include book reviews as part of its services. Databases already available in the library may also include full-text sources that publish reviews of reference books. A common limiter available in databases is the ability to limit search results to book reviews. A free source of book reviews might be a library catalog of a consortium or large library as many library catalogs now include book reviews.

The most useful reviews are those that describe the source, critically examine it, and compare it to similar sources. Reviews provide the reference collection manager with valuable assistance in choosing reference resources when the resource itself cannot be examined. When considering the acquisition of an online reference source, the librarian can frequently arrange for a trial. This is invaluable in determining the potential usefulness of an online reference source, particularly if the trial can be made available to the user groups most likely to use this particular source.

Guides to Reference Sources

The ALA issued the most famous guide to reference sources in the United States. This source was first published in 1902 as the *Guide to the Study and Use of Reference Books*, edited by Alice Kroeger, with the most recent print edition published in 1996 as *Guide to Reference Books*, edited by Robert Balay. Librarians relied on the various editions of this guide for more than 100 years. This series was so heavily used that the print book was frequently referred to by the editor's last name. In 2008, ALA launched an online version. The *Guide to Reference* was a searchable database of more than 16,000 reviews of both print and electronic reference resources. It aimed to provide information about the best sources, rather than just the newest sources. In March 2015, ALA Publishing announced that the *Guide* was being discontinued as a subscription database. Although no longer published, the print editions can be used to identify older titles of value.

ALA has also published *Reference Sources for Small and Medium-Sized Libraries*, most recently in 2014. The target audience for this guide is school and public libraries.

Subject-oriented guides to reference books can be very helpful when a librarian is building a more extensive reference collection in a particular subject. A few examples of this type of publication are the *ALA Guide to Sociology and Psychology Reference*, *Introduction to Reference Sources in the Health Sciences*, and *Information Resources in the Humanities and the Arts*.

Older guides may be useful for reviewing the existing reference collection. For instance, *The New Walford* is a three-volume set that was issued one volume at a time, beginning in 2005. The three volumes are *Volume 1: Science, Technology, and Medicine* (2005), *Volume 2: Social Sciences* (2008), and *Volume 3: Arts, Humanities, and General Reference* (2008). This British counterpart to the *Guide to Reference Books* includes entries for print and electronic reference sources.

Guides to reference sources are useful for both collection development and reference work. As a collection development tool, they can be used as a resource for evaluating the content of the reference collection and as a guide to the selection of new resources. They can also guide the reference librarian to the most appropriate source to answer a question in a subject area with which the librarian is not familiar. The remainder of Part II will expand on the various types of reference sources, describing the aspects of each type and the strategies for using these sources.

REFERENCE COLLECTIONS IN TRANSITION

Reference collections have been in transition ever since the first electronic reference sources became available in the early 1970s. They will continue to transition as libraries downsize their print collections and acquire an ever-increasing variety of online resources. In fact, some librarians refer to their print collection as the legacy print collection, implying that the print collection has become something of an antique. Nevertheless, publishers continue to issue print reference books, and libraries continue to buy them. Until librarians no longer see the need to provide a print reference collection, both print and electronic reference collections must be developed and maintained to effectively support all the types of reference services that are available to assist library users.

REFERENCES

ALA Publishing. 2015. "Guide to Reference to Cease Publication." News release, March 17. http://www.ala.org/news/press-releases/2015/03/guide-reference-cease-publication.

Anson, Catherine, and Ruth R. Connell. 2009. *E-book Collections*, SPEC Kit 313. Washington, DC: Association of Research Libraries.

Bleiler, Richard, and Jill Livingston. 2010. *Evaluating E-Resources*, SPEC Kit 316. Washington, DC: Association of Research Libraries.

Cordell, Rosanne. 2014. "Optimizing Library Services—Managing the 21st-Century Reference Collection." *Against the Grain* 26 (4): 53–54.

DeLong, Linwood. 2007. "Subscribing to Databases: How Important Is Depth and Quality of Indexing?" *The Acquisitions Librarian* 19 (37/38): 99–106.

Fernandes, Maria Isabel. 2008. "Ready Reference Collections: Thoughts on Trends." *Community & Junior College Libraries* 14 (3): 201–10.

Hill, Heather, and Jenny Bossaller. 2012. "Public Library Use of Free E-resources." *Journal of Librarianship and Information Science* 45 (2): 103–12.

Hodgkin, Adam. 2002. "Integrated and Aggregated Reference Services: The Automation of Drudgery." *D-Lib Magazine* 8 (4). http://www.dlib.org/dlib/april02/hodgkin/04hodgkin.html.

Kessler, Jane. 2010. "Print Reference Collection in New York State: Report of a Survey." *Journal of the Library Administration and Management Section* 6 (2): 32–44.

Landsman, Margaret. 2005. "Getting It Right—The Evolution of Reference Collections." *The Reference Librarian* 91/92: 5–22.

Leonard, Elisabeth. 2014. *The State of Reference Collections.* N.p.: SAGE.

Levine-Clark, Michael, and Toni M. Carter, eds. 2013. *ALA Glossary of Library and Information Science.* Chicago: American Library Association, s.v. "reference source".

Liestman, Daniel. 2001. "Reference Collection Management Policies: Lessons from Kansas." *College & Undergraduate Libraries* 8 (1): 79–112.

Neufeld, M. Lynne, and Martha Cornog. 1986. "Database History: From Dinosaurs to Compact Discs." *Journal of the American Society for Information Science* 37 (4): 183–90.

Pearson. 2014a. *Pearson Student Mobile Device Survey 2014. National Report: College Students.* http://www.pearsoned.com/wp-content/uploads/Pearson-HE-Student-Mobile-Device-Survey-PUBLIC-Report-051614.pdf.

Pearson. 2014b. *Pearson Student Mobile Device Survey 2014. National Report: Students in Grades 4–12.* http://www.pearsoned.com/wp-content/uploads/Pearson-K12-Student-Mobile-Device-Survey-050914-PUBLIC-Report.pdf.

Polanka, Sue. 2010. "Interactive Online Reference." *Booklist* 106 (9/10): 116.

Richardson, E.C. 1893. "Reference-Books." *Library Journal* 18 (7): 254–57.

Singer, Carol A. 2012. *Fundamentals of Managing Reference Collections*, ALA Fundamentals Series. Chicago: American Library Association.

Tatomir, Jennifer Nasasia, and Joanna Catarina Tatomir. 2012. "Collection Accessibility: A Best Practices Guide for Libraries and Librarians." *Library Technology Reports* 48 (7): 36–42.

Wilcox, Carolyn. 2009. "The Reference Roller Coaster." *Choice* 47 (3): iv.

LIST OF SOURCES

Accessible Archives. Malvern, PA: Accessible Archives. http://www.accessible-archives.com/. [subscription required]

AGRICOLA. Washington, DC: U.S. Department of Agriculture. http://agricola.nal.usda.gov/.

ALA Guide to Sociology and Psychology Reference. 2011. Chicago: American Library Association.

Amazon.com. Seattle: Amazon. http://www.amazon.com/.

American Reference Books Annual. 1970–. Edited by Shannon Graff Hysell. Santa Barbara, CA: Libraries Unlimited.

Angelo, Joseph A. Jr. 2006. *Encyclopedia of Space and Astronomy*. New York: Facts on File.

ARBAonline. Santa Barbara, CA: Libraries Unlimited. http://www.arbaonline.com/. [subscription required]

Berg Fashion Library. New York: Oxford University Press. http://www.bergfashionlibrary.com/. [subscription required]

Best Free Reference Web Sites Combined Index. 1999–. RUSA ETS Emerging Technologies Section. http://www.ala.org/rusa/sections/mars/marspubs/marsbestindex.

Booklist. 1905–. Chicago: American Library Association. 22 issues per year.

Booklist Online. Chicago: American Library Association. http://www.booklistonline.com/. [subscription required for full access]

Books In Print. New York: R.R. Bowker. http://www.booksinprint.com/. [subscription required]

Charleston Advisor: Critical Reviews of Web Products for Information Professionals. 1999–. Denver: The Charleston Advisor. Quarterly. http://www.charlestonco.com/index.php. [subscription required for full access]

Choice: Current Reviews for Academic Libraries. 1964–. Middletown, CT: Association of College and Research Libraries. 11 issues per year.

Choice Reviews Online. Middletown, CT: Association of College and Research Libraries. http://www.ala.org/acrl/choice/cro. [subscription required]

Consumer Health Complete. Ipswich, MA: EBSCO. http://search.ebscohost.com/. [subscription required]

Credo Reference. Boston: Credo Reference. http://search.credoreference.com/. [subscription required]

Encyclopedia of Associations. Farmington Hills, MI: Gale Cengage Learning. Available online as part of *Gale Directory Library*.

ERIC. Washington, DC: U.S. Department of Education. http://eric.ed.gov/.

Federal Register. 1936–. Washington, DC: Office of the Federal Register. Daily. https://www.federalregister.gov/.

Gale Directory Library. Farmington Hills, MI: Gale Cengage Learning. http://www.cengage.com. [subscription required]

Google Scholar. http://scholar.google.com/.

Guide to Reference Books. 1996. 11th ed. Edited by Robert Balay. Chicago: American Library Association.

Guide to the Study and Use of Reference Books: A Manual for Librarians, Teachers and Students. 1902. Edited by Alice Bertha Kroeger. Boston: Houghton Mifflin Company.

Hip Hop Archive. Cambridge, MA: Hip Hop Archive and Research Institute. http://hiphoparchive.org/.

Homeland Security Digital Library. Monterey, CA: Naval Postgraduate School Center for Homeland Defense and Security. https://www.hsdl.org/.

Human Anatomy on File. 2003. New York: Facts on File. [subscription required]

IMDb: Internet Movie Database. N.p.: IMDb.com, Inc. http://www.imdb.com/.

Independent Voices: An Open Access Collection of an Alternative Press. Saline, MI.: Reveal Digital. http://voices.revealdigital.com/.

Information Resources in the Humanities and the Arts. 2013. Edited by Anna H. Perrault and Elizabeth S. Aversa, 6th ed. Santa Barbara, CA: Libraries Unlimited.

Internet Archive. San Francisco: Internet Archive. https://archive.org/.

Introduction to Reference Sources in the Health Sciences. 2014. Edited by Jeffrey T. Huber and Susan Swogger, 6th ed. Chicago: Neal-Schuman.

Kelley Blue Book. Irvine, CA: Kelley Blue Book. http://www.kbb.com.

Library Journal. 1876–. New York: Library Journals, LLC. 20 issues per year. http://lj.libraryjournal.com/.

Media History Digital Library: Online Access to the Histories of Cinema, Broadcasting & Sound. N.p.: Media History Digital Library. http://mediahistoryproject.org/.

NCJRS: National Criminal Justice Reference Service. Washington, DC: U.S. Department of Justice. https://www.ncjrs.gov/.

The New Walford Guide to Reference Resources. 3 vols. London: Facet, 2005–2008.

Occupational Outlook Handbook. 1949–. Washington, DC: U.S. Bureau of Labor Statistics. http://www.bls.gov/ooh/.

Project Gutenberg. Salt Lake City: Project Gutenberg Literary Archive Foundation. https://www.gutenberg.org/.

Project Muse. Baltimore: Johns Hopkins University Press. http://muse.jhu.edu/. [subscription required]

PubMed. Bethesda, MD: National Library of Medicine. http://www.ncbi.nlm.nih.gov/pubmed/.

Reference & User Services Quarterly (RUSQ). 1997–. Chicago: American Library Association. https://journals.ala.org/rusq.

Reference Sources for Small and Medium-Sized Libraries. 2014. Edited by Jack O'Gorman, 8th ed. Chicago: American Library Association.

Reference Universe. Sterling, VA: Paratext. http://reference.paratext.com/. [subscription required]

Rock and Roll, Counterculture, Peace and Protest: Popular Culture in Britain and America, 1950–1975. Marlborough, UK: Adam Matthew Digital. http://www.rockandroll.amdigital.co.uk/. [subscription required]

RoJaRo. Oslo: RoJaRo. http://www.rojaro.com/.

SBRnet: Sports Business Research Network. Princeton, NJ: Sports Business Research Network. http://www.sbrnet.com/. [subscription required]

School Library Journal. 1954–. New York: Media Source. Monthly. http://www.slj.com/.

Science Online. New York: Facts on File. http://www.fofweb.com/Science/. [subscription required]

Spangenburg, Ray, and Kit Moser. 2012. *African Americans in Science, Math, and Invention*. Revised edition. New York: Facts on File.

Statistical Abstract of the United States. 1872–2012. Washington, DC: U.S. Census Bureau. http://www.census.gov/compendia/statab/.

The World Factbook. 1981–. Washington, DC: U.S. Central Intelligence Agency. https://www.cia.gov/library/publications/the-world-factbook/.

WorldWideScience.org. Oak Ridge, TN: WorldWideScience Alliance. http://worldwidescience.org/.

SUGGESTED READINGS

Brumley, Rebecca. 2009. *Electronic Collection Management Forms, Policies, Procedures, and Guidelines Manual with CD-ROM.* New York: Neal-Schuman Publishers.

This compilation of policies, procedures, guidelines, and forms from academic and public libraries provides a treasure trove of information to assist the reference collection manager. It includes resources for administration, collection development, equipment, accessibility, copyright, and position descriptions.

Detmering, Robert, and Claudene Sproles. 2012. "Reference in Transition: A Case Study in Reference Collection Development." *Collection Building* 31 (1): 19–22.

Detmering and Sproles describe changes made to the University of Louisville reference collection policies and print collection as a result of changing reference practices, budget limitations, and the implementation of a learning commons. The librarians revised the collection development policy and used it to evaluate serials and standing orders, weed the reference collection, and plan for the future development of the collection. They concluded, "Since neglect can cause the collection to quickly spiral out of control, the new collection development approach will make it easier to update and maintain the collection to ultimately better serve the needs of users."

Francis, Mary. 2012. "Weeding the Reference Collection: A Case Study of Collection Management." *The Reference Librarian* 53 (2): 219–34.

The reference librarians at Dakota State University undertook a weeding project of their reference collection. Francis notes, "A bloated reference collection focused on the needs of patrons from 20 years ago offers little service to the current patrons" (220). She details the steps taken during this process, from developing a reference collection development policy to analyzing whether they met their goals.

Hill, Heather, and Jenny Bossaller. 2013. "Public Library Use of Free E-Resources." *Journal of Librarianship and Information Science* 45 (2): 103–12.

Hill and Bossaller describe a study concerning the use of free electronic resources by public libraries. Although the study was not exclusively about reference materials, it explored the use of free reference sources, including their use in answering ready-reference questions. The authors urged public libraries to add freely available online resources to their collections, due to budgetary realities, as a way to diversify their collections, and in support of projects such as *Project Gutenberg* and the *Internet Archive.*

Husted, Jeffrey R., and Leslie J. Czechowski. 2012. "Rethinking the Reference Collection: Exploring Benchmarks and E-Book Availability." *Medical Reference Services Quarterly* 31 (3): 267–79.

Husted and Czechowski described a project implemented at the University of Pittsburgh's Health Sciences Library System to discover whether it was possible to replace their print reference collection with an online collection, of particular interest to them as their user population was spread throughout five campuses and more than 15 hospitals. After comparing the available electronic resources with several standard lists of reference books, they decided that an all-online reference collection could not be established as too few electronic versions of the titles on the benchmark lists were available at that time.

Kessler, Jane. 2013. "Use It or Lose It! Results of a Use Study of the Print Sources in an Academic Library Reference Collection." *The Reference Librarian* 54 (1): 61–72.

The University at Albany, State University of New York, implemented a study to determine the extent of use of its reference collection. Kessler discusses the procedures used for the study, which found that only 7.1 percent of the volumes in the reference collection were used at least once during the fall semester.

King, Nathaniel. 2012. "Nice vs. Necessary: Reference Collections in ARL Member Libraries." *The Reference Librarian* 53 (2): 138–55.

King describes the results of a survey of some members of the Association of Research Libraries about collection development policies, selection of reference materials, weeding, and use of the reference collection. The survey revealed that 67 percent of responding libraries had a reference collection development policy, although the policies were usually infrequently updated. Preference for the format of reference sources was strongly in favor of electronic, with 70 percent answering they preferred electronic resources and 27 percent responding "depends on the item."

Larson, Jeannette. 2012. *CREW: A Weeding Manual for Modern Libraries*. Austin: Texas State Library and Archives Commission. https://www.tsl.texas.gov/ld/pubs/crew/index.html.

The CREW guide to weeding was written primarily for small- and medium-sized public libraries, but is also useful for other libraries. It explains the entire process of weeding, from planning to disposing of unwanted materials. One chapter focuses on weeding reference collections.

Leonard, Elisabeth. 2014. *The State of Reference Collections*. N.p.: SAGE. http://www.sagepub.com/repository/binaries/pdfs/StateofReference.pdf.

This SAGE White Paper compiles information about reference collection development and reference services in libraries worldwide, although 90 percent of the respondents were from North America. The information was gathered through an international survey, focus groups, and interviews. Among the topics included in the volume are: the types of resources that are considered to be reference, whether reference budgets were increasing or decreasing, the transition from print to electronic resources, and selection criteria.

Managing Electronic Resources: A LITA Guide. 2012. Edited by Ryan O. Weir. Chicago: ALA TechSource.

The chapters in this edited volume focus on various aspects of acquiring and managing electronic resources. Of particular interest are Chapter 3, "Acquiring Electronic Resources", and Chapter 4, "Licensing Electronic Resources and Contract Negotiation".

Singer, Carol A. 2012. *Fundamentals of Managing Reference Collections*. Chicago: American Library Association.

This volume summarizes the basics of managing a print and an online reference collection. It is divided into nine chapters: "Reference Collection Fundamentals"; "Reference Collection Development Policies"; "Staffing Models for Reference Collection Management"; "Selecting Reference Materials"; "Acquisitions, Budgets, and Licenses"; "Collection Maintenance"; "Weeding the Reference Collection"; "Reference Collection Development and Consortia"; and "Discovery and Access". The book also includes a "Reference Collection Development Policy Template".

Chapter 14

Licensing Electronic Sources

Rick Burke

INTRODUCTION

Acquiring print resources is a straightforward process; once a librarian has determined what materials will be added to the collection, an order is placed, and when the materials arrive, they are cataloged and placed on the shelf. The library generally pays list price for the item, unless the publisher offers a preprint discount for early orders or the librarian goes through a book vendor who offers a discount, and multiple titles may be ordered at once. Once acquired, the item remains in the collection until it is weeded.

Acquiring electronic sources, including databases, eJournals, eBooks, and services such as discovery systems, is more complicated. Pricing is based on anticipated usage, often calculated by the number of patrons the library serves. For example, in an academic setting, student FTE, which is the calculated total full-time equivalent enrollment, is a common pricing model. For public libraries, population served or total library cardholders might be employed. In a corporate library, the cost might be based on the number of researchers served or it may be an arbitrary "custom" price. In a hospital library, the number of beds is, surprisingly, a common pricing formula. And, for school libraries, student FTE models similar to those in the academic library market may apply, but typically at much lower price points. The same goes for community colleges, which usually obtain special two-year college pricing, which is an exception to the standard academic library pricing.

In addition, the vendor will require the librarian to sign and abide by a set of licensing terms that outline permissible use of the resource in areas such as off-site or remote access, interlibrary loan, and course reserves. As noted later in this chapter, there are major areas of concern in licensing that are evolving as well as areas that were once contentious but are now more settled, such as interlibrary loan issues.

Thus, the librarian needs to work with the vendor to negotiate a price and licensing terms for each resource acquired. In addition, since online resources are usually licensed for only a year at a time, the resource must be renewed on a regular basis, often spurring another round of negotiations. Licensing of electronic resources is a cycle of ongoing activity for librarians.

Large libraries may have an acquisitions librarian devoted to licensing eResources; this librarian will develop expertise in the area of licensing, and will be responsible for negotiating with vendors to ensure a fair price for the resource and license terms that protect the library's interests. However, most libraries are not large enough to have a dedicated librarian for this purpose, and the director or a reference librarian will be called upon to select eResources and negotiate with vendors. Even in large libraries, reference librarians will be expected to work with acquisitions librarians as they negotiate licenses to ensure that the final usage conditions meet the needs of the library's patrons. Libraries in a consortium may acquire many, but not all, of their resources through the consortium (see Chapter 5 for more on consortia). However, even then, librarians are still responsible for understanding and adhering to the license terms negotiated by the consortium. Thus, all types of librarians in all types of libraries benefit from understanding the basics of eResource licensing.

The major considerations in licensing electronic resources include pricing models and contract terms. In addition to providing an introduction to these considerations, this chapter discusses negotiation strategies and the role of consortia in assisting libraries in eResource acquisition.

PRICING MODELS

Vendors use a variety of models to price their products. These models vary with what the market will bear, the type of library for which they are priced, and the type of consortium for which they are priced. Some vendors will adopt a one-model-fits-all approach, which might be favorable for some libraries or consortia, but unfavorable for others. Most often, vendors use a pricing model based on the number of patrons served. As will be noted later, the practice of providing a custom quote is also quite widespread. In such instances, particularly in the corporate or special library market, a vendor may arbitrarily set a high price for large, corporate, for-profit institutions. There is no apparent model for this other than that the market will bear the price, much like a corporate business traveler will willingly pay a premium for a better seat and meal.

In addition, the vendor's goal is to sustain revenue growth year over year, which might prompt a change to a new pricing model at some point. This means that librarians need to be prepared to renegotiate price when models shift, as the price increases can be significant. Thus, it is important for librarians to understand the variety of pricing models in order to be prepared for all possibilities.

Basic Pricing Models

The most common pricing models are those based on the population served. These are used in all types of libraries and often form the basis of more complicated models used in specific types of libraries, where additional factors add another dimension to the pricing. Other less commonly used models are also listed in the following, such as simultaneous use, multiple product discounts, and multiyear pricing commitments.

- *Patrons served*: The most common pricing model is one based on the number of patrons served. The vendor uses student enrollment, population served, the number of researchers on staff, or similar measures of size, and sets ranges or tiers to which a cost is assigned. Another variation on this model is to have maximum and minimum costs (or "floors and ceilings") so that the cost of the lowest tier is a minimum acceptable to the vendor and the highest tier does not unfairly penalize institutions with the largest population (see Tables 14.1 and 14.2 for examples).
- *Patrons served plus additional factors matrix*: Probably the second most common model used by vendors, this model adds another factor to the basic tiered model, creating a matrix by which a price is calculated. Additional factors include the type of institution, the number of products licensed or purchased, and limits on simultaneous usage (see Tables 14.3, 14.4, and 14.5 for examples).
- *Simultaneous users*: In this pricing model, the library pays for access on the basis of how many people can be logged in at one time. Librarians often opt for this model when the price for unlimited usage would be prohibitive. This model was more popular in the early years of licensing but has become less common over time.
- *Multiyear pricing*: In this model, costs decrease if the librarian makes a longer-term commitment (e.g., a three-year commitment, rather than a year at a time).

TABLE 14.1 Academic Libraries: Pricing Model Based on Enrollment Tiers

Maximum Price: ______________________

Minimum Price: ______________________

FTE	$
1–1,000	$9,995
1,001–2,000	$13,945
2,001–5,000	$16,775
5,001–10,000	$27,495
10,001–20,000	$37,340

TABLE 14.2 Public Libraries: Pricing Model Based on Population Tiers

Population Served	Library Price	Consortium Price
Less than 7,500	$775	$762
7,501–15,000	$953	$937
15,001–30,000	$1,737	$1,708
30,001–50,000	$2,443	$2,402
50,001–75,000	$3,707	$3,645
75,001–150,000	$4,886	$4,804

TABLE 14.3 Academic Library: Pricing Model Based on Enrollment and Institution Type

FTE	Four-Year Institutions	Art Schools	Law Schools	Medical Schools	Miscellaneous Schools
1–999	$845	$510	$637	$510	$510
1,000–2,999	$1,657	$510	$637	$510	$510
3,000–4,999	$2,533	$510	$637	$510	$510
5,000–11,999	$4,122	$510	$637	$510	$510
12,000–24,999	$5,270	$510	$637	$510	$510
25,000–39,999	$6,791	$510	$637	$510	$510
40,000–999,999	$8,075	$510	$637	$510	$510

TABLE 14.4 Academic Library: Pricing Model Based on Enrollment and Multiple Subscriptions

FTE	w/Academic eBook	w/out Academic eBook
1–2,499	$1,500	$2,250
2,500–5,999	$3,000	$4,500
5,000–7,499	$4,845	$7,268
7,500–9,999	$6,565	$9,848

TABLE 14.5 Academic Library: Pricing Model Based on Product Quantity

FTE	Price per Journal				
	1 Journal	2–10 Journals	11–20 Journals	21+ Journals	All Journals
1–999,999	$452	$428	$404	$380	$309

Variations for Academic Libraries

In setting prices for academic libraries, vendors often use variations on the earlier models.

- *Cost per FTE*: Rather than using price tiers, the vendor sets a cost per student. For example, if a resource costs $3.00/student, a library serving 1,000 students would pay $3,000.
- *FTE tiers plus budget tiers*: Another variation is one that uses library acquisition budget tiers alongside enrollment tiers (see Table 14.6 for an example). This

TABLE 14.6 Academic Library: Pricing Model Based on Enrollment and Budget

FTE	Budget ($)				
	1–499,999	500,000–749,999	750,000–999,999	1,000,000–2,499,999	2,500,000–9,999,999
1–1,999	$709	$1,241	$1,772	$2,304	$2,832
2,000–3,999	$756	$1,323	$1890	$2,457	$3,020
4,000–999,999	$945	$1,654	$2,363	$3,072	$3,776

model is less common, but in many ways is most fair to libraries as it factors into the cost what the library budget can likely afford. However, because library budgets are not reported in a uniform fashion, most vendors do not use this model. For example, some libraries might have a separate electronic resource budget, while others do not; this makes it difficult for the vendor to apply a common budget figure across its customer base.

- *Carnegie classification*: This model is becoming more common for vendors whose primary market is the academic library market. The Carnegie classifications, which classify institutions based on size, degrees offered, and level of research activity, were refined into many more categories several years ago, making it possible for vendors to more precisely classify a library and assign a cost accordingly ("Classification Description" 2015). Some vendors still utilize the previous broader Carnegie classifications or the more recent basic classification categories. One drawback to this model is that Carnegie categories do not apply outside of the U.S. market, which means vendors must construct multiple pricing models for different geographical regions. More seriously for libraries, Carnegie classifications do not capture the institution's budget and affordability issues. For example, a consortium with many very small schools where some schools grant advanced degrees might get lumped into a higher price category than it would under a more equitable pricing model, such as the FTE model options.

Variations for Public Libraries

In setting prices for public libraries, vendors often use variations on the earlier models that take into account the presence of branch libraries.

- *Cost per person with minimums per branch*: Here, the vendor not only sets a cost per patron served, similar to the cost per student described earlier, but also sets a minimum that will be charged for a branch if the per-patron calculated total is less than the minimum (see Table 14.7 for an example).
- *Internal/remote access*: In some cases, vendors will charge one price for access within the library and a higher price if the library offers remote access to the database (e.g., allowing cardholders to log in from home).
- *Pricing per license*: In this model, each instance of a resource installation has a per-license fee; the more licenses purchased, the less the cost per license. This is somewhat similar to the afore-mentioned simultaneous use model in that each license instance might represent one user.

TABLE 14.7 Public Library: Pricing Model Based on Population and Branches

Population Served	Library Price	Library Minimum per Branch	Consortium Price	Consortium Minimum per Branch
Less than 15,000	$0.063/person	$810.00	$0.06/person	$780
15,001–50,000	$0.055/person	$1,818.25	$0.05/person	$1,725
50,001–200,000	$0.032/person	$3,872.25	$0.03/person	$3,685
200,001–500,000	$0.024/person	$7,675.50	$0.023/person	$7,290
500,001–1,000,000	$0.017/person	$14,847.25	$0.016/person	$14,125
Greater than 1,000,000	$0.014/person	$21,280.00	$0.013/person	$20,260

Variations for Consortia

When consortia negotiate with vendors on behalf of their members, they may negotiate a per-library price using one of the earlier models. However, in some cases, vendors will offer a consortia-based pricing model.

- *Percentage of participating total FTE*: This model has become quite rare. A consortium will be given a total cost for all subscribers. The consortium will total the enrollment of the purchasing libraries and then calculate a percentage of the whole for each participant based on their enrollment.
- *Per-site equal share*: This model is often used where one price applies to an eBook collection or other one-time purchases. It is dependent on having solid participation commitments from member libraries. If a library were to initially commit to participate and then later withdraw, it would raise the cost for all the other libraries, possibly triggering further shifts in participation or causing the deal to collapse altogether. Thus, this model is very dependent on strong collaborative commitments.

Custom Quotes

In many cases, the vendor will offer a librarian a custom quote. This all-too-common approach is not a model because the pricing is not transparent. What librarians and consortia directors seek is transparency in pricing so that the model can easily be explained to administrators who hold the purse strings of the library budget. Custom quotes are typically opaque; however, with a thorough negotiation approach, one might be able to uncover enough information to shed light on how a custom quote is calculated for a particular vendor, thus raising the veil on why a resource costs a given amount.

Price Predictability

Effective pricing models are key to streamlining the acquisition process for electronic resources. Librarians and their consortia want discounts and savings, but they equally want price predictability. Librarians need to be able to predict costs and plan their annual acquisitions budgets accordingly. Unlike custom quotes, transparent pricing models facilitate a librarian's or consortium's ability to easily determine the cost of a resource and make collection decisions (see Box 14.1 for an example).

Box 14.1 Activity: Determining eResource Pricing

JSTOR, a popular vendor for eJournals, provides a transparent and easy-to-use price calculator on their website. Go to http://purchase.jstor.org/quotecart. Complete the information on that Web page, and it will lead to http://purchase.jstor.org/quotecart/products.php, where a collection can be selected with its cost (it does not factor in consortial discounts). Also, note that for academic libraries, JSTOR uses the earlier broad Carnegie classifications to allocate pricing; smaller libraries or those that fall outside the standard Carnegie classifications would be better off calling a JSTOR representative for a quote.

Other vendors, such as the large database aggregators, have a very large set of wildly different resources, so for those vendors, offering a pricing calculator like JSTOR's would be a significant challenge. In the meantime, libraries need their consortia precisely for vendors like these (and other less-diversified vendors) to help bring order from the chaos that is electronic resource pricing.

A final note about the pricing of eResources is that it is very elastic. Prices can be unpredictable from year to year. eResources are unlike almost any other commodity, with higher-than-average inflation rates and often a lack of transparency. Multiple-year licenses help libraries and consortia ameliorate this, as does pricing transparency.

THE ROLE OF CONSORTIA IN PRICING

Because of their added clout and economy of scale, consortia can often arrange lower prices for member libraries. At one time it was assumed that the greater number of libraries licensing a resource, the lower the price, but in today's consortial marketplace, that is not a given. Discounts may be applied because consortia bring an economy of scale in a number of ways, such as consolidated ordering, invoicing, or licensing. In addition, with the growth of geographically unbound consortia with large numbers of libraries, vendors have become more reluctant to increase discounts based solely on the number of subscribing or purchasing libraries. For example, if a consortium can provide the added value of consolidated invoicing or licensing, then other discounts might be negotiable, as these save vendors valuable time and effort.

As discussed in Chapter 5, consortia can be organized in a number of different ways. Thus, pricing may vary from consortium to consortium:

- *All-in purchasing*: Some consortia are organized to acquire resources for all their libraries. This will most likely occur where the consortium is made up of like library types, for example, a consortium of research libraries. It can also occur in a consortium that has a tightly knit collaborative collection development program.

- *Opt-in purchasing*: In these consortia, the consortium negotiates a deal with the vendor, and librarians can decide whether their library will participate in the purchase. This has become more common as central funding for consortial acquisitions has diminished. Opt-in purchasing complicates negotiation for pricing because the consortium cannot predict the number of orders that will be placed for any given resource. If a clear pricing model is in place, negotiation will take place over the amounts that will be used to calculate final costs, such as cost per tier or factors for matrix pricing.

In addition to negotiating reasonable prices for the current year, consortia may be able to negotiate "price caps," or agreed-upon limits to future price increases, to provide price predictability. These promised annual increases may be lower than those that librarians can negotiate for an individual library. It should be noted that these price caps may still outpace the rate of inflation and place an unsustainable budget burden on libraries, a burden that consortia work hard to ameliorate.

Librarians expect a speedy response from their consortia when they are doing their acquisitions and considering a variety of electronic resources to acquire. They assume that the consortium can go to the vendor and obtain a price quickly and transparently. With clear price models in hand, the acquisitions process is streamlined for both the consortium when it groups and places a large number of orders, and for the librarian, who can quickly obtain a price.

Librarians should keep in mind that a consortium is a neutral partner in the acquisition process. Consortia that negotiate a large number of eResource offers must try to treat all vendors equally. When a library purchases a resource directly, it will follow its usual criteria for selection and evaluate each product accordingly. As a neutral party, the consortium will most likely negotiate the best price and terms, but will not apply selection criteria or quality evaluation on each resource it offers. While it will seek to offer only quality resources, by offering a plethora of products, the consortium enables the local librarian the opportunity to compare and contrast similar resources, and apply the evaluation criteria most relevant to the library's needs when making any purchase or subscription decision.

LICENSE TERMS AND CONDITIONS

The license between the library and the vendor determines the terms and conditions that govern the relationship for a particular resource or set of resources. The area of license terms and conditions is important and time consuming for both librarians and vendors alike. Librarians need lawyer-like skills to decipher vendor licenses.

Over the years, consortial groups like the NorthEast Research Libraries Consortium and California Digital Library have developed model licenses to serve as templates for license term negotiation. The most recent model license to emerge was generated by the Center for Research Libraries in November 2014. This model updates an earlier version and reflects what consortia have learned from their negotiations since the late 1990s. There is also the Shared Electronic Resource Understanding (SERU) from NISO, the National Information Standards Organization, which is a "handshake agreement" that takes the approach that copyright law prevails just as it did in the print environment, and thus no actual license needs to be signed by both parties. Unfortunately, most publishers and librarians have not adopted SERU.

Box 14.2 Key Considerations in eResource Licensing

1. *Authorized users*: This determines who is eligible to use the resource and can be specific to the type of library. For academic libraries, authorized users are typically full- and part-time students, full- and part-time faculty, full- and part-time staff, and walk-in users. For public libraries, it could include registered patrons (i.e., library cardholders), walk-in patrons, and other persons affiliated with the institution. In a hospital library setting, the authorized users may be limited to physicians only or might also include nurses and other associated medical staff. In a special library, such as a research institute or corporate library, the authorized users may be restricted to research staff and employees; walk-ins would not be authorized users.
2. *Means of access*: IP authentication is the most common form of authentication for access. For libraries that offer off-site access, the license should stipulate whether authentication services such as Shibboleth or Athens are permitted.
3. *Concurrent use*: Unlimited use is the norm, but use may be restricted to a "number of seats" to cap user access.
4. *ADA compliance*: The vendor should commit to compliance with the Americans with Disabilities Act (ADA) to ensure equal access for patrons with disabilities. One way to confirm compliance is to see whether they have completed a Voluntary Product Accessibility Template indicating compliance with federal Section 508 standards on technology accessibility (United States Access Board 2015).
5. *Filtering software*: Some libraries, particularly school and public libraries, need to restrict access to obscene content in order to comply with the Children's Internet Protection Act. The license should allow for the use of technology protection measures in such instances.
6. *Remote access*: Remote access is standard in licenses for academic libraries, but may be an issue in public libraries if the vendor also licenses a resource to the consumer market (e.g., genealogy databases). To reduce competition with that consumer sector, it may not permit remote access to the library's instance of the resource.
7. *Interlibrary loan*: The license should stipulate whether interlibrary loan is allowed and by which means (e.g., print, fax, secure electronic transmission, or simple electronic transfer).
8. *Course packs and reserves*: In academic libraries, the license should state whether material can be included in course packs and reserves.
9. *Copying*: The license should state whether patrons can print, e-mail, and/or download materials and whether there are limits as to quantity.
10. *Fair use*: The vendor should acknowledge fair use rights.
11. *Cancellation*: The license should state what happens if a library cancels a subscription, in particular whether it is granted post-cancellation perpetual use rights and, if so, to what content. For multiyear eJournal package licenses, it should include a budget hardship opt-out clause.
12. *Governing law*: The governing law should be that of the state where the institution is located or the license should "remain silent" (i.e., not specifically say).
13. *Usage statistics*: The license should state whether usage statistics are available and whether they are compliant with COUNTER, a joint initiative by librarians, consortia, and vendors to standardize eResource usage statistics.
14. *Mobile access*: The license should state whether the vendor provides a no-cost mobile device app for access to the resource or if this will be an additional cost.

Although this chapter will not analyze specific model licenses, Box 14.2 highlights key parts of a license. Librarians should pay particular attention to these areas in a negotiation in order to ensure that license terms meet the needs of their patrons (for more guidance, see Dygert and Langendorfer 2014; Lemley, Britton, and Li 2011).

An additional concern that arises when considering license terms is that of confidentiality. Some vendors will include a nondisclosure clause governing the discussion of the cost of the resource. The International Coalition of Library Consortia opposes this practice. Its "Statement of Current Perspective and Preferred Practices for the Selection and Purchase of Electronic Information: Update No. 2, Pricing and Economics" (2004) states, "Non-disclosure language should not be required for any licensing agreement, particularly language that would preclude library consortia from sharing pricing and other significant terms and conditions with other consortia." The more librarians are able to communicate with one another about vendor offers, the better they are able to weigh the costs and benefits of any individual offer. An open market will result in better licensing terms.

One of the consequences of removing nondisclosure clauses might be further standardization of pricing across the marketplace. Such standardization eliminates the possibility of negotiating a unique price point that fits the specific circumstances of a particular library or consortium. Libraries and consortia are different from one another, and if a standard pricing model does not address the needs of a certain institution or consortium, then the only room for negotiation will be in other non-price-related areas. These other areas might include perpetual post-cancellation access rights, fewer digital rights management restrictions (e.g., more liberal download quantity allowances or the use of content on multiple devices), or a multiyear contract to increase price predictability.

NEGOTIATION: AN OVERVIEW

Negotiation is a skill that every selection, acquisitions, or eResources librarian should acquire. In order to gain the most leverage for the library and its users, librarians often need to negotiate optimal terms with vendors (or turn to a trusted consortium to do the negotiation, but even then, it is helpful to understand the approach the consortium representative will take).

Essentially, negotiation:

1. is a basic means for getting what one wants from others,
2. occurs when there are differences between the needs of the buyer and seller, and
3. is a "back-and-forth," "give-and-take" process which often involves a "compromise," a settlement in which each side gives something up in order to gain something else.

In eResource licensing, there are typically two things that are being negotiated:

- *Pricing negotiation* seeks to reach equilibrium between what the vendor charges and what libraries are willing to pay.
- *License negotiation* seeks to reach equilibrium between the ideal terms for the library and the ideal terms for the vendor.

Box 14.3 provides examples of circumstances when a library and a vendor might negotiate on price and license terms.

Box 14.3 Negotiation Scenarios

Here are some examples of negotiations a librarian might come across in the context of different types of resources. If the library is part of a consortium, the consortium may report they are experiencing such scenarios and attempting to deal with them in a way that is most beneficial for their libraries:

- *Budget crisis*: Most academic library budgets are static or declining due to the inability to keep pace with inflation. According to a 2012 study by ARL, which represents what were historically the most well-funded academic libraries, "the percentage of university funds allocated to academic libraries shrank for the 14th straight year in 2009, dipping below 2 percent for the first time" (Kolowich 2012). The report goes on to state that this downward trend is applicable to both public and private universities in the United States. This fact is used as leverage in negotiating eResource renewals or for offers of new products. Many librarians are faced with unsustainable budget circumstances, where the only option is to cancel something else in order to acquire something new, or to renew something with an inflation rate that outpaces budget increases. If faced with the option of no sale and no revenue (or a cancellation), a vendor may be more flexible on pricing and terms.
- *Past concessions*: Librarians can compare a vendor's current position with concessions they have made in past negotiations in order to explore what can be sustained for future offers. One consortium did this successfully with an eBook offer. Small school pricing was negotiated at a time when the vendor was new to the consortial market; as their product matured, their pricing changed, but for the good of the relationship, they maintained historic pricing that allowed smaller schools to stay in the deal.
- *Access fees*: Many eResource purchases, particularly purchases of archival collections or back files, are purchases in name only. Many vendors charge ongoing annual access fees in order to maintain these collections and, in some instances, to update them annually with new content. These access fees may be reasonably priced, but even so, they collectively add up to a new burden on library budgets. Despite a "purchase," the library is saddled with annual access fees that from a budgetary perspective look much like annual subscription fees. When negotiating such purchases, librarians can try to get these fees reduced or incrementally reduced over time to help provide the library some price predictability and sustainability.

Approaches to Negotiation

Librarians benefit from deciding at the outset which of two approaches to negotiation to employ: adversarial or relationship based. The adversarial approach views the negotiation as a win–lose proposition. This approach can lead to a better result for a difficult pricing negotiation initially, but it tends to burn bridges in the relationship with the other party. Librarians should keep in mind the long view; in most cases, librarians and vendor representatives are in a long-term business relationship. If the librarian batters the vendor into submission one year, the next time a renewal comes up, he or she is not likely to have a successful negotiation.

If librarians want to obtain short-term goals, such as a good price, but also want to build the foundation of a positive long-term relationship so that they feel assured of access to a resource at a reasonable cost with reasonable terms in the future, a better approach to negotiation is the relationship-based "win–win" approach. This approach is built on relationships and constructive compromise. The classic book advocating this approach to negotiation is *Getting to Yes*, by Roger Fisher, William Ury, and Bruce Patton (2011). Box 14.4 outlines the basic principles of "win–win" negotiation in the context of licensing electronic resources.

Box 14.4 Win–Win Negotiation Strategies

1. Prepare for your negotiation.
   a. Determine your objectives.
   b. Set a timetable.
   c. Assemble a team if you are working with others.
   d. Develop a strategy, such as who takes a lead in the negotiation and what roles other team members might play.
2. Do your homework.
   a. Research the vendor, the product, the price model, and license terms and conditions ahead of time.
   b. Know the hierarchy of the power structure of the vendor's sales force so that you can work with someone with decision-making authority.
   c. Know your vendor's desired timeline and know that you may be able to extract concessions if they are time constrained to "get a deal" (this is often related to time-based sales targets, much like one might see in other industries).
3. Be a good listener.
4. Aim high. Do not be afraid to ask for your ideal solution.
5. Be patient.
   a. Spell out what you expect to achieve in the negotiation so that you can frame the negotiation with the vendor from the start.
   b. Do not accept the first offer.
   c. Do not negotiate against yourself!
   d. Focus on the other side's point of view.
   e. Seek transparency.
6. Be willing to meet in the middle.
   a. Make sure both parties are satisfied.
   b. Do not make unilateral concessions; always ask for a concession in return for making any concession to your negotiating partner.
   c. Successful negotiators consider it a good process when each side walks away with the feeling that they obtained 70 percent of what they set out to achieve.
7. If the negotiation is heading toward failure, be willing to walk away.
   a. Have a plan B. Is there an alternate product or vendor you can work with instead?
8. Do not allow your perception of the vendor representative's personal behavior to deter your focus away from your original goals in the negotiation. In other words, do not take things personally.
9. Use data to support your negotiating position.
10. Have a sense of humor! Nothing eases tensions and builds relationship as well as techniques that engender a relaxed atmosphere of trust.
11. Be easy to work with and always highlight what you are doing to help your vendor partner. Library vendors are people who have jobs to do too, and when you offer to help them with a need that they have, they will often move heaven and earth to thank you for your assistance.

Another nuance to negotiation is stated by Michael Wheeler (2013) of the Harvard Business School. In some ways, negotiation is like jazz: it can go in many different directions and is never predictable. The most successful negotiators are those that can improvise. Such negotiators use cleverness, an ability to turn a problem inside-out, a sense of humor, and an ability to stick to a theme while allowing the process to take its course. Real-world examples include diplomats like Richard Holbrooke, who negotiated the Balkans peace agreement in the late 1990s, or George Mitchell, who negotiated peace in Northern Ireland. Such negotiations are truly much more difficult than a license negotiation, but the elements for success are the same: a win–win approach coupled with an ability to see the other party's position and improvise to get to a mutual goal. In some instances, this might mean that neither party's first or second option is reached, but both parties can agree on a new, unforeseen third option.

Looking at negotiation in the context of consortia reveals some examples of these practices. In the early days of consortia (discussed in more detail in Chapter 5), when there were more centrally funded all-in consortia, such as legislatively funded statewide consortia purchasing on behalf of every library in their state, the win–lose approach was often used with some success. Vendors wanted the large pot of money represented by such a consortium, and they knew going into the process that the consortium could deliver all the libraries at once. This level of certainty up front made the stakes clearer and the negotiation more direct.

However, since the recession that began in 2008, there has been a great deal of consortial consolidation and a greater instance of opt-in consortial deals, where individual libraries can elect whether to subscribe to a resource offered by the consortium, leading to uncertainty about how many libraries will actually purchase a resource. With shrunken library budgets and severely diminished central funding (where it existed in the first place), the options are more limited than before. As a result, consortia often need a more nuanced approach, where the consortium acknowledges the risks of an eResource offer not obtaining significant pickup initially, yet wants to convince the vendor that such an offer is worth the risk. The vendor appreciates that the consortium can provide it an opening to new markets (i.e., libraries not reached by their perhaps-limited sales force) and also needs to acknowledge that it might take two or three years for enough libraries to sign up to produce increased revenue results. In turn, the consortium agrees to help the vendor market its resources while still obtaining the best possible terms for its libraries.

This scenario calls for the win–win negotiation approach noted earlier. Relationship building is key to having the ability to make ongoing offers from multiple vendors available to a consortium's libraries. A strong relationship assures both the consortium and its libraries that, even with turnover in a vendor's sales or marketing force, or with turnover in consortial staff, the business relationship will persist and be sustainable over time.

When to Walk Away

Negotiations usually go well, but there are times when a librarian should walk away. The following list provides some examples but is by no means comprehensive. Poor communication or an inability to even begin to understand each party's positions can lead to a walkaway scenario. Here are some other more specific examples:

- *Unreasonable price increases*: A for-profit business always seeks to grow faster than the rate of inflation, but if a vendor cannot justify a price increase and provide some transparency to substantiate that increase, librarians should consider walking away from the deal. For example, if a resource increases three times its previous price, it is time to renegotiate or find an alternative product.
- *No interlibrary loan or e-reserve rights*: In an electronic environment, accessibility and sharing is natural and expected. This right is increasingly granted by most vendors as compared with the early years of site licensing, but if it is not, librarians should reconsider licensing the product.
- *Restricted list of authorized users*: Librarians want to provide online resource access to their remote users as well as to walk-in users. Both of these should be included with any license. On a similar note, some academic institutions want to offer alumni access and should be sure to ask for that class of users to be included; this is not typical in licenses, but has become more prevalent in recent years.

SPECIAL CIRCUMSTANCES FOR NEGOTIATION

Negotiations can vary for different types of resources or packages. There are nuances to an eJournal negotiation that are different from those for a database or aggregations of databases. Likewise, there are numerous approaches to eBooks that vary from subscription packages to patron-driven acquisition to outright purchase of collections, and the negotiation of access rights, terms, and costs can be quite different. eJournal packages provide a good example of these complexities.

eJournal packages have always been an area of concern for librarians. In the "big deal," a library is granted access to a large number of titles from a particular publisher. In these packages, title usage is typically very high for a core set of titles, but then trails off into a long tail of lower-use titles. Some librarians object to paying for all the lower-use titles in order to get access to the higher-use titles. However, by packaging these titles into more or less standard packages, publishers say they are able to reduce their title management overhead and costs, and they pass savings to libraries in the form of discounted package costs with reduced annual price increases. Also, for most of these packages, staff in large research libraries and consortia will negotiate multiyear contracts in exchange for reduced annual increases and better overall terms.

Publishers argue that many journals actually lose money and that the reason some journals are priced so high is that they are subsidizing the financial "losers" in the portfolio. Those "money-losing" titles might be inherently valued niche titles representing certain disciplines (e.g., certain humanities titles as compared with prestigious science and technology titles), thus the publisher cannot cease publication or sale of those journals. Also, many publishers act as third parties to help publish and distribute professional society titles or university press titles that would otherwise lack marketing clout and reach, and they need to absorb the cost of that business arrangement through the redistribution of pricing to provide the necessary subsidization. At the same time, librarians perceive some publishers as perpetuating extraordinary price increases for some of these titles, which often complicates ongoing negotiations and the sustainability of related offers.

For some libraries, especially smaller and mid-sized academic libraries, the big deal may work well. For other libraries, especially large research libraries, it tends to be viewed as problematic. Individual libraries need to weigh the advantages and disadvantages of the eJournal packages in making a decision whether to subscribe. In a consortial context, the big deal poses a negotiating conundrum since there are clearly advantages and disadvantages to the model. Plus, consortia that agree to such a multiyear package are making a significant financial commitment on behalf of their libraries, and they need to be sure that it is sustainable and fair over the full number of years covered by the contract.

Thus, the big deal provides an opportunity to exercise one's negotiation skills to the maximum. While it is a challenge, it is also an opportunity to be creative and offers options that the vendor might not have anticipated, but that might be beneficial to the overall goals of the deal. Consortia can obtain significant discounts for their libraries in such instances, but they have to be consultative with the libraries and provide clear communication of the advantages and consequences of such deals to assure that they are acceptable and sustainable over time.

FINAL THOUGHTS

Whether one is negotiating directly with a vendor or is part of a consortium that negotiates on the library's behalf, the lessons in this chapter are relevant. It is essential for librarians to gain an understanding of the library acquisitions landscape and hone their negotiation skills.

The marketplace is dynamic, and librarians can obtain better value and more "bang for the buck" by studying the marketplace and knowing the options and vendors well. Librarians should read the literature, such as the *Charleston Advisor*, to obtain honest reviews of potential eResource acquisitions. In addition, they can attend conferences such as the Charleston Conference or Electronic Resources and Libraries to hear industry leaders speak and to discuss the latest trends in the field. Librarians can also work with colleagues or a consortium to offer local workshops or events that help guide colleagues in the navigation of this complex acquisitions arena.

If a library is a member of a consortium, librarians should participate in its governance or committees and take advantage of the opportunity to learn and contribute. Librarians should judge the consortium critically and not be afraid to challenge the terms of a consortial offer if they have insights that could improve the benefit of that offer for member libraries. Librarians who are active in scholarly communication, online discussions, or publications should share their expertise and insights with their consortium, such as by offering workshops or participating in discussion panels to share with their colleagues the latest thinking on the shifting licensing environment.

A common tendency among librarians is to want to avoid being "tainted" by the wheeling and dealing of the greater business world. It is easy to view libraries as somewhat sheltered idealistic havens that preserve knowledge and have a higher purpose than that of the day-to-day business world. However, as noted in this chapter, in this new electronic resource environment, the most successful path to effective collection development and provision of library services will be one where a thorough grasp of the library business marketplace is employed. Knowing how the business works, the meaning of license terms, who in the hierarchy of library vendors to talk to, and what forces are driving the greater marketplace are all are keys to success.

REFERENCES

California Digital Library. 2015. "Licensing Toolkit." Updated April 30. http://www.cdlib.org/services/collections/toolkit/.

Center for Research Libraries. 2014. "LIBLICENSE: Licensing Digital Content." http://liblicense.crl.edu/licensing-information/model-license/.

Charleston Advisor: Critical Reviews of Web Products for Information Professionals. 1999–. Denver: The Charleston Advisor. Quarterly. http://www.charlestonco.com/index.php. [subscription required for full access]

Charleston Conference. http://www.charlestonlibraryconference.com/.

"Classification Description." 2015. The Carnegie Classification of Institutions of Higher Education. Accessed October 4. http://carnegieclassifications.iu.edu/descriptions/basic.php.

COUNTER. http://projectcounter.org/.

Dygert, Claire, and Jeanne M. Langendorfer. 2014. "Fundamentals of E-Resource Licensing." *The Serials Librarian* 66 (1–4): 289–97.

Electronic Resources and Libraries. http://www.electroniclibrarian.com/.

Fisher, Roger, William Ury, and Bruce Patton. 2011. *Getting to Yes: Negotiating Agreement without Giving In*, 3rd ed. New York: Penguin.

International Coalition of Library Consortia. 2004. "Statement of Current Perspective and Preferred Practices for the Selection and Purchase of Electronic Information: Update No. 2, Pricing and Economics." http://icolc.net/statement/statement-current-perspective-and-preferred-practices-selection-and-purchase-electronic.

Kolowich, Steve. 2012. "Smaller Servings for Libraries." *Insider Higher Ed.* February 21. https://www.insidehighered.com/news/2012/02/21/library-budgets-continue-shrink-relative-university-spending.

Lemley, Trey, Robert M. Britton, and Jie Li. 2011. "Negotiating Your License." *Journal of Electronic Resources in Medical Libraries* 8 (4): 325–38.

National Information Standards Organization. 2015. "Shared Electronic Resource Understanding." http://www.niso.org/workrooms/seru.

NorthEast Research Libraries Consortium. 2012. "Model License." http://nerl.org/nerl-documents/nerl-model-license.

United States Access Board. 2015. "Background." Accessed October 4. http://www.access-board.gov/guidelines-and-standards/communications-and-it/about-the-section-508-standards/background.

Wheeler, Michael. 2013. *The Art of Negotiation: How to Improvise Agreement in a Chaotic World.* New York: Simon and Schuster.

SUGGESTED READINGS

Ashmore, Beth, Jill E. Grogg, and Jeff Weddle. 2012. *The Librarian's Guide to Negotiation: Winning Strategies for the Digital Age.* Medford, NJ: Information Today.

The authors provide a practical guide to win–win negotiation for a variety of circumstances. In addition to vendor negotiations, chapters address the role of consortia, the big deal, and negotiation with funding sources, administrators, and patron communities.

Dygert, Claire, and Robert Van Rennes. 2015. "Building Your Licensing and Negotiation Skills Toolkit." *The Serials Librarian* 68 (1–4): 17–25.

The authors outline the elements of a license and provide advice for novice negotiators.

Fisher, Roger, William Ury, and Bruce Patton. 2011. *Getting to Yes: Negotiating Agreement without Giving In*, 3rd ed. New York: Penguin.

Now in its third edition, this book is the classic on win–win negotiation.

Gruenberg, Michael L. 2014. *Buying and Selling Information: A Guide for Information Professionals and Salespeople to Build Mutual Success*. Medford, NJ: Information Today.

Written by an experienced vendor representative, this book explores negotiation from the standpoint of both vendors and librarians. It is recommended not only for the advice it offers librarians, but also for the insights into vendor perspectives.

Johnson, Peggy. 2013. *Developing and Managing Electronic Collections: The Essentials*. Chicago: ALA Editions.

In addition to licensing and negotiation, Johnson addresses eResources budgeting, evaluation, selection, and management. Each chapter includes an extensive bibliography.

Wheeler, Michael. 2013. *The Art of Negotiation: How to Improvise Agreement in a Chaotic World*. New York: Simon and Schuster.

Although not written specifically for librarians, Wheeler's practical advice on negotiation is applicable to many situations, including eResource licensing.

Chapter 15

Search Strategies for Online Resources

Melissa A. Wong

INTRODUCTION

Early online databases utilized complex search and retrieval systems, and individual researchers, for the most part, did not have the time or inclination to learn the necessary codes and formulas for successful searching. In addition, because the companies that provided these early databases charged for each search conducted as well as the number of minutes spent in the database, librarians were reluctant to give access to novice searchers who could quickly rack up considerable charges with inefficient searching. As a result, the use of early information retrieval systems was limited to trained and experienced reference librarians.

In time, these early mediated systems developed end-user versions that could be easily searched by individuals without specialized training. Now, the large majority of these databases have migrated to the Web, and there has been a vast expansion of the world of end-user searching far beyond the scope of local workstations and far beyond the walls of the reference room. In place of highly structured search command languages, most of these services provide a point-and-click interface with a "fill in the box" search window designed for easy searching by the end user. These point-and-click interfaces resemble Web search engines such as *Google* and *Yahoo!*. Results are displayed on the screen for review, and with a few more clicks, very often the user will be connected to the full text of the source online, ready to be read, downloaded, imported into the user's own database, or printed.

One consequence of the change in the primary audience for electronic resources is a change in the way reference librarians use their expertise and understanding of databases. A few years ago, their role was to serve as an intermediary between the complex database search system and the person needing the information. Now it is to serve as coach and tutor for the end user conducting the search. Another critical role is to guide the user to the appropriate information resource.

In any of these roles, an understanding of the concepts and mechanics of information retrieval is essential for reference librarians. It can be argued that it is more important to fully understand a search system when one is a coach because of the consequences of an error. If, as an experienced searcher, one misremembers a feature, the resulting search failure is readily apparent and can be corrected immediately. If one makes a similar error as a coach, the inexperienced user may never realize the error or the implications of the error, never understanding why the search failed.

This chapter examines the deep structure of databases and explains the concepts and mechanics of information retrieval. In addition, because librarians increasingly use free Internet sources for reference work, the chapter presents strategies for effectively searching the Web.

TYPES OF DATABASES

Many types of databases can be in libraries, including catalogs, indexes and abstracts, eJournal collections, and reference tools. Although similar search strategies can be used in all types of online resources, librarians should understand the different content found in these resources.

Catalogs

A *catalog*, sometimes referred to as an *online public access catalog, OPAC*, or *online catalog*, lists items available in a library's collection, including their location, call number, and circulation status (whether they are checked out or available). In addition to books, the catalog will list videos, music, audiobooks, and other materials. The catalog may list the periodicals a library subscribes to, although it will not list specific articles within a publication. In addition to maintaining a local catalog, libraries may participate in a regional, statewide, and/or national catalog, all of which exist to identify the materials available within specific libraries. Catalogs are discussed in more detail in Chapter 16.

Indexes and Abstracts

An *index* is a database that lists the contents of periodicals, and sometimes other types of publications, such as conference proceedings and book chapters, in order to provide access to articles by author, title, and subject. If the database also contains short summaries of the articles, called abstracts, it is technically called an *abstract*; however, in reality, the term "index" is often used to refer to any database that is primarily intended to provide subject access to the contents of periodicals.

Because of the space limitations of the print format, indexes traditionally contained only the bibliographic record for an item. However, now that indexes are primarily offered via the Web, they may offer not only citations and abstracts, but also the full text of articles. These are often referred to as *full-text databases*, although they may not contain the full text of all the indexed articles due to copyright restrictions.

Indexes are created by commercial companies and sold to libraries, thus they reflect materials available somewhere in the bibliographic universe, not the holdings of a specific library. This can confuse patrons, since an index available on the library's Web page may list articles in journals not available at the library where the patron is searching.

Indexes typically cover a specific subject area. For example, *America: History and Life* indexes journals on the history of the United States and Canada, while *PsycINFO* covers literature in psychology and the behavioral and social sciences. In addition, indexes can be aimed at a particular audience. For example, both *PubMed* and *Consumer Health Complete* provide coverage in the area of health and medicine, but *PubMed* is intended for physicians and biomedical researchers and indexes scholarly journals, while *Consumer Health Complete* is aimed at patients and caregivers and contains encyclopedia and magazine articles, book chapters, and videos. Indexes are discussed in more detail in Chapter 17.

eJournal Collections

The term "eJournal" may be used to describe a journal that is published only online, but usually refers to any online access to articles from any type of periodical, including journals, magazines, or trade publications. So, although somewhat of a misnomer to librarians who understand the differences in types of periodicals, the term "eJournal" is often used for electronic access to any kind of periodical.

Libraries have access to eJournals in many ways. In some cases, libraries subscribe to individual eJournal titles or bundles of titles directly from the publisher and access the contents of titles through the publisher's website. In other cases, libraries subscribe to an eJournal collection like *JSTOR*, which pulls together content from multiple publishers. Open-access efforts have also provided online access to journal literature through single-title websites, collections of open-access titles like *PLOS*, and repositories for individual articles like *PubMed Central*.

Reference Tools

Libraries also provide access to a wide range of reference tools in online formats, including encyclopedias, dictionaries, and collections like *Credo* and *Oxford Reference*. These resources, many of which are discussed in detail in Chapters 18–28, can be free or subscription based, and vary widely in their content. What they all have in common is that they are databases that can be searched by patrons and librarians in order to locate information.

STRUCTURE OF ONLINE DATABASES

Regardless of content, a *database* is a set of information items, called *entries*, formatted into defined structures with additional elements designed to assist retrieval. An entry can be a basic bibliographic citation with the authors' names and the source; it can be an enhanced citation including subject headings and abstracts, or it can be the full text of an article or report. In addition to text, entries can be media items such as photos, musical selections, or video clips.

Each element of an entry, such as the author's name or the title of the work, is assigned to a *field*. Fields are defined, organized, and labeled according to the rules of the database. Typically, each field has a particular format for the elements within it. For example, an author's name is likely to be structured with the surname first, followed by a comma and some elements of the forenames. This structure for names is ubiquitous, appearing in the telephone directory, personal address books, endnotes, and the like. The more formal term for the kinds of structures and elements used to organize and index information is "metadata."

The term "metadata" is defined as "data about data" or "data associated with data." People encounter, use, manipulate, and create metadata many times a day every day. One example is seen in the organization and arrangement of the daily newspaper. Each part of the newspaper is assigned to a section and, in the world of print, a page. Online, articles are grouped into browsable categories such as "Local News," and each article has a particular URL. The section is a metadata element, as is the page number. These metadata elements are shown in the "What's Inside" index that newspapers put on the front page. In the case of a newspaper where the full text is online, this index is more likely displayed as a menu along the top or left side of the newspaper's website. Each article is composed of many elements, and each element has a role to play in the display, arrangement, and retrieval of the article. For example, pieces of metadata are attached to the headline. Some of it drives the display so that the headline appears in a larger, bolder font than the body of the article. Hidden elements of the headline metadata allow the newspaper's users to search for words in the headline and retrieve the needed article.

In the robust online databases found in libraries, the kinds and roles of metadata grow in complexity. This database design with metadata elements is the result of very deliberate decisions by database producers and has consequences for searching. Figure 15.1 shows a made-up example of how a typical entry from a telephone directory could be structured in a database. From this simple example, one can see the kind of decision making that is required to build a database with enough structure for it to be functional. The developers have to anticipate all the forms of the information and take into account all the possible variations.

Field labels allow for three essential tasks: sorting, formatting, and searching. The sorting can be imagined as a series of sets of slots. Each record will be sent through the appropriate slot at each level for further sorting. At each level, the sorting becomes finer. For example, in print directories, the initial sort would be

Record Number:	qs122333
Record Type:	residential
Surname:	Hunkle
Forename:	Walter
Middle Initial:	A
Title:	DDS
Street:	123 Maple Avenue
City:	Hometown
State:	NE
Telephone:	555-123-4567

FIGURE 15.1 Sample database entry

at the record type, which determines the segment of the directory; the second level would be alphabetical by surname; the third level would be alphabetical by forename; and so on. Decisions about how to deal with compound surnames or hyphenated forenames would be built into the sorting software. In a print source, the arrangement of entries is static; in an online database, entries can be sorted dynamically, depending on the needs of the user. In the earlier example, results could be displayed by name or by address.

Once the records are sorted, the field labels would be used to determine formatting. In a print directory, the name of a person or organization might be in bold, at the furthest left place in the column. Additional information, such as an address and phone number, might be set in lighter typeface and indented under the name. In an online database, the title of an article might appear at the top of the record in bold, with the author, source, and date of publication appearing underneath in a smaller typeface.

Finally, correctly populated fields of metadata enable accurate searching. When searching for a name in a print directory, users will first turn to the correct section of the directory, then search alphabetically, trusting that the entries are displayed in the correct order. In an online database, metadata allows one to search within specific fields, so one can search for books authored by Malala Yousafzai, rather than books about her (or vice versa).

When applied to a database of bibliographic citations, this database-building process becomes very complex. Even a very basic metadata structure within an index has to deal with the huge variety of names, journal titles, languages, abbreviations, volume and issue numbering, and pagination. All of the relevant data elements must have a field that supports their form. For example, ISSN numbers need to be 8 characters long, ISBN numbers 10 (or 13, depending on the date of the item). To be of more use, the database structure must be explicitly built and labeled to support subject headings, descriptors, identifiers, and other elements that can also be added to the record. These elements are usually the results of human indexing.

Raising Cultural Awareness in the English Language Classroom

Frank, Jerrold

English Teaching Forum, v51 n4 p2-11, 35 2013

This article discusses how teachers can incorporate cultural knowledge into English language classes, exploring elements of culture, intercultural phenomena, and high-context and low-context cultures. Activities offered by the author to raise cultural awareness include web quests, role plays, cultural observations, and culture journals.

Descriptors: Second Language Instruction, English (Second Language), Cultural Awareness, Language Teachers, Consciousness Raising, Cultural Context, Learning Activities, Teaching Methods, Web Sites, Computer Uses in Education, Role Playing, Observation, Journal Writing

US Department of State. Bureau of Educational and Cultural Affairs, Office of English Language Programs, SA-5, 2200 C Street NW 4th Floor, Washington, DC 20037. e-mail: etforum@state.gov; Web site: http://www.forum.state.gov

Download full text

ERIC Number: EJ1020809

Record Type: Journal

Publication Date: 2013

Pages: 11

Abstractor: As Provided

Reference Count: 16

ISBN: N/A

ISSN: ISSN-1559-663X

Publication Type: Journal Articles; Reports - Descriptive

Education Level: N/A

Audience: Teachers

Language: English

Sponsor: N/A

Authoring Institution: N/A

Identifiers: N/A

FIGURE 15.2 Sample entry from *ERIC*

Figure 15.2 shows a sample database entry. Some metadata fields, such as those for the descriptors, record type, and language, are labeled, while others, such as the article's title and author, are not.

THE ROLE OF THE SEARCH ENGINE AND INTERFACE

A database is a collection of information in the form of metadata. To be searchable, an online database needs a *search engine* that determines how search queries will be handled. Although the term search engine is usually used to describe tools that search the free Web, such as *Google* and *Bing*, any electronic database with a search feature could be said to have a search engine. In addition, since the goal of database vendors is to create a product that can be searched by a nonexpert, databases are given a search screen, or *interface*, through which users can access the database and determine the search capabilities of the system.

The search engine of a database determines how the database searches metadata to produce a list of results. For example, if a user conducts an author search, the database would search the author field. In addition, most databases will search related fields like those for editors and contributors, in order to create a comprehensive list of a writer's works available in the database. This is why, for example, one can search a catalog for the author "Jared Diamond" and retrieve titles for which he served as author, editor, and contributor.

Every search engine has a *default search* that determines how it handles search queries and displays results. For example, if a user enters a two-word query like "dog training," the default search determines whether the two words are searched separately or as a phrase and whether a word variation like "dogs" would be retrieved.

The interface dictates how search boxes, limiters, and other features display on the screen. Many interfaces offer both a basic search screen with a single search box and an advanced search screen that provides numerous additional options. Interfaces may also offer features designed to make searching easier, such as autocomplete, where the database anticipates the word a user is typing and offers complete search terms, and a "did you mean?" spell-check. The interface will also dictate how results are displayed, such as listing entries in alphabetical, date, or relevance order, and placing facets, recommended search terms, or similar entries near the results list.

In some cases, a vendor creates a unique interface designed to maximize access to content in a specific database. However, interface design is a complex undertaking, and many vendors create a general interface that is used for most of the databases they offer; thus, online resources can look virtually the same but have very different content. This can be confusing for patrons, who may tell the librarian, "I've already searched there" when in fact they have unknowingly searched a different database than the one the librarian is recommending.

SEARCH STRATEGIES FOR DATABASES

In online databases, the fields, data elements, and structure of a database interact with the search engine capabilities in highly specific ways to create information retrieval possibilities. Most of the decisions a searcher makes in the search strategy are made to achieve the appropriate balance between the two aims of information retrieval: precision and recall. *Precision* refers to getting only relevant material. *Recall* refers to getting all the relevant material. In a world where language is unambiguous and indexing is perfect, precision and recall would be the same. But in this world, because language is ambiguous and indexing imperfect, precision and recall are largely incompatible goals. For example, the word "program" is used to represent multiple different concepts. This affects precision because a search on the term "program" for one of these concepts will retrieve unrelated material that refers to other meanings of the term, which thus reduces precision. On the other hand, because of synonyms and changes in terminology over time, there are often a multitude of terms to describe a single concept. Searching for every possible term to achieve perfect recall is a demanding task. As a result, search strategies are a compromise between precision and recall. Whether aiming to improve precision or recall, some of the more important tools librarians can use for effective searching are field searching, controlled vocabulary, Boolean logic, proximity operators, and truncation and wildcards.

Field Searching

Because the individual parts of a record are organized in fields, it is possible to limit a search to a particular field. For example, searching for "Toni Morrison" in the author field of an online catalog will retrieve a list of books authored *by* Morrison, but not books *about* Morrison. Common field searches include author, title, date, language, and type of publication or media. In addition, databases may offer search options specific to a particular type of content. For example, *American National Biography* offers the option to search for people by place of birth or occupation, while *ProQuest Dissertations & Theses Global* has an option to search by advisor.

In most interfaces, the basic search screen offers few to no field search options, while the advanced search screen offers numerous field search options. In addition, when displaying a list of search results, many interfaces now offer the ability to refine one's results by *facets* such as type of publication and date. These facets are really field searches with a new look and name, designed to improve the search experience for novice users. Box 15.1 offers a practice activity using search fields.

Box 15.1 Activity: Using Search Fields

WorldCat is a free database of the holdings of libraries worldwide. Go to *WorldCat* at http://www.worldcat.org and review both the initial search screen and the advanced search screen. Next, try to locate the following:

1. A film version of the ballet *Coppelia*.
2. Spanish-language children's books about soccer.
3. Books about Amish life and culture published within the past five years.

Questions for Reflection and Discussion:

1. What search options are available on the initial search screen?
2. What additional search options are available on the advanced search screen?
3. What search options were most useful to you in the practice searches?
4. When looking at a list of results, what facets did *WorldCat* offer to further refine your search?

Controlled Vocabulary

Catalogs and indexes are meant to provide enhanced access to information resources by allowing users to identify resources on a particular topic. Therefore, records include *subject headings* that describe the content of the item. In theory, the person creating the catalog or index can label the item with any terms he or she wants; however, this would get messy very quickly, as different people choose different terms to describe the same idea (e.g., should the database use the term "Indians," which might be most recognizable to a young child; "Native Americans," the term commonly used in the United States; or "First Nation Peoples," a term used primarily in Canada?). Therefore, catalogs and indexes use a set of *controlled vocabulary* to create consistent subject headings.

A well-known set of controlled vocabulary that is used by most libraries in the United States to catalog books is the *Library of Congress Subject Headings* (LCSH). However, there are other sets of controlled vocabulary. For example, *PubMed*, a database of medical literature, uses *Medical Subject Headings* (*MeSH*). Just as *MeSH* provides a controlled vocabulary more appropriate to the medical literature, most indexes use a set of controlled vocabulary specific to their content. Often this specialized controlled vocabulary provides more nuanced access to the literature of a particular field.

A master list of the controlled vocabulary that shows the definitions of controlled vocabulary terms and the relationships between terms is called the "thesaurus." Thesauri are arranged in a hierarchy of broader and narrower terms that allows the user to identify the most precise term for his or her topic; *see* and *use* references direct users to preferred entries. Figure 15.3 shows a hierarchy of terms that could be created for controlled vocabulary related to fruit. In this case, "fruit" is the broader term that encompasses "citrus" and other types of fruit; narrower subject headings exist for specific types of citrus and pome fruit, while see references direct the user from the popular term "Chinese gooseberry" to the preferred term "kiwifruit."

- Fruit
  - Chinese Gooseberry – *use* Kiwifruit
  - Citrus
    - Grapefruit
    - Oranges
    - Lemons
    - Limes
  - Eggfruit – *use* Lucuma
  - Kiwifruit – *use for* Chinese Gooseberry
  - Kumquats
  - Lucuma – *use for* Eggfruit
  - Pome
    - Apples
    - Pears

FIGURE 15.3 Example term hierarchy from a thesaurus

In an online database, a link to the thesaurus can usually be found from both the basic and advanced search screens. Box 15.2 provides a practice activity using thesauri to identify controlled vocabulary.

Box 15.2 Activity: Using a Database Thesaurus

The *Educational Resources Information Clearinghouse* (*ERIC*) is an index to books, articles, conference proceedings, and other literature in the field of education. Go to *ERIC* at http://www.eric.ed.gov and click on "Thesaurus." Use the thesaurus to answer the following questions:

1. When searching *ERIC*, what is the difference between "home schooling" and "home instruction"?
2. How does the *ERIC* thesaurus define "learning disabilities"?

Your library may also offer access to *ERIC* through a subscription-based service from EBSCO, ProQuest, or another vendor. Although the thesaurus will be the same as in the free version, the vendor may offer a richer thesaurus browsing experience. Try the same searches again. How does your experience differ?

PubMed is an index to literature in the field of medicine. Go to *PubMed* at http://www.pubmed.gov and click on "MeSH Database" to access the thesaurus. Use the thesaurus to answer the following questions:

1. What is the official subject heading for a sore throat?
2. Look up "myocardial infarction." What is the broader term? What are the narrower terms?
3. In *MeSH*, what is the preferred subject heading for "learning disabilities," and what is its definition? How does this definition compare to the one in *ERIC*?

Boolean Logic

Boolean logic is a form of symbolic logic named after George Boole, the 19th-century English mathematician who developed it. Boolean logic uses common words as logical operators in very specific ways to create and manipulate sets. Some of these Boolean operators are *and*, *or*, and *not*.

The Boolean operator *or* is used to create a set by making an item eligible for inclusion if it meets at least *one* of the stated criteria: an item would be included in a set if it meets the condition A *or* the condition B *or* the condition C, and so on. In creating a set of citrus fruit, one might use the following Boolean string: oranges *or* grapefruit *or* lemons *or* limes *or* kumquats. This set is more inclusive than a set that has a single criterion for acceptance, for example, oranges. One way to visualize Boolean logic is with Venn diagrams. In these diagrams, shadings indicate the results of each of the operators. The Venn diagram for *or* is shown in Figure 15.4.

The Boolean operator *and* is used to make a more restrictive set by requiring that an item meet *both* the conditions stated: an item would be included only if it meets condition A *and* condition B. One could use the Boolean *and* to create a set containing only those books written by Isaac Asimov that contained the word "robot." The Boolean string would be "Isaac Asimov *and* robot." The Venn diagram for *and* is shown in Figure 15.5.

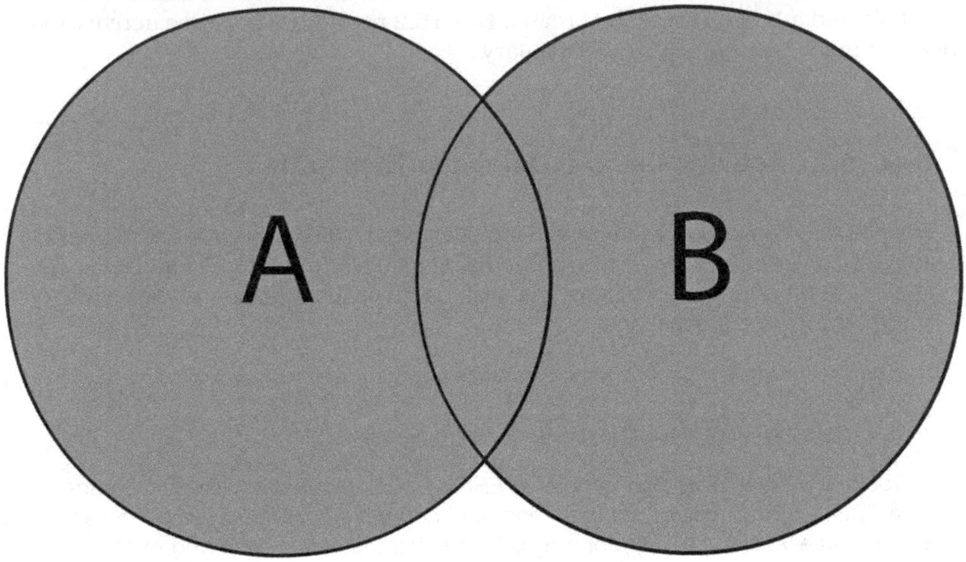

FIGURE 15.4 A Venn diagram for the Boolean operator *or* (A *or* B). The shaded area represents the items that would be retrieved.

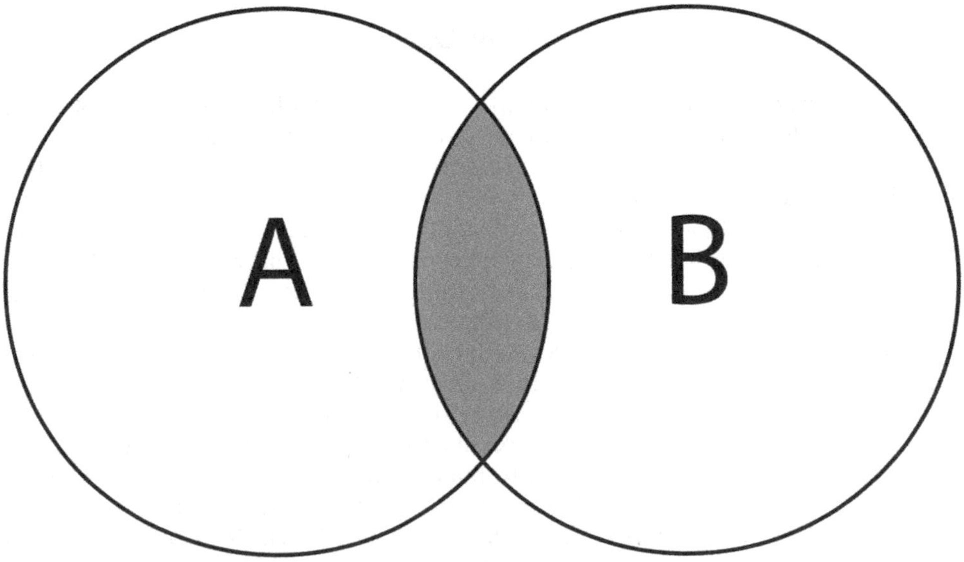

FIGURE 15.5 A Venn diagram for the Boolean operator *and* (A *and* B). The shaded area represents the items that would be retrieved.

The Boolean *and* and the Boolean *or* are concepts that the beginning searcher may have trouble keeping straight. The use of the terms is somewhat at odds with the ordinary usage of the English words "and" and "or." In ordinary English usage, "or" implies a choice where to select one item is to exclude the others, whereas the Boolean *or* expands and includes all of the items. An example from a restaurant can highlight this difference. On a breakfast menu, one might be offered toast or a muffin or a bagel. From the customer's perspective, the English "or" means the customer may select one item from the "breakfast bread" set. Viewing this menu from the restaurant's perspective, it has used the Boolean *or* ("toast" *or* "muffin" *or* "bagel") to create the set "breakfast breads," but it expects the customer to select only one choice. From a database's perspective, the same search string would be a request to retrieve any articles that used at least one of these terms, and it would return all the articles that met the criteria (or, all the bread in the restaurant!).

The Boolean *and* and the English "and" produce different outcomes as well. The English "and" works through addition: it adds all the items joined by the "and." The Boolean *and* selects items that include all the named elements. To highlight this difference, one can look at another restaurant example. In a restaurant that allows one to choose one item from column A *and* one from column B *and* one from column C, the result of an order will be a plate that contains three items. The result of a Boolean search for A *and* B *and* C is one item that contains all three elements, an unlikely dish in any restaurant.

Box 15.3 When Librarians Shop for Groceries

If you send a reference librarian to the store with a Boolean list of "sugar" *and* "flour" *and* "eggs," you will get a cookie.

The Boolean operator *not* (sometimes *and not*) is also used to make a more restrictive set. It first creates a set of items that meet condition A and then *removes* from the set those items that also meet condition B. To create a set of trees that are not deciduous, one would use the Boolean *not* to exclude deciduous from the set of trees. The Boolean string would be "trees *not* deciduous." The Venn diagram for *not* is shown in Figure 15.6.

Boolean operators can be used in combination. For example, if the librarian is seeking professional resources about reference services to children, he or she might use the search, "reference *and* children *or* youth." However, this search could be interpreted by the database in one of two ways, leading to two very different sets of results:

- If the database reads the search string from left to right, it will create a set of articles about "reference *and* children" and then add all the articles about "youth" (based on the *or* statement). This will produce search results in which a large number of articles are about youth, but not necessarily about reference services for youth.
- If the database prioritizes *or* searches first, it will create a set of articles about "children *or* youth," then limit that set to only the articles that mention "reference" (based on the *and* statement). This will produce a small set of results that is on topic for the librarian's needs.

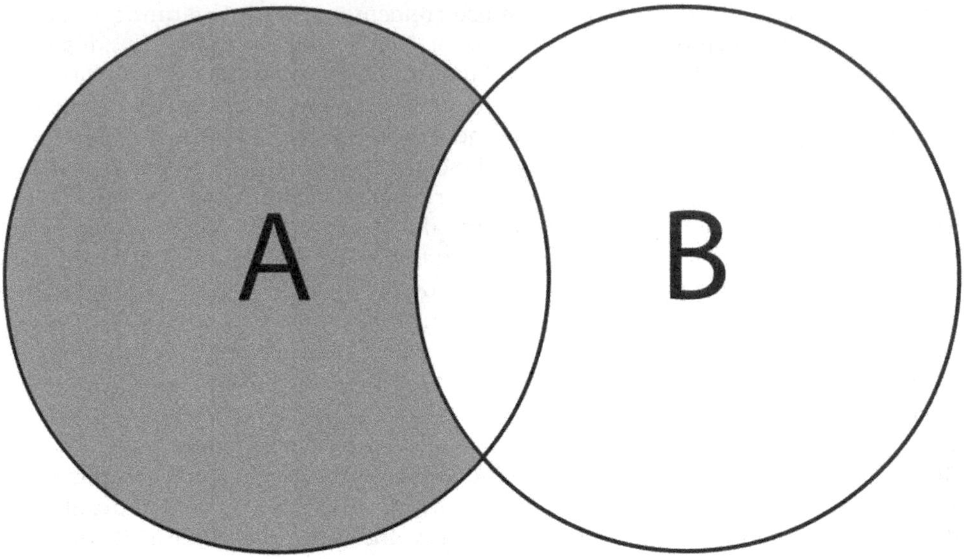

FIGURE 15.6 A Venn diagram for the Boolean operator *not* (A *not* B). The shaded area represents the items that would be retrieved.

Extending the earlier example, the search string "children *or* youth *and* reference" would produce different results because the order of operations has been changed. Librarians can use the help menu in a database to determine how a database will interpret a search query with multiple Boolean operators. However, a more efficient method is to tell the database which action should be done first by placing it in parentheses. In this example, the correct search query would be "reference *and* (children *or* youth)" or "(children *or* youth) *and* reference."

Box 15.4 Activity: Predicting the Results of Boolean Operators

Consider these statements:

- (mice *or* rats) *and* pets
- (mice *or* rats) *not* pets
- mice *or* rats *and* pets
- (mice *and* rats) *and* extermination
- (mice *or* rats) *and* extermination
- (mice *or* rats) *and* food
- (mice *or* rats) *and* food *not* extermination

Questions for Reflection and Discussion:

1. What kind of documents would be retrieved with each set of statements?
2. Imagine that a patron was interested in having a small rodent, such as a mouse or hamster, as a pet, but had not yet selected what type of animal to get. What search string(s) would you recommend to find information about selecting such a pet?

Boolean operators form the essential machinery for making computerized information retrieval precise and effective. With Boolean logic, one can manipulate databases containing a million records to produce the single item that contains all and only the information specified by the user. It is most effective on databases that have a higher proportion of structured text and relatively little unstructured or "free" text. Box 15.4 provides practice using Boolean logic.

Proximity Operators

Proximity operators enable the user to state how close search terms should appear to one another. The most common use of proximity operators is to create a phrase, such as "gun control" or "eating disorders." In almost all databases, phrase searches are created by enclosing the search terms in quotation marks.

Proximity operators can also be used to indicate that search terms should be found "with" or "near" one another, if not actually adjacent. In most databases, *with* (or *w*) indicates that words should be found in the order indicated, while *near* (or *n*) indicates that words can be found in any order. A combination of the operator and a number are used to indicate how close the words should be. The following examples illustrate the use of proximity operators when searching.

- "Electronic health records"—locates articles that use the exact phrase "electronic health records."
- Electronic *and* "health records"—locates articles that use the exact phrase "health records" anywhere in the record (e.g., in the title) and the term "electronic" anywhere in the record (e.g., in the abstract).
- Electronic *w5* "health records"—locates articles with the term "electronic" followed by the exact phrase "health records" within five words (e.g., in a title like "As Hospitals Move into the Electronic Era, Health Records Go Digital").
- Electronic *n5* "health records"—locates articles with the term "electronic" and the exact phrase "health records" within five words of one another (e.g., in a title like "Hospitals Move Health Records Online in Electronic Patient Care Systems").

Using quotation marks to create phrases is one of the simplest and most powerful tools in a librarian's search arsenal. The *with* and *near* operators are less common in everyday searching, but can be useful tools when searching the full text of books or other data-rich resources.

Truncation and Wildcards

Truncation refers to shortening a word or eliminating some characters from a longer term to pick up variants. In truncation, the database is told to retrieve all those items that share a common sequence of characters, even if they do not share all the same characters. For example, when a user searches for the truncated term "librar," the database will retrieve items that contain the term "library" or "libraries" or "librarians" or "librarian" or "librarianship." The symbols used to indicate truncation will vary from system to system. The asterisk (*) is one symbol that is commonly used, but others, including the question mark (?), the exclamation mark (!), and the plus sign (+) are also used in different systems.

Truncation can take place to the left, to the right, or in the middle of the core characters. Truncation can also involve the replacement of several characters or a single character. In the previous example, because the truncation occurred to the right of the core characters, it is called right-hand truncation. It can be further described as a multiple-character truncation. If the truncation occurs to the left of the core characters, it is left-hand truncation. For example, left-hand truncation with the core characters "ship" would retrieve records containing the terms "librarianship," "guardianship," "statesmanship," "leadership," "starship," and more. When truncation occurs in the middle of the core characters, it is called a *wildcard*. An example would be "Labo#r" where the "#" is the wildcard symbol. If this were a single-character substitution system, in which the symbol can stand

TABLE 15.1 Chart of Operators for Common Interfaces

	EBSCOhost	ProQuest	Gale Infotrac
Boolean Operators			
and *example*: earthquakes *and* Illinois	and	and	and
or *example*: Burma *or* Myanmar	or	or	or
not *example*: Asimov *not* robots	not	not	not
Proximity Searching			
Phrase *example*: "alternative spring break"	"____"	"____"	"____"
Words in Order *example*: alternative w5 spring break	W# (e.g., W5)	PRE/# P/# (e.g., PRE/5)	W# (e.g., W5)
Words in Any Order *example*: reform n8 "income tax"	N# (e.g., N5)	NEAR/# N/# (e.g., N/5)	N# (e.g., N5)
Truncation and Wildcards			
Plural (may be automatic) *example*: librarian* = librarian, librarians	automatic	*	*
Truncation *example*: librar* = library, libraries, librarian	*	*	*
Wildcard Ex: wom#n, defen?e, sul?ur	? (single letter) # (multi-letter)	? (single letter) *# (e.g., *5)	? (single letter) * (multi-letter) ! (0–1 letters)

for either nothing or a single character, this term would pick up items that contained the terms "labor" or "labour." If it were a multiple-character system, in which the symbol can stand for more than one alternate character, the set could include "labor," "labour," "laborer," and "labourer."

Frequently, systems allow one to select a single-character or multiple-character truncation or wildcard method in order to tailor the search to one's needs. Truncation and wildcard searching allow the user to acknowledge and compensate for some amount of uncertainty in the source information, as well as for other more predictable variations in the database. At the same time, the searcher must take care to avoid unwanted hits, such as "readjustment" from a search for a truncated term such as "read*."

While the Boolean operators *and*, *or*, and *not* are used consistently in most databases, the symbols used for proximity, truncation, and wildcards vary widely. Librarians can use the help menu of a database to determine the correct symbols to use. Table 15.1 shows the symbols used in many common interfaces. Boxes 15.5 and 15.6 provide practice activities related to searching.

Box 15.5 Activity: Using Boolean Operators

GreenFILE is an index to scholarly journals and government documents in the environmental sciences. Go to *GreenFILE* at https://www.ebscohost.com/academic/greenfile. Search for information about one or more of the following:

1. Environmentally friendly building materials
2. Toxins from mines
3. Simple living

Questions for Reflection and Discussion:

1. What Boolean search strings were most helpful for finding information about each topic?
2. Did you try other search strategies, and if so, what strategies were most helpful?

Box 15.6 Activity: Learning about a New Database

An important skill for librarians is the ability to analyze a new database and learn to search it effectively. You can do this by reading promotional literature from the publisher, reading the help screens, and conducting practice searches. For this activity, go to your library's list of databases and select an unfamiliar database.

1. Use the help menu to locate a description of the database. What kind of information can be found in this database? Who is the intended audience? What kinds of patrons would benefit from using this database?
2. Review the basic and advanced search screens. What kinds of searches can be conducted in this database? Are there any search options that are unique or particularly appropriate for the topics covered by this database? What operators and search limits are available?
3. Next, try some practice searches. Are the results what you expected? If not, can you determine why?
4. Do you like this interface? Why or why not?

SEARCHING THE WEB

While the commercial databases offered by libraries are highly structured compilations of carefully vetted information, the Web is not. Anyone can publish on the Internet, either through the creation of a formal Web page or blog or by posting to one of the innumerable bulletin boards and websites dedicated to discussion or user-generated content. No process exists to vet this information as accurate, reliable, or up to date; thus, high-quality information exists side by side with urban legends, rumors, half-truths, and deliberately misleading information. And while individual websites may be well curated and organized, the Web as a whole does not have an overarching organizational system designed to facilitate information retrieval.

Despite these drawbacks, the Web can serve as an excellent source of information for almost any need. Educational organizations, government agencies, companies, organizations, and even individual authors provide free, reliable information on almost any topic imaginable, sometimes in more detail than one can find in commercially published sources.

Web Directories

Directories provide a list of websites, often recommended as high-quality sites, organized into browsable categories. Once the predominant way to locate sites on the Internet, general Web directories that cover all subject areas have largely given way to search engines. However, some directories devoted to specific topics continue to be available. For example, the Association for Library Service to Children maintains *Great Websites for Kids*, which recommends sites in eight categories, including "Animals" and "History & Biography." *MedlinePlus*, a website from the National Library of Medicine that provides reliable health information for patients and caregivers, includes a directory of organizations that provide health information.

Librarians should be familiar with website directories that are relevant to their patrons' needs, since such sites can ease the search for reliable information online. Chapters 16–28 recommend many such sites in a variety of topical areas.

Search Engines

Search engines crawl the Web on a regular basis, following links and indexing Web pages as well as resources like PDF documents, images, and videos. The goal of most search engines is to index as much of the Web as possible, although some search engines will focus on selected types of information, and no search engine has indexed the entire Web (the phrase "deep web" or "hidden web" is often used to refer to those pages a search engine cannot access, e.g., those behind corporate firewalls or within proprietary databases like the ones offered by libraries).

When a user queries a search engine, the search engine then uses its vast index of the Web to present the user with a list of results. Because the Web is so large and searches can easily return thousands and even millions of results, search engines attempt to rank results so that the first few results are the ones most likely to meet a user's need with high-quality relevant information. The exact algorithms used to rank a set of results are a closely guarded secret for any search engine, but are generally based on a combination of the presence and placement of keywords and popularity, with popularity measured by how often other high-quality sites link to the particular site.

Because search engines are free to users, the companies that provide them are often supported by advertising revenue. In addition to websites retrieved from the search engine's index, a results page will display ads, often placed at the top and sides of search results and designed to look very similar to actual search results.

Google indexes billions of Web pages and features a simple search interface with a single box for inputting text. The display of search results includes ads, which are clearly labeled as such, and the opportunity to limit results by facets such as images, videos, news, and shopping. A list of suggestions is offered to help users refine their search both during the search and as part of the results. In some cases, *Google* will respond to a search by providing information that it thinks will answer a user's query. For example, a search for "Pantages Theatre" results in not only links to the official home page and sites with information about the theater, but also a sidebar with an address, map, and schedule of upcoming shows. *Google*'s SafeSearch option allows the user to block potentially objectionable content from search results.

Bing also features a simple search box, but has a more elaborate home page that features an image of the day, complete with embedded relevant searches to inspire browsing, and links to current news stories. Search results include links and images, ads, search suggestions, and in some cases, a sidebar of related information. *Bing* also features a SafeSearch option as well as a Search History feature.

DuckDuckGo bills itself as a search engine that does not track users. A simple search box provides recommendations as users search. Search results include a brief definition of the topic with an image, links, clearly labeled ads, and the ability to limit to videos or images. A particularly useful feature of *DuckDuckGo* is that in the case of searches for specific places, such as the Pantages Theatre, it labels the official site in the list of results.

Specialized search engines provide access to niche material on the Web. Many such search engines exist, and only a few examples will be given here. The *Wayback Machine* provides access to archived copies of Web pages and can be useful for locating material that no longer exists in its original location, such as a Web page that was taken down or past versions of pages. *Wolfram Alpha* is a computational search engine that provides statistics, facts, and other numerical data, rather than links to external pages. A source link at the bottom of the results provides citations for and links to source material.

SEARCH STRATEGIES FOR THE WEB

Most search engines offer a simple search box, and it may not be obvious whether one can use Boolean operators and other advanced search strategies. The lack of an advanced search page or help menu may further stymie librarians accustomed to the more complex search possibilities offered by databases. However, most search engines do offer some advanced search options; one can often find more detailed information by searching for the name of the search engine and a phrase like "search help" or "advanced search" (e.g., Bing search help, Google advanced search).

Boolean Operators and Truncation

Search engines typically permit the use of Boolean operators. The most common strategy is to use quotation marks to create a phrase (e.g., "gun control"). In addition, usually the *or* operator can be used, while a dash is used to eliminate results, similar to the *not* operator (e.g., bats-baseball). Truncation is often applied without any express action on the part of the searcher. Each search term is matched to a set of terms that have the same stem; these multiple variants on the stem are then searched in the search engine's index.

Limiting by Site and URL

Each address on the Web must be registered to assure its uniqueness. Naming conventions govern the appearance of the domain name or URL. In the United States, the top-level domain names have one of several main endings: .edu, .org, .com, .gov, .net, and so on. Each ending lets the user anticipate the kind of organization or service that is available through that website. Although the categories are not absolute, in general, ".edu" is used for educational organizations, ".org" for nonprofit organizations, ".com" for commercial sites, ".gov" for units of government, and ".net" for organizations that support Internet access and Web services.

In other parts of the world, there are similar patterns governing domain name conventions. In countries outside of the United States, domain names generally include an abbreviation for the country of origin as well as an element designating the kind of service provider. For example, the URL for a commercial site in Australia might look like http://mycompany.com.au.

Many search engines allow one to limit a search to a particular domain name, such as .edu, or URL. For example, in *Google*, the search "admissions site:.edu" would limit the search for admissions to Web pages from educational institutions, while the search "flu prevention site:cdc.gov" would limit the search for information on preventing the flu to Web pages from the Centers for Disease Control and Prevention.

Other Types of Search Limits

In addition, search engines will offer specialized search options to facilitate searching for specific types of information. For example, *Bing*'s image search returns only image files and includes the ability to limit by attributes such as color, size, and usage rights. *Google Shopping* returns only items available for purchase and includes the ability to filter results by price, color, brand, and other features. *socialmention*, a search engine for social media, allows one to limit by social media platform, hashtag, and timeframe.

PUTTING IT ALL TOGETHER: LOCATING INFORMATION ONLINE

Searching for information online is a complex process that involves the following steps:

1. Conducting the reference interview
2. Deciding where to search

3. Developing a search query
4. Searching, revising, and searching again
5. Saving and managing search results

Conducting the Reference Interview

The first step in any successful reference transaction is a reference interview to ensure that the librarian accurately understands the patron's information need. Strategies for a successful reference interview are given in Chapter 3. In addition, some chapters in Part II of this book provide tips for particular types of reference interviews, such as those related to readers' advisory, business, and legal questions.

Deciding Where to Search

Based on information gained in the reference interview, the librarian next selects an appropriate resource to search for information. If the patron needs a basic explanation of a scientific term, the most appropriate place might be an online encyclopedia. If the patron needs scholarly journal articles, the most appropriate place would be a subscription-based index or open-source article repository. If the patron is seeking a list of all the television adaptations of the show *The Office*, a fan site or *Wikipedia* might provide the most comprehensive up-to-date answer. In selecting an appropriate resource, librarians should consider not only the depth and amount of information needed, but also the age and educational level of the patron, the subject of the query, the need for a specific format such as a book or DVD, and whether the patron needs an immediately available item or can wait for an interlibrary loan.

Developing a Search Query

Once the librarian has selected a resource, he or she will need to create a search query. This can be done by brainstorming keywords or using the thesaurus to identify appropriate controlled vocabulary, and linking terms into a query using Boolean operators, truncation, and so on. In addition, the librarian should consider whether the database offers any limiters or search features that would be useful for the given query.

For example, if the patron is searching for information about whether elephants show grief when a member of the group dies, a brainstormed list of search terms might include elephants, grief, mourning, emotion, death, die, and dying. These could be combined into a simple search string such as *elephants and grief and death* or a more complicated search string such as *elephants and (grief or mourn* or emotion) and (death or die or dying).*

A few quick searches in the selected database can often be helpful in developing a search query. For example, one can put in a few keywords combined with Boolean *and* to get a very rough and ready estimate of the quantity of materials that may be of interest in a database. Scanning a few records retrieved in this way can point the way to improving the search. One record may have a subject heading or descriptor that encapsulates an aspect of the search topic more effectively than the keywords with which one began. This can also confirm that the database is likely to be productive because it has records with appropriate and relevant subject headings.

Searching, Revising, and Searching Again

Once searching begins in earnest, librarians should keep in mind that the first search is rarely the best search. Rather, it represents a starting point from which the librarian can critically evaluate search results for clues about improving the search. A search that brings back only a few results may indicate that the librarian has not yet identified the best search term to describe the topic; he or she can continue to brainstorm alternate vocabulary or consult the thesaurus for subject headings. The librarian should also consider whether a broader search term or even another database would yield better results. On the other hand, a search that brings back an overwhelming number of results may indicate that the librarian needs to narrow the search through the use of additional terms or database limiters.

Librarians can also use a strategy of *citation pearl growing* to build a set of relevant results. Once an on-topic record has been located, it can serve as a jumping-off point for further searches. Most obviously, librarians can use the subject headings from one record to identify additional relevant records. Many databases will suggest "articles like this one" to assist patrons in identifying promising material. Librarians can also run additional searches for selected authors or within likely journals or other publications.

Librarians can also remind patrons to mine footnotes and bibliographies to identify additional materials on their topic. A few databases will assist patrons in doing this, most notably *Web of Science*, which allows one to trace articles through footnotes going both forward and backward in time. *Google Scholar* is also working to link articles through citations, as are some databases from EBSCO and ProQuest.

In the case of complex searches, librarians may find it helpful to keep notes about the search process. Inevitably, as the search for an elusive piece of information progresses, one forgets where one has searched and which search terms have been tried. Jotting notes about the databases and search queries that have been used can prevent frustration and the potential for unwittingly repeating unsuccessful searches. Some databases offer a *search history* feature that allows the user to not only see a list of all searches that have been attempted, but also repeat searches, combine search queries, and compile sets of results from multiple searches.

Saving and Managing Search Results

For simple queries, such as the definition of a word, it may be sufficient for the librarian to point to an entry on the screen or help the patron print a brief record. In the case of more complex searches, the librarian may want to assist the user in saving records for later use. Most databases allow the user to collect records in a "folder" to print, e-mail, or download at the conclusion of a search session. Librarians can also assist patrons in using reference management tools like *EndNote* and *Zotero* to collect and manage citations.

HELPING PATRONS LOCATE INFORMATION ONLINE

Although librarians can use their extensive knowledge of the library's resources to select an appropriate database or reference tool to search for a given topic, patrons may not have the necessary experience to do the same. Therefore, one of the responsibilities of reference librarians is to present the library's resources in such a way that patrons can identify appropriate resources to search for information.

Many libraries provide an alphabetical or subject-based list of databases. These pages can direct patrons to appropriate resources, although they rely on the patron to browse pages and lists to identify the most appropriate places to search. Lists that combine catalogs, indexes, reference tools, and reliable websites provide more comprehensive access to the library's resources, but as lists grow, they become more cumbersome to use. In addition, such pages may require that library users understand the difference between a catalog, index, and reference tool and what kind of information can be found in each.

Another option for helping users locate the resources most relevant to their information needs is librarian-authored guides. Librarians have long made bibliographies or research guides for patron use, first as print handouts and later as Web pages. These guides, often devoted to a particular topic, list recommended reference tools and indexes, search strategies, and general advice germane to the topic. Guides can also provide readers' advisory, guidance on citation styles, and even information on local services. A popular product for authoring Web-based guides is *LibGuides*, a service that hosts a library's guides and provides templates to ease the process of organizing and formatting entries, linking to databases and websites, and updating content as needed. In addition, *LibGuides* allows librarians to reuse content across multiple guides, share content with colleagues, and integrate multimedia and social media.

Recognizing that lists and guides may not be enough to enable patrons to make full use of the library's resources, librarians are turning to federated search and discovery tools. Federated search and discovery systems attempt to go one step further by providing patrons with a single search box through which to search multiple resources, including the library's catalog, subscription databases, local repositories and digital collections, and even selected websites. As Michael Levine-Clark, John McDonald, and Jason S. Price (2014, 249) note, "Searching across multiple resources at once makes it much easier to find information, especially for students who might not understand the difference between an article index and a library catalog, and even for more experienced researchers who may not know the best subject-specific resource for locating articles. With the growth of interdisciplinary research, discovery services make it easier to gather information from a variety of disciplinary viewpoints at once."

The technology underlying federated searching and discovery systems differs, resulting in different search experiences for patrons. In federated searching, the patron's query is relayed to selected databases; each database is searched and then a list of results is displayed to the user (in some cases, a list of the databases searched is displayed with the number of results found, an attempt to simplify the presentation of results, although this requires the patron to enter each database to see the list of actual results). Early federated search efforts suffered from slowness and an inability to de-duplicate or rank records, resulting in a potentially overwhelming list of disorganized results (Wang and Mi 2012, 232–33). More recent federated searching products have increased search speed and provided improvements in de-duplication as well as more advanced search features and faceted results (Wang and Mi 2012, 234). Currently available products include *MetaLib* and *360 Search*.

Discovery services, on the other hand, create an index of content and associated metadata from selected sources, allowing for a richer, faster search experience as well as better de-duplication and results ranking. Current products include *Summon Service*, *EBSCO Discovery Service*, *WorldCat Discovery Services*, and *Primo Central*.

CONCLUSION

Today's modern databases offer robust search options for patrons and librarians alike. For patrons, interface designers offer simple search boxes combined with features like auto-complete, spell-check, and faceted searching that enable even novice searchers to refine their search results. For librarians, these same interfaces permit the use of sophisticated strategies like Boolean operators, truncation, and wildcard searching that can improve the precision and recall of searches.

REFERENCES

Levine-Clark, Michael, John McDonald, and Jason S. Price. 2014. "The Effect of Discovery Systems on Online Journal Usage: A Longitudinal Study." *Insights* 27 (3): 249–56.

Wang, Yongming, and Jia Mi. 2012. "Searchability and Discoverability of Library Resources: Federated Search and Beyond." *College & Undergraduate Libraries* 19 (2–4): 229–45.

LIST OF SOURCES

360 Search. Ann Arbor, MI: ProQuest. http://www.proquest.com/products-services/360-Search.html. [subscription required]

America: History and Life. Ipswich, MA: EBSCO. https://www.ebscohost.com/academic/america-history-and-life. [subscription required]

American National Biography. 1999. New York: Oxford University Press. Supplements, 2000–. Available online: http://www.anb.org. [subscription required]

Association for Library Service to Children. *Great Websites for Kids.* American Library Association. http://gws.ala.org/.

Bing. http://www.bing.com/.

Consumer Health Complete. Ipswich, MA: EBSCO. https://www.ebscohost.com/public/consumer-health-complete. [subscription required]

Credo Reference. Boston: Credo Reference. http://search.credoreference.com/. [subscription required]

DuckDuckGo. https://duckduckgo.com/.

EBSCO Discovery Service. Ipswich, MA: EBSCO. https://www.ebscohost.com/discovery. [subscription required]

EndNote. Philadelphia: Thomson Reuters. http://endnote.com/.

ERIC. Washington, DC: Institute of Education Sciences. http://eric.ed.gov. Available online from EBSCO, ProQuest and other vendors.

Google. http://www.google.com.

Google Scholar. https://scholar.google.com/.

Google Shopping. https://www.google.com/shopping?hl=en.

GreenFILE. Ipswich, MA: EBSCO. https://www.ebscohost.com/academic/greenfile.

JSTOR. Ann Arbor, MI: JSTOR. http://www.jstor.org/. [subscription required]

LibGuides. Miami, FL: Springshare. http://libguides.com. [subscription required]

Library of Congress Subject Headings. Library of Congress. http://authorities.loc.gov/.

Medical Subject Headings. National Library of Medicine. https://www.nlm.nih.gov/mesh/.

MedlinePlus. http://www.nlm.nih.gov/medlineplus/.

MetaLib. Des Plaines, IL: ExLibris. http://www.exlibrisgroup.com/category/MetaLib Overview. [subscription required]

Oxford Reference. New York: Oxford. http://www.oxfordreference.com/. [subscription required]
PLOS. https://www.plos.org/.
Primo Central. Des Plaines, IL: ExLibris. http://www.exlibrisgroup.com/category/Primo Central. [subscription required]
ProQuest Dissertations & Theses Global. Ann Arbor, MI: ProQuest. http://www.proquest.com/products-services/pqdtglobal.html. [subscription required]
PsycINFO. Washington, DC: American Psychological Association. http://www.apa.org/pubs/databases/psycinfo/. [subscription required]
PubMed. http://www.ncbi.nlm.nih.gov/pubmed.
PubMed Central. http://www.ncbi.nlm.nih.gov/pmc/.
socialmention. http://www.socialmention.com/.
Summon Service. Ann Arbor, MI: ProQuest. http://www.proquest.com/products-services/The-Summon-Service.html. [subscription required]
Wayback Machine. Internet Archive. https://archive.org/index.php.
Web of Science. Philadelphia: Thomson Reuters. http://wokinfo.com/. [subscription required]
Wikipedia. https://www.wikipedia.org/.
Wolfram Alpha. http://www.wolframalpha.com/.
WorldCat. http://www.worldcat.org.
WorldCat Discovery Services. Dublin, OH: OCLC. http://www.oclc.org/worldcat-local.en.html. [subscription required]
Yahoo!. http://www.yahoo.com.
Zotero. Roy Rosenzweig Center for History and New Media. https://www.zotero.org/.

SUGGESTED READINGS

Beall, Jeffrey. 2011. "Academic Library Databases and the Problem of Word-Sense Ambiguity." *The Journal of Academic Librarianship* 37 (1): 64–69.
Beall looks at how word-sense ambiguity, or the fact that one word can have multiple meanings, affects precision in searching as well as efforts like machine translation and text mining. This is a thoughtful exploration of a contemporary problem in information management.

Bell, Suzanne S. 2015. *Librarian's Guide to Online Searching: Cultivating Database Skills for Research and Instruction*, 4th ed. Santa Barbara, CA: Libraries Unlimited.
Bell provides an excellent guide to online databases and search strategies. Following early chapters on search strategies, including field searching, operators, and controlled vocabulary, Bell provides chapters on core database titles and discipline-specific search strategies for the humanities, social sciences, sciences, statistics, and more. Chapters include excellent examples and practice activities.

Hines, Kristi. 2016. "40 Advanced and Alternative Search Engines." *Kissmetrics*. Last accessed January 5. https://blog.kissmetrics.com/alternative-search-engines/.
Hines provides an excellent list of specialized search engines, including those for images, video, social media, documents, and news.

Lilly, Paul. 2014. "Best Search Engine: Google, Bing, and DuckDuckGo." *MaximumPC*. November 18. http://www.maximumpc.com/best-search-engine-2014/#page-1.
Ostensibly an analysis of which is the best search engine, Lilly rates each on a number of factors. He uses practice searches to illustrate both how the search engines work and the unique features of each one, making this an informative article for those new to the topic.

Pope, Julia T., and Robert P. Holley. 2011. "Google Book Search and Metadata." *Cataloging & Classification Quarterly* 49 (1): 1–13.

The authors discuss the importance of good metadata in helping users discover resources and explore the problem of high rates of error in the metadata used in *Google Books*.

Robbins, Jennifer Niederst. 2012. *Learning Web Design: A Beginner's Guide to HTML, CSS, JavaScript, and Web Graphics*, 4th ed. Sebastopol, CA: O'Reilly.

For those who want more detailed information on the structure of the Internet and Web pages, Chapter 2, "How the Web Works," provides a brief accessible introduction.

Uyar, Ahmet, and Farouk Musa Aliyu. 2015. "Evaluating Search Features of Google Knowledge Graph and Bing Satori: Entity Types, List Searches, and Query Interfaces." *Online Information Review* 39 (2): 197–213.

The authors examine efforts by major search engines, particularly *Google* and *Bing*, to deliver not just Web pages in response to a user's query, but actual content that answers the implied question.

Chapter 16

Bibliographic Sources

Linda C. Smith

USES AND CHARACTERISTICS

Knowledge of bibliographic sources is essential for assisting users in identifying resources on various topics. In addition, many of the most challenging questions that a reference librarian faces are bibliographic puzzles involving the verification of incomplete or inaccurate information when a user wants to find a particular book or other resource in the library. The librarian must then determine the following:

1. Do the library's catalog records show that the library owns the item?
2. If not, is the user looking for an item that really exists? That is, has it actually been published? Or is the user looking for a type of item not indexed in the catalog?
3. Is the user's information correct, or only partially correct? For example, could the author's name be misspelled?
4. If the information is not completely correct, did the user get the information about the item from a reliable source, or has it perhaps been garbled in an oral communication?

The librarian must decide what path to take to recreate the information in correct form or to verify that the information is correct. A seemingly simple question may turn into a puzzle requiring the use of multiple sources, including catalogs and bibliographies.

The process of bibliographic control generally means providing two different kinds of access to information: bibliographic access, letting the user know of the existence of the work; and physical access, letting the user know where the work can be found. To achieve the aims of bibliographic control, three major types of reference sources have evolved: bibliographies, library catalogs, and shared cataloging networks. In general, bibliographies list works or parts of works regardless of their physical location. Library catalogs aim to list the works located in or accessible online from one or more libraries. Shared cataloging networks serve both functions, providing complete machine-readable cataloging copy and a list of libraries that own the item reflected in the catalog record.

Patrick Wilson in *Two Kinds of Power* (1968, 13) defines universal bibliographic control as the creation of an "exhaustive inventory" of all the works that have ever been published. Although extremely noble, such an aspiration toward universal bibliographic control is unattainable and has become even more elusive given the proliferation of self-published works (Hadro 2013). However, progress has been made through the cooperative efforts of national libraries, national standards organizations, and the efforts of the shared cataloging networks in various countries. Especially in the digital realm, there is increasing interest in extending the access provided by bibliographic control to encompass archival and museum collections as well as library collections (Marcum 2014).

Types of Bibliographies and Catalogs

In the print environment, a bibliography is a list of works compiled on some common organizing principle, such as authorship, subject, place of publication, or chronology. The primary arrangement of the list is usually alphabetical, although a subject classification scheme, such as the Dewey Decimal Classification System, may be used. Secondary arrangement schemes may also be employed, such as by date when the primary arrangement is by author. As explained in Chapter 15, electronic resources provide a superior bibliographic product because most fields or elements of the bibliographic record are searchable and extremely precise queries can be formulated.

National bibliographies list the materials published in a particular country. In addition, the scope may be enlarged to include works written about the country or in the language of the country, regardless of the place of publication. Material written by the citizens of the country, wherever published, may also be included. Trade bibliographies are produced by commercial publishers and serve to provide the information necessary to select and acquire recently published materials. The predominant form of trade bibliography is the in-print list. Subject bibliographies are lists of materials that relate to a particular topic.

The terms "current" and "retrospective," as applied to bibliographies, refer to the time period covered by the items selected for inclusion in the bibliography. A current bibliography lists books or other items published close to the time at which the bibliography is compiled. A retrospective bibliography covers materials published during an earlier time period. Compilations of current bibliographic sources turn into retrospective sources when the time period covered recedes into the past.

Library catalogs exist to serve the users of a particular library by listing the holdings and location of materials accessible to users in that library. Union catalogs (or union lists) identify the material held in the collections of more than one library. Library consortia may create union catalogs for their member libraries. In the case of union lists of serials, it is quite common to find not only the list of libraries holding a particular title, but also a record of which volumes each library holds.

Kinds of Information Contained in Bibliographies and Catalogs

The data elements in a bibliography entry depend largely on the intent of the publication. Current national bibliographies exist in part to facilitate the international exchange of cataloging data in a standardized format. Therefore, the entries reflect the information available in machine-readable cataloging records. In addition to author, title, and publication data, each entry usually includes subject headings, content notes, and suggested classification numbers. Name entries, both personal and corporate, are standardized. Ordering information such as price is often included.

Because trade bibliographies are produced for the use of book dealers, they contain information that is essential for book purchases. Examples include price, availability, publishers' addresses, and International Standard Book Number (ISBN). The International Standard Serial Number (ISSN) serves a similar role, uniquely identifying each serial title.

Use of bibliographies depends on the type of information needed. If one needs simply to verify the existence of an item, a source giving short entries may be sufficient. If one needs both to identify and to locate copies, a union list is necessary. If the intent is to purchase materials, information such as price, ISBN, and availability is definitely required.

The content of catalog records reflects the cataloging code in use by the organization creating the records. Increasingly, catalog records are being enriched with additional content such as tables of contents, images of book jackets, narrative summaries of the book's contents, and even excerpts from book reviews.

EVALUATION

Evaluation of bibliographies and library catalogs is primarily concerned with the following criteria: authority, accuracy, scope, access points, and currency of the included material.

Authority

Authority concerns the qualifications of the compiler or sponsor. Compiling a national or trade bibliography is a massive undertaking, usually involving the resources of a major publisher, national library, or governmental agency. Therefore, the issue of authority usually concerns the compilers of smaller subject bibliographies or resources found on the Web. Do the compilers have the educational background or academic stature to justify their roles in compiling these bibliographies? Does the organization sponsoring the bibliography have a particular political agenda or viewpoint?

Accuracy

To accomplish bibliographic control, the accuracy of the bibliographic data describing each item is essential. In catalogs, this also entails standardization of forms of entry for authors and subjects. A basic tenet of cataloging is the principle of collocation, which means that similar materials are gathered together at a single location. An essential requirement for achieving collocation is maintenance of authority control, whether of authors' names, subjects, or titles. For example, author-name authority control ensures that all existing permutations of an author's name are linked so that all works written by that individual are gathered together at a particular location in the catalog. Subject authority control has as its objective the gathering together in one place of items on a particular topic. The sheer size of the bibliographic universe has made authority control one of the biggest challenges in cataloging today (Gorman 2004).

Scope

The scope of any reference tool is of primary importance when evaluating its usefulness. Parameters determining scope can include place of publication, language, time period, type of materials, format, or subject. For retrospective sources, *Guide to Reference Books* (see Cargill 1996) gives clear and concise descriptions of the scope. For currently published works, the introductory material in a print source or the "about" section of a website should be studied.

Access Points

A print bibliography or catalog will have a primary form of arrangement, such as by author, possibly supplemented by one or more indexes. For online sources, options for searching and limiting are generally much more numerous. For example, the typical card catalog generally had entries for authors, titles, and subjects interfiled alphabetically. Online catalogs likewise enable searching not only by author, title, and subject, but also by keyword and other elements of the record such as ISBN/ISSN. It may also be possible to limit the search by such elements as date, format, or language.

Currency

Currency refers to the delay, or lack thereof, between the date of publication and the time at which the publication is entered in the bibliography. Publications designed for the book trade should offer the most recent information to fulfill the intent of their publications: providing information on currently available materials. Book trade publications may also list publications announced for publication but not yet published.

SELECTION

Many of the sources discussed in this chapter would be found in most libraries. Most often, the choice is fairly clear-cut; only one source will fill a particular need. Occasionally, there may be a choice between format, print or electronic, with the latter likely more expensive. In that case, the librarian needs to assess whether the cost is justified by added value for reference work, perhaps due to greater currency or more access points to the content. As more resources become freely available on the Web, the librarian may also need to determine whether a purchased or licensed resource provides information or search capabilities not yet matched through freely available sources. For example, the Online Computer Library Center (OCLC) provides both *WorldCat.org* on the open Web and *WorldCat* as a licensed resource.

IMPORTANT GENERAL SOURCES

The following discussion covers those bibliographic compilations that provide the most comprehensive coverage of books or serials or both. The focus is tools that continue to be updated. For guidance to retrospective titles, such as the *National Union Catalog, Pre-1956 Imprints*, the *Guide to Reference Books* provides an effective means for identifying and learning about the vast array of bibliographic sources that have been published. This section covers *WorldCat* and digital initiatives, followed by sections on library catalogs, current bibliography, sources of purchasing information, serial sources, and recommended lists.

WorldCat

The most important bibliographic source in today's library is produced by the shared cataloging network OCLC. Founded in 1967 as the Ohio College Library Center, OCLC is a "global library cooperative that provides shared technology services, original research and community programs for its membership and the library community at large" (OCLC 2016). The cooperative encompasses thousands of library members in more than 100 countries. As of early 2016, OCLC's *WorldCat*, the world's largest and most comprehensive catalog of library resources, includes more than 360 million bibliographic records (albeit with some duplication) with a new record added every 10 seconds. These records represent more than 2.3 billion items held by participating libraries. Coverage encompasses books, serials, audiovisual materials, musical scores, maps, archives/manuscripts, and electronic resources. These records are accessible in two ways: through the licensed database *WorldCat*, and freely available to the world in the form of the simpler *WorldCat.org*. Given its scope, *WorldCat* can be used to identify materials available in a subject area, in a particular format, or by a particular author; to verify citations; and to locate libraries holding a title.

In 2005, OCLC announced the Open WorldCat Initiative, with the goal of making library holdings more visible on the Web (McCullough 2015). *WorldCat.org* opens up *WorldCat* so that any Web user can search the database and link to online catalog records. *WorldCat.org* offers a single search box, faceted browsing (refining an initial search by year, audience, content, format, language, author, or topic), and a general streamlining of the interface. The Advanced Search page allows combination of terms and limits by year, audience, content, format, and language. Libraries holding an item are also displayed as part of the search results. In addition, OCLC worked with partners such as *Wikipedia* to include links from title-level book displays back to *WorldCat.org*, and from there to local libraries.

The licensed version of *WorldCat* has a sophisticated advanced search, allowing selection from more than 20 options when entering search terms, including author, title, or subject as words or phrases as well as elements such as publisher and series. Limiting options include year, audience (any, juvenile, not juvenile), content (e.g., fiction, biography), format, language, and location. Retrieval results provide detailed bibliographic information, bring together different editions and formats of the title searched, and identify holding libraries.

Digital Initiatives

As projects to digitize large numbers of books proceed, one can supplement searches of the document surrogates found in catalog records with a search of the full text of a growing number of books. Launched in 2004, *Google Books* is currently the most ambitious digitization project, allowing a simple Web search of book contents or an advanced search on combinations of fields such as keyword or phrase, language, title, author, publisher, subject, and publication date. While acknowledging concerns that have been raised about the lack of quality in the metadata (James and Weiss 2012; Pope and Holley 2011), Dorothy A. Mays argues that *Google Books* can enrich what a library can offer its patrons. She notes that in addition to books, "there is a wealth of non-monograph ephemera, including government documents, retail catalogs, maps, city reports, directories, and illustrations that can be mined for genealogical and historical research" (Mays 2015, 23). Google scans two types of materials: pre-1923 works that are in the public domain and books published in 1923 or after that are likely still under copyright protection. The pre-1923 books are fully searchable and almost always can be read in their entirety online. In the case of books published in 1923 or after, what can be viewed depends on the copyright status of the book. Full view is possible if the book is out of copyright or if the publisher or author has asked to make the book fully viewable. Limited preview of selected pages is possible if the author or publisher has given permission. Otherwise, a "snippet view" is provided: information about the book plus a few sentences to display the search term or terms in context. If no text is available online, then basic bibliographic information about the book is provided. Entries for each book include a "find in a library" link to *WorldCat.org* (Chen 2012). A court decision in October 2015 clarified the legality of *Google Books* (Meyer 2015).

Other noteworthy projects providing access to digitized content include the *HathiTrust Digital Library* and the *Digital Public Library of America* (*DPLA*). Started in 2008, *HathiTrust* is a partnership of academic and research institutions offering a collection of millions of titles digitized from libraries around the world. It is characterized by a robust search engine that provides the option of searching the full text or the catalog with well-organized metadata. Eamon P. Duffy (2013) documents the ways in which this library metadata benefits search strategies. The *DPLA* launched in the spring of 2013. It collocates the metadata of millions of publicly accessible digital assets, unifying access to previously siloed collections of digitized content from libraries, archives, museums, and historical societies.

Naomi Eichenlaub (2013) highlights the common challenges faced by such efforts to broaden access to content through digitization: copyright, orphan works (a copyrighted work for which the copyright owner cannot be contacted), and the quality of metadata and the content resulting from the digitization process. Despite these barriers, such projects dramatically extend access not only to records of materials, but also to the contents of many more of the items themselves.

LIBRARY CATALOGS

For many years, the library catalog was the primary means of locating and accessing items in a library's collection; indeed, the function of the catalog was to display the holdings of a particular library. Over the past several decades, however, the catalog's function has evolved so that it not only reflects the library's collection, but also acts as an access mechanism to resources beyond the library, whether housed in other libraries in a consortium or available in electronic form. Although the records that make up a library's catalog may be drawn from a shared cataloging network such as OCLC, such records may be tailored to the specific library's collection, such as through the addition of a local call number or volume holdings statement. Consulting a database like *WorldCat* answers the question "Does an item exist?" Consulting the local catalog answers the questions "Does the library own or provide access to the item?" and "Where can the item be found?"

A library's catalog is cumulative, including materials held in a collection, regardless of date of publication or date of acquisition. In a library consortium, the contents of the catalog may be a combination of several libraries. In these instances, the catalog is known as a union catalog. When the catalog is not fully representative of a library's collection, this fact should be made clear to users and librarians. For example, if an academic library maintains an institutional repository including the research output of scholars affiliated with the institution such as electronic theses and dissertations, the contents are not necessarily included in the library's catalog. The library catalog may also not fully represent the library's holdings of eBooks and eJournals, so the user should be made aware of other finding tools for such content. As noted in Chapter 15, implementation of Web-scale discovery systems seeks to combine catalog access with access to other resources such as online databases.

Historically, the catalog provided three major types of access points for a given item: author, title, and subject. Authority control ensures that author names and subject headings are represented consistently. The *Library of Congress Authorities* includes authority headings for subject, name, title, and name/title combinations. Given the ease of access to catalogs across the world, as demonstrated by *LibWeb: Library Servers via WWW*, it is important to be aware that libraries in other countries do not necessarily conform to the authority control practices followed by the Library of Congress. The *Virtual International Authority File* is a collaborative effort that identifies the authoritative form of a given name in different countries.

For bibliographic verification tasks, most often it is preferable to search *WorldCat* rather than individual library catalogs. Either successful or negative search results cost the librarian very little time. However, the presence of locally produced cataloging copy that might not be present in *WorldCat* occasionally merits searching catalogs individually. Subject bibliographers may wish to search a local collection to determine its holdings in a particular area of strength. In addition to the online catalog, conditions of use, hours of operation, and other worthwhile information may be found on a library's website.

Online catalog design has become more user centered. Such catalogs are characterized as "next generation" (Yang and Wagner 2010, 694–95), with features that may include: single search box, state-of-the art Web interface, enriched content (book cover images, user tags, reviews), faceted navigation (refining results based on dates, languages, formats, locations, etc.), relevancy ranking of search results, did you mean . . . ?, and recommendations of related materials. Such catalogs take lessons from online booksellers like *Amazon*, which include more information about each title than a typical catalog provides and seek to involve users in activities like providing reviews of titles.

United States

Currently the products and services of the Library of Congress and the shared cataloging network OCLC are the dominant elements in the provision of bibliographic control in the United States. The *Library of Congress Online Catalog* is a database of more than 18 million catalog records for books, serials, manuscripts, maps, music, recordings, images, and electronic resources in the Library of Congress collections.

Great Britain, France, and Canada

The *British Library Catalogue* includes millions of records for books, journals, newspapers, printed maps, scores, electronic resources, sound archives, and other items in the Library's collections. *Catalogue* is now part of *Explore the British Library*, which also supports search of the British Library website and freely available articles. The *Catalogue Général* of the Bibliothèque Nationale de France (BnF) contains records for books and periodicals, sound recordings, videos, multimedia, electronic materials stored on physical media, graphic documents, documents digitized by the BnF, and portions of other collections such as cartographic materials and microfilms. *AMICUS*, Canada's national catalog, includes holdings of published materials held at Library and Archives Canada (LAC) and at more than 1,300 libraries across Canada. It contains more than 30 million records for books, magazines, newspapers, government documents, theses, sound recordings, maps, and electronic texts, as well as items in braille and large print.

CURRENT BIBLIOGRAPHY

Current bibliographic sources are heavily used by librarians because they provide a timely list of books and other media at the time of publication and often in advance of publication. Librarians use these listings to perform the core functions of libraries: selection, reference, and cataloging. Subject access to newly published books allows both librarians and users to determine those books that have been published on the topic of interest. In addition, reference librarians use them to answer reference questions, including the verification of bibliographic citations. National bibliographic agencies have a broader societal ambition when producing current bibliographic sources: to capture the record of the national publishing output for posterity.

U.S. Bibliography

In the United States, the only title being published that meets the definition of a current bibliography is the *American Book Publishing Record* (*ABPR*), a monthly publication from Grey House Publishing. *ABPR* provides full cataloging information for more than 10,000 new titles as they are published. It is arranged by the Dewey Decimal Classification System, with author and title indexes complementing the primary arrangement. Separate sections for adult fiction and juvenile fiction are arranged alphabetically by main entry author or title. In addition, the subject guide, arranged alphabetically, directs the user from the subject headings to the corresponding Dewey Decimal Classification System numbers. The annual *ABPR*, published in March, is compiled from the 12 monthly issues.

Current Bibliographies from Great Britain, France, and Canada

British National Bibliography (*BNB*) has been the national record of publishing in the United Kingdom and the Republic of Ireland, covering the books and new journal titles published or distributed in the United Kingdom and Ireland since 1950. It also lists forthcoming book titles and hand-held electronic publications deposited with the Legal Deposit Office of the British Library since 2003. The coverage of the *BNB* has always been selective, with an emphasis on mainstream monographs available through normal book-buying channels. It is freely available on the British Library website. Records include author, title, subject headings, Dewey Decimal classification, publication details, physical description, language, ISBN, and price.

The current national bibliography of France is *Bibliographie Nationale Française* (*BNF*), which records titles received by the Bibliothèque Nationale de France through legal deposit. *BNF* has five sections listing books ("Livres"), publications in series ("Publications en série"), audiovisual materials ("Audiovisuel"), printed music ("Musique"), and cartographic materials ("Cartographie"). Its primary arrangement is by Universal Decimal Classification (UDC). Indexes by author, title, and subject heading complement the classified arrangement. It is freely available online from the Bibliothèque Nationale de France website.

Canadiana is the current national bibliography of Canada. Its listings are composed of cataloging records for a wide variety of publications produced in Canada, including books, periodicals, sound recordings, microforms, music scores, pamphlets, government documents, theses, educational kits, video recordings, and electronic documents. Legal deposit applies to all publishers in Canada, who are required to send copies of items to LAC as they are published. In addition, *Canadiana* lists titles published outside Canada that are of special interest because they are about Canadian topics or because they are written by Canadian authors. *Canadiana* can be searched free of charge through *AMICUS*, the Canadian national catalog.

SOURCES OF PURCHASING INFORMATION

In-print lists identify titles that are currently available from publishers. Because books may remain in print for a number of years, the current list can also be useful in identifying material published much earlier. In reference work, in-print lists are often used to determine whether an announced book has been published, whether a later edition of a work has been published, or what volumes of a series are still in print. The primary advantage of the in-print list is that it consolidates book purchasing information from thousands of publishers into one integrated list.

Other resources are rivaling the in-print list in usefulness. Almost all publishers worldwide now produce catalogs available through the Web. Frequently, these electronic catalogs provide more accurate up-to-date information than that available from in-print lists. *Amazon* and *Barnes & Noble* provide easily searchable basic bibliographic and pricing information for millions of books in multiple formats, videos, and CDs. However, as Melissa De Fino (2013) cautions, *Amazon*'s data are not organized or indexed in a way that is conducive to research, but rather designed to improve sales. The quality, search capability, and organization of bibliographic information important to researchers are lacking. Accurate and objective metadata is what sets library catalogs apart from commercial databases like *Amazon*.

Currently a business unit of ProQuest, Bowker, dominates the in-print list field. The Web-based *Books In Print* offers information on more than 20 million book, audiobook, eBook, and multimedia global titles, including in-print, forthcoming, and out-of-print items. It is available at two subscription levels: U.S. Editions for U.S. publications and Global Editions for the U.S., UK, Canadian, European, and Australian publications. It offers multiple search options. The basic search includes subject, title, author, publisher, series title, and character options. Advanced search allows even more precise searching through combinations of various fields and a variety of limits such as language, country of publication, age range, date range, and Dewey range. In addition to detailed bibliographic and order information, records for titles may include reviews and suggestions of similar titles.

Grey House Publishing issues a number of titles, based on the Bowker data, in print form. *Books In Print* (*BIP*) is an annual listing of books available from U.S. publishers, with a midyear supplement. *Forthcoming Books*, published four times a year, lists books projected to be published within the next several months. *Subject Guide to Books In Print* arranges the content of *BIP* according to the *Library of Congress Subject Headings* (*LCSH*) assigned to the books. *Children's Books In Print* and the *Subject Guide to Children's Books In Print* list material selected by age level. Other titles cover specific formats: *Books Out Loud: Bowker's Guide to Audiobooks* and *Complete Video Directory* are examples.

SERIAL SOURCES

The most comprehensive source of bibliographic information about serials is *Ulrichsweb*, a database with entries for more than 300,000 serials of all types, including academic and scholarly journals, eJournals, peer-reviewed titles, popular magazines, newspapers, newsletters, and more. Entries in *Ulrichsweb* provide data such as ISSN, publisher, frequency, language, subject, indexing and abstracting coverage, full-text database coverage, and reviews written by librarians. The status of each title, whether active or ceased, is clearly indicated as is whether or not the contents are refereed. The basic search prompts for title, ISSN, or search term; advanced search allows one to enter additional terms and limit by status (e.g., active, ceased), serial type, content type, and language.

Newspapers currently published in the United States and Canada are listed in the *Gale Directory of Publications and Broadcast Media*. In addition to newspapers, this directory includes information about magazines, journals, college publications, radio and television stations, and cable stations and systems. It is published annually in five volumes. The first two volumes (United States and Canada) and volume 5 (international) are arranged geographically, with the print and broadcast entries alphabetically under the place of publication. The third volume includes indexes by publisher and subject as well as listings by category such as ethnic publications and women's publications. The fourth volume has a regional market index. This directory is available online as part of the *Gale Directory Library*.

A series of publications from Oxbridge Communications replicates the coverage offered by other serial directories and expands coverage into other areas such as newsletters. *The Standard Periodical Directory* includes more than 59,000 U.S. and Canadian periodicals; *The National Directory of Magazines* provides production specifications and rates for more than 20,000 U.S. and Canadian publications; and the *Oxbridge Directory of Newsletters* covers more than 13,000 consumer, association, and business newsletters. All these titles are produced in print and are accessible online through *MediaFinder* database.

In recent years, there has been growth in open-access journals, publications that make the full text of their articles freely available on the Web. The *Directory of Open Access Journals* has been developed to simplify identification of and access to these scientific and scholarly journals. As of mid 2016, the directory included 9,078 journals from 130 countries, with 6,242 searchable at the article level.

RECOMMENDED LISTS

Recommended lists are highly selective evaluative bibliographies, used by librarians in three integral ways: building a collection to meet the needs of users, measuring (evaluating) the library collection against these standard lists, and advising readers. In carrying out these activities, one must keep in mind that recommended lists are created for an average collection, whereas the librarian is collecting for a particular library with a unique user population. A few examples of some well-known recommended lists are discussed in this chapter. Chapter 13 can be consulted for lists of reference books, and Chapter 24 provides thorough coverage of tools for readers' advisory use.

Seven *Core Collections* databases are available online from EBSCO, and subsets including the most highly ranked titles are also distributed in print by Grey House Publishing: *Children's Core Collection*, *Middle & Junior High Core Collection*, *Senior High Core Collection*, *Young Adult Fiction Core Collection*, *Graphic Novels Core Collection*, *Fiction Core Collection*, and *Public Library Core Collection: Nonfiction*, with the latter two recommending titles for a general adult audience. Titles included are selected by the *Core Collections* team employed by EBSCO and the *Core Collections* Advisory Group, comprising public, academic, and school librarians who are experts in their fields. Entries in each database include complete bibliographic information, an annotation and subject headings, grade level and Dewey classification, recommendation level, and links to reviews, similar books, and other books by the author.

Resources for College Libraries (*RCL*) covers more than 85,000 titles targeted at an undergraduate audience in a broad range of subjects, including the traditional liberal arts and sciences curriculum, business, computer science, education, engineering, and health sciences. *RCL* resources are selected by subject specialists, including both academic librarians and faculty members. Primarily a collection development tool, the database provides titles of print and electronic books, websites, and databases. The database is searchable by keyword, subject, title, author, Library of Congress Classification, and via a hierarchical framework of *RCL* subject categories.

Magazines for Libraries is an annotated list by subject of more than 5,200 periodicals, both print and electronic journals. Selection is limited to those titles considered to be most useful for the average elementary or secondary school, public, academic, or special library. *Magazines for Libraries* also serves as a readers' advisory tool for the user who wants to select a magazine in a subject area of particular interest. Annotations from *Magazines for Libraries* are included in *Ulrichsweb.* The *Magazines for Libraries Update* blog includes annotations for selected open-access and niche titles of interest.

Oxford Bibliographies consists of subject modules covering the literature on specific topics, primarily in the humanities and social sciences. Each collection has its own editor in chief and editorial board. Each bibliography identifies the essential literature of its topic, providing introductory overviews, identifying standard works if they exist, and providing evaluative and comparative annotations of relevant books, articles, primary sources, online resources, and other formats of material deemed essential to an overview of the subject. Broad subject areas range from management to medieval studies to music. Examples of specific bibliographies within these subject areas are "organization culture," "feudalism," and "folk music."

SEARCH STRATEGIES

Verification is necessary when trying to identify, and eventually locate, a given item. Often the bibliographic information presented by a library user to the reference librarian is so incomplete that a good deal of ingenuity must be used to locate a copy. The sources of incomplete citations can vary from partial information gathered from a chance reference on a television or radio talk show to a poorly constructed bibliography in a scholarly book. Practice and experience make the process easier, but there are a number of factors to keep in mind when deciding where to start.

For most bibliographic quests, a search begins with *WorldCat.* The speed, ease of searching, and depth and breadth of coverage make this the first choice in almost all cases. However, a study by Jeffrey Beall and Karen Kafadar (2005) and a follow-up study by Christine DeZelar-Tiedman (2008) demonstrate that there are still a significant number of bibliographic records, especially for old and rare materials, found in the *National Union Catalog, Pre-1956 Imprints* that are not found in a search of *WorldCat.* To fully answer a question, the librarian may need to look at several tools and may well find pieces of the bibliographic puzzle in each of them. Knowledge of these sources will assist the librarian in deciding which tools to examine and, in some cases, may narrow the search to only one tool that will give a particular type of information.

The search in Box 16.1 illustrates several points. First, one should note that current English usage indicates that the word *homeschooling* should be spelled as one word, yet *LCSH* uses two words. When one goes back and checks the electronic *Books In Print* entry for the book, the entry shows only one subject heading: Education—Aims and Objectives. At no place in the *Books In Print* entry does the

Box 16.1 Search Strategy: A Book on Homeschooling

An out-of-town researcher appeared at a university library's reference desk. A colleague at her home institution had recommended a book by Eva Boyd. The book was about a single mother who homeschooled her son, who then completed college by age 17. She remembered neither the date of publication nor the title of the book. The first step was searching the university library's own catalog. Because the university had a strong collection in the field of education, it was assumed that the book would turn up immediately as a result of an author search. No author with the name of Eva Boyd appeared in the list of authors. A widening of the catalog search to include the holdings of the consortium of which the library was a part resulted in one book by Eva Jolene Boyd on the subject of stagecoach travel in the American West, *That Old Overland Stagecoaching.* A search of *WorldCat* and *Books In Print* on the Web turned up more books by the same Eva Jolene Boyd. Finally, the librarian revised her strategy on *WorldCat*. A subject search on "Home Schooling" and keyword author search "Eva" produced two matches, including *About Face* by Eva Seibert. The alternative title is "How both sons of a single mother were homeschooled and admitted to college by the time they were twelve." The record indicated that the book was self-published, and only two holding libraries were listed, neither close by. The librarian turned to *Amazon* to determine whether a copy was available inexpensively. Several sources for purchase were identified with two copies priced at $10.00 or less.

concept "home schooling" appear. Had the librarian relied on only one source, this query would never have been answered. This case shows how resourceful and creative reference librarians must be when tackling complex bibliographic questions. Name and title variations, or uncertainties regarding specific editions of works or which libraries might own these editions, are just a few of the difficulties that may arise from a seemingly simple request for a book. Often, the librarian must carefully question the user and consider all available resources to successfully answer bibliographic reference questions.

The future of bibliographic sources and the capabilities they offer reference librarians will be shaped by new developments in bibliographic control. In November 2006, the Library of Congress convened the Working Group on the Future of Bibliographic Control. Its final report, titled *On the Record*, concluded that: "The future of bibliographic control will be collaborative, decentralized, international in scope, and Web-based. Its realization will occur in cooperation with the private sector, and with the active collaboration of library users. Data will be gathered from multiple sources; change will happen quickly; and bibliographic control will be dynamic, not static" (2008, 4).

REFERENCES

Beall, Jeffrey, and Karen Kafadar. 2005. "The Proportion of NUC Pre-56 Titles Represented in OCLC WorldCat." *College & Research Libraries* 66 (5): 431–35.

Cargill, Mary. 1996. "Bibliography." In *Guide to Reference Books*, 11th ed., edited by Robert Balay, 1–105. Chicago: American Library Association.

Chen, Xiaotian. 2012. "Google Books and WorldCat: A Comparison of Their Content." *Online Information Review* 36 (4): 507–16.

De Fino, Melissa. 2013. "Amazon for Technical Services Librarians: Making Order of the Jungle." *Technical Services Quarterly* 29 (4): 280–91.

DeZelar-Tiedman, Christine. 2008. "The Proportion of NUC Pre-56 Titles Represented in the RLIN and OCLC Databases Compared: A Follow-Up to the Beall/Kafadar Study." *College & Research Libraries* 69 (5): 401–6.

Duffy, Eamon P. 2013. "Searching HathiTrust: Old Concepts in a New Context." *Partnership: The Canadian Journal of Library and Information Practice and Research* 8 (1). https://journal.lib.uoguelph.ca/index.php/perj/article/view/2503#.Vq1vNUYj5qE.

Eichenlaub, Naomi. 2013. "Checking in with Google Books, HathiTrust, and the DPLA." *Computers in Libraries* 33 (9): 4–9.

Gorman, Michael. 2004. "Authority Control in the Context of Bibliographic Control in the Electronic Environment." *Cataloging & Classification Quarterly* 38 (3–4): 11–22.

Hadro, Josh. 2013. "What's the Problem with Self-Publishing?" *Library Journal* 138 (7): 34–36.

James, Ryan, and Andrew Weiss. 2012. "An Assessment of Google Books' Metadata." *Journal of Library Metadata* 12 (1): 15–22.

Marcum, Deanna. 2014. "Archives, Libraries, Museums: Coming Back Together?" *Information & Culture* 49 (1): 74–89.

Mays, Dorothy A. 2015. "Google Books: Far More Than Just Books." *Public Libraries* 54 (5): 23–26.

McCullough, John. 2015. "OCLC and Discovery." In *Reimagining Reference in the 21st Century*, edited by David A. Tyckoson and John G. Dove, 327–33. West Lafayette, IN: Purdue University Press.

Meyer, Robinson. 2015. "After 10 Years, Google Books Is Legal." *The Atlantic*. October 20. http://www.theatlantic.com/technology/archive/2015/10/fair-use-transformative-leval-google-books/411058/.

OCLC. 2016. "About OCLC." Last accessed January 30. http://www.oclc.org/en-US/about.html.

Pope, Julia T., and Robert P. Holley. 2011. "Google Book Search and Metadata." *Cataloging & Classification Quarterly* 49 (1): 1–13.

Wilson, Patrick. 1968. *Two Kinds of Power: An Essay on Bibliographic Control*. Berkeley: University of California Press.

Working Group on the Future of Bibliographic Control. 2008. *On the Record*. Washington, DC: Library of Congress. https://www.loc.gov/bibliographic-future/news/lcwg-ontherecord-jan08-final.pdf.

Yang, Sharon Q., and Kurt Wagner. 2010. "Evaluating and Comparing Discovery Tools: How Close Are We towards Next Generation Catalog?" *Library Hi Tech* 28 (4): 690–709.

LIST OF SOURCES

Amazon. http://www.amazon.com.

American Book Publishing Record. Amenia, NY: Grey House Publishing. Monthly with annual cumulation.

AMICUS. Ottawa: Library and Archives Canada. http://amicus.collectionscanada.gc.ca/aaweb/aalogine.htm.

Barnes & Noble. http://www.barnesandnoble.com.

Bibliographie Nationale Française. Paris: Bibliothèque Nationale de France. http://bibliographienationale.bnf.fr/.

Books In Print. Amenia, NY: Grey House Publishing. Annual with semiannual supplements.

Books In Print. Ann Arbor, MI: ProQuest. http://www.proquest.com/products-services/Books-in-Print.html. [subscription required]

Books Out Loud: Bowker's Guide to Audiobooks. 2016. Amenia, NY: Grey House Publishing. Annual.

British Library Catalogue. London: British Library. http://explore.bl.uk/primo_library/libweb/action/search.do?mode=Basic&vid=BLVU1&tab=local_tab&.

British National Bibliography. London: British Library. http://bnb.bl.uk/.

Canadiana. Ottawa: Library and Archives Canada. http://www.bac-lac.gc.ca/eng/services/canadiana/Pages/canadiana-national-bibliography.aspx.

Catalogue Général. Paris: Bibliothèque Nationale de France. http://catalogue.bnf.fr/index.do.

Children's Books In Print. 2016. 46th ed. Amenia, NY: Grey House Publishing. Annual.

Children's Core Collection. 2015. 22nd ed. Amenia, NY: Grey House Publishing. Also available online from EBSCO as part of *Core Collections.*

Complete Video Directory. 2016. Amenia, NY: Grey House Publishing. Annual.

Core Collections. Ipswich, MA: EBSCO. https://www.ebscohost.com/public/core-collections. [subscription required]

Digital Public Library of America. http://dp.la/.

Directory of Open Access Journals. https://doaj.org/.

Explore the British Library. London: British Library. http://explore.bl.uk/.

Fiction Core Collection. 2016. 18th ed. Amenia, NY: Grey House Publishing. Also available online from EBSCO as part of *Core Collections.*

Forthcoming Books. 2016. Amenia, NY: Grey House Publishing. Quarterly.

Gale Directory Library. Farmington Hills, MI: Gale Cengage Learning. http://solutions.cengage.com/BusinessSolutions/Gale-Directory-Library/. [subscription required]

Gale Directory of Publications and Broadcast Media. 2016. 152nd ed. Farmington Hills, MI: Gale Cengage Learning. Annual. Also available online as part of *Gale Directory Library.*

Google Books. http://books.google.com.

Graphic Novels Core Collection. 2016. Amenia, NY: Grey House Publishing. Also available online from EBSCO as part of *Core Collections.*

Guide to Reference Books. 1996. 11th ed. Edited by Robert Balay. Chicago: American Library Association.

HathiTrust Digital Library. https://www.hathitrust.org/.

Library of Congress Authorities. Library of Congress. http://authorities.loc.gov.

Library of Congress Online Catalog. Library of Congress. https://catalog.loc.gov/.

Library of Congress Subject Headings. Library of Congress. http://authorities.loc.gov/.

LibWeb: Library Servers via WWW. http://www.lib-web.org/.

Magazines for Libraries. 2014. 23rd ed. Edited by Cheryl LaGuardia. Ann Arbor, MI: ProQuest. Also available online as part of *Ulrichsweb.*

Magazines for Libraries Update. Ann Arbor, MI: ProQuest. http://www.proquest.com/blog/mfl/.

MediaFinder. New York: Oxbridge Communications. http://www.mediafinder.com/. [subscription required]

Middle & Junior High Core Collection. 2015. 12th ed. Amenia, NY: Grey House Publishing. Also available online from EBSCO as part of *Core Collections.*

The National Directory of Magazines. 2016. New York: Oxbridge Communications. Annual. Also available online as part of *MediaFinder.*

National Union Catalog, Pre-1956 Imprints. A Cumulative Author List Representing Library of Congress Printed Cards and Titles Reported by Other American Libraries. 1968–1981. 754 vols. London: Mansell.

Oxbridge Directory of Newsletters. 2016. New York: Oxbridge Communications. Annual. Also available online as part of *MediaFinder.*

Oxford Bibliographies. Oxford: Oxford University Press. https://global.oup.com/academic/product/oxford-bibliographies-9780199799701?cc=us&lang=en&. [subscription required]

Public Library Core Collection: Nonfiction. 2015. 15th ed. Amenia, NY: Grey House Publishing. Also available online from EBSCO as part of *Core Collections.*

Resources for College Libraries (RCL). Ann Arbor, MI: ProQuest. http://www.proquest.com/products-services/Resources-for-College-Libraries.html. [subscription required]

Senior High Core Collection. 2014. 20th ed. Amenia, NY: Grey House Publishing. Also available online from EBSCO as part of *Core Collections.*

The Standard Periodical Directory. 2016. New York: Oxbridge Communications. Annual. Available online as part of *MediaFinder.*

Subject Guide to Books In Print. Amenia, NY: Grey House Publishing. Annual.

Subject Guide to Children's Books In Print. Amenia, NY: Grey House Publishing. Annual.

Ulrichsweb. Ann Arbor, MI: ProQuest. http://www.proquest.com/products-services/Ulrichsweb.html. [subscription required]

Virtual International Authority File. https://viaf.org/.

Wikipedia. https://www.wikipedia.org/.

WorldCat. Dublin, OH: OCLC. http://www.oclc.org/en-US/worldcat.html. [subscription required]

WorldCat.org. Dublin, OH: OCLC. http://www.worldcat.org/.

Young Adult Fiction Core Collection. 2015. Amenia, NY: Grey House Publishing. Also available online from EBSCO as part of *Core Collections.*

SUGGESTED READINGS

Bell, Suzanne S. 2015. *Librarian's Guide to Online Searching: Cultivating Database Skills for Research and Instruction*, 4th ed. Santa Barbara, CA: Libraries Unlimited.

This text has a helpful chapter on searching bibliographic databases, with a focus on *WorldCat* as well as a library's own catalog.

Chambers, Sally, ed. 2013. *Catalogue 2.0: The Future of the Library Catalogue.* Chicago: ALA Neal-Schuman.

This collection of papers provides a state-of-the-art examination of the library catalog and an exploration of where it may be headed.

Hall, Danielle. 2004. "Mansell Revisited." *American Libraries* 35 (4): 78–80.

Hall highlights the decrease in usage of the *National Union Catalog* by U.S. libraries, coinciding with the growth of *WorldCat.* She provides a brief history of this ambitious publication project, commenting that "even as the project progressed, the profession recognized that this 'greatest single instrument' would be the last great bibliographic effort in a paper format."

Kornegay, Rebecca, Heidi E. Buchanan, and Hildegard B. Morgan. 2009. *Magic Search: Getting the Best Results from Your Catalog and Beyond.* Chicago: American Library Association.

The authors explain the *Library of Congress Subject Heading* system, particularly the subdivisions and how they can be used to improve keyword search results.

Krummel, D.W. *Bibliographies: Their Aims and Methods.* London: Mansell Publishing, 1984.

This basic text discusses the various types of bibliographic study and the evaluation of bibliographies.

Mann, Thomas. 2015. *The Oxford Guide to Library Research*, 4th ed. New York: Oxford University Press.

Three chapters in this guide provide guidance on search strategy specific to bibliographic sources: "Subject Headings and the Library Catalog," "Published Subject Bibliographies," and "Locating Materials in Other Libraries."

Taylor, Arlene G., and Daniel N. Joudrey. 2009. *The Organization of Information*, 3rd ed. Westport, CT: Libraries Unlimited.

This introductory text gives an excellent overview of the principles of organizing recorded information of various types. Within a broad context, the authors enable the reader to see how organization facilitates use.

Chapter 17

Indexes and Abstracts

Linda C. Smith

USES AND CHARACTERISTICS

A library's catalog generally does not provide access to the entire contents of a library's collection. The catalog may confirm the holdings of a periodical title but not its contents, a poetry collection but not individual poems, the title of an author's collected works but not an individual essay, and newspaper titles but not individual news stories. Indexes and abstracts can more fully reveal resources not covered in the general catalog as well as the existence of additional resources not held in a given library's collection. With the availability of online catalogs, indexes, and abstracts in electronic form, more efforts are being made to provide direct links among them. For example, when the user of an index locates the record of a journal article likely to be of interest, information about the library's holdings of that journal title should be directly accessible. As more material becomes available in electronic form, mechanisms for index entries to link directly to the full texts of the publications indexed are likewise being developed.

Indexes such as periodical indexes usually list the authors, titles, or subjects of publications without comment. Abstracts, on the other hand, present a brief summary of content. Many abstracting services rely on author abstracts (or translations thereof) rather than having staff read each article and abstract it (a very costly practice). Abstracts serve as an aid in assessing the content of a document and its potential relevance, and they continue to be valued (Nicholas, Huntington, and Jamali 2007). Although indexes and abstracts existed before 1900, there was a dramatic growth in their number during the 20th century, as the scholarly community demanded improved access to a growing number of publications. The advent of the Web made it possible for librarians to subscribe to indexing and abstracting databases that the user could search and view over the Web, dramatically expanding their availability and usefulness.

In the first two decades of the 21st century, increasing questions have been raised about the future of indexes and abstracts, especially those covering specialized subject areas (Chen 2010; Tucci 2010). A growing number of publications are available in full text online, with the entire text searchable for occurrences of the keywords sought, potentially reducing the need for document surrogates such as indexes and abstracts. Nevertheless, Dennis Auld (1999) argues that the skills of classifying, indexing, aggregating, and structuring content still are needed in the Web environment. Traditional databases remain superior in their ability to describe, organize, and connect information in a consistent structured way. Indexes and abstracts are often thought of as value-added services because a human indexer has analyzed the document content and developed a document surrogate, including indexing terms. It is assumed that this effort benefits the user by improving retrieval performance, enabling the identification of the best set of items for the user's purposes: "Abstracts are one antidote to information overload. Indexing is another. . . . The value added by well-written abstracts and appropriate thesauri are more important than ever" (Ojala 2012, 5).

Publishers of indexes and abstracts are introducing a number of enhancements to better meet user needs: inclusion of abstracts in what were formerly only indexing services; inclusion of full-text articles in what were formerly only abstracting services; marketing of different subsets of a service to meet the needs of different sizes and types of libraries; creation of rich networks of links between indexes and multiple full-text resources; and enhanced retrospective coverage. Library users increasingly demand rapid access to full texts, and indexes and abstracts are evolving to support that. This has led to what can seem to be a bewildering array of choices for librarians seeking to make selections among competing indexes and abstracts, increasing the need for careful evaluation.

EVALUATION

As reference librarians use the tools in reference work, they evaluate indexes and abstracts and choose those that will best reveal the contents of their own collections or that will refer users to needed information beyond library walls. Important characteristics to consider are format, scope, authority, accuracy, access points, and any special features that enhance effectiveness or ease of use.

Many of the indexes and abstracts discussed in this chapter are devoted to a particular type of publication, such as periodicals, newspapers, or dissertations. More specialized services devoted to indexing and abstracting the literature of a discipline often try to encompass many different types of publications to provide more comprehensive coverage in one source. Other differences arise if there are restrictions on place and language of publication of the source materials. Some indexes and abstracts cover only English-language material; others try to identify material relevant to a particular subject area in any language and from any part of the world. To determine the scope, it is necessary to rely on database descriptions found in documentation provided by the database producer or vendor. Many publishers of periodical indexes are now posting lists of indexed journals on their websites, making comparison among competing services easier (Chen 2006).

Format

While some indexes and abstracts still have a print counterpart, most current indexes exist only in electronic form with much more powerful search capabilities, including more access points and the possibility of refining searches by using Boolean logic to combine terms (see Chapter 15 for a discussion of search strategy). However, because many databases do not cover the literature before the mid-1960s, searches of indexes and abstracts for older literature must rely on the print versions, where they exist for the period of interest.

Scope

Several characteristics define the scope of indexes and abstracts, including the publication dates covered and the types of materials indexed. The time covered does not necessarily coincide with the period of publication because the publisher may go back and index some older material valuable to the users of the index. For example, *Science Citation Index* has now extended its coverage back to 1900, although it originally began publication in the 1960s. An advantage of searching indexes and abstracts online is that the contents are automatically cumulated, with updates as often as daily.

Types of materials covered are another aspect of scope. Indexes and abstracts differ in the number of publications covered and the depth or specificity of the indexing. General periodical indexes tend to index all substantive articles from the periodicals selected for indexing, whereas subject-specific indexes and abstracts are more likely to index selectively from a much larger list of periodicals, with indexers identifying those articles of most relevance to the subject scope of the service. Some indexes and abstracts are more inclusive in the types of articles indexed, indexing such things as letters to the editor and editorials, whereas other services restrict their coverage to research articles. As the number of electronic-only and, more recently, open-access journals has grown, publishers of indexes and abstracts have had to develop criteria for covering such titles.

Authority

The reputation of the publisher or sponsoring organization and the qualifications of the editorial staff determine the authority of indexes and abstracts. Publishers of indexes include commercial firms, professional associations, and government agencies. EBSCO, Gale Cengage Learning, and ProQuest are the major commercial publishers of indexes and abstracts. The Modern Language Association, publisher of *MLA International Bibliography*, is an example of a professional association, and the National Agricultural Library, publisher of *AGRICOLA*, is an example of a government agency.

Accuracy

The quality of indexing and accuracy of bibliographic citations affect the usefulness of indexes. Questions to consider include the following: Are all authors associated with an indexed item included in the author index? Are all major facets of the content of the article represented by entries in the subject index? Accuracy can also apply to both author and subject indexing. Author names should be spelled in the index as they are spelled in the work. Unfortunately, indexing guidelines for some indexes and abstracts dictate that only initials of given names be retained, even when a fuller form of the name appears on the original publication. This can make it difficult, when searching authors, to distinguish between different authors who share a common surname and initials. Accuracy of subject indexing depends on the indexer's ability to represent the content of a publication using terminology drawn from the controlled vocabulary (thesaurus or list of subject headings) to be used in indexing. Cross-references should be included where needed to lead from a form not used to the proper form or to link related terms. Some indexes include augmented titles, where the indexer supplements the original article title with additional terms to characterize the article's content more completely. Abstracts should provide an accurate summary of the original article's content.

Access Points

Indexes and abstracts in electronic form generally offer many options for searching in addition to author name and subject. These may include such elements as keywords from title and abstract, journal title, and author affiliation. Documentation provided by the publisher can be studied to learn more about the structure of a database record and which elements can be searched or used to limit the results.

Special Features

When indexes and abstracts are evaluated, any special features that enhance their usefulness should be noted. Examples include a list of periodicals or other sources indexed and a published list of subject headings. The list of sources indexed is helpful in providing a clear indication of the materials covered as well as complete bibliographic information for those materials not available locally. This can be helpful in acquiring documents, whether ordering copies for inclusion in the library's collection or making requests through interlibrary loan or a document delivery service. A published list of subject headings can help in formulating effective search strategies because the user can see a comprehensive list of terms available to the indexer and thus have a better chance of locating the appropriate terms to search. This is especially the case for those lists of subject headings that include scope notes or instructions for indexers, explaining how particular terms are to be used in indexing (and hence in searching). A growing number of indexing and abstracting services are developing approaches to ease the task of locating the full text of documents covered by their services, such as including the full text of documents as page images or searchable full text.

When a library subscribes to multiple indexing and abstracting databases and full-text resources, it can be a challenge to determine whether the full text of an article cited in one database is available in another resource. Link-resolving software makes this task easier by creating a bridge between databases, enabling users to easily go from a journal citation in one database to the full text of the journal article in another database (Breeding 2012).

SELECTION

Indexes and abstracts are often expensive reference tools. Selection of titles for a particular collection must take into account the characteristics of that collection as well as the needs of users for access beyond what is already provided by the library's catalog. *Ulrichsweb*, described in Chapter 16, can be searched for serial type "abstract/index." In addition, for each periodical listed, *Ulrichsweb* provides an indication of the indexes and abstracts that include the periodical in their coverage.

Needs of Users

Indexes and abstracts selected for a particular library collection should reflect the types of information and publications that library users wish to access. Given the increasing availability of full text online as part of indexing and abstracting databases, selection of such a database also gives users access to these full-text documents in electronic form. General periodical indexes and newspaper indexes could be useful in libraries of all types. Selection of indexes devoted to particular subject areas will reflect the subject interests of the library's users. Citation indexes, with their emphasis on scholarly literature, will be of most use in academic and special libraries. Indexes to special types of materials are also likely to be found most often in academic and special libraries. Selection of indexes to reviews should reflect user demand for this information. Indexes to literary forms can prove useful wherever collected works and anthologies make up part of the collection. Usage of indexes and abstracts in electronic form can be measured, providing a tool to guide the choice of which resources to retain and which to cancel when licenses come up for renewal (International Coalition of Library Consortia 1999; Pesch 2006).

Cost

The discussion of licensing in Chapter 14 identifies a number of factors affecting the cost of indexes and abstracts. As explained in Chapter 5, increasingly libraries are gaining access to electronic databases through participation in consortial licensing arrangements, which may reduce the price paid by each participating library.

Most of the major index publishers have several products, usually for different types of libraries and often in different size packages, so librarians can choose which package they need and can afford. For example, EBSCO has three general titles for public libraries (*MasterFILE Complete*, *MasterFILE Elite*, and *MasterFILE Premier*) and three general titles for academic libraries (*Academic Search Complete*, *Academic Search Elite*, and *Academic Search Premier*) as well as products for elementary, middle, and high school library use. They differ in the number of periodical titles indexed, the number of titles in full text, the types of titles (scholarly vs. popular; intended age level), and supplementary materials included together with the indexed titles (e.g., *MasterFILE* databases include the full text of selected reference books, primary sources, and photos, maps, and flags in addition to periodicals).

Uniqueness

Although overlap in sources indexed is one indicator of the degree of uniqueness of indexes, the access points and search capabilities provided by the indexes must also be considered. Two indexes could cover many of the same periodicals, but the subject indexing provided may give the user different ways of approaching the content in each. Thus, examination of overlap in materials covered must be supplemented by an assessment of the approaches provided to those materials by the different indexes.

Although many indexes and abstracts are available on only a single system, others may be available on more than one, such as *MLA International Bibliography*, which is distributed by EBSCO, Gale Cengage Learning, and ProQuest. In such a case, librarians need to consider the selection factors for electronic sources discussed in Chapter 13, including the user interface, branding and customization, and accessibility.

Full-Text Coverage

Given the growing demand for the full text of periodicals, newspapers, and other publications in electronic form, criteria for selecting these resources deserve special consideration. Unfortunately, "full text" does not have a standard definition when applied to electronic publications with print counterparts. At the article level, "full text" may include the main text but not any sidebars or illustrations (Chen 2005). At the issue level, "full text" may include major articles but omit such things as letters to the editor, short columns, book reviews, and advertisements. At the journal level, one expects "full text" to cover all the issues of the publication, including any supplements. As Walt Crawford (2000) notes, these differences may result in a loss of important context for the content.

Factors to consider in comparing full-text databases include which titles are covered in various subject areas (and whether any are unique, not covered elsewhere), coverage dates, currency, policy on inclusion of article types and illustrations, whether text is searchable or only displayable, indexing, output formats, and pricing. Delivery of full text in a Web environment also opens up the possibility of creating links among articles, reflecting the relationships among them.

As journal publishers experiment with the electronic medium, the situation becomes even more complex. Because of possible differences between the electronic and print versions of the same title, indexing and abstracting services may have difficulty deciding which version to index. Reference librarians also need to be aware of the different models of supplying full text that have emerged in the Web environment: publisher-supplied full text; third-party or aggregator-supplied full text; and distributed "linked" full text, in which an indexing or abstracting service links to publisher-supplied full text (Tenopir 1998).

IMPORTANT GENERAL SOURCES

This chapter describes some of the most widely held general periodical indexes, newspaper indexes, subject-oriented indexes, citation indexes, indexes for special types of materials, indexes of reviews, and indexes for different literary forms. Only a few of the indexing and abstracting services devoted to coverage of the literature of a specific subject area can be mentioned in this chapter as examples.

General Periodical Indexes

General periodical indexes are held by all types of libraries. They index periodicals covering current events, hobbies, popular culture, and school curriculum–related areas. The *Readers' Guide to Periodical Literature* has filled this need since 1901 (Biggs 1992). It continues to be published in print quarterly with an annual cumulation, providing subject and author access to articles in 300 of the most popular and important periodicals published in the United States and Canada. In May 2011, EBSCO purchased H.W. Wilson, publisher of *Readers' Guide* and several other indexes, and now provides online access to *Readers' Guide* with coverage beginning in 1983 as well as to *Readers' Guide Retrospective: 1890–1982*. The *Alternative Press Index*, which began publication in 1969, seeks to provide subject indexing for more than 300 journals and newspapers covering alternative or radical points of view. It is available online through EBSCO.

EBSCO, Gale Cengage Learning, and ProQuest all produce multiple databases that index periodicals and provide increasing quantities of full text, with products ranging from those for school libraries to those intended for large academic and public libraries. These competing products continue to change their coverage, both of titles indexed and of titles available in full text, and search capabilities. Therefore, librarians need to follow these developments to determine which approaches to providing access to periodicals best meet the needs of the library's users and which are affordable. Increasingly, these databases encompass material in addition to periodicals, such as selected reference books. Box 17.1 compares the coverage of the most comprehensive multidisciplinary database offered by the three major vendors as of early 2016.

Box 17.1 Comparison of Major Multidisciplinary Databases

EBSCO, *Academic Search Complete:*
Nearly 13,600 journals indexed; more than 8,800 journals in full text; additional content includes reports, books, and more than 60,000 videos from the Associated Press.

Gale Cengage Learning, *Academic OneFile:*
More than 17,000 journals, books, news sources, and reports indexed; more than 8,100 in full text.

ProQuest, *ProQuest Central:*
More than 20,000 journals indexed; more than 85 percent of content in full text; additional content includes news, market information, dissertations, and preprint working papers.

Comparison among these offerings should consider not only how many of their titles are full text but also how far their backfiles extend, how many of their titles are unique, and how many of their titles are peer reviewed. In addition, librarians need to be aware that the most recent issues of a journal may be embargoed. To protect subscriptions, journal publishers may not immediately release the full text of their most recent issues for inclusion in these aggregated collections.

Google released *Google Scholar* in a beta version in 2004 to enable Web-based search of the scholarly literature. Because it is simple to use, free, and available to anyone with access to the Web, *Google Scholar* has rapidly gained in popularity.

Nevertheless, a number of questions have been raised. As Badke (2009, 49) notes, *Google Scholar* "is not like the carefully structured, library-based databases we treasure." Concerns include that its selection criteria for "scholarly" materials are unknown, its scope and currency are unknown, and its formatting of citations for items retrieved is very nontraditional (Badke 2013). Nevertheless, it provides a way to search across many disciplines and sources simultaneously. Recognizing that many of their users are turning to *Google Scholar* despite its potential shortcomings, librarians are partnering with Google to include links to their resources as part of *Google Scholar* search results (Google 2016). In addition to being interactive with a library's link resolver to provide full-text access, *Google Scholar* expands the full-text collection of the library beyond what is accessible through paid subscriptions and database content via its ability to ferret out free full text for open-access titles (Chen 2013).

Major retrospective indexing projects are becoming available in electronic form, overcoming a long-standing weakness of most online indexes. For example, *Periodicals Index Online* from ProQuest provides access to citations for more than 18 million periodical articles from more than 6,000 journals from as early as 1665 in the arts, humanities, and social sciences, including titles in several non-English, Western European languages. Libraries can gain access to the digitized full text of more than 750 of these journals through *Periodicals Archive Online* from ProQuest.

Although indexes like *Readers' Guide* include some magazines of interest to children, other products are targeted specifically at children. Examples include EBSCO's *Primary Search*, a full-text database covering nearly 100 popular elementary school magazines; EBSCO's *Middle Search Plus*, with the full text of more than 170 popular middle school magazines; Gale Cengage Learning's *InfoTrac Junior Edition*, with 300 indexed journals, of which 230 are full text; and *InfoTrac Student Edition*, with 1,200 indexed journals, of which 1,100 are full text. In addition to the journal content, these resources include supplementary reference material useful to students such as encyclopedias, dictionaries, and biographical sources.

Two indexes provide good coverage of Canadian periodicals. *CPI.Q*, or *Canadian Periodicals Index Quarterly*, available from Gale Cengage Learning, indexes nearly 1,300 Canadian periodicals (both English and French) from 1980 to the present, with full text from more than 700 periodicals. This resource also covers more than 130 newspapers, including the *Toronto Star* and *The Globe and Mail*, as well as reference material related to Canada. ProQuest's *Canadian Business & Current Affairs* (*CBCA*) *Complete* combines full text and indexed content from four *CBCA* database subsets (Business, Current Events, Education, and Reference). Coverage includes full text of nearly 640 periodicals and daily news sources (more than 480 of which are Canadian), plus indexing to an additional 1,100 other titles (more than 95% Canadian). Indexed coverage begins in 1971, and full-text content begins in 1985.

As library users become more diverse, libraries need to consider databases in languages other than English. *Informe Académico* from Gale Cengage Learning provides a wide range of full-text Spanish- and Portuguese-language scholarly journals and magazines both from and about Latin America.

Newspaper Indexes

Many library users want access to newspaper coverage of national and international topics, as well as regional and local news. The effect of technology on newspaper indexing has been considerable, with an increasing number of full-text newspapers in electronic form. More recently, the Web has developed into a rich and diverse source of current news. These changes have made it possible to make much fuller use of news sources in answering reference questions, especially those on current events.

Gale Cengage Learning (*InfoTrac Newsstand*), ProQuest (*Canadian Newsstand, ProQuest Newsstand, ProQuest Historical Newspapers*), and EBSCO (*Newspaper Source, Newspaper Source Plus*) all offer coverage of newspaper resources. *InfoTrac Newsstand* provides access to more than 1,100 major U.S. national, regional, and local newspapers as well as leading titles from around the world. It also includes thousands of images, radio and TV broadcasts, and transcripts. *ProQuest Newsstand* has 1,500 titles available, including both U.S. newspapers and titles from around the world, and libraries can select which titles to subscribe to. *Canadian Newsstand* offers access to the full text of nearly 300 Canadian newspapers, including *The Globe and Mail. ProQuest Historical Newspapers* offers digital archives of major newspapers dating back to the 18th century. *Newspaper Source* contains the full text of more than 40 national (U.S.) and international newspapers as well as full text for more than 300 regional (U.S.) newspapers as well as television and radio news transcripts for several major broadcast networks. *Newspaper Source Plus* expands coverage to include more than 1,200 full-text newspapers, more than 130 newswires, and more than 40 news magazines.

NewsBank is another producer of multiple databases covering newspaper titles, as well as newswires, Web editions, blogs, videos, broadcast transcripts, business journals, periodicals, government documents, and other publications. For example, *Access World News* offers extensive coverage at local, regional, national, and international levels. Other vendors providing access to news databases via the Web include LexisNexis and Factiva.

Publishers are creating other specialized online products to complement coverage of indexes for general newspapers. For example, *Ethnic NewsWatch* from ProQuest is a full-text database with articles from more than 340 newspapers, magazines, and journals published by the ethnic minority press in the United States, including African American, Caribbean, African, Arab/Middle Eastern, Asian/Pacific Islander, European/Eastern European, Hispanic, Jewish, and Native People. Nearly one-fourth of the articles are in Spanish. Coverage begins with 1990; *Ethnic NewsWatch: A History* provides coverage for the period 1959–1989.

At present, news sources freely available on the Web are most valuable for the access they provide to very current news from around the world. Newspapers, news magazines, wire services, and broadcast networks are among the sources of news on the Web (Pew Research Center 2015). Google has entered the arena of providing access to news with its *Google News* service, a computer-generated news service that aggregates headlines from more than 50,000 news sources worldwide, groups similar stories together, and displays them according to each reader's interests.

Subject-Oriented Indexes

Multidisciplinary databases such as *Academic Search Complete, Academic OneFile*, and *ProQuest Central* can provide some coverage of publications from many difference subject areas, but indexes focused on a specific subject area often enable more complete and effective searching of the literature in that subject area. One index commonly found in public and academic libraries is ProQuest's *PAIS International*. It contains citations to journal articles, books, government documents, statistical directories, research reports, conference papers, Web content, and more. *PAIS International* includes publications from more than 120 countries throughout the world, with coverage back to 1977. In addition to English, some of the indexed materials are published in French, German, Italian, Portuguese, Spanish, and other languages. It does not index journals cover to cover, but selects articles relevant to public policy. The scope of *PAIS* includes public policy, business, legal, economic, social science, and related literature. In introducing a library user to this index, it is helpful to point out the types of publications indexed, given that different strategies may be needed to locate periodicals, books, and documents in the library's collection. For users seeking to go back further in time, *PAIS International with Archive* covers the period from 1915 to 1976.

EBSCO, Gale Cengage Learning, and ProQuest all have a range of databases indexing the literature of broad subject areas as well as some more specialized in focus. In many cases, they have acquired databases originally developed by another publisher, such as EBSCO's purchase of H.W. Wilson. The company websites can be consulted for a listing and descriptions of available subject-oriented indexes. While some subjects are covered by a unique database available from a single vendor, such as the *ATLA Religion Database* from EBSCO, other subjects are covered by competing products. For example, Gale Cengage Learning's *Business and Company ASAP*, ProQuest's *ABI/INFORM*, and EBSCO's *Business Source Complete* are rich sources of business journal literature as well as related reference material.

The relative value of general periodical indexes, periodical indexes with a more specific subject focus, and Web resources will vary by discipline. Specialized subject databases often include coverage of a range of publication types, such as conference proceedings and books, as well as journals, where these are important to the discipline. In addition, the subject indexing may draw on a specialized thesaurus reflecting concepts and terminology specific to that discipline. See Table 17.1 for examples of some widely used subject-oriented indexes. See Chapters 25, 26, and 28 for more discussion of indexes for business, medical, and legal materials.

Citation Indexes

The periodical indexes described thus far allow the user to find articles written by the same author or indexed under the same subject heading. Citation indexes allow the user to locate items based on a different type of relationship: the links created when authors cite earlier works by other authors (or even some of their own previously published works). The primary use of a citation index is to find, for a particular publication known to the searcher, later items that have cited it. Thomson Reuters publishes three indexes that allow the user to carry out such searches in broad subject areas: *Science Citation Index*, *Social Sciences Citation Index*, and *Arts & Humanities Citation Index*, searchable singly or in combination online as *Web of Science*. All three are international in scope, covering many journals published outside the United States as well as the major U.S. titles in each subject area. Coverage of other types of publications has been expanded with the addition of *Conference Proceedings Citation Index* (in two parts, one for science and one for social science/humanities) and *Book Citation Index* (in two parts, one for science and one for social science/humanities). Citation networks are an inherently hypertext approach to navigating the literature. *Web of Science* has three types of internal links among records in the database: "cited references" lead to the

TABLE 17.1 Major Subject-Oriented Indexes

Humanities and Arts	
Art	*Art Source*
Film	*Film & Television Literature Index*
Literature	*MLA International Bibliography* *Literature Resource Center*
Music	*Music Index*
Religion	*ATLA Religion Database*
Social Sciences	
Education	*ERIC*
History	*America: History and Life*
	Historical Abstracts
Library and Information Science	*Library & Information Science Source* *Library and Information Science Abstracts (LISA)*
Political Science	*PAIS International*
Psychology	*PsycINFO*
Sociology	*Sociological Abstracts*
Women's and Gender Studies	*GenderWatch* *LGBT Life*
Sciences	
Agriculture	*AGRICOLA*
Biology	*Biological Abstracts*
Chemistry	*SciFinder*
Engineering	*Compendex*
Geology	*GeoRef*
Physics	*Inspec*

items cited by a publication (going backward in time), "times cited" links lead to the items citing a publication (going forward in time), and "related records" identify other publications that have overlapping items cited with the publication of interest. *Web of Science* also provides external links to the full text of journal articles indexed in the database. If the library subscribes to a given journal, then the user can link from the record in *Web of Science* to the full text of the journal article. Box 17.2 provides an example of a search using *Web of Science*.

Box 17.2 Search Strategy: The Filter Bubble

A media studies student has recently come across the video of a 2011 TED talk by Eli Pariser titled "Beware Online 'Filter Bubbles'" and wanted to investigate the topic further as the focus for a paper he had to write for a course on Social Aspects of Media. A *Google* search led to the *Wikipedia* page for "filter bubble," which noted that Pariser coined the term and elaborated on the concept in his 2011 book *The Filter Bubble: What the Internet Is Hiding from You.* Now the student needed to locate more scholarly research on the topic and sought advice through his college library's e-mail reference service. The librarian who handled the question recognized *Web of Science* as a likely tool for such a search, since it would enable the student to locate more recent scholarly publications citing and discussing Pariser's premise. Completing a cited reference search in *Web of Science* using "Pariser E" as the cited author and 2011 as the cited year, she found citations to both the TED talk and the book as the cited work. Recent article titles included "Exposure to Ideologically Diverse News and Opinion on Facebook," and "Automating the News: How Personalized News Recommender System Design Choices Impact News Reception." She e-mailed the student instructions on how to repeat the cited reference search and navigate the links in *Web of Science* and encouraged him to contact the reference desk again if he had further questions.

The dominance of *Web of Science* in the citation searching arena has now been challenged by both fee-based and freely available resources. Elsevier's *Scopus* not only has particular strengths in coverage of the scientific and medical literature but also covers journals in the social sciences and arts and humanities. Some discipline-specific indexes as well as full-text journal databases have introduced citation-searching capabilities (Herther 2015). Finally, *Google Scholar* includes a "cited by" link as part of the bibliographic information for items retrieved through a search. Péter Jacsó (2010) cautions that citation counts displayed in *Google Scholar* are often in error because they are generated automatically and not through the careful editorial process exercised in compiling *Web of Science* and *Scopus*. Yet *Google Scholar* has merit in retrieving citations made by documents not readily found elsewhere, such as online theses, technical reports, and course syllabi. An exhaustive search for cited references requires searching more than one resource. Librarians are becoming more involved in assisting in gathering citation as well as "altmetric" (new metrics based on the Social Web) data, so familiarity with citation indexes is becoming increasingly important (Roemer and Borchardt 2015).

Indexes for Special Types of Materials

The indexes discussed thus far in this chapter provide good coverage of periodicals and newspapers but are not helpful for gaining access to some other special types of materials that may be important in certain library collections. Academic library users frequently want access to dissertations. Indexes devoted to these and other special types of materials, such as conference proceedings and research reports, can be useful for both collection development and reference work. This section describes the indexes for dissertations. Other indexes to special materials are described in more specialized guides to reference sources, such as books on patent searching (Hunt, Nguyen, and Rodgers 2007).

Research for the doctorate is reported in dissertations, many of which are deposited with ProQuest to enable their use outside the institution in which the research was originally completed. The *ProQuest Dissertations & Theses Global* database provides historic and ongoing coverage for North American works and growing international coverage, with many dissertations available in full text. Increasingly, universities are encouraging students completing a dissertation to deposit it in electronic form, and the *Networked Digital Library of Theses and Dissertations* website supports a global search for electronic theses and dissertations.

Indexes of Reviews

Reference librarians may be asked to assist the user in locating reviews of books. Although periodical indexes can sometimes help with such requests, it may be more efficient and effective to use indexes specifically designed for this purpose. Four tools available to libraries include EBSCO's *Book Review Digest Plus* and *Book Review Digest Retrospective*, Gale Cengage Learning's *Book Review Index Plus*, and EBSCO's *Book Index with Reviews*. *Book Review Digest*, with coverage since 1905, provides excerpts of and citations to reviews of current juvenile and adult fiction and nonfiction in the English language. It continues to be published in print but is more easily consulted online, where it exists in two parts: *Book Review Digest Retrospective: 1905–1982*, covering 300,000 books, and *Book Review Digest Plus*, with coverage from 1983 forward. For the current database, contents include at least a citation to every book review from more than 5,000 indexed journals. Excerpts from reviews or full reviews are included for many books. *Book Review Index Plus* contains entries for more than 5 million reviews from 1965 to the present. Citations are drawn from thousands of periodicals and newspapers. *Book Index with Reviews* includes citations for reviews of thousands of books, music, eBooks, audiobooks, and movies, with more than 700,000 reviews in full text. Of course, there are several freely available sources of book reviews on the Web, including online bookseller sites such as *Amazon* and *Barnes & Noble*. Chapter 24 identifies many sites useful for readers' advisory. The book review index databases identified in this section remain valuable for the wide range of sources of book reviews that they index and for their retrospective coverage of books both in and out of print.

Indexes for Different Literary Forms

Library collections in school, public, and academic libraries generally include many collected works: poetry anthologies, collections of plays or short stories, and collections of essays. Unless the contents of these volumes are analyzed during the cataloging process and the analytical entries made searchable directly in the library's catalog, the user of the catalog cannot easily determine whether the library holds an anthology that includes a particular play, short story, poem, or essay. EBSCO publishes three indexes that provide access to the contents of collections by author and subject: *Essay and General Literature Index*, *Play Index*, and *Short Story Index*.

Essay and General Literature Index is an author and subject index to essays published in collections, with particular emphasis on materials in the humanities and social sciences. It is now online in two parts: a retrospective index covering the period 1900–1984 and a regularly updated index for the period from 1985 forward.

Play Index contains entries for approximately 34,000 plays, published individually or in collections, dating from 1949 to present, and is updated on a weekly basis to incorporate new content. The scope includes one-act plays, plays in verse, musicals, radio and television plays, classic drama, and monologues. Various limits can be placed on the search, including age level, number of female and male cast members, and genre.

Short Story Index is now online in two parts: a retrospective index covering the period 1915–1983 and a regularly updated index for the period from 1984 forward. *Short Story Index* is searchable by author, title, subject, keyword, date, literary technique, and source, or by any combination of terms, making it easy for users to find what they are looking for. Additionally, subject access helps narrow searches even further by theme, locale, narrative technique, or device. A print volume is published annually by Grey House Publishing.

Indexes to poetry anthologies provide author, title, and subject indexing to poems printed in collections. In addition, titles such as *The Columbia Granger's Index to Poetry in Anthologies* provide access by first line and last line because that may be the information the user remembers rather than the poem's title. The most recent print edition of *The Columbia Granger's* covers anthologies published through May 31, 2006, including 85,000 poems by 12,000 poets. Several of the anthologies are collections of poetry translated from other languages, as well as poems published in Spanish, Vietnamese, and French. Because the most recent edition does not cover all anthologies indexed in the previous editions, the latter should be retained to allow access to poems found only in older anthologies.

Online, *The Columbia Granger's World of Poetry* includes 250,000 poems in full text in English and other languages and 450,000 citations. Search options include title, first line, last line, full text, subject, and author. Other reference material includes biographies and bibliographies on poets and commentaries on poems. Gale Cengage Learning's *LitFinder* provides a repository of full-text literature including 140,000 full-text poems; 800,000 additional poem citations and excerpts; 7,100 full-text stories; 3,800 full-text essays; 1,700 full-text plays; and 2,000 full-text speeches, as well as related reference material. Basic and advanced search modes allow users to search by keyword, author, subject, work title, work date, nationality, gender, century, and more.

SEARCH STRATEGIES

In performing searches of indexes and abstracts and in guiding library users in search strategy development, today's reference librarian must be able to locate the appropriate databases and take full advantage of the search capabilities. This requires a sophisticated understanding of specifics regarding content, organization, and interface. Almost anyone can find something from an electronic index without any knowledge of searching. It requires skilled searching to find precisely what is needed rather than everything with the same general descriptor.

The reference interview is an important part of assisting library users in accessing indexes and abstracts. Many users may be familiar only with *Google* or other

Web search engines. As a starting point for database selection, it is important to determine the subject of interest and direct the user to the most appropriate indexes for the subject and type of material desired. Because online databases are often limited in the time period covered, library users must be aware that using only these tools for literature searching may lead to inadequate coverage of the published literature.

If a library user is in search of an article that is known to have appeared in a certain periodical, but for which no other information is available, the librarian can consult an index or abstract that covers the periodical in order to identify the complete bibliographic information and possibly a link to the full text. The entry for the periodical in *Ulrichsweb* provides notations to indicate coverage by indexes and abstracts. Because many indexes and abstracts cover periodical titles only selectively, it may be necessary to look in more than one index to find the particular article sought. Indexes may also differ in time lag for indexing the same article. For topical searches, it is likewise necessary to identify the index or indexes most likely to provide the best coverage of the topic. As noted in Chapter 13, Box 13.5, electronic resources must be organized in order to be discoverable and accessible. Reference librarians are frequently involved in the redesign of the library's user interface or the part of the library's Internet presence that provides access to electronic resources in order to assist library users in identifying the most appropriate databases or other online sources for their needs.

For the first-time user of an index, some instruction may be necessary. This is also an opportunity to advise on search strategy. It may also be necessary to explain how to interpret the various components of a bibliographic citation as well as how to locate materials in the library's collection. Chapter 15 provides additional discussion of search strategies for indexes and abstracts. Knowing the scope of the various indexes and abstracts is essential in selecting the most appropriate sources when verifying a citation or searching for information on a subject. Awareness of the conventions used by a particular database for author indexing is essential to doing a thorough search for works by an author. Familiarity with the approaches to subject indexing used in each index or abstract is necessary to select the sources most likely to have the terminology required in searching a particular subject. If the librarian is unfamiliar with the topic sought, it may be necessary first to check reference books such as encyclopedias and dictionaries to develop a list of related terms under which to search. Indexing vocabularies are not standardized, so it may be necessary to reformulate a subject search when checking multiple indexes and abstracts. Access to online sources allows the use of terms appearing in titles, abstracts, and possibly full text in addition to terms selected from controlled vocabularies.

In order to simplify access to multiple indexing and abstracting databases, as discussed in Chapter 15, many libraries are implementing some type of federated searching or Web-scale discovery. As Mark Dehmlow (2015, 2) cautions, "Because of the nature of merging billions of scholarly records into a single system, discovery systems will never be able to provide the same experience as a native A&I system." Discovery systems and indexing and abstracting databases are serving two separate needs: discovery systems provide quick access to full text, while indexing and abstracting databases provide "precision discipline-specific searching for expert researchers" (Hawkins 2013). At present, records from all indexing and abstracting databases licensed by the library may not be integrated into a library's discovery system. Ideally, in the future, discovery systems can be enhanced to guide users back to indexing and abstracting databases based on terms in their search queries when they need to go beyond what can be found easily through the discovery system.

Because discovery systems cannot take advantage of unique features in particular databases, most expert searchers prefer to exploit the specific access points and search features provided by individual databases in order to produce thorough comprehensive searches. As Miriam Drake (2008, 22) observes, "effective information finding . . . requires users to know the type and quality of required information, to have extensive knowledge of sources, to understand how to build effective search strategies, and to have the experience to evaluate results." Knowing that user needs vary, the librarian should seek to understand the kind and

Box 17.3 Search Strategy: Earth Day

A college student in an environmental policy class came to the reference desk looking frustrated. She explained that she was trying to locate sources that would be useful in writing a paper comparing the first Earth Day celebration with those held in 2015 and planned for Earth Day 2016. She had tried some Web searching using *Google* but was overwhelmed with the amount of material that was retrieved when she searched on "Earth Day." She had also tried the "easy search" option (a Web-scale discovery system) on the library's home page but still was getting far too many matches to wade through. The librarian checked *Wikipedia* and confirmed that the first Earth Day celebration took place on April 22, 1970; April 22, 2016, would be the 46th anniversary. He explained that most databases had limited retrospective coverage, so the student might need to use print indexes to locate material contemporary with the first Earth Day.

Together they reviewed the categorized lists of databases available through the library's online gateway. Under General Interest, the librarian pointed out that the student might be interested in exploring the discussion of recent Earth Day events in a range of databases with varying perspectives. He suggested that NewsBank's *Access World News*, ProQuest's *Ethnic NewsWatch*, and EBSCO's *Academic Search Complete* would be good starting points for her research. He showed her how to limit the search by date and search for "Earth Day" as subject. She was excited to see the lead article in *Access World News* from the December 15, 2015, issue of *The Chronicle Herald* (Halifax, Nova Scotia, Canada) on plans by the UN Secretary General to hold a climate pact signing on Earth Day 2016. *Ethnic NewsWatch* included articles from many different ethnic perspectives; *Academic Search Complete* included both newspapers and periodical articles and President Barack Obama's statement on the 45th anniversary of Earth Day from the *Compilation of Presidential Documents*. For material on the original Earth Day, the librarian turned to *Readers' Guide Retrospective: 1890–1982*, this time limiting the search to 1970 and searching on the subject "Earth Day." This yielded several relevant articles in general magazines. In *ProQuest Historical Newspapers*, a search for articles discussing "Earth Day" on April 22, 1970, turned up the full text of articles from such newspapers as the *New York Times*, *Boston Globe*, *Chicago Tribune*, *Los Angeles Times*, and *The Washington Post*. The librarian also did a subject search on the online catalog for "Earth Day," finding a biography, *The Man from Clear Lake: Earth Day Founder Senator Gaylord Nelson* (2004), including a chapter on the history of Earth Day. Satisfied that she had several promising leads to resources for her paper, the student went to one of the public terminals to spend time exploring the electronic sources in more depth.

quality of information desired by the user before starting an index search. If the user just wants general, non-scholarly articles on a subject, then multidisciplinary periodical and newspaper indexes are places to begin. Should the user's interest be more specialized, however, the librarian can assist the user in finding appropriate subject-oriented indexes and developing strategies to exploit their capabilities.

REFERENCES

Auld, Dennis. 1999. "The Future of Secondary Publishing." *Online & CD-ROM Review* 23 (3): 173–78.

Badke, William. 2009. "Google Scholar and the Researcher." *Online* 33 (3): 47–49.

Badke, William. 2013. "Coming Back to Google Scholar." *Online Searcher* 37 (5): 65–67.

Biggs, Mary. 1992. "'Mom in the Library': *The Readers' Guide to Periodical Literature*." In *Distinguished Classics of Reference Publishing*, edited by James Rettig, 198–210. Phoenix: Oryx Press.

Breeding, Marshall. 2012. "E-resource Knowledge Bases and Link Resolvers: An Assessment of the Current Products and Emerging Trends." *Insights* 25 (2): 173–82.

Chen, Xiaotian. 2005. "Figures and Tables Omitted from Online Periodical Articles: A Comparison of Vendors and Information Missing from Full-Text Databases." *Internet Reference Services Quarterly* 10 (2): 75–88.

Chen, Xiaotian. 2006. "Overlap between Traditional Periodical Indexes and Newer Mega Indexes." *Serials Review* 32 (4): 233–37.

Chen, Xiaotian. 2010. "The Declining Value of Subscription-Based Abstracting and Indexing Services in the New Knowledge Dissemination Era." *Serials Review* 36 (2): 79–85.

Chen, Xiaotian. 2013. "Journal Article Retrieval in an Age of Open Access: How Journal Indexes Indicate Open Access Articles." *Journal of Web Librarianship* 7 (3): 243–54.

Crawford, Walt. 2000. "Here's the Content—Where's the Context?" *American Libraries* 31 (3): 50–52.

Dehmlow, Mark. 2015. "A & I Databases: The Next Frontier to Discover." *Information Technology & Libraries* 34 (1): 1–3.

Drake, Miriam A. 2008. "Federated Search: One Simple Query or Simply Wishful Thinking?" *Searcher* 16 (7): 22–25, 61–62.

Google. 2016. "Library Support." Accessed January 2. http://scholar.google.com/scholar/libraries.html.

Hawkins, Donald T. 2013. "Information Discovery and the Future of Abstracting and Indexing Services: An NFAIS Workshop." *Against the Grain*. August 6. http://www.against-the-grain.com/2013/08/information-discovery-and-the-future-of-abstracting-and-indexing-services-an-nfais-workshop/.

Herther, Nancy K. 2015. "Advanced Citation Searching: Moving from Single Sourced Research to a Potential Future of Unlimited Connections." *Online Searcher* 39 (3): 44–48.

Hunt, David, Long Nguyen, and Matthew Rodgers, eds. 2007. *Patent Searching: Tools & Techniques*. Hoboken, NJ: Wiley.

International Coalition of Library Consortia. 1999. "Guidelines for Statistical Measures of Usage of Web-Based Indexed, Abstracted, and Full-Text Resources." *Information Technology & Libraries* 18 (3): 161–63.

Jacsó, Péter. 2010. "Metadata Mega Mess in Google Scholar." *Online Information Review* 34 (1): 175–91.

Nicholas, David, Paul Huntington, and Hamid R. Jamali. 2007. "The Use, Users, and Role of Abstracts in the Digital Scholarly Environment." *Journal of Academic Librarianship* 33 (4): 446–53.

Ojala, Marydee. 2012. "An Abstract Concept." *Online* 36 (2): 5.
Pesch, Oliver. 2006. "Ensuring Consistent Usage Statistics, Part 1: Project COUNTER." *Serials Librarian* 50 (1–2): 147–61.
Pew Research Center. 2015. "Digital: Top 50 Online News Entities (2015)." http://www.journalism.org/media-indicators/digital-top-50-online-news-entities-2015/.
Roemer, Robin Chin, and Rachel Borchardt. 2015. "Altmetrics, Bibliometrics: Librarians and the Measurement of Scholarship." *American Libraries* 46 (9/10): 29.
Tenopir, Carol. 1998. "Linking to Full Texts." *Library Journal* 123 (6): 34, 36.
Tucci, Valerie. 2010. "Are A&I Services in a Death Spiral?" *Issues in Science and Technology Librarianship* 61 (Spring). http://www.istl.org/10-spring/viewpoint.html.

LIST OF SOURCES

ABI/Inform. Ann Arbor, MI: ProQuest. http://www.proquest.com/products-services/abi_inform_complete.html. [subscription required]
Academic OneFile. Farmington Hills, MI: Gale Cengage Learning. http://assets.cengage.com/pdf/bro_academic-onefile.pdf. [subscription required]
Academic Search Complete. Ipswich, MA: EBSCO. https://www.ebscohost.com/academic/academic-search-complete. [subscription required]
Academic Search Elite. Ipswich, MA: EBSCO. https://www.ebscohost.com/academic/academic-search-elite. [subscription required]
Academic Search Premier. Ipswich, MA: EBSCO. https://www.ebscohost.com/academic/academic-search-premier. [subscription required]
Access World News. Naples, FL: NewsBank. http://www.newsbank.com/libraries/schools/solutions/us-international/access-world-news. [subscription required]
AGRICOLA. Washington, DC: Department of Agriculture. http://agricola.nal.usda.gov/.
Alternative Press Index. Baltimore: Alternative Press Center. http://www.altpress.org/mod/pages/display/8/index.php?menu=pubs. Available online from EBSCO. [subscription required]
Amazon. http://www.amazon.com.
America: History and Life. Ipswich, MA: EBSCO. https://www.ebscohost.com/academic/america-history-and-life. [subscription required]
Art Source. Ipswich, MA: EBSCO. https://www.ebscohost.com/academic/art-source. [subscription required]
Arts & Humanities Citation Index. Philadelphia: Thomson Reuters. http://thomsonreuters.com/en/products-services/scholarly-scientific-research/scholarly-search-and-discovery/arts-humanities-citation-index.html. Available online as part of *Web of Science.* [subscription required]
ATLA Religion Database. Chicago: American Theological Library Association. https://www.atla.com/about/who/Pages/Directions-HQ.aspx. Available online from EBSCO. [subscription required]
Barnes & Noble. http://www.barnesandnoble.com/.
Biological Abstracts. Philadelphia: Thomson Reuters. http://thomsonreuters.com/en/products-services/scholarly-scientific-research/scholarly-search-and-discovery/biological-abstracts.html. [subscription required]
Book Citation Index. Philadelphia: Thomson Reuters. http://wokinfo.com/products_tools/multidisciplinary/bookcitationindex/. [subscription required]
Book Index with Reviews. Ipswich, MA: EBSCO. https://www.ebscohost.com/public/book-index-with-reviews. [subscription required]
Book Review Digest. Amenia, NY: Grey House Publishing. Annual. [subscription required]
Book Review Digest Plus. Ipswich, MA: EBSCO. https://www.ebscohost.com/public/book-review-digest-plus-h.w.-wilson. [subscription required]

Book Review Digest Retrospective: 1905–1982. Ipswich, MA: EBSCO. https://www.ebscohost.com/public/book-review-digest-retrospective. [subscription required]

Book Review Index Plus. Farmington Hills, MI: Gale Cengage Learning. http://www.cengage.com/search/productOverview.do?Ntt=book+review|14183411691360546253640681638309622139&N=197+4294917650&Ntk=APG|P_EPI&Ntx=mode+matchallpartial. [subscription required]

Business and Company ASAP. Farmington Hills, MI: Gale Cengage Learning. http://solutions.cengage.com/Gale/Catalog/Fact-Sheets/bcprof.pdf. [subscription required]

Business Source Complete. Ipswich, MA: EBSCO. https://www.ebscohost.com/academic/business-source-complete. [subscription required]

Canadian Business & Current Affairs (CBCA) Complete. Ann Arbor, MI: ProQuest. http://www.proquest.com/libraries/academic/databases/cbca.html. [subscription required]

Canadian Newsstand. Ann Arbor, MI: ProQuest. http://www.proquest.com/products-services/canadian_newsstand.html. [subscription required]

The Columbia Granger's Index to Poetry in Anthologies. 2007. 13th edition. Edited by Tessa Kale. New York: Columbia University Press.

The Columbia Granger's World of Poetry. New York: Columbia University Press. http://www.columbiagrangers.org/. [subscription required]

Compendex. Amsterdam, The Netherlands: Elsevier. https://www.elsevier.com/solutions/engineering-village/content/compendex. [subscription required]

Compilation of Presidential Documents. Government Publishing Office. https://www.gpo.gov/fdsys/browse/collection.action?collectionCode=CPD.

Conference Proceedings Citation Index. Philadelphia: Thomson Reuters. http://thomsonreuters.com/en/products-services/scholarly-scientific-research/scholarly-search-and-discovery/conference-proceedings-citation-index.html. [subscription required]

CPI.Q, Canadian Periodicals Index Quarterly. Farmington Hills, MI: Gale Cengage Learning. http://www.gale.com/pdf/facts/cpiq.pdf. [subscription required]

EBSCO. https://www.ebscohost.com/.

ERIC. Washington, DC: Institute of Education Sciences. http://eric.ed.gov/.

Essay and General Literature Index. Ipswich, MA: EBSCO. https://www.ebscohost.com/academic/essay-general-literature-index. [subscription required]

Essay and General Literature Index Retrospective: 1900–1984. Ipswich, MA: EBSCO. https://www.ebscohost.com/academic/essay-general-literature-retrospective. [subscription required]

Ethnic NewsWatch. Ann Arbor, MI: ProQuest. http://www.proquest.com/products-services/ethnic_newswatch.html. [subscription required]

Ethnic NewsWatch: A History. Ann Arbor, MI: ProQuest. http://www.proquest.com/products-services/ethnicnewswatch_hist.html. [subscription required]

Factiva. http://www.dowjones.com/products/product-factiva/.

Film & Television Literature Index. Ipswich, MA: EBSCO. https://www.ebscohost.com/academic/film-television-literature-index. [subscription required]

Gale Cengage Learning. http://www.cengage.com/search/showresults.do?N=197.

GenderWatch. Ann Arbor, MI: ProQuest. http://www.proquest.com/products-services/genderwatch.html. [subscription required]

GeoRef. Alexandria, VA: American Geosciences Institute. http://www.americangeosciences.org/georef/georef-information-services. Available online from EBSCO and other vendors. [subscription required]

Google. http://www.google.com.

Google News. http://news.google.com.

Google Scholar. https://scholar.google.com.

Historical Abstracts. Ipswich, MA: EBSCO. https://www.ebscohost.com/academic/historical-abstracts. [subscription required]

Informe Académico. Farmington Hills, MI: Gale Cengage Learning. http://galesupport.com/nj_support_portal/ifme.html. [subscription required]

InfoTrac Junior Edition. Farmington Hills, MI: Gale Cengage Learning. http://www.gale.com/pdf/facts/itjr.pdf. [subscription required]

InfoTrac Newsstand. Farmington Hills, MI: Gale Cengage Learning. http://www.gale.com/pdf/facts/ITCN.pdf. [subscription required]

InfoTrac Student Edition. Farmington Hills, MI: Gale Cengage Learning. http://www.gale.com/pdf/facts/itstu.pdf. [subscription required]

Inspec. London: The Institution of Engineering and Technology. http://www.theiet.org/resources/inspec/. Available online from EBSCO and other vendors. [subscription required]

LexisNexis. http://www.lexisnexis.com/en-us/gateway.page.

LGBT Life. Ipswich, MA: EBSCO. https://www.ebscohost.com/academic/lgbt-life. [subscription required]

Library & Information Science Source. Ipswich, MA: EBSCO. https://www.ebscohost.com/corporate-research/library-information-science-source. [subscription required]

Library and Information Science Abstracts (LISA). http://www.proquest.com/products-services/lisa-set-c.html. [subscription required]

Literature Resource Center. Farmington Hills, MI: Gale Cengage Learning. http://gdc.gale.com/gale-literature-collections/literature-resource-center/. [subscription required]

LitFinder. Farmington Hills, MI: Gale Cengage Learning. http://gdc.gale.com/gale-literature-collections/litfinder. [subscription required]

MasterFILE Complete. Ipswich, MA: EBSCO. https://www.ebscohost.com/public/masterfile-complete. [subscription required]

MasterFILE Elite. Ipswich, MA: EBSCO. https://www.ebscohost.com/academic/masterfile-elite. [subscription required]

MasterFILE Premier. Ipswich, MA: EBSCO. https://www.ebscohost.com/academic/masterfile-premier. [subscription required]

Middle Search Plus. Ipswich, MA: EBSCO. https://www.ebscohost.com/us-middle-schools/middle-search-plus. [subscription required]

MLA International Bibliography. New York: Modern Language Association. https://www.mla.org/Publications/MLA-International-Bibliography. Available online from EBSCO, Gale Cengage Learning, and ProQuest. [subscription required]

Music Index. Ipswich, MA: EBSCO. https://www.ebscohost.com/academic/music-index. [subscription required]

Networked Digital Library of Theses and Dissertations. http://search.ndltd.org/.

NewsBank. http://www.newsbank.com/.

Newspaper Source. Ipswich, MA: EBSCO. https://www.ebscohost.com/public/newspaper-source. [subscription required]

Newspaper Source Plus. Ipswich, MA: EBSCO. https://www.ebscohost.com/public/newspaper-source-plus. [subscription required]

PAIS International with Archive. Ann Arbor, MI: ProQuest. http://www.proquest.com/products-services/pais-set-c.html. [subscription required]

PAIS International. Ann Arbor, MI: ProQuest. http://www.proquest.com/products-services/pais-set-c.html. [subscription required]

Periodicals Archive Online. Ann Arbor, MI: ProQuest. http://www.proquest.com/products-services/periodicals_archive.html. [subscription required]

Periodicals Index Online. Ann Arbor, MI: ProQuest. http://www.proquest.com/products-services/periodicals_index.html. [subscription required]

Play Index. Ipswich, MA: EBSCO. https://www.ebscohost.com/academic/play-index. [subscription required]

Primary Search. Ipswich, MA: EBSCO. https://www.ebscohost.com/us-elementary-schools/primary-search. [subscription required]

ProQuest. http://www.proquest.com/libraries/.

ProQuest Central. Ann Arbor, MI: ProQuest. http://www.proquest.com/libraries/academic/databases/ProQuest_Central.html. [subscription required]

ProQuest Dissertations & Theses Global. Ann Arbor, MI: ProQuest. http://www.proquest.com/products-services/pqdtglobal.html. [subscription required]

ProQuest Historical Newspapers. Ann Arbor, MI: ProQuest. http://www.proquest.com/products-services/pq-hist-news.html. [subscription required]

ProQuest Newsstand. Ann Arbor, MI: ProQuest. http://www.proquest.com/products-services/newsstand.html. [subscription required]

PsycINFO. Washington, DC: American Psychological Association. http://www.apa.org/pubs/databases/psycinfo/. [subscription required]

Readers' Guide Retrospective: 1890–1982. Ipswich, MA: EBSCO. https://www.ebscohost.com/academic/readers-guide-retrospective. [subscription required]

Readers' Guide to Periodical Literature. Amenia, NY: Grey House Publishing. Quarterly with annual cumulation. Available online from EBSCO. [subscription required]

Science Citation Index. Philadelphia: Thomson Reuters. http://thomsonreuters.com/en/products-services/scholarly-scientific-research/scholarly-search-and-discovery/science-citation-index-expanded.html. Available online as part of *Web of Science.* [subscription required]

SciFinder. Columbus, OH: Chemical Abstracts Service. http://www.cas.org/products/scifinder. [subscription required]

Scopus. Amsterdam, The Netherlands: Elsevier. http://info.scopus.com. [subscription required]

Short Story Index. Amenia, NY: Grey House Publishing. Annual. Available online from EBSCO. [subscription required]

Short Story Index Retrospective: 1915–1983. Ipswich, MA: EBSCO. https://www.ebscohost.com/academic/short-story-index-retrospective. [subscription required]

Social Sciences Citation Index. Philadelphia: Thomson Reuters. http://thomsonreuters.com/en/products-services/scholarly-scientific-research/scholarly-search-and-discovery/social-sciences-citation-index.html. Available online as part of Web of Science. [subscription required]

Sociological Abstracts. Ann Arbor, MI: ProQuest. http://www.proquest.com/products-services/socioabs-set-c.html. [subscription required]

Thomson Reuters. http://thomsonreuters.com/en.html.

Ulrichsweb. Ann Arbor, MI: ProQuest. http://www.proquest.com/libraries/academic/discovery-services/Ulrichsweb.html. [subscription required]

Web of Science. Philadelphia: Thomson Reuters. http://wokinfo.com/. [subscription required]

Wikipedia. http://www.wikipedia.org.

SUGGESTED READINGS

Bell, Suzanne S. 2015. *Librarian's Guide to Online Searching: Cultivating Database Skills for Research and Instruction*, 4th ed. Santa Barbara, CA: Libraries Unlimited.
Following early chapters on search strategies, Bell provides thorough coverage of core database titles for the humanities, social sciences, sciences, statistics, and more.

Breeding, Marshall. 2015. *The Future of Library Resource Discovery.* Baltimore: NISO. http://www.niso.org/apps/group_public/download.php/14487/future_library_resource_discovery.pdf.
This paper provides an overview of the current resource discovery environment, including gaps in the coverage of abstracting and indexing resources by the

discovery services and the potential role of such resources in discovery services going forward.

Cleveland, Donald B., and Ana D. Cleveland. 2013. *Introduction to Indexing and Abstracting*, 4th ed. Santa Barbara, CA: Libraries Unlimited.

This book provides a complete introduction to the subject and covers the many recent changes in the field. It provides practical examples of the procedures for indexing and abstracting and includes numerous resource lists helpful for practitioners as well as students.

Keyser, Pierre de. 2012. *Indexing: From Thesauri to the Semantic Web*. Oxford: Chandos.

Keyser describes various traditional and novel indexing techniques, giving a broad and comprehensible introduction to indexing. Chapters include coverage of subject headings and thesauri; automatic indexing vs. manual indexing; indexing special materials such as images and music; taxonomies and ontologies; tagging; topic maps; indexing the Web; and the semantic Web.

Mann, Thomas. 2015. *The Oxford Guide to Library Research*, 4th ed. New York: Oxford University Press.

Several chapters in this guide provide helpful discussions on search strategy for effective use of indexes and abstracts. See in particular chapters on "Subject Headings and Descriptors in Databases for Journal Articles," "Keyword Searches," "Citation Searches," and "Special Subjects and Formats."

Roemer, Robin Chin, and Rachel Borchardt. 2015. *Meaningful Metrics: A 21st-Century Librarian's Guide to Bibliometrics, Altmetrics, and Research Impact.* Chicago: Association of College and Research Libraries.

Starting with historical background on bibliometrics and altmetrics, and continuing with descriptions of the core tools and emerging issues in the future of both fields, *Meaningful Metrics* is a helpful resource on the current scholarly metrics movement.

Chapter 18

Sources for Facts and Overviews

Melissa A. Wong

INTRODUCTION

Patrons are often looking for answers to factual questions such as:

- "What are the tallest mountains in Africa?"
- "What colleges are located in and near San Antonio, Texas?"
- "How did Ohioans vote in the 2000 presidential election?"

Questions like these arise in school assignments, at work, and in everyday conversation. Although many times these questions seemingly can be answered with a quick Internet search, patrons who contact the library want to ensure that they are using the most reliable information available.

Other times, patrons are looking for a basic explanation or overview of a topic. Librarians field questions like:

- "How are true north and magnetic north different?"
- "What happened during the Great Chicago Fire?"
- "How can earthquakes be measured?"

Again, patrons who contact the library are looking for a complete and trustworthy answer as well as one at an appropriate level of written and topical sophistication.

Although questions that require facts and questions that require overviews initially appear to be completely different in nature, they can often be answered using a similar set of tools: almanacs, handbooks, yearbooks, directories, and encyclopedias. Pre-Internet, most libraries had a substantial collection of these sources in order to answer a wide range of questions on all types of subjects. Today, many staple sources of previous years have gone out of print, and librarians and patrons often turn to the Internet for quick answers to easy questions. However, when patrons need up-to-date, reliable, and complete information, librarians can point them to a collection of reliable sources that includes print titles, subscription-based online resources, and free websites.

USES AND CHARACTERISTICS

Almanacs

Almanacs were first published as early as the second century as calendars, containing days, weeks, and months, and astronomical data such as the phases of the sun and moon. Over time, these calendars expanded to include many topics relevant to everyday life, such as the weather forecast, the expected harvest, and religious and political information. By the 17th and 18th centuries, almanacs had developed into a form of folk literature, with notations of anniversaries and interesting facts, home medical advice, statistics of all sorts, jokes, and even fiction and poetry. The most famous American almanac was Benjamin Franklin's *Poor Richard's Almanack* (published by him in 1732–1757), which, in its title, recalled one of the most popular and long-lasting of English almanacs, that of "Poor Robin" (founded ca. 1662). *The Old Farmer's Almanac* was first published in 1792 by Robert Bailey Thomas, continuing from Franklin's almanac, and is still published today (Morrison 1992, 313–14).

Modern-day almanacs are collections of facts, statistics, and lists gathered together in a convenient format for easy reference. Coverage typically includes facts about people and organizations, current and historical events, countries, geographical data, political and historical data, statistics, practical information such as ZIP codes and first aid treatment, and popular culture items such as sports and entertainment. Even though much of this information may be available from other sources, almanacs provide a type of "one-stop shopping" as they consolidate, summarize, and synthesize information on various topics. The most well-known general almanac is *The World Almanac and Books of Facts*, first published as a booklet in 1868, discontinued in 1876, and revived in 1886.

Although most almanacs are broad in geographical and subject coverage, many of the best-known general almanacs emphasize a particular country, such as the *Canadian Almanac & Directory*, or state, such as the *Texas Almanac*. Some almanacs are focused on a given field and will provide a glimpse of the state of the world in regard to that particular topic, as well as show trends in that area. They are a significant source for statistical information and often contain citations for their sources of information. Additionally, they can be utilized for biographical or directory information.

Handbooks and Manuals

The terms *handbook* and *manual* are used almost interchangeably. Although some reference works of this type actually do explain how to do something (e.g., how to format a citation to a journal article or repair a car), these books are more than just "how to" books.

A handbook generally covers a limited area of knowledge and can be used by people interested in gaining in-depth knowledge about a specific topic. Handbooks generally pertain to a specific subject, such as chemistry or physics, and contain quick facts, charts, formulas, tables, statistical information, historical background, and perhaps lists of organizations connected to the subject. A handbook can serve as a handy guide to a particular subject, with all of the critical information that one might need for a particular field in one book. Often, large amounts of information about a subject are compressed into a single volume.

Some handbooks are geared to those who have a basic knowledge of the subject area and may contain information and language that may be difficult for casual readers to comprehend. Because they are updated frequently, handbooks may include information about new developments. References to additional information are usually included.

Handbooks organize bits of important data that will enable the reader to do something. For instance, the *CRC Handbooks* (the most important in the physical sciences) provide the data needed for the equations necessary for doing scientific experiments. The *Diagnostic and Statistical Manual of Mental Disorders* (*DSM-5*) is the diagnostic manual for psychiatry and provides all of the necessary diagnostic criteria for diagnosing a patient. The *Physicians' Desk Reference* (*PDR*) provides physicians with the necessary information to prescribe medications.

In addition to the multitude of specialized handbooks available, there are many subject handbooks that are guides to various scientific fields and to religion, history, literature, and social sciences. These are often referred to as *companions*, such as *The Oxford Companion to Philosophy*, or take the form of single-volume encyclopedias, such as the *Encyclopedia of Insects*.

Manuals, much like handbooks, deal with very specific subject matter and are narrow in scope. They typically provide step-by-step instructions on how to do specific tasks. They can show one how to rebuild a carburetor, conduct a scientific experiment, apply for financial aid, correctly format papers or cite information in a bibliography, and so on. One example of a manual frequently found in public libraries or linked from their Web pages is Chilton's automotive repair guides. There are more than 40,000 from 1910 onward of these types of manuals on how to repair automobiles.

Encyclopedias

The encyclopedia has long been the quintessential reference tool—a source that seems to cover any topic imaginable and the one many people remember learning to use at an early age. More than any other book, the encyclopedia has long been associated with an educated mind. In the 20th century, traveling salesmen sold encyclopedias door to door, and many families bought an encyclopedia for their school-aged children. The home encyclopedia set provided ready access to information for school reports and symbolized the family's commitment to education and knowledge. Libraries purchased encyclopedias to provide ready access to information on a wide range of topics, supporting both student research and general information seeking.

As personal computers become more widespread, families and libraries could purchase online encyclopedias, first on CD-ROM and later online. These early online encyclopedias that largely replicated the content of their print equivalents have given way to robust online products that provide enhanced multimedia content and access to supplementary resources such as newspaper and magazine articles, primary documents, and curricular tools. At the same time, free, volunteer-authored encyclopedias have emerged on the Internet. The popularity of resources like *Wikipedia* and the *Encyclopedia of Life* are further evidence of people's desire to access introductory information on a wide variety of topics.

Whether the encyclopedia is a multivolume work such as the *World Book*, a single volume on one specific subject, or an online multimedia resource, the goal remains implicit: to provide a summarized compendium of multidisciplinary knowledge in a verifiable, organized, and readily accessible manner that allows its users to meet their information needs first on a general level and then on a specific level by pointing them to more detailed sources of information.

Because of the broad nature of information available in encyclopedias, they can be used to answer a variety of types of reference questions, including factual questions about dates, people, and statistics. However, librarians and patrons most often turn to encyclopedias for general background information, such as an explanation of photosynthesis or construction techniques used to build the Golden Gate Bridge. Encyclopedias are unique in that they give definitions, explain phenomena, and provide illustrations. Children's encyclopedias are particularly helpful in this regard, given that they typically provide simplified explanations accompanied by illustrations. Subject-specialized encyclopedias can provide a comprehensive review of a specialized subject or insight on a topic from a particular vantage point. For example, *Brill's Encyclopedia of Hinduism* can be used to look up not only information about Hindu religious practices, but also topics like gift giving and travel and their significance in Hindu culture.

Encyclopedias are often used as "pre-research" tools, providing not only succinct overviews of topics, but also cross-references to related topics that allow the novice to make connections and to see that all information lies in a broader context. In addition, encyclopedias may identify important controversies and unanswered questions that can prove fruitful research avenues, particularly for students. Encyclopedias also may include bibliographic citations to more in-depth information found in outside sources, further assisting the patron in the research process.

Jacques Barzun (1992, 73) notes that "encyclopedias should be 'learned' and not blindly used: The childhood faith in *the* encyclopedia that happened to be the one large book of knowledge in the house should be replaced by a discriminating acquaintance with others." Barzun's comments aptly describe the mixed perceptions many people have of encyclopedias. Although few would dispute their convenience, others, particularly those in academe, may not view them as scholarly works and may encourage students not to overuse them when engaging in research. Barzun's advice seems particularly appropriate today, when traditional print multivolume sets with recognizable names have given way to robust online products that combine multiple encyclopedia titles in two or more languages with multimedia and a choice of user interfaces. In addition, free online titles can supplement the library's print and online holdings. The responsibility of the librarian is to have the "discriminating acquaintance" with encyclopedias that allows him or her to direct the user to the right encyclopedia for the information need.

Directories

Directories provide contact information for people, organizations, and businesses. They may also provide descriptive information, such as services offered, names of executives, the number of employees or members, or sales figures. Although print directories are often organized by name for easy access to a known entry, they also can be organized by location, subject, or other appropriate category to enable browsing. Print directories may also have an index to facilitate further access. Online directories provide keyword searching and browsing across a variety of access points and can be considerably quicker to search than their print counterparts. In addition, they will offer the ability to print and even download entries for later use.

Yearbooks

Yearbooks provide information dealing with a particular year, often organized by characteristics such as subject area or geographical boundary. Since most yearbooks are released annually, they are sometimes referred to as *annuals*. Yearbooks are useful for an overview of trends that occurred in a particular year as well as factual information about the events, organizations, people, places, and trends that had an effect on the lives of people living during the time period. Many yearbooks, such as *The Statesman's Yearbook*, provide detailed statistical data.

Although a general almanac also provides some of the same information as a yearbook, the yearbook's presentation of the information is different. Almanacs are full of bits of data on a wide spectrum of topics, whereas a yearbook can provide more in-depth information on a specific topic. A general almanac will satisfy a sports fan wanting box scores from the most recent World Series, but a yearbook will be a more suitable tool for a fan wanting a game-by-game description of the series.

Traditionally, general encyclopedias issued yearbooks that supplemented the main set and reviewed a specific year, such as *Britannica Book of the Year*. These yearbooks contained a chronology of the year, biographies of newsmakers, obituaries, sports news, current statistical data, and articles about events of the year. Even as they weed print encyclopedias in favor of online products, larger libraries and those with a research focus should consider retaining older yearbooks since they provide a valuable snapshot of past years.

EVALUATION

One of the most important considerations for librarians answering factual and background questions is that the information be accurate. Attentiveness to accuracy is paramount whether the librarian is using a print source, an online database the library subscribes to, or a free website. Although one would like to believe otherwise, all reference works can contain errors and misinformation. Copy editors overlook typographical errors, and even the most diligent editors and authors can get their facts wrong.

When assessing resources for accuracy, reference librarians can read reviews, compare data in different sources, and rely on personal expertise. The longtime reputation of a work is also a guide, subject to continual reevaluation. When evaluating specific titles, librarians can consider coverage and objectivity, authority, currency, and the physical format or interface.

Coverage and Objectivity

Because encyclopedias have numerous contributors and because, in the case of general encyclopedias, they cover a broad range of subjects, users may initially assume that encyclopedias maintain an objective viewpoint. However, without examining an encyclopedia's prefatory material as well as its text and images, a librarian would be naive to make such an assumption. Although the publishing industry has made great strides in the past decade to eliminate gender- and racially biased language or stereotyped images from its publications, bias has not been eliminated entirely.

When reviewing an encyclopedia, a librarian should pay careful attention to what an article includes or omits. A librarian should also be concerned with balanced coverage and language. With respect to controversial issues such as the death penalty or abortion, does the article present both sides? Is inflammatory language used, or is the article entirely neutral in its treatment? A librarian must also consider photographs, illustrations, sounds, and digital images when evaluating an encyclopedia for objectivity. Do images portray women solely in traditional settings? Do multimedia encyclopedias developed in the United States devote equal media space to all ethnic groups?

With regard to multivolume general encyclopedias, coverage should be even across all subjects; however, it is important to note that some subjects, by their very nature, will be given greater emphasis. For example, general encyclopedias published in the United States contain far more information about the United States than they do about any other country. In a children's encyclopedia, articles about popular animals such as sharks and lions will be more detailed than those about lesser-known animals. When assessing whether an encyclopedia is balanced with respect to subject coverage, one merely has to examine the length and depth of articles written on a variety of subjects.

Almanacs, because they cover a broad range of topics and provide factual data, are often assumed to be both balanced and objective. However, librarians should familiarize themselves with specific titles and recognize that despite the wealth of information they contain, all almanacs must be selective. For example, *Whitaker's Almanack* was founded in London in 1868 and emphasizes the United Kingdom, while *The World Almanac* and *Infoplease* emphasize the United States.

Authority

With any reference source, authority, or the staff responsible for the content, has immense value when making a selection decision. An examination of a source's prefatory remarks can reveal much about its authority and, thus, its worthiness. With regard to encyclopedias, manuals, and handbooks, the editorial board and contributors are deemed to be specialists in their respective fields. The editorial staff serves to review and revise authors' contributions so that they conform to the editorial guidelines typically set forth by the publishers. For example, there must be conformity in style and length. Author credit appears either at the beginning or at the end of each article, and a separate list of authors and their credentials can generally be found within the publication or site. Some articles may not provide an author credit; therefore, one might conclude that the editorial staff, in concert with a subject expert, wrote those pieces.

Directories may rely on self-reported data or may compile data from other sources. Many almanacs, yearbooks, and handbooks are composed, at least in part, of secondhand information. The statistics should be recent and from identified sources. Identification should be complete enough to lead to the original source where additional information might be located. Reference works without documentation are of questionable reliability.

Currency

Almanacs, yearbooks, and directories are published annually; however, even recently published print and online works can be out of date. A 2016 almanac will contain statistics and events from 2015 at best, and even in such a small publication, not all information will be updated each year. For example, a user recently asked for the salary that members of Congress receive. The answer varied in two reputable online almanacs. In one of the almanacs, that piece of information had not been updated in five years. This problem is even more pronounced in larger reference works. It is a Herculean and economically infeasible task to revise a multivolume general encyclopedia yearly. Consequently, publishers tend to update only a portion of the encyclopedia with each new edition.

Online resources have no limitations, other than those imposed by their producers, on the level and frequency of updates, and most publishers update their online versions more frequently than their print counterparts. For example, within days of American Pharaoh winning the Belmont Stakes, *Encyclopaedia Britannica* had updated not only the entry on the Triple Crown, but also entries for trainer Bob Baffert and jockey Victor Espinoza. Again, however, librarians should take care to confirm time-sensitive information in more than one appropriate source.

Physical Format

The key to evaluating a resource in terms of its physical format lies in understanding one's target audience. In encyclopedias for adults, a plethora of photographs and illustrations and a dearth of content might indicate a lack of substance; however, in the case of encyclopedias for children, this scenario would be welcome, particularly if the photographs and illustrations are current and targeted to a child's viewpoint. Manuals, even those for adults, can be expected to have extensive examples, and titles that outline step-by-step directions or procedures should have well-rendered images.

Page layout also figures prominently. Minimal or excessive "white space," poor placement of illustrations, and incorrect choice of fonts for headers and text would again detract from content, no matter how scholarly or substantive it may be.

Print encyclopedias typically follow a common format: alphabetical arrangement with associative cross-references and indexes. Bibliographies often follow articles or sections within long articles. Alphabetization can vary between the word-by-word method, where *San Salvador* comes before *sandman*, and the letter-by-letter method, where *sandman* comes before *San Salvador*. Most encyclopedias provide *see* references to direct users to preferred entries, for example, from a variant spelling of a name to the correct spelling, while *see also* references at the end of articles direct users to related entries.

In larger works, the arrangement of volumes also impacts usability. Children's encyclopedias are often arranged so that one volume encompasses an entire letter of the alphabet, ensuring, for example, that entries beginning with M are not split between two volumes, which can be confusing for younger users. Although the alphabetical arrangement is the most common, it is not the only possible arrangement. Some encyclopedias aimed at young children, such as *The New Children's Encyclopedia*, organize each volume around a broad topic, such as continents or technology. Most manuals and handbooks are also arranged topically. The *Encyclopedia of*

American History is arranged chronologically, with individual volumes devoted to a specific time period and the entries within organized alphabetically.

Indexes are critical tools, especially in almanacs and handbooks because they contain lots of bits of information organized in categories. In an almanac, the first page may list the types of topics covered. Both a very specific index and a very general, or quick reference, index may also be available. The index in a fact book should be helpful, accurate, and internally consistent in style and terminology, and it should complement the overall arrangement of the work. Some yearbooks include a cumulative index that covers more than the current volume. This is an extremely useful feature if, for example, the exact date of an event is unknown.

Interface

In selecting an online resource, the librarian should give careful consideration to the interface used for searching and reading. The design needs to be age appropriate, user friendly, and intuitive. Interfaces must readily and effortlessly guide their users to desired information; otherwise, the resource will be of little value. Good search features include a well-designed main page with multiple search possibilities, browsing capabilities, and organization by categories. Resources targeted at a wide range of age ranges may even offer a choice of interfaces. For example, *Britannica School* offers different search screens for elementary, middle, and high school users.

Ease of access to information in electronic resources is theoretically superior to locating information in print versions. With the presence of robust Boolean-based search engines, the inclusion of controlled vocabulary and indexing, and hyperlinked cross-references, one can, in effect, access any word contained in a resource through keyword searching. Using Boolean operators such as *and*, *or*, and *not* and phrase searching can make a search more precise and productive; however, because not all users have experience using Boolean logic, many titles allow for natural language searching, where the user types in a question such as "What was England's role in the American Civil War?" and the search engine returns articles containing any of the question's keywords (England, American, Civil, and War). Although this latter method lacks precision and yields a number of false hits, the user will presumably retrieve some relevant articles that could lead to other related information. Most products automatically spell-check searches and offer alternate spellings of words, which can greatly ease a user's search for information and rank retrieved articles for relevance, thus allowing the user to quickly discard irrelevant information.

SELECTION

Even libraries with minimal budgets should have a few standard sources in their ready-reference collection, including a good almanac, general and subject-specific encyclopedias, and appropriate handbooks and manuals. When considering titles, librarians can consult the standard reviewing sources discussed in Chapter 13. In addition to purchasing print titles and online databases, librarians should bookmark freely available authoritative titles, such as *Infoplease* and the free *Encyclopaedia Britannica*, in order to provide quick and easy access to reliable information by both librarians and patrons (see Box 18.1 for an example of evaluating a website for addition to the collection).

Box 18.1 Activity: *Encyclopedia of Life*

Access the *Encyclopedia of Life*, a community-edited encyclopedia for life science, at http://eol.org. Search for at least three organisms and review the entries you find.

Questions for Reflection and Discussion:

1. How thorough were the entries you reviewed?
2. What can you learn about the author(s) of each entry?
3. What can you learn about the source(s) of information?
4. How would you rate this encyclopedia using the evaluative criteria discussed in the chapter: accuracy, coverage and objectivity, authority, currency, and interface?
5. Would you use this source for reference, and if so, for what types of questions?

Audience

Subject matter, writing style, and presentation all determine a title's audience. Clearly, the *Dictionary of Mechanical Engineering* sees its audience as adults who have a professional interest in engineering. *Worldmark Encyclopedia of the Nations* is appropriate for readers at the ninth grade level and above. The *Scholastic Encyclopedia of the Presidents and Their Times*, with its short entries, numerous illustrations, and larger print, is aimed at young readers. Some titles aim to serve a wide audience and can be used by children, young adults, and adults. Although targeted at primary and secondary school students, *World Book Encyclopedia* prides itself as being suitable as a "family reference tool." Many librarians find *World Book* useful for adult users seeking an illustration or a simple explanation of a topic.

In addition to age, the academic, occupational, and recreational needs of a library's patrons will influence decisions about which works to purchase. Librarians in public libraries often get requests for information about how to make or repair household items and machinery. Some of the standards in this area are now available online, such as *HowStuffWorks*. Automobile repair manuals are also in demand, and all but the smallest public library will have at least one such manual. However, if the budget allows, librarians can subscribe online to a large number of manuals through *ChiltonLibrary*, rather than having to purchase and shelve individual manuals. Reference works relating to hobbies and games—for example, bird-watching, various kinds of collecting, craft work, and card games—are also standard tools in public library reference departments. Other common specialized almanacs, yearbooks, and handbooks in public libraries relate to questions of health, investments, consumer affairs, legal matters, and popular entertainment. Many of these are discussed in Chapters 25 (business sources), 26 (medical sources), and 28 (legal sources).

Academic libraries may have a general almanac and encyclopedia, but because they generally serve a different clientele, they will concentrate on acquiring scholarly and educational encyclopedias and handbooks that support teaching and research. A graduate student in library science would obviously benefit from access to the *Encyclopedia of Library and Information Sciences*, and the library and information science librarian would undoubtedly choose that for inclusion in the reference collection. Because the University of California at Davis has a prominent enology program, it would necessarily follow that its university library would acquire encyclopedias and handbooks about wine and winemaking.

School libraries generally have smaller collections, and the intellectual level of the student body affects the books selected. Elementary school libraries in particular will opt for titles aimed at children, such as *The World Almanac for Kids*, precisely because they contain less detailed information. Special libraries have as many specialized handbooks in their field as budgets will allow.

Almanacs, encyclopedias, and yearbooks consist of information that may be treated more extensively in other sources. The decision of whether to rely on the almanac and yearbook to supply information or to purchase specialized sources depends on budget, similar sources available, and the frequency of demand for the type of in-depth information. For example, *The World Almanac* has a table outlining votes by state in the last presidential election; this information would suffice for a school library or small branch library, but a research library supporting a program in political science would need more in-depth sources.

The presence of certain subject handbooks and encyclopedias may bolster areas underrepresented in the circulating collection or may augment the broad, general information contained in a traditional, multivolume encyclopedia. Online encyclopedias might add further depth to a collection by providing users with sound and video images that supplement the text and can be used in the classroom or student presentations.

Cost

Cost plays a major role in the acquisition of any library material. Almanacs, yearbooks, handbooks, and even single-volume encyclopedias tend to offer very good value at a low cost. However, cost may be a determinant. Some general reference departments in public and academic libraries and many school libraries can afford to purchase a moderately priced yearbook such as *The Statesman's Yearbook* but not the more expensive *The Europa World Year Book*. Multivolume encyclopedias, by their very nature, can be viewed as investment pieces. In addition to the oft-substantial cost of purchasing a print set, annual updates and supplements are often purchased as separate items.

Subscription rates for online products vary according to the number of users a library serves, although institutions often can get a discount by purchasing as part of a consortium or by subscribing to multiple products from the same vendor. Multi-title databases such as *Credo Reference* and *Oxford Reference* also can be an economical way of expanding the library's collection of handbooks and subject encyclopedias as well as other types of resources.

Choosing between Print and Online Options

Many standard titles are available in both print and electronic formats. Librarians need to consider whether to acquire resources in print, online, or a combination of both. In addition, reliable free websites such as *Infoplease* and the *Stanford Encyclopedia of Philosophy* abound and can often replace costly print and subscription-based sources. Reliance on free websites can also save valuable collection space; in previous decades, most libraries needed to acquire and save a substantial number of print "telephone books" from local and distant cities in order to provide contact information for individuals and businesses. Almost all libraries have been able to weed such collections thanks to the emergence of websites like *AnyWho* and *Yelp*.

Online titles offer the ability to both search and browse content, providing enhanced access. Features such as "Today in History," prominent links to timely topics, and trivia or puzzle-type games all add visual appeal and encourage users, particularly children, to explore the resource. Online encyclopedias in particular are often enriched with additional illustrations, multimedia such as video and audio clips, primary source materials, and even magazine and journal articles. These additional features can make the online version a very attractive purchase, although it is important to verify that such features enhance the educational value of the encyclopedia and are not merely shallow or distracting.

Generally, one would think that the subscription sources would be easier to search and have better formatting and access. Certainly some free websites, even those with reliable information, suffer from a busy interface, poor search options, and intrusive advertisements. However, this is not always the case, and it may be that a subscription source is not any better than a freely available website.

Despite the many attractive features of online products, librarians should not overlook the value of print editions, particularly for almanacs and handbooks. When finding quick factual information, many times it is faster to grab the print almanac behind the reference desk and flip to the chart or page (assuming there is a good index) than it is to go online, find the resource, and navigate through it. Additionally, it may be easier to browse a print title. For example, when citing an unusual source, using the print version of *The Chicago Manual of Style* allows one to quickly skim through many examples, while the online version presents one example at a time.

Ultimately, librarians need to examine a variety of issues in choosing between print and online counterparts. In addition to cost and access issues, librarians need to consider shelf space, preservation goals, and user needs. A large academic or public library may subscribe to online encyclopedias in order to provide its users access to information from homes and offices. A small school library with limited computer workstations, however, might find a print encyclopedia provides the best access since multiple volumes can be used simultaneously. In the end, libraries will want to achieve the balance of print and online titles that best serves their particular users.

IMPORTANT GENERAL SOURCES

This section focuses on standard almanacs and encyclopedias typically purchased by school, public, or academic libraries. Later sections in this chapter discuss specialized titles such as handbooks and manuals, almanacs and encyclopedias for children, subject encyclopedias, and directories and yearbooks.

Multi-Title Databases

In recent years, the emergence of databases that aggregate access to tens or hundreds of reference titles has changed the way most librarians collect and access almanacs, handbooks, and encyclopedias. Rather than selecting numerous print titles, librarians can subscribe to an online collection that covers multiple subject areas and offers a unified search interface for access to an individual title, multiple titles in a selected subject area, or all titles in the collection. Aggregator reference databases are ideal for checking a fact, clarifying the definition of a term, or finding a succinct overview of a topic since most of the content comes from one- and two-volume subject encyclopedias as well as other standard reference tools. In some cases, more in-depth content is available, making these a potential source of pre-research information. Boxes 18.2 and 18.3 illustrate the utility of multi-title databases.

Credo Reference provides access to hundreds of subject-specialized encyclopedias and handbooks in all subject areas as well as general encyclopedias such as the *Britannica Concise Encyclopedia* and *The Columbia Encyclopedia*, quotation books, and dictionaries. *Credo* is organized into core collections that target the needs of school (350 titles appropriate for students in grades 7–12), academic (600 titles across all disciplines), and public (700 titles that target users of all ages) libraries. Libraries can also subscribe to additional collections to expand holdings in particular subject areas, such as dentistry, Judaism, and linguistics.

Box 18.2 What Is a Millennium?

A search for the definition of "millennium" in *Credo Reference* illustrates the strength of multi-title reference databases. A simple keyword search yields 4,419 results; using the advanced search option to limit to "in a heading" yields a more manageable 129 entries. Because these entries are taken from a variety of dictionaries, encyclopedias, and handbooks, they define the word and its significance in different contexts, providing a richer understanding of the word.

- The *Good Word Guide* notes that millennium and its plural millennia are frequently misspelled and provides readers a mnemonic to help with correct spelling. The source goes on to note the popular misconception that the "new millennium" began in the year 2000 and explains why it correctly began in 2001.
- The *Macquarie Dictionary* provides a straightforward definition of a millennium as a thousand years along with written and audio pronunciation guides. It also notes the etymology of the word and that millennia or millenniums can be used as the plural form.
- *The Hutchinson Unabridged Encyclopedia with Atlas and Weather Guide* defines millennium as an event that was celebrated on January 1, 2000, and briefly outlines some of those celebrations in England and other countries.
- The *Cambridge Dictionary of Christian Theology* addresses the significance of the word in Christianity, citing specific Biblical passages and explaining how it has been interpreted both literally and figuratively.
- The *Dictionary of Computing* offers an entry on the "millennium bug," the concern that some hardware and software stored only two-digit dates and were not ready for the advent of the year 2000.
- Other entries reference the United Nations' (UN) Millennium Declaration, London's Millennium Dome, and England's Millennium Bridges as important architectural features that were built to celebrate the year 2000, and two works of art titled "Millennium."

Box 18.3 Activity: Searching Multi-Title Databases

Use *Credo*, *Oxford Reference*, or *Encyclopedia.com* to search for the following terms.

- Airplane
- Craftsman
- Iceberg
- Reich

Questions for Reflection and Discussion:

1. How many definitions did you find?
2. How did the definitions differ based on the original source?
3. If possible, use more than one database. Did either source provide unique definitions?

Credo's interface offers browsing by subject or title, a basic and advanced search option, and "Mind Map," a brainstorming tool where users can enter a search term and see related terms in a dynamic, visual display. In the search results, a faceted menu offers an easy way to narrow results by subject, title, or type of reference: dictionary, quotation, and so on. The interface can be branded with the library's logo and links to external resources like the library's Web page and virtual reference service.

Oxford Reference, which is most suitable for academic and adult users, provides access to entries from more than 135 titles in Oxford's *Companions*, *Dictionaries*, and *Encyclopedias* series. A basic search screen is supplemented by a robust browse option that highlights 19 subject areas; in each subject area, *Oxford Reference* provides an overview of the subject and links to timelines, maps, images, and interesting trivia, for example, the subject "Health and Medicine" highlights links to body mass index and a list of phobias and phobic stimuli. Users can also jump to specific types of reference tools such as dictionaries and quotation books. In the search results, a faceted menu allows narrowing by subject or to entries in specific titles. One notable feature for students is the availability of 270 "timelines" that provide a chronological listing of events with links to appropriate entries and cross-references to other timelines and subject areas. The interface can be branded with the library's logo.

Another notable multi-title option is *Gale Virtual Reference Library*. Although librarians must build their own collection, all titles are available through a single interface. Users can search the entire collection, within a specific subject area, or within an individual title. A simple but effective browse option allows users to see cover images and jump to specific titles of interest. Given Gale Cengage Learnings's extensive reference offerings, with a little effort, librarians can build a robust online collection of resources across a wide variety of subjects and age levels.

In the realm of free resources, *Encyclopedia.com* offers access to more than 100 encyclopedias and dictionaries from Gale and Oxford. Sponsored by Gale Cengage Learning, this is a reliable site for overviews on a wide variety of topics. A simple search interface returns entries from multiple titles, allowing users to compare information from a variety of subject viewpoints.

Almanacs

According to *Merriam-Webster Online Dictionary* (2015), there are two kinds of almanacs. The traditional type is defined as "a publication containing astronomical and meteorological data for a given year and often including a miscellany of other information." The other is "a usually annual publication containing statistical, tabular, and general information."

The Old Farmer's Almanac, published in print since 1792, is an example of the first type of almanac. It provides traditional almanac content, including astronomical information, weather forecasts, and gardening tips. A freely available companion site has been online since 1996. The weather pages offer detailed seven-day forecasts for thousands of cities and towns across the United States and Canada. A searchable weather history database contains weather conditions for 2,000 locations in the United States and Canada for any date from 1946 to the present. Gardening pages include frost charts, planting tables, and source lists for seeds and flowers. Astronomy pages offer charts and tables for various celestial events, including moon phases, comet and meteor appearances, and rise/set times for the sun, moon, and planets. Cooking pages, household pages, forums, and a country store are also available.

Examples of the second type of almanac are *The World Almanac and Book of Facts* and *Infoplease*. Both have some information the other does not, and librarians should check both depending on the information sought.

The World Almanac and Book of Facts began in 1868 as a publication of the *New York World* newspaper. It is a perennial best seller for both home and library use. Although it prominently bears the date of the following year, the almanac is usually published annually at the end of November. An introductory section contains a list of "Number Ones" such as the wealthiest person and most populous country as well as feature articles on the year's important topics. For example, the 2015 edition included articles on Ebola, American veterans, and the 2014 elections. Organized topically, the bulk of the almanac contains a wealth of information on topics such as health, sports, politics, world countries, arts and entertainment, and science. *The World Almanac* also includes numerous timelines for both recent and historical events; a center section contains a series of colored plates of countries' flags and maps of countries and time zones.

The World Almanac has three indexes: a quick reference index composed of keywords for some of the most sought-after information in the almanac, a more complete general index that provides keyword access to information throughout the almanac, and a thumb index that uses black marks on page edges to indicate the location of major sections of the almanac. A user can find the population of Botswana, for example, by using the general index to search for "Botswana" or by using the thumb index to turn to Nations of the World, an alphabetically arranged summary of information about countries.

Infoplease, a reputable online almanac, had its origins in the *Information Please Almanac*, first published in 1947 (this title later became the *Time Almanac* and ceased publication in 2013). The almanac information is integrated with the *Random House Unabridged Dictionary* and *The Columbia Encyclopedia* into a single reference source with a wealth of facts. The search page offers several ways to find information, including a keyword search, an index of topics, and a browsable directory of information divided into the following categories: World, United States, People, History and Government, Science and Health, Calendar and Holidays, Business, and the Fifty States. Additional links provide easy access to commonly used resources, including a dictionary, thesaurus, crossword puzzle helper, conversion calculator, periodic table, and perpetual calendar. The site is continuously updated, offering more recent information than can be found in the paper edition. However, there are annoying pop-up ads from time to time.

The famous trivia book *Guinness World Records* (formerly *The Guinness Book of Records*) is also a useful reference work. The first American edition was published in 1956, and it has appeared annually since then. The records in the book are for every type of extreme: largest and smallest, worst and best, widest and narrowest, oldest and newest, and the like. Librarians will find the subject index essential when using *Guinness* to answer a specific query, but patrons can also browse. Each two-page spread is given over to a topic like "birds" or "cars," with similar topics grouped together. The Web-based version features only a selection of the records; users can browse by category (e.g., "Natural World" or "Travel & Transport") or search by keyword.

Encyclopedias

The best known of the traditional encyclopedias, *Encyclopaedia Britannica* was also the most detailed and scholarly. Britannica's online products, available in versions for school, public, and academic libraries, maintain the high standards that were the hallmark of the print version. *Britannica School*, aimed at K–12 libraries (discussed in more detail later in this chapter), and *Britannica Library*, aimed at public libraries, draw articles from three separate encyclopedias written for different reading levels. In *Britannica Academic*, the most advanced of the three online products, signed articles are authored by experts in the field. In all three products, textual content is supplemented with over 90,000 full-color images, maps, videos, and audio clips. Content is updated daily with at least 1,200 updates per month. In addition to a prominent search box, all Britannica interfaces offer the ability to browse topics, media, biographies, and a world atlas. Special features include interactive timelines, access to the *Merriam-Webster's Collegiate Dictionary* and pop-up word definitions, featured media, and eye-catching links like "This Day in History" and "Can You Guess?" Interfaces are mobile friendly for use on smartphones and tablets.

For public libraries, *Britannica Library* offers interfaces for children, young adults, and adults, and includes access to thousands of magazine and journal articles. For academic libraries, *Britannica Academic* offers additional enhanced content beyond the encyclopedia, including primary source materials, magazine and journal articles, classical works, a daily newsfeed with articles from the BBC and *New York Times*, and the World Data Analyst, which provides up-to-date statistical profiles of countries worldwide.

Britannica also offers a free version of its encyclopedia under the name *Encyclopaedia Britannica*. Although more limited in content than the subscription-based products, the free version contains substantial articles on thousands of topics, images and multimedia, the ability to search or browse content, and engaging features such as quizzes and lists. Thus, the free *Encyclopaedia Britannica* is an excellent resource for librarians to verify facts and locate background information.

For Canadian audiences, *The Canadian Encyclopedia* does an admirable job of including information on a wide variety of Canadian personalities, places, events, and achievements. Previously published in print and as a CD-ROM, the encyclopedia is now produced as a free website available in both English and French. The site also offers the *Encyclopedia of Music in Canada* and selected content from *Maclean's* magazine. Features such as interactive maps, timelines, and exhibits invite the user to explore the site.

In the realm of free resources, *Wikipedia*, the online encyclopedia that anyone can author and edit, is undoubtedly the most well-known. Authors are asked to maintain a neutral point of view, include only verifiable information, and provide references. Unlike more traditional encyclopedias, there is not an editorial system that certifies articles or their authors prior to "publication." Instead, *Wikipedia* assumes that other user-authors will check for and correct erroneous information. Each article includes a discussion page, where authors can explain a change they have made or otherwise discuss the article's content. Lengthy guidelines and policies set expectations for appropriate content, writing style, and reliable sources.

Because of the open authorship, reviews of *Wikipedia* have been mixed. An early study published in *Nature* found that science articles in *Wikipedia* were nearly as accurate as those in *Britannica* with three errors per article on average for *Britannica* and four for *Wikipedia* (Giles 2005). Studies also have found that errors and vandalism are quickly fixed. At the same time, studies have noted that *Wikipedia's* articles can provide uneven treatment of topics; thus, while the information given in an article is generally accurate thanks to eager fact checkers and editors, the same article can be missing important aspects of a topic that a more conventional source would include (Read 2006). Studies have also found that controversial topics are particularly prone to repeated editing, making their accuracy and objectivity at any given time suspect (Wilson and Likens 2015). In addition, as the encyclopedia has become more ubiquitous, concerns have arisen about a Western bias in content (Giles 2013) and efforts to pay public relations firms and experienced editors to edit *Wikipedia* entries to promote products or remove unflattering information (Pinsker 2015).

One of the advantages of *Wikipedia* is its sheer size; in mid-2015, the site had nearly 4.9 million articles in its English-language version, doubling in size from seven years earlier. *Wikipedia* covers topics from the scholarly (phenomenology) to the mundane (San Pedro, California) to the trivial (a comparison chart of characters from eight different versions of the television show *The Office*). Thus, the encyclopedia can be a source of information on even the most unusual of topics. In addition, *Wikipedia's* open editing structure means articles can be updated almost simultaneously with world events.

Although librarians should be wary of consulting *Wikipedia* for ready-reference factual information, the encyclopedia can be a valuable resource for general background information and pre-research information. Bibliographies and cited references, when present, can direct researchers to additional sources of information, and careful reading of the discussion page associated with a topic can reveal diverse points of view worthy of further study. Box 18.4 provides an opportunity to examine *Wikipedia* in more detail.

Box 18.4 Activity: Comparing Encyclopedias

Compare coverage in *Wikipedia* and a general encyclopedia using three topics:

- A controversial topic such as vaccinations or climate change.
- An event or person that was recently in the news.
- A topic about which you have some in-depth knowledge.

Questions for Reflection and Discussion:

1. Which source is more up to date?
2. Which source is more balanced and objective?
3. In each source, how would you rate the quality and style of writing?
4. Which source offers more helpful guidance for further study?

SOURCES FOR CHILDREN AND YOUNG ADULTS

Reference works for children, particularly encyclopedias, abound. Typically, the format of these titles mirrors those targeted to adults although pages may be more colorful and lavishly illustrated. For young students in particular, font sizes may be larger, and there may be less text on a page so as not to overwhelm the reader. However, the principal difference between the titles for children and adults lies in content. Because young readers represent a variety of abilities and audiences, one finds a variety of titles to choose from in both print and electronic formats.

Almanacs

The World Almanac for Kids appears annually in print and has a corresponding website. It offers a plethora of "kid-friendly" information on such topics as animals, the environment, nations, population, religion, birthdays and holidays, and mythology, and has sections on sports, books, and states as well as a U.S. history timeline. The site also offers a games area with puzzles, educational games, and quizzes.

Another online almanac for children is *Factmonster.com.* Drawing on the contents of *Infoplease*, the freely available website offers information in various categories: World, United States, People, Science, Math and Money, Word Wise, and Sports. The Cool Stuff area includes information on art, architecture, business, entertainment, fashion, holidays, music, and worldwide dating and marriage customs. *Factmonster.com* also offers a Games and Quizzes area and a Homework Center. The Word Wise section includes information on children's literature, language facts, and a handy grammar and spelling resource. This reference also has a Reference Desk area. One can search all the information on the site through a simple keyword search box on the home page.

General Encyclopedias

In the realm of encyclopedias for children, some print titles continue to exist, even as online products grow richer and more popular. Of the general multivolume sets for children, the most prominent is the *World Book Encyclopedia*. The 2016 revision has 22 volumes. Articles vary in length and treatment depending on the subject matter and intended audience. The "mouse" article targets young readers and includes age-specific vocabulary, whereas the "cell" article targets advanced readers. Many of the lengthier articles, like the one on leaves, use a graduated approach; that is, authors use simple concepts and vocabulary at the beginning of the article and build toward incorporating more advanced ideas and vocabulary at its conclusion. Technical terms are italicized and their meanings given within the context of the sentence or within parentheses. Articles are arranged alphabetically using the word-by-word method, and cross-references play a significant role.

World Book is heavily illustrated. The 2016 revision has more than 25,000 illustrations, the vast majority in color, including photos, illustrations, and maps. QR codes link to video content available online. *World Book* conveys much of its information in tables and charts that are set apart from the text on a given page. This method makes the layout more visually appealing and acts as a vehicle for helping readers digest what they have read thus far. For example, the "tree" article has 23 illustrations covering, among other things, the parts, growth cycle, and uses of trees; instructions on correctly planting and growing a tree; and a guide to more than 75 tree species that includes an illustration of each tree with and without leaves and detailed views of the leaf, seed, and bark.

World Book is also available electronically through a suite of products known as *World Book Online*. The online version contains the complete contents of the print set plus thousands more articles, as well as additional illustrations and multimedia. *World Book Kids* is aimed at younger students and features a simple search and the ability to browse articles, along with games and fun activities. *World Book Student* is intended for elementary and middle school students. Optimized for tablets, it also features a dictionary and atlas, a citation builder, current news articles, and the ability to create an account and save content. For teachers, content is correlated to Common Core and state standards, and many articles are labeled by Lexile level, a measure of reading difficulty. *World Book Advanced*, for high school students, includes all of the content and features of *World Book Student* along with access to thousands of eBooks, periodical articles, and primary sources. World Book also offers a version for English-language learners, struggling readers, and adult learners. *World Book Discover* features specially written articles, a visual dictionary in multiple languages, a text-to-speech option, and a section on "Life Skills" with information on topics like health care and applying for jobs. For public libraries, a version called *World Book InfoFinder* combines the features of *Student*, *Advanced*, and *Discover* into one product.

As discussed earlier in this chapter, Britannica's online products offer rich textual material supplemented by extensive illustrations and multimedia. For children, *Britannica School* offers interfaces for elementary, middle, and high school audiences. Each interface draws on content from one of three age-appropriate encyclopedias, although once an article has been located, students can adjust the reading level and complexity of the content while remaining in their chosen interface. Options to change the font size and have text read aloud further improve accessibility for students with special needs. *Britannica School* also offers pop-up word definitions and the ability to translate articles into 50 languages. On-screen tools make it easy for students to bookmark, save, and print content. In addition to articles and multimedia content, *Britannica School* offers access to primary source documents for classroom and research use. At the high school level, there are resources to assist students with the research and writing process, book reviews, and presentations. Teachers can take advantage of a Lesson Plan Builder and standard correlations to integrate content into the classroom.

Another major online title for children and young adults is *Scholastic Go!* (formerly *Grolier Online*). *Go!* is based on two venerable encyclopedias that have now ceased publication, the *New Book of Knowledge* and the *Encyclopedia Americana*, with supplemental content from additional science, social science, and Spanish-language encyclopedias. The site offers more than 120,000 articles, each labeled with Lexile level and correlated to educational standards, along with interactive maps, videos, articles from more than 1,100 newspapers in 73 languages, and links to vetted Web resources. Users can choose from five interfaces designed for elementary, middle, and high school students as well as adult patrons and educators; depending on the interface used, content is pulled from one of three collections distinguished by reading level.

A few general encyclopedias are suitable for younger and/or struggling readers. World Book offers the *Discovery Encyclopedia*, a 13-volume set that focuses on high-interest topics and informational text that aligns with the Common Core State Standards. Most articles are brief, but special feature articles on high-interest topics contain more detailed treatments. Pages are colorful, and articles are heavily illustrated. Although aimed at grades four to eight, it is most appropriate for elementary school users. Britannica offers the *Britannica Student Encyclopedia*, a 16-volume set to support homework and in-class assignments. Although also heavily illustrated, pages are less busy than those of the *Discovery Encyclopedia*. This set is also most appropriate for elementary school users.

Single-Volume Encyclopedias

Many excellent single-volume encyclopedias are available for children, many focusing on a specific subject area. These can be kept in a noncirculating reference collection to provide breadth of coverage for students working on school assignments or seeking an answer to a specific question, or they can be integrated with the circulating collection to provide reading material for students interested in a particular topic.

The New Children's Encyclopedia has more than 4,000 entries organized into broad topics like "Space" and "The Human Body." Entries feature simple explanations and flashcard-style facts, often integrated into engaging timelines, charts, and illustrations. Excellent cross-section diagrams accompany articles on topics like the planet Earth and fossil fuels.

The *Scholastic Encyclopedia of the Presidents and Their Times* provides four- to six-page profiles of all the U.S. presidents arranged in chronological order. Profiles are heavily illustrated and include biographical and campaign information along with brief descriptions of contemporary events, the culture of the time, and the individual's policies and initiatives. Appendices provide tables of election results and a history of the White House. *The Kingfisher Animal Encyclopedia* covers 2,000 animals and is organized by classification. Each section includes information about a group of animals and profiles of specific species. Entries on specific species include common and scientific names, environment and distribution, size, and behavior. Kingfisher makes many encyclopedias for children, including *The Kingfisher History Encyclopedia* and *The Kingfisher Science Encyclopedia*.

SPECIALIZED SOURCES

Specialized Almanacs

Numerous specialized almanacs are published, although some of these could easily be called either handbooks or yearbooks. In fact, one can now find an almanac or handbook for nearly every subject, from cults to politics to pseudonyms. A few examples give an indication of the wide variety available. *The Almanac of American Politics* provides biographical information and political records of state governors and members of Congress. Published every two years, it is organized by state and, within each state, by congressional district. The *Library and Book Trade Almanac* (formerly *The Bowker Annual*) consists of reports written by library and information industry professionals about events of the previous year, topics of current importance, and activities of national associations and government agencies. In addition, it includes statistics, directories, awards, and other information of interest to librarians. The *NEA Almanac of Higher Education* highlights current information on employment conditions in higher education, including national salary data, trends in bargaining, and faculty workload. The *Sports Illustrated Sports Almanac* includes extensive statistics and coverage of sporting events for the preceding year with commentaries from staff writers.

Books of Days

A "book of days" provides a list of important events and the dates on which they occurred. Edited by Steven Anzovin and Janet Podell, *Famous First Facts* describes itself as an alphabetical subject list of "first happenings, discoveries, and inventions in American history." Firsts included are quite diverse, from the invention of the tape measure to the first appearance of billiards in the United States. Five indexes, by subject, years, days of the month, personal names, and geographical areas, expand the usefulness of the work. *Famous First Facts*, now in its seventh edition, can be used to establish historical fact, to identify anniversaries, and to gather information about a specific place or time. The index to days of the month serves as a "book of days" for the United States. *Notable Last Facts* includes an eclectic selection of the last of something (event, person, place, or thing), such as the last game played by Red Sox legend Ted Williams or the last works of a major author. The volume has broad topic areas and includes both individual lasts and those that can be grouped together.

Other "books of days" are common in reference collections. *American Decades* is a set of 11 volumes spanning the period 1900–2009. Each volume begins with a chronology of the decade, and the subject chapters concentrate on the important aspects of the period under consideration by providing biographies of prominent individuals, statistics, and information on arts, music, literature, government and politics, business, science and technology, and more. The set includes bibliographies and indexes. *Chase's Calendar of Events* lists birthdays of famous people (living and dead), festivals, historical anniversaries, presidential proclamations, special events, and the like for every day of the year. It contains more than 12,500 entries. Brief biographical information is included with each name, and the name and telephone numbers of event organizers are given where applicable. *Chase's* also lists the winners of many popular awards, such as television's Emmy Awards. *Today in*

History, a website from the Library of Congress, highlights an event from American history with digitized items from the American Memory historical collections. *This Day in History*, from the History Channel, also profiles a notable historical event on a daily basis.

Style Manuals

A standard handbook in almost all reference collections is the style manual. A style manual is consulted by writers, students, and librarians to help determine the format of papers, bibliographies, footnotes, and endnotes. Such a manual may also include helpful information of interest to authors and others concerned with publishing, such as information on the bookmaking process and copyright law and the rules of spelling and grammar.

One of the most commonly used style manuals is *The Chicago Manual of Style*. The manual is subdivided into numbered entries. References in the index, except for tables and figures, are to entry numbers rather than page numbers. Since 2006, users have been able to subscribe online to *The Chicago Manual of Style Online*, which provides a searchable interface to the popular Chicago Style Q&A, updated advice on style issues from the editorial staff, and the content of *The Chicago Manual of Style*. Although the full online version requires a subscription, information on basic citation formats is available for free. *A Manual for Writers of Research Papers, Theses, and Dissertations*, by Kate L. Turabian, is adapted from *The Chicago Manual of Style* and is aimed primarily at students. Although there is generally a style guide for each discipline, the other commonly required style manuals are the Modern Language Association's *MLA Handbook for Writers of Research Papers* and the *Publication Manual of the American Psychological Association*.

An excellent free guide to citing sources is Purdue University's *Online Writing Lab* (*OWL*). *OWL* provides a quick reference guide to citation formats for Chicago, MLA, and APA styles along with directions on formatting manuscripts and bibliographies. Although libraries will still need the print publications or their online equivalents for access to comprehensive information, *OWL* is a handy reference for verifying basic citation formats and may be particularly useful when working with patrons in virtual reference settings.

Libraries can also subscribe to bibliographic management systems, such as *EndNote*, *NoodleTools*, *RefWorks*, and *Zotero*. Once a patron creates an individual log-in, these systems allow him or her to create a personal database of citations and then insert references in papers and create bibliographies using almost any citation style. Some of them, such as *RefWorks*, allow for importing citations directly from databases, further saving the time of the user.

Etiquette Books

Because many library users ask for assistance in solving practical problems of day-to-day living, etiquette books, another type of handbook, are a part of most public and academic library reference collections. Long considered the standard, *Emily Post's Etiquette*, currently edited by Peggy Post, has a subject arrangement covering such topics as "Greetings and Introductions," "Table and Party Manners," and "The Finer Points of Tipping." It has an excellent index. *Miss Manners' Guide to Excruciatingly Correct Behavior* is another excellent guide. *Miss Manners*, written by Judith Martin, is also organized by subject and well indexed but differs from *Emily Post's Etiquette* in that it consists of letters written to "Miss Manners" and her responses to the letters.

When Henry M. Robert discovered associations, societies, and other organized groups needed rules of etiquette to govern their conduct at meetings, he wrote his classic reference work on parliamentary procedure, *Robert's Rules of Order*. It was originally published in 1876, and many editions have appeared since then (Watstein 1992). *Robert's Rules of Order Newly Revised* has been updated to incorporate new rules, interpretations, and procedures made necessary by the evolution of parliamentary procedure. A companion volume, *Robert's Rules of Order Newly Revised in Brief*, offers guidance in applying the rules.

Handbooks

Handbooks also solve educational, professional, or research problems. Both *Credo Reference* and *Oxford Reference* provide access to numerous handbooks in all subject area; a few well-known titles will be discussed.

In the sciences, the *CRC Handbook of Chemistry and Physics*, published since 1913, is a basic reference work for chemistry and physics. Composed primarily of tables, it describes or defines the structure, formulas, and phenomena of chemistry and physics. Physicists, chemists, and students of physics and chemistry use the handbook for research and study, and reference librarians consult it to answer questions for them.

Literary handbooks are commonplace in most reference departments. *Benét's Reader's Encyclopedia* is a useful one-stop guide to authors, titles, plots, characters, literary terms, movements, and other information sought by book enthusiasts. Oxford University Press produces a series of respected "Oxford Companion" handbooks. Some of these companions, such as *The Oxford Companion to American Literature* and *The Oxford Companion to Canadian Literature*, serve as comprehensive guides to the literature of a particular country. These guides include historical themes and trends, biographies of writers, summaries of plots, and descriptions of literary awards, journals, societies, and so forth.

SUBJECT ENCYCLOPEDIAS

Subject encyclopedias, unlike their single- or multivolume counterparts having a broader scope, give more in-depth coverage to a specific field of knowledge. Varying in price and size, subject encyclopedias can deliver depth and breadth of information not covered in general encyclopedias and can easily be used to augment the reference collection of a library.

Inexpensive single-volume titles such as *A Native American Encyclopedia* or *The Concise Encyclopedia of Poultry Breeds*, although highly specialized, can function as cost-effective alternatives that facilitate ready-reference access to subjects underrepresented in the overall library collection. Some midsized sets, such as the *Worldmark Encyclopedia of the Nations* or *Women in World History*, can also add immediate depth to a library's circulating collection for a reasonable cost. Specialized multivolume sets address their subjects in even greater detail, but can be expensive to collect and update. The *McGraw-Hill Encyclopedia of Science and Technology* is a case in point; the 11th edition has a list price of $3,700 as of 2015.

Although there are numerous high-quality subject encyclopedias, the limits of a single chapter allow for discussion of only a few representative titles. Perhaps the most important subject encyclopedia is the 22-volume *McGraw-Hill Encyclopedia of Science and Technology*. Unsurpassed in scope and coverage, the 11th edition, published in 2013, contains more than 7,000 articles, 2,500 of which are new or revised, and more than 13,000 illustrations. Articles are authored by experts, including a number of Nobel Prize winners, from universities, industry, and government organizations. In spite of having so many world-renowned experts, the *McGraw-Hill Encyclopedia of Science and Technology* is written to accommodate a wide variety of readers, from the layperson to the specialist. Specific disciplines, such as meteorology and physics, are covered in broad survey articles. Each entry begins with a definition and a general overview of the topic. The entry then progresses from the general to the specific in an effort to provide comprehensive coverage of the topic. Bibliographies typically come at the end of an article. Pure science remains the focus; there are no articles devoted to sociological or historical aspects of science or technology.

The *McGraw-Hill Encyclopedia of Science and Technology* is available online under the name *AccessScience*. From the initial screen, users can browse alphabetically or by topic, search the encyclopedia, or jump straight to multimedia resources. An advanced search screen allows Boolean searching and a variety of search limits. The online version includes more than 3,000 biographies; users can browse by name or scientific discipline. A Nobel Prize section provides a list of all prize winners, including those for literature, peace, and economics, with links to relevant articles. *AccessScience* enhances the textual content of the print set with a number of multimedia features designed for the nonexpert. Images, animations, and videos can be viewed online or downloaded for use in the classroom. A section for educators provides curriculum maps to further facilitate classroom use. *AccessScience* also offers a widget that can be embedded in course management systems and a mobile version for tablets and smartphones.

A second important science encyclopedia is *Grzimek's Animal Life Encyclopedia*. The 17-volume set contains more than 700 articles and 12,000 color illustrations. *Grzimek's* is arranged taxonomically by class, order, and family, which can be confusing for the novice user. However, finding aids abound. Each volume includes a table of contents and index for the volumes in that class; for example, the five volumes on mammals have the same table of contents and index reprinted in each volume. Volume 17 contains a cumulative index. Each article provides an overview of a family (e.g., slit-faced bats), including biology, habitat, behavior, and conservation status, followed by more detailed information on individual species. Information is presented in both narrative and tabular form, and each article is accompanied by at least one distribution map. Articles end with a list of resources for further study. *Grzimek's* is available online as part of *Gale Virtual Reference Library*.

The McGraw-Hill Encyclopedia of Science and Technology and *Grzimek's* are both suitable for high school students and adults. For younger children, a potential purchase is the *Student Discovery Science Encyclopedia*. Aimed at children in kindergarten through sixth grade, this 13-volume encyclopedia contains 2,100 entries and 3,300 illustrations covering all areas of science. In addition, it offers 60 science experiments and activities that can be used in the classroom or at home, suggestions for science fair projects, and a homework help section.

The *Encyclopedia of Religion*, most recently revised in 2004, is available in print and online. The 15-volume set contains approximately 3,300 articles on religion and spiritual practice. The *Encyclopedia of Religion* takes a valuable cross-cultural approach, highlighting practices and beliefs in different faiths and countries. Because of this cross-cultural approach and because one of the goals of the encyclopedia is to place religion in the context of daily life, the content is relevant to users interested in art, history, sociology, and other fields. Articles are arranged alphabetically, and longer articles include a table of contents. Cross-references and bibliographies, many with annotations, are located at the end of articles. Composite articles start with an overview of a topic (e.g., Afterlife) followed by articles that explore the topic in the context of a particular faith or place (e.g., Afterlife: Oceanic Concepts, Afterlife: Jewish Concepts). Interestingly, this edition retained approximately 50 prominent articles in their original form, providing updates in a second article subtitled "Further Considerations." All articles are signed and dated. Volume 15 contains an index.

The five-volume *Worldmark Encyclopedia of the Nations* is another essential title for most libraries. Country information is contained in four volumes that are organized by continent, with country entries organized alphabetically within each volume. Each entry starts with basic country facts, followed by detailed information organized under 50 subheadings. These subheadings are numbered and are consistent across all entries to aid users in finding the desired information. Information is presented primarily in narrative form, although some tabular data are given. Illustrations are black and white and consist of the coat of arms and flag, as well as a map of each country. A full-color regional map is printed at the front of each volume. Volume 1 provides detailed information about the United Nations, as well as information on polar regions, tables of statistical data, and an index (unfortunately, its location in the first volume is counterintuitive to most users, and it is easily overlooked). Although librarians would want to verify some information in a more up-to-date source, the *Worldmark Encyclopedia of the Nations* continues to be an excellent source for succinct background information about a nation's history, politics, economy, and culture.

A companion work is the *Worldmark Encyclopedia of Cultures and Daily Life*, a five-volume title that focuses on ethnic and cultural groups. Arranged alphabetically by culture or nationality, the encyclopedia uses frequent cross-references to direct the user to related articles and, in the case of groups with more than one popular name, to the main entry. Each entry contains basic facts such as the group's population, location, and religion as well as detailed descriptions of characteristics like language, clothing, folklore, rites of passage, educational traditions, family life, and work. Both *Worldmark Encyclopedia of the Nations* and *Worldmark Encyclopedia of Cultures and Daily Life* are available through *Gale Virtual Reference Library*.

In the arts, two prominent titles are Oxford's *Grove Art Online* and *Grove Music Online*. *Grove Art Online* is based on the 34-volume *Dictionary of Art*, a venerable encyclopedia covering art and artists from all time periods and regions of the world. The 45,000 articles are authored by experts and include bibliographies and cross-references to related articles. The online version includes thousands of images as well as links to additional images available on the Web, a dictionary of art terms, and access to additional Oxford resources on art. Libraries that want additional depth of coverage can subscribe to *Oxford Art Online*, which provides access to the *Benezit Dictionary of Artists* in conjunction with all the resources of *Grove Art Online* and additional research tools such as timelines and subject guides.

Grove Music Online brings together content from five encyclopedias and two music dictionaries with additional material written solely for the online platform. Its 50,000 articles, authored by experts, and 30,000 biographies include bibliographies, music samples, and cross-references. Libraries also have the option of subscribing to *Oxford Music Online*, which provides the content of *Grove Music* with additional articles and research tools

FOREIGN-LANGUAGE AND NON-ENGLISH-LANGUAGE ENCYCLOPEDIAS

Increasingly, encyclopedia publishers are offering content in Spanish, French, and other languages. Non-English-language encyclopedias may be based on a publisher's other encyclopedia titles and typically include general content with additional articles appropriate to the language of publication, translation dictionaries, news articles, and a wealth of multimedia images and videos. These encyclopedias can be valuable additions to libraries supporting bilingual and multilingual communities, English-language learners, and students studying other languages. Offerings from Britannica, World Book, and Scholastic can be purchased as a stand-alone resource or combined with other online holdings for seamless access in multiple languages.

Britannica offers two French-language products, *Universalis Online* for young adults and adults and *Universalis Junior Online* for elementary school children. Britannica also publishes the *Spanish Resource Center*. This online, Spanish-language product includes two encyclopedias, *Enciclopedia Moderna* for young adults and adults and *Britannica Escolar* for elementary school students. For libraries seeking broader coverage, Britannica's *Global Reference Center* offers content in French, Spanish, Chinese, Korean, and Japanese.

World Book publishes the Spanish-language *Enciclopedia Estudiantil Hallazgos* for younger readers and *Hispánica Saber* for older readers. It also offers the French-language *L'Encyclopédie Découverte* and the Arabic-language *Kids eLearn*, both for elementary school-aged users. Scholastic offers Spanish-language content built into its *Scholastic Go!* product.

DIRECTORIES

As noted earlier, many librarians now depend on free online sources for contact information for people, businesses, and organizations. However, because specialized directories can provide more comprehensive coverage, in-depth entries, and, in the case of online products, a robust search interface, subscription-based directories are common in all types of libraries. In addition to the following directories listed, Chapter 22 discusses directories of government agencies and Chapter 25 discusses directories for businesses and corporations.

Multi-Title Sources

As with handbooks and encyclopedias, libraries can choose to subscribe to a database that provides unified access to a multitude of directory titles. *Gale Directory Library* offers access to more than 30 titles, including the *Encyclopedia of Associations*, *Publishers Directory*, the *Directory of Special Libraries and Information Centers*, and the *Research Centers Directory*. Users can search a specific title or the entire collection by name, keyword, or subject. In addition to e-mailing or printing results, users can export a list of entries for use in Excel or mailing lists.

For librarians who need in-depth coverage and want to identify available directories, *Directories in Print* indexes and describes approximately 16,000 directories, rosters, mailing lists, and other types of contact files. The volume is available in print and through *Gale Directory Library*.

Telephone Directories

Patrons are often seeking contact information for individuals and businesses. *AnyWho* is a free website that provides both a "white pages" for locating individuals and a "yellow pages" for locating businesses. When seeking individuals, *AnyWho* allows searching by the full or partial name; searches can be limited by a city and/or state, but these are not required. *AnyWho* also provides a "reverse" lookup option, allowing the user to search an address or phone number to get the associated name. When seeking businesses, *AnyWho* allows searching by name or type of business (e.g., dance, plumbing). Entries include address, phone number, website, a map, and basic information about the services offered. Other sites that provide free directory information include *Switchboard*, which covers the United States, and *Infobel*, which is international in scope.

Associations

Directories of associations provide contact and profile information for nonprofit organizations. They can be used to answer specific questions, such as when an organization was founded or how many members it has, or to identify organizations on a topic of interest, such as lighthouses or ultimate frisbee.

The three *Encyclopedia of Associations* titles provide comprehensive directory coverage for organizations. The *Encyclopedia of Associations: National Organizations of the U.S.* and *Encyclopedia of Organizations: International Organizations* are organized by subject, while the *Encyclopedia of Organizations: Regional, State, and Local Organizations* is organized geographically. Entries generally consist of a name and contact information, a description of the association's activities, the name of a chief executive, the annual budget, and a list of conferences, meetings, and publications. All three are available online through *Gale Directory Library*, where they can be searched collectively or individually.

For librarians seeking coverage of Canadian associations in particular, *Associations Canada* is available in print and online. Entries, many of which are in both French and English, include contact information, a description, the names of chief executives, budget figures, and a list of conferences, meetings, and publications.

Education

Questions about educational institutions and programs are common in most reference settings, especially in academic and school libraries. *Peterson's Four Year Colleges* provides information on more than 2,500 accredited four-year institutions in the United States and Canada. College descriptions are arranged alphabetically by state or province, and contain information such as name, address, phone number, fax number, website URL, acceptance rates, majors, current tuition, and available student activities. A special section provides additional in-depth narrative profiles for more than 400 selected colleges and universities. Indexes provide access to institutions by name, majors, cost range, and entrance difficulty. A prefatory section provides advice on the college application and admissions process.

Graduate education is covered by *Peterson's Graduate & Professional Programs*, a six-volume set. Contact and informational profiles are provided for more than 44,000 graduate programs in more than 500 fields. These include programs offered by institutions in the United States as well as those accredited by U.S. accrediting bodies in other countries. Across all the volumes in this set, three kinds of entries appear: basic profiles, displays, and close-ups. The basic profiles are the heart of each volume, and every program listed has a profile that includes information such as name, address, degrees offered, student demographics, entrance requirements, and faculty research interests. Some profiles have a display at the end of their listing containing information that the school or program wants to emphasize to potential applicants. Some profiles also have a cross-reference to an in-depth close-up of their program, submitted by the schools themselves. These descriptions are found at the end of subject sections in the individual volumes and appear in a standard format that includes information on programs of study, research facilities, financial aid, costs, and how to apply.

Another excellent source of information on higher education is *The College Blue Book*, which profiles more than 11,800 universities and postsecondary institutions in the United States and Canada. In its print form, this resource is organized in six thematic volumes that can largely stand by themselves. Volume 1 contains narrative descriptions of more than 4,100 colleges and universities. The entries are arranged alphabetically by state and Canadian province, and include contact and descriptive information. Volume 2 includes tabular data for colleges, with information about tuition, accreditation, enrollment, faculty, and administration. Volume 3 is an index of degrees offered by colleges in various subject areas. Volume 4 profiles more than 6,700 postsecondary occupational and vocational schools. A directory of grant, scholarship, fellowship, and loan opportunities is provided in Volume 5. Volume 6 gives detailed profiles of nearly 1,000 institutions that offer distance education programs in the United States and Canada. The *College Blue Book* is available through *Gale Virtual Reference Library*, where users can browse individual volumes or search the set by keyword.

Peterson's also offers a website, simply titled *Peterson's*, with free information on undergraduate, graduate, and online programs. Users can search for a specific institution or use an advanced search feature to locate schools by institution type, location, major, or a combination of factors. School profiles include contact information, lists of degrees and majors, demographic and admissions data, the cost of tuition and fees, and lists of extracurricular activities. Like the print publications, the site also provides advice on the application and admissions process and tips for college success.

Another free website for college information is *College Navigator*, offered by the U.S. Department of Education. Institutional profiles include contact information, programs offered, and a wealth of data, including student demographics, admission rates, retention and graduation rates, and campus safety statistics. Most notable is that this site offers detailed information on tuition and fees, available financial aid, net price for students from different income brackets, and loan default rates.

For questions with an international scope, *The Europa World of Learning* covers more than 33,000 educational institutions outside of the United States and Canada, including colleges and universities, museums, art galleries, and research organizations. *The Europa World of Learning* is available in print and online. In the online version, users can search by institution name, keyword, or location, or browse by country. National profiles provide an overview of each country's higher education system, including history and structure. Institutional profiles provide contact information, the names of key personnel, and a brief description of activities and publications.

Grants

Individuals seeking funds to advance their education and organizations seeking funds to support the development of new initiatives may need assistance in identifying potential funding sources. Whether users have specific questions, such as the giving interests of a particular foundation, or need to develop a list of foundations to approach, directories of foundations and grants are valuable resources for all types of libraries.

The most comprehensive resource covering private grant giving to nonprofit organizations is the *Foundation Directory Online*. Subscriptions can be customized through a number of different packages, with the top-level option profiling more than 100,000 grant makers, including foundations and corporate giving programs. Detailed entries include foundation name, address, telephone number, contact person, establishment date, principal donors, assets and expenditures, areas of giving, and application procedures. Users can search by foundation or corporate name or use advanced search options to identify grant makers by giving area, geographical focus, trustee or officer names, and type of grant offered. *Foundation Directory Online* also offers the option to search foundations' IRS 990 forms by keyword and a database of past grants that have been given.

For users seeking less comprehensive information, *Foundation Directory Online Free* has basic information on grant makers in the United States and can be searched by name as well as location to identify grant makers in a given city, state, or ZIP code. A print version is also available and comes in two parts: *The Foundation Directory*, which profiles the top 10,000 foundations in terms of annual giving, and *The Foundation Directory Part 2*, which profiles the next 10,000 in terms of giving. Finally, the publisher offers print and online versions of *Foundation Grants to Individuals*, an extensive resource covering private grant giving to individuals.

Information about grant-giving organizations can also be found in the *Annual Register of Grant Support*. This one-volume directory profiles public and private foundations, government agencies, corporations, community trusts, unions, educational and professional associations, and special interest organizations that are involved in grant giving. The directory is divided into a number of broad topical funding areas that are further divided into more specialized categories. Entries include contact information for the funding entity, website URL, amount of funding for awards, areas of interest, eligibility requirements, and application process. Subject, organization and program, geographical, and personnel indexes give users access options to identify the best funding opportunity.

The federal government provides two free online portals to locate government grants and assistance. The *Catalog of Federal Domestic Assistance* (*CFDA*) provides information on all federal funding programs that are available to individuals, state and local governments, private organizations, and nonprofit groups. This directory can be searched by functional area, agency, program title, applicant eligibility, deadlines, program number, grant, and keyword. *Grants.gov* is a searchable database of grants from 26 federal agencies. Users can search by keyword and limit results based on agency, subject category, and eligibility status; there is also an option to browse available grants. While *CFDA* lists the existence of federal programs, *Grants.gov* has the most recent information on currently available grants and application procedures. In addition, it allows individuals and organizations to register and apply online.

Publishers and Booksellers

As repositories of books and other materials, libraries are closely connected to the publishing industry. Both librarians and library users are interested in information about publishing and publishers. It is not surprising that questions about contacting and locating publishers would be common in the reference setting.

A good example of a comprehensive directory of publishers in the United States and Canada is the *Literary Market Place*. In its two-volume print form, *Literary Market Place* is an annual publication with more than 12,500 entries for various entities in the publishing industry. Volume 1 provides information on publishers, editors, industry associations, events such as conferences and workshops, and trade publications. Volume 2 is a directory of supporting services that includes entries for marketers, advertisers, promoters, suppliers, and services such as translation and illustration. Entries provide name, address, contact information, website, key personnel, affiliated offices, and a brief descriptive annotation. Indexes for companies and personal names serve as quick reference directories and refer back to the main entries. For users needing broader coverage, the *International Literary Market Place* lists 13,000 entities in 180 countries. Both *Literary Market Place* and *International Literary Market Place* can be found as a Web-based product called *LiteraryMarketPlace.com.*

The *American Book Trade Directory* is a comprehensive directory of book retailers and wholesalers in the United States and Canada. It lists more than 20,000 retailers, wholesalers, antiquarians, and dealers in foreign-language books, arranged geographically by state or province and then by city. The entries provide store or business name, address, contact information, owner/manager, stocked volumes, and subject strengths. A standard alphabetical index and a store-type index provide access to the directory content.

Libraries

Of special interest to librarians are directories of libraries. They can answer questions such as the number of people employed at the Library of Congress or whether Uganda has a national library.

The *American Library Directory* lists libraries in North America, covering libraries of all types, consortia arrangements, and key library personnel. An online version can be searched by name, location, special collections, and personnel; advanced search options allow users to identify libraries using criteria such as size, budget, automation system, population served, and annual circulation. Entries themselves consist of the library name and branches, address, contact information, names of key personnel, collection size, subject strengths, automation information, budget and expenditures, population served, and annual circulation. In print, the *American Library Directory* consists of an annual two-volume set. The first volume covers libraries in the United States and is organized by state and then city. The second volume covers Canadian libraries, consortia, and other institutions that are related to libraries such as library schools and state library agencies. This volume includes organization and personnel indexes.

For those seeking more specific information about specialized collections, the *Directory of Special Libraries and Information Centers* can be helpful. This resource covers more than 37,500 special libraries, including collections in corporations, museums, foundations, professional organizations, hospitals, and learned societies. It is arranged alphabetically by the name of the collection or library; indexes provide geographical, subject, and personnel access points. The entries contain elements such as name, address, contact information, parent organization, director name, and founding date. The directory is available online through the *Gale Directory Library*.

YEARBOOKS

The *Britannica Book of the Year* includes vast statistical information in the "World Data" section, a collection of current facts and figures for the countries and dependencies of the world. In addition, a "World Affairs" section provides narrative updates for individual countries, while additional articles provide updates on cultural topics such as fashion and literature. The *Book of the Year* also includes brief biographies of notable figures, obituaries, and a timeline of noteworthy events. As with almanacs, it is important to note that the date given on the spine reflects the publication year; the data come from the preceding year (i.e., the 2015 *Book of the Year* actually reflects data and events from 2014). World Book's annual *Year Book* contains approximately 250 articles on influential people and major events of the year. In addition, it provides special reports on contemporary topics. For example, the *Year Book 2015* contained an article on the history of Ukraine's independence and events leading up to that year's conflict with Russia.

Two excellent yearbooks with an international scope are *The Europa World Year Book* and *The Statesman's Yearbook*. Both consist of an initial section on international organizations, followed by alphabetically arranged countries of the world. Both aim to give a concise but complete description of organizations and countries and to emphasize the political and economic aspects of the world. However, each has unique characteristics.

Europa is published annually in three volumes. The first volume contains international organizations and the first part of the alphabetically arranged survey of countries; the remaining volumes contain the remainder of the alphabet. International organizations are described in terms of structure, function, and activities. Names of important officials, budget information, and addresses are given. Information about individual countries is divided into three parts: introductory survey, statistical survey, and directories. The introductory survey has short essays on location, climate, language, religion, recent history, government, defense, economic affairs, and education. The statistical survey provides summary data about the country and is followed by separate directories for government, the press, religion, finance, and other areas. Entries for some of the industrialized countries include directories for periodicals, banks, and trade unions.

The inclusion of this varied information makes *The Europa World Year Book* a one-stop reference work. The yearbook contains a short index to territories of the world. Statistical tables compare life expectancy, population, gross national product, and other topics among countries of the world. *The Europa World Year Book* obtains information from the institutions listed as well as from many other sources such as national statistics offices, government departments, diplomatic missions, and UN publications. The publisher of *The Europa World Year Book* also publishes nine regional surveys; these surveys are similar in content to *The Europa World Year Book* but include more detailed information and a bibliography. *Europa World Plus* enables online searching of *The Europa World Year Book* together with the nine regional surveys. In addition to search and browse options, the interface supports retrieval of comparative statistics from data included in the country profiles.

The Statesman's Yearbook, published annually since 1864, is a one-volume book. It includes country profiles covering key historical events, territory and population, social statistics, climate, constitution and government, government chronology, recent elections, current administration, current leaders, defense, international relations, economy, energy and natural resources, environment, industry, international trade, communications, social institutions, religion, culture, diplomatic representatives, and a list for further reading. The volume also has a chronology of world events from the previous year. *The Statesman's Yearbook Online* supports searching and browsing the contents of the volume and is updated throughout the year.

A freely available Web-based resource that offers a bit of what *Europa* and *Statesman's* offer is *The World Factbook*. Made available by the U.S. Central Intelligence Agency, it provides brief data and small maps for each country. This site provides a reliable resource for information on independent states, dependencies, areas of special sovereignty, uninhabitable regions, and oceans. Each entry typically includes concise physical and demographic statistics, an outline of government, and an economic overview, as well as communications, transportation, and military information. Although *The World Factbook* does not have a search feature, once at an individual country's page, librarians can use a browser's built-in "Find" option to search the text on the page for specific facts. Embedded links make it easy to compare data points across multiple countries. While it does not compare in coverage to *Europa* or *Statesman's*, *The World Factbook* will have sufficient information for many libraries' needs.

As is true for almanacs, there are many yearbooks on special topics. Sometimes topical yearbooks update either a special or a general encyclopedia. The *McGraw-Hill Yearbook of Science and Technology*, for example, is an annual review of the previous year's scientific accomplishments and advancements that supplements the *McGraw-Hill Encyclopedia of Science and Technology*. The yearbook is arranged alphabetically by topic and includes bibliographies, cross-references, and an index.

Other yearbooks review the activities of organizations or groups. These annuals furnish statistics, directories, facts, and trends about a specific group and are often published as a handbook for the group's members. For example, the *Yearbook of the United Nations* summarizes events of a designated year, provides texts of important UN documents, and lists member nations and important officeholders.

SEARCH STRATEGIES

The first step in developing a search strategy is to determine the nature of the question. If the patron needs a simple factual answer, an almanac, handbook, directory, or yearbook may be an appropriate resource; encyclopedias can also be used to verify factual information, but are most useful when a patron needs a concise overview of a topic or is seeking background information.

Other factors influence the choice of source. If current information is required, frequently updated databases or websites are preferable. For difficult or hard-to-find information, the search capabilities of electronic resources make them better choices. On the other hand, for quick facts or simple information, books are often faster. Reference works with a national or regional slant usually have more information about these geographical areas, while subject encyclopedias can provide more in-depth information or a unique perspective on a topic. It is important to remember, especially when relying on fact books, that more than one source can answer the same question. Often, comparing information in two or more sources may be the best way to serve the user.

"How many animals are endangered?" is a question particularly suited to an almanac. *Infoplease* has a table listing the total number of endangered species in groups such as mammals, fish, and insects. *The World Almanac* has a similar table as well as an additional table listing selected endangered species by their common name, scientific names, and range. Both cite the original source as the U.S. Fish and Wildlife Service, providing the patron with an avenue for further research and fact-finding.

"I would like to attend college in Sydney, Australia. What schools are located there?" Because the patron is looking for a list of institutions, a directory would be an optimal choice. *The Europa World of Learning* would allow the patron to search by the name of the city and obtain a list of schools. Alternately, the patron could browse to the entry on Australia to learn about the country's educational system and then link to a list of schools located in the territory of New South Wales, enabling him or her to identify schools located in and around Sydney.

"I am writing a report about Martin Luther King. My teacher said that he wrote a speech about a dream. Where can I find it?" Not only does *Britannica Library* provide an article about Dr. King as well as links to the text of his "I Have a Dream Speech," but it also includes a video clip of Dr. King delivering that speech. The student would benefit from reading and listening to this speech and might gain a better understanding of the impact Dr. King had on U.S. history.

"Where can I read about the structure of DNA?" Because of the specificity of this question, a subject encyclopedia would be the first place to look. In particular, the *McGraw-Hill Encyclopedia of Science and Technology* lends itself to this question

Box 18.5 Search Strategy: Ancient Civilizations Report

A student approaches the librarian and asks for assistance researching a brief report that is due the next day. A reference interview reveals that he needs to write about an ancient civilization and has not yet chosen a topic. The librarian suggests starting with *The World Almanac and Book of Facts*. Turning to the World History section, she shows him a timeline of human civilizations that begins with a one-page discussion of "Earliest Civilizations: 4000–1000 BCE."

After reading the entry, the student decides he is interested in researching Mesopotamia or civilizations in the Indus Valley; he requests additional information about both. The librarian uses *Credo Reference* to access the *National Geographic Almanac of World History* and finds substantial entries that identify distinctive features of each civilization. The student reads both entries and decides to write about the ancient city of Mohenjo-Daro.

Finding no available books in the circulating collection, the librarian again turns to reference sources. A further search of *Credo* results in two articles about Mohenjo-Daro from the *World History Encyclopedia*, while a search of *Oxford Reference* locates a lengthy article from *The Oxford Companion to Archaeology*. Because Mohenjo-Daro had distinct architectural features, the librarian also searches *Grove Art Online* and locates an article about architecture and art in the ancient city.

because it is the standard for in-depth information on science and technology. For younger users, *World Book* would provide comparable information written at a level they would better understand.

Oftentimes, librarians will use more than one almanac or encyclopedia to completely answer a patron's question. As Boxes 18.5 and 18.6 illustrate, librarians can use a general source for introductory information and then specialized sources to find more in-depth or focused information.

Box 18.6 Search Strategy: What Would You Like to Know about Giraffes?

A library user approaches the desk and asks for information on giraffes. The free *Encyclopaedia Britannica* provides a short article accompanied by photos and a video. After reviewing the article, the user indicates that more information is needed. Which source would be the best?

If the patron is a child, *World Book* would be a good choice. In the print version, the article is almost two pages long and is accompanied by multiple illustrations. The article addresses physical appearance and reproduction, as well as the family life of giraffes, how they move, and their interaction with people. In addition to two photos of giraffes, one of which shows how giraffes bend to the ground to lick salt or drink, there is an illustration of the giraffe's skeleton, an illustration of its footprints, and a world map showing distribution. Although there is no bibliography, the article is signed. *World Book Student* provides a similar article, and while there are fewer illustrations, it includes videos of giraffe behavior.

For an older student, *Britannica Library* provides a moderate-length article with two photos and a video. This article has more detail than its print counterpart and lists the nine subspecies of giraffes. *Grzimek's Animal Life Encyclopedia* has 12 pages on the Family Giraffidae, which includes giraffes and okapis. The article includes in-depth information and numerous photos. One section provides scientific names and descriptions for the nine subspecies, as well as photos illustrating their markings and a short discussion of current scientific debates about whether all nine are truly distinct subspecies.

In addition to a brief article on giraffes, *AccessScience* has a lengthy article on the order Artiodactyla that includes a detailed discussion of unique features of the ankle joint, skulls and teeth, and cranial appendages. There is also an analysis of how the order has evolved and the relationship of giraffes to other animals. *Oxford Reference* provides access to the *Encyclopedia of Mammals*, which contains a detail-rich article about giraffe physiology and behavior. Further exploration reveals links to poetry and literary references to giraffes, an entry for the constellation Camelopardalis, which represents a giraffe, and a discussion of "camelopard" as an archaic name for a giraffe, opening up further avenues of exploration for the patron.

Wikipedia provides an extensive article with a table of contents, an illustration with the complete scientific classification and conservation status, numerous photos (including one of the tongue and one of giraffes bending down to drink), a map of the distribution of all nine subspecies, and an illustration of the skeleton. The article provides information on evolution, anatomy and morphology, behavior, and conservation, and giraffes in art and culture. The entry ends with a list of references and links to further information on other sites. By consulting two additional free encyclopedias, the *Encyclopedia of Life* and *Wildscreen Arkive*, the librarian is able to locate numerous additional images and videos as well as links to further information.

REFERENCES

Barzun, Jacques. 1992. *The Modern Researcher*, 5th ed. New York: Houghton Mifflin.
Giles, Jim. 2005. "Internet Encyclopaedias Go Head to Head." *Nature* 438 (December 15): 900–901.
Giles, Jim. 2013. "Wiki-opoly." *New Scientist* 218 (April 13): 38–41.
Merriam-Webster Online Dictionary. 2015. "Almanac." http://www.merriam-webster.com/dictionary/almanac.
Morrison, Margaret. 1992. "All Things to All People: *The World Almanac*." In *Distinguished Classics of Reference Publishing*, edited by James Rettig. Phoenix: Oryx. 313–21. https://archive.org/details/DistinguishedClassicsOfReferencePublishing.
Pinsker, Joe. 2015. "The Covert World of People Trying to Edit Wikipedia—for Pay." *The Atlantic*. August 11. http://www.theatlantic.com/business/archive/2015/08/wikipedia-editors-for-pay/393926/.
Read, Brock. 2006. "Can Wikipedia Ever Make the Grade?" *The Chronicle of Higher Education* 53 (October 27): A31–A36.
Watstein, Sarah. 1992. "Demystifying Parliamentary Procedure: *Robert's Rules of Order*." In *Distinguished Classics of Reference Publishing*, edited by James Rettig. Phoenix: Oryx. 211–19. https://archive.org/details/DistinguishedClassicsOfReferencePublishing.
Wilson, Adam M., and Gene E. Likens. 2015. "Content Volatility of Scientific Topics in Wikipedia: A Cautionary Tale." *PLoS One* 10 (8): 1–5.

LIST OF SOURCES

AccessScience. New York: McGraw-Hill. http://www.accessscience.com/. [subscription required]
The Almanac of American Politics. 1972–. Bethesda, MD: Columbia Books and Information Services. Biennial.
American Book Trade Directory. 1915–. Medford, NJ: Information Today. Biannual.
American Decades. 1994–2011. 11 vols. Farmington Hills, MI: Gale Cengage Learning. Available online as part of *Gale Virtual Reference Library*.
American Library Directory. 1923–. 2 vols. Medford, NJ: Information Today. Annual. Available online: http://www.americanlibrarydirectory.com/. [subscription required]
Annual Register of Grant Support. 1967–. Medford, NJ: Information Today. Annual.
AnyWho. YP Intellectual Property LLC. http://www.anywho.com.
Anzovin, Steven, and Janet Podell. 2015. *Famous First Facts*, 7th ed. Amenia, NY: Grey House Publishing.
Associations Canada. 1991–. Toronto: Grey House Publishing Canada. Annual. Available online: http://www.greyhouse.ca/assoc.htm. [subscription required]
Atkins, Tony, and Marcel Escudier. 2013. *Dictionary of Mechanical Engineering*. London: Oxford University Press. Available online as part of *Oxford Reference*.
Bates, Marcia J., and Mary Niles Maack, eds. 2009. *Encyclopedia of Library and Information Sciences*, 3rd ed. Boca Raton, FL: CRC Press. Available online: http://www.tandfonline.com. [subscription required]
Benét's Reader's Encyclopedia. 2008. 5th ed. New York: Collins.
Brahms, William, ed. 2005. *Notable Last Facts: A Compendium of Endings, Conclusions, Terminations, and Final Events through History Organized in a Single, Easy-to-Use Reference*. Haddonfield, NJ: Reference Desk Press.
Brill's Encyclopedia of Hinduism. 2014. Edited by Knut A. Jacobsen. Boston: Brill. Available online: http://referenceworks.brillonline.com/browse/brill-s-encyclopedia-of-hinduism. [subscription required]

Britannica Academic. Chicago: Encyclopaedia Britannica. http://info.eb.com/products/britannica-academic-edition/. [subscription required]

Britannica Book of the Year. 1938–. Chicago: Encyclopaedia Britannica. Annual.

Britannica Escolar. Chicago: Encyclopaedia Britannica. http://info.eb.com/products/britannica-escolar/. [subscription required]

Britannica Library. Chicago: Encyclopaedia Britannica. http://info.eb.com/products/britannica-public-library-edition/. [subscription required]

Britannica School. Chicago: Encyclopaedia Britannica. http://info.eb.com/products/britannica-school/. [subscription required]

Britannica Student Encyclopedia. 2015. 16 vols. Chicago: Encyclopaedia Britannica.

Burnie, David. 2011. *The Kingfisher Animal Encyclopedia.* New York: Kingfisher Encyclopedias.

Canadian Almanac & Directory. 1847–. Toronto: Grey House Publishing Canada. Annual.

The Canadian Encyclopedia. Historica Foundation. http://www.thecanadianencyclopedia.com.

Catalog of Federal Domestic Assistance. http://www.cfda.gov.

Chase's Calendar of Events. 1995–. New York: McGraw-Hill. Annual. (Formerly *Chase's Annual Events,* 1954–1994.)

The Chicago Manual of Style. 2010. 16th ed. Chicago: University of Chicago Press. Available online: http://www.chicagomanualofstyle.org/home.html. [subscription required for full access]

ChiltonLibrary. Farmington Hills, MI: Gale Cengage Learning. http://chilton.cengage.com/home/library. [subscription required]

The College Blue Book. 1923–. 6 vols. Farmington Hills, MI: Gale Cengage Learning. Annual. Available online as part of *Gale Virtual Reference Library.*

College Navigator. National Center for Education Statistics. https://nces.ed.gov/collegenavigator/.

Commire, Anne, and Deborah Klezmer, eds. 1999–2002. *Women in World History: A Biographical Encyclopedia.* 17 vols. Farmington Hills, MI: Gale Cengage Learning. Available online as part of *Gale Virtual Reference Library.*

CRC Handbook of Chemistry and Physics. 1913–. Boca Raton, FL: CRC Press. Annual. Available online as part of *CRCnetBASE.*

CRCnetBASE. Boca Raton, FL: CRC Press. http://www.crcnetbase.com/. [subscription required]

Credo Reference. Boston: Credo Reference. http://search.credoreference.com/. [subscription required]

Diagnostic and Statistical Manual of Mental Disorders, Fifth Edition (DSM-5). 2013. Washington DC: American Psychiatric Association. Available online: http://psychiatryonline.org/. [subscription required]

Directories in Print. 1989–. 2 vols. Farmington Hills, MI: Gale Cengage Learning. Annual. Available online as part of *Gale Directory Library.*

Directory of Special Libraries and Information Centers. 1963–. 3 vols. Farmington Hills, MI: Gale Cengage Learning. Annual. Available online as part of *Gale Directory Library.*

Discovery Encyclopedia. 2011. 13 vols. Chicago: World Book.

Enciclopedia Estudiantil Hallazgos. Chicago: World Book. http://www.worldbook.com/online-learning-encyclopedia/world-book-enciclopedia-estudiantil-hallazgos. [subscription required]

Enciclopedia Moderna. Chicago: Encyclopaedia Britannica. http://info.eb.com/products/spanish-reference-center/. [subscription required]

Encyclopaedia Britannica. http://www.britannica.com/.

Encyclopedia of Associations: International Organizations. 1961–. 3 vols. Farmington Hills, MI: Gale Cengage Learning. Annual. Available online as part of *Gale Directory Library.*

Encyclopedia of Associations: National Organizations of the U.S. 1961–. 3 vols. Farmington Hills, MI: Gale Cengage Learning. Annual. Available online as part of *Gale Directory Library*.

Encyclopedia of Associations: Regional, State, and Local Organizations. 1987–. 5 vols. Farmington Hills, MI: Gale Cengage Learning. Annual. Available online as part of *Gale Directory Library*.

Encyclopedia of Life. http://eol.org/.

Encyclopedia.com. Farmington Hills, MI: Cengage Learning. http://www.encyclopedia.com/.

EndNote. Thomson Reuters. http://endnote.com/.

The Europa World of Learning. 1947–. 2 vols. London: Routledge. Annual. Available online: http://www.worldoflearning.com. [subscription required]

The Europa World Year Book. 1926–. 2 vols. London: Routledge. Annual. Available online as *Europa World Plus*: http://www.europaworld.com/pub/. [subscription required]

Factmonster.com. Boston: Information Please. http://www.factmonster.com.

The Foundation Directory. 1960–. New York: Foundation Center. Annual. Available online as part of *Foundation Directory Online*.

Foundation Directory Online. New York: Foundation Center. https://fconline.foundationcenter.org/. [subscription required]

Foundation Directory Online Free. New York: Foundation Center. https://fdo.foundationcenter.org/.

The Foundation Directory, Part 2. 1990–. New York: Foundation Center. Annual. Available online as part of *Foundation Directory Online*.

Foundation Grants to Individuals. 1977–. New York: Foundation Center. Annual. Available online: http://gtionline.foundationcenter.org/. [subscription required]

Gale Directory Library. Farmington Hills, MI: Gale Cengage Learning. http://www.cengage.com. [subscription required]

Gale Virtual Reference Library. Farmington Hills, MI: Gale Cengage Learning. http://www.cengage.com. [subscription required]

Global Reference Center. Chicago: Encyclopaedia Britannica. http://global.eb.com. [subscription required]

Grants.gov. http://www.grants.gov.

Grove Art Online. New York: Oxford University Press. http://www.oxfordartonline.com/public/book/oao_gao. [subscription required] Also available as part of *Oxford Art Online*.

Grove Music Online. New York: Oxford University Press. http://www.oxfordmusiconline.com/public/book/omo_gmo. [subscription required] Also available as part of *Oxford Music Online*.

Grzimek's Animal Life Encyclopedia. 2003–2004. 2nd ed. 17 vols. Farmington Hills, MI: Gale Cengage Learning. Available online as part of *Gale Virtual Reference Library*.

Guinness World Records. 1956–. New York: Guinness World Records. Annual. Available online: http://www.guinnessworldrecords.com.

Hams, Fred. 2015. *The Concise Encyclopedia of Poultry Breeds.* London: Southwater.

Hart, James D., and Phillip W. Leininger. 2013. *The Oxford Companion to American Literature.* 6th ed. New York: Oxford. Available online as part of *Oxford Reference*.

Hispánica Saber. Chicago: World Book. http://www.worldbook.com/online-learning/online-for-schools/language-sites. [subscription required]

Honderich, Ted. 2005. *The Oxford Companion to Philosophy.* 2nd ed. New York: Oxford. Available online as part of *Oxford Reference*.

HowStuffWorks. http://www.howstuffworks.com/.

Infobel. http://www.infobel.com.

Infoplease. http://www.infoplease.com.
International Literary Market Place. 1966–. Medford, NJ: Information Today. Annual. Available online: http://www.literarymarketplace.com.
Jones, Lindsay, ed. 2005. *Encyclopedia of Religion.* 2nd ed. 15 vols. Detroit: Macmillan Reference. Available online as part of *Gale Virtual Reference Library.*
Kids eLearn. Chicago: World Book. http://www.worldbook.com/online-learning/online-for-schools/language-sites. [subscription required]
The Kingfisher History Encyclopedia. 2012. New York: Kingfisher Encyclopedias.
L'Encyclopédie Découverte. Chicago: World Book. http://www.worldbook.com/online-learning/online-for-schools/language-sites. [subscription required]
Library and Book Trade Almanac 2016. 61st ed. Medford, NJ: Information Today.
Literary Market Place. 1967–. 2 vols. Medford, NJ: Information Today. Annual. Available online: http://www.literarymarketplace.com.
Martin, Judith. 2005. *Miss Manners' Guide to Excruciatingly Correct Behavior (Freshly Updated).* New York: Norton.
McGraw-Hill Encyclopedia of Science and Technology. 2013. 11th ed. 22 vols. New York: McGraw-Hill. Available online as part of *AccessScience.*
McGraw-Hill Yearbook of Science and Technology. 1962–. New York: McGraw-Hill. Annual.
MLA Handbook for Writers of Research Papers. 2009. 7th ed. New York: Modern Language Association of America.
Nash, Gary B., ed. 2009. *Encyclopedia of American History.* 11 vols. New York: Facts on File.
NEA Almanac of Higher Education. 1984–. Washington, DC: NEA Communications Services. Annual.
The New Children's Encyclopedia. 2013. New York: DK Publishing.
NoodleTools. http://www.noodletools.com/.
The Old Farmer's Almanac. 1792–. Dublin, NH: Yankee Publishing. Annual. Available online: http://www.almanac.com.
Online Writing Lab. Purdue University. https://owl.english.purdue.edu/owl/.
Oxford Art Online. New York: Oxford University Press. http://www.oxfordartonline.com/public/. [subscription required]
Oxford Music Online. New York: Oxford University Press. http://www.oxfordmusiconline.com/public/. [subscription required]
Oxford Reference. New York: Oxford. http://www.oxfordreference.com/.
Peterson's. https://www.petersons.com/.
Peterson's Four-Year Colleges. 1970–. Lawrenceville, NJ: Peterson's. Annual.
Peterson's Graduate & Professional Programs. 1966–. 6 vols. Lawrenceville, NJ: Peterson's. Annual.
Physicians' Desk Reference. 1946–. Montvale, NJ: Thomson PDR. Annual. Available online: http://www.pdr.net/.
Post, Peggy. *Emily Post's Etiquette.* 2011. 18th ed. New York: William Morrow.
Pritzker, Barry M. 2000. *A Native American Encyclopedia: History, Culture, and People.* New York: Oxford.
Publication Manual of the American Psychological Association. 2009. 6th ed. Washington, DC: American Psychological Association.
RefWorks. https://www.refworks.com/.
Resh, Vincent H., and Ring T. Cardè. 2009. *Encyclopedia of Insects.* 2nd ed. Amsterdam: Elsevier. Available online as part of *Credo Reference.*
Robert's Rules of Order Newly Revised. 2011. 11th ed. Cambridge, MA: Da Capo Press.
Robert's Rules of Order Newly Revised in Brief. 2011. 2nd ed. Cambridge, MA: Da Capo Press.
Rubel, David. 2013. *Scholastic Encyclopedia of the Presidents and Their Times.* New York: Scholastic Reference.

Scholastic Go! http://teacher.scholastic.com/products/grolier/. [subscription required]

Spanish Resource Center. Chicago: Encyclopaedia Britannica. http://info.eb.com/products/spanish-reference-center/. [subscription required]

Sports Illustrated Sports Almanac. 1992–. New York: Sports Illustrated. Annual.

Stanford Encyclopedia of Philosophy. Stanford University. http://plato.stanford.edu.

Student Discovery Science Encyclopedia. 2011. 13 vols. Chicago: World Book.

Switchboard. http://www.switchboard.com/.

Taylor, Charles. 2012. *The Kingfisher Science Encyclopedia.* New York: Kingfisher Encyclopedias.

Texas Almanac. Texas State Historical Association. http://texasalmanac.com/.

This Day in History. History Channel. http://www.history.com/this-day-in-history.

Today in History. Library of Congress. http://memory.loc.gov/ammem/today/.

Toye, William, and Eugene Benson. 2006. *The Oxford Companion to Canadian Literature.* 2nd ed. New York: Oxford. Available online as part of *Oxford Reference.*

Turabian, Kate L. 2013. *A Manual for Writers of Research Papers, Theses, and Dissertations.* 8th ed. Chicago: University of Chicago Press.

Turner, Barry, ed. *The Statesman's Yearbook.* 1864–. Basingstroke, Hampshire: Palgrave Macmillan. Annual. Available online: http://www.statesmansyearbook.com/public/. [subscription required]

Universalis Junior Online. Chicago: Encyclopaedia Britannica. http://info.eb.com/products/universalis-junior-online/. [subscription required]

Universalis Online. Chicago: Encyclopaedia Britannica. http://info.eb.com/products/universalis-online/. [subscription required]

Whitaker's Almanack. 1868–. London: A&C Black. Annual.

Wikipedia. http://www.wikipedia.org.

Wildscreen Arkive. Wildscreen. http://www.arkive.org/.

The World Almanac and Book of Facts. 1868–1876, 1886–. Mahwah, NJ: World Almanac Books. Annual. Available online: http://www.infobasepublishing.com/. [subscription required]

The World Almanac for Kids. 1996–. Mahwah, NJ: World Almanac Books. Annual.

World Book Encyclopedia. 2016. 22 vols. Chicago: World Book.

World Book Online. Chicago: World Book. http://www.worldbook.com/. [subscription required]

The World Factbook. Central Intelligence Agency. https://www.cia.gov/library/publica tions/the-world-factbook/.

Worldmark Encyclopedia of Cultures and Daily Life. 2009. 2nd ed. 5 vols. Farmington Hills, MI: Gale Cengage Learning. Available online as part of *Gale Virtual Reference Library.*

Worldmark Encyclopedia of the Nations. 2007. 12th ed. 5 vols. Farmington Hills, MI: Gale Cengage Learning. Available online as part of *Gale Virtual Reference Library.*

Year Book. 1962–. Chicago: World Book. Annual.

Yearbook of the United Nations. 1946/1947–. New York: United Nations. Annual.

Yelp. http://www.yelp.com.

Zotero. Roy Rosenzweig Center for History and New Media. https://www.zotero.org/.

SUGGESTED READINGS

Jacobs, A.J. 2004. *The Know-It-All: One Man's Humble Quest to Become the Smartest Person in the World.* New York: Simon & Schuster.

Entertaining and informative, this book describes the author's attempt to read the entire *Encyclopaedia Britannica* and what he learned in the process.

Katz, Bill. 1998. *Cuneiform to Computer: A History of Reference Sources*. Lanham, MD: Scarecrow Press.

For those interested in the origins and evolution of almanacs, encyclopedias, and other reference sources, this book provides an in-depth introduction.

Rettig, James. 1992. *Distinguished Classics of Reference Publishing*. Phoenix: Oryx Press. https://archive.org/details/DistinguishedClassicsOfReferencePublishing.

This wonderful history of famous reference books includes many of the works discussed in this chapter, including *The Chicago Manual of Style*, *Encyclopaedia Britannica*, *The Encyclopedia of Associations*, *Emily Post's Etiquette*, *Guinness Book of Records*, *Robert's Rules of Order*, *The Statesman's Yearbook*, the *World Book Encyclopedia*, and *The World Almanac*.

Chapter 19

Dictionaries

Stephanie R. Davis-Kahl

USES AND CHARACTERISTICS

Purpose: Past and Present

Dictionaries have long been the tool by which people from all walks of life find definitions, pronunciations, usage, and etymology of words. According to the *Encyclopaedia Britannica*, "a dictionary lists a set of words with information about them" (Read 2005, 257). They are fascinating glimpses into how words and their meanings are shaped by aspects of our culture and society such as commerce, technology, entertainment, trends, politics, and globalization: "Dictionaries, [. . .] are often all too human products, able to reflect the social and cultural assumptions of the time in which they are written, and telling, as a result, their own stories of society, culture, innovation and ideals. Who writes a dictionary—and when and where—are factors which, in significant ways, will change and influence the kind of dictionary that is produced" (Mugglestone 2011, xii). In the last century, dictionaries have expanded their reach from using words to integrating images and visual information, audio, and multimedia, all excellent developments for a wide range of users, including children, teachers, librarians, and English-language learners. By far, the most exciting development in the dictionary's long history is the now-ubiquitous availability of dictionaries on the Web and as apps, extending the value, accessibility, and versatility of the dictionary as a format in and of itself. However, with progress comes tension, as the commercial viability of print dictionaries has come under scrutiny recently for even the most venerable and highly regarded dictionary, the *Oxford English Dictionary* (*OED*; Flanagan 2014). Funding for another well-respected and award-winning publication, the *Dictionary of American Regional English* (*DARE*), is uncertain at this writing (Flood 2015).

Although a short word list from the seventh century BCE was found in central Mesopotamia, the dictionary as we know it today in the 21st century has its roots in Greece and later in Italy, from the first century CE into the Middle Ages. In the early Middle Ages, manuscripts often included *glosses*, marginal or interlinear notes, to define or translate words. Oftentimes, glosses from different works were collected and printed as a stand-alone publication. Clerics, spelling reformers, and teachers heavily influenced the development and creation of dictionaries. These could be divided into two schools of thought: the first stressed standardizing the language (that is, dictionary as authority, a *prescriptive* approach), whereas the second emphasized recording language as it was used by the people (that is, dictionary as reflection of reality, a *descriptive* approach). An excellent example of the divergence between the two perspectives is illustrated by the reaction to one of the first dictionaries compiled in America, Caleb Alexander's *The Columbian Dictionary of the English Language*, published in 1800. According to the *Encyclopaedia Britannica*, "it received abuse from critics who were not yet ready for the inclusion of American words" (Read 2005, 280).

Although Britain's contribution to the evolution of the dictionary is exemplified best in the massive and incomparable *OED*, it is worth noting that dictionaries created up until the 18th century were authored by amateur lexicographers. John Kersey the Younger published *The New English Dictionary* in 1702, the first work to be compiled by a professional lexicographer. Another major name in the history of dictionaries is Samuel Johnson, a poet and critic, whose *Dictionary* included quotations showing the usage of the word as well as a definition. Johnson's *Dictionary* went through multiple editions and was even imported to America for schoolchildren.

Kinds of Information Found in Dictionaries

The goal of a dictionary usually dictates layout, breadth, and depth of coverage, and the information included in each entry. A standard general dictionary will contain pronunciation (including syllabication and emphasis), definitions, function, variant spellings, and an example of usage. Entries may also include more in-depth information, such as etymological history, dates of use, and—depending on the objective, scope, and size of the publication—an illustration or photograph. A specialized subject or discipline-focused dictionary will go into more detail in its definition, examples, and usage but may omit elements found in a general dictionary such as pronunciation. Dictionaries are generally organized alphabetically, but visual dictionaries, in which the focus is on associating terms with their corresponding objects, are often organized by subject. Dictionaries in electronic form can include enhancements such as links for cross-references, audio samples of correct pronunciation, or visual representations of synonyms.

Types of Dictionaries

General dictionaries are one of two types: abridged and unabridged. An *abridged* dictionary is usually based on a larger work, such as the two-volume *Shorter Oxford English Dictionary on Historical Principles*, which has fewer than 3,900 pages, whereas the full 20-volume *OED* has 22,000 pages. The goals of an abridged dictionary are convenience, conciseness, and selectivity. An *unabridged* dictionary strives to be comprehensive in its goal to record and reflect the usage and definition of words in use at the time of the dictionary's creation. Also, an unabridged dictionary provides more information about its contents than an abridged dictionary. While an abridged dictionary may include only a word's definition, part of speech, pronunciation, and usage, an unabridged dictionary may include variant spellings, word etymology and dates of use, lengthy notes about usage including examples, synonyms or word history, and color pictures. Specialized types of dictionaries focus in depth on particular aspects of words, such as etymology or synonyms (see Box 19.1). Examples of these specialized types are discussed later in this chapter.

Box 19.1 Specialized Dictionaries

Etymological dictionary. An etymological dictionary gives the history of individual words with linguistic derivation and examples from writings of the past.

Slang dictionary. A slang dictionary defines terms used in ordinary informal speech. These terms may include jargon, obscenities, or ephemeral words that go in and out of use quickly.

Thesaurus. A thesaurus contains synonyms and antonyms, usually without definitions. Its purpose is to provide writers with alternate or more specific words.

Dual-language dictionary. A dual-language dictionary has two sections, the first being a dictionary of terms in one language with definitions in a second language. The second section is the reverse, with terms in the second language and definitions in the first language.

Dialect dictionary. A dialect dictionary gives regional variants and usage for words within a language. It may include some slang.

Usage dictionary. A usage dictionary prescribes how a word should be used, based on the way it has been used in the past.

EVALUATION

When evaluating dictionaries, an assessment of their authority and accuracy is essential. Scope considerations include both the number and the content of entries, and also paramount is the clarity of definitions and examples. Because a growing number of titles are available in electronic form, a comparison of the features of print and electronic formats becomes important in relation to the user community's needs.

Authority

Authority can be difficult to ascertain in the case of large, unabridged, comprehensive dictionaries because they are usually the product of editorial staffs of publishers. As a consequence, investigating the authority of the publisher is usually a more productive endeavor. In the United States and Canada, several publishers are well known for the quality of their previously published work: Houghton Mifflin Harcourt, Merriam-Webster, NTC/Contemporary, Oxford University Press, Random House, Macmillan USA, and World Book. Internationally, Dorling Kindersley (DK) is noted for its visual dictionaries, and Cambridge University Press is noted for its overall reputation and quality of content. In addition, attention should be paid to university presses, which often publish dictionaries of regional interest, with a focus such as slang or regionalisms. In general, judging the authority of a dictionary can be informed by professional or user reviews; reviews in the library literature; posting queries to mailing lists or blogs; and browsing catalogs or bookstores. Publishers are seeking to make dictionaries "more accessible, more inviting, more popular with individual users" but without "sacrificing the imprimatur of authority" (Dahlin 1999, 34).

Accuracy and Currency

The three key factors in judging a dictionary's accuracy and currency are spelling, definition, and usage. Spelling should be up to date, keeping pace with how a word's spelling might have changed in common use. The inclusion of variant spellings is also important for loanwords that have been subsumed into a language from other languages or dialects, such as the word *airplane*, which is an alteration of the French word *aéroplane*. Typically, dictionaries also demonstrate where hyphens should go if necessary. This is a helpful feature especially with terms that sometimes appear as a single word, for example, e-mail, home page, and website. Definitions of words should be succinct and clear, without using the word itself. It is important to note here that some dictionaries organize definitions chronologically, whereas others order definitions by the most to the least commonly used. In addition, a comprehensive unabridged dictionary will include several, if not many, definitions, but a general desk dictionary will usually limit itself to commonly used definitions. The same holds true for usage, which is fundamental to understanding how the word is used in context, not only grammatically but also in modern connotations. For example, the word "cookie" has three definitions listed in *The American Heritage Dictionary of the English Language* (2011, 403):

1. A small, usually flat and crisp cake made from sweetened dough.
2. *Slang* A person, usually of a specified kind: *a lawyer who was a tough cookie.*
3. *Computer Science* A collection of information, usually including a username and the current date and time, stored on the local computer of a person using the World Wide Web, used chiefly by websites to identify users who have previously registered or visited the site.

Some dictionaries create their own usage examples, and others use phrases or sentences from literature, poetry, science, or news to demonstrate usage.

Format

The Web has brought along another wave of evolution in dictionaries. In contrast to dictionaries that were once static representations of language and word use, publishers and communities are now taking advantage of the fluid and mobile nature of technology and putting it to excellent use. An article published in *Booklist* in 2003 reported that pre-Internet, Merriam-Webster would receive about 1,000 letters every year from dictionary users with new definitions, corrections, and questions. At the time of the article, the company received 1,000 e-mails per month. In addition, "the company can observe which words are most frequently looked up online at any given time" (McQuade 2003, 1688).

A plethora of free and subscription-based dictionary websites are active on the Internet. Some are from standard publishers and include additional online content. An example is *Merriam-Webster Online*, which includes extras such as word games, word of the day, free downloads such as dictionary toolbars, and links to free and fee-based apps. In evaluating and selecting which online dictionaries to link from a library website, criteria to consider are similar to criteria used to evaluate print dictionaries with the additional factors of ease of navigation, ease of printing, and quick response time. Crowdsourced dictionaries such as *Urban Dictionary* and meta-dictionaries that bring together several different sources such as *Wordnik* are other examples of new uses and formats for dictionaries as a source not only of definitions, but also of correct and colloquial usage of words and phrases.

Major dictionary publishers have developed apps for mobile phones and tablets. App-based dictionaries create a new set of usability issues for developers and users. Readability on a small screen, ease of navigation, cost, links between words, integration of audio and graphics, and internal/external linking to related terms in addition to the criteria listed later are all factors for librarians to consider. An important consideration to some is choosing an off-line app vs. an online app. An off-line app requires the user to download the dictionary's database, which may cause storage space constraints, as opposed to searching an app's online database. Comprehensiveness of a dictionary's database may also be sacrificed in an off-line app. Functionality of a dictionary app, regardless of whether off-line or online, is analogous to print. Readability of text is vital, as is the ability to enlarge text or change the layout of a screen. Complexity of entries might be constrained on an app due to small screens, so users may not be able to access features such as images, usage examples, or word origins. However, one advantage of a dictionary app is the capacity to say a word to search it and to hear the pronunciation spoken. Some apps have translations or thesauri built in, while others provide only a basic definition.

In print, online, and mobile app dictionaries, aesthetics make a difference. Because dictionaries are traditionally text with some pictures (if any), layout is a key factor in assessing usability. Good use of white space, color choices, use of boldface or italics for emphasis, use of different fonts, and size of typeface all have an impact on the ease of locating a definition and readability. In some cases, how a page looks may seem frivolous; however, for users who are visually impaired or who just prefer not to squint over a screen or page of small words, user-friendly aesthetics will improve the user experience and comprehension of the text, page, or screen. Accessibility is also key for readers with visual disabilities. Effective layouts help screen readers "read" pages aloud, and the ability to enlarge or change the background color is also beneficial.

Scope

No matter the format, a dictionary's scope is often communicated in its introduction or an "about" section, usually written by the primary author or lead editor. In addition to explaining the purpose and content of the dictionary, the introduction often contains information such as abbreviations and acronyms, pronunciation guides, names of contributors, and how the dictionary came to be compiled and published. This information will help gauge whether the dictionary will supplement or replace other items in the current reference collection, and its content will help decide whether the dictionary is age appropriate (i.e., children, college students) and contains a useful amount of information. For instance, language derivation is less important for children than visual representations and a clear pronunciation guide. Last, some dictionaries may include charts, tables, and timelines that make up a sort of miniature ready-reference collection. Such information is definitely helpful but, for many libraries, not a requirement for selection, given that libraries will have other materials such as almanacs and encyclopedias that include such information.

Comparing Similar Dictionaries

In evaluating dictionaries that cover similar topics, regions, or time periods, an excellent rule of thumb is to choose a few words, look them up in each dictionary, and compare the elements of the dictionary entry discussed earlier in this chapter. The words selected should represent commonly used terms, slang, technical jargon, and rarely used words. Other considerations include the presence of a chart or legend explaining the abbreviations used to represent word derivation, part of speech, stress marks, and regionalisms.

SELECTION

With the many varieties of dictionaries available, assessing the value of a particular dictionary is vitally important. Ideally, this process should begin with an exploration of user needs. No matter the type of library, there are often several choices for purchasing dictionaries. Therefore, in the public library setting, the librarian must consider the needs of children, adolescents, adults, and senior citizens. Also important is the demographics of the community; as the ethnic makeup of the community changes, so do the reading and reference needs of library users. In a school library, dictionaries (as all reference works in general) should be useful for a range of ages, learning styles, reading levels, curricula, and topics. In addition, teachers' and administrators' needs should be addressed, so a more comprehensive dictionary or a dictionary specific to education may be a good purchase depending on other factors such as cost. In academic libraries, considerations include type of institution. For example, a research university's students, faculty, and staff will differ from those of a school of art and design. In any academic library, the balance between curriculum and research needs is key to creating a responsive reference collection. There is no one-size-fits-all solution to selecting dictionaries, especially when considering more specialized, subject-focused dictionaries. Fortunately, publishers provide a wide range of options for dictionaries, so libraries have many choices.

Sources for Reviews

Selecting dictionaries for purchase takes time to compare and contrast individual titles and to decide whether an online resource will best fit the needs at hand. Luckily, there are several sources that aid librarians by providing objective opinions. Academic librarians with access to *Resources for College Libraries* (*RCL*) and *Choice* will find those sources helpful for their well-written, succinct, and authoritative reviews. *RCL*, a collection of "core bibliographies, together covering approximately 85,000 titles," focuses on selecting books and electronic resources deemed "essential for all academic libraries" with an emphasis on supporting undergraduate studies across a wide variety of disciplines (American Library Association 2015). Reviews are written by academic librarians and faculty, and are peer reviewed to ensure that the sources selected fit the *RCL* criteria. *RCL* is published thanks to a partnership between the Association of College and Research Libraries (ACRL), *Choice*, Bowker, and ProQuest.

Choice, also published by ACRL, is a well-regarded source of reviews of newly published monographs, electronic resources, and websites. According to the *Choice* website, its "primary mission is to assist librarians who build collections at the undergraduate level by providing concise, critical reviews of current scholarly books and electronic resources" (Association of College and Research Libraries 2009). Reviews are written by academic librarians and faculty, and are published online, in print, and as "*Choice* Reviews on Cards" suitable for distribution to faculty and colleagues to aid in collective collection development. Academic librarians may also wish to consult discipline-specific journals for reviews of reference works specific to specialized fields of study.

Public and school librarians have several sources for reviews. *Booklist* is a magazine providing reviews of publications and products in print and electronic media. *Booklist* also sponsors webinars and blogs, and also includes classroom activities, author interviews, and more features that aid librarians in both readers' advisory and collection building. *Library Journal* is another source for reviews of many different types of sources, both print and electronic. In addition, general sources such as *Amazon* can be helpful in understanding what consumers look for in a dictionary.

Electronic Options

Electronic options for dictionaries include both freely available and subscription-based titles and mobile apps. Features of some specific titles are discussed in the following section. Electronic dictionaries may be single titles or aggregations of titles that can be searched simultaneously. The best-known title available by subscription is the *OED Online*, the electronic version of the *OED*. An example of a single freely available title is Joan M. Reitz's *ODLIS: Online Dictionary for Library and Information Science*, based on the print *Dictionary for Library and Information Science*. The online version supports browsing by initial letter in a word or phrase and searching either headwords or headwords and definitions. Like many subject-specific titles, entries include only definitions. Extensive hyperlinks connect terms within a definition to entries elsewhere in the dictionary. In addition, several entries include links to other websites for additional explanations of terms.

Increasingly, multiple dictionaries are available as part of collections in electronic form. *Credo Reference* aggregates access to more than 600 titles from more than 70 publishers in its Academic Core collection and in its Public and School Core collections. Among the titles aggregated are English-language dictionaries, bilingual dictionaries, and subject dictionaries in areas such as art, business, medicine, and law. Several sources of quotations are also included. Oxford University Press is making increasing numbers of titles from its rich collection of reference material available in electronic form. Its collection of English-language and bilingual dictionaries in the *Oxford Reference* collection online includes more than 295,000 "concise definitions and in-depth, specialist encyclopedic entries on the subjects of slang, semiotics, rhetoric, abbreviations, etymology, phrase & fable, and usage" (Oxford University Press 2015).

Tools are also available to facilitate simultaneous searching of freely available dictionaries on the Web. In addition to *Wordnik* (described earlier), *OneLook Dictionary Search* indexes words in more than 1,000 online dictionaries and provides a range of search options in addition to exact match, such as **bird* to find words and phrases that end with *bird*. When a word is searched, the resulting list of matches identifies the titles of sources that provide a definition, allowing the user to select the one(s) likely to be most authoritative.

Selection tools for finding mobile dictionary apps are as easy as visiting a device's online app store. User reviews can be helpful as an initial filter for quality, ease of searching, ease of navigation, and comprehensiveness. There are also occasional reviews of dictionary apps from technology and education blogs, which give a more nuanced and in-depth view of selected apps. In general, dictionary apps are free or low cost, so testing different apps on different devices is not cost prohibitive. One notable exception is *The American Heritage Dictionary* app, which costs $24.99. For hardcore dictionary users, the cost is most likely worth it given the stellar reputation of the text and the number of words included in the fifth edition (more than 300,000). Updates to the dictionary are included in the initial price.

IMPORTANT GENERAL SOURCES

This section focuses on several kinds of dictionaries and related tools that are found in typical school, public, or academic library reference collections. Under each category, a few representative titles are described. For information on titles not discussed here, the reader can consult the sources for reviews listed earlier and relevant articles in the "Suggested Readings" section.

Unabridged Dictionaries

Though unabridged dictionaries are expensive to develop and maintain, the quality ones continue to keep high standards in comprehensiveness, description, and usage. First, a note on the prodigious use of the name "Webster" in the dictionary world is required. Though Merriam-Webster purchased the copyright from Noah Webster in 1843, the name "Webster" is still used by multiple publishers. The name "Webster" has become a sort of colloquialism for the word "dictionary," and this is reflected in the publishing world.

Noah Webster's first unabridged dictionary, *An American Dictionary of the English Language*, appeared in 1828, and the first Webster's dictionary published by Merriam was released in 1847. The latest in the modern series of the Webster's unabridged dictionary, *Webster's Third* (first published in 1961), is infamous for the decision of its editors to be descriptive in its style and content, rather than prescriptive. Traditionalists were unsupportive of the inclusion of colloquial and slang words, but others welcomed the change as a true reflection of how new words and phrases contribute to the English language. (For more on the controversy, see the Suggested Readings.)

Its most current edition, titled *Webster's Third New International Dictionary of the English Language, Unabridged*, was published in 2002. The print edition includes a CD-ROM and a complimentary one-year subscription to *Merriam-Webster*

Unabridged online. Each edition contains nearly a half-million entries with pronunciation, part of speech, definition, example of usage, etymology, labels (obsolete, slang, dialect, regional), cross-references, and more. In the matter of pronunciation, description over prescription also holds true; entries reflect "general cultivated conversational usage, both formal and informal, throughout the English-speaking world" (Merriam-Webster 2002, 4a). The 2002 edition of *Webster's* also included a new label especially for scientific and technical terms: international scientific vocabulary (ISV). ISV labels denote current, in-use words with uncertain language of origin, such as "endoscope" and "cholesterolemia" (Merriam-Webster 2002, 16a). The dictionary is also available as an app, either for free or for a fee.

Another authoritative publisher of unabridged dictionaries is Random House. A revised single-volume edition of the *Random House Webster's Unabridged Dictionary* was published in 2005 with an updated word list, definitions, and etymologies. In addition, the dictionary includes illustrations, maps, and supplements in the form of lists, tables, timelines, style guides, and more. A CD-ROM version is also available. Like other dictionary publishers, Random House also boasts an ever-growing database of new words, new uses for words, and updated definitions.

Etymological Dictionaries

The *OED* is by far the most comprehensive etymological dictionary available. The story of the *OED* is a fascinating history of an incredible human achievement that began in 1857 and continues to the present day (see "Suggested Readings" at the end of this chapter). The publication has had countless contributors throughout its development and reflects the technology of its time; it was made available in microfilm in 1971, on CD-ROM in 1992, and on the Web in 2000. The most recent edition in print was published in 1989, combining the text of the first edition, published between 1884 and 1928, with four supplements published between 1972 and 1986. Three volumes of supplements, the *Oxford English Dictionary: Additions Series*, were subsequently published in 1993 and 1997. The master copy of the *OED* was digitized in the late 1990s (previous editions had been typeset in hot metal), paving the way for both the CD-ROM and online editions. The second edition contains nearly 300,000 main entries, a 15 percent increase over the first edition, but more importantly, the second edition also contains 34 percent more text, with expanded citations, usage examples, and notes. The *Additions Series* not only contained new words such as "acid house," but also added new meanings to older words; for example, to the entry for the word "read," editors added the following definition: "To interpret or translate (genetic information); *spec.* to extract genetic information from (a particular sequence of nucleic acids), or to extract from a given sequence the genetic information necessary to synthesize (a particular substance)" (Simpson and Weiner 1993, 1: 220). The *OED Online* is now the home for the second edition and the *Additions Series*, and on its website, the Help section lists the new words added to the database on a quarterly basis. The quarterly updates to the *OED Online*, which began in 2000, are considered to be its third edition. The *OED Online* can be considered as a database with extensive searching options, from simple word and proximity searching to Boolean searching across one or more fields (e.g., headword, definition, and etymology) in the dictionary entries. The quotations illustrating word usage are also searchable.

Though the full 20-volume second edition is usually out of the price range of most public and school libraries, Oxford University Press has several smaller options for these libraries. The *Shorter Oxford English Dictionary on Historical Principles* is a two-volume set that is currently in its sixth edition, published in 2007. The purpose of the *Shorter OED* is to provide a "historical dictionary of modern English" (Trumble and Stevenson 2002, vii). It is also available as a fee-based app. The *Oxford Dictionary of Word Histories* was published in 2002 and provides narrative descriptions of words, tracing their development through other languages and time periods to present-day English, including regionalisms and older spellings. The *Shorter OED* and the *Oxford Dictionary of Word Histories* are excellent options for those libraries that choose not to purchase the full *OED*.

Another choice is Eric Partridge's *Origins: An Etymological Dictionary of Modern English*. Though not as comprehensive as the *OED*, it is equally informative and useful as a single-volume etymological dictionary. The most attractive aspect of *Origins* is its focus on current and modern language, with more than 20,000 words, as well as lists of prefixes and suffixes. Another title related to etymology is Julia Cresswell's *The Insect That Stole Butter?: Oxford Dictionary of Word Origins*, published by Oxford University Press.

Desk Dictionaries

Desk dictionaries are usually single volume and more concise than an unabridged dictionary. Content is more focused on current usage and more up to date, with rare, technical, and obsolete words and definitions omitted. Etymologies are usually abbreviated or do not appear in a desk dictionary, and appendices usually contain supplemental lists of things such as weights and measures, abbreviations, names, and dates. The biggest difference between the desk dictionaries discussed in this section is layout; any of the works listed would be excellent choices for home, school, or office.

The American Heritage Dictionary of the English Language is published by Houghton Mifflin Harcourt and is well known for its readable and aesthetically pleasing layout. Words are in boldface, printed with a dark blue ink, and appear in syllabicated form, distinguishing them from accompanying pronunciation, part of speech, definitions, brief etymological note (when included), usage example, and variant forms (also when included). Illustrations are in both black and white and color, and nearly every page has a mini-guide to pronunciation. The updated fifth edition, published in 2011, includes more than 10,000 new words, including "ginormous" and "cloud" in the technology sense, and more than 4,000 new images. "The Usage Panel," a group of more than 200 researchers, scholars, writers, journalists, and others "in occupations requiring mastery of language," supports the development of the dictionary (Houghton Mifflin Harcourt 2015). The dictionary is also available for a fee as an app for both iOS and Android devices.

The *Merriam-Webster's Collegiate Dictionary* is part of the Merriam-Webster family of publications. The strength of the *Collegiate Dictionary* lies in its content, taken from the Merriam-Webster word database. The 11th edition, published in 2014, contains about 10,000 new words, more examples of usage, idioms, and updated definitions. Illustrations are black-and-white drawings, and entries include the usual pronunciation, brief etymology, and usage examples. Considering that the 10th edition of the *Collegiate Dictionary* was published in 1993, the new additions and changes to the 11th edition are significant. The 11th edition comes with the dictionary on CD-ROM and a free year's subscription for consumers (not libraries or schools) to the *Collegiate Dictionary* online, which includes the *Collegiate*

Thesaurus, *Collegiate Encyclopedia*, and *Merriam-Webster's Spanish-English Dictionary*. With Merriam-Webster's stellar reputation, libraries may want to investigate a subscription to the Merriam-Webster online products in addition to or instead of purchasing print, depending on factors such as user needs and budgets. An extensive subset of the *Collegiate Dictionary* is freely available at *Merriam-Webster Online*. The app version includes Voice Search, an integrated thesaurus, and user-generated Favorites.

Funk & Wagnalls New International Dictionary of the English Language was published in early 2005 and is a two-volume set, setting it apart from other desk dictionaries. In the introduction, editors share their three major objectives: "To present the fundamental facts and characteristics of the language accurately, fully and interestingly. . . . To present adequately the significant contributions to English made in the United States, [and] To secure the widest possible coverage of both established word stock of English and of the rapidly expanding vocabularies of the arts, sciences, trades, and professions" (*Funk & Wagnalls*, 2005, iv). To this end, definitions are succinct and easy to understand; entries include pronunciation, usage, brief etymology notes, and variant spellings when necessary. A mini-guide to pronunciation appears on each odd-numbered page of the book, and black-and-white line drawings serve as illustrations. Although the readability and layout are not as contemporary as *Merriam-Webster's Collegiate*, *Funk & Wagnalls* organizes its definitions with the most currently used appearing first, followed by other less-used definitions. This not only allows editors the flexibility to shape the dictionary's content to the language but also allows the user to learn the word in chronological context.

Two well-regarded titles from Oxford University Press, the *New Oxford American Dictionary* and the *Canadian Oxford Dictionary*, emphasize coverage of current American and Canadian English, respectively. The *New Oxford American Dictionary* has entries organized around core meanings, supplemented by illustrative, in-context usage examples. The *Canadian Oxford Dictionary* entries provide the meaning most familiar to Canadians first. Among the words defined are 2,200 unique Canadian words. Coverage also includes 5,500 biographical entries and 5,600 place names.

School Dictionaries

Dictionaries for children and young adults are published by nearly every reputable dictionary publisher, including Oxford University Press, Houghton Mifflin Harcourt, Macmillan, Merriam-Webster, and World Book, leaving readers to decide between a visual and a textual focus. Visual dictionaries can be exciting ways to introduce new words to children, with bright colors, images, and simple definitions. Textual dictionaries may be more appropriate for older children, depending on reading ability and grade level. In each case, important criteria for selection include clear layout, easy-to-understand definitions, and enough words to interest and educate a child using the dictionary. Large print and the highlighting of main words are both helpful at this level, as are simple examples of usage. Dictionaries are available for specific age groups, organized alphabetically and by subject, both with their advantages and drawbacks. For settings serving children and young adults, having a few of both types of dictionaries is a wise choice. Because use of the word "children's" or "student" in the title does not always correspond to a specific age range or grade level, evaluation of such a dictionary should include determining the target audience. For example, Merriam-Webster has a series of four titles: *Merriam-Webster's Primary Dictionary* and *Merriam-Webster's First Dictionary* (grades K–2; last published in 2005 and 2012, respectively), *Merriam-Webster's Elementary Dictionary* (grades 3–5; last published in 2014), *Merriam-Webster's Intermediate Dictionary* (grades 6–8; last published in 2011), and *Merriam-Webster's School Dictionary* (grades 9–11; last published in 2015).

DK Merriam-Webster Children's Dictionary combines the design strengths of DK with the lexicographic strengths and the reputation of Merriam-Webster. The collaboration between the two publishers results in an easy-to-read and informative reference work, with design and images from DK and text based on *Merriam-Webster's Elementary Dictionary*. For older readers, *The American Heritage Student Dictionary* is focused on providing more detailed information such as etymology and usage notes. The *World Book Dictionary* is a two-volume set with more than 225,000 entries and 3,000 illustrations. Words likely to be used by students are clearly defined, and usage examples are included.

Dual-Language Dictionaries

In the case of dual-language dictionaries, the options available include everything from mini-abridged dictionaries for travelers to comprehensive dictionaries for scholars and academics to dictionary apps and translation apps. Specialized dictionaries for those traveling on business, dictionaries for students studying abroad, and dictionaries devoted to single subjects such as food are also abundant. In the case of foreign languages, the authority of the publisher is key. Cassell's, HarperCollins, Cambridge University Press, and Larousse have excellent reputations in the world of dual-language dictionaries, and Oxford University Press also publishes dual-language dictionaries suitable for a range of readers. In addition to print titles available from Oxford, *Oxford Language Dictionaries Online* includes bilingual dictionaries in French, German, Spanish, Italian, Russian, and Chinese with up-to-date translations of words and phrases, illustrative examples, and native speaker audio pronunciation of words.

Visual dictionaries are a well-established format for dual-language dictionaries and useful to both language learners and travelers. As previously noted, DK is a well-known publisher in this area. DK's *5 Language Visual Dictionary* includes English, French, German, Spanish, and Italian. The book is organized by broad categories, including people, appearance, health, home, services, shopping, food, and leisure. Each image is accompanied by the word printed in a different font according to its language. Images are all in color and are pleasing to the eye. The book also includes helpful short phrases, such as "Do you have any vegetarian dishes?" and "Where can I park?" An index of all the words in the dictionary, arranged alphabetically by language, is also included. This type of book would be an excellent addition to any type of library with either foreign-language or English-language learners. The *Merriam-Webster's Compact 5-Language Visual Dictionary* is equally robust, with more than 1,100 pages with illustrations and words (with masculine, feminine, and neutral versions notes) organized clearly into broad categories such as "House and Do-It-Yourself," "Transportation," and "Animal Kingdom."

A large number of dual-language dictionaries in many languages can be accessed on the Web, including online counterparts by the major publishers listed earlier (see List of Sources for specific sites). A number of free websites can serve as aids to translating from one language into another as well, such as *Word Reference.com*, *Reverso.com*, and *Translate.Reference.com*. Translation apps are now commonplace, including *Google Translate*, *iTranslate*, *and iTranslate Voice*, which allows voice-to-voice translation. One unique element of *Google Translate* is Words Lens, which allows the user to take pictures of words for a translation using the built-in camera.

Dialect and Regionalisms Dictionaries

One of the most fascinating types of dictionaries is that which chronicles the evolution and use of language from a specific geographical area. Three such works are the *DARE*, the *Dictionary of the American West*, and the *Dictionary of Smoky Mountain English*. The first is legendary in its scope: 10 years, 1,000 communities, nearly 3,000 informants, and 80 field-workers, ultimately totaling more than 2 million responses to the survey created by the American Dialect Society (ADS). The ADS had planned *DARE* since the beginning of the society in the late 1800s and held on to this goal through the Depression and two World Wars, finally appointing an editor in the 1960s. Thanks to federal funding, the editors and staff developed a survey (included in an appendix) to record the use of English throughout the country. Responses from informants, a listing of whom is included, complemented other primary and secondary sources of usage, such as oral histories, diaries, letters, regional fiction, and newspapers. *DARE* contains entries for single words, phrases, and compounds, with each entry including parts of speech, etymology, geographical and usage labels, definitions, and cross-references for variant spellings. At now six volumes (the sixth was published in 2013), it lives up to its goal of "testify[ing] to the wondrous variety and creativeness of human language, and specifically of the English language as it is used regionally in the United States" (Cassidy, Hall, and Von Schneidemesser 2013, xxii). *DARE* continues its work with plans to begin a new round of fieldwork and to continue developing the Digital *DARE*, the subscription-based online edition. *DARE* received the Dartmouth Medal from the American Library Association (ALA) in 2013, and Joan Houston Hall, editor of *DARE*, received the 2013 Emory Medal from Emory University. The Emory Medal is the university's highest honor and is awarded for "achievement of the highest distinction in a field of learning, the arts, the professions, or public and community service" (Emory University 2013).

Michael Montgomery and Joseph Hall's *Dictionary of Smoky Mountain English*, published in 2004, achieves a similar level of comprehensiveness for the "traditional and contemporary folk language of Appalachia" (Montgomery and Hall 2004, vii). Based on the lifework of Joseph Hall, a trained phonetician who studied Appalachian English over his entire career, the book chronicles and identifies two centuries' worth of words, phrases, and definitions from three generations of members of the Appalachian community. In fact, Hall's work was consulted by the editors of *DARE*. Like *DARE*, other primary and secondary sources, such as documents, recordings, and transcripts from archives, historical societies, and libraries were also used to create the word and definition list. Entries include definitions, usage examples and their supporting citations, variant spellings, labels, and cross-references. The book also includes fascinating historical material, such as informative chapters about the grammar and syntax of the Great Smoky Mountain areas.

Win Blevins's *Dictionary of the American West* began as a pamphlet for book editors unfamiliar with the vernacular of the American West. As the author researched and wrote, his goal expanded to "restore some of the full richness of the history of the West" (Blevins 2001, vii). The book is fascinating given that the American West was home to a wide diversity of people: Native Americans, Mormons, Hispanics, French-Canadians, Mexicans, slaves, and immigrants from Europe, to name a few. The book's entries include definitions, some black-and-white illustrations and photos, a history of how the word came to be used, and occasionally, examples of use. The book's introduction is a captivating overview of the history of the area, and it also lists books on the topic of the American West.

For readers more interested in modern English, two sources from Houghton Mifflin cater to the contemporary English-language learner. *The American Heritage Dictionary for Learners of English* is for students of all ages, and *The American Heritage Thesaurus for Learners of English* is directed at high school–level readers and above. Both focus on building vocabulary, and the textual layout supports this goal. The text is easy to read, and examples are easy to understand while imparting a word's meaning at the same time. The *Thesaurus* includes an appendix of irregular verbs and idiomatic uses of prepositions, and the *Dictionary* includes several appendices useful for quick reference, such as lists of state capitals, units of measure, and the periodic table of elements. Both would be suitable for public, school, and university libraries serving multi-language communities. *The Oxford Advanced American Dictionary for Learners of English*, published in 2011, contains not only definitions, but also words in context and an Academic Word List for students. This book is also available as a Kindle title.

Slang and Euphemism Dictionaries

The most entertaining types of dictionaries are those that keep a record of the various words in our language that do not appear, as a rule, in general dictionaries. The word "slang" has several synonyms, including *vernacular, colloquialism, mumbo jumbo, vulgarity, lingo,* and *jargon.* In general, slang is either language used by a specific group, such as teenagers, or language that is informal and conversational, used for added effect. Euphemisms are closely related to slang at first glance, given that both are colloquialisms, but the difference is that euphemisms seek to restate or deflect a harsh, perhaps too-realistic, term or phrase. For example, the term "person of interest," when used by police, usually equates with the word "suspect" or "witness." Both slang and euphemisms can be geographical and occupation based as well.

Words, at least the ones used in conversation, are a fascination for people. Publications recording the rise and fall of slang and euphemisms exist for libraries as well as for consumers' personal libraries. Aaron Peckham, the creator of *Urban Dictionary*, released a print edition of the online dictionary in addition to calendars and flash cards, titled *Urban Dictionary: Freshest Street Slang Defined.* Two titles offer a look into how colorful language evolved over time: Rob Chirico's *Damn!: A Cultural History of Swearing in Modern America* traces our use of expletives through the latter part of the 20th century, using pop culture, politics, and the media as primary sources. Rosemarie Ostler's *Dewdroppers, Waldos, and Slackers: A Decade-by-Decade Guide to the Vanishing Vocabulary of the Twentieth Century* is broader in scope and provides more of a historical look at slang generally. *Dictionary.com* has a site dedicated to slang, and the site *Internet Slang Dictionary & Translator* searches both words and acronyms used frequently in texting. Several apps for both Android and iOS assist with defining slang terms and acronyms, such as *Chat Slang* (which includes a list of text slang for parents), and specialized slang for specific occupations, foreign languages, or topics.

More traditional reference sources for current colloquialisms are available as well. Jonathon Green published his comprehensive and celebrated *Green's Dictionary of Slang* in 2010, with more than 100,000 definitions and more than 400,000 citations. The three-volume set was named an Outstanding Reference Source by ALA's Reference and User Services Association, was a 2011 *Booklist* Editor's Choice, and was named as a Best Reference Book by *Library Journal* in 2011. Another standard source for American slang, currently in development, is the *Random House Historical Dictionary of American Slang*, to be completed in four volumes. For librarians who seek to show the development of the English language in America from colonial times to the present day, this would be an excellent source. *The Routledge Dictionary of Modern American Slang and Unconventional English* provides an authoritative source for contemporary American slang with 25,000 entries accompanied by citations and examples of usage. The second edition of *The New Partridge Dictionary of Slang and Unconventional English*, a two-volume set, contains more than 60,000 entries and is unique in its international focus, bringing in entries from several English-speaking countries around the world. Entries include not only definitions, but dates and citations to common usage as well. *New Partridge* begins in 1945, but readers who want a historical perspective on slang can consult the old *Partridge*, which remains the best record of British slang antedating 1945.

A source that provides a different geographical perspective is R.W. Holder's *How Not to Say What You Mean: A Dictionary of Euphemisms*. Published by Oxford University Press, the fourth edition of this resource covers American and British euphemisms, both contemporary and traditional. The most interesting aspect of this dictionary is the number of words shared by both countries. Each entry contains the main word, definitions, usage examples or citations, and notes, such as "obsolete" or "American." Ewart James's *NTC's Dictionary of British Slang and Colloquial Expressions* also covers modern English in Britain, including terms from America. Terms in *NTC's Dictionary* were culled not only from individuals but also from television, movies, and radio. Verification of terms came from reference sources (including the *OED*), newspaper stories, and old movies. Besides the standard entry information (word, definition, usage, and citation), entries also include notes to further contextualize the word, such as "cant," to denote crime jargon, and "taboo," to denote unacceptable speech. C.J. Moore's *How to Speak Brit: The Quintessential Guide to the King's English, Cockney Slang, and Other Flummoxing British Phrases*, and *British English from A to Zed: A Definitive Guide to the Queen's English*, edited by Norman W. Schur, Eugene Ehrlich, and Richard Ehrlich, while less scholarly, are more portable guides to the usage of British colloquialisms.

McGraw-Hill's Conversational American English: The Illustrated Guide to the Everyday Expressions of American English edited by Richard Spears stands out from the rest with its focus on English-language learners. The book contains more than 3,000 expressions organized by broad theme, such as "Making Friends," "Polite Encounters," and "Small Talk." The goal of the dictionary is to help new English speakers not only understand the idiomatic phrases being used in conversation, but also use English correctly in conversation. Spears has also compiled *McGraw-Hill's Dictionary of American Slang and Colloquial Expressions*, which provides definitions of more than 12,000 slang and informal expressions. For librarians looking for an abridged slang dictionary, either *The American Heritage Dictionary of Idioms*, which contains 10,000 expressions, or the *Dictionary of Contemporary Slang*, by Tony Thorne, which contains more than 7,000 words in its updated fourth edition published in 2014, would be worthwhile investments.

Thesauri and Usage Guides

A thesaurus is an invaluable tool to anyone who writes for work or pleasure and for English-language learners. Essentially a dictionary of synonyms and antonyms, a thesaurus helps novice and expert writers alike add variety and clarity to their work.

First published in England in 1852 by physician Peter Mark Roget, *Roget's International Thesaurus* is the standard thesaurus of choice. Currently in its seventh edition, *Roget's* is organized not alphabetically but instead by category. Fifteen classes of words contain more than 1,000 categories, and 325,000 synonyms, antonyms, and phrases serve to guide readers, writers, and speakers to the best word or phrase for their purpose. Classes are broad, including "Place," "Natural Phenomena," "Measure and Shape," "Behavior," and "Language." Categories are more detailed; for example, under the class "Mind and Ideas," categories include "Comparison," "Discrimination," "Judgment," and "Theory and Philosophy". Cross-references and quotations help to add meaning and context to each category and each entry, and an alphabetical index helps users to locate specific words when necessary. Lists of words without synonyms appear in sidebars throughout the book with their related class; for instance, names of muscles and bones appear in the "Body" class. The layout of the book is clear and helpful to the reader, with main words in bold and numbered for easy location. Editor Barbara Ann Kipfer holds an MPhil and PhD in linguistics from the University of Exeter and is a lexicographer for several Roget's publications, including the *Roget's 21st Century Thesaurus* and *The Concise Roget's International Thesaurus*, both desk versions of the original.

In addition to *Roget's*, Oxford University Press has entered the thesaurus market with its usual quality and authority. The *Oxford American Writer's Thesaurus* is suitable for middle school and high school students, as is the *American Heritage Student Thesaurus*. For college students, the *Merriam-Webster's Collegiate Thesaurus* or *Roget's* is suitable, and online, both *Merriam-Webster Online* and *Dictionary.com* include a thesaurus search option in addition to the dictionary. For new speakers of English, the *Oxford Learner's Thesaurus* is an excellent complement to any of the dictionaries referenced in this chapter.

Academic libraries invest heavily in general thesauri but should also be aware of discipline-specific works that will aid students and scholars in their research. The *Thesaurus of Psychological Index Terms*, published by the American Psychological Association (APA), was last published in print in 2007, but the APA posts updates of new terms to its website. Likewise, the eighth edition of the *Thesaurus of Aging Terminology*, published by the AARP in 2005, is also available online. *The Art and Architecture Thesaurus*, published by the Getty Research Institute of the J. Paul Getty Trust, is now searchable online.

Usage guides are another important resource for writers. These go one step further than a general desk dictionary by providing quotations and citations illustrating grammar and word use. Two examples published in the last decade are given here. The third edition of *Garner's Modern American Usage*, published by Oxford University Press in 2009, not only includes nouns, verbs, adjectives, idioms, and exclamations, but also explains distinct jargon such as "commercialese" and "computerese" and figures of speech such as the "zeugma." In addition to examples of word and phrase use, *Garner's* includes a lengthy bibliographic timeline of usage guides and a bibliography of sources used to gather examples. The third edition of *Common Errors in English Usage*, based on the popular website of the same name, is a good choice for new or native English learners for its readable and authoritative approach to improving speaking and writing.

Abbreviation and Acronym Dictionaries

Dictionaries of abbreviations and acronyms are key sources for any type of library, especially those that serve writers, researchers, journalists, or students. The sheer number of abbreviations and acronyms in the United States alone is mind-boggling, so a quality dictionary is an essential reference tool. The two largest and perhaps most comprehensive publications are Gale's *Acronyms, Initialisms & Abbreviations Dictionary* and its counterpart, *Reverse Acronyms, Initialisms & Abbreviations Dictionary*. Each is a multivolume set covering abbreviations and acronyms from specific subjects and disciplines, associations, organizations, companies, and periodical titles. The latter is organized alphabetically by abbreviation, and the former is organized alphabetically by organization name. Published annually, the two sets easily stand alone as core sources. There are also numerous publications for special subjects, such as medicine, politics, business, and law. Because abbreviations dictionaries are usually compiled and published by publishing houses within specific disciplines or industries, the information is usually authoritative and credible. There are several online acronym dictionaries, including *AcronymFinder.com* and *Dictionary.com*'s abbreviations finder, which is based on *The American Heritage Abbreviations Dictionary*.

Quotation Dictionaries

Another core source for any reference collection is a dictionary of quotations. Questions from users often focus on the source of a particular quotation or on how a quotation appeared originally; reasons for researching quotations can vary from a planned toast at a wedding to a speech for a class or event or even to the settling of a bet. The challenge with answering a quotation question is the frequent misinformation provided by the user. However, if a quotation book has a decent index, quotations can be easy to locate and verify. In addition to the two sources noted in this section, librarians may also like to supplement their collections with more focused quotation books, such as dictionaries of song lyrics, movie quotations, political speeches, or Shakespeare, or of quotations specific to weddings, graduations, birthdays, retirements, and other special occasions.

The core quotations source is *Bartlett's Familiar Quotations*, now in its 18th edition, published since 1855. With 25,000 quotations from more than 2,000 authors, *Bartlett's* covers a wide variety of subjects, time periods, and people, from the Bible and Shakespeare to contemporary figures such as Maya Angelou and Steve Jobs. It is arranged chronologically and includes an author index and a keyword index to provide and enhance access. Its moderate price puts it within the reach of many libraries' budgets, and for the content and history contained in *Bartlett's*, it should be part of every library's collection.

Other publishers have emulated *Bartlett's* and developed their own quotation books. Oxford University Press has an impressive array of choices, from the general and comprehensive to the specialized. The *Oxford Dictionary of Quotations*, now in its eighth edition, is another core source for libraries of any type. Like *Bartlett's*, sources of quotations come from traditional works and from elements of modern culture. An excellent keyword index helps the reader locate authors and verify quotations, and informative sidebars contribute to the comprehensive nature of the work. Citations provide context for quotations, and cross-references help readers find quotations on related topics. Oxford also publishes many other quotation dictionaries focusing on literature, science, politics, law, business, humor, and other specific topics, industries, or occupations.

SEARCH STRATEGIES

Questions about definitions of words or phrases can be among the most important interactions between librarian and user. Sometimes just giving an example of how to correctly use a word or illustrating a word's definition with a sentence can help a reader understand a topic in a whole new way. Librarians need to be cognizant of both the tools and the many ways users can approach them. The key to understanding how to use a specific dictionary is to make a list of words and look them up in different dictionaries to compare and contrast the clarity, completeness, and credibility of the sources and to experience firsthand how the same words are treated in different dictionaries. The introduction and any "how to use this book" section are valuable tools to review so that the information in the book can be used to its fullest extent. For some of the more subject-specific dictionaries and word books, this is crucial to understanding the organization and access methods of the information within the book.

Just as one must work to become familiar with the scope and organization of print titles, the features and search capabilities of electronic sources, both freely available and subscription based, need to be explored so that an informed choice can be made as to when turning to the Web is likely to be more efficient and effective than consulting print sources. Depending on the source, electronic format dictionaries may allow users to differentiate between exact and "near" spellings and to search other elements of an entry (definition, quotations, word usage, word history) in addition to the entry word. The capability to simultaneously search multiple sources increases the chances of locating the information sought. Enhancements such as audio pronunciation go beyond the capabilities of print resources, as do visual representations of words and their synonyms and antonyms.

Readers of all ages, from children to adults to senior citizens, have a need for dictionaries, which can explain the wide variety of print and online dictionaries available today. Reference librarians have the enviable task of getting to know the character and strengths of the dictionaries, quotation books, and thesauri in their collections for the benefit of the users in their community. As the example in Box 19.2 illustrates, it is important to develop an appreciation for the range of answers that different sources can provide for even a seemingly simple definitional question. Understanding why the information is sought and how it will be used can be helpful in developing a search strategy to guide the user to the sources most likely to be helpful in responding to a particular word-related question.

Box 19.2 Search Strategy: Defining "Suffragette"

In seeking a definition, it would be natural to begin with a desk dictionary such as *Merriam-Webster's Collegiate Dictionary*, where one finds the following definition for suffragette:

> "*n* (1906): a woman who advocates suffrage for women." (2006, 1248)

This is not particularly informative. *The American Heritage Dictionary of the English Language* adds a bit more detail but still requires the user to look further if unfamiliar with the meaning of "suffrage":

> "An advocate of women's suffrage, especially in the United Kingdom." (2011, 1742)

The *OED Online* provides a more detailed definition, accompanied by numerous examples of the word's use in context, beginning with a quotation from the 1906 *Daily Mail*:

> "A female supporter of the cause of women's political enfranchisement, *esp*. one of a violent or 'militant' type."

Thus far, only general dictionaries have been consulted. A search of subject-specific dictionaries yields definitions reflecting the particular perspective of each. Some examples include the following:

> In the *Dictionary of American Government and Politics*, the term does not appear; however, there is a nearly two-page entry on women's suffrage that begins, "The term 'women's suffrage' refers to the economic and political reform movement aimed at extending the suffrage, or right to vote, to women. Its origins are often traced back to the United States in the 1820s" (Watts 2010, 329).

According to *The SAGE Dictionary of Sociology* (2006, 294), "This 19th-century term denotes the right to vote in elections. The feminine 'ette' ending was added to denote those women who in the early part of the 20th century campaigned to have voting rights extended to women."

Finally, one can turn to a usage guide, *The American Heritage Guide to Contemporary Usage and Style* (2005), to differentiate between "suffragist" and "suffragette":

> "The word *suffragist*, meaning an advocate of the extension of political voting rights, especially to women, is used of both men and women. The word *suffragette*, which refers only to female suffragists, became popular in the early 20th century and was favored by many female British suffragists as well as some groups and individuals who mocked women's attempts to gain suffrage. In the United States, however, the word *suffragist* was preferred by advocates of women's suffrage, who regarded *suffragette* as a sexist diminutive."

REFERENCES

The American Heritage Dictionary of the English Language. 2011. 5th ed. Boston: Houghton Mifflin Harcourt.

American Library Association. 2015. "Selection Policy, Resources for College Libraries." http://proquest.rclweb.net/learn_more/selection_policy.html.

Association of College and Research Libraries. 2009. "Selection Policy, Choice." http://www.ala.org/acrl/choice/selectionpolicy/.

Blevins, Win. 2001. *Dictionary of the American West: Over 5,000 Terms and Expressions from Aarigaa! to Zopilote*, 2nd ed. Seattle: Sasquatch Books.

Cassidy, Frederic G., Joan Houston Hall, and Luanne Von Schneidemesser, eds. 2013. *Dictionary of American Regional English*. Cambridge, MA: Belknap Press of Harvard University Press.

Dahlin, Robert. 1999. "You're as Good as Your Word." *Publishers Weekly* 246 (46): 33–37.

Emory University. 2013. "2013 Emory Medalists Honored for Achievements, Dedication." http://news.emory.edu/stories/2013/11/upress_emory_medalists/campus.html.

Flanagan, Padraic. 2014. "RIP for OED as World's Finest Dictionary Goes Out of Print." *The Telegraph*. April 20. http://www.telegraph.co.uk/culture/culturenews/10777079/RIP-for-OED-as-worlds-finest-dictionary-goes-out-of-print.html.

Flood, Alison. 2015. "Cash Crisis Threatens Dictionary of US Regional English." *The Guardian*. April 17. http://www.theguardian.com/books/2015/apr/17/cash-crisis-threatens-dictionary-of-us-regional-english.

Funk & Wagnalls New International Dictionary of the English Language. 2005. Comprehensive Millennium Edition. Naples, FL: Literary Guild World Publishers.

Houghton Mifflin Harcourt. 2015. "The Usage Panel." https://ahdictionary.com/word/usagepanel.html.

McQuade, Molly, 2003. "Defining a Dictionary." *Booklist* 99 (18): 1688.

Merriam-Webster. 2002. *Webster's Third New International Dictionary of the English Language, Unabridged*. Springfield, MA: Merriam-Webster.

Montgomery, Michael B., and Joseph S. Hall, eds. 2004. *Dictionary of Smoky Mountain English*. Knoxville: University of Tennessee Press.

Mugglestone, Lynda. 2011. *Dictionaries: A Very Short Introduction*. New York: Oxford University Press.

Oxford University Press. 2015. "Language Reference, Oxford Reference." http://www.oxfordreference.com/page/languagereference/language-reference.

Read, Allen Walker. 2005. "Encyclopaedias and Dictionaries." *Encyclopaedia Britannica*, 15th ed., 18: 257–86. Chicago: Encyclopaedia Britannica.

Simpson, John, and Edmund Weiner, eds. 1993. *Oxford English Dictionary: Additions Series*. New York: Oxford University Press.

Trumble, William R., and Angus Stevenson. 2002. *Shorter Oxford English Dictionary on Historical Principles*, 5th ed. New York: Oxford University Press.

LIST OF SOURCES

5 Language Visual Dictionary. 2003. New York: DK Publishing.

Abbreviations Dictionary. http://www.dictionary.com/abbreviations.

AcronymFinder.com. http://www.acronymfinder.com.

Acronyms, Initialisms & Abbreviations Dictionary: A Guide to Over 300,000 Acronyms, Initialisms, Abbreviations, Contractions, Alphabetic Symbols, and Similar Condensed Appellations. 2015. 49th ed. Farmington Hills, MI: Gale Cengage Learning.

Alexander, Caleb, and American Imprint Collection (Library of Congress). 1800. *The Columbian Dictionary of the English Language: In which Many New Words, Peculiar to the United States, and Many Words of General Use, Not found in Any Other English Dictionary, Are Inserted . . . : To which Is Prefixed, a Prosodial Grammar, Containing, a Short Dissertation on Vowels and Consonants: To the Whole Is Added Heathen Mythology, Or, a Classical Pronouncing Dictionary*. Printed at Boston: By Isaiah Thomas and Ebenezer T. Andrews.

The American Heritage Abbreviations Dictionary. 2007. 3rd ed. Boston: Houghton Mifflin.

The American Heritage Dictionary for Learners of English. 2002. Boston: Houghton Mifflin.

The American Heritage Dictionary of Idioms. 2013. 2nd ed. Boston: Houghton Mifflin Harcourt.

The American Heritage Dictionary of the English Language. 2011. 5th ed. Boston: Houghton Mifflin Harcourt.

The American Heritage Dictionary of the English Language. 2015. [mobile app] Boston: Houghton Mifflin Harcourt.

The American Heritage Guide to Contemporary Usage and Style. 2005. Boston: Houghton Mifflin.

The American Heritage Student Dictionary. 2013. 3rd ed. Boston: Houghton Mifflin Harcourt, 2013.

The American Heritage Student Thesaurus. 2013. Updated ed. Boston: Houghton Mifflin.

The American Heritage Thesaurus for Learners of English. 2002. Boston: Houghton Mifflin.

The Art and Architecture Thesaurus. The Getty Research Institute. http://www.getty.edu/research/tools/vocabularies/aat.

Bartlett's Familiar Quotations: A Collection of Passages, Phrases, and Proverbs Traced to Their Sources in Ancient and Modern Literature. 2012. 18th ed. Boston: Little, Brown.

Blevins, Winfred. 2008. *Dictionary of the American West: Over 5,000 Terms and Expressions from Aarigaa! to Zopilote*. 2nd ed., expanded and rev. Fort Worth, TX: TCU Press.

Booklist. Chicago: American Library Association. http://www.booklistonline.com/. [subscription required for full access]

Canadian Oxford Dictionary. 2004. 2nd ed. Don Mills, ON: Oxford University Press.

Chat Slang. 2014. [mobile app] Minneapolis, MN: Sharpened Productions.

Chirico, Rob. 2014. *Damn!: A Cultural History of Swearing in Modern America*. Durham, NC: Pitchstone Publishing.

Choice. Middletown, CT: Choice/Association for College and Research Libraries. http://www.ala.org/acrl/choice/home. [subscription required]

Common Errors in English Usage. 2013. 3rd ed. Sherwood, OR: William, James & Co.

The Concise Roget's International Thesaurus. 2011. 7th ed. New York: Harper.

Credo Reference. Boston: Credo. http://www.credoreference.com. [subscription required]

Cresswell, Julia. 2009. *The Insect That Stole Butter?: Oxford Dictionary of Word Origins*, 2nd ed. New York: Oxford University Press.

Dictionary of American Regional English. 1985–2013. 5 vols. Cambridge, MA: Belknap Press of Harvard University Press. Available online: http://www.daredictionary.com. [subscription required for full access]

Dictionary.com. http://dictionary.reference.com/.

DK Merriam-Webster Children's Dictionary. 2015. New York: Dorling Kindersley.

Funk & Wagnalls New International Dictionary of the English Language. 2005. Comprehensive Millennium Edition. Naples, FL: Literary Guild World Publishers.

Garner, Bryan A. 2009. *Garner's Modern American Usage*, 3rd ed. New York: Oxford University Press.

Google Translate. 2015. [mobile app] Mountain View, CA: Google, Inc.

Green, Jonathon. 2010. *Green's Dictionary of Slang*. London: Chambers.

Holder, R.W. 2007. *How Not to Say What You Mean: A Dictionary of Euphemisms*, 4th ed. New York: Oxford University Press.

Internet Slang Dictionary & Translator. NoSlang.com. http://www.noslang.com/.

iTranslate. 2015. [mobile app] Pischeldorf, Austria: Sonico GmbH.

iTranslate Voice. 2015. [mobile app] Pischeldorf, Austria: Sonico GmbH.

James, Ewart. 1999. *NTC's Dictionary of British Slang and Colloquial Expressions*. Lincolnwood, IL: NTC.

Johnson, Samuel, William Strahan, and Pre-1801 Imprint Collection (Library of Congress). 1755. *A Dictionary of the English Language: In Which the Words Are Deduced from Their Originals, and Illustrated in Their Different Significations by Examples from the Best Writers: To Which Are Prefixed, a History of the Language, and an English Grammar*. London: Printed by W. Strahan, for J. and P. Knapton.

Kersey, John. 1702. *The New English Dictionary*. London: Printed for H. Bonwicke & R. Knaplock.

Library Journal. New York: Library Journal. http://lj.libraryjournal.com/. [subscription required for full access]

Merriam-Webster Dictionary. 2015. [mobile app] Springfield, MA: Merriam-Webster.

Merriam-Webster Online. Springfield, MA: Merriam-Webster. http://www.merriam-webster.com/.

Merriam Webster's Collegiate Dictionary. 2014. 11th ed. Springfield, MA: Merriam-Webster.

Merriam-Webster's Collegiate Thesaurus. 2010. 2nd ed. Springfield, MA: Merriam-Webster.

Merriam-Webster's Compact 5-Language Visual Dictionary. 2010. Springfield, MA: Merriam-Webster.

Merriam-Webster's Elementary Dictionary. 2014. Updated & expanded ed. Springfield, MA: Merriam-Webster.

Merriam-Webster's First Dictionary. 2012. Springfield, MA: Merriam-Webster.

Merriam-Webster's Intermediate Dictionary. 2011. Rev. and updated ed. Springfield, MA: Merriam-Webster.

Merriam-Webster's Primary Dictionary. 2005. Springfield, MA: Merriam-Webster.

Merriam-Webster's School Dictionary. 2015. Springfield, MA: Merriam-Webster.

Merriam-Webster's Spanish-English Visual Dictionary. 2014. Springfield, MA: Merriam-Webster.

Montgomery, Michael, and Joseph Hall. 2004. *Dictionary of Smoky Mountain English*. Knoxville: University of Tennessee Press. Available online: http://artsandsciences.sc.edu/engl/dictionary/dictionary.html.

Moore, C.J. 2014. *How to Speak Brit: The Quintessential Guide to the King's English, Cockney Slang, and Other Flummoxing British Phrases*. New York: Gotham Books.

New Oxford American Dictionary. 2013. 3rd ed. New York: Oxford University Press.

The New Partridge Dictionary of Slang and Unconventional English. 2013. 2nd ed. New York: Routledge.

OED Online. Oxford: Oxford University Press. http://www.oed.com. [subscription required for full access]

OneLook Dictionary Search. http://www.onelook.com.

Online Dictionary for Library and Information Science (ODLIS). Santa Barbara, CA: ABC-CLIO. http://www.abc-clio.com/ODLIS/odlis_A.aspx.

Ostler, Rosemarie. *Dewdroppers, Waldos, and Slackers: A Decade-by-Decade Guide to the Vanishing Vocabulary of the Twentieth Century*. 2005. New York: Oxford University Press.

Oxford Advanced American Dictionary for Learners of English. 2011. New York: Oxford University Press.

Oxford American Writer's Thesaurus. 2012. 3rd ed. New York: Oxford University Press.

Oxford Dictionary of Quotations. 2014. 8th ed. Oxford: Oxford University Press.

Oxford Dictionary of Word Histories. 2002. New York: Oxford University Press.

Oxford English Dictionary. 1989. 2nd ed. 20 vols. New York: Oxford University Press.

Oxford English Dictionary. Additions Series. 1993–1997. 2 vols. New York: Oxford University Press.

Oxford Language Dictionaries Online. Oxford: Oxford University Press. http://www.oxforddictionaries.com/us/. [subscription required for full access]

Oxford Learner's Thesaurus: A Dictionary of Synonyms. 2012. 4th ed. Oxford: Oxford University Press.

Oxford Reference. Oxford: Oxford University Press. http://www.oxfordreference.com/. [subscription required]

Partridge, Eric. 2008. *Origins: An Etymological Dictionary of Modern English*. New York: Routledge.

Peckham, Aaron. 2012. *Urban Dictionary: Freshest Street Slang Defined*. New ed. Kansas City, MO: Andrews McMeel Pub.

Random House Historical Dictionary of American Slang. 1994–2007. 1st ed. 3 vols. New York: Random House.
Random House Webster's Unabridged Dictionary. 2005. 2nd ed., rev. and updated ed. New York: Random House.
Reitz, Joan M. 2004. *Dictionary for Library and Information Science.* Westport, CT: Libraries Unlimited.
Resources for College Libraries. Chicago: American Library Association. Available online from ProQuest. http://www.rclweb.net/. [subscription required]
Reverse Acronyms, Initialisms & Abbreviations Dictionary: A Companion Volume to Acronyms, Initialisms & Abbreviations Dictionary, with Terms Arranged Alphabetically by Meaning of Acronym, Initialism or Abbreviation. 2015. 49th ed. Farmington Hills, MI: Gale Cengage Learning.
Reverso.com. http://www.reverso.com.
Roget's 21st Century Thesaurus in Dictionary Form: The Essential Reference for Home, School, Or Office. 2008. 3rd ed. Bridgewater, NJ: Baker & Taylor.
Roget's International Thesaurus. 2011. 7th ed. New York: HarperCollins.
The Routledge Dictionary of Modern American Slang and Unconventional English. 2013. New York: Routledge.
The SAGE Dictionary of Sociology. 2006. Thousand Oaks, CA: SAGE.
Schur, Norman W., Eugene Ehrlich, and Richard Ehrlich. 2013. *British English A to Zed: A Definitive Guide to the Queen's English,* 3rd ed. New York: Skyhorse.
Shorter Oxford English Dictionary. 2015. [mobile app] San Diego: MobiSystems.
Shorter Oxford English Dictionary on Historical Principles. 2007. 6th ed. 2 vols. New York: Oxford University Press.
Spears, Richard. 2011. *McGraw-Hill's Conversational American English: The Illustrated Guide to the Everyday Expressions of American English.* New York: McGraw-Hill.
Spears, Richard. 2006. *McGraw-Hill's Dictionary of American Slang and Colloquial Expressions.* New York: McGraw-Hill.
Thesaurus of Aging Terminology. 2005. 8th ed. Washington, DC: AARP. http://assets.aarp.org/rgcenter/general/thesaurus.pdf.
Thesaurus of Psychological Index Terms. 2012. Washington, DC: American Psychological Association.
Thorne, Tony. 2014. *Dictionary of Contemporary Slang,* 4th ed. London: Bloomsbury.
Translate.Reference.com. http://translate.reference.com/.
Urban Dictionary. http://www.urbandictionary.com.
Watts, Duncan. 2010. *Dictionary of American Government and Politics.* Edinburgh, Scotland: Edinburgh University Press.
Webster, Noah. (1828) 1970. *An American Dictionary of the English Language.* New York: Johnson Reprint Corp.
Webster's Third New International Dictionary of the English Language, Unabridged. 2002. Springfield, MA: Merriam-Webster.
Wordnik. San Francisco, CA: Planetwork NGO. http://www.wordnik.com.
World Book Dictionary. 2011. 2 vols. Chicago: World Book.
WordReference.com. Weston, FL: WordReference.com. http://www.wordreference.com.

SUGGESTED READINGS

Battistella, Edwin L. 2008. "Groping for Words: A Guide to Slang and Usage Resources." *Choice* 46: 619–31.

This bibliographic essay offers a wide-ranging discussion of some of the many books on grammar, pronunciation, spelling, diction, and punctuation. The scope includes guides to both American and British English, as well as slang and dialect. Concluding sections of the article discuss "grammar as entertainment" and "language and the Web."

Brewer, Charlotte. 2007. *Treasure-House of the Language: The Living OED*. New Haven, CT: Yale University Press.

This book brings the history of the *Oxford English Dictionary* forward from the completion of the first edition in 1928 to its current electronic form in the 21st century.

Kendall, Joshua C. 2008. *The Man Who Made Lists: Love, Death, Madness, and the Creation of Roget's Thesaurus*. New York: Berkley Books.

This biography of Peter Mark Roget (1779–1869) traces Roget's life and the thesaurus project that occupied his retirement years, with the first edition published in 1852.

Landau, Sidney I. 2001. *Dictionaries: The Art and Craft of Lexicography*. 2nd ed. London: Cambridge University Press.

Landau offers a description of how dictionaries are researched and written, with particular attention to how computers have changed modern lexicography. The final chapter addresses legal and ethical issues.

Martin, Rebecca A., and Sarah McHone-Chase. 2009. "Translation Resources on the Web: A Guide to Accurate, Free Sites." *College & Research Libraries News* 70: 356–59.

This article provides a selected annotated list of sites useful as aids in translating from one language into another. Resources are grouped under headings for online dictionaries, online translator services and directories, gateways to glossaries, and blogs.

Mulac, Carolyn. 2002. "Other People's Words: Recent Quotation Books." *Booklist* 98 (21): 1870–72.

In order to highlight the range of specialized quotation books that are available for purchase, this article looks at 20 titles, ranging from *African American Quotations* to *The Ultimate Dictionary of Sports Quotations*. Annotated entries are grouped by broad topic.

Mugglestone, Lynda. 2011. *Dictionaries: A Very Short Introduction*. New York: Oxford University Press.

The "Very Short Introductions" series from Oxford University Press is a gem of a collection, and the slim, 134-page volume on dictionaries is no exception. In six chapters, Mugglestone covers not only the basic facts about dictionaries, but also their cultural, social, and historical significance.

Skinner, David. 2012. *The Story of Ain't: America, Its Language, and the Most Controversial Dictionary Ever Published*. New York: HarperCollins.

David Skinner has written an entertaining and vivid history of the controversial *Webster's Third*. The editor of *Webster's Third*, Philip Gove, courted furor and dismay from readers when he and the editorial board of the dictionary decided to completely overhaul and revolutionize the content of the venerated source, including the addition of the word *ain't*.

Steinmetz, Sol. 2010. *There's a Word for It: The Explosion of the American Language Since 1900*. New York: Harmony Books.

Steinmetz, a lexicographer with several books to his name, investigates and illuminates all the various ways the English language has changed and grown over the past 114 years. Organized by decade, each chapter begins with a succinct history lesson for the reader, then lists out by year the new words in use.

Winchester, Simon. 2003. *The Meaning of Everything: The Story of the Oxford English Dictionary*. New York: Oxford University Press.

Winchester provides an interesting history of the first edition of the *Oxford English Dictionary*, including prior efforts to document the English language beginning in the 17th century. He describes the people and processes involved in the project over a 70-year period concluding with the completion of the first edition in 1928.

Chapter 20

Geographical Sources

Jenny Marie Johnson

> Geography matters, not for the simplistic and overly used reason that everything happens in space, but because *where* things happen is critical to knowing *how* and *why* they happen. (Warf and Arias 2009, 1)

INTRODUCTION

Geography identifies, connects, describes, and explains the wheres of life; it studies the whys of the wheres of life. Geography focuses on the interactions of humans with the physical world, looking for answers to questions about how the world impacts human activities and how human activities impact the world. Geographers examine connections between places, looking for similarities, transfers, and impacts. Geography is a discipline that faces two ways, reflective of components of earth science (physical geography) and social science (human geography). The unifying factors within the discipline all reflect the core understanding that place/location/space is the most important underlying and connective factor.

During the past 20 years, tools of geographical analysis and ways of geographical thinking have been discovered and adopted by many disciplines. This "spatial turn," the exploration of spatial questions within non-geography disciplines, has been driven largely by the deployment and use of geographic information system (GIS)–fueled analysis techniques. The University of Virginia Library's *Spatial Humanities* is an extensive website discussing spatial humanities with essays on how the spatial turn is being expressed and taken advantage of in a number of humanities and non-geography social sciences. Barney Warf and Santa Arias's *The Spatial Turn: Interdisciplinary Perspectives* (2009) also includes a number of examples of the application of geographical processes and attention to the importance of space or place. Students and researchers in many disciplines have realized that space, and connections or transfers between spaces are important. So it will be difficult to predict or anticipate the geographical knowledge base or prior experience of individuals who come to a reference desk or engage in a reference chat session.

Seekers of geographical information sources often are looking for maps, atlases, aerial photography, or data. Much of the data collected about human activities and environmental happenings have a spatial component. Census data of any kind, such as human or animal populations, crop yields, or building facilities, all have an element of where, as do data collected about geologic phenomena and meteorological events. Data users may need assistance in determining appropriate methods of spatial analysis to discover connections and correlations while map, atlas, and aerial photography users may need help interpreting their selected resources.

EVALUATION

The ability to robustly evaluate geospatial information sources differs greatly from format to format. For atlases, in particular world atlases, there may be multiple publications available, which can be critically examined and compared through multiple facets. But most other resources will have no selection to choose from; only one title or publication might have been produced, or only one organization is creating and publishing materials. Prime examples of this situation are topographic maps and aerial photographs, both of which are usually sole-sourced by or through government agencies. In these cases, materials are not so much evaluated for quality but rather for how they do or do not meet information and data needs. Additionally, they need to be considered critically for the appropriateness of repurposing or reusing them for purposes not originally intended.

GAZETTEERS

Gazetteers are alphabetical place-name lists that include locational information. They can be used to answer questions like "Where is the Firth of Forth?" In addition, finding geographical location data for places is critical for the vast majority of reference questions that involve geospatial information. There are three basic forms of gazetteers: list, dictionary, and encyclopedic. The list is the simplest form; entries include the place-name and location information such as an area on an alphanumeric grid, a page number, and indication of location (usually via alphanumeric grid) on the page, or a latitude/longitude pair. List gazetteers may serve as indexes for specific print publications, such as state highway maps or atlases, and will include only locations that appear in that publication. Dictionary and encyclopedic gazetteers are not tied to specific maps and are not intended to serve as an index to a particular publication. Entries include location information and other descriptive information. Location information may be latitude/longitude pairs but could also be county and state, direction and distance from a major city, or an indication of a general region. Encyclopedic gazetteers will generally include more and lengthier entries than dictionary gazetteers. Neither kind of gazetteer should be considered all inclusive; preface or introductory text should explain the purpose of the gazetteer and how inclusionary decisions were made. Gazetteers are a kind of resource that retains its usefulness even though it may be dated. Older gazetteers often contain places that no longer exist or names that have fallen into disuse, and thus should not be considered automatic candidates for withdrawal from a collection.

GEOnet Names Server (*GNS*), hosted by the National Geospatial-Intelligence Agency, contains more than 9 million names for more than 5 million places worldwide except for the United States, its dependent areas, and Antarctica. The server describes itself as "the official repository of standard spellings of all foreign geographical names, sanctioned by the United States Board on Geographic Names (US BGN)." The database is updated weekly. Besides official names, it includes a large number of variant names and spellings. There are two search interfaces: a Web map service viewer and a text-based search that allows limits by country and type of location. The results table includes place-names, latitude/longitude pair, an indication of the province or country the location is in, the type of location, and links to the location displayed through *Google Maps* and *MapQuest* (see Figure 20.1). The database has its roots in gazetteers published by the United States Army Mapping Service and the Board on Geographic Names (BGN) beginning in the 1940s. The early gazetteers produced by these agencies often indexed place-names found on specific sets of U.S.-produced topographic map sets for areas and countries that were of particular interest at the time. The postwar gazetteers all are subtitled "Official Standard Names Gazetteer" and generally expand beyond the names included in a specific map set. Because *GNS* is available online cost-free, there probably is no reason to search for and expend funds on purchasing the old print volumes. But these print volumes are still very useful. If a place-name is misspelled when input, for example, Hesinki instead of Helsinki, no results are displayed, and the user is not given an opportunity to browse a list of place-names. The print volumes preserve list browsability; this is especially important when working with place-names, such as those transcribed from handwritten immigration records, where spelling is uncertain or cannot be confirmed.

The comparable gazetteer for the United States, and Antarctica and undersea features, is the *Geographic Names Information System* (*GNIS*), which is hosted by the United States Geological Survey (USGS). As with *GNS*, *GNIS* is a product of the

GeoNames Search Results

Total Number of Names in query: 234
Total Number of Features in query: 62
Records 1 through 150

Page 1 Next >>

The geographic names in this database are provided for the guidance of and use by the Federal Government and for the information of the general public.
The names, variants, and associated data may not reflect the views of the United States Government on the sovereignty over geographic features.

Name (Type)	Geopolitical Entity Name (Code)	First-Order Administrative Division Name (Code)	Latitude, Longitude DMS (DD)	MGRS	Feature Designation (Code)	Display Location Using
Ḥamad al Gharāb (Approved - N) Ḥamad (Generic) حمد الغراب (Non-Roman Script - NS) حمد (Generic)	Syria (SY)	Ḥimş (SY11)	34° 00' 26" N, 038° 40' 06" E (34.007265, 38.66838)	37SDT6937863011	plateau (PLAT)	Google Maps MapQuest
Ḥamad al Ghurāb (Approved - N) حمد الغراب (Non-Roman Script - NS)	Syria (SY)	Ḥimş (SY11)	33° 58' 37" N, 038° 40' 17" E (33.976967, 38.671448)	37SDT6965159651	area (AREA)	Google Maps MapQuest
Wādī al Ḥamadā (Approved - N) Wādī (Generic) وادي الحمدا (Non-Roman Script - NS) وادي (Generic)	Syria (SY)	Dayr az Zawr (SY07)	35° 47' 34" N, 039° 54' 42" E (35.792772, 39.911553)	37SEV8237261347	wadi(s) (WAD)	Google Maps MapQuest
Ḥamad as Sajr (Approved - N) حمد السجر (Non-Roman Script - NS)	Syria (SY)	Ar Raqqah (SY04)	35° 32' 55" N, 039° 23' 00" E (35.548611, 39.383333)	37SEV3474533952	area (AREA)	Google Maps MapQuest
Ḥamad 'Assāf (Approved - N) حمد عساف (Non-Roman Script - NS)	Syria (SY)	Ar Raqqah (SY04)	35° 50' 22" N, 039° 27' 45" E (35.839411, 39.46252)	37SEV4177066236	populated place (PPL)	Google Maps MapQuest
Bīr Ḥamād al Qadr (Approved - N) Bīr (Generic) بير حماد القدر (Non-Roman Script - NS) بير (Generic) Bi'r Ḥamād al Qadr (Variant - V)	Syria (SY)	Ar Raqqah (SY04)	35° 54' 47" N, 039° 17' 49" E (35.912978, 39.296954)	37SEV2679374337	water well(s) (WLL)	Google Maps MapQuest

FIGURE 20.1 *GEOnet Names Server* search results

BGN, and it is the federal government's list of official geographical names for use on maps and in other publications. A wide variety of feature types are included; only named roads and highways appear to be excluded. Results tables include feature name, type (class) of feature, county and state, latitude and longitude, elevation, USGS topographic map name, and the date when the feature was entered into the database. Most of the feature names are derived from USGS topographic maps. Additional names were harvested from smaller-scale maps and from BGN files. This database is not a static database. Additional sources have been consulted to further enhance the database including federal, state, and local government agencies; commercial publications and databases; specialty websites such as genealogical websites; and services that support first responders. Clicking on the feature name in the results table will display a "detail report" including information about the entry's source. *GNIS* does not include links to online maps so, unlike *GNS*, locations cannot be displayed immediately on a map.

The *JewishGen Communities Database* and *JewishGen Gazetteer* are two of many databases made available through JewishGen, an affiliate of the Museum of Jewish Heritage. The databases vary substantively in size and scope. *JewishGen Communities*, using data compiled by JewishGen, focuses exclusively on 6,000 Jewish communities in Europe, North Africa, and the Middle East. Because of its limited contents, this database may be frustrating for users. *JewishGen Gazetteer* includes 1.8 million locations, possibly creating a different kind of frustration, found in 54 countries of Europe, North Africa, the Middle East, and Central Asia. The Gazetteer has its foundations in *Shtetl Finder* (Cohen 1980) and *Where Once We Walked: A Guide to the Jewish Communities Destroyed in the Holocaust* (Mokotoff and Sack 1991). This core has been extensively augmented by BGN data. The helpful information contained in the introductory sections of the two print foundation works regarding data discovery and compilation is, unfortunately, not included anywhere on the JewishGen website. Although dated, the release notes for the two databases may help in determining which may be more appropriate. Both databases offer the same flexibilities in search. Five search options are available, ideal for working with murky place-names: phonetically like (Beider-Morse Phonetic Matching), sounds like (Daitch–Mokotoff Soundex), exact spelling, starts with, and contains. Additionally, users can select different displays of relative distance and direction from the country's capital city, a specific latitude and longitude pair, or a specified selected city when searching both databases. Results from the *JewishGen Communities Database* include other names and the town, district, or province, and country of the requested location; hovering over an icon displays additional information about historical population and displays the place-name in non-Roman scripts. The Gazetteer results include links to map displays and a secondary search that will display other towns within a 10-mile radius of the selected town. Because of the phonetic and sounds like search aspects, *JewishGen Gazetteer* may be helpful for anyone, regardless of ancestry, searching for locations in Europe, North Africa, the Middle East, and Central Asia.

MAP READING AND INTERPRETATION

Maps are an awkward mix of primary and secondary sources. A manuscript map by George Washington recording a survey of Mount Vernon is obviously a primary source. An aerial photograph of a small town in central Illinois is a primary source. But is a USGS topographic quadrangle of that same town, produced using data from that aerial photograph and field surveys, a primary source (see Figure 20.2)?

For certain, a map produced in 2014 using data about automobile ownership in 1912 as reported by *Automobile Journal* is a secondary source. But what about a map published by the Miroslav Krleza Lexicographical Institute, located in Zagreb, in 1991 showing late 20th-century ethnic group distribution in the Republic of Croatia and the Republic of Bosnia and Herzegovina? Joni Seager (2015) takes on this question in her Web-based article "'Mapping' Primary and Secondary Sources," but the question of primary vs. secondary source still is not clear except in that it needs to be determined for each cartographic item.

FIGURE 20.2A Watson, Illinois. Segment of 1981 USDA aerial photograph. Courtesy of the University of Illinois at Urbana-Champaign Map Library

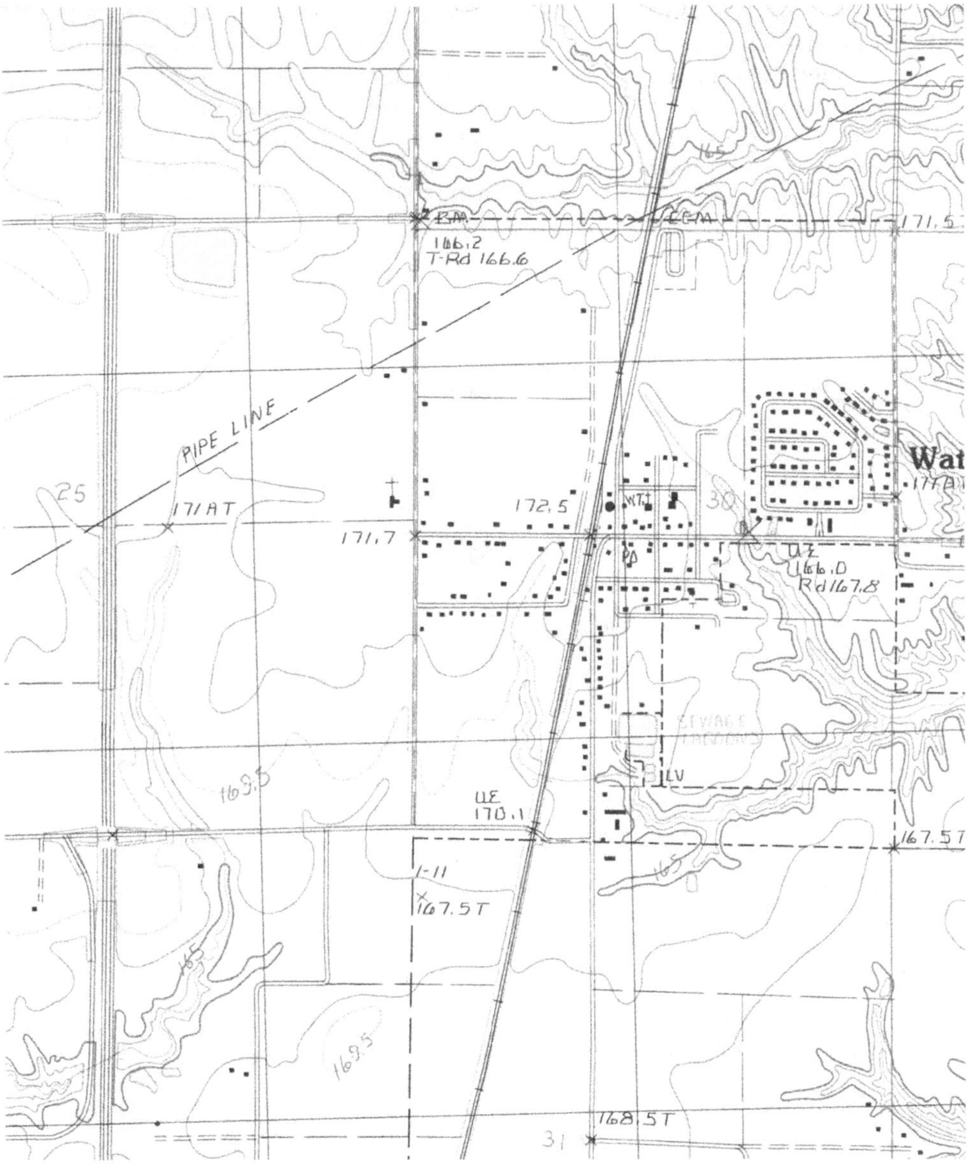

FIGURE 20.2B Watson, Illinois. Segment of USGS Effingham South, Illinois, topographic quadrangle (provisional edition, 1985), compiled from 1981 USDA photography

It must be remembered that maps are always made for a reason; regardless of being a primary or a secondary source, a map is never made just to make a map. Maps may appear to be "scientific," but they always have a viewpoint. The reason for the map, the perspective of the map maker (individual or organizational), and the context of production all play into the many decisions made about what data to show, how to manipulate that data, and how the data are symbolized.

Part of map creation is the process of data selection and generalization. Not everything can be shown to every last detail. So for a map to do its job, whatever that job might be, a map needs to "lie," usually through lies of omission, combination, and displacement. The amount of generalization can depend heavily on the scale of the map. Map scale is a ratio of a distance between two points on a map and the distance between the same two points in the physical world. As with any ratio, this ratio has no units attached, so a scale of 1:24,000 could be interpreted as 1 inch on the map equals 24,000 inches in the physical world or the distance covered by 1 pencil length on the map equals the distance covered by 24,000 pencils of the same length in the physical world. Besides as a ratio, scale can be expressed verbally ("Scale approximately 6 miles to an inch") or graphically through a bar scale.

Maps can be divided into large-, medium-, or small-scale groups. Large-scale maps show the most detail, while small-scale maps show the least amount of detail. The amount of area shown is inversely related; if looking at two maps printed on the same size piece of paper, the large-scale map will show less area than the small-scale map. The distinction between large- and small-scale maps, especially when working with potential cartographic materials users, is critical. Novice users often ask for a "small-scale map," which they think means that they will get a detailed map of a small area when actually they will get a very reduced, very general map of a large area. When working with this kind of conversation starter, it might be useful to find a way to restate the user's question perhaps as "You are looking for a map with a lot of detail?" to elicit additional information (see Table 20.1).

Determining scale of a map on a computer screen, or sometimes of a map that has been photocopied, can be difficult. In both of these cases, a ratio or verbal scale should be considered questionable because it is so easy to change the size, and thus the scale, on a screen and because maps can be reduced or enlarged during reproduction. Look for a graphic or bar scale in these instances because it will change as the map is altered.

Map projection, the mathematical method to transform a three-dimensional (3-D) ellipsoid into a 2-D image, is often ignored by map users but should not be because the selection of projection by the map producer can impact how maps look and what can be done with them. Depending on the projection chosen, distance, size, shape, or direction will be distorted. No projection is perfect; no projection can maintain all four of these characteristics at the same time.

An Album of Map Projections by John Snyder and Philip Voxland (1989) is available both in print and online from the USGS as a PDF. No prior knowledge of map projections and no advanced math skills are necessary to use this work (although the math is explained in an appendix). Each projection is illustrated and described including information about distortion and appropriate or intended usage. The

TABLE 20.1 Large–Small Scale

Scale Group	Sample Scales	Denominator	Land Area Shown	Details Shown
Small	1:2,500,000 1:1,000,000	↑	↑	↓
Large	1:63,360 1:24,000	↓	↓	↑

layout for each projection follows the same pattern, making it easy to compare. Also included are a glossary and a very useful "Guide to selecting map projections." This work should be considered any time a question about using maps from different sources occurs. Differences in projection may be the explanation for why maps might not be overlaying or lining up correctly.

Describing location is another tricky aspect of map use because there are so many different ways to indicate where a feature is on Earth. Three different coordinate systems appear in the margins of standard USGS topographic maps: geographical coordinate system (latitude–longitude), Universal Transverse Mercator, and state plane coordinate system (see Figure 20.3). Additionally, for most of the United States west of the 13 original states, it is essential to understand the Public Land Survey System (PLSS) comprising townships and sections, which are indicated on USGS topographic maps. This is the system used to describe much of the rural land in the United States. County plat books, which show rural landownership, rely on PLSS to locate parcels, and documents used in land sales often include PLSS designations. The Wisconsin State Cartographer's Office has

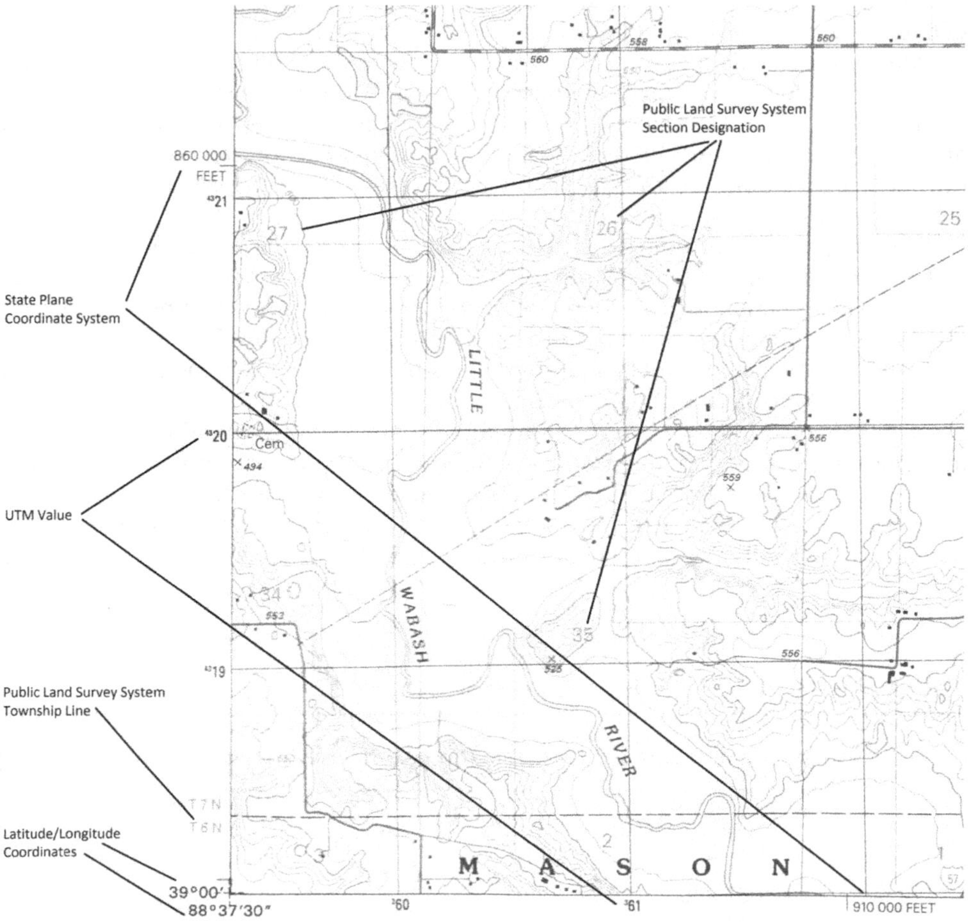

FIGURE 20.3 Location systems on USGS topographic quadrangles

developed a number of Web pages introducing PLSS. Although they are intended for a Wisconsin-oriented audience, the information is general enough that it can be used to understand the application of PLSS throughout the United States.

Map users need to understand appropriate map use. They might think that a USGS topographic quadrangle could be used to measure the distance between a railroad and a parallel-running highway. This is not an appropriate use because symbols are not always placed exactly where the feature is located in the physical world. Symbols are often displaced because otherwise they would lie on top of each other. Also for readability, symbols sometimes are disproportionally large or exaggerated in comparison with the map scale. On dot maps, often used to show raw numbers such as number of chickens, the dots cannot be interpreted as indicating exactly where the chickens roost.

To be able to appropriately answer questions regarding cartographic materials, the librarian needs to have a foundational understanding about map use, map interpretation, and map creation. Works such as Jon Kimerling's *Map Use: Reading, Analysis, Interpretation* (2012) will help take some of the mystery out of making usage decisions and interpreting maps. Kimerling and his coauthors take the view that in order to be able to appropriately use maps, map users should understand how maps are made. The heavily illustrated text is divided into three sections: map reading (understanding how the complex environment is represented through an abstract graphic); map analysis (the description and analysis of features and patterns on a map); map interpretation (using maps to understand the environment). *Map Use* can be read completely or used as a quick information fix. *Map Use* devotes entire chapters to map fundamentals such as scale, projection, grid coordinate systems, and methods for showing land surfaces. Foundational ideas are described in straightforward language that does not require prior technical knowledge.

Cartography textbooks can also serve some of the same needs. Arthur Robinson's *Elements of Cartography* (1995), Borden Dent's *Cartography: Thematic Map Design* (2009), and Terry Slocum's *Thematic Cartography and Geovisualization* (2009) all will be easy to locate in library collections.

Mapping It Out: Expository Cartography for the Humanities and Social Sciences by Mark Monmonier (1993) is not written in the popular tone of *Map Use* but still effectively conveys essential information about map creation and thus map reading. *Mapping It Out* is intended to support the work of authors who need to create maps that go beyond a simple location map. The section on map copyright and permissions to reuse maps may be a good beginning place for researchers and authors who are looking for guidance in matters of cartographic illustrations. Copyright for maps is no different than copyright for other published materials, yet map users often do not stop to think that a map is as much of an intellectual work deserving protection as a work of literature.

ATLASES

An atlas is a group of maps bound together; these maps may or may not, especially those in very early atlases, have been designed or intended to be incorporated into a volume together. Think of an atlas as a "convenience store" containing a broad array of geographical information tied together through focus on place or a specific topic.

Evaluating Atlases

Evaluating atlases becomes a challenge when there is only a single title available, for instance, a historical atlas of Massachusetts or a national atlas of Azerbaijan. For some places and atlas types, there might be two or three options available; some states in the western United States have two topographic atlases available from different publishers, and there are two predominant U.S. road atlases published on a regular basis, one by Rand McNally and the other by American Automobile Association (AAA). In cases where choice is limited, the user simply needs to be aware of and accommodate possible biases.

For world atlases, many more choices are available so titles can be compared in order to find the publication that best suits needs and budgets. A wide array of characteristics should be considered whenever examining an atlas, regardless of geographical scope.

- *Balance of coverage*: Coverage should be geographically balanced, proportional to area in the "real world."
- *Index*: A tabular index of place and feature names is essential; inclusion of variant names is highly desirable.
- *Currency*: Political situations, names, and boundaries should be up to date if the atlas is a current publication.
- *Accuracy*: Names should be spelled correctly and appear in appropriate locations. Features should be in the right locations. The index should guide the user to the correct pages.
- *Legibility/understandability*: Symbols, line weights, type styles, and color should all assist in reading the maps.
- *Scale and projection*: A scale statement should appear on map; it is helpful if the projection is identified.
- *Authority*: The reputation of the publisher and its track record of long-standing publications are helpful in predicting the usability of new editions.
- *Physical attributes*: An atlas should have a sturdy binding that allows the volume to lay completely flat without obscuring in the gutter any map that flows across pages.

In addition, an atlas should be more than 50 percent maps; text and other information sources can be included, but the maps should be the primary object. *Kister's Atlas Buying Guide* (1984), while mostly devoted to describing atlases available in the early 1980s, includes good advice on comparing and evaluating world atlases.

World Atlases

Three predominant and long-standing world atlas titles are *The Times Comprehensive Atlas of the World*, *National Geographic Atlas of the World*, and *Goode's World Atlas* (Veregin 2010). *The Times* and the *National Geographic* atlases are large folio-sized volumes with price tags to match. The *Goode's* atlas, intended for an education-based audience, is highly portable and suitable for quick desk reference. All three of these atlases capably meet the need to locate places and features worldwide. Because of the difference in physical size, the scope and level of detail included in *The Times* and the *National Geographic* atlas is much greater than that in the *Goode's*. The index section of *The Times* includes more than 200,000 names; *National Geographic* includes more than 150,000; and *Goode's* more than 30,000.

Area coverage balances are weighted a little differently between the three. *The Times* places greater emphasis on Europe and includes more coverage of Africa than the *National Geographic*. Both the *National Geographic* and *Goode's* highlight the United States. All three atlases include thematic maps showing topics such as climate, population, and weather. *Goode's* includes additional thematic maps at the continental level.

Numerous other world atlases are available from publishers such as Oxford University Press and Dorling Kindersley as well as other atlases published by *The Times* and *National Geographic*. These publications can easily be identified through resources such as Amazon.com and OCLC *WorldCat*.

The arena of Web-based world atlases is not as clear-cut. Searching the Web for "world atlas" will retrieve a number of possibilities. They are useful for quick dips, finding out something about a country or viewing a simple map of a nation. Web-based atlases have their place—find an atlas, click on Africa, check to make sure that Sudan is the country east of Chad, and read about current events and possibly see some photographs. Web-based atlases are not useful for in-depth searching of place-names. They lack the highly designed or composed maps that are found in a printed atlas. The maps included in Web-based "atlases" are often rudimentary or crude looking in comparison with those of *The Times*, *National Geographic*, and *Goode's*. Advertising on free sites may be intrusive. Often the statistical and demographic text included is lifted directly from the Central Intelligence Agency's (CIA) *The World Factbook*. *The World Factbook* is cleaner in design than many of the free Web-based atlases and includes digital versions of long-established CIA base and briefing maps. Additionally, *The World Factbook* is a trusted resource with clear indication of data age.

National Atlases

National atlases typically are published by national or quasi-governmental agencies. Most are oversized volumes and portray elements of a country's history, geography, economic structure, and demographics. Some national atlases include general maps with an accompanying tabular place and feature name index, but this should not be presumed. National atlases are a best-face-forward presentation. Often they include cartographic treatment of topics that are core to the country's identity. For example, the *National Atlas of Japan* includes a map showing the mean date of the first flowering of the Japanese cherry tree, the *National Atlas of Sweden* includes 15 maps about snow, and the *National Atlas of Sri Lanka* includes bar graphs on a map of coconut and spices showing hectares of land producing cinnamon, pepper, cloves, cardamom, and nutmeg.

The United States produced one print national atlas in 1970, *National Atlas of the United States*, edited by Arch Gerlach. Like all national atlases, this large book was intended to be many things to many users; it "was designed to be of practical use to decision makers in government and business, planners, research scholars, and others needing to visualize country-wide distribution patterns and relationships between environmental phenomena and human activities" (vii). Most of the atlas is thematic maps divided into five sections: physical, history, economic, social cultural, and administrative. Also included are 22 pages of general reference maps and a place-name index containing 41,000 names. The data mapped generally are from the mid- to late-1960s. The atlas was never completely revised. The USGS, the atlas complier/publisher, occasionally distributed separate map sheets as revisions or completely new content. The entire 1970 *National Atlas of the United States*, except for the gazetteer section, has been scanned by the Library of Congress, Geography and Map Division, and is available through the Library's *American Memory* website. Also at this website are commercially produced statistical atlases for the United States from 1870, 1880, and 1890.

Between 1997 and fall 2014, the United States' national atlas was available online as a cooperative multiagency project led by the USGS at a site identified as *nationalatlas.gov*. This site was taken off-line in October 2014, and the functions and content of *nationalatlas.gov* were merged into the USGS's *National Map* product, in particular in the Small-Scale Collection. Small-scale data sets that were originally developed for the *National Atlas* can be downloaded. Additionally, a large number of maps, considered "legacy products," can be viewed and printed.

Road atlases that provide national-level coverage should be remembered as an easily accessible and portable view of locations and connections between locations. Publishers are somewhat specialized in the regions and countries they map. Rand McNally produces an annual road atlas for the United States, Canada, and Mexico, as do the AAA and Michelin. Michelin also produces a large number of road atlases for countries and regions of Europe. Guia Roji publishes road atlases of Mexico. Map Studio, which originally specialized in maps of South Africa, has branched out to produce materials, including atlases, for all of Africa.

State Atlases

Like countries, there are state-level thematic atlases and road/topographic atlases. The thematic atlases usually are produced by educational institutions or private agencies in commemoration of a particular historical event. There has been no systematic or coordinated effort to prepare comparable thematic atlases for all states, and contents and production values will vary greatly. In the same way that national atlases highlight topics of particular concern to a nation, state atlases will treat topics of special interest as well as standard topics such as demographics and economics.

DeLorme, in its Atlas and Gazetteer series, produces road/topographic atlases for all states. The look and feel of these atlases is highly consistent, showing roads and trails, topography, populated places, and recreational areas. Each state volume has an alphabetical town index at the front. Benchmark Maps produces a similar atlas series focusing on the western United States. MapArt Publishing creates road atlases for Canadian provinces.

It must be remembered that many atlases have enduring value. Just because an atlas is older does not automatically mean that the information being conveyed has reduced value. Outdated or old information found in atlases will resonate with anyone doing historical research.

GENERAL MAPS

Maps are often divided into two broad categories, general or reference and thematic or special purpose. General maps could be considered multipurpose maps with an emphasis on locations and areas. Natural and man-made features may be shown. Sometimes general maps that include very little detail are used as the geographical base layer for thematic maps. Thematic maps show the spatial distribution of topical data such as water quality, locations of oil wells and pipelines, average income, predominant field crop, and racial distribution. Thematic maps often appear in atlases or illustrate articles.

CIA Maps

The CIA has created a series of general interest maps, formatted to fit on an 8.5- × 11-inch sheet of paper, which are freely available to the public to view and download as either a PDF or a JPG file from the CIA website. Maps found through the *Maps of CIA* website are for countries and often are available in three information formats: administrative, physiographic, and transportation. In addition, the CIA's *The World Factbook* offers region, continent, and world maps.

The *Perry-Castañeda Library Map Collection* at the University of Texas at Austin makes available through its website an extensive collection of older CIA maps, along with many other maps in the public domain. The oldest CIA maps available tend to be from the 1980s although there are a few from the 1970s. Maps are available in either JPG or PDF, sometimes in both formats. The collection FAQ explains viewing, printing, downloading, and usage requirements.

CIA maps will be useful for school projects and for paper, book, and lecture illustrations. The streamlined nature of the information lends itself to quick looks for information and easy answers to questions such as "I need a map showing all of the countries in Africa so I can study for a test" and "My daughter is doing a poster about our family in Poland for a fifth grade international fair. Do you have a map she can use?"

Google Maps/Google Earth

Google has developed two free map applications that have begun to converge in the functionalities that they offer. Many library users will already be familiar with Web-based *Google Maps*. *Google Maps* is intended to fill the need for a road map explorer. It allows users to find specific addresses and get directions. The display can be toggled between a map and a satellite/air photo-based image. For some very large structures, such as regional shopping malls, museums, and airports, *Google Maps* includes "indoor" maps. Because of privacy concerns, Google has been somewhat notorious for its mobile car-based photograph units that collect images showing building fronts along streets. An icon can be clicked on to display how a location appears "from a car." In some places, more than one Street View might be available. *Google Maps* also includes directory and contact information, daily hours, reviews, and other photos of the location besides the Street View photos.

Google Earth, also a free product, expands on the functionalities of *Google Maps* with increased navigational functionality and extraterrestrial coverage such as maps of the Moon and Mars. While *Google Maps'* default view is a map, *Google Earth* defaults to imagery. Zoom far enough in, and the imagery is displayed as a 3-D image that can be zoomed, panned, and rotated to view the same location from multiple angles. This allows interesting 360° views of cultural icons such as the courtyards of Westminster Palace or the back side of Disney World's Mount Everest.

Teaching with Google Earth, part of the Pedagogy in Action project at Carleton College, may be useful in learning to navigate and explain its display possibilities.

TOPOGRAPHIC MAPS

Topographic maps are an essential information resource for answering many questions. They include an astounding breadth of information including topography, surface water, land cover, transportation networks, boundaries, and location systems. All areas or locations covered by a topographic map set will be mapped to the same standards, using the same or very similar symbols, and to the same level of detail. Of course, because these map sets cover large areas and are complex and labor-intensive to produce, the dates of the maps within a set may vary greatly, and users need to be aware of age differences. But this variability is decreasing and the date windows narrowing as production becomes increasingly digital.

Because of their sweeping content, topographic maps are used for many different purposes: predicting the flows of floodwaters, mudslides, or volcanic eruptions; rediscovering abandoned rural locations such as one-room schools and cemetery plots; hiking, camping, and outdoor recreation; and as base or foundation maps for geological, botanical, or environmental data. The look-and-feel and scale of coverage will differ between countries, but generally there are some color conventions that transcend national boundaries. Green usually indicates vegetation, and blue stands for water. Brown, but sometimes black or orange, is often used for topography.

National priorities and programs for topographic map production differ greatly. An essential, and often difficult, first step to providing guidance in a search for topographic maps is determining what might have been produced. Since national mapping programs may differ greatly, it cannot be assumed that Country C produces maps at the same scales as Country U or that all of Country I's maps will be available for purchase. Convincing, or showing, a potential map user that the product she or he wants for a particular place does not exist is always more difficult than determining that products are available. Fortunately, there are a few works that can assist in identifying product existence and gaps.

World Mapping Today (Parry and Perkins 2000) reviews the status of national mapping programs with an emphasis on single-sheet maps and topographic map sets, although other resources such as atlases may appear. Countries appear in alphabetical order within continent groupings, and entries provide basic descriptions of mapping agencies, a list of references including publishers' catalogs and websites, contact information for mapping organizations and publishers, a list of "currently" available publications, and a set of graphic indexes for map sets. Nearly 20 years after its publication, *World Mapping Today* remains useful because it documents the trajectory of mapping programs. Mapping programs rarely migrate, although their home organization may be renamed, so it is possible to discover which agencies are producing what kinds of maps using foundational information from *World Mapping Today*.

Maps for America (Thompson 1987), focusing on the cartographic publications of the USGS, informs about and illustrates map symbols, possible errors or anomalies that could impact map reading and interpretation, different kinds of maps and data, and sources for maps and data. The USGS has available online a full-text PDF of the first edition. The key chapters on map symbols and interpretation are essentially the same between editions so using an older edition online in lieu of the most recent, albeit also dated, third edition is completely acceptable.

U.S. Topographic Maps

The standard 1:24,000-scale (7.5-minute) topographic series was geographically completed, requiring 57,000 map sheets, for the conterminous United States in 1991. For decades, libraries in the United States received USGS-produced topographic maps of the United States through the Federal Depository Library Program (see Chapter 22). But this distribution ended in 2009 when the USGS ceased producing printed topographic maps. The paper topographic map collections housed in libraries, while still very valuable, should be considered a legacy collection and retained for their high historic value.

For current topographic mapping, users will need to access digital maps through the US Topo program, part of the *National Map*, a nationwide repository of integrated data from federal, state, and local sources. PDFs of topographic maps can be downloaded via *The USGS Store* website. The search is simple, revolving around zooming into a map of the United States to locate the area/topographic quadrangle desired, clicking on the quadrangle, and then following simple navigational instructions to download. The download will include multiple layers that can be turned on and off, making it possible to create maps that show exactly what the map user needs or wants. Superseded (analog) editions of maps can also be downloaded for free from *The USGS Store*. These older maps are not dynamic in that layers cannot be turned on and off; the image viewed appears exactly like the printed map that was scanned to create the image file. More than 255,000 topographic maps from 1884 to the present are available for download.

An alternative entry point into historical (pre-US Topo, pre-2006) USGS topographic maps is the *Historical Topographic Map Explorer*, a joint project of the USGS and Esri that came online in summer 2014. Searching involves typing in a place-name and then clicking on the resulting map to indicate the specific location desired. A timeline of maps that cover the selected location, color-coded by scale, will appear along the bottom of the screen. Clicking on a map title will cause it to become a layer on top of the base map. As with *The USGS Store*, PDFs can be downloaded for free. This interface allows users to zoom and pan and, most interestingly, change the opaqueness of map layers so that it is easy to "see through" a top map to one "below" and find differences. This is an invaluable tool for historians and anyone interested in landscape change as expressed through USGS topographic maps.

SPECIAL TYPES OF MAPS

In order to answer some questions, maps created for specific tasks or in an earlier era may need to be repurposed or viewed through a different contextual lens. This is an accepted and long-established practice. Users may need to be guided to materials that are suited to their needs.

Fire Insurance Maps

Questions about "my house, "my neighborhood," or "my town" are perpetual favorites. Requestors want to know about the age of their house, what was on a vacant lot in the next block, or where stores or recreational facilities were located. Family historians may have stacks of letters that they are using to build a picture of "the old neighborhood." Fire insurance maps, often called Sanborn fire insurance maps after the predominant producer, show building footprints, are color coded for construction material, and include information about the number of floors and building use (see Figure 20.4). Their original purpose was to assist in writing fire insurance policies, but they have been repurposed to support historical research. Generally they are available for cities in the United States from the 1870s through the middle of the 20th century.

Fire Insurance Maps in the Library of Congress (Library of Congress 1981) and *Union List of Sanborn & Other Fire Insurance Maps* (Hoehn 2012), both originally

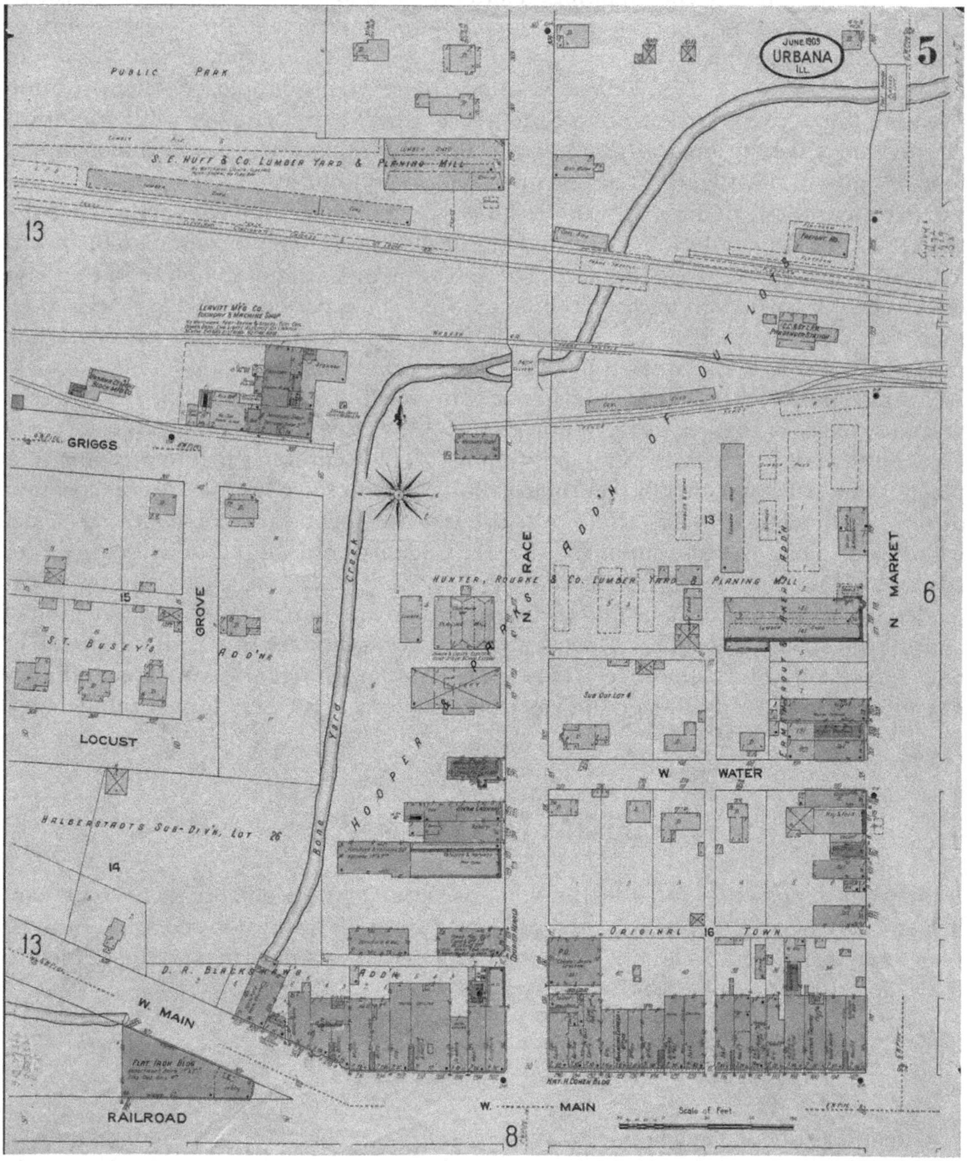

FIGURE 20.4 Urbana, 1909 Sanborn fire insurance map, sheet 5. Courtesy of the University of Illinois at Urbana-Champaign Map Library.

print titles but now available through the Web, help identify what maps are available and where they are. Copies of fire insurance maps were deposited at the Library of Congress as part of the copyright process. Between 1955 and 1978, the Library of Congress distributed duplicate copies to major libraries throughout the United States. *Fire Insurance Maps in the Library of Congress* is a checklist of the division's entire collection of 12,000 cities covered by more than 700,000 map sheets. The introductory text, including a list of libraries where duplicates were sent, contains an introduction to fire insurance maps and the Sanborn Map Company as well as a symbol key. More than 6,000 sheets have been scanned and are available through links from the division's online checklist.

Union List of Sanborn & Other Fire Insurance Maps lists fire insurance maps holdings at libraries other than the Library of Congress and California State University, Northridge, both of which have their own lists. This list is not a comprehensive, complete list of all fire insurance maps everywhere; its focus is on substantial collections. In its current Web-based version, which expands on the content of the original print, the *Union List* incorporates links to websites for scanned Sanborn maps and a bibliography. A caveat about the *Union List*: when it was compiled, the Bureau of the Census had an office in Jeffersonville, Indiana, with a large collection of Sanborn maps. Note that the *Union List* includes "Formerly" wherever this office is indicated as a holder; that is because the office was closed, and the maps were moved to a now unknown location.

Antiquarian Maps

Library users ask to see old (antiquarian) maps for a number of reasons, many of which are not at all geographical in nature. Early maps, specifically pre-mid-19th-century items, often are highly decorative or decorated. Zephyrs will occupy corners; whales, sea monsters, and sailing ships navigate the high seas; mythical kings sit on thrones in unexplored Africa and Asia. Sometimes the decoration is less fanciful and relates to the region mapped—the inside of a native American lodge house, baskets of crops and bundles of furs, residents in native dress, exotic (to the map maker) indigenous species. Old maps can be used to dress a play's set or to provide a background pattern for a website. They can be used to research or make a statement about (primarily European) knowledge of the rest of the world. Of course, old maps can be used for more "typical" geographical information tasks such as locating places, tracing name changes, and tracking boundary shifts.

A large number of glossy, color, coffee table–like books reprint assortments of antiquarian maps. These titles usually revolve around a specific region or time period and could be useful to have on hand to quickly show a possible antiquarian map user different forms or genres of antiquarian maps. Between these accessible works and the increasing number of images available online, there probably is little reason for a library that does not already have a collection of antiquarian maps to begin developing one.

The number of libraries making images of antiquarian maps available online has exploded in the past 10 years (see Table 20.2). Some libraries have collections that range widely through geography and history, while others focus on specific places and regions. Of course, each site works a bit differently from the others, and some sites require multiple steps and additional open windows to view images and download files. Depending on the needs of the reader, the images available online

TABLE 20.2 Sampling of Sites Containing Antiquarian Map Images

Site	Coverage	Download Options
Library of Congress http://www.loc.gov/maps	Worldwide coverage, emphasis on the United States, 1200–present	Direct download options of different file size and resolution
Office of Coast Survey, National Oceanic and Atmospheric Administration http://www.nauticalcharts.noaa.gov/	United States only, 1700s–present. nautical charts; Civil War maps; landform sketches	Direct download
New York Public Library http://www.nypl.org	Worldwide coverage, emphasis on New York City, 1700s–	Direct download options of different file types
Boston Public Library http://www.bpl.org/research/nblmapcenter.htm	Worldwide coverage, 1400s–present.	Direct download; printer friendly or full-size file
Stanford University Library http://library.stanford.edu/subjects/rare-maps	Four collections—California as an island; 1700s–1800s North and South America; Africa 1480s–1900; worldwide items from a dealer's listing 1400s to mid-20th century	Direct download of multiple-sized files and resolutions for North/South America and African collections only
American Geographical Society Library https://uwm.edu/libraries/agsl/	Worldwide coverage with emphasis on Wisconsin, 1400s–present	Direct download of low-resolution images
Osher Map Library http://www.oshermaps.org/	Worldwide coverage, 1400s–present	Direct download of low-resolution files
David Rumsey Map Collection http://www.davidrumsey.com/	Worldwide coverage, focus on 18th- and 19th-century North/South America	Direct download options of different file size and resolution

will either satisfy the need with no other steps necessary, will necessitate that the user download and manipulate or print the image, or will whet the user's appetite to see the original object.

Working with a specific need such as "I would like to see a map of the world produced by Homann Heirs" is quite a bit different from answering "I need a map with sea monsters." Producers and places will be indexed and can be searched;

non-geographical elements typically are not indexed or even noted in cataloging, necessitating visual scanning of images to identify those that will fill the stated need. It will be helpful when answering questions such as the latter to have a general sense of the progression of the history of cartography and the evolution of "scientific" maps that did not fill empty/unexplored/unknown areas with non-geographical graphics.

A large number of resources available will assist in building a knowledge foundation in the history of cartography. *The History of Cartography* Project at the University of Wisconsin–Madison is publishing, through the University of Chicago Press, a monumental, multivolume *The History of Cartography*. The volumes are organized by time period and region, and the deep and fulsome chapters are authored by an international panel of experts. This series is a touchstone in the field and a necessity if fielding a large number of questions on the history of cartography. The University of Chicago Press currently is making available online full text of the first three volumes at no cost.

For a gateway into Web-based resources focusing on the history of cartography, *Map History/History of Cartography* contains more than 100 Web pages of links to thousands of sites. The site is curated by Tony Campbell, a former map librarian at the British Library, and is regularly updated. The site includes lists of sites that contain images of maps as well as links to articles about all aspects of the history of cartography and interacting with antiquarian maps. The expanse of the site may feel daunting, but it is one of the most complete access points for history of cartography on the Web.

Many print options focus on the history of cartography, some scholarly and others for the interested lay reader. Bagrow's *History of Cartography* (1985) has long been central to the field because of its broad coverage, and the journal *Imago Mundi* focuses exclusively on the history of cartography through publication of articles, reviews, and bibliographies of recently published works.

AERIAL PHOTOGRAPHY AND REMOTELY SENSED IMAGERY

Aerial photography and satellite imagery are two kinds of remotely sensed images. Remote sensing is collecting data without touching the object being surveyed. Remote sensing of Earth uses cameras and electromagnetic sensors to collect data that are often processed and interpreted later in a location different than where the data were recorded. The equipment used to capture remote sensing data is mounted on a wide variety of platforms ranging from a human handheld camera to satellites orbiting Earth just outside of the atmosphere to probes sent through space by NASA. The data collected are along the portion of the electromagnetic spectrum that includes ultraviolet, visible light, and infrared radiation.

Since the 1930s, the United States, in particular the Department of Agriculture, has been instrumental in photographing the United States from the air. Photography was used to collect data for land use and land cover, to estimate crop production, and to identify areas of soil erosion. Technological advances from World War II, in particular the development of color infrared film, became available for civilian use. Early photography was in black and white, but color infrared (false color) and natural color photography have become available more recently. Federally driven aerial photography projects continue to predominate for the coverage of much of the nation. Federal photography produced during the past 50–60 years can be purchased through the Department of Agriculture's Aerial Photography Field Office. The cutoff date of availability at the Field Office is a rolling date. Photographs older than the cutoff are available through the National Archives and Records Administration (NARA), Cartographic and Architectural Records Division, and possibly at regional NARA facilities.

Finding collections and archives of aerial photographs can be tricky. A basic Web search for the name of a state along with "aerial photographs" or "aerial photography" could fill all needs for older photography. Some state universities such as the University of Minnesota, at *Minnesota Historical Aerial Photographs Online*, and Pennsylvania State University, through *Penn Pilot: Historical Aerial Photographs of Pennsylvania*, have scanned large collections and are making images available online. But search results may also be full of websites for companies that create aerial photography on demand/under contract. The chapter on noncommercial state and regional aerial photograph sources in *The Aerial Photo Sourcebook* (Collins 1998) will help focus the search for publicly accessible collections. Keep in mind that not all collections have been scanned and that there will be great variability in the kinds of assistance available to distant users.

A number of options are available for viewing and possibly downloading current or more recent imagery. *Google Earth* has imagery available generally from the early 1990s to the present. Zoom in sufficiently, and a small clock icon with a date will appear in the lower left corner (the icon also appears in the tool bar at the top of the image). Clicking on the clock causes a time slider bar to appear in the upper left corner making it possible to select different years of imagery for viewing. One advantage of *Google Earth's* display of images, unlike the reference image used in *Google Maps*, is that the date the image was collected appears at the bottom of the window. Images can be zoomed and panned until they are exactly what the user wants and then saved as a JPG.

The USGS's *EarthExplorer* allows searching and viewing, but a free user name and password must be created, working through a daunting form, to download high-resolution images as zip files; preview JPG images can be copied. The *EarthExplorer* interface is not exactly intuitive, but it does provide access to a wide variety of federal imagery products. Another entry point for federal remote sensing data is the *Earth Resources Observation and Science (EROS) Center*. Selecting the "Find Data" or "Remote Sensing" tabs on the Center's home page will take the reader to descriptions of remote sensing products and links for searching and downloading.

Many different aspects need to be considered in the context of each other when interpreting imagery: pattern, shadow, shape, site and association, size, texture, and tone and color. *Basic Photo Interpretation* (Rasher and Weaver 1990), distributed by the U.S. Department of Agriculture, Soil Conservation Service, may be helpful when thinking about these interpretation facets and about aerial photography as a possible resource. The text is accompanied by an extensive set of photographs and overlays providing an opportunity for experiential learning. Also consider seeking out any of the standard texts on aerial photography and remote sensing interpretation such as *Aerial Photography and Image Interpretation* (Paine and Kiser 2012) or *Fundamentals of Remote Sensing and Airphoto Interpretation* (Avery and Berlin 1992). Natural Resources Canada provides a very brief introduction and online overview of aerial photograph interpretation that includes sample photographs with different kinds of features identified. Additionally, some of the basics of image interpretation can be explored through the *Remote Sensing Core*

Curriculum website. This appears to be a work in progress because not all sections are fleshed out or contain content.

GEOGRAPHIC INFORMATION SYSTEMS

A GIS is a combination of hardware, software, data, people, and organizations that captures, stores, manages, retrieves, analyzes, and displays geospatial information. Data from multiple sources can be incorporated to answer queries. While the anticipated analysis response from a GIS is usually a map, it can also be a single number or a table. A GIS is often visualized as a stack of data layers, each with a unique theme, that are geographically aligned. Data in a GIS have geographical and attribute (or thematic or descriptive) components; attributes in different data tables have relationships to other attributes if they share a common spatial reference.

Because of the increase in questions being fielded by reference desks about GIS, librarians increasingly need a foundational knowledge base in geographical information science and geospatial data use and interpretation. There are a number of ways to begin becoming acquainted with the capabilities of GIS. MOOCs can provide both librarians and patrons a place for hands-on exploration of GIS capabilities in a guided manner. Esri, a vendor of GIS software, is another source of training.

Esri makes a *GIS Dictionary* available through its website. The definitions are short but sufficient and are illustrated as needed. Some of the definitions are specific to Esri software, but that should not preclude use of the dictionary for more general GIS-related needs. Concepts from GIS basics ("what is a base layer?") to map design and construction ("do you know what billboarding is?") along with image processing, hardware and programming concepts, spatial statistics, and more are all included. Having this website at hand will assist in making connections between assistance requestors and appropriate resources.

The suite of GIS products available from Esri, ArcGIS, is one of the most widely adopted GIS software platforms in the United States. Some other commercial packages to be aware of include MapInfo, TerrSet, and Smallworld. QGIS and GRASS are two free/open-source packages that have been widely adopted, and ERDAS IMAGINE is used for image manipulation.

Geospatial data for use in GIS have one of two different underlying data structures: raster, arranged in a grid with cells of equal size and shape, and vector, x/y location coordinates for points that sometimes may have relationships with other points to create lines and polygons. Attribute data that describe qualities of locations, such as dates, measurements, values, and names, are stored in data tables separate from the locations described in raster or vector data. Data come from many different sources. It might be "born digital," or it could be converted through scanning or digitization from paper. The United States Bureau of the Census is one of the United States' largest attribute (the decennial census) and location (TIGER/Line files) data producers. The bureau also makes available a simple *Census Data Mapper* Web-based utility to map, view, and print county-level demographic statistics (see Figure 20.5). A variety of small-scale, national-level data can be downloaded from the *National Map*. *Geoplatform.gov* acts as a geospatial data clearinghouse for data from federal agencies as well as from other levels of government and mapping communities. Many states have state-level geospatial data

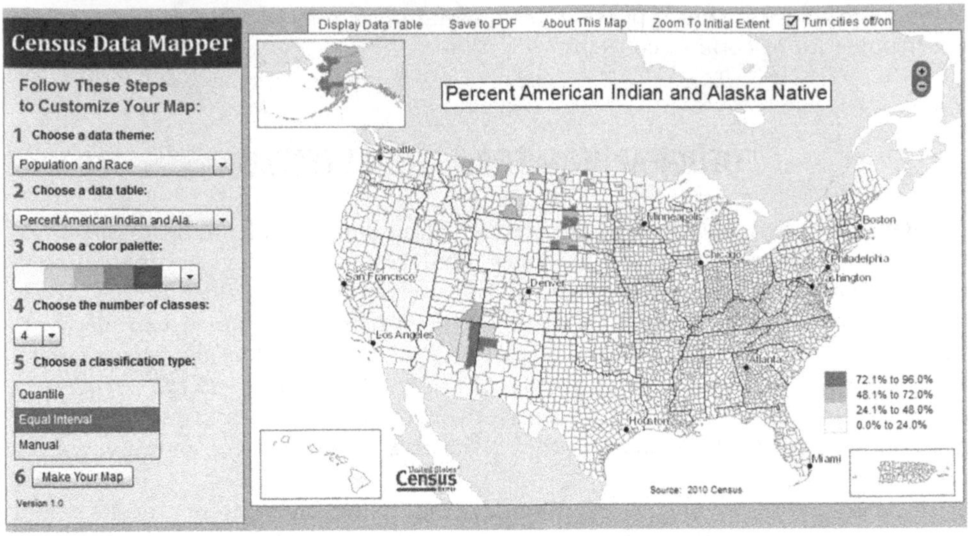

FIGURE 20.5 Census Data Mapper

clearinghouse websites for more state-specific or state-generated data. Additionally, counties, municipalities, colleges, and nonprofit organizations may have data that they are willing to share.

No single institution can be expected to own all of the data that its community of learners and researchers will want to investigate and use. Making connections is key to assisting those interested in using GIS in their work.

OTHER TYPES OF GEOGRAPHICAL SOURCES

In addition to maps, patrons with geographical questions may be seeking factual or descriptive information about countries or cultures. The following section discusses resources that can be used to answer these types of queries.

Countries and Cultures

The World Factbook, a free resource from the CIA, provides extensive factual information about 267 countries and entities as well as brief descriptions of their history and government. Factual information covers geography, people, government and international relations, economy, energy, transportation, and the military. Interactive tables allow users to select a data point and compare countries in alphabetical or ranked order. Simple maps, an image and description of the country's flag, and an audio clip of the national anthem supplement textual information. *The World Factbook* can be used to answer questions like "What is the voting age in Liberia?" and "How many airports are there in Brazil?"

The Europa World Year Book, available in print and online, provides country and regional profiles. Country profiles include an in-depth discussion of a country's history and economy, a chronology and historical events, a directory of government officials, and extensive statistical information in the areas of people, economy, industry, and natural resources. Regional profiles include maps, chronologies, statistics, a list of organizations active in the area, a discussion of history and economy, and essays on specialized topics. For example, the entry on sub-Saharan Africa includes an essay on China's involvement in the area. The online version of *The Europa World Year Book* provides updates on recent world events and an interactive tool for accessing comparative statistics.

The Statesman's Yearbook is another excellent choice for country information. Available in print and online, it provides extensive factual information on 194 countries plus states and dependencies. Entries cover topics such as government, economy, transportation, people, culture, and international relations. There are also chronologies and brief biographical profiles of past leaders. In the online version, the home page provides links to world chronologies, updates on recent events, and a comparison tool that can be used to compare two or more countries across a wide variety of data points.

Worldmark Encyclopedia of the Nations and *Worldmark Encyclopedia of Cultures and Daily Life*, discussed in Chapter 18, are excellent sources for descriptive information about countries and cultures. Both are appropriate for a high school through adult audience. General encyclopedias like *Encyclopaedia Britannica* are also a reliable source of information about countries and cultures.

For patrons seeking travel-specific information, the U.S. Department of State provides a website with information on travel to other countries. Country profiles include a list of embassies and consulates; entry, exit, and visa requirements; safety; local laws; healthcare; and in-country transportation. In addition, the website lists current Travel Alerts and Travel Warnings. Travel Alerts warn readers about political events, disease outbreaks, or other conditions that may affect travel in the country or region. Travel Warnings are more serious and caution travelers to reconsider visiting a country or area. Both Alerts and Warnings contain a description of the situation and safety tips.

Books and Periodicals

Patrons seeking a more in-depth discussion of a country, location, or geographical topic can also be directed to books and periodicals. Monographs with a geographical slant may be found throughout a library's collection. Librarians should consult their online catalog using appropriate keywords and subject headings.

Geographical journal articles are indexed by *GeoBase* (both human and physical) and *GeoRef* (physical) as well as indexes that are more specialized such as *America: History and Life*. *Current Geographical Publications*, which provides access to tables of contents of current geographical journals through links to publisher websites or PDFs of table-of-contents pages, is also available.

Resources for Children

Geographical resources for children provide maps as well as information about countries and cultures. As with other types of resources for children, geographical works for younger readers will be written at a lower reading level and heavily illustrated. In addition, resources may focus on high-interest topics for children such as daily life, dress and other customs, and education.

The *National Geographic Student World Atlas* is organized by continent; each section contains multiple maps, including political, climate, population, and elevation maps, and a special section on a geographical feature of the region such as Europe's waterways and the Amazon rainforest in South America. A prefatory section includes world maps on climate, vegetation, migration, languages, food, natural resources, and more. The *Student World Atlas* also has a section that teaches map reading skills and a table of countries with area, population, capital, languages, and an image of the flag. Another excellent choice for middle and high school students is the *DK Student Atlas*. For younger readers, the *Children's World Atlas* features regional maps with brief introductions and illustrations of daily life and notable geographical features.

Students, and their teachers, may also ask for a "printable" or "outline" map of a specific country or state. Printable maps are designed for printing on a standard printer and are often intended for quick reference by students, while outline maps are usually black-and-white maps of a country or continent, sometimes unlabeled, designed for use in the classroom and school projects. The *Perry-Castañeda Library Map Collection* links to numerous printable and outline maps.

Students may also ask for a historical map of a country or region. In this case, the student may not need a true antiquarian map, but rather one that shows the historical boundaries of a country, the expansion of an empire over time, or the routes of human migration. The *Atlas of World History* (O'Brien 2010) contains more than 450 maps organized by time period. Introductory essays to each section review the era's socioeconomic, cultural, and religious themes and give context to the maps. An extensive index includes alternate name forms to facilitate finding locales by both current and historical name. The *Perry-Castañeda Library Map Collection* also links to numerous historical maps.

For students seeking information about countries and cultures, ProQuest's *CultureGrams* provides a wealth of information about more than 200 countries and dependencies. The resource can be browsed by keyword or through a series of maps. Once the patron has selected a country of interest, encyclopedia-style entries cover history, government, land and climate, society, and customs and courtesies. An infographic describes the "average person" based on factors such as income and family size. Entries are written for a middle to high school audience. A *Kids* module, written at a level appropriate for an elementary school audience, provides shorter entries that focus on daily life and fun facts. *CultureGrams* also has additional modules that cover the U.S. states and Canadian provinces in detail.

Gale publishes the *Junior Worldmark Encyclopedia of the Nations* and *Junior Worldmark Encyclopedia of World Cultures*. Both follow the same format as the similarly titled volumes aimed at older students and adults, but are more heavily illustrated and written at a level appropriate for upper elementary and middle school students.

MAKING CONNECTIONS

Reference and access services for cartographic materials center on making connections between the reader and cartographic items that are appropriate to answer the reader's information needs. On the surface, this seems no different than any other kind of reference transaction, but the twist is that many map collections have very localized depths of coverage, holding materials that either are not available elsewhere or items that might possibly be elsewhere but cannot be located because of lack of cataloging and access mechanisms. Collections of contemporary 20th- and 21st-century maps generally have similar foundation materials, maps published by mainstream publishers and available from mainstream vendors. These usually are not the items that potential map users need extended assistance identifying and locating. The items sought are more specific and focused on particular spaces in specified times. Providing access and making connections to these materials rely greatly on the generosity of strangers, individuals, and organizations that are investing in cataloging cartographic materials through mainstream utilities such as OCLC (more than 4 million map format records as of May 2014) or scanning and making items in the public domain Web-available.

Guide to U.S. Map Resources (Thiry 2006) will assist in identifying collection specializations. Although nearly a decade old, basic institutional information will still be valid. Entries include lists of geographical and subject strengths, special collections, and ranges of chronological coverage as well as information on depository programs that the library participated in, size of collection, and how the collection is cataloged and accessed. *Guide to U.S. Map Resources* could simply be employed to find the largest map collections in a state. But the "Geographic/Subject/Special Collection Index" is of great value for identifying libraries to contact for specific needs. For instance, under the heading "Northwest Territory," three libraries are listed that self-identified as holding substantial collections for the region, giving a quick starting point for finding maps of the upper Midwest in the 18th century.

The Western Association of Map Libraries (WAML) and the Association of Canadian Map Libraries and Archives (ACMLA) both maintain a list of map libraries in their principal membership regions. There are a number of organizations in North America that can either assist in answering geographical and cartographic queries or refer librarians to local specialists:

- Association of American Geographers (AAG)—More than 10,000 members with shared interests in the theory, methods, and practice of geography, 60 specialty groups with specific focus.
- Association of Canadian Map Libraries and Archives (ACMLA)—Professional group for Canadian map librarians, cartographic archivists, and others interested in geographical information in all formats.
- American Geographical Society (AGS)—Advances and promotes geography in business, government, science, and education; enhancing geographical literacy.
- Map and Geospatial Information Round Table (MAGIRT) of the American Library Association—Leads and inspires information professionals at all levels of expertise in their work with map and geospatial information resources, collections and technology in all formats, through community, education, and advocacy.
- North American Cartographic Information Society (NACIS)—Specialists from private, academic, and government organizations along with people whose common interest lies in facilitating communication in the map information community.
- Western Association of Map Libraries (WAML)—Map librarians and others with an interest in maps and map librarianship encouraging high standards in every phase of the organization and administration of map libraries.

Journals and newsletters from these organizations include reviews and lists of new publications. The AAG has a Web page specifically devoted to listing new publications received by its book review editors, and MAGIRT's *base line* includes an extensive list and reviews of new publications as well as cartographically focused Web resources in nearly every issue.

CARTOGRAPHIC MATERIALS CITATIONS

Cartographic materials usage is expanding to many disciplines well beyond expected earth and social sciences users, as many humanities fields, and traditionally less-spatially oriented social sciences, experience a "spatial turn" in the questions that are being posed and answered. Thus, this expansion of use is being experienced by individuals who are not practiced in identifying elements that will best describe or are necessary to describe cartographic materials. To many users, it may seem that creating an appropriate citation describing a stand-alone map, a map from an atlas, an aerial photograph, or a geographical data website will be difficult because maps look so different from "normal" research materials. Additionally, standard citation guides do not include a chapter or suggestions on citing these kinds of materials.

This critical gap in cartographic materials use is filled by *Cartographic Citations: A Style Guide* (Kollen, Shawa, and Larsgaard 2010). Although slender, this essential guide is packed with foundation forms that can be easily adjusted to fit standard citation styles and many real examples of how the forms can be applied to describe a wide variety of cartographic information resources. The citation forms include those for manuscript maps, printed maps from a variety of sources, atlases, 3-D models, remotely sensed images including both aerial photography and satellite images, and computer files including satellite images, software, geospatial data, and websites. The "Explanation of map citation elements" and glossary will assist in selecting information and guide in its transcription.

Cartographic materials citation guides are also appearing as part of library websites; many are based on *Cartographic Citations*. All display a standard template and show a limited number, often only one, of examples. *Maps and Atlases: Citing Maps* from the North Carolina State University Libraries is an easily navigated distillation of *Cartographic Citations*. Western Washington University Library's *Citing Maps* LibGuide includes examples that follow both the MLA and APA formats. Brock University Map, Data & GIS Library's *How to Reference Geospatial Data, Maps, Atlases, Air Photos* places emphasis on Web-based and digital resources.

CONCLUSION

The user experience of cartographic/geographical information resources users has changed greatly in the past 20 years. Web-based resources have seemingly taken away the necessity of a visit to the library. Yet at the same time, this treasure trove of riches may entice users to journey to a specialized collection because their curiosity or need has been whetted by seeing a low-resolution JPG. Regardless of what is available at hand in a reference collection or through the Web, answers to many questions still must rely on making personal connections between researchers and curators. Geographical information resources have always been clustered with concentrations of materials on specific areas located in or near those areas or in proximity to individuals or programs that specialize in specific areas. What is new is that searchers may be coming to cartographic resource collections with greater knowledge or higher expectations because of what they have been able to locate and preview through the Web. As acculturated by the Web and distributed information resources, researchers are also increasingly independent and willing to move forward in their search on their own once they have been shown the next steps in their research journey.

Box 20.1 Search Strategy: Chisholm and a *Field of Dreams*

A library user comes to the desk curious about Chisholm, Minnesota. He had read *Shoeless Joe* by W. P. Kinsella and recently saw the movie *Field of Dreams* and noted in the credits that filming had not been done in Chisholm but rather in Galena, Illinois. He would like to see maps and photographs of Chisholm between 1909 and 1965, the time period that Doc "Moonlight" Graham lived and practiced medicine in Chisholm. The user has looked at *Google Maps* and knows where Chisholm is located but does not know where to go next for more detailed or period appropriate maps.

The librarian may want to revisit *Google Maps* to check where Chisholm is located. Knowing this in advance might smooth the path through other resources. Another quick check is to simply Google "Chisholm Minnesota map." Unfortunately, no old maps appear in the results, but keep this kind of search in mind because it may point to other possible resources.

Remembering that many times map reference work relies on the kindness of others, checking *WorldCat* for maps of Chisholm could be a good first step. Doing a subject search for "Chisholm Minn" limited to the maps format results in slightly fewer than 20 matches. Most postdate 1965, but a few fall into the desired time period. The patron could be referred to the University of Minnesota-Twin Cities, University of Wisconsin-Milwaukee, and the Library of Congress Geography and Map Division. The University of Minnesota-Twin Cities could be especially fruitful because it is the largest map collection in the state. Many map collections are incompletely cataloged, so it is worth taking the time to call or e-mail to inquire about other possible holdings.

Chisholm is located on the Iron Range in St. Louis County, in northeast Minnesota; the largest nearby city and county seat is Duluth. A branch of the University of Minnesota is also located in Duluth. Searching the Web for the St. Louis County Historical Society, its archives are housed at the Kathryn A. Martin Library (KAML) Archives and Special Collections of the University of Minnesota-Duluth Library as part of the Northeast Minnesota Historical Center Collections. The LibGuides created by KAML include links to other possible information resources including the Iron Range Research Center and the Minnesota Historical Society (MHS).

The Iron Range Research Center is located in Chisholm. Maps are included in the Center's Archival Collections, and some are available for viewing online including a plat map originally created in 1938 and revised in 1953.

The online *Union List of Sanborn and Other Fire Insurance Maps* indicates that the MHS holds Sanborn fire insurance maps of Chisholm from 1904, 1909, 1912, 1921, and 1928. The MHS has not scanned its Sanborn holdings; they are not available for viewing online. According to the MHS LibGuide about maps, it has more than 19,000 maps and 2,000 atlases for Minnesota, making it quite likely that maps of Chisholm might be available either as separate items or as part of an atlas's contents.

This sizable focused collection in combination with the collection of Sanborn maps makes contacting MHS an essential step.

Although perhaps they do not display the level of detail the patron might want, the USGS *Historical Topographic Map Explorer* should be considered an important resource, especially for examining a time sequence. Iron ore extraction, primarily through open-pit mining, has changed the landforms in the area surrounding Chisholm. Topographic maps show the expansion of the named mines and changes in roads that enter Chisholm. Additionally, the topographic maps show locations of landmark buildings within Chisholm including Lincoln, Roosevelt, and Washington elementary schools, the junior and senior high schools, the post office, water tower, and churches.

The requestor now has a number of options of places to contact to inquire about maps: University of Minnesota-Twin Cities, University of Minnesota-Duluth, Iron Range Research Center, Minnesota Historical Society. But he also asked about photographs.

What is meant by "photographs" could be subject to interpretation and should be clarified; aerial photographs (vertical) or building facades and streetscapes (oblique)? Searching the Web for "Minnesota air photos," the best option presented is Minnesota Historical Aerial Photographs Online (MHAPO) from the John R. Borchert Map Library at the University of Minnesota. MHAPO supports searches for locations by place-name and displays the center points of aerial photographs color-coded by decade of flight. The center points are clickable to display JPEG images. Within the time period requested, photographs flown in 1939, 1948, and 1961 are available. As with the historical topographic maps, historical aerial photographs are an essential resource for exploring chronological change.

Finally, consider that the patron might be interested in photographs of building facades and streetscapes in Chisholm. The fastest way, although not the most reliable, to begin to find photographs might be to do a simple *Google* search. Make sure to include the word "Minnesota" or else the search might result in photographs of Shirley Chisholm or the Chisholm Trail (the cattle trail from Kansas to Texas). The Minnesota Historical Society has collections of images that can be viewed online. The Iron Range Research Center and University of Minnesota-Duluth also have images online but very few of the city of Chisholm. The Research Center's scanned photos are primarily of mines, and the university's photos are retrieved because the index term "Chisholm" refers to either Archibald Mark Chisholm, one of the founders of Chisholm who later moved to Duluth, or the A. M. Chisholm Children's Hospital. Although few photographs of the City of Chisholm appear online, it would be worthwhile for the patron to inquire about materials currently not available through the Web.

At the end of all of this searching, hopefully interactively with the requestor, there is a bouquet of possibilities for the baseball movie fan to follow up on. He has seen, on screen, images of mid-20th-century aerial photographs and perhaps a few maps, and he has a number of other options depending on his interest, needs, and time constraints. He should be encouraged to contact all of the possible collections because often special collections materials are not completely cataloged.

To the reference librarian, this interaction may be oddly dissatisfying or disquieting. Was the question truly answered? Given the resources available through the Web, it *was* better answered than it might have been 20–25 years ago. Then librarians were really only able to use directories of collections and institutions to find contact information to give to their patrons or perhaps use themselves. Now, depending on the resources available to organizations with collections, library patrons might have an opportunity to get a taste of a collection's contents or even to digitally preview the needed items before visiting or sending an e-mail to inquire about purchasing a copy.

Box 20.2 Search Strategy: Hama, Syria, on Antiquarian Maps

A nonaffiliate patron sends the reference desk an e-mail indicating that he would like to see Hama, Syria, on an old map. There's no other information. How old is old? When asked via return e-mail, the patron indicates that he might be interested in multiple maps and that old is just that, old.

If the collection does not include a large number of antiquarian, or facsimile, maps of the Middle East, the way to tackle this might be through some of the websites created by collections that do have sizable holdings of antiquarian maps and atlases.

First, though, verify the location of Hama, Syria. *Google Maps* works fine for this. Hama is located north of Homs and a bit southeast of the island of Crete (but not on the coast, inland). Knowing where other landmasses and features are relative to where you are looking can be helpful. When looking at *Google Maps*, notice that Hama is spelled Hamah. This small discrepancy from how the patron spelled it, plus knowing that names can change through time, should spur the searcher on to a quick look at the *Wikipedia* article for Hama. Scrolling through, note the number of different names including Hamath, Amatuwana, Amat, Hamata, Epiphania, Emath, Emathous. Additionally, Hama is located on the left bank of the Orontes River. Background reading completed, it is time to look at some maps.

A good first stop might be the Library of Congress. "Syria" would be a good first search. Most of the 20 maps resulting seem to be 20th-century U.S. federal government publications. But one, from 1900 of the Euphrates Valley, does include the name Hamah, although in a very unsatisfying way because the name is split by a gap between map panels. An important thing to remember about working with geographical places and regions is that every place is part of another, often larger, region. Try expanding the search to Middle East. Check the facets at the left side of the results page; at the Library of Congress, searching Middle East can produce some surprising results because of the keyword nature of the search. There are 43 maps created between 1600 and 1899 of the Middle East in the digital collection. Sort the results by date and visually spot-check looking for Hama or one of the other names.

A similar approach can be used at other sites. The Boston Public Library has a clickable alphabetical list of locations with five maps of Syria, 1482–1783, and 12 maps of the Middle East predating 1900 (some of which also appear in the Syria results). At the David Rumsey site, there are an overwhelming number of results when searching for Syria. Some of them will not fit the need because they point toward maps of Palestine, which do not extend far enough north.

The patron is e-mailed the information about where an assortment of maps that might fit his needs can be found. Included are some suggestions about searching as well as tips about different names and looking along the Orontes River and an invitation to the patron to e-mail again if he has other questions, thus leaving the door open for further contact. Sadly, as in most asynchronous e-mail-based interactions, the patron never communicates about his success with any of the websites.

On the surface, this question does not seem all that tricky—find a map, look for a name. But the difficulty can be knowing when to stop. How much specific guidance should a remote user be given, especially if the materials referred to are not in the collection but are miles away and belong to somebody else? How much time should be taken? How should follow up be handled? There is no good rule of thumb. Each librarian, through experience and by the examples of others, will develop his or her personal sense of how much is enough.

REFERENCES

Seager, Joni. 2015. "'Mapping' Primary and Secondary Sources." *TeachingHistory.org*. Accessed October 1. http://teachinghistory.org/history-content/ask-a-historian/25244.

Warf, Barney, and Santa Arias, eds. 2009. *The Spatial Turn: Interdisciplinary Perspectives*. New York: Routledge.

LIST OF SOURCES

America: History and Life. Ipswich, MA: EBSCO. https://www.ebscohost.com/academic/america-history-and-life. [subscription required]

American Automobile Association. http://www.aaa.com.

American Geographical Society. https://www.amergeog.org/.

American Geographical Society Library. https://uwm.edu/libraries/agsl/.

Aerial Photography. Department of Agriculture. http://www.fsa.usda.gov/programs-and-services/aerial-photography/index.

ArcGIS. http://www.arcgis.com.

Association of American Geographers. http://www.aag.org/.

Association of Canadian Map Libraries and Archives. http://www.acmla-acacc.ca.

Association of Canadian Map Libraries and Archives. 2014. "Canadian Map Libraries & Archives." http://www.acmla-acacc.ca/institutions.php.

Avery, Thomas E., and Graydon L. Berlin. 1992. *Fundamentals of Remote Sensing and Airphoto Interpretation*, 5th ed. New York: Macmillan.

Bagrow, Leo. 1985. *History of Cartography*, 2nd ed., revised and enlarged by R.A. Skelton. Chicago: Precedent.

Benchmark Maps. http://www.benchmarkmaps.com/.

Boston Public Library. "Norman B. Leventhal Map Center." http://www.bpl.org/research/nblmapcenter.htm.

Brock University Map, Data, GIS Library. 2015. *How to Reference Geospatial Data, Maps, Atlases, Air Photos*. Accessed October 1. http://www.brocku.ca/maplibrary/guides/How-to-Reference.pdf.

Census Data Mapper. Bureau of the Census. https://www.census.gov/geo/maps-data/maps/datamapper.html.

Children's World Atlas. 2011. Rev. ed. New York: Dorling Kindersley. Available online as part of *Gale Virtual Reference Library*.

Citing Maps. Western Washington University. http://libguides.wwu.edu/c.php?g=308303&p=2063297.

Cohen, Chester G. 1980. *Shtetl Finder: Jewish Communities in the 19th and Early 20th Centuries in the Pale of Settlement of Russia and Poland, and in Lithuania, Latvia, Galicia, and Bukovina, with Names of Residents*. Los Angeles: Periday.

Collins, Mary Rose. 1998. *The Aerial Photo Sourcebook*. Lanham, MD: Scarecrow Press.

CultureGrams. Ann Arbor, MI: ProQuest. http://www.proquestk12.com/productinfo/culturegrams.shtml. [subscription required]

Current Geographical Publications. University of Wisconsin-Milwaukee Libraries. http://guides.library.uwm.edu/c.php?g=56532.

David Rumsey Map Collection. http://www.davidrumsey.com.

DeLorme. http://www.delorme.com/.

Dent, Bordon D. 2009. *Cartography: Thematic Map Design*, 6th ed. New York: McGraw-Hill Higher Education.

DK Student Atlas. 2015. 8th ed. New York: Dorling Kindersley.

Earth Resources Observation and Science (EROS) Center. United States Geological Survey. http://eros.usgs.gov/.

EarthExplorer. United States Geological Survey. http://earthexplorer.usgs.gov/.

Encyclopaedia Britannica. http://www.britannica.com/.

ERDAS IMAGINE. http://www.hexagongeospatial.com/products/producer-suite/erdas-imagine.

Esri. http://www.esri.com/.

The Europa World Year Book. 1926–. 2 vols. London: Routledge. Annual. Available online as *Europa World Plus*: http://www.europaworld.com/pub/. [subscription required]

Gale Virtual Reference Library. Farmington Hills, MI: Gale Cengage Learning. http://www.cengage.com. [subscription required]

GeoBase. Atlanta: Elsevier. https://www.elsevier.com/solutions/engineering-village/content/geobase. [subscription required]

Geographic Names Information System (GNIS). United States Board on Geographic Names. http://geonames.usgs.gov/domestic/index.html.

GEOnet Names Server (GNS). United States Board on Geographic Names. http://geonames.nga.mil/gns/html/.

GeoPlatform.gov. Federal Geographic Data Committee. https://geoplatform.gov/.

GeoRef. Alexandria, VA: American Geosciences Institute. http://www.americangeosciences.org/georef/georef-information-services. [subscription required]

Gerlach, Arch C., ed. 1970. *National Atlas of the United States*. Washington, DC: Department of the Interior, Geological Survey. http://memory.loc.gov/ammem/gmd html/census3.html.

GIS Dictionary. Esri. http://support.esri.com/en/knowledgebase/Gisdictionary/browse.

Google Earth. http://www.google.com/earth/.

Google Maps. http://www.maps.google.com/.

GRASS. https://grass.osgeo.org/.

Guia Roji. http://www.guiaroji.com.mx/.

Historical Topographic Map Explorer. United States Geological Survey and Esri. http://historicalmaps.arcgis.com/usgs/.

The History of Cartography. University of Chicago Press. http://www.press.uchicago.edu/books/HOC/index.html.

The History of Cartography Project. University of Wisconsin-Madison. http://www.geography.wisc.edu/histcart/.

Hoehn, Philip. 2012. *Union List of Sanborn & Other Fire Insurance Maps*. University of California Berkeley. http://lib.berkeley.edu/EART/sanborn_union_list.

Imago Mundi. 1935–. New York: Taylor & Francis. Biannual.

Iron Range Research Center. Minnesota Discovery Center. http://www.mndiscoverycenter.com/research-center/.

JewishGen Communities Database. JewishGen. http://www.jewishgen.org/Communities/Search.asp.

JewishGen Gazetteer. JewishGen. http://www.jewishgen.org/Communities/LocTown.asp.

Junior Worldmark Encyclopedia of the Nations. 2012. 6th ed. 10 vols. Farmington Hills, MI: Gale Cengage Learning. Available online as part of *Gale Virtual Reference Library*.

Junior Worldmark Encyclopedia of World Cultures. 2012. 2nd ed. 9 vols. Farmington Hills, MI: Gale Cengage Learning. Available online as part of *Gale Virtual Reference Library*.

Kathryn A. Martin Library Archives and Special Collections. University of Minnesota Duluth. http://www.d.umn.edu/lib/archives/archives-special-collections.htm.

Kimerling, A. Jon. 2012. *Map Use: Reading, Analysis, Interpretation*, 7th ed. Redlands, CA: Esri Press.

Kister, Kenneth F. 1984. *Kister's Atlas Buying Guide*. Phoenix: Oryx.

Kollen, Christine, Wangyal Shawa, and Mary Larsgaard. 2010. *Cartographic Citations: A Style Guide*, 2nd ed. Chicago: Map and Geography Round Table, American Library Association.

Library of Congress. 1981. *Fire Insurance Maps in the Library of Congress: Plans of North American Cities and Towns Produced by the Sanborn Map Company: A Checklist.* Washington, DC: Library of Congress.

Library of Congress. Geography and Map Division. http://www.loc.gov/rr/geogmap/.

Map and Geospatial Information Round Table. American Library Association. http://www.ala.org/magirt/front.

Map and Geospatial Information Roundtable. *base line*. 1980–. American Library Association. http://www.ala.org/magirt/publications/baseline. Annual.

Map History/History of Cartography. 2015. http://www.maphistory.info/.

Map Studio. http://www.mapstudio.co.za/.

MapArt Publishing. http://www.mapartmaps.com/.

MapInfo. http://www.pitneybowes.com/us/location-intelligence/geographic-information-systems/mapinfo-pro.html.

Maps and Atlases: Citing Maps. North Carolina State University Libraries. http://www.lib.ncsu.edu/maps/citingmaps.html.

Maps of CIA. Central Intelligence Agency. https://www.cia.gov/library/publications/resources/cia-maps-publications.

Michelin. http://travel.michelin.com/.

Minnesota Historical Aerial Photographs Online. University of Minnesota Libraries. https://www.lib.umn.edu/apps/mhapo/.

Mokotoff, Gary, and Sallyann Amdur Sack. 1991. *Where Once We Walked: A Guide to the Jewish Communities Destroyed in the Holocaust.* Teaneck, NJ: Avotaynu.

Monmonier, Mark. 1993. *Mapping It Out: Expository Cartography for the Humanities and Social Sciences*. Chicago: University of Chicago Press.

National Archives and Records Administration. http://www.archives.gov/.

National Atlas of Japan. 1990. 2nd ed. Tokyo: Geographical Survey Institute.

National Atlas of Sri Lanka. 2007. Colombo: Survey Department, Sri Lanka.

National Geographic Atlas of the World. 2014. 10th ed. Washington, DC: National Geographic Society.

National Geographic Student World Atlas. 2014. 4th ed. Washington, DC: National Geographic Society.

National Map. United States Geological Survey. http://nationalmap.gov.

Natural Resources Canada. "About Aerial Photography." http://www.nrcan.gc.ca/earth-sciences/geomatics/satellite-imagery-air-photos/air-photos/9681.

New York Public Library. http://www.nypl.org.

North American Cartographic Information Society. http://www.nacis.org.

O'Brien, Patrick, ed. 2010. *Atlas of World History*, 2nd ed. Oxford: Oxford University Press.

Office of Coast Survey, National Oceanic and Atmospheric Administration. http://www.nauticalcharts.noaa.gov/.

Online Maps and Photos. University of Wisconsin-Milwaukee Libraries. http://uwm.edu/libraries/agsl/online-maps-photos/.

Osher Map Library. http://www.oshermaps.org/.

Paine, David P., and James D. Kiser. 2012. *Aerial Photography and Image Interpretation*, 3rd ed. Hoboken, NJ: Wiley.

Parry, Robert B., and C.R. Perkins. 2000. *World Mapping Today*, 2nd ed. London: Bowker-Saur.

Penn Pilot: Historical Aerial Photographs of Pennsylvania. Pennsylvania Geological Survey and Pennsylvania State University. http://www.pennpilot.psu.edu/.

Perry-Castañeda Library Map Collection. University of Texas at Austin Libraries. http://www.lib.utexas.edu/maps/.

QGIS. http://www.qgis.com.

Rand McNally. http://www.randmcnally.com/.

Rasher, Michael, and Wayne Weaver. 1990. *Basic Photo Interpretation: A Comprehensive Approach to Interpretation of Vertical Aerial Photography for Natural Resource Applications.* Washington, DC: Department of Agriculture.

Remote Sensing Core Curriculum. http://www.r-s-c-c.org/.

Robinson, Arthur. 1995. *Elements of Cartography*, 6th ed. New York: Wiley.

Sanborn Fire Insurance Maps. California State University Northridge. http://www.csun.edu/geography-map-library/sanborn-fire-insurance-atlas-collection.

Sanborn Fire Insurance Maps. Library of Congress. http://www.loc.gov/rr/geogmap/sanborn/.

Slocum, Terry A. 2009. *Thematic Cartography and Geovisualization*, 3rd ed. Upper Saddle River, NJ: Pearson Prentice Hall.

Smallworld. http://www.gedigitalenergy.com/geospatial/catalog/smallworld_network.htm#sa6.

Snyder, John, and Philip M. Voxland. 1989. *An Album of Map Projections.* US Geological Survey Professional Paper 1453. Washington, DC: Government Printing Office. http://pubs.usgs.gov/pp/1453/report.pdf.

Spatial Humanities. University of Virginia Library. http://spatial.scholarslab.org/.

St. Louis County Historical Society. http://www.thehistorypeople.org/default.asp.

Stanford University Library. http://library.stanford.edu/subjects/rare-maps.

Teaching with Google Earth. 2014. Pedagogy in Action: The SERC Portal for Educators. Carleton College. http://serc.carleton.edu/sp/library/google_earth/index.html.

TerrSet. https://clarklabs.org/.

Thiry, Christopher J.J., ed. 2006. *Guide to U.S. Map Resources*, 3rd ed. Lanham, MD: Scarecrow Press.

Thompson, Morris M. 1979. *Maps for America: Cartographic Products of the U.S. Geological Survey and Others.* United States Geological Survey. http://pubs.er.usgs.gov/publication/70045412.

Thompson, Morris M. 1987. *Maps for America: Cartographic Products of the U.S. Geological Survey and Others*, 3rd ed. Reston, VA: Geological Survey.

TIGER Products. Bureau of the Census. https://www.census.gov/geo/maps-data/data/tiger.html.

The Times Comprehensive Atlas of the World. 2014. 14th ed. London: Times Books.

Travel. Department of State. http://www.state.gov/travel/.

Turner, Barry, ed. *The Statesman's Yearbook.* 1864–. Basingstroke, Hampshire: Palgrave Macmillan. Annual. Available online: http://www.statesmansyearbook.com/public/. [subscription required]

United States Board on Geographic Names. *Official Standard Names Gazetteers.* Publisher varies, 1955–1978.

The USGS Store. United States Geological Survey. https://store.usgs.gov.

Veregin, Howard, ed. 2010. *Goode's World Atlas*, 22nd ed. Skokie, IL: Rand McNally.

Wastenson, Leif, Gudrun Lindberg, and Måns Rosén. 2000. *National Atlas of Sweden.* Uppsala, Sweden: National Atlas of Sweden.

Western Association of Map Libraries. http://www.waml.org.

Western Association of Map Libraries. "Principal Region Map Collections." http://www.waml.org/maplibs.html.

Wisconsin State Cartographer's Office. "Public Land Survey System." http://www.sco.wisc.edu/plss/public-land-survey-system.html.

The World Factbook. Central Intelligence Agency. https://www.cia.gov/library/publications/the-world-factbook/.

Worldmark Encyclopedia of Cultures and Daily Life. 2009. 2nd ed. 5 vols. Farmington Hills, MI: Gale Cengage Learning. Available online as part of *Gale Virtual Reference Library*.

Worldmark Encyclopedia of the Nations. 2007. 12th ed. 5 vols. Farmington Hills, MI: Gale Cengage Learning. Available online as part of *Gale Virtual Reference Library*.

SUGGESTED READINGS

Dodsworth, Eva. 2012. *Getting Started with GIS: A LITA Guide*. LITA Guides 18. New York: Neal-Schuman.

Intended to be a training package for library staff, this book provides an introduction to GIS and online mapping applications, including examples, tutorials, a glossary, and chapter bibliographies. There is also a companion website.

Ehrenberg, Ralph E. 2006. *Mapping the World: An Illustrated History of Cartography*. Washington, DC: National Geographic.

Ehrenberg's book is an example of the many highly illustrated compilations and anthologies of historical maps available. This title is notable because it was compiled and written by a former chief of the Geography and Map Division of the Library of Congress, and many of the maps included come from the division's collections.

Farrell, Barbara, and Aileen Desbarts. 1984. *Guide for a Small Map Collection*, 2nd ed. Ottawa: Association of Canadian Map Libraries.

This slender volume gives straightforward advice on working in all aspects of map librarianship. Because of its age, there are no pages devoted to GIS or accessing geospatial data, and some of the library-related technologies are dated. But, at its core, this title presents foundational information on caring for and accessing cartographic collections still relevant 30 years after publication.

Johnson, Jenny Marie. 2003. *Geographic Information: How to Find It, How to Use It*. Westport, CT: Greenwood.

This volume provides descriptions and usage guidance for a wide range of geographical information resources including maps, atlases, remotely sensed images, aerial photograph, gazetteers, GIS, and general reference sources.

Kerski, Joseph J., and Jill Clark. 2012. *The GIS Guide to Public Domain Data*. Redlands, CA: Esri.

Kerski and Clark's book is an aid to finding, acquiring, and using public domain geospatial data with practical advice for solving problems and evaluating data and data sources. An accompanying website, http://spatialreserves.wordpress.com, expands on the book's contents with blog-post discussions of current geospatial data situations.

Larsgaard, Mary Lynette. 1998. *Map Librarianship: An Introduction*, 3rd ed. Englewood, CO: Libraries Unlimited.

Larsgaard offers a comprehensive and heavily documented overview of all aspects of cartographic materials librarianship. This seminal text includes chapters on acquisitions, classification, cataloging, physical care, reference services, public relations, and education.

Monmonier, Mark. 1996. *How to Lie with Maps*, 2nd ed. Chicago: University of Chicago Press.

This book, containing brief, quickly read chapters, will serve as a reminder that data must be manipulated to create maps and that not all manipulations are easy to identify or on the level. It will assist the reader in developing both map reading and critical map assessment skills with explanations of map fundamentals and the "lies" necessary to create maps.

Tyner, Judith A. 2015. *The World of Maps: Map Reading and Interpretation for the 21st Century*. New York: Guilford.

Concise, readable explanations presented by a master cartographic educator make this title amenable to either a quick dip to answer a specific question or an extended chapter-length read. Technical topics are covered in a nontechnical manner without losing core content or context.

Chapter 21

Biographical and Genealogical Sources

Jeanne Holba Puacz

USES AND CHARACTERISTICS

From investigating potential corporate board members to learning about presidents for school reports, from exploring personal genealogical relationships to researching figures for dissertations, biographical questions abound at the reference desk. At all types of libraries and for all sorts of reasons, users ask questions about the lives of others. While the questions may focus on the lives of local personages or family members, they will more commonly focus on the lives of the famous and the infamous.

In order to best determine what sources are most appropriate and most helpful for the users of a particular library, it is necessary to evaluate both the sources available and the needs of the users. Source evaluation and selection should encompass such considerations as scope, accuracy, currency, format, and cost. The types of questions commonly received, the depth of response generally required, and the age and educational level of the average user are often included in an evaluation of user needs.

In addition to classic biographical sources such as *Current Biography*, the *Who's Who* titles, and *Encyclopedia of World Biography*, a number of excellent electronic sources have evolved, which greatly reduce the time required for many biographical searches. Sources such as *Biography in Context*, *Biography Reference Bank*, and *Biography Reference Center* allow simultaneous searching of numerous biographical sources, and many of the results are available in full text. These sources allow cumulative access to and searching of multiple editions, titles, and series.

Box 21.1 Sources of Interest in Biography

> Man's sociality of nature evinces itself . . . [in] the unspeakable delight he takes in Biography.
>
> —Thomas Carlyle
> (Carlyle 1876, 27)

> For one who reads, there is no limit to the number of lives that may be lived, for fiction, biography, and history offer an inexhaustible number of lives in many parts of the world, in all periods of time.
>
> —Louis L'Amour
> (L'Amour 1989, 21)

When pursuing biographical information, search strategy will be affected by a number of factors. How much information is needed, how quickly it is needed, and by whom it is needed must all be considered. The number and type of sources consulted for an elementary student will, obviously, be more limited than the sources consulted for a graduate student. The subject of the biographical search and what is already known about the subject will also impact the search process. Information concerning a well-known historic figure is often readily available, even if the user is unsure about the spelling of the name, the time period, or the subject area in which the biographee was most influential. Unfortunately, searches for information pertaining to lesser-known individuals can be significantly hampered by such a lack of knowledge.

Although it is true that, as William Katz has said, "answering reference questions may involve the resources of the whole library, and, for that matter, libraries and collections elsewhere" (Katz 2002, 2), there are a number of standard sources with which any student of reference should become familiar. In addition to the classic biographical sources, standard encyclopedia and indexing sources can be extremely useful when pursuing information about people. Many specialized biographical sources exist, so many that it is impossible to know all of them. Therefore, numerous excellent guides to biographical sources have been produced to assist librarians in locating specialized sources to meet the needs of their users. Primary sources, such as vital records, city directories, and census data may be necessary for some types of questions. However, because this goes beyond reference to research, it is important for the reference librarian to know when to direct users to this type of source and where to direct them so that they can obtain the documents they need.

Although a number of biographical sources may be considered universal, in that they include persons regardless of their nationality, their subject of interest, or whether they are living or dead, many sources consulted in biographical research are subdivided into a variety of categories. These subdivisions can be classified by the type of information the source provides, the type of persons included in the source, or the format of the source itself. The strengths and limitations of each category of source, as well as the goal of the user's research, must be considered when choosing the sources to be consulted.

Direct vs. Indirect

Biographical sources are typically designated as either direct or indirect. This designation refers to the type of information that the sources provide. Direct sources provide information within the source itself, whereas indirect sources indicate which titles should be consulted in order to locate the needed information. Direct sources are often further classified as being either directory sources or dictionary sources. In general, directory sources provide basic and brief information about the biographee. Titles of the *Who's Who* variety are classic examples of biographical directories. More detailed, essay-length descriptions of the person of interest are provided by those sources commonly referred to as biographical dictionaries. *Current Biography* and *American National Biography* exemplify the category of biographical dictionary. Indirect sources provide very little biographical information within the body of the source; rather, they indicate which works the searcher should consult to obtain additional information. Indexes, such as *Biography and Genealogy Master Index* and *Biography Index Past and Present*, are illustrations of indirect biographical sources. These titles provide just enough information about the person of interest for identification purposes and then point the user to supplementary data.

Although the categorizations of direct and indirect are very common when describing biographical sources, there are many works that can be classified as both direct and indirect. Sources that provide any type of bibliography, list of works consulted, or recommended sources for further reading at the end of a biographical entry easily qualify for both categories. *Encyclopedia of World Biography* and *Contemporary Authors* provide both direct and indirect access to information. *Biography in Context* and *Biography Reference Bank*, which are electronic sources that provide aggregated and cumulative coverage of numerous and varied biographical sources, also provide both types of information.

Current vs. Retrospective

Biographical sources are frequently categorized by the type of persons included in the work and are commonly designated as being either current or retrospective. Persons included in the current sources are generally assumed to be living at the time of publication. The *Who's Who* variety of source serves as a representative example of current sources. Retrospective sources are understood to provide information about persons from the past and to include only those who are deceased. *Dictionary of American Biography* (*DAB*) and *American National Biography* are two such retrospective sources. A number of sources provide information on both current and retrospective figures. *Current Biography* profiles only current individuals, but provides access to obituaries for deceased individuals who were previously profiled by the publication and a citation for the issue of *Current Biography* in which that profile appeared. *Biography in Context* and *Biography Reference Bank* regularly include both living and deceased individuals.

International vs. National

Biographical sources are often classified as either international or national in scope. *Who's Who in the World* and *Encyclopedia of World Biography* are international in coverage and include persons regardless of their ethnicity or country of birth. National sources restrict their coverage to individuals born in the nation in question and, as is becoming more common in today's shrinking world, to those persons of prominence in, or importance to, the nation being covered. *Who's Who in America* and *American National Biography* are two examples of sources that are limited nationally in their scope. Sources may be further restricted to cover only a particular region of a country, such as with *Who's Who in the Midwest* or to cover only a particular field of interest, such as *American Men and Women of Science* (*AMWS*).

Alternative Sources

While persons included in major biographical works have, obviously, obtained some level of fame, the area in which they have achieved their status may dictate into which sources they are placed. Those of long-standing fame, such as classical Greek poets, or of outstanding achievement, such as past presidents of the United States, are likely to be included in the selective and well-respected dictionary sources, while those of sport or entertainment fame may be restricted to sources with good coverage of individuals of broad popular interest, such as *Current Biography* and *Biography.com*.

Newspapers and magazines can serve as excellent sources of biographical information, particularly for those persons who are newly famous, fleetingly famous, or famous for notorious or criminal reasons. Although perpetually of interest, the notorious are often excluded from many of the standard biographical sources. However, this does nothing to lessen the interest of the general public, and periodicals can often fill the gap. In the past, limited indexing made locating periodical articles challenging and time-consuming, with *Biography Index* traditionally being a quality resource for locating articles about people. Periodical indexes have made great strides both in content and format, and periodical articles are increasingly available (see Chapter 17). These indexes act as an excellent supplement to the traditional sources by providing access to very current information before the standard sources have been updated. *Biography in Context*, which integrates periodical coverage, primary sources, and websites into their biographical entries, has recognized the value of these source types to biographical research and has attempted to facilitate access. It should be noted that while some periodical indexes offer full-text access to referenced articles, they may be limited in their retrospective coverage; if older articles are required, a lack of full-text coverage may slow the process.

Encyclopedias can also act as supplementary biographical sources and should not be overlooked (see Chapter 18). Encyclopedia articles can provide concise and helpful overviews concerning the person sought and are quite useful for historical figures. Encyclopedias, particularly those created for young people, are often an excellent source for pictures. Valuable information may also be included in topical encyclopedia articles for subjects related to the field of interest of the individual in question; therefore, it is important that the index or search features of the encyclopedia be consulted. Important references to the life, work, and influence of a person may be missed if these access points are overlooked.

The Web can serve as another outstanding alternative for very current information or difficult-to-locate persons. In addition to some of the well-known biographical websites, such as *Biography.com* and *Infoplease Biography*, a wealth of additional biographical information may be gleaned from the Web. Personal websites of the famous (and infamous), company websites that provide profiles of corporate officials, and access to the content of smaller local newspapers via their websites are a few examples of potential Web resources that may be tapped. Social networking sites, such as Facebook and LinkedIn, where users are encouraged to post and share autobiographical information, are an evolving type of biographical resource that has the potential to provide more complete access to lesser-known individuals. Collaborative Web sources, such as *Wikipedia*, may also serve as supporting sources in biographical searches. While collaborative sources and general Web searching are likely to produce some results for most searches, they may or may not be results of quality. Although numerous sites containing quality information are available, many other Web sources lack editorial control. Thus, it is important to view each site critically and evaluate it for such qualities as accuracy, reliability, and currency. Although users may contend otherwise, searching accepted electronic biographical sources of known quality is often far more efficient than general Web searching.

EVALUATION

A staggering amount of biographical information is available, and myriad new works are updated and published yearly. It is imperative for librarians to carefully evaluate the sources available and to work diligently to direct users to those sources deemed to be of the highest quality. Whether adding a print source to the traditional reference collection or an electronic source to the Web-based collection, librarians should strive to ensure that users are consulting sources that are current, accurate, comprehensive, and easy to use.

Currency

When evaluating the currency of a work, it is important to consider how quickly, how often, and how thoroughly the work is updated. The entries in retrospective sources generally do not need regular updating and will be updated only if significant new information about a historical figure is discovered. However, because lives and fortunes can change very quickly, it is extremely important for current sources to be regularly and thoroughly updated. Dated entries have the serious potential consequence of providing incorrect information to the researcher. While many directory sources have regularly scheduled updates, other dictionary sources are updated less frequently, offering updates and revisions only when a new edition is released. Some dictionary sources that are published serially, such as *Contemporary Authors* and *Current Biography*, periodically include revised entries to keep the information provided more accurate. Print sources, by their nature, cannot be updated as often or as quickly as electronic sources. However, it must be noted that, just because it is possible to update electronic sources more quickly and more often, this does not necessarily mean that the sources are updated or indicate how thorough those updates may be. During the evaluation process, careful attention should be paid to the editorial policy regarding updates.

Accuracy and Authority

Issues of accuracy and authority can be considered on several levels. When evaluating any reference work, it is important to investigate what kinds of reviews the source received upon publication and whether the work has been included in the standard guides to reference works. The reputation of the publisher of the work can also serve as a good indicator of the overall quality. Gale, Oxford, ProQuest, EBSCO, and Marquis Who's Who are some of the best-known and most trusted names in biographical reference publishing.

A consideration that is somewhat unique to biographical works encompasses the source of the biographical data. Often, the biographees themselves are asked to provide the information included in the entry. Theoretically, self-compiled information will be superior as it will be most accurate. However, the accuracy and legitimacy of the information provided is dependent upon the honesty and thoroughness of the individual entrant. While the entrant may not actually provide factually incorrect information, the information may be, effectively, edited to provide a more flattering, if not more complete, picture. If the information located in a source seems at all questionable or incomplete, it is highly advisable to consult additional sources in an effort to provide the user with the most complete answer possible.

Scope and Comprehensiveness

The scope statement of the source will indicate which individuals are eligible for inclusion. A clearly worded and well-defined statement of scope will help to lend legitimacy to the source and its entries. Common ways to limit scope include whether the entrants are living or deceased, whether the entrants are residents of a particular country or region, and whether the entrants are employed in a particular field or profession. Inclusion of as many individuals as possible who meet the stated scope results in a more comprehensive source. If prominent individuals who meet the stated scope are overlooked, the overall legitimacy of the source will suffer. Likewise, if individuals who do not meet the qualifications set down by the scope statement are included, the quality of the source could and should be questioned.

Format

The usefulness of a source, even a source that contains information of the highest quality, may be greatly diminished if the source is difficult to use. The source and its information can be rendered useless if it is inaccessible due to poor organization or lack of access points. The number and type of available indexes in a print source will greatly impact the overall effectiveness of the work. Electronic sources have great potential in terms of searching and accessibility. Many sources allow for searching essentially all of the fields of the record, searching a number of factors in combination to refine the search, or even searching the entire contents of the database by keyword (see Figure 21.1). This search power of electronic sources should be exploited to the fullest so that searchers can locate the information of interest quickly and effectively. The ability of electronic sources to allow for cumulative searching of multiple editions of a title, such as with *Biography and Genealogy Master Index*, is an excellent and time-saving advantage for any searcher. Likewise,

People Search				
Search for:		in	Name	▼
And:		in	Place of Birth	▼
And:		in	Place of Death	▼
More Options:				
Occupation:	▼			
Nationality:	▼			
Ethnicity:	▼			
Gender:	Male ▣		Female ▣	
Birth Year:	is ▼			
Death Year:	is ▼			

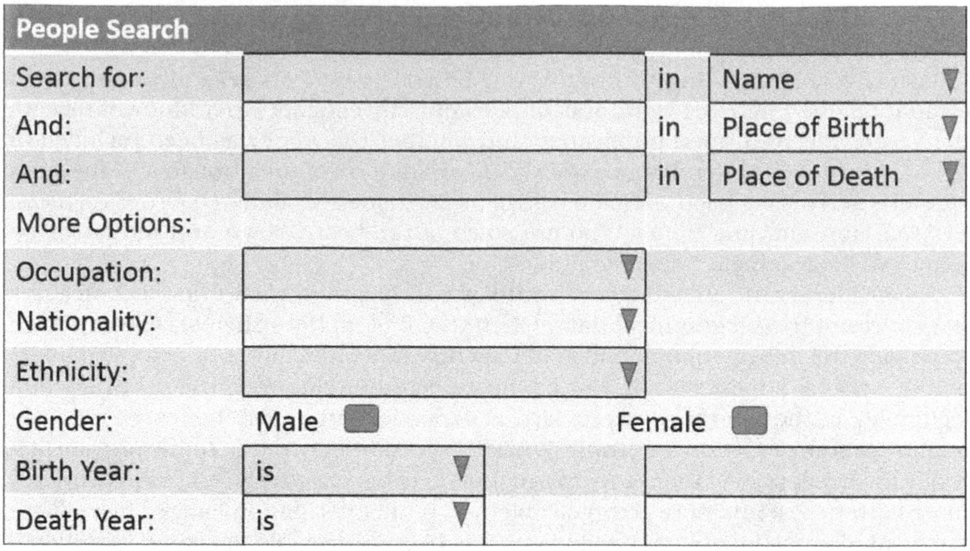

FIGURE 21.1 Example of a search screen that enables searching a combination of multiple fields

the ability to search a large number of biographical sources at one time, as allowed for by the large aggregate sources such as *Biography Reference Bank*, *Biography in Context*, and *Biography Reference Center*, can make the process of biographical searching fast, easy, and effective. Some librarians find the variety of works included in the aggregate sources somewhat detrimental. There are many different source types, of varying breadth and depth, so there is no guarantee of consistency in information located for included individuals. However, for most, the increased efficiency and convenience of such sources outweigh these concerns. Additionally, supporting contextual information, such as that provided in *Biography in Context*, can be exceedingly helpful to patrons who are trying to understand the overall impact of the person of interest on society.

Careful attention should be paid to the spelling of names when using electronic sources. Unlike print sources, where the traditional alphabetical arrangement of the source and/or its index may help the searcher to stumble upon the correct entry even if the spelling is inaccurate, electronic sources are less likely to return a result if the name is spelled incorrectly. Increasingly, sources will offer close matches, suggest alternative spellings, or offer an alphabetical browse feature in order to assist the searcher in locating the correct individual.

Box 21.2 Biographical Details

Discretion is not the better part of biography.

—Lytton Strachey
(Adams 2003, xi)

Cautions

A number of cautions should be taken into account when discussing biographical sources. Many early biographical works, particularly those from 19th- and early 20th-century America, were essentially vanity publications. Prominent citizens would be offered inclusion in the source for a fee, and the publishers would profit. While these works are now useful to scholars as historical snapshots of the era and the locale, they are not legitimate and unbiased biographical sources. A large number of vanity publications continue to exist in the biographical realm; any publication that requires an individual to purchase a copy of the title before he or she is included or that offers to include an individual for a fee should be viewed as suspect. Librarians may be questioned about such sources by users who have received invitations for inclusion; tact should be employed when discussing these invitations and titles.

Quality and completeness of information included in biographical entries has varied greatly over time. Whether done deliberately or subconsciously, biographers can be selective in their coverage. The Victorian era was notorious for including only acceptable and complimentary information about its biographical subjects. Obituaries, which can serve as another important source of biographical information, are also often considered to be more complimentary than complete. For this reason, among others, knowing what sources have been consulted during the creation of a biographical work and knowing where to look to locate additional information can be quite helpful to the biographical researcher. As it is often necessary to consult multiple works in order to obtain a clear picture of an individual, particularly an individual from the past, references and recommendations for sources of further information are an important component of many, and especially retrospective, works.

SELECTION

Although the type and depth of information needed can vary greatly by library, it is interesting to note that a number of classic biographical sources are useful in most libraries. Sources such as *Who's Who in America*, *Current Biography*, and *Biography and Genealogy Master Index* can be just as useful to a corporate librarian as to a school media specialist. The succinct information provided in a directory such as *Who's Who in America* may provide the answer to a simple ready-reference question. The essay format and excellent coverage of popular figures from *Current Biography* may provide the supplemental information needed for a more in-depth query. *Biography and Genealogy Master Index* provides efficient and effective direction to those pursuing biographical research.

Needs of Users

Although some sources are useful at multiple levels, the needs of the users of specific types of libraries will impact each library's selection of biographical tools. Dictionaries that are written at an appropriate level for the students being served and that provide illustrations are likely to be more useful than directories in a school library. Such dictionary sources will be far more useful to students as they work to complete reports and projects on prominent individuals. Dictionaries are also likely to be more useful than directories to the student users of academic libraries. However, the directory sources may be extremely useful to the staff and faculty users of the library. Identifying researchers specializing in a particular field, locating colleagues at different educational institutions, and obtaining contact information for potential donors are just a few of the possible uses for biographical directories at academic libraries. Directories that provide very current contact information and brief biographical data are often the most useful biographical sources for users of special libraries. The narrative entries provided by dictionary sources are likely to provide substantial retrospective information and, thus, be less useful in these settings. As it is difficult to anticipate the broad range of questions that may be faced in a public library, it is important to provide a cross section of sources. Both dictionary and directory sources, in a progression of difficulty and detail, should be made available for use.

Cost

Unfortunately, libraries are not financially able to provide all of the sources that might be helpful to their users. Therefore, in addition to evaluating sources for quality and usefulness, the prices of the sources must be considered. Some classic biographical sources offer abridged versions that may be sufficient for smaller libraries with limited budgets. For example, the *Almanac of Famous People* acts as a significantly abridged version of *Biography and Genealogy Master Index*, covering more than 30,000 of the larger work's 17 million plus entries. The uniqueness of works considered for a collection should be taken into account and titles with similar scope statements should be studied closely; it is unlikely that smaller libraries truly need or can easily afford titles that duplicate coverage.

Electronic versions of some sources may be available at reduced prices for those libraries that hold the print version of the source, thus providing additional access without significant extra cost. While still costly, electronic aggregate sources that provide full-text access to numerous classic biographical sources may enable libraries to provide access to more sources than they would otherwise be able to afford in print. Consortial pricing, which may result in a substantial discount in price, should be investigated for those sources that may be useful to multiple libraries in an area. A number of quality biographical sources are available free of charge on the Web. For example, *Biography.com* and *Infoplease Biography* are free resources that can be used by libraries of any budget to supplement their collections.

IMPORTANT GENERAL SOURCES

While it is not possible to provide a detailed description of every biographical source, a number of regularly used sources of widely accepted worth are discussed in this chapter. Several of the Additional Readings at the end of this chapter can be used to identify more specialized biographical sources suitable for particular collections.

Directories of the Who's Who Format

Who's Who directories, in one variation or another, are traditionally used biographical sources. They provide succinct, noncritical access to biographical facts for currently prominent individuals including name, age, education, family, and contact information. The original *Who's Who* was first published in England in the

19th century and limited entry to those of British citizenship. The source retains its British focus to this day, although now also includes foreigners influential in Britain. It should be noted that this is the original work of this type and is the only *Who's Who* title that is not qualified by some additional designation, such as *Who's Who in America* or *Who's Who in the Midwest. Who's Who* includes more than 33,000 influential people in British public life today.

Who's Who in America, which began approximately 50 years after the original *Who's Who*, is a premier source for basic information about more than 90,000 eminent Americans. "Americans," for this source, includes those from the United States, Canada, and Mexico. Inclusion in *Who's Who in America* is restricted to those deemed to be of "reference interest" and is dictated by an individual's achievements. Achievement may be measured by positions of leadership or responsibility held, significant creative or educational works, public speaking, publishing, or noteworthy contributions to the community. These are the same criteria used to measure all entrants into the Marquis Who's Who sources; however, achievements for those being considered for *Who's Who in America* are generally at the national level. Government officials at the national or state level, upper-level administrators from academic institutions, and key personnel from major businesses are generally ensured inclusion. Those selected for inclusion are sent a questionnaire and are asked to provide information about their life, family, career, and achievements, which is compiled in a standardized format. It should be noted that although the *Who's Who* sources have generally been found to be reliable, the answers provided by the biographees may not undergo any editorial review or revision, and the depth of content and currency for entries can vary significantly.

Marquis Biographies Online provides aggregate searchable access to 24 Marquis Who's Who titles, including *Who's Who in America*. Also included are regional titles based on the *Who's Who in America* format that cover the East, Midwest, South and Southwest, and West and topical *Who's Who* titles that are limited by profession or vocation, by gender, or by ethnic identity. The *Who's Who* directories are current sources and aim to include only those who are among the living. *Who Was Who* and *Who Was Who in America* provide reprints of entries for those individuals who are the subject of continued reference interest even after they have died. Access to 110,000 entries from Who Was Who in America, from 1607 to the present, is available via *Marquis Biographies Online*. In total, more than 1.5 million individuals are included in this database, which may be searched by 15 fields including name, occupation, gender, degrees, colleges or universities, year of graduation, hobbies, and religion. These fields may be searched individually or in combination to create specific search statements.

Many countries of the world produce some type of *Who's Who* directory, providing information about their prominent citizens. For example, *Canadian Who's Who* includes more than 13,000 biographies of persons of current national interest. The online *Canadian Who's Who* provides access to an additional 11,000 archived biographies as well as to supplemental video content. *Who's Who in the World* and *The International Who's Who* provide access to individuals who are prominent in a broader scope, including heads of state, politicians, writers, artists, businesspeople, and religious leaders. *World Who's Who*, which is available electronically, provides information for almost 60,000 men and women of note from around the world and provides access to the entries from *The International Who's Who*. Each entry includes an individual's date and place of birth, nationality, marital/family information, education, career background, awards and honors, artistic achievements, publications, leisure interests, and contact information. Coverage of the content of *Who's Who in the World* is available via *Marquis Biographies Online*.

A specialized directory useful for finding biographical information on contemporary scholars is *AMWS*. *AMWS* includes biographical entries on nearly 151,000 living scientists from the United States and Canada. Entries include birthdate and place, field of specialty, education, career history, awards, memberships, research/publication information, and contact information. *AMWS* is available online independently, as part of *Biography in Context*, or through the *Gale Virtual Reference Library*. It should also be noted that significant information about current scholars, such as contact information, research interests, publications, awards, and fellowships, is readily available by visiting the websites of the academic institution with which that scholar is affiliated.

Indexes

Biography and Genealogy Master Index includes citations from more than 2,000 publications that provide biographical information. Currently, the index provides access to more than 17 million citations relating to almost 5 million individuals. The number of citations is continually rising, as an estimated 450,000 new entries are added every year and existing citations are retained, not removed. Although the source provides little biographical data within its entries, just name, birth, and death dates, it effectively points the researcher to where biographical information is published. As the print source is updated with supplement volumes twice a year and exists in multiple volumes, the cumulative searching offered by the electronic version is quite beneficial, saving both time and effort. A note of caution regarding *Biography and Genealogy Master Index* lies in the method of including names. Names and dates are included as they appear in the title that has been indexed; no attempt is made at authority control. Therefore, a single individual may have multiple entries under various forms of the same name (see Figure 21.2).

Results for Basic Search: (Riley, James Whitcomb)		
Mark	☐	Riley, James Whitcomb (1849-1916) 102 Citations
Mark	☐	Riley, James Whitcomb (1849-) 1 Citation
Mark	☐	Riley, James Whitcomb (d1916) 1 Citation
Mark	☐	Riley, James Whitcomb 1 Citation
Mark	☐	Riley, James Whitcomb (1852?-1916) 1 Citation
Mark	☐	Riley, James Whitcomb (1853-) 1 Citation
Mark	☐	Riley, James Whitcomb (1853-1916) 4 Citations
Mark	☐	Riley, James Whitcomb (1854?-1916) 1 Citation

FIGURE 21.2 An example of search results that lack authority control and consist of multiple forms of entry for the same individual

Biography Index provides access to more than 1 million book and article citations. These citations not only are limited to biographies and autobiographies, but also include interviews, obituaries, letters, diaries, memoirs, juvenile literature, reviews, and bibliographies. Coverage includes persons from the past and the present, of all nationalities, and from all fields of interest. Unlike *Biography and Genealogy Master Index*, authority control is employed to ensure easy access to individuals regardless of possible name variations. The source, which has ceased publication in print, is now available online, individually as *Biography Index Past and Present* or via *Biography Reference Bank*. As with *Biography and Genealogy Master Index*, the online source may be searched cumulatively and is updated daily. Retrospective coverage of the online version now goes back to 1946, covering the full span of the corresponding print index.

Biographical Dictionaries

Current

Current Biography, which began publication in 1940, is a useful biographical source, enduringly popular with users and librarians. Complete with photographs, family life, and physical descriptions of the biographees, *Current Biography* provides accurate and quite readable essay-length biographies of international personalities. Subjects often tend to have had some impact on American life and are often important figures in popular culture. The print source is published monthly, with about 20 profiles in each issue as well as brief obituaries for past entrants who are recently deceased. The monthly issues are gathered into an annual yearbook that also contains additional current and cumulative indexing. The title is also available electronically as *Current Biography Illustrated*, and the database contains the entire contents of all print issues, more than 31,000 articles and obituaries in total. The source is also included in *Biography Reference Bank*.

Containing profiles of almost any published American writer, including novelists, poets, columnists, cartoonists, and screen and television writers, *Contemporary Authors* is an extremely comprehensive choice for biographical information about authors. Produced by Gale since 1962, it references more than 145,000 authors. Described as a bio-bibliographical guide, the work contains biographical details, references to recent news about the author, biographical and critical references, and more. Modern writers and significant writers from the early 20th century from around the world are included, and, when possible, biographical information is provided directly from the entrant. It should be noted that several different series of *Contemporary Authors* are published, and the print volumes and their indexes may be cumbersome for novice users. The online version is significantly easier to use and may provide more current entries than the print format. The source is available online individually or as a part of *Biography in Context*. *Contemporary Authors* is also offered online as part of Gale's *Literature Resource Center*.

Newsmakers is designed to provide profiles of prominent contemporary individuals from various backgrounds and professions. Like *Current Biography*, *Newsmakers* covers all fields, from government and business to entertainment and sports. Issues appear quarterly, covering about 200 newsmakers each year. Gathered annually into a cumulative volume, the content is indexed by name, nationality, occupation, and subject. A separate obituaries section provides concise profiles of recently deceased newsmakers. Also published by Gale, *Contemporary Black Biography* focuses on important persons of African heritage. Each volume contains at least 55 biographies. Name, occupation, nationality, and subject indexes are included in each volume. Both *Newsmakers* and *Contemporary Black Biography* are available online through the *Gale Virtual Reference Library* or as part of *Biography in Context*.

Current and Retrospective

Encyclopedia of World Biography contains more than 7,000 biographical sketches of current and historical figures. In addition to the more expected historical entrants, movie, television, and music stars are included. The text is eminently readable and, thus, quite accessible to students as well as the general public. Illustrations and bibliographical references are provided for many of the entries, and extensive indexing is available. The source is well organized and easily usable in print, but it is also available online and as part of *Biography in Context*.

African American National Biography contains more than 4,000 entries written and signed by distinguished scholars under the direction of editors in chief Henry Louis Gates Jr. and Evelyn Brooks Higginbotham. The time span is almost 500 years, from 1528 to the present day. The scope includes slaves and abolitionists; writers, artists, and performers; politicians and businesspeople; athletes; and lawyers, journalists, and civil rights leaders. Each entry is followed by a section of suggestions for further reading. Indexes allow access by category or area of renown and by birthplace. There are also lists of African American prizewinners, medalists, members of Congress, and judges. The regularly updated entries are available online as part of the *Oxford African American Studies Center*. *Contemporary Hispanic Biography* presents biographical information pertaining to prominent individuals of Latino heritage. The source includes Hispanics of various nationalities and in numerous fields, including art, music, and literature to science, politics, and business. The source is available online and as part of the *Gale Virtual Reference Library*.

Retrospective

DAB is a massive work containing narrative biographical accounts for more than 19,000 prominent deceased Americans. All entries are evaluative, written by scholars, and focus on the public life of the featured individual. Some personal information is also included, as are bibliographical references for further reading. The first volumes of this source were published in the late 1920s, with the index following in the late 1930s; updates and supplements provide coverage through 1980. A comprehensive index, published in 1990, has six sections including subject of the biography, birthplace, schools and colleges attended, occupations, topics discussed in the biography, and contributors' names. Although long accepted as an excellent reference source, it should be noted that it has been criticized for its lack of diversity; entries for women and minorities are quite limited. As it is now quite dated, researchers should consult additional sources, when possible, to guarantee accuracy and thoroughness. Continuing biographical coverage of prominent individuals in the tradition of the *DAB*, *The Scribner Encyclopedia of American Lives* includes entries covering 1998–2006 and is available both in print and online via the *Gale Virtual Reference Library*.

Compared with *DAB*, *American National Biography* is an equally massive, but far more recent, biographical work focusing on significant deceased Americans. Foreigners who have had a significant impact on the country are included. Providing new entries for approximately 10,000 of the figures covered in *DAB*, *American National Biography* also includes entries for more than 7,000 figures not included in that source. As *DAB* stopped updating its coverage in 1980, many of the 7,000 are persons who died after that date. However, *American National Biography* has also worked to include those persons overlooked by *DAB*, especially women, minorities, and precolonial figures. Entries are signed, quite lengthy, include bibliographical references, and may also include illustrations. Four indexes are provided in the print edition: subject, contributors, birthplace, and "occupations and realms of renown." Originally published in 1999, the title is available in print and online. The online version is revised, updated, and expanded semiannually to ensure accuracy. Access points that may be searched singly or in combination go beyond the print indexes to also include fields such as gender, birth and death dates, occupation, and limits to special collections (e.g., Black History, Women's History, Asian Pacific American Heritage, Hispanic Heritage, American Indian Heritage). Serious scholars who are researching figures included in both *ANB* and *DAB* should consult both entries; these sources, although written from different perspectives and in different eras, are both works of significant scholarship and are viewed by many as complementary.

Dictionary of National Biography, the inspiration for *DAB*, was originally published in the late 1800s in an attempt to profile deceased persons of distinction from Great Britain and Ireland. A new edition of the *Dictionary of National Biography*, titled *Oxford Dictionary of National Biography*, was released in 2004, with a supplement released in 2009. This edition continues to focus on deceased Britons, but foreign-born persons who have achieved significance in Britain are also included. The revised source contains in excess of 59,000 biographies, more than 16,000 of which are new to this edition. The popular and the scholarly, the ancient and the modern, are all included in this revision. This edition has received excellent reviews for its content, coverage, and quality of writing. In the online format, search options include searches by person, full text, bibliographic references, contributors, or images. Selected biographies are also grouped by theme, such as "Astronomers royal," "Climbers of Mount Everest," and "Poets laureate." Online updates are done three times per year, including new biographies, themes for reference, illustrations, and corrections and additions to articles already published.

The major source for historically important Canadians is the *Dictionary of Canadian Biography* (*DCB*). The 15 volumes of this work published to date cover Canadian history from 1000 to 1930, with additional volumes in progress. The *DCB* is arranged chronologically rather than alphabetically. Each volume contains essays about individuals who contributed to a specific period of Canadian history. Entries in the *DCB* average several hundred words in length, and all conclude with citations for further reading and research. Free online access to the contents of the set, including biographical content from the forthcoming volumes, is available. The online *DCB* supports searching by name or keyword and limiting by date range, gender, or occupation.

Developed by the Australian National University, the *Australian Dictionary of Biography*, which is available in print or online, contains more than 12,000 entries on persons who were important in Australian history or who represent the diverse nature of the Australian experience. Coverage currently extends to 1990, with plans to extend coverage to prominent individuals who died in subsequent decades.

Browsing may be done by name or occupation, and the advanced search feature enables searches based on dates and place of birth/death, religious influence, cultural heritage, occupation, and gender. Entries include physical description, family details, distinctions gained, career, occupation, and religious affiliation.

World Biographical Information System Online (*WBIS Online*) offers access to 8.5 million biographical entries. Entries are compiled from more than 10,000 printed works including K. G. Saur's *Biographical Archives*. Sources represented include those published from 1559 until the present. International in scope, entrants represent all countries, professions, and areas of renown. *WBIS Online* includes index listings as well as digitized copies of many original biographical articles.

Retrospective sources may also focus on particular ethnic or gender groups or professions. Examples include *Dictionary of Scientific Biography* (*DSB*) and its supplement *New Dictionary of Scientific Biography*. The *New Dictionary of Scientific Biography* includes more than 700 new biographies, treating scientists deceased since 1980 or overlooked in the original *DSB*. In addition, a number of original articles have been updated to reflect more recent scholarship. More women and African Americans have been included as well as more scientists from Middle Eastern and Asian countries. Articles describe work and career and conclude with a bibliography of works by and about the scientist. The two publications exist in an online version called the *Complete Dictionary of Scientific Biography* and are available as part of the *Gale Virtual Reference Library*. *Notable American Women* provides scholarly essays on historically significant American women. Together, the series provides content on women from 1607 through the 20th century. Modeled on the *DAB*, each entry contains a fairly lengthy life history covering personal and career events. Each entry concludes with a list of primary and secondary sources for further research, and indexes by occupation are provided. Electronic access is available from Alexander Street Press and via *Credo Reference*.

Aggregate Sources

Although general aggregators of online reference sources, such as *Credo Reference*, include a growing number of biographical titles, several aggregate sources devoted to biographical information provide even richer coverage. *Biography in Context*, an easy-to-use online source, provides access to more than 700,000 biographies and integrates contextual articles to clarify the overall impact of the featured individuals. In this source, 50,000 biographies are added or updated annually, and daily updates are made to reflect current events. It is universal in scope, including current and historical figures from around the world and from all areas of interest. Biographical information from more than 170 titles from Gale and its partners, such as *Newsmakers*, *Contemporary Authors*, and *Contemporary Black Biography*, are indexed and made available full text. Full-text articles from hundreds of magazines and newspapers are included in this comprehensive database as are websites, illustrations, and audio/video clips. This media-rich content does much to ensure that the researcher will find something at the desired level on the individual in question. The database is regularly updated to include new content and to update existing entries. Quick name searching, advanced searching, and biographical facts searching (by birth/death years and places, nationality, ethnicity, occupation, gender) make this a useful tool for novice searchers and librarians alike. The convenience and time savings of searching so many standard and accepted reference works at one time are quite significant, as are the collection development implications; libraries that might be unable to afford a fraction of these biographical sources in print may be able to access all of them full-text online via this database.

Biography Reference Bank is an aggregate source from H.W. Wilson, online from EBSCO. This source provides biographical information for more than 700,000 individuals, with more than 3.5 million total records. *Biography Index, Current Biography*, Wilson's *World Authors Series, Junior Authors & Illustrators Series*, and more are combined with biographical content from other Wilson databases and selected biographical material from other reference publishers (e.g., Greenwood Publishing and Oxford University Press) to provide the substance for this resource. In addition to narrative biographies, more than 35,000 images and links to more than 600,000 full-text magazine articles are provided, as are interviews, reviews, speeches, and obituaries. This extensive database allows searching by name, profession, place of origin, gender, ethnicity, birth and/or death date, titles of works, and keywords. As with *Biography in Context*, the overall convenience and time that may be saved by accessing these numerous valuable titles via one interface and one search is quite substantial.

Similar in function to *Biography in Context, Biography Reference Center* provides access to both brief and extensive biographies as well as to related supporting articles. The title boasts more than 460,000 full-text biographies as well as access to the content of *Biography Today* and *Biography*. Also available is some supplemental content from a number of respected reference titles such as *American National Biography, Notable American Women*, and *Congressional Biographies*. Keyword searching is supported, and users can also opt to locate biographies by browsing a variety of categories, including occupation, nationality, publication, and more than 30 genre categories, including actors, artists, athletes, authors, current world leaders, explorers, and scientists. *Biography Reference Center* is available independently or via *EBSCOhost*.

Free Web Resources

Biography.com is an outgrowth of the Arts & Entertainment channel's popular *Biography* television program. Providing access to more than 7,000 biographical entries, the database is not limited to those who have been featured on the program; however, the coverage and content for those who have been featured is much more complete. Although emphasizing coverage of figures in popular culture, historical figures and scholars are also included. This user-friendly and familiar site is a worthwhile free source of legitimate biographical information. *Infoplease Biography*, an affiliate of the *Infoplease Almanac*, provides access to more than 30,000 brief biographical entries. These listings can be searched by name, browsed by occupational category, or browsed by race and ethnicity. The *Biographical Dictionary* is a database that provides timeline entries for numerous individuals of current interest. This source is a community-based wiki and notes that users can edit the biographical entries or even create entries for themselves. Thanks to this communal wiki model, the scope of the entries is quite broad, and the database can be a useful starting point for research. However, as with any collaboratively created website, findings should be evaluated for accuracy and authority.

SEARCH STRATEGIES

When developing a search strategy to locate biographical information, a number of factors should be considered, such as what the user knows about the individual being sought, what the user is hoping to learn about the individual, and at what level the information is needed. Whether the person is well known or obscure, whether the coverage should be scholarly or popular, whether the user is sure of the spelling or unsure of even the name, there are sources and strategies that can be employed to attempt to locate the required information.

When the subject of the search is well known, it is possible, even likely, that the problem will not lie in being able to find something about the individual; rather, it will lie in finding too much. When there is an abundance of information available, the librarian may find it wise to assist the user in evaluating the search results to determine which sources are most appropriate. When the individual sought is not well known, finding anything may become an issue, and it may be necessary to employ sources with a regional or local focus. If the user knows very little about the individual being sought, it can be very difficult to narrow the search or even to be sure that the located results are actually for the correct person. It is extremely important for the librarian to obtain any and all information possible from the user. Information that the user may feel is insignificant or information that the user is hesitant to share because he or she is unsure of its accuracy may well be the information that the librarian will need in order to conduct a successful search. It may also happen that a user claiming to need biographical information about an individual in fact needs information related to that person's work instead. Thus, a thorough reference interview, investigating everything from where the user heard of the individual, to any variations on the name or spelling of the name, to what the user is actually hoping to find, is essential, and no detail obtained should be discounted as unimportant.

Biographical information exists in a range of depth and completeness, from thorough, scholarly articles to popular, gossipy coverage. In order to perform a successful reference transaction, it is necessary for the librarian to ascertain the level of coverage desired by the user. It is unlikely that an elementary school student would find an article from the *DAB* useful and readable, or that a graduate student would find a single profile from *Current Biography* sufficient for term paper research; however, it is equally unlikely that a librarian can assume what level of coverage is most appropriate for a specific user. Therefore, in order to avoid misunderstandings and assumptions that could leave the user feeling uncomfortable, the librarian should try to investigate the level and depth of coverage desired during the interview process. If the user is hesitant to clarify the level needed, the librarian may wish to consider offering a number of sources at varying levels of complexity. The user can then choose the desired source, thus indicating to the librarian the type of coverage preferred if additional information is necessary.

Factual Data

If the user is looking for brief factual data, such as birth or death dates, full name, education, or contact information, biographical directories are excellent sources. If the individual is famous, basic information such as nationality and whether the individual is still alive may be known to the user and the librarian. If so, it may be possible to go without hesitation to the appropriate directory, such as *Who's Who* for those of British nationality and *Who's Who in America* for those from North America. *Marquis Biographies Online* is a noteworthy possibility for locating living North American figures. As this source includes the regional and many of the subject-specific *Who's Who* titles, multiple sources can be consulted quickly and easily. In addition to biographical directories, encyclopedia articles may well prove an effective resource for general factual data about well-known individuals.

Single-volume universal biographies, which do not restrict by time, place, or subject and include both the living and the dead, have long served as effective starting points when little is known about the individual sought. Titles of this type include *Merriam-Webster's Biographical Dictionary*, providing very brief biographical information for about 30,000 world figures, and *Chambers Biographical Dictionary*, with entries for 18,000 individuals. Because *Merriam-Webster's Biographical* has not been updated on a regular basis, it may be most useful for historical figures. *Chambers Biographical*, updated and expanded in 2011, is more current and as such should be more useful for contemporary figures. Both sources are available electronically, *Merriam-Webster's* via *Biography in Context* and *Chambers* via *Credo Reference*. *Biography in Context* and *Biography Reference Bank*, regularly updated electronic aggregate sources, may now be the best options to serve in their stead for individuals from all periods.

When the subject in question is not known to the librarian and the user can provide little detail, the librarian may find it efficient to consult an indirect source, such as *Biography and Genealogy Master Index*, in order to determine in which titles the individual will be found. If available, an electronic source such as *Biography in Context* can act as both an indirect and direct source for this type of question. A single search in such a source can provide the searcher not only with results for directory information but also with dictionary-type information as well as references to additional content in the event that the user decides to pursue the subject further.

Narrative Biographies

If the user is looking for essay-length coverage, biographical dictionaries should be consulted. Again, if the figure is well-known, it may be possible to progress directly to an appropriate source. Important historical figures of British descent may be available in the *Oxford Dictionary of National Biography*; historical figures of American heritage may be found in either the *DAB* or *American National Biography*. If the person sought is fairly well known, but the nationality of the person is in question, a source such as *Encyclopedia of World Biography*, which is international in scope, may provide an entry. If the figure sought is well known, but currently famous or popular, sources such as *Current Biography* or even *Biography.com* may be most appropriate. As noted earlier, if very little is known about the figure being sought, an indirect source such as *Biography and Genealogy Master Index* or an aggregate source that provides both direct and indirect access to information, such as *Biography in Context* or *Biography Reference Bank*, should be consulted early in the search in order to locate information with a minimum of lost time and fruitless searching.

If the user is hoping to locate detailed or exhaustive coverage of an individual, a number of steps will be required. Indirect biographical sources should be consulted to obtain references to articles that are available in the standard biographical reference sources. Then, the articles located should be consulted for any bibliographic references or recommendations that may be included. Information about the individual of interest may also be available in non-biographical periodical articles. Sources such as *Biography Reference Bank*, *Biography in Context*, *Biography Reference Center*, or even a general periodical index, can provide access to such articles. If the user is hoping to obtain as much information about the person in question as possible, the existence of a full-length biography or autobiography of the individual should be investigated. The library catalog, available union catalogs such as *WorldCat*, and biographical bibliographies (e.g., Daniel Burt's *The Biography Book* and related titles listed in this chapter's Suggested Readings) may be consulted to determine whether such a work is available.

Subject Inquiries

A number of sources are designed to help searchers locate information on individuals prominent in a particular subject area or vocation. Sources such as *Contemporary Authors*, *Something about the Author*, *American Men and Women of Science*, *Grove Art* and *Grove Music* (available via *Oxford Art Online* and *Oxford Music Online* respectively) are just a few of the numerous subject-specific sources available. These specialized sources, due to their more limited scope, are often able to include a larger number of entrants from the field and information at a greater level of detail. If the profession or field of the individual sought is known to the user, these subject-specific sources may be a good starting point for the search. If it is not known whether a subject-specific source is available, a guide to biographical sources (see Suggested Readings) should be consulted for further information. A number of excellent subject-specific free websites also may be consulted for biographical information. *Union List of Artist Names* (*ULAN*), *Internet Movie Database* (*IMDB*), *All Music Guide*, *POTUS: Presidents of the United States*, and *The First Ladies* are just a few of the subject-specific free websites that can provide reliable biographical information. Professional directories, although limited in the biographical information they provide, may also serve a purpose in biographical searching. These directories often provide an opportunity to verify the name, licenses, and educational credentials of individuals who are not included in more standard biographical sources.

Authors and writers are particularly well covered in many general biographical sources. Additionally, there are a number of excellent sources that focus on this vocation. If the subject of the search can be considered a writer by any definition, *Contemporary Authors* should be checked for coverage. *Dictionary of Literary Biography*, a related work to the *Contemporary Authors Series*, is also an excellent source of biographical information for literary figures. These sources, which provide thorough cross-referencing, can be quite valuable when dealing with questions of pseudonyms. *Contemporary Authors*, *Contemporary Authors New Revisions Series*, *Dictionary of Literary Biography*, and more are available electronically via Gale's *Literature Resource Center*. As this aggregate source also includes works focusing on literary criticism, it is a particularly effective resource for those searching not only for biographical information about an author but also for critical information about the author's works. *Contemporary Authors* and

Contemporary Authors New Revisions are also included in *Biography in Context*, which may be more widely available than *Literature Resource Center*, especially in smaller libraries.

It is not uncommon for a librarian to be asked to help a user identify an individual who fits a particular set of biographical criteria. Often related to school assignments, librarians may be faced with the challenge of finding an individual of a certain race or ethnicity who is prominent in a particular field or profession. Searches of this type have been, historically, difficult and labor-intensive. However, with the powerful search capabilities and excellent access points of the electronic biographical sources, such searches have become much simpler, as illustrated in Box 21.3. *American National Biography*, *Oxford Dictionary of National Biography*, *Biography in Context*, *Biography Reference Center*, and *Biography Reference Bank*, among others, allow searching by a variety of criteria such as gender, vocation, ethnicity, religion, place of birth, date of birth, and date of death.

Box 21.3 Combining Criteria in Biographical Searching

An elementary student was assigned to write a report on a male photojournalist of African American descent. Such a task seemed hopeless to the student and his grandmother when they approached the reference desk; however, with the assistance of *Biography in Context*'s Person Search, an appropriate individual was identified in a matter of minutes. The librarian used the various options in the search interface to specify Occupation=photojournalist, Ethnicity=African American, and Gender=male. The search resulted in 10 matches, including John H. White, a photojournalist for the *Chicago Sun-Times*. The search yielded links to three articles on White in *Contemporary Black Biography*, *Contemporary Authors Online*, and *Who's Who among African Americans.*

Images

If a picture of the subject is required, there are a number of sources that may be useful. While some may feel that images are only sought by schoolchildren writing reports, a vast amount of information that may not be readily available elsewhere can be gleaned from the image of an individual. Details of a person's appearance are not regularly included in many of the traditional sources; however, the searcher may observe that information firsthand if an image is available. Standard biographical sources, such as *Encyclopedia of World Biography* and *Current Biography* generally provide images of their entrants. *Encyclopedia of World Biography* and *Current Biography* may be searched electronically: the *Encyclopedia* via *Biography in Context* and *Current Biography* via *Biography Reference Bank* or individually. With many electronic sources, such as *Biography in Context*, *Biography Reference Bank*, *American National Biography*, and *Oxford Dictionary of National Biography*, it is possible to limit the search to entries with illustrations. Encyclopedias, especially those designed for young people, can serve as an excellent source for images. Web search tools, such as *Google Images*, may provide quick electronic access to hard-to-find pictures. Images relating to the work of the individual in question, such as campaign posters and political cartoons, may provide additional insight and perspective. When dealing with requests for images, the librarian may be faced with the dilemma of having to explain to users why no photographs exist for certain figures of historical significance. It is important for the librarian to remain patient and tactful when explaining the time limitations of photographic technology and to offer artists' renderings as a possible alternative.

Box 21.4 Images as a Form of Biographical Information

A good portrait is a kind of biography . . .

—Alexander Smith
(Smith 1863, 292)

Recently Deceased

Individuals who are recently deceased may, for a brief period, still be listed in the current sources; however, after they are removed from the current sources, it may take some time before they are included in the retrospective. During this gap, it may be necessary to consult alternative sources. Electronic resources that are regularly updated, particularly sources that include newspaper, magazine, or journal articles, may fill this need. Biographical sources that index periodicals, such as *Biography Reference Center*, *Biography in Context*, and *Biography Reference Bank*, as well as general periodical indexes, may be extremely useful.

Obituaries

Obituaries can provide a wealth of biographical information on the famous as well as on the lesser known. Obituaries for famous individuals may be accessed in a number of ways. The *New York Times Obituaries Index* is a standard source to use when searching for obituaries of the well known. The index is available in print, or obituaries can be searched online from the *New York Times* Web archive. The online *New York Times* archive may be searched for citations free of charge; however, full-text coverage must be purchased. *Current Biography* provides short obituary notices with references to the *New York Times* obituaries for past biographees. The content of *Current Biography*, and thus, the obituaries, is available electronically. *Biography and Genealogy Master Index* may also be used to find some obituary references. Often obituaries will be published even for lesser-known figures, particularly in the person's local newspaper. Historically, the obituaries published in these small-town newspapers became quite inaccessible over time. While the newspaper itself may have been preserved in microform, access to the contents of said paper was often quite limited due to a lack of indexing. Currently, a number of retrospective indexing and digitization projects are helping to save these valuable records from obscurity. Librarians should be sure to investigate this possible avenue of access for obituaries published in local papers. Because newspaper websites may make their obituary sections freely available, searches using a Web search engine such as *Google* may also yield a needed obituary.

Local and Lesser-Known Personalities

If the user is attempting to locate information on local or lesser-known personalities, it will be necessary to alter the search strategy and sources employed. As users can pose queries about anyone and comparatively few persons are ever included in biographical reference sources, biographical requests for the local and lesser-known can be quite daunting. However, it is important to remember that virtually all persons are listed somewhere, even if only in local sources. Locally compiled and created resources, particularly local newspapers, are excellent potential sources. Vital records, city directories, or yearbooks from local institutions may also provide biographical insights. Until recently, using such sources necessitated research visits and interlibrary loan requests. Now, as many libraries and institutions have begun creating databases of local history information and records, much information is available via the Web. Visiting the websites of the libraries in the area where the individual lived or achieved prominence should give some indication as to what information is available electronically, or, if not yet available online, what is available in print. If sources are available to be consulted remotely, the librarian should explain their accessibility and worth to the user to ensure the user's ability to exploit them. If the sources are not available for use remotely, the librarian should again explain what sources are held, what they may contain, and what options exist for consulting those sources, including interlibrary loan, requesting photocopies, or site visits. *Facebook*, *LinkedIn*, and other social networking sites that invite users to share autobiographical information may serve as excellent sources of biographical information for the lesser known. Even if the persons in question have not been included in the standard biographical sources, they may have chosen to share details on these sites. Similarly, collaboratively created Web sources, such as *Wikipedia*, may provide significant amounts of information about minor celebrities. As with any information that is obtained from sources that are not under consistent editorial control, the information located on social networking and collaborative sites should be evaluated fully for accuracy.

Genealogical Information

Genealogical queries are a subset of biographical questions and are quite popular, especially in public libraries and in libraries that house a special collection focusing on family or local history. Because of their popularity, it is necessary for all reference librarians, even those not choosing to specialize in this field, to be familiar with some of the basic genealogical sources. A number of excellent electronic options exist when searching for genealogical information, including both freely available and subscription tools.

Subscription databases, such as *Ancestry Library Edition* and *HeritageQuest Online*, provide extensive coverage and access to works of genealogical research. *Ancestry Library Edition* includes access to Census data, draft registrations, passenger and immigration lists, and the *Social Security Death Master File*, also known as the *Social Security Death Index*. *HeritageQuest* is also helpful for U.S. Census information and is notable for indexing thousands of genealogical texts and journals. *FamilySearch*, a free resource from the Church of Jesus Christ of Latter-Day Saints, shares introductory information about conducting genealogical research and also provides access to various databases of genealogical information. Accessible content includes the catalog of the Church's Family History Library, indexes of birth and marriage registers that have been transcribed from microfilm, and the *International Genealogical Index*. *Cyndi's List of Genealogy Sites on the Internet* provides a categorized index to genealogical resources on the Web, serving as a free starting point for online research. *Mocavo*, a relatively new search site, has emerged with the intention of indexing freely available websites to increase access to publicly available genealogy content.

Numerous genealogical sites and tools have been created and posted by volunteers. Projects such as the *RootsWeb* and the *USGenWeb* are examples of tools created by dedicated genealogical volunteers. *RootsWeb* hosts a multitude of surname discussion groups and also provides access to significant primary source material. Primary sources such as obituaries, tax lists, and local histories, which have been scanned or transcribed, are made available on their site. *The USGenWeb Project* is facilitated by volunteers and is organized by state and county. The project provides access to geographically arranged genealogical discussions and content. *Find a Grave*, a moderated site containing much crowd-sourced information about graves and cemetery records, is another example of a large volunteer-driven resource. There are many dedicated and skilled genealogists posting content to the Web; however, as with any resource, all located content should be evaluated for accuracy and authority. Self-published family history websites, which are often posted by amateur researchers, may be inconsistent, incomplete, or inaccurate, and should be approached with caution.

As when searching for information on local personalities, genealogical requests may necessitate consultation of primary source materials, and the reference request may quickly move into the realm of research. Primary source materials such as birth, death, and marriage certificates, census records, and tombstones provide a wealth of genealogical and biographical information, but can be very time-consuming and labor-intensive to locate and consult. The responsibility of the librarian in this realm usually does not lie in conducting the research for the user; rather, it lies in conveying to the user the types of sources that may be available, the information that they may contain, and suggestions on how to locate and obtain the records. Libraries, genealogical groups, and historical societies often hold a wealth of archival sources that may be available to visiting researchers. Additionally, many of these organizations are working to make digitized content available electronically from their websites. As noted, *Ancestry Library Edition*, *HeritageQuest*, and *FamilySearch* all provide access to some primary source documents. The National Archives and Records Administration hosts a *Resources for Genealogists* site that provides access to and information about immigration records, land records, census information, military service records, and more.

The National Archives and Records Administration also provides a more detailed guide to immigration information on its *Immigration Records* page. For immigrants to the United States, naturalization records may be available from the U.S. Citizenship and Immigration Service (USCIS). USCIS hosts a website, *Genealogy*, which details the available records and how they can be requested. Immigration records may also be available from the immigrant's port of entry to the United States. Large and historically significant ports of entry, such as Ellis Island and Castle Garden, host websites providing online access to records and information.

Land and property ownership records can provide valuable genealogical information. *Land Records*, from the National Archives and Records Administration, provides information and tips about locating and obtaining records of land transfers from the U.S. government to private ownership. *General Land Office Records*, from the Bureau of Land Management, provides some access to federal land conveyance records. *Sanborn Maps*, which were originally used to assess fire insurance risk, provide detailed histories of many U.S. localities. While archives often hold paper copies of their local *Sanborn Maps*, the collection is available electronically as *Digital Sanborn Maps* from ProQuest.

Fictional Personalities

Reference questions may arise that are presumed to be biographical in nature but, in fact, focus on a fictional personality instead of an actual person. While the librarian may determine that the name in question is that of a fictional personality, it may require some tact when conveying this information to a user who believes the person to be real. Literary characters, gods, or epic heroes may be the focus of such inquiries. General and subject encyclopedias, such as those focusing on literature, folklore, mythology, and religion, may be helpful when searching for references to fictional figures. *The New Century Cyclopedia of Names* has entries for places, events, literary works, and fictional and mythological characters, as well as for important people from the past. Individuals who were alive at some point but who have since attained legendary status, such as saints, folk heroes, and outlaws, may also pose unique challenges. It should be noted that biographical studies of saints are often quite glorified, frequently to the point that it is considered hagiography. Legends surrounding folk heroes and outlaws (and especially outlaws who have evolved into folk heroes) are often quite exaggerated as well, and careful checking will be required to verify occurrences as fact.

Book-Length Biographies

Biographical queries are perennially popular at the reference desk, and some users do not wish to stop their investigation with a few mere articles. Recommendations for book-length biographical works may also be requested. This type of request may be considered both a biographical and a readers' advisory request. Both factual and fictionalized book-length biographies exist, and the librarian should take care to ascertain which type of coverage interests the user. Standard readers' advisory sources, such as those discussed in Chapter 24, may be useful, and readers' advisory tools with a biographical or historical focus should also be consulted. *The Biography Book* provides recommendations for factual biographies, biographical novels, fictional portraits, and even juvenile biographies, while *What Historical Novel Do I Read Next?* and *Historical Figures in Fiction* will, obviously, focus on fictionalized accounts. Recommendations for hundreds of memoirs, biographies, and autobiographies are available through *Read on—Biography* and *Read on—Life Stories*. Theatrical and cinematic adaptations of biographies may also be of interest to users. *The Biography Book* provides references to both, and free Web sources, such as the *Internet Movie Database*, may also be helpful.

Box 21.5 Search Strategy: Seeking Mr. Rogers

A media studies student had an assignment to write a paper on an individual who was influential in television programming for children. She chose Mr. Rogers, recalling her own experience as a child watching the *Mister Rogers' Neighborhood* program. Searching for "Mr. Rogers" in *Wikipedia*, she found an article on Fred Rogers that included his full name ("Fred McFeely Rogers") and his birth and death dates (March 20, 1928—February 27, 2003). Not satisfied with this article and its associated references and external links, she e-mailed the reference librarian at her college library for assistance in locating more complete and authoritative sources. The librarian began by consulting the online version of *Biography and Genealogy Master Index* and discovered several variant forms of his name: Rogers, Fred; Rogers, Fred (1928–); Rogers, Fred (1928–2003); Rogers, Fred (McFeeley) (1928–); Rogers, Fred (McFeely) (1928–2003); Rogers, Fred M. (1928–); Rogers, Fred M. (1928–2003); Rogers, Fred McFeely (1928–); Rogers, Fred McFeely (1928–2003). Scanning the entries associated with each of these variant forms, the librarian identified the sources likely to provide the most substantive information (in contrast to briefer *Who's Who* type entries). These included *Contemporary Authors*, *The Scribner Encyclopedia of American Lives*, *Encyclopedia of World Biography*, and *Current Biography Yearbook.* Because Mr. Rogers died a few years earlier, the librarian also checked *American National Biography* online and found a detailed biographical sketch together with a photograph. This entry concluded with a very helpful bibliography including various published sources and a three-hour documentary by PBS, *Fred Rogers: America's Favorite Neighbor*. The librarian sent the student an e-mail summarizing her search strategy and recommended sources. The student replied with a "thank you" e-mail and a further request for help in locating the documentary. The librarian did a title search in *WorldCat* and found more than 400 holding libraries. Although the college library did not have a copy, the librarian was able to direct the student to a copy in the video collection at the local public library.

REFERENCES

Adams, Diana. 2003. Introduction to *Eminent Victorians*, by Lytton Strachey, xi. New York: Barnes & Noble.

Carlyle, Thomas. 1876. *The Carlyle Anthology*. Edited by Edward Barrett. New York: Henry Holt.

Katz, William. 2002. *Introduction to Reference Work*, 8th ed. Boston: McGraw-Hill.

L'Amour, Louis. 1989. *Education of a Wandering Man*. New York: Bantam.

Smith, Alexander. 1863. *Dreamthorp: A Book of Essays Written in the Country*. London: Strahan & Co.

LIST OF SOURCES

All Music Guide. http://www.allmusic.com.

Almanac of Famous People. 2011. Detroit: Gale Research. Available online as part of *Biography in Context.*

American Men and Women of Science. 2012. Detroit: Gale Research. Available online as part of *Gale Virtual Reference Library* and *Biography in Context.*

American National Biography. 1999. New York: Oxford University Press. Supplements, 2000–. Available online: http://www.anb.org. [subscription required]

Ancestry Library Edition. Ann Arbor, MI: ProQuest. http://ancestrylibrary.proquest.com. [subscription required]

Australian Dictionary of Biography. http://adb.anu.edu.au.

Biographical Dictionary. http://www.s9.com.

Biography and Genealogy Master Index. Farmington Hills, MI: Gale Cengage Learning. http://assets.cengage.com/pdf/fs_bgmi.pdf. [subscription required]

Biography in Context. Farmington Hills, MI: Gale Cengage Learning. http://solutions.cengage.com/InContext/Biography/. [subscription required]

Biography Index Past and Present. Ipswich, MA: EBSCO. https://www.ebscohost.com/academic/biography-index-past-and-present. [subscription required]

Biography Reference Bank. Ipswich, MA: EBSCO. https://www.ebscohost.com/us-high-schools/biography-reference-bank. [subscription required]

Biography Reference Center. Ipswich, MA: EBSCO. https://www.ebscohost.com/us-high-schools/biography-reference-center. [subscription required]

Biography.com. http://www.biography.com.

Burt, Daniel S. 2001. *The Biography Book: A Reader's Guide to Nonfiction, Fictional, and Film Biographies of More Than 500 of the Most Fascinating Individuals of All Time.* Westport, CT: Oryx Press.

Burt, Daniel S. 2003. *What Historical Novel Do I Read Next?* Detroit: Gale.

Canadian Who's Who. Toronto: University of Toronto Press. http://canadianwhoswho.ca. [subscription required]

Castlegarden.org. The Battery Conservancy. http://www.castlegarden.org/.

Chambers Biographical Dictionary. 2011. London: Chambers Harrap. Available online as part of *Credo Reference.*

Church of Jesus Christ of Latter-Day Saints. 1988. *International Genealogical Index United States.* Salt Lake City: Church of Jesus Christ of Latter-Day Saints, Genealogical Dept. Available online as part of *FamilySearch.*

Complete Dictionary of Scientific Biography. 2008. Farmington Hills, MI: Charles Scribner's Sons. Available online as part of *Gale Virtual Reference Library.*

Contemporary Authors Series. 1962–. Farmington Hills, MI: Gale Cengage Learning. Available online as part of *Biography in Context* and *Literature Resource Center.*

Contemporary Black Biography. 1992–. Farmington Hills, MI: Gale Cengage Learning. Available online as part of *Biography in Context.*

Contemporary Hispanic Biography. 2002–. Farmington Hills, MI: Gale Cengage Learning. Available online as part of *Gale Virtual Reference Library.*

Credo Reference. Boston: Credo Reference. http://credoreference.com. [subscription required]

Current Biography. 1940–. Ipswich, MA: EBSCO. Available online as part of *Current Biography Illustrated* and *Biography Reference Bank.*

Cyndi's List of Genealogy Sites on the Internet. http://www.CyndisList.com.

Dictionary of American Biography. 1928–1937. New York: Scribner. Supplements, 1944–1980. Available online as part of *Biography in Context* and *HathiTrust Digital Library.*

Dictionary of Canadian Biography. 1966–2006. Toronto: University of Toronto Press. Available online: http://www.biographi.ca/en/index.php.

Dictionary of Literary Biography Complete Online. Farmington Hills, MI: Gale Cengage Learning. Available online as part of *Literature Resource Center*.

Dictionary of Scientific Biography. 1970–1980, 1990. New York: Scribner. Available online as part of *Gale Virtual Reference Library* and *HathiTrust Digital Library*.

Digital Sanborn Maps. Ann Arbor, MI: ProQuest. http://sanborn.umi.com/. [subscription required]

Encyclopedia of World Biography. 1998. Farmington Hills, MI: Gale Cengage Learning. Supplements, 1999–. Available online and as part of *Biography in Context*.

FamilySearch. http://familysearch.org/.

Find a Grave. http://www.findagrave.com/.

The First Ladies. https://www.whitehouse.gov/1600/first-ladies.

Gates, Henry Louis Jr., and Evelyn Brooks Higginbotham. 2013. *African American National Biography*. New York: Oxford University Press. Available online as part of *Oxford African American Studies Center*.

General Land Office Records. Bureau of Land Management. https://www.glorecords.blm.gov.

Google Images. http://images.google.com.

Grove Art. Oxford: Oxford University Press. Available online as part of *Oxford Art Online*.

Grove Music. Oxford: Oxford University Press. Available online as part of *Oxford Music Online*.

Hartman, Donald K., and Gregg Sapp. 1994. *Historical Figures in Fiction*. Phoenix: Oryx.

HeritageQuest Online. Ann Arbor, MI: ProQuest. http://www.proquest.com/products-services/HeritageQuest-Online.html. [subscription required]

Immigration Records. National Archives and Records Administration. http://www.archives.gov/research/immigration/.

Infoplease Biography. http://www.infoplease.com/people.html.

The International Who's Who. 1935–. London: Europa. Available online: http://www.worldwhoswho.com. [subscription required]

Internet Movie Database (IMDB). http://www.imdb.com/.

Land Records. National Archives and Records Administration. http://www.archives.gov/research/land/.

Literature Resource Center. Farmington Hills, MI: Gale Cengage Learning. http://gdc.gale.com/gale-literature-collections/literature-resource-center/. [subscription required]

Marquis Biographies Online. New Providence, NJ: Marquis Who's Who. http://www.marquiswhoswho.com/. [subscription required]

Merriam-Webster's Biographical Dictionary. 1995. Springfield, MA: Merriam-Webster. Available online as part of *Biography in Context*.

Mocavo. https://www.mocavo.com/.

The New Century Cyclopedia of Names. 1954. New York: Appleton-Century-Crofts.

New Dictionary of Scientific Biography. 2007. Farmington Hills, MI: Charles Scribner's Sons. Available online as part of *Gale Virtual Reference Library*.

New York Times Obituaries Index. 1858–. New York: New York Times. http://www.nytimes.com/pages/obituaries/index.html.

Newsmakers. 1988–. Farmington Hills, MI: Gale Cengage Learning. Available online as part of *Biography in Context* and *Gale Virtual Reference Library*.

Notable American Women: 1607–1950. 1971. Cambridge, MA: Belknap Press of Harvard University Press. Available online as part of *Credo Reference* and *Alexander Street Press*.

Notable American Women: A Biographical Dictionary Completing the Twentieth Century. 2004. Cambridge, MA: Belknap Press of Harvard University Press. Available online as part of *Credo Reference* and *Alexander Street Press.*

Notable American Women: The Modern Period. 1971. Cambridge, MA: Belknap Press of Harvard University Press. Available online as part of *Credo Reference* and *Alexander Street Press.*

Oxford African American Studies Center. Oxford: Oxford University Press. http://www.oxfordaasc.com/. [subscription required]

Oxford Dictionary of National Biography. 2004. Oxford: Oxford University Press. Supplements 2009–. Available online: http://www.oxforddnb.com. [subscription required]

POTUS: Presidents of the United States. http://potus.com/.

Reisner, Rosalind. 2009. *Read on—Life Stories: Reading Lists for Every Taste.* Santa Barbara, CA: Libraries Unlimited.

Resources for Genealogists. National Archives and Records Administration. http://www.archives.gov/research/genealogy/other-websites/database-links.html.

Roche, Rick. 2012. *Read on—Biography: Reading Lists for Every Taste.* Santa Barbara, CA: Libraries Unlimited.

RootsWeb. http://www.rootsweb.ancestry.com/. [subscription required]

The Scribner Encyclopedia of American Lives. 1998–. Farmington Hills, MI: Charles Scribner's Sons. Available online as part of *Biography in Context* and *Gale Virtual Reference Library.*

Social Security Administration. *Social Security Death Master File.* Washington, DC: Government Publishing Office. http://www.ntis.gov/about/index.aspx. Available as *Social Security Death Index (SSDI)* online as part of *Ancestry Library Edition.*

Something about the Author. Farmington Hills, MI: Gale Cengage Learning. http://gdc.gale.com/gale-literature-collections/something-about-the-author-online/. [subscription required]

Statue of Liberty—Ellis Island. http://www.libertyellisfoundation.org/.

Union List of Artist Names (ULAN). Getty Research Institute. http://www.getty.edu/research/tools/vocabularies/ulan/.

U.S. Citizenship and Immigration Services. *Genealogy.* http://www.uscis.gov/genealogy.

The USGenWeb Project. http://usgenweb.org/.

Who Was Who: A Companion to Who's Who, Containing the Biographies of Those Who Died during the Period. 1916–. London: A & C Black. Available online: http://www.ukwhoswho.com. [subscription required]

Who Was Who in America, 1897–2007. 1942–. New Providence, NJ: Marquis Who's Who. Available online as part of *Marquis Biographies Online.*

Who's Who. 1849–. London: A & C Black. Available online: http://www.ukwhoswho.com. [subscription required]

Who's Who in America. 1900–. New Providence, NJ: Marquis Who's Who. Available online as part of *Marquis Biographies Online.*

Who's Who in the Midwest. 1949–. New Providence, NJ: Marquis Who's Who. Available online as part of *Marquis Biographies Online.*

Who's Who in the World. 1972–. New Providence, NJ: Marquis Who's Who. Available online as part of *Marquis Biographies Online.*

World Biographical Information System Online. Berlin: De Gruyter. http://db.saur.de/WBIS.

World Who's Who. New York: Routledge. http://www.worldwhoswho.com. [subscription required]

WorldCat. Dublin, OH: OCLC. http://www.worldcat.org.

SUGGESTED READINGS

Mann, Rupert. 2006. "Searching the *Oxford Dictionary of National Biography.*" *The Indexer* 25 (1): 16–18.

Mann, electronic publication manager for the *Oxford Dictionary of National Biography*, explains how the option to "Search for biography of person" can exploit the metadata associated with each name to enable retrieval on alternative forms, such as maiden and married surnames. While the index stores variants in the spelling of names that appear in the historical record (e.g., searching "shakspere" will lead to "Shakespeare"), misspellings will not yield a match.

Roche, Rick. 2012. *Read on—Biography: Reading Lists for Every Taste.* Santa Barbara, CA: Libraries Unlimited.

Roche provides an annotated readers' advisory guide to 450 book-length biographies that include both recently published and classic titles. Organized by features such as character, story, language, setting, and mood, the title will assist in the identification of relevant titles for readers. The work also includes a brief history of biography as a literary form.

Reference and User Services Association. 2007. *Guidelines for a Unit or Course of Instruction in Genealogical Research at Schools of Library and Information Science.* http://www.ala.org/rusa/resources/guidelines/guidelinesunit.

These guidelines provide an outline of the expertise needed to support library users undertaking genealogical research, including basic genealogical research methodology and major genealogy research resources. Notes accompanying the guidelines identify several sources useful in developing this expertise.

Reference and User Services Association. 2007. *Guidelines for Developing a Core Genealogy Collection.* http://www.ala.org/rusa/resources/guidelines/guidelinesdeveloping.

These guidelines describe the services, resources, and staff necessary to create and maintain a collection suitable for genealogical research. They are designed to help libraries build core genealogy collections and plan for basic genealogical reference assistance.

Searing, Susan E. 2007. "Biographical Reference Works for and about Women, from the Advent of the Women's Liberation Movement to the Present: An Exploratory Analysis." *Library Trends* 56 (2): 469–93.

Searing compiled a database of more than 400 English-language biographical dictionaries and collective biographies devoted to women and published in the period 1966–2006. This database was analyzed to identify trends in subject content over this period. She also highlights problems with some sources, including duplicative content, subjectivity, and factual errors and omissions. A bibliography of sources used in this study, grouped by decade, is available at: https://www.ideals.illinois.edu/bitstream/handle/2142/3534/SearingWomensBiogRef-final.pdf?sequence=2.

Skarl, Susie. 2014. "This Is Your Life." *College & Research Libraries News* 75 (7): 394–406.

Skarl provides a guide to authoritative online biographical sources for notable individuals, both living and deceased, in an effort to aid students in their research. Noted sites include those from nonprofit organizations, government entities, universities, and media outlets. The guide does not intend to be comprehensive; but, rather, to serve as a gateway to information about noteworthy individuals.

Szucs, Loretto Dennis, and Sandra Hargreaves Luebking. 2006. *The Source: A Guidebook to American Genealogy*, 3rd ed. Provo, UT: Ancestry. Also available online: http://www.ancestry.com/wiki/index.php?title=The_Source:_A_Guidebook_to_American_Genealogy.

This guide was designed to help genealogists select, locate, and use primary and secondary sources in their research. It can also serve as an introductory guide for new genealogists and provide tips for more experienced researchers.

Wleklinski, Joann M. 2010. "Get a Life." *Online* 34 (1): 40–44.

Wleklinski evaluates a number of online biography resources, such as Gale's *Biography Resource Center* (now *Biography in Context*) and H.W. Wilson's *Biography Reference Bank*. Biographical results from the general Web search tool, *Google*, are also analyzed.

Chapter 22

Government Information

Sarah Erekson and Mary Mallory

INTRODUCTION

Government information offers an exciting unique area of reference service. It is pervasive electronically, and it has its own Internet domains and specialized classification schemes. Similarly to other publishers and information providers, governments produce resources and publications that educate, enlighten, and entertain, although in the case of governments, the original purpose is not for profit. Most importantly, government information exists to accomplish a particular civic mission, that is, to record openly a government's activities and inform the public. The result is that government information covers nearly every imaginable topic.

Government documents are used by officials, the general public, statisticians, social workers, scientists, students, retirees, teachers, parents—in short, by almost anyone who has an information need. That is why, in addition to formal government depositories, most libraries, regardless of type, size, or location, function as providers of government information to users. Many library practitioners use government information every day. It is not just for specialists anymore, and of course, it never was.

This chapter focuses on current strategies for discovering, locating, and using government information. It also discusses the most indispensable government documents and information sources. U.S. federal government information sources are stressed, with related sources and tools from nongovernmental or commercial sources discussed as appropriate. Canadian government information is covered in its own section. Selected state, local, and intergovernmental sources, such as the United Nations (UN), are also then discussed. Strategies for reference and research services using government information are discussed throughout.

GOVERNMENT INFORMATION: A BRIEF HISTORY

Government information has existed since governments were first formed. The *U.S. Constitution*, in Article 1, Section 5, contains the first mention of U.S. government information, calling on Congress to keep and publish a journal of its proceedings. By 1795, Congress was distributing copies of laws to the states, and in 1813, it passed the first law authorizing systematic printing of government materials. Congress founded the Government Printing Office within the legislative branch in 1861. Throughout this historical period, most executive agencies submitted annual reports to Congress about their activities. These appeared as part of the *United States Serial Set.*[1] The *Serial Set* was a shifting composition of congressional publications, messages, and communications from the president and other executive agencies, or anything else chartered or commissioned by Congress, and was the primary vehicle for publishing and distributing *all* federal government information. Soon, the *Serial Set* and other documents began to be sent more widely to states, historical societies, and universities, and this geographical, institutional pattern served as an early model for the establishment of federal depository libraries throughout the country.

In 1895, the General Printing Act advanced this idea much further: it streamlined and expanded the arrangement into a system of depositories of public documents called the Federal Depository Library Program (FDLP), through which documents were distributed, free of charge, to designated libraries throughout the nation. This act also mandated the creation of a catalog of all such documents, the first effort at systematic ongoing bibliographic control of government documents; by this time, more and more executive branch documents were being printed separately from the *Serial Set*.

During the 20th century, the federal government itself expanded quickly and, with it, the production of government information. The depository library enterprise also continued to mature. However, public access was implicit only until 1962 when Congress passed a law specifically requiring depository libraries to allow all members of the public to have access to the documents. The program continued to evolve. The bicentennial era, 1976–1977, saw the beginning of nonprint formats, primarily microfiche, and distributed cataloging. All bibliographic records for government documents began to be included in the Online Computer Library Center (OCLC) database, ultimately resulting in the integration of government documents records into online library catalogs. Government agencies are now making documents and other content directly available in electronic format via the Web, and the renamed Government Publishing Office (GPO) is managing, preserving, and making content accessible through *FDsys*, the agency's digital system. At present, the FDLP continues to offer selected tangible documents to depository libraries, although libraries are not required to collect these.[2]

The creation of the *Federal Information Preservation Network* (*FIPNet*), part of the National Plan for U.S. Government Information, represents another step toward ensuring access into the future to this vast national asset, including both tangible and digital documents. *FIPNet is* envisioned as a collaborative network dependent upon local participation and decentralization.

USES AND CHARACTERISTICS

U.S. government documents are officially defined as "informational matter which is published as an individual document at Government expense, or as required by law" (44 United States Code 1901). Basic government information sources include the laws and official records of government entities, such as the *United States Statutes at Large*, the *Congressional Record*, the *United States Code* (*USC*), the *Federal Register*, the *Code of Federal Regulations*, the *Public Papers of the President*, and the *United States Reports*. Government information also includes information of a more administrative nature, such as the Department of the Interior's *Annual Performance Plan and Report* or Department of State's *Foreign Per Diem Rates by Location* for federal employee travel outside the country. In the course of carrying out their responsibilities, government agencies often produce demographic and economic data, such as reports from the *Census of Population and Housing* and *USA Trade Online*. Government information may be technical or scholarly in nature, as in the case of the myriad research studies included in the U.S. Geological Survey's *Bulletins* and *Professional Papers*, or specific titles, such as *The Art of Empathy: Celebrating Literature in Translation*, published by the National Endowment for the Arts. Many documents are informational matter for general use by the public, such as *Dietary Guidelines Consumer Brochure*, produced by the U.S. Department of Agriculture. The percentage of current U.S. federal government information available online is extremely high and trending ever closer toward 100 percent. GPO's emphasis is on discovery and stewardship of government information, regardless of format, and it continues to work hard in the areas of identification of materials, cataloging and metadata, preservation, and ensuring perpetual access to government information in all formats.

On a significantly smaller scale, state governments produce a similar range of state government information. State governments may have agencies that are responsible for managing depository programs, although many of these now rely upon electronic formats to satisfy legal requirements and provide no-fee information access to depositories and the public. Local governments, foreign-country governments, and intergovernmental organizations (IGOs), such as the African Union or the North Atlantic Treaty Organization, create government information, although the output and volume of these entities vary greatly. Nonetheless, e-publishing, websites, databases, and e-government services have increased the availability of all levels of government information and resulted in better access for many.

The UN, the most prominent IGO, has maintained a formal depository program since 1946, and similar to the FDLP, selected libraries housed onsite collections and retained specialists to provide reference service. Today, electronic collections and repositories yield far greater numbers and types of resources and can offer greater and more efficient access, but may require a greater range of unique knowledge to be used effectively.

Organization of Documents

Federal government documents in physical formats use a unique classification system called the Superintendent of Documents system, referred to as SuDocs. Unlike Dewey or Library of Congress, the SuDocs system is based on issuing agency; that is, provenance, rather than subject. Class numbers are based on

TABLE 22.1 Example of a SuDocs Number

L				Department of Labor
	35			Occupational Health and Safety Administration (OSHA)
		.8		Handbooks, manuals, and guides
			:N 14	Cutter for title word "Nail"
				Nail Gun Safety: A Guide for Construction Contractors

agency, subagency, and publication series, type, or form. For example, the SuDocs number for *Nail Gun Safety: A Guide for Construction Contractors*, L 35.8:N 14, is constructed as follows:[3]

SuDocs numbers are devised and assigned by GPO to materials in all formats. Although some libraries have classified and integrated documents into the regular collections using the Library of Congress or Dewey classification schemes, the SuDocs system is universal and used in many standard bibliographies, such as *Catalog of U.S. Government Publications*. For libraries that catalog government documents and information, the standard SuDocs number can then be searched in the online catalog. The system allows the user to find a particular item and/or browse an agency or subagency's publications on the shelves, and depending upon the integrated library management system in use, it should be possible to create a browsable SuDocs shelflist, regardless of format. Understanding and use of the SuDocs system remains essential for reference, classification, and access purposes. It comprehensively illustrates every U.S. government unit, relationships within these units, changes over time, and the publishing output of the units, historically and currently. Consequently, it is an invaluable tool for identifying and locating federal government information. This is similarly true of the UN Document Symbols scheme for its resources.

Web domain names also represent an authoritative type of information organization. Most U.S. government information is at the .gov domain, although the U.S. Department of Defense uses .mil for most of its websites. Quasi-governmental entities, such as the Smithsonian Institution, may use another; Smithsonian's is .edu. The UN uses the .org domain. Most state governments use either a variation on their postal abbreviation and .us or the state name with .gov. Other national-level governments generally use their assigned country extension.

It is important to remember that nongovernmental sites, perhaps a university or even a private company, may host digital versions of government documents. These may not be official versions, but depending upon the user and the purpose, such digital versions may in reality be more than sufficient.

Uses of Government Information

Librarians rely on a broad range of federal government information. Standard types of reference tools include compendiums, directories, yearbooks, handbooks, bibliographies, indexes and abstracts, periodicals, and maps. Often electronic now, these are used to answer factual questions about the government, its personnel, its activities, and the nation. Government information also contains a wealth of historical and current information about the country, geographical and political units, and its people. In the following section, major types of reference activity utilizing government documents are highlighted.

A major category of reference use of documents is bibliographic verification, or supplying bibliographic information about a particular document. The question may take the form of "What is the *Serial Set* volume number of House Document 91–102?" or "This citation for *The Great Lakes Triangle* says the call number is ED 202716, what does that mean?" Furthermore, certain government publishers tend to use numbering systems that are independent of SuDocs classification or that have been acquired by libraries through providers other than the FDLP, such as the National Technical Information Service (NTIS) documents. Upon identification of the item or source, the question becomes how to find the desired document within the library's tangible collection or online. Similarly, government reports and statistical tables are cited daily in newspapers and other media, and a librarian may be asked to find the original source.[4] Increasingly, search engines can often identify current known-item requests, but standard government information catalogs may be required. Familiarity with major government surveys, series, abbreviations, and acronyms is fundamental to this process.

Answering questions about legislation and public laws is standard practice in government information reference service. A user may be looking for a specific fact, such as the date the president signed a bill into law, or may want to review a known discrete source, such as a public law, a House report, or committee hearings on a bill. Frequently, the testimony of a particular individual at the hearing is requested. A user may be interested in the status of proposed legislation or may want either a succinct overview or in-depth coverage of a particular legal or public policy or program. Usually, current information is needed, but historical queries are common. Standard congressional information tools may provide answers to ready-reference or basic requests, although in some cases congressional publications must be consulted. Locating official versions of these publications, whether in print or in electronic format, can be straightforward, as long as an accurate citation is available or can be fairly easily ascertained. Each legislative measure—that is, bill or resolution—has a legislative history, whether brief or extensive, and the process of ascertaining this information or tracking current legislative proposals has become much less time-consuming and cumbersome as a result of the development of excellent electronic tools and databases, including both free and fee-based resources. These are discussed specifically later in the section on legislation.

Historical uses of government information are also extremely important. Local collections and digital resources are heavily utilized, and referrals to other libraries and archives occur frequently. Another major type of assistance revolves around statistical information and data sets (covered in Chapter 23).

Librarians and E-Government

Government information reference work may require an instructional component. Because certain bibliographic tools are specific to particular genres of government information, users may be unaware of these or unfamiliar with the content, organization, and best approaches to using any given tool. Librarians frequently find themselves in the position of teaching users about unique reference sources and helping them to acquire government information access skills. Librarians also may need to instruct users on technology, such as software unique to government sources.

Combining these two types of instruction, library professionals provide e-government service. That is, they help users interact with governments electronically by connecting to government websites, communicating with government agencies and staff, contacting elected officials through e-mail, and submitting forms for government programs and services.

Common e-government information needs requested at libraries revolve around: government programs and services, specific legal questions or research, permits and licenses, laws and regulations, government forms, and assistance from a government agency (Fisher, Becker, and Crandall 2010). However, the term "e-government" also includes other aspects of government information and technology use. For example, it breaks down barriers for business and industry to interact with the government. Another benefit of e-government is that it facilitates efficiency and transparency.

In 2007, Darrell M. West did a survey of state and federal e-governments in the United States. He analyzed more than 1,500 state and federal websites on factors like accessibility, security and privacy policies, readability, and service functions. Some of the issues he identified were making services that are reliable, secure and private, accessible to people with disabilities, adaptable to various devices, fully functional, and at a reading level of most users. Nearly 10 years later, these are still major hurdles in e-government. However, now there are also issues surrounding the sustainability, preservation, transparency, and the role of libraries in e-government.[5] In the 2014 Center for Research Libraries forum, "Leviathan: Libraries and Government Information in the Age of Big Data," James A. Jacobs posited that "The simple fact is: no one knows how much born-digital U.S. Federal government information has been created, or where it all is, or how much of it is being preserved." The role of librarians in helping organize, provide access to, and preserve the electronic government information is not fully defined. While one role may be directing patrons to *IRS.gov*, other e-government reference may provide users with tutorials on how to apply for grants online using *Grants.gov*. Other services may be available such as searching the online city council proceedings about new food truck regulations. To determine what kinds of e-government services can be reasonable for a library to provide, librarians can use the American Library Association's *E-Government Toolkit*.

EVALUATION

Government information sources may be the only authoritative source on a subject. There may be no similar sources with which to compare its currency and accuracy. Evaluation of reference tools from the government therefore depends mainly on comparing features, format, indexing, ease of use, local need, and price, as well as the inclusion of complete and accurate citations to the original sources. Space constraints must be considered as well. Scientific studies, government-funded research and its report literature, and administrative records of government agencies also present unique and original information. These considerations must be accounted for in the evaluation process.

Commercially published reference sources provide background, present additional factual information, and offer analyses on politics, socioeconomic matters, and public officials, even critiques, and help to supplement the vast array of government-produced information tools. For instance, a user interested in legislation might prefer the *CQ Magazine*, weekly coverage that surveys current public policy, significant legislation, and other activities of Congress and includes major votes and other activities, to the often-more-difficult task of examining the primary source materials found in *Congress.gov*, a legislative research system discussed later in the chapter.

Government information should be evaluated as to its nature and purpose. For instance, much agency government information is by nature designed to be strictly factual and may be considered accurate. Proceedings, records, and most statistical undertakings are relatively straightforward, and the research involved is done by career staff, scientists, and statisticians. Other government information, but perhaps less than one might think, is potentially subject to disagreement, depending on politics and interpretations of specific issues.

SELECTION

The dramatic reduction of government information in print format has clearly altered the selection and acquisition of government information. The traditional method of acquiring government documents was for a library to be part of the FDLP, through which some 1,000 depository libraries would select "classes" (a designation for a particular title or series or type of publication from a particular government entity) of depository item numbers and receive these from GPO at no cost. The law requires libraries to house and retain the materials and make them available to the general public. GPO continues to produce a number of "essential titles" in print, and most depository libraries receive them.

Because of the preponderance of online government information, selection of government information by depositories is becoming a two-part process: first, identify those titles beyond the essential titles necessary to receive in tangible formats, and second, identify what online government information requires localized discovery tools. However, though much information is available online and in tangible formats through depository programs, there are hundreds of thousands of government documents that are not distributed through depository programs. These include U.S. federal and UN documents and publications. Acquisition of government information, especially local, state, and international publications, is an important skill that continues in the digital publishing environment. In most cases, these other levels of government do not have persistent URLs or assurances that the electronic materials will have permanent access. This may mean that long-term access to these publications is in jeopardy if the only way libraries provide access to these publications is by pointing to websites.[6]

To a degree, government information selection is not significantly different from any other selection process: one must be aware of the needs of local users. Although most federal depositories will want to own the essential titles, decisions of what else to acquire are informed by local needs. Librarians in rural libraries located among public lands might make sure that they are receiving in print, if available, pertinent publications from the U.S. Forest Service or the Bureau of Land Management. Similarly, librarians in the Delaware suburbs of

Philadelphia might want to make sure that they receive *Census of Population and Housing* volumes not only about Delaware but about Pennsylvania and Maryland as well. When items are electronic-only, librarians will use similar logic to decide whether they would like local catalog records for particular electronic documents. Although the basic government information sources are easily identified and are discussed later in this chapter, the less common sources needed by users of a particular library have to be identified through librarians' alertness and sensitivity to their users' needs, and reliance upon standard government information collection tools.

GENERAL SOURCES ON THE U.S. FEDERAL GOVERNMENT

Government-produced reference sources fall into many categories. The section identifies sources that can be used to locate information on and publications from a wide variety of federal government entities.

The Federal Depository Library Program and the GPO

As mentioned earlier, the standard system of acquiring and providing access to federal government information is the FDLP. Administered through the GPO, the FDLP distributes tangible and electronic materials, and provides bibliographic records. GPO offers a number of tools for accessing government publications. The essential finding tool for federal documents is the *Catalog of U.S. Government Publications*. Although it does not include all unclassified documents, the *Catalog* represents the most complete bibliography available. The free online *Catalog* contains bibliographic records created since 1976 and is updated on a daily basis. In addition to keyword, title, and SuDocs class number searches, the system supports depository item and GPO stock number searches, among other options. In many cases, the *Catalog* links to online copies of publications. In addition, a "Locate in a Library" option allows the user to enter a state or area code and identify which depository libraries should own the item based on their item selection profile.

FDsys is another GPO tool. *FDsys* provides full-text access to Congressional documents and other publications. These are considered authentic electronic versions of government titles. *FDsys* is growing and evolving conceptually; all three branches of the U.S. Government are covered, although selectively, and it is an extremely valuable repository.

As of spring 2016, the GPO is planning to replace *FDsys* with a new online portal called *govinfo*, currently in beta. This new system allows basic and advanced searches, searching by citation, and a variety of browsing options, including alphabetical, by collection, by date, by committee, and by government author. *govinfo* also highlights new content and has a section of featured content related to current events.

Many government publications can also be found in local libraries using *WorldCat*. However, in a library in which documents are not cataloged and entered into an online catalog, the *Catalog* may function as the primary access tool to the library's physical U.S. documents collection, especially of older material, assuming the SuDocs arrangement.

General and Agency Websites

The U.S. General Services Administration's *USA.gov* tool functions as the official primary portal to federal government information online. In English and Spanish versions, *USA.gov* offers broad access to government information based on topics and services. Besides the comprehensive Index, the following categories are featured: Government Agencies and Elected Officials; Benefits, Grants, and Loans; Health; Housing and Community; Jobs and Unemployment; Money and Shopping; and Travel and Immigration. Other services, such as Disasters and Emergencies, and Military and Veterans are found on an extended list. Links to contact information for the president, members of Congress, federal agencies, governors, state legislators, state agencies, and tribal governments are readily accessible, and two other highly valuable points of access, Jobs and Kids, are prominently placed. Internships and volunteer opportunities are promoted in the Jobs section. All depository libraries, all public libraries, and any other type of library that deals directly with the public should maintain a link to this portal, and anyone working in a user services environment should be familiar with it.

USA.gov indexes millions of government Web pages at all levels of government. *FDsys* is equally useful along these lines. If the query is about government "services," *USA.gov* should be the starting point. In general, both resources can be more than adequate for known-item searches. It is important to note that these have some potential for subject searching, with significant exceptions: several major categories of government information remain outside the reach of search engine indexing (for instance, some of the technical reports servers), or their nature usually does not lend itself to discovery via a general search engine (bills and bill status, laws and codes, and specific statistical information). So although recent government monographs that appear on government websites are somewhat easily found using these search engines, and increasingly, historical documents through services such as *HathiTrust*, many types of government information require knowledge of, and skills with, the specialized sources to be discussed in this chapter. Depending upon the type of query, federal government agency websites may be just as useful, more up to date, and more convenient. In other cases, specialty Web domains may provide quick access to information from an amalgamation of federal agencies or focus on specific federal resources. The portal *Drought.gov* represents this kind of dedicated resource of government information.

Directories

One standard way to obtain information about the federal government is to consult its official handbook, the *United States Government Manual*, which has been published annually since 1935 and is now online. The *Manual* describes the federal government (see Figure 22.1) and provides mission statements, descriptive information, organizational charts (see Figure 22.2), and directory information for legislative, judicial, and executive agencies and offices, as well as for independent boards, commissions, committees, and quasi-official agencies. Entries cover dates of establishment, key personnel, major subagencies, and programs and services. It is a convenient source for locating contacts, including those for public information inquiries and regional offices.

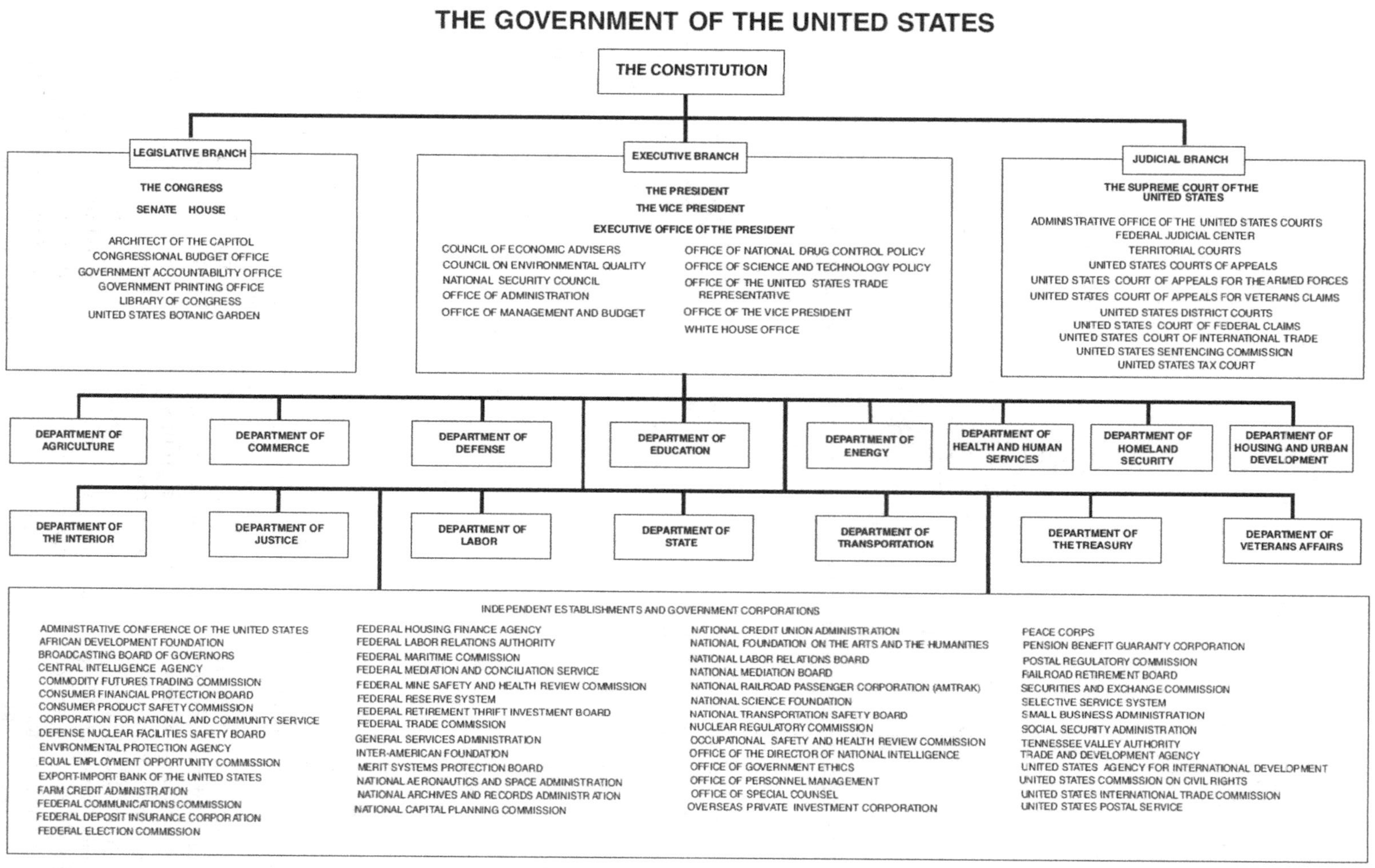

FIGURE 22.1 Organizational chart of the U.S. Government

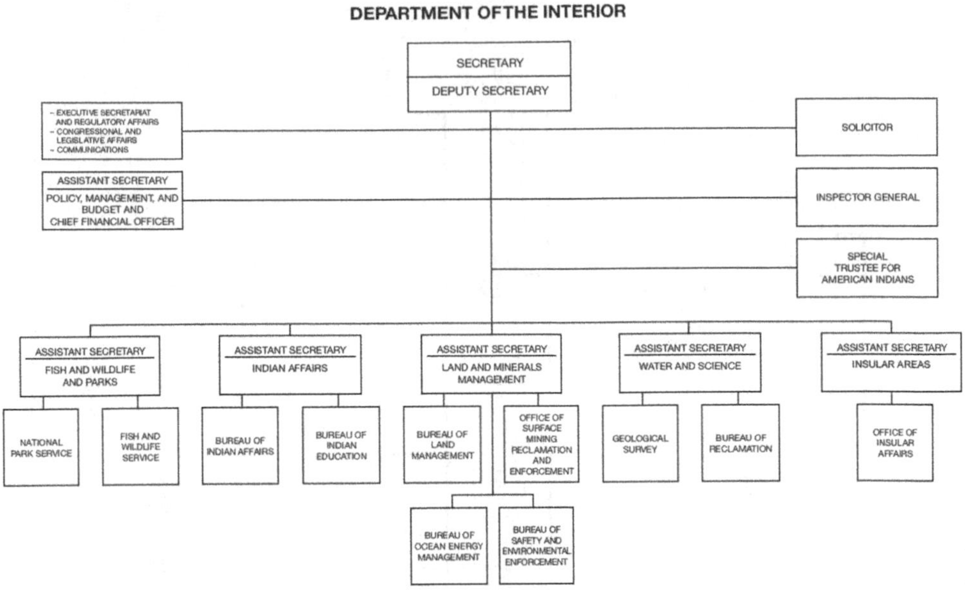

FIGURE 22.2 Organizational chart of the Department of the Interior

The websites of the House of Representatives and the Senate are a rich source of directory information as well, although they too can be inconsistent in their coverage, generally relying on individual representative and senator websites for directory information. The traditional government handbook that covers Congress is the comprehensive biennial *Official Congressional Directory*. It can be thought of as a directory for use *by members* of Congress, as well as for those seeking information *about* the Congress. A major portion of this one-volume tool (also available online) provides brief biographies and committee appointments of senators and representatives and directory information for them, their office staff, and congressional committee staff. It includes descriptions and maps of congressional districts and zip codes. Although the *United States Government Manual* presents useful descriptions of agencies and their programs, the *Official Congressional Directory* usually provides more personnel information.

Various other directories are published commercially, so unlike nearly all sources discussed in this chapter, they are not free online or available via the FDLP. In some instances, these provide directory information deeper than that is provided free online. Some are descriptive, such as the *Washington Information Directory*, which includes brief information about the programs or purpose of an agency or congressional committee, as well as the address, telephone number, and names of directors or committee members and staff. The *Washington Information Directory* also covers nongovernmental groups interested in federal activities; these include associations, lobbying organizations, and foundations.

Individual federal agencies sometimes publish their own directories, phonebooks, guides, or handbooks that give the user more detailed information about the programs, services, and organization of an agency and that also may provide factual material for reference purposes. One example is the *Social Security Handbook*, which tells what the Social Security Administration programs encompass and how to apply for benefits. The *Federal Depository Library Directory* is a useful tool in situations when a query received from a distance may be better answered by a specialist at the requestor's local depository. Moreover, as with all reference transactions, the cardinal rule in government information reference situations is "If you can't answer the question or find the source, ask a colleague."

Historical Indexes and Guides

One of the trickiest aspects of working with government information is discovering that historical publications, especially items that were quite possibly never descriptively cataloged, have not been scanned and placed online, *and* predate the *Catalog*'s creation in 1895. For these items, specialized historical indexes are necessary. A number of private and government-sponsored ventures attempt to index government publications before 1895. An example is Benjamin Poore's *A Descriptive Catalogue of the Government Publications of the United States, September 5, 1774–March 4, 1881*. An excellent annotated list of such titles is available on the National Archives' site, *Library Resources for Administrative History: Indexes to Legislative and Executive Publications*.

When using these older catalogs, it is important to remember that for the first century of the nation, most government publications were published in the *Serial Set* as previously mentioned. So historical catalogs are often used in conjunction with the *Tables of and Annotated Index to the Congressional Series of United States Public Documents* or the *Checklist of United States Public Documents 1789–1909*, each of which provides a bridge between the catalogs and the actual place within the *Serial Set* where each item is located.

Another useful source for tracking historical government publications is the *Guide to U.S. Government Publications*, popularly known as "Andriot" after its founder. It is arranged by SuDocs number and therefore by agency and includes defunct and discontinued agencies and classes alongside the current ones. It is a valuable tool for understanding publication patterns of historical and current agencies.

Specialized Catalogs and Indexes

The preceding sources are mostly broad and relatively comprehensive access points to government information. However, several types of government information needs may require more than the useful realm of Web search engines and general catalogs or indexes, especially for in-depth or comprehensive research. The two most obvious examples are tracking legislation and regulatory actions (covered later in this chapter) and finding statistical data (covered in Chapter 23). This section focuses on important examples of other types of government information that require specialized tools, including archival material, technical reports, and patents and trademarks.

Although most government information that the reference librarian deals with is public and relatively widely accessible (publications and websites designed for public consumption on some level), there are also endless amounts of archival material, and material considered by the government to be of a more private nature, especially information that concerns specific individuals or entities or is considered politically sensitive. Most of these records of the government are held by the National Archives and Records Administration (NARA) and its network of regional archives, more than 20 facilities spread out across the nation.

NARA's *National Archives Catalog* is the major point of entry to use, followed by its *Guide to Federal Records in the National Archives of the United States*. Available as a Web version, this is a general index and finding aid to what is held by the National Archives. The *Guide* does not attempt to describe individual items and pieces, but does *outline* NARA's holdings. For instance, a person researching the Tennessee Valley Authority (TVA) could use the guide to see the general types of materials held by NARA from the TVA, where they are located, and what format they are in, as well as to obtain the details to identify the relevant records. Many more popular archival records have been microfilmed, and microfilm copies are available at many of the regional archives. Some of these are now available electronically, in most cases by subscription.

The Freedom of Information Act (FOIA) requests result in files and collections of information. As an example, a selection of FBI releases are accessible at its *FBI Records: The Vault* site, formerly referred to as the *FBI FOIA Library* site. A few of the prominent individuals, groups and incidents include Josephine Baker, Bertolt Brecht, Amelia Mary Earhart, Albert Einstein, Martin Luther King Jr., John Winston Lennon, the Highlander Folk School, People for the Ethical Treatment of Animals, and the Ruby Ridge shooting incident. These files may also serve as the foundation for unique and more expansive resources, often fee-based, such as the Assassination Archives and Research Center. These can be highly useful to specialists in the reference environment as well.

For questions about accessing federal records, the following titles should be helpful. *Your Right to Federal Records: Questions and Answers on the Freedom of Information Act and the Privacy Act* and *A Citizen's Guide on Using the Freedom of Information Act and the Privacy Act of 1974 to Request Government Records* both outline the procedures that individuals can use to obtain access to federal records and agency files.

FOIA notwithstanding, librarians should be aware that nearly all government information on file in any format in archives or databases about private individuals or entities is barred by law from being released to anyone because of privacy restrictions. In no instance, often not even via law enforcement search warrant or subpoena, can anyone get access to someone else's income tax returns, social security or welfare records, census questionnaires, or any other documents related to their participation in government programs.

Scientific and technical reports represent another type of government publication for which specialized indexes may be the better finding aid or e-repositories may be available, either subscription-based or free. A recent trend is registration for basic access and subscription fees for advanced options to these now digital collections.

The premier example, NTIS reports are mostly government-funded projects. The first year of publication was 1899, and at present, there are more than 3 million reports covering more than 350 subject areas. For the most part, depositories and other libraries purchased these comprehensively or selectively, usually in microform, and the collections were arranged by NTIS-assigned "accession numbers." At present, the best option for access to reports is NTIS's *National Technical Reports Library*, which is open to all users, both domestic and international. Other useful repositories include *Technical Report Archive and Image Library* (TRAIL) and *HathiTrust*. It is also worthwhile to do a Web search for any known technical report as reports indexed by NTIS can sometimes be found elsewhere on the Web.

Patents and trademarks are a unique genre and also require separate discovery tools. In fact, patent and trademark research is sufficiently specialized to merit its own set of Patent and Trademark Resource Centers. Although these libraries remain the best places to conduct patent and trademark research, one can now accomplish fairly extensive patent and trademark research on the Web. However, accurately finding the information requires knowledge of patents and trademarks as well as an understanding of how they are indexed and classified. The basics are covered in the companion publications *General Information Concerning Patents* and *Protecting Your Trademark: Enhancing Your Rights through Federal Registration, Basic Facts about Trademarks*, which describe the nature of patents and trademarks and how the United States Patent and Trademark Office (USPTO) handles them. The USPTO website now has searchable databases of all patents and trademarks ever issued. In addition, Google has uploaded the majority of patents from USPTO into its own patent search database.

LEGISLATIVE INFORMATION

Law and its creation delineate a major area of government information reference service. Primary legal sources are published by government, available to depositories, and are in the purview of the government information professional. This section focuses on the most important information needs that occur related to statutory, administrative, and in brief, judicial law. Legal materials are discussed in greater detail in Chapter 28.

The Legislative Process

It is incumbent on the government information provider to acquire and maintain an in-depth understanding of the legislative process (depicted visually in *The Legislative Process*). Comprehension of this process and an awareness of the resultant publications ensure that librarians are able to locate the most authoritative information.

Statutes begin as legislative proposals, usually in the categories of "bills" or "resolutions." Although the ideas behind legislative proposals and bills do not always originate in Congress, only members of Congress may introduce a measure, and it is at this step that the formal life cycle of a measure begins. Upon introduction, each House or Senate bill or resolution is printed and numbered sequentially within a specific Congress, and here lies the first publication that a user may need: the text of a bill as introduced. The number and session of the pertinent Congress is printed as part of the header of the bill, and if provided, the bill's "Short Title" appears at the beginning of the bill text. The sponsor and cosponsors are listed.

The numbering is important, given that the bill will often be referenced by number. For instance, the first bill introduced in the Senate during a session of Congress will be given the number "S.1," and the second bill will be "S.2," and so on. Likewise, the first bill introduced in the House will be numbered "H.R. 1." Note that each session of Congress lasts for two years, between the elections that occur during each even-numbered year; so "S.1" for the 114th Congress will either become law or die by the end of the two-year duration of the 114th Congress. If it does not become law, a new version (which could be identical) would need to be introduced again in the next Congress, at which time it would receive a new number and begin the process anew. Further, each two-year session of Congress consists of a "first" and "second" session, usually one for each calendar year to comply with the Constitutional mandate for Congress to meet at least once each year. Action does continue from the first to the second session *within* each Congress.

It is common for high-profile legislation to be given a popular though unofficial name. A recent example is "Obamacare," actually the Patient Protection and Affordable Care Act. If a user requests the text of a bill using the popular name, the first task for the librarian will be to figure out exactly which bill is being requested.

Once a bill has been introduced, it is usually referred to a congressional committee. The committee may hold hearings on the bill, and usually a transcript of these is published. Such committee hearings are popular congressional publications, containing the oral and/or written testimony of both legislators and experts on the subject at hand. Contentious issues usually have several experts testifying on both sides of an issue, making hearings of particular use to students, the public, and casual and serious researchers alike.

If the committee decides to move the measure to the next stage, consideration by the full chamber, the bill is "reported" out of committee and accompanied by a written Senate or House report. The report, "to accompany H.R. [bill no.]" or "S. [bill no.]," contains the latest version of the proposed legislation and may include more detailed information, such as an overview of the proposal, a cost estimate, and supplemental views. These committee reports are, along with hearings, the other major committee publications. The discussion therein often renders the legislation in something closer to plain language and provides insight into the intent of the legislation (in fact, in reviewing a law, the judicial branch may actually examine the committee report to better understand what the law is trying to accomplish). More in-depth analyses about a policy, subject, or issue may also be authorized, and these studies are published as committee prints.

Once a bill is sent to the entire chamber for consideration, usually after it has come back out of a committee, it may be debated on the floor of the chamber and then voted on. These debates appear in the *Congressional Record*, and the vote activity is recorded there as well. If passed, it is sent to the other chamber to follow a similar path. Upon passage by both chambers, it is sent to the president for consideration. Note that occasionally the same legislation, or extremely similar legislation with a few differences, could make its way through both chambers concurrently. If this is the case and both bills pass their respective chambers, a "conference" of senators and representatives is appointed to iron out the differences between the two bills and make a single piece of legislation to send to the president. The result and details of the conference are published in "conference reports." The results of the conference are then sent back to each chamber to consider for passage by all members. These conference reports can be popular, especially for more contentious legislation where the House and Senate may not agree on some major provision, where the conference becomes the compromise.

Finally, once signed by the president, the legislation is known as a "public law" and is assigned a sequential number based on the Congress (e.g., Public Law 114–5). Each public law is eventually compiled sequentially into the bound series the *United States Statutes at Large*. At this point, it is usually cited using its *Statutes at Large* citation rather than its public law citation.

As indicated previously, there are numerous steps in the process by which a formal bill or resolution becomes a public law. Upon completion, the entire process is often referred to as a law's *legislative history*. Judith Schiek Robinson (1998) cites a potential 153 steps in the process, as well as "the undocumented political activities interwoven at every stage" (5). At each stage of this activity, information is produced, and in most cases, the congressional publications noted previously are issued as the primary and official mechanisms for disseminating that information. Bills and resolutions, hearings, reports and committee prints, floor debates, votes, presidential actions, laws, and other congressional publications are the tangible representations and textual records of the legislative process.

Legislative Research: Guides and Indexes

The Library of Congress's *Congress.gov* and the congressional section of *FDsys* are the permanent, no-fee electronic gateways to bills and resolutions, legislative actions, congressional publications, and related information. *Congress.gov* has the full text of most congressional publications, except congressional hearings, and its "Bill Summary and Status" section, which begins coverage with the 93rd Congress in 1973/1974, includes bill text and comprehensive bill tracking along with coverage of congressional actions. The full text of appropriate congressional actions, including committee reports and links to pages in the *Congressional Record*, began with the 104th Congress in 1994.

The comprehensive search options of *Congress.gov* include searching legislation by bill number or keyword, sponsor, assigned committee, or stage in the legislative process. Once a bill is found, *Congress.gov* offers an abundance of information: title, text, and sponsors/cosponsors; related bills; bill status; cost estimates related to the legislation provided by the Congressional Budget Office; useful summaries of the legislation from the Congressional Research Service; detailed legislative histories with links to publications; and even subject terms. If one understands the legislative process as outlined, *Congress.gov* is easy and complete.

Alternatively, GPO's *FDsys* also covers legislation, with browsable and searchable collections of congressional bills, documents, hearings, reports, and the *Congressional Record*, as well as the *Public and Private Laws* and the *Unites States Code*. Most information in *FDsys* goes back to the 104th Congress in 1994. In addition to the electronic versions of congressional publications, tangible versions are maintained by all regional and many selective federal depository libraries.

Tracing older legislation using free depository materials is more time-consuming, but viable. The former print serial *Digest of Public General Bills and Resolutions*, which the Library of Congress's Legislative Reference Service compiled from the 74th Congress (1936) through the 101st Congress (1990), did much the same as *Congress.gov*'s "Bill Summary and Status." The *Digest* is accessible in digital format via *HathiTrust*. The *Calendars of the United States House of Representatives and History of Legislation* and the *Senate Calendar of Business* are also helpful in obtaining historical bill tracking. Beginning with the 104th Congress, 1995–1996, these can be found on *FDsys*; selected issues of both of these resources also appear in *HathiTrust*. Or if available locally, the print format editions are still essential when investigating earlier legislation.

ProQuest Congressional is a subscription service offering near real-time access to congressional activity. Furthermore, more detailed coverage and indexing of historical legislation and congressional documents is provided.

CQ products are likely to appeal to those who desire readable background information on political activities, but not necessarily primary documents from Congress. These users can consult *CQ Magazine, CQ Almanac, and CQ Researcher*. These three major publications cover Congress, the presidency, the Supreme

Court, issues, and politics. *CQ Magazine* discusses major legislation, events, and issues. It also furnishes roll-call votes. At the end of the year, information from *CQ Magazine* is reorganized by subject and summarized in chronological order in the *Almanac. CQ Magazine* and *CQ Almanac* provide the user with a well-organized, succinct, and readable account of national politics and congressional, presidential, and judicial consideration of major issues affecting the American public. They are excellent resources to obtain an overview of the major legislation that one is likely to be researching on *Congress.gov* and elsewhere. *CQ Researcher*, on the other hand, offers in-depth, unbiased coverage of political and social issues, including regular coverage of topics as diverse as health, international affairs, education, the environment, technology, and the economy.

Of course, new media are covering Congress as well. Various blogs such as *GovTrack* and *Twitter* feeds from reporters, scientists, and even representatives feature congressional news as well, from every conceivable political angle. Box 22.1 illustrates how the various guides and indexes support tracking legislative history.

Box 22.1 Search Strategy: Tracking Current Legislation

A user read on a blog that Congress passed a law that would ensure that safe drinking water was available throughout the world, and she would like to find out more. A search of "drinking water" in *Congress.gov*'s current Congress bill-text section yielded a moderately long list. Browsing this list, the librarian found "H.R.2030: To provide 100,000,000 people with first-time access to safe drinking water and sanitation on a sustainable basis by 2015 by improving the capacity of the United States Government to fully implement the Senator Paul Simon Water for the Poor Act of 2005." It appeared that this might be the law the user had in mind, but a quick glance showed that it was only in committee and had not become law.

However, the result inspired the librarian to investigate further the "Senator Paul Simon Water for the Poor Act of 2005." By using *Congress.gov*'s option to search all legislation, the librarian quickly located the right bill, H.R. 1973 of the 109th Congress. Looking at the "Actions" tab section allowed the user to trace the bill's passage through Congress. The user was happy to see that her representative, Susan A. Davis, Democrat from the 53rd District in California, was a cosponsor of the bill, along with 100 other cosponsors. It had initially been referred to the House Committee on International Relations and eventually had been signed by President George W. Bush as Public Law (P.L.) 109–260 on December 1, 2005.

Information provided in the congressional actions and bill summary sections allowed her to readily learn more details about the legislative process, an overview of the purpose of the bill, and cost estimates. Note that legislation can be reported in the press at various stages, and a bill's particular status at any given time is not always made clear. Within *Congress.gov*, direct links to *Congressional Record* remarks and activities and the relevant House Report 109–260 were available within the "Actions" section, allowing her to see the remarks made on the floor of the House at the time of introduction and also the tally of the final House vote. From *Congress.gov*, the user was also able to access the full text of both the bill and the public law in *FDsys*. In general, a nearly identical process would be followed to obtain the same information in another legislative resource, such as *FDsys*, *ProQuest Congressional*, or information available in the CQ suite of titles.

Compilation and Codification of Statutes

In addition to tracing legislation from a bill to a public law, another frequent need is to find an older law or to find the current status, or codification, of statutory law on a particular subject. These two needs are filled by the use of two key sources, the *United States Statutes at Large* and the *United States Code*.

Laws enacted by each Congress are compiled into the bound volumes called the *United States Statutes at Large*. The *Statutes at Large* provide a chronological arrangement of the laws in the exact order that they have been enacted, with the text of the law as passed. Each volume contains a subject and title index. A user looking for the text of the Civil Rights Act of 1964 could find the 1964 volumes and use the indexes to locate the text. Once found, the law will include the original bill number and a brief legislative history of that bill, with major actions only. This strategy of finding laws requires knowing when the law was enacted in order to locate the correct volume. If it is a famous piece of legislation, it would likely be simple to nail down the year of passage through a quick Web search. If it is less well known, a more traditional method would be to use one of several reference books that cite laws by popular name, such as *Shepard's Acts and Cases by Popular Names*, and then use the citation to find the text of the law in the *Statutes at Large*.

FDsys contains all public laws back to 1995. Note that public laws from the current Congress will not be bound as the newest volume of the *Statutes at Large* until after the end of the current session of Congress, but these newest laws do appear in *FDsys* exactly as they will look in the *Statutes* volume and also contain the *Statutes* citation. The *United States Statutes at Large* is the official record of laws passed by Congress as they are passed (see Figure 22.3).

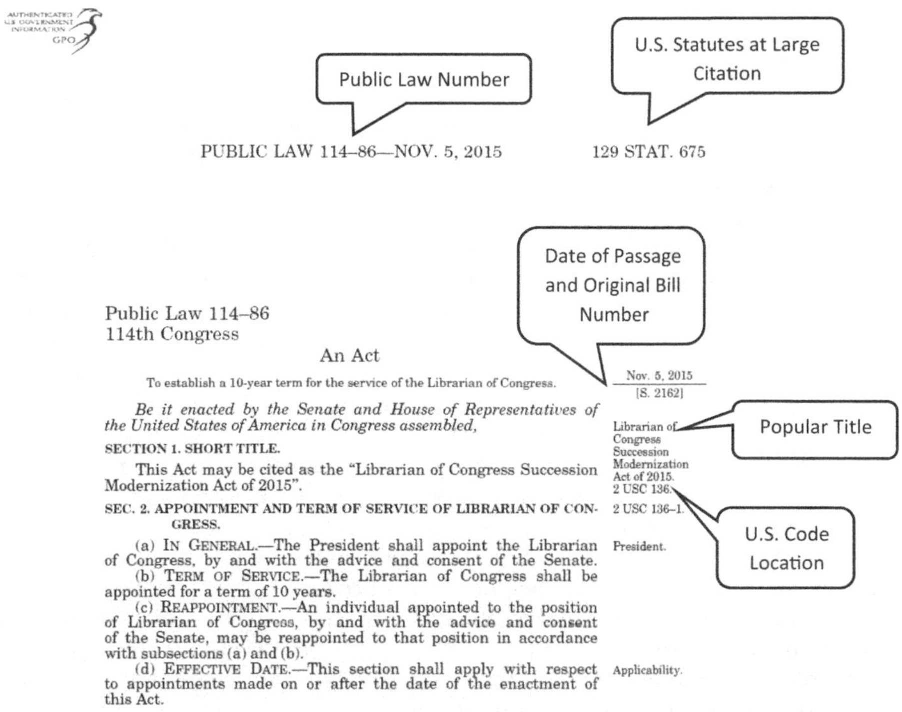

PUBLIC LAW 114–86—NOV. 5, 2015 129 STAT. 675

Public Law 114–86
114th Congress

An Act

To establish a 10-year term for the service of the Librarian of Congress.

Nov. 5, 2015
[S. 2162]

Be it enacted by the Senate and House of Representatives of the United States of America in Congress assembled,

SECTION 1. SHORT TITLE.

Librarian of Congress Succession Modernization Act of 2015. 2 USC 136.

This Act may be cited as the "Librarian of Congress Succession Modernization Act of 2015".

SEC. 2. APPOINTMENT AND TERM OF SERVICE OF LIBRARIAN OF CONGRESS.

2 USC 136–1.

President.

(a) IN GENERAL.—The President shall appoint the Librarian of Congress, by and with the advice and consent of the Senate.

(b) TERM OF SERVICE.—The Librarian of Congress shall be appointed for a term of 10 years.

(c) REAPPOINTMENT.—An individual appointed to the position of Librarian of Congress, by and with the advice and consent of the Senate, may be reappointed to that position in accordance with subsections (a) and (b).

Applicability.

(d) EFFECTIVE DATE.—This section shall apply with respect to appointments made on or after the date of the enactment of this Act.

FIGURE 22.3 Example of a public law from the *United States Statutes at Large*

The current law of the land is contained in the *United States Code*. The *Code* is the codification by subject matter of the general and permanent laws of the United States at a given time. It is divided by broad subjects into 50 titles and published by the Office of the Law Revision Counsel of the U.S. House of Representatives. It has been published in print every six years since 1926, with annual supplements published between editions. The *United States Code* is now on *FDsys*.

EXECUTIVE BRANCH PUBLICATIONS

The executive branch includes the Office of the President and numerous agencies and departments. The president may make law, although such overt lawmaking is generally limited to executive orders, which detail some function of how the government will operate and do not often have large policy implications, and proclamations, which tend to be more ceremonial. Executive branch agencies and departments are responsible for enforcing the laws enacted by Congress.

Presidential Documents

All presidential actions, such as executive orders and proclamations, along with the text of speeches, press conferences, bill-signing ceremonies, and other activities, are recorded in the *Compilation of Presidential Documents*, available in *FDsys*, which is eventually compiled into the bound *Public Papers of the President*. Of course, the White House's website is also a good source for information about presidential activity and publications.

Regulatory Documents

A key method of enforcing laws is via rules and regulations, by which executive agencies and departments issue detailed requirements pertaining to statutory law and its actual implementation. Central to the regulatory process is the publishing of *proposed* rules and regulations, followed by a public comment period, and completed with the publication of *final* rules. The comment period is normally 30, 60, or 90 days. In addition, the agency must list the name and telephone number of a person to contact for further information. Most agencies accept comments electronically or in writing. The publishing and distribution of the proposed regulations give citizens, officials, and experts the opportunity to comment on and critique them in advance of the final ruling. It is just as common for users to seek proposed rules as final versions. These administrative rulings, notices, and comments, as well as presidential executive orders and proclamations, appear in the daily *Federal Register*. *Federal Register* notices can also be announcements of meetings, opinions, or other miscellaneous information, such as the availability of an environmental impact statement or a research grant.

Federalregister.gov, the online version, allows for advanced searching and provides other tools for tracking specific areas of regulation. The website presents the same information as the print publication, but has various value-added features such as the ability to link to enabling Public Laws and *United States Code* sections, electronically comment via *Regulations.gov*, create an account to save rules for later, and subscribe to searches to get notifications on topics or announcements of the publications.

Final rules and regulations, and presidential executive orders and proclamations, are incorporated into the *Code of Federal Regulations* (*CFR*), the codification of the general and permanent rules from executive departments and agencies of the federal government. The *Federal Register* publishes rulemaking as it occurs, much as the *United States Statutes at Large* compiles laws as they are passed. Likewise, the *CFR* compiles and codifies all current, in-force regulations into a subject arrangement, just as the *United States Code* does for statutory law. The latter titles, then, are the source for current in-force laws and regulations. *FDsys* has direct links to the daily *Federal Register* and the current and historical volumes of *CFR* from its central Web page and also allows a variety of searching options, such as by agency and proposed or final rule.

When a library user needs regulations for an agency and its programs, the research may start with the *CFR*. For example, a library patron may be interested in locating the most recent regulations related to personal ownership and operation of a drone. It is possible to search the *CFR* database by keyword or to browse the subject-based volumes. The GPO and NARA Office of the Federal Register also have an "unofficial" constantly updated version of the *CFR*, entitled the *e-CFR*.

JUDICIAL BRANCH PUBLICATIONS

Courts may issue decisions on some aspect of law that is unclear or disputed. Such decisions, when considered significant by the courts, are published and make up what is called "case law." The Supreme Court's *United States Reports* have been the only judicial decisions that were (and still are) printed by the U.S. Government as government documents. Other court decisions, when they were published at all, have traditionally been published by private publishers, and access required subscriptions to large, expensive sets or databases. Government information specialists and others now have the option of using *Public Access to Court Electronic Records* (*PACER*). Case and docket information from federal appellate, district, and bankruptcy courts, and *PACER* Case Locator form this centralized system. Case law and other legal materials are discussed in Chapter 28.

CANADIAN GOVERNMENT INFORMATION

Like their U.S. counterparts, Canadian government documents and other officially disseminated information products are up to date, authoritative, readily accessible online, and indispensable as reference tools. The Canadian government's official website, *Canada.ca*, is in both English and French. Resembling *USA.gov*, the site's organization is user friendly, even for novices such as tourists or other visitors, and well organized. It achieves the near impossible by providing ready access through this initial page to the most significant and in-demand types of information, including jobs, immigration, travel, business, health, and taxes; online forms and services; the prime minister's website; and publications and reports. The footer has a "Government" section listing a series of convenient links based on the government's organization and functions.

Unlike their U.S. counterparts, Canadian government documents and information sources are no longer disseminated to the public in tangible formats. The Depository Service Program (DSP) used to administer a program somewhat analogous to the GPO's FDLP. However, due to several conditions, like website consolidation and streamlining, budget cuts, and the political climate, the program ceased distribution of tangible materials to the depository libraries in Canada, England, and the United States in 2013.[7]

Now, the DSP administers an online-only documents dissemination program. Libraries can access cataloging metadata and permanent electronic URLs to items in the Government of Canada Publications *Catalogue*. The catalogue contains more than 275,000 Government of Canada publications, including more than 150,000 that can be downloaded for free. In addition, through basic and advanced search functions, users are able to readily search publications by date and language and browse serial publications and the *Weekly Acquisitions Lists*. The latter is the source for identifying electronic publications from federal departments and the Parliament. Records for items in the *Weekly Acquisitions List* provide URLs for items and may be downloaded. Lists of documents in the *Weekly Acquisitions List* become issues of the *Weekly Checklist* or the *Supplementary Checklist*. The archived *Weekly Checklist* online goes back to 1995; the archived *Supplementary Checklist* has issues back to 1997.

Canadian Government Information Guides

In light of the changes to the Canadian Depository Services Program and Canada's government information moving to electronic-only publishing, many previously published reference guides no longer give an accurate portrait of the information services landscape in Canada today. *Info Source* is a series of publications containing information about the Government of Canada's access to information and privacy programs.

Canadiana is a one-stop shop for digitized primary source materials of Canadian history, including government information, a boon to genealogists, students, and scholars. The site is a Trusted Digital Repository, meaning that it has gone through a certification process to assure the library and archival communities that these scanned materials will be preserved and accessible. *Canadiana* is made up of several digital collections including Héritage scanned archival collections; Early Canadiana Online, scanned manuscripts and early printed materials; and the Canadiana Discovery Portal, which includes documents, archival materials, and other digitized holdings from many memory institutions.

Canadian Legislative Documents

The *Canadian Parliamentary Guide/Guide Parlementaire Canadien* is an annual publication that details the current membership of the legislative and judicial branches of the government. It includes biographical information on the members of the Senate and House of Commons, the Supreme Court and Federal Court of Canada, and the provincial legislatures. Canadian government representatives abroad and foreign representatives in Canada, members of boards and commissions, results of general elections dating back to 1867, members of the Privy Council, and members of the royal family are also listed.

For general information about the parliamentary system of government in Canada, refer to recent texts such as *The Canadian Regime: An Introduction to Parliamentary Government in Canada* (Malcolmson and Myers 2012). For a detailed discussion of the process through which bills become laws, refer to a specialized guide such as *Canadian Official Publications* (Bishop 1981).

The *Parliament of Canada* website includes extensive and current information about Parliament and its processes. "About Parliament," and its "How Parliament Works" section links to "How Canadians Govern Themselves" and "Our Country, Our Parliament," which provides overviews of the government structure and the legislative process. Primary sources from Parliament, including bills and debates, are now published online and are widely accessible using the *Parliament of Canada* website. *LEGISinfo*, available on the website, is an outstanding tool for finding information about legislation currently before Parliament. *Canadian Parliamentary Historical Resources*, a digital collection from the Library of Parliament, has the Debates and Journals of both houses from the 1st Parliament to the 35th Parliament (1867–1996). Publications from more recent Parliaments can be searched through the *Parliament of Canada* website.

The *Canada Gazette*, the official newspaper of the Government of Canada, is now published online. *Part I* contains notices and proposed regulations; *Part II* gives the text of official regulations; and *Part III* publishes Acts of Parliament.

Other Sources about Canadian Governance

The *Canadian Almanac & Directory*, from Grey House Publishing Canada, is an expansive compendium of directory information for governmental and nongovernmental organizations, and it includes coverage for municipalities. From abbreviations and airline companies to the Yukon government and zoological gardens, it is a convenient source for quick facts, basic statistics, and street and e-mail addresses, as well as URLs, if available. Color plates of flags, arms and emblems, honors, and a map of Canada add to this important tool. Many of the sections have been revised to include the new territory of Nunavut.

Governments Canada, also published by Grey House, is a directory of government officers from the federal, provincial, and municipal governments in Canada. Other features include analysis of election spending and a glossary of acronyms.

While previously covered sources may help librarians find information about Canadian legislation, regulation, and organization, other sources may elaborate on recent changes to government transparency and access to information.[8] The importance of networking and utilizing local resources cannot be overemphasized on the road to success as a government information specialist. For example, Queen's University Library has a well-organized, convenient set of links in its *Government Information* site that highlight the main government divisions and the major tools, publication series, and other types of information and data resources. The list provides nearly one-stop access to the basics. Another useful site is the University at Buffalo Libraries' *Canadian Federal Government* guide.

STATE, LOCAL, OTHER NATIONAL, AND INTERNATIONAL GOVERNMENT PUBLICATIONS

Just as U.S. and Canadian government information have nuances and require expertise, providing access to international, foreign national, state, and local government information also requires specialized knowledge of the systems that produce and disseminate government information at those levels of governance.

State Government Information

While much of federal government information is managed by the GPO and its FDLP, the coordination of state information may or may not be controlled or systematized. Some states offer depository programs wherein libraries can receive state government publications. Other states may have systems similar to the current Canadian Depository Services Program and have moved to all-electronic production and dissemination.

Bibliographies of state government publications have a venerable heritage as a separate publishing endeavor, beginning with R. R. Bowker's four-volume set, covering the years 1899 through 1908, titled *State Publications; a Provisional List of Official Publications of the Several States of the United States from Their Organization.* Adelaide Hasse's *Index of Economic Material in the Documents of the States of the United States*, 1908–1919, continued the tradition. From 1910 to 1994, the most comprehensive bibliography of state government information sources was the *Monthly Checklist of State Publications* from the Library of Congress. It was compiled by Collection Services of the Library of Congress Exchange and Gift Division. Typically, bibliographic information and price were given for monographs, annuals, and monographic series, arranged by state and issuing agency. This massive undertaking ceased in the mid-1990s, as state governments increasingly used Web publishing. It is useful for the verification of legacy state documents.

Most state governments publish directories to their agencies and officials. Like their federal counterparts, state agency websites contain directory and other factual information, which is in some cases extensive. Web searching should turn these up, although a useful, freely accessible list of links to state government is *State and Local Government on the Net. Book of the States*, published biennially, also offers a wealth of factual information about individual states in one place that may be unmatched online. *Book of the States* is the standard ready-reference source to check for recent information on state officials, state legislatures, and the state judiciary, as well as on state elections and finances. Whether seeking information on the qualifications of secretaries of state, the methods for the removal of judges and filling of vacancies, or allowable state investments, this source is the place to start. Tables abound; state excise tax rates, motor vehicle laws, and time series data on state minimum wages are examples. State mottoes, flowers, songs, birds, and so forth are also given, although a quick review of a state website may also provide this type of information.

The amount and variety of state information in electronic format has increased rapidly. Legislative information, business and economic data, and agency reports are representative of the types of information that are currently available to the public on the Web. Using these electronic sources to answer questions about state issues has become the norm. Librarians should be aware of how their own state catalogs and distributes its documents and what the best sources are for identifying those documents. The Government Documents Round Table's *State Depository Library Systems* listing can be used to identify state systems.

While legal resources are covered in greater detail in Chapter 28, states usually mimic the federal government in the publication of their state statutory law and state administrative (or regulatory) law. The titles, however, may not correspond directly to the titles of federal publications. "Statutes" can mean different things at different levels. For instance, the Illinois equivalent to the *United States Statutes at Large* is called *Laws of the State of Illinois* and its equivalent to the *United States Code* is called the *Illinois Compiled Statutes.* In recent years, making the primary legal materials of states available online has been advocated by professional organizations and users. While electronic versions of state legal materials may be available, states that have passed the Uniform Electronic Legal Materials Act have assurances that those materials are accessible, authenticated, and preserved.

Local Government Information

In the large arena of government information librarianship, the documents that are closest to home may be the hardest to obtain or to access. Local governments, like state governments, may not have obligations or mandates to "deposit" their works with libraries. Local government structures may be different from the three-branch system of checks and balances at the federal level. For example, legislative and executive functions may not be as strictly separated as they are at state or federal levels. Also, there may be a number of layers of governance at a local level; local taxing bodies or districts may overlap.[9] Finally, producers of local information may be unaware of the partnership potential for information dissemination with libraries. At these local and regional levels, there may not be an awareness about the long-term access, subject expertise, and scholarship that working with librarians can bring. If the attitude is "it's available on our website" and "we don't need to waste server space with these capital plans that are ten years old," then there is a real need for government information specialists to step in and help preserve access to local government information within their communities.[10]

That said, some cities and municipalities have repositories for local publications. Sometimes these fall into the category of archives; other times, these materials are kept at the public library.

Foreign Governments and Intergovernmental Organizations

Available in print and online, the *Worldwide Government Directory with International Organizations* is an excellent guide to foreign governments and international or intergovernmental organizations (IGO). This volume is especially useful as finding equivalent information free online for foreign government entities can be difficult or impossible. This directory provides names, addresses, and telephone numbers for foreign governments and their major agencies, as well as major IGOs. Still, collections of Web links for IGOs and other national-level governments, such as the *List of IGOs: Getting Started* and *List of Foreign Governments: Getting Started,* both from Northwestern University Library, or *Web Sites of National Parliaments,* from the Inter-Parliamentary Union are useful sources. Going straight to the websites of IGOs or foreign governments may help users get statistics, publications, and other information quickly.

Foreign governments and most IGOs vary widely in the availability of catalogs of their materials. *International Government Information and Country Information:*

A Subject Guide and *Guide to Official Publications of Foreign Countries* provide a good starting point for the publishing activities of foreign governments, and the librarian may do well by seeking out a foreign country's national bibliography and reviewing the official country website for more recent publications.

Both foreign and IGO documents may have been cataloged and be discoverable via a library catalog or a union catalog. The United Nations, the largest IGO, does have several access tools and a database of its publications and documents. The *Official Document System of the United Nations* is freely available, and it both indexes and has the full text, except for sales publications, of UN materials from 1993 forward, with selected older material. The *UNBISNET* catalog, also free, indexes (with selected full text) UN materials from 1979 forward. Older materials are being added. At present, the UN depository program is in a transitional phase, and more and more publications will be disseminated in digital format only. Another prominent IGO for libraries is the European Union, whose *ECLAS* catalog provides bibliographic access to EU documents.

SEARCH STRATEGIES

Current government information is nearly all online and mostly free. Locating a known, recent government publication can usually be accomplished through a general Web search or the library's discovery tools, including the online catalog. FDLP members may have loaded MARCIVE's e-records packages, known as, for example, Documents without Shelves. It may even be accomplished efficiently with a search of a government Web search service such as *USA.gov*. When an item is known, or characteristics are known but the title is not, a civics-informed strategy often may be successful, namely, navigating to the website of the appropriate government agency or branch and browsing for the desired information.

The *Catalog of U.S. Government Publications* continues to be a key bibliographic tool for verifying and locating government publications. If a Web search is unsuccessful or inappropriate, or if the needed item is older, search the *Catalog*. The *Catalog* benefits from the usual bibliographic advantages, such as subject headings and author information featuring the issuing agency. GPO aggressively catalogs online documents and includes links in the *Catalog*. GPO is also adding bibliographic records for legacy titles. As indicated previously, a number of specialized tools exist to aid the search for historical government information as well.

As suggested previously, many government information needs require the use of specialty tools. When Web searches, local discovery tools, and the *Catalog* are unsuccessful in locating the item sought, identify and utilize the appropriate tool. When seeking technical reports or archival documents, use tools such as the *NTIS Bibliographic Database* or *The National Archives Catalog*.

Legislation, bill history, and congressional documents are frequently needed. When specific legislation or information about a bill is sought, search *Congress.gov*, which provides easy access to bills, their text, their status in the legislative process, and documents related to the bill. *Congress.gov*, along with *FDsys*, leads to key congressional publications: committee hearings, committee reports, and the *Congressional Record*. *Congress.gov* and *FDsys* are also used to find the text of laws passed, known as public laws, and compiled into the *United States Statutes at Large*. To find the text of current law in force, search the *United States Code* via *FDsys*.

Regulations are a type of law whereby executive agencies explain how they will enforce laws passed by Congress. To locate the documents of the regulatory process, characterized by a draft rule, a comment period, and a final rule, search the *Federal Register*, accessible via *FDsys*. Regulations are then compiled and codified into the *CFR*; to find currently in-force regulations, search the *CFR* via *FDsys*. Case law, the decisions of courts and the third type of law, is generally best found in law libraries by legal specialists, but recent Supreme Court opinions and the opinions of other federal courts can be found via their websites.

For Canadian government information, pursue a strategy similar to that for the United States. Start with the official Canadian government website and also search the *Weekly Checklist* for Canadian government documents. Canadian legal information may be widely accessed via Parliament's website.

State laws, legislation, court decisions, and regulations are usually found via state-specific sources somewhat akin to federal sources. The reference librarian should learn the appropriate tools for the state or states of interest to the library's clientele.

By developing knowledge of sources of government information and associated search strategies, reference librarians can ensure public access to government information. Given the range of material published by the government, librarians in any setting can enhance service to their users by more fully integrating government information sources and assistance into reference services.

NOTES

1. For an interesting explanation and discussion of the *Serial Set*, see Virginia Saunders, "U.S. Congressional Serial Set: What It Is and Its History" (2000). Ms. Saunders was probably the foremost expert on the *Serial Set* until her death in 2009.
2. The FDLP lists those documents, which continue to be available in print on its *Essential Titles for Public Use in Paper or Other Tangible Format* website.
3. For more discussion of the Superintendent of Documents Classification system, see *Superintendent of Documents (SuDocs) Classification Scheme* on the FDLP website.
4. For an analysis of how often this happens as well as approaches to locating the documents cited, see Kline (2013).
5. For more discussion on issues of e-government implementation, see Dawes (2010) and Rose and Grant (2010).
6. Digital preservation standards and practices continue to evolve. One organization assessing, certifying, and assuring libraries of the trustworthiness and permanence of digital repositories is the Center for Research Libraries. For an overview of one library's approach, see Oehlerts and Liu (2013).
7. For historical background, a complete discussion of the early history, evolution, problems, and status of the Canadian Depository Services Program through the late 1980s can be found in Dolan (1989). The author describes the official origins of the program, the role of various agencies, and the pressures that combined to form the system in place until recently. Also, archived issues of the *Weekly Checklist* 13–49, 13–50, and 13–51 focused on the history of the Depository Services Program. For more background on the changes to the Depository Services Program in Canada, see Smugler (2013) and Wakaruk (2014).
8. See also Conteh and Roberge (2013), Larsen (2013), Larsen and Walby (2012).
9. See Stanton (2013).
10. See Wilson and Richey (2005).

REFERENCES

Center for Research Libraries. *Digital Preservation.* https://www.crl.edu/archiving-preservation/digital-archives.

Conteh, Charles, and Ian Roberge. 2013. *Canadian Public Administration in the 21st Century.* Boca Raton, FL: CRC Press.

Dawes, Sharon S. 2010. "Stewardship and Usefulness: Policy Principles for Information-Based Transparency." *Government Information Quarterly* 27 (October): 377–83.

Dolan, Elizabeth Macdonald. 1989. *The Depository Dilemma: A Study of the Free Distribution of Canadian Federal Government Publications to Depository Libraries in Canada.* Ottawa: Canadian Library Association.

E-Government Toolkit. 2008. American Library Association. http://www.ala.org/advocacy/advleg/federallegislation/govinfo/egovernment/egovtoolkit.

Essential Titles for Public Use in Paper or Other Tangible Format. 2013. Federal Depository Library Program. April 29. http://www.fdlp.gov/requirements-guidance/collections-and-databases/1443-essential-titles.

Fisher, Karen E., Samantha Becker, and Michael Crandall. 2010. "eGovernment Services Use and Impact through Public Libraries: Preliminary Findings from a National Study of Public Access Computing in Public Libraries." Paper presented at 43rd Hawaii International Conference on System Sciences, Koloa, HI. January 5–8. http://www.computer.org/portal/web/csdl/doi/10.1109/HICSS.2010.451.

Jacobs, James A. 2014. "Government Records and Information: Real Risks and Potential Losses." Paper presented at Leviathan: Libraries and Government Information in the Age of Big Data. Chicago, IL. April 24–25. https://www.crl.edu/sites/default/files/d6/attachments/events/Jacobs%20Slides%204-18.pdf.

Kline, Sims D. 2013. "Documents in the News: A Review of Articles in the *New York Times.*" *DttP: Documents to the People* 41 (Summer): 22–26.

Larsen, Mike. 2013. "Access in the Academy: Bringing ATI and FOI to Academic Research." Vancouver, BC: British Columbia Freedom of Information and Privacy Association. https://fipa.bc.ca/wordpress/wp-content/uploads/2014/06/Access-in-the-Academy.pdf.

Larsen, Mike, and Keven Walby, eds. 2012. *Brokering Access: Power. Politics, and Freedom of Information Process in Canada.* Vancouver, BC: UBC Press.

The Legislative Process. 2015. Congress. Last accessed December 26. https://www.congress.gov/legislative-process.

Oehlerts, Beth, and Shu Liu. 2013. "Digital Preservation Strategies at Colorado State University Libraries." *Library Management* 34 (1–2): 83–95.

Robinson, Judith Schiek. 1998. *Tapping the Government Grapevine: A User-Friendly Guide to U.S. Government Information Sources*, 3rd ed. Phoenix: Oryx Press.

Rose, Wade R., and Gerald G. Grant. 2010. "Critical Issues Pertaining to the Planning and Implementation of E-Government Initiatives." *Government Information Quarterly* 27 (January): 26–33.

Saunders, Virginia. 2000. "U.S. Congressional Serial Set: What It Is and Its History." Government Printing Office. September 20. http://www.access.gpo.gov/su_docs/fdlp/history/sset/index.html.

Smugler, Sherrie. 2013. "Facing Change: A Perspective on Government Publications Services in Canadian Academic Libraries in the Internet Age." GODORT Occasional Paper 9. American Library Association. http://wikis.ala.org/godort/index.php/GODORT_Occasional_Papers.

Stanton, Dan. 2013. "State and Local Documents Spotlight: A Whole Lotta Local Going On." *DttP: Documents to the People* 41 (Fall): 14–16.

Superintendent of Documents (SuDocs) Classification Scheme. 2015. Government Publishing Office. http://www.fdlp.gov/catalogingandclassification/cataloging-articles/1791-superintendent-of-documents-sudocs-classification-scheme.

U.S. Constitution. National Archives. http://www.archives.gov/exhibits/charters/constitution_transcript.html.

Wakaruk, Amanda. 2014. "What the Heck Is Happening Up North? Canadian Government Information, Circa 2014." *DttP: Documents to the People* 42 (Spring): 15–20.

West, Darrell M. 2007. "State and Federal E-Government in the United States." http://www.brown.edu/academics/taubman-center/sites/brown.edu.academics.taubman-center/files/uploads/egovt07us.pdf.

Wilson, Yvonne, and Debora Richey. 2005. "State and Local Documents Round-Up: A Basic Primer on Collecting Local Government Publications." *DttP: Documents to the People* 33 (Winter): 9–11.

LIST OF SOURCES

Annual Performance Plan and Report. Department of the Interior. https://www.doi.gov/bpp.

Assassination Archives and Research Center. http://aarclibrary.org/.

Bishop, Olga B. 1981. *Canadian Official Publications*. Guides to Official Publications, vol. 9. Oxford: Pergamon.

Book of the States. 1965–. Lexington, KY: Council of State Governments. Annual.

Bowker, R. R. (Richard Rogers). 1899–1908. *State Publications; a Provisional List of Official Publications of the Several States of the United States from Their Organization*. New York: Publishers Weekly.

Bulletins. U.S. Geological Survey. https://pubs.er.usgs.gov/browse/usgs-publications/B.

Calendars of the United States House of Representatives and History of Legislation. Government Publishing Office. https://www.gpo.gov/fdsys/browse/collection.action?collectionCode=CCAL.

Canada Gazette: Parts I, II, and III. Government of Canada/Gouvernement du Canada. http://www.gazette.gc.ca/.

Canada.ca. Government of Canada/Gouvernement du Canada. https://www.canada.ca/index.html.

Canadian Almanac & Directory. 1847–. Toronto: Grey House Publishing Canada. Annual.

Canadian Federal Government. University at Buffalo Libraries. http://libweb1.lib.buffalo.edu/guide/guide.asp?id=129.

Canadian Parliamentary Guide/Guide Parlementaire Canadien. 1909–. Toronto: Grey House Publishing Canada. Annual.

Canadian Parliamentary Historical Resources. Library of Parliament. http://parl.canadiana.ca/.

Canadiana. Canadiana.org. http://www.canadiana.ca/en/home.

Catalog of U.S. Government Publications. Government Publishing Office. http://catalog.gpo.gov/.

Catalogue. Government of Canada Publications. http://publications.gc.ca/site/eng/ourCatalogue.html.

Census of Population and Housing. Census Bureau. http://www.census.gov/prod/www/decennial.html.

A Citizen's Guide on Using the Freedom of Information Act and Privacy Act of 1974 to Request Government Records: First Report. 2002. Government Printing Office. https://www.gpo.gov/fdsys/pkg/CRPT-107hrpt371/html/CRPT-107hrpt371.htm.

Code of Federal Regulations. 1938–. Washington, DC: National Archives and Records Administration. Revised annually. https://www.gpo.gov/fdsys/browse/collection Cfr.action?collectionCode=CFR.

Compilation of Presidential Documents. Government Publishing Office. https://www.gpo.gov/fdsys/browse/collection.action?collectionCode=CPD.

Congress.gov. http://congress.gov.

Congressional Record. 1873–. Washington, DC: Congress, Daily when Congress is in session. https://www.gpo.gov/fdsys/browse/collection.action?collectionCode=CREC. Also available via *Congress.gov*.

CQ Almanac. 1945–. Washington, DC: Congressional Quarterly, Annual. http://www.cqpress.com/lib/cq-almanac-online.html. [subscription required]

CQ Magazine. 1946–. Washington, DC: Congressional Quarterly. Weekly. http://library.cqpress.com/cqweekly/. [subscription required]

CQ Researcher. 1991–. Washington, DC: Congressional Quarterly. Weekly. http://www.cqpress.com/product/Researcher-Online.html. [subscription required]

Dietary Guidelines Consumer Brochure. 2011. Department of Agriculture. http://www.choosemyplate.gov/sites/default/files/printablematerials/DG2010Brochure.pdf.

Digest of Public General Bills and Resolutions. 1936–1990. Washington, DC: Library of Congress, Congressional Research Service, 74th Cong., 2nd sess.–101st Congress, 2nd sess. Two cumulative issues, occasional supplements, and a final edition for each session. Ceased.

Drought.gov. National Integrated Drought Information System. http://www.drought.gov/drought/.

e-CFR: Electronic Code of Federal Regulations. Government Publishing Office. http://www.ecfr.gov/cgi-bin/ECFR?page=browse.

ECLAS: European Commission Libraries Catalogue. European Commission Libraries. http://ec.europa.eu/eclas/.

FBI Records: The Vault. Federal Bureau of Investigation. https://vault.fbi.gov/.

FDsys. Government Publishing Office. http://www.gpo.gov/fdsys/.

Federal Depository Library Directory. Government Publishing Office. http://catalog.gpo.gov/fdlpdir/FDLPdir.jsp.

Federal Information Preservation Network (*FIPNet*). Government Publishing Office. https://www.gpo.gov/PreserveFedInfo/.

Federal Register. 1936–. Washington, DC: National Archives and Records Administration. Daily. https://www.federalregister.gov/.

Foreign Per Diem Rates by Location. Department of State. https://aoprals.state.gov/web920/per_diem.asp.

General Information Concerning Patents. Patent and Trademark Office. http://www.uspto.gov/web/offices/pac/doc/general/.

Google Patents. http://patents.google.com.

Government Information. Queen's University Library. http://library.queensu.ca/gov.

Governments Canada. Toronto: Grey House Publishing Canada. Annual.

govinfo. Government Publishing Office. http://www.govinfo.gov.

GovTrack. Civic Impulse, LLC. https://www.govtrack.us/.

Grants.gov. http://www.grants.gov/.

Guide to Federal Records in the National Archives of the United States. 1998. 2nd ed. 3 vols. Washington, DC: GPO. http://www.archives.gov/research/guide-fed-records/.

Guide to Official Publications of Foreign Countries. 1997. Compiled by American Library Association Documents Round Table International Documents Task Force. 2nd ed. Bethesda, MD: Congressional Information Service.

Guide to U.S. Government Publications. 1953–. Farmington Hills, MI: Gale. (Commonly called "Andriot.")

Hasse, Adelaide Rosalia. 1908–1919. *Index of Economic Material in the Documents of the States of the United States*. Washington, DC: Carnegie Institution of Washington. Various volumes for individual states.

HathiTrust Digital Library. https://www.hathitrust.org/.

House of Representatives. http://house.gov.

Illinois Compiled Statutes. Illinois General Assembly. http://www.ilga.gov/legislation/ilcs/ilcs.asp.

Info Source. Ottawa: Government of Canada. http://www.infosource.gc.ca/.

IRS.gov. Internal Revenue Service. https://www.irs.gov/.

Laws of the State of Illinois. https://www.illinois.gov/Government/Pages/LawsAndConstitution.aspx.

LEGISinfo. Ottawa: Library of Parliament. http://www.parl.gc.ca/LEGISinfo/.

Library Resources for Administrative History: Indexes to Legislative and Executive Publications. National Archives. http://www.archives.gov/research/alic/reference/admin-history/publication-indexes.html.

List of Foreign Governments: Getting Started. Northwestern University Library. http://libguides.northwestern.edu/ForeignGovernmentList.

List of IGOs: Getting Started. Northwestern University Library. http://libguides.northwestern.edu/IGO.

Malcolmson, Patrick, and Richard Myers. 2012. *The Canadian Regime: An Introduction to Parliamentary Government in Canada*, 5th ed. Toronto: University of Toronto Press.

Monthly Checklist of State Publications. 1910–1994. Washington, DC: Library of Congress. Monthly. Ceased.

Morrison, Andrea M., and Barbara J. Mann. 2004. *International Government Information and Country Information: A Subject Guide*. Westport, CT: Greenwood Press.

National Archives Catalog. National Archives and Records Administration. http://www.archives.gov/research/arc/.

National Endowment for the Arts. 2014. *The Art of Empathy: Celebrating Literature in Translation*. https://www.arts.gov/publications/art-empathy-celebrating-literature-translation.

National Technical Reports Library. National Technical Information Service. http://www.ntis.gov/products/ntrl/.

NTIS Bibliographic Database. National Technical Information Service. http://www.ntis.gov/products/ntis-database/.

Official Congressional Directory. Government Publishing Office. Biennial. https://www.gpo.gov/fdsys/browse/collection.action?collectionCode=CDIR.

Official Document System of the United Nations. New York: United Nations. http://documents.un.org/.

PACER, Public Access to Court Electronic Records. Administrative Office of the U.S. Courts. http://www.pacer.gov.

Parliament of Canada. http://www.parl.gc.ca/default.aspx?Language=E.

Poore, Benjamin Perley. 1885. *A Descriptive Catalogue of the Government Publications of the United States, September 5, 1774–March 4, 1881*. Washington, DC: Government Printing Office.

Professional Papers. U.S. Geological Survey. https://pubs.er.usgs.gov/browse/usgs-publications/PP.

ProQuest Congressional. Bethesda, MD: Congressional Information Service/ProQuest. http://congressional.proquest.com/congressional/search/basic/basicsearch. [subscription required]

Protecting Your Trademark: Enhancing Your Rights through Federal Registration, Basic Facts about Trademarks. Patent and Trademark Office. http://www.uspto.gov/sites/default/files/trademarks/basics/BasicFacts.pdf.

Public Access NTRL. National Technical Information Service. https://ntrl.ntis.gov/NTRL/login.xhtml.

Public Papers of the President. 1929–1933. 1945–.Washington, DC: Government Publishing Office. (Equivalent volumes for many earlier presidents and FDR published by various private publishers.) http://www.archives.gov/federal-register/publications/presidential-papers.html.

Regulations.gov. http://www.regulations.gov/.

SAGE Knowledge. Thousand Oaks, CA: SAGE Publications. http://sk.sagepub.com/

Senate. http://senate.gov.

Senate Calendar of Business. Government Publishing Office. https://www.gpo.gov/fdsys/browse/collection.action?collectionCode=CCAL.

Shepard's Acts and Cases by Popular Names: Federal and State. 1999. 3 vols. Colorado Springs, CO: Shepard's. Cumulative supplements.

Social Security Handbook. 1960–. Social Security Administration. https://www.socialsecurity.gov/OP_Home/handbook/handbook-toc.html.

State and Local Government on the Net. Jeffersonville, IN: Hello Metro. http://www.statelocalgov.net/.

State Depository Library Systems. Government Documents Round Table. American Library Association. http://wikis.ala.org/godort/index.php/State_Depository_Library_Systems.

Supplementary Checklist of Canadian Government Publications. Government of Canada Publications. http://publications.gc.ca/site/eng/supplementaryChecklist/supplementaryChecklist.html.

Tables of and Annotated Index to the Congressional Series of United States Public Documents. 1902. Washington, DC: Government Printing Office.

Technical Reports Archive and Image Library (TRAIL). http://www.technicalreports.org/trail/search/.

Twitter. http://www.twitter.com.

UNBISNET: United Nations Bibliographic Information System. New York: United Nations. http://unbisnet.un.org/.

United States Code. Government Publishing Office. https://www.gpo.gov/fdsys/browse/collectionUScode.action?collectionCode=USCODE.

United States Government Manual. 1935–. Washington, DC: Office of the Federal Register, Annual. https://www.gpo.gov/fdsys/browse/collection.action?collectionCode=GOVMAN.

United States Reports. 1790–2009. Supreme Court. http://www.supremecourt.gov/opinions/boundvolumes.aspx.

United States Serial Set. 1817–. Washington, DC: Congress.

United States Statutes at Large. 1789–. Washington, DC: Government Publishing Office. Annual. https://www.gpo.gov/fdsys/browse/collection.action?collectionCode=STATUTE.

USA Trade Online. Census Bureau. https://usatrade.census.gov/.

USA.gov. General Services Administration. http://www.usa.gov.

Washington Information Directory. 1975/1976–. Washington, DC: Congressional Quarterly. Annual. Available online as part of *SAGE Knowledge*.

Web Sites of National Parliaments. Inter-Parliamentary Union. http://www.ipu.org/english/parlweb.htm.

Weekly Acquisitions List. Government of Canada Publications. http://publications.gc.ca/site/eng/weeklyAcquisitionList/lists.html.

Weekly Checklist of Canadian Government Publications. Ottawa: Government of Canada. http://publications.gc.ca/site/eng/weeklyChecklist/weeklyChecklist.html.

White House. https://www.whitehouse.gov/.

WorldCat. http://www.worldcat.org.
Worldwide Government Directory with International Organizations. 1981–. Washington, DC: CQ Press. Annual.
Your Right to Federal Records: Questions and Answers on the Freedom of Information Act and the Privacy Act. General Services Administration. http://www.gsa.gov/graphics/staffoffices/Your_Right_to_Federal_Records.pdf.

SUGGESTED READINGS

Drake, Miriam A., and Donald T. Hawkins, eds. 2016. *Public Knowledge: Access and Benefits*. Medford, NJ: Information Today.

Chapters in this book discuss the challenges in collecting, preserving, updating, and disseminating the large quantities of information generated daily by public sources. Of particular interest is the chapter by James A. Jacobs and James R. Jacobs on "Beyond LMGTFY*: Access to Government Information in a Networked World."

DttP: A Quarterly Journal of Government Information Practice and Perspective. 1972–. Chicago: American Library Association, Government Documents Round Table. Quarterly.

Formerly *Documents to the People* (*DttP*), this is the official publication of the Government Documents Round Table. It is an important source for articles, news items, and other information on government publications, technical reports, and maps; related governmental activities; documents librarianship; and Round Table matters, as well as other professional organizations, such as the Council of Professional Associations on Federal Statistics.

Free Government Information (*FGI*). http://freegovinfo.info/.

Every government information specialist and depository librarian's favorite blog, *FGI* focuses on open government information through collaboration, education, advocacy, and research among librarians, government agencies, nonprofits, researchers, journalists, and so on.

GODORT Exchange. American Library Association. http://wikis.ala.org/godort/index.php/Exchange.

The Education Committee of the Government Documents Round Table (GODORT) of the American Library Association (ALA) is responsible for the *GODORT Exchange*, which offers hundreds of instructional guides, most of them librarian created. These can be useful for training purposes and to learn more about specific components of documents reference work or about specific resources.

Hartnett, Cassandra J., Andrea L. Sevetson, and Eric J. Forte. 2016. *Fundamentals of Government Information: Mining, Finding, Evaluating, and Using Government Resources*, 2nd ed. Chicago: ALA Neal-Schuman.

This publication is the go-to-source for new and seasoned depository librarians and other practitioners who provide government information references services, whether basic or advanced. A quick look or a longer consult can help any stymied reference librarian confronted with a request for government information.

Sevetson, Andrea, ed. 2013. *The Serial Set: Its Make-Up and Content*. Bethesda, MD: ProQuest.

This recent compilation discusses various subjects, formats, and time periods covered in the *United States Serial Set*.

Sunlight Foundation. http://www.sunlightfoundation.com/.

This organization is dedicated to protecting and expanding access to government information.

Welch, Susan, John Gruhl, Sue Thomas, and MaryAnne Borrelli. 2014. *Understanding American Government*, 14th ed. Boston: Wadsworth/Cengage Learning.

This title is an outstanding engaging textbook on American government and politics. An introductory chapter on the role of government in America is followed by chapters covering such topics as units of government (e.g., Congress, the Presidency, the Judiciary) and important issues such as civil liberties and civil rights.

Chapter 23

Sources for Data and Statistics

Celina Nichols McDonald

INTRODUCTION

Humans have been collecting and analyzing data since ancient times. The earliest known data collection dates to 4500 BCE, when the Babylonians collected economic data and recorded it on clay tablets (Grajalez et al. 2013). Since the mid-1970s, many libraries have provided users access to machine-readable data files, initially using diskettes and remote services like Dialog. With the increase in available data and user interest, librarians had to acquire a new set of data-related skills in order to assist their patrons and manage their collections.

The data boom continued, and today a vast amount of data are available to library users through a variety of sources. Patron needs for statistics and data have grown more common and simultaneously more complex. While in the past librarians expected to be able to pull a book or a CD-ROM and show the data to the patron, today growing numbers of patrons need direct access to the numeric information in data sets for their own analyses.

Data and statistical literacy are increasingly important to the institutions that libraries serve.

- K–12 institutions are introducing data literacy into their curriculums.
- Undergraduates are learning how to create and analyze data using sophisticated software.
- Graduate students and faculty continue to rely heavily on data sets in their research.
- Public and private sector businesses use data and statistics for many of their decisions.

For many librarians, data and statistics reference questions can be an intimidating and time-consuming prospect. There is an overwhelming body of information available, which can make it difficult to find the right content for the user's needs.

This chapter can serve as a general introduction to the sources and strategies librarians can use when responding to data and statistical questions. It can also serve as a reference to more in-depth sources for addressing more complex needs.

WHAT ARE DATA AND STATISTICS?

Many people use the terms "data" and "statistics" interchangeably, but a more nuanced understanding of the two terms and their differences is informative. Statistics can be data and data can be statistics, but neither is exclusively synonymous with the other. This chapter will use definitions from the *Oxford English Dictionary*, which defines data as "related items of (chiefly numerical) information considered collectively, typically obtained by scientific work and used for reference, analysis, or calculation" (*OED Online* 2015a). Statistics are defined as "a numerical characteristic of a sample (as opposed to a characteristic of the population from which it is drawn)" (*OED Online* 2015b).

Data can be better understood by considering the processes that shape it from collection to dissemination. The collection of information via a variety of methods, including surveys, measurements, tests, and other media, begins the data life cycle. After the information is collected, it typically undergoes a cleaning process to remove duplicates, exclude inaccurate or unreadable information, and, in general, ensure the quality of the information that will become the final released data set. After the data are cleaned, they are converted into a numerical format for uses such as calculation or analysis. One common outcome at this stage in the process is the use of analysis techniques so the data can be presented as a statistical aggregate that can be used as evidence to support or reject a hypothesis. The last step in the process is dissemination, traditionally referring to the statistical analysis published in a scholarly paper but increasingly involving the sharing of the data set itself. Once the numeric information has been published, others may reuse either the data set or the resulting statistics and create new data from it, repeating the cycle (as in the example of meta-analyses that synthesize the results of many previous studies to draw conclusions about the strength of evidence for a position). While traditionally librarians have been involved in the data life cycle only post-publication, increasingly libraries are creating data repositories for their institutions, and consequently they are being included much earlier in the process, sometimes even at the point of the design of the study.

In addition to the definitions established earlier, librarians should understand how the terms are defined in different disciplines to ensure that there is no miscommunication when a patron asks for assistance. For example, sociologists may use the *Blackwell Dictionary of Sociology*, which defines data as "facts that social scientists gather, analyze, and interpret" (Johnson 2000a). In medicine, *The Dictionary of Nursing Theory and Research* defines data as "pieces of information (numerical and/or verbal) collected during a research study comprising the empirical evidence" (Powers and Knapp 2010a). The common thread throughout the disciplines is that data are the initially unprocessed information collected in the course of a study that is then aggregated or synthesized to support an interpretation.

Like data, the word "statistics" has a variety of meanings to different groups. The *Dictionary of Nursing Theory and Research* defines a statistic as "a summary measure of the data for a sample, such as a sample mean, a sample standard deviation, or a sample correlation coefficient" (Powers and Knapp 2010b). By contrast, the *Blackwell Dictionary of Sociology* defines statistics as "a set of mathematical

TABLE 23.1 Common Data and Statistical Words and Concepts

Term	Definition
Big data	A large collection of data. Frequently used to refer to a collection of data that requires specialized software to analyze.
Codebook	A book or file that contains information about how a study or survey's data were collected, processed, and analyzed.
CSV	A type of file format that can be used by most mathematical software. CSV stands for comma separated value, wherein a comma is used to demarcate different fields.
Data cleaning	To prepare data for analysis by reviewing the content to ensure the data are accurate and in a format that can be analyzed.
Data mining	Searching large data collections to find new information such as previously undiscovered relationships between data sets.
Data set	Collection of related data such as data from a survey.
Meta-analysis	A systematic review of data or statistics that have been analyzed previously.
Raw data	Unprocessed numeric information that has not been cleansed or analyzed.
Text mining	Similar to data mining, text mining occurs when someone searches large collections to find new relationships between content.

techniques used to organize, analyze, and interpret information that takes the form of numbers" (Johnson 2000b).

In addition, to understand the definitions of data and statistics as they apply to different subjects, librarians should learn common terms and phrases that are used when people talk about numeric information (see Table 23.1 for a list of terms and their definitions). Understanding these terms will greatly facilitate the librarian's communication with users as well as clarify the characteristics of users' requests that will be used to develop a search strategy for the data they need.

TYPES OF DATA AND STATISTICS

Official and Unofficial

Several different schemes can be used to categorize data and statistics. The source of the data is one such scheme. Although data and statistics are produced by a wide variety of sources, the most meaningful distinction is between official and unofficial sources.

Official data and statistics are those collected by government agencies. A patron looking for population, business, agriculture, and environmental statistics will find a treasure trove of official information to meet his or her information needs. For example, users can find a wide range of general data on Canada, the United States, and Mexico collected by Statistics Canada, the U.S. Census Bureau, and Instituto Nacional De Estadística y Geografía, respectively. More targeted data are often available from specialized government entities, such as weather data gathered by the National Oceanic and Atmospheric Administration or the Uniform Crime Reports (UCR) program from the Federal Bureau of Investigation. Most official publications are available for free in electronic formats. Many tangible publications are also distributed for free to federal depository libraries (see Chapter 22).

Official sources are not limited to national government sources. Official data and statistics are also collected by local town/city, county, parish, provincial, and state governments. Additionally, the United Nations (UN), an intergovernmental organization, provides extensive access to official data and statistics from around the world.

While official data and statistics originate with government entities, unofficial data and statistics encompass all other publishers, including researchers, nonprofit and for-profit companies. There is a great deal of variety in the data that are collected by unofficial sources. Businesses collect market research data on customers and their preferences; academic researchers in every discipline collect data to support claims in their research; and nonprofits collect data to support their missions.

It is important to note that the use of the term "unofficial" does not imply that the data and statistics are unreliable, but merely that they do not emerge from the operating needs of a government entity. For example, many businesses subscribe to databases from companies such as Nielsen (United States), Abacus Data (Canada), and Research International (United Kingdom) to conduct market research. An example of an authoritative and significant unofficial data source is the Roper Center. Created in 1957, the Roper Center has become one of the most important sources for data on the American public's opinion of political candidates (Hart 2015). In years when there are presidential elections, librarians are likely to field questions from patrons seeking information about public opinion polls cited by a news source. Along with Gallup, Roper is a valuable tool for politicians and the public to measure the success of a campaign.

Box 23.1 Search Strategy: Searching for Budget Information

A public library patron wants to find the United States' budget from 2000 to 2015. Although there are many ways to access the information, there are three free, official, and publicly available resources. The Government Publishing Office publishes the *Budget of the United States Government* annually in print and electronic format. Additionally, users can visit *Data.gov* to access the *Public Budget Database*, which contains data back to 1962. Many different software programs, free and proprietary, can read files in both formats. Additionally, the data dictionary is available on the *Data.gov* site for the budget. Users can easily download, extract, and format data in a way that meets their needs.

Public, Restricted Access, and Inaccessible Data

Another important factor to consider when helping patrons find and use data and statistics is the accessibility of the numeric information, which can be categorized as public, restricted, or inaccessible. All data, official and unofficial, fall in this spectrum of accessibility. Public data are the easiest type of data and statistics to access because there are no impediments to their use. Many sources for official data and statistics make content publicly accessible. Online accessible resources such as *Data.gov*, *Open Government*, and *UNdata* make public data available to everyone. All of these are good general online sources for data and statistics. All of them cover a wide variety of subjects and are good one-stop sources when a librarian is uncertain of where to find official content.

Librarians should be careful not to overlook print publications, as many valuable sources of data and statistics are made publicly available in nonelectronic formats. The U.S. Census Bureau and the UN continue to print some of their publications. Examples of this include data and statistics from the U.S. Census Bureau, National Center for Health Statistics, and the Bureau of Justice Statistics, where the majority of the content is open access, including print publications that are disseminated to federal depository libraries or are available for purchase. Even when electronic access is available, some library users who are visually impaired prefer to use print versions because they find it easier to read. In Canada, although the government has transitioned to an electronic-only system, some publications can be printed for users with special needs.

Restricted access content requires the user to meet some requirements for access, which may include subscription products such as *ProQuest Statistical Insight* or *Country Data Online*, or those that require membership in an institution such as the Inter-University Consortium for Political and Social Research (ICPSR) or the Minnesota Population Center's Integrated Public Use Microdata Series. Common reasons for restricted access are:

- Privacy/security concerns
- Subscription-only materials
- Researcher/producer's discretion

Other content may require the user to apply for access, ranging from quick questionnaires that simply identify the user to in-depth application processes requiring references and/or a certain professional standing.

At times, data may exist but be impossible for the user to access for any of a number of reasons. Many data sets are completely inaccessible to all users due to privacy concerns, such as individuals' U.S. Census forms, which are completely unavailable for 72 years after data collection. Other data may be inaccessible to users without a formal government security clearance due to national security concerns. Researchers may also have to implement privacy safeguards that protect subjects of their study by making some data permanently inaccessible.

Micro, Aggregated, and Secondary Data

Another way to understand different types of data is to consider the stage of the data life cycle that produced it. Microdata, aggregated, and secondary data represent different data life cycle phases. When the data are initially collected, each individually collected unit (an individual's survey question response, the result of an experimental trial on a single subject, etc.) is called microdata. At this stage, no changes have been made to the data, and personally identifiable information is often still included; for this reason, microdata is the type of data most likely to be subject to access restrictions.

After gathering all of the microdata, the next step in the process is to clean up the data so it can be aggregated and analyzed. Typically, this means removing irrelevant, inaccurate, or duplicate data, stripping out personally identifiable information as needed, and organizing the data into a form that is easier for the researcher to work with. After the data are processed, the researcher will use various statistical techniques to analyze the data for the purpose that they were gathered. Data analysis can lead to a variety of outcomes such as facts (the observed mass of the Higgs boson), statistics (mortality rates broken down by demographic categories), or analytical conclusions (evidence supporting the effectiveness of a public health campaign).

After analysis, the results of the study are published, but the data life cycle continues. After publication, the data set itself is often shared so other researchers can make use of it to verify the researcher's conclusions or to use it in a new study as secondary data, perhaps for a purpose unanticipated by the initial study. The statistically analyzed data can also be reused as secondary statistics, often by combining it with the results of other similar studies to generate more statistically significant conclusions.

For most reference librarians, the user need most frequently encountered is to find data and statistics that they can then put to secondary use for their own research project. The user's specific needs will help determine the type of data most appropriate for his or her purposes. Understanding the data life cycle will make it easier for librarians to determine whether micro, aggregate, or secondary data will be most useful for their user.

Cross-Sectional, Time Series, and Longitudinal Data

Cross-sectional, longitudinal, and time series data relate to how long data are collected. A cross-sectional data set is collected at a single point in time. Survey responses, measurements taken on a single experiment, and information collected from travelers' customs declaration forms collected at the end of a flight from Amsterdam to Moscow are all examples of cross-sectional data. In libraries, cross-sectional data might be obtained from a brief customer satisfaction survey conducted over the course of a week. Frequently, reference questions will call for cross-sectional data.

Time series data are collected in regular intervals over a period of time. An example of time series data is the data gathered by the STAR*D trial, which studied the efficacy of different depression treatments. Data were gathered from participants in 12-week intervals until the depression went into remission. Researchers followed up with the patients again, 12 months after they went into remission.

Longitudinal data are collected over an extended period of time, often spanning multiple decades. Longitudinal data are often the most difficult to find because of the expense and level of commitment by an institution required to ensure the success of a study that may span decades. As a result, longitudinal data sets are some of the most frequently reused, with the data collected from a single longitudinal study often leading to dozens of publications, even years after the original study was published. Census data are a prominent example of an ongoing longitudinal data set.

Box 23.2 Search Strategy: Video Game Statistics

An eighth-grade class is learning about descriptive statistics. The school librarian is asked to help a student find information about the video game industry.

Like patrons, many librarians turn to Google when they need to conduct a quick search for information. A search for "video game statistics" will find more than 26,000,000 results. Among the first results will be a link to the Entertainment Software Rating Board (ESRB) and the Entertainment Software Association (ESA). If the reference librarian is uncertain about which resource is the best source, he or she can review a report's citations. A review of the works cited by the ESRB's report *Video Game Industry Statistics* (Entertainment Software Rating Board 2015) will reveal that their report relies on information from other groups, including the ESA's *2015 Essential Facts about the Computer and Video Game Industry* (Entertainment Software Association 2015). If the user needs only users, sales, and industry information, the ESA report is a better source because it is a "primary" source for that information. If the user would like a broader view of the video game industry, the ESRB report will be more useful because it includes information on a broader number of topics.

EVALUATION OF SOURCES

When evaluating any type of material for the reference collection, it is important to have a collection development policy in place with set criteria for evaluating potential acquisitions and withdrawals. In this regard, data and statistics are no different from any other type of publication. Thematically, the criteria by which data and statistical publications are evaluated mirrors other parts of reference collections; however, there are some aspects that are unique to statistical and data resources. It is not enough to just look at the group that gathered the data, who funded the study that led to its collection, and the institution it was published by; a truly thorough review will also examine the data's content and the methods by which they were collected. Understanding data collection methods and best practices is especially important for librarians because in recent years many studies have been debunked because they were based on faulty data. Since a library's reputation is based in large part on the credibility of the resources it provides, librarians should take the steps needed to provide quality resources to minimize the chances of their users' research being invalidated due to a reliance on faulty data.

Authority

Previous chapters have discussed the importance of the author and the publisher in establishing the authority of a source. In addition to these considerations, librarians should look at the funding source when evaluating data and statistics. In many professions, people judge the value of research based on who funded it. For example, in a 2012 study published by the *New England Journal of Medicine*, researchers found that doctors trusted NIH-funded studies more than those that received funding from pharmaceutical companies (Kesselheim et al. 2012). Studies funded by pharmaceutical companies were generally distrusted due to the potential conflict of interest between the researcher's objectivity and the funding agent's business objectives.

Citations of a data set can also be a useful tool in establishing its authority, as it provides a general measure of how a data set is regarded within its discipline. *Data Citation Index*, a database published by Thomson Reuters, is a useful tool for determining how often a data set has been cited and by whom. Exploring the citing articles to understand the context of the citation can also inform the librarian on the quality of the data.

Accuracy

It is important to assess data collection methods as carefully as possible when evaluating data and statistical materials. When presenting data to patrons, it may be helpful for the librarian to be able to explain factors that might complicate its accuracy. For example, longitudinal studies may suffer from data collection methods that vary from year to year, resulting in improper comparisons across time. If possible, librarians should determine whether a study or data set has been contradicted or revised by later research, as in the high-profile case of a study published in *Lancet* (Wakefield et al. 1998) linking vaccinations to autism, which was later debunked. Some data sets include "data quality flags" that identify any variables that have been edited for analysis due to incomplete or illegible responses.

Currency

Collected data are almost invariably linked to the time that they were collected. Thus, it is extremely important to understand the user's needs and whether current or historical data will answer their questions. Both the date of the data's collection and that of its publication are valuable pieces of information. If the 1990 census data set was published in 1991, the librarian may need to see whether a more recent edition or corrected copy supersedes the original edition. If the data are the products of research, it can be important to determine whether they have been debunked by later studies. One way to ascertain this is to look up the article produced by the study and see whether they have been retracted. One widely followed blog, *Retraction Watch*, provides up-to-date and comprehensive information on retracted articles.

Scope and Comprehensiveness

The scope and comprehensiveness of the collection should be determined by the level of service the library intends to provide surrounding data and statistics (see Box 23.3). A collection development policy should be established that deals with levels of service and criteria for including and excluding materials from the collection. The policy should include formats collected, the subject scope to be covered,

Box 23.3 Levels of Service

The early 1990s saw a dramatic increase in demand for data services as a result of the 1990 Decennial Census being distributed to Federal Depository Libraries. Since 1991, when Jim Jacobs's seminal article about data services was published, librarians have been trying to define the right level of data and statistical support to provide their uses. Because authors differ on the number of levels and what services are provided for each stage, this section introduces a simplified version of the levels of service.

Level One: Basic Services

The library acquires, catalogs, and helps users search for materials held by other institutions. Users have access to computers with an office suite, such as Microsoft Office or LibreOffice, both of which include programs that help people work with numeric information. Reference librarians at these institutions should be knowledgeable of general resources and where a patron can go to get more advanced assistance. The library may purchase materials from Facts on File, Inc., which is recommended for K–12 users. For complex questions, librarians refer patrons to other departments or organizations that provide specialized support. This level of service would be appropriate at small public, school media, special, and academic libraries, where there is little demand for data and statistics.

Level Two: Intermediate Services

At this level, the library subscribes to general data and statistical databases as well as popular subject-specific databases. The library also purchases data sets on request and makes specialized software packages available on the public-use computers. The library does not provide technical support or guidance regarding the software's use; however, librarians do offer consultations to library patrons who need help finding data and statistics. Librarians have access to and can help patrons search databases for content. Reference librarians at these institutions should be knowledgeable of the general resources as well as the more popular sources. This level of service can typically be found at large public research, academic, and special libraries.

Level Three: Advanced Services

The library subscribes to an extensive number of databases providing subject-specific data and statistical information. At least one dedicated data services librarian works with researchers to curate original research for the library's collection, and an employee provides statistical analysis support to researchers. This may include helping the researcher design the study, clean data, and process them in specialized software. This level of service is generally found at large research, academic, and special libraries.

When making decisions regarding the level of service to be provided by the library, librarians should carefully examine their users' needs and their financial resources before developing a formal policy and plan for providing the services, no matter how simple, because they will inform all staff and guide acquisitions decisions.

criteria and schedule for weeding, and a preservation plan to ensure that data do not become corrupted or otherwise unusable.

Format

Data and statistical information can be categorized as analog (published in a tangible format, e.g., print or microform) or digital (requiring the use of a computer to access, e.g., via the Internet or CD-ROM), with various delivery mechanisms for each:

A librarian must carefully weight considerations with both analog and digital data and statistics when evaluating sources. In many cases, the librarian has no choice as to the format of the data. Print publications are becoming more difficult to find, while increasing numbers of data and statistical publications are being released in electronic formats. Several key U.S. titles such as the *Statistical Abstract of the United States*, *Employment and Earnings*, and the *Digest of Education Statistics* are available only electronically, and Canada now releases its official publications exclusively online.

When data exist in both formats, another consideration is the ease of use. With analog data, if the user wants to reuse and analyze the data using a computer, they will have to manually enter the data; with larger data sets, this may be prohibitively cumbersome. Analog materials are less frequently updated, so users who rely on current data often find them less useful. However, analog data are less prone to corruption and are less vulnerable to becoming unusable through changes in technology. Printed data are in most cases connected to an identifiable publisher (Congressional Information Services, the U.S. Census Bureau, etc.), and as a result its authority may be easier to determine. Print materials may also be preferred by some patrons with vision impairment or who process printed information more easily.

In general, however, electronic sources for data are more popular because numeric information is easier to import into statistical analysis tools for reuse or analysis. This makes it possible to process huge amounts of data or link data from different sources; such projects are often infeasible with printed data. Electronic data sources can be accessed more quickly, and the distributed nature of the Internet means that a much broader range of data can be included in a library's collection than would be possible in a physical space.

The chief drawback of electronic data is the tendency of technological changes to make formats and carriers obsolete, placing a burden on a library that collects such data sets to convert or move data from one format to another. The popularization of data delivered via CD-ROM expanded greatly in the early 1990s when the Government Printing Office distributed the 1990 Census on CD-ROM. At the time, CD-ROMs were considered a long-term stable storage solution. Later studies, however, have shown the usable life of a CD-ROM to be anywhere from 15 months (Zurkirch and Reichart 2000) to 5 years (Lawrence, Connaway, and Brigham 2001). Furthermore, CD-ROMs have subsequently become less popular in general, leading many libraries to lack the technology needed to use them. Many notebook computers are being made without an optical disc drive, which is required to use CD-ROMs. Electronic materials that are not properly managed are also susceptible to corruption, both accidental and intentional. Data stored on a remote server that the library does not control can become inaccessible, should the administrator decide to remove them or place restrictions on their use.

SELECTION

Needs of Users

Users at all types of libraries have rapidly evolving needs for data and statistics. To determine appropriate collection policies, libraries of different types may rely on different tools or measurements to evaluate their users' needs. For example, a school librarian, in addition to getting demographic information about the students, should obtain course syllabi to understand what kind of projects the students will be bringing to the library and anticipate their needs. Public libraries, with a more diverse set of users, will need to base their selection decisions on a more complicated set of criteria, examining both their community as a whole and library users in particular. Many librarians avoid tracking patron-specific data due to privacy concerns, so they must pursue alternate means of gathering data on user needs. For example, tracking reference questions and materials' circulation and in-house use can help the librarian gain insight into the topics of interest, formats, level of technical expertise, and so on, of their users. Any analysis of the library's user demographics and their needs should be included in the collection development policy.

Cost

Different types of data and statistical sources are associated with different cost considerations. As is often the case, the primary distinction is between print and electronic formats. On a basic level, print content has a single up-front cost, while electronic content, even if purchased, generally comes with an annual access fee. Another cost that should be considered for both formats is the cost of maintaining the collection; acquiring and cataloging the data, storing it, and ensuring long-term access (particularly for digital formats, which will likely need to be migrated periodically to remain usable) all have associated costs. While electronic data in many formats can be used with basic text editors or common spreadsheet programs, others may require the purchase or licensing of specialized software needed to access or manipulate the data. There may be additional costs depending on the library's level of service and the user's needs.

Storage and Organization

Storage and organization of statistical resources is complicated. Data and statistical information is commonly classified by the subject of the information rather than collocating all data and statistics in a single area. Library staff members may prefer to create a central data and statistics collection, particularly in the electronic domain. However, the staff then needs to be careful about selectors communicating with each other to minimize overlap and gaps in the collection.

Traditionally, tangible data and statistical materials have been housed by format, usually at or near information services desks. In institutions where the library has taken on a more active role in acquiring digital sources of data or curating those generated by their institution's researchers, a much more complex set of considerations could include the hardware, database architecture, and user interface design needed to store, organize, and make the data accessible. Even some smaller libraries, particularly those with archives, serve as an institutional repository for organizational data and statistics. If the library is itself collecting and storing data and statistics, attention must be given to the organization and access to materials stored on library servers. This is an extensive topic, and librarians with the responsibility of supporting an institutional repository should refer to a more in-depth work on data curation such as *Research Data Management: Practical Strategies for Information Professionals* (Ray 2014).

Supplemental Tools

When acquiring electronic data sets and statistics, librarians also need to consider what technology and supplemental tools may be needed, particularly if they plan to offer data services beyond the most basic level. For example, most data sets come with a codebook that explains the fields in the data, the questions that were used in data collection, how the data were acquired and processed, and so on. Users need this information to make sense of the data, and it should be in a format that can be loaded into SPSS or other specialized data analysis tools.

Providing access to specialized software is also important. Some are cost-prohibitive for most patrons, and many require expertise in order to use effectively.

One area of data analysis that has seen significant growth in recent years is text mining. Although people in different fields, especially biomedicine, have been text mining since the 1990s, in recent years, the practice has expanded to the humanities and social sciences disciplines (Hearst 1999). Some free tools are available, such as the *Google Books Ngram Viewer*, which allows users to numerically analyze the frequency of words and phrases used in a corpus of millions of books going back to 1800. Other text mining projects may require access to content from specific subscription databases and use of special statistical software. In these cases, the library staff must negotiate with the vendor for the researcher to make use of the database's content beyond the access allowed by general license agreements. In some cases, researchers who are unaware of this condition may attempt to download whole collections from a vendor database in violation of the library's license agreement, which can result in a disruption in service (Van Noorden 2012).

Because of the increase in text mining, libraries and publishers are being compelled to learn how to allow complete access to collections without losing control of the copyrighted materials. Typically, the library must subscribe to the database and purchase additional access to allow the researcher to download the corpus to be analyzed. This access must be negotiated carefully on a case-by-case basis, typically initiated by a user's request, but due to the cost of enhanced access, the library will usually want to purchase the content outright for it to be cost-effective. Text mining is a new frontier for librarians, where even text can be transformed into numerical information. *The Text Mining Handbook: Advanced Approaches in Analyzing Unstructured Data* by Ronen Feldman and James Sanger (2007) is a seminal introductory title, which can help reference librarians deepen their understanding of text mining.

IMPORTANT GENERAL SOURCES

The goal of this chapter is to highlight some key guides and sources that reference librarians will frequently use to answer patron questions. Due to the vast range of available sources and frequency with which useful sources are introduced, it is not possible to list all information sources or even list all of the best ones. Data and statistical guides and sources change frequently as more and more people find ways to share numeric information online. If a reader is unable to access a source, the Internet Archive's *Wayback Machine* website can often be used to gain access to archived websites, including older versions of existing websites as well as sites that have been deleted.

While data and statistics are increasingly available for use, there has been a marked decrease in the number of general guides to resources. One particular area that has not kept pace with the information boom is print guides. The rapid expansion, rapid rate of change, and instability of online content have caused authors to be reluctant to attempt a print publication. Therefore, many print publications tend to be older and out of date; however, there are a significant number of excellent online guides. One standout guide is *Data & Statistics Research Guides* from Michigan State University, which includes information for finding data and statistics in overlooked areas such as the arts, religion, and linguistics. Canadian librarians may find that the University of Ottawa's *Data and Statistics* provides guidance for finding and using official Canadian statistics. For users searching for international data and statistics, *International Statistics and Data* from the University of Illinois at Urbana-Champaign is an online guide with an extensive collection of links to data in other countries and from a variety of sources.

Books dedicated to finding data and statistics are rare because they quickly become outdated. As a result, there are only a few books that can guide librarians to different resources. One book that is very useful is the *Reference Guide to Data Sources* by Julia Bauder, an essential title for the reference shelf. It is organized by subject and serves as a guide to finding data from a variety of sources from the United States and other nations, both general and specialized.

Statistics Sources: A Subject Guide to Data on Industrial Business, Social, Educational, Financial and Other Topics for the United States and Internationally, an annual bibliographic guide to official and unofficial statistics, can be a good publication for libraries of all types and sizes to have in their collections. A two-volume set, *Statistics Sources*, is a comprehensive guide that can help a librarian quickly identify the best source for statistical information.

Another regularly published guide that can be an asset to all types of libraries, especially public and school media libraries, is *Datapedia of the United States: American History in Numbers* (Kurian and Chernow 2007) because it is an easy way to access data and statistics about the United States from 1789 to 2003. The book is highly recommended because it has many tables, is easy to read, and full of citations, which readers can then use to access the source materials.

Finding guides to unofficial resources tends to be more difficult than guides for official sources. Unofficial resources tend to be more unstable than official sources. If a reference librarian needs help finding unofficial sources, the *World Directory of Non-Official Statistical Sources* is a useful guide to keep in the reference collection.

OFFICIAL RESOURCES

The resources included in this section are official data and statistics resources from the originating agency or another government body. Official numeric information that is accessed through an aggregator such as *Data-Planet* is explored as unofficial resources. Official resources can help reference librarians assist users of all ages and reading levels find data and statistics about:

- Population and demographics
- Economics, industry, finance, and business
- Health and vital statistics
- Energy (fossil fuels, renewable, natural)
- Environment, forestry, water, fish, and wildlife
- Agriculture, livestock, and crops

Almost all official data and statistics resources are available online for free to the general public, making them essential and affordable sources for content. Official information is especially strong for subjects in the social sciences such as anthropology, business, political science, economics, education, the environment, history, geography, and psychology. Because official data cover a multitude of subject areas and dates, there is a tremendous amount of information, which can make it difficult to find official data on a particular topic. This section of the chapter will focus on data and statistical products from the United States, Canada, and the UN. Because of the affordability, scope, and relevance to a wide range of users of different reading levels and abilities, there will be a greater focus on official resources than on unofficial sources. Readers are encouraged to consult the *Reference Guide to Data Sources* by Julia Bauder to get a more complete list of data and statistical sources.

U.S. Resources

More than 100 U.S. federal departments and agencies publish data and statistics, 13 of which are considered the primary producers. These agencies are listed in Table 23.2 with information on their major data-gathering programs and publications. Many data and statistics questions that a reference librarian will be asked revolve around population, business, workforce, education, health, agriculture, and criminal justice. Because of the depth and breadth of the data and statistical information available from the U.S. government, a few agencies are highlighted in more detail later.

For general informational needs, *Data.gov* and *FedStats* can also help a librarian find the data and statistics he or she needs. *Data.gov* serves as a single access point to more than 188,000 data sets on a variety of subjects such as agriculture, business, environment, education, health, and criminal justice. Librarians at academic institutions may find *Data.gov* of greater assistance than those at public and school libraries. Starting in May 2015, *FedStats* (continuing an older site, FedStats.gov, a URL that is no longer in use) has become a portal for identifying agencies that provide useful statistics. The original *FedStats* was a database that could be used to search multiple statistical products from across all federal agencies and departments. The new *FedStats* provides information about the different federal statistical programs, but has limited search capabilities for people who are searching for actual publications.

The U.S. Census Bureau is one of the most important sources for statistics about the U.S. population, government, and business. In addition to the familiar *Census of Population and Housing*, they collect and publish valuable data in the *Economic Census* and *Census of Governments*. In addition to conducting censuses, they

TABLE 23.2 Primary U.S. Federal Agencies That Produce Statistics and Data and Their Major Publications.

Agency	Description
Bureau of Economic Analysis	Regional, national, and international trade data.
Bureau of Justice Statistics	Arrest, crime incidence, law enforcement, and penal data and statistics.
Bureau of Labor Statistics	Labor, compensation, employment, and unemployment statistics; workforce, career, and industry data and statistics; *Consumer Price Index.*
Bureau of Transportation Statistics	State and national transportation statistics including rail, air, and motorway statistics.
Census Bureau	Censuses of population and housing, economic, and governments; *American Community Survey.*
Economic Research Service	USDA crop, food supply, consumption, and market data and statistics.
Energy Information Administration	Energy use, trade, and market data and statistics.
National Agricultural Statistics Service	Crop and livestock data and statistics; *Census of Agriculture.*
National Center for Education Statistics	K–12, secondary, and postsecondary data and statistics; student achievement and assessment data and statistics; school, library, and school district data and statistics.
National Center for Health Statistics	Birth, mortality, and health data and statistics; includes data for specific ailments and conditions as well as current issues such as obesity.
National Center for Science and Engineering Statistics	Science and engineering statistics including demographic profiles of the workforce.
Social Security Administration Office of Research, Evaluation, and Statistics	Social security recipient and program data and statistics.
Statistics of Income IRS	Individual, nonprofit, and for-profit taxation information.

continuously gather information through surveys such as the *American Community Survey.* Their content is published in tangible and electronic formats. One of their most well-known publications is the *Statistical Abstract of the United States*, which was published in print format annually until 2012 when it ceased to be published by the U.S. Census Bureau. The *Statistical Abstract* is a valuable ready-reference resource that serves as a place to find the most commonly used statistics such as state population counts, demographic information, mortality statistics, employment, and industry. *American FactFinder* is an online tool that makes it possible to search multiple data sets and statistics from a variety of programs, including the *Census of Population and Housing*, *Census of Governments*, and *Economic Census*. Although the database is a valuable resource, it is important to note that it only provides access to the two most recent decennial censuses. To find data published before 2000, librarians can use *DataFerrett* to access some, but not all, historical content. Librarians can access older data and statistics from free and subscription databases, which will be explored more fully later in the chapter.

The Census Bureau also conducts surveys for or with other federal agencies and departments such as the *American Housing Survey* for the Department of Housing and Urban Development and the *Current Population Survey* with the Bureau of Labor Statistics (BLS). A complete listing of surveys is available from the Census Bureau's website.

The BLS provides numeric information about employment, compensation, and consumer trends. Major publications include the *Consumer Price Index*, *Employment and Earnings*, *Employment Cost Index*, and *Monthly Labor Review*, all of which were published in print until 2007 and 2008 when they became electronic-only publications. One of their most frequently cited sources is *Employment and Earnings* (E&E), which contains city, state, and national employment, unemployment, and compensation statistics. For reference librarians who are helping people learn about the cost of different products and services, the *Consumer Price Index* is a valuable publication. In addition to providing data and statistics about the workforce, the BLS produces *Employment Cost Index*, which contains information about total expenditures by employers per employee. One publication that is not marketed as a statistical publication, but is a good source for data and statistics, is the *Occupational Outlook Handbook* because it provides easy access to important statistics about different professions, which many library users find useful when they research potential career paths.

The National Center for Health Statistics is a valuable official source for health statistics and data. They publish a multitude of reports such as the *National Vital Statistics Reports* and the *National Health Statistics Reports*, which contain birth, death, and other health statistics for the United States. They also publish annual reports that focus on current trends and issues through *Health, United States* which is an annual publication that is available in print and on the agency's website. People who would like to build custom tables that contain the information they need will find *Health Data Interactive* a useful online tool for health statistics. Users can build custom tables by report, subject, geographical location, race, age, and urban/rural.

The National Center for Education Statistics is an excellent source for data and statistics on education topics. One of the best sources to consult is the *Digest of Education Statistics*, a yearly publication that is currently published only in electronic format. The publication contains statistics derived from many different surveys and programs conducted throughout the year. The *Digest of Education Statistics* is a compilation of statistics about all levels of education from prekindergarten to secondary education, public and private schools, staffing, libraries, crime in schools, achievement, and employment. *The Condition of Education* is another good source for data and statistics about current issues such as crime in schools.

In addition to its regular publications, the National Center for Education Statistics has developed online tools for its different survey programs. Someone who is searching for data about a school district can use *Search by School District*.

Someone else who wants to find statistics related to students' academic achievements in different subjects can consult the Data Explorer on the *National Assessment of Educational Progress* website.

For librarians who are asked questions about U.S. food production, costs, nutrition, or people's eating habits, two excellent sources of data and statistics are agencies within the U.S. Department of Agriculture (USDA): the Economic Research Service and the National Agricultural Statistics Services. The National Agricultural Statistics Services collects and disseminates information about the agricultural industry such as livestock and crop data and statistics. For example, the National Agricultural Statistics Services conducts the *Census of Agriculture* every five years. As with many publications, the most recent census is currently available as an electronic file or can be searched for via the *Quick Stats* database. The Economic Research Service publishes reports about farm productivity, market data for specific crops such as rice and wheat, and data about people's access to and consumption of food. The easiest way to find and use current data and statistics from the Economic Research Service is to visit its website's *Data Products* page, which has a full listing of files, applications, and charts. School media librarians may find the *Atlas of Rural and Small-Town America, Food Access Research Atlas, and Food Environment Atlas* particularly useful. The user-friendly, brightly colored atlases are well designed for middle and high school students. They can create subject- and location-specific maps, which can then be exported as images or PDF files. For research-oriented questions, librarians can consult the USDA's *Economics, Statistics and Market Information System*, a database that provides access to reports and data sets from five USDA agencies and Cornell University. Users can access and download historical and current publications about crop, livestock, and market data and statistics.

The Bureau of Justice Statistics publishes data and statistics about crime, criminals, victims, court cases, and incarceration. Of all the departments and agencies that produce data and statistics, the Bureau of Justice Statistics content can be easy to find, but difficult to use. Many library patrons may find the content too advanced or technical for their needs. Most of their publications, even older publications, are published only electronically. Users who prefer print can purchase a hard copy using the National Criminal Justice Reference Service website. Young readers in particular may have a hard time with the content because of the frequent use of technical terms. On the other hand, the data and statistics are well organized by topic, and it is easy to browse for relevant publications. For example, recent years have seen an increased interest in statistics about the number of civilians killed by police officers. Many people tried to find data using the Federal Bureau of Investigation's UCR program. Although the UCR program provides extensive data in publications such as *Crime in the United States, Law Enforcement Officers Killed and Assaulted, Hate Crime Statistics*, and the *National Incident-Based Reporting System*, it is easier to find arrest-related death statistics through the Bureau of Justice Statistics. Users can browse to data from their Arrest-Related Deaths and Deaths in Custody programs.

Canadian Sources

In contrast to their southern neighbors, Canada has a centralized system for collecting and disseminating data. Most official Canadian data and statistics are collected and disseminated by Statistics Canada, which provides access to content on a broad variety of topics, including agriculture, business, crime and justice, economics, education, energy, health, income, labor, population, science, transportation, and the environment. In addition to Statistics Canada, 11 other agencies generate data and statistics (see Table 23.3). For many librarians from all types of libraries, Statistics Canada's data and statistics can meet most, if not all, users' needs.

One of the most important products Statistics Canada has created is *CANSIM*, "Canada's key socioeconomic database." Through *CANSIM*, it is possible to download full data sets from many of its surveys. Users can type in a search or browse by subject and survey to find relevant content. All librarians can find information that will help them and their users, but librarians at research and academic libraries will find CANSIM especially helpful because of the access it provides to large data sets. Librarians and their users should avoid harvesting data, however, because it is in violation of *CANSIM* policies, which can result in loss of access. Some of the questions that can be answered using *CANSIM* are:

- How does the educational attainment of First Nations people from 2010 to 2014 compare with that of others?
- What percentage of Canadian households used energy-saving lightbulbs in 2013 in comparison with 2007?
- How much is the Canadian dollar worth compared with the U.S. dollar for the last five months?

TABLE 23.3 Significant Producers of Canadian Data and Statistics

Agency/Department	Description
Bank of Canada	Banking and financial statistics
Blue Water Bridge Canada	Traffic and toll data for the Blue Water Bridge
Canada Revenue Agency	Individual and business income statistics
Canadian Grain Commission	Grain data and statistics including exports and tax
Immigration and Refugee Board of Canada	Refugee data and statistics
Military Grievances External Review Committee	Military grievance data and statistics
National Defence and Canadian Forces Ombudsman	National defense data and statistics
National Energy Board	Energy market and use data and statistics
Natural Resources Canada	Forest and natural resources data and statistics
Office of the Commissioner of Official Languages	Language use data and statistics
Parole Board of Canada	Parole statistics
Statistics Canada	National statistics office for Canada; population, education health, economic, criminal justice, and agricultural data and statistics

One resource that many librarians will find essential is the reference section of the Statistics Canada website. On the reference page, users can find guides, codebooks, dictionaries, and reference publications such as *Canada Year Book*. The *Canada Year Book* is a comprehensive collection of tables and statistics from all the censuses, surveys, and statistics collections published by Statistics Canada. Subjects covered include publications and surveys on topics including agriculture, education, economics, crime and justice, labor, and transportation. Although users can access archival copies of the *Canada Year Book* online, new editions ceased to be published in 2012.

Canada at a Glance is a small quick reference publication for current statistics in the most common areas such as population, agriculture, health, education, commerce, justice, and travel. *Canada at a Glance* is one of the few publications that are still published in print, in addition to the electronic version.

For historical data and statistics, the *Historical Statistics of Canada* is a good publication for reference collections because it contains statistics from 1867 to the mid-1970s. Available in print and online, *Historical Statistics of Canada* provides easy access to official statistics from the start of the nation. The online version makes the information available in a variety of formats including tables that can be downloaded and then manipulated by almost all statistical software, including Microsoft Excel.

In addition to the data and statistics available from Statistics Canada, the Government of Canada has *Open Data*, which like *Data.gov* serves as a single portal to official data from all branches of the government. Statistical information can also be found from federal agencies and divisions such as the Canada Revenue Agency.

United Nations

The United Nations (UN) is one of the best resources for international data and statistics. Although the UN has its own statistics division, UN-affiliated organizations like the World Health Organization, International Monetary Fund, World Bank, and United Nations Educational, Scientific and Cultural Organization (UNESCO) also publish statistics.

The goal of the UN's Statistics Division is to be the "apex entity of the global statistical system." In that capacity, the division collects and disseminates data and statistics about and for the international community. Several databases and publications can help a librarian answer data and statistics questions.

For a librarian or library user who prefers accessing content online, *UNdata* is an interorganizational database that makes it possible to search UN and partner organizations' statistical publications. When they use *UNdata*, users can also search for statistics from organizations such as the UNESCO Institute for Statistics, International Monetary Fund, United Nations Population Division, and World Health Organization. In addition to the search function, a glossary, list of included data sets, and country information are available via *UNdata*.

Another excellent online resource is *UN COMTRADE Database*, a database with more than 1.5 billion records that serves as a comprehensive source for international trade data. Highly technical, *COMTRADE* is recommended for advanced users. For most data and statistics questions reference librarians receive, *UNdata* will meet the patron's needs.

In addition to its databases, the UN and its affiliates continue to publish materials in print and electronic formats. One such publication is the *Statistical Yearbook*, an annual report that strives to be a comprehensive collection of statistics assembled from UN divisions and affiliated organizations. The *Statistical Yearbook* is divided into four parts called:

- World and region
- Population and social statistics
- Economic activity
- International economic relations

In addition to being available in print, every edition of the *Statistical Yearbook* published since 2006 is available electronically, making it convenient for users to download and analyze its data.

Two other vital UN Statistics Division publications are the *World Statistics Pocketbook* and *Monthly Bulletin of Statistics*. Both publications are good multidisciplinary statistical sources, potentially useful to library users with a wide range of needs. The former is a compilation of statistics for 224 counties and locations around the world. Agriculture, finance, health, tourism, labor, and population are among the subjects covered in the *World Statistics Pocketbook*. The *Monthly Bulletin of Statistics* comprises 50 tables of economic, population, labor, energy, and transportation statistics for more than 200 countries. Published for more than 80 years, the *Monthly Bulletin* is now available in print and electronic formats. Online users also have the option of downloading tables.

In addition to the general sources already mentioned, the UN and its affiliates publish subject-specific statistics. For example, the *Energy Statistics Yearbook*, *Demographic Yearbook*, and *International Trade Statistics Yearbook* are annual compendiums that have a smaller target audience than the general sources. Many UN publications are available in different tangible and digital formats. The most recent editions of the publications are available for purchase. It is also possible to purchase historical materials. For example, librarians can purchase the *Demographic Yearbook* for 1948–1997 in CD-ROM format.

For official international statistics, the UN affiliates publish a significant number of useful statistics and data. UNESCO Institute for Statistics publishes titles like the *Global Education Digest*, an annual publication with statistics that assess children's access to education, identify achievement gaps, and explain environmental factors affecting student learning. Another affiliate that publishes valuable information is the World Health Organization. Its publication, the *World Health Report*, a biennial publication with health statistics from 194 participating countries, may be of particular use to librarians in all sorts of libraries. Librarians who work with students from middle school to graduate school can find the content useful to answer questions such as:

- What is life expectancy for males and females in Afghanistan?
- What country has the lowest rate of infant mortality?
- What country has the highest number of people infected with the HIV virus?

The statistics from the World Health Organization can also be accessed using the *Global Health Observatory Data Repository*. In this database, users can download and customize the tables included in the *World Health Report* as well as content from other sources.

Dozens of other UN divisions and affiliates provide access to data and statistics. Librarians are encouraged to visit the UN Statistics Division website. There are links to a number of resources from different UN divisions, affiliates, and nations from around the world.

Sources for Children and Young Adults

For school librarians, helping their users find and use suitable data and statistics sources can be problematic. Most official sources focus on adult users when they design websites and publish materials. Subscribing to new content can be economically infeasible or require a great deal of red tape because cities and counties make decisions for all schools. Here are some free official online sources for data and statistics that are accessible to young readers:

- *USDA for Kids*: The USDA's page for food, crop, livestock, and agricultural information including links to games, information about research, and guides for educators.
- *Statistics in Schools*: The U.S. Census Bureau's website is a resource for educators who wish to teach their students about data and statistics. It includes information about activities, games, apps, and resources, which can be used to educate students on statistics.
- *Data.gov in the Classroom*: Links to educational resources from the U.S. federal government that can help educate students on how to find and use data, and includes lesson plans, activities, and links to official and unofficial data sources.
- *Teachers' Guide to Data Discovery*: Website from Statistics Canada to help teachers educate their students on data, including a lesson plan and links to resources.
- *Secretary-General's Envoy on Youth*: UN portal to help educate and engage young people in the UN. Includes information about the UN as well as links to statistics about children.

In addition to these sources, there are a number of other resources available. School librarians should stay abreast of current trends in their profession by reading professional publications and signing up for listservs, where they can communicate with and receive advice from their peers.

UNOFFICIAL RESOURCES

A tremendous number of subscription and free databases make data and statistics available. Even databases that are primarily text focused, such as *ProQuest Legislative Insight*, can provide data in the form of text. The databases included in this section will focus on providing access to data and statistics, feature interdisciplinary content, and support library users at all types of libraries. The goal is to highlight those databases that many libraries should include in essential or high-priority lists.

Subscription-Based Databases

Data-Planet is a helpful database for reference librarians to have access to. Available as either *Data-Planet Statistical Datasets* or *Data-Planet Statistical Reference*, both interfaces provide access to the same content. The primary difference between the two is the ability to customize tables. First-time users for both databases will probably be able to find and extract relevant information, but the user interfaces may require adjustment. For example, if someone who is using *Data-Planet Statistical Datasets* wants to create a time series chart that correlates arrest rates, unemployment, and government policies, he or she can select the following facets from the list:

(1) Arrests by race from 1980 to present
(2) Presidencies during that time by political party
(3) Unemployment statistics

By default, the chart will display data for the largest data set, which in this case goes back to 1900. In addition, the unemployment statistics are monthly, so the easiest way to remove the surplus data is by downloading and modifying the data using Microsoft Excel or another statistical software package. Because of its complexity, *Data-Planet Statistical Datasets* is recommended for academic and research institutions, where students, professors, and researchers frequently work with large data sets.

Another excellent database is *ProQuest Statistical Insight*, which provides electronic access to official and unofficial data and statistics from a multitude of sources, including the United States, Canada, and the UN. For example, *Statistical Insight* includes content from the *American Statistics Index*, *Statistics Reference Index*, and the *Index to International Statistics*, all of which have also been published in microfiche. Furthermore, *ProQuest Statistical Insight* serves as a single access point for data from federal and international agencies. This can help a reference librarian to answer:

- Students who need downloadable content that they can import into Microsoft Excel to create charts and graphs for their class assignments
- Users who want to see how different states rank for field crop production, by type of crop
- Users around the world who are interested in Senate election results

Two other products many librarians find useful are *ProQuest Statistical Abstracts of the World* and *ProQuest Statistical Abstract of the United States*, both of which can replace discontinued products like the Census Bureau's *Statistical Abstract*.

In many public and academic libraries, the institution subscribes to several business databases that may be useful in answering statistical questions. One such database is Standard & Poor's *NetAdvantage*, which provides access to data on individual companies, industries, and the Daily Price Record, which provides information on stocks, bonds, and futures prices. Many other business databases provide valuable data for researchers (see Chapter 25). Business librarians consider these databases essential, and in fact, for some academic libraries, they are mandatory because the departments they serve may lose accreditation if the library does not subscribe to the databases. More specialized business databases are the Roper Center's *iPOLL* and *Gallup*, which supply public opinion data and statistics.

In addition to the databases that provide access to newer and/or specialized content, there are several sources for historical statistics. Librarians from the United States may find *Historical Statistics of the United States* (Carter et. al. 2015) from Cambridge University Press to be a helpful database. This database provides access to statistical content that can be difficult to find in other sources. For example, users can find crime and arrest information back to 1910. Law enforcement agencies did not start to regularly record crime data and statistics until 1930 when the FBI was given the responsibility.

The last database to be highlighted in this section is the ICPSR, which is not truly a subscription database; however, the institution must pay a membership fee and belong to the consortium to be able to have full access to its data repository. ICPSR is a repository for research data. Although many universities and colleges participate, federal agencies also use and deposit content. Librarians who receive advanced questions that seem to have no easy-to-find solution are advised to search ICPSR to ascertain whether any of the data sets contain the content the library user needs. For example, undergraduate students who need data about how sentencing affects inmates' actions can find that information at ICPSR. Much of the data is curated from research projects conducted by academics, government entities, and researchers. To be included in the ICPSR database, data must meet several requirements including the types of files and information that must be submitted with the data. This is a valuable resource for large academic libraries and a must-have for many researchers. Members include academic, government, and special libraries from around the world. Although ICPSR has existed since 1962, in recent years, increasing numbers of faculty, graduate, and undergraduate students have sought access to data available through ICPSR.

Free Sources

Since the early 2000s, there has been a marked increase in the number of open-access online data repositories, which totally change the data and statistics landscape. While governments and intergovernmental organizations previously had a monopoly on free data and statistics, universities, consortia, academics, and publishers are entering the market in growing numbers. Because many of the resources included in this section are specialized and have narrow scopes, reference librarians will find these resources helpful when trying to find data and statistics that cannot be found in any of the usual places.

Two examples of highly specialized databases are the *Global Terrorism Database* and the *Suicide Attack Database*. Although both are open-access databases, they deal with a specialized subject and target audience. The *Global Terrorism Database* was created by the National Consortium for the Study of Terrorism and Responses to Terrorism, which was created by the University of Maryland and Department of Homeland Security.

No section on open-access unofficial data and statistics sources is complete without the mention of the Minnesota Population Center at the University of Minnesota, which provides access to United States and international demographic data resources through the Integrated Public Use Microdata Series (IPUMS). All of the content is available for free, but users must register for access if they want to download any of the information. Through IPUMS, registered users can access IPUMS-USA, IPUMS-International, Current Population Survey, Integrated Health Interview Series, and the North Atlantic Population Project. This database can be very useful when one is unable to find data and statistics elsewhere. For example, a student asking for maternal and infant mortality statistics for Sierra Leone may have difficulty finding that information on the UN's website, but the information is readily available using IPUMS. Users can create their own tables and then download the data set.

Simmons College's School of Library and Information Science hosts the *Open Access Directory* (*OAD*), which helps users find open-access content online from official and unofficial sources. *OAD* is most useful when trying to find data that seem outside of the scope of most databases. For example, if an archaeologist needs help finding data and statistics, the *OAD* can help because it provides a link to the Archaeology Data Service. It can also help connect users to unique types of repositories such as *Databrary*, an online video data library from New York University.

A site that is similar to the *OAD* is the *Registry of Research Data Repositories* (*re3data.org*). *re3data.org* is an international registry of data collections from around the world. Additionally, the registry lists repositories for audiovisual, images, word documents, and other types of data files. Users can search using its search function, or they can browse by subject, country, or type of content.

SEARCH STRATEGIES

Librarians have many ways to approach finding data if they know the source of the data needed. Starting with the source is frequently the most direct way to find the data. For example, if a librarian gets a question about the number of barrels of crude oil imported by the United States in the previous month, starting directly at the Department of Energy website is likely to yield quick results.

If the librarian is not sure of the best source for the data, depending on users' needs, he or she can do several things. One of the most common ways is to use Google. Librarians can conduct keyword searches, and then depending on the type of source that is needed, they can focus to a specific site or type of site by typing "site:." Using the site facet, librarians can search for .com, .org, .edu, .gov, and so on, by typing "site:.com" with the preferred domain ending as the last part of the search.

Another way to search is to conduct a general search for a secondary source. For example, if a patron needs farm industry information, and is unsure whether it is available through NASS (National Agricultural Statistics Service), the Economic Research Service, the BLS, or the Census Bureau, he or she may wish to consult a secondary source or statistical aggregator database such as *Data-Planet*, *FedStats*, or *ProQuest Statistical Insight*. For Canadian libraries, the *Statistics Canada* website makes it possible for users to search multiple agencies at once to ascertain which agency has published the most useful information.

The reference interview for patrons seeking data and statistical information should draw out some specific pieces of information not commonly needed in other cases. The appropriate units of analysis or observation for the user's question should be understood by the librarian, although it is not necessary to use those terms with the user. The time period to be analyzed is also of great importance and should be established as soon as possible.

CONCLUSION

As library users gain experience and facility with data and statistics, their queries are becoming more advanced. Therefore, there is an increasing need for librarians who have a deeper understanding of data and statistics and can provide the appropriate level of support. While not all librarians need to be data experts, they still need to understand the types and usage of data; know how it can be evaluated, accessed, and manipulated; and be able to recommend general sources of data. Providing and facilitating access to data and statistics presents a valuable opportunity for librarians to develop stronger relationships with their users and demonstrate the value of their library to its community.

REFERENCES

Feldman, Ronen, and James Sanger. 2007. *The Text Mining Handbook: Advanced Approaches in Analyzing Unstructured Data.* Cambridge: Cambridge University Press.

Grajalez, Carlos Gómez, Eileen Magnello, Robert Woods, and Julian Champkin. 2013. "Great Moments in Statistics." *Significance* 10 (6): 21–28.

Hart, Darlene. 2015. "The Roper Center." *Roper Center.* Accessed October 14. http://www.ropercenter.uconn.edu/.

Hearst, Marti A. 1999. "Untangling Text Data Mining." In *Proceedings of the 37th Annual Meeting of the Association for Computational Linguistics on Computational Linguistics*, 3–10. Association for Computational Linguistics. http://dl.acm.org/citation.cfm?id=1034679.

Jacobs, Jim. 1991. "Providing Data Services for Machine-Readable Information in an Academic Library: Some Levels of Service." *Public Access-Computer Systems Review* 2 (1). https://journals.tdl.org/pacsr/index.php/pacsr/article/view/6033/5665.

Johnson, Allan G. 2000a. "Data." *The Blackwell Dictionary of Sociology.* Malden, MA: Blackwell Publishers.

Johnson, Allan G. 2000b. "Statistics." *The Blackwell Dictionary of Sociology.* Malden, MA: Blackwell Publishers.

Kesselheim, Aaron S., Christopher T. Robertson, Jessica A. Myers, Susannah L. Rose, Victoria Gillet, Kathryn M. Ross, Robert J. Glynn, Steven Joffe, and Jerry Avorn. 2012. "A Randomized Study of How Physicians Interpret Research Funding Disclosures." *New England Journal of Medicine* 367 (12): 1119–27.

Lawrence, Stephen R., Lynn Silipigni Connaway, and Keith H. Brigham. 2001. "Life Cycle Costs of Library Collections: Creation of Effective Performance and Cost Metrics for Library Resources." *College & Research Libraries* 62 (6): 541–53.

OED Online. 2015a. "Data, N." Oxford University Press. http://www.oed.com/view/Entry/296948?redirectedFrom=data.

OED Online. 2015b. "Statistics, N." Oxford University Press. http://www.oed.com/view/Entry/189322?redirectedFrom=statistics&.

Powers, Bethel Ann, and Thomas R. Knapp. 2010a. "Data (Datum Sing.)." *Dictionary of Nursing Theory and Research.* New York: Springer Publishing Company.

Powers, Bethel Ann, and Thomas R. Knapp. 2010b. "Statistic." *Dictionary of Nursing Theory and Research.* New York: Springer Publishing Company.

Ray, Joyce M., ed. 2014. *Research Data Management: Practical Strategies for Information Professionals.* Charleston Insights in Library, Archival, and Information Sciences. West Lafayette, IN: Purdue University Press.

Van Noorden, Richard. 2012. "Trouble at the Text Mine." *Nature* 483 (7388): 134–35.

Wakefield, Andrew J., Simon H. Murch, Andrew Anthony, John Linnell, D.M. Casson, Mohsin Malik, Mark Berelowitz, et al. 1998. "Ileal-Lymphoid-Nodular Hyperplasia, Non-Specific Colitis, and Pervasive Developmental Disorder in Children." *The Lancet* 351 (9103): 637–41.

Zurkirch, Manfred, and Inge Reichart. 2000. "Environmental Impacts of Telecommunication Services." *Greener Management International* 32: 70.

LIST OF SOURCES

Abacus Data. http://abacusdata.ca/.

American Community Survey. Census Bureau. https://www.census.gov/programs-surveys/acs/.

American FactFinder. Census Bureau. http://factfinder.census.gov/.

American Housing Survey. Census Bureau. http://www.census.gov/programs-surveys/ahs.html.

Archaeology Data Service. http://archaeologydataservice.ac.uk/.

Atlas of Rural and Small-Town America. Department of Agriculture. http://www.ers.usda.gov/data-products/atlas-of-rural-and-small-town-america.aspx.

Bauder, Julia. 2014. *Reference Guide to Data Sources*. Chicago: American Library Association.

Budget of the United States Government. Bureau of the Budget, and Office of Management and Budget. https://www.gpo.gov/fdsys/browse/collectionGPO.action?collectionCode=BUDGET.

Bureau of Justice Statistics. http://www.bjs.gov/.

Bureau of Labor Statistics. http://www.bls.gov.

Canada at a Glance. 1995–. Ottawa: Statistics Canada. Annual. Available online: http://www5.statcan.gc.ca/olc-cel/olc.action?objId=12-581-X&objType=2&lang=en&limit=0.

Canada Revenue Agency. http://www.cra-arc.gc.ca/menu-eng.html.

Canada Year Book. Statistics Canada. http://www65.statcan.gc.ca/acyb_r000-eng.htm.

CANSIM. Statistics Canada. http://www5.statcan.gc.ca/cansim/home-accueil?lang=eng.

Carter, Susan B., Scott Sigmund Gartner, Michael R. Haines, Alan L. Olmstead, Richard Sutch, and Gavin Wright. 2015. *Historical Statistics of the United States: Millennial Edition*. Cambridge: Cambridge University Press.

Census Bureau. http://www.census.gov/.

Census of Agriculture. Department of Agriculture. http://www.agcensus.usda.gov/.

Census of Governments. Census Bureau. https://www.census.gov/econ/overview/go0100.html.

Census of Population and Housing. Census Bureau. http://www.census.gov/prod/www/decennial.html.

The Condition of Education. Department of Education. http://nces.ed.gov/programs/coe/.

Consumer Price Index. Bureau of Labor Statistics. http://www.bls.gov/cpi/.

Country Data Online. East Syracuse, NY: PRS Group. https://www.prsgroup.com/about-us/our-two-methodologies/our-data. [subscription required]

Crime in the United States. Department of Justice. https://www.fbi.gov/about-us/cjis/ucr/ucr-publications.

Current Population Survey. Census Bureau. http://www.census.gov/programs-surveys/cps.html.

Data & Statistics Research Guides. MSU Libraries. Michigan State University. http://libguides.lib.msu.edu/datastatguides.

Data and Statistics. Library. uOttawa. http://uottawa.libguides.com/friendly.php?s=DataandStatistics-en.

Data Citation Index. Eagan, MN: Thomson Reuters. http://wokinfo.com/products_tools/multidisciplinary/dci/. [subscription required]
Data Products. Department of Agriculture. http://www.ers.usda.gov/data-products.aspx.
Data.gov. http://www.data.gov/.
Data.gov in the Classroom. https://www.data.gov/education/datagov-classroom.
Data-Planet: The Universe of Data. Bethesda, MD: Conquest Systems. http://homepage.data-planet.com/. [subscription required]
Databrary. New York University. https://nyu.databrary.org/.
DataFerrett. Census Bureau. http://dataferrett.census.gov/.
Demographic Yearbook. United Nations Statistics Division. http://unstats.un.org/unsd/demographic/products/dyb/dyb2.htm.
Department of Agriculture. http://www.usda.gov.
Digest of Education Statistics. Department of Education. https://nces.ed.gov/programs/digest/.
Economic Census. Census Bureau. http://www.census.gov/econ/census/.
Economics, Statistics and Market Information System. Department of Agriculture and Cornell University. http://resolver.library.cornell.edu/misc/aqz4687.
Employment and Earnings Online. Bureau of Labor Statistics. http://www.bls.gov/opub/ee/.
Employment Cost Index. Bureau of Labor Statistics. http://www.bls.gov/news.release/eci.toc.htm.
Energy Statistics Yearbook. United Nations Statistics Division. http://unstats.un.org/unsD/energy/yearbook/default.htm.
Entertainment Software Association. 2015. "2015 Essential Facts about the Computer and Video Game Industry." http://www.theesa.com/wp-content/uploads/2015/04/ESA-Essential-Facts-2015.pdf.
Entertainment Software Rating Board. 2015. "Video Game Industry Statistics." http://www.esrb.org/about/video-game-industry-statistics.aspx.
FedStats. http://fedstats.sites.usa.gov/.
Food Access Research Atlas. Department of Agriculture. http://www.ers.usda.gov/data-products/food-access-research-atlas.aspx.
Food Environment Atlas. Department of Agriculture. http://www.ers.usda.gov/data-products/food-environment-atlas.aspx.
Gale Virtual Reference Library. Farmington Hills, MI: Gale Cengage Learning. http://www.cengage.com. [subscription required]
Gallup. http://www.gallup.com/home.aspx.
Global Education Digest. UNESCO Institute for Statistics. http://www.uis.unesco.org/Education/Pages/global-education-digest.aspx.
Global Health Observatory Data Repository. World Health Organization. http://apps.who.int/gho/data/view.main.
Global Terrorism Database. University of Maryland. http://www.start.umd.edu/gtd/.
Google. http://www.google.com
Hate Crime Statistics. Department of Justice. https://www.fbi.gov/about-us/cjis/ucr/ucr-publications.
Health Data Interactive. Centers for Disease Control and Prevention. http://www.cdc.gov/nchs/hdi.htm.
Health, United States. Centers for Disease Control and Prevention. http://www.cdc.gov/nchs/hus.htm.
Historical Statistics of Canada. Statistics Canada. http://www5.statcan.gc.ca/olc-cel/olc.action?objId=11-516-X&objType=2&lang=en&limit=0.
Instituto Nacional De Estadística y Geografía. http://www.inegi.org.mx/.
Integrated Public Use Microdata Series. University of Minnesota and Minnesota Population Center. https://www.ipums.org/.

Inter-University Consortium for Political and Social Research. https://www.icpsr.umich.edu/icpsrweb/landing.jsp.

International Statistics and Data. University Library. University of Illinois at Urbana-Champaign. http://www.library.illinois.edu/doc/researchtools/guides/statistics/interstats.html.

International Trade Statistics Yearbook. United Nations Statistics Division. http://unstats.un.org/unsd/tradekb/Knowledgebase/International-Trade-Statistics-Yearbook-ITSY.

iPOLL. Ithaca, NY: Roper Center for Public Opinion Research. http://ropercenter.cornell.edu/ipoll-database/. [subscription required]

Kurian, George Thomas, and Barbara Ann Chernow. 2007. *Datapedia of the United States: American History in Numbers*, 4th ed. Lanham, MD: Bernan Press. Available online as part of *Gale Virtual Reference Library.*

Law Enforcement Officers Killed and Assaulted. Department of Justice. https://www.fbi.gov/about-us/cjis/ucr/ucr-publications.

Monthly Bulletin of Statistics Online. United Nations Statistics Division. http://unstats.un.org/unsd/mbs/app/DataSearchTable.aspx.

Monthly Labor Review. Bureau of Labor Statistics. http://www.bls.gov/mlr/.

National Assessment of Educational Progress. Department of Education. http://nces.ed.gov/nationsreportcard.

National Center for Education Statistics. Department of Education. http://nces.ed.gov.

National Center for Health Statistics. Centers for Disease Control and Prevention. http://www.cdc.gov/nchs/.

National Health Statistics Reports. Centers for Disease Control and Prevention. http://www.cdc.gov/nchs/products/nhsr.htm.

National Incident-Based Reporting System. Department of Justice. https://www.fbi.gov/about-us/cjis/ucr/ucr-publications.

National Oceanic and Atmospheric Administration. http://www.noaa.gov/.

National Vital Statistics Reports. Centers for Disease Control and Prevention. http://www.cdc.gov/nchs/products/nvsr.htm.

NetAdvantage. New York: S&P Global Market Intelligence. https://www.netadvantage.standardandpoors.com/. [subscription required]

Ngram Viewer. Google Books. https://books.google.com/ngrams.

Nielsen. http://www.nielsen.com/us/en.html.

Occupational Outlook Handbook. Bureau of Labor Statistics. http://www.bls.gov/ooh/.

Open Access Directory. Simmons College. http://oad.simmons.edu/oadwiki/Main_Page.

Open Data. Government of Canada/Gouvernement du Canada. http://open.canada.ca/en/open-data.

Open Government. Government of Canada/Gouvernement du Canada. http://open.canada.ca/en.

ProQuest Legislative Insight. Ann Arbor, MI: ProQuest. http://www.proquest.com/products-services/legislativeinsight.html. [subscription required]

ProQuest Statistical Abstract of the United States. Ann Arbor, MI: ProQuest. http://www.proquest.com/products-services/statabstract.html [subscription required]

ProQuest Statistical Abstracts of the World. Ann Arbor, MI: ProQuest. http://www.proquest.com/products-services/proquest-statistical-abstracts-world.html. [subscription required]

ProQuest Statistical Insight. Ann Arbor, MI: ProQuest. http://cisupa.proquest.com/ws_display.asp?filter=Statistical%20Overview [subscription required]

Quick Stats. Department of Agriculture. http://www.nass.usda.gov/Quick_Stats/.

Registry of Research Data Repositories (*re3data.org*). http://www.re3data.org.

Retraction Watch. http://retractionwatch.wordpress.com/.

Secretary-General's Envoy on Youth. United Nations. http://www.un.org/youthenvoy/.

Statistical Abstract of the United States. 1878–2012. Census Bureau. https://www.census.gov/library/publications/time-series/statistical_abstracts.html.
Statistical Yearbook. United Nations Statistics Division. http://unstats.un.org/unsd/syb/.
Statistics Canada. http://www.statcan.gc.ca/start-debut-eng.html.
Statistics in Schools. Census Bureau. http://www.census.gov/schools/census_for_kids/.
Statistics Sources. 1992–. 2 vols. Farmington Hills, MI: Gale Cengage Learning. Available online as part of *Gale Virtual Reference Library*.
Suicide Attack Database. University of Chicago. http://cpostdata.uchicago.edu/search_new.php.
Teacher's Guide to Data Discovery. Statistics Canada. http://www5.statcan.gc.ca/olc-cel/olc.action?objId=12-593-X&objType=2&lang=en&limit=0.
UN COMTRADE Database. United Nations. http://comtrade.un.org/.
UNdata. United Nations Statistics Division. http://data.un.org/.
USDA for Kids. Department of Agriculture. http://www.usda.gov/wps/portal/usda/usdahome?navid=FOR_KIDS.
Wayback Machine. Internet Archive. https://archive.org/web/.
World Health Report. World Health Organization. http://www.who.int/whr/.
World Directory of Non-official Statistical Sources. 2007. 5th ed. London: Euromonitor.
World Statistics Pocketbook. United Nations Statistics Division. http://unstats.un.org/unsd/pocketbook/.

SUGGESTED READINGS

Bauder, Julia. 2014. *The Reference Guide to Data Sources*. Chicago: American Library Association.

This is a good introductory book that explains key concepts in data and provides an in-depth listing of a wide range of data sources. The book is organized by subject and is indexed, with a helpful appendix on citing data. The first chapter is especially helpful, exploring the different types of data, publishers, and the process of searching for data. The rest of the book is useful to refer to for specific reference needs. The listing of sources includes a substantial description of each agency and the data it provides.

Geraci, Diane, Chuck Humphrey, and Jim Jacobs. 2012. *Data Basics: An Introductory Text*. Ann Arbor, MI: Inter-University Consortium for Political and Social Research. http://3stages.org/class/2012/pdf/data_basics_2012.pdf.

Data Basics is an important monograph by pioneers in the area of data and statistics services for libraries. It provides a good introduction to data services and provides valuable insight for librarians intending to offer such a service. It lays a solid foundation for understanding data and statistics and their position in libraries, examining the entire life cycle of data, and provides one of the best overviews of preservation issues with data currently available.

Kellam, Lynda M., and Katharin Peter. 2011. *Numeric Data Services and Sources for the General Reference Librarian*. Chandos Information Professional Series. Oxford: Chandos Publishing.

A more advanced look at data and its use, *Numeric Data Services and Sources* examines the data life cycle in detail. This book can be very helpful for a library that wishes to provide advanced data services. The book's intended audience is academic librarians.

Rice, Robin C., and John Southall. 2016. *The Data Librarian's Handbook*. Chicago: American Library Association.

This forthcoming book is expected to be a useful guide for librarians involved in the data curation process.

Chapter 24

Readers' Advisory Services and Sources

Neal Wyatt[1]

INTRODUCTION

Discovery tools shape how the seemingly ineffable is defined and found. Companies such as Netflix, Match.com, and Pandora have invested millions in such processes, telling subscribers they know what makes a movie enjoyable, a partner desirable, and one song evocative of another. Book discovery is part of this same movement. Amazon.com, both on its bookstore site and via *Goodreads*, offers author and title suggestions based upon mathematical formulas and circles of influence. Celebrities of all kinds, and through an ever-expanding range of outlets, also venture to tell readers what is worth exploring. Where do librarians fit into a conversation fueled by big data, circles of influence, and celebrity recommendations?

Readers' advisory (RA) librarians occupy the space between discovery and suggestion. Their work is interwoven into the primary reason most users visit the library: to access and discover books. A 2010 OCLC study found that 75 percent of Americans identified "books" as the first thing they thought of when thinking about libraries, and a third of the study's respondents said that the "top purpose" of a library was to "provide books" (De Rosa et al. 2011, 38, 40). A 2013 Pew Research Center study found that the primary reasons for visiting a library were to "borrow print books" and to "browse the shelves for books or media" (Zickuhr, Rainie, and Purcell 2013, 6).

Advisors help readers learn the addictive joys of books such as J. K. Rowling's *Harry Potter and the Sorcerer's Stone* when they are young and the sustaining pleasures of books such as David McCullough's *1776* and Elizabeth Strout's *Olive Kitteridge* when they grow older. RA librarians help readers discover underappreciated gems, as well as the books lighting up social media and racing up the best seller lists. They suggest titles to readers based upon conversations about what readers like and dislike and what they desire in their reading experiences. Author by author, book by book, RA librarians assist readers in negotiating the most complex process of discovery—understanding what one likes to read and why.[2]

EDUCATION, PLACEMENT, AND DUTIES OF READERS' ADVISORY LIBRARIANS

A 2013 *Library Journal* (*LJ*) study found that most RA librarians are self-taught (Thornton-Verma and Schwartz 2014).[3] They learn to practice RA through trial and error and in-house training, reading RA books and articles, attending conference sessions, and modeling peers. In addition to book- and reading-related skills, advisors must be accomplished in many of the same areas such as reference, collection development, and cataloging librarians, as each contributes to the ways readers borrow, access, and discover books. Like reference librarians, advisors study to be expert searchers, practiced in the art of developing nuanced and intricate search strategies. Like collection development librarians, advisors acquire a thorough knowledge of the publishing industry, familiarize themselves with the various publisher imprints, and understand the cycles of the publishing calendar. Like catalogers, RA librarians learn to characterize the essence of a wide variety of books succinctly and master the operations of a rich and user-friendly controlled vocabulary.

While there is a nascent movement to bring RA services to those who use academic libraries, and while school librarians are in the vanguard of the service in K–12 institutions, RA is most widely practiced in public libraries.[4] RA staff can be based within the public services department, working alongside of, and often in the same role as, reference librarians. Indeed, in many libraries, RA service is part of a range of responsibilities that public service/reference librarians undertake. In a smaller number of libraries, there are librarians who devote most of their attention to RA services, while reference services are delivered from a separate location. In addition to public services librarians, advisors can be based within the collection development or technical services departments, working as selectors and catalogers as well as frontline librarians. Regardless of where they are housed, advisors must collaborate with other departments of the library in order to offer the best service to readers. Multiple aspects of library operations—from circulation policies to the selection of the integrated library system (ILS) to what the service desks are termed—shape the form and extent of RA duties.

What are those duties? RA librarians talk with patrons about books and reading. They do so at the service desk, in the stacks, and via online forums and social media. Advisors suggest books to readers, based upon a system of appeal terms. They identify read-alikes, read-arounds, and sure bets; create displays; and develop reading guides of all types.[5] Advisors read widely, venturing far beyond their own personal preferences. They monitor publishing trends and keep abreast of popular authors and titles. They track changes in genres and nonfiction types and note emerging authors just starting to gain attention (see Box 24.1 for guidance). RA librarians advocate for the importance of reading in the lives of those they serve and strive to create an environment in which reading and book discovery is a familiar and accessible service of the library.

Box 24.1 Activity: Creating a Reading Plan

Advisors need to be readers, and strategic ones at that. Developing a reading plan to ensure wide exposure to key authors, genres, and subgenres is an important part of fulfilling the role of advisor. There are many ways to create a reading plan, and the following are descriptions of four approaches. For each book read, advisors should think about why the book is popular, consider its central appeals, speculate as to what kinds of readers will enjoy it, and identify possible read-alikes. It is also helpful to discuss discoveries with colleagues and fellow fans.

Five-Book Challenge

First devised by Ann Bouricius (2000, 67–68), this reading plan asks that advisors read any five books they wish in a given genre over the course of a year. Joyce Saricks (2009, 335–350) offers a genre-spanning list of suggestions for those needing help getting started.

Reading through the Best Seller List

Used by Saricks to train her departmental staff, this reading plan asks that advisors start with the current *New York Times* Hardcover Fiction Best Seller List and read every book on it that is written by an author the advisor has yet to read. As the list does not change radically week to week, over a month or two, the advisor will have read at least one book by every author on the list. Once the advisor has read through the list, keeping up with newly added authors is relativity easy. The same process can be applied to other lists such as hardcover nonfiction and young adult.

Reading Pathways

This reading plan, a feature on *Book Riot*, is an easy way to become familiar with an author's style, interests, and genre affiliations. Pick three books by one author and read them in a row. This is a particularly good approach for learning more about key authors or to sample an author who writes in a range of genres. Once done, pick another author and keep going.

Classic Sure Bet/New Sure Bet

Sure bets are books that hold wide appeal for a wide range of readers. They are good books to have in the proverbial RA back pocket, and reading them instills confidence and advances RA knowledge in a very strategic manner. Pick one classic sure bet, a title genre fans often reference and adore. Then pick a new sure bet, one published in the last year that is in the same genre as the classic title. Read both back to back, starting with the classic. Once done, pick another pair and keep reading.

Question for Reflection and Discussion:

1. What might be other ideas for reading plans that ensure both depth of knowledge and awareness of contemporary trends?

READERS' ADVISORY THEORY: APPEAL

Appeal is the foundational theory of RA work. It is a set of terms that describes the multiple attractions readers have to books and with the reading experience. More broadly, it is a framework advisors use to translate what a reader enjoys about one book into a set of descriptors that can be applied to others. Advisors use appeal to help readers better understand their reading interests as well as to make suggestions, identify read-alikes and sure bets, and understand genres. Prior to the development and widespread adoption of appeal, many advisors struggled to routinely develop satisfying suggestions and identify a range of authors who pleased readers. Instead they made suggestions based upon genre classification, subject headings, popularity, their own reading preferences, or a vague intuition that one book felt similar to another. Before appeal was standardized, an advisor might have suggested, for example, Jane Austen's *Pride and Prejudice* to readers of Emily Brontë's *Wuthering Heights* as both are highly regarded classics of roughly the same time period and both explore domestic life and courtship. The fact that Austen's novel is witty, sprightly, and straightforward and Brontë's is seething, dark, and complex would not have been considered as important as it should.

Systems of appeal are most frequently expressed as a list of elements with accompanying descriptions and definitions. Currently, there are three systems of appeal commonly used by advisors.

Joyce Saricks and Nancy Brown

Joyce Saricks and Nancy Brown (1989) developed the most widely used system of appeal. It consists of four elements—pacing, characterization, story line, and setting—and was first formally published in their landmark book *Readers' Advisory Service in the Public Library* (51–52). Pacing captures how quickly a novel progresses through the story arc and readers' perception of that speed. Characterization refers to the types of characters in a novel and the manner in which they are brought to life. Are they developed over time through their dialogue, actions, and inner thoughts, or are they fully formed and described from the outset and easily understood and known? Story line encompasses several elements including the point of view from which the story is told and the amount of dialogue in a novel. This latter concern was Saricks and Brown's effort to distinguish novels of action from those that revolve around relationships. They believed that books with a great amount of dialogue were "talking" books, those in which characters and their relationships were the center focus. Story line is most centrally concerned, however, with the authors' treatment of, and intentions toward, the story itself. Treatment refers to the kind of story being told. One author might approach an espionage novel, for example, from the standpoint of the mission, tracing the elements of spy craft and emphasizing the danger and escape. Another author could pen an espionage novel with a stress on the moral ambiguity of the situation and the cost of the mission on the agent's psyche. Intention refers to the author's approach, be it a serious examination of an issue, a romp, or a soap opera. Setting, as Saricks and Brown wish the term to be understood, does not only mean place or time but also background detail, the description and detail that sets the book into a particular world. Settings readers notice tend to be rich and expansive, such as the archaeological and mythical details of ancient Egypt that so enhance the Amelia Peabody series by Elizabeth Peters, rather than those that are thin and imprecise, such as the version of London depicted in Daniel Silva's novels.

Saricks has continued to study appeal and has published further editions of *Readers' Advisory Service in the Public Library* and columns on appeal in *Booklist* magazine.[6] Through these outlets, she has revised some of the terminology she and Brown first developed, changing the term "setting" to frame and adding the concepts of tone and mood as well as language and style to her list of appeal elements. Saricks's term "frame" has been widely adopted, and many advisors use it in place of the word "setting" as frame more clearly marks a distinction between setting as "time and place" and setting as "background detail." Building off of the work of Catherine Sheldrick Ross (discussed later), Saricks uses the term "mood" to define the emotional state of the reader. She defines tone as the feeling an author creates in a book. Like Ross, Saricks believes that readers' moods are critical and can almost entirely account for a reader not enjoying a suggestion. She also holds that tone can be as important as pacing in the determination of what a reader will enjoy (Saricks 2010, 21). Saricks uses the terms "language" and "style" to account not only for the fundamentals of writing quality and "stylistic flourishes" but also for a wider range of language and style concerns, such as language that is "clever, natural, ornate, polished, lyrical, smart, witty, breezy, or pun-filled" and styles that are "anecdotal, journalistic, scholarly, complex, unusual, or experimental" (2013, 19).

Nancy Pearl

Nancy Pearl (1999, xii–xiii), who created the concept of the One City One Book community reading program and directed the Washington Center for the Book at the Seattle Public Library, defines four elements of appeal: setting, story, character, and language. What might strike advisors first about Pearl's framework is its seeming correspondence to Saricks and Brown's. Both include a stress on setting, story, and characters. However, Pearl defines these terms differently. In her framework, setting refers to both the geographical and temporal locations of a novel and the degree to which a particular place or time is fully evoked (rather than the Saricks/Brown's use of the word to also mean tone or frame). Pearl uses story to indicate "what happens" and "what happens next" aspects of the novel. It is this use of the term that has become the most widely adopted definition within RA service. Few advisors, even if they use the term "story line," understand that term to mean anything more than a story summary. Pearl's use of the term "character" does overlap with Saricks and Brown's, but her interest is in whether or not the most important part of a novel is its characters, rather than the events in which they feature. "Language" indicates style and word craft. In Pearl's use of the term, it means writing of a particularly high quality.

Pearl has used the divisions between her appeal terms to create a metaphor that describes the way a reader engages with a book. The "doorway" system of appeal posits that all books have a front door, the main entrance through which readers connect to a given work (Pearl 2012, 18). While all books have all four doorways, the size of the doors frequently operates on a sliding scale. For example, a large story doorway often decreases the aperture of the language doorway. Sometimes appeal elements work hand in hand, however. A sizable setting doorway might require an equally large language doorway, creating a French door effect. Pearl discusses books in terms of their doorways, linking works with large setting doorways to each other in ways that are similar to how Saricks links books with quick pacing and twisty plots to one another.

Catherine Sheldrick Ross

In 1982, professor Catherine Sheldrick Ross began interviewing avid readers. Over the course of two decades, she and her graduate students interviewed more than 300 readers, developing a rich collection of data addressing why people read, how they select titles, and the elements that contribute to enjoyment. Based upon these data, Ross (2001a, 2001b) has created an appeal framework that includes 11 elements: mood, cost, physical size, subject, treatment, impact, character, pacing, action, setting, and ending.[7]

Mood, which Ross frequently expresses as the "reading experience wanted" (2001a, 17), is the central revelation found through her interviews. Ross posits that readers choose titles based upon their emotional state at the time of selection. If readers are under stress when making selection choices, they tend to gravitate toward books that offer reassurance and validation. If they are in a state of equanimity, then readers are more likely to seek new experiences (e.g., unfamiliar authors or genres) and are able to enjoy books that challenge their beliefs or offer less predictable stories.

Cost addresses the effort it takes to read a book. If a novel requires a great deal of background knowledge or uses obscure vocabulary, for example, it can be more difficult, or costly, in terms of the degree of work. If a book is very long, it also has a higher cost in terms of commitment. If a novel is deeply depressing or harrowing, it exacts an emotional cost. Related to cost is the concern some readers have regarding the physical size of a book. Individual readers may not enjoy slim volumes, as there is not enough content to sustain them, while others dislike thick tomes, as they take too long to read and require too much continued attention.

Subject, treatment, impact, character, pacing, action, setting, and ending are more traditional appeal elements, several of which Saricks and Brown as well as Pearl have also identified. As was the case with Pearl, however, some terms vary in meaning across each of the appeal frameworks. Ross understands subject to encompass what she terms the "what's-this-book-about-question" (Catherine Sheldrick Ross, pers. comm.), which includes not only its story but also its genre or nonfiction type. Ross's term "treatment" aligns with part of Saricks and Brown's aspect of "story line" in that both address the approach an author takes to the story. Ross also includes the emotional content of the book under a consideration of treatment (an aspect Saricks terms "tone"). Impact is related to both treatment and mood, and addresses the emotional effect a book has on a reader and readers' preferences in that regard. Some readers do not enjoy ironic books or those with black humor. Others do not enjoy works they consider saccharine. Character includes not just a concern for dimensionality vs. stereotypes but also the actual kind of characters in the novel, such as strong female heroines, alpha males, or zany private detectives.

Ross uses the concept of pacing to address the level of engagement a reader has with the unfolding story. She also gathers here a concern about dialogue vs. descriptions of events, people, and places. Action addresses how the story is developed, through its unfolding events or the thoughts and development of its characters. These concerns of pacing and action are echoed by Saricks and Brown as well as Pearl, as each, using different terms, makes a distinction between books in which story, character, or language is the principal attraction.

In discussing "setting," Ross addresses what she terms "the nature of the world represented" (2001b, 92). Like Pearl, this concept covers the level of detail and description of the geographical and temporal setting, but moving beyond both Pearl and Saricks and Brown, Ross means the term to define the similarity between the fictional world and a reader's reality in terms of the essential truths of the novel. Ending addresses the way a novel concludes, such as happily, predictably, or unresolvedly.

Other Contributions

While Saricks and Brown, Pearl, and Ross have developed the most widely used and known explanations of appeal (see Table 24.1), others have contributed much to the conversation surrounding why a reader enjoys and selects a particular book. Annelise Mark Pejtersen (1978) discussed what today would be termed appeal in her 1978 article, "Fiction and Library Classification." Pejtersen questioned the functionality of an alphabetical arrangement of fiction and suggested instead that readers would be better served by a classification system reflective of content, mood, and style. Betty Rosenberg (1982) also offered an array of appeal factors in *Genreflecting: A Guide to Reading Interests in Genre Fiction.* While Rosenberg scattered her appeal terms throughout her explorations of genres, she brought attention to many elements now familiar to advisors such as action, characterization, setting, and tone. The 2007 article "Redefining RA: An RA Big Think," part of *LJ's* three-year long examination of RA service, offered a set of further considerations, including the unpacking and expansion of the terms "story line" and "frame" and the addition of new concepts such as "design" and "format" (Wyatt 2007, 40–41).

The differences between Saricks and Brown, Pearl, and Ross, and the other practitioners and academics who have suggested appeal schematics are less important than the concept of appeal itself. Learning an appeal framework, applying

TABLE 24.1 Appeal Term Summary

The following are the most widely used appeal terms in contemporary RA. Be aware that a common term, such as setting, may hold different meaning between frameworks.

Joyce Saricks/ Nancy Brown	Nancy Pearl	Catherine Sheldrick Ross
Pacing	Setting	Mood
Characterization	Story	Cost
Story line	Character	Physical size
Setting [frame]	Language	Subject
Tone/mood		Treatment
Language/style		Impact
		Character
		Pacing
		Action
		Setting
		Ending

it to one's own reading preferences (see Box 24.2), and developing a customized approach to appeal based upon interactions with patrons are critical steps in studying to be an advisor.

Box 24.2 Activity: Understanding Your Own Appeal Preferences

It is critical that advisors understand the appeal framework and how it describes and classifies the reading experience. To practice appeal, try this exercise first devised by Debra Wordinger and further explained by Saricks (2005a, 35). It offers advisors a chance to consider their own reading preferences and practice applying appeal terms to those preferences. It also illustrates the powerful ways appeal serves to classify the reading experience and the difficulty readers may have expressing their likes and dislikes.

Getting Started

- List three to five books you have deeply enjoyed and three to five books you have not.
- For each title, list as many reasons why as possible. Be specific. For example, rather than saying "I liked the story" push further and list "I enjoyed the Cinderella, ill-treated and then made good, aspects of the story."
- Continue examining each title and listing reasons for your response. Consider all aspects of why you did or did not enjoy the work.
- Once you have exhausted your own mental list of reasons, look at the appeal summary list of terms (Table 24.1) and make sure each has been addressed. Continue expanding your profile as needed.
- Review your notes, looking for similar comments and appeal terms in your analysis of each book you enjoyed and each you did not.
- List the areas of positive overlap and apply appeal terms to each. Are there repeated instances of several appeal terms?
- List the areas of negative overlap and apply appeal terms to each. Again, are there repeated instances of appeal concepts? Are they in opposition to the aspects you enjoyed? Do they deepen your understanding of what you enjoy or change how you understand your preferences?
- Are there appeal terms that do not seem to matter to your reading preferences?

Creating the Profile

- List three to five books you count as outstanding examples of books you deeply enjoy. For each, summarize the reasons why they are favorites, using appeal terminology.
- List the most important appeal elements as indicated by the frequency each was a reason you enjoyed a given title.
- List the aspects of books you do not enjoy, again using appeal terminology.

Putting the Profile to Use

Exchange profiles with classmates. Read each other's work and ask questions to clarify meaning and point out areas that are not as precise as others. Revise accordingly and then exchange profiles again, using them as the basis to suggest new titles to one another. Discuss why each title was offered and why it might be enjoyed.

READERS' ADVISORY PRACTICE: THE CONVERSATION

RA service fundamentally involves the sharing of books between two readers, one of whom happens to be the advisor. Traditionally, the process of talking with readers and making book suggestions has been termed an "interview," aligning the process with the reference interview. In many ways, the RA conversation is similar to a reference interview, and readers of M. Kathleen Kern and Beth S. Woodard's Chapter 3 in this text will find much overlap as well as good guidance.[8] Both the reference interview and the RA conversation blend art and craft. To do either well requires a certain degree of deftness, but for each, the processes can be learned, and skill and adroitness can be acquired through practice. Both the reference interview and the RA conversation require a willingness to be open to possibilities and to think creatively. Each also demands skill, knowledge, confidence, and most of all, a positive, welcoming, and professional approach. Ultimately, however, the RA conversation is different from a reference interview, with different starting points, processes, expectations, and outcomes.

Foremost is a difference in goals. Unlike a reference interview in which a patron seeks assistance finding an answer to an information query, the RA conversation is not focused upon informational outcomes but on the experience itself. At its best and most felicitously practiced, the RA conversation achieves several objectives. The offering of book suggestions is the most obvious result. However, RA conversations should also provide readers the opportunity to share books and reading experiences and to have their interests in reading supported and reflected back. Conversations should help readers articulate their reading likes and dislikes and teach readers how to browse the collection and evaluate and select titles. Conversations should also teach readers, and then continually reinforce the concept, that the library is a place where reading—of any kind and of any type—is appreciated and encouraged. Finally, conversations should invite readers back to the library and, it is to be hoped, back to further conversations, so that they feel sustained in a lifetime of reading. These goals of suggestion, support, and education shape the RA conversation. While many interactions with patrons ultimately conclude with book suggestions, a conversation that does not close with suggestions can be equally successful. RA conversations can conclude with an advisor teaching a patron to use a database or a website, with an invitation to join the library's book discussion group, or with the advisor promising to send a title list to the reader later on that week.

Even given the divergence of goals and outcomes between reference and RA encounters, the broad outline of the RA conversation shares much with the steps governing the reference interview. As such, advisors are well served following many of the best practices developed for the provision of reference services. The Reference and User Services Association's (RUSA) "Guidelines for Behavioral Performance of Reference and Information Service Providers" (2013) offers expansive recommendations for how advisors should generally proceed through the conversation and establish rapport. Basing the RA conversation upon its general structure, it is possible to identify four parts of the RA counterpart: initiating the conversation, appeal identification, title suggestion, and an invitation to continue the conversation.

Initiating the Conversation

Most patrons are not taught that RA is a part of the library's core mission. RA services of all kinds are less obvious, and often less obviously promoted, than traditional information-seeking services, computer access, and circulation services.

Few libraries have dedicated RA desks and few have staff devoted solely to RA services.[9] For these reasons, and many more, it is very common to encounter readers who do not know that asking for help finding a book to read for pleasure—beyond the basics of location or availability—is a service they can expect from the library. Accordingly, one of the largest challenges advisors face is starting conversations. Few readers will approach a service desk labeled "Information" or "Reference" and ask what to read now that they have finished all the George R. R. Martin books. It is incumbent upon advisors to be proactive and help readers begin such conversations.

Start by meeting readers where they are. Walk around the library and approach readers at the new bookshelf, at display locations, and in the stacks. Offer assistance by asking, "Are you finding everything you're looking for?"[10] Readers are likely to be more open to RA services when they encounter a librarian in the stacks or near book displays. Meeting patrons in these locations is also less awkward for RA librarians. It is easier for advisors to begin talking about the books in front of them or walk patrons around a corner and pull a book off the shelf than it is to leave the service desk and walk across the open floor, perhaps even to another floor, to find a title. Even if patrons initially refuse the offer of assistance, they have learned that librarians are happy to offer reading suggestions.

Increasingly, advisors are using online services to initiate conversations. Many libraries offer form-based RA, and some are providing RA through social media as well.[11] The advantages of these types of RA services are many. They allow readers to request assistance at a direct point of invitation (the form or site itself) so they know that such requests are part of the library's services. They allow readers to think more carefully about what they desire, lessening concerns over articulating likes and dislikes. Additionally, form-based RA allows advisors time to find suggestions without the pressures of patrons waiting for them to do so or while other patrons wait in line.

Determine Needs/Appeal Identification

Once a reader has entered into a discussion with an advisor, the next step is to determine needs. Some readers might simply want to talk about books and authors they enjoy, while others may wish to continue the conversation from a book discussion the previous night. Many, however, will be seeking something to read and will ask for help in that process. The rest of this discussion assumes that an advisor is helping a patron with this type of inquiry. The first step is to prompt for appeal descriptions. Ask open-ended questions that guide readers toward sharing features of works they have enjoyed. Prompts such as: "What are some [books/authors] you have enjoyed in the past?" and "Tell me about a book you have recently enjoyed" often work because they allow readers to share what they can articulate, directing their attention toward the aspects of a work they most enjoyed. The opposite question, "Tell me about a book you have recently disliked," works just as well and allows readers the freedom to admit that they found a book wanting.

If readers cannot describe a particular book or author, ask them to describe a movie or television show they have recently enjoyed. As all forms of storytelling share a basis of appeal, movies and television shows can provide an equally useful place to start a conversation, as do books. For example, advisors can learn just as much about a reader by discovering whether that reader enjoys *Broadchurch* or *The Bridge* as knowing the reader enjoys the Ian Rutledge mysteries by Charles Todd or the Harry Bosch mysteries by Michael Connelly.

Advisors can also offer options to help readers describe their desired experience. Pose contrasting pairs of features such as, "Are you in the mood for a book that is fast and thrilling with a great story, or would you enjoy one filled with interesting characters and fewer adventures?"

Once readers begin to talk about the kind of reading experience they are seeking, listen carefully for appeal clues. Readers will not necessarily use appeal terminology, but they will say things that relate to appeal such as:

- I could not put the book down. I stayed up all night reading.
- I was fascinated by ideas in the book; it really got me thinking about cloning.
- I fell in love with the book; it was so wonderful, comforting, and special.
- I liked the characters. They were interesting and complicated.
- It was scary. That was great.
- It was a super story, very twisty and surprising.
- I was really captured by how evocative and poetic it was. I think I paid attention to each sentence. It took a while to read but I loved it.
- It was a quick read. It kept me entertained on the plane.

Advisors should next translate those descriptions into the appeal framework and determine what the reader is emphasizing. A reader who says something similar to "It was a quick read. It kept me entertained on the plane and was twisty and surprising" is stressing pacing and story over other concerns. A reader who says, "I was really captured by how evocative and poetic it was. I think I paid attention to each sentence. It took a while to read but I loved it" is stressing style. Based on what the reader shares, advisors next create an appeal summary of what the reader is seeking. This process is critical to do well and with care. Advisors should take time to confirm that they have understood the reader by restating the appeal elements. Advisors might say, "It sounds like you enjoy books that keep you turning the pages and have gripping and clever plots. Is that right or are you in the mood for something else?" Giving readers an out by including something similar to "or are you in the mood for something else" allows them to correct the appeal summary without having to challenge the authority of the librarian—an action many might be reluctant to do.

After the opening segment of the conversation, once readers have shared what they desire, advisors need to determine whether there are certain formats, types, or genres in which readers are particularly interested. Knowing the genre a reader enjoys can help narrow choices, but do not assume that a single genre is the limit of the suggestion range. Genre blends are common and regularly introduce readers of one genre to the pleasures of another. Also do not assume that fiction is the only area of the collection upon which to draw. There are many narrative nonfiction titles that will please readers, and films, audiobooks, and graphic novels all make excellent suggestions as well. Indeed, suggesting that fans of Diana Gabaldon's Outlander books consider watching the Michael Mann version of *The Last of the Mohicans* can be just as pleasing as suggesting Deborah Harkness's novel *A Discovery of Witches*.

Advisors should also determine whether readers wish to avoid any topics, treatments, or certain levels of sex, violence, or profanity. However, the question itself is a tricky proposition as it can unintentionally suggest that the advisor thinks there are books that should be avoided and knows the level of sex, violence, and profanity in every title offered. This thorny problem is best approached by simply asking readers whether there is anything they do not want to read (rather than listing possible affronts) and then suggesting that once a few titles are identified that readers check reviews to find more specific information.

Title Suggestion

It is at the point of making suggestions that many new advisors feel the most trepidation. It can be a daunting undertaking. With practice and experience, the process does become easier, but there will always be titles and authors that stump even the most experienced advisor, titles advisors cannot find anything about, or those so unique that they are hard to match with other works. With the right approach, however, making suggestions can be deeply enjoyable as advisors and readers share the pleasures of discussing books and discover new titles to explore.

Equipped with an appeal profile, an idea of the authors and titles enjoyed in the past, and any specifics to avoid, advisors can proceed to think of, search for, and find suggestions. The variety of methods for doing so are too lengthy to detail here and vary by advisor based upon their own depth and breadth of reading, the in-house tools at their disposal (e.g., key author templates and genre sure bet lists), the RA resources their library owns or they can access, and the actual holdings of their collection. There is, however, a body of time-tested advice advisors typically share with each other:

- Relax. Readers do not expect advisors to have encyclopedic information on every book ever written. Making suggestions is part of a conversation, not a speed-round on a game quiz show.
- Just as in reference service, there are many tools that contain answers to RA questions. Readers do not expect advisors to know a list of suggestions off the top of their heads for every book ever written, and advisors should not expect that of themselves.
- Keep the search focused on the specific appeal elements the reader mentioned.
- Focus on the reader. Advisors should keep their own reading tastes out of the equation unless they directly overlap with the reader's. Even then, avoid comments such as "I love Lee Child and know you will too" as this leaves the reader little room to disagree.
- Suggest proven reader-tested title and author matches. Even if readers have already read them, it helps confirm appeal and lets readers know the advisor is on the same page as the reader. Suggesting such titles also helps further narrow the search once readers comment upon their particular favorites.
- Focus on award winners, sure bets, and fan favorites within a few connected genres that are known for sharing the appeals the reader enjoys. For example, crime novels of all types (thrillers, suspense, and mysteries) are often engrossing and fast-paced reads.
- Collaboration is encouraged. It is always appropriate to ask for assistance from coworkers. It is also perfectly fine to e-mail a colleague in another library or post a query to an RA discussion list.
- It is absolutely appropriate to offer to send readers a list of suggestions at a later date to allow for more time to conduct research.

Invitation to Continue the Conversation

Every RA conversation should conclude with an invitation to continue the dialogue. Invite readers to share what they think of the suggestions with a closing sentence such as "I hope you come back and let me know what you think. If you really enjoy any of these, we can find more, and if you do not like some of them, that will help me pinpoint better suggestions—we have lots to choose from." Advisors can also mention they will keep an eye out for further titles and will be happy to share more the next time they see the patron. Doing so sets the stage for further conversations and establishes the library as a part of the patron's reading life. Advisors also might wish to point out any additional RA services the library offers as part of wrapping up a session. For example, if the library offers a form-based RA service, let the reader know that suggestions can be received via e-mail as well. Advisors can also share guides to authors and genres or free book-based newsletters that the library makes or offers, so that the reader has something else to take home or read online. Box 24.3 offers practice integrating each aspect of the RA conversation.

Special Concerns

Book Judgment

As Catherine Sheldrick Ross, Lynne (E.F.) McKechnie, and Paulette M. Rothbauer (2006, 10–16, 181–204) have shown through their studies of readers, the selection of a book can be a disheartening process. It is difficult for many readers to know what makes a book enjoyable and thus the search for such elusive titles can be fruitless and frustrating. Beyond the difficulties of selection, reading itself is a culturally weighted issue. Many people have opinions on what is a "good" book, from talk show hosts to magazine editors to next-door neighbors. Few readers are lucky enough to reach adulthood without someone telling them what they are reading is "bad," be that a parent, teacher, friend, or complete stranger.

Advisors have to work against this baggage. They need to help readers become comfortable in their reading choices and confident in the selection process. As such, their work is guided by the core philosophy that all types of reading are to be supported in the library and that all types of books—from the most denigrated "pulp" paperback novel to the most lauded award-winning biography—are valuable to the readers who enjoy them. Betty Rosenberg created the standard philosophical tenet that supports this idea in RA service: "never apologize for your reading tastes" (1982, 5). The professional correlation to Rosenberg's law is that advisors should never make others feel as if they have a need to apologize for their reading tastes either. "Advisors act as appreciators rather than critics" is the way Joyce Saricks frames it (2007, 33).

When working at a service desk or talking with readers in the stacks, advisors should take care to respond to readers in a positive way regardless of the kind of book they are seeking. This means that an advisor's reaction to learning that a reader enjoys fantasy novels, armchair travel, or biographies must be the same as learning they enjoy mysteries, memoirs, or science fiction. An individual advisor might think that Chick Lit is silly or that Westerns are pulp, but those opinions have no place in a professional transaction and frankly no place within RA service. All kinds of reading provide opportunities for enjoyment, learning, and reflection.

Box 24.3 Activity: Identifying Read-Alikes and Places to Start Reading

An advisor meets a reader in front of the new book display and asks whether he can help the patron find a specific title. The reader responds that she is looking for the newest book by Julia Quinn, but it seems all the copies are checked out. The librarian offers to help find books in the same style and manner of Quinn, and the reader is happy to hear a few suggestions.

Questions for Reflection and Discussion:

1. Given that the librarian is in front of the new bookshelf, how might that shape the start of the RA conversation?
2. What are some of the questions the librarian needs to ask the reader?
3. How will the librarian know which appeal elements are most important to the reader?
4. What will the librarian need to know about Quinn's books in order to make suggestions?
5. What resources might identify read-alikes?
6. What are some ways the librarian can successfully end the conversation?

The Flipside

What if the reader does not want a read-alike but rather requests help getting started with a selected author? An RA librarian comes upon a patron sitting in the stacks, with every book by Stephen King pulled out and scattered on the floor. The advisor asks whether the reader needs any help and gets the reply "How do you tell which one is the best? A friend told me I would love Stephen King but how am I supposed to know where to start?"

Questions for Reflection and Discussion:

1. What might be some ways the advisor can immediately ease the reader's frustration?
2. How do appeal elements factor into this question?
3. What aspects about the reader's preferences and King's body of work would help determine the best starting title?
4. Who might have created the most useful guides to aid in answering this question?
5. What elements in a review or an RA resource would provide help in determining an answer to the reader's question?
6. How many choices of starting titles might the librarian offer? What might be a good way to introduce each different title?
7. How should the advisor conclude the conversation?

One never knows what book will trigger the creation of a lifetime reader or what work will open a new world of discovery. It is the advisor's job to actively support all reading explorations and interests.

To that end, advisors should school their facial expressions as much as possible, always reacting with interest to a reader's preferences. Advisors should curb any negative verbal reactions as well. While it is to be hoped that no advisor would respond to a reader with an astonished, "Really?" it is easy to unthinkingly express comparable thoughts during an off-the-cuff and on-the-fly conversation.

For example, saying something similar to "I don't know that author, we don't have many fans of science fiction here" or "We keep books like that in the paperback spinner" have the same effect and tell readers that what they read is not valued in the library. One moment of negative judgment, however unintended, can have the consequence of teaching the reader that the library is another place that offers disapproval. To counter any unintentional responses, advisors should practice positive replies (see Box 24.4) and develop a toolkit of phrases that they feel comfortable using.

Box 24.4 Positive Replies

Develop phrases that are honest and apply to all types of reading. Such responses let readers know they are in good company and affirm their reading choices. Generic responses might include:

- That is a very popular [genre/author].
- I have heard lots of buzz about that [book/author].
- I am so happy to hear you enjoyed [title/author].
- The hold list for that title is very long; you are in great company!

If advisors happen to be fans of the author/genre/type a reader mentions, then even more enthusiastic responses are appropriate:

- I just [finished/started] that. Tell me what you thought about it.
- [Author] is one of my favorites too!
- I really enjoy [genre/type] as well. Tell me about some of your favorites.
- I just read a great review about [title]. I cannot wait to read it. What did you most enjoy?

The point is to develop responses that feel authentic and natural so that immediate positive reactions become instinctual.

Wrong Answers

Given the multiple variables in an RA conversation, it should not be surprising that there are no right answers in the suggestion process, only possibilities. The fact that there are no right answers, however, does not mean that there are not wrong answers. Stephen King is not a read-alike for Sarah Addison Allen. Fans of hard-core science fiction will likely not be pleased with time travel based on a magic ring. Both of these "wrong" answers arise from not listening carefully to the reader, not applying appeal, and not understanding the genre or type of book under discussion.

An inexperienced advisor, unaware of appeal or genre conventions, could mistakenly pair King and Allen because each has included ghosts in their writing. However, King's version of a haunting is very different than Allen's. King writes dark, anxious, and violent books, while Allen writes supportive, gentle, and gracefully airy works. The fact that each has populated a title with spirits is not enough to create a read-alike between the authors and ignores the fact that both authors feel very differently to read and create markedly different effects in readers. Suggesting King to Allen fans, particularly when those fans discuss the gentle and lyrical nature of Allen and how her books leave them feeling settled and happy is an RA mistake and is an example of not listening to readers and not applying appeal elements. Suggesting a book that features time travel via a magic ring to hard-core science fiction fans is an example of not understanding the fundamental tenets of a genre. Science fiction readers expect events to be based on possible science. Time travelers can make use of a wormhole or a time machine, but conjuring a magic ring and using it to jump between time and place is the realm of fantasy novels.

Suggesting books to readers and supporting their reading interests is not work to be undertaken lightly with the thought that connections between titles can be casually made. Any book will not do. It must be a book within a range of correct possibilities. It does a disservice to the reader to approach RA service with the mindset that all mysteries set in an English village are the same, for example, or any book with time travel will suit a reader who likes time travel. The RA conversation may be less formal in its tone than a traditional reference interview but its standards for excellence are not less exacting.

READERS' ADVISORY SOURCES

Uses and Characteristics

RA resources aid in the identification of read-alikes, sure bets, key authors, and genre conventions. Resources also assist advisors in the ongoing work of keeping abreast of publishing trends and forthcoming titles. RA resources answer questions such as:

- What is the best book by Dan Simmons?
- Can I start this series with its most recent title or do I have to go back to the beginning?
- Who writes just like Hilary Mantel?
- What was the name of that book [celebrity of the moment] talked about yesterday?
- What is slipstream fiction?

For a field that covers every aspect of the library's collection, RA resources are a concentrated body of literature. ALA Editions (or one of its imprints) and Libraries Unlimited (LU) publish the majority of the print resources used by advisors. The major library information vendors, such as EBSCO and Gale, produce the standard RA databases. Trade review sources are also concentrated to four primary publications: *Booklist*, *Kirkus Reviews*, *LJ*, and *Publishers Weekly*. Consumer reviews remain fairly centralized as well, although the business of book reviewing is in flux as publications struggle to balance the space they can afford to allot to reviews with the revenue such reviews generate. According to Nora Rawlinson, editor of *EarlyWord*, "National book review coverage has diminished greatly in the last few years, with only *The New York Times* still publishing a weekly standalone book section (plus daily reviewing). Among popular magazines, *Entertainment Weekly* still publishes a review section in each issue while both *USA Today* and *People* have reduced their sections. National Public Radio (NPR) also has a separate and influential book section online, which includes reviews that don't appear on the air" (pers. comm.). For variety and range in RA resources of all kinds, librarians can look toward the multitude of Internet sites.

Crafting a collection of RA tools is an interesting exercise in collection development because it is, unfortunately, largely a collection used only by staff. Imagine a special collection the public never saw or only understood existed as represented by a single database. It would be unthinkable. Yet libraries routinely buy RA guides that never move beyond the desks of advisors. S. R. Ranganathan's first law of library science is that "books are for use" (1963, 26). This applies to RA resources as well. Perhaps one explanation for patrons not understanding that RA services exist is that there are few books on the shelf helping them explore RA themselves. To the extent it is possible, collection development of RA titles should include circulating copies for public use. These books overflow with invitingly described suggestions arranged in such a way that readers can learn more about their appeal profiles and find titles to enjoy. Library-favorite websites and book review journals should be shared as well.

Evaluation

Format

RA resources have four primary formats: books, subscription databases (and related catalog enhancement services), print journals (and their online counterparts), and a wide variety of free sources on the Web. Each offers different benefits. RA books include annotations written by readers' advisors who know how to craft descriptions that go beyond story summary to detail appeal and offer read-alikes. Subscription databases have a variety of access points and indexing that supports complicated searches accounting for a range of factors important to readers. Print journals and their Web editions offer advanced notice of forthcoming titles with content specifically directed toward librarians. Because of their diversity in approach, topic, and content, free Web resources offer advisors information that is rarely covered in a more formal printed text or database, giving RA librarians advance notice on what fans are reading and thinking. RA librarians are well served by including all four formats in their work, as it is in their combination that advisors can most successfully keep abreast of title information, increase their knowledge of genres and key authors, and offer suggestions readers will enjoy.

Authority

The qualifications of those creating and/or contributing to an RA resource are of critical importance. As many advisors are self-taught, the resources they use to help readers are among those they use for continuing education. As such, these sources have significance beyond the ways they are used in any individual RA encounter: they shape how RA services are understood and practiced. RA librarians should evaluate resources based upon the approach they take and the guidance they provide in addition to other standard elements of assessment.

Librarians or groups of librarians write most print RA resources. Many of these authors have been working as RA or collection development librarians for years and have developed a thorough knowledge of a genre, its development, appeal, and key titles. These librarians have worked with readers, making suggestions in the stacks and online, and have also spent a great deal of time thinking and writing about books and RA best practices. When considering the authority of a print resource, advisors should determine the experience and expertise of the authors. Do they have experience working with readers or developing collections? Have they worked in a public library? For how long? Alternatively, are they nationally known for their expertise in an area, based upon their academic research or a highly regarded online site they have maintained for years?

The authority of a database rests largely on the reputation of its publisher; the accuracy, timeliness, and thoroughness of its bibliographic entries; the depth of its indexing; and the reliability of its read-alike suggestions. Having practicing RA librarians involved in its production as either contributors or on an advisory board is also a factor to note. Sustained use is likely the best indicator of reliability and accuracy, however. Advisors using databases quickly learn which offer suggestions that are appeal based and please readers and which do not.

The old joke that anything one reads online must be true applies to free online RA resources as well. Many are produced by librarians and other experts in the publishing world with deservedly strong reputations, but a number are little more than personal musings, which, while interesting, are not sufficiently authoritative to base a suggestion upon alone. As is true with all Web sources, advisors should practice rigorous evaluation before relying upon them for RA information. The four primary trade journals offering book reviews for public libraries are uniformly highly regarded and should be considered standard and authoritative resources.

Scope

Scope varies by format, but each type of RA resource should be evaluated based upon its date range, material types included, content of entries, and the thoroughness of indexing. Advisors work with both front and backlist titles, and thus the required date range will vary by inquiry. Books and databases offer the deepest coverage, including older titles that are still relevant to readers. Journals and websites typically focus only upon new and forthcoming titles. Advisors also work with a wide range of materials. The term "reader" has become a hypernym, gathering listener, viewer, and gamer under the general scope of someone experiencing a story. Patrons routinely seek information on fiction and nonfiction, audiobooks, film, and TV series, and resources that cover each of these areas are increasingly useful.

Central to evaluation as well is the depth of content. What is possible to include varies based on the format of the resource, with databases having the most complete entries, followed by books. Journals typically offer the most complete bibliographic data, including imprint, publication date, ISBN, format, and price. A story summary/review including appeal should be considered a standard of all RA resources regardless of format. Summaries or reviews that do not include appeal might be useful for purposes other than RA, but without an indication of such elements as pacing, characterization, tone, style, and setting, their RA use is limited. To the extent a resource is designed to aid advisors in making suggestions, reliable read-alikes, with an explanation as to why a title is suggested as a read-alike, should also be considered standard. RA usefulness is further enhanced when entries suggest the best starting point for a series or author and list all the awards a title has won. Full series information is expected in database entries. Databases should additionally be evaluated based upon the more expansive content possible for entries. Full reviews, ideally from all four trade journals, are of key consideration as are jacket covers (of sufficient size to see enough detail to visually recognize the book).

Indexing is only an evaluative element of databases and books although the ease of searching a website or blog should be considered as well. At a minimum, books should be indexed by author, title, series, and genre/subgenre. A higher standard of indexing includes an index of appeal, award winners, subject/theme, and other specialized entry points such as an index to book discussion titles. Databases offer the deepest indexing possible. In addition to the standards governing books, databases can be evaluated based upon the expansiveness of their genre and subject tracings and the extent to which they support searching by starred reviews, geographical and temporal setting, and keyword.

Currency

All book resources are in some ways out of date the moment they are published due to the volume and speed of the publishing cycle. However, because librarians rely upon their backlist holdings to form the spine of the collection, many book resources do not age as quickly as might be feared. Titles by authors who have ceased writing can serve equally well for suggestions and read-alikes as the hottest title by a debut author. That being said, currency remains an important consideration. Older resources will neither include titles that become sure bets and genre classics after the resource is published nor include new titles that serve as excellent read-alikes for an older title. Readers tend to focus on what is new, and if advisors rely upon dated resources to suggest titles, they risk seeming out of touch. Currency is also a concern when benchmark author examples are dated. This is particularly troublesome for advisors who are not sufficiently familiar with a genre to recognize passé choices. Finally, older resources may include a higher percentage of out-of-print materials and titles no longer held by the library, leading to frustrations for advisor and reader alike. Best practice is to update as new editions become available and retain older editions as well.

Review journals and websites are often the most current resources an advisor can use. Journals routinely publish reviews months prior to street date release and many websites are as current. Databases should mirror library review sources in their currency. It is not unreasonable to expect a subscription database to routinely include full records for titles two to three months in advance of publication.

Selection

RA resources are generally not comprehensively reviewed in the library media. Many of the print resources are written by librarians connected to the journals themselves, making reviews inappropriate. RA databases are not routinely reviewed either, often gaining focused attention only when major updates have been made or new databases are introduced. Few free websites are formally reviewed, if even mentioned, by the library media. This dearth of review attention requires selectors to seek other ways of identification and selection.

Reviewing examination copies is a time-tested method. Publisher exhibits at conferences offer selectors an opportunity to inspect print books. If conference attendance is not possible, consider interlibrary loan or visiting a neighboring library with significant RA holdings. Given the generalized nature of book descriptions, little can replace examination. It can often be the only way to ascertain the nature of the resource, the depth of genre coverage, and the extent of whole collection coverage.[12] Conferences also provide the occasion to compare each of the major RA databases and examine catalog enhancement services. Database providers are typically willing to arrange in-library trials as well. Each database should be compared for cost, usefulness, accuracy, appeal indexing, search capabilities, ease of use, and catalog integration. As most libraries will purchase only one RA database, its selection should additionally be carefully considered in terms of expected usage and anticipated value to patrons and staff. Enhancement services can be viewed by searching subscribing libraries' catalogs. Advisors should perform typical searches to see the range of material supplied and, as with databases, carefully consider what aspects will support their work and enrich patrons' experiences.

Asking advisors about the resources they find most useful is another excellent method of selection. The RA community is an active and friendly one, always ready to offer opinions about the most useful resources and tools. If selectors cannot examine sources, posting a query to a RA discussion list such as Fiction_L or CODES-L is likely to elicit a number of opinions. This method is useful for books and databases but is likely most useful for the identification and selection of free Internet resources. The scope of such resources is so vast that the insight of other advisors who have found useful sites is critical.

Beyond examination and community feedback, selection should also take into account cost as well as service-level expectations. Price is a factor of every selection decision as is the number of copies of a resource a library system needs. Libraries offering robust RA service require RA collections at every location that support both staff and public use. If multiple copies of print titles are beyond a library's budget, then the creation of a publicly available ready-reference RA collection allows both patrons and staff to access necessary resources. Consider purchasing circulating subscriptions to select library journals as well as consumer magazines focused upon books and publishing. Not only do such resources support RA services, but they also support community members interested in reading and authorship. As they acquire materials, selectors must align resources with the service expectations of the RA program, ensuring that RA is not offered without the proper resources to fulfill the requirements of readers and the needs of advisors.

IMPORTANT GENERAL SOURCES

These resources address the collection needs of public libraries intending to offer robust RA services for adults. RA for children and teens are specialized fields with specific service goals and resources. Those interested in learning more about the provision and resources of either can do so by consulting works such as *Serving Teens through Readers' Advisory* by Heather Booth (2007) and *Readers' Advisory for Children and 'Tweens* by Penny Peck (2010).

Books

Genre Bibliographies

Genre bibliographies introduce the history and subdivisions of a genre as well as list its key authors, essential titles, and important series. They are indispensable tools as they provide a depth of knowledge beyond what advisors can often gain based solely upon their own reading (see Box 24.5). The basic format of a genre bibliography is a title listing (including author, title, publisher, date, and ISBN) followed by a brief annotation. As the name suggests, such works are organized by genre or subgenre, depending on the breadth of the resource, but can include

Box 24.5 Search Strategy: Learning about a Genre

An advisor realizes that she does not know enough about historical fiction titles to feel comfortable helping fans of the genre and decides to undertake a mini-genre study of her own. Not knowing where to start, she does a search using "guides to historical fiction" as her search string. The first hit is to a library page entitled "A Guide for Historical Fiction Lovers." On the site, she sees that Sarah Johnson is listed as an expert, so she searches for "Sarah Johnson" and "historical fiction" and finds Johnson's blog *Reading the Past*. On the site, she learns that Johnson is a reference and RA librarian, reviews for *Booklist*, has won an ALA award, and belongs to the National Book Critics Circle. She also finds that Johnson has written two books on the genre, *Historical Fiction* and *Historical Fiction II*. Hoping to find more guides, the librarian looks in the Libraries Unlimited and the ALA Editions' online catalogs and discovers *The Readers' Advisory Guide to Historical Fiction* by Jennifer S. Baker as well as two more general guides, *Genreflecting* and *The Readers' Advisory Guide to Genre Fiction* by Joyce Saricks. Checking the library's catalog reveals that all of the books are owned by neighboring libraries, so she puts the books on hold. While she waits, she returns to Johnson's blog and reads sample posts and explores the lists of sites Johnson follows. In the process, the librarian develops a list of titles she wants to read. She also searches for "Historical Fiction" "Genre Study" and finds an 18-page guide from the Adult Reading Round Table, complete with benchmark titles and further reading. When her requested books arrive, she reads Baker's and Johnson's introductions to the genre and uses the books to build a list of key authors and develop a reading list for her own study.

divisions by appeal. Appeal classifications, when used, are not specific enough to determine read-alikes. Further reading is sometimes included in an entry, but appeal-specific suggestions are rare.

The standard genre bibliography is *Genreflecting*, edited by Cynthia Orr and Diana Tixier Herald (2013). Betty Rosenberg, one of the key figures in contemporary RA service, first wrote this classic RA resource in 1982. Long considered a core text in the field, the seventh edition includes an introduction to RA services followed by lengthy chapters on historical fiction, mysteries, thrillers, Westerns, romances, women's fiction, fantasy, horror, science fiction, mainstream fiction, and nonfiction as well as shorter sections on Christian and urban fiction and graphic novels. The Genreflecting Advisory Series, a spin-off of *Genreflecting*, offers volumes focused upon individual genres.

Read on . . . is another well-regarded series of genre bibliographies. Each title is arranged by broad appeal classification and then further divided into booklist or display topics. Annotations are longer than those in *Genreflecting*, and their arrangement and approach is more imaginative and quirky. The dual classification, by broad appeal and then by topic, can be used to make starting suggestions, but the entries do not include specific read-alikes. This amiable and eminently browsable series is particularly notable for the way it provides an accessible entry point into the vast scale of genre collections.

Read-Alike Guides

Read-alike guides differ from genre bibliographies in that their main purpose is to suggest specific appeal-based read-alikes for key titles and authors. They are foundational tools of RA as they provide actionable suggestions to advisors and readers based upon key authors, essential titles, and important series. Similar to genre bibliographies, read-alike guides additionally offer a depth of knowledge about a given genre beyond what advisors learn based only upon their own reading histories and preferences. Like their bibliographic counterparts, they are also typically genre based and include history and subgenre information. Annotations tend to be longer than those found in genre bibliographies and include appeal elements in their descriptions. Because of their approach and the requirement of developing read-alikes for featured titles, these guides include less extensive title listings than genre bibliographies although many are supplemented with suggested reading lists.

The standard read-alike guide is *The Readers' Advisory Guide To* series published by ALA Editions. Each title in the series is devoted to a particular genre and includes chapters that address the genre's appeal, history, development, and subgenres. Chapters cover such topics as the RA conversation, marketing the collection, keeping up to date, key awards, whole collection RA, and resources for further reading. Also included is a crash course in the genre designed to help advisors get quickly up to speed in an area they do not know well. The core of each book is a set of chapters devoted to key titles and authors with read-alikes, extensive annotations, and appeal descriptions of both the main book and the read-alikes.

Now Read This by Nancy Pearl and colleagues addresses mainstream fiction and is published by Libraries Unlimited. It is unique not only in that it suggests nongenre titles but also in that it details Pearl's appeal framework: story, character, setting, and language. There are currently three volumes in the series covering books published from 1978–1998, 1990–2001, and 2002–2009. Story summaries in the first and second volumes are very brief, while the third volume includes longer entries. Further reading suggestions are based upon topic and kind of reading experience rather than specifically stated appeal terms. The most recent volume was written by Nancy Pearl and Sarah Statz Cords and includes suggestions for nonfiction reading as well as fiction titles.

What Do I Read Next? is a long-running series produced by Gale, which provides suggestions for further reading in eight genres. Entries include a story summary, listing of story type, major characters, subjects, locales, and series name where applicable. Also included is a selected list of other titles by the author, information on where the title was reviewed, and a brief list of further suggested reading based upon style and theme.

Journals

Professional review journals offer advisors a number of RA resources. Most critically, they allow advisors to stay ahead of the publishing curve by reading about forthcoming titles before they appear in popular magazines, thus preparing advisors for the moment readers learn about a title themselves. Journals also provide advisors with appeal-rich reviews. Their comments about pacing, setting, depth of characterization, and other appeal aspects allow advisors to learn about the appeal profile of a book prior to publication. Some review sources, most notably *Booklist* and *LJ*, often suggest read-alikes within the body of the review itself as well. Beyond these invaluable services, trade review journals provide additional RA resources worth noting.

Booklist features the "At Leisure" column by Joyce Saricks. In monthly columns, Saricks discusses fundamental RA skills, appeal, genres, displays, and ways of thinking about the practice of RA. *Booklist* also has a very robust website, through which advisors can access Saricks's column, as well as excellent blogs to aid advisors, gathered under the umbrella site *The Booklist Reader*. Additionally, *Booklist* offers expansive genre showcase pieces that offer title suggestions as well as a rich array of additional features.

Kirkus Reviews provides a quick scan of best-selling titles, with a thumbs up or down as to whether they think the book is worth buying, checking out from the library, or skipping altogether. Readers might well disagree, but advisors will appreciate the easy once-over take and may well find it helps identify sure bets.

LJ offers a host of RA material both online and in its pages. In addition to the outstanding "Prepub Alert," which provides advance notice of upcoming titles with hints as to the degree of splash they might make, there is a newsletter devoted to prepublication news about audiobooks (*LJ Audio in Advance*). Additionally, there are a number of columns devoted to a myriad of RA concerns, including "RA Crossroads," "The Reader's Shelf," and "Books for Dudes." *LJ* also provides occasional genre guides with reading suggestions, explanations as to what makes the genre popular, and elements to consider when suggesting titles.

Publishers Weekly offers buying guide overviews that supply genre, topic, and subject profiles. It also includes their indispensable "Tip Sheet," a weekly e-mail (and Web page) that features highlights from the journal as well as a list of the best books of the week.

Advisors need to keep up with what their readers see as well and that means following popular consumer media such as the books section of *The New York Times*, *The Los Angeles Times* (and the *LA Times* "Jacket Copy"), *NPR*, and *Entertainment Weekly*. It also means being alert to the local sources within a given community, such as the free weekly paper and local radio.

Databases and Catalog Enhancement Services

RA databases have become foundational tools for advisors. Currently, EBSCO's *NoveList* and Gale's *Books & Authors* are the most widely used. While they differ in approach and additional content, both allow advisors to quickly look up a title and find subject, genre, and setting information as well as a basic story summary. Both also provide read-alike suggestions and include trade reviews. *NoveList* is particularly notable for its innovative appeal indexing, multi-point searching, depth of subject headings, and range of coverage (including audiobooks). *Books & Authors* offers an inviting "Who, What, Where, When" search process, which allows for inputs based on character, subject, location, and time period and graphically displays the overlapping results.

Advisors are increasingly seeking to extend the valuable information found in RA databases by placing it directly within the bibliographic record, where readers tend to center their explorations of a title. Furthermore, advisors are eager to encourage readers to share their own read-alike suggestions and reviews as doing so helps widen and extend the RA conversation. As a consequence, RA cataloging enhancement has begun to combine the content from databases such as *NoveList* with social reading and cataloging products to create expanded RA-rich records. *NoveList* has partnered with *Goodreads* in this regard, while ProQuest has partnered with *LibraryThing*. Other companies such as BiblioCommons also offer RA-enriched bibliographic records. Many of these companies offer further RA products such as customizable e-mail reading lists (*NoveList's NextReads*) and recommendation engines tied to library holdings (*LibraryThing for Libraries' BookPsychic*).

Given that many libraries participate in system, regional, or statewide joint purchases, the selection of an RA database is often not a local one. Additionally, catalog enhancement services are frequently folded into decisions about ILS and online catalog additions, complicating the choice of a product by removing it from the sole domain of RA librarians. When advisors are able to consider an RA database purchase as a stand-alone product or are given a voice in the ILS package, there are key elements to consider including the strength and depth of appeal indexing, the quality of annotations, the presence of reviews from trade journals, and the validity of the read-alike suggestions.

Internet Resources

Readers' Advisory and Book-Centric News

There is a wealth of book news resources on the Internet that advisors can consult, created by librarians, authors, publishers, trade journals, trade associations, and various media outlets. Some of these sites can be invaluable, and it is strongly suggested that advisors practice a continuous effort of website curation and establish RSS feeds to discover resources that enhance their work. One key librarian-oriented site is *EarlyWord*. It serves as a daily update for RA and collection development librarians, offering a usefully arranged and thoughtfully selected overview of important publishing news of the day. Among its features are posts alerting advisors to titles they should have on their radar, books garnering large hold queues, book adaptations, RA alerts, and reports from librarians on their reaction to advance reader copies. *EarlyWord* also links to a number of sites featuring forthcoming title information, lists of when monthly and weekly magazines publish reviews, and links to sites that focus on titles receiving consumer media coverage.

Collaborative Readers' Advisory Aids

The RA world is a highly collaborative one, full of advisors willing to help each other find a suggestion or unravel a question (see Box 24.6 for an example search relying upon this collaborative nature). Three resources are particularly worth tracking: Fiction_L, The Adult Reading Round Table (ARRT), and CODES Conversations. Fiction_L is perhaps the best example of the open and collaborative atmosphere of RA. Begun in 1995, it is an electronic mailing list to which queries about read-alikes, title identification, book groups, genre studies, and more are shared with a large community of librarians who help by offering suggestions and sharing best practices. Fiction_L's rich archive is searchable by date of post and keyword

Box 24.6 Search Strategy: A Read-Alike for Donna Tartt's *The Goldfinch*

An advisor encounters a reader in the stacks, aimlessly pulling books off the shelf and putting them back. The advisor offers assistance saying, "Can I help you find anything to read or are you content to browse on your own?" The patron accepts the offer responding, "I could use some help. I cannot find anything I think I would like." The following dialogue takes place:

Advisor: "That happens to me all the time too. Tell me what you enjoyed about the last book you read and we can work from there."
Reader: "I liked *The Goldfinch* a lot, but I thought some of it was pretty slow."
Advisor: "What parts did you like?"
Reader: "That it was about a boy growing up, maybe, and that it was kind of moody with really great writing."
Advisor: "That is a great description. Are you searching for another book like that?"
Reader: "Yes, that would be good, or something with just a really meaty story to it—but not too slow."
Advisor: "All right, let's see what we can find. Since *The Goldfinch* was very popular with our readers here in the library, we made a list of reading suggestions for fans. We can start there and then look for more titles too." The advisor shows the list to the reader. Since the guide is annotated, there is sufficient appeal-based description for the reader to identify a book she wants to check out. The librarian consults the catalog, sees the book is on the shelf, and walks with the reader into the stacks to pull it. Along the way the advisor says, "Would you like more books or are you happy just checking out this one?"
Reader: "I would like something else. Since this one is about a painting, maybe something not about art?"
Advisor: "Certainly, let's do a quick search of read-alikes online and see what we find."

The advisor searches for "read-alikes Goldfinch" and finds a page authored by Wayne Roylance listing suggestions by the staff of New York Public Library. One of the suggestions is David Mitchell's *The Thousand Autumns of Jacob De Zoet*, which the reader thinks she will like based on the description. It is on the shelf too. As they go to pull the book, the reader thanks the advisor who responds, "We are always happy to help. If you don't like these, come back and we will find you something else. We have plenty of options. And if you do like them, let us know and that will help us find you even more great titles to enjoy."

and supports Boolean constructions, making it an RA resource for book displays and read-alikes in its own right. ARRT posts exhaustive reports from its lengthy genre studies and offers resources to aid in book discussions. They also create a Popular Fiction List to use as a reading plan and orientation guide to key authors. CODES Conversations, run by the Collection Development and Evaluation Section (CODES) of RUSA, gather hundreds of librarians together for a two-day electronic e-mail conversation related to specific topics such as "RA as a Technical Service" and "Working with Titles You Have Not Read." A summarized report is sent to all subscribers, and the full conversation is archived. In addition to these dedicated RA tools, many advisors post read-alike lists on their library websites. Searching for a particular book or specific author along with terms such as "read-alike[s]" or "if you like" will often return a number of librarian-crafted read-alike suggestions.

Book Sites

The Millions is an online magazine devoted to literary and general fiction. It includes an eclectic and far-ranging collection of essays, reviews, commentaries, links, and lists. Advisors should not miss the "Most Anticipated" posts in which *The Millions* surveys the literary landscape of the year, offering a reading list of key authors far in advance of publication date (see Box 24.7 for one RA use of this site).

Fantastic Fiction provides a cornucopia of book-related information based on author bibliographies, new titles, and forthcoming releases. Most title pages include suggested further reading (although appeal reasons are not given), series information, and a full range of available formats. The true gem of the site, however, is the list of 250 top authors. For each author, the site provides his or her newest book, a full backlist broken by series where applicable, and a list of titles the author recommends, with brief reasons as to why the recommendation has been made.

Box 24.7 Search Strategy: Finding a New and Unusual Title

A reader approaches the reference desk and asks the librarian on duty whether the library owns a copy of *Night Film* by Marisha Pessl. The librarian checks the catalog and sees that all copies are checked out and asks whether the reader wants to put the book on hold. The following dialogue takes place:

Reader: "Yes, thanks. How long is the wait going to be?"

Librarian: "I would think you should have a copy by late next week."

Reader: "Great, thanks for doing that."

Librarian: "My pleasure. While you wait for it to come in, would you like some suggestions of other books you might enjoy?"

Reader: "You do that?"

Librarian: "Absolutely, it's part of our job here. If you have a minute and want to tell me a bit about what you like to read, I would be happy to help you find a few books to take home and try today."

Reader: "Sure. I wanted *Night Film* because a friend told me how unique it was. I am always looking for different kinds of books, books not everyone is reading yet, although I suppose I am behind the curve with *Night Film* since I have to wait for it."

Librarian: "So if I could find you a unique and new book that might be what you want? Something under the radar?"

Reader: "Yeah, and something really well written too."

Librarian: "Can you tell me some authors you think write really well?"

Reader: "Oh, you know, writers like Colm Tóibín and Elizabeth Strout."

Librarian: "Perfect. I can find you some books we have in the library today and perhaps a few titles to think about putting on hold now so you will get them first when they come out."

Reader: "That would be great."

Librarian: "Okay, let's start with a website I think you will like. It is called *The Millions* and it has a very interesting list of its most anticipated books coming out in

	the next six months—so you can get a jump on new titles. They would have included both Tóibín and Strout in their roundup when their latest books came out so you should find writers you enjoy. Why don't you scan this post and jot down any that seem like good possibilities. Let me know when you are done and we can also find you some books you can take home today."
Reader:	"Great." The reader finds two forthcoming titles of interest, Jenny Erpenbeck's *The End of Days* and *Family Furnishings* by Alice Munro. Both are already on order, and the librarian is able to put them on hold for the reader, who is high enough in the holds queue to get a copy the day they are released.
Librarian:	"Now let's find something for you to take home today. This is a book database called *NoveList*. We can search for *Night Film* and find other similar titles you might like." The librarian shows the reader how to look up titles and points out the appeal indexing. The reader picks "literary fiction," "intricately plotted," and "compelling" as search terms. Together they scan the results, dipping into each record to skim the reviews. The reader picks *The Luminaries* and *The Weight of Water* as good choices. Doing the search reminds the advisor of Donna Tartt's *The Little Friend* so he pulls up its record and shows it to the reader. Based on the reviews, the reader decides to check it out as well. A quick check of the catalog confirms that two of the books are on the shelf, and the librarian walks the reader to each and pulls them for checkout. As the librarian hands the books to the reader he says, "I hope you enjoy these, but if you don't like any of them, please come back and let us know—we can find lots of others you may enjoy."
Reader:	"That's great! Thanks so much."

Book Riot offers a variety of book-related features. It is the quirky kind of book site readers can get lost in for hours only to emerge with a list of titles they want to borrow. The content on *Book Riot* also supports display ideas, offering a seemingly endless number of suggestions on how to think about book groupings. Of particular note are the "Reading Pathways," a three-book sequence designed to introduce a reader to an author. It is an idea advisors might want to model as well as a good place to start one's own reading explorations.

Beyond these general and omnibus sites, there is a range of specific genre sites such as *Reading the Past*; *RA for All: Horror* (both written by librarians); *Stop, You're Killing Me*; *All about Romance*; and *Smart Bitches Trashy Books*. Such sites help advisors identify sure bets and new titles. Some offer read-alike suggestions as well, and all help RA librarians stay current with genre developments.

While the number of excellent sites far exceeds the space allotment of this chapter, three additional resources are also specifically worthy of close attention by advisors. *IndieBound* is the website of independent bookstores. Its aim is to promote its members, but advisors refer to it monthly to see what has made the "Indie Next List," a group of titles suggested by booksellers who hand-sell books much as advisors do. The list includes a description that often includes appeal terms. *LibraryReads* is a group that models much of what *IndieBound* has done, from a library perspective. Each month they release a list of 10 titles to note, as selected by librarians across the country. *Bookmarks Magazine* offers a ranked list of the most reviewed books from around the Web. They also post a list of weekly reviews, including those from local papers. Taken as a whole, these resources will help advisors stay abreast of genre development and new releases, ensuring that they note titles as they begin to gain sustained attention and coverage.

Awards

Key librarian-selected awards include the Notable Books List, The Reading List, and The Listen List. All three select books that are a pleasure to read or listen to based upon reader-centered criteria. Notable Books focuses upon general and literary fiction, nonfiction, and poetry. The Reading List offers a winner and four shortlist titles in eight genre classifications and supplies read-alikes for each winning title. The Listen List offers 12 audiobook titles, as well as listen-alikes, in both fiction and nonfiction. In a given year, the list may also include poetry or plays. A panel that includes librarians selects the Andrew Carnegie Medals for Excellence in Fiction and Nonfiction. These awards offer a single winner title in both areas as well as a long and short list.

Other literary and nonfiction awards include the Pulitzer Prize, the Man Booker Prize, the Nobel Prize, the National Book Awards, the National Book Critics Circle Awards, the Costa Book Awards, the *Los Angeles Times* Book Prize, the *Kirkus* Prize, the Governor General's Literary Awards, the many PEN Literary Awards, and the Baileys Women's Prize for Fiction.

Other genre awards to note include the Hugo and the Nebula Awards (science fiction and fantasy), the Arthur C. Clarke Award (science fiction), the World Fantasy Award (fantasy), the Edgar Awards (mystery), the International Thriller Writers Thriller Awards (thriller/suspense), the RITA Awards (romance), the Bram Stoker Award (horror/dark fantasy), the Walter Scott Prize (historical fiction), and the Spur Awards (Westerns).

Additionally, year-end "best of" roundups are also of great use to advisors. Key lists include those issued by the library trade journals, the *New York Times*, *NPR*, and *Entertainment Weekly*. Beyond these, there are multiple lists available addressing various genres and formats that should be routinely consulted as they are released.

Social Reading and Personal Library Catalogs

Social reading and cataloging supports much of the online conversation about books and book selection. Two sites currently predominate: *Goodreads* and *LibraryThing*. Both allow users to catalog their own books, post personal reviews, and conduct conversations with fellow members. *Goodreads* is decidedly more social than *LibraryThing*, while *LibraryThing* has a much stronger system for cataloging. Advisors should be aware of both services as they provide opportunities to learn about levels of interest in, and readers' reactions to, specific titles. Advisors can further use such sites to share books with patrons, create an online presence within a community of dedicated readers, and create groups that support book discussion.

Suggestion Engines

A number of types of services seek to offer book suggestions, from those that scan through Twitter to sites that use appeal to suggest titles. In this latter category, two are of particular note: *AllReaders* and *Whichbook*. *AllReaders* supports searching based on an expansive list of features related to type of story and character. Options range from the quirky (whether the main character has super powers) to the appeal based (e.g., the percentage of character development). *AllReaders* also lets users select primary, secondary, and tertiary topic options. Users can select main character gender, profession, age, and other features and do the same for the main adversary (including selecting whether the villain is a "monster of some sort"). Setting and writing style are options as well, including the amount of dialogue present. *Whichbook* allows users to set sliding scales for a range of book categories such as happy/sad, funny/serious, and safe/disturbing or attributes such as short/long, conventional/unusual, and larger than life/down to earth. A second mode allows users to select character, plot, and setting. Suggestions sets can be quirky, but advisors should monitor developments in this field as suggestion engines offer new appeal considerations and modes of searching well worth incorporating into the standard appeal framework. They also can supply well-crafted read-alikes advisors might never have found without such exploration.

CONCLUSION

Practicing RA well, with skill, care, and attention, is an undertaking central to the mission of public and school libraries and is an added benefit for those using academic libraries. Many of the terms staff, directors, and board members wish to associate with libraries, words such as "service," "enjoyment," "community," "education," and "enlightenment," are fulfilled when advisors help patrons discover books they relish.

The process of successfully pairing reader and book depends upon a protocol that includes listening to and engaging with the reader, understanding the dynamics of appeal, and practicing the steps of the RA conversation. It involves the deft use of the right resource at the right time and a deep knowledge of popular authors, titles, and genres. It further depends upon understanding that the provision of RA service is a cycle that has no real end and is instead a continuous process of reading, sharing, and learning—such that one conversation can enhance another and that one book can connect outward to many others in a chain of read-alikes. Critically, it requires a thoughtful professional approach that situates RA services within the same high standards librarians have traditionally demanded of themselves in the provision of reference services. There might not be a more daunting question than "can you help me find something good to read?" but there are not many questions as potentially joyful and important within a library either.

NOTES

1. The author wishes to disclose that she publishes with several of the sources cited.
2. For ease of reading, and because novels were the initial subject of RA, this chapter uses the terms "reader," "reading," and "novel" to represent the individuals, activities, and objects of RA work. However, these terms are intended to be understood in their broadest context with listening, watching, looking, and playing understood as activities "readers" undertake and audiobooks, nonfiction, graphic novels, films, music, and games as the additional subjects of RA work.
3. The specific survey data accompanies Thornton-Verma and Schwartz's article (2014) in the form of an online report: http://lj.libraryjournal.com/2014/02/library-services/the-state-of-readers-advisory/#. For further discussion of RA education, see Van Fleet (2008).
4. For discussion of academic RA and how RA is practiced in K–12 institutions, see Behler (2011) and Nesi (2012).

5. Read-alikes are titles that share similar appeal. Read-arounds are titles that amplify or extend the subjects and themes of a book. They are not based upon appeal. Sure bets are titles that please a wide range of readers. They are typically titles that have strong story lines and well-developed characters.
6. See Saricks and Brown (1997) and Saricks (2005b). See also a range of appeal references throughout the "At Leisure with Joyce Saricks" columns in *Booklist* magazine.
7. Ross (2001a, 2001b) uses slightly different explanations and terms in her discussions of appeal over the course of her research, as she refines concepts and gathers new data. These two sources contain the most complete explanations of her theories and findings, although each presents those findings in different forms. I have elected to use her most common terms when summarizing her work. However, students should be aware that it is entirely possible to list Ross's concepts in different ways, and thus the number of appeal terms accounted to her (and the terms themselves) can vary.
8. Ross, Nilsen, and Radford (2009) offer more excellent guidance on this topic.
9. According to the data collected by the *Library Journal* RA survey (Thornton-Verma and Schwartz 2014), only 9 percent of survey respondents report having a full-time RA librarian on staff or having an RA service desk.
10. Joyce Saricks and Nancy Brown, interviewed by Neal Wyatt, August 12, 2014. This is the question Saricks and Brown found most useful when approaching readers.
11. Hollands's (2006) article lays out much of the groundwork for asynchronous RA. For examples of RA forms and social media use, see the online RA forms of Williamsburg Regional Library (http://www.wrl.org/books-and-reading/adults/looking-good-book); the Seattle Public Library's Facebook RA sessions (e.g., https://www.facebook.com/SeattlePublicLibrary/photos/a.381987691338.168821.7511741338/10151095134766339); and Twitter programs (e.g., https://twitter.com/search?q=%23SEAreads%20%23bookmatch&src=typd) and the Pickerington Public Library Tumbler page (http://pickeringtonlibrary.tumblr.com/).
12. Whole collection RA includes the entire scope of the collection (fiction, nonfiction, poetry, music, audiobooks, films, and digital collections), as well as those resources available freely online.

REFERENCES

Behler, Anne. 2011. "Leisure Reading Collections in College and University Libraries: Have Academic Librarians Rediscovered Readers' Advisory?" In *Reference Reborn: Breathing New Life into Public Services Librarianship*, edited by Diane Zabel, 133–42. Santa Barbara, CA: Libraries Unlimited.

Bouricius, Ann. 2000. *Romance Reader's Advisory: The Librarian's Guide to Love in the Stacks*. Chicago: American Library Association.

De Rosa, Cathy, Joanne Cantrell, Matthew Carlson, Peggy Gallagher, Janet Hawk, and Charlotte Sturtz. 2011. *Perceptions of Libraries, 2010: Context and Community: A Report to the OCLC Membership.* Dublin, OH: OCLC. http://www.oclc.org/content/dam/oclc/reports/2010perceptions/2010perceptions_all.pdf.

Hollands, Neil. 2006. "Improving the Model for Interactive Readers' Advisory Service." *Reference & User Services Quarterly* 45 (3): 205–12.

Nesi, Olga M. 2012. *Getting Beyond "Interesting": Teaching Students the Vocabulary of Appeal to Discuss Their Reading.* Santa Barbara, CA: Libraries Unlimited.

Pearl, Nancy. 1999. *Now Read This: A Guide to Mainstream Fiction, 1978–1998.* Englewood, CO: Libraries Unlimited.

Pearl, Nancy. 2012. "Check It Out with Nancy Pearl: Finding That Next Good Book." *Publishers Weekly* 259 (March 19): 18–19.

Pejtersen, Annelise Mark. 1978. "Fiction and Library Classification." *Scandinavian Public Library Quarterly* 11 (1): 5–12.
Ranganathan, S. R. 1963. *The Five Laws of Library Science.* Bombay, India: Asia Publishing House.
Reference and User Services Association. 2013. "Guidelines for Behavioral Performance of Reference and Information Service Providers." American Library Association. http://www.ala.org/rusa/resources/guidelines/guidelinesbehavioral.
Rosenberg, Betty. 1982. *Genreflecting: A Guide to Reading Interests in Genre Fiction.* Littleton, CO: Libraries Unlimited.
Ross, Catherine Sheldrick. 2001a. "Making Choices: What Readers Say about Choosing Books to Read for Pleasure." *Acquisitions Librarian* 25: 5–21.
Ross, Catherine Sheldrick. 2001b. "What We Know from Readers about the Experience of Reading." In *Readers' Advisor's Companion*, edited by Kenneth D. Shearer and Robert Burgin, 77–95. Englewood, CO: Libraries Unlimited.
Ross, Catherine Sheldrick, Lynne (E. F.) McKechnie, and Paulette M. Rothbauer. 2006. *Reading Matters: What the Research Reveals about Reading, Libraries, and Community.* Westport, CT: Libraries Unlimited.
Ross, Catherine Sheldrick, Kirsti Nilsen, and Marie L. Radford. 2009. *Conducting the Reference Interview: A How-To-Do-It Manual for Librarians*, 2nd ed. New York: Neal-Schuman.
Saricks, Joyce G. 2005a. "At Leisure with Joyce Saricks: Writing a Reader Profile; or, What I Like and Why." *Booklist* 102 (October 1): 35.
Saricks, Joyce G. 2005b. *Readers' Advisory Service in the Public Library*, 3rd ed. Chicago: American Library Association.
Saricks, Joyce G. 2007. "At Leisure with Joyce Saricks: RA Today." *Booklist* 103 (February 15): 33.
Saricks, Joyce G. 2009. *The Readers' Advisory Guide to Genre Fiction.* Chicago: American Library Association.
Saricks, Joyce G. 2010. "At Leisure with Joyce Saricks: Tone and Mood." *Booklist* 106 (April 1): 21.
Saricks, Joyce G. 2013. "At Leisure with Joyce Saricks: Updating Appeal—Language and Style." *Booklist* 109 (March 1): 19.
Saricks, Joyce G., and Nancy Brown. 1989. *Readers' Advisory Service in the Public Library.* Chicago: American Library Association.
Saricks, Joyce G., and Nancy Brown. 1997. *Readers' Advisory Service in the Public Library*, 2nd ed. Chicago: American Library Association.
Thornton-Verma, Henrietta, and Meredith Schwartz. 2014. "The State of Readers' Advisory." *Library Journal* 139 (February 1): 30.
Van Fleet, Connie. 2008. "Education for Readers' Advisory Service in Library and Information Science Programs: Challenges and Opportunities." *Reference & User Services Quarterly* 47 (3): 224–29.
Wyatt, Neal. 2007. "Redefining RA: An RA Big Think." *Library Journal* 132 (April 15): 40–43.
Zickuhr, Kathryn, Lee Rainie, and Kristen Purcell. 2013. *Library Services in the Digital Age.* Washington, DC: Pew Internet. http://libraries.pewinternet.org/2013/01/22/Library-services/.

LIST OF SOURCES

Adult Reading Round Table. http://arrtreads.org.
Adult Reading Round Table. "Popular Fiction List." Available online as part of *Novelist* or by contacting ARRT directly.
ALA Editions. http://www.alastore.ala.org/SearchResult.aspx?CategoryID=198.

All about Romance. http://www.likesbooks.com/.
AllReaders. http://allreaders.com/.
Andrew Carnegie Medals for Excellence in Fiction and Nonfiction. http://www.ala.org/awardsgrants/carnegieadult/.
Arthur C. Clarke Award. http://www.clarkeaward.com/.
Baileys Women's Prize for Fiction. http://www.womensprizeforfiction.co.uk/.
Baker, Jennifer S. 2015. *The Readers' Advisory Guide to Historical Fiction*. Chicago: ALA Editions.
BiblioCommons. http://www.bibliocommons.com/.
Book Riot. http://bookriot.com/.
Book Riot. "Reading Pathways." http://bookriot.com/category/reading-pathways/.
Booklist. 1905–. Chicago: American Library Association. Twice monthly, September–June; monthly, July–August.
The Booklist Reader. http://www.thebooklistreader.com/.
Bookmarks Magazine. http://www.bookmarksmagazine.com.
BookPsychic. http://www.bookpsychic.com/.
Books & Authors. Farmington Hills, MI: Gale Cengage Learning. http://gdc.gale.com/gale-literature-collections/books-and-authors/. [subscription required]
Booth, Heather. 2007. *Serving Teens through Readers' Advisory*. Chicago: American Library Association.
Bram Stoker Award. http://horror.org/awards/stokers.htm.
CODES Conversations. http://www.ala.org/rusa/sections/codes/convos.
CODES-L. http://lists.ala.org/sympa/lists/divisions/rusa.
Costa Book Awards. http://www.costa.co.uk/costa-book-awards/welcome/.
EarlyWord: The Publisher | Librarian Connection. http://www.earlyword.com/.
EBSCO. https://www.ebsco.com/.
Edgar Awards. http://www.theedgars.com/.
Entertainment Weekly: Books. http://www.ew.com/ew/books/.
Fantastic Fiction. http://www.fantasticfiction.co.uk/.
Fiction_L. http://www.mgpl.org/read-listen-view/fl/flmenu/.
Fiction_L: Booklists. http://www.mgpl.org/read-listen-view/fl/flbooklists/.
Gale. http://www.cengage.com/search/showresults.do?N=197.
Genreflecting series. 1999–.Various eds. Santa Barbara, CA: Libraries Unlimited.
Goodreads. https://www.goodreads.com/.
Governor General's Literary Awards. http://ggbooks.ca/.
Hugo Awards. http://www.thehugoawards.org/.
"Indie Next List". http://www.indiebound.org/indie-next-list.
IndieBound. http://www.indiebound.org/.
International Thriller Writers Thriller Awards. http://thrillerwriters.org/programs/thriller-awards/.
Johnson, Sarah L. 2005. *Historical Fiction: A Guide to the Genre*. Westport, CT: Libraries Unlimited.
Johnson, Sarah L. 2009. *Historical Fiction II: A Guide to the Genre*. Westport, CT: Libraries Unlimited.
Kirkus Prize. https://www.kirkusreviews.com/prize/.
Kirkus Reviews. 1933–. New York: Kirkus Media. Biweekly.
Libraries Unlimited. http://www.abc-clio.com/LibrariesUnlimited.aspx.
Library Journal. 1876–. New York: Media Source. 22 issues per year.
Library Journal: Books for Dudes. http://reviews.libraryjournal.com/category/readers-advisory/books-for-dudes/.
Library Journal: LJ Audio in Advance. http://lj.libraryjournal.com/forms/LJsub.php (newsletter subscription site).
Library Journal: Prepub Alert. http://reviews.libraryjournal.com/category/prepub/.

Library Journal: RA Crossroads. http://reviews.libraryjournal.com/category/readers-advisory/ra-crossroads/.

Library Journal: The Reader's Shelf. http://reviews.libraryjournal.com/category/readers-advisory/readers-shelf/.

LibraryReads. http://libraryreads.org/.

LibraryThing. https://www.librarything.com/.

LibraryThing for Libraries. https://www.librarything.com/forlibraries/.

The Listen List. http://www.ala.org/rusa/awards/listenlist.

The Los Angeles Times: Books. http://www.latimes.com/books/.

The Los Angeles Times Book Prize. http://events.latimes.com/bookprizes/31-year-anniversary/.

The Los Angeles Times: Jacket Copy. http://www.latimes.com/books/jacketcopy/.

Man Booker Prize. http://www.themanbookerprize.com/.

The Millions. http://www.themillions.com/.

National Book Awards. http://www.nationalbook.org/.

National Book Critics Circle Awards. http://bookcritics.org/awards/.

National Public Radio: Books. http://www.npr.org/books/.

Nebula Awards. http://www.sfwa.org/nebula-awards/.

The New York Times: Books. http://www.nytimes.com/pages/books/index.html.

The Nobel Prize. http://www.nobelprize.org/.

Notable Books List. http://www.ala.org/rusa/awards/notablebooks.

NoveList. Ipswich, MA: EBSCO. http://www.ebscohost.com/novelist. [subscription required]

NoveList: NextReads. http://www.ebscohost.com/novelist/our-products/nextreads. [subscription required]

Orr, Cynthia, and Diana Tixier Herald, eds. 2013. *Genreflecting: A Guide to Popular Reading Interests*, 7th ed. Santa Barbara, CA: Libraries Unlimited.

Pearl, Nancy. 2002. *Now Read This II: A Guide to Mainstream Fiction, 1990–2001.* Englewood, CO: Libraries Unlimited.

Pearl, Nancy, and Sarah Statz Cords. 2010. *Now Read This III: A Guide to Mainstream Fiction.* Santa Barbara, CA: Libraries Unlimited.

Pearl, Nancy, Martha Knappe, and Chris Higashi. 1999. *Now Read This: A Guide to Mainstream Fiction, 1978–1998.* Englewood, CO: Libraries Unlimited.

Peck, Penny. 2010. *Readers' Advisory for Children and 'Tweens.* Santa Barbara, CA: Libraries Unlimited.

PEN Literary Awards. http://www.pen.org/literary-awards.

People. http://www.people.com/people/.

ProQuest. http://www.proquest.com/libraries/.

Publishers Weekly. 1872–. New York: PWxyz, LLC, Weekly.

Publishers Weekly: Tip Sheet. http://www.publishersweekly.com/pw/by-topic/industry-news/tip-sheet/index.html.

Pulitzer Prize. http://www.pulitzer.org/bycat.

RA for All: Horror. http://raforallhorror.blogspot.com/.

Read On . . . : Reading Lists for Every Taste. 2006–. Barry Trott, series ed. Santa Barbara, CA: Libraries Unlimited.

The Readers' Advisory Guide To. 2012–. Joyce Saricks and Neal Wyatt, series eds. Chicago: ALA Editions.

The Reading List. http://www.ala.org/rusa/awards/readinglist.

Reading the Past. http://readingthepast.blogspot.com/.

RITA Awards. http://www.rwa.org/p/cm/ld/fid=525.

Roylance, Wayne. 2014. "Read Alikes for Donna Tartt's *The Goldfinch.*" New York Public Library. April 16. http://www.nypl.org/blog/2014/04/16/read-alikes-goldfinch-donna-tartt.

Saricks, Joyce G. 2004–. "At Leisure with Joyce Saricks." *Booklist*. Chicago: American Library Association. Monthly.
Smart Bitches Trashy Books. http://smartbitchestrashybooks.com/.
Spur Awards. http://westernwriters.org/spur-awards/.
Stop, You're Killing Me! http://www.stopyourekillingme.com/.
USA Today: Books. http://www.usatoday.com/life/books/.
Walter Scott Prize. http://www.bordersbookfestival.org/walter-scott-prize.
What Do I Read Next? 1990–. Various eds. Farmington Hills, MI: Gale Cengage Learning.
Whichbook. http://www.openingthebook.com/whichbook/.
World Fantasy Award. http://www.worldfantasy.org/awards/index.html.

SUGGESTED READINGS

Dali, Keren. 2014. "From Book Appeal to Reading Appeal: Redefining the Concept of Appeal in Readers' Advisory." *The Library Quarterly* 84 (1): 22–48.

Dali extends the considerations of appeal by exploring the distinction between book-oriented and reader-oriented appeal elements and by situating appeal within a wider consideration of reading practices.

Hollands, Neil. 2006. "Improving the Model for Interactive Readers' Advisory Service." *Reference & User Services Quarterly* 45 (3): 205–12.

Hollands wrote the classic article on form-based RA in which he explained the service, argued for its implementation, and challenged traditional assumptions about the provision of RA. The article includes details of what is widely regarded as the first online reading preferences form and explores how Hollands's library set up and managed an asynchronous RA service.

Langemack, Chapple. 2003. *The Booktalker's Bible: How to Talk about the Books You Love to Any Audience*. Westport, CT: Libraries Unlimited.

A noted expert in the art of booktalking, Langemack's book remains the foundational guide to the practice. Chapters address audience and messaging, marketing, key rules, title selection, composition, length, appeal, and performance. Attention is given to booktalking to adults, children, and teens in an array of environments.

May, Anne K., Elizabeth Olesh, Anne Weinlich Miltenberg, and Catherine Patricia Lackne. 2000. "A Look at Reader's Advisory Services." *Library Journal* 125 (September 15): 40–43.

This classic and influential article reports the findings of a "secret shopper" study conducted at 54 community libraries and/or library districts. The results of the study serve to illustrate the various ways RA occurs when it is not an institutionalized practice supported by training and education.

Orr, Cindy. 2013. "Readers' Advisory Services." In *Reference and Information Services: An Introduction*, edited by Kay Ann Cassell and Uma Hiremath, 3rd ed., 285–302. Chicago: Neal-Schuman.

This survey chapter provides an overview of RA services. Orr reviews the history of RA, the place of RA within a range of library services, and how RA differs from reference. She discusses the RA conversation, common situations, and RA best practices. The chapter includes a helpful review of key tools, methods of keeping current, and a detailed further reading list.

Orr, Cindy. 2015. *Crash Course in Readers' Advisory*. Santa Barbara, CA: Libraries Unlimited.

Orr offers a fresh and accessible introduction to the field by reviewing the research on reading and readers, outlining the tools and techniques of RA, and discussing how to create a reader-centered library. She further reviews best practices, supplies an exhaustive reading list, and examines the current and future state of RA.

Ross, Catherine Sheldrick. 2014. *The Pleasures of Reading: A Booklover's Alphabet.* Santa Barbara, CA: Libraries Unlimited.

Using the alphabet as an organizing skeleton, Ross explores 30 areas related to reading and readers' advisory service. The chapters are uniformly accessible, inviting, and illuminating. They serve not only as an introduction to a number of RA elements but also as a model way of thinking deeply and broadly about the field.

Ross, Catherine Sheldrick, and Mary K. Chelton. 2001. "Readers' Advisory: Matching Mood and Material." *Library Journal* 126 (February 1): 52–55.

This classic *LJ* article condenses Ross's research on readers and appeal and makes it more straightforward and accessible. Included are Ross's basic findings, their implications for libraries, and guidance on how advisors can apply them to RA interactions.

Ross, Catherine Sheldrick, Lynne (E. F.) McKechnie, and Paulette Rothbauer. 2006. *Reading Matters: What the Research Reveals about Reading, Libraries, and Community.* Westport, CT: Libraries Unlimited.

A survey of reading and reading practices from an academic perspective, this essential text explores the history of reading, how readers develop, the reading experience, and the importance of reading. It provides critical background on why RA service is important and the factors that should influence its provision. The chapters include case study examples, lists of suggestions for how librarians can improve the reading environment, and a bibliography for further reading in each topic area.

Saricks, Joyce G. 2005. *Readers' Advisory Service in the Public Library*, 3rd ed. Chicago: American Library Association.

This is the foundational text in the field. First published in 1989 and cowritten with Nancy Brown, it is the book that helped shape the future and direction of contemporary RA service. It first defined appeal in a standardized form, detailed the duties of RA librarians, and outlined the range of RA services. Not only does Saricks's book, now in its third edition, still provide the most complete explanation of appeal, but also it reviews the tools of RA, discusses how to conduct the RA conversation, offers guidance on the necessary background for advisors, and considers ways to market RA services.

Saricks, Joyce G. 2009. *The Readers' Advisory Guide to Genre Fiction.* Chicago: American Library Association.

In this classic text devoted to genre studies, Saricks applies appeal concepts to genres, grouping 15 genres into "Adrenaline," "Emotion," "Intellect," and "Landscape" categories, and listing major appeal elements for each. Chapters provide a definition of each genre, characteristics and appeals, key authors, and sure bets. Chapters also address whole collection RA, the RA conversation, and trends.

Thornton-Verma, Henrietta, and Meredith Schwartz. 2014. "The State of Readers' Advisory." *Library Journal* 139 (February 1): 30. http://lj.libraryjournal.com/2014/02/library-services/the-state-of-readers-advisory/#_.

The authors report the results of a November 2013 survey of 694 libraries designed to map the current state of RA practice. Findings illuminate the importance of RA in libraries, the difficulties librarians have keeping up with new titles and trends in genres, and the lack of formal RA education in library and information science programs. The article includes a link to the full survey and data.

Trott, Barry, and Neil Hollands. 2011. "Contemporary and Future Roles for Readers' Advisory in Public Libraries." In *Reference Reborn: Breathing New Life into Public Services Librarianship*, edited by Diane Zabel, 117–31. Santa Barbara, CA: Libraries Unlimited.

In their overview of RA practices and services, Trott and Hollands detail traditional and new methods of RA service, discuss the benefits of RA in libraries as a countermeasure to declining reference queries, and explore eight elements shaping the future of RA. Among these are whole collection, changes in genres and technology, the future of appeal, and methods of marketing.

Wyatt, Neal. 2014. "We Owe Our Work to Theirs: Celebrating the Twenty-Fifth Anniversary of *Readers' Advisory Service in the Public Library*." *Reference & User Services Quarterly* 54 (2): 24–30.

This entry in *RUSQ's* RA Column presents an examination of *Readers' Advisory Service in the Public Library* on the occasion of its 25th anniversary. It provides a detailed account of the formulation of appeal and explores how the times in which Saricks and Brown worked shaped both appeal and the provision of RA service. Also included are excerpts from an audio interview with Saricks and Brown.

Zickuhr, Kathryn, Lee Rainie, and Kristen Purcell. 2013. *Library Services in the Digital Age*. Washington, DC: Pew Internet. http://libraries.pewinternet.org/2013/01/22/Library-services/.

The Pew Research Center is a nonpartisan think tank that conducts public opinion surveys and research on American attitudes toward a number of issues, including libraries and reading. This 2013 survey, centered on e-reading, explores the demographics of readers, reading habits, and format preferences.

Chapter 25

Business Sources

Celia Ross

INTRODUCTION

Anyone working at a general reference desk should anticipate facing numerous queries related to business. Many topics fall under the umbrella of business, and questions range from broad subjects like marketing, finance, and management to more specific areas such as pharmaceuticals, manufacturing and retail, consumer trends, and everything in between. Although the subject of business is often carved out as a separate area of reference service, it is, in fact, very multidisciplinary. Business questions that overlap with fields such as engineering, psychology, medicine, and public policy are not uncommon.

Entrepreneurs, business owners, students, researchers, and others are looking for business information, some for "real-world" applications (and "real-world" profit) and others for more scholarly purposes. These information seekers are turning to public, academic, and specialized libraries for assistance, often after trying—and failing—to find the information they are looking for with an Internet search.

Finding business information can be a challenge even for a business research specialist because it is seemingly everywhere—in proprietary business databases, on company and government websites, in business publications—and nowhere, once a search for a specific answer is under way. The increasing spread and ubiquity of business-related questions combined with the complexity and challenges involved in answering them make knowledge of business information sources and research strategies important and valuable components of any general reference librarian's repertoire.

This chapter will introduce strategies for successfully handling business questions and emphasize a variety of business reference resources, including databases, websites, and print resources. It will highlight key resources, some free and many commercially produced, that all reference librarians should be familiar with.

STRATEGIES FOR BUSINESS REFERENCE

Types of Business Reference Questions

Before discussing search strategies and resources in more detail, it is important to consider the overall process of business reference, which begins with the question itself. Business reference questions can come in many shapes, sizes, and degrees of complexity, but typically their essence can be broken into a few broadly defined general categories:

- Company information
- Industry information
- Consumer information
- Financial or investing information

Of course there are other categories in addition to these, including international questions, small business questions, and legal questions. However, starting with these broadly defined areas can provide a solid foundation upon which to build a search strategy for a particular question and ultimately enhance one's understanding of business reference resources. Box 25.1 provides some examples.

Box 25.1 Search Strategies: Categorizing Business Reference Questions

The following questions have been simplified using the categories listed earlier:

- Who are the top executives at Apple, Inc.? *Company*
- How can I find information on the smoothie industry? *Industry*
- What is the target market for the Fitbit and other wearable fitness products? Who else makes products like Fitbit? *Consumer/Industry/Company*
- What was the stock price of Kmart on Black Friday in 2000? *Investing*
- What are the quarterly sales and EBIT for every Starbucks in Chicago? *Company/ Financial*

Some of these questions, especially the last two, will turn out to be quite challenging once the search for the answer gets under way, but by categorizing them, you have given yourself and your patron something to work with and reduced some of their initial complexity. As you become more familiar with business reference, you'll know which resources to start with based upon how you have categorized the question.

See Boxes 25.5 and 25.6 later in the chapter for more discussion on the last two questions, respectively.

Box 25.2 Activity: Putting Categories to Use

Work with your classmates to come up with additional examples of business questions and then work collaboratively to apply categories to them. Keep the questions available and review them again once you have explored some of the resources covered later in this chapter.

The Business Reference Interview

It can be challenging for patrons, and librarians, too, to know where to begin when it comes to business reference. Because business questions can cover such a wide range of topics and because the questions presented are often an amalgam of multiple questions, an important first step is to parse out a complex business question into its more specific component parts. A thorough reference interview will help identify the general categories and subcategories at the root of the question (strategies for the reference interview are outlined in Chapter 3). Just as with any reference situation, communication and dialogue can enhance the overall interaction and provide the context and details necessary for a successful outcome.

Beyond the standard reference interview queries, questions that can help direct the business reference search include:

- What are some keywords you would use to describe this company or industry?
- Do you have an example of a company that operates in this industry?
- Do you have an example of some relevant data that we could track back to its source?
- If we could find exactly what you are looking for right now, what would it look like?

It is also important not to focus too narrowly on the specifics of a question at first and instead to consider the broader topics involved. Define the scope of the question and brainstorm a list of relevant terms, whether broader or narrower. Keep in mind that the more granular a question, the more difficult it will be to find an answer. Many business reference questions are multilayered, and trying to answer everything at once can impede the process. Chip away at each piece of the puzzle rather than setting out to find everything all together at once. Box 25.3 provides an example of how to approach a reference question.

In addition to clarifying the question at hand, the librarian should gauge the patron's expectations and determine his or her research goals as well as the situation in which the information will be used. These goals and situations can vary widely and will influence the trajectory of the search. For example, small business owners and local governments are turning to their public libraries to start and build companies, to grow their personal and regional economy, and possibly play on a national or global stage, while students from a business school or from elsewhere on campus may be trying to do an assignment for a class. Higher-level researchers may need long runs of standardized data going back over time. Each type of requester may pose a similar question yet require different data to meet their needs. Asking some directed closed- and open-ended questions from the start will help guide the steps needed to find the appropriate answer for each situation.

It is important to understand that there are some types of business reference questions that cannot be answered due to their proprietary nature rather than a deficiency in an institution's collections or the research skills of the librarian. There frankly is no simple process, even with access to every business resource available, to easily and accurately answer many business reference questions. Even with access to a wide array of business resources and a skilled business research professional's guidance, most business reference questions, even the seemingly straightforward examples, will take time to answer.

Successfully answering a business reference question will involve an interplay between understanding these core components of the question and identifying appropriate resources based on their functionality and content. Business research is often more of a hunt for clues than for answers. Focus at first on finding sources of data rather than the specific answers being sought. Once the general topic or topics of the question have been identified (using some of the categories noted earlier), then the appropriate resource(s) can be determined, and the search for clues and answers can begin.

Box 25.3 Search Strategy: Looking for Information about Nike's Target Market

A student is looking for information on running clothes and, specifically, Nike's target market. After determining that the student is working on a class assignment, the librarian suggests the student say more about the project. The following dialogue takes place:

Student: "I have information about Nike as a company, but I can't find anything specifically about their customers or about their running clothes."

Librarian: "Let's break this question into a few parts. We'll look for general information on Nike and their consumers using article databases which we'll search together. We'll also look for information about running clothes in general or maybe the overall sportswear or fitness apparel market."

Student: "Yes, I'm interested in fitness apparel and things like workout clothes or athletic clothes like the kind Nike and Under Armour make."

Librarian: "Great. You're already helping with some of the terminology and names of competitors. I can point you to some databases that might have some information on athletic apparel and then we can look for articles mentioning Nike and consumers. As we search, we'll keep an eye out for additional keywords and related companies and any other clues that might help."

Student: "This sounds like it will take a lot of time. I thought you could just point me to one place where I could find the answer."

Librarian: "Well, business research takes some time and you usually have to search and then re-search some of the databases looking for clues. Often you won't find an exact answer and you'll have to extrapolate and make some logical guesses based on what you *can* find. Companies like Nike and Under Armour don't want their competitors to be able to find out all about their strategies and business practices, so they don't publicize this kind of information or make it easy to find. The good news is, this kind of research is like any skill and the more you do it, the better you'll get at it. The next time you have an assignment like this, you'll be that much farther up the learning curve."

Student: "OK. We better get started then. The paper is due tomorrow."

Asking "Who Cares?"

A framework that works well with many types of business questions is to consider "Who cares?" about the main themes that have been identified. This is notably critical when dealing with any kind of industry-related question, but the "Who cares?" framework can be helpful in most business reference situations. Asking "Who cares?" is industry agnostic and can be applied whether the question relates to oil prices or the stock market, wearable technology, agribusiness, or apps. Asking "Who cares?" can lead to the discovery of useful clues and can answer questions such as:

- Are there industry or consumer groups that focus on this topic?
- Are there databases that include coverage of this industry or these types of companies?
- Are there scholarly papers on this topic?
- Are there government agencies or municipal groups that collect data in this area?
- Has a research guide been created that addresses this subject?
- Is there a known expert or other go-to resource in this field?

Asking and then identifying "Who cares?" will uncover relevant players and industry terminology as well as help refine and finesse the search. Further investigation of the clues found along the way can lay the groundwork for successfully answering the research question(s) at hand.

Search Strategies

Once the question of "Who cares?" has been posed, then comes the challenge of looking for the answer(s). Begin with a combination of article databases and the open Internet. Whether the topic is a particular product and its target market, a company's supply chain, business ethics, or a specific executive, there is no limit to the topics an article or open Internet search will work for. Article and Internet searching can often turn up a number of relevant clues that will be useful throughout the course of the search.

Articles from magazines, trade publications, and journals are a familiar source of information to librarians, but they are often overlooked in the hunt for business information when people, perhaps mistakenly, believe that the answer they are looking for must be held only within a specialized company or industry database. By providing bits and pieces of information about a company, an industry, a person, or a product, among other things, articles can play a key role in identifying "Who cares?" about the question at hand. These bits of information, in turn, can provide clues that will guide the ongoing search. Articles, especially those from trade journals or local newspapers, are often one of the few resources for information on private companies, industries made up of small private companies, and certain types of products or specific brands. The key to a successful article search on business topics is to brainstorm on keywords that relate to the topic and then adding terms like "statistics," "data," "trends," or "attitudes" and similar vocabulary to the search. If possible, start with some of the specialized business article databases highlighted later in this chapter to begin this search. These same strategies can be applied to an Internet search in order to turn up relevant trade associations and other potential sources of data. A persistent and creative search in article databases and on the open Internet should be an automatic step when doing business research, regardless of the topics involved.

As mentioned earlier, remember to parse out the main themes rather than searching for everything all at once. As the search progresses, be on the lookout for synonyms to the main keywords that have been identified (e.g., clothing or apparel; utilities or energy; bonds or corporate finance). Incorporate these keywords into the search in order to expand or narrow the scope as necessary and always be on the lookout for other potential clues, such as references to a particular study, a relevant competitor or process, or an expert or association.

Google Scholar falls somewhere between an article database and the free Internet and can provide potential business research leads and information. Use *Google Scholar* to search for keywords to see what kinds of papers have been published and what data sources they utilize. Even without full access to some of the sources listed, it will be helpful to know what resources are relevant. Mine the bibliographies of papers and use the "Cited by" feature to locate similar research. *Google Scholar* can provide a welcome respite, too, from searching the open Internet, where some industry keyword searches will return only commercial sites. Use the "Library Links" feature in the advanced settings of *Google Scholar* so that search results highlight and connect to any library or other institutional content available to the user.

The "Who cares?" framework can also be used to identify library guides and other research tools that may provide useful suggestions. The Business Reference and Services Section (BRASS) of the Reference and Users Services Association (RUSA) of the American Library Association (ALA) has a "Business Reference Essentials" guide that serves as a great starting point and includes links to research guides, blogs, periodicals, and associations on the topic of general business research. Another way to identify potentially useful guides is to search relevant keywords (e.g., bonds or finance) and add in the phrase "library guide" or just "library." Limiting a search in *Google* to "site:.edu" will bring up only academic library guides and is another helpful strategy. Even if the resources highlighted on another institution's guide are not available to the patron, a good guide will still inform an understanding of the topic and provide indications as to whether the search is moving along the correct trajectory.

When using this kind of "Who cares?" brainstorming to identify likely sources of information, the key to success will be a combination of creativity, search prowess, perseverance, and timing. And while article database and open Internet searching will provide clues that can be incorporated into an overall search, specialized business databases are a crucial component to successful business research, so be sure to become familiar with the resources highlighted next. See Box 25.4 for an example of how to incorporate "Who cares?" into a reference interaction.

IMPORTANT GENERAL SOURCES

Some key resources will form the foundation of a solid business reference collection and serve as useful starting points for many business reference questions. The next section highlights a number of these by business topic and/or functionality.

Box 25.4 Search Strategy: "Who Cares?"

A small business owner approaches the reference desk and indicates that he is looking for information on parking garages. The following dialogue takes place:

Patron: "I'm trying to find out how often parking garages change their lighting systems. Ideally, I'd like to know the numbers by year and by state."

Librarian: "Okay, let's get started by thinking about the parking garage industry and also the lighting industry and try to determine what groups are out there who track relevant data. I'm going to search *Google* for: *parking garages association* to see what turns up."

Patron: "Oh, look, there's a National Parking Association and I see a Parking Market Size report on their page. And a technology report—do you think that might include lighting?"

Librarian: "We can look through and see. Also, you may wish to call them to see if you can speak to someone who knows this industry inside and out. They may be able to clarify whether or not the kind of data you're looking for is tracked in the first place and, if so, where the data gets collected."

Patron: "Can we go back to that first result page? I also saw an International Parking Institute. Oh, and they have an Emerging Trends report. That looks good."

Librarian: "Great! Now you have another potential source to reach out to. Let's think beyond parking garages now and focus on lighting in general for commercial spaces. We'll search on: buildings and lighting and trends."

Patron: "There's something by a facilities organization on lighting controls and retrofitting. And something about adaptive controls, too."

Librarian: "Good, now we're getting some more terminology. Let's keep those keywords in mind as we do some searching in this database that contains articles from trade and industry publications. But we'll start simple, first, and try just *parking lights*."

Patron: "Oh, look, there's a magazine that focuses on buildings and I see a heading for parking lots and garages. That one abstract says there was a report that names companies who improved their lighting efficiency that I want to look for later. Still nothing on how many garages changed their lighting by year, though. Or by geography."

Librarian: "That's not too surprising since the more granular we try to go with any kind of data, the harder it will be to find. After we do a little more searching in the article database, how about we identify the parking garages in our town and find out what we can on who owns them? It looks like there is one company who runs the public parking garages and there is a campus parking office for the university in town. They will be worth reaching out to and you can ask them about their own lighting practices and see if they know of any other sources of this kind of data."

Patron: "That's a good idea. I've already got a contact at the university. I'll see if I can find someone at the company who runs the public parking garages, too."

Librarian: "Sounds good. In the end, it might be that every garage does things differently and that there is no single source of data for frequency of lighting changes. But you may be able to get a sense from talking to some of these people of how often lighting systems are upgraded or of trends in adaptive controls. Then you can make some educated guesses about percentages of parking garages who deal with this and come up with a rough number."

Patron: "Thanks."

Librarian: "You're welcome. Please come back if you aren't finding what you need or if you'd like to brainstorm further."

Many of these resources could be listed in multiple categories; for the most part, they are listed under the area in which they have the strongest content. Some databases contain a combination of formats and subjects and are discussed first.

Multi-Content Databases

Some business resources have a little bit of everything in them, including company and industry profiles, articles, and directory information. These kinds of resources can be good starting points in a business information search.

OneSource includes coverage of public and private companies as well as subsidiaries and provides company hierarchy information. It also aggregates content from other vendors and provides analyst reports, industry overviews, news articles, company filings and financials, and more. *OneSource* offers powerful screening options and covers both public and private companies. Geographical coverage depends on the subscription.

Gale Cengage Learning's *Business Insights: Global* database includes online access to a number of business reference titles, including *Business Rankings Annual*, *Market Share Reporter*, *Notable Corporate Chronologies*, the *International Directory of Company Histories*, and *Ward's Business Directory*. It also contains full-text articles from trade journals and some company, country, and industry comparison and screening tools. Additional content includes financial and investment reports.

Mergent Online focuses primarily on publicly traded companies, although a *Mergent Intellect* module is available as an add-on containing Dun & Bradstreet's private company data. *Mergent* (originally *Moody's*) has been collecting data and rating publicly traded companies since 1900. *Mergent Online* covers U.S. and international companies and includes country economic reports. Company profiles include history, financial statement data going back over 15 years, and management profiles, and come with a number of exportable report-building and screening options. An add-on module covers defunct, merged, or bankrupt companies, executive biographies, and corporate calendars. The stand-alone *Mergent Archive* database contains PDF versions of historical *Moody's/Mergent* manuals. A *Mergent Horizon* add-on focuses on company suppliers, partners, and business customers.

Statista covers a wide variety of industries and consumer demographics, aggregating data from a number of free and fee-based sources into one intuitive interface. Country coverage focuses on Europe, the United States, and other developed countries, although data related to emerging countries can be found, too. Data sources are thoroughly cited on the off chance users want to follow up on a lead to search for additional data; each page points to related results for further exploration. Some data on larger companies and defined industries are compiled into what are referred to as *Statista* dossiers. Some free data are available, but for full content and downloading capabilities, a subscription is required.

NetAdvantage, from S&P Global Market Intelligence, pulls together a number of Standard & Poor's reference publications, including stock reports, corporation records, a register of public companies, and a register of private companies. It also includes an online version of their popular industry surveys (discussed in more detail in the General Industry Resources section of this chapter). *NetAdvantage* can be used for public company financial and market information, including charting and screening capabilities, some private company directory data, and mutual fund screening.

MarketLine, from Progressive Digital Media, provides a wide range of company and industry profiles covering many individual countries as well as regional and global reports. Most of the company profiles include a Strengths, Weaknesses, Opportunities, Threats (SWOT) analysis, and many of the industry reports include a Porter's Five Forces analysis (Buyer Power, Supplier Power, New Entrants, Threat of Substitutes, and Degree of Rivalry). Some subscriptions include access to additional databases including Country Statistics, Financial Deals, and company and investment screening tools.

Business Articles and Other Periodical Resources

Article searching, as mentioned earlier, is a key part of thorough business research. Some databases specifically target business publications. ProQuest's *ABI/Inform* contains scholarly journals, trade publications, working papers, press releases, newspapers, and other sources of business information, much of it available full text. Similarly, EBSCO's *Business Source* suite of products offers full-text access to a number of business publications and research tools including market reports, country reports, and company reports. Various versions are offered, including *Business Source Complete* and *Business Source Premier*. Content varies by version; some include EBSCO's *Regional Business News* product and/or the full text of the *Harvard Business Review*.

Many general article and news databases such as *Factiva*, *LexisNexis*, Gale Cengage Learning's *General* and *Academic OneFile*, and *NewsBank* can contain relevant information, as can subject-specific article databases such as *PsycInfo* and *EconLit*. As mentioned earlier, *Google Scholar* should also not be overlooked as a potential source of business information.

SOURCES FOR COMPANY INFORMATION

Business reference questions often involve looking for company information. A patron may want to identify companies in a particular industry, prepare for a job interview, identify a company's competitors or suppliers, or learn more about a company's products and services. More often than not, basic information about a company such as the headquarters location or an executive's name can be found with a simple Internet search. The company information questions that are brought to the reference desk will be more challenging and may lean toward competitive intelligence queries such as a company's supply chain strategies or marketing practices. Because of this, understanding company information resources and what can and cannot be found in them plays a key role in becoming adept at business reference.

Determining whether a company is publicly traded, private, or a subsidiary of a larger parent company is an important first step in company research.[1] The *Hoovers* website is one place to check for basic company information, including whether one company is a subsidiary of another. Another quick way to check whether a company is public or not is to perform an Internet search for the company's name and add in the word "ticker."[2] If the company is public, generally its ticker symbol will come up as well as links to additional information about its performance in the stock market. This information is often labeled "Investor Relations" or "For Investors" (more about searching for investor relations information is provided later in the chapter).

Be aware that while some databases cover both public and private companies, some cover only public companies and a search for a private entity or a subsidiary company will turn up nothing. In general, it will be much more difficult to find a great deal of information on private companies.

There are many strategies for finding company information and numerous resources that are part of the company information landscape. While there is no single best practice for this kind of searching, the University of Florida Business Library has a useful step-by-step *Company Research* guide that can direct the process.

Article Databases

Whether a company is public, private, or subsidiary, an article search is always recommended. As mentioned earlier, articles are often one of the only sources of information for private and subsidiary companies. In addition to the general article databases listed earlier, librarians can identify local newspapers and business publications and search those. Two publishers, Crain Communications and American City Business Journals (ACBJ), each produce a number of publications focusing on a specific city. Crain's covers fewer areas and focuses on Midwestern cities such as Chicago, Detroit, and Cleveland. Crain's also publishes *Crain's New York Business*. ACBJ covers more than 60 market areas including larger cities such as Atlanta, Boston, Phoenix, and San Francisco, and smaller cities such as Buffalo, Dayton, Santa Barbara, and Wichita.

Company Directories

While many databases listed in this chapter are useful for finding company information, some databases are better than others to search for companies that meet certain criteria (e.g., number of employees, industry, sales, or geography) and export the resulting data. If a patron needs to generate a list of companies, company directory databases offer the filtering and export capabilities that will help them make the most of the data. Some business directories are available in print format, although many publishers are moving to online-only availability and ceasing print. Most online directories include only the most recent listings. For historical business research purposes, a print directory may be the only resource that can provide snapshots of specific past time periods. Some business databases contain specialized directories providing lists of companies that operate in a certain industry or in a certain state. Often directories will identify private companies in addition to public companies, albeit with limited phone book entry–type information.

Examples of key company directories include *OneSource*, mentioned earlier, and Infogroup's *ReferenceUSA*. *ReferenceUSA* provides powerful screening and crisscross capabilities (using a number to look up an address or vice versa) for more than 12 million public and private U.S. businesses. *ReferenceUSA* also offers a New Businesses directory and more, including consumer research and mapping capabilities, which will be covered later in the Sources for Consumer Information section.

Bureau Van Dijk's *Orbis* includes coverage of millions of companies across the globe, many of them private. Companies can be screened by a number of different criteria including keywords from the business description. Unique among many company directory tools, *Orbis* retains coverage of inactive companies so that historical research going back to about the mid-1990s is possible.

The *Leadership Directories* focus on providing contact information at various companies, government organizations, nonprofits, and law offices. The print versions of the *Leadership Directories* are colloquially known as the "Yellow Books," although various *Leadership Directories* are also available online. Some are general company directories while others focus on the energy industry, transportation, and health. Additional products include lists of charitable donors; chief information officers; and meeting, event and conference planners.

The *Million Dollar Directory* covers millions of private (and public) companies in more than 200 countries. Information includes founding dates and in some instances sales estimates, officer names, state of incorporation and titles, and functions of company officers.

Ward's Business Directory of U.S. Private and Public Companies, available through Gale Cengage Learning, focuses on approximately 100,000 domestic companies of which about 90 percent are private. Entries include a company description and contact information as well as some ranking information and other screening capabilities.

The *Thomas Register of American Manufacturers* is a useful resource for identifying who makes, distributes, or supplies a product. The online version can be sorted by state and searched for computer-aided design models; it also contains manufacturing industry news, white papers, some technical illustrations, and other information.

LexisNexis's *Corporate Affiliations* database, sometimes referred to as "Who Owns Whom?", profiles public and private companies and provides a visual representation of their affiliates, subsidiaries, and divisions. Coverage is strongest for U.S. companies and includes information such as founding dates and top competitors.

Websites, Annual Reports, and SEC Filings

When searching for company information, reviewing the company's website is recommended. Retail and other consumer product sites often focus on the ecommerce side of their mission and serve primarily as a sales portal, but a careful search for an "About Us" section (or a link to "For Investors" or "Investor Relations" for public companies as mentioned earlier) can lead to information about the corporate side of the business.

Most public companies will make their annual report available somewhere on their website as well as link to their filings with the Securities & Exchange Commission (SEC). Both the annual report and its SEC-filing counterpart, the 10-K, contain valuable information about the company. An annual report serves as an informational tool for the company's shareholders. It generally will contain pictures and graphics and can give its reader a sense of the company's style and culture. An annual report will also contain a "Letter to Shareholders" from the CEO that can provide insight into a company's vision and future plans. The 10-K is a less colorful document than the annual report but will contain useful information in the form of a Business Description section and other data about the company. Additional clues can be found on the website in the form of links to subsidiaries or information about executives or specific initiatives the company is pursuing. A useful resource for making the most of the information found in an annual report is IBM's *How to Read Annual Reports.*

Some websites offer searchable annual reports and SEC filings. *AnnualReports.com* can be searched by company, stock exchange, and industry or sector. *Rank and Filed* bills itself as "SEC Filings for Humans" and provides a visual look at companies and when they file, what they file, their stock ownership, executives and boards of directors, and more. A quick company lookup can lead to a graph that illustrates all of the other companies whose stock are owned by the company's officers and directors. *SEC Live* offers the ability to highlight text in filing documents, make notes, and export financials.

SOURCES FOR FINANCIAL AND INVESTING INFORMATION

For a librarian without a background in corporate finance or accounting, finding information related to a company's financial or investment performance can be a challenge. Two useful resources that can serve as primers in this area are William G. Droms and Jay O. Wright's *Finance and Accounting for Nonfinancial Managers: All the Basics You Need to Know* (2015) and the *Guide to Financial Statements* from IBM.

Two popular databases for investment research are *Value Line* and *Morningstar.* The *Value Line Investment Survey* divides companies into categories based on their market capitalization size.[3] Companies are further divided by industry sector. Industries and companies are ranked according to a proprietary *Value Line* analysis. Online subscriptions also offer mutual fund coverage and "special situations" surveys that focus on a more aggressive and risk-oriented investment strategy, among other content. *Value Line* also offers instructional material for individual investors. *Morningstar* is another source of stock price and other market information as well as personal finance guides and tools. It is well known for its coverage of mutual funds and also includes information on other types of funds as well as bonds. Both *Value Line* and *Morningstar* feature investment and market news as well as commentary and analysis.

Some websites offer company investment and financial data. *Big Charts* contains current and historical stock quotes and allows for screening and comparison of companies, as do sites like *Yahoo! Finance* and *Zacks Investment Research.*

Global Financial Data's *GFDatabase* contains historical data, some going back to the early days of currency and finance, on economic indicators, global markets, and indices. The interface is fairly straightforward considering the amount of data it contains, and results are easy to export. Additional modules covering individual stocks as well as global real estate are also available.

Often business researchers need raw data points; these can be daily stock prices,[4] bond ratings, currency exchange rates, revenue data, and so on. These kinds of data requests can quickly turn unwieldy, whether because a consistent run of data going back a number of years is needed or because it involves complicated financial or economic data points or some combination of these challenges. These types of requests are less likely to occur in public library settings or in smaller academic libraries, but an awareness of some of the big names in finance databases is useful nonetheless. Four key players on the financial and market information database landscape include the S&P Global Market Intelligence's

Capital IQ database, as well as *Bloomberg*, *Eikon* (formerly *ThomsonONE*), and *FactSet*. Many of these products are used in professional settings such as investment firms and banks. Because of their wide use in professional settings, many academic institutions with large business or finance programs will subscribe to at least one of these products in order to provide their students with some exposure to them. All of these products focus on global markets, including corporate and municipal bonds, real estate, and technical financial analysis of U.S. and international stocks. Regardless of one's knowledge or expertise in these areas, each of the aforementioned databases involve a relatively steep learning curve in order to understand proprietary search functions, Excel add-in functionality, and other interface features.

Other big names in finance data products, especially in PhD-level institutions with finance and economic data research needs, include *Compustat Research Insight*, from S&P Global Market Intelligence, the *Center for Research in Security Prices* (*CRSP*) *U.S. Stock Databases*, *Datastream* from Thomson Reuters, and *Wharton Research Data Services* (*WRDS*). *Compustat* provides historical coverage of company annual and quarterly income statements, balance sheets, cash flows, and other data. North American and Global versions are available. *CRSP* data allow researchers to do historical research on company stock performance and ties together entities through its proprietary identification system. *Datastream* combines company financial information with time series economic data. Data sources are aggregated from a number of different suppliers and include specialized content such as earnings estimates and environmental, social, and governance data. Lastly, *WRDS* is not a specific database, per se, but a platform that can be used by researchers to manipulate and view large data sets, such as those produced by *Compustat* and *CRSP*, both of which are available as subscriptions via *WRDS*. Institutions subscribe to *WRDS* and then can select their data sets à la carte. Most, if not all, business schools with a PhD program will have at least some access to data via *WRDS*. All of the data available through *WRDS* requires advanced knowledge of Web querying and statistical analysis, so this is not the kind of tool that would be used for a quick stock price lookup and the like.

Private Equity, Venture Capital, and Mergers and Acquisitions

A lot of investing occurs outside of the stock market. Private equity firms are funding established companies to help them grow, and venture capitalists are looking for start-up companies to take a chance on as an investment. Between companies themselves, mergers and acquisitions are happening, sometimes resulting in a whole new entity or sometimes just a larger parent company.

The resources covered in this section focus on the private equity and venture capital markets[5] as well as mergers and acquisitions.[6] Note that these types of resources can provide clues as to whether a private company has acquired another company, been bought themselves, or been invested in, so they are useful in private company research.

One free resource covering the venture capital market is *CrunchBase*. Because *CrunchBase* focuses on start-ups, it often includes information on companies that are too new to be covered in directory or other company research databases. Users can see which companies are being invested in and by whom, which are getting the most money, and who is giving away the most in funding. Because the start-up industry is focused on technology, companies covered lean heavily on the tech side, but *CrunchBase* is still a useful tool to explore for all types of companies.

Bureau van Dijk's *Zephyr* database is similar to *Orbis*, mentioned earlier in the Company Directory section, except that it focuses on mergers and acquisitions. *Zephyr* can be searched by company, industry, geography, and more. Rumored and announced deals are included in addition to a history of completed deals. Data are gleaned from various news sources, and financials are included where possible.

Lastly, *PrivCo* is a private company financial intelligence database that focuses on private companies and investors as well as private equity, venture capital, and mergers and acquisitions deals. If public companies have acquired a private entity, these types of deals are also covered. *PrivCo* can be searched by company location, industry, revenues, employee growth, and more. Reports include a company profile, growth rates, some financial data, lists of competitors, and information about owners and investors as well as any related deals and other funding activity. *PrivCo* also offers a freely available *Knowledge Bank* section, which contains helpful overviews on private company valuation, explanations of public and private mergers and acquisitions, private company life cycles, bankruptcy and restructuring, and more.

Investor Education Sites and Publications

Personal finance and investing are subjects where a librarian's advice should be limited to making recommendations regarding trusted sources. Just as librarians steer clear of giving medical or legal advice, so, too, should they avoid making investment picks for their patrons. Many resources are available for those wanting further edification and instruction regarding investing and personal finance. This section will focus primarily on online resources, although print and eBooks on financial topics should not be overlooked, so a catalog search is also recommended.

Investopedia is a useful go-to source for all kinds of investment topics. Descriptions are clear, and terminology is linked to definitions. Ads on the site distract somewhat but are not overwhelming to users. In addition to providing overviews of topics from stock market basics to wealth management, it offers tutorials and exam preparation information for users who wish to take their financial skills to the next level. Similar edification can be found on the Motley Fool's *Fool's School* site, which offers a 13-step guide to investing and a "Getting Started" section covering financial and market concepts. Both *Investopedia* and the *Fool's School* offer glossaries and dictionaries.

The *Investor's Clearinghouse* is produced by the Alliance for Investor Education, a nonpartisan organization that strives to create greater understanding of investing, investments, and the financial markets for all. The site offers resources for older investors, young investors, and teachers. It also has financial planning information and investing basics as well as information on how to avoid scams. More complicated topics such as bonds, futures, and mutual funds are also covered. *Path to Investing*, from Securities Industry and Financial Market Association, is a similar resource for users who want to familiarize themselves with the basics of the market. The Financial Industry Regulatory Authority also has an *Investor Education Foundation*, which aims to provide "underserved Americans with the knowledge, skills and tools necessary for financial success throughout life." Note that the *Investor Education Foundation* has partnered with ALA and is behind the *Smart Investing @yourlibrary* campaign, including grants and other resources.

A number of news sites also provide useful information for anyone interested in investing or personal finance. Print publications like *Barron's*, the *Wall Street Journal*, and the *Financial Times* all have robust websites full of market information and news as well as tools and guides for subscribers. The *New York Times's DealBook* is another key publication in market news. *Bloomberg Businessweek* (formerly known as *BusinessWeek*) is no longer available as a print publication but is a key online source for business and market news. *Institutional Investor* and *Kiplinger* round out this array of financial news sources.

Historical Stock Prices and Other Historical Market Information Resources

Many of the investment sites noted earlier like *Yahoo! Finance* and *Morningstar* offer daily, weekly, and monthly stock prices going back a number of years. Finding historical stock prices can be a challenge, however, if the company in question has undergone changes over time such as merging with another company or ceasing to exist. See Box 25.5 for a helpful example of this kind of scenario.

Traditionally, microform versions of newspapers such as the *New York Times* and *Wall Street Journal* were the go-to resources for basic historical stock price research because the business section of each would contain a record of that

Box 25.5 Search Strategy: Finding a Historical Stock Price

A good example of a seemingly straightforward historical stock price question was presented in Box 25.1: What was the stock price of Kmart on Black Friday in 2000?

After confirming that the patron is indeed referring to the Friday after the U.S. Thanksgiving holiday and searching the Web to find the actual date it occurred in 2000 (November 24), the next logical step would be to use one of the many stock price tools available and simply look up Kmart. However, most stock price databases will not contain stock information for Kmart on this date.

A little digging will turn up news of the merger of Kmart and Sears in 2006. Out of this merger, the company now called Sears Holdings (ticker symbol SHLD) was formed, and Sears and Kmart each became obsolete. Immediately, their respective ticker symbols, S and KM, no longer were tied to them. Further complicating things, Kmart filed for bankruptcy in early 2001, not long after Black Friday, so Kmart's status as "inactive" may have happened even sooner than the merger date.

Mergers and bankruptcies and similar kinds of changes in a company's status are clues to the researcher that standard stock price tools, even some of the fee-based database tools, are unlikely to have the information they are seeking. Instead, they will have to turn to a specialized tool such as the *Daily Stock Price Record* or dig through old newspaper microfiche.

Kmart's stock closed at $6.06 (sometimes reported as 6-1/6) on Friday, November 24, 2000, according to *NetAdvantage*.

day's stock and other market prices. Unfortunately, beginning around 2006, many newspapers, including the *New York Times* and *Wall Street Journal*, stopped printing daily stock prices, and thus their microform versions will not help if a post-2006 price is being sought.

The *Daily Stock Price Record* from Standard & Poor's has been a trusted resource for historical stock prices since the early 1960s. Three editions cover stocks traded on the New York Stock Exchange, the American Stock Exchange, and the NASDAQ market. Listings in the print version are alphabetical by company. Online access to stock prices for defunct and inactive companies is available through S&P Global Market Intelligence's *NetAdvantage* and *Capital IQ* products, mentioned earlier. Similarly, *Mergent Online* offers an inactive company module that contains stock price information for those entities.

For clues about a company's past and changes it might have undergone, a search of news sources should provide helpful clues. Additionally, publications like the *Capital Changes Reporter* and the *Directory of Obsolete Securities* can help. Now published by CCH and available in print and online, *Capital Changes Reporter* contains a chronological history of the stock's changes in corporate capital structure, including name changes, mergers, spin-offs, bankruptcy filings, stock splits, and other information that may help to determine an old stock's current worth. The *Directory of Obsolete Securities*, published by Financial Information Incorporated, can be used to determine the value of a stock at the time of a merger or acquisition and will indicate whether a company has become obsolete due to a name change, merger, acquisition, bankruptcy, or other factors. The print publication is still available as a stand-alone volume or as part of a subscription package called *Library Reference Service*.

The *Stocks, Bonds, Bills & Inflation* yearbook does not cover individual company stock prices but instead focuses on the entire market collectively including large and small companies, government bonds, treasury bills, and inflation. Previously published by Ibbotson and now owned by Morningstar, this source gives rates of return on the capital markets in the United States from 1926 onward. Another useful source for historical market data is the *Commodity Research Bureau Yearbook*. It contains information on more than 100 U.S. and international commodities, including seasonal patterns and historical data for the past 10 years.

Company and Industry Ratios

Industry and financial ratios can help determine how well a company is performing relative to its peers. Company ratios are generally calculated using numbers from a company's financial statements, so getting specific ratios for a private company or a subsidiary is often not possible. However, if financial ratios exist for a public company or for an industry, these can be used as a benchmark or extrapolation point for a private company. Keep in mind that some of the ratios will be strongly influenced by the size of a company and the scale of its operations, so avoid directly comparing a small company with a large one and vice versa.[7]

Ratios can indicate a company's financial stability, its efficiency overall, its profit, and other measures. Averaging out these numbers across companies in the same industry can provide similar insights into an industry. Patrons will often want a source that provides industry ratios so that the comparisons can be made without having to do the actual calculations. Steven Bragg's *Business Ratios and Formulas: A Comprehensive Guide* (2012) presents definitions and formulas for calculating ratios as well as explanations of each and their appropriate use. Rosenfeld Library at the University of California Los Angeles has a guide to *Financial Ratios*, which points users to data sources for specific types of ratios. Three core print titles, *Industry Norms & Key Business Ratios*, Leo Troy's *Almanac of Business and Financial Ratios*, and *RMA Annual Statement Studies* are also useful sources of information on this topic. *BizStats* from BizMiner provides some free business statistics and financial ratios.

Company Rankings and Market Share

Often a patron will want to know where a company ranks among its peers/competitors or how much of the industry's market share is owned by the company. This information is challenging to find for a number of reasons, including the fact that industries can be difficult to define and that companies can do more than one thing but will not necessarily break out their performance in all areas and make the data available for general consumption. Many times a ready-made ranked list of companies and their market shares will not be found, but instead will have to be constructed by the patron using a variety of sources.

Business Rankings Annual from Gale Cengage Learning is one of the few resources available that focuses on company and product ranking data. This publication is available in a searchable online form through *Business Insights: Global* database (mentioned earlier in the Multi-Content Databases section) as well as through their *Gale Directory Library* product. Also available through *Business Insights: Global* and the *Gale Directory Library* is the *Market Share Reporter*. Both resources aggregate articles reporting market share and ranking information from across various business publications and trade journals. If a relevant entry is found in either database, it can be used as a pointer toward additional resources, such as an updated ranking, or to provide additional keywords and terminology for later searching. For example, a search in *Business Rankings Annual* on the company Costco turns up an entry for Top Home Furnishing Retailers with sales estimates from a 2013 issue of *Home Furnishings News*. A search in *Market Share Reporter* on Costco finds an entry for Top Appliance Retailers with sales figures and market share percentages from a 2013 issue of *TWICE: This Week in Consumer Electronics*. These publications could now be searched for additional information or the other companies on the list explored.

Mentioned earlier, both Crain Communications and ACBJ publish an annual *Book of Lists* for the cities they focus on. These can be useful resources for finding lists of companies that have been compiled throughout the year in the rest of the publication. Very specialized lists including area executives who are paid the most money, the state's largest manufacturers, the leading small business lenders in the region, and the top healthcare institutions are compiled in these titles. Each individual publication's website will sometimes make some of the list content available, as well, but in general, librarians should add the relevant *Book of Lists* to the collection, especially if the library is located near one of the major metropolitan areas covered.

Additional information on rankings or market share can sometimes be found by doing an article or Internet search. Searching terms like "top or best or ranking" and "("market size" or "market share" or "share of industry")" and relevant keywords can lead, if not to an actual ranked list or market share data to start, to useful clues that can help to guide the rest of the search.

Company Organizational Charts

A patron may ask for a company's organizational chart or "org chart" for short. An org chart illustrates the various positions, titles, and departments within a company and the hierarchical reporting structure. These documents are not generally made available outside of the company's walls since they are considered proprietary due to the information they contain related to the company's overall organization and internal operations. One strategy for locating an org chart equivalent is to search the open Internet for the phrase "org chart" and the company's name. Sometimes limiting the results of the search to the Microsoft PowerPoint format can also point to unofficial charts. Most freely available charts will have been crowd-sourced or will come from an unverified source, so it is important to understand that they are not official documents. Some sites like *The Conference Board* and *The Official Board* offer org charts for a fee.

When faced with an org chart request, it can be useful for the patron to construct his or her own unofficial chart. To do this, use the company's website, directory databases, and other sources noted earlier in this chapter to identify some of the key executives and other personnel.

Using Social Media for Company Research

Social media sources such as *LinkedIn*, *YouTube*, and *Twitter* should also be considered as potential sources of information on companies and executives.[8] Many companies have a social media presence that can provide insights into their marketing and other strategies. Searching *Twitter* for mentions of a company name or a product can turn up useful clues, as can looking on *LinkedIn* for executives' profiles. A search in *YouTube* can sometimes provide a glimpse onto a factory floor or demonstrate a new manufacturing technology.

SOURCES FOR INDUSTRY INFORMATION

Industry research questions are a mainstay of business reference. Strategies for answering industry questions were presented in the Asking "Who Cares?" section, and mastering those strategies should be considered the core component of one's business research skill set.

Although they may start as seemingly straightforward, industry questions can be a challenge, especially if an industry is niche, new, or dominated primarily by private companies. Often the industry in question comprises all three of those characteristics. Many questions that do not start off with a focus on industry will shift gears during the course of the search because it will be necessary to search for industry information in order to fully understand a company and/or consumers.

General Industry Resources

Some databases and other business resources cover many industries, others only a few. Some databases cover very narrow, niche types of industries, while others include only broadly defined industries. The Strategies for Business Reference section provides tips for using article databases and the open Internet for industry research. Many of the databases mentioned in the Multi-Content Databases section, such as *MarketLine* and *Statista*, also include industry information.

Gale Cengage Learning's *Business Insights: Global* (*BI:G*) was mentioned earlier but is worth noting again here. *BI:G* contains content from the *Encyclopedia of American Industries*, the *Encyclopedia of Global Industries*, and the *Encyclopedia of Emerging Industries*, which are also available as print products. Each of these titles provides insights into their respective topics, including local and suburban transit in the United States, global aquaculture, boutique wineries, and green construction. Because these are print publications, some of the editions have not been updated in a few years. Librarians should check the publication date of entries and supplement with additional sources when necessary.

The *Standard & Poor's Industry Surveys* provide a solid overview of about 50 broadly defined North American industries. Each survey contains a glossary of industry-related terms, an industry profile, pointers to key publications and associations in the industry, a look at the industry's current environment, key industry ratios and statistics, an overview of how the industry operates, and a useful section on how to analyze that particular industry. Industry Surveys are available in print and through *Capital IQ* and *NetAdvantage*; a *Global Industry Surveys* module is also available.

The *Freedonia Focus Report Collection* from the Freedonia Group primarily covers industry sectors such as energy, construction and building materials, electronics, chemicals, industrial/manufacturing, and packaging. Other sectors include consumer products, pharmaceuticals/life sciences, and service industries. This is a good database for finding coverage of somewhat niche industries, and the reports cover market size, product and market forecasts, industry composition, major players, and trends.

IBISWorld provides access to more than 700 U.S. and global industries, including everything from shoe stores to pawnshops to gold ore mining and all industries in between. It is a popular resource because of its coverage of very niche industries. Each report contains information on key economic drivers for the industry, as well as supply- and demand-related industries. Industry outlook, the competitive landscape, and major companies are included as well as key statistics. *IBISWorld* has been expanding to include a searchable Risk Ratings reports section, which covers the risk level for each industry based on an assessment of its operating conditions, including revenue outlook and key drivers.

Plunkett Research Online publishes a number of industry almanacs that give a useful snapshot to anyone trying to get a quick overview on an industry's trends, statistics, and major players. The online version allows for various screening and reporting options. Many Plunkett almanacs are available in print. Industries include apparel, textiles and fashions, manufacturing and robotics, entertainment and media, and consulting.

For additional tips on resources and strategies, the University of Florida Business Library has a useful *Industry Research Tutorial* and Harvard's Baker Library has a number of helpful industry research guides. Similar guides can be identified through an Internet search on words such as "industry research" or on relevant industry keywords and adding in the words "library" and "guide." In *Google*, a search can also be limited to site:.edu to retrieve only academic sites.

Industry Classification Codes

In addition to the "Who cares?" framework, industry codes and classification systems can serve as useful tools to identify potential sources of industry information. In the United States, the North American Industry Classification Codes (NAICS) and the Standard Industrial Classification System (SIC) codes broadly classify the industry areas in which a company operates. These codes and others can be useful tools when doing research on an industry or looking into a company's competitors. The quickest way to look up NAICS classifications (and to find their corresponding SIC codes) is to use the U.S. Census *North American Industry Classification System* site.

A company can have more than one SIC or NAICS code: a primary code to identify its main area of business and additional codes to indicate other areas of activity. Note that using SIC and NAICS codes will not necessarily produce an exhaustive, comprehensive list of an industry's players; these codes are just one of many industry research tools, and not every industry has a related code.

There are other general classification systems as well as more specialized ones. NAICS and SIC are the closest to universal schemes compared with others likely to be found in the typical business reference setting. While not all industry resources utilize NAICS or SIC codes in their indexing, being aware of these classification systems enables the best use of those that do. It should also be noted that many, if not most, databases that include industry coverage have their own industry classifications and headings; these usually are just industry names and not numerical codes.

Additional codes that may be encountered in a business reference transaction include Harmonized Tariff and Schedule B codes used in import and export research related to foreign trade. *Trade.gov* has a helpful FAQ on Schedule B and Harmonized System numbers.

Specialized Industry Databases

Many database products target specific industries, such as technology, sports, energy, healthcare and medicine, and automotive. Many of them are available for library use, but because of the nature of this kind of specialized industry information, these databases are often cost prohibitive and may not be found in a public library setting or smaller academic settings. A few examples of these types of databases include the *Automotive News Data Center* and *Power eTrack*, which focuses on the alternative and other energy industries.

Industry Report Vendors and Other Report Aggregator Sites

Patrons doing an open Internet search will often stumble across expensive market research reports that seem to have all the information they need, and then be disappointed when they discover their library does not have it. While most libraries will not subscribe to these kinds of reports nor be able to afford to purchase them individually, they can still serve as useful sources for looking at the industry in question. There is often a free registration feature that will provide access to the table of contents for the report and possibly some snippets of data or mentions of the companies covered in the report.

SOURCES FOR CONSUMER INFORMATION

Finding data on consumers' attitudes, buying habits, demographics, and so on is almost always a challenge. As with industry research, often a successful consumer and market information search will involve searching in article databases and on the open Internet; however, many databases do cover consumers and their markets, as well as some print resources.

Many consumer information databases offer mapping capabilities, such as CIVICTechnologies' *Business Decision* and *Business Decision Academic* databases, Gale Cengage Learning's *DemographicsNow*, Esri's *Business Analyst*, *ReferenceUSA's Consumers/Lifestyles* and *New Movers/Homeowners* modules, Geographic Research's *SimplyMap*, and *Social Explorer*, distributed by Oxford University Press. These products provide geographically based demographic and consumer data, like households with income over a certain amount in specified ZIP codes or which state buys the most frozen pizza, or other information that may help the user paint a more robust picture of the target market or consumer product being researched. They can also be used in business location analysis and research. Each of these resources requires some amount of training and exploring to fully make use of all its functionality and content.

Databases like *Passport* from Euromonitor contain profiles of consumer-focused markets such as food, beverages, apparel, beauty and personal, retail, and travel. *Passport* covers more than 200 countries and provides historical and forecast market data for consumer products as well as demographic, economic, and marketing statistics for each country. Market share and brand share data for numerous products are included, and quick top-level economic data can be pulled to compare trends across countries and time. But the real wealth of information comes from the consumer data side of the product; for example, users can find out how much people spent on pet food or on diapers in France as compared with the whole world.

Mintel is another resource focused on industries from a consumer perspective. In addition to covering the consumer side of industry sectors such as automotive, financial services, household care, and technology, *Mintel* categorizes its reports by themes such as Healthy Lifestyles, Austerity and Value, and Premium and Luxury. There are also demographic categories such as Millennials, Mothers, Singles, and Teens. *Mintel* reports focus primarily on the U.S. and UK markets, although there is some international coverage. Reports are robust and include brand analysis, purchase and price information, packaging data, market size, forecast information, and more.

The U.S. Census Bureau's *American Factfinder* database is a freely available source for population, housing, economic, and geographical information. Much of the data is available down to ZIP code and census tract levels and includes coverage of not only the decennial census, but also other census surveys, including the economic census, annual economic surveys, and the annual American Community Survey.

Some databases, like *Ad$pender*, *Advertising Red Books*, and *SRDS Business Media Advertising Sources*, focus more on advertising. Companies are not required to report how much they spend on advertising, but *Ad$pender* is one of the few products available that tracks advertising spending by brand, product category, and outlet (e.g., television, radio, billboard). It is owned by Kantar Media, who also own the Standard Rate and Data Service (SRDS) suite of products, among other advertising and marketing resources. The *Advertising Red Books*, sometimes referred to simply as the *Red Books*, track companies that spend more than $200,000 annually on advertising and provide some ad spending, agency, and brand data, and other top-level company information. The *Advertising Red Books* database contains profiles of more than 10,000 advertising agencies and includes a list of the accounts represented by each agency and fields of specialization. *SRDS Business Media Advertising Source* provides information and analysis on all kinds of media products, including consumer magazines, business publications, TV and radio stations, and newspapers. Advertising rates, circulation data, and profile information on audience markets, including Designated Marketing Areas and Metro Survey Area maps, are included. When used creatively, they can provide a great deal of target market insight and other useful information.

Statista should be highlighted here for its wealth of consumer information. From social media habits to wine consumption and more, *Statista* is worth a search when looking for anything related to consumers. Similarly, *eMarketer* provides a lot of consumer data regarding online habits. A robust demographics section includes Internet users by age and race as well as frequency of use. Consumer attitudes about various online industries and mobile technologies and social media are also included. A digital atlas shows the total population, total number and percentage of Internet users, households with broadband, and mobile phone users on a country-by-country basis. Data are forecast out for five years.

Other useful databases for consumer data include *MRI+*, which provides information on demographics, lifestyles, product, brand usage, and advertising media preferences reported by a sample of more than 25,000 U.S. consumers. The *SRDS Local Market Audience Analyst* cross-tabulates demographic attributes such as age, gender, and income against those groups' likelihood to participate in a variety of activities (what they call lifestyles). These lifestyle activities are anything from traveling for business to exercising, hunting, and owning a dog. Data is survey based and broken out by lifestyles (e.g., so one can look up who says they ride a bike to work), by geographical area (e.g., so one can see what people in Spokane like to do), and by demographic attributes (e.g., so one can see what women ages 22–35 do compared with men ages 36–45). *Simmons OneView* provides survey data on the demographic, psychographic, and media use characteristics of users of products, brands, and services. Like *MRI+*, academic access to the surveys is generally embargoed by at least two years.

In addition to Kantar mentioned earlier, a few other names are big players in the consumer market research sector, and business librarians should be aware of them. They include *Nielsen*, *NPD*, and *IRI*, all of which offer some freely available publications on consumer trends and analysis on their websites. *Nielsen* is a familiar name to many, famous for their "Nielsen ratings," which measure television audiences. The Nielsen Company has expanded to include all types of consumer research. Some consumer panel and retail scanner *Nielsen* data are now available to researchers through a partnership with the University of Chicago's Kilts Center for Marketing. For online consumer analytics focused on website statistics including visitor data and ownership, *Compete PRO* and *MediaMetrix* are powerful industry-level tools.

Additionally, *Crimson Hexagon* is a professional tool available in some advanced research settings and can be used to analyze social media posts from Twitter and other sources. Finally, adding "NPD or IRI or comScore or Kantar" to a search for consumer statistics may unearth nuggets of data in an article search.

ADDITIONAL SOURCES

International Information

Understanding a country is often key to understanding a particular company, its products, customers, suppliers, and other stakeholders. Many industries function across international borders, as well, so tracking down information on the global market is important. The following resources are strong in their coverage of country economic indicators and/or business and industry topics globally.

The *World Bank Data* site is freely available online and is an important source for all kinds of data related to international socioeconomic development. Some of the data, such as the *World Development Indicators* and *Global Development Finance*, are used to be available only as fee-based products but are now included in this open-access resource. Data can be searched by country, topic, or indicator, and much of the data is available in time series form.

GlobalEDGE from Michigan State University is an excellent free portal to global industry information. The site can be searched by country, trade bloc, industry, and state as well as by the economic classifications of emerging or frontier markets.

Business Monitor Online covers a wide range of industry sectors, including agribusiness, autos, commercial banking, defense and security, freight and transport, information technology, infrastructure, metals, oil and gas, pharmaceuticals, power, real estate, retail, shipping, and water. *Business Monitor Online* also covers political risk, finance, economic indicators, macroeconomic performance, and the business operating environment for a number of countries, including emerging markets and industrialized countries.

The Economist Intelligence Unit (EIU), part of the Economist Group that publishes the *Economist* magazine, offers an *EIU.com* product that covers business conditions, economic forecasting, and other data for more than 200 countries. Additionally, some versions of *EIU.com* include analysis and background information for eight industry areas: automotive; food, beverages, and tobacco; consumer goods and retailing; healthcare and pharmaceuticals; energy and electricity; telecommunications and technology; financial services; and travel and tourism. *ViewsWire*, another offering from the suite of products available from EIU, is a business intelligence product that includes coverage of the political and regulatory environment as well as economic and financial indicators for more than 195 countries, with an emphasis on those countries that are considered emerging markets.

The *EMIS Insights* database delivers news, company, and financial data on more than 70 emerging markets in Asia, Latin America, Central and Eastern Europe, the Middle East, and Africa. The *OECD iLibrary* from the Organisation for Economic Co-operation and Development produces reports and statistics on its members, mostly high-income countries, that cover a wide variety of subjects, including economics, trade, government finance, and health.

Susan Awe's *Going Global: An Information Sourcebook for Small and Medium-Sized Businesses* (2009) provides practical information for businesses that are considering expanding into foreign markets. The *International Business* guide from ALA BRASS is an excellent guide to finding more information on this topic and includes coverage of the resources mentioned here and many more.

Small Business and Entrepreneurship

Small business and entrepreneurship are increasingly popular and vital areas of research in libraries. Often, these topics go beyond the scope of the types of company and industry research that a general academic or public library reference desk can support, such as patent searching,[9] business financing or legal questions, and deep dives into trends in innovation. However, like any challenging business research topic, there are always ways to creatively approach these types of questions and provide the patron with some useful material. In fact, many of the resources and strategies that have been covered in this chapter will be useful in assisting small business and entrepreneurial patrons. Additionally, the following resources focus specifically on small business.

EBSCO's *Small Business Reference Center* includes full-text articles from trade publications as well as eBooks on managing meetings and projects, budgeting, marketing, and more. The *Small Business Reference Center* also includes sample business plans, U.S. tax forms, videos, and case studies. EBSCO also publishes *Entrepreneurial Studies Source*, which leans more toward company profiles (from *MarketLine*) as well as some videos and reference and periodical titles. Gale Cengage Learning's *Small Business Resource Center* includes titles on how to start, finance, or manage a small business and also includes access to the *Business Plans Handbook* and the *Encyclopedia of Small Business*. Users can browse for information on business types, such as bakeries, design services, gift shops, or health clubs and topics such as customer service, payroll tax, and pricing. *ProQuest Entrepreneurship* includes start-up plans and templates as well as business plan examples, eBooks, periodicals, case studies, videos, and industry overviews. Working papers, conference proceedings, dissertations, and blog entries related to entrepreneurship can also be found in *ProQuest Entrepreneurship*.

The U.S. government's *Small Business Administration* (SBA) site is another useful resource. Users can find information on starting and managing a business, on loans and grants, and on contracting with the government. Users can also find pointers to local resources, such as state branches of the SBA, as well as help for veteran business owners or export assistance. A learning center provides online tutorials on a range of topics including market research, growing an established company, and legal requirements for small businesses.

Billed as the "Counselor to America's Small Business," SCORE is a nonprofit organization that works closely with the SBA and provides mentoring services for entrepreneurs from seasoned business experts. Mentors can be searched for online or SCORE will work to help pair people. Local and regional SCORE chapters also often partner with area libraries to offer small business workshops.

The *Business Plans and Profiles Index* from the Carnegie Library of Pittsburgh provides a useful index to business plans available online and indexes print resources for business plans, such as the *Business Plans Handbook*. Use the site to find sample plans as well as for pointers to other helpful small business research websites. Two nonprofit organizations to be aware of who have a focus on small business and entrepreneurship are the Kauffman Foundation and the Global Entrepreneurship Monitor.

Finally, a great print resource that is useful for this area of research is *Small Business and the Public Library: Strategies for a Successful Partnership* (2011) by Luise Weiss, Sophia Serlis-McPhillips, and Elizabeth Malafi. The authors provide inspiration and actionable ideas for outreach to small business patrons and emphasize that libraries can highlight their value to the community through this kind of outreach.

Nonprofit Organizations

While most business research tends to focus on either large corporations or small business entities, questions involving nonprofit organizations can arise. *Guidestar* can be used to search for nonprofit organizations by name, location, and subject categories such as arts, culture and humanities, education and research, or environment and animals. Some financial data are included, as well as overviews of each organization, key personnel, and U.S. Internal Revenue Service (IRS) form 990s, which contain information about top-paid executives and outside consultants for the organization, among other information.

The Urban Institute focuses on research in nonprofit organizations, among other areas, and oversees the *National Center for Charitable Statistics* (NCCS). For researching the charitable activities of various corporations as well as identifying available grants for nonprofits, the *Foundation Directory Online* (FDO) is a useful resource. While the FDO is a fee-based product, the Foundation Center offers additional tools and information related to philanthropy, grants, and other nonprofit activity. Another organization focused on research in philanthropy is the *Association for Research on Nonprofit Organizations and Voluntary Action* (*ARNOVA*). *ARNOVA* offers information from a theoretical and applied perspective and hosts an annual conference as well as publications and special interest groups related to nonprofit and philanthropic studies.

The Chronicle of Philanthropy covers jobs, statistics, and other news related to the topic and is considered a key publication for nonprofit leaders, fund-raisers, and grant makers. *The Chronicle* is published in print monthly and provides daily updates on its website. The website also includes tools and guides related to running and researching nonprofits.

The *Free Management Library* provides a collection of articles and guides for individuals and organizations looking for information or education on management topics, whether nonprofit or not. *BoardSource* is a similar resource with a focus on nonprofit governance. Much of the *BoardSource* content is available only to members, but a Community Resources section points to publications that are freely available.

Charity Navigator helps users evaluate a charity's reputation and overall efficiency based on a number of criteria including expenses, CEO salary, privacy policies, scope of the charity, use of government support, and data transparency. Users can register for free to use these advanced screening criteria or browse by ratings. The *Charity Navigator* does not accept money from rated charities. *Give.org* is from the Better Business Bureau's Wise Giving Alliance (BBB WGA) and produces similar reports about national charities, evaluating them against their Standards for Charity Accountability. The intention is to serve donors and help them to make informed giving decisions, but it is a useful site for researchers as well. It should be noted that charities that have met the BBB WGA standards can opt to sign a license and pay a fee to use the BBB Accredited Charity seal.

Box 25.6 Search Strategy: Stumper Scenarios

Box 25.1 posed the stumper, "What are the quarterly sales and EBIT for every Starbucks in Chicago?"

At first glance, this was classified into the categories of Company Information and Financial Information. Because of the financial component, a likely approach would be to look for Starbucks in the databases covered in the Multi-Content Databases section, such as *Mergent Online*, to see whether EBIT jumps out. More probable, unless the librarian had either a corporate finance background or a predilection toward finance acronyms, would be to start with a quick search in one of the Finance and Investment Education resources to clarify what EBIT stands for. According to *Investopedia*, EBIT means earnings before interest and tax, and there are some "see also" references, including operating earnings, operating profit, and operating income. These are useful synonyms to use while searching.

However, a reference interview reveals that it is not just EBIT for Starbucks that the patron wants, but EBIT for each individual Starbucks in Chicago. Some brief skimming of Starbucks's financials will show that there are not sections that break out financials beyond those for the entire company. This is where the Company Information part of the question kicks in. Some creativity will be required, and some collaboration with the patron as well. Does she know how many Starbucks there are in Chicago? A search on "Chicago" in Starbucks's most recent annual report does not turn up any hits and neither does a search on Illinois. Further skimming shows that store counts are broken out by country only. These are some potential flags that the information the patron is asking for is not going to be found.

At this point, the librarian should show the patron what has (and has not) been found and brainstorm acceptable alternatives. With some extrapolation based on the number of states or major cities within the United States, the patron might be able to come up with a rough estimate of how many Starbucks there are in Chicago, but it will be just that: a rough estimate. The patron could apply that calculation to further (and more roughly) estimate the EBIT for those Chicago Starbucks. But the patron will need to understand that this is likely as specific as she can get. Individual store operations are highly proprietary, and a company does not want its competitors to know how well (or how poorly) a precise location is doing.

EVALUATION AND SELECTION

A common misconception about business reference is that expensive databases are required to successfully answer any business-related query. Many times, with some brainstorming and creative application of the "Who cares?" framework, useful, non-database, sources of information can be identified and relevant pieces of data found. A related myth is that only databases contain business information and that access to lots of business databases equates to access to all business answers. As mentioned earlier, sometimes a business research question simply is not going to be answered, regardless of the array of business databases the librarian has access to. In the scenario in Box 25.4, no databases were used, only open Internet searching, and even though the answer was not found, many helpful clues were uncovered. This type of outcome is not a failure, just a business reference reality.

It should also be considered that many sources of business information have no obvious connection to the business discipline itself. There are numerous databases and publications specifically marketed as business research products, but there is no official definition of what makes a resource a "business" resource. The wide variety of companies, industries, and other areas related to the subject of business means that almost anything, when viewed through the proper lens, can be considered a possible business resource. This is helpful to keep in mind when reviewing an existing collection for potential business reference resources that may have been previously overlooked. Do not overlook the business information that can be found through general article databases, through freely available government and municipal sites, and other seemingly nonbusiness resources. However, most libraries will want to invest in some specialized sources for business like those described in this chapter.

Like business reference questions, business reference resources also come in many shapes, sizes, and degrees of complexity. In addition to categories like company information, industry information, financial or investing information, or consumer information that a resource may cover, consider that business reference resources can be differentiated by other more functionality-focused nuances. Subject coverage and other content can overlap among resources, but each will have particular areas of strength, whether it is their interface, their depth of coverage of a certain discipline or topic, their ability to export data in a particular way, or their unique material or expansive scope.

Some business reference resources are better than others, depending on the task at hand. Some may cover multiple industries or geographical areas, others may have a specialized subject focus or unique data formatting features. For example, if a patron requires a list of companies by size and industry by ZIP code, or a researcher needs a run of historical stock prices for a set of companies, then only certain databases have this functionality. Or if a patron is focused on clean energy, there are particular resources that focus on this industry and its main players. If a patron needs an in-depth overview of a well-known company's history, a search for books, an article database search, and a company profile database search may be the best strategy. Often, it will be necessary to search in multiple resources, all while keeping an eye out for clues or pointers toward other potential sources of information.

Cost

Cost is always a consideration when evaluating sources, and some business information resources have very high price tags. Rather than focusing on the quantity of business databases and books, librarians should consider how each complements the other and how they collectively serve to support their respective audiences. Budgets as well as users' needs will vary depending upon whether the setting is academic, public, or corporate. Regardless of their expense, the selection of business resources must take into account the overall needs of users as well as the existing collection to determine overlapping content from other resources. Cost–benefit analysis should also include a consideration of the learning curve involved in thoroughly utilizing the resource in question and the number of users it would serve. Librarians should also consider how users would access the resource, whether it is a physical print publication, an online database, or a tool that needs a dedicated terminal or some other specialized software or expertise to run.

Beyond an investment of money in business information sources, librarians should factor in an investment of time for training and other professional development related to business. Training should focus on specific database interfaces and content as well as on business reference in general. Business information sources are only as valuable as they are utilized. The best business resource is a skilled information professional who can think creatively about how to approach any question.

Uniqueness

Commercially published business information tools often offer at least some level of unique content—how unique it is may be a factor in pricing. Some business databases produce their own content, while others aggregate information from multiple sources. As mentioned earlier, content among business reference databases can overlap, so it is important to compare and contrast to avoid duplication and double-spending.

A good business librarian will, over time, become something of a "database whisperer" and be able to creatively exploit the databases and other available resources. Becoming familiar with some of the many business database products starts with understanding not only the database's subject coverage but also some of the underlying content and how the business information is organized in each (see Box 25.7). For example, a business database's content may be comprising primarily articles from news, trade, and scholarly publications or contain pre-compiled company or industry profiles. Some databases are especially strong in their coverage of consumers or consumer markets, others have mapping capabilities and demographic data. Some cover only the United States, others have an international or global or regional focus. There are databases that contain directory information and can screen for companies by various criteria such as the number of employees, industry, and revenue. Other databases have business plan templates and other information that makes them especially suited for small business topics. A few of the (generally more expensive) databases contain investment information including stock and bond data, corporate financials, mergers and acquisitions, venture capital and private equity, and other financial market and investment information. Also, many business databases have interfaces that are more on par with professional-level use, and so the learning curve can be steep. Reference librarians can help the patron to focus more on the overall business research process rather than getting frustrated or distracted by a specific interface or data point and reiterate that business research, like any skill, takes time and practice before any ease or expertise emerges.

Box 25.7 Activity: Speed Date a Database

Take a look at the library and research collections you have access to and see what kind of business resources are available and how they are arranged. If possible, "speed date" some of the databases by looking up a company or industry or two. If you are stumped on what company to pick, think of your favorite grocery store or airline. Or look up your bank or the company that makes your cell phone. What cable company or Internet provider do you use? You know more about business than you may realize!

Questions for Reflection and Discussion:

1. What are your initial thoughts on the database's appearance?
2. What about the database's content and functionality?
3. What will your patrons think of this database?
4. How can you highlight its strengths and make it accessible to them?

The more time you spend exploring these resources, the better you will get at knowing which one to turn to for which business reference situations. This may be the beginning of some long-term research relationships!

In terms of building a business reference collection, remember that no single resource will exhaustively cover all business reference topics. Librarians should consider their user base and strive to include one or two databases that fall into some of the categories mentioned in the previous paragraph. A robust business reference database collection might include, for example, one or two business article databases, one or two databases with company or industry information, one or two databases with international content, one or two directory databases, one or two finance and investment databases, and one or two small business databases. It can be helpful to identify a peer institution and compare business collections and seek inspiration from innovative subject guides for collection and access ideas. Reaching out to other librarians, either directly or via some of the channels mentioned in Box 25.9, to request feedback and insights on business collection development is also recommended. For more on business database holdings at various academic institutions, see Kim and Wyckoff (2016).

Reviewing Tools

A number of reviewing tools focus on business resources or occasionally cover business-related topics. The BRASS *Selected Core Resources for Business Reference* is a curated guide to resources in topics ranging from banking and electronic commerce to healthcare management, taxation, and more. BRASS also selects and publishes an annual list of the year's *Outstanding Business Reference Sources* in the Winter volume of the *Reference & User Services Quarterly* journal.

The University of Florida Business Library's *Business Books: Core Collections* has been a useful tool highlighting selections of the best business and economics books published since 2000. These lists can be used to compare against local holdings and provide a robust resource on the readings on the major aspects of business, including consumer behavior, accounting, and management.

Best of the Business Web is published by Robert Berkman, a coeditor of the *Information Advisor's Guide to Internet Research.* Monthly newsletters covering business research sites get sent out to registered users. Quarterly *iFocus* reports are published on themes such as Private Company Financials and Consumer Demographics. Subscribers can access one free report per year, and the others are available for a small fee.

A number of journals include coverage of business reference resources including the *Journal of Business & Finance Librarianship* and *Business Information Review.* Standard reviewing sources such as the *Charleston Advisor* and *Choice Reviews Online* include coverage of business databases and major titles in business, economics, and other relevant social science disciplines.

The *Sudden Selector's Guide to Business Resources* (Bergart and Lewis 2007) focuses on the topic of business reference within the context of collection development. It highlights key publishers, associations, and other useful resources to help business selectors learn to build and maintain their collection.

CONCLUSION

Business research, like any skill, is mastered through practice over time. As a librarian's familiarity with researching business topics grows, certain databases and other resources will come to mind when faced with a business question. To become adept at business reference, it is less important to exhaustively know the content and functionality of every single business database than to approach each question with creativity and flexibility. Business information is everywhere, as are business questions. Any librarian should expect to face at least a few business

Box 25.8 Search Strategy: Putting It All Together

Review the questions you and your classmates were prompted to gather in Box 25.2. Select one or two and brainstorm ways you might approach them and the resources you would use. Then work individually on the questions and regroup later to discuss your findings.

Questions for Reflection and Discussion:

1. Do these questions seem as daunting as they did before reading this chapter?
2. What databases did you end up using? What roadblocks did you hit?

Box 25.9 Other Professional Resources

Identifying library guides was suggested earlier in this chapter as a strategy for finding information on challenging business reference topics. Behind these guides are the people who created them. Individually and collectively, these intrepid business librarians are an amazing source of information and support and should not be overlooked.

The BRASS division of ALA's RUSA has been referred to already in this chapter. One of the core missions of BRASS is to assist business librarians in the work that they do. Additionally, getting involved with BRASS is a great way to expand your professional development and leadership horizons. For ALA members with an interest in business reference, BRASS is a welcoming and supportive ALA home base. The Special Libraries Association (SLA) has a similar group of helpful and productive business librarians in the form of their Business and Finance Division (B&F). Both BRASS and SLA's B&F are key organizations for anyone looking for business reference assistance or for guidance with the profession of business librarianship in general.

Another key resource for business librarians is the *BusLib-L* e-mail group. A Listserv log-in is required, but members of the list have access to a wealth of business information in the form of the *BusLib-L* searchable archives, as well as the more than 1,500 members who make up the group and who are ready and willing to share their vast knowledge of complicated business research topics.

Finally, some resources are helpful for keeping up on business resources, for inspiration on how to show others how to do business research, and as examples of intuitive and streamlined presentations of business information resources. *BizRefDesk*'s tagline is "Land of the Free and the Good." It is a bare-bones blog maintained by Wharton Lippincott librarian Terese Terry. Useful, reputable sources for industry and economic data are posted frequently and can be browsed by a number of categories. Chad Boeninger is the librarian behind Ohio University's (OU) *Business Blog*, which he uses to highlight the best databases and other resources for business researchers. OU students are the main target audience, but helpful instructional videos that guide users through the ins and outs of market research using specific databases serve as great examples and templates for librarians to replicate for their own patrons. Many public libraries also produce great examples of business research guides, such as the New York Public Library's *Business Research Guide: Market Research.*

reference questions at some point in their career. Hopefully the resources and strategies covered in this chapter will help when the time comes. See Box 25.8 for some tips on how to put it all together.

NOTES

1. For a helpful explanation of the difference between public and private companies, see "What's the Difference between Publicly- and Privately-Held Companies?" (2015) as well as the *Investopedia.com* dictionary entries for "Public Company," "Private Company," and "Subsidiary."
2. For more information on ticker symbols, see "The Evolution of Ticker Symbols" (Cussen 2011).
3. See the *In-Depth Guide to Reading a Value Line Research Report* (2013). The guide refers to the print format but will give readers insights into overall *Value Line* content.
4. A useful explanation of what an adjusted closing price of a stock is can be found at "How Do I Calculate the Adjusted Closing Price for a Stock?" (Balasubramaniam 2015).
5. For a helpful overview of this topic, see "What Is the Difference between Private Equity and Venture Capital?" (2015).
6. For a helpful overview of mergers and acquisitions, see Ben McClure's "The Basics of Mergers and Acquisitions" (2015).
7. Common size analysis can be used to translate a company's financial statements into percentages so that it can be compared with other companies, regardless of size. For more information, see "The Common-Size Analysis of Financial Statements" (Fuhrmann 2013).
8. For more on the use of social media in business reference, see Berkman (2015), Brown (2011), and Falls and Deckers (2011).
9. Patent searching goes beyond the scope of this chapter, but some good library guides exist and can be useful starting points if the topic comes up. Try an Internet search for "patent searching library guide" to see examples.

REFERENCES

Balasubramaniam, Kesavan. 2015. "How Do I Calculate the Adjusted Closing Price for a Stock?" *Investopedia.com.* Last accessed November 1. http://www.investopedia.com/ask/answers/06/adjustedclosingprice.asp.

Berkman, Robert. 2015. *Find It Fast: Extracting Expert Information from Social Networks, Big Data, Tweets, and More*, 6th ed. Medford, NJ: Information Today.

Brown, Scott. 2011. "Social Media for Company Research: A Few of the Best Tools." *Business Information Review* 28 (3): 163–74.

Cussen, Mark P. 2011. "The Evolution of Ticker Symbols." *Investopedia.com.* August 17. http://www.investopedia.com/financial-edge/0811/the-evolution-of-ticker-symbols.aspx.

Dictionary. Investopedia.com. http://www.investopedia.com/dictionary/.

Falls, Jason, and Erik Deckers. 2011. "How to Use Social Media for Research and Development." *Entrepreneur.* December 6. http://www.entrepreneur.com/article/220812.

Fuhrmann, Ryan C. 2013. "The Common-Size Analysis of Financial Statements." *Investopedia.com.* November 14. http://www.investopedia.com/articles/investing/111413/commonsize-analysis-financial-statements.asp.

In-Depth Guide to Reading a Value Line Research Report. 2013. *Value Line.* http://www3.valueline.com/pdf/The_In-Depth_Guide_to_Reading_a_Value_Line_Research_Report.pdf.

Kim, Kyunghye, and Trip Wyckoff. 2016. "What's In Your List?: A Survey of Business Database Holdings and Funding Sources at Top Academic Institutions." *Journal of Business & Finance Librarianship* 21 (2): 135–51.

McClure, Ben. 2015. "The Basics of Mergers and Acquisitions." *Investopedia.com.* Last accessed November 1. http://www.investopedia.com/university/mergers/.

"What Is the Difference between Private Equity and Venture Capital?" 2015. *Investopedia.com.* Last accessed November 1. http://www.investopedia.com/ask/answers/020415/what-difference-between-private-equity-and-venture-capital.asp.

"What's the Difference between Publicly- and Privately-Held Companies?" 2015. *Investopedia.com.* Last accessed November 1. http://www.investopedia.com/ask/answers/162.asp.

LIST OF SOURCES

ABI/Inform. Ann Arbor, MI: ProQuest. http://www.proquest.com/products-services/abi_inform_complete.html. [subscription required]

Academic OneFile. Farmington Hills, MI: Gale Cengage Learning. http://assets.cengage.com/pdf/bro_academic-onefile.pdf. [subscription required]

Ad$pender. New York: Kantar Media. http://kantarmedia.us/product/adspender. [subscription required]

Advertising Red Books. New York: Redbooks. http://www.redbooks.com/. [subscription required]

American City Business Journals. American City Business Journals. http://acbj.com/brands/bizjournals. [subscription required for full access]

American Factfinder. Census Bureau. http://factfinder.census.gov/faces/nav/jsf/pages/index.xhtml.

AnnualReports.com. http://www.annualreports.com/.

Association for Research on Nonprofit Organizations and Voluntary Action (ARNOVA). Indianapolis: ARNOVA. http://www.arnova.org/.

Automotive News Data Center. Crain Communications. http://www.autonews.com/section/datacenter?cciid=internal-anhome-dcnav. [subscription required]

Awe, Susan. 2009. *Going Global: An Information Sourcebook for Small and Medium-Sized Businesses.* Santa Barbara, CA: Libraries Unlimited.

Baker Library. "Industry Research." Harvard University. http://www.library.hbs.edu/guides/.

Barron's. Dow Jones and Company, Inc. http://online.barrons.com/. [subscription required for full access]

Bergart, Robin, and Vivian Lewis. 2007. *Sudden Selector's Guide to Business Resources.* Chicago: ALCTS/American Library Association.

Best of the Business Web. Rochester, NY: Best of the Business Web. http://www.bestbizweb.com/.

Big Charts. MarketWatch. http://bigcharts.marketwatch.com/.

BizRefDesk. http://www.bizrefdesk.com/.

BizStats. Camp Hill, PA: BizMiner/The Brandow Company. http://bizstats.com/.

Bloomberg. New York: Bloomberg. http://www.bloomberg.com/professional/education/. [subscription required]

Bloomberg Businessweek. Bloomberg. http://www.bloomberg.com/businessweek. [subscription required for full access]

BoardSource. Washington, DC: BoardSource. https://www.boardsource.org/eweb/. [subscription required for full access]

Bragg, Steven M. 2012. *Business Ratios and Formulas: A Comprehensive Guide*. Hoboken, NJ: Wiley.

Business Analyst. Redlands, CA: Esri. http://www.esri.com/software/businessanalyst. [subscription required]

Business and Finance Division. Washington, DC: Special Libraries Association. http://bf.sla.org/.

Business Blog. Ohio University Libraries. http://www.library.ohiou.edu/subjects/businessblog/.

Business Decision. CIVICTechnologies. http://civictechnologies.com/businessdecision/. [subscription required]

Business Decision Academic. CIVICTechnologies. http://civictechnologies.com/businessdecision/. [subscription required]

Business Information Review. 1984–. Thousand Oaks, CA: Sage. Quarterly. http://bir.sagepub.com/.

Business Insights: Global. Farmington Hills, MI: Gale Cengage Learning. http://solutions.cengage.com/BusinessSolutions/Business-Insights-Global/. [subscription required]

Business Monitor Online. New York: Business Monitor International. http://www.bmiresearch.com/platform. [subscription required]

Business Plans and Profiles Index. Carnegie Library of Pittsburgh. http://www.carnegielibrary.org/research/business/bplansindex.html.

Business Rankings Annual. Farmington Hills, MI: Gale Cengage Learning. http://find.galegroup.com/gdl/help/GDLeDirBRAHelp.html. Available online as part of *Gale Directory Library* and *Business Insights: Global*. [subscription required]

Business Reference and Services Section. American Library Association. http://www.ala.org/rusa/sections/brass.

Business Reference and Services Section. 2015. *Business Reference Essentials*. American Library Association. October 22. http://brass.libguides.com/BusinessReference.

Business Reference and Services Section. 2015. *International Business*. American Library Association. July 13. http://brass.libguides.com/internationalbusinesscore.

Business Reference and Services Section. *Selected Core Resources for Business Reference*. American Library Association. http://brass.libguides.com/.

Business Source Complete. Ipswich, MA: EBSCO. https://www.ebscohost.com/academic/business-source-complete. [subscription required]

Business Source Premier. Ipswich, MA: EBSCO. https://www.ebscohost.com/academic/business-source-premier. [subscription required]

BusLib-L. https://sites.google.com/site/buslibl/.

Capital Changes Reporter. Riverwoods, IL: Wolters Kluwer. https://www.cchgroup.com/capitalchanges. [subscription required]

Capital IQ. New York: S&P Global Market Intelligence. http://www.spcapitaliq.com. [subscription required]

Center for Research in Securities Prices US Stock Databases. Chicago: University of Chicago. http://www.crsp.com/products/research-products/crsp-us-stock-databases. [subscription required]

Charity Navigator. Glen Rock, NJ: Charity Navigator. http://www.charitynavigator.org/.

Charleston Advisor: Critical Reviews of Web Products for Information Professionals. 1999–. Denver: The Charleston Advisor. Quarterly. http://www.charlestonco.com/index.php. [subscription required for full access]

Choice Reviews Online. Middletown, CT: Association of College and Research Libraries. http://www.ala.org/acrl/choice/cro. [subscription required]

The Chronicle of Philanthropy. https://philanthropy.com/. [subscription required for full access]

Commodity Research Bureau (CRB) Yearbook. 1994–. Chicago: Commodity Research Bureau. Annual. http://www.crbyearbook.com/.

Compete PRO. Boston: Compete, Inc. https://www.compete.com/products/compete-pro/. [subscription required]

Compustat Research Insight. New York: S&P Global Market Intelligence. http://www.compustat.com. [subscription required]

The Conference Board. New York: The Conference Board. https://www.conference-board.org/. [subscription required for full access]

Corporate Affiliations. Dayton, OH: LexisNexis. http://www.corporateaffiliations.com/. [subscription required]

Crain's New York Business. Detroit: Crain Communications. http://www.crain.com/publications/index.html. [subscription required for full access]

Crimson Hexagon. Boston: Crimson Hexagon. http://www.crimsonhexagon.com/. [subscription required]

CrunchBase. San Francisco: AOL. https://www.crunchbase.com/. [subscription required]

Daily Stock Price Record: American Stock Exchange. 1962–. New York: Standard & Poor's. Annual. Available online as part of *NetAdvantage* and *Capital IQ*.

Daily Stock Price Record: NASDAQ. 1993–. New York: Standard & Poor's. Annual. Available online as part of *NetAdvantage* and *Capital IQ*.

Daily Stock Price Record: New York Stock Exchange. 1962–. New York: Standard & Poor's. Annual. Available online as part of *NetAdvantage* and *Capital IQ*.

Datastream. New York: Thomson Reuters. https://forms.thomsonreuters.com/datastream/. [subscription required]

DealBook. New York: New York Times Company. http://www.nytimes.com/pages/business/dealbook/index.html.

DemographicsNow. Farmington Hills, MI: Gale Cengage Learning. http://solutions.cengage.com/BusinessSolutions/Demographics-Now/. [subscription required]

Directory of Obsolete Securities. South Plainfield, NJ: Financial Information Incorporated. http://www.fiinet.com/products/libraries-universities. [subscription required]

Droms, William G., and Jay O. Wright. 2015. *Finance and Accounting for Nonfinancial Managers: All the Basics You Need to Know*, 7th ed. New York: Basic Books.

EconLit. Nashville: American Economic Association. https://www.aeaweb.org/econlit/. [subscription required]

Eikon. New York: Thomson Reuters. http://thomsonreuters.com/en/products-services/financial/trading-platforms/thomson-reuters-eikon.html. [subscription required]

EIU.com. St. Louis: The Economist Group. http://www.eiu.com/. [subscription required]

eMarketer. New York: eMarketer. http://www.emarketer.com/. [subscription required]

EMIS Insights. London: Euromoney Institutional Investor. http://www.securities.com/emis/. [subscription required]

Encyclopedia of American Industries. Farmington Hills, MI: Gale Cengage Learning. http://solutions.cengage.com/Gale/Catalog/Fact-Sheets/EncyAmericanIndustries.pdf. Available online as part of *Business Insights: Global*.

Encyclopedia of Emerging Industries. Farmington Hills, MI: Gale Cengage Learning. http://assets.cengage.com/pdf/fs_Emerging-Industries.pdf. Available online as part of *Business Insights: Global*.

Encyclopedia of Global Industries. Farmington Hills, MI: Gale Cengage Learning. http://assets.cengage.com/pdf/fs_Ency-Global-Industries.pdf. Available online as part of *Business Insights: Global*.

Entrepreneurial Studies Source. Ipswich, MA: EBSCO. https://www.ebscohost.com/academic/entrepreneurial-studies-source. [subscription required]

Factiva. New York: Dow Jones and Company. http://new.dowjones.com/products/factiva/. [subscription required]

FactSet. Norwalk, CT: FactSet Research Systems Inc. http://www.factset.com/. [subscription required]

Financial Times. http://www.ft.com/home/uk. [subscription required for full access]
Fool's School. Alexandria, VA: Motley Fool. http://www.fool.com/school.htm.
Foundation Directory Online. New York: Foundation Center. https://fconline.foundationcenter.org/. [subscription required]
Free Management Library. Authenticity Consulting. http://managementhelp.org/.
Freedonia Focus Report Collection. Cleveland: Freedonia Group. http://www.freedoniagroup.com/FocusReports.aspx. [subscription required]
Gale Directory Library. Farmington Hills, MI: Gale Cengage Learning. http://access.gale.com/nslsgdl/. [subscription required]
General OneFile. Farmington Hills, MI: Gale Cengage Learning. http://solutions.cengage.com/Gale/Catalog/Fact-Sheets/genOneFile.pdf. [subscription required]
GFDatabase. San Juan Capistrano, CA: Global Financial Data. https://www.globalfinancialdata.com. [subscription required]
Give.org. BBB Wise Giving Alliance. http://www.give.org/.
Global Industry Surveys. New York: S&P Global Market Intelligence. http://www.spcapitaliq.com/our-capabilities/our-capabilities.html?product=industry-surveys. Available as part of *Capital IQ* and *NetAdvantage*. [subscription required]
GlobalEDGE. Michigan State University. http://globaledge.msu.edu/.
Google. http://www.google.com.
Google Scholar. http://scholar.google.com.
Guide to Financial Statements. IBM. http://www.ibm.com/investor/help/guide/.
Guidestar. Williamsburg, VA: Guidestar USA. http://www.guidestar.org/.
Hoovers. Short Hills, NJ: Dun & Bradstreet. http://www.hoovers.com/. [subscription required for full access]
How to Read Annual Reports. IBM. http://www.ibm.com/investor/help/reports/.
IBISWorld. Los Angeles: IBISWorld. http://www.ibisworld.com. [subscription required]
iFocus Reports. Rochester, NY: Best of the Business Web. Quarterly. http://www.bestbizweb.com/ifocus-reports.html.
Industry Norms & Key Business Ratios. 1989–. Murray Hill, NJ: Dun & Bradstreet Credit Services. Annual.
Information Advisor's Guide to Internet Research. 2014–. Medford, NJ: Information Today. 10 issues per year. http://www.informationadvisor.com/.
Institutional Investor. New York: Institutional Investor. http://www.institutionalinvestor.com/. [subscription required for full access]
International Directory of Company Histories. 1998–. Farmington Hills, MI: Gale Cengage Learning. Annual. Available online as part of *Business Insights: Global*.
Investopedia. http://www.investopedia.com/.
Investor Education Foundation. Financial Industry Regulatory Authority. http://www.finrafoundation.org/.
Investor's Clearinghouse. http://www.investoreducation.org/.
IRI. Chicago: IRI. http://www.iriworldwide.com/.
Journal of Business & Finance Librarianship. 1990–. Florence, KY: Taylor & Francis Group. Quarterly. http://www.tandfonline.com/toc/wbfl20/current.
Kiplinger. Washington, DC: Kiplinger Washington Editors. http://www.kiplinger.com/. [subscription required for full access]
Knowledge Bank. New York: PrivCo. http://www.privco.com/knowledge-bank. [subscription required for full access]
Leadership Directories. New York: Leadership Directories. https://www.leadershipdirectories.com/Hub/Business.aspx. [subscription required]
LexisNexis. Dayton, OH: LexisNexis. http://www.lexisnexis.com/en-us/products/lexisnexis-academic.page. [subscription required]
Library Reference Service. South Plainfield, NJ: Financial Information Incorporated. http://www.fiinet.com/products/libraries-universities. [subscription required]

LinkedIn. https://www.linkedin.com/.
Market Share Reporter. Farmington Hills, MI: Gale Cengage Learning. http://find.galegroup.com/gdl/help/GDLeDirMSRHelp.html. Available online as part of *Gale Directory Library* and *Business Insights: Global*. [subscription required]
MarketLine. New York: Progressive Digital Media. http://advantage.marketline.com/. [subscription required]
MediaMetrix. Reston, VA: comScore. https://www.comscore.com/Products/Audience-Analytics. [subscription required]
Mergent Archive. New York: Mergent. http://www.mergent.com/solutions/print-digital-archives/mergent-archives. [subscription required]
Mergent Horizon. New York: Mergent. http://www.mergent.com/solutions. [subscription required]
Mergent Intellect. New York: Mergent. http://www.mergent.com/solutions/private-company-solutions/mergent-intellect. [subscription required]
Mergent Online. New York: Mergent. http://www.mergent.com/solutions. [subscription required]
Million Dollar Directory. New York: Mergent. http://www.mergentmddi.com/. [subscription required]
Mintel. Chicago: Mintel Group. http://www.mintel.com/. http://www.morningstar.com/.
Morningstar. Chicago: Morningstar. http://www.morningstar.com/. [subscription required for full access]
MRI+. New York: GfK MRI. http://www.mri.gfk.com/en/gfk-mri.html. [subscription required]
National Center for Charitable Statistics. Washington, DC: Urban Institute. http://nccs.urban.org/.
NetAdvantage. New York: S&P Global Market Intelligence. https://www.netadvantage.standardandpoors.com/. [subscription required]
New York Public Library. 2013. *Business Research Guide: Market Research*. http://www.nypl.org/collections/nypl-recommendations/guides/market-research.
New York Times. http://www.nytimes.com/.
NewsBank. Naples, FL: NewsBank. http://www.newsbank.com/. [subscription required]
Nielsen. http://www.nielsen.com/us/en.html.
Nielsen Consumer Panel Data & Retail Scanner Data. Kilts Center for Marketing, University of Chicago. http://research.chicagobooth.edu/nielsen/. [subscription required]
North American Industry Classification System. Census Bureau. http://www.census.gov/eos/www/naics/concordances/concordances.html.
NPD. Port Washington, NY: NPD Group. https://www.npd.com/wps/portal/npd/us/home/. [subscription required]
OECD iLibrary. Washington, DC: Organisation for Economic Co-operation and Development. http://www.oecd-ilibrary.org/. [subscription required]
The Official Board. Saint Cloud, France: The Official Board. http://www.theofficialboard.com. [subscription required for full access]
OneSource. Concord, MA: Avention. http://www.avention.com/. [subscription required]
Orbis. London: Bureau Van Dijk. http://www.bvdinfo.com/en-gb/our-products/company-information/international-products/orbis. [subscription required]
Passport. London: Euromonitor International. http://www.euromonitor.com/passport. [subscription required]
Path to Investing. Securities Industry and Financial Market Association. http://www.sifma.org/education/sifma-foundation/path-to-investing/.
Plunkett Research Online. Houston: Plunkett Research. http://www.plunkettresearchonline.com/. [subscription required]
Power eTrack. London: GlobalData. http://power.globaldata.com/. [subscription required]
PrivCo. New York: PrivCo. http://www.privco.com/. [subscription required]

ProQuest Entrepreneurship. Ann Arbor, MI: ProQuest. http://www.proquest.com/products-services/pq_entrep.html. [subscription required]

PsycInfo. Washington, DC: American Psychological Association. http://www.apa.org/pubs/databases/psycinfo/index.aspx. [subscription required]

Rank and Filed. http://rankandfiled.com/.

Reference & User Services Quarterly (*RUSQ*). 1997–. Chicago: American Library Association. Quarterly. https://journals.ala.org/rusq/index.

ReferenceUSA. Papillion, NE: Infogroup. http://www.referenceusa.com. [subscription required]

Regional Business News. Ipswich, MA: EBSCO. https://www.ebscohost.com/academic/regional-business-news. [subscription required]

RMA Annual Statement Studies. Philadelphia: Risk Management Association. Available online through *Avention.*

Rosenfeld Library. 2014. *Financial Ratios.* University of California Los Angeles. http://www.anderson.ucla.edu/rosenfeld-library/business-topics.

SCORE. https://www.score.org/.

SEC Live. Seattle, WA: SEC Live. http://www.seclive.com/.

Simmons OneView. Costa Mesa, CA: Experian. http://www.experian.com/marketing-services/simmons-oneview.html. [subscription required]

SimplyMap. New York: Geographic Research. http://geographicresearch.com/simplymap/. [subscription required]

Small Business Administration. https://www.sba.gov/.

Small Business Reference Center. Ipswich, MA: EBSCO. https://www.ebscohost.com/public/small-business-reference-center. [subscription required]

Small Business Resource Center. Farmington Hills, MI: Gale Cengage Learning. http://assets.cengage.com/pdf/fs_Small-Biz-RC.pdf. [subscription required]

Smart Investing @yourlibrary. American Library Association and FINRA. http://smartinvesting.ala.org/.

Social Explorer. New York: Oxford University Press. http://www.socialexplorer.com/. [subscription required]

SRDS Business Media Advertising Source. New York: Kantar Media. http://next.srds.com/media-data/business. [subscription required]

SRDS Local Market Audience Analyst. New York: Kantar Media. http://next.srds.com/media-data/consumer-demographics. [subscription required]

Standard & Poor's Industry Surveys. http://www.spcapitaliq.com/our-capabilities/our-capabilities.html?product=industry-surveys. Available online as part of *Capital IQ* and *NetAdvantage.* [subscription required]

Statista. New York: Statista. http://www.statista.com/. [subscription required for full access]

Stocks, Bonds, Bills & Inflation. Chicago: Morningstar. http://corporate.morningstar.com/ib/asp/subject.aspx?xmlfile=1414.xml.

Thomas Register of American Manufacturers. New York: Thomas Publishing Company. http://www.thomasnet.com/.

Trade.gov. US Department of Commerce. http://www.trade.gov.

Troy, Leo. 1970–. *Almanac of Business and Financial Ratios.* Englewood Cliffs, NJ: Prentice-Hall. Annual.

Twitter. https://twitter.com/.

University of Florida Business Library. 2015. *Business Books: Core Collections.* October 30, 2015. http://businesslibrary.uflib.ufl.edu/businessbooks.

University of Florida Business Library. 2015. *Company Research.* September 23, 2015. http://businesslibrary.uflib.ufl.edu/companyresearch.

University of Florida Business Library. 2015. *Industry Research Tutorial.* October 1, 2015. http://businesslibrary.uflib.ufl.edu/c.php?g=114645&p=746469.

Urban Institute. http://www.urban.org/.
Value Line Investment Survey. http://www.valueline.com/.
ViewsWire. London: Economist Group. https://www.eiu.com/handlers/PublicDownload.ashx?mode=m&fi=country-analysis/viewswire.pdf.
Wall Street Journal. http://www.wsj.com/.
Ward's Business Directory of U.S. Private and Public Companies. Farmington Hills, MI: Gale Cengage Learning. http://assets.cengage.com/pdf/fs_Wards-On-GDL.pdf. Available online as part of *Gale Directory Library* and *Business Insights: Global.* [subscription required]
Weiss, Luise, Sophia Serlis-McPhillips, and Elizabetrh Malafi. 2011. *Small Business and the Public Library: Strategies for a Successful Partnership.* Chicago: ALA Editions.
Wharton Research Data Services. Philadelphia: Wharton University of Pennsylvania. https://wrds-web.wharton.upenn.edu/wrds/. [subscription required]
World Bank Data. World Bank Group. http://data.worldbank.org/.
Yahoo! Finance. http://finance.yahoo.com/.
YouTube. https://www.youtube.com/.
Zacks Investment Research. Chicago: Zacks. http://www.zacks.com/. [subscription required for full access]
Zephyr. London: Bureau van Dijk. https://zephyr.bvdinfo.com/. [subscription required]

SUGGESTED READINGS

Heckman, Lucy. 2011. *How to Find Business Information: A Guide for Businesspeople, Investors and Researchers.* New York: Praeger.
A helpful introduction, this title includes good coverage of business guides, including some older seminal publications in the field. Other chapters cover finding industry and company information, the stock market, insurance, accounting and taxation, marketing and advertising, management, small business, and entrepreneurship. Appendices cover acronyms and abbreviations, major business libraries, business-related government agencies, and major stock and securities exchanges.

Moss, Rita W. 2012. *Strauss's Handbook of Business Information: A Guide for Librarians, Students, and Researchers*, 3rd ed. Santa Barbara, CA: Libraries Unlimited.
A business reference standard, *Strauss's Handbook* provides an overview of basic resources and then covers specific topics such as company information, industry information, credit and banking, and real estate. Appendices decode acronyms and abbreviations, point to sources for business case studies, and identify key economic indicators, among other helpful topics.

Phelps, Marcy. 2011. *Research on Main Street: Using the Web to Find Local Business and Market Information.* Medford, NJ: CyberAge Books.
This general guide presents a straightforward introduction to finding information on local businesses and includes some sample questions and answers. Strategies such as interviewing, and sources, including many free websites, are presented for finding information on demographics, economics, companies, people, and issues.

Ross, Celia. 2013. *Making Sense of Business Reference: A Guide for Librarians and Other Research Professionals.* Chicago: ALA Editions.
This book attempts to demystify the process of business reference and is described by the author as "part business reference source guide, part business reference therapy." General business reference strategies and sources are covered as well as those useful in company research, industry research, investment research, consumer and market research, business statistics, international business, and

small business. An appendix includes a collection of "stumpers" that feature business reference questions and sample strategies for answering them.

Wasserman, Paul, Verne Thompson, and Virgil Burton III, eds. 2015. *Encyclopedia of Business Information Sources*, 32nd ed. Farmington Hills, MI: Gale Cengage Learning.

This annual publication presents a wide variety of terms and topics such as adhesives, affluent market, and baking industry, all arranged alphabetically. Each entry points to relevant abstract and indexing sources, directories, ratio sources, handbooks, databases, periodicals, research centers, trade associations, and more. Note that this title is available through Gale Cengage Learning's *Small Business Resource Center.*

Chapter 26

Health and Medicine Sources

Maura Sostack

INTRODUCTION

It would be difficult to find someone who has not, at some point during her lifetime, sought out medical or wellness information. Health talk is everywhere. Consider the fact that media outlets employ health news journalists (Association of Health Care Journalists 2015), a number of who are physician reporters (Linden 2010). In late 2014, a simple *Google* phrase search for "consumer health information" produced 404,000 hits. The "Social Life of Health Information" research findings reveal that individuals not only seek health information online, but post their medical conditions via Twitter tweets, Facebook, and blogs as well (Fox 2011). Physicians, nurses, pharmacists, and other healthcare providers all need access to up-to-date medical information to care for their patients (Del Fiol, Workman, and Gorman 2014), while biomedical researchers rely heavily on bibliographic databases, such as *MEDLINE*, to inform their work (Niu 2010; Wessel, Tannery, and Epstein 2006).

This chapter provides an introduction to reference sources for questions related to health and medicine. It begins with brief descriptions of medical terminology, the hidden problem of health literacy, and allied health, nursing, and medical education, licensure, and credentialing. The chapter then looks at five discrete use cases for medical and health information after which evaluation and collection development methods are described. Sources are explained and search strategies provided to acquaint librarians with varying patron-dependent approaches to answering a health- or medical-related query.

MEDICAL TERMINOLOGY

Librarians providing health or medical reference services in a public library or a hospital-based patient resources center may encounter questions like the following during a reference interview:

- "I find it difficult to make a fist and my hands are very stiff lately. My doctor told me I have osteoarthritis."
- "My doctor prescribed a drug to help with my arthritis pain. On the prescription note, he wrote 'take this medicine bid.'"
- "I just watched the movie *Pride of the Yankees*, and now I see where the term Lou Gehrig's disease comes from."
- "My sister has smoked four packs of cigarettes a day for the last 40 years and was recently told she has developed COPD."

During surgical rounds, a hospital-based clinical librarian might be asked the following by the attending surgeon:

- "I need all the evidence-based information you can find me about transoral robotic surgery versus open procedures for a partial glossectomy."

Medicine, like all professions, has its own language. For the uninitiated, medical terminology can be confusing and even intimidating. However, it can help to recognize that medical vocabulary includes terms built from Greek and Latin word parts. The four-word parts are:

- *Root*: Core or fundamental meaning of a word.
- *Prefix*: Attached to the beginning of the word root and provides additional information.
- *Suffix*: Attached to the end of the word and provides additional information.
- *Combining vowel*: Usually the letter O and placed between two word roots or the root and suffix.

Thus, the word "osteoarthritis" could be deconstructed:

- *Oste*: Is of Greek derivation and means "bone."
- *Arth*: Is a word root meaning "joint."
- *O*: Is the combining vowel.
- *itis*: Is a suffix meaning "inflammation."

Therefore, "osteoarthritis" means "inflammation of the bone and joint." The word "glossectomy" is from the root word "gloss," which is of Greek derivation and means "tongue," and the suffix "ectomy," which means excision or removal. "Glossectomy" is the surgical removal of the tongue.

Not all medical vocabulary is built from Greek or Latin word parts. Medical eponyms are the names of individuals, places, or things. "Lou Gehrig's disease" is the eponym for the medical term "amyotrophic lateral sclerosis." Medical acronyms are formed from the first letter of several words. "COPD" is the acronym for the medical term "chronic obstructive pulmonary disease." In some cases, medical abbreviations are shortened forms of a word or phrase. "BID" means twice a day, from the Latin *bis in die*.

Understanding these common origins of medical terminology can help librarians negotiate the reference interview and search for health information. Both Barbara Cohen's *Medical Terminology: An Illustrated Guide* (2013) and Danielle LaFleur and Myrna LaFleur-Brooks' *Basic Medical Language* (2013) offer an informative overview. Librarians who provide a high volume of health and medical reference services, particularly those in medical libraries, may find it helpful to enroll in a medical terminology course.[1] A number of free Web-based medical terminology resources include medical acronyms, eponyms, abbreviations, and, to assist with pronunciation, talking dictionaries.

HEALTH LITERACY

The Institute of Medicine (IOM) defines health literacy as "the degree to which individuals have the capacity to obtain, process, and understand basic health information and services needed to make appropriate health decisions" (2004, 2). However, 90 million U.S. adults cannot accurately and consistently locate, match, and integrate information from newspapers, advertisements, or forms ("Adult Literacy" 1993). Linda Murphy-Knoll writes, "Low health literacy is so common in America that it puts at risk countless numbers of patients who cannot comprehend the information required to seek or receive quality healthcare" (2007, 205). Population-based survey findings for both adult and health literacy research have shown that population groups considered to be at risk—age of 65 and older ("Quick Guide" 2007), individuals who have not completed high school, and minority populations—are more likely to have health literacy challenges. Even highly educated individuals have difficulty understanding admission forms, discharge instructions, and medication regimes. Generally speaking, the majority of health information is written at an 8th- through 11th-grade reading levels. And when emotions run high, as they do when a patient or caregiver is dealing with illness, these materials can be difficult to decipher. Box 26.1 provides additional information about health literacy.

Some information providers specialize in easy-to-understand medical information. "Easy-to-Read" is a subset of *MedlinePlus*. Free to all, this great resource provides access to consumer health resources on a wide variety of topics written

Box 26.1 Activity: Understanding Health Literacy

To better understand the scope of the problem of limited health literacy, watch "Health Literacy and Patient Safety: Help Patients Understand," a 23-minute video produced by the American Medical Association Foundation (https://www.youtube.com/watch?v=cGtTZ_vxjyA).

Questions for Reflection and Discussion:

1. For patients who lack health literacy skills, what problems do they encounter?
2. When helping patrons who are seeking health information, what can librarians do to ensure the patron can read and understand the information?

at second-, fifth-, and eighth-grade readings levels. The Plain Language Action and Information Network is a group of U.S. federal employees from various agencies who support the use of clear communication in government writing. Their *Improving Health Literacy* Web page provides information and links to health literacy resources. The National Patient Safety Foundation's *Ask Me 3* educational program was designed to help improve communication between patients and their healthcare providers. *Ask Me 3* refers to three questions every patient should ask their healthcare provider:

1. What is my main problem?
2. What do I need to do?
3. Why is it important for me to do this?

The Agency for Healthcare Research & Quality (AHRQ), part of the U.S. Department of Health & Human Services, has developed a list of questions patients should ask prior to, during, and after seeing their healthcare provider. In addition, a free interactive "Question Builder" tool is available to help patients to prepare for healthcare appointments. The pharmaceutical giant Pfizer has partnered with a number of national organizations and taken the lead in developing easy-to-read consumer health resources. The Taubman Health Sciences Library at the University of Michigan created an interactive *Plain Language Medical Dictionary*. Users can search or browse for a term, and its plain language equivalent appears.

MEDICAL, NURSING, AND ALLIED HEALTH PROFESSIONALS

There are more than 100 different healthcare jobs and careers including doctors, nurses, medical assistants, aides, physician assistants, and dietitians, and all have their own educational, licensing, and credentialing requirements. This section serves as an introduction to the health professions, with a focus on medical and nursing education. Librarians working in a public library setting may field reference questions from patrons who are interested in pursuing a medical or nursing career. For librarians who work in hospital-based or academic medical center libraries, the information on accreditation, education, and credentialing will add to the understanding of those they serve.

Types of Medical Professionals

When answering questions about health and medicine, it can be helpful to understand the type of medical professionals that work within the healthcare system.

- *Allied health professionals*: A diverse group of healthcare providers that include occupational, physical, and respiratory therapists; speech and language pathologists; dietitians, radiology technicians, and laboratory personnel.
- *Clinician*: A health professional who works directly with patients. Clinicians are distinguished from other types of health workers, such as those involved in biomedical laboratory work.
- *Dentist*: An individual educated, trained, and licensed to practice dentistry and/or oral surgery. Dentists treat diseases and conditions of the teeth and gums.

In the United States, a dentist's post-nominal credential is doctor of medicine in dentistry (DMD).

- *Nurse*: An individual educated, trained, and licensed to practice nursing. In the United States, a nurse's post-nominal credential is either registered nurse (RN) or licensed practical nurse.
- *Pharmacist*: An individual educated, trained, and licensed to dispense prescription medications. In the United States, a pharmacist's post-nominal credential is doctor of pharmacy (Pharm.D.).
- *Physician*: An individual educated, trained, and licensed to practice medicine. In the United States, a physician's post-nominal credentials are either medical doctor (MD) or doctor of osteopathy (DO). Many refer to physicians as doctors, that is, "My doctor prescribed an antibiotic for my strep throat." MDs practice allopathic medicine, which emphasizes the treatment of diseases and illness through the use of drugs and medications. Allopathic medicine tends to focus on a specific body part and is concerned with the process of disease. DOs practice osteopathic medicine, which emphasizes preventive care, the integration of the body's systems, and allowing the body to heal without overusing medications.
- *Podiatrist*: An individual educated, trained, and licensed to practice podiatric medicine. Podiatrists diagnosis, treat, and prevent foot disorders. In the United States, a podiatrist's post-nominal credential is doctor of podiatric medicine (DPM).
- *Resident*: Is a physician in training. The individual has graduated from medical school with a DO or MD degree and is employed, usually at a community or academic health system, in post-medical school training. The residency period lasts three to seven years depending on the type of medical specialty training.

Accreditation

Accreditation is proof that a university, college, school, or program has met minimum educational standards as set forth by a recognized reviewing agency. These agencies develop criteria and conduct periodic onsite evaluations to determine whether a program meets required standards. In health-related professions, accreditation standards are developed by practicing healthcare professionals and reflect what a person needs to know to be successful within that health profession.

Nurses

There are three educational roads an individual can travel to become a nurse:

1. Hospital-based RN diploma program.
2. Community college or university associate's program whereby an individual earns an associate's degree in nursing (ADN).
3. University baccalaureate program whereby an individual earns a bachelor of science in nursing degree (BSN).

The Commission on Collegiate Nursing Education is the accrediting agency for baccalaureate, graduate, and residency programs in nursing. The Accreditation Commission for Education in Nursing (ACEN) is responsible for specialized accreditation of practical, diploma (hospital-based), associate, baccalaureate, and master's level programs as well as clinical doctorate and postmaster's certificate programs. The ACEN provides a wonderful resource for librarians: an interactive, Web-based program finder. To assist patrons, librarians can search by state or country and narrow results by program type. The American Association of Colleges of Nursing also provides a list of accredited baccalaureate, master's, doctor of nursing practice, and postgraduate programs.

After successfully completing educational requirements, an individual is required to pass a licensing exam to practice nursing. The National Council for State Boards of Nursing develops and administers the NCLEX-RN licensing examination. Eligibility requirements to sit for the NCLEX-RN licensing examination fall within the purview of the state where an individual wishes to practice nursing. Once licensed, nurses may become certified in specialty practice areas. The American Nurses Credentialing Center offers 12 nurse practitioner, 10 clinical nurse specialist, and 27 specialty certification programs.

Physicians

Medical education programs within the United States that lead to an MD degree are accredited through the Liaison Committee on Medical Education (LCME). The LCME is jointly sponsored by the Association of American Medical Colleges and the American Medical Association. It offers a free list of accredited MD programs in the United States and Canada on its website. The Commission on Osteopathic College Accreditation of the American Osteopathic Association (AOA) accredits osteopathic medical schools, and a list of U.S.-based schools can be found on the American Association of Colleges of Osteopathic Medicine's website.

After successfully completing four years of medical school training, individuals must complete post-medical school training, also known as residency. MD residency programs are accredited through the Accreditation Council for Graduate Medical Education (ACGME). This nonprofit organization evaluates and accredits residency programs throughout the United States. Osteopathic residency programs are currently administered and accredited through the AOA and the American Association of Colleges of Osteopathic Medicine. In July 2014, the AOA and the ACGME agreed that AOA-accredited residency training programs will transition to ACGME accreditation. By 2020, all DO and MD residency programs will be administered through a single accreditation system.

After completing medical school and residency training, a physician must obtain a license to practice medicine from the state in which he or she plans to practice. Medical licensure requirements are state specific. The Federation of State Medical Boards is a national nonprofit that represents 70 medical and osteopathic boards in the United States. The National Board of Medical Examiners develops and manages the United States Medical Licensing Examination examinations. The National Board of Osteopathic Medical Examiners administers the NBOME COMLEX-USA examination series.

MDs may become certified in a medical specialty and subspecialty through standards established by 24 American Board of Medical Specialties (ABMS) certifying boards. The ABMS's *Certification Matters* website provides free access to check physician certification. *Board Certified Docs* is a subscription service published by Elsevier. It has been designated by the ABMS as its official display agent and primary source verification of its data. DOs may earn board certification in an osteopathic specialty or subspecialty through the AOA Board Certification program.

USES OF HEALTH AND MEDICAL INFORMATION

Health and medical information can be categorized into five discrete "use cases," each with unique, yet sometimes overlapping, sources. When librarians encounter a health-related question at the reference desk, considering which "use case" the query best matches can help the librarian determine which sources and search strategies to use in the search for information.

1. *Consumer health information*: Users of health and wellness information include patients, someone who receives healthcare services; caregivers, a term reserved for a family member or close friend who cares for individuals who are physically or mentally ill (caregivers usually have no formal clinical training and often are not paid for their services); and the general public.
2. *Patient education materials and discharge instructions at the point-of-care (POC)*:[2] Educating patients at the POC is an essential component of the clinician/patient encounter. Users of these materials include allied health professionals, dentists, nurses, pharmacists, and physicians as well as dental, medical, nursing, and pharmacy students and residents. Patients and their families, along with caregivers, are the recipients. The vast majority of these materials are distributed in print format.
3. *Medical information at the POC*: From physicians keeping a print copy of a differential diagnosis handbook stashed in their white coats, to residents using symptom checker software on their tablets, the availability of referential clinical information at the POC has always been a mainstay of clinical practice. Users include allied health professionals, dentists, nurses, pharmacists, and physicians as well as dental, medical, nursing, and pharmacy students and residents.
4. *Biomedical research information*: Biomedical researchers are individuals who experiment, observe, test, and analyze diseases. They may work at large universities, in private industry, and with state and federal agencies. Researchers most often have postgraduate degrees, and many have dual PhD and MD degrees. Biomedical scientists are individuals employed by hospitals and independent laboratories. Virology, medical microbiology, clinical chemistry, cytology, and histopathology are broad areas of biomedical laboratory work. Both professions require biomedical research information to inform their experimental and clinical work.
5. *Healthcare business, economic, and technology information*: Hospital and health system executives, health economists, and health informaticists are the primary audience for this type of information.

This chapter will provide an introduction to three types of health and medical information: consumer; professional, including both POC and biomedical research sources; and executive, including resources on the business of healthcare and contemporary issues in healthcare.

CONSUMER HEALTH INFORMATION

Pew Research Center findings reveal that 82 percent of Internet users say they have looked online for health information within the past year and 77 percent of these health information seekers say they began their last session using a general search engine such as *Google*, *Bing*, or *Yahoo!* ("Health Fact Sheet" 2015).

Unfortunately, once these information seekers find something that piques their interest, they may not check the source or date of the health information they find. Pew Research also shows that the vast majority of these health information seekers feel overwhelmed and confused by the amount of information they find and frustrated by their inability to find what they were looking for.

With the March 23, 2010, passage of the Patient Protection and Affordable Care Act (P.L. 111–488), colloquially referred to as "Obamacare," there is increased emphasis on patients' active, rather than passive, participation in issues concerning their health status. Yet active, meaningful participation is difficult for the one in five U.S. adults who function at a basic or below basic literacy level (National Assessment of Adult Literacy 2003).

The more-than-65-years-of-age population will constitute almost 20 percent of the total U.S. population by 2030 (U.S. Census Bureau 2010). Six out of ten baby boomers will manage multiple chronic illnesses ("Baby Boomers" 2007) and require access to timely, reliable, and accurate healthcare information to make timely and appropriate healthcare decisions.

Information-seeking behavior by a member of the general public typically looks like this: sitting at a computer terminal in a local public library, a library patron googles the phrase "how do I lower my cholesterol?" and retrieves 35 million results in .55 seconds. The patron scans the page and clicks on the first hit, *WedMD*, and scans the website. Puzzled by the advertisements for cholesterol-lowering medicines that appear on the page, the patron hits the browser back button and clicks the *health.harvard.edu* link. The patron reads the article abstract but must purchase access to read the full text of the article published in the *Harvard Health Letter*. Frustrated, the patron calls over the reference librarian for assistance. At the librarian's disposal are a number of consumer health resources.

Evaluation of Consumer Health Resources

Numerous groups and associations have developed criteria for evaluating consumer health resources. These criteria can guide librarians as they select materials for the collection, including websites that might be linked on a library's Web page. In addition, these criteria can be shared with patrons during the reference interview and in instructional sessions. The list of "20 Questions for Evaluating Consumer Health Information" in Box 26.2 provides a framework to determine the accuracy, authority, objectivity, currency, and coverage of a consumer health website. Box 26.3 provides an opportunity to practice using this framework.

Selection of Consumer Health Resources

Allocated budget dollars, institutional strategic imperatives, and patron needs/requests guide the consumer health collection development process (Spatz 2014). Four additional collection development questions include:

1. How will consumer health information and reference services be provided?
2. Will there be a physical and virtual space, including a website?
3. If there is a physical space, what percentage of budget dollars will be allocated to print vs. online licensed resources?
4. If there is a physical library space with onsite reference, how will it be staffed? For example, are budget dollars allocated to employ a librarian with the Medical Library Association's Consumer Health Information Specialization?

Box 26.2 20 Questions for Evaluating Consumer Health Information

1. What is the URL?
2. Who runs the site?
3. Why was the site created?
4. What do the site creators want from the reader?
5. Who is paying for the site?
6. Are there advertisements on the website?
7. If so, are the advertisements in line with the site's purpose?
8. Does the information on the website favor the site's owner?
9. Is a celebrity used to promote the information on the website (if there is a celebrity endorsement, librarians should check whether the celebrity has medical credentials)?
10. Is the health and wellness information posted on the website reviewed by medical experts?
11. Where did the information come from?
12. Are there bibliographic references provided?
13. Does the information on the site make unbelievable claims?
14. Is the site up to date?
15. Is there a way to contact the site's owner through its website?
16. Is there a privacy statement?
17. Do users need to register to access information?
18. Do users need to pay to access information?
19. If so, does the site require users register and store debit or credit card information?
20. What happens to personal information if the user registers?

Box 26.3 Activity: Evaluate a Consumer Health Website

Using the 20 questions in Box 26.2, evaluate one or more of the following consumer health websites:

- GenF20Plus (http://www.genf20.com)
- Harvard Health (http://www.health.harvard.edu/)
- Healthy People 2020 (http://www.healthypeople.gov/)
- Healthyroads (https://www.healthyroads.com/)
- Kripalu Center for Yoga & Health (http://kripalu.org/)
- Suzanne Somers (http://www.suzannesomers.com/)
- U.S. Anti-Doping Agency (http://www.usada.org/)

Questions for Reflection and Discussion:

1. During your evaluation process, did you find the website provided enough information that you were able to answer all 20 questions?
2. If you could not answer all 20 questions, were the missing pieces of information problematic enough that you could not recommend the site?

Three additional questions hospital or academic medical center librarians need to consider are:

1. Will the clinical library be open to patients, caregivers, and/or the general public?
2. Has the hospital or academic medical center allocated space and resources for a patient and consumer health library, separate and distinct from its clinical library space?
3. For-profit companies such as Elsevier, Krames, and Milner Fenwick license patient education materials. Have budget dollars to license patient education resources been allocated to the library or another hospital or academic medical center department?

It is important for librarians to understand the difference between patient education and consumer health resources. Patient education materials are given to a patient at the POC by a nurse or medical assistant and are part of a patient's discharge instructions. Patient education materials are licensed resources and can be embedded within an electronic medical record (EMR). EBSCO, Elsevier, Krames, and Wolters Kluwer are four of the major information software and services vendors that publish and license these materials. Consumer health materials do not contain discharge instructions, and numerous high-quality print and Web-based materials are available free of charge.

Core title and resource lists, developed by experts in consumer health collection development, are available from the Medical Library Association's Consumer and Patient Health Information Section (CAPHIS). These lists can be used by reference librarians to identify print and electronic titles for the collection. Librarian selectors for *Doody's Core Titles in the Health Sciences*, discussed later in this chapter, also evaluate and rate consumer health titles.

Important General Resources

MedlinePlus is universally considered by consumer health, hospital, and academic medical librarians as the "gold standard" for consumer health information. *MedlinePlus* is a product of the National Institutes of Health and is maintained by the National Library of Medicine (NLM). *MedlinePlus* does not accept third-party advertising, and content is available free of charge.

From the *MedlinePlus* home page, information is arranged into three main categories:

1. *Health Topics*: More than 950 topics are searchable by body systems; disorders and conditions; diagnosis and therapy; demographic groups; and health and wellness issues.
2. *Drugs & Supplements*: Users can search the A to Z list for prescription and over-the-counter medications by generic or brand name. Another A to Z list provides information about herbs and dietary supplements. Drug information is provided by the American Society of Health-System Pharmacists.
3. *Videos & Tools*: This is a very interesting and entertaining part of *MedlinePlus*. Users can view animated videos about anatomy and physiology, as well as prerecorded Webcasts of surgery videos. The interactive "Health Check Tools" section contains risk calculators, questionnaires, and health assessment quizzes. The "Games" section provides links to third-party interactive health games.

MedlinePlus provides access to the *A.D.A.M. Medical Encyclopedia*, which includes more than 4,000 articles about symptoms, diseases, and surgical procedures. This encyclopedia also contains medical photographs and illustrations. Each entry is reviewed by A.D.A.M.'s content review board and contains references, the author's credentials, and the date of the last update.

Of particular interest to reference librarians, at the bottom of the home page are links to "Organizations" and "Directories." As librarians know, for every topic or subject, there usually is a journal, a newsletter, and an organizational entity associated with that topic. Healthcare is no different. The "Organizations" link provides an A to Z list of organizations that provide health information such as the Alzheimer's Association, the American Academy of Cosmetic Dentistry, and the ALS Association. The "Directories" link has resources to find health professionals, services, and facilities as well as consumer health libraries and information centers, searchable by state or Canadian province.

Polypharmacy is defined as the use of four or more medications. The more medications taken, the greater chance of a medication error. Pills look alike or have a similar shape or color, or one forgets what that "little pink pill" is actually for. An important aspect of reference work is to point patrons to the right resource to help them visually identify medications. A number of websites, including *Drugs.com*, *RxList*, *Pill Identifier* from the AARP, and NLM *Pillbox*, provide free access to interactive pill identifier "wizards."

As mentioned previously, the more-than-65-years-of-age population will constitute almost 20 percent of the total U.S. population by 2030 and 6 out of 10 baby boomers will be managing multiple chronic illnesses. In the first of a series of consumer healthcare articles entitled "Six Killers," the *New York Times* (2007) identified the "leading causes of illness and death in the United States today: heart disease, cancer, stroke, chronic obstructive pulmonary disease, diabetes and Alzheimer's disease, in that order." Because these diseases tend to be progressive and cause health problems later in life, librarians need to have reliable health resources targeted for senior health issues.

One of the best online resources for the 65 years and older population is the National Institutes of Health's *NIH Senior Health* website. It was developed by the National Institute on Aging and the NLM. The American Geriatrics Society provides both expert and independent reviews of some materials found on the site. Senior-friendly features include dark font against a light background, large sans-serif font, and the ability to change the screen contrast and enlarge the font. The primary senior health topics include:

1. Bones and Joints
2. Cancer
3. Diseases and Conditions
4. Healthy Aging
5. Heart and Lungs
6. Memory and Mental Health
7. Treatment and Therapies
8. Vision and Hearing

Senior-specific health topics can also be searched using the A to Z list found on the site's home page. Box 26.4 provides an opportunity to explore *NIH Senior Health* in more depth.

Box 26.4 Activity: Senior Health Topics Research

You were recently hired by a large public library system to serve as the system's Consumer Health Reference librarian. A library patron tells you her sister was recently diagnosed with early onset Alzheimer's disease and her mother suffers from chronic obstructive pulmonary disease (COPD). She wants more information about both disease processes. You find her a comfortable seat near you and decide to quickly check *NIH Senior Health*.

Questions for Reflection and Discussion:

1. As you read through the Alzheimer's disease and COPD information on *NIH Senior Health*, what additional questions might you ask the patron when you resume the reference interview?
2. Was there information you found that you might not want to share immediately with your patron until you have conducted a more thorough reference interview?

The American Board of Internal Medicine Foundation created the Choosing Wisely program as a conversation starter between clinicians and patients regarding the overuse of medical tests and procedures. More than 300 recommendations can be found on the *Choosing Wisely* website.

PubMed Health is a service of the NLM and provides plain language summaries and free full-text access to a select number of systematic reviews from the Cochrane Collaboration, AHRQ, the National Cancer Institute, and the National Institute for Health and Care Excellence (NICE) guideline program.

The CAPHIS Top 100 Committee reviews consumer health websites used to produce their highly regarded *Top 100 List: Health Websites You Can Trust.* The Top 100 List is divided into 10 categories and can be used to locate additional sites for reliable consumer-oriented medical information.

1. General Health
2. Women's Health
3. Men's Health
4. Parenting & Kids
5. Senior Health
6. Specific Health
7. For Health Professionals
8. Drug Information Resources
9. Complementary & Alternative
10. Other Useful Health Sites

Providing Consumer Health Reference Services

Public librarians are on the front lines of consumer health reference work. The vast majority of public library patrons are looking for information about a disease, condition, or treatment. Quite often, public librarians are caught in the middle of patient/doctor miscommunication; therefore, a thorough health reference interview is key to providing timely and accurate information. Barriers and challenges include:

- Health issues evoke strong, complicated emotional responses. Patrons may be upset, confused, and somewhat angry.
- Patrons may have hidden literacy problems.
- Patrons ask questions not for themselves, but for a friend or relative. The librarian is now dealing with second-hand information.
- The librarian may be hesitant to ask probing personal questions.

Chapter 3 provides guidance for the reference interview, including in situations where the patron may be asking for a friend or family member. Additional tips for the health reference interview include:

- If possible, move the conversation to a private space within the library.
- Practice active listening skills.
- Be mindful of clues to possible low literacy problems.
- If low literacy is suspected, gently ask: "How happy are you with the way you read?"
- Never interpret medical information. Make sure the patron understands you are not a healthcare provider, but a provider of healthcare information.
- At no time should a librarian interpret the information found or make any direct or indirect inferences regarding diagnosis.
- Use both verbal and printed disclaimer statements. For example, "Materials in ABC Library represent the opinions of the authors and are intended to complement, not substitute for the advice of your healthcare professional."

The Reference and User Services Association's "Health and Medical Reference Guidelines" also provide advice for the reference interview.

PROFESSIONAL MEDICAL INFORMATION

Healthcare providers need reliable, accurate, and up-to-date clinical information at the POC. Characteristic information-seeking behavior by a hospital-based clinician may look like this:

- A pulmonologist (a physician who specializes in lung diseases) sends a text message to the hospital-based librarian and asks: "I am teaching third year medical students about various drug therapies for asthma. Can you do a *MEDLINE* search for review articles going back five years?"
- During daily patient care rounds in the hospital's intensive care unit, an intensivist, a physician who specializes in critical care medicine, asks the clinical librarian to find evidence-based practice guidelines discussing the use of beta lactam antibiotics for the treatment of severe sepsis.

Biomedical researchers also have sophisticated medical information needs. For example, a researcher with a PhD in epidemiology may request a comprehensive literature search on published studies discussing the use of chest X-rays to affirm an asthma diagnosis in adults. This is a comprehensive, highly sensitive literature search for quality studies to answer the narrowly focused question, "What is the added value of chest radiography to affirm an asthma diagnosis in adults?" Biomedical researchers use information gleaned from literature searches to inform their own research and to create clinical practice guidelines (CPGs) for clinicians to use at the POC.

Medical librarians have at their disposal a number of resources to answer clinical and research questions. Some of these are electronic POC resources, while others are biomedical bibliographic databases.

Evaluation and Selection of Medical Resources

For almost four decades, the Brandon/Hill lists were the most widely used collection development instruments utilized by hospital-based medical and nursing school librarians. Librarians Alfred Brandon and Dorothy Hill developed three lists:

1. Brandon/Hill Selected List of Print Books and Journals for the Small Medical Library, published from 1965 through 2004 (Hill and Stickell 2001)
2. Brandon/Hill Selected List of Print Nursing Books and Journals, published from 1979 through 2004 (Hill and Stickell 2002)
3. Brandon/Hill Selected List of Print Books and Journals in Allied Health, published from 1984 through 2004 (Hill and Stickell 2003)

One drawback of the Brandon/Hill lists, as all libraries transitioned to a mixed print and electronic resources model, was they listed only print resources. However, although publication of the lists ceased over a decade ago, many hospital-based librarians still use the lists as a guide in their collection development process.

When the Brandon/Hill lists ceased publication, the void was filled by *Doody's Core Titles in the Health Sciences (DCT)* from Doody Enterprises (Fischer 2005). Basic and premium versions of DCT are available on an annual subscription basis. The basic edition includes a title list organized by subject area for 121 healthcare specialties and the ability to search and filter results. Entries include title scores and "Essential Purchase" recommendations made by librarian selectors. The premium edition includes all the features of the basic edition, plus the full reviews and star ratings of all titles in Doody's Review Service. Library selectors score each title on five collection development criteria:

1. Authoritativeness of author and publisher
2. Scope and coverage of subject matter
3. Quality of content including timeliness
4. Usefulness and purpose
5. Value for the money

Founded in 1946, Rittenhouse Book Distributors provides print and electronic books in medicine, nursing, and allied health. Librarians can access the "Browse Categories" section of the Rittenhouse website and filter results by "Display Doody Star Rated Titles Only." If budgets are tight, this free service can be used as part of a librarian's collection development process.

The World Health Organization's Regional Office for the Eastern Mediterranean publishes the *List of Basic Sources in English for a Medical Faculty Library*, which can be used to identify core titles in a variety of subject areas. *Essential Nursing Resources* (*ENR*) is a product of the Interagency Council on Information Resources in Nursing. Hospital and academic medical center librarians find the *ENR* a useful nursing collection development resource. In addition, the Nursing and Allied Health Resources Section (NAHRS) of the Medical Library Association published the "NAHRS 2012 Selected List of Nursing Journals," which can be used to guide selection.

Databases

MEDLINE is internationally recognized as *the* database for biomedical research. A product of the NLM, *MEDLINE* contains more than 21 million references to journal articles in the life sciences with a focus on biomedicine. *MEDLINE* records are indexed using NLM's Medical Subject Headings (MeSH). More than 5,600 journals, in more than 40 languages, are indexed in *MEDLINE*. A number of *MEDLINE* citations contain links to free full-text articles archived in *PubMed Central* and other sites like *Biomed Central*, making *MEDLINE* a useful resource for even small libraries with limited journal holdings. If articles are not available freely, users can link from a *MEDLINE* citation to the publisher or other full-text provider.

NLM licenses *MEDLINE* to a number of database providers and publishers including:

- Elsevier, as a subset of the *Embase* database
- EBSCO, searchable via the EBSCOhost platform
- OVID Technologies, searchable via the OVID platform
- Thomson Reuters, searchable via Web of Science platform

In addition, since 1997, *MEDLINE* has been available free of charge via the *PubMed* platform. Medical and large academic libraries may prefer to offer *MEDLINE* through one of the earlier-mentioned commercial interfaces that can integrate *MEDLINE* with other databases and the library's eJournal holdings; however, the free *PubMed* version offers a robust search interface and is an excellent option for libraries with limited budgets. Box 26.5 provides practice searching *PubMed*.

Box 26.5 Activity: Searching *PubMed*

Remember our pulmonologist, preparing to give a lecture to third-year medical students about drug therapies for asthma? The following is a step-by-step narrative review search strategy:

Step 1: Go to the *PubMed* home page (http://www.ncbi.nlm.nih.gov/pubmed).
Step 2: Click on the MeSH Database link.
Step 3: Type the word *Asthma* in the MeSH Search box.
Step 4: Click the Search button.
Step 5: The first of the 11 asthma-related MeSH terms is called *Asthma*. Click on the *Asthma* MeSH term link.

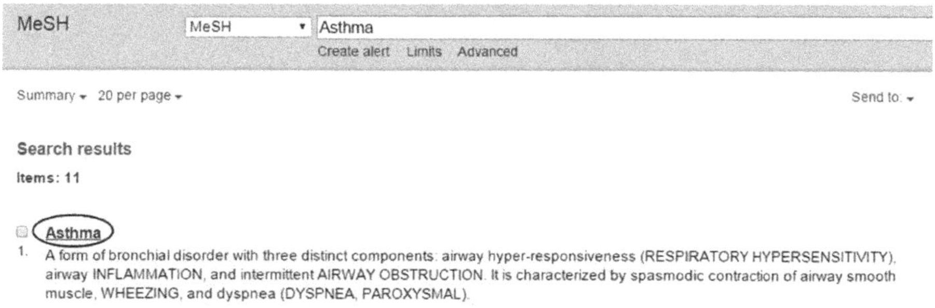

FIGURE 26.1 Asthma MeSH Term Link

Our physician is interested in journal articles where drug therapies for asthma is the major topic of the article. We see that there are a number of MeSH subheadings associated with the MeSH term "Asthma."

Step 6: Select the "drug therapy" subheading. We do not want a lot of "noise" so we further refine our search.
Step 7: Select "Restrict to MeSH Major topic."
Step 8: Select "Do not include MeSH terms found below this term in the MeSH hierarchy."

We have now made our selections and are ready to search *PubMed*.

Step 9: Click the "Add to search builder" button.
Step 10: Click the "Search *PubMed*" button.

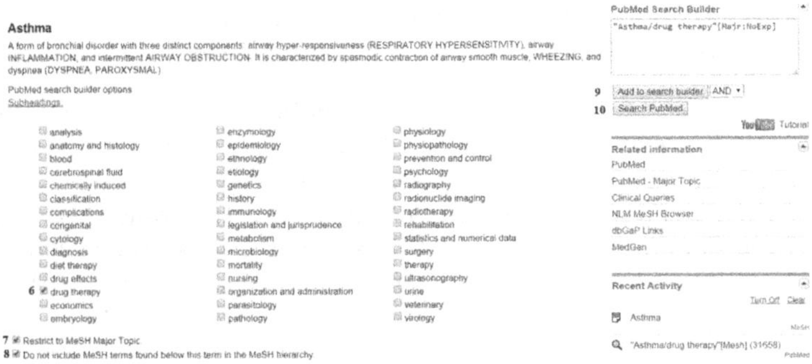

FIGURE 26.2 Applying search limits in *PubMed*

After executing our *PubMed* search, we can apply additional limits. Our physician is interested in review articles published within the past five years in core clinical journals.

Step 11: Under "Article Types," click the "Review" link.
Step 12: Under "Publication Dates," click the "5 years" link.
Step 13: Under "Journal Categories," click the "Core clinical journals" link.

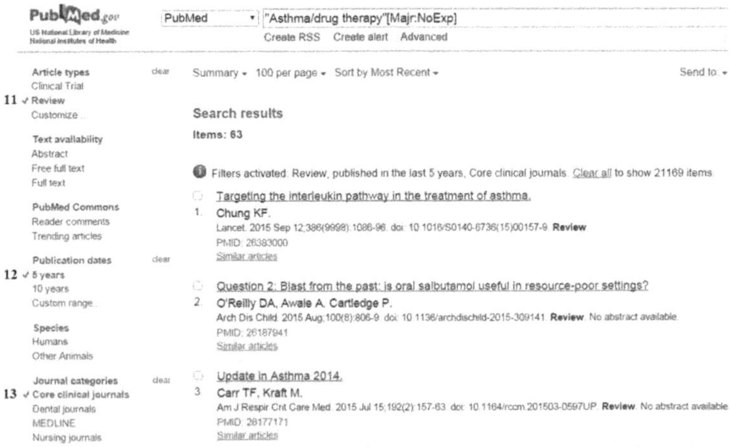

FIGURE 26.3 Filtering search results in PubMed

It is completely acceptable to use preset database limits as part of a search strategy to find background information on a disease process.

With almost 4 million citations and 5,000 journals indexed dating back to the late 1930s, the *Cumulative Index to Nursing and Allied Health Literature* (CINAHL) is widely regarded as the definitive nursing and allied health database. It includes citations to journal articles, books and book chapters, conference proceedings, and practice guidelines. In addition, for those seeking nursing literature, *MEDLINE* indexes more than 760 nursing journals, and searches can be limited to the nursing journals subset.

Point-of-Care Resources

For clinicians at the POC, biomedical researchers, and senior executives, also known as C-suite executives,[3] the phrase "find me the evidence" works its way into almost every health and medical-related reference interview and request. The need to access the best available evidence quickly at the POC, along with the rapid adoption of mobile technology by clinicians, spawned a new type of healthcare electronic resource information tool: the clinical decision support eResource, also known as a POC eResource (the differences between databases and POC eResources are summarized in Table 26.1). These clinical support eResources offer digested summaries, many of which are evidence based, on clinically relevant healthcare topics. Instead of clinicians doing their own primary research, information services companies, publishers, and nonprofits are doing it for them and writing a research summary. This summary informs how a clinician makes clinically sound decisions at the POC.

Numerous well-regarded clinical decision support eResources are available. Although these require a subscription and are most likely to be found in a

TABLE 26.1 At a Glance: Databases vs. POC Resources

	Databases	POC Resources
Content	Citations, abstracts, and full text for journal articles and conference proceedings.	Summaries or structured evidence reviews on a clinical topic.
Purpose	Conduct topic-specific, in-depth research.	Assist clinicians in making patient care decisions.
Role in healthcare	In-depth research results sourced to write systematic reviews and meta-analyses that, in turn, inform clinical practice guideline development.	Systematic reviews and clinical practice guidelines are the building blocks used to produce digested summaries available through online POC resources.
Search options	Boolean and proximity operators, truncation, controlled vocabulary, field searching, hedge limits.	Simple search box employing natural language search techniques.

medical library or large academic library supporting a medical school, some provide patient-appropriate information or limited free content that may be of interest to patrons in all types of libraries.

ACP Smart Medicine was developed by the American College of Physicians and is the only clinical decision support tool developed by a professional society, rather than a for-profit information services or publishing company. Content is developed specifically for internal medicine practitioners. An EBSCO product, *DynaMed*, is a clinical decision support tool that provides clinicians access to more than 3,200 topics and practice guidelines at the POC. Owned by Wiley-Blackwell, *Essential Evidence Plus* is an evidence-based POC clinical decision support tool providing access to more than 13,000 topics, guidelines, and diagnostic calculators.

JAMAevidence, an American Medical Association product licensed through McGraw-Hill, is a portal to evidence summaries and clinical decision-making tools and calculators. *TRIP Database* (TRIP originally stood for Turning Research into Practice) is a clinical search engine that simultaneously searches evidence-based sources of systematic reviews, practice guidelines, and critically appraised topics and articles. And finally, *UpToDate* is an evidence-based clinical decision support resource. Research is synthesized with evidence-based recommendations for use at the POC.

For nurses, there are two well-regarded POC tools: Elsevier's *Mosby's Nursing Consult*, a portal to evidence-based nursing resources and drug monographs, and EBSCO's *Nursing Reference Center*, an evidence-based resource that includes care sheets and POC drug information.

Evidence-Based Medicine

What is evidence-based medicine (EBM)? In a 1996 editorial published in the journal *BMJ*, David Sackett, one of the "godfathers" of the evidence-based medicine movement, described EBM as ". . . the conscientious, explicit, and judicious use of current best evidence in making decisions about the care of individual patients. The practice of evidence based medicine means integrating individual clinical expertise with the best available external clinical evidence from systematic research" (1996, 71). Sackett's definition continues, "Increased expertise is reflected in many ways, but especially in more effective and efficient diagnosis and in the more thoughtful identification and compassionate use of individual patients' predicaments, rights, and preferences" (see Figure 26.4).

Sackett makes reference to individual patients and individual "clinical expertise." Two decades later, this definition of EBM has changed, and the scope broadened to include the use of evidence in guidelines and policies that apply to entire populations. The phrase "is there any evidence to show . . ." or "what does the evidence say . . ." permeates every decision-making level of any healthcare system.

So where do librarians go to find the evidence? EBM research begins with a well-built clinical question that contains four distinct components, referred to as PICO:

- **P** = Patient(s) or population
- **I** = Intervention
- **C** = Comparator
- **O** = Outcome

FIGURE 26.4 Evidence-based medicine triad

Librarians and biomedical researchers collaborate to write PICO questions, harvest search terms, select databases to search, and choose date parameters. Librarians search bibliographic biomedical databases and cull information from research organizations, government agencies, and clinical trial data repositories. Citation results are imported into bibliographic software programs like *EndNote* or *Mendeley* for evaluation by researchers. Figure 26.5 provides an example of a PICO question using the example of a biomedical researcher seeking information about the use of a chest X-ray to confirm a diagnosis of asthma.

A number of organizations work to promote EBM and provide evidence-based reviews. As noted earlier, the AHRQ is part of the U.S. Department of Health & Human Services. Its mission is to "produce evidence to make health care safer, higher quality, more accessible, equitable, and affordable, and . . . to make sure that the evidence is understood and used" ("About AHRQ" 2015). Since 1997, AHRQ has awarded five-year contracts to healthcare research institutions in the United States and Canada to function as evidence-based practice centers (EPCs). As of November 2014, there were 11 AHRQ-designated EPCs. Researchers at EPCs search biomedical literature on a variety of clinical and healthcare services topics and publish their research results in evidence reports. These evidence reports, among other things, inform CPGs. They can be accessed via the *Evidence Reports* section of the AHRQ website.

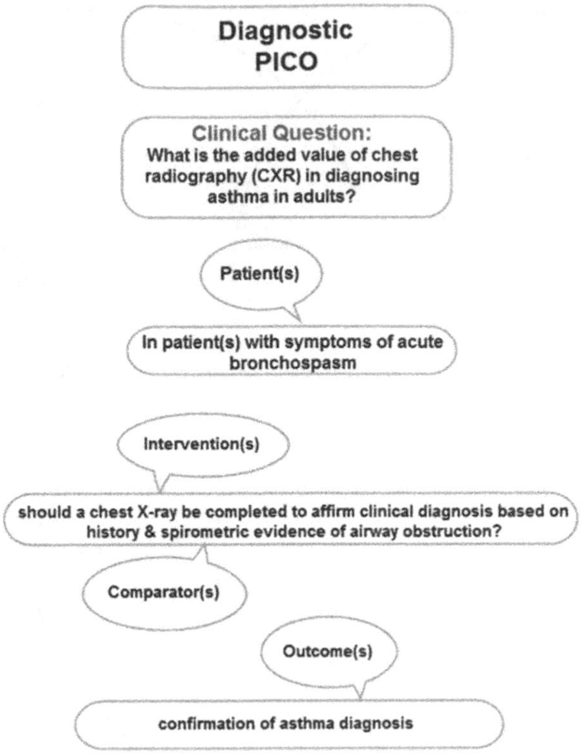

FIGURE 26.5 Example of a PICO search

Founded as a not-for-profit in 1993, the Cochrane Collaboration is international in scope with a mission to "promote evidence-informed health decision-making by producing high-quality, relevant, accessible systematic reviews and other synthesized research evidence" ("About Us" 2015). Members of Cochrane Review Groups research and publish systematic reviews on specific clinical topics. These systematic reviews are used by clinicians worldwide, at the POC, to make evidence-based treatment decisions. Of particular interest to librarians is the Collaboration's Information Retrieval Methods Group (IRMG). The IRMG recognizes that "a broad and sensitive literature search to retrieve the maximum number of relevant published and unpublished studies is a crucial component of an unbiased systematic review" ("Information Retrieval Methods Group" 2015). Cochrane reviews can be accessed through the *Cochrane Database of Systematic Reviews*, as part of the *Cochrane Library* from Wiley.

Joanna Briggs Institute (JBI) is an international not-for-profit division of the School of Translational Science at the University of Adelaide, South Australia. The institute conducts research on health-related topics, with a focus on nursing practice, and publishes its results in journals *JBI Systematic Reviews and Implementation Reports*, *Evidence Summaries*, and *Best Practice Information Sheets* (BPIS), available as part of the *Joanna Briggs Institute EBP Database* from Ovid.

Located in Hamilton, Canada, the Health Information Research Unit (HIRU) is a component of the Clinical Epidemiology and Biostatistics Department at McMaster University. HIRU's mission is to "improve the effectiveness and efficiency of health care by providing innovative evidence-based information products and systems to health professionals, patients, policy makers, and the public" (Health Information Research Unit 2015). One of their products, *McMaster Plus*, is a database created by the McMaster Health Knowledge Refinery. Studies published in journal articles are selected and indexed using a critical appraisal process. Studies are then rated by clinicians who work at the POC using McMaster's Online Rating of Evidence system. PLUS ratings are used to help select content published in POC electronic resources such as *BMJ Clinical Evidence* and *DynaMed*.

Clinical Practice Guidelines

Evidence-based research findings inform the writing and publication of CPGs. Many healthcare organizations author their own CPGs, but the retrieval process, via medical society and association websites, is very often time consuming. What was needed was a one-stop shopping experience. AHRQ established, in partnership with the American Medical Association, the National Guideline Clearinghouse. The goal of the clearinghouse is to make it easier for clinicians and patients to access, free of charge, evidence-based CPGs. The Clearinghouse updates its Web-based content on a weekly basis.

With offices in London and Manchester, England, the NICE guidelines are evidence-based POC recommendations for healthcare provided in England. Most NICE guidelines are available free of charge. *DynaMed*, EBSCO's subscription-based POC clinical decision support resource, does an excellent job gathering and organizing CPGs by topic. Created in 1984, and supported by the AHRQ, the U.S. Preventive Services Task Force (USPSTF) comprises experts in preventive and evidence-based medicine. The task force makes evidence-based recommendations about preventive services such as screenings, counseling services, and preventive medications. The *USPSTF Information for Consumers* provides evidence-based recommendations for patients and caregivers with information on ways to prevent illness and stay healthy.

Clinical Trial Repositories

A clinical trial is a research study designed to evaluate new drugs or treatments, prevention measures, diagnostic tests, and prognostic tools. Retrieval of results reported in trial repositories and republished in journal articles, conference abstracts, or posters is an integral part of an EBM literature search. *ClinicalTrials.gov* is a global repository of clinical trial studies, limited to human participants. The U.S. National Institutes of Health maintains this trial repository.

Database Hedges

Regardless of preferred searching platform, *MEDLINE* is the bibliographic database of choice to begin an EBM literature search. High recall is the end goal, and to achieve this, librarians need to use validated search hedges. A hedge is a combination of controlled vocabulary and natural language words and phrases used to search for American and British spellings of concepts and terms. The purpose of using a hedge, rather than preset filters found in bibliographic databases, is to improve search recall of clinically important studies.

Librarians and researchers collaborate to create and validate hedges. Many are publicly available. The most well-known is the McMaster Hedge Project. Using hedges developed at McMaster University, *PubMed Clinical Queries* provides a quick way to find evidence in *MEDLINE* via the *PubMed* search platform. The *Clinical Queries* page is designed to filter one search by three clinical research areas: Clinical Study Categories, Systematic Reviews, and Medical Genetics. While quick and convenient, a search in *Clinical Queries* cannot take the place of information retrieved from comprehensive mediated literature searches.

PROFESSIONAL HEALTHCARE INFORMATION

Numerous executives work within the hospital and healthcare realm:

- *Chief medical officer* (CMO): An executive or C-suite position responsible for all physician services at a hospital(s) or health system. A CMO is either an MD or DO and in many instances has a master's in business administration (MBA) and Fellow of the American College of Healthcare Executives certification.
- *Chief medical information officer or chief medical informatics officer* (CMIO): An executive responsible for healthcare technology systems and services. A CMIO is usually an MD or DO with formal training, advanced degree, or certifications in healthcare informatics.
- *Chief nursing officer* (CNO): A healthcare executive in charge of all nursing services at a hospital(s) or health system. A CNO is an RN and quite often has an MBA and a master's in nursing.
- *Chief nursing information officer or chief nursing informatics officer* (CNIO): An executive who functions as a liaison between clinical information technology and nursing informatics. The CNIO is an RN with advanced degrees in both clinical nursing and informatics.

It is essential for librarians to be well versed in resources on the business aspects of healthcare. Healthcare executives will contact librarians to request information about healthcare reform, health information technology (HIT), institutional accreditation, and continuing education and certification programs. The following are resources librarians should become familiar with, as they are vital sources of business information.

Evaluation and Selection of Healthcare Business Information

Doody's Core Titles evaluates and rates titles in health economics and the delivery of healthcare. Two essential healthcare business journals are *Health Affairs* and the *Milbank Quarterly*. *Health Affairs* publishes feature articles, editorials, and blog postings on health policy, quality, reform, and spending issues. Since 1986, The Milbank Memorial Fund, a healthcare research policy organization, has published the *Milbank Quarterly*. This peer-reviewed journal publishes original healthcare policy research and editorials.

Health Insurance

During the Great Depression of the 1930s through the early 1940s, hospital admissions dropped, as did hospital and physician profits. Hospitals began to offer health insurance plans. In December 1929, Baylor University Hospital enrolled public school teachers, at 50 cents a month, for guaranteed 21 days of hospital care. This model grew into the Blue Cross Hospital Insurance Plan.

U.S. Presidents Theodore Roosevelt, Franklin D. Roosevelt, and Harry S. Truman proposed national healthcare programs. None were successful until 1965, when President Lyndon B. Johnson signed the Social Security Amendments of 1965 (P.L. 89–97: Title XVIII and XIX of the Social Security Act) creating Medicare and Medicaid. This was the first time in U.S. history Americans 65 years of age and older and low-income individuals and families were guaranteed health insurance coverage.

Administered by the Centers for Medicare and Medicaid (CMS), an agency within the U.S. Department of Health and Human Services, Medicare is a complicated alphabet soup of insurance coverage options. The best place to begin a Medicare and Medicaid information search is the U.S. federal government's Medicare and Medicaid websites.

Signed into law in 1997, and reauthorized in 2009, the Children's Health Insurance Program (CHIP) provides health insurance coverage for children and their families who cannot afford private health insurance or qualify for Medicaid. The best place to learn about CHIP is *InsureKidsNow*, the website operated and maintained by CMS.

Enacted into law on March 23, 2010, the Patient Protection and Affordable Care Act is referred to as the Affordable Care Act, the ACA, or colloquially as "Obamacare." Key provisions eliminate lifetime limits on insurance benefits, prohibit rescission of health policies, and require insurance companies to cover preventive health services and immunizations.

The ACA's unique characteristic is its multiyear rollout or implementation schedule. The Kaiser Family Foundation (KFF) created a very simple implementation timeline accessible via its website. Also found on the KFF website is a wealth of nonpartisan healthcare reform research and information. In addition, both the U.S. White House and the *HealthCare.gov* websites provide information for individuals, families, providers, and insurers.

The individual mandate is a key provision of the Affordable Care Act. Effective January 2014, individuals not coved by a healthcare insurance plan are required, by law, to buy health insurance or pay a penalty tax. Health Insurance Exchanges (HIEs), also known as Marketplaces, function as a marketplace for individuals and small businesses looking to purchase health insurance. The National Conference of State Legislatures website is a great jumping-off point to learn about HIEs in all 50 states as is the CMS-run *HealthCare.gov* website. The activity in Box 26.6 explores resources on the ACA in more depth.

Health Information Technology

HIT is the electronic management of patient healthcare information. During his 2004 State of the Union Address, U.S. President George W. Bush stated "By computerizing health records, we can avoid dangerous medical mistakes, reduce costs, and improve care." Through widespread adoption and use of EMRs, HIT proponents believe that patient care quality and safety will dramatically improve and delivery of healthcare will become more efficient (Nguyen, Bellucci, and Nguyen 2014).

Box 26.6 Activity: ACA Updates

Select one of the following scenarios:

- You are the newly minted medical reference librarian at a four-hospital health system. The chief nursing officer walks into your library and asks you to recommend a few websites that she can easily access to keep her updated on ACA changes.
- You are the newly minted consumer health librarian for a medium-size public library system. Your patron, an MBA student concentrating in healthcare administration, is researching a portion of the ACA rollout schedule.

Questions for Reflection and Discussion:

1. Using the 20-point consumer website evaluative criteria, would you recommend the Kaiser Family Foundation's *Health Reform* (http://kff.org/health-reform) to both the chief nursing officer and the MBA student? Why or why not?
2. Would you recommend *Healthcare.gov* instead of *Health Reform*? Why or why not?

On February 17, 2009, the U.S. Congress passed the American Recovery and Reinvestment Act (ARRA) of 2009. Also known as "the Stimulus," it provides $19 billion to promote the adoption and use of HIT through the Health Information Technology for Economic and Clinical Health Act, which was enacted as part of the ARRA. The following are the go-to resources for EMR implementation and other HIT issues that directly impact both patients and providers. Addressing a Joint Session of Congress, on February 24, 2009, U.S President Barack Obama stated, "Our recovery plan will invest in electronic health records and new technology that will reduce errors, bring down costs, ensure privacy, and save lives."

HealthIT.gov is maintained by the U.S. federal government as a one-stop shopping information resource for patients, providers, and researchers concerned with the secure use and sharing of health information. Founded in 1961, the Healthcare Information and Management Systems Society (HIMSS) is a not-for-profit organization focused on the use of HIT. HIMSS publishes the quarterly digital-only *Journal of Healthcare Information Management.*

In 1928, the American College of Surgeons established the Association of Record Librarians of North America, which eventually became the American Health Information Management Association (AHIMA). The AHIMA is the certifying body for HIM professionals including registered health information administrator (RHIA) and registered health information technician (RHIT) as well as coding, privacy and security, and document improvement certifications. The official publication of the AHIMA, the *Journal of AHIMA* publishes best practices in health information management, as well as coverage of emerging issues in patient data security and privacy.

Business and Financial News Services

Four major healthcare financial news service providers publish a mix of subscription and free newsletters and magazines:

- ASC Communications (publisher of the Becker's Healthcare series)
- FierceMarkets

- HealthLeaders Media
- Kaiser Family Foundation (KFF)

Becker's Healthcare offers five trade publications that focus on the business and legal issues of healthcare delivery: *Becker's ASC Review*, *Becker's Infection Control & Clinical Quality*, *Becker's Spine Review*, *Becker's Hospital Review*, and *Becker's Dental Review*. Fierce Markets Healthcare is a marketing and lead generation company that publishes healthcare management news eResources including: *Fierce Healthcare*, which provides daily news for healthcare executives and administrators; *Fierce HealthIT*, which provides daily news for hospital chief information officers, technology officers, and IT administrators; *Fierce EMR*, a weekly publication about the use of EMR systems in healthcare; and *Fierce Mobile Healthcare*, a weekly newsletter covering telemedicine and telehealth, remote monitoring, RFID, and smart phone and tablet use in healthcare settings.

HealthLeaders Media, a division of Business & Legal Resources, publishes magazines, newsletters, and intelligence reports covering a wide array of healthcare business topics. *HealthLeaders Media Online* website is continually updated Monday through Friday and covers major healthcare business topics such as healthcare physician, nurse, and executive leadership, finance, quality, HIT, rural and community hospitals, and health insurance plans. *HealthLeaders Media Daily News & Analysis* is a free e-newsletter for senior healthcare executives. *HealthLeaders* magazine is published 10 times per year and free of charge. E-mail registration is required to access these titles.

Kaiser Health News (*KHN*) is a nonprofit news service covering healthcare policy and politics. *KHN* is an independent arm of the KFF. The site accepts no advertising.

Institutional Accreditation

Accreditation of direct patient care institutions means that these organizations accept review of their policies, procedures, and outcomes against nationally accepted standards of care. Depending on the type of service, such as outpatient day surgery or inpatient hospital stay, individuals may check their healthcare provider's accreditation status by doing the following:

- Check provider websites.
- Call the healthcare provider's Office of Patient Advocacy, Office of Patient Relations, or Compliance Department.
- Call the State Survey Agency, where care is provided. The CMS website provides access to a State Survey Agency Directory.

ADDITIONAL RESOURCES

Healthcare Foundations and Private Research Organizations

Healthcare foundations and research organizations sometimes produce publicly available reports that can be useful to patrons. Established in 1991, the Henry J. Kaiser Family Foundation is a private, independent, nonprofit organization that develops its own health policy analysis research and manages its journalism and communications programs. All Kaiser products are available free of charge. The IOM, established in 1970, is the health division of the National Academies. It is an independent nonprofit organization. Much of the healthcare research performed by the IOM originates with requests from the U.S. Congress, federal agencies, or public and private organizations. Established by the founder of Johnson & Johnson, the Robert Wood Johnson Foundation (RWJF) provides grants with the goal to improve the health and healthcare of all Americans. Grant awards go to projects to combat childhood obesity, expand health insurance coverage, and improve the cost and quality of healthcare. Reports and research produced by the RWJF are available free of charge.

The National Network of Libraries of Medicine

Whether one is a consumer health librarian working in a public library setting, a clinical librarian providing information to clinicians at the POC, or part of a biomedical research team, one of the most important resources available is the National Network of Libraries of Medicine (NN/LM). The NN/LM is composed of a nationwide network of hospital and health science libraries and information centers. NN/LM members are supported through eight regional offices called Regional Medical Libraries (RMLs). RMLs offer e-learning and in-person classes to support the effective use of NLM information products and services, such as *MedlinePlus*. Most of these learning opportunities are free. Many NN/LM hospital and health science libraries have consumer health collections and provide interlibrary loan services to public libraries. A number of these libraries employ consumer health librarians who provide reference services to the general public and assist public librarians in answering difficult health questions.

SUMMARY

Information needs for health and medical information come from inside and outside the healthcare system because health happens everywhere. And the need for timely and accurate healthcare information happens everywhere. Patients, caregivers, and the general public tend to access consumer health information via the Internet, and librarians can play a role in directing them to reliable, up-to-date sources. Inside the healthcare system, clinicians at the POC need access to digested, evidence-based summaries on topics of clinical relevance. To inform their work, biomedical researchers need access to bibliographic databases and clinical trials repositories. Healthcare executives, concerned with the "business of healthcare," have information needs regarding healthcare, information technology, and credentialing. It is incumbent on librarians to choose the right resource for the clientele they serve.

NOTES

1. Many community colleges offer two and three credit courses taught from an anatomical perspective. For-profit educational centers also offer medical terminology courses as part of medical transcription certification programs. Please check the Association for Healthcare Documentation Integrity (AHDI) for accreditation status of these for-profit centers.

2. The term "point of care" abbreviated to "POC" means the location at which patient services and care, either inpatient or outpatient, are delivered.
3. Senior executives are referred to as C-suite executives since most senior-level titles at any company, whether at for- or nonprofit organizations, begin with the letter C, as in chief operating officer, chief executive officer, chief nursing officer, and so on.

REFERENCES

"About AHRQ." 2015. Agency for Healthcare Research. Department of Health & Human Services. http://www.ahrq.gov/cpi/about/index.html.

"About Us." 2015. *The Cochrane Collaborative.* http://www.cochrane.org/about-us.

"Adult Literacy in America: A First Look at the Findings of the National Adult Literacy Survey." 1993. Washington, DC: United States Department of Education.

The American Recovery and Reinvestment Act of 2009. Pub. L. No, 111–5, 123 Stat. 115.

Association for Healthcare Documentation Integrity. http://www.ahdionline.org/.

Association of Health Care Journalists. 2015. "History of AHCJ." http://healthjournalism.org/about-history.php.

"Baby Boomers to Challenge and Change Tomorrow's Health Care System: More than Six out of 10 Baby Boomers Will Be Managing Multiple Chronic Illnesses by 2030." 2007. American Hospital Association. http://www.aha.org/presscenter/pressrel/2007/070508-pr-boomers.shtml.

Bush, George W. 2004. "Address before a Joint Session of Congress on the State of the Union." 40 *Weekly Compilation of Presidential Documents* 94 (January 20).

Cohen, Barbara Janson. 2013. *Medical Terminology: An Illustrated Guide*, 7th ed. Philadelphia: Lippincott Williams & Wilkins.

"Consumer Health Information Specialization." 2015. Medical Library Association. http://www.mlanet.org/p/cm/ld/fid=329.

Del Fiol, Guilherme, T. Elizabeth Workman, and Paul N. Gorman. 2014. "Clinical Questions Raised by Clinicians at the Point of Care: A Systematic Review." *JAMA Internal Medicine* 174 (5): 710–8.

Fischer, Karen S. 2005. "Doody's Core Titles in the Health Sciences (DCT)." *Journal of the Medical Library Association* 93 (3): 409.

Fox, Susannah. 2011. "The Social Life of Health Information." Pew Research Center: Washington, DC. http://www.pewinternet.org/2011/05/12/the-social-life-of-health-information-2011/.

"Health Fact Sheet." 2015. Pew Research Center. Accessed September 25. http://www.pewinternet.org/fact-sheets/health-fact-sheet/.

Health Information Research Unit. 2015. McMaster University. http://hiru.mcmaster.ca/hiru/.

"Health Literacy and Patient Safety: Help Patients Understand." 2007. American Medical Association Foundation, 23 minutes. https://www.youtube.com/watch?v=cGtTZ_vxjyA.

Hill, Dorothy R., and Henry N. Stickell. 2001. "Brandon/Hill Selected List of Print Books and Journals for the Small Medical Library." *Bulletin of the Medical Library Association* 89 (2): 131–53.

Hill, Dorothy R., and Henry N. Stickell. 2002. "Brandon/Hill Selected List of Print Nursing Books and Journals." *Nursing Outlook* 50 (3): 100–13.

Hill, Dorothy R., and Henry N. Stickell. 2003. "Brandon/Hill Selected List of Print Books and Journals in Allied Health." *Journal of the Medical Library Association* 91 (1): 18–33.

"Information Retrieval Methods Group." 2015. *The Cochrane Collaboration.* http://irmg.cochrane.org.

Institute of Medicine. 2004. *Health Literacy: A Prescription to End Confusion.* Washington, DC: National Academies Press.

LaFleur, Danielle S., and Myrna LaFleur-Brooks. 2013. *Basic Medical Language*, 4th ed. St. Louis: Elsevier.

Linden, Tom. 2010. "Reporting by TV Docs in Haiti Raises Ethical Issues." *Electronic News* 4 (2): 60–64.

Murphy-Knoll, Linda. 2007. "Low Health Literacy Puts Patients at Risk: The Joint Commission Proposes Solutions to National Problem." *Journal of Nursing Care Quality* 22 (3): 205–9.

National Assessment of Adult Literacy. 2003. *A First Look at the Literacy of America's Adults in the 21st Century.* Washington, DC: Department of Education. http://nces.ed.gov/naal/pdf/2006470.pdf.

Nguyen, Lemai, Emilia Bellucci, and Linh Thuy Nguyen. 2014. "Electronic Health Records Implementation: An Evaluation of Information System Impact and Contingency Factors." *International Journal of Medical Informatics* 83 (11): 779–96.

Niu, Xi. 2010. "National Study of Information Seeking Behavior of Academic Researchers in the United States." *Journal of the American Society for Information Science and Technology* 61 (5): 869–90.

Obama, Barack. 2009. "Address before a Joint Session of the Congress." *Daily Compilation of Presidential Documents*, 2009 DCPD No. 200900105 (February 24).

Patient Protection and Affordable Care Act, 42 U.S.C. § 18001 et seq. (2010).

"Quick Guide to Health Literacy and Older Adults." 2007. Department of Health & Human Services. http://www.health.gov/communication/literacy/olderadults/literacy.htm.

Sackett, David L. 1996. "Evidence Based Medicine: What It Is and What It Isn't." *BMJ* 312 (7023): 71–72.

"Six Killers." 2007. *New York Times.* April 8. http://www.nytimes.com/2007/04/08/health/08hbox.html.

Social Security Amendments of 1965, Pub. L. No. 89–97, 79 Stat. 286.

Spatz, Michele. 2014. *The Medical Library Association Guide to Providing Consumer and Patient Health Information.* Lanham, MD: Rowman & Littlefield.

U.S. Census Bureau. 2010. *The Next Four Decades: The Older Population in the United States: 2010 to 2050.* Washington, DC: Department of Commerce.

Wessel, Charles B., Nancy H. Tannery, and Barbara A. Epstein. 2006. "Information-Seeking Behavior and Use of Information Resources by Clinical Research Coordinators." *Journal of the Medical Library Association* 94 (1): 48–54.

LIST OF SOURCES

Accreditation. Centers for Medicare and Medicaid. http://www.cms.gov/Medicare/Provider-Enrollment-and-Certification/SurveyCertificationGenInfo/Accreditation.html.

Accreditation Commission for Education in Nursing. http://www.acenursing.org/.

Accreditation Council for Graduate Medical Education. https://www.acgme.org/acgmeweb/.

ACP Smart Medicine. http://smartmedicine.acponline.org/. [subscription required for full access]

A.D.A.M. Medical Encyclopedia. 2015. *MedlinePlus.* https://www.nlm.nih.gov/medlineplus/encyclopedia.html.

Agency for Healthcare Research and Quality. http://www.ahrq.gov/.

American Association of Colleges of Nursing. http://www.aacn.nche.edu/.
American Association of Colleges of Osteopathic Medicine. http://www.aacom.org/home.
American Board of Medical Specialties. http://www.abms.org/.
American Health Information Management Association. http://www.ahima.org/.
American Medical Association. http://www.ama-assn.org/ama.
American Nurses Credentialing Center. http://www.nursecredentialing.org/default.aspx.
American Osteopathic Association. http://www.aacom.org/become-a-doctor/med-students/career-planning/self-to-program/residencies.
Ask Me 3. The National Patient Safety Foundation. http://www.npsf.org/?page=askme3.
Association for Healthcare Documentation Integrity. http://www.ahdionline.org.
Association of American Medical Colleges. https://www.aamc.org/.
Becker's ASC Review. 2001–. Chicago: Becker's Healthcare. 9 issues per year. http://www.beckersasc.com/.
Becker's Dental Review. Chicago: Becker's Healthcare. http://www.beckersdental.com/.
Becker's Hospital Review. 2008–. Chicago: Becker's Healthcare. Monthly. http://www.beckershospitalreview.com/.
Becker's Infection Control & Clinical Quality. 2008–. Chicago: Becker's Healthcare. http://www.beckershospitalreview.com/quality.
Becker's Spine Review. 2009–. Chicago: Becker's Healthcare. http://www.beckersspine.com.
Best Practice Information Sheets. The Joanna Briggs Institute. The University of Adelaide. http://joannabriggs.org/bpis/jbi-BPIS.html.
Bing. http://www.bing.com.
Biomed Central. http://www.biomedcentral.com/.
Board Certified Docs. Atlanta: Elsevier. http://www.boardcertifieddocs.com/abms/static/home.htm. [subscription required].
Certification Matters. American Board of Medical Specialties. http://certificationmatters.org/.
Choosing Wisely. http://www.choosingwisely.org/doctor-patient-lists/.
ClinicalTrials.gov. https://clinicaltrials.gov/.
The Cochrane Collaboration. http://www.cochrane.org/.
Cochrane Database of Systematic Reviews. London: The Cochrane Collaboration. http://community.cochrane.org/editorial-and-publishing-policy-resource/cochrane-database-systematic-reviews-cdsr. Available as part of *Cochrane Library.*
Cochrane Library. Hoboken, NJ: Wiley. http://onlinelibrary.wiley.com/cochranelibrary/search. [subscription required]
Commission on Collegiate Nursing Education. http://www.aacn.nche.edu/ccne-accreditation.
Commission on Osteopathic College Accreditation. American Osteopathic Association. http://www.osteopathic.org/inside-aoa/accreditation/Pages/default.aspx.
Consumer and Patient Health Information Section. Medical Library Association. http://caphis.mlanet.org/.
Cumulative Index to Nursing and Allied Health Literature. Ipswich, MA: EBSCO. https://health.ebsco.com/products/the-cinahl-database. [subscription required]
Doody's Core Titles in the Health Sciences. Oak Park, IL: Doody's Enterprises. http://www.doody.com/dct/default.asp. [subscription required]
Drugs.com. http://www.drugs.com/.
DynaMed. Ipswich, MA: EBSCO. https://dynamed.ebscohost.com/. [subscription required]
Easy-to-Read. *MedlinePlus.* http://www.nlm.nih.gov/medlineplus/all_easytoread.html.
Embase. Elsevier. https://www.elsevier.com/solutions/embase-biomedical-research.
EndNote. Thomson Reuters. http://endnote.com/.
Essential Evidence Plus. Hoboken, NJ: Wiley. http://www.essentialevidenceplus.com/. [subscription required]

Essential Nursing Resources. 2012. 26th ed. Silver Spring, MD: Interagency Council on Information Resources in Nursing. http://icirn.org/.

Evidence Reports. Agency for Healthcare Research and Quality. http://www.ahrq.gov/research/findings/evidence-based-reports/search.html.

The Federation of State Medical Boards. http://www.fsmb.org/.

Fierce EMR. Washington, DC: FierceMarkets. Weekly. http://www.fiercemarkets.com/market/healthcare.

Fierce Healthcare. Washington, DC: FierceMarkets. Daily. http://www.fiercemarkets.com/market/healthcare.

Fierce HealthIT. Washington, DC: FierceMarkets. Daily. http://www.fiercemarkets.com/market/healthcare.

Fierce Mobile Healthcare. Washington, DC: FierceMarkets. Weekly. http://www.fiercemarkets.com/market/healthcare.

Google. http://www.google.com.

Health. National Conference of State Legislatures. http://www.ncsl.org/research/health.aspx.

Health Affairs. 1981–. Bethesda, MD: Project HOPE. Monthly. http://www.healthaffairs.org/.

"Health Literacy." Pfizer. http://www.pfizer.com/health/literacy.

Health Reform. The Henry J. Kaiser Family Foundation. http://kff.org/health-reform/.

Health Reform Implementation Timeline. The Henry J. Kaiser Family Foundation. http://kff.org/interactive/implementation-timeline/.

Healthcare Information and Management Systems Society. http://www.himss.org/.

HealthCare.gov. https://www.healthcare.gov/.

HealthIT.gov. http://healthit.gov/.

HealthLeaders. 2006–. Brentwood, TN: HealthLeaders. 10 issues per year. http://www.healthleadersmedia.com/magazines.

HealthLeaders Media Daily News & Analysis. 2006–. Brentwood, TN: HealthLeaders. Daily. http://www.healthleadersmedia.com/news.

HealthLeaders Media Online. http://www.healthleadersmedia.com.

The Henry J. Kaiser Family Foundation. http://kff.org/.

Institute of Medicine. http://iom.nationalacademies.org/.

InsureKidsNow.gov. http://www.insurekidsnow.gov/.

JAMAevidence. New York: McGraw-Hill. http://jamaevidence.com/. [subscription required]

Joanna Briggs Institute EBP Database. Ovid. http://resourcecenter.ovid.com/site/pdf/jbi/JBI_2pg_fs_0912_FINAL.pdf.

Journal of AHIMA. Chicago: American Health Information Management Association. 11 issues per year. http://journal.ahima.org/.

Journal of Healthcare Information Management. 1998–. Chicago: Healthcare Information and Management Systems Society. Quarterly. http://www.himss.org/jhim.

Kaiser Health News. Washington, DC: Kaiser Family Foundation. http://kaiserhealthnews.org/.

Liaison Committee on Medical Education. http://www.lcme.org.

List of Basic Sources in English for a Medical Faculty Library. 2013. 15th ed. Geneva: World Health Organization: Regional Office for the Eastern Mediterranean. http://applications.emro.who.int/dsaf/EMPUB_2013_EN_1536.pdf.

McMaster Hedge Project. http://hiru.mcmaster.ca/hiru/HIRU_Hedges_home.aspx.

McMaster Plus. http://hiru.mcmaster.ca/hiru/HIRU_McMaster_PLUS_projects.aspx.

Medicaid.gov. http://www.medicaid.gov/.

Medicare.gov. https://www.medicare.gov/.

MEDLINE. https://www.nlm.nih.gov/pubs/factsheets/medline.html.

MedlinePlus. http://www.nlm.nih.gov/medlineplus/.

Mendeley. https://www.mendeley.com/.
Milbank Quarterly. 1923–. New York: Milbank Memorial Fund. Quarterly. http://www.milbank.org/the-milbank-quarterly.
Mosby's Nursing Consult. Atlanta: Elsevier. http://www.nursingconsult.com/nursing/index. [subscription required]
National Board of Medical Examiners. http://www.nbme.org/.
National Board of Osteopathic Medical Examiners. http://www.nbome.org/.
National Cancer Institute. http://www.cancer.gov.
National Council for State Boards of Nursing. https://www.ncsbn.org/index.htm.
National Guideline Clearinghouse. http://www.guideline.gov/.
National Institute for Health and Care Excellence. https://www.nice.org.uk/guidance.
National Library of Medicine. http://www.nlm.nih.gov/.
National Network of Libraries of Medicine. http://nnlm.gov/.
NIH Senior Health. http://nihseniorhealth.gov/.
Nursing and Allied Health Resources Section. Medical Library Association. http://nahrs.mlanet.org/home/.
Nursing Reference Center. Ipswich, MA: EBSCO. http://www.ebscohost.com/nursing/products/nursing-reference-center. [subscription required]
Pill Identifier. AARP. https://www.nlm.nih.gov/medlineplus/encyclopedia.html.
Pillbox. National Library of Medicine. http://pillbox.nlm.nih.gov/pillimage/search.php.
The Plain Language Action and Information Network. http://www.plainlanguage.gov/populartopics/health_literacy/index.cfm.
Plain Language Medical Dictionary. The Taubman Health Sciences Library. University of Michigan. http://www.lib.umich.edu/plain-language-dictionary.
PubMed. http://www.ncbi.nlm.nih.gov/pubmed.
PubMed Central. http://www.ncbi.nlm.nih.gov/pmc/.
PubMed Clinical Queries. http://www.ncbi.nlm.nih.gov/pubmed/clinical.
PubMed Health. http://www.ncbi.nlm.nih.gov/pubmedhealth/.
"Questions to Ask Your Doctor." 2012. Agency for Healthcare Research and Quality. http://ahrq.gov/patients-consumers/patient-involvement/ask-your-doctor/index.html.
Reference and User Services Association. 2015. "Health and Medical Reference Guidelines." American Library Association. http://www.ala.org/rusa/resources/guidelines/guidelinesmedical.
Rittenhouse Book Distributors. https://www.rittenhouse.com/Rbd/Web/Default.aspx.
Robert Wood Johnson Foundation. http://www.rwjf.org/.
RxList. http://www.rxlist.com.
State Survey Agency Directory. 2015. Washington, DC: Centers for Medicare and Medicaid. https://www.cms.gov/Medicare/Provider-Enrollment-and-Certification/SurveyCertificationGenInfo/downloads/state_agency_contacts.pdf.
Top 100 List: Health Websites You Can Trust. Medical Library Association. http://caphis.mlanet.org/consumer/top100all.pdf.
TRIP Database. http://www.tripdatabase.com/.
UpToDate. Boston: Wolters Kluwer. http://www.uptodate.com/home. [subscription required]
U.S. Preventive Services Task Force. http://www.uspreventiveservicestaskforce.org/Page/BasicOneColumn/28.
USPSTF Information for Consumers. http://www.uspreventiveservicestaskforce.org/Tools/ConsumerInfo/Index/information-for-consumers.
The White House. http://www.whitehouse.gov/healthreform.
Yahoo! http://www.yahoo.com.

SUGGESTED READINGS

Bell, Suzanne S. 2015. *Librarian's Guide to Online Searching*, 4th ed. Santa Barbara, CA: Libraries Unlimited.

It is essential for anyone conducting online mediated literature searches to understand the structure of databases. No one does this better than Suzanne Bell. Her "Searcher's Toolkit," the seven basic skills needed for effective searching, is presented in clear, concise language. Her visual representations as well as exercises and points to consider make this the best online searching text in its class.

Groopman, Jerome E. 2007. *How Doctors Think*. Boston: Houghton Mifflin.

This book enables the reader to understand how physicians process information gleaned from their patients and how they understand illness. According to Groopman, for the most part, doctors get it (diagnosis) right, but when they get it wrong, the fallout can be monumental. Most diagnostic errors are due to doctors' perceptions of and sometimes stereotypical beliefs about their patients. Much of what is written about the doctor–patient dialogue is from the patient's perspective meaning, how do patients more effectively communicate with, and become partners with, their healthcare team. Groopman's tome offers much needed insight into how doctors process information. And this insight, in turn, can help patients.

Huber, Jeffrey T., and Susan Swogger. 2014. *Introduction to Reference Sources in the Health Sciences*, 6th ed. Chicago: ALA Neal-Schuman.

This guide to reference sources is essential for anyone considering a career providing medical or health sciences reference services. The authors present their information in four parts: Health Reference in Context, the Reference Collection, Bibliographic Sources, and Information Sources. Published in 2014, this edition includes new chapters on health information-seeking behaviors, point-of-care, and global health sources. There is also an increased emphasis and focus on highlighting electronic resources since these resources are ubiquitous in medical reference work. In the preface, the authors state the important caveat: "Since there is no consensus as to what constitutes 'basic works' the materials represent the authors' candidates for such a list."

Kohn, Linda T., Janet M. Corrigan, and Molla S. Donaldson, eds. 1999. *To Err Is Human: Building a Safer Health System*. Committee on Quality of Health Care in America; Institute of Medicine. Washington, DC: National Academy Press.

On November 29, 1999, the Institute of Medicine (IOM) released its groundbreaking *To Err Is Human* report. In it, the IOM made a staggering pronouncement: medical errors account for upward of 98,000 hospital deaths in the United States each year, and most of these errors are preventable. The findings of this report ushered in what is known as the patient safety era whereby patients and their families must be part of the care process. This report was one of the first to put the spotlight on health literacy issues.

Nordenström, Jörgen. 2007. *Evidence-Based Medicine in Sherlock Holmes' Footsteps*. Malden, MA: Blackwell Publishers.

Understanding the EBM process can be overwhelming. This very useful, easy-to-read book provides an introduction to the basic concepts of evidence-based medicine. This fun (yes fun!) text takes the reader through the literature searching process to a step-by-step approach to critically appraising results.

Osborne, Helen. 2013. *Health Literacy from A to Z: Practical Ways to Communicate Your Health Message*, 2nd ed. Burlington, MA: Jones & Bartlett Learning.

Osborne's text was included in the 2015 edition of the essential collection of *Doody's Core Titles*. Chapters are organized around "Starting Points" with an introduction to key concepts, followed by "Strategies, Ideas and Suggestions" that contain how-to tips. "Stories from Practice" discuss real-life health literacy experience, and "Sources to Learn More" include a bibliography of books, journal articles, podcasts, and other resources. This is an extremely practical and easy-to-read book, and librarians providing consumer health reference will find Osborne's strategies and ideas invaluable.

Sanders, Lisa. 2010. *Every Patient Tells a Story: Medical Mysteries and the Art of Diagnosis*, 1st ed. New York: Broadway Books.

Consumer health as well as medical and health science librarians would do well to read Sanders's dramatic text about the technological tools and skills doctors possess to diagnose illnesses. Despite these abilities, doctors are still challenged with getting to the heart of their patient's health stories.

Spatz, Michele. 2014. *The Medical Library Association Guide to Providing Consumer and Patient Health Information*. Lanham, MD: Rowman & Littlefield.

Spatz covers all aspects of consumer health information services: from ethical issues to needs assessments; from budgeting and funding to strategic partnerships, to meeting the needs of diverse groups such as children, teens, LGBT individuals, and patients with low literacy. This book provides a foundation from which to build effective and efficient consumer health reference services.

Sultz, Harry A., and Kristina M. Young. 2014. *Health Care USA: Understanding Its Organization and Delivery*, 8th ed. Sudbury, MA: Jones & Bartlett Learning.

The eighth edition of this classic text provides a wide-ranging overview of the U.S. healthcare system. New to this edition are analyses of the progress and impact of the Affordable Care Act, and new information on efforts to reduce medical errors such as the Institute for Health Care Improvement's 100,000 Lives Campaign. Readers are provided with historical overviews of Medicare and Medicaid programs and the role that managed care plays as the primary method of insuring most Americans.

Wischnitzer, Saul, and Edith Wischnitzer. 2011. *Top 100 Health-Care Careers: Your Complete Guidebook to Training and Jobs in Allied Health, Nursing, Medicine, and More*, 3rd ed. Indianapolis: JIST Works.

A well-organized healthcare career guidance manual, this book contains a detailed overview of 100 jobs including educational requirements, admission test and financial aid, salary range, and certification requirements. The authors provide a directory of education and training programs for each of the 100 featured jobs and include advice on choosing and planning a career in healthcare.

Wood, M. Sandra. 2014. *Health Sciences Librarianship*. Lanham, MD: Rowman & Littlefield.

This text is useful to those tasked with managing the day-to-day operations of a medical or health sciences library. Chapters are organized in four main parts: The Profession, The Collection, User Services, and Administrative Services. The authors emphasize how technological advances have changed the role of the health science librarian, specifically the expectation of virtual reference services and 24/7 access to resources. Additionally, the authors discuss the "library without walls" concept and the idea of embedded librarianship.

Chapter 27

Primary and Archival Sources

Shelley Sweeney

The palest ink is better than the best memory.

—Chinese proverb

INTRODUCTION

Although primary sources and archival records were opened up for research in the 1800s, they were more or less inaccessible to all but the most privileged and dedicated scholars. Today most such records are open to everyone. They are attractive to students interested in experiential learning and creating mash-ups, scholars who are including more original resources in their research, and members of the public who have more time on their hands and have such hobbies as genealogy and local history. But what has led to the democratization of primary sources and archival records is the advent of the Internet and the digitization of resources. Suddenly, instead of users having to physically get to archives in obscure locations during short opening hours, they can go online and get access to millions of photographs, documents, audio recordings, and myriad other formats, whenever it is convenient to them. However, because of the newness and unfamiliarity of these resources, many users in all types of libraries require reference assistance, and this is where the reference librarian comes in.

Primary and Archival Sources

Primary or archival sources can be used to respond to a wide variety of reference requests. But what exactly are "primary" or "archival" sources? Unfortunately, not all historians and teachers agree on the definition. However, the Society of American Archivists' (SAA) *Glossary* defines a primary source as "material that contains firsthand accounts of events and that was created contemporaneous to those events or later recalled by an eyewitness" (Pearce-Moses 2005). Such materials can include:

- Diaries
- Memoirs
- Oral history interviews
- Newspaper articles about contemporaneous events
- Records of court cases
- Official government documents
- Ephemera

Primary sources are often contrasted with secondary sources, which are sources that are produced after the event by someone who did not experience the event. Secondary sources can contain summaries, interpretations, authorial opinions, and commentary, and are often compilations of information from various sources. Scholarly publications, textbooks, encyclopedias, and journals would be typical formats of secondary sources. Sometimes secondary sources can contain primary sources within them, such as histories that contain eyewitness accounts.

Archival records are defined as "materials created or received by a person, family, or organization, public or private, in the conduct of their affairs that are preserved because of the enduring value contained in the information they contain or as evidence of the functions and responsibilities of their creator" (Pearce-Moses 2005). The key consideration is that these materials were produced in the normal course of daily activity and record or support that activity in some way. Typical formats of such materials include:

- Textual records, such as correspondence
- Photographs
- Maps
- Architectural plans
- Drawings and sketches
- Sound recordings
- Audiovisual records

Figure 27.1 provides an example of an archival photograph; such "old" photographs can be extremely useful for adding color to student essays and illustrating texts on historic topics. The records can be analog or digital; increasingly, archives are "born digital." Artifacts, microforms, and published materials can sometimes be considered part of archival sources, although typically artifacts are collected by museums and microforms and published materials by libraries. It usually depends on the relationship between the materials. If, for instance, an archival collection included design drawings and correspondence for the creation of a medal, an archive might keep the medal as part of the collection. Likewise with literary archives, it is not unusual for an archive to keep the final published version of a work with drafts of the same.

Although a single item might be considered an archive, typically archives consist of a group of materials that have organic relationships between the component parts based on the activities of the creator or creators. The fact that archival records are typically a grouping of materials affects everything from how they are described, to how they are retrieved, to how they are used. This will be explored further.

FIGURE 27.1 Métis woman with child, 1880, Connie Macmillan Collection, from the University of Manitoba Archives & Special Collections, the Libraries, Acces sion Number: UM_pc284_A11-086_001_0001_002_0001.

Primary sources can be published summaries of selected archival documents, often referred to as "calendars." In the British tradition, these so-called calendars provide the substance of the selected documents in chronological order, which can save a great deal of time when researchers need to pin down the exact documents they need (Sweetman 2008). In addition, if the documents are in a foreign or ancient language, the calendar will provide a translation. These calendars provide very rigorous and specific descriptions that can obviate the need to consult the originals and can be used as primary sources. In the North American tradition, however, the calendars are more likely to be simple lists pointing the researcher to the appropriate materials.

Primary sources can also be published compilations of selected archival documents; this can include facsimiles, which attempt to reproduce the original records as closely as possible. These publications reproduce important series of documents relating to a particular event, such as the Anglo-Chinese opium wars (Waley 1958), or the correspondence of someone important, such as American President Theodore Roosevelt (Roosevelt 1951–1954). Although such publications were more popular in the 20th century, it is still fairly common for organizations and authors to publish important documents, although increasingly, these compilations of archival texts are being produced online. For example, InteLex's *Past Masters* includes the complete letters of Jane Austen.

Other Words for Primary and Archival Sources

Primary sources are almost always called just that: "primary sources." In rare circumstances, they can also be referred to as original sources or evidence. Archival sources can be referred to in a number of different ways by both users and creators: archival materials or collections, archives, the archive, records, documentation, documents, papers, and manuscripts, among others. They are often referred to as being rare, unique, and original. Furthermore, although users are unlikely to use this term, Canadian and international archivists and archival websites often refer to a creator's "fonds." This term refers to all the archival records created or collected by a person, family, or organization. American archivists are more likely to refer to "record groups" or "collections."

Although all archives are primary sources, not all primary sources would necessarily be considered archives. A verbatim interview in a stand-alone publication could be considered a primary source but neither the interview nor the publication would be considered archival. They lack all the defining characteristics of an archive: they were not created in the conduct of daily activity, and they were not selected to be permanently retained, although the publication might have been selected by a librarian for the importance of its contents.

In general, users do not care whether they are accessing primary or archival sources. They just want the answer to their questions. It is usually only professors and teachers who will specify that their students need to use primary sources. For the purposes of this chapter, references to primary sources will be considered separately from original archival sources that have not been published or digitized.

USES

The types of reference requests that primary and archival sources can best help answer will likely fall into five categories. The users:

1. Have been given an assignment that requires they use primary sources.
2. Want to know a specific fact or facts that cannot be found in more traditional reference sources.
3. Have specific goals in mind but are unsure what records might meet their needs.
4. Are looking for specific known records or specific types of records.
5. Are looking for records that will help enforce their rights.

When referring a patron to primary or archival sources, the reference librarian should mentally categorize the reference request according to the type of use, because determining the best resources will depend upon the category. A good reference interview will elicit the scope of the user's question and the level or amount of information required, and particularly the deadline by which to have the information. It also helps a great deal to know what outcomes the users are hoping for. Are they going to write five-page papers, or are they writing a *magnum opus* and require as much information as possible no matter how long it takes them to acquire it? All of the information solicited will help the reference librarian decide whether primary or archival sources are best used to answer the information need.

Box 27.1 Search Strategy: Examples of Questions for Primary and Archival Sources

"My teacher wants us to go through old newspapers and find stuff about soldiers from our town during the Second World War." (Category 1)
"My professor wants me to use primary sources to do an assignment on the Civil Rights movement and the paper's due tomorrow." (Category 1)
"I want to find out whether X ever held a position in Y company." (Category 2)
"Can you tell me when X graduated from university?" (Category 2)
"I am going to write the history of the Garden Club of Allegheny County and would like to find as much information about it as I can." (Category 3)
"I am researching my family tree and I want to know more about the X family of New York City." (Category 3)
"Do you know where I can find the records of Walter Cronkite?" (Category 4)
"Where would I find papers relating to Harriet Tubman?" (Category 4)
"I would like to find the marriage certificate of X. She died in 1875 in Austin, Texas." (Category 4)
"I need to prove I attended Residential School to receive compensation." (Category 5)
"I have to provide evidence of my birthdate to get my pension." (Category 5)

Class Assignments

Primary sources are fairly easy and straightforward to use when a class assignment requires a student to use them, or for quick and ready reference. Archival sources, because of the amount of records, the hierarchies, the complex relationships between the various parts of the collections, the indirect nature between descriptions and contents, and the lack of granularity in the descriptions, can be tricky, and often time consuming and laborious to use. In addition, there is no guarantee that the records will have what the student is looking for or enough information to fulfill a class assignment. Certainly when there is a time limit, primary sources are best, but digitized archival sources might also be appropriate for class assignments, depending on the request.

Searching for Facts

If the information need is to determine a specific fact, either primary sources or archival sources could be employed. If the required fact is about a person, family, or organization, and popular reference sources cannot answer the question, then potentially the private papers of those entities might have the answer. Correspondence written by the person, family, or representative of an organization to another entity would also be good to consult.

If the user needs an answer about a specific event, then primary sources would be a good place to start. If these did not provide the answer, then the user would need to tie the event to a particular person, family, or organization, and employ archival sources.

Seeking Specific Goals

The same decision would need to be made if the user has specific goals in mind but is unsure what records to use. Where requests are broad, the reference librarian needs to assist researchers in narrowing down their requests. For instance, "I want to find the causes of the American Civil War" is too broad for archival records unless the user wants to spend a significant amount of time, even years, on the request. In that case, contemporary newspapers might be appropriate, but such a request would still be time consuming. A more specific request, such as "I want to know how Union soldiers viewed the American Civil War," could be answered by reading letters from soldiers.

A request such as "I want to know how many women worked in Chinese laundries in San Francisco in the 1920s" is so narrow and so specific that it quite likely will not result in any answers because of the lack of records. Depending on the user's needs, the researcher could consider looking at the 1930s instead, when the Chinese Consolidated Benevolent Association and the Chinese Hand Laundry Alliance were formed, in case these institutions might have produced records on their members. There may also have been government inquiries into the laundry business that produced records. It is important to keep in mind that the absence of information about women might just mean that women were not considered important enough to include in the records.

Thus, unless users are planning on spending significant amounts of time, they will not be able to quickly answer general historical questions through examining primary or archival sources. For detailed histories, fresh analyses of historical issues, specific questions, and to enforce rights, however, normally archival records are the *only* materials that can satisfy such requests.

Box 27.2

History, to be above evasion or dispute, must stand on documents, not opinions.

—Lord Acton

Looking for Known Records

When a researcher comes to a reference librarian asking for specific records or record types, it is always good to probe a bit deeper through a reference interview to ensure users understand what they are asking for. Once assured that they know the records will answer their needs, the librarian can assist them to find the institution that would most likely hold the records.

Looking for Records to Enforce Rights

This is a special category. Normally when people are looking for records to enforce their rights, there is a court case involved, and all typical sources of records have been exhausted. Reference librarians should send the users to the most appropriate archival institution because it is unlikely that the records are going to be online somewhere.

IDENTIFYING RECORDS

Linking Topics to Records

For all searches, if the researcher does not yet have a good understanding of his or her topic, the librarian should advise the user to read secondary sources, if any exist, and extract all names of people, families, and organizations that appear in the literature. The researcher should also confirm all the changes in names of these entities. For example, in the past, women often changed their names when they got married. It is important to know both their single and married names. Organizations often change their names over time, reflecting changes in purpose. Or, as businesses are amalgamated with other businesses, they will have variations in their names. The researcher should also look for language or naming that is unique to the topic. For instance, in the early part of the 20th century, people from Czechoslovakia were referred to as Bohemians. Then they were referred to as Czechoslovaks. Over time and particularly once the country split into two separate countries in 1993, people were referred to as Czechs and Slovaks. It is critical to know all names associated with the topic because archival records are organized by the name of the creator or, in some instances, by the name of the donor. This is referred to as the provenance of the archive.

This seemingly arcane practice of identifying all archival records by their creators is not simply to recognize the importance of who created the records, although that is critical to determining the value of the records, but because the creator's name is the only certain way to consistently identify archival materials. There is no title on archival records, the dates may not be precisely known, and the number of subjects is often too many to narrow down to only a few. But if one knows who created the materials, what his life story is, and particularly what functions he performed during his lifetime, then the contents of the archive might be inferred.

In addition to determining the names of all of the people connected to the topic, the user should note all the locations associated with those people, keeping in mind that place-names may have changed over time. This will help the librarian identify the institutions most likely to hold relevant records. The context of creation, then, is everything.

Finally, by consulting secondary scholarly works, the researcher will be able to compile a list of the archival sources that other scholars have cited; these citations will provide helpful shortcuts to archival records to give some impetus to the search.

The Value of Records

Archival records, and to a lesser extent primary sources, are valued for their impartiality. Because the records were created in the normal course of daily activity, they were neither written for an audience nor with the intent to present a particular point of view; they are, in other words, unmediated. They will still reflect the biases of their creators however, and acknowledging the context of creation is very important in determining those biases. This must be taken into account when researchers use the materials. Additionally, the records will also reflect the biases

Box 27.3 Search Strategy: Determining Likely Topics Covered by Archival Records

Cesar Chavez was an American farmworker who became a well-known civil rights leader and championed the rights of farmworkers through unionization beginning in 1952. Chavez died in 1993. Delving into his life, one would expect to find information in his papers about civil rights, the unionization and labor movements, the Mexican American population in California, the history of California between 1952 and 1993, immigration, and the lives and struggles of farm laborers, among other topics. Thus if users were interested in the lives and struggles of farmworkers in California in the 1960s, they would ask themselves: who was involved with these farmworkers? One person would be Cesar Chavez, so they could consult his papers.

Knowing the life history of Amelia Earhart, an American pilot, aviation pioneer, and author, who mysteriously disappeared during a round-the-world flight in 1937, would give one a good indication of what one might expect to find in her private papers. One might look for information on female pilots, early aviation history, the role and public reaction to female pilots, the mechanics of early flight, and the commercial aspects of aviation in the 1920s and 1930s, for instance. Users interested in unusual careers for women in the early 20th century might have a difficult time in coming up with the name Amelia Earhart, but reading biographies of outstanding American women would probably lead them to her name and hence her papers.

The Hudson's Bay Company is a retail store based in Canada, which started off life as a fur-trading company after receiving an English royal charter in 1670. The company at one time was one of the largest landowners in the world, owning huge swaths of territory in Western Canada. Knowing its history even superficially, one would expect to find information about British attitudes toward North America, the fur trade, international shipping and selling, and modern retailing and corporate ownership. Plunging further into the company's history, however, reveals that employees of the company were expected to keep detailed records of their daily business and general observations and that these records can and do provide information on the local indigenous populations, weather, the geography of Hudson Bay and all the areas surrounding it where fur was traded, the lives of fur trappers, and a whole lot more. Researchers wanting to investigate the effects of global warming in Canada over a sustained period of time would ask themselves who or what organization was creating records in the 1700s that might have included observations of the weather? This would lead them to the Hudson's Bay Company archives.

and opinions of the archivists that determined whether they would be acquired or not, and if acquired, how they would be described and made available.

Archivists talk about the *evidential* and *informational* value of archives. The evidential value of a record is, according to the SAA *Glossary*, "the quality of records that provides information about the origins, functions, and activities of their creator" (Pearce-Moses 2005). The informational value is: "the usefulness or significance of materials based on their content, independent of any intrinsic or evidential value" (Pearce-Moses 2005). The glossary gives a good example of the difference between evidential and informational value. Census records are evidence of a government's enumeration of its citizens, but genealogists use those same census records in order to find information about their relations.

Archivists also refer to the *authenticity* and *reliability* of archival records. The authenticity of records refers to the fact that they are what they purport to be based on internal and external evidence, such as their formats and physical characteristics, the way they are structured, and the information they hold. Archivists also refer to the unbroken line of custody for archives; that is to say, they can trace who held the records from the original creator to the time when the archives received them. That custody provides some measure of assurance that the records were indeed created by the person, persons, or organization identified as the creator(s). The reliability of records indicates that they are worthy of trust. Primary sources are less likely to provide evidence because they have been stripped of their context or they never had any context beyond publication to begin with. They do, however, have information that can be utilized.

Selecting the Most Appropriate Types of Records

Once the librarian has a good grasp of what the researcher needs, and the user knows all the names and geographical locations connected to the topic, the next step is to determine the best resource the researcher can use. There are two types of resources that a librarian can point users to: reproductions of records, or descriptions of those records, held by a variety of commercial and noncommercial organizations; and original records in various formats that were collected by institutions. In both cases, records can be analog or digital.

Reproductions

The easiest option for users is to use records that have been published or are online. A professional has already selected the documents for their relevance or for their importance to a particular topic. With published individual documents, the records are usually transcribed, so there is no need for the researcher to have to deal with cursive writing or strange fonts. Increasingly, cursive is becoming more and more difficult for younger members of society to read who have not been taught cursive. In addition to published or online primary and archival sources being easy to read, quite often the historical context and significance of the documents will be outlined in an introduction. There can be commentary on each document included as well, with a helpful index at the end. All of these tools make these publications a gentle way to introduce neophytes to the use of primary and archival documents. Calendars can also be considered primary sources without requiring the demands of using original documentation.

Reproductions of records can be found in analog format most often in libraries and rare book rooms and in electronic format on the websites of archives and through commercial online databases licensed by libraries. Organizations also mount reproductions of their records; for example, the United Nations has mounted treaties on its website.

Published physical texts of documents can be found in library catalogs, and when they are grouped around a person, family, or organization or are on a particular topic, they will have subject headings to assist in discovering them. Christine Bone, associate librarian at the University of Manitoba Libraries (pers. comm.), notes that the subdivision "Archives" should be attached in the subject heading field to the name of a particular person, family, or organization that created the records. The heading "Archives" can also be attached more broadly to classes of persons, ethnic groups, types of organizations, and so on. The subdivision "Sources" is generally added to historical subject headings when the item contains predominantly primary sources, that is to say, published primary or archival records *about* a subject. Alternatively, if the documents are of a specific format, that term may be used instead, for example "Diaries" or "Correspondence." "Personal narratives" can be used with wars and other events. With organizations and types of industries, "Records and correspondence" will be added to distinguish these types of records (although a search using "Correspondence" would capture this too). The term "Letters" can also be used for very general correspondence not associated with any particular person, organization, or event, so it would be less useful in finding archival materials, but might be helpful as a last resort.

So, the subject terms that will capture most published primary and archival sources are:

- Archives
- Sources
- Diaries
- Correspondence
- Records and correspondence
- Personal narratives
- Letters

Using words such as "papers," "letters," and "documents" in a keyword search along with the subject of interest is also a possible way to track them down, particularly if there has been inconsistent use of subject terms.

Digital reproductions of records can be in commercial databases or freely available. Commercial databases typically group materials by theme or subject. They may be licensed by libraries for patron use, or in some cases, individual researchers can pay for access by subscription. Free resources would be those offered by archives, libraries, research centers, and consortia on their websites. Many university libraries and research centers provide links to these reproductions. For example, a regional group calling itself the Triangle Legal History Seminar, connected to a number of universities, provides a page on *Legal History on the Web*, which provides an exhaustive list of links to dozens of sources of primary materials on legal history.

Original Records

When reproductions are not available, researchers, and the librarians helping them, locate original records. How can the librarian determine which repository would be appropriate to send users to, either physically or virtually? This is when the researcher's background work focusing the topic, collecting the names of all the people, families, and organizations connected to the topic, and finding the geographical locations where these entities carried out their activities becomes essential.

Do the records actually exist? If they exist, have they been kept? If they have been kept, have they been donated or sold to a public institution? If they have been deposited in, or sold to, a repository, can one find that institution? If one can find the place where have they been placed, have they been processed and cataloged? All of these questions have to be answered in the affirmative to determine whether records are available for research. There is absolutely no way to tell whether records might have been created or not, but one can make an educated guess. Governments are required to create records, prominent individuals often create records in their daily activities, and certain types of private organizations, such as religious organizations, typically create records. One can only hope that the organizations or people kept the records they created. Whether they decided to donate the records, keep the materials in their family or organization, or destroy them is completely unknowable. There is an economic incentive to place records in public institutions. Most archives can provide tax receipts for the value of records of private individuals and organizations. And some wealthier institutions purchase records.

Finding the institution where records have been placed can sometimes be challenging. Private individuals and organizations do not always make sensible decisions about where to deposit their records. And there exist enormous backlogs of unprocessed late-20th-century records which were acquired by archives in great volumes in a very short period of time. Thus, even if logic tells one that an institution should have appropriate records for a reference request, it does not mean that those records either exist or are available. One must accept that archival research is more challenging than research into primary sources or published material, but the thrill of the chase is often, for researchers, a huge part of the allure.

Primary sources often end up being acquired by special collections within libraries or special libraries and are often discoverable through library catalogs. Archival sources can be found in a variety of institutions, including special collections departments within libraries, and in a significant number of cases, the collections can be found only through a search of the institutions' own websites.

However, to begin a search for collections of really prominent individuals, the librarian can conduct a *Google* search such as "where are archives relating to X?" This will likely bring up a number of sites that have archival material relating to that person. "Where are archives relating to Harriet Tubman?" for instance, brings up links to records relating to Tubman African American abolitionist and humanitarian, from the National Archives and Records Administration (NARA) and the Library of Congress, among others. Or "where are the archives of Walter Cronkite?" in a *Google* search will instantly bring up the location of the records of the prominent television newscaster at the Briscoe Center for American History at the University of Texas at Austin. For organizations, it is best to check the website of that organization first. Even if the organization does not maintain its own archives, they may have information about where their records are kept.

For collections of people who are not prominent and defunct organizations, generally one can say that the place where the entities carried out their activities will determine where the users should start their search. For example, one would expect to find the archives of the Hawaiian government in Hawaii, and one would expect to look for the papers of prominent Hawaiians in Hawaiian repositories, at least in the first instance. As to how to determine the type of organization that might hold the records, there is an overlying structure that provides pointers as to what institutions might hold the actual records the users need. Carrying the previous example forward, one would expect to find the archives of the Hawaiian government at the Hawai'i State Archives. The personal papers of prominent

Hawaiians, particularly those who likely would have deposited after institutions were created in Hawaii, might be found in a variety of institutions, such as the University of Hawai'i at Mānoa Library.

Important institutions at the national level in the United States are the Library of Congress and the NARA. The Library of Congress was established in 1800 originally to collect books, but by 1897, the new Manuscript Division acquired 25,000 manuscripts, which became the basis for collecting the records of private individuals. NARA was established considerably later in 1934 and is responsible for collecting federal government records or private records with a strong federal connection. NARA is also responsible for the confusingly named Presidential Libraries, which primarily house the archives of each president. Below the national level, almost every state has a state archives, or often a state archives and library combined, for government records, and a state historical society for private records. In a number of states, the state archives and the historical society are combined. State archives particularly in the south also have significant holdings of private records. Many of the larger cities have their own archives, or departments responsible for records management that will also look after archives. Sometimes private records at the city level will be held by history centers located within municipal public libraries. The majority of universities will have archives, most housed in the library. Some will have only university archives that collect university records, and some will have only a special collections department that collects private records, but a significant number will have both. Religious organizations usually have archives at all administrative levels except individual churches.

A number of major businesses have archives, such as the Ford Motor Company (although the records are now cared for by the Henry Ford, essentially a museum) and the Coca-Cola Company, but many business archives exist to serve only their parent organizations, and much of their work has to do with patent and trademark rights, so it is sometimes difficult for external researchers to get access to these archives. In addition to business archives, there are a number of archives that serve parent organizations, such as the NSDAR archives of the Daughters of the American Revolution and the archives of the Boy Scouts of America, held by the National Scouting Museum.

In Canada, the National Library and the National Archives merged to form Library and Archives Canada in 2004. The National Library collected literary manuscripts, music archives, and maps in particular. In Canada, all governmental archives made a special point of collecting private records of interest; this is something Canadian archivists refer to as "total archives." That collection effort did not stop nongovernmental libraries and archives from collecting private records, a role that has become increasingly important as today many governmental institutions have sharply cut back on their collecting of private records. University archives, religious archives, and municipal archives are the major collectors outside of federal and provincial archives. There are very few independent business archives. Many companies have placed their records with public institutions, such as the Hudson's Bay Company archives at Archives of Manitoba, and the Eaton's Company archives at the Archives of Ontario, both provincial archives.

Internationally, similar structures can be found in most countries, although they will have individual differences among them. In Britain, for instance, many of the major estates have significant family archival holdings.

Thus, one can see that archives are closely associated with organizations. With the exception of universities, which tend to have broad collecting mandates, most records are kept by their creating institutions: religious records by religious organizations, government records by governments, business records by businesses, and so on. Various websites and guides can help users look for appropriate institutions. However, a general Web search is a good place to start. Many archives have a strong presence on the Internet, and that is the best place for researchers to begin their searches. Many institutions also have restricted hours, and special conditions for individual holdings based on donor restrictions and privacy concerns. In addition, a number of larger archives now store their collections in off-site storage after they ran out of space in their main facilities. This can result in a day or longer wait time after materials have been requested. Making contact with the facilities in advance will overcome these issues and will also help pinpoint the best materials to use for the request in advance of the visit. Staff might be able to predict the likelihood of finding the required information in the selected materials and can possibly assist in forwarding the researcher to a more appropriate location, saving the researcher a wasted trip.

Descriptions of Records

Once the librarian and the user have pinpointed the institution that holds the records of interest, then the librarian can either assist the user in navigating the descriptions of records or the user will do the searching on his or her own and will be responsible for selecting the records that best suit the user's needs. Some institutions will have the descriptions of their records online, some will have in-house databases of descriptions, and some will still have manual systems. For online and database descriptions, users will likely be able to search the descriptions. With manual systems, there will likely be indexes to the contents. In virtually every case, users will be searching for the names of the individuals they have identified connected to their topic, although archives have begun to add subject headings to the descriptions of their holdings, and many have created thematic Web pages.

At the top level, each named collection will be described through such information as biographical sketches of the creators, dates of the records, extent and type of records, and the scope and contents of the collection. In Canada, archivists will refer to these global descriptions as "RAD descriptions," which refers to fonds or collection-level descriptions according to the Canadian standard, the *Rules for Archival Description* (Bureau of Canadian Archivists 2008). Figure 27.2 provides an example of a global-level description.

Below these high-level descriptions will be finding aids, inventories, or file lists. These aids assist the user in determining the specific contents of each collection. See Figure 27.3 for an example of a file-level inventory.

Finding aids and inventories describe the contents of the collection using hierarchical levels of description such as the following:

- Group/fonds
- Subgroup/sousfonds
- Series
- Subseries
- File
- Item

Hamilton Family fonds	
Call Number:	Mss 14, Pc 12, Tc 70 (A.79-21, A.79-41, A.79-52, A.79-56, A.79-65, A.80-08, A.80-25, A.81-09, A.86-56)
Title:	Hamilton Family fonds.
Dates:	1919–1986.
Extent:	2.5 m of tcxtual records and other material
Biographical sketch:	Dr. T.G. (Thomas Glendenning) Hamilton was born in Agincourt, Ontario in 1873. In 1883, his family moved west to Saskatchewan and was among the first pioneer families to settle in Saskatoon. After his father died in 1891, his mother moved the family to Winnipeg where young T.G. Hamilton attended Manitoba College. He graduated from medical school in 1903, completed his internship at the Winnipeg General Hospital in 1904, and commenced practice in the district of Elmwood within Winnipeg. In 1915, he was President of the Manitoba Medical Association. Hamilton also served on the Public School Board for nine years, one year as chairman. He was also elected a member of the provincial legislature in 1914–1915. In 1918, soon after his young son's death, he began to experiment with psychic phenomena. His aim was the investigation of paranormal phenomena such as rappings, psychokinesis, ectoplasms, and materializations under scientific conditions that would minimize any possibility of error. His work became known in the United Kingdom, Europe, and the United States. In 1923, T.G. Hamilton was appointed to the Executive of the Canadian Medical Association as a representative for Manitoba; he held thie position until 1931. Between 1926 and 1935, he presented eighty-six lectures and wrote numerous articles that were published in Canada and abroad. Dr. Hamilton's wife, Lillian, carried on his paranormal experimentations following his death in 1935.
Custodial history:	The fonds was donated to University of Manitoba Archives & Special Collections by T.G. and Lillian's daughter, Margaret Hamilton Bach, and her daughters in several instalments between 1979 and 1986.
Scope and content:	The fonds is primarily related to Dr. T.G. and Lillian Hamilton's investigations of psychic phenomena spanning the years 1918 to 1945. The subject matter of the records includes rappings, clairvoyance, trance states and trance charts, telekinesis, wax molds, bell-ringing, transcripts and visions, as well as teleplasmic manifestations. The records are in the following various formats: scrapbooks, seance attendance records and registers, affidavits, automatic writings, correspondence, speeches and lectures, newsclippings, journal articles, books, photographs, glass plate negatives and positives, prints, slides, tapes, manuscripts, and promotional materials related to major publications. All positive prints taken from the photographic negatives have been retained with the written records of the experiments which they illustrate. Almost all the glass plate negatives were photographed for archival purposes, and the black and white glossy print collection is also available. A library of related books and journals which accompanied the collection has been separately catalogued and is available.
Restrictions:	There are no restrictions on this material.
Finding aid:	Printed finding aids are available in the Archives reading room

FIGURE 27.2 Global-level description of the Hamilton Family collection at the University of Manitoba Archives & Special Collections

		Seance Attendance Registers:
Box	Folder	
8	1	March 29, 1925–December 9, 1926—includes MSS & typed formats.
	2	Jan 20, 1927–Dec 29, 1929. Typed format, 1927 only.
	3	Jan 5, 1930–Feb 19, 1933.
	4	Feb 22, 1933–May 22, 1935.
	5	May 8, 1935–June 8, 1936. Original notes by Gladys and Dr. Bruce Chown.
		Seance Directories:
Box	Folder	
8	6	Index April 1923–September, 1927.
	7	R.L.S. seance output index, April 1923–July 1925.
	8	"Book I—R.L.S. directory 1923–1927", MSS & typed format.
Box	Folder	
9	1	"Book II—R.L.S. Alone 1923–1925".
	2	"Book III—Directory 1925–1927".
	3	"Book IV—Directory 1927".
		Affidavits for Seance Sittings:
Box	Folder	
	4	May 13, 1928—Bell Ringing.
	5	September 23, 1928—Bellchords & Teleplasm.
	6	November 4, 1928—Spurgeon Face.
	7	November 25, 1928—5 Faces.

FIGURE 27.3 File-level inventory for the Hamilton Family collection at the University of Manitoba Archives & Special Collections

A series is an intellectual grouping of like materials. "Correspondence," for example, might be a typical series title. File lists are simple lists of files in a collection without any attempt to distinguish groupings. A number of Canadian and other international archives employ something called the series system, which focuses descriptions on the series level and then links each series to all the creators and to all the files that belong to the series. This is particularly useful for describing government archives where names, functional responsibilities, and composition of departments frequently change. In these systems, users will begin by searching series descriptions.

It is important to remember two things: item-level finding aids are very rare and are usually confined to special formats, such as photographs and maps, and not every archive has had the funds to retrospectively re-catalog its collections when it has changed access systems. Thus an archive can have some holdings described by a published guide, and other holdings described by a card catalog, paper finding aids, and/or online finding aids.

Using Archives at the Institution

> I get slightly obsessive about working in archives because you don't know what you're going to find. In fact, you don't know what you're looking for until you find it.
>
> —Antony Beevor (quoted in Orr 2009)

If the librarian directs the researcher to a suitable institution, the archivists or librarians at the repository will guide the researcher through the access process. They will also explain the nature and meaning of any restrictions that might apply to any of the records the user is interested in. If it is a factual question and can be answered in a relatively brief period of time, most institutions will provide the answer directly to the researcher. If, however, the reference question requires a significant amount of time or decisions need to be made along the research path (is this information important enough to continue the search here?), then the repositories' staff will request the researcher physically come to the archives or library and do the research himself or herself or will suggest that a research assistant be hired to do the research on the user's behalf.

SOURCES BY COUNTRY OR REGION

The following discussion presents important websites and databases of primary and archival sources according to American, Canadian, UK, European, and International categories, followed by thematic categories. Sources related specifically to genealogical research are discussed in Chapter 21; newspaper sources are discussed in Chapter 17. Databases and websites are growing exponentially, as archives, libraries, research centers, and commercial entities rush to provide access to these previously inaccessible resources. As universities in particular see these resources as one of the few ways to distinguish their institutions, they are making significant efforts to digitize their collections. This list provides a useful starting point of major collections of materials.

As has been noted, there is a strong geographical component to archival resource discovery. The following list separates institutions by country. The general rule is that one can expect to find the records of a country or its citizens in that country; however, unfortunately that is not always entirely true. North American universities often see their collecting mandates as very broad and hence acquire records from international sources.

United States

The NARA has holdings dating back to 1775, numbering literally billions of records of all types. Naturally, for a collection so large, there are a number of online tools and helpful instructional pages. In addition to an online catalog, there are a microfilm catalog and a number of archival databases that provide access to special formats. There is also a specialized guide to federal records. In addition to these finding aids, there is a specialized tool for researching veterans' service records. Actual copies of some of NARA's records have been digitized in conjunction with a number of organizations, such as Google and the University of Texas at Austin, and are held on those sites. A number of iconic documents, including the Constitution, the Louisiana Purchase, and Thomas Edison's patent application for the lightbulb, are available on NARA's website on the *America's Historical Documents* page.

The Library of Congress website provides a wealth of information on the holdings of the Library of Congress. The main thrust of the collection is American history and culture through historic newspapers, sound recordings, prints, photographs, and U.S. legislative information, and through the veterans' history project and website archiving. Finding aids to personal papers such as the Alexander Graham Bell family papers, the Jackie Robinson papers, and the Frank Lloyd Wright papers, indicate what users might find if they come to the Library of Congress. However, the overwhelming majority of papers described were created by men, giving a decidedly lopsided view of American history. The Library of Congress's *American Memory* website presents selected collections that have been digitized. There is a cautionary note: the library migrated some of its collections to a new system. Collections that have been migrated no longer appear in internal *American Memory* search results and browse lists. To search all Library collections (including *American Memory*), one must use the general search and browse options.

The Smithsonian, a complex of 19 museums and 9 research centers and affiliates, provides both descriptions of holdings and online collections through its website, *Smithsonian*. Included are the Archives of American Art, the Smithsonian Archives, and the Smithsonian Libraries. In addition, many of the museums have their own archives, such as the National Museum of the American Indian (NMAI), that go beyond the archives of the actual individual institution. *The Archive Center* of the NMAI actively collects the records of contemporary Native American artists, writers, activists, and organizations. Photographs from the archives can be accessed from the general Collections Search website.

ArchiveGrid was begun by the Research Libraries Group and contains more than 4 million archival material descriptions held by more than 1,000 different archives, libraries, museums, and historical societies, mostly in the United States but also around the world. One can easily see which organizations are included. What is less obvious is that the material that is included is archival material that was cataloged for library catalogs and so therefore often more nearly resembles published primary sources. From the Folger Shakespeare Library, for example, one can see a description of a handwritten book of recipes from 1675 from Thomas Sheppey, with a list of chief Rosicrucians added to the back. This would be useful for anyone researching food, customs, perhaps appropriate props for plays or films, the individuals named in the recipe book, and so on. But is this the only item the Folger holds from this individual? Does the recipe book make up a part of a larger collection? Where did it come from, and how did the Folger get it? Answers to these questions would make the item more useful to any serious scholars. The *Digital Public Library of America* is a portal that provides integrated access to more than 10 million digitized items from libraries, archives, and museums throughout the United States. The website supports searching by topic, place, and date.

Web-based directories can assist in locating particular types of collections of primary and archival sources. The *Repositories of Primary Sources* lists and provides links to more than 5,000 websites describing holdings of manuscripts, archives, rare books, historical photographs, and other primary sources for the research scholar. Unfortunately, as of January 1, 2015, the list was no longer being updated or maintained. *State Archives and Libraries* provides links to various state archives. Although many of the links are broken, the site provides the names of the state repositories that researchers can use in Internet searches. The *Lavender Legacies Guide* produced by the SAA's Lesbian and Gay Archives Roundtable is a good site for finding repositories that hold significant amounts of records relating to the lesbian and gay communities in North America. The *Directory of Corporate Archives in the United States and Canada* produced by the SAA's Business Archives Section includes companies that maintain their historical records themselves, as well as other sources of company records.

Canada

Library and Archives Canada is the main repository for federal government records and many private records of national importance. The institution has suffered severe cutbacks in recent years, but more recently has been undergoing significant improvements under new leadership. An improvement in the user interface with the *Library and Archives Canada* website has made searching easier. There is a general search tool for descriptions of archival resources with accompanying finding aids as well as specialty portals for the most popular types of uses including genealogy and family history, censuses, military records, and portraits. The site is available in Canada's official languages, French and English.

Most of the provinces and territories in Canada have provincial archival organizations that maintain databases that include collection-level descriptions. Although the coverage varies from database to database, these portals are generally important sources to find records held by small- and medium-sized archival institutions, particularly those that are unable to support their own descriptive databases. Generally it is better however when seeking information from larger organizations such as university archives to go straight to the websites of those institutions as the holdings will be fuller and more up to date than what is included in these portals. A common portal called *Archivescanada.ca* is coordinated by the Canadian Council of Archives (CCA) and is hosted by Library and Archives Canada, but it lacks ranked results and faceted searches, making it difficult to use. The CCA does provide access to an online *Directory of Archives*, which provides names of institutions and contact information. It has not been recently updated, however, so should be used only as a starting point.

A major source of radio broadcasts and television footage is the archives of the Canadian Broadcasting Company (CBC), the national public radio and television broadcaster. The *CBC Digital Archives* provides excellent online access to its most popular broadcasts. It also has a music archive of original CBC commissions, a library of CBC publications, and a photo collection made up primarily of publicity shots taken by the CBC's own photographers in the 1950s, 1960s, and 1970s. The CBC Archives is an important resource of information on Canadian personalities and events.

Images Canada provides central search access to the thousands of images held on the websites of participating Canadian cultural institutions. This is an odd mix of 15 repositories of greatly varying sizes including Library and Archives Canada and the Canadian Aviation Museum as well as the Sir Alexander Galt Museum & Archives and the Earth Sciences Information Center, from National Resources Canada. The size of the images is unfortunately quite small, and not all of the images can be blown up to see details, particularly with images from the Glenbow Museum, which viewers must purchase to get any detail.

A number of websites not only cover primarily published literature but also include gray literature and ephemera. Canadiana.org had been systematically microfilming, and now scanning, Canada's published heritage since 1978. *Early*

Canadiana Online includes government publications. The *Canadiana Discovery Portal* provides access to digital collections from many Canadian libraries, museums, and archives, but the overwhelming majority of material on the site is published, although it does include gray literature and ephemera. The *Héritage* collection is composed of scans of nearly 20,000 microfilms of archival and published records held by Library and Archives Canada. Digitized versions of the debates of the Senate and House of Commons from 1867 to 1993 can also be found there.

United Kingdom

The National Archives provides a strong search tool that allows users to search the records from the Archives as well as more than 2,500 archives across the United Kingdom (UK). Users can also narrow the search down to just those held by the National Archives. As might be expected from the National Archives, the results are excellent.

A Directory of Rare Book and Special Collections in the UK and Republic of Ireland, edited by B.C. Bloomfield (1997), lists information on approximately 1,200 libraries, archives, museums, and private holdings providing details on the contents of these institutions as well as their locations and contact information. Although the majority of this information is about published books, manuscripts held by these institutions are also included.

Europe

Archives Portal Europe provides for a federated search across 60 million descriptive units of archives contained in 865 institutions as well as important details such as their location, access conditions, and hours of service. *Europeana* allows users to explore millions of items from a range of Europe's leading galleries, libraries, archives, and museums. Items include books and manuscripts, photos and paintings, television and film, sculpture and crafts, diaries and maps, sheet music, and recordings. The Czech Republic has produced *Manuscriptorium*, a sub-aggregator of *Europeana*, which provides access to "historic book resources," including manuscripts, incunabula,[1] early printed books, maps, charters, and university theses. Materials display in their original language although the interface is in 11 different languages. *Manuscriptorium* is both a catalog of descriptions of online holdings and a collection of a smaller number of digitized images.

European History Primary Resources is a joint initiative of the Library and the Department of History and Civilization of the European University Institute in Florence, Italy. It provides a one-stop location for visiting archives and libraries of primary and archival sources throughout Europe. Brigham Young University has also produced a handy website called *EuroDocs—Online Sources for European History*, which gathers together links to a huge number of websites of digitized primary sources.

Other Countries

Many sites all over the world feature the archives of that country, particularly offered by national institutions. The drawback, of course, is that users must understand the language of the country. However, one website that is close to home and provides access in English is at the Library of Congress. The Library of Congress, with support from UNESCO, has created the *World Digital Library*. In addition to books, there are archival materials from a wide variety of institutions, such as the Bibliothèque nationale de France and the Tetouan Asmir Association of Morocco. The strength of the website is that it provides all navigation tools, bibliographic information, and content descriptions in seven languages: Arabic, Chinese, English, French, Portuguese, Russian, and Spanish. Additionally, the metadata and descriptions can be listened to using text-to-voice conversion in all of these languages.

RESOURCES BY SUBJECT

Many websites and subscription-only online databases focus on specialized subjects, providing an easier way for users interested in subjects or topics, rather than individuals, to do their research. Many of these databases include materials from both the United States and Canada and occasionally other countries. Most sites are a hybrid of archival, primary, and published sources. Even the archival material on these sites would be considered more primary sources, however, for though the publishers cite the origins of the material, they present each document on its own as if it were a publication. It would take a great deal of digging to get back to the repository, where the original is described to see what other records might enhance the user's understanding of the context. The great strength of these databases is the ability to search across materials because of the detailed metadata attached to each image. These websites are mostly digitized documents, although occasionally there may be descriptions and actual finding aids as well.

Gale Cengage Learning refers to its *Artemis Primary Sources* as an "integrated research environment" that allows users to search across eight primary source collections including: *Indigenous Peoples: North America*; *17th and 18th Century Burney Collection*; *Eighteenth Century Collections Online*; *The Making of Modern Law: Trials, 1600–1926*; *The Making of Modern Law: Legal Treatises, 1800–1926*; *The Times Digital Archive, 1785–2008*; *Nineteenth Century Collections Online*; and *The Sunday Times Digital Archive*. *Artemis* adds frequency and term-relationship tools to assist users in analyzing content. The search engine is easy to use, the results are impressive, and the display of the results is relatively easy to decipher.

ProQuest has its own subscription database of archival documents on American history from the 18th to the 20th century called *ProQuest History Vault*. Although the main emphasis is on Southern, African American, and women's history, there is also material relating to political science, military and diplomatic history, immigration, and so on.

American Foreign Policy

For general historic U.S. government documents, there are a number of websites to explore (see Chapter 22). In addition, however, there has been a growing interest in foreign policy and security. Official publications from the American government, for instance, the book series *Foreign Relations of the United States*, are published by the Office of the Historian in the Department of State. This series presents the official record of major U.S. foreign policy decisions and significant diplomatic activity and includes declassified records from foreign affairs agencies.

The series began publication in 1861. *HeinOnline* provides access to these volumes from 1861 to 1980, or users can go to the *Historical Documents* website of the U.S. Department of State Office of the Historian and search the volumes covering the presidencies from the Truman administration to the Carter administration from 1945 to 1980.

ProQuest provides subscription access to the *Digital National Security Archive*, which consists of declassified documents dealing with U.S. foreign policy and intelligence and security issues from post–World War II to the 21st century. From this site, there is free access to the intriguingly named "CIA Family Jewels Indexed." This file, dating from 1973, documents the domestic activities that the CIA was engaged in that were outside of its charter and therefore illegal, such as assassinations, interrogations, surveillance, and break-ins. *The National Security Archive* at George Washington University provides access to unpublished and published declassified documents on issues including U.S. national security, foreign policy, diplomatic and military history, and intelligence policy.

African Americans

Although *Black Thought and Culture: African Americans from Colonial Times to the Present* by Alexander Street Press presents primarily published material by leaders within the black community, it also contains pamphlets, letters, and other primary sources. The collection is intended for research in black studies, political science, American history, music, literature, and art. Adam Matthew's *Slavery, Abolition and Social Justice 1490–2007* is designed as an important portal for slavery and abolition studies, bringing together documents and collections dating from 1490 to 2007. Another good site is Vanderbilt University's *Ecclesiastical & Secular Sources for Slave Societies*, which preserves and makes available endangered ecclesiastical and secular documents relating to Africans, people descended from Africans in the Americas, Chinese, and Indigenous groups.

American History

A number of commercial online resources provide information on American history. Alexander Street Press offers *Early Encounters in North America: Peoples, Cultures and the Environment*, which documents the relationships among peoples and their environment in North America from 1534 to 1850. *North American Immigrant Letters, Diaries, and Oral Histories* provides access to private records about immigration to America and Canada, including letters, diaries, pamphlets, autobiographies, and oral histories, and dates from around 1840 to the present, although the predominant dates are from 1920 to 1980. The search engine for this resource is very powerful, with a nice display of all the contextual information up front for search results, although as with *Early Encounters*, one does not see or hear the original records but only transcriptions.

Sage Knowledge has produced *Historic Documents*, which is an online version of the Historic Documents print editions. Published annually since 1972, the Historic Documents volumes present transcriptions of approximately 100 documents covering the most significant events of the year. Because these are single documents, it makes it very difficult to get a sense of the context. The *New Deal Network* is devoted to documents and photographs of the new deal under Franklin Roosevelt when the U.S. government responded to the Great Depression by enacting laws that saw a significant number of public projects created to employ the unemployed between 1933 and 1938.

Human Rights

Many websites have sprung up, particularly in the last decade, featuring human rights archives and primary sources. Often these sites have been created by university libraries to assist in the preservation and dissemination of human rights materials for academics and students. These types of records are fragile not only because of the circumstances of their creation, often in countries struggling with poverty and extreme environmental conditions, but also because the records themselves are often the targets of destruction. These archives are not necessarily always physical. In some cases, the organizations have been digitizing the documents and returning them to their country of origin. In others, such as the U.S. Secretary of Defense's *Conflict Records Research Center*, they have been holding onto the physical records of the Saddam Hussein regime, a move not entirely without controversy. The access conditions for each of these archives vary widely, depending upon the sensitivity of the information, their dates, and so on.

The Columbia University Libraries' *Center for Human Rights Documentation & Research* holds a variety of archival collections including records of Amnesty International USA and Human Rights Watch. The center also holds the *Human Rights Web Archive*, a searchable collection of archived copies of human rights websites created by nongovernmental organizations, national human rights institutions, tribunals, and individuals. Collecting began in 2008 and has been ongoing for active websites. The Duke University Libraries' *Human Rights Archive* has been partnering with human rights organizations and individuals since 2006, acquiring records and papers of human rights advocates. Their collections are as diverse as Radio Haiti records and the Southern Poverty Law Center collection of extremist literature. Iraqi secret police records were seized by Kurds in 1991 after the defeat of the Iraqi armed forces in the Gulf War. Approximately 18 metric tons of files were digitized by the U.S. Defense Intelligence Agency with the possibility of gathering evidence of genocide against the Iraqi regime. Although the 5.5 million document collection was eventually returned back to the Kurds, the digitized images were deposited with the University Libraries at the University of Colorado Boulder in a collection known as the "Iraqi Secret Police Files" and are available for research via an Institutional Review Board. The University of Texas Libraries of the University of Texas at Austin maintains the *Human Rights Documentation Initiative*, which helps to preserve vulnerable records of human rights activities around the world. Significant holdings include the Free Burma Rangers, the Genocide Archive for Rwanda, and the Guatemalan National Police Historical Archive.

The University of Southern California's *Shoah Foundation* has an archive of nearly 52,000 testimonies of survivors and witnesses to the Holocaust, but the foundation is also incorporating collections of testimonies on the Cambodian, Rwandan, and Armenian genocides. The *Human Rights Collection*, at Archives & Special Collections at the Thomas J. Dodd Research Center of the University of Connecticut, includes such archives as the U. Roberto (Robin) Romano digital photographs of child labor and the African National Congress Oral History Transcripts Collection.

The *National Research Centre for Truth and Reconciliation* at the University of Manitoba in Winnipeg is the site for the records of the Truth and Reconciliation Commission of Canada. This includes recorded testimonies of survivors of the Canadian Indian Residential School system and digital copies of records relating to the schools from the federal government and churches, as well as records relating to the Settlement process, which established the commission. There are in excess of 5 million records and more than 6,000 testimonies. The collection will continue to grow, as the Centre has a mandate to continue seeking out and adding records relating to residential schools as well as to Indigenous people in Canada in general.

Indigenous Peoples

A number of key websites in North America and internationally are dedicated to preserving records relating to indigenous peoples. In the United States, *The Plateau Peoples' Web Portal* provides access to archival records held in Washington State University's Libraries, Manuscripts, Archives and Special Collections, the Museum of Anthropology, and private donors. In Canada, the *Reciprocal Research Network* at the University of British Columbia holds museum items focused on Northwest Coast museum collections as well as nearly 300,000 photographs, including historic photos, from 24 partner institutions including the American Museum of Natural History, the Smithsonian Institution, and the Pitt Rivers Museum, University of Oxford. The Métis National Council's *Historical Online Database* is a Web-interfaced database that contains genealogical information on individuals of the historic Métis Nation. The website also contains scans of many of the original documents represented in the database; many of the documents were created by other organizations and institutions.

Internationally, the *Australian Institute of Aboriginal and Torres Strait Islander Studies* provides access to its holdings through the Mura catalog. The catalog provides descriptions about original photographs, rare serials, photographs, moving images, and sound recordings on Australia's indigenous population. Two hundred people who were in care or were child migrants were interviewed by the National Library of Australia for the *Forgotten Australians and Former Child Migrants Oral History Project*. Advocates or people who worked in the welfare system were also interviewed. In New Zealand, there are Māori archives held by a number of institutions including Archives New Zealand, the National Library of New Zealand, and the University of Auckland. Archives New Zealand has a small number of original records online. Descriptions of records on the Māori can be found by using that search term on the Archives' website.

A number of online subscription databases relate to indigenous people. *American Indian Histories and Cultures* from Adam Matthew includes manuscripts, artwork, photographs, and newspapers dating from contact to the mid-20th century. It is a handsome and easily navigated site with excellent presentation of materials from the Newberry Library's Edward E. Ayer Collection. The *American Indian Law Collection* from HeinOnline covers American Indian Law, including treaties, federal statutes and regulations, federal case law, tribal codes, constitutions, and jurisprudence. This library also features rare compilations edited by Felix S. Cohen that are newly accessible online. Gale's *Indigenous Peoples: North America* assembles sources from collections at Canadian and American institutions and provides insight into the cultural, political, and social history of Native Peoples from the

17th into the 20th century. Included are manuscripts, newspapers from various tribe and Indian-related organizations, and materials such as Bibles, dictionaries, and primers in Indigenous languages. Alexander Street Press provides access to biographies, autobiographies, oral histories, reference works, manuscripts, and photographs in the database *North American Indian Thought and Culture.* Again, the coverage is North American.

Women

An excellent general site for finding resources on women is the *Women's History Research in Archives* guide at UW-Madison Libraries. It provides links to sites on professional women, women of color, Jewish women, lesbian archives, and websites devoted to women's archives in different parts of the United States and around the world. Alexander Street Press has two online resources relating to women. *North American Women's Letters and Diaries: Colonial to 1950* includes transcriptions of both published letters and diaries from individuals writing from Colonial times to 1950, and unpublished materials. Represented are most age groups, life stages, ethnicities, and geographical regions. It includes approximately 300 biographies. There are a small number of digitized materials. *Women and Social Movements in the United States 1600–2000* brings together images, documents, scholarly essays, and commentaries on women's reform activities.

SOURCES FOR SPECIFIC MEDIA

Sometimes users are looking for particular media or formats, such as oral histories or sound and moving image archives. This is a popular way for organizations to group primary and archival sources, particularly with photographs. The following section provides information about sources for these various types of materials. General sources discussed earlier will also include these types of media.

Digital Archives

The Internet Archive *Wayback Machine* is hosted in the United States. It is a service that allows people to visit archived versions of sites on the World Wide Web. Visitors to the *Wayback Machine* can type in a URL, select a date range, and then begin surfing on an archived version of the Web. This is an extremely useful resource, but the harvesting has not been consistent, so not all changes to a website will necessarily be represented, and often links to external and even sometimes internal Web pages are broken.

Oral Histories

Oral History Online from Alexander Street Press is a database of English-language oral histories, including Ellis Island oral history narratives and exclusive Black Panther Party interviews. The interface is not always easy to use as some links to resources take the user to the collecting institution where it is necessary to conduct another search. *American Rhetoric* is a massive multimedia site that contains more than 5,000 full-text, audio, and video versions of public speeches, sermons, legal proceedings, lectures, debates, interviews, and other recorded media events, and 200 short audio clips from well-known speeches, movies, sermons, popular songs, and media events by politicians, actors, preachers, athletes, singers, and other noteworthy personalities. Significant American political and Hollywood speeches of the 20th century are also included. The *G. Robert Vincent Voice Library* at Michigan State University houses an enormous collection of spoken word recordings, dating back to 1888. Not all recordings are available to listen online, but researchers can hear the recordings at the library.

Photographs

A number of free and commercial sites are dedicated to providing access to historic photographs. Many of the sites provide access to both still and moving images. The *AP Images* photo archive features state, regional, and national photos from North America as well as international photos. The historical section in particular features iconic photographs of people, places, objects, and events in various themed categories such as sports and entertainment. *Artstor* provides access to nearly 2 million digital images that cover the arts, architecture, humanities, and the sciences from museums, photo archives, scholars, and artists. Although *Artstor* bills itself as an image library, there are a number of primary source collections, including Magnum Photos, the Thomas K. Seligman Archive, and a selection from the Condé Nast Archive of Photography.

Flickr is a free photo-sharing service. A number of archives and libraries have established photostreams. One of the most important is the Library of Congress, which has uploaded nearly 23,000 images from its collections. Unfortunately, the results from searching Flickr for primary or archival images are hit and miss. Few libraries and archives have really taken to the site to disseminate their holdings. But searching on the *Flickr Commons*, launched in 2008, provides an easier way to discover primary and archival images. The quality of the images and the metadata is sometimes lacking, but can be a good place to start for a beginner.

Two for-profit organizations provide access to professional-level photographs and films for a price. *Getty Images* is an American stock photo company with an archive of 80 million still images and illustrations as well as 50,000 hours of stock film footage. An important component of this archive is the inclusion of the entire inventories of Archive Photos of New York, which included archive images from the *New York Times*, *Metronome*, *National Geographic*, Hulton Picture Archive, and George Eastman House. Users must pay to use these images. There is a section of royalty-free images, but they are merely illustrative and thematic with no authoritative historic content. However, users can find historic photos under the term "editorial" with thematic categories such as archival, editorial, sports, and entertainment, taken by professional photographers. The searching of metadata is very powerful, and, of course, the quality of the photography is very impressive. The website *mptv* also provides still images taken by professional photographers. Most of the content of *mptv* and *Getty Images* is aimed at professionals who are willing to pay significant prices to license images. George Eastman House has its own historic *Photography Collection*, which contains a selection from its large photo collection. Daguerreotypes, 19th-century British and French photography on paper, and American 19th-century holdings have been uploaded onto *Flickr Commons* and are freely available. Although the images online are a very small portion of the overall collection of George Eastman House, the metadata is extensive and excellent, and the searching is better for it.

Millions of images, both photos and drawings, from *Life* magazine dating back to as early as the 1860s have been uploaded into *Google Images* and can be searched by adding "source:life" to any *Google* image search or searched from the *Life* photo archive page. Most of these images were never published. These images can be used for personal, noncommercial use without having to pay for the use. *U.S. Government Photos and Images* is a convenient way to access the National Archives, Library of Congress, U.S. Department of Agriculture National Agricultural Library Special Collections, and Smithsonian historic images. Most of the photographs from other government departments are relatively current but could be considered primary sources for activities of the U.S. federal government. Most images are in the public domain and can be used without permission.

Sound and Moving Images

A number of websites exist for accessing moving images that could be considered primary sources. On *YouTube*, if the phrase "old commercials" is entered into the search bar, advertisements from 1940 to 1970 will be retrieved, including television advertisements. The *Internet Archive* includes films, video, community video, television shows, and advertisements on its site. Many titles created by U.S. corporations, nonprofit organizations, trade associations, community and interest groups, and educational institutions from the Prelinger Archives, begun by Rick Prelinger of New York City, are included. *Metavid—Open Video Archive of the US Congress* is a community-based archiving project to provide access to more than 1,000 hours of U.S. House and Senate floor footage. The Office of the Clerk of the U.S. House of Representatives also provides access to their floor proceedings back to 2009 through its *HouseLive* site. U.S. Senate *Floor Webcast* has its own Webcasts of its proceedings going back to 2012. Both of these sites are searchable.

The *Museum of the Moving Image* includes photographs, fan magazines, and marketing materials, although this website does not feature the actual digitized items, but only descriptions of them. However, the site does have *The Living Room Candidate*, which is an archive of more than 300 commercials featuring U.S. presidents from every presidential election since 1952. The *Pinewood Dialogues* are interviews with various creative figures in film, television, and digital media. *The Open Video Project*, sponsored by the Interaction Design Laboratory at the School of Information and Library Science, University of North Carolina Chapel Hill, is a growing repository of both clips and full digital video and digitized video in the historical, documentary, educational, public service, and ephemeral arenas. Although the purpose of this project is to provide video for research such as developing face recognition software and testing algorithms for automatic segmentation and summarization, complete metadata is provided for each segment or video; thus, this can be used to access the original films held by the contributing repositories. *ResearchChannel* on *YouTube* provides one-stop shopping for videos from research and academic institutions on such topics as the history of multiple sclerosis and anthropogenic biomes. The videos are a mixture of documentaries and oral interviews.

CONCLUSION

Major publishers and a number of archives and libraries have tried to bridge the gap between users who are accustomed to searching by subject and the standard arrangement of archival resources listed by creator by developing websites focused on a particular subject. If users are trying to complete assignments, or they do not need a specific answer, these websites are usually sufficient. These websites can also be good places to start a more in-depth search. But for specific answers and for any intensive research that relies on facts related to specific people and events, archives are usually the only way to find the answers. By using a method of matching topics to persons, and then matching the persons to a geographical place, the reference librarian can often determine where likely collections will reside and point the users there online first and then to the physical location as a follow-up.[2]

NOTES

1. Incunabula, or incunables, are books printed before 1501. The date of 1500 is arbitrary, but incunabula are generally the earliest printed books printed using wooden blocks or movable type, although many authors use incunabula only for those printed with movable type.
2. Thanks to Cheryl Avery, Megan Butcher, Kyle Feenstra, Frank Van Kalmthout, James Kominowski, Kristen Kruse, Regina Landwehr, Anne Lindsay, Leon Miller, and Lewis St. George Stubbs, for their valuable insights. Also thanks to Michael Moir for his helpful tips.

REFERENCES

Bureau of Canadian Archivists. 2008. *Rules for Archival Description.* Ottawa: Bureau of Canadian Archivists.

Orr, Deborah. 2009. "Antony Beevor: 'History Has Not Emphasised Enough the Suffering of French Civilians during the War.'" *The Independent.* June 6. http://www.independent.co.uk/news/world/europe/antony-beevor-history-has-not-emphasised-enough-the-suffering-of-french-civilians-during-the-war-1696148.html.

Pearce-Moses, Richard. 2005. *A Glossary of Archival and Records Terminology.* Chicago: Society of American Archivists.

Roosevelt, Theodore. 1951–1954. *Letters.* Edited by Elting E. Morison. 8 vols. Cambridge: Harvard University Press.

Sweetman, H. S. 2008. *Calendar of Documents Relating to Ireland Preserved in Her Majesty's Public Record Office.* Burlington, ON: TannerRichie.

Waley, Arthur. 1958. *The Opium War through Chinese Eyes.* Stanford, CA: Stanford University Press.

LIST OF SOURCES

America's Historical Documents. National Archives and Records Administration. http://www.archives.gov/historical-docs/.

American Indian Histories and Cultures. Chicago: Adam Matthew. http://www.amdigital.co.uk/m-collections/collection/american-indian-histories-and-cultures/. [subscription required]

American Indian Law Collection. Getzville, NY: HeinOnline. https://help.heinonline.org/2011/10/american-indian-law-collection-now-available/. [subscription required]
American Memory. Library of Congress. http://memory.loc.gov/ammem/index.html.
American Rhetoric. http://www.americanrhetoric.com/.
AP Images. New York: Associated Press. http://www.apimages.com/historical-photo-archive. [subscription required for full access]
Archive Center. National Museum of the American Indian. http://nmai.si.edu/explore/collections/archive/.
ArchiveGrid. Dublin, OH: OCLC. http://beta.worldcat.org/archivegrid/.
Archives of Manitoba. http://www.gov.mb.ca/chc/archives/.
Archives of Ontario. http://www.archives.gov.on.ca/en/index.aspx.
Archives Portal Europe. The Hague, Netherlands: APEx project. http://www.archives portaleurope.net/.
Archivescanada.ca. Ottawa: Canadian Council of Archives. http://www.archives canada.ca/.
Artemis Primary Sources. Farmington Hills, MI: Gale Cengage Learning. http://gale.cengage.co.uk/gale-artemis/gale-artemis-primary-sources.aspx. [subscription required]
Artstor. New York: Artstor. http://www.artstor.org/index.shtml. [subscription required]
Australian Institute of Aboriginal and Torres Strait Islander Studies. http://www.aiatsis.gov.au/main.html.
Black Thought and Culture: African Americans from Colonial Times to the Present. Alexandria, VA: Alexander Street. http://alexanderstreet.com/products/black-thought-and-culture. [subscription required]
Bloomfield, B.C., ed. 1997. *A Directory of Rare Book and Special Collections in the UK and Republic of Ireland*. London: Library Association.
Canadiana Discovery Portal. Canadiana.org. http://search.canadiana.ca/?usrlang=en.
CBC Digital Archives. CBC/Radio Canada. http://www.cbc.ca/archives/.
Center for Human Rights Documentation & Research. Columbia University Libraries. http://library.columbia.edu/locations/chrdr.html.
The Coca-Cola Company. http://www.coca-colacompany.com/history/.
Conflict Records Research Center. Department of Defense. http://crrc.dodlive.mil/about/.
Digital National Security Archive. Ann Arbor, MI: ProQuest. http://nsarchive.chadwyck.com/marketing/index.jsp. [subscription required]
Digital Public Library of America. http://dp.la.
Directory of Archives. Canadian Council of Archives. http://www.cdncouncilarchives.ca/directory.html.
Directory of Corporate Archives in the United States and Canada. Society of American Archivists. http://www2.archivists.org/groups/business-archives-section/directory-of-corporate-archives-in-the-united-states-and-canada-introduction.
Early Canadiana Online. Canadiana.org. http://eco.canadiana.ca/.
Early Encounters in North America: Peoples, Cultures and the Environment. Alexandria, VA: Alexander Street. http://alexanderstreet.com/products/early-encounters-north-america-peoples-cultures-and-environment. [subscription required]
Ecclesiastical & Secular Sources for Slave Societies. Vanderbilt University. http://www.vanderbilt.edu/esss/.
EuroDocs—Online Sources for European History. Harold E. Lee Library. Brigham Young University. http://cudocs.lib.byu.edu/index.php/Main_Page.
European History Primary Sources. European University Institute. http://primary-sources.eui.eu.
Europeana. http://www.europeana.eu/.

Flickr. https://www.flickr.com/.
Flickr Commons. http://www.flickr.com/commons.
Floor Webcast. U.S. Senate. http://www.senate.gov/floor/.
Foreign Relations of the United States. Getzville, NY: HeinOnline. http://heinonline.org/HeinDocs/Foreign%20Relations%20of%20the%20US.pdf. [subscription required]
Forgotten Australians and Former Child Migrants Oral History Project. National Library of Australia. http://www.nla.gov.au/oral-history/forgotten-australians-and-former-child-migrants-oral-history-project.
G. Robert Vincent Voice Library. Michigan State University Libraries. http://vvl.lib.msu.edu/.
Getty Images. http://www.gettyimages.ca/. [subscription required for full access]
The Henry Ford. http://www.thehenryford.org/.
Héritage. Canadiana.org. http://heritage.canadiana.ca/.
Historic Documents of 2014. Thousand Oaks, CA: Sage. http://www.cqpress.com/product/Historic-Documents-of-2014.html. [subscription required]
Historical Documents. Office of the Historian. U.S. Department of State. https://history.state.gov/historicaldocuments.
Historical Online Database. Métis National Council. http://metisnationdatabase.ualberta.ca/MNC/.
HouseLive. Office of the Clerk. U.S. House of Representatives. http://houselive.gov/.
Human Rights Archive. Duke University Libraries. http://library.duke.edu/rubenstein/human-rights/.
Human Rights Collection. Archives & Special Collections at the University of Connecticut Libraries. http://doddcenter.uconn.edu/asc/dodda2z/subjectarea.cfm?Area=8.
Human Rights Documentation Initiative. University of Texas Libraries. University of Texas at Austin. http://www.lib.utexas.edu/hrdi.
Human Rights Web Archive. Columbia University Libraries. http://hrwa.cul.columbia.edu/.
Images Canada. Library and Archives Canada. http://www.imagescanada.ca/index-e.html.
Indigenous Peoples: North America. Farmington Hills, MI: Gale Cengage Learning. http://www.cengage.com/search/productOverview.do?Ntt=Indigenous+Peoples%3A+North+America|133117818019578271561928728850118397207 3&N=197&Ntk=APG%7CP_EPI&Ntx=mode+matchallpartial. [subscription required]
"Iraqi Secret Police Files." University Libraries. University of Colorado Boulder. http://ucblibraries.colorado.edu/archives/collections/international.htm.
Lavender Legacies Guide. Society of American Archivists. http://www2.archivists.org/groups/lesbian-and-gay-archives-roundtable-lagar/lavender-legacies-guide.
Legal History on the Web. Triangle Legal History Seminar. http://law.duke.edu/legal_history/portal/primary-sources.html.
Library and Archives Canada. http://www.bac-lac.gc.ca/.
Library of Congress. http://www.loc.gov/.
Life Photo Archive Hosted By Google. http://images.google.com/hosted/life.
The Living Room Candidate. Museum of the Moving Image. http://www.livingroomcandidate.org/.
Manuscriptorium. National Library of the Czech Republic. http://www.manuscriptorium.com.
Māori. Archives New Zealand. http://archives.govt.nz/gallery/v/Walter%20Nash%20Exhibition/Maori.
Metavid—Open Video Archive of the US Congress. http://metavid.org/.
mptv. http://mptvimages.com.
Museum of the Moving Image. http://www.movingimage.us/.

The National Archives. http://discovery.nationalarchives.gov.uk/.
National Archives and Records Administration. http://www.archives.gov/.
National Research Centre for Truth and Reconciliation. University of Manitoba. http://umanitoba.ca/centres/nrctr/.
National Scouting Museum. Boy Scouts of America. http://www.bsamuseum.org/.
The National Security Archive. The George Washington University. http://www2.gwu.edu/~nsarchiv/.
New Deal Network. http://newdeal.feri.org.
North American Immigrant Letters, Diaries, and Oral Histories. Alexandria, VA: Alexander Street. http://alexanderstreet.com/products/north-american-immigrant-letters-diaries-and-oral-histories. [subscription required]
North American Indian Thought and Culture. Alexandria, VA: Alexander Street. http://alexanderstreet.com/products/north-american-indian-thought-and-culture. [subscription required]
North American Women's Letters and Diaries: Colonial to 1950. Alexandria, VA: Alexander Street. http://alexanderstreet.com/products/north-american-womens-letters-and-diaries. [subscription required]
NSDAR Archives. National Society Daughters of the American Revolution. http://www.dar.org/archives/nsdar-archives.
The Open Video Project. School of Information and Library Science. University of North Carolina at Chapel Hill. http://www.open-video.org/.
Oral History Online. Alexandria, VA: Alexander Street. http://alexanderstreet.com/products/oral-history-online. [subscription required]
Past Masters: Full Text Humanities. Charlottesville, VA: InteLex Corporation. http://www.nlx.com/home. [subscription required]
Photography Collection. George Eastman Museum. https://www.eastman.org/photography.
Pinewood Dialogues. Museum of the Moving Image. http://www.movingimagesource.us/dialogues/all.
Plateau Peoples' Web Portal. http://plateauportal.wsulibs.wsu.edu/html/ppp/index.php.
ProQuest History Vault. Ann Arbor, MI: ProQuest. http://www.proquest.com/libraries/academic/primary-sources/historyvault.html. [subscription required]
Reciprocal Research Network. http://www.rrncommunity.org/.
Repositories of Primary Sources. http://webpages.uidaho.edu/special-collections/Other.Repositories.html.
ResearchChannel. YouTube. https://www.youtube.com/user/ResearchChannel.
Shoah Foundation. University of Southern California. https://sfi.usc.edu/.
Slavery, Abolition and Social Justice 1490–2007. Chicago: Adam Matthew. http://www.amdigital.co.uk/m-collections/collection/slavery-abolition-and-social-justice/. [subscription required]
Smithsonian. http://www.si.edu/.
State Archives and Libraries. Clear Digital Media. http://statearchives.us/index.htm.
U.S. Government Photos and Images. http://prod.usa.gov/Topics/Graphics.shtml.
WayBack Machine. Internet Archive. https://archive.org/web/.
Women and Social Movements in the United States 1600–2000. Alexandria, VA: Alexander Street. http://womhist.alexanderstreet.com/. [subscription required]
Women's History Research in Archives. University of Wisconsin-Madison Libraries. http://researchguides.library.wisc.edu/c.php?g=177948&p=1168872.
World Digital Library. Library of Congress. http://www.wdl.org/en/.
YouTube. https://www.youtube.com/.

SUGGESTED READINGS

Archivists are very good at writing books and articles aimed at other archivists, but there is very little written by archivists for those outside the profession. The following texts are by leaders in the field and cover everything from basic archival practice, to theory, to the importance of archives to society.

Cook, Terry. 1997. "What Is Past Is Prologue: A History of Archival Ideas since 1898, and the Future Paradigm Shift." *Archivaria* 43 (Spring): 17–63.

This particular article by the giant of archival science, Terry Cook, is written for the archival practitioner, but is a seminal work that explores the evolution of thinking about archives that will give non-archivists good insight into the archival profession.

Duranti, Luciana, and Patricia C. Franks, eds. 2015. *Encyclopedia of Archival Science.* Lanham, MD: Rowman & Littlefield.

This work promises to be the definitive reference work on archival science, with definitions of all major aspects written by experts in the field. This likely will not present theories and concepts in plain language, but for those interested in learning more without having to wade through lengthy articles, this will be the place to start. This reference work will be a good way for librarians to dip into archival theory without drowning in jargon.

Harris, Verne. 2007. *Archives and Justice: A South African Perspective.* Chicago: Society of American Archivists.

Verne Harris, who was a director of the South African History Archive and archivist for South Africa's Truth and Reconciliation Commission, has been the head of the Memory Programme at the Nelson Mandela Foundation's Centre of Memory and Dialogue since 2004. This is a volume of his best writing about archives during the period of postapartheid democracy. The third and fourth sections on "Politics and Ethics" and "Pasts and Secrets," respectively, will be of particular interest to those who are interested in the power of archival records in building toward a democracy.

Jimerson, Randall C. 2009. *Archives Power: Memory, Accountability, and Social Justice.* Chicago: Society of American Archivists.

This text revolves around the role of the archivist, but the context of that role will be important for librarians who are wondering about the importance of archives. Randall Jimerson considers the intersection between archives, memory, identity, accountability, and social justice. He feels there is a renewed emphasis on remembrance, evidence, and documentation in order to make governments accountable and transparent.

Kraue, Magia Ghetu, and Elizabeth Yakel. 2007. "Interaction in Virtual Archives: The Polar Bear Expedition Digital Collections Next Generation Finding Aid." *American Archivist* 70 (2): 282–314.

This article provides practical insights into finding aids and how they might be enhanced to make archival materials more accessible by using direct and indirect interactions between users and archivists. There have been few improvements to the traditional finding aid over the years, particularly once Encoded Archival Description allowed archivists to place their finding aids on the Web. This article indicates what might be possible in the future.

Millar, Laura, and Association of British Columbia Archivists Small Archives Committee. 1994. *A Manual for Small Archives*, 2nd ed. Vancouver: Association of British Columbia Archivists.

This textbook, although dated, provides a very good overview of archival practice for people who may be responsible for an archives but do not have any training. As such, this work is useful for reference librarians who might want to get an overview of archives practice. The language is straightforward, easy to understand, and is based on foundational archival principles. Millar herself writes extensively for the archival profession and has a great deal of experience consulting for archives internationally.

O'Toole, James M., and Richard J Cox. 2006. *Understanding Archives and Manuscripts*. Chicago: Society of American Archivists.

Part of the Archival Fundamentals Series II published by the Society of American Archivists, this is an American text for students and beginning practitioners. It gives a good overview of the history of the archival profession, the organization of archival records, and the theory and practice of archives in an increasingly electronic world.

Posner, Ernst. 1972. *Archives in the Ancient World*. Cambridge, MA: Harvard University Press.

This is an older work, but still a classic by an important member of the archival profession. Posner was educated in Europe and brings that sensibility to his coverage of the history of archives, of recordkeeping and archiving practices, of the changing nature of archival materials, of different societal uses, and so on. This book provides a broad perspective on archiving and gives other information professionals a sense of what has made archival practice so different from librarianship.

Chapter 28

Legal Sources

Paul D. Healey

INTRODUCTION

Law and legal issues permeate American life. For this reason, legal questions are very common at the reference desk of almost any library. In the past, it was generally not possible for librarians to provide much in the way of legal reference service, except at specialized law libraries, because legal reference materials were expensive, were highly technical in nature, and required a lot of shelf space.

The Web has changed much of this. Legal materials of all kinds are a natural fit for the online world, and most legal materials are easier to work with and more current online than they were in book form. Although specialized legal research tools used by attorneys are still very expensive and difficult to use, most basic legal materials, such as statutes, cases, and regulations, are freely available in authoritative forms on the Web. The result is that librarians in all kinds of libraries now have access to the tools and information required to provide basic reference service for legal questions.

Unfortunately, access to legal information is not the only problem that arises with legal reference questions. At least two other major issues must be considered. First, there exists the possibility of personal legal liability for a reference librarian who does not handle a legal reference question in the right way. Second, the highly technical and complex nature of many legal questions remains a formidable barrier to providing appropriate legal information.

This chapter begins by looking at the professional issues that arise when handling legal information requests, including the possibility of liability, and discusses how to handle them appropriately. This is followed by a discussion of the technical nature of legal information, in order to provide the reader with some background on these issues. Finally, an overview is provided of the array of print, online, and Web-based resources that are currently available for providing legal reference service.

PROFESSIONAL ISSUES IN PROVIDING LEGAL REFERENCE

As with any area of reference, good legal reference service requires some familiarity with available resources and an understanding of how those resources might serve a user's needs. With legal reference, however, additional issues arise. How a user intends to use legal information and how the reference librarian interacts with that user are very important.

Legal Liability

Legal reference is relatively unique in that it is one area of reference service where the librarian's actions could conceivably lead to legal liability. This is because it is theoretically possible that providing legal reference service could be construed as giving legal advice and thus constitute the unauthorized practice of law.[1] As of the date of this writing, no reference librarian has ever been charged with unauthorized practice of law for providing legal reference services, but the risk, if theoretical, is still real.[2]

Before exploring the nature of this potential liability, and how to avoid it, it may be helpful to explore why library users are searching for legal information and how this affects the liability issue. Put simply, people who seek legal information can be divided into two groups: those who are searching for legal information for some general purpose, and those who are looking for legal information in order to pursue their own legal interests.

First, people who are seeking legal information for some general purpose, but are not pursuing their own legal interests, are generally not a matter of concern. In this case, someone might want legal information in order to write a paper on a legal topic, or to inform himself or herself about some legal issue. The key distinction is that the information request is not related to the individual's own legal interests. The issue of liability arises only when the librarian's reference activities involve acting like a lawyer by providing legal information that could be seen as legal advice. When the request does not involve this issue, it does not raise the possibility of liability. Because of this, people who are seeking legal information for some reason other than pursuing their own personal legal interests do not present a liability issue for the librarian and can be treated like any other reference service user.

The second group consists of library users who are seeking legal information in order to pursue their own legal interests. These people may be engaged in a variety of activities. They might be involved in litigation, such as a divorce or an eviction action. Alternatively, they might be doing such things as drafting their own will, or handling legal matters related to running a business, or pursuing legal action based on social issues. The possibilities for involvement in legal issues are many and varied. The key issue here is that, in seeking legal information, the library user is seeking that information in order to protect or pursue his or her personal legal interests.

It is this fact that raises the liability issue for librarians. Although one might imagine that it would be clear-cut what activities constitute the practice of law, and thus what activities would be the unauthorized practice of law if performed by a nonlawyer, in fact, the practice of law has never been clearly defined.[3] Each jurisdiction has a definition of legal practice, but those definitions are unfortunately vague about details. The giving of legal advice is one of the activities that appears in all definitions of the practice of law. Again, giving advice is only broadly defined, but in some instances could include providing legal information.

Legal reference activities raise the issue of liability because providing legal information might be considered giving legal advice. Unfortunately, although many researchers have pursued the topic over the years, no one has been able to draw a clear line between what constitutes appropriate legal reference service and what constitutes legal advice (for further reading on this issue, see Healey 2002).

Avoiding Liability

Since the specter of potential liability has been raised, one needs to consider it. Fortunately, the answer is simple, at least in concept. In order to avoid liability, librarians should present themselves as an expert on finding information, but not as experts on the information they find. This is a dictum with plenty of gray areas, but the distinction is crucial.

Although the concept of giving legal advice remains frustratingly undefined, at its heart is the concept of one person advising another person what to do to protect their legal interests. Why would this come up at the reference desk? Because if a reference librarian were to suggest to a library user what form might meet his or her need, or what area of law to research, that could constitute advising the user on how to pursue his or her own legal interests, and thus constitute legal advice. As a librarian responding to a legal reference question, the key point is to avoid exercising any kind of legal judgment in providing legal information.

Under this set of requirements, it is clearly acceptable for a librarian to answer questions that might be referred to as ready reference. A specific request for a statute or a form, when the item requested is clearly identified, should never pose a problem because it does not involve a legal judgment. Similarly, answering a request for information on a legal topic is not a problem when the answer is to refer the user to a resource that can be explored to answer his or her question. However, getting involved in the question itself, including offering opinions on appropriate approaches to the problem or possible answers, should be strictly avoided.

One of the potential dangers to a librarian who is not careful is the urge to relate personal experiences when responding to questions. A librarian who has been through a divorce or written a will might be tempted to offer his or her perspective on the question being asked based on that experience. The message here is to strictly avoid such an urge. Simply restrict oneself to providing the information the user is seeking.

Other Professional Issues

In addition to liability, other professional issues arise when providing legal reference service to people who are pursuing their own legal interests. While none of these rises to the level of a liability issue for the librarian, the ethical problems they create are quite real. These issues are also not unique to legal questions, but are definitely important in this context.

The first issue is confidentiality. Librarians have a strong ethic of confidentiality at the reference desk (for more on confidentiality in the reference transaction, see Chapter 2). In the case of legal questions, the library user may be dealing with an issue that is extremely personal, and potentially embarrassing or difficult. Under the circumstances, protecting confidentiality becomes crucial. Talking about a user's question with others could not only prove embarrassing or difficult for the user, but could in some cases lead to harm. Imagine a person trying to find a legal way out of an abusive domestic relationship. Loose talk about that person's situation could actually lead to harm. Confidentiality with legal reference questions is a must.

The second issue is conflict of interest. While this issue is rare at the reference desk, in a legal dispute, it is not unreasonable to assume that people on different sides of a legal dispute might seek information at the same reference desk. In such a situation, it is important both to treat library users fairly and equally, and to refrain from becoming personally involved in the issue. This problem also reinforces the need for confidentiality.

A third issue is reliance and harm. In law, reliance takes place when people believe that they can trust advice they have been given. If they rely on erroneous advice, they could be harmed in some way. Many library users see reference librarians as educated and informative. Fortunately, most users readily accept and trust the information they get at the reference desk. For most purposes, this is desirable, and it is desirable in legal reference, so long as users understand that they are being given information and not advice.

If library users seeking legal information get the impression that the librarian is an expert on law, and the librarian offers an opinion or advice, they may rely on him or her to their detriment. This is particularly a problem in specialized law libraries, where many of the librarians are, in fact, legally trained. However, even in a nonlaw library, it would be possible for a librarian to act in such a way that the library user gets the impression that he or she is getting expert information. Even if it did not lead to allegations of giving legal advice, it would be unfortunate if this led to reliance and subsequent harm. It is far better to simply supply information as requested and let users make their own assessment of the information they receive and decide how to use it.

A Restrained Approach to Legal Reference

Librarians are dedicated to providing access to information for all library users, generally striving to answer reference questions fully and completely. To hold back information or skimp on a response feels wrong as a professional. However, the legal and professional issues discussed earlier demonstrate that it is theoretically possible for a librarian answering legal reference questions to cause problems for users and even get into legal trouble, by being accused of unauthorized practice of law. The result is a requirement that librarians take a more restrained approach to answering legal reference questions.

In answering legal reference questions, librarians should strive to provide the information that is requested, but nothing more than what is requested. Librarians should refrain from expressing an opinion about the legal issue, or from suggesting issues or approaches to research. This approach protects both the librarian and the user.

When presented with a legal question, a librarian should provide complete, fair, and balanced information to the extent possible. The librarian should avoid becoming involved in the question or the research, avoid putting himself or herself forward as an expert on the topic, and avoid giving any kind of advice.

Box 28.1 Responding to Requests for Legal Advice

Library users with legal questions often do not understand that librarians cannot give them a direct answer. Because of this, users sometimes become frustrated. Here are some suggestions on how to respond to legal questions.

When a user asks a question that would require a legal answer (e.g. "How do I file for divorce?" or "What is the law on . . ."), the best response is to remind the user that you cannot answer the question itself, but you can help him or her find information on it.

Examples of good responses include:

- "I can't answer that question for you, but I can show you some materials that might let you find the answer."
- "That's a legal question, and I'm not a lawyer. However, we do have some legal resources that might help. Let me show them to you."
- "Legal questions are quite complicated. We have some materials that I can show you that might help."

The important point is to make sure that users don't feel that you have answered a legal question for them. Keep in mind the following ideas when dealing with legal questions:

- Do not get personally involved. Even if you have experienced a similar legal situation, stay in role as a librarian and restrict yourself to helping the user find information.
- Another library may have better resources. If there is a reasonably close law library open to the public, you may want to refer the user to that library.
- Do not be shy about suggesting that a user seek legal counsel. Often a user has already considered this option and rejected it, but once the person encounters the difficulty of doing legal research or representing himself or herself, the user may reconsider.

BASIC CONCEPTS IN LEGAL INFORMATION

As has been mentioned, law is a very complicated and technical subject. While it is best that librarians take a restrained approach to answering legal reference questions, some knowledge of the structure of law and the structure of legal materials will be useful in locating information in response to a legal question.

The Structure of Law in the United States

Legal materials and the publication of legal information are closely tied to the structure of American government. Most educated Americans understand the structure of government, but it is worth reviewing, with an eye to how that structure affects the publication and availability of legal information.

In the United States, the government makes laws. The federal government and 50 sovereign state governments all have lawmaking authority. Fortunately, all of those governments are structured in roughly the same way and generally make law in the same form. The federal and state governments are each set up by, and operate under, a constitution, and in each case, the constitution calls for three branches of government, with a legislature, a court system, and an executive branch.

The American system is what is known as a federal system. This means that rather than being one country with subdivisions, the United States consists of 50 separate states, each with the sovereign power to make law, united under a federal government, which can also make laws. The federal government is intended to have limited lawmaking powers. Speaking broadly, the U.S. Constitution empowers the federal government to handle matters that affect the entire country, such as the military and relations with other countries; to manage the relations between the separate states; and to regulate affairs in certain specific areas listed in the Constitution, such as copyright and bankruptcy. All other lawmaking is reserved to the states.

Each state government has a broad mandate for lawmaking, and most matters affecting day-to-day life are regulated by state law. The only limit on this power is that the states cannot make laws that violate the federal or their state constitution, and they cannot intrude on areas that are reserved to the federal government. If a state does make law that intrudes on an area of federal interest, the federal law will be controlling. This is referred to as the federal supremacy clause. Apart from these exceptions, the states can make law on any matter that they choose. Thus, everything from marriage and divorce, to business regulation, to criminal laws is mostly a state law matter.

In this system, all three branches of government make law. The legislature makes law in the form of statutes, the judiciary makes law in the form of case law, and the executive branch makes law in the form of regulations. This is true for the federal government and for each of the 50 states. The states are further divided into smaller governmental units, usually called counties; the incorporation of towns or cities introduces additional governmental bodies. These smaller units of each state can often also make law, referred to as ordinances or local laws.

Jurisdiction

The structure of American government creates a complicated landscape for law. For any given legal issue, the first question to answer is usually that of jurisdiction. Jurisdiction is defined as the official power to make laws or legal decisions and is delineated by sovereign body, geography, and other factors. Any given form of law, whether a statute, a case, or a regulation, is controlling only in its own jurisdiction.

One of the primary divisions in jurisdiction is between federal and state laws. For example, if someone wants to find information on filing for bankruptcy, the relevant jurisdiction is federal, because the U.S. Constitution reserves bankruptcy as a federal matter. On the other hand, if someone wants information about divorce, the answer will lie in state law, because divorce is a state matter. Of course, each state has its own jurisdiction, so someone who lives in Illinois will want information on Illinois divorce law, rather than from some other state.

These examples are just for purposes of illustration. An extended discussion of jurisdiction is beyond the scope of this chapter (for further reading on this topic, see Healey 2014). However, being sensitive to jurisdiction as an issue is important in rendering legal reference services.

Type of Law

A very common question asked at the reference desk is some variation of "I would like the law about X." Finding that law has two parts. The first is determining the relevant jurisdiction as described earlier. The second question has to do with type, or actual form, of law involved. This could be a constitution, a statute, a case, a regulation, or a local ordinance of some kind. This section describes each of these in turn.

Constitutions

The most fundamental form of primary legal material is a constitution, an agreement between all of the people to set up a government. Constitutions have several functions. First, they set up the form of government. The federal and state constitutions each lay out the three branches of government and decree how people will be elected or appointed to posts in those branches. The constitution also decrees what the powers of the government will be and in what areas it will be allowed to make and enforce laws. Finally, the constitution sets out liberties for the people. These liberties cannot be taken away by any law or action of the government. A constitution is a fundamental form of law and governs many disputes about the propriety of other laws.

Statutes

Statutes are what most people commonly think of as the law. Statutes are created by the legislature. Legislation at the federal level is limited to the areas listed in the U.S. Constitution, while state legislation can be on almost any topic not otherwise precluded by the U.S. or the state constitution. For this reason, each state makes its own law on such areas as business relations, family and divorce, alcohol and drugs, and transportation and driving.

Case Law

Case law is law made by the courts in the form of legal decisions by appellate courts. The American legal system has a large and active body of case law. Case law, and its importance, results from two aspects of the American judiciary. The first is the ability of the courts to interpret legislation and review statutes for their constitutionality. The second is because courts can actually make law, called common law, in areas where there is no legislation.

Both federal and state courts have the power to review any statute to be sure it does not violate provisions of the relevant constitution. This is a basic protection built into the American system of government and is a major part of the checks and balances between the branches of government. If a court finds that a law violates some provision of the constitution, it can invalidate all or part of the statute.

Courts in the United States also have the power to interpret legislation when the meaning of a statute is not clear. State courts can do this only in relation to statutes from their state, while federal courts are restricted to interpreting federal statutes. Once an appellate court has interpreted a statute, the court's decision must be followed in understanding and interpreting the law. This is why annotated codes are so important. A researcher must have access to the case law that has interpreted a particular statute in order to fully understand the statute and how it works.

In the United States, there are areas of law that are generally not governed by legislative statutes or rules. These areas of law, most commonly torts, contracts, and property, are instead governed by law made by the courts. When the courts make law in areas where there is no statute, the resulting body of law is referred to as common law. Common law consists of the assembled appellate decisions on that area of law from the appellate courts in that jurisdiction.

The body of common law in America is extensive and very difficult to work with. Cases are not organized by topic in the way statutes are, and any one case can be affected by subsequent cases that overrule, limit, or interpret it. Private publishers have developed professional tools to help with case research, but these are very expensive and can be difficult to understand and use. For this reason, a user who wants to do extensive case research is probably best referred to a law library for assistance.

Regulations

Regulations are often the overlooked form of primary law. This is unfortunate, because regulations are a very important form of law and are widespread in the United States. Regulations are made by the executive branch of government, and their function is to provide details for the enforcement of a statute. Regulations have traditionally been somewhat difficult to locate. The Web is changing this, but access to regulations can take some effort.

Ordinances and Local Laws

In addition to federal and state laws, local governments make laws. Local governments can include county, township, and municipal bodies. The nature of these local units, and the lawmaking powers they have, varies widely from state to state. Local laws, often referred to as ordinances, can cover such issues as zoning and business regulation, or minor crimes. Perhaps not surprisingly, local law has been the most difficult to find for research purposes, although again the Web is improving this situation.

Several private publishers provide the service of codifying local ordinances at the request of a local government. This is important because it provides a published code of local ordinances that can be distributed and consulted. In addition, most of these private publishers place their codes on the Web, which provides free access to all. Many libraries will want to obtain a copy of their relevant local ordinances, but will also want to be aware of what local ordinances they can find online, particularly for local governments that they would not normally pay to acquire.

Legal Issue

Like any other topic, when a library user asks a law-related question at the reference desk, the question might involve finding a simple fact or discrete item, what might be called ready reference, or it might require more involved research. Sometimes, a patron will ask for a discrete item for which there is a citation or reference. In this case, it is a matter of locating the item. Often, however, the reference question is not about a particular item, but about a legal issue. In such a case, all of the matters discussed earlier, such as jurisdiction and type of law, must be determined for the user to get the right information. Identifying the legal issue at hand is important as a way of determining the type of legal material needed. It would be impossible to provide a comprehensive guide to researching all legal issues. However, Figure 28.1 provides a brief overview of the jurisdiction and type of law for some common legal issues.

Note for Any Issue:

If the question involves litigation on any topic in state or federal courts, the patron will also need information on court rules of procedure and evidence, and potentially also jury instructions and local court rules. Litigation rules are an entire set of procedures that must be followed, in addition to the subject matter of the suit.

Issue:	Bankruptcy
State or Federal:	Federal
Type of Law:	Statute (Title 11 of the *U.S. Code*), with case law interpretation
Notes:	Personal exemptions are sometimes covered by state statute.

Issue:	Contracts
State or Federal:	State
Type of Law:	Case law
Notes:	Commercial disputes may be covered by the *Uniform Commercial Code*, which is part of the state's statutes.

Issue:	Criminal
State or Federal:	State (most commonly) or Federal
Type of Law:	Statute, with case law interpretation
Notes:	People facing criminal charges should be strongly encouraged to seek legal counsel.

Issue:	Debt (Credit, Collections, Foreclosure)
State or Federal:	State or Federal, possibly a combination
Type of Law:	Statutes and regulations
Notes:	Many issues will involve the Fair Debt Collection Practices Act (FDCPA), 15 U.S.C. § 1692, or the Consumer Finance Protection Bureau.

Issue:	Divorce and Custody
State or Federal:	State
Type of Law:	Statute, with case law interpretation
Notes:	Very common legal question; generally lots of self-help materials available.

Issue:	Employment Discrimination
State or Federal:	State or Federal (most commonly)
Type of law:	Statute, with case law interpretation

FIGURE 28.1 Determining legal issue jurisprudence and type of law for some common legal issues

Issue:	Employment (Other than Discrimination)
State or Federal:	State
Type of Law:	Statute, with case law interpretation
Issue:	Housing Discrimination
State or Federal:	State or Federal (most commonly)
Type of Law:	Regulations (mostly) and Statute
Notes:	"Section 8," now called the Housing Choice Voucher Program, refers to Section 8 of the Housing Act of 1937 (42 U.S.C. § 1437f)
Issue:	Intellectual Property (Copyright and Patent)
State or Federal:	Federal
Type of Law:	Statute, with case law interpretation
Issue:	Landlord-Tenant
State or Federal:	State
Type of Law:	Statutes
Notes:	Most states have a specific landlord-tenant statute. However, case law might be relevant.
Issue:	Professional Malpractice (a form of tort)
State or Federal:	State
Type of Law:	Case law
Notes:	Usually medical or legal, but other professions as well, particularly licensed professions.
Issue:	Torts (Accidents, Injuries, etc.)
State or Federal:	State
Type of Law:	Case law
Issue:	Wills, Estate Planning, Probate
State or Federal:	State
Type of Law:	Statute
Notes:	Many states have a separate probate code. Also, if going to court, there may be special probate court procedural rules.

FIGURE 28.1 (Continued)

TYPES OF LEGAL MATERIALS

A distinction should be made between two fundamentally different forms of legal materials: primary and secondary. In one sense, the difference between primary and secondary legal materials is quite simple. Primary legal materials are the law, while secondary legal materials are everything else. Although this distinction can be expressed simply, it would benefit from some further explanation.

Primary Legal Materials

Primary legal materials are those that constitute the law itself; they are items that can be used as controlling law or precedent in their jurisdiction. The three forms of primary legal materials that are referred to most commonly are statutes, court cases, and regulations. In addition, a full description of primary legal materials would include constitutions and local laws and ordinances.

Secondary Legal Materials

Secondary legal materials are those that have the law as their subject, but are not themselves law. A vast and varied array of secondary legal materials is available, both in print and online. The majority of these secondary legal materials are both extremely expensive and highly technical in nature. For this reason, they are generally not available except in specialized law libraries.

Some secondary legal materials that all librarians should know about include some basic tools. These include legal encyclopedias and legal dictionaries, which would be reasonable to find in a nonlaw library, and a vast number of websites that offer legal information for free or at a low cost.

Secondary legal materials can, and most commonly do, provide reference to primary authority, but they are not the law itself. For example, even though a legal encyclopedia may cite a primary authority on a particular point, the encyclopedia is not the law, or precedent. The function of secondary legal materials is to explain the law and direct the user to the relevant primary law. As such, secondary legal materials are very important for research, but they are not the law itself.

Attorney Oriented Materials

A number of secondary legal publications are used by legal professionals that would normally be found only in a specialized law library, or in a subscription database. These resources are useful and popular with legal professionals and scholars, and so they are often referred to in other sources. Based on such a reference, a library user might ask for these secondary sources at the reference desk. If that resource itself is needed, it will be necessary to refer the user to a law library. However, sometimes the information the secondary source provides can be found in other ways. As a result, it might be useful to describe a few of the most common secondary sources and what they do.

Treatises

Legal treatises are written by experts to provide an in-depth explanation of a particular area of law. While legal treatises are migrating online into subscription databases, as of the time of this writing, most are still in print form. Large law libraries will contain most of the prominent legal treatises. If the treatise is in print form, it might be possible to obtain it through interlibrary loan.

American Law Reports

American Law Reports, often referred to as *ALR*, is a set of more than 15,000 articles, called annotations, on specific legal issues. Each annotation contains an explanation of the issue and citation to all related legal authority. *ALR* is currently published by West Publishing and can be found in most law libraries.

Restatements

Restatements are published by the American Law Institute, a body of legal scholars and leading practitioners. Restatements are created for each area of common law, and they attempt to do for the common law what a code does for statutes. In other words, the restatement looks at the common law across all 50 states and summarizes the law in the form of a set of rules. Restatements are useful to scholars and the courts as a way of assessing what the most common form of the common law is for a given topic.

Looseleaf Practice Sets

Legal publishers have produced a wide variety of publications intended to assist lawyers as they practice in a particular area of law. These sets have traditionally been referred to as looseleafs because they were published in a physical format that allowed for the insertion of new pages within each volume. Many legal practitioners use the term "looseleaf" to mean any practice aid set.

Looseleafs will commonly provide editorial and expert information on the topic, along with references and summaries of the relevant law, and often forms, practice checklists, reference materials, and other helpful material. Many looseleafs come with a current awareness service on that topic. Looseleafs require a subscription to be kept up to date. Many looseleafs have migrated online and are available through subscription databases provided by their publisher.

Subscription Legal Databases

As mentioned earlier, the major private legal publishers make their materials available through online subscription databases. These databases are tools aimed at legal professionals and tend to be very expensive. Although it is unlikely that a nonlaw library will have access to any of these, it might be helpful to know something about them because of their prominence in the legal publishing field. As of this writing, there are three major legal database providers.

West Publishing, now a subsidiary of Thomson Reuters, has been the premier publisher of American law since the 19th century. West started *Westlaw*, its online legal database, in the 1970s in competition with *LexisNexis*. *Westlaw* contains all of the primary law from all U.S. Jurisdictions, as well as a vast array of secondary sources published by West and Thomson Reuters. *Westlaw* also benefits from having the proprietary Key Number System, the only comprehensive topical index to American case law. *Westlaw* is generally considered to be the most popular legal database.

Bloomberg Law, a relative newcomer to the legal database field, describes itself as an integrated legal research and business intelligence solution. In addition to providing primary legal materials and some professional finding aids, the database includes materials from the Bureau of National Affairs, which was acquired by Bloomberg in 2011.

LexisNexis was the original online legal database, launched in 1973. It contains primary law from the federal government and all 50 states, along with a vast array of other legal materials, including material published by its parent company, Reed Elsevier.

One subscription legal database that might be available in an academic or large public library is *LexisNexis Academic*. This product by Lexis is aimed at universities, colleges, and large public libraries. It provides access to Lexis news and legal databases, and contains case law, statutes, regulations, and some law review articles, as well as access to the Shepard's Case Citator. If an institution subscribes to *LexisNexis Academic*, it should be the librarian's primary tool for answering legal reference questions.

EVALUATION AND SELECTION OF LEGAL MATERIALS

Most librarians will want to have access to some legal materials. The blossoming of free Web-based materials makes this even more compelling. This section will discuss how to evaluate legal materials being considered for the collection, and then some considerations for selection.

Evaluating Legal Materials

Because of the wide array of legal materials, both primary and secondary, that are available, it is crucial that potential sources be evaluated carefully. A number of factors should be considered when evaluating legal materials, including authority, currency, completeness, and bias or slant.

Authority

It is very important that legal information come from authoritative sources, particularly with primary legal materials. Authoritative sources include the government itself, state bar associations,[4] accredited law schools, intergovernmental and quasi-governmental organizations,[5] and established legal publishers with a solid reputation. Before purchasing or relying on a legal source, it would be best to check the authority of its publisher or provider.

Currency

Laws are constantly being changed, and many legal concepts and issues exist in a state of flux. Because of this, it is essential that any legal material be current. In the case of law, out-of-date materials are not only less useful, but can actually be harmful as well. For example, if a library user were to consult a statute book from the library's shelves that is out of date, it is possible that the relevant law has been changed in a way that could seriously affect the user. For this reason, out-of-date legal materials should generally be removed from a library's collection, unless they are being retained for archival or historical purposes. Providing out-of-date legal materials can be much worse than providing nothing at all.

Completeness

In order for legal materials to be fully useful, they must provide complete access to the relevant law. For example, many statutes have been interpreted by courts in a way that affects how they are understood and used. As such, having a current set of statutes is only part of the required information, because access to the relevant case law is also needed to fully understand the statute. Completeness is an important issue, one that most libraries cannot solve fully without access to specialized legal materials. However, when evaluating a Web-based resource, completeness should be considered.

Bias or Slant

Because law is such a fundamental topic, and because aspects of law are often controversial, bias or slant in legal materials is always possible. This comes up most commonly with websites and publications produced by advocacy and special interest organizations. Contentious areas of the law, such as abortion, gun rights, taxation, and child custody issues have all seen biased information on the law offered by organizations on one side of the issue or the other. Certainly many if not most such organizations provide a fair and balanced view of the law in their area of concern, but some do not. Librarians must be on the lookout for bias when evaluating such materials.

Selection of Legal Materials

Primary legal materials, particularly statutes, cases, and regulations, have traditionally been available for free or at a low cost directly from the government. In book form, the biggest challenge presented by these materials has been the enormous amount of shelf space they can take up and the administrative hassles of keeping them up to date. Primary legal materials are also available from private publishers, who include a variety of research aids and added information. These privately published versions of the law are very expensive and are generally collected only by specialized law libraries and practitioners.

This dichotomy remains true as legal materials have made the transition into online forms. If anything, statutes, cases, and regulations are even more widely available than ever on government websites. Private publishers now publish all or most of their materials online as well, although they do so in subscription databases that are, once again, very expensive and generally subscribed to only by dedicated law libraries and law firms.

For most libraries, privately published legal materials will be too expensive to collect and keep updated. In addition to their expense, privately published legal materials tend to be complex tools designed for use by trained legal professionals. As such, they can have limited utility for regular library users.

Thus, most librarians will rely on free websites for access to the statutes, cases, and regulations of their state and of the federal government. Some librarians may want to collect selected secondary materials as well, such as legal dictionaries and encyclopedias, and perhaps some legal self-help books on particular topics.

Print Sources

Print resources for legal reference are mostly a dying breed. Law libraries still have many print resources because some resources, particularly specialized treatises, are not yet available online. However, most of those resources are too specialized to be of interest to a library that does not specialize in law. Most of the legal resources that nonlaw libraries routinely collected, such as statutes, are now available online, and often for free.

One of the perennial problems with print resources is updating. Because the law changes so often, book resources are often out of date. Arguably having an outdated legal resource, such as a state code, on the shelf is worse than having no resource at all, because an out-of-date resource can mislead a user as to the letter of the law. Happily, Web resources have helped make such printed legal materials unnecessary for most libraries.

Primary Legal Materials in Print

Because primary legal materials are government publications, they can often be found in print for a reasonable cost, or even free. However, even if they are provided for free or for low cost under a depository program, primary materials in print take up valuable shelf space and must be regularly updated to be useful. As a result, many libraries, even law libraries, no longer collect primary legal materials in print.

Probably the most common primary legal item found in print is the U.S. Constitution. Because it is a relatively short document, it can be found both published on its own in various forms and included in many other publications. For instance, all statute sets, both federal and state, contain the text of the U.S. Constitution. As a matter of providing reference service, it might be worthwhile to locate those items in print in the library that contain the text of the U.S. Constitution. However, the Constitution is also widely available online for free, both from the government and from other sources.

State constitutions tend to be rarer, but again are included in state statute sets. In addition, a state constitution might be available in pamphlet form for free from the state government and could be a useful reference item. As with the U.S. Constitution, state constitutions are readily available online, usually on the state legislature Web page as well as other sources.

GENERAL AND SECONDARY LEGAL RESOURCES

This section discusses general resources for legal reference that can be useful in the library. Most of these resources are Web based, but some are in print. This section will cover affordable secondary materials in print, online legal dictionaries and encyclopedias, free websites, general research guides, federal law research guides, legal forms, and referral resources. Box 28.2 provides advice on helping a patron with legal questions utilizing primarily free legal resources.

Secondary Legal Materials in Print

Most secondary legal materials in print will be too expensive, and in many cases too hard to use, to be of interest to a public or academic library. However, there are

Box 28.2 Where to Start?

Helping a library user get started on a legal question can be daunting. A good place to start is to determine whether a user is seeking information about some aspect of law or is seeking a particular item, such as a specific case or a form. If a user is looking for a particular item, you can use the resources in the following sections of this chapter to help them. If a user does not have a particular item that he or she is looking for, it is best to start with general information, even if the question sounds fairly specific.

Example: A user at the reference desk is looking for information on how to file for divorce.

Tactic 1: Start general. If your library has a legal encyclopedia, you might start there. If not, suggest online encyclopedias such as that at *Nolo*, or the Legal Information Institute's *Wex*. Suggest that the user start by getting background information.

Tactic 2: Look for state or local self-help resources. Your state might have an online legal self-help site that has information on filing for divorce in your state. Such resources can be very useful.

Tactic 3: Offer attorney referral and legal aid resources. The user may not be aware that low-cost or free legal help is potentially available.

some basic relatively low-cost items that any library might want to obtain in print form. These include a legal dictionary or encyclopedia, and legal self-help books.

Legal dictionaries define legal terms and can be very useful for pursuing any legal topic. The most popular legal dictionary is *Black's Law Dictionary*, published by Thomson Reuters and available in hardcover for less than $100. Online legal dictionaries are also available, often for free, but a print version is a handy resource for any reference desk.

Many librarians will also find it useful to have access to a general legal encyclopedia. The *Gale Encyclopedia of American Law*, third edition, is a good choice for most libraries and is available in print or as an eBook. There are also legal encyclopedias aimed at legal professionals, such as *American Jurisprudence 2nd* or *Corpus Juris Secundum*, both published by Thomson Reuters, but these are both very expensive and aimed at a technically trained audience.

Legal self-help books are intended to explain the law to laypersons and often guide nonlawyers through a legal process. Although such books are not without controversy and even resistance from the bar, there is no risk to a library for providing them as part of its collection.

The most prominent publisher of self-help legal books is Nolo, which provides books on a wide variety of legal topics, including many that are state specific. Nolo's publications are generally considered authoritative and are available through the Nolo website.

Other self-help resources may be available from a local legal services office or county or state bar association. Often, these groups have pamphlets and short books they distribute for free or low cost that they might be willing to provide to the library.

Online Legal Dictionaries and Encyclopedias

Some online legal dictionaries and encyclopedias are available for free. While these sources can be quite good, they are generally not as comprehensive as purchased products. *Wex*, from Cornell University Law School, is both a dictionary and an encyclopedia. In addition, the previously mentioned Nolo provides some very good information on their website for free. Among other things, they provide a *Free Dictionary of Law Terms and Legal Definitions* as well as a fairly extensive legal encyclopedia with information on a broad variety of topics under the name *Free Legal Articles & FAQs*. These resources are excellent for quick reference and basic legal information:

Free Websites

Several free online resources provide a broad spectrum of reliable authoritative legal information. These sites are worth noting here in general, although they will each appear later in the chapter in relation to specific kinds of material. These are great go-to sites to have on hand when providing legal reference services.

The Legal Information Institute (*LII*) is produced and maintained by the law library at Cornell University Law School. It was one of the first general resources made available on the Web and continues to be one of the most useful and robust. It is basically a portal, in that most of the material it supplies is via links to other sources. This is an excellent first stop when looking for legal information.

FDSys, which stands for Federal Digital System, is a site maintained by the U.S. Government Publishing Office (GPO). It provides access to legal materials from all three branches of the federal government, and much more besides.

Lexis Web is one good specialized legal search engine. This free search engine, provided by LexisNexis, searches legal sites that have been verified by Lexis.

General Research Guides

Other sites provide guidance in finding basic legal information. Most not only cover federal law topics, but also provide good information at the state level. Most of these guides offer links to resources by specific jurisdiction.

The American Association of Law Libraries, through their Legal Information Services to the Public Special Interest Section, offers the free *Public Library Toolkit*. These are toolkits aimed at average public libraries for answering legal reference questions. The toolkits would work well in most academic libraries too, particularly if they are open to the public. There are specific toolkits for each state. Another good basic source of state law information is the *LII*'s "Law by Source: State" page.

Federal Law Research Guides

These guides are designed to provide access to the broad variety of federal legal resources on the Web. Both of the guides here are produced by major law schools and are generally kept up to date.

The *LII* has a page called the "Federal Law Collection." This provides a comprehensive set of links to federal resources. New York University School of Law, through its Hauser Global Law School Program, has produced *A Guide to the U.S. Federal Legal System Web-Based Public Accessible Sources*. This resource was produced and is maintained by law librarian Gretchen Feltes. It nicely mixes links with explanatory material and is also quite comprehensive.

Legal Forms

Forms are used widely in legal issues, both in court actions and in transactional situations such as contracts and wills. Traditionally, forms have been hard to come by, but once again, the Web is making things more available. Keep in mind that there is not always a form for every legal situation, and not all forms are available on the Web. For local forms, it is usually best to check the website of the local clerk of court. Also remember that librarians should never select a particular form for a user or help a user fill it out. Those activities could constitute the unauthorized practice of law.

The *FindLaw* website has a very comprehensive page of links to forms, called *State Specific Legal Forms for All States*. *LLRX.com* is a site oriented toward legal professionals, but it has good resources for everyone. Its page of forms is very rich and has forms from almost all jurisdictions, some down to county level.

Referral Resources

These resources can help with finding a lawyer or a public law library. If a library handles lots of legal questions from the public, it would be a good idea to contact local referral sources, or nearby law libraries, to discuss when and how librarians can make referrals.

If there is a law school in the vicinity, it would be good to check with it about its policy for public access. Not all law schools, even publicly funded ones, are open to the public. A good alternative is a state, court, or county law library. Most of these are open to the public. Again it is a good idea to check with the library first to get to know its access policies. *WashLaw*, from Washburn University School of Law, has a list of "State, Court, and County Law Libraries" and a list of "Law School Library & State Law Library Catalogs," which can be used to identify local law libraries.

It is almost always a good idea to refer users to a lawyer if it becomes clear that they are trying to handle a legal problem without help. Users who meet income guidelines might even qualify for free legal representation. Most state bar associations have a referral service that is often a good first stop. Otherwise, "Find an Attorney" at *AttorneyPages* and "Find a Lawyer" at *FindLaw* are good alternatives. For referrals to legal aid, librarians can use *LSC Programs*.

PRIMARY LEGAL RESOURCES

This section of the chapter provides information about finding the law itself, specifically constitutions, statutes, case law, regulations, and local ordinances. Information about the type of law is provided, as well as suggested sources for finding a particular type of law.

Constitutions

Because constitutions serve such a fundamental purpose, it is fairly common to get requests for them. Fortunately, there are plenty of sources for constitutions on the Web.

The U.S. Constitution is widely available on the Web. For an official version, a good site is the *U.S. Constitution* page at the National Archives. The U.S. Constitution has been heavily interpreted and analyzed over the course of its existence. Although the material is very complex, the U.S. Congress provides a very good annotated version of the Constitution at *U.S. Constitution Annotated.*

Each state's official government website should have that state's constitution in full text. Most commonly, this will be on the state legislature's site.

Statutes and Legislative Materials

Legislation is created by the legislative process. The documentation of the legislative process, referred to as legislative history, is often used to determine the intent of the legislature in creating a particular law (for more on researching legislative history, see Chapter 22). The legislative process produces individual laws, which are published as session law and made publicly available. Relevant individual session laws are then compiled by topic into a code.

Session Law and Codes

In each legislative session, bills are introduced by legislators and considered by the legislative body. Those bills that successfully pass through that process emerge as individual laws. These individual laws are called session laws and are collected for publication in a session law set. The session law set is an official publication of the legislature and contains each law passed in chronological order. This set is published after each legislative session. Session laws are also available on the legislature website.

The session law set is a permanent record of the laws passed in each legislative session, but session law has some problems for those who want to understand what the current law is. To begin with, session law is published in chronological order, which means that there is no topical organization of the law. Also, any given session law may be amended or repealed by a later session law, but there will be no indication of this change in the original law. For these reasons, a further tool is needed to understand what the law is now.

Once session law has been published in the session law set, it is codified. In codification, the individual laws from all legislative sessions are arranged by topic. Any amendments to prior laws are placed in context, and repealed laws are edited out. The result is a publication of all legislation currently in force, arranged by topic and called a code. The code allows a user to see the legislative law on a particular topic as it exists right now, regardless of when the underlying pieces of session law were passed, and without any former language that has been repealed or amended.

It is important to note that not all session law ends up in the code. While most legislation will be included, at least while it is still in force, some session laws are not suitable for codification and are not included. One category of legislation that does not get codified is session laws that by their nature change yearly. The most prominent examples of this would be appropriation session laws and the annual budget. Another category of laws that are not codified are those of minor import, sometimes referred to as private laws. Private laws are session laws that affect only a small number of persons or entities, and therefore do not have general effect.

Some examples would be laws that name a public building or that grant citizenship to a foreign national as a reward for rendering service to this country (for more information, see Mantel 2008).

The code is therefore the primary tool for consulting statutes. Because new laws are passed regularly, a code must be updated regularly. An out-of-date code is not only less useful, but can actually be dangerous also, because code sections important to the researcher may have been changed subsequent to its publication. Virtually all state legislature websites now contain the current state code, although usability varies. In addition, most states still publish their code in print for a reasonable price.

Annotated Codes

Because the courts in America have the power to interpret legislation, finding the language of a statute may be only part of the answer to a user's question. In order to fully understand a code section, the researcher will need to be aware of any court decisions that have interpreted or otherwise directly affected that statute. Private publishers have solved this problem by publishing something called an annotated code. An annotated code contains all of the language of the official code, but each code section is interspersed with notes about court decisions that have interpreted that section, along with references to other related materials. Annotated codes are available for the federal *United States Code* and for each of the 50 states.

An annotated code is obviously a very useful tool for statutory research. Unfortunately, annotated codes are very expensive in print form and require a substantial annual subscription fee to be kept up to date. Annotated codes are also available as part of a subscription to one of the major legal databases, but this is also prohibitively expensive for most libraries. For library users doing substantial research in statutes, it might be worthwhile to refer them to a law library that has access to the relevant annotated code.

Federal Statutes

Congress.gov is generally the best place to start federal legislative research. It can be searched by bill number or title as well as keyword. Entries provide a summary and the full text of legislation in addition to a list of sponsors, and actions and votes taken. *Congress.gov* also provides browsable lists of public laws passed in each two-year session of Congress and access to the *United States Code.*

While *Congress.gov* is the official source of the *United States Code*, it is also widely available on the Web, as are other federal legislative materials. A good source, although it is not official, is the *LII*. Box 28.3 provides further advice on locating statutes.

State Statutes

Each state's legislature website will have the most recent version of the state code, and usually will have much more legislative material as well, such as bills, past versions of the code, and other legislative materials. Two resources that

Box 28.3 Finding a Statute

Asking for the text of a particular statute is a common reference question. Unfortunately, the way legislation and statutes work can make finding the statute itself complicated.

Issue 1: Session law vs. code. As discussed earlier, statutes begin life as session, a single law that is published in a session law set. From there, it is codified, meaning it is placed in topical context in the code. Unfortunately, it is very common for people to request a session law, when what they really want is the code.

For example, a user might want to read some part of the Americans with Disabilities Act. However, this title refers to the session law. Almost always users want to see provisions of it in the code. It is important to be clear as to which form of the law the user wants.

Issue 2: Popular names. Many session laws are given a popular name, especially at the federal level. Popular names always refer to the session law. As with the example earlier, popular names do not indicate where a session law is codified. Fortunately, most code publishers provide a popular names table that will cross-reference the session law with its location in the code. If no popular names table is available, a *Google* search can often find the information.

Issue 3. Searching codes. Searching online for a code section can be very frustrating. Many state legislature sites have limited search capabilities. Even in well-developed databases, searching for code sections is frustrating because codes inevitably do lots of cross-referencing, which leads to many false hits in a search.

The best approach to searching a code is to use a finding aid such as the index, if available, or the table of contents.

provide access to all or most state codes are *State Home Page and Legislature Links* from MultiState Associates and *State Law and Code Links* from FreeAdvice.

Case Law

Case law has always been the most difficult form of primary legal material to work with. This is because, as mentioned earlier, case law is not published in a way that organizes it by topic, and because when a case is affected by later cases, such as by being overruled or limited in scope, those changes are not reflected in the original case.

Case law is published in books called reporters. Reporters issue cases in the order they are issued by the courts. Traditionally case law was published by the court itself in an official reporter. In addition, private legal publishers, most notably West Publishing, publish case law from state and federal courts. Case law is also published in private legal databases, as discussed later.

This is another area that the Web has changed. Most courts now publish their cases online, on the court website. However, the problems of organization and updating remain, and online publication of cases tends to only go back a few years, meaning many years of cases are not available on a court website.

The good news is that case law is now more available than ever, and mostly for free. The bad news is that the tools required to find cases by topic and update the treatment of those cases are still mostly the purview of private publishers whose products are very expensive.

Case Citation

Cases are identified and located by their citation. A case citation includes the names of the primary parties involved, information about the reporter in which the case is published, the court issuing the case, and the year. Although all of this information is present in a case citation, the highly technical nature of the citation system can make this very confusing.

For purposes of illustration, a standard case citation looks like this:

Garratt v. Dailey, 279 P.2d 1091 (Wash. 1955)

The citation provides the names of the parties (*Garratt v. Dailey*), the location of the case in the reporter set (279 P.2d 1091), and in the parentheses, the jurisdiction (the Supreme Court of Washington) and the year the decision was rendered (1955).

The reporter information in a case citation is key to locating the case in order to read it. In the earlier example, the reporter information—279 P.2d 1091—is parsed as follows: The central abbreviation P.2d indicates that the reporter being referenced is from the second series of the *Pacific Reporter*, a publication of state case law published by the West Publishing company. The first number, 279, indicates that the case is in volume 279 of the second series of the *Pacific Reporter*. The final number, 1091, is the beginning page number of the case in volume 279.

West Publishing established a national set of reporters in the 19th century for all state and federal case law, and references to their reporters are the most commonly found citations.[6] However, many cases, including the example here, are published in two reporters: the relevant West reporter, and the official reporter of the issuing court, which in this case is the Washington Supreme Court. The citation to this case in the official reporter looks like this:

Garratt v. Dailey, 46 Wash. 2d 197 (1955)

In this case, the reporter information indicates that the case appears in volume 46 of the Washington Reports, second series, starting on page 197. The text of the case in this reporter will be identical to that in the West *Pacific Reporter*. Finally, many case citations will contain the citation information for both the official reporter and the West reporter. Such a cite looks like this, with the official reporter information listed first:

Garratt v. Dailey, 46 Wash. 2d 197, 279 P.2d 1091 (Wash. 1955)

It is interesting to note that, with a few exceptions, this system of designating cases by reporter volume and starting page number continues to dominate, in spite of the fact that cases are now published almost exclusively online. As of this writing, several jurisdictions have designed online citation systems, but no one system has emerged as dominant, and in most jurisdictions, the reporter system is still the only citation system in use.

One final note on finding a case by its citation: when presented with a case citation, do not hesitate to try *Google*. Many cases are published on the Web in various forms, and searching the citation will often find them. In particular, check *Google Scholar*, which, as described in the following case law resources, provides access to case law from most jurisdictions. Box 28.4 provides additional advice on locating court decisions.

Box 28.4 Where's That New Case?

Legal cases often make the news, and library users often want to read the decision itself. The Web has made legal decisions much more available than they were previously, but there are still challenges.

Challenge 1: Case name and citation. News reports very rarely include full citation information for a legal decision. In that event, the most important information to look for is the last name of one or more of the parties, along with the identity of the issuing court. These two pieces of information will usually allow you to search the court's website for the opinion.

Challenge 2: Trial court decisions. Published case law is made up of appellate court decisions. Trial court decisions are not considered legal precedent and therefore are not published. In addition, many trials are decided without any kind of a written opinion. For instance, a jury verdict is simply a finding of guilty or not guilty in criminal cases, or liable or not liable in civil cases. No other opinion exists. Even when a judge issues the trial court decision, it is often a similar finding, without a written decision.

Trial court judges sometimes do issue written opinions, but there is no system of publication or distribution for such decisions. While trial court decisions are usually a public record, traditionally the only way to access them has been to go to the courthouse and view the case file. However, this situation may change in the future. Most courts are adopting online docket systems, and these often contain all documents filed in a case. If such documents are viewable by the general public, it would then be possible to find trial court decisions online.

Court Rules and Dockets

Many people doing research on a legal topic may be involved in litigation. In addition to access to other forms of law, they will need access to court rules and dockets. Court rules are the rules that the courts follow during litigation and appeals. There are generally separate sets of rules for civil litigation, called the rules of civil procedure; criminal litigation, called the rules of criminal procedure; the production of evidence, called the rules of evidence; and appeals of court decisions, called the rules of appellate procedure. These bodies of rules are generally the same throughout the jurisdiction. In other words, there is one set of rules of civil procedure for all of the federal courts and one set for the courts in each state. However, in addition to these jurisdiction-wide rules, there are often local court rules that govern the administration and conduct of local courts.

In addition to rules, each court will have a docket system. The docket is primarily a scheduling and deadline system, but modern online systems will also include the actual documents filed at each stage of the litigation. Dockets can be used to check on the progress of particular litigation and to find and download documents that have been filed in a case, such as motions, briefs, and orders. Dockets are public records, but many are not free. For example, the federal court docket system, *PACER*, charges a small per-page fee for downloading documents.

Court rules, and often docket access, can usually be found on the website of the particular court involved. If in doubt as to which site to consult, start with the state's Supreme Court or state courts website. At the federal level, the *Court Website Links* provides an interactive map of federal courts. Rules and dockets for many courts, both state and federal, are also available on *LLRX Court Rules, Forms and Dockets.*

Case Law

Google Scholar provides access to case law from most jurisdictions. Select case law under the *Google Scholar* search bar. U.S. Supreme Court opinions are among the most commonly sought legal cases. Most prominent or famous U.S. Supreme Court cases are available on the Web and can be found using *Google Scholar.* In addition, the U.S. Supreme Court website has a directory of where to find opinions, both online and in print, at *Where to Obtain Supreme Court Opinions.*

For a U.S. Circuit Court of Appeals decision, *Google Scholar* is once again a good choice. Other sources tend to be limited to decisions from the past 10 to 20 years. Each circuit court of appeals has its own website, and most have at least some decisions available. The previously mentioned *Court Website Links* can be used to locate the website of the desired circuit court. Other partial databases of U.S. Circuit Court of Appeals decisions include the *Opinion Summaries Archive* from FindLaw, which has cases from 2000 to the present, and *Public Library of Law*, which has cases from 1950 to the present.

It is not possible to provide specific access to each state's court resources in this chapter. For recent court opinions for a particular case, it is best to check that state's court website. The National Center for State Courts has a helpful page of links to all state court websites, including individual courts in most states. It is a good starting point for finding state court opinions online. *Google Scholar* has an extensive collection of state court decisions and allows searchers to pick a particular jurisdiction for searching.

Regulations

Regulations are promulgated by executive agencies when the legislature passes a statute that requires regulations in order to be properly enforced. Laws that direct an agency to promulgate regulations are referred to as enabling legislation; an agency can make regulations only when an enabling statute directs them to.

In many ways, regulations at both the federal and state levels are published in the same way as legislation. There is an initial publication of the regulation, much like session law, and then current regulations are gathered by topic into a code, referred to as an administrative code. In the case of regulations, however, there is actually a two-step process for the initial publication of regulations. Regulations are first published as proposed regulations; there is generally then a comment period, during which anyone can send comments on the proposed regulation to the agency. After the comment period, the regulations are issued in final form, and it is these final regulations that are codified.

Proposed and final regulations are published in a publication of the executive branch, usually referred to as a register. At the federal level, regulations are published in the *Federal Register*, which is published each day that the executive branch operates. All proposed and final regulations, requests for comments, and other materials of the executive branch of the federal government appear in the *Federal Register*. Most states have a similar publication, although state registers are often published weekly rather than daily.

Each jurisdiction also has an administrative code, which contains all of the regulations currently in force arranged by topic. As with statute codes, administrative codes are regularly updated and will normally be the preferred source for regulations. At the federal level, the regulatory code is called the *Code of Federal Regulations*.

Executive agencies not only draft rules, but also enforce their rules. This means that agencies have their own court systems, called administrative courts, which render decisions. Sometimes these decisions are published on the Web, but often they are not. Administrative action is a fairly advanced topic for research, and again someone with such a question is probably best referred to a law library.

When library users are searching for a particular rule, it might be worth inquiring whether they need the text of the rule itself or are looking for what the rule requires. The reason for this is that regulations can be very dense and hard to parse, making the effect of a regulation hard to discern. Because of this, the agencies that promulgate and enforce the rules often provide practical accessible information on a rule's effect on their website.

As an example, a library user who wants to see the regulations on what items are prohibited from being carried aboard airlines is much better served by going to the Transportation Security Agency's website, where a very helpful set of pages describes what items are prohibited. Such situations are quite common, and searching an agency's website for information is often more useful than searching for the regulation itself.

Federal regulations are the most commonly requested regulations at the reference desk. Federal regulations cover such topics as taxation, business activities, discrimination of all kinds, housing assistance, and health care. Fortunately, all current federal regulations are available for free from websites maintained by the federal government. *Regulations.gov* is a site the federal government has set up to encourage public participation in the regulation drafting process. It provides a good first stop for regulations research. The *Federal Register* is available from the GPO from 1994 onward through the *FDSys* website. The current *Code of Federal Regulations* is available on the GPO on a page referred to as the *eCFR*. This version of the *CFR* is updated daily, and although it is not an official version of the *CFR*, it is produced by the office that produces the official *CFR* and can be trusted. Finding the relevant federal agency can be a challenge. Fortunately, *USA.gov* has a fairly comprehensive directory.

State governments also issue regulations, working in a manner very similar to the federal government. Of course, each state is different, so librarians would be advised to do a little research to discover the rules about resources available for their state. A good starting point for finding state rules is the website of the Administrative Codes and Registers Section of the National Association of Secretaries of State, *Administrative Rules*.

Ordinances and Local Law

Ordinances and local laws have historically been the hardest laws to find. The Web has helped immensely as many local communities now put their ordinances and laws on their websites. Prior to the Web, and continuing today, several private publishers have served as publishers of local ordinances for municipalities. While these were previously published only in book form, they are now commonly also published on the Web. Because publishers have only the ordinances and codes that they publish, librarians may wish to determine which sites have the ordinances relevant for their library.

Municipal Code Corporation is the largest publisher of local law and has the most comprehensive site with *Code Library*. A number of other municipal law publishers provide partial or regional coverage. *Municipal Codes* from Code Publishing has partial coverage, as do *Codes Online* and *Online eCode360 Library*. *Code Library* from Coded Systems also offers partial coverage, mostly for Western states.

CONCLUSION

Reference questions about legal issues are very common in most libraries. Helping users with legal questions can be daunting, both because of the complex nature of legal issues and legal materials, and because of fears of liability. However, with proper preparation, such questions can be handled effectively and fruitfully.

While the possibility of liability arising from answering legal reference questions is real, such a possibility is highly unlikely. The best way to minimize this risk is to refrain from being an expert or having an opinion about the actual legal issue being researched. Instead, the librarian should concentrate on being an expert at finding the information sought.

The amazing array of legal resources available on the Web has made effective legal reference a possibility in any library. The most important starting point for the librarian is to understand the basic structure of legal materials. With that in hand, most legal questions can be handled effectively using Web resources. For very complex or difficult issues, the user can be referred to an expert, either a specialized law librarian or a legal professional.

Like any other area of expertise, facility with legal materials comes with practice and experience. Mastering legal materials can be very rewarding and extremely useful to the user who needs the librarian's research expertise.

NOTES

1. This issue also potentially applies to providing reference service on medical issues, and indeed in any area of knowledge that relates to a licensed profession, if the act of providing information could reasonably be seen as providing the professional expertise of the licensed profession. For more information on this, see Paul D. Healey (2008).
2. This assertion is based on searches of the literature and of news and legal databases by the author first performed in 1994 (Healey 1995, 519–21) and regularly updated since then through December 2014.
3. The actual definition of the practice of law varies from state to state, although most states base their definition, at least in part, on the American Bar Association's *Model Definition of the Practice of Law* (2003).
4. Most state bar associations have a close relationship to, and often serve in some ways as an arm of, the state supreme court. State bar associations often act on

behalf of the state supreme court in disciplining lawyers and setting rules for legal practice. As a result, materials published by state bar associations are generally considered authoritative.

5. Examples include the Uniform Law Commission, which drafts suggested laws for all 50 states; the National Center for State Courts and the National Conference of State Legislatures, which provide guidance and resources for state court systems and state legislatures respectively; and the American Law Institute, which gathers legal experts and government officials to provide guidance on legal issues.
6. *Wikipedia* has a brief but good explanation of the West National Reporter System, which includes abbreviations, maps, and dates of coverage ("National Reporter System" 2015).

REFERENCES

American Bar Association. 2003. *Model Definition of the Practice of Law*. http://www.americanbar.org/groups/professional_responsibility/task_force_model_definition_practice_law.html.

Healey, Paul D. 1995. "Chicken Little at the Reference Desk: The Myth of Librarian Liability." *Law Library Journal* 87 (Summer): 515–33.

Healey, Paul D. 2002. "Pro Se Users, Reference Liability, and the Unauthorized Practice of Law: Twenty-Five Selected Readings." *Law Library Journal* 94 (Spring): 133–38.

Healey, Paul D. 2008. *Liability Issues for Librarians and Information Professionals*. New York: Neal-Schuman.

Healey, Paul D. 2014. *Answering Legal Reference Questions: How and Where to Find the Answers*. Chicago: ALA Editions.

Mantel, Matthew. 2008. "Private Bills and Private Laws." *Law Library Journal* 99 (Winter): 87–100.

"National Reporter System." 2015. *Wikipedia*. Last accessed October 12. http://en.wikipedia.org/wiki/National_Reporter_System.

Pacific Reporter. 1883–. Eagan, MN: West Publishing.

LIST OF SOURCES

Administrative Rules. National Association of Secretaries of State. http://www.administrativerules.org/administrative-rules/.

American Jurisprudence. 2004–2015. 2nd ed. Eagan, MN: Thomson Reuters. Available online as part of *Westlaw*.

American Law Institute. http://www.ali.org/.

American Law Reports. 2005–2016. 6th ed. Eagan, MN: Thomson Reuters. Available online as part of *Westlaw*.

Black's Law Dictionary. 2014. 10th ed. Eagan, MN: Thomson Reuters.

Bloomberg Law. http://www.bna.com/bloomberglaw.

Code Library. Coded Systems. http://www.codedsystems.com/codelibrary.html.

Code Library. Municipal Code Corporation. http://www.municode.com/library/.

Code of Federal Regulations. Government Publishing Office. http://www.ecfr.gov.

Codes Online. Sterling Codifiers. http://www.sterlingcodifiers.com/#codes.

Congress.gov. http://www.congress.gov/.

Consumer Finance Protection Bureau. http://www.consumerfinance.gov/.

Corpus Juris Secundum. 2003–2016. Eagan, MN: Thomson Reuters.

Court Website Links. United States Courts. http://www.uscourts.gov/about-federal-courts/federal-courts-public/court-website-links.

FDSys. Government Publishing Office. http://www.gpo.gov/fdsys/.
"Federal Law Collection." *Legal Information Institute*. Cornell University Law School. http://www.law.cornell.edu/federal.
Federal Register. Government Publishing Office. http://www.gpo.gov/fdsys/browse/collection.action?collectionCode=FR.
"Find a Lawyer." *FindLaw*. http://lawyers.findlaw.com/.
"Find an Attorney." *AttorneyPages*. http://attorneypages.com/.
FindLaw. http://www.findlaw.com/.
Free Dictionary of Law Terms and Legal Definitions. Nolo. http://www.nolo.com/dictionary/.
Free Legal Articles & FAQs. Nolo. http://www.nolo.com/legal-encyclopedia.
Gale Encyclopedia of American Law. 2011. 3rd ed. Farmington Hills, MI: Gale Cengage Learning. Available online as part of *Gale Virtual Reference Library*.
Gale Virtual Reference Library. Farmington Hills, MI: Gale Cengage Learning. http://www.cengage.com/. [subscription required]
Google. https://www.google.com/.
Google Scholar. https://scholar.google.com/.
A Guide to the U.S. Federal Legal System Web-Based Public Accessible Sources. Hauser Global Law School Program. New York University. http://www.nyulawglobal.org/globalex/United_States1.htm.
"Law by Source: State." *Legal Information Institute*. Cornell University Law School. http://www.law.cornell.edu/states/.
"Law School Library & State Law Library Catalogs." *WashLaw*. http://www.washlaw.edu/lawcat/.
Legal Information Institute. Cornell University Law School. http://www.law.cornell.edu/.
LexisNexis. San Francisco, CA: LexisNexis. http://www.lexisnexis.com/. [subscription required]
LexisNexis Academic. San Francisco, CA: LexisNexis. http://www.lexisnexis.com/en-us/products/lexisnexis-academic.page. [subscription required]
Lexis Web. LexisNexis. http://lexisweb.com/.
LLRX Court Rules, Forms and Dockets. LLRX. http://www.llrx.com/courtrules.
LSC Programs. Legal Services Corporation. http://www.lsc.gov/find-legal-aid.
Municipal Codes. Code Publishing. http://www.codepublishing.com/elibrary.html.
The National Center for State Courts. http://www.ncsc.org/.
National Conference of State Legislatures. http://www.ncsl.org/.
Nolo. http://www.nolo.com.
Online eCode360 Library. General Code. http://www.generalcode.com/codification/ecode/library.
Opinion Summaries Archive. FindLaw. http://caselaw.findlaw.com/summary/.
PACER. Administrative Office of the U.S. Courts. https://www.pacer.gov/.
Public Library of Law. http://www.plol.org/Pages/Search.aspx.
Public Library Toolkit. Legal Information Services to the Public Special Interest Section. American Association of Law Libraries. http://www.aallnet.org/sections/lisp/Public-Library-Toolkit.
Regulations.gov. http://www.regulations.gov/#!home.
Restatements. American Law Institute. http://www.ali.org/projects/.
State Constitution Page. Constitution Society. http://www.constitution.org/cons/usstcons.htm.
"State, Court, and County Law Libraries." *WashLaw*. Washburn University School of Law. http://www.washlaw.edu/statecourtcounty/.
State Home Page and Legislature Links. MultiState Associates. http://www.multistate.com/site.nsf/state.
State Law and Code Links. FreeAdvice. http://law.freeadvice.com/resources/statecodes.htm.

State Specific Legal Forms for All States. FindLaw. http://www.uslegalforms.com/findlaw/.

Uniform Commercial Code. https://www.law.cornell.edu/ucc.

Uniform Law Commission. http://www.uniformlawcommission.com/.

United States Code. Congress. http://uscode.house.gov/.

United States Courts. http://www.uscourts.gov/Home.aspx.

U.S. Constitution. National Archives. http://www.archives.gov/exhibits/charters/constitution_transcript.html.

U.S. Constitution Annotated. Congress. http://www.congress.gov/constitution-annotated.

USA.gov. https://www.usa.gov/federal-agencies/a.

WashLaw. Washburn University School of Law Library. http://www.washlaw.edu/.

Westlaw. Eagan, MN: Thomson Reuters. http://legalsolutions.thomsonreuters.com/law-products/westlaw-legal-research/. [subscription required]

Wex. Legal Information Institute. Cornell University Law School. http://www.law.cornell.edu/wex/.

Where to Obtain Supreme Court Opinions. Supreme Court of the United States. http://www.supremecourt.gov/opinions/obtainopinions.aspx.

SUGGESTED READINGS

Healey, Paul D. 2002. "Pro Se Users, Reference Liability, and the Unauthorized Practice of Law: Twenty-Five Selected Readings." *Law Library Journal* 94 (Spring): 133–38.

This article surveys the literature that addresses the issue of providing legal reference services to members of the public. As the article shows, there is a broad diversity of opinion as to whether legal reference service constitutes legal advice and where the line between reference service and legal advice might be.

Healey, Paul D. 2008. *Liability Issues for Librarians and Information Professionals.* New York: Neal-Schuman.

This book addresses the concept of liability for librarians. Legal issues arising from providing legal reference services are covered in Chapter 7.

Healey, Paul D. 2014. *Answering Legal Reference Questions: How and Where to Find the Answers.* Chicago: ALA Editions.

This book covers much of the information covered in this chapter, only in much greater detail. It also includes an appendix that lists Web-based legal resources for all 50 states and the federal government.

How to Research a Legal Problem: A Guide for Non-Lawyers. American Association of Law Libraries. http://www.aallnet.org/sections/lisp/howtoresearchlegalproblem-final.pdf.

In this guide, law librarians explain the research process for nonlawyers. The guide is a free service of AALL.

Locating the Law. 2011. 5th ed., rev. Public Access to Legal Information Committee. Southern California Association of Law Libraries. http://www.aallnet.org/chapter/scall/locating.htm.

Although aimed at California librarians and California law, this free publication contains some excellent information on providing reference services on legal topics.

Public Library Toolkit. Legal Information Services to the Public Special Interest Section. American Association of Law Libraries. http://www.aallnet.org/sections/lisp/Public-Library-Toolkit.

This Web resource provides information on collecting and using legal materials for public and academic libraries. In addition to general information, the guide provides a specific toolkit for each state.

Part III

The Future of Reference Service

Chapter 29

Creating the Future of Reference Service

Amy VanScoy

INTRODUCTION

The chapters of this book have covered all manner of knowledge and skills concerning reference service. You have learned about the reference interview, strategies for searching, and a wide variety of reference sources. However, there is more to reference service than knowledge and skills. It is also a way of thinking. Excellent reference service includes attitudes and beliefs that make professional practice more than simply a series of behaviors.

Some shared attitudes and values have been covered in this book, such as putting the patron at the center of the interaction and the importance of equal access for all patrons. However, the profession's shared values are not the only ones that will guide your practice; you will develop a personal philosophy of reference. Your attitudes and beliefs will be influenced by your reflection, your vision for reference service, and the kinds of experiences you have as a practitioner.

Throughout this book, you have been absorbing the wisdom of reference experts. They have shared both broad and deep knowledge. But now that you are at the end of the book, it is time to take what you know and go make a difference in your professional work. As you develop your own expertise, you need to develop your personal reference philosophy that will shape and guide your practice. This philosophy will articulate what you believe about information seeking and reference service. It will guide your daily practice and help you communicate to others the values, attitudes, and beliefs that inform and motivate what you do. You can think of your career as a journey to create the future of reference service based, not on policies and procedures, but on values, attitudes, and beliefs about reference service. This chapter will guide you in reflecting on reference practice and creating a vision for reference service with the goal of developing a reference philosophy to help create the future you envision.

BE YOUR OWN FUTURIST

Much has been said and written about the future of reference service. Listening to and reading the predictions of futurists in the profession can provide food for thought and lively conversation with colleagues. However, these speculations about the future may be only marginally helpful to a practicing librarian because they can fall short of the core principles of reference service. Speculations about whether or not reference desks will exist or what new technologies will be used to provide service do not contribute to high-level thinking about reference practice. They reduce practice to the level of furniture and technological fads. These concepts are not the basis for a real vision for practice and how it can be continuously improved. In addition, it is critical not to sit back and listen to what the futurists tell you will or should happen. In today's world, change tends to come from below, from people on the front lines who see opportunities for improvement.

THEMES TO CONSIDER IN ENVISIONING THE FUTURE

Creating a vision is the first step in any strategic planning exercise. As you plan your career, envisioning the impact you want to have is key for charting a course toward your desired future. As part of this process, it might be useful to reflect on some key themes—the user/professional interaction, technology, entrepreneurship and creativity, social justice and allyship, the confines of space, and the search process in context.

User/Professional Interaction

The interaction between the patron and the information professional has always been the fundamental part of reference service. This is such a given that it is easy to lose sight of the interaction and focus energy on the opportunities and challenges of technologies, physical spaces, and other issues that are more concrete. However, the user/professional interaction needs attention for continuous improvement.

A key component of the user/professional interaction is interpersonal relations. Marie L. Radford's (2006) and Radford and Lynn Silipigni Connaway's (2009) research has demonstrated the importance of relationship building in reference service. Using extensive virtual reference data, Radford and Connaway developed a model for success in virtual reference that includes both a content dimension (whether the interaction addressed the user's information need) and a relational dimension (whether the interaction addressed the user's interpersonal need). They found that both the relational and content dimensions were important for success in reference service, with the relational dimension actually being more important to the user. In the past few years, we have seen a resurgence of interest in relationship-building initiatives, such as embedded librarians and community reference, both of which are intended to build and strengthen relationships between the professional and his or her local clientele.

Another key aspect of interacting with users is listening. Listening gets its own step in the reference interview guidelines, but sometimes librarians do not recognize it as a professional skill, claiming, "I didn't really do anything. All I did was listen." However, good listening is a significant professional skill. While the librarian who is listening may appear passive, listening is an active state, and much work is happening during this activity. Listening supports the concept of the reference dialogue (Doherty 2006) by allowing the user to take some control and shape the direction of the interaction. In talking through her research issue with the listening librarian, a course of action or new insight may occur to the user.

An essential skill related to good listening is empathy. Although empathy is often associated with emotions and sympathy, cognitive empathy is about trying to understand another person. This understanding allows the librarian to grasp the other's reasoning and provide them with service that really meets their needs, rather than the needs you assume they have. Empathy is increasingly viewed as a skill that can be learned, not a personal characteristic. Young (2015, 38) breaks down the practice of empathy into two parts. The first part is "develop empathy," which you do through listening and thinking about what you heard. The second part is "apply empathy," which you do through trying to use the other person's reasoning process when creating something or collaborating with them (rather than relying on your own ideas of what makes sense) and through supporting them via your products or services. Developing and applying empathy allows you to understand the user's mindset and to provide them with better service.

Relationship building, good listening, and empathy are only a few of the many aspects of interacting effectively with users. The most important point is that the interpersonal aspect is of critical importance in reference service and should be actively considered when envisioning the future.

Technology

Discussions of the future of reference service nearly always involve discussions of technology. Technology has always been an important tool in providing reference service, even when that technology was not digital, and envisioning the future of reference service definitely requires exploration and creative thinking about technology. However, the applications or devices themselves are not where the improvement in reference service lies. The improvement lies in how you exploit these applications and devices and, in addition, how you use these applications or devices to think differently about your practice. You should approach new technologies not as specific tools that you could implement, but as new ways to think about what you do. Think about the latest gadget that your patrons are using as a window into what they like, how they want to interact, and how they see their world.

For example, years ago, when people started flocking to Second Life, a collaborative virtual world, librarians went there, too. They explored the virtual world, set up in-world professional communities, and created libraries and reference desks. When Second Life succumbed to the next online fad, there was some scoffing about how silly these reference desks in Second Life had been. If you view this experimentation as being solely about staffing a reference desk in a virtual world, then the experiment does appear to be a bit of a failure. However, if you view it as a group of professionals investigating what their users are doing, meeting users where they are, and exploring, experimenting, and pushing the boundaries of the traditional environment where reference service occurs, then the Second Life experiment may well have been a total success.

- What did librarians learn about virtual worlds?
- What did they learn about their users?
- How did their beliefs about reference service and interactions with users change as a result of this experimentation?

The answers to these questions are much more important than how many reference interactions actually occurred at the reference desks in Second Life.

Keep in mind that technology does not necessarily improve reference service. Recall Dave Tyckoson's words from Chapter 1 that technology is "a tool that enhances library service," but he continues, "it does not fundamentally change the nature of that service." Like the card catalog or an iPad, cool new technology is simply a tool that you can exploit to provide better service. Be suspicious of a conference presentation that claims that a particular technology will revolutionize your service. Instead, seek out presenters who propose discussing how a new technology might help you think outside the box about your work or presenters who discuss how the technology can give you insights into how your patrons use technology.

Thinking about new technology not just as a tool to be evaluated, but also as a way to better understand your users is a mind-set that requires practice. Box 29.1 provides an example of this way of thinking.

Box 29.1 Case Study: Reddit

Reddit (www.reddit.com) is an online forum used by millions of people. The largest group of users is young adult males, but as this group represents only 15 percent of the total users, the reddit community is diverse (Duggan and Smith 2013). Users post and comment on information, images, and questions, and there is a sense of community with shared acronyms and behavior patterns. What can librarians learn from reddit? Misguided librarians might investigate the site and then reject it as a means of communication not suitable for reference service. Others might try to figure out how they can answer user questions within the reddit format. But the real questions to ask are:

- Why is reddit so popular?
- What about this particular format draws millions of people every day to share and ask for information?
- What does reddit tell us about our current users?
- What does it tell us about their issues and concerns?
- What does it tell us about how they like to communicate?

The answers to these questions might provide new ideas for creating new services or modifying existing services to appeal to the information-sharing and -seeking behaviors of some users.

Developing an attitude of experimentation with technology may be the best way to keep your practice on the cutting edge and fend off the routine and disappointment that leads to burnout. For some librarians, experimentation with technology comes naturally. For those who do not feel a thrill at the discovery of a new smartphone app, remember that it is not really about the technology, it is about the users. So, find some users who are thrilled by new technology and tap into their excitement. Seek out a coworker using a device you do not recognize. Identify a blog or twitter account that discusses or reviews new technologies. Find out what young people in your area are using by chatting with a few who visit your library regularly, asking to have some time with the teen advisory board, or charging your young adult services librarian to investigate for you. Look outside the library literature to people and publications in computer science or education. And always be thinking, "how could I use this to provide better service?"

Entrepreneurship and Creativity

Creating a future for reference service requires an entrepreneurial spirit. Creating the change you want to see in reference service requires creative thinking and initiative. Of course, any new initiatives require critical analysis and careful planning before implementation, but those creative ideas have to come from somewhere.

There is a common misperception that creativity is a trait of only certain people or that it spontaneously occurs, as if by magic. In reality, creativity occurs as a result of concerted effort over time. "Creative people" are the ones who consistently apply themselves to the task—gathering and processing new information, interacting with and reflecting about this new information, and setting aside and revisiting their ideas.

Box 29.2 Generating Creativity through an Idea File

There are many strategies for developing creative ideas. An incredibly simple but effective strategy is the "idea file" suggested by Robert Boice (1994).

- Create an "idea file"—a simple file folder for something you want to think creatively about: for example, reference services, programming or events, instruction, or a conference presentation.
- Every time you think of or run across a related idea, jot down the idea and put it in your idea file. Ideas may come from professional articles, articles from other fields, blogs, tweets, and even science fiction films!
- Every week, go through your folder, reading and reorganizing the ideas in your file. Move them around, grouping ideas together to see them in different ways. Feel free to jot additional thoughts on any idea in the file.

Eventually, the act of rereading and reorganizing the ideas will create connections between the ideas and will help you see them in new ways. These connections and insights will be the seeds of innovative services, inspiring lesson plans, clever programs, and useful presentations.

Like creativity, entrepreneurship is not a gift, but a skill. What can we learn from entrepreneurs that we can apply to reference service? One concept is that of "failing fast." The worst thing you can do with a start-up company is to fail slowly. This draws out the agony and prevents you from moving on to something that might be more successful. This is not a familiar concept for librarians. Librarians tend to carefully examine an issue, do the necessary research, bring everyone to consensus, and wait until they are absolutely sure of success before launching a new service. Often services are launched as pilot projects with limited hours and a limited duration. This cautious approach may occasionally save a library from a failed initiative, but it consumes significant time and resources that could have been spent on simply giving the service a try. Failing fast in reference service might look like jumping on some new technology, blasting out advertising via every possible channel, and jumping into the new service 100 percent with every staff member on board. If patrons love it, great! Then time can be spent on figuring what they really love about it and how it can be maintained. If patrons hate it, no problem! At least you will know quickly that it was a bad idea, and you can turn your time and resources to something else. Of course, failing fast requires a culture that supports innovation and risk taking. Librarians need to feel supported in being creative and entrepreneurial.

Another key concept for innovative thinking is that it is OK to be wrong. As conscientious stewards of community resources, librarians are sometimes reluctant to experiment with new services or programs. As wrongness expert Kathryn Schulz says, "Wrongness is a vital part of how we learn and change. Thanks to error, we can revise our understanding of ourselves and amend our ideas about the world" (2010, 5). Experimentation, even with its associated risk of being wrong, is an excellent way to learn what works for our users. So future information professionals, do not be afraid to be occasionally wrong! An attitude of perseverance and acceptance of mistakes can lead to continuous improvement and innovation in reference service.

Social Justice and Allyship

An important aspect of librarianship in general and particularly for reference service is social justice. While this has been a common thread through the history of reference service, recently it has received more explicit attention. In Chapter 2 on Ethics, you read about the professional value on equal access to information. The "digital divide" limits some users' access to information. Simply by helping a user to log into a computer and navigate to a website, you may have helped to narrow this divide. Offering financial literacy programming and being patient with users who are not tech-savvy are ways that librarians facilitate equal access.

Beyond treating all users as equal in your practice, you can be a force for social good. Not all users share your understanding that libraries are places where they belong. Making a family feel welcome in your library conveys that libraries are for everyone. As the "face" of the library, professionals providing reference service are in a unique position to notice opportunities and create a "safe space" atmosphere for all users.

Librarians are in a powerful position to serve as allies—members of a dominant social group that actively work to dismantle systems of oppression. A key element of successful allyship is working with members of the community to help them help themselves. Because librarians value listening and dialogue and have excellent skills in this area, they are particularly suited to being good allies. In a useful resource called *Community Tool Box*, the Work Group for Community Health and Development (2014) provides a concrete and substantial discussion of allyship and how you can work toward being an effective ally. According to the *Community Tool Box*, "we need to get to know people, find out what they're up against, and support them in their struggles. That's a lot of what allies do—get involved and support people, instead of staying on the sidelines."

For libraries to be effective institutions for social justice, professionals must develop the cultural competence necessary to effectively serve the wide variety of users they will encounter. Patricia Montiel Overall's (2009, 192–98) cultural competence model for LIS professionals provides a framework for self-evaluation and concrete examples of steps professionals can take to develop in this area. Overall identifies three domains of cultural competence and provides strategies for improving one's competence in each area, such as examining one's own cultural identity (cognitive), engaging in conversation with people from other cultures (interpersonal), and translating library signage (environmental). What cultural competence skills do you need to develop to build the kind of inclusive reference service you want to see in the future?

The Confines of Space

Librarians sometimes see reference service as happening solely at a "reference desk." While this is changing somewhat with the idea of mobile services, it has not completely changed. Librarians sometimes neglect to view an interaction with a user as reference service when it does not occur at the reference desk, but perhaps in the context of instruction or in a building outside the library. It is important to realize that reference service can happen outside the confines of your regular shift at the reference desk.

Most librarians have experienced the "feeding frenzy" sensation. When they leave the traditional reference desk to help a user at a computer, suddenly all the users around them are asking questions. Librarians liken this experience to being in shark-infested waters—once the users smell blood, they attack. This phenomenon demonstrates how important it is to get out in the areas where users are looking for and using information. This may be as simple as leaving the reference desk to help a user in the stacks, or it may be as far afield as providing service, for example, in a community center, a faculty office, or a laboratory.

When people agonize about "reference is dead," they really mean that reference desks, as monolithic pieces of furniture, are dead. Reference service thrives beyond the reference desk, in the library building, in the community, and in the world. Successful reference desks often do not look like those of the past—they may be combined with other services, be replaced by other types of furniture, or be more like an Apple Store Genius Bar with librarians moving about the space. So move out of your comfort zone and expand your notion of the "reference area" to include the entire library, the entire school, or the entire community.

The Search Process in Context

It is becoming clear that the future of reference service involves more than searching for and locating information. Information seeking is one component of a broader activity for users—a broader activity that information professionals have the skills and knowledge to improve. If you think about the context for the user's information seeking, you can begin to see opportunities to fill.

When searching was extremely difficult, users needed the help of a professional to locate bits of information in esoteric reference books or to locate scholarly papers in unintuitive databases. Today, searching for and locating information still has its challenges, but users with reasonable information literacy skills can often manage this task. Some have perceived this change as a crisis for reference service, but it is really an opportunity.

A useful model for thinking about how to expand reference service beyond its traditional context is Carol Kuhlthau's information search process model (2004). Kuhlthau's model describes the stages of the search process through which users progress—initiation, selection, exploration, formulation, collection, and presentation—including the thinking and feeling of the user and the actions that he or she takes. Although librarians have always helped users at all stages of the information search process, by necessity, most of their attention has been focused on the Collection stage, when users were searching for and locating information. As access to information has become easier, professionals now have the opportunity to focus more on pre-searching activities, such as topic selection and focus reformulation, or post-searching activities like managing information and presenting results. These activities may be even more intellectual and less mechanical than search and retrieval. As these stages of the search process are associated with more challenging affective states for patrons, such as uncertainty, frustration, and disappointment, supportive reference assistance might be most welcome.

Experienced librarians usually have a proud story about the time they asked a user to tell them about a topic and, through the ensuing conversation, helped the user to clarify and develop their thinking about the topic. The reference interview is not simply a diagnostic tool to inform searching, but also an opportunity for synergy in thinking about the user's information need. Simple encouragements like handing users some markers to sketch out their topic on a whiteboard or handing them some sticky notes to jot down their ideas can encourage users to take advantage of professionals' skills and knowledge about the pre-searching phase. Pre-searching activities like topic selection can be enhanced as well by providing and instructing users in concept mapping software and other applications that enhance creativity and clarify thinking.

Post-searching activities can include providing and instructing users in the use of citation management or note-taking software (e.g., NoodleTools) or instructing users in evaluation criteria and ensuring that they are applying these criteria. There are lots of productivity apps that can help users to organize and present their ideas. For example, providing access to and support for apps, such as Gingko (an online notecard system), could be a way of supporting information use and communicating to users the vital and extensive role of reference professionals. Thinking beyond the Collection stage to the other stages of the information search process can create opportunities and help you provide useful service.

THINKING LIKE A REFERENCE LIBRARIAN

In other professions, the focus of professional work has shifted from knowledge and skills to professional thinking. While knowledge and skills are certainly important, focusing on how professionals who provide reference service think about their work is also important and may provide the greatest opportunity for professional development after the novice phase. In the few studies of professional thinking, issues such as a focus on the user, a varied and uncertain work environment, focus on learning, importance of engagement, and development of reference expertise are key dimensions of the experience of the expert librarian (VanScoy 2013).

Thus, in moving through one's career, it is important to continue to develop new skills and knowledge by reading the professional literature; attending webinars, conferences, and training; and maintaining professional dialogue with both local and distant colleagues. However, it is also important to continue to develop one's professional thinking. Professional thinking is the values, attitudes, and beliefs of the librarian. The key to examining and developing your professional thinking is reflective practice.

Reflective Practice

Reflective practice may sound like a buzzword, but it prevents you from simply going through the motions of your work and helps you to practice reference deliberately and mindfully. In general, it means thinking about and questioning your practice. As a professional, it can be easy to submit to the pressure to constantly produce. If there are no questions or projects that demand your attention, you will likely have projects you have been meaning to get around to. In this fact-paced line of work, it can be hard to take time to reflect and ask yourself the kinds of probing questions that lead to creative ideas and improvement in service.

Reflective practice might manifest itself as thinking about a reference interaction after it is finished and asking yourself whether it went well or went poorly, deciding what you did effectively and what you could have done better, and then considering what you might do in the future to improve your practice. You can go further than this, as well, by examining how your values, attitudes, and beliefs affected your practice. But how do you know how they affected it, if you do not know what they are?

Developing Your Reference Philosophy

It is important to examine your values, attitudes, and beliefs about reference service. These things affect your practice whether you are aware of them or not. Throughout this book, you have been presented with scenarios that challenge you to think about what you would do in a given situation. These scenarios are designed to prompt you to think about, for example, your values, attitudes, and beliefs in terms of ethics and social justice. You have also been presented with various orientations toward reference service, such as Wyer's (1930) "conservative," "moderate," and "liberal" levels of service.

Information professionals have diverse beliefs about the purpose of reference service. Table 29.1 (VanScoy, 2012) lists some different roles a librarian may play based on her reference philosophy. Some of the purposes in the table may resonate with you.

TABLE 29.1 Roles for Reference Librarians

Roles for Reference Librarians	Professional Beliefs Motivating These Roles
The information provider	The goal of reference is to provide answers to questions.
The instructor	The goal of reference is to teach skills in library and information use.
The communicator	The goal of reference is a flow of accurate information and a human connection between the user and the resources.
The relationship builder	The goal of reference is a productive, long-term relationship between librarian and user.
The guide/the advisor	The goal of reference is to guide and advise users.
The counselor	The goal of reference is to develop lifelong information in users through mentoring or coaching.
The partner	The goal of reference is a balance of power and expertise between librarian and user.

As Kern and Woodard say in Chapter 3 "Knowledge of technique is essential, but each librarian will develop his or her own style." What will be your style? A useful exercise might be to write a "reference philosophy" with the same deliberate reflection as a teacher writes a "teaching philosophy." A teaching philosophy usually begins with a discussion of what the instructor believes about learning. How does it happen? What makes learning happen? How does teaching facilitate learning? This section of the philosophy may refer to specific theories. The next section discusses how the instructor's beliefs about learning influence his or her teaching. This section usually includes some specific examples of what the instructor does in the classroom because of his or her beliefs. The teaching philosophy can also talk about how the instructor assesses his or her teaching and how the instructor has improved and developed. A teaching philosophy statement has multiple uses. Most importantly, producing the statement is an opportunity for the instructor to deliberately reflect on his or her teaching. It also allows the instructor to articulate his or her philosophy, so that it can be shared with others. In practical terms, it can be shared with a prospective employer, so that the employer can see what the instructor believes and how this belief is manifested in practice.

A reference philosophy is useful for the same reasons. Taking the time to reflect on one's practice and articulate one's beliefs may be enlightening. One's attitudes, values, and beliefs about reference service change over time, so doing this exercise as a student in an LIS program, as an early career librarian, and later as an expert librarian could provide satisfying evidence of your professional development and journey from novice to expert. While an employer is unlikely to request a reference philosophy statement, a job candidate who clearly articulates his or her values, attitudes, and beliefs about reference service and describes in detail how these manifest themselves in his or her past experience is likely to seem a more competent candidate than an applicant who has not reflected on these things. Box 29.3 provides questions to guide your reflection as you develop a reference philosophy.

Box 29.3 Activity: What Is Your Reference Philosophy?

First, consider your beliefs about users and their experience of information seeking and use.

- What are your beliefs about information seeking and use?
- What are your beliefs about the user experience?
- Are there concepts about the user experience from this book or other courses that really speak to you (e.g., the Information Search Process model, library anxiety, the imposed query)?

Second, consider your beliefs about reference service.

- How can reference service address the needs, problems, and challenges of information seeking and use that you described earlier?
- Which techniques introduced by this book support your beliefs about reference service (e.g., searching, listening, communicating, instruction, relationship building)? Are some techniques more important than others? If so, which ones and why?
- What do you think about the balance between instructing users and providing them with information?
- What do you think about developing relationships with users?

Next, consider how these beliefs influence your practice or how you would like them to influence your practice.

- How do these thoughts manifest themselves in your practical experience?
- If you do not have work, volunteer, or field experience in libraries, what practical experience do you have that might be related, such as tutoring or customer service?

Finally, consider how you assess the quality of your reference service.

- By what standards do you judge your practice?
- What areas for improvement have you identified and how did you go about improving your practice as a result?

The process of articulating a reference philosophy goes back to thinking like a librarian and acting upon your values, attitudes, and beliefs. If you believe that instruction is of critical importance, but you notice that in all of your virtual reference transcripts you provide URLs with little instruction, how can you reconcile belief and practice? If instruction truly is important, how can you increase the instructional aspects of your virtual reference work?

In addition, you may have practices that were dictated to you by training or library policies. As a staff member or student worker, you may have been instructed to practice in a certain way. But as a librarian, you need to develop a sense of professional judgment, decide what the profession should be, and work to make it that way. This begins with reflecting about what you have been told to do and reconciling it with your professional beliefs. Consider again an example from virtual reference: If you have been told that a virtual reference transaction should take 15 minutes or less, and to transfer any user to another medium after 15 minutes, consider the values, attitudes, and beliefs behind this policy. Does this policy reflect your values, attitudes, and beliefs? If not, you should work to communicate this and make changes that will improve service to your users.

Developing a Portfolio

Another mechanism for reflecting on your practice is developing a portfolio of your work. This is an effective practice from teaching and other professions, where professionals consider their values, attitudes, and beliefs and gather evidence to support them. The exercise of compiling a portfolio of your professional work should not simply be to show others what a fantastic job you are doing, but also to reflect on your values, attitudes, and beliefs, and demonstrate how they manifest themselves in practice.

Box 29.4 Create a Reference Service Portfolio

Your reference service portfolio not only provides evidence of your experience providing reference service, but also demonstrates that you have thought carefully about what it means to provide good service and that you engage in reflective practice and assessment.

What might go into a reference service portfolio?

- Transcripts of your virtual and/or e-mail reference interactions. Do not just choose the best ones or the ones where you found the answer. Choose ones that demonstrate specific values. For instance, if you feel that relationship building is a key component of reference service, find an example of a transcript in which you made an extra effort to develop a relationship with the user. Accompany the transcript with a brief reflection about how your behaviors reflected your beliefs and how this improved the experience in some way for the user.
- Summaries of consultations with users in which you describe in detail the user, his or her need, what you did with the user, and the end result, including the impact of your service.
- Examples of Web pages or online tutorials you have developed. Explain how these pages or tutorials anticipate user needs and demonstrate your reference philosophy.
- Reports from supervisors or even fellow students who have observed you providing reference service.

Developing Your Professional Brand

Users still sometimes associate information professionals with reference books and do not understand the broad range of expertise they have. Even some library administrators retain this conservative view, insisting that reference desks are no longer being used, so reference service is no longer necessary. While this is frustrating, it is not a reason to give up on the vital work that you do. Try to see these frustrating encounters as opportunities, even teachable moments. Develop an "elevator speech" that succinctly and pleasantly reveals the mission of the contemporary reference professional.

Creating a personal brand for your reference service may be an effective way to do this. Using your professional Web page, your presentations and service activities, your Twitter feed, and other tools, you can create an image for yourself as the kind of information professional you want to be. This brand can be helpful in communicating your value in cover letters and job interviews. It is an ongoing, always developing process, but it will keep you fresh and help keep you focused on your professional mission.

Box 29.5 Activity: Creating Your Professional Brand

What is your existing brand?

What you are communicating about yourself now? Search for yourself online and analyze what you find about yourself.

- Do pages about you show up at the top of the results list? If not, you may want to work on optimizing pages so that potential employers see your work first.
- What kinds of pages exist that communicate your work? Have you created a professional website, a professional blog, a LinkedIn profile, a Twitter feed, or a student profile page?
- What message do these pages convey about you as an information professional? Do they reflect your reference philosophy or your professional attitudes and values?

How can you improve your brand?

After searching for yourself, you may have already come up with some ideas, such as creating a professional website or setting up a LinkedIn profile. As you are creating and editing pages about yourself, however, think about your reference philosophy and other professional attitudes and beliefs. How can you communicate these attitudes and beliefs through your online presence?

- Make a statement on your website that communicates your philosophy.
- Include excerpts of your work or testimonials from users or supervisors that illustrate these beliefs in practice.
- Add photographs to your site if you feel that some aspects of your philosophy might be better communicated with images.
- Ask colleagues to endorse you on LinkedIn.
- Create a professional Twitter feed where you tweet about things that support your reference philosophy and your brand.
- Include ideas from your brand in your cover letters to reinforce the impression that potential employers have seen online.
- Make sure that your brand is consistent across all of your professional sites and profiles.

Your professional brand will involve much more than reference service. All professionals need a broad range of knowledge and skills in order to be flexible and to succeed in today's multifaceted positions; however, your reference philosophy should play some role in this suite of expertise. If you do not see yourself providing reference service as a major part of your work, consider how your reference philosophy contributes to the kind of work you plan to do—how does an understanding of the user experience or expert searching skills contribute to your future work? How do you want to portray yourself to potential employers? How do you want to be viewed by your future colleagues? How do you want to be perceived when you give workshops, present at conferences, or blog about your work? Here are some images that might resonate with you: tech savvy, ally and advocate, nexus for scholars on campus, dynamic and innovative, inspiring instructor, creative problem solver.

CONCLUSION

Reference service is and will continue to be a vibrant and essential service in libraries and information agencies. Systems will continue to improve and become more intuitive, and information will become easier to find. However, the interaction between the user and the information professional will remain a key offering of libraries and information centers. Beyond this certainty, the future of reference service is up to you to envision and create. As M. Kathleen Kern, experienced reference librarian and former president of the American Library Association's Reference and User Services Association, has written: "Take the action of trying the new, but don't lose sight of the purpose. Know that your actions shape the future" (2014, 284). Use the knowledge and skills in this book, along with your thinking and reflection about them, to create your vision of the future of reference service.

REFERENCES

Boice, Robert. 1994. *How Writers Journey to Comfort and Fluency: A Psychological Adventure*. Westport, CT: Praeger.

Doherty, John J. 2006. "Reference Interview or Reference Dialogue?" *Internet Reference Services Quarterly* 11 (3): 97–109.

Duggan, Maeve, and Aaron Smith. 2013. "6% of Online Adults Are Reddit Users." *Pew Research Internet Project*. Pew Research Center. http://www.pewinternet.org/2013/07/03/6-of-online-adults-are-reddit-users/.

Kern, M. Kathleen. 2014. "Continuity and Change, or, Will I Ever Be Prepared for What Comes Next?" *Reference & User Services Quarterly* 53 (4): 282–85.

Kuhlthau, Carol C. 2004. *Seeking Meaning: A Process Approach to Library and Information Services*, 2nd ed. Westport, CT: Libraries Unlimited.

Overall, Patricia Montiel. 2009. "Cultural Competence: A Conceptual Framework for Library and Information Science Professionals." *The Library Quarterly* 79 (2): 175–204.

Radford, Marie L. 2006. "Encountering Virtual Users: A Qualitative Investigation of Interpersonal Communication in Chat Reference." *Journal of the American Society for Information Science and Technology* 57 (8): 1046–59.

Radford, Marie L., and Lynn Silipigni Connaway. 2009. "Thriving on Theory: A New Model for Virtual Reference Encounters." Presented at the American Society for

Information Science and Technology 2009 Annual Meeting, Vancouver, British Columbia, Canada. http://www.oclc.org/research/activities/synchronicity/ppt/asist09-thriving.ppt.

Schultz, Kathryn. 2010. *Being Wrong: Adventures in the Margin of Error*. New York: Harper Collins.

VanScoy, Amy. 2012. "Inventing the Future by Examining Traditional and Emerging Roles for Reference Librarians." In *Leading the Reference Renaissance: Today's Ideas for Tomorrow's Cutting-Edge Services*, edited by Marie L. Radford, 79–94. New York: Neal-Schuman.

VanScoy, Amy. 2013. "Fully Engaged Practice and Emotional Connection: Aspects of the Practitioner Experience of Reference and Information Service." *Library & Information Science Research* 35 (4): 272–78.

Work Group for Community Health and Development. 2014. "Section 5. Learning to Be an Ally for People from Diverse Groups and Backgrounds." Community Tool Box. http://ctb.ku.edu/en/table-of-contents/culture/cultural-competence/be-an-ally/main.

Wyer, James I. 1930. *Reference Work: A Textbook for Students of Library Work and Librarians*. Chicago: American Library Association.

Young, Indi. 2015. *Practical Empathy: For Collaboration and Creativity in Your Work*. New York: Rosenfeld Media.

Index

Note: Page numbers with f, t, or b indicate figures, tables, and boxes respectively.

About the Contributors

MARCIA A. BRANDT, School Library Information Specialist, Herscher (Illinois) Community Unit School District #2

RICK BURKE, Executive Director, SCELC (Statewide California Electronic Library Consortium)

NICOLE A. COOKE, Assistant Professor, School of Information Sciences, University of Illinois at Urbana-Champaign

STEPHANIE R. DAVIS-KAHL, Scholarly Communications Librarian and Professor, Illinois Wesleyan University

SARAH EREKSON, Librarian II, Government Information and Municipal Reference Librarian, Chicago Public Library

PAUL D. HEALEY, Senior Instructional Services Librarian and Associate Professor of Library Service, College of Law, University of Illinois at Urbana-Champaign

WENDY HOLLIDAY, Head of Teaching, Learning, and Research Services, Cline Library, Northern Arizona University

JOANN JACOBY, Associate University Librarian for User Services and Associate Dean of Libraries, University of Illinois at Urbana-Champaign

JENNY MARIE JOHNSON, Map and Geography Librarian and Associate Professor of Library Administration, University of Illinois at Urbana-Champaign

M. KATHLEEN KERN, Reference Team Lead, National Defense University Libraries

EMILY J. M. KNOX, Assistant Professor, School of Information Sciences, University of Illinois at Urbana-Champaign

ELISABETH LEONARD, Executive Market Research Manager, SAGE Publishing

LILI LUO, Associate Professor, School of Information, San Jose State University

MARY MALLORY, Coordinator, Government Information Services, Access & Collections and Associate Professor, University Library, University of Illinois at Urbana-Champaign

CELINA NICHOLS McDONALD, Government Documents, Law, & Criminology Librarian, University Libraries, University of Maryland

JEANNE HOLBA PUACZ, Adjunct Lecturer, School of Information Sciences, University of Illinois at Urbana-Champaign

CELIA ROSS, Associate Librarian, Ross School of Business, University of Michigan

LAURA SAUNDERS, Assistant Professor, School of Library and Information Science, Simmons College

CAROL A. SINGER, Professor, Library Teaching & Learning Department, Bowling Green State University

MAURA SOSTACK, EBM Librarian, Evidence-Based Medicine Center, Elsevier Health Sciences

SHELLEY SWEENEY, University Archivist, Head of Archives & Special Collections, University of Manitoba Libraries

ROSALIND TEDFORD, Director for Research and Instruction Services, Z. Smith Reynolds Library, Wake Forest University

DAVE A. TYCKOSON, Associate Dean, Henry Madden Library, California State University, Fresno

AMY VANSCOY, Assistant Professor, Department of Library & Information Studies, Graduate School of Education, University at Buffalo

BETH S. WOODARD, Staff Development and Training Librarian and Associate Professor of Library Administration, University Library, University of Illinois at Urbana-Champaign

NEAL WYATT, Readers' Advisory Columnist, *Library Journal*

About the Editors

LINDA C. SMITH, professor and associate dean for academic programs in the School of Information Sciences at the University of Illinois at Urbana-Champaign, teaches courses in information organization and access, reference, and science reference, both face-to-face and online. She is a past president of both the Association for Library and Information Science Education and the Association for Information Science and Technology and is a recipient of the Isadore Gilbert Mudge Award from the Reference and User Services Association for distinguished contribution to reference librarianship.

MELISSA A. WONG has been an online instructor for the School of Information Sciences at the University of Illinois since 2001, teaching courses in reference, instruction, management, and academic librarianship. Previously, she worked as an academic librarian for 14 years, including 6 years in various positions at the University of Southern California and 8 years as library director at Marymount College Palos Verdes. She earned her master's degree in library science at the University of Illinois at Urbana-Champaign.